CW00819446

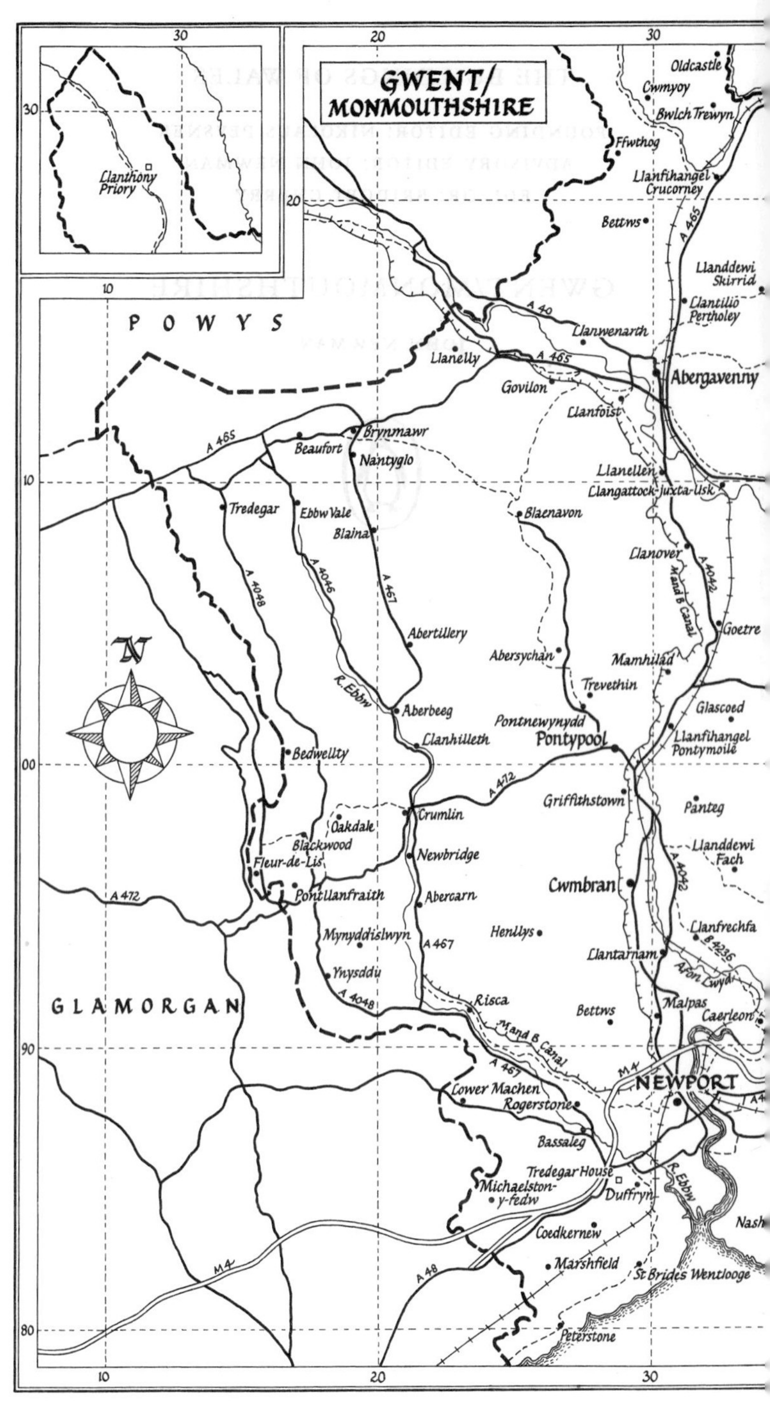
GWENT/
MONMOUTHSHIRE
Llanthony Priory
Oldcastle
Cwmyoy
Bwlch Trewyn
Ffwthog
Llanfihangel Crucorney
Bettws
A 465
Llanddewi Skirrid
Llantilio Pertholey
POWYS
A 40
Llanwenarth
Llanelly
A 465
Govilon
Abergavenny
Llanfoist
Brynmawr
Beaufort
Nantyglo
A 465
Llanellen
Llangattock-juxta-Usk
Tredegar
Ebbw Vale
Blaina
Blaenavon
Llanover
M and B Canal
A 4042
A 4048
A 4046
A 467
Abertillery
Goetre
Abersychan
Mamhilad
Trevethin
Glascoed
R. Ebbw
Aberbeeg
Pontnewynydd
Pontypool
Llanhilleth
Llanfihangel Pontymoile
Bedwellty
A 472
Griffithstown
Panteg
Crumlin
Oakdale
Blackwood
Llanddewi Fach
Newbridge
Fleur-de-Lis
A 4042
Cwmbran
A 472
Pontllanfraith
Abercarn
Llanfrechfa
Henllys
B 4236
Mynyddislwyn
A 467
Llantarnam
Afon Lwyd
Ynysddu
Risca
GLAMORGAN
A 4048
Bettws
Malpas
Caerleon
M and B Canal
A 467
M4
NEWPORT
Lower Machen
Rogerstone
Bassaleg
Tredegar House
R. Ebbw
Michaelston-y-fedw
Duffryn
Nash
Coedkernew
M4
A 48
Marshfield
St Brides Wentlooge
Peterstone

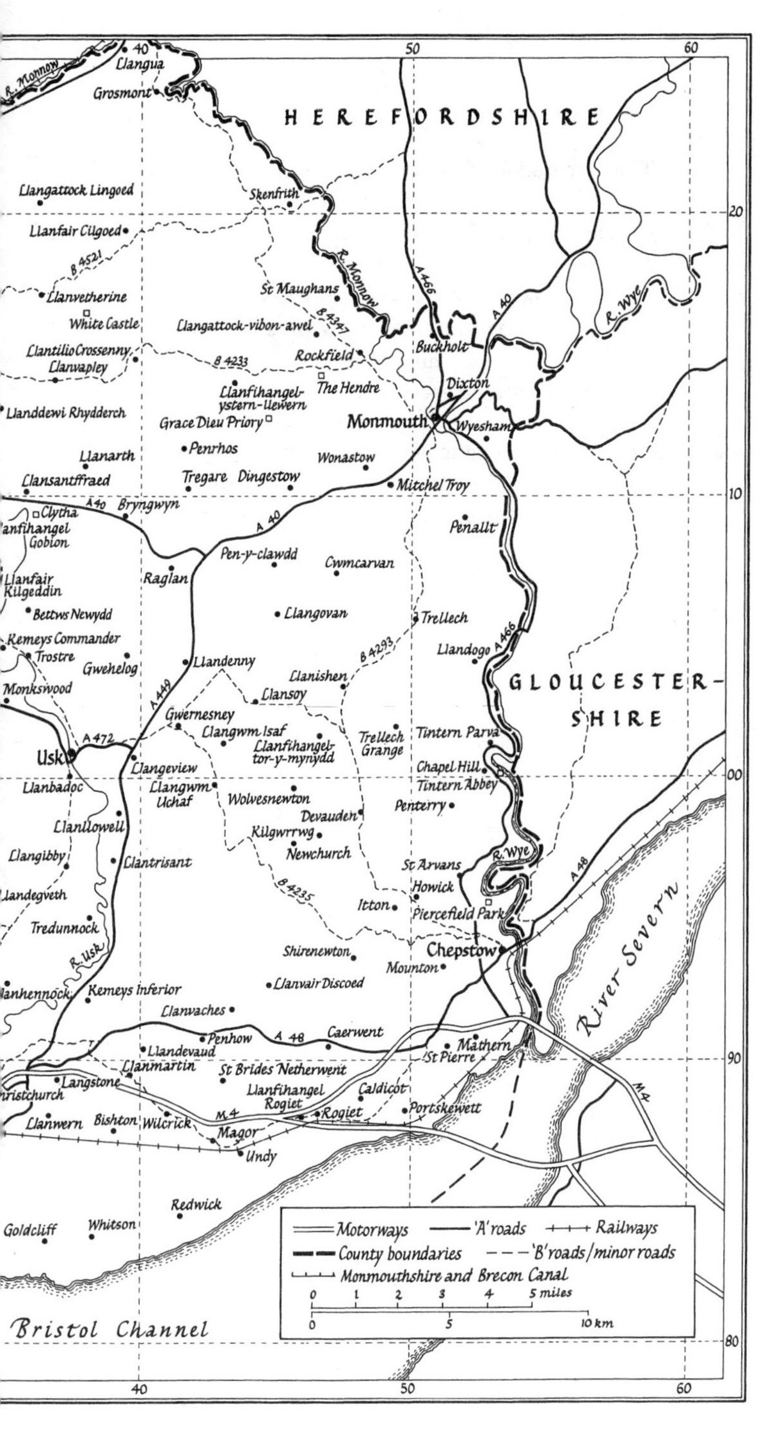

HEREFORDSHIRE
GLOUCESTERSHIRE
R. Monnow
R. Wye
R. Usk
River Severn
Bristol Channel
Llangua
Grosmont
Skenfrith
Llangattock Lingoed
Llanfair Cilgoed
Llanvetherine
White Castle
St Maughans
Llangattock-vibon-awel
Llantilio Crossenny
Llanvapley
Rockfield
The Hendre
Buckholt
Dixton
Llanfihangel-ystern-llewern
Llanddewi Rhydderch
Grace Dieu Priory
Monmouth
Wyesham
Penrhos
Llanarth
Wonastow
Llansantffraed
Tregare
Dingestow
Mitchel Troy
Clytha
Llanfihangel Gobion
Bryngwyn
Penallt
Pen-y-clawdd
Cwmcarvan
Raglan
Llanfair Kilgeddin
Bettws Newydd
Llangovan
Trellech
Remeys Commander
Trostre
Gwehelog
Llandenny
Llandogo
Llanishen
Monkswood
Llansoy
Gwernesney
Llangwm Isaf
Llanfihangel-tor-y-mynydd
Trellech Grange
Tintern Parva
Usk
Llangeview
Chapel Hill
Tintern Abbey
Llanbadoc
Llangwm Uchaf
Wolvesnewton
Penterry
Devauden
Llanllowell
Kilgwrrwg
Newchurch
Llangibby
Llantrisant
St Arvans
Howick
Llandegveth
Itton
Piercefield Park
Tredunnock
Shirenewton
Chepstow
Mounton
Llanhennock
Kemeys Inferior
Llanvair Discoed
Llanvaches
Penhow
Caerwent
Mathern
Llandevaud
St Pierre
Llanmartin
St Brides Netherwent
Langstone
Christchurch
Llanfihangel Rogiet
Caldicot
Portskewett
Llanwern
Bishton
Wilcrick
Rogiet
Magor
Undy
Redwick
Goldcliff
Whitson
A 466
A 40
A 449
A 472
A 48
M 4
B 4521
B 4347
B 4233
B 4293
B 4235
Motorways
'A' roads
Railways
County boundaries
'B' roads/minor roads
Monmouthshire and Brecon Canal
0 1 2 3 4 5 miles
0 5 10 km
40
50
60
20
10
00
90
80

The preparation of this book has been greatly helped
by grants from
THE TRUSTEES OF THE DAVIES CHARITY
from
THE BOARD OF CELTIC STUDIES OF THE
UNIVERSITY OF WALES
and from
CADW: WELSH HISTORIC MONUMENTS

Assistance with photographs has been generously provided by
THE ROYAL COMMISSION ON THE ANCIENT
& HISTORICAL MONUMENTS OF WALES

Gwent/Monmouthshire

BY

JOHN NEWMAN

WITH CONTRIBUTIONS BY

FRANCES LYNCH

WILLIAM MANNING

AND

STEPHEN HUGHES

THE BUILDINGS OF WALES

PENGUIN BOOKS
UNIVERSITY OF WALES PRESS

PENGUIN BOOKS
Published by the Penguin Group
Penguin Books Ltd, 27 Wrights Lane, London W8 5TZ, England

Penguin Putnam Inc., 375 Hudson Street, New York, New York 10014, USA
Penguin Books Australia Ltd, Ringwood, Victoria, Australia
Penguin Books Canada Ltd, 10 Alcorn Avenue, Toronto, Ontario, Canada M4V 3B2
Penguin Books (NZ) Ltd, Private Bag 102902, NSMC, Auckland, New Zealand

Penguin Books Ltd, Registered Offices: Harmondsworth, Middlesex, England

First published 2000

ISBN 0 14 071053 1

Made and printed in Great Britain by Butler & Tanner Ltd, Frome and London
Set in 9/10pt Monotype Plantin

TO MARGARET
THIRTY YEARS ON

CONTENTS

LIST OF TEXT FIGURES AND MAPS

MAPS

Marginal page references in Roman type indicate where relevant text figures appear elsewhere in the book.

ACKNOWLEDGEMENTS FOR THE PLATES

We are grateful to the following for permission to reproduce photographs:

Architectural Review: 120
Cadw: Welsh Historic Monuments. Crown copyright: 49, 50
Martin Charles: 122–6, 128
Christopher Dalton: 106

All other photographs are reproduced by kind permission of the Royal Commission on the Ancient & Historical Monuments of Wales.

The plates are indexed in the indexes of artists and places, and references to them are given by numbers in Roman type in the margins of the text.

MAP REFERENCES

Marginal references printed in italic type against place names in the Gazetteer indicate the position of the place in question on the index map (pp. ii–iii), which is divided into sections by the 10-kilometre reference lines of the National Grid. The reference given here omits the two initial letters (formerly numbers) which in a full grid reference refer to the 100-kilometre squares into which the country is divided. The first two numbers indicate the *western* boundary, and the last two the *southern* boundary, of the 10-kilometre square in which the place in question is situated. For example, Raglan (reference 4000) will be found in the 10-kilometre square bounded by grid lines 40 (on the *west*) and 50, and 00 (on the *south*) and 10; Blaenavon (reference 2000) lies in the square bounded by grid lines 20 (on the *west*) and 30, and 00 (on the *south*) and 10.

Text locations

Buildings are located within each place in the Gazetteer by distance in miles and by compass direction from the parish church, unless otherwise stated.

FOREWORD

Work on the present volume has followed hard on the heels of Glamorgan. *Although much in the new county was thereby rendered familiar, particularly in the industrial Valleys, much appeared surprisingly different: the impressive evidence of Roman occupation, the abundant medieval castles, the many aisled churches and even some late medieval fittings, rich* C17 *plaster ceilings, lavish decorative timberwork in* C16 *and* C17 *farmhouses, Georgian market towns; all this and more had little or no counterpart further west.*

On the other hand, I was not starting from scratch. This volume has had the benefit of substantial research by Richard Haslam, who generously made available his notes and collections. Specialist authors have made important contributions: Frances Lynch on prehistoric monuments, Professor William Manning on Roman sites, and Stephen Hughes on the substantial remains of past industrial activity. They have written the relevant Gazetteer entries and sections of the Introduction. Funds which covered the research for the volume were administered by Ned Thomas when he was Director of the University of Wales Press. I am grateful to him and to his successor, Susan Jenkins, for their assistance and interest. Extra funding from Cadw through the Civic Initiatives (Heritage) Grant Scheme has been provided, first for Glamorgan *and now for this volume, through the good offices of John Carr, former chief executive of Cadw, and is gratefully acknowledged.*

Library preparation was undertaken with enthusiasm and enterprise by Robert Scourfield, who during twelve months in 1993–4 combed a remarkable range of published and unpublished material. His researches have greatly enriched the following pages. I am grateful, too, for his continuing interest in the progress of the book, and for passing on further useful nuggets. Thanks are also due to Vernon Hughes, who kindly loaned me his extracts from the Builder.

At an early stage my path was smoothed by Elisabeth Whittle, who put me in touch with some key local experts. Jeremy Knight, doyen among the county's antiquaries, also gave encouragement, information and a memorable tour of Caerleon. Others who took us to see buildings and sites about which they were especially knowledgeable were Maurice Broady (the work of Celtic Studios), Alan Brooks (Victorian stained glass), Michael Eastham (monuments at St Mary, Abergavenny), George Francis (buildings around Chepstow by Eric Francis), Anne Rainsbury (Caldicot Castle) and Jim Russell (Cwmbran). All helped me to see and understand what I would otherwise have missed. Exceptionally helpful owners of historic houses were Anthony Bosanquet, Robin Herbert (who put on a splendid, if rainswept, tour), Grant Muter and Michael Walsh. Thanks are gratefully recorded to them and to all who readily allowed us to visit houses, churches, chapels and other buildings not normally open. And here it should be pointed out that the description of a building in these pages does not necessarily imply that it is accessible to the public.

At Monmouth Keith Kissack was endlessly helpful and was kind enough to read and comment on my draft text on the town. Others who read drafts and thereby improved the final text are Annette Burton (Usk), David Freeman (Tredegar House), John Kenyon (Raglan Castle) and Frank Olding (Abergavenny). Dr David Robinson did this and more for several major buildings; his guidance over Chepstow Church and Castle, and Llanthony Priory, was particularly valuable.

Two people undertook especially formidable assignments. Peter Howell read a draft of the entire Gazetteer, and his expostulations over gaps and gaffes led to much double-checking and several return visits. Bridget Cherry, as editor, brought to bear on everything her expertise as a medievalist, her growing familiarity with Wales, and her sympathy for the reader who needs to understand.

*Thanks are due to Gareth Dowdell, director of the Glamorgan–Gwent Archaeological Trust, for giving access to Edith Evans's unpublished archaeological survey of medieval churches, to Richard Suggett for transmitting material held by the Royal Commission on the Ancient & Historical Monuments of Wales, and to Julian Orbach for sharing discoveries made while listing. I had the good fortune to discuss with George McHardy the Gwentia collection of mid-*C19 *drawings of churches belonging to the Society of Antiquaries of London. Margaret Richards supplied information from the archives at Badminton.*

Those who kindly provided information drawn from personal knowledge or private research include Adrian Barlow (C. E. Kempe), Tye Blackshaw (J. P. Seddon), Paul Davis (vernacular houses in the Valleys), Dr Ian Dungavell (The Hendre), Dr Angela Gaffney (war memorials), David W. Lloyd (the development of towns), Mick Morden and Norman Robson-Smith (postwar schools), Dr Richard Morris (Caldicot Castle), the late Dale Owen (Percy Thomas Partnership), Liz Pitman (the Brutes), Peter Price (Roman sites), Dr Aileen Reid (Henry Crisp), John Roberts (PSA Projects Cardiff), Susan Smith (R. G. Thomas) and Dr Chris Wakeling (Nonconformist churches). Others whose information or advice I want to acknowledge are Dr Tim Ayers, Annette Burton, Elizabeth Evans, former conservation officer of Monmouthshire County Council, Roger Evans, former MP for Monmouth, Michael Kerney, Tom Lloyd, David Park, Malcolm Parry, Arthur Price, Dr Margaret Scott, Chris Samuel of the Church in Wales and Rachel Stock of the Civic Trust. Many others have answered queries and provided information about buildings in their care. In spite of all this help, many gaps and, I fear, some mistakes still remain. Corrections and supplementary information will be welcomed by author and publisher, and incorporated in a subsequent reprint or edition.

The illustration of the book owes a great debt to Peter White, Secretary of the Royal Commission on the Ancient & Historical Monuments of Wales, who allowed us to reproduce Commission photographs, and to Iain Wright, who took most of them. Martin Charles captured the qualities of several recent buildings. Reg and Marjorie Piggott prepared the maps, and Alan Fagan drew many of the text figures. Alison

McKittrick coordinated the text illustrations with an eagle eye. Copy-editing was once again in the capable hands of Caroline Palmer.

Thanks are due to Allan Braham for his companionship. The Dedication acknowledges the vital contribution made by my wife to the whole enterprise. Without her it could not have been done; with her, it has seemed like a series of holidays.

INTRODUCTION

What's in a name? The answer to that must be that a name embodies history. So the apparently indecisive title of this book – *Gwent/Monmouthshire* – alludes to a thousand years of change in the governing of south-east Wales, and also to its ambivalent position as a part of the Principality, yet unusually closely tied to England.

The name Gwent is derived from Caer-went, the Celtic form of the Roman Venta Silurum, a fact which reflects the continuity between Roman settlement in the area and the subsequent Celtic kingdom of Gwent, which was bounded by the River Wye to the E and to the W by the River Usk. That kingdom was eliminated shortly after 1066 at the Norman subjugation of south-east Wales, and replaced by several small and shifting Marcher lordships, including those of Gwynllŵg, which controlled the mountainous area immediately W of the River Usk, and Abergavenny to the N. Although these lordships were in the hands of Normans and their English descendants, the Welsh name of Gwent continued to be unofficially applied to the entire area.

The Act of Union of 1536, whereby the Tudor dynasty extended its rule over Wales as well as England, abolished the lordships and established in their place thirteen shires on the English model. The area which had informally been known as Gwent now became Monmouthshire, with Monmouth as its county town. This disposition proved durable over more than four centuries, and was superseded only in 1974. Then eight new counties took the place of the former thirteen, taking account of the drastic differences in population which had developed in different parts of Wales as a result of industrialization since the early C19. In this reshuffle Monmouthshire was the only one of the thirteen counties to remain an entity, neither subdivided nor amalgamated. Yet, such was the desire to link this administrative change to an emphasis on Welshness, that the virtually unchanged* entity had to change its name, and Gwent was reborn. Within the newly named county of Gwent were five new subdivisions: the county borough of Newport and four districts, three of them small in area – Torfaen, Islwyn and Blaenau Gwent – covering the populous industrial Valleys, and one, Monmouth, large, covering the rural eastern two-thirds of the old county.

Finally, in 1996, the subdivision into five became much more significant when it was made the basis of a single tier of local

* The Rhymney Valley was ceded to Mid Glamorgan, but Brynmawr and Llanelly were gained from Powys.

government. The county of Gwent was abolished, and five unitary authorities were established along the lines of the former districts. Islwyn, however, was redrawn as the borough of Caerphilly, incorporating part of Glamorgan, and, bewilderingly, Monmouth district was renamed as the county of Monmouthshire. So today Gwent does not officially exist, and Monmouthshire has shrunk to two-thirds its former size. Local loyalty, however, keeps both names vigorously alive, so there seems to be no alternative to calling a book on the buildings of the former county of Monmouthshire by both these historic and still resonant appellations.

In addition, a word of explanation is needed about the perception that Monmouthshire has been somehow a semi-detached part of Wales. (Alec Clifton-Taylor even used to reproach Sir Nikolaus Pevsner for omitting it from *The Buildings of England.*) This perception seems to have originated in a provision of the second Act of Union, of 1543, which for legal purposes apportioned twelve of the thirteen Welsh counties to four Welsh circuits, but placed Monmouthshire in the Oxford circuit. The county was also a little more strongly represented in the Westminster Parliament than any other. On this slim foundation it became common to find official references to 'South Wales and Monmouthshire'. Only after the Local Government Act of 1972, as Monmouthshire, and from 1974, under the revived name of Gwent, did it become indisputable that the county was fully a part of Wales.

Nevertheless, as is shown not least by the history of its architecture, the nearness of Bristol had a major effect on the county's economy and culture. Immigration into the county from England has been and continues to be substantial. Welsh speaking, though normal in the Valleys until the later C19, thereafter rapidly declined. The valiant efforts of individuals, most notably Lady Llanover, could not hold back the ebbing tide. In the twentieth century the Welsh language has been thoroughly in retreat, much more so than in some other parts of Wales, so that in the 1991 census less than 3 per cent of the residents of Gwent reported that they could speak Welsh. Today, even among the farming community, West Country accents are more commonly heard than Welsh ones. The anglicizing of Welsh place names has produced more bizarre hybrids here than anywhere else in Wales. In this book the principle has been generally adopted to spell names as they are currently conventionally spelt, however indefensible linguistically the form may be.

LANDSCAPE AND BUILDING MATERIALS

Gwent/Monmouthshire is quite a small county; of the thirteen counties into which Wales was subdivided in 1536, only three were smaller. Yet, with a population of 434,244 in 1991, it is more heavily populated than any other part of the country except Glamorgan.

Among Welsh towns, Newport is exceeded in size only by Cardiff and Swansea, and of the South Wales industrial valleys, two of the longest and most heavily developed, Ebbw Vale and the Sirhowy Valley, are in the county. Then there is Cwmbran, Wales's major post-war New Town. Improved road communications since the 1960s, above all the M4 motorway linking Wales to England across the Severn Bridge and Crossing, have helped to concentrate Welsh industrial growth around Newport. Housing estates continue to spring up close to the motorway all along its line.

This activity, however, has taken place in the W and S of the county. The centre, N and E remain rural, a close-textured, hedge-enclosed countryside in which scattered churches and farmsteads maintain much of the medieval and Tudor pattern of settlement, when the spread of corn-growing led to enclosure of the lowlands. The towns planted in the late C12, Abergavenny, Chepstow, Monmouth and Usk, continue to serve as market centres.

The general configuration of the landscape can be likened to an amphitheatre. The arena is the Vale of Usk, though the Vale is hardly anywhere flat, but threaded by miniature twisting ridges and valleys as the River Usk pursues its winding way SE-wards from Abergavenny and its tributary the Olway Brook meanders SW-wards from Monmouth.

The Vale is bounded on all sides, more or less firmly, by hills. To the N two isolated mountains appear in every view, the shapely, symmetrical Sugarloaf, and Skirrid with its cloven outline. Beyond
them extends an out-lier, the beautiful, steep-sided Vale of Ewyas, 1
enfolding Llanthony Priory. To the E the ground rises by means of dramatically wooded slopes to the Trellech ridge, and beyond it the gorge of the River Wye, which forms the county boundary in this direction. To the W is the long, even ridge which terminates at its northern end in the crouching form of the Blorenge, and beyond which lie the industrial Valleys. Interrupted at Pontypool, the ridge rises again to the S and forms a splendid backdrop to Cwmbran, before dying away as the River Ebbw flows SE-wards to join the River Usk SW of Newport. Finally, to the S, the ridge over which spread the eastern suburbs of Newport rises steadily to become a steep flank to the lower Usk Valley, and then to stretch across E-wards, covered by the extensive tracts of ancient Wentwood.

That leaves only two parts of the county beyond the confines of the 'amphitheatre'. To the W lie the Ebbw and Sirhowy valleys, their industrial bottoms and steep lower slopes starkly contrasting with lonely upland ridges, farmed or forested. Finally, the southern borderland is something quite different: the flat Severnside Levels, criss-crossed with drainage dykes, and dotted with surprisingly ambitious medieval churches. This, and the band of undulating country N of it, rising towards Wentwood, formed Gwent Iscoed (beneath the wood), as it was called, most easily tamed first by the Romans, then by the Normans. And now again, at the end of the C20, as mentioned above, it is here that the communication corridor brings greatest pressure for development.

Building Materials

This is not a county of high-quality building stones. Yet almost everywhere there is usable STONE, and in one or two localized sites freestones could be found. The geologically oldest stone, the Old Red Sandstone of the Devonian series, is the most widespread, occurring everywhere in the north-eastern and central parts of the county. In colour it varies from a strong purple to mauve and even grey. Blocks can also be found in a great range of sizes, from the megaliths used in a few medieval church towers to hand-sized pieces. The choicest stone, which could be cut for mouldings, was the pinkish-grey type quarried in the neighbourhood of Tintern, and used for all the buildings at Tintern Abbey, for dressings for Roger Bigod's late C13 works at Chepstow Castle and for the late C16 remodelling of Raglan Castle. Old Red Sandstone was the standard building material for medieval churches and post-medieval farmhouses throughout the north-eastern half of the county, though the rough-textured walls which resulted would originally have been given a coating of lime-mortar render. One type of Old Red Sandstone, of strong purple hue, could be used as ashlar. This can be seen in the early C14 N aisle at Skenfrith and the show front of Newton Court, Dixton, of *c.* 1800. More practical was the Victorian preference for giving Old Red Sandstone a hammerdressed or rock-faced texture, as for example at Abergavenny Town Hall.

Next in age is the Carboniferous Limestone which appears so dramatically in the cliffs of the lower Wye Valley between Tintern and Chepstow. Here it is quite a dazzling white, and white or grey limestone could be quarried in the hills S of Wentwood. Local limestone was used by the Romans in small, roughly squared blocks at Caerleon and Caerwent, and seems to have been extensively reused in the late C11 in the keep at Chepstow Castle. Other, later, buildings at Chepstow are constructed of Carboniferous Limestone, most conspicuously the early C18 Thomas Powis Almshouses, where its rough, irregular surface conflicts with the precision of the classical design. Carboniferous Limestone can be found used in combination with Old Red Sandstone at Newport Castle, and other late medieval buildings in the vicinity, for example Llanwern Church and Church House, Christchurch. These too were doubtless originally intended to be rendered.

A brown Dolomitic Limestone, still quarried for road stone at Penhow, occurs in an irregular band running N-wards from there across the Vale of Usk. It lent itself best as rubble-stone for farm buildings and walls; but *Prichard & Seddon* used it in polychromatic effects, as at Llanfrechfa Vicarage, and Holy Trinity, Pontnewydd, Cwmbran. Its rugged qualities were well exploited in the 1920s in the Arts and Crafts village at Llanover. Here frost-split stone slates complete the picture. This traditional local roof covering has been replaced almost everywhere in the late C18 and C19 by the thin, machine-cut slates from North Wales, all too mean and inappropriate on a stout, rough-walled Monmouthshire farmhouse.

The stone which is associated with the Coal Measures of the Valleys on the W border of the county is Pennant Sandstone. The exploitation of first iron and then coal in the Valleys from the late C18 led to the quarrying of Pennant Sandstone on an enormous scale. The major quarry in the county was at Newbridge, where the quarry cliffs are still a conspicuous sight. The stone occurs in a variety of sombre hues, grey ('blue'), brown and green, sometimes with rusty iron-staining. Its texture is hard, making it impossible to cut to a smooth face, and it can be used only as random walling or in shallow courses. In the later C19 it was normal to give it a rock-faced tooling. Virtually all the C19 and early C20 buildings of the Valleys towns and settlements, chapels and churches, community buildings and terraced housing alike, employ Pennant Sandstone in one way or another. Dressings, however, have to be of some other material, normally Bath stone or brick.

The only stone indigenous to the county which could be used in squared ashlar blocks was a Triassic Sandstone, of coarse texture and yellowish hue. This stone outcropped mainly in the SE of the county, at Sudbrook, Portskewett, and around Caldicot, and was locally popular from the late C11 until the C14, when it seems to have been largely worked out. It occurs conspicuously in the late C11 castle keep at Chepstow and in the priory church there, and very splendidly in the round keep at Caldicot Castle, of a century later. Subsequent parts of Caldicot Castle continued to use it, but sizeable blocks were not always easy to come by. A related sandstone was used for the finest display of ashlar stonework in the county, the C15 parts of Raglan Castle. This is quite finely textured and has weathered extremely well. Its source has been located about 5 m. (8 kilometres) to the E, at Redbrook in the Wye Valley, just over the county boundary.

For mouldings and dressings, stones of higher quality were often imported. Plenty was available across the Bristol Channel. At Chepstow Castle, from the earliest phases, Oolitic Limestone from Dundry near Bristol was employed. Later, Bath stone was widely used, as for the exuberant enrichments at Tredegar House in the 1660s. In the West Country the heyday of Bath stone's popularity extended from the early C18 to the early C19. In Monmouthshire this is reflected by a few prestigious buildings completely faced with Bath stone ashlar: the Shire Hall, Monmouth, of 1724, Soane's exquisitely finished Piercefield Park, 1792–3, and Clytha Park, of the 1820s. During the Victorian period Bath stone continued to be the most popular stone for dressings, though much was of poor quality, as cheapness became an overriding consideration in rapidly expanding Newport and the Valleys. Where a better colour match was sought, dark greenish Forest of Dean Sandstone was paired with Pennant, and pink sandstones from Cheshire and Shropshire were brought in to dress Old Red Sandstone.

BRICK, where it occurs, has a somewhat exotic air in this predominantly stone county. The Romans used brick sparingly, for example in the amphitheatre at Caerleon, and Roman brick was reused to striking effect in the late C11 at Chepstow Castle. It next occurs at Raglan Castle, in the 1460s, where it was employed internally in a few places not intended to be seen. The early C17 saw its growth in popularity. It can be found again at Raglan, in the castle, used in the same way as before, but at Castle Farm for exposed walling throughout. This probably belongs to the 1630s. An important early brick house of about the same time was Pentrebach, Llantarnam. Brick finally came into its own from the 1660s, when it was used as the walling material at Tredegar House and stables. Over the ensuing half-century or so brick was used for farmhouses and barns, mainly in a localized area of the Vale of Usk NE of Raglan. This is where the great red brick Victorian mansion of The Hendre can be found, the successor no doubt to such a red brick farmhouse. In Monmouth brick was used in the mid C18 for several handsome town houses.

All the brick mentioned so far is of a warm orangey-red hue. Very different is the yellow brick made from clay exposed by coalmining. Ebbw Vale was one of the largest producers of yellow pressed brick, used in the later C19 to dress Pennant Sandstone buildings. The manner of its use demonstrates that it was seen as a cheap substitute for Bath stone. Similar hard, shiny red brick was normally imported, in particular from Cattybrook near Bristol. It can be seen, for example, in several board schools and council schools of *c.* 1900, at Newport, Pontnewynydd and Abersychan.

Exposed TIMBER outside and in was normal in house-building from the late Middle Ages until the mid C16. Thereafter stone walling took over, so that today surviving external timber-framing is extremely rare. What has survived much better is the substantial oak carpentry used for doors and windows in farmhouses up to *c.* 1700. These timber members, used unusually lavishly in Monmouthshire, it seems, have the bulk and mouldings associated with stonework. Internally, the achievements of local carpenters and joiners are even more memorable. Massive, richly moulded ceiling beams and joists, and handsome timber partitions are characteristic features of these houses.

PREHISTORIC REMAINS

BY FRANCES LYNCH

Gwent is not a geographical unity: in the W there are the moorland ridges and narrow industrialized valleys which are essentially a continuation of the Glamorgan valley systems; in the N there is a small corner of the grand open country of the Black Mountains, and in the S a swathe of marshland bordering the Bristol Channel. But perhaps the most characteristic scenery lies between the broad valley of the Usk and the narrow twisting gorge of the Wye. Central to this band of undulating, well-wooded, rich agricultural land is the low basin of the Olway Brook, overlooked by several fortified hilltops. To the N the land between the rivers Trothy and Monnow would seem equally suitable for early settlement, yet no visible monuments survive.

The valley of the Usk, an important thoroughfare giving access to Breconshire and central Wales, and the low hills between Chepstow and Caerleon, overlooking the Severn Levels and relatively easily reached from the E, show the greatest exploitation by prehistoric man. However, recent fieldwork has shown that the coastal marshlands were far from deserted, and that their specialized resources were well used at several periods in the past.

The Stone Age

Slight but significant evidence for the presence of small bands of hunters in the Palaeolithic and Mesolithic periods comes from this coastal region, then a broad, shallow valley. Hand-axes from the mud flats and a levallois flake from Chepstow show man's presence in the area more than 100,000 years ago. More immediate evidence of man's stalking and hunting activities in the warmer woodland of the Mesolithic is found on the modern shoreline near Goldcliff, where flint microlithic arrowtips and fossilized human footprints have been found.

Early farming settlements have not been found in Gwent, but the distribution of the surviving tombs of this period suggests that these colonizers had settled chiefly near the valley of the Usk. This distribution and the design of tomb favoured in the region relates both to the coastal areas of Glamorgan and to the Cotswolds, and is no doubt also connected with the group of Cotswold-Severn tombs in Breconshire, in the area around Talgarth. These tombs, part of a tradition of monumental building which was widespread in western Europe in the fourth millennium B.C., were the communal burial places, and no doubt also the religious foci, of the earliest farming communities in the region. The chambers were built of large stones, the ground plan varying according to the traditions of the particular group or tribe, and they would be covered by a large mound of earth or stones – a very much more permanent structure than the wooden houses in which these farmers lived.

Only four of these 'megalithic' tombs are known in Gwent, but the recent discovery of the fourth near Chepstow offers hope of more finds, and of more information about their date and the background of those who built them. The plan of the chambers at Thornwell Farm, Chepstow, and at Gaer Llwyd, Newchurch, which have characteristic antechambers, confirms an affinity with the Cotswold tombs; the unusual terminal chamber at Portskewett and the badly ruined one at Cleppa Park, Duffryn, are consistent with this type, but despite some limited excavation there is no precise evidence for their date of construction. Analogy with similar tombs elsewhere would suggest that they were built towards the end of the fourth millennium B.C. and could have remained in use for perhaps a thousand years.

Stone axes were a vital tree-felling tool for the Neolithic farmer, and their distribution, too, emphasizes the importance of the Usk Valley at this time. At least two hoards of stone axes have been found at Newport and another comes from Llangenny across the Powys border, where the river enters Breconshire. These hoards, which included flint axes from England and dolerite ones from

Preseli, suggest a trade in these tools which no doubt passed up the river in boats. Single finds from Cwmbran, Mynyddislwyn and the Abergavenny area confirm the W-ward emphasis of settlement, with only the single examples from Chepstow and St Brides Netherwent to indicate a presence at the mouth of the more restricted Wye Valley and in the coastal hills.

The Bronze Age

The succeeding Bronze Age saw many changes, not only in technology but also in social life. The communality of the Neolithic period was replaced by a much greater individualism and hints of a sharper social stratification, in many places to be connected with the appearance of weapons as symbols of prestige and power. The background to these changes is very complex, and their adoption in different parts of the country uneven. Both internal change and foreign contacts combining with a new economic structure must have played a role in the emergence of a new society – sharply defined in Wessex, less aggressively new in the W.

The changes are reflected most clearly in the graves of the period which, beside the individually laid out body, often include a distinctive and prestigious 'beaker' pot and what are clearly personal, private possessions. So far no round mound in Gwent has revealed such an early burial, but several have been found in Glamorgan and in the Cotswolds.

The Early Bronze Age round barrow is normally one of the commonest surviving antiquities but they are relatively rare in Gwent. A few characteristic summit cairns may be seen on the ridges above Lower Machen and Blaenavon, out-liers of the much larger group on the Glamorgan moors. Finds such as a cremation urn from Tredunnock and a fine dagger from St Brides Netherwent show that rich burials were made in the Usk Valley and in the coastal hills, but agriculture has reduced the covering mounds to virtual invisibility.

Only two barrows have been scientifically excavated in Gwent: that at Crick, Caerwent, and the almost obliterated monument at St Brides Netherwent. In the former, the cremation burials, one dating from the construction of the mound, the other added later, were simple, but the mound was quite elaborately constructed with an encircling wall containing two cup-marked stones, though nothing of this can be seen on the site at present. The mound at St Brides was originally simpler but was later enlarged with a similar kerb. The large bronze dagger found with the cremated bones and the lumps of flint, clearly dug from the chalk, indicate both an unusual level of wealth and a close connection with the rich society across the Severn in Wessex. The former, of Camerton Snowshill type current around 1400 B.C., is a rare find for Wales, where daggers were not the preferred status symbol, and it underlines the fact that this coastal area of Gwent has always been a borderland between two cultures.

Bronze Age ritual activity was very closely linked with aspects of death and burial, but may also have had other dimensions connected

with the sky and the calendar. Such religious sites, normally taking the form of circles of tall stones or rings of boulders, are rare in Gwent. The most interesting group is that on Gray Hill, Llanvair Discoed, a flat-topped moorland area overlooking the coastal plain where contemporary burial monuments seem to have been most common. Here there are two tall standing stones, a ruined circle and several small cairns. Another well-known group of stones, undoubtedly of Bronze Age date though their purpose is unknown, is the line of three called 'Harold's Stones' at Trellech. A single 3
large stone survives at Druidstone House, Michaelston-y-fedw, said to be the central stone in a large circle, now destroyed. The ridge between the Ebbw and the Rhymney is an area where much must have been lost beneath later developments, for several bronze implements have been found there.

Casual finds of bronze implements, like those of the earlier stone axes, can indicate the main areas of prehistoric settlement and, through the analysis of their design and manufacture, can reflect trading contacts and the influence of distant markets. The earliest bronze implements are rare, but analysis of some of the flat axes indicates a connection with the metal industry of southern England, from which the St Brides Netherwent dagger also came. In the Middle Bronze Age (1400–1200 B.C.), however, native Welsh industries come to the fore, and the early palstaves from Gwent clearly belong to a group found mainly in the Marches and NE Wales. The impact of foreign styles and techniques seen clearly at Pennard, Glamorgan, and in the upper Severn Valley at the beginning of the Late Bronze Age is reflected in Gwent in a scabbard from Caldicot and a French Urnfield bracelet from Usk.

In the full Late Bronze Age (800–600 B.C.) Gwent became the centre of a thriving local industry producing 'South Welsh' socketed axes – the standard tool of the period. These small, utilitarian and rather roughly finished tools are found in large numbers, both as single finds and as hoards in Glamorgan and Gwent, and also across the Severn in Somerset. Some of the hoards include broken tools and unworked metal and must have been the property of the metalworkers themselves. Such men must have relied on scrap for their raw material, and it has been suggested that scrap metal was imported in the Late Bronze Age from northern France. At Tintern a hoard of Breton axes, a type with such a high lead content that they may have been ingots rather than functional tools, confirms this trading link.

Like the Neolithic houses before them, Bronze Age settlement sites are difficult to find. However, two unexpected discoveries in marshland environments have recently revealed domestic activity of Late Bronze Age date. At Chapel Tump on the Wentlooge marshes, pottery and postholes have defined a small circular house, and at Caldicot excavation for a new lake beside the castle exposed worked timbers, piles and a plank from a sewn boat, debris from a nearby settlement thrown into a silted creek.

Fortified hilltop settlements of the later prehistoric period are the most numerous antiquity in Gwent and perhaps provide the most interest for visitors. These villages, surrounded by earthen or stone ramparts and deep ditches, mark a notable change in the settlement history of Britain, suggesting as they do a period of unrest, with warring tribes and military citadels. This change has traditionally been associated with the advent of new people in the Iron Age, but excavation has revealed a longer, native history to many of these sites, which began as palisaded enclosures of the Late Bronze Age. This was a period when deteriorating weather created an internal economic crisis and led to the enclosure and defence of the remaining workable land. The more permanent earthen defences still visible today are often only the later phases of a long sequence of habitation. None of the relatively few excavated sites in Gwent has produced positive evidence of a Late Bronze Age origin, but several show a history of structural development which may have early beginnings.

The Iron Age

There are over twenty hill-forts worthy of note in Gwent; most of them are in the southern half of the county, and they range from large, multivallate enclosures like Gaer Fawr, Llangwm Uchaf, and Campswood Camp, Gwehelog, to small, single-banked farmsteads like Rhiwderin, Bassaleg, or Y Gaer, Trellech. While it is possible that some may have early beginnings, the only dated sites in Gwent are relatively late. Radiocarbon dates suggest that Twyn y Gaer, Ffwthog, in the N of the county was first defended in the C5 B.C., well within the pre-Roman Iron Age, while the wheel-thrown pottery and other goods from Llanmelin, Llanvair Discoed, and Sudbrook, Portskewett, indicate that these sites were being extensively remodelled only shortly before the Roman invasion. Some of the smaller ones, such as Gaer Hill, Penterry, may even be post-Roman in date, though this has yet to be proved by excavation. Roman material reported from Gaer Fawr and from the virtually destroyed Camp Hill, Bryngwyn, certainly implies a continued occupation of these hilltops despite the attraction of the sophisticated life at Caerwent.

While most of the hill-forts, like other earlier monuments, lie S of Abergavenny, there are two important sites, Twyn y Gaer,
4 Ffwthog, and Pentwyn, Bwlch Trewyn, on the southern fringe of the Black Mountains. These two forts stand out from the others in Gwent geographically and because of their connections, proved by excavation at Twyn y Gaer, with the Marcher camps to the N. In central Gwent, on the hills above the Usk and around the Olway Brook basin, there is a group of large, multivallate forts with impressive ramparts and complex entrances. At Gaer Fawr there is evidence to suggest two periods of defence, and at Coed y Bwnydd, Bettws Newydd, a section across the defences showed alterations associated with two different kinds of house within the enclosure.

However, the bulk of the monuments are concentrated in the coastal areas, where both large and small enclosures may be found. The social mix has recently been enlarged by the discovery on the Goldcliff mudflats of a group of unusual rectangular, wicker-walled houses of Iron Age date. Houses of this shape and situation have not been found before, and a preliminary interpretation suggests that they may relate to a specialist cattle economy, working the salt marshes in the summer months. However, in 1999 another group of three wicker-walled houses was discovered deep below the alluvium at Magor, raising the possibility that such houses were more widespread and less specialized than originally thought.

There is a notable group of hill-forts at the mouth of the Wye and another around Newport commanding the river crossings and the coast. They form part of a series lying along the fertile coastal strip from Gloucester to Glamorgan, which are strongly defended but relatively small compared to the large forts of the hinterland of Herefordshire and Gloucestershire. Some of these centres, such as Sudbrook and Llanmelin, seem to have been remodelled late in the Iron Age, perhaps by people pushing westward from south-east England. Others, such as Lodge Farm camp, Caerleon, seem to be older and may have been the military and political centres of people longer established in the area. The foundation of the major Roman base at Caerleon, just below Lodge Farm camp, underlines its strategic importance, and hints, perhaps, at its political significance, though others have preferred to see Llanmelin as the native tribal capital abandoned in favour of the Romanized town of Caerwent.

ROMAN REMAINS

BY WILLIAM MANNING

The county of Gwent includes two of the most notable Roman sites in Britain, the legionary fortress of Caerleon and the tribal capital at Caerwent. Both have remarkable and well-preserved 5, 6
Roman structures, but once the visitor has seen them, he has seen almost all of the visible Roman remains in the county. Of the important early military site at Usk, nothing whatever is to be seen above the ground; and for an area which saw a great deal of military activity in the Roman period, there is a surprising lack of forts or marching camps. It is known from the historian Tacitus that the conquest of the Iron Age tribe of the Silures was a prolonged and difficult affair, but the foundation of the fortress at Usk in *c.* A.D. 55 must mean that the eastern part of their territory, including Gwent, was overrun relatively quickly. It is to the period of military consolidation which followed this conquest that the fortress at Usk and the fort at Abergavenny belong. Other forts may possibly have existed at Caerleon and Caerwent, but certain proof is lacking. By *c.* A.D. 75 the conquest of Wales was complete, and the earlier military arrangements were replaced by a system of forts which, in one form or another, was to survive for a century or more. In the S of Wales military control was exercised through the Second Augustan Legion based at Caerleon, which formed the keystone p. 137
of a series of more or less regularly spaced auxiliary forts linked by carefully engineered roads. Only two of these forts lay within

Gwent, both in the Usk Valley, at Usk itself, where a smaller fort replaced the earlier legionary fortress, and at Abergavenny. This paucity of military occupation must indicate that most of Gwent was regarded as pacified, and this is confirmed by the creation of a civilian administration for the Silures with its capital at Caerwent, late in the C1 A.D. Whether the new Roman tribe covered the same area as its Iron Age predecessor may be doubted. The continued existence of Roman forts in Breconshire suggests that the hinterland at least remained under military control, while the legionary fortress at Caerleon and its associated territory will also have remained outside the control of the new civilian administration.

p. 146 Caerwent (*Venta Silurum*) was among the smaller and less spectacular of the provincial capitals of Roman Britain, and in this it probably reflected the relative backwardness of the territory which it administered. The Silures appear to have been among the least Romanized of all the tribes to whom nominal self-government was granted, and this is reflected in the rarity of small towns and even of villas in the county. Admittedly, Gwent has been less subject to the intensive ploughing which in other areas has often led to the discovery of rural settlements, while the prevalence of pasture means that aerial photography has been less productive than might otherwise have been the case. But despite these factors it remains true to say that Roman sites are surprisingly rare in the county. A few rural settlements – at Usk, at Great Bulmore E of Caerleon, and probably at Abergavenny and Monmouth – and a handful of stone buildings which may have been villas, mainly around Caerleon and Caerwent, are all that are known. To these may be added a few industrial sites, most notably the leadmining settlement at Lower Machen, extensive iron-working around Monmouth and a pottery at Caldicot. Clearly, other Roman sites remain to be discovered, but it is most unlikely that they will greatly change this general picture. Gwent was on the edge of the Roman world, divided between, on the one hand, the army, with its great centre at Caerleon, surrounded as it must have been by a sprawling settlement of discharged legionaries and their descendants, traders and natives, and on the other, the civilian administration, representing the Romanized element of the Silures centred at Caerwent. Beyond the strip of coastal plain around these two centres the degree of Romanization fell away rapidly, with the old style of country life continuing in most ways much as it did before the Roman invasion.

THE MIDDLE AGES

From the six centuries between the departure of the Romans from south-east Wales and the arrival of the Normans, virtually no visible evidence survives of the social, agricultural and religious activity which can be deduced from written sources. Offa's Dyke, formed by the king of Mercia in the later C8 to define his lowland territory from the uplands to the W, is by far the most prominent feature in the area, but lies to the E of the River Wye, in what is now Gloucestershire and Herefordshire. The kings of Gwent held sway until the C11 over the land between the rivers Wye and Usk. Several *clas*, or monastic churches, are known to have existed, and as many as forty-two medieval church sites can claim to be of pre-Norman origin. But we look in vain for any parallel to the great collections of Celtic crosses further W in Glamorgan. At Caerwent a disc cross-head was recently found, and in the church at St Arvans is preserved part of the disc head and part of the shaft, decorated with interlace, of a C10 cross.

Castles

During these centuries substantial parts of the great stone buildings of the Romans survived, at Caerleon and Caerwent and perhaps elsewhere. The challenge they presented was taken up after the Norman invasion of 1066. William the Conqueror, in granting lands on the Welsh border to his most trusted henchmen, ensured that the borderland, or Marches as it came to be called, would come under Norman control. The numerous earthwork castles of the late C11 and C12, mostly mottes, and a few ringworks, bear witness to the struggles necessary before that control was secured. Of these, the great motte at Caerleon, thrown up before 1087, is the most impressive. At Chepstow, however, on a rocky ridge p. 169 overlooking the lowest crossing point on the Wye, William fitz Osbern, Earl of Hereford, took the step of erecting a stone castle, in the few years before his death in 1071. Similar rectangular stone keeps had already been erected in Normandy, and in England two much larger and more complex stone keeps were started soon after the Conquest: Colchester, and the White Tower of the Tower of London. Nevertheless, the keep at Chepstow, built of finely squared blocks, with a mid-height band of reused Roman brick, clearly emulates Roman construction. It has even been suggested that the chip-carved diaper pattern in the tympanum of the entrance doorway imitates *opus reticulatum*; and the same could be said of the painted decoration of the niches in the internal walls, a white and red lattice pattern, traces of which, remarkably, survive. The keep was not so much a stronghold as a splendid ceremonial hall, but its position, its stone walls and the at least partly stone-walled enclosure to the E (the present middle bailey), must have given the castle both great security and an air of menace.

Several other castles built in the C12 have, or had, rectangular stone keeps. The keep at Monmouth is a smaller version of that at Chepstow, but is undated. The taller, squarer keep at Usk was probably 7 built by the de Clares soon after 1174. Typical of small C12 stone castles in south-east Wales is an arrangement whereby a rectangular keep is set astride a polygonal enclosure wall. This is the form of the original White Castle, probably built 1184–6, and of the extremely small Penhow Castle. The latest rectangular keep was at Grosmont, thought to be as late as *c.* 1201–5, for Hubert p. 240 de Burgh.

By the turn of the C13, however, the advantages of a quite different form of castle structure were becoming accepted. This is the drum tower, used both as a circular free-standing keep and as a strong point in an enclosure wall, and much more efficient than the square tower or turret in providing a comprehensive field of vision for defenders with crossbows. Royal builders in both France and England employed it: Philip Augustus at the Louvre, Richard I in Normandy at Château Gaillard, and in England King John at Corfe 1201–4. In South Wales the lead was taken by William Marshal, who in 1189, through marriage to the de Clare heiress, acquired Pembroke in the far W, and in Gwent both Chepstow and Usk. Recent discoveries at Chepstow Castle have provided powerful evidence that the outer gatehouse there, with its round-arched entrance and portcullis between two drum towers, may have been built *c.* 1189, and so was significantly innovative for gatehouse design in general. Round towers became in the early C13 extremely popular among Welsh castle-builders. Marshal himself built the greatest of them all, the free-standing keep at Pembroke Castle *c.* 1190. However, in the years shortly before his death in
1219 he built two more locally, the impressive circular Garrison
p. Tower in the walled enceinte at Usk, and the more modest tower
590 at Caerleon, close to the bridge over the River Usk. It was
Marshal too, or perhaps one of his sons, who strengthened the
middle bailey wall at Chepstow with two bold drum towers.

p. The finest array of drum towers is at Caldicot Castle. On the
155 pre-existing motte was built a great circular keep, echoing the
keep at Pembroke. The bailey wall is punctuated by three round-
fronted towers, and there may originally have been more. The W
tower incorporates a flank entrance protected by a portcullis, an
24 unusual feature also paralleled at Pembroke. At Skenfrith Castle
p. there is a free-standing circular residential tower within a high-
533 walled trapezoidal enclosure with circular angle towers, built for
Hubert de Burgh 1220–2. Hubert's gateway and curtain wall at
Grosmont also make use of towers of curved form, and show that
by the early 1220s he had adopted the prevailing fashion. Other
circular towers, presumably of the early C13, can be found at
Llanvair Discoed Castle and Pencoed Castle, Llanmartin. An
unusually complete expression of the idea is in the virtual recon-
p. struction of White Castle for Henry III, from the mid 1250s.
597 It was provided with a very large outer bailey, its gatehouse with
D-fronted twin towers, its walls punctuated by four towers, three
of them cylindrical, and a splendid inner bailey gatehouse with
twin round towers, the inner bailey walls strengthened with four
more cylindrical towers. The rebuilding of White Castle was the
only work of fortification in Gwent which seems to have been undertaken for fear of the great Welsh prince, Llywelyn ap Gruffudd,
who in 1262 pushed as far S as Brecon and attacked Abergavenny
in 1263.

Chepstow Castle can boast the last and one of the most spec-
23 tacular of all the cylindrical towers in the county. Marten's Tower,
built by Roger Bigod, Earl of Norfolk, *c.* 1286–93, with great spurs
at its base, and a rich little chapel and carved demi-figures at its

crown, stands at one corner of the outer bailey, beside the main approach to the castle. It was intended not only as a display, of strength and splendour at the same time, but also as a private suite of lodgings on four levels. Edward I had stayed at Chepstow in 1284, and this great residential tower may well have been intended to house the monarch appropriately on some future occasion. Bigod's other works at Chepstow were primarily concerned with ceremonial feasting. One of the younger Marshals in the second quarter of the C13 had already undertaken a splendid remodelling of the hall in the keep, introducing two-light N windows with handsomely moulded and shafted rere-arches, and a two-bay transverse arcade resting on magnificent stiff-leaf corbels to 22
support a new upper W chamber. Bigod continued this top storey across the full length of the keep; but his main work was a new hall and kitchen range on the N side of the lower bailey, under way as early as 1271. Of the hall, little remains, just enough to indicate the delicacy of its enrichment. The hall porch, however, is largely intact, even with extensive areas of internal heraldic wall paintings, known to have been executed 1292–3. Much more evocative of the scale and complexity of Bigod's provisions for feasting are the service arrangements. The kitchen itself is a grand room, lit and ventilated by tall, two-light traceried openings to N and S. The service passage, between the kitchen and the flight of stairs leading up to the hall, extends to the cliff-face, where a stair under a rib vault leads down to a great storage room under the hall. Everything is nobly scaled and ingeniously planned, so it is appropriate that the name of the designer mason is known, Master *Ralf*.

Bigod also strengthened the defences at the W end of Chepstow Castle, and, probably 1272–8, built a defensive wall for the town, the Port Wall, strengthened with a series of low D-shaped towers. Much of the wall survives, though the town gate was reconstructed in the early C16. Abergavenny and Monmouth are also known to have had stone walls, and Newport stone gates, three of them, but all that survive are, at Monmouth, a drum tower of *c.* 1297, and, much more important even in a national context, the Monnow Bridge and gate. This is the only survivor in Britain of a fortified 25
gateway on a town bridge, a type of structure still found in some numbers on the Continent. The bridge is said to have been built in 1272, the gate was part of the strengthening of the town walls between 1297 and *c.* 1315.

New building and improvement of castles continued during the C14 and C15. The main stronghold of the de Clares in the locality in the early C14 was Usk Castle. But it seems that a start was made on a powerful new castle at Llangibby, in a more commanding position 3 m. (5 kilometres) further S, either by the last de Clare, who perished at Bannockburn in 1314, or by the royal favourite Hugh le Despenser, who was briefly in possession of the de Clare estates until his fall in 1326. The present ruins deeply embedded in woodland show that the castle would have consisted of a great keep-gatehouse with round angle turrets, a separate fortified 27
dwelling tower, admirably provided with garderobes, and an extremely large but lightly fortified bailey. The towers clearly develop

ideas pioneered in the great castle of the de Clares at Caerphilly, of the 1270s and '80s.

At Caldicot Castle, probably in the 1330s or '40s, the de Bohuns built a handsome new residential entrance gatehouse. This is rectangular in plan, with small, square side turrets, and preserves fragments of a good deal of sculptural enrichment. Defensibility was clearly not the main concern, and enough remains of the upper hall and its vaulted stair to show that lavish entertainment mattered more. However, there was already at Caldicot a well-appointed chamber in the SE tower, fitted up in the late C13, and a suite of rooms abutting the curtain wall was added beside the SE tower about the time the gatehouse was built. Of the extensive building work at Caldicot for Thomas Woodstock, Edward III's youngest son, documented as having been carried out in the 1380s, little can be identified; but Woodstock certainly rebuilt a long stretch of the N wall of the bailey, and 1385–9 erected a polygonal residential tower over the postern gate, the so-called
28 Woodstock Tower. This is not only itemized in the surviving accounts but also bears a most unusual 'signature', a stone in the jamb of the postern gate inscribed 'Thomas'.

What remains at Abergavenny Castle of the early C14 hall and lodging block of the Hastings family is much less eloquent. At Grosmont the two mid-C14 residential blocks built by the Earls of Lancaster have been so reduced that only one significant feature survives. But this is something rare and extraordinary, a perfectly
26 preserved and exquisitely elegant chimneystack, an epitome of courtly comfort.

Newport Castle, though now unpropitiously situated in the middle of the modern town and heavily restored, retains its medieval form largely intact. It seems to have been built in the late C14 for the Earl of Stafford, and remodelled in the mid C15 for his descendant, created Duke of Buckingham in 1444. It consists of three polygonal towers set in line on the muddy bank of the River Usk and linked by short stretches of curtain wall. The central tower, larger than the others, stands over a watergate. Behind this river frontage there seems never to have been much else. So this was not primarily a fortified residence but, it has been suggested, the western headquarters of a great estate, where the lord or his receiver might occasionally appear in state and collect rents and dues from his tenants. The mid-C15 alterations created what must have been a grand vaulted central room. The S tower had stacked residential accommodation.

Also of this period is the outer ward of Usk Castle, fortified with mural towers, one of them round, and a curious gatehouse, with an outer entrance archway linked by stairs to the far higher level of the outer ward. But all this, let alone the works of this period at Penhow Castle, and the much-ruined Pencoed Castle, Llanmartin, and Cas Troggy, Newchurch, pales in comparison with the great mid-C15 castle at Raglan.

p. Raglan Castle, which had previously belonged to the Bloet
494 family, was grandiosely rebuilt in two stages some time between 1432, when Sir William ap Thomas bought the manor, and 1469,

when his son Sir William Herbert, Earl of Pembroke, was executed.
According to family tradition, ap Thomas built the great hexagonal
tower, the so-called Yellow Tower of Gwent, probably originally 42
five storeys high and encircled by a moat. The Yellow Tower stood,
an independent strong point outside the bailey enclosure, in the
manner familiar in mid Wales from Bronllys and Tretower, Powys,
but on a far larger scale. However, ap Thomas had fought at the
battle of Agincourt, and French parallels for the Yellow Tower
have also been cited, both for its impressive ashlar masonry and
for its sheer scale. The great tower at Largoët in Britanny is particularly
relevant, as it was provided with a double bascule (i.e.
pivoting) timber bridge very similar to that at the Yellow Tower.
This bridge type was even taken by Sir William Herbert as a family
badge (*see* Usk Church). The tower was provided with gunloops
as well as arrow loops. The South Gate, which provides entrance
into the bailey, now the Fountain Court, immediately to the SW of
the Yellow Tower and its moat, was clearly built at the same time;
however, it is a mere rectangular gabled structure, provided with
drawbridge and portcullis, lacking any aspect of threat.

Sir William ap Thomas's power extended no further than South
Wales, but his son, William Herbert, became both extremely
wealthy by overseas trade and increasingly powerful as the Yorkist
cause prospered, and after the accession of Edward IV he was
granted both a new lordship of Raglan and the English earldom of
Pembroke. His magnificent enlargement of the castle, probably
1461–9, was commensurate with these honours. The work of the
1460s is extremely similar to the first phase in its ashlar masonry,
in its use of hexagonal towers and in details such as the forms of
windows and provision of low-sited gunloops as well as arrow loops.
(Indeed, it has been argued by Anthony Emery that the entire castle
shows such ambition and such consistency that it must all be
William Herbert's work.) But in concept the virtually new castle of
the 1460s, for such it was, comprehensively subverted its predecessor.
A new, much more powerful, twin-towered gatehouse NE 43
of the Yellow Tower gave entry into a new courtyard, the Pitched
Stone Court, with two more mighty hexagonal towers at its outer
angles. A richly decorated, two-storey range of state apartments with
lofty bay windows was wrapped round behind the Yellow Tower, 46
dependent on its protection but extending as far as the South Gate.
The bascule bridge to the tower was replaced by an elaborate
masonry one. The SW, Fountain, Court was completely reconstructed
with a strongly fortifiable outer wall, but with sumptuously
decorated guest lodgings facing on to the court. Chapel and hall 44,
(the latter rebuilt in the C16) retained their positions, which prob- 45
ably went back to the days of the Bloets, in the range between the
courts. The service ranges lay on two sides of the Pitched Stone
Court, but of these only the Kitchen Tower survives, and it is clear
that the NW range was incomplete at the time of Herbert's death.

The French character of the 1460s castle is marked, and once
again its builder had campaigned in France in his youth. The
machicolation of the gatehouse and towers in particular is so
similar to the duc d'Orléans's early C15 fortifications N of Paris,

such as Pierrefonds and La Ferté Milon, that one wonders whether the masons did not have some French pattern to hand. The grandly broad and architecturally emphasized flight of stairs in the Fountain Court is reminiscent of the French emphasis on prominent and spacious stairs, though the arrangement here, with a straight, not a turning flight giving access to two levels of apartments l. and r., is in principle the same as in the English collegiate layout developed, for example, at New College, Oxford, in the late C14.

Herbert made one other modification to the Yellow Tower, constructing a platform for cannon around its base, thus acknowledging the impracticality of the gunloops. This hints at one reason why Raglan Castle stands at the end of a tradition. The development of cannon rendered the high-towered castle obsolete for defensive purposes. This adds irony to the tragedy of Raglan's destruction during the Civil War in 1645, a victim of bombardment by the very cannon for which it had made such early provision. But Raglan was for another reason the last great fortified castle to be built, not just in Gwent but in the whole of Wales. The power of the Marcher lords was on the wane, particularly after the establishment of the Tudor dynasty in 1485. The Act of Union of 1536, which replaced the lordships with shires under civil administration, was merely the end of a process. From the early C16 the gatehouse and the porch survived as symbols of gentility, but the fortifiable tower was seen no more.

Unfortified Medieval Houses

The pillage and destruction wrought by Owain Glyndŵr's rebellion 1402–5 must have destroyed much more than the castles mentioned by Adam of Usk, the contemporary local chronicler. The C13 chapel at Crick Manor, Caerwent, is a rare manorial survivor, as are the tower absorbed into Kemeys Manor, Kemeys Inferior, apparently of the C13, and that at Itton Court of the C14. Reconstruction of the countryside may have taken several decades to get under way. The early C15 N block at the bishop of Llandaff's palace at Mathern, of *c.* 1419, is exceptional. Otherwise what remains of unfortified houses of the late Middle Ages must belong to the late C15 and early C16. Most of Mathern Palace as it now stands, an inner gatehouse range and chapel, is attributed to Miles Salley, bishop 1500–16. It is undistinguished work. The remains of an early C16 priest's house are at Magor. The only manorial open hall is at Great Cil-lwch, Llantilio Crossenny. It retains an arch-brace and collar-beam roof, and the screens passage arrangement, but no original fenestration.

In towns there are a few tantalizing survivals. At Chepstow, St Anne's, a stone's throw from the castle, is a substantial stone gabled range which retains a two-light upper window, and higher up the hill, in Bank Street, there is part of a two-bay rib-vaulted undercroft. At Abergavenny there is a single enriched post from the timber-framed jettied front of a town house. This was modernized in the late C16 for the Vaughan family of Tretower, Powys, when oriel windows were added. The Murenger's House, Newport, also with oriel windows, is entirely of the later date, and a similar house, much altered, at Agincourt Square, Monmouth, is dated 1624. There is also the timber-framed front in New Market Street, Usk. These are a reminder that urban building in timber was normal during the Middle Ages and up to the early C17.

The most eloquent late medieval houses, however, are to be found in the rural N of the county, and are now no more than substantial farmhouses. Most complete is Llwyncelyn, Cwmyoy, which 55 had an open hall and at the upper end, in a cross wing, a parlour p. also open to the roof. Enrichment includes an aisle-truss, a North 210 Wales feature, and moulded arch-braced roofs with wind-braces. Blaengavenny, Llantilio Pertholey, retains its hall with arch-braced roof, more plainly treated, and evidence that it had stone-mullioned windows. The late medieval house of this scale with the most telling stone details is Old Court, Llangattock Lingoed, where there are a transomed two-light hall window, a shorter two-light upper window and two doorways. Elsewhere evidence is more fragmentary: a parlour wing at The Innage, Mathern, and groups of pointed stone doorways in otherwise unintelligible houses, Cwrt Henllys, Henllys, and Llanddewi Court, Llanddewi Skirrid.

Monastic Foundations

The Norman Marcher lords who built castles, William fitz Osbern at Chepstow and Monmouth, Hamelin de Ballon at Abergavenny, in the late C11 or early C12 founded Benedictine priories alongside, as dependencies of great abbeys in their native France. At Usk a Benedictine nunnery was founded soon after 1174 by Richard 'Strongbow' de Clare. The only Benedictine foundation not associated with a Marcher stronghold was Goldcliff, founded in 1113 on the shore of the Severn Estuary. Llanthony Priory was 1 another early C12 foundation, but the site in the Vale of Ewyas was chosen for its wild solitude for a community of Augustinian canons. The Cistercians, who founded three houses in Gwent, chose less lonely spots. Tintern on the River Wye, colonized from L'Aumône in 1131, was the earliest Cistercian foundation in Wales, and remained favoured and wealthy throughout the Middle Ages. The other two were considerably later, Llantarnam founded in the late 1170s, Grace Dieu as late as 1217 and never, it seems, properly established. The boroughs which grew up beside the Marcher castles ensured the partial survival of the priory churches at Abergavenny, Chepstow and Usk, when their parochial use was continued after the Dissolution. Otherwise, the churches at Tintern and Llanthony remain as eloquent ruins, together with something of their claustral buildings. Other, later, urban foundations were an Augustinian friary at Newport, 1377, of which nothing survives, and a hospital at Usk, of which there is a late medieval fragment.

Medieval Churches

Another of the innovations introduced by the Normans was the stone-built parish church. The late C11 therefore marks an epoch in ecclesiastical building, and its development in Gwent over the ensuing four centuries can be considered as a whole.

NORMAN. The major C12 churches were those of the monastic foundations. Chepstow priory church, begun by William fitz Osbern before his death in 1071, must have been a grand work of early Norman architecture. The base of one complex pier indicates that there was an impressive crossing tower. Five of the six bays of the nave survive, a full three-storeyed composition originally vaulted, though most of the articulating detail has been shorn off. What
8 remains of the W front, however, is richly decorated with shafted openings and zigzag, and must be early C12. At Monmouth enough remains only to show that the C12 nave had arcades with cylindrical piers. At Usk the crossing tower survives on stout shafted piers with scallop caps, surprisingly austere for a late Norman work.

The finest surviving C12 work, however, is at what was then a
p. 426 parish church, St Woolos, Newport. Here the five-bay nave, which seems to be a work of the 1140s, has cylindrical piers with scallop caps, but unmoulded arches and clerestory windows immediately above their heads. The W doorway, by contrast, is an exotic piece,
9, 10 the shafts perhaps reused Roman material, the capitals carved with crude leaves and figures, the arch lavishly enriched with zigzag and billet. Since the doorway was clearly never external, the narthex-like W chapel must already have been there in some form by the mid C12. A comparison with the similar feature at Llantwit Major, Glamorgan, an important Celtic site, may suggest that the strange plan of St Woolos reflected the presence of a Celtic church here too.

Other parish churches which may have been aisled in the C12 are Caerleon, largely rebuilt in the C19, and Christchurch, where the S aisle doorway has a fine display of zigzag decoration. Other ambitious building in the Norman period is indicated by towers at Caldicot, Magor and Redwick. These all stand centrally, between chancel and probably originally aisleless nave. At Penhow the little S tower may be Norman in origin. Most C12 churches, however, were mere single cells or consisted of chancel and aisleless nave. The abandoned church at Runston, St Pierre, is a remarkably unaltered example. Portskewett is also fairly complete. About twenty small parish churches still retain a C12 window or doorway, all quite plain except the shafted and roll-moulded doorway at Whitson. The most richly decorated small Norman buildings, however, are (or were) non-parochial chapels: St Thomas Overmonnow, Monmouth, heavily restored but still impressive, and
p. 376 the totally reconstructed Malpas, a cell of Montacute Abbey. The chancel arch was the focal feature of both, with outward-pointing zigzag at Overmonnow, with triple shafting at Malpas.

The characteristic C12 church fitting, here as throughout England and Wales, is the FONT. A number survive in churches which show no Norman fabric. The grandest type is the square bowl on colonnettes. At St Woolos, Newport, a fine carved fragment, with Herefordshire school carving, is incorporated into the C19 font. Standard examples are at Usk and Whitson, and others, perhaps of the early C13, are at Redwick and Undy. A local speciality is a cup-shaped bowl decorated with concentric semicircles on a roll moulding. Examples are at Abergavenny, Bettws Newydd, Goetre and Llansantffraed, presumably all made in the same workshop.

TRANSITIONAL AND EARLY ENGLISH. The move towards a
Gothic style is well seen in the church at Llanthony Priory, which 11
was probably constructed within the period *c.* 1189–1217. It con- pp.
sists of an aisleless presbytery, transepts with paired E chapels (later 340–1
altered), a crossing tower and aisled nave. Pointed arch-forms predominate, but round-headed openings occurred in the eastern half. The handling of the nave elevation, with linked triforium and clerestory, shows influence from Wells, but the arcade merely has continuous chamfers, handsome but simple. Throughout there are triple wall-shafts, with scallop caps of Norman character, but embryonic leaf caps occur in the crossing area over the canons'
choir. Display was reserved for the twin-towered W front, where 13
there is much shafting. The claustral buildings, though fragmentary, were clearly built well into the C13. The evidence of clustered shafts at the entry to the chapter house shows that, and the fully developed stiff-leaf capitals in the slype.

One parish church is Transitional in style. This is Marshfield,
which retains a chancel arch and S doorway with stiff-leaf capitals 14
very similar to those provided in the early C13 at Llandaff Cathedral, *c.* 6 m. (10 kilometres) away, but also has undercut zigzag on the doorway.

At Tintern Abbey rebuilding of the C12 monastic buildings on a larger scale started early in the C13, boosted by a generous land grant by the younger William Marshal, lord of Chepstow, in 1223–4. The C13 works are sadly ruined, but enough remains to indicate the splendid nature of the rebuilding. The once rich arcading of the cloister walk has all gone. The refectory, in accordance with Cistercian practice, was the grandest room. Enough remains to show that the entrance to it from the cloister was through a many-shafted doorway flanked by shafted recesses for basins. The refectory itself had richly decorated upper walls. Paired
plate-traceried windows survive in the E wall; but they formed 12
only an outer skin, for it is clear that there was also an inner veil of bar-traceried openings corresponding to the windows. All this must belong to the mid C13. Of the monks' day room the walls survive and evidence for a vault on a central row of octagonal piers, while the vault of the warming house is half intact, over traces of a remarkable four-way fireplace. These rooms, naturally, were relatively plain. The rectangular chapter house must have been another impressive room, of which too little is left. Of the C13 infirmary and abbot's lodging, both on an imposing scale, the remains are too scanty to convey their architectural character. On the other hand, the outer gatehouse chapel (St Anne's) retains high quality detail of the mid C13.

Before discussing Tintern Abbey further, some E.E. parish churches should be mentioned. At Caerwent, Grosmont and Mathern are impressive chancels with compositions of lancets. Grosmont's was largely reconstructed by *J. P. Seddon* in 1869–70,
but he did not touch the fine double piscina there with miniaturized 15

Geometrical tracery and dogtooth enrichment. The much-altered
chancels at Christchurch and Michaelston-y-fedw must once have
been similar. As for aisled naves, the parish churches of the Three
16 Castles have the most impressive: five-bay at Grosmont with
cylindrical piers, four-bay at Skenfrith of similar design, and four-
bay at Llantilio Crossenny with octagonal piers. Grosmont and
Llantilio are cruciform churches with crossing towers. At Grosmont
the crossing piers and arches look early C13 (much restored), but
the octagonal bell-stage and tower must belong to the early C14.
The only other E.E. aisled nave is at Mathern, with complex piers
of lozenge plan with attached shafts. At Usk priory church a N
aisle was added in the C13 for parochial use. Its fine four-bay
arcade survives, with cylindrical piers, the E one embellished with
slender cylindrical shafts. Of W towers datable to the C13 only
two impress in scale, the massive but extremely plain tower at
Christchurch, and the tower at Skenfrith, with triple-chamfered
tower arch and later upper stages.

GEOMETRICAL AND DECORATED. The rebuilding of the
pp. church at Tintern Abbey from 1269 marks an epoch, both because
540–1 of the grand scale of the work and because of its remarkable survival.
It was constructed over a little more than thirty years to a design
which remained structurally consistent but accommodated decorative developments, particularly in the forms of the window tracery.
In plan a simple Latin cross, the church has an aisled presbytery,
transepts with eastern aisles and an aisled nave. There are no towers.
In elevation a happy balance is kept between strength and height.
19 The piers are of the clustered form with round shafts in the four
cardinal directions, and lesser shafts of Purbeck marble, now lost,
on the diagonals. Bases and caps are moulded, and there are rich
filleted mouldings on the arcade arches. The triforium is plain, the
clerestory has simple two-light windows with hexfoils at their
heads. Foliage carving was used very sparingly, on the little cor-
18 bels which support the wall-shafts for the vaulting, and on the
vault bosses, some of which survive loose. They show both stiff-leaf
and naturalistic foliage, as one would expect in the last decades of
the C13. The size of the four axial windows and their tracery patterns
20 must always have been arresting. Today only the seven-light W
window survives intact, but the design of the eight-light E window
p. has been reconstructed on paper. It is clear that this was a pure
546 Geometrical design, of which the E window of the Angel Choir at
Lincoln Cathedral of *c.* 1260 is the classic version, while the W
window combines cusped intersecting tracery with encircled groups
of trefoils in a way that is clearly moving towards Dec complexity
and invention. It is closely paralleled by windows in the West
Country (e.g. Exeter Cathedral choir) and in London (St Etheldreda,
Holborn, *c.* 1284). The W doorway composition, immediately
below, must have been exquisite, with delicate filleted mouldings,
diaper background and central figure sculpture. Two other features
surviving in the cloister represent the incipient Dec style, the doorway to the bookroom in the E walk, which has continuous mould-
21 ings instead of shafts, and the multicusped processional doorway
in the S walk, here as elsewhere a feature on which special effort

was lavished. It is sad that the large, undercut, dogtooth-derived square flowers which form a continuous frame to the doorway have all been mutilated.

Work on the embellishment of the church seems to have gone on well into the C14. Many fragments of a sumptuous pulpitum survive, and a recent paper reconstruction of its complete design makes clear that it must have dated to *c.* 1320. During the C14 major works were put in hand remodelling the infirmary and providing the abbot with greatly expanded lodgings, but barely more than footings survive.

At other monastic sites work was going on at this period. At Llanthony part survives of a handsome gatehouse to the outer court, at Llantarnam a splendid eleven-bay barn, and at Abergavenny part of the dormitory range on the S side of the church.

New-built Dec churches are rare. That at Trellech, rebuilt in its 17
entirety after 1296, is the largest and most impressive. It has nave arcades typical of the C13, with cylindrical piers. The window tracery is mostly very simple, but perhaps based on some of the minor windows at Tintern Abbey. The grand W tower, though clasped by a continuation of the lean-to aisles, has a tall and wide arch to the nave, moulded with no fewer than six waves. The reticulated W window is on a scale to match, and there is a crowning stone spire. The steeple of the former priory church at Monmouth is similar, also with a large reticulated W window, and a stone spire, rebuilt in the C18. The crossing tower and spire at Grosmont have already been mentioned. As for reticulated tracery, a particularly memorable pattern, in which the reticulation is allowed to create a wavy head to the window opening, is found at three Severnside churches, Redwick, Caldicot and Rogiet. Influence from Wells and Bristol can be assumed. At Llanwenarth the reticulated E window is conventional. At Redwick much of the body of the church is of the early C14, with octagonal nave arcade piers. At Skenfrith the N aisle was handsomely widened. But there are only two further complete Dec churches to mention, both quite small. At Llanfihangel Rogiet the church was probably built when the two fine early C14 monuments were set up. The chancel arch is set on what were once handsome head corbels. At Mitchel Troy there are nave arcades with mouldings continuous through piers and arches, and an eccentric, slope-topped aisle E window. Mention of Dec sculpture in churches must include the green
men at Llantilio Crossenny and Llangwm Uchaf. 35,

PERPENDICULAR. During the C15 and early C16 much enlarg- 36
ing and improvement of churches went on. Especially fine is the group of churches on the Severnside Levels which shows strong influence from Somerset. Two imposing, almost identical towers,
probably early C15, are at Peterstone and St Brides Wentlooge. 29
They have diagonal buttresses with many set-offs and at the top
panelled battlements, pinnacles and sculptured figures. At Peterstone 30
the aisled nave is clearly contemporary and of equal ambition. At St Brides, however, the body of the church is later, with somewhat debased Perp forms. The other noble Perp tower in this area is at Nash, carrying a contemporary stone spire.

At Magor the nave was rebuilt with aisles extended E-wards to clasp the central tower. It has arcades of Somerset type, with four shafts and four hollows, and capitals carved with angels. Magor was also given a tall, enriched N porch. Porches of similar character, wholly or in part constructed out of imported Somerset limestone ashlar, are at Caldicot, Redwick, Caerwent, and, not quite so ambitious, at Peterstone. Though tall, these porches are not two-storeyed, but had internal stairs giving access, apparently, for
31 dressing high-level images. At Usk the two exquisite vaulted porches added to the parochial aisle of the priory church bear the badge of Sir William Herbert of Raglan. A much more modest vaulted porch is at Tintern Parva. Other significant Perp works are the
32 outer aisle walls and porch at Mathern, a handsome design, and the impressive W tower there, with diagonal buttresses, added by Bishop Marshall of Llandaff (1478–96). Other tall towers with diagonal buttresses are at Raglan, perhaps datable to the 1460s, and St Woolos, Newport, probably built under the patronage of Jasper Tudor, and so of *c.* 1485–95. Another, less tall, is part of the complete Perp rebuilding of the little church at Llanwern.

To complete a survey of towers it is necessary to mention a number that were probably built well on in the C16. These form a group, plain, strongly built, unbuttressed but constructed of large squared blocks of coarse local sandstone. That at Cwmcarvan is datable *c.* 1525. Others are at Itton, Llanarth, Llandenny, Llanfrechfa, Llanover, Llantarnam and Trevethin. In the far NW is a group of towers with timber-framed top stages, a type familiar across the border in Herefordshire: Llangua, Rockfield, St Maughans, and, the only large-scale one, Skenfrith. All but the last have been drastically reconstructed.

LATE MEDIEVAL MONASTIC BUILDING. In the century before the Dissolution there continued to be activity at the monastic houses. At Monmouth the prior's lodging was rebuilt. One range survives, with an oriel window on strongly characterized head corbels. At Llanthony, Court Farm, SW of the church, may have begun life as the prior's lodging. There are traces inside of a richly moulded timber ceiling. A rear wing has small heated rooms at three levels. This unusual arrangement is similar to what survives at the enigmatic late medieval house at Caldicot which goes under the name of Llanthony Secunda, and may have belonged to a grange of the priory. At Usk there is a very simple precinct gateway, and part of a
48 remarkable carved timber frieze from the priory itself, now mostly at Cefntilla, Llandenny. It is datable to the time of the last prioress in the early 1530s and incorporates Renaissance forms in its foliage trails.

Several important fittings survive in ex-monastic churches. At Usk is a Perp screen with a cove of Devon type. At Abergavenny both sets of choir stalls are intact, though their canopies are only partly so. One set is datable 1493/1516. Also at Abergavenny, and utterly
33 unforgettable, is the over-life-size timber figure of a reclining Jesse from what must have been a truly monumental Jesse tree.

LATE MEDIEVAL CHURCH FITTINGS AND MONUMENTS. The most commonly surviving late medieval fitting is the FONT. Normally the font bowl is octagonal or hexagonal, on a stem of the same plan and a splayed foot. Only a few fonts are further enriched. The most splendid, though worn, is at Chepstow, with little flying buttresses round the stem. At Tregare the bowl, now a replica, was decorated with hearts enclosing IHS. Otherwise the decoration is standardized – quatrefoils, shields and panelling – as at Portskewett, Bryngwyn and Llanarth. The only medieval font cover, flat with blind tracery, is at Llanfair Kilgeddin.

The late medieval fitting which caused most disturbance to the fabric of churches was the ROOD LOFT on its SCREEN. Most churches retain doorways and stairs inserted to give access to the lofts, and windows inserted to light them. At Llangwm Uchaf the N tower seems to have been built in relation to the rood. Of timber screens there is little to see. Apart from the one at Usk, they include Gwernesney (rearranged), Llanfair Kilgeddin (probably brought in), Skenfrith and Rockfield (fragments). But two complete rood lofts on their screens still survive *in situ*. The most complete and authentic, unrivalled indeed in England and Wales for its completeness, is at Bettws Newydd. The decorative loft front here is of 37
a fairly simple design. The screen and much more elaborate loft at Llangwm Uchaf, its front enriched with band upon band of stylized foliage, was substantially reconstructed and enriched with polychromy by *J. P. Seddon* 1876–8, with Patrishow, Powys, as his model. At Mamhilad there is a loft of the simpler type, re-erected as a W gallery, at Llangattock Lingoed a richly carved bressumer. At Kemeys Commander the screen and rood beam remain, and were clearly constructed together with the fabric of the little church. There is similar, less extensive, evidence at Trostre. The skeleton of the loft survives at Llangeview, and fragments at Redwick. There are decorated floor tiles at Tintern Abbey, C13, Llangattock-juxta-Usk, dated 1456, and at Monmouth, dated 1465; two beautiful C15 alabaster panels of Midlands manufacture survive at Llansantffraed; at Bedwellty there is a timber cupboard or cope chest, and at Skenfrith, a cope.

Late medieval WALL PAINTINGS survive only at Llangibby, where there are two fragmentary schemes with large-scale figures. Otherwise there is only the enrichment in strong reds and blues of the mouldings of the N arcade at St Brides Wentlooge. STAINED GLASS in churches is even more scrappy. The most numerous fragments are at Mathern, where they fill a whole window, and at Skenfrith. The only coherent panel is in a house, the St George at Great Cil-lwch, Llantilio Crossenny. The most important glass is German, inserted into the late C18 R.C. chapel at Llanarth and identified as early C16 work of the Cologne school.

To turn to medieval MONUMENTS is to find much more. The great series of tombs at the former priory church at Abergavenny, commemorating members of the Hastings and Herbert families, makes it one of the places of pilgrimage for students of medieval sculpture, especially since their conservation 1994–8. Here are effigies of the finest quality in timber, limestone and alabaster, 38–
spanning from the mid C13 to the early C16. Most of the tombs 41
are free-standing, but two are wall monuments with architectural backplates. Several tomb-chests retain some of the weeper figures,

and there are two alabaster panels of religious subjects, such as rarely escaped the zeal of post-Reformation iconoclasts.

Elsewhere, carved tomb slabs of the C13 can be seen at St Pierre and Pen-y-clawdd, where there is a relief of a priest under a foliate cross. The slabs at Llangattock-juxta-Usk and Llanvetherine (another priest) are probably a little later. At Christchurch is an incised slab showing a civilian and wife (†1376). Effigies in the round are miserably mutilated. Most interesting are those at Llanfihangel Rogiet, probably contemporary with the early C14 church. The three at St Woolos, Newport, are hardly more than torsos. The damaged figure of a priest at Caldicot is oddly embedded in the porch. The effigy of a civilian at Usk has been relegated to the churchyard. At Llanmartin the wall monument with a panel of lively children seems to be a composite, partly *c.* 1510, partly *c.* 1541. Of greatest technical interest is the early C14 effigy of a knight at Grosmont which has been abandoned unfinished – a very rare survival.

Before leaving medieval churches, what remains in CHURCHYARDS must be mentioned. Almost all have something left of the late medieval churchyard cross. Most of these are of a standard design (Raglan is an exception). Best-preserved and something
34 quite out of the normal run is the cross at Mitchel Troy, which has shields and ballflower up its shaft, and so must date from the C14. No cross retains its carved head *in situ*, though heads with carved scenes of the Crucifixion or Virgin and Child are at Llanarth Court (reset on a modern cross) and Caerwent (loose in the church).

Three simple LYCHGATES, presumably late medieval, survive, just a roof on stone side walls, at Llandenny (restored), Mitchel Troy and Penallt.

FROM THE SIXTEENTH CENTURY TO *c.* 1830

Historically, the 1530s mark a watershed. The Reformation, followed by Henry VIII's break with the papacy and establishment of himself as head of the Anglican Church, was immediately followed by the Dissolution of the Monasteries between 1536 and 1540. Church-building was thereby largely halted, and vast amounts of monastic property came into the hands of secular landowners, leading to the widespread destruction or conversion of abbeys and priories. Also in 1536 the Act of Union, supplemented by a second Act in 1543, abolished the numerous small Marcher lordships and recast the local government of Wales along English lines in thirteen shires. It was at this point that power began to pass from the great aristocratic families of Herbert and Somerset to the gentry, who were now serving as sheriffs and justices of the peace.

Gentry Houses c. *1500 – 1750*

Surviving C16 GENTRY HOUSES are hard to date and in many cases extremely fragmentary. Some medieval features remained in

use, such as the imposing gatehouse, a status symbol now rather
than a serious piece of fortification. The open hall, however, was
abandoned, except at the highest social level, and houses became
multi-storeyed throughout. The most impressive early to mid-C16
structures are the GATEHOUSES at St Pierre and Pencoed Castle, 47
Llanmartin. Both are three-storeyed, with full-height projecting
turrets at their forward angles, moulded entrance arches and
simple rubble vaults. Two-storeyed RESIDENTIAL RANGES with
mullioned windows of four or five arched lights under hoodmoulds are at Tredegar House and Pentrebach, Llantarnam,
both, like Pencoed Castle, built for branches of the widespread
Morgan family. Similar ranges which seem to have originated in
the late 1550s are at Llanvihangel Court, Llanfihangel Crucorney,
and Roger Williams's town mansion at Usk. Kemeys Manor,
Kemeys Inferior, notable for its finely laid rubble-stone walling,
is the most complete example of this type. Another finely constructed, though much-altered, house, probably of the mid C16, is
Llanwenarth House, Govilon. Its great height, three full storeys
with a full-height porch, marks it out as exceptional. Comparison
can, however, be made with a nearby house in Glamorgan,
Llancaeach-fawr, Gelligaer.

Later in the century, branches of the Morgan family built
MANSIONS on a larger scale but still without any sense of architectural coherence: at Pencoed Castle, Llanmartin, a three-storey
range faced with sandstone ashlar, at Llantarnam Abbey, said to
have carried the date 1588, but sweepingly reconstructed in the
1830s (*see* below, p. 65), and Plas Machen, Lower Machen, p.
reduced in size in the C19. By far the most important work of this 372
period was at Raglan Castle, where the third Earl of Worcester 49
reconstructed the hall and service ranges and formed a magnificent new suite of state rooms in two upper storeys. The hall was
entirely late medieval in character, as its polygonal multi-light dais
window most eloquently proclaims. Yet the carved achievement of
arms set in the dais-end wall is datable after 1570, and the chimneypiece in the long gallery after 1572. Work was still going on in 50
the years immediately before the Earl's death in 1589. In the state
apartments, in particular the long gallery, the chimneypiece and
bench consoles in a classical idiom are of Bath stone, and were
probably imported ready-made from Bristol. A magnificent timber
chimneypiece and overmantel now at Badminton, Gloucestershire,
and an overmantel at Troy House, Mitchel Troy, probably came
from Raglan. Terraces and an elaborate water garden, of which
the outlines survive, were also created beyond the castle walls to
the N. The recasting of the moat surrounding the Great Tower to
form a sunken promenade, with shell-lined niches for statues of
Roman emperors, may belong to the fourth Earl's time. In these
ways defensibility gave way to recreation. The fifth Earl (first
Marquess), who succeeded in 1628, built a 'little town' of service
buildings to the NE. The red brick Castle Farm is what survives
of these.

New ideas about GENTRY HOUSE DESIGN IN THE EARLY C17 not only affected decoration, but led to a radical regularization of

51 the plan and the composition of elevations. Moynes Court, Mathern,
1608–10, a lodge built by the bishop of Llandaff $\frac{1}{4}$m. (0.4 kilometre) away from his episcopal palace, has a compact, double-pile
plan, and a completely symmetrical front, deftly uniting five bays
under three gables with a central porch, and even the chimneystacks grouped symmetrically. The house is devoid of decoration,
53 but does not need it, so satisfyingly is it composed. Treowen,
Wonastow, built shortly before 1627, is larger, taller and designed
on the same principles, though its external effect has been seriously
compromised by the removal of half its top storey. Here the two-
storey porch is decorated with crudely proportioned pilasters and
p. strapwork. The original room layout largely survives, typical of its
603 time in not taking the external symmetry into the interior. A
remarkably large proportion of the ground storey was devoted to
54 service uses, and a grandly spacious open-well stair leads to the
great chamber over the hall. Tantalizing fragments are all that
remain of what must have been a rich array of joinery chimneypieces and ceiling plasterwork. The best piece is the hall screen,
52 dated 1627. Third and largest of this group is Llanvihangel Court,
p. Llanfihangel Crucorney. This, as has been noted above, incorpo-
290 rates a mid-C16 range, but its enlargement in the early C17 created
a virtually new house. Here the entrance front has the hall recessed
between twin-gabled projections. Symmetry was taken so seriously
that the off-centre hall doorway was placed in the side wall of the
r. projection, to make it invisible in the frontal view – a widespread device in the first decade of the C17, found for example at
Chastleton, Oxfordshire, and Burton Agnes in the East Riding of
Yorkshire. Here, too, carefully considered external composition
was thought to make decorative enrichment unnecessary, but
inside no fewer than five rooms have enriched plaster ceilings, in a
variety of thin-ribbed patterns. They seem to be essentially
original but were restored or remade in the late C19.

Plaster ceilings of greater richness and authenticity remain in
62 the fragment of Troy House, Mitchel Troy, built for Sir Charles
Somerset, son of the fourth Earl of Worcester, probably *c.* 1611 –
the date on the enriched stone gateway into the walled garden
there. Two more, datable after 1603, are in Roger Williams's house
at Usk. At Cefntilla, Llandenny, 1616, the hall overmantel is of
plaster, displaying an achievement of arms flanked by crudely
executed soldiers. Simple decorative plasterwork survives in an
upstairs room at the Murenger's House, Newport, and also at
Gunter Mansion, Abergavenny, where there are vine scrolls and
cherub heads. It is tempting to relate the latter to the fact that a
Catholic chapel is known to have been fitted up in the house during the C17. Joinery comparable to what remains at Treowen can
be found in surprising abundance at Great House, Penpergwm,
Llangattock-juxta-Usk, and in one room at Trostrey Court, Trostre,
where there is also a contemporary staircase. Other much-altered
gentry houses of this period are Penllwyn, a secondary house of
the Morgans at Pontllanfraith, Lower Dyffryn at Grosmont,
where the bones of a contemporary walled garden also survive,
Great Pool Hall, Llanvetherine, a partly timber-framed house dated

1619, and the large red brick addition to Pentrebach, Llantarnam, perhaps built by Edward Morgan before 1606, but which subsequently suffered the indignity of conversion into a barn.

The destruction of Raglan Castle after the siege of 1646 and the subsequent transfer by the Somerset family of their principal seat to Badminton in Gloucestershire had less effect on the power structure of the leading families in Monmouthshire than might have been expected. In particular, it was still the Somersets, raised to the dukedom of Beaufort in 1682, and the senior branch of the Morgans who led the way in great house-building.

These RESTORATION HOUSES embrace a new, classical image, symmetrical, of course, but essentially rectangular in plan, even on the largest scale, with casement windows of upright proportions and a crowning hipped roof. The type had been developed in and around London from *c.* 1630, and was employed by Inigo Jones. By the 1650s it was moving out into the provinces, but
William Morgan's reconstruction of Tredegar House in this image 65
from the mid to late 1660s shows him well abreast of fashion. Yet, if Sir Howard Colvin's persuasive stylistic arguments are correct, he called in to design it the provincial carpenter-architects *Roger* and *William Hurlbutt* of Warwick. Morgan's ambition, half-achieved, was to rebuild his early C16 house range by range, so that it retained
its courtyard plan. The two executed ranges are treated with pro- p.
jecting angle pavilions, a rare feature concurrently employed by the 565
Hurlbutts at their major new house, Ragley Hall, Warwickshire. But the extraordinary array of stone dressings and carved decoration which enriches the exterior of the red brick house must reflect William Morgan's taste. The twisted, foliage-clad columns which
carry the pediment of the principal doorway are the most exuberant 67
feature.

The Somersets, after their removal to Gloucestershire, retained vast landed estates in South Wales and continued to exercise political power. At Monmouth in 1673 the first Duke of Beaufort, as he was soon to become, built on the site of the castle keep Great Castle
House, a compact, upstanding house under a steep hipped roof. 70
The broad end bays slightly project, and the mullion-and-transom windows do not all achieve classical proportions. Furthermore, the doorway and window above are framed by thin pilasters carrying a stilted semicircular pediment and bulgy urns; so a good deal of early C17 character remains. The enormous three-storey, thirteen-bay
block which the Duke added 1681–4 to Troy House, Mitchel Troy, 71
for the use of his eldest son is very different in feeling, sober but pompous through sheer scale. The central five bays are crowned by a large, plain pediment, reinforcing the classical spirit of the house.

Also at Monmouth are two more, smaller houses of similar character. Drybridge House, with a front of two storeys and five bays under a big hipped roof, bears a datestone of 1671. The builder, William Roberts, held a post in the Office of Works and later was Paymaster during Hugh May's remodelling of Windsor Castle. So here was a direct link with the metropolitan centre of architectural innovation. Unfortunately, fanciful elaboration of the design in the 1860s makes the original character of the house hard to discern. The removal of render from Priory Farm, Monmouth, has recently revealed it as having a red brick front, also of two storeys and five bays, under a pitched rather than hipped roof, and the date 1672 has been reported. There are stone quoins and dressings for the classically proportioned windows. Still in Monmouth, Chapel House and No. 5 Monk Street carry the idiom on into the early C18. Both have flared hipped roofs. Elsewhere in the county there is one more house to add to the group, Trewyn, Bwlch Trewyn, a seven-bay example said to have carried the date 1692.

There is just as much innovation in the treatment of the interiors of these houses. In plan, only Great Castle House, Monmouth, aims at the symmetry of room layout essential to the design ideal derived by Inigo Jones from the great C16 Italian architect and theorist Andrea Palladio. Great Castle House seems to have been an official residence rather than a dwelling house. In others of these houses the placing of the staircase immediately behind the entrance hall on or near the central axis, as at Tredegar House, Troy House, Mitchel Troy, and Chapel House, Monmouth, is all that is achieved.

The INTERNAL DECORATION of these houses continued to give opportunities primarily to the carver, joiner and plasterer, who could provide a handsome timber stair balustrade, moulded wall-panelling and enriched plaster ceilings. But all their forms show a decisive change towards grander scale and more classical mouldings. This is demonstrated with irresistible swagger at Tredegar House, where the interior was probably largely complete by 1680.
66 Carved timberwork, decorative plaster ceilings and inset paintings all play their part. Twisted columns and colonnettes are prominent.

The nearest rival to this spectacular display is at Great Castle House, Monmouth, probably of the same years, the mid to late
64 1670s. Here the plaster ceilings take pride of place, two with thick, deep wreaths, and one virtuoso effort, with dangling swags and serried rows of leaves encrusting the ceiling beams. By contrast, Troy House, Mitchel Troy, 1681–4, retains only one internal feature, the ducally expansive open-well staircase with twisted balusters. Chapel House, Monmouth, has a wreathed plaster ceiling and a staircase with twisted balusters clearly influenced by the Beaufort houses nearby.

Impressive late C17 open-well stairs can be found at Llanvihangel Court, Llanfihangel Crucorney, where too the balusters are twisted, and Great Pool Hall, Llanvetherine. The latter is dated 1665 but may have been brought in. Others on a lesser scale are at Penhow Castle, Langstone Court, Wernddu, Llantilio Pertholey, and Skirrid Mountain Inn, Llanfihangel Crucorney, still with flat, shaped
63 balusters; but most remarkable is the open-well stair at Kemeys Manor, Kemeys Inferior. Here, on the upper landing, three doorways are enframed by rich but naive plasterwork, foliage-clad twisted columns from which emerge demi-angels. Timber stairs of this period on a dog-leg plan are at Court Farm, Llanover, and Artha, Tregare, with flat, shaped balusters, the latter dated 1678.

Artha, Tregare, is the most completely decorated small house of this period, with dates 1676–9. There are a Corinthian overmantel, pedimented door-cases and plaster ceilings enriched with rosettes and cherub heads. At Llwyn-y-gaer, Tregare, also no doubt of the 1670s and perhaps by the same plasterer, are two ceilings, one with five wreaths, and an overmantel with twisted, vine-clad colonnettes. Other farmhouses with a little decoration on a plaster ceiling or two are Old Trecastle Farm, Llangovan, and Winston Court, Llanvetherine; and the White Hart Inn, Llangibby, has some too. At a slightly higher social level, the best survivor is a ceiling at Manor Farmhouse, Portskewett. But there are scraps of what may have been schemes of some ambition at Great Cil-lwch, Llantilio Crossenny, The Argoed, Penallt, and Great Pool Hall, Llanvetherine. Finally, mention should be made of the plaster relief bust of Charles II at the King's Head, Monmouth.

No house of this period was complete without a STABLE. The 68
stables built at Tredegar House *c.* 1684–8, probably to the design of the *Hurlbutts*, are almost as magnificent as the house. Since they face the entrance court they were clearly intended to impress visitors. They even have a central pediment, which is more than the house can boast. Stables which preserve handsome late C17
stalls are the brick-fronted range at Llanvihangel Court, Llanfihangel 61
Crucorney, and the simple stone range at The Argoed, Penallt.

THE EARLY EIGHTEENTH CENTURY. The magnificent
wrought-iron gates by *William* and *Simon Edney* that close the 69
forecourt at Tredegar House were made 1714–18, completing the great project which had been begun fifty years earlier. Otherwise, the early C18 was not a period of much activity in country house building. The major new house at the beginning of the century was the Hanbury family's Pontypool Park, but its character inside and out was thoroughly transformed a century later. One Gibbsian
Baroque overmantel remains. It must be of the late 1720s or '30s. 78
Pontypool Park has the other pair of outstanding wrought-iron gates in the county. These traditionally were a gift to John Hanbury from the Duchess of Marlborough for acting as her husband's executor at his death in 1721. (A routine marble chimneypiece in the house is said to have come from the same source.) The most handsome early C18 frontage is at Itton Court, a conventional seven-bay composition with a central three-bay pediment and a hipped roof. Bath stone quoins and window dressings give it a cachet. The garden front of Cornwall House, Monmouth, said to have been built in 1752, repeats the composition, but has a Diocletian window in the pediment, sparing white dressings and rich red brick walls. Glandŵr, in the street at Grosmont, dated 1742, is a reduced version of the formula without the pediment or the dressings. The only Palladian house in the county, Coldbrook, Abergavenny, of *c.* 1746–53, has been pulled down.

Farmhouses c. *1500 – 1700*

The farmhouses built in south-east Wales *c.* 1500–1700 characteristically exploited timber not stone, stout oak rather than friable sandstone. Farmers who flourished during the century or more of rapidly increasing agricultural prosperity which began in the second quarter of the C16 invested not in large houses, but in substantial ones, and many were attracted by the rich effects produced by moulding massive timbers. Several hundred such houses survive, even though in all cases altered and in many heartlessly modernized. Sir Cyril Fox and Lord Raglan in their three pioneering volumes, *Monmouthshire Houses*, surveyed no fewer than 470 houses, and subsequently nearly a hundred more have been identified, mostly in the western uplands, which they did not investigate in detail. The earliest date on a farmhouse is 1599, so until tree-ring analysis can be applied to some examples of the earlier house types, dating must remain approximate.

The open hall house, it seems, continued to be built through the first half of the C16. Cruck-truss construction was used, with framed side walls, though in what were probably the latest examples, the internal partitions also were framed, so that crucks were used only in the gable-ends. The only completely surviving houses of this type, where the hall is accompanied by a parlour at one end and service rooms at the other, both subsequently floored over
56, at eaves level, are Little Pit Cottage, Llanarth, and The Pant,
57 Llanfihangel-ystern-llewern. Both of these combined framed partitions with cruck-truss end gables. There is evidence that Lower Tal-y-fan, Dingestow, was similar in plan but fully of cruck construction with arch-braces. This was doubtless one of the earliest of these houses, perhaps of the 1480s.

Later alteration of these little houses, in particular the flooring over of the hall, and encasing of the walls in stone, has left them hard to interpret. In particular, it is not clear whether any originally consisted only of hall and service end, without a parlour, since it is impossible to say whether a later parlour is an addition or a replacement. The best-preserved cruck-truss houses on this curtailed plan are Pool Farm, Llangattock-vibon-awel, and the recently identified Chapel Farm, Blaina. Cruck trusses of the largest dimension were used in barns, as can still be seen in the much-mutilated six-bay barn at Upper Tre-rhiw, Llantilio Crossenny, and the five-bay barn at Cwrt-y-brychan, Llansoy. At Lower Llantrothy, Dingestow, enough survives to suggest that the entire farmstead was of cruck construction.

The desire for greater privacy, which led to the horizontal subdivision of the open hall and the concurrent building of new houses two-storeyed throughout, seems to have taken hold in Monmouthshire from the mid C16. However, whereas to the N, in Montgomeryshire and Herefordshire, framed timber construction was further developed, here, after the mid C16, even a partly timber-framed building such as Great Pool Hall, Llanvetherine (1619), is a rarity. The Walks, Penrhos, probably late C16, is unique in having originally been completely timber-framed, with an upper room open to a hammerbeam roof. Timber-framed barns, on the other hand, are not uncommon in the N of the county, as for example the large barn at Llanvihangel Court, Llanfihangel Crucorney, where the framing is now completely exposed. Instead, storeyed farmhouses of every size were built with thick rubble-stone walls, but with internal partitions and window frames and door-frames of timber. Only in the SE of the county do

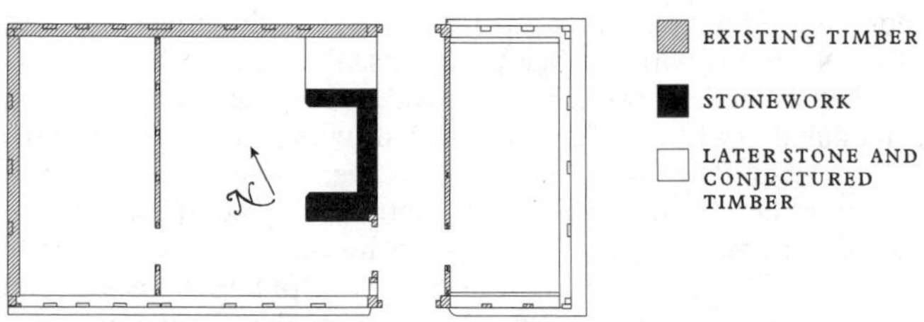

Little Pit Cottage, Llanarth

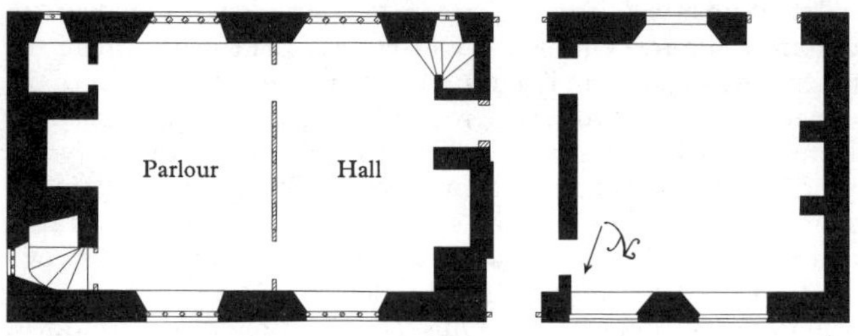

Berllan-deg, Llanhennock

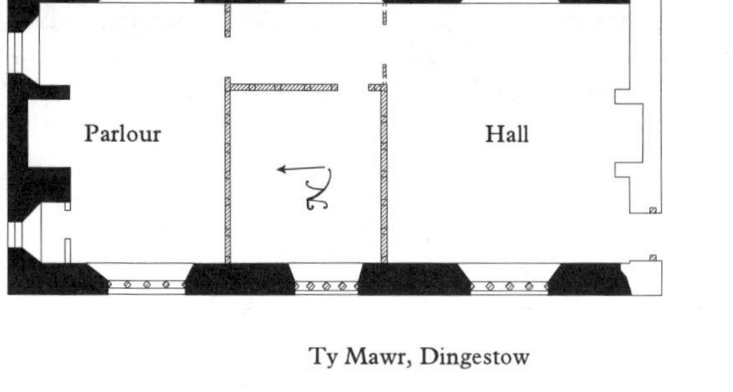

Ty Mawr, Dingestow

Rural house plans, sixteenth and early seventeenth century (after Fox and Raglan)

all-stone storeyed houses occur, below gentry level. Influence from Gloucestershire may be assumed.

The all-stone houses normally have windows with arched lights and may include some of the earliest storeyed farmhouses in the county. At Howick the finely constructed little mid-C16 house of two full storeys has what was soon to become a typical plan for timber-detailed houses. It is of two units. The original entrance was in a gable-end, beside the hall fireplace, with a stair forming the third element in the entrance wall. Beyond the hall lies a narrow unheated room. Upstairs the two rooms are similarly arranged.

For storeyed houses with timber details, a closely similar two-unit plan is found, with timber partitions. An exceptionally richly finished example of two full storeys is Persondy (i.e. the parsonage), p. 379 Mamhilad. Ty Llwyd, Llangwm Uchaf (with heated inner room), was another. Pontesgob Cottage, Ffwthog, exemplifies the plan at the other end of the scale, where there is just one full storey and an inhabited roof space. Many such houses were subsequently extended. The usual way of doing this was to add a passage and third room behind the hearth, thus making the original entrance doorway internal within the passage. Cefn Maen, Raglan, is a good example. It was also, of course, possible to build a house of the full three units with cross-passage in one campaign, though few C16 examples survive. One is the Old House, Llangovan, where the inner downstairs room is a heated parlour with its own stair to the upper storey, and two service rooms lie beyond the cross-passage. Here, unusually, the service end is cross-gabled, like an embryonic wing. Another example is Dan-y-bwlch, Bwlch Trewyn, single-storeyed with attics. Here the service rooms lay at the inner end, and the space beyond the cross-passage was a windowless cow-house. This, then, was a longhouse. Similar, but with a stone cross wall to the cowhouse, is the unusually well preserved Cwmdows, Newbridge. These, especially Old House, represent the type of house which for Fox and Raglan epitomized what they called the 'regional style'. Although entry beside the hall hearth was the norm, entrance doorways in a long wall or in the opposite gable-end were sometimes used. In extending such houses different strategies had to be employed. At Cefn Gwyn, Llanddewi Rhydderch, for example, a two-unit house entered in the gable-end, opposite the hall fireplace, was given a parlour extension in 1637 beyond the entrance doorway, even though that positioned the parlour beyond the cross-passage.

Where original windows survive in these houses they have close-spaced mullions set lozenge-wise and were clearly not intended to be glazed. Windows of this sort, which were obsolete in dwelling houses by the end of the C16, are found in unusually planned examples which probably started out as ambitious late C16 additions to earlier houses, Coldbrook, Llandenny, and Parlour Farm, Dingestow. Only when there was some constraint did builders abandon the principle, presumably inherited from the cruck-truss tradition, that all rooms should lie in line under a continuous roof ridge with ridgetop chimneystacks.

From *c.* 1600 new planning ideas begin to appear, and a new interest in building high. Fox and Raglan single out Allt-y-bela, Llangwm Uchaf (now miserably derelict), as the harbinger of the new ways. Here, to a later C16 house of one storey and a floored roof space (subsequently heightened to two storeys) was added in 1599 a three-storeyed gabled parlour wing with large glazed windows, vertically aligned with one another, and a crown of imposing lozenge-plan chimneystacks. There is a full-height timber newel stair in a turret-like extension. Trevela, Llangwm Uchaf, dated 1601, is a complete house in the same spirit (though much extended in the late C20). It consists of a two-room range of three storeys, with a short wing formed of a full-height porch and newel stair. The two-storey porch, hitherto a gentry feature, is found on a number of ambitious early C17 farmhouses. It may be combined with the stair, as at Cwm Mawr, Llanellen, and Trivor, St Maughans, or it may stand alone, as at Upper Dyffryn and Kingsfield, both at Grosmont, and the Manor House, Llanfihangel Gobion. In these houses the entrance is not into a passage but directly into the hall. At the two

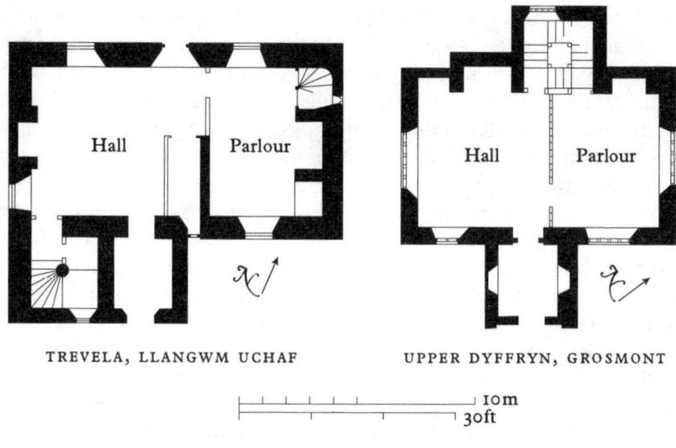

Rural house plans, early seventeenth century (after Fox and Raglan)

Grosmont houses the stairs are set at the back in a square tower 58
flanked by chimney-breasts, for here the fireplaces are set not in the end gables but in the long side of the house. Another house which takes this liberty in siting the hearths is Nant-y-banw, Llantrisant, dated 1625. The plan of Nant-y-banw is an irregular cross, conditioned by the sloping site. A new feature which encouraged such siting is the cider cellar, normal in new houses and additions from *c.* 1600, and more accessible from an external door when the site sloped.

Several DETACHED KITCHENS survive. They seem to be of the later C17 in date, and so perhaps reflect greater specialization in room uses at that time when the convenience of cooking in the hall was losing its appeal. Three widely distributed examples can be mentioned, at Cwm Bwchel, Cwmyoy, Brook Cottage, Caerwent, and Llwynau, Llantrisant.

An effect of height in early C17 houses was also created by a new preference for high-ceilinged rooms. In a few houses this is very marked, as at Ty-mawr, Llanfihangel Pontymoile. But even more towering are added wings, normally providing one room each on two storeys plus an attic, and gabled in three directions. Windows are normally aligned vertically under the gable. Typical examples are at Penyclawdd Farm, Pen-y-clawdd, and Cwm Mawr, Llanellen. At Little Llwygy, Cwmyoy, it was even possible to provide gables in all four directions.

All this experimentation did not mean that the traditional three-unit range with cross-passage behind the hall fireplace was abandoned in the early C17. Llwynau, Llantrisant, perhaps as late as 1652, has this plan in its longhouse form. Berllan-deg, Llanhennock, is a well-preserved example clearly of this period, not least because the hall and parlour units have a higher roof ridge than the passage and service end. An important revision of this plan omitted the cross-passage and placed an unheated storeroom in the central unit. This was done in 1640 at Ty Mawr, Dingestow, and in 1673 at Town Farm, Grosmont. The former has a gable-end entry and a detached kitchen close by, the latter an entry in the centre of the
59 long side. At both, in a significant development, regular four-light windows are disposed symmetrically in both long walls.

By the last quarter of the C17 metropolitan and gentry preferences were beginning to be adopted by Monmouthshire farmers. Symmetry was certainly one of them, but the double-pile plan was another, and the siting of service functions in rooms projecting at the rear perhaps a third. The hipped roof and the enlargement of windows so that they were taller than wide were other signs of what was in effect the breakdown of a local tradition. Of the double-pile plan, High House, Penrhos, dated 1675, provides a precocious example. The Skirrid Mountain Inn, Llanfihangel Crucorney, combines a double pile of only one full storey with an open-well stair and a hipped roof. The hipped roof is found at Artha, Tregare, on the parlour wing dated 1676–9, and also at Upper Red House, Llanfihangel-ystern-llewern, the latter a rare example of a lobby-entry plan. Clydach House, Llanelly, of 1693, built for an ironmaster, has a symmetrical, classically proportioned front, a double-pile plan and central open-well stair. Great Marlborough, Grosmont, must have been a particularly decorative example of the type. Contemporary five-bay, single-pile ranges of similar appearance are at Treworgan, Llandenny, and New House, Llangibby, the latter even attempting a central pedimental feature, as does the smaller Llwyn-y-celyn, Shirenewton, dated 1705.

DECORATIVE TIMBERWORK. From the later C16 many of the builders of even the smallest houses delighted in enriching their timberwork with mouldings. Window and door-frames were chamfered. The sunk chamfer was popular *c.* 1590–1630, as it was in stone in neighbouring Glamorgan, but throughout the middle decades of the C17 the ovolo took its place. Ceiling beams and joists could take a much more elaborate treatment, with repetitive sequences of hollows, steps, quarter-rounds and the occasional wave. In some houses the hall was the most richly decorated room, in others the parlour. In a few, similar treatment extended to the principal chamber upstairs. The timber partitions which were the almost universal room dividers could also have mouldings applied to the angles of their plank-like studs. Uninhibited
60 ensembles can be found at Persondy, Mamhilad, at Coldbrook, Llandenny, at Parlour Farm, Dingestow, and at Llantellen, Skenfrith, to name only a few of the most memorable. The other characteristic decorative feature is the shaped door-head, created by inserting a thin shaped board into the head of the door-frame.

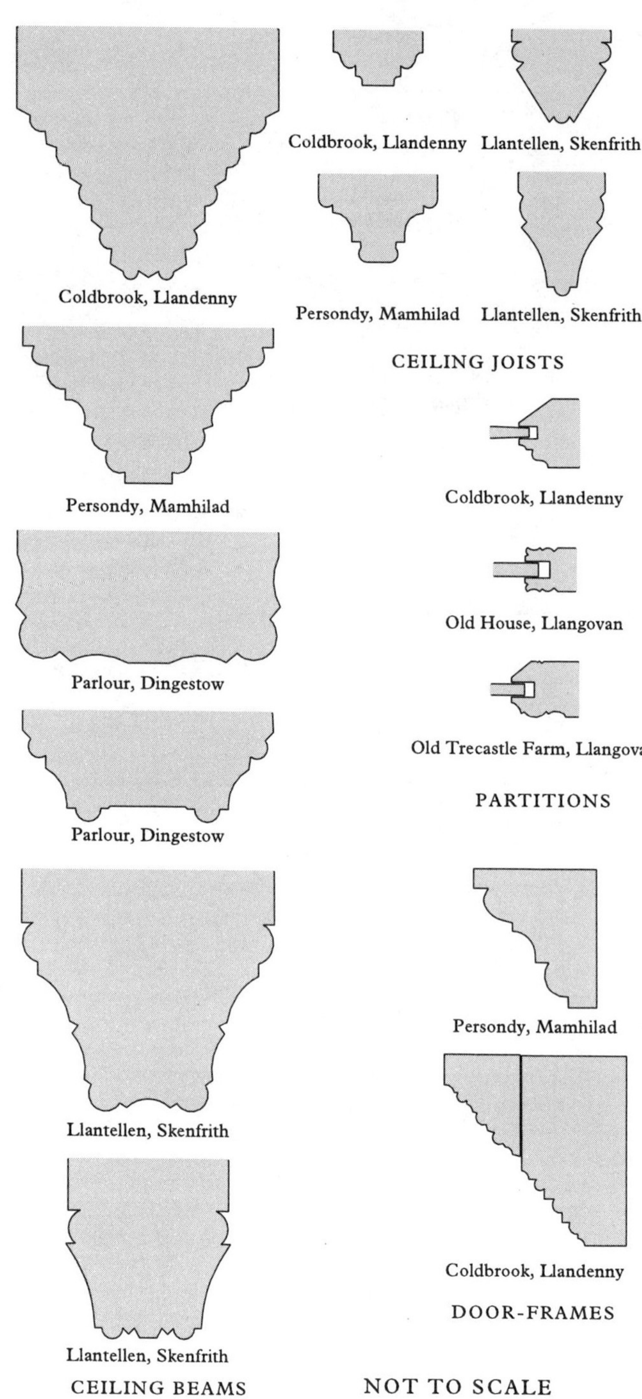

Rural houses: timber mouldings (after Fox and Raglan)

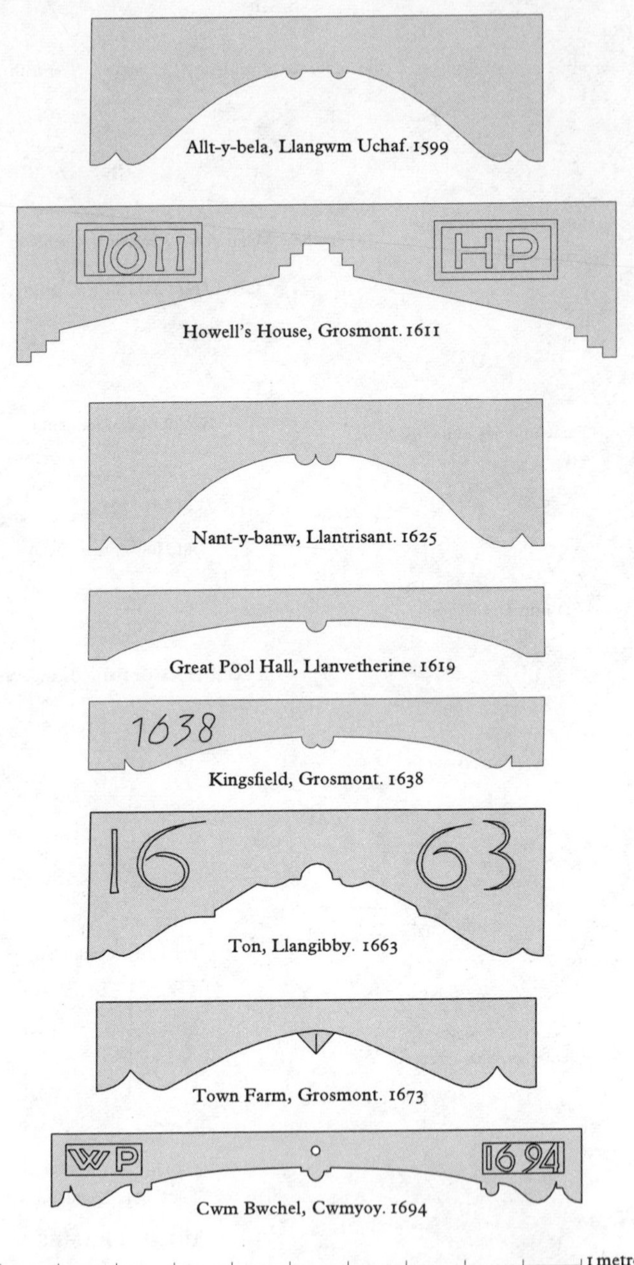

Allt-y-bela, Llangwm Uchaf. 1599

Howell's House, Grosmont. 1611

Nant-y-banw, Llantrisant. 1625

Great Pool Hall, Llanvetherine. 1619

Kingsfield, Grosmont. 1638

Ton, Llangibby. 1663

Town Farm, Grosmont. 1673

Cwm Bwchel, Cwmyoy. 1694

Rural houses: shaped door-heads, dated examples (after Fox and Raglan)

Such door-heads were sometimes used externally, but are normally found inside, in partition doors or doors on staircase landings; the group of four on the upstairs landing at Whitehouse Farm, Clytha, epitomizes their use. The typical shape is a pair of scrolls sweeping up to a pair of central knobs. It is found in the earliest dated example, of 1599 at Allt-y-bela, Llangwm Uchaf. Other, generally fussier, shapes are found. Several bear dates, spanning the entire century up to 1694.

In the 1660s and 1670s a fashion took hold for incised patterns of Jacobean character. Examples are the timber porches at High House, Penrhos (1675), and Llwyn-y-gaer, Tregare, and internal features at Ton, Llangibby (1663), and Artha, Tregare (1678). At Cwm Bwchel, Cwmyoy, an enriched doorway is dated 1694. For plasterwork, *see* above, pp. 30–1.

FARMSTEADS. Occasional examples can be found of two farmhouses grouped in a single farmstead, in what has been termed the 'UNIT SYSTEM'. Upper Hafodarthen, Llanhilleth, is the best-preserved. At Llanddewi Court, Llanddewi Fach, the two houses are now joined into one. At Ty Mawr, Ffwthog, all but the porch of the earlier house has been demolished. Such a grouping implies that the needs of an extended family were being catered for.

Numerous FARM BUILDINGS of the C17 and C18 survive, though they are not systematically mentioned in the Gazetteer. An authoritative survey is required, before too many more are mutilated or destroyed. Particularly well-preserved farmsteads, with more than one early building, are at Llanddewi Court, Llanddewi Fach, and Great Tre-rhiw, Llantilio Crossenny. The largest and finest BARNS, naturally, were built for gentry families with large estates. At Pencoed Castle, Llanmartin, is a great group of three. At Tredegar House the two surviving barns originally formed a single one over 250 ft (76 metres) long. At Kemeys Manor, Kemeys Inferior, the barn is dated 1597. The most beautifully constructed is the noble eight-bay barn at Pant-glas, Trellech. But the many C17 barns which survive bear witness to the widespread cultivation of corn in this period of greatest agricultural prosperity. Stables, cart-houses and granaries were often added to barns. The outstanding group, of the C16 to judge by the four-centred-headed stone openings, is at Hygga, Trellech, where seven-bay barn and stable-cum-shippon face each other across the yard, and a circular stone dovecote stands nearby. A few other capacious free-standing DOVECOTES can be found, as in the village centre at Llanvair Discoed, and at Llantellen, Skenfrith. These are square, but the fine brick dovecote, of *c.* 1700, at Trewyn, Bwlch Trewyn, is octagonal. Many a farmhouse, however, made do with a group of nesting boxes in a gable-end.

Post-Reformation Churches

Although the Reformation led to a vast amount of destruction not only of monastic buildings but also of fittings in churches, church-building is unlikely to have come to a complete standstill during the rest of the C16. In particular it is probable, as has been mentioned already, that a number of substantial towers were built or completed during the post-Reformation period, evidence of the increasing popularity of bell-ringing. Unfortunately, dates and documentation are lacking. The earliest dated piece of POST-REFORMATION CHURCH-BUILDING is the W-ward extension at Langstone dated 1622, which may have been intended to provide space for a gallery. Only after 1700 was anything significant put in hand, and then only when circumstances forced it. Thus, at Chepstow it was the collapse of the crossing tower of the former monastic church in 1701 which led to the building, in 1705–6, of a new tower within the W bay of the nave. The surveyor, *Stephen Harvey*, made use of a good deal of Romanesque masonry to support his tower, but externally applied various naive classical motifs. Much more medieval in spirit is the spire added to the crossing tower at Llantilio Crossenny in 1708–9. The ex-monastic church at Monmouth had its spire renewed *c.* 1743 by *Nathaniel Wilkinson*. By then the entire body of Monmouth church had been rebuilt to a classical design by *Francis Smith* of Warwick, 1736–7. Until its sweeping Gothicization in the 1880s, this was the one major Georgian church in the county. That leaves as the sole representative of the C18, the large but aisleless nave at Nash, reconstructed probably *c.* 1740, with fanciful Baroque detailing, in particular on the S porch.

From the early C19 token acknowledgement was given to Gothic as the appropriate ecclesiastical style, as is shown in the churches built for ironworking communities at Blaenavon in 1805 and Pontypool, 1820 by *Watkin George*. The large church built in 1835–6 at the newly established town of Tredegar was by contrast designed by a London architect, *John Jenkins*, in a style part classical part neo-Norman. These years have little else to show, just the minimal Gothic of Holy Trinity, Whitebrook, Llandogo, 1835, and *Edward Haycock*'s meagre churches at Abersychan (1831–2) and Llandevaud (1843).

The generally utilitarian character of church restoration at this period is shown in the bald reconstruction of Mynyddislwyn church *c.* 1819, the crude remodelling of the church at Llangattock-juxta-Usk by the county surveyor *John Upton*, in 1827, and the thin little tower at St Arvans. The most extensive work in this spirit was the drastic remodelling of St Mary, Abergavenny, in 1828, but this in turn was swept away by Victorian improvements, so that only Maddox's plaster groin vault in the chancel survives.

POST-REFORMATION FITTINGS provide rather more to see. The early C17 was the golden age of preaching, and the 1630s the decade when PULPITS were installed in churches far and wide. In
74 Monmouthshire the best survivor is at Caerwent, dated 1632, where the jewelled ornament includes a miniature representation of Llandaff Cathedral, and a hortatory text is inscribed round the cornice. The pulpit at Penallt may be of 1634, and that at Trellech, dated 1639, has been simplified. Later pulpits are at Llangibby, large and handsome, and at Usk, part of a three-decker. Immediately after the restoration of the Monarchy in 1660, and the re-establishment of the Anglican Church, a number of parishes
75 re-equipped themselves for baptism. FONTS at Llandenny and Skenfrith are dated 1661, at Llangibby and Tredunnock, 1662,

the bowl at Buckholt, 1663. Then there is a gap until 1673, the date on the font at Llantrisant. All these are polygonal, and most are simply decorated. Incised floral decoration and idiosyncratic lettering on the fonts at Llandenny and Llangibby suggest that they may be products of the same workshop as the remarkable sundial now in the church at Trellech, though that bears the rather later date of 1689. Later fonts to note are at Michaelston-y-fedw, with a serpent twined up its stem, and at Blaenavon, 1805, 79
appropriately made of cast iron.

The siting of the altar against the E wall of the chancel and its enclosure by wooden rails was promoted by Archbishop Laud in the 1630s. Many ALTAR RAILS survive, of the late C17 and early C18. The arrangement envisaged by Laud, whereby the altar was railed in on three sides, survives at Trellech. Elsewhere altar rails run straight across the chancel, with central gates. Two rails are dated, at Llanvapley, 1724, and Penallt, 1743, both with turned balusters. Undated examples with twisted balusters are at Llangeview, Llangibby, Llanvetherine and Usk. Others with turned balusters are at Bryngwyn, Gwernesney, Llanfihangel-tor-y-mynydd, Llanover, Skenfrith and Wilcrick.

PEWS are generally unimpressive. Skenfrith has two types: C16 open pews with embryonic poppyheads, and a couple of Jacobean box pews. The most impressive ensemble is at Llangattock Lingoed, two C17 sets with a little incised decoration, one dated 1634. At Llantilio Pertholey there are C17 pews recently brought in. Ensembles of box pews are found at Llangeview, late C18, together with a squire's pew and family monument, at Nash, *c.* 1792, and 82
Llandegveth (probably early C19).

ROYAL ARMS were required to be displayed in churches from the time that Henry VIII declared himself Defender of the Faith until early in Queen Victoria's reign. A good range from the late C17 onwards survives. The earliest dated arms are at Trellech, 1683, a small but robust relief carving. Similar is the undated arms at Llangua. Much larger examples painted on panel or canvas are at Rockfield, 1700, Penallt and Abergavenny, 1709, and Dixton, 1711. After that, there is nothing until the early C19. That at Chepstow is dated 1841. Most memorable is the swagger early C19 arms at 80
Llanover.

POST-REFORMATION MONUMENTS. Monmouthshire is rich in locally made floor slabs and tablets. In the later C16 even men of substance had to make do with local products. At Skenfrith, a Steward of the Duchy of Lancaster (†1557) has a tomb-chest with merely incised full-length figures, though the figures of his children and armorial displays on the tomb-chest are in relief. Likewise, the first Principal of Jesus College, Oxford, †1584, is commemorated at Abergavenny by a monument signed by the ambitious local sculptor *John Gildon*, whose cavalier way with the classical vocabulary is discernible here, but seen in its utmost glory over the border at Bosbury in Herefordshire.

A particular local speciality of the early to mid C17 is the series of large stone slabs carved in shallow relief with boldly stylized figures in civilian costume, which may have come from a single

73 workshop. Most memorable is the undated slab at Llanfihangel
Crucorney, on which the figures kneel in twisting poses. On the
other slabs the figures are frontal and impassive. Dated examples
are at Llantilio Crossenny, 1620 and 1621, Llanvetherine, †1621,
Llanelly, 163[?] and 1646, Grosmont, 1636 and bearing the initials
I. B., which may be a signature, and Llangattock-juxta-Usk,
†1644. Some slabs bear later dates, presumably relating to later
deaths in the family, but the only such slab which seems to have
been made substantially later is at Abergavenny, 1699.

The earliest clearly imported monument, one which shows a
well-understood classicism, is the canopied monument of the second
Earl of Worcester, †1549, at Chepstow. Its arcaded superstructure,
to which Corinthian three-quarter columns are applied, bearing a
full entablature and strapwork cresting, looks like high-quality West
Country work of the 1570s or '80s. The monument at St Woolos,
Newport, to Sir Walter Herbert of St Julian's, †1568, with Ionic
half-columns, is similar in character. The monuments at Raglan to
the third and fourth Earls of Worcester (†1589 and 1628) were
originally doubtless splendid objects, which may have been London-
made, but Civil War vandalism soon reduced them to little more
than the torsos of the recumbent effigies. Other fragmentary
remains of once-handsome monuments are in the Morgan chapel
at Llantarnam and the Kemeys chapel at Michaelston-y-fedw. Only
four substantial, largely intact, early C17 monuments remain, that
at Chepstow, dated 1620, heavily repainted, that at Abergavenny,
†1631, with damaged recumbent alabaster effigies, the standing
wall monument at Wonastow, †1637, and, best-preserved, at
Abergavenny, with kneeling figures facing each other across a
prayer desk, erected after 1660.

Monumental BRASSES, all small engraved plaques, are at
Mathern, 1560s, Llanover, 1610, Llangattock-juxta-Usk, †1625,
and Llangattock-vibon-awel, †1629.

For the first examples of metropolitan quality one must look to
BAROQUE MONUMENTS. Fine white marble cartouches enfolding
flowers, putto heads or skulls within their scrolly drapery surrounds
76 can be found at Llangibby, 1685, Llandenny, †1710, Chepstow,
†1713 and Monmouth, †1715. The larger and more architectural
wall monument at Lower Machen, which includes veiled putto
heads and palm fronds, was supplied in 1717 by *Edward Stanton*,
for the mausoleum newly erected at the church there by a branch
of the Morgans. Also there is a double wall monument erected
shortly after 1731, with particularly vivid huntsman supporters.
77 But by far the finest piece is the pedimented wall monument at
Trevethin for the ironmaster John Hanbury, †1734. It was clearly
designed by *James Gibbs*, and the lively bust carved by *Rysbrack*,
as comparison with a closely similar documented monument in
Westminster Abbey shows. Of what is probably Bristol workmanship, the best early example is the oval cartouche at Llanfihangel
Crucorney, †1695, framed by twisted columns and topped by a
broken pediment carrying putti. Bristol work still Baroque in spirit
as late as 1767 is at Monmouth, by *James Paty jun.*, featuring a
yellow marble sarcophagus of curvaceous outline.

The NEOCLASSICAL STYLE first clearly shows itself at Llantarnam, †1775, where on a wall monument a black pyramid is set between urns. In the mausoleum at Lower Machen a weeping putto and veiled urn are set on a sarcophagus, †1792. Such motifs recur for the next half-century on smaller wall monuments and tablets in churches all over the county. Weeping willows and broken columns are other favourite emblems of mourning. Several Bristol firms must have grown prosperous by supplying such items, none more so than *Tyley*.

Work by leading London sculptors remains rare after 1800. Monuments by *Sir Richard Westmacott* can be seen at Monmouth, an early work (†1796), with naval imagery, and, more impressively,
at Bassaleg to a Morgan of Tredegar, †1808. In tune with the 87
mood of the times, its mourning family is grouped below a draped sarcophagus. Also at Bassaleg is a nearly contemporary monument supplied by *Coade & Sealy*, †1806, but this is no more than a version of the well-known antique figure known as the Cleopatra, presumably intended here as a generalization of grief. The only other familiar name is *Flaxman*, whose characteristic relief group at Llantilio Crossenny (†1819) is again of a mourning family. Still in the mid C19, the Merthyr-Tydfil-born sculptor *Joseph Edwards* was purveying grief-racked groups. His monument at Dingestow dated 1853 has a life-size mourner slumped in the lap of Faith, and his smaller one at St George's, Tredegar, of 1860, a family group. The deathbed scene at Tintern Parva (†1839) is signed by *Woolcott* of Bristol. Other monuments including figures of Virtues are at Llantrisant (†1804), by *Reeves & Son* of Bath, and at Monmouth (†1837) by *T. Smith* of London, the latter including the three Theological Virtues and a medallion portrait of the deceased.

Eighteenth-century Public Architecture

PHILANTHROPY found an outlet during the Stuart and Georgian periods in the establishment of schools and almshouses. The SCHOOLS founded at Monmouth in 1614 and Usk in 1621 were rebuilt in the C19, but there survives the unusually imposing building erected in 1724 at Caerleon for the Charles Williams Charity School. Then there is a gap of a century until the little Neoclassical school of 1820 at Llantilio Crossenny, and the semi-Gothic ironworks school of 1816 at Blaenavon.

ALMSHOUSES of the period are hardly less modest. Of the two examples at Chepstow, that of 1614 was given a Tudoresque remodelling in the early C19, but the Thomas Powis Almshouses of 1716 survive unaltered. Their constricted, hillside site forced the building into an L-plan without symmetry. The Roger Edwards Charity Almshouses at Llangeview, 1825–6 by *Edward Haycock*, are also on an L-plan, minimally Gothic, but with a loggia on iron posts.

CIVIC BUILDINGS make more of a show. Pride of place goes to
the Shire Hall at Monmouth, with its giant Ionic pilasters. This 72
dates to 1724, and was designed by an otherwise unknown architect or master craftsman from Bristol called *Fisher*. One would like

to know more about him, as the building shows a knowledge of Vanbrughian Baroque. Only one of the several town halls and market halls can match the Shire Hall for urban pomp. The Town Hall at Usk, 1771 and later, has a certain presence, though clearly built in several phases. The Market Hall of 1730 at Pontypool has an old-fashioned, domestic look. The little Town Hall of 1829–32 at Grosmont retains the traditional arrangement, with the hall above an open ground stage. The Assembly Rooms at Chepstow of 1807 have paired Tuscan columns and large round-headed windows to the upstairs room. The only building in this group to rise to the monumental was the Market Hall at Monmouth, completed in 1839 to the design of the local architect *G. V. Maddox,* and his major work. The noble Greek Doric columns in its Bath stone lower storey survive, but its remarkable top stage, incorporating an Ionic temple front, is unfortunately gone. Maddox laid out, as
96 part of the same scheme, a riverside bypass, Priory Street, supported on brick vaults with sandstone arcading which accommodated slaughterhouses. Its shallow curving frontage reaching away into the distance makes a sublime sight, in the C18 Burkean sense. Of Monmouth's other building which may have had a certain sublimity, the County Gaol by *William Blackburn,* 1789, only a small fragment is left. In a different class, but worth mentioning here, is the Legionary Museum, Caerleon, built 1847–50 to house the early finds from the Roman fortress. The architect, *H. F. Lockwood,* came from Hull. His Greek Doric portico is a fitting match for Maddox's Monmouth market. Its interior, now rebuilt, was originally toplit, *à la Grecque.*

Late Georgian Houses and Landscapes

From the 1790s, country houses began to be built in some numbers, although most of them are quite modest in scale. NEOCLASSICAL COUNTRY HOUSES include some of the most satisfying pieces of architecture in the county. Yet, sadly, what was once the premier
86 house is now reduced to a pathetic ruin. Piercefield Park was built to *Soane*'s design in 1792–3, a reticent, crisply detailed rectangular block which made no concession to the romantic landscape (*see* below, p. 46) in which it was set. The subtle rhythms of its five-bay pilastered façade are closely related to his slightly earlier Shotesham Park, Norfolk. Even today in its ruined state, the refinement of Soane's design, executed in sharply cut Bath stone ashlar, can be admired. From 1795 *Joseph Bonomi* added temple-
88 like flanking pavilions and fitted up rich interiors, but his work remains in an even more fragmentary condition. The effect of the semicircular columned porch added by Bonomi can be gauged from the contemporary Gwy House, Chepstow, 1796 (now Chepstow Museum). Whitson Court, completed *c.* 1795, has a comparable composition, a rectangular main block with low flanking service wings. Here the parts are unified by ground-floor blind relieving arches. The architect of this competent piece is unknown.

Local taste in Neoclassical house design is better represented by several houses of lesser pretension. They are tall and block-like, and

have full-height bows projecting from one or from two adjacent
façades, depending on what views there were to admire from the
windows. The finest is Newton Court, Dixton, *c.* 1799–1802, both 85
because the bows are so bold and because the walls are faced with
purple Old Red Sandstone ashlar in a *tour de force* of mason-craft.
The others in the group are Bertholey House, Llantrisant, begun
c. 1795 and long a ruin, Tŷ Uchaf, Llanover, an addition of *c.* 1792
in red brick to an earlier house, and, somewhat later, the white
rendered Glen Usk, Llanhennock, built probably *c.* 1820. No
architect's name is known for any of these houses, though Newton
Court has much in common with houses across the border in
England by Anthony Keck of King's Stanley, Gloucestershire.
Llanarth Court, a mansion on a much larger scale, built shortly
before 1793, also has full-height window bows, but was so thoroughly
remodelled in 1849–50 by *W. G. & E. Habershon* as to be to all
intents and purposes a mid-C19 house. The remodelling destroyed
what must have been the house's historically most significant feature,
a portico '*à la* Paestum'. The early 1790s was very early for the
imitation in this country of the primitive Greek Doric order found
in the celebrated early temples at Paestum S of Naples. However,
an almost equally early example of such primitivism does survive
in the Nelson Temple, erected on The Kymin, Wyesham, in 1800 90
to celebrate Nelson's naval victories over the forces of Napoleon.
This double-sided alcove carrying a seated statue of Britannia is
flanked by baseless, unfluted (i.e. primitivist) Doric columns.

The copying of the Greek orders became as fashionable in early
C19 house design as in public architecture. But whereas Greek
Doric columns were felt to lend weight to anything from a market
hall to a Baptist chapel, private houses might equally exploit the
greater elegance of the Ionic order. The two most impressive early
C19 country houses in the county both have splendid Ionic entrance
porticoes. Clytha Park, 1820–8 by *Edward Haycock* of Shrewsbury, 92
has much more than that. Its full-height Ionic portico is contrasted
with a half-height Doric one wrapped round a window bow. Hilston
Park, St Maughans, begun soon after 1838, is more conventional,
the bays of its broad façade defined by pilaster-like antae, its grand
portico Ionic. Croft-y-bwla, Monmouth, by *G. V. Maddox*, probably
c. 1830, is a crisp villa with a single-storey Greek Doric porch.

Neoclassical INTERIORS provide several breathtaking spatial
effects. The main internal spaces at Clytha House are first a circular 93
entrance hall, its enriched saucer dome carried on an entablature
and attached primitivist scagliola columns, and then an expansive
clerestory-lit staircase with an exquisite metal balustrade. The drastic
remodelling of Pontypool Park from *c.* 1801 made its exterior no
more impressive than it had been before, but internally the space
was opened up by a remarkable sequence of arches, groin-vaulted
corridors and lobbies. The grandly scaled staircase with scrolled
metal balustrade may be a mid-C18 feature enlarged. Two staircases
in other houses of the period demand mention. Machen
House, Lower Machen, 1831, has an extraordinary free-flying
circular stair, its exquisitely thin steps radiating from a mighty newel
post. The staircase at Blackbrook House, Skenfrith, a house built

1797–1800, is equally vertiginous, but rises more conventionally in a bowed flight to an expansive balcony.

Several smaller houses show the influence of John Nash's ITALIANATE VILLA STYLE, inaugurated in 1802 at Cronkhill, Shropshire, in which symmetry may be sacrificed in favour of picturesque grouping. Court St Lawrence, Llangovan, probably built before 1818, and Penhein, Llanvair Discoed, of after 1813, both cautiously embrace these ideas, as does the lodge at Whitson Court, where there is an early tradition that Nash was personally involved. The most sophisticated essay in this idiom is *Robert Lugar*'s Wyelands, Mathern, built, it seems, shortly before 1824.

This was the period in which the classical tradition was increasingly challenged by an alternative approach to architectural design. This is readily summed up in the words GOTHIC REVIVAL, but was inspired not only by a new admiration for medieval buildings but also by greater sensitivity to nature, in particular to landscape. The earliest signs of a new attitude were seen at two of the most important medieval ruins, both owned by the Dukes of Beaufort.
p. In the early 1750s the fourth Duke cleared and turfed the site at
538 Tintern Abbey, and a decade or so later his successor at last gave protection to the ruins of Raglan Castle. From the mid C18 the valley of the River Wye, with Tintern midway along its length, became one of the most popular areas in Britain for travellers in search of picturesque beauties. At Piercefield Park soon after 1752 Valentine Morris began to lay out a clifftop walk with alcove seats, from which travellers could admire views, sublime rather than picturesque, over the sinuous course of the Wye.

Elsewhere, views were sought from hilltop FOLLIES. The Hanburys of Pontypool Park erected two, the circular castellated folly tower at Trevethin in 1762 (rebuilt 1993–4), and the Shell
91 Hermitage in the park at Pontypool itself. The Hermitage is an above-ground grotto, a late example, since it dates from the 1830s, designed by a certain *G. S. Tit* of Bath, and was restored to splendour
89 1994–6. By far the most fantastic folly is Clytha Castle, built in 1790 by *John Davenport*. Its L-plan, defined by two circular towers and a square one with a higher turret, provides contrasted groupings from different directions, and its gauche Gothic details are so oversized that they can easily be made out at a distance. At the park entrance to Clytha in 1797 a much more daintily detailed Gothic gateway was erected, although the next generation, as we have seen, turned to Grecian for the rebuilding of the house.

John Davenport was a landscape gardener, who designed Clytha Castle as part of his landscaping of the park. The most beautiful LANDSCAPED PARKLAND in the county is at Llanthony Priory, where what remains of the poet Walter Savage Landor's tree-planting activities 1807–13 still enhances that lovely valley. The only other extensive landscaped park is at Llanarth Court, where a Brownian scheme of 1792 by *Samuel Lapidge* was softened and elaborated in 1805 by *J. C. Loudon*, and further modified in 1849. The garden at Machen House, Lower Machen, formed in the 1830s, is on a miniature scale by comparison, an excellent example of the 'gardenesque' style popularly associated with the name of Loudon.

It boasts two lakes, a cascade, and a 'Willow Pattern' bridge, and is enclosed by an embattled wall with turrets. The similar but later garden at Bedwellty House, Tredegar, is less eventful, and notable mainly for rocky features constructed of artificial stone.

INDUSTRIAL STRUCTURES

BY STEPHEN HUGHES

Early industry developed in two separate areas in the county. From the late C16 the Wye Valley, on its eastern boundary, became a centre of ironworking, stimulated both by the proximity of coal and iron reserves across the river in the Forest of Dean, and by accessibility to Bristol, then the second city of Britain. In the hills to the W of the county, ironworking forges had started into action even earlier, though here too it was only in the late C16 that anything approaching productive industry was established, primarily by the Hanburys of Pontypool.

The future lay with the western area. Here from the 1780s far more efficient, multi-furnace, coke-fired ironworks were constructed, the earliest at Blaenavon. Although by the 1830s supremacy had passed to the two great ironworks across the county boundary at Merthyr Tydfil in Glamorgan, iron production in the county continued to develop until the 1860s, but then declined. The only successor still active is the great tinplate works at Ebbw Vale.

Meanwhile, coalmining quickly took the place of ironworking as the principal extractive industry across the whole of the South Wales coalfield, of which only the eastern third lay in Monmouthshire. Coal mines dominated the Valleys from the mid C19 until the second quarter of the C20, when the industry went into sharp decline. The widespread closure of mines in the 1980s and '90s has brought this industrial story firmly to a conclusion.

The success of these industries had depended crucially on effective transport of goods to the coast. Horse-drawn tramroads, canals and railways have all left their mark. The growth of Newport dates from the beginning of the C19, when for a time it was the busiest port in South Wales, until overtaken by Cardiff. Also crucial to the economic prosperity of South Wales as a whole, and of Monmouthshire in particular, was the construction of effective transport links to England. The rail link was made in the 1880s, when the Severn Tunnel was excavated – a heroic enterprise. The road connection was far slower to come; the M4 motorway and bridge are works of the 1960s.

Ironworks

Extensive traces survive of charcoal-fired C17 ironworks, mainly producing wire, in the remote and rural valleys of two small tributaries of the River Wye, the Angidy at Tintern, and the Whitebrook at Llandogo. Of four known sites, three preserve features such as ponds impounded by stone dams, ironmasters' houses and terraces of workers' houses. One site, Abbey Tintern blast furnace, Tintern, has been excavated and laid out for display.

In the W of the county one important early site has been identified, at Abercarn, where a tall, charcoal-fuelled blast furnace with charging-house survives. It is datable to the mid C18, and is thus the earliest well-preserved furnace in South Wales.

The great era of coke-fuelled ironworks in the Heads of the Valleys area on the border of Glamorgan and Monmouthshire
p. extended from *c.* 1790 to the 1830s, when the biggest ironworks in
124 the world could be found there. The multi-furnace ironworks
108 developed at Blaenavon from 1788 was the earliest in Britain (and perhaps, except for Sweden, in the world). Much of the blast furnaces survives, together with parts of two casting-houses and formally laid out workers' housing, all dating from the earliest years. Blaenavon ironworks produced pig iron. Of Garnddyrys Forge, opened nearby in 1816 to convert the pigs into wrought iron, only substantial earthworks remain visible. Forgeside Ironworks, opened across the valley in 1860 to replace the original works, has been mostly swept away, but leaving terraces of workers' housing as its main memorial. Nevertheless, much that can still be seen in Blaenavon town close to the early works and in its surrounding landscape recalls the pioneering days.

At Ebbw Vale the ironworks was founded in 1790 and steadily developed into a major enterprise. An exceptionally intact bank of at least six blast furnaces survives. They are of the early and mid C19, but are partly buried in a later charging-bank. The site of what must have been the most imposing early C19 ironworks in South Wales is also tantalizing. This was the British Ironworks at Abersychan, built in 1826–7 to the design of *Decimus Burton*. Its handsome composition is known from an engraving, but the works closed in 1883, and only the offices, the angle pavilions of a quadrangle, survive, in a much-altered state.

IRON PRODUCTS. In the C19 the Monmouthshire ironworks produced both steam engines and structural cast-ironwork. One mid-C19 engine survives *in situ* at Glyn Pits, Pontypool. Of structural iron, a good deal can still be found, for example in Nantyglo, Roundhouses Farm and towers, 1816 or 1838, the service court at Tredegar House, *c.* 1828, and the stables at Pontypool Park, 1831. Iron roof trusses are at the Cattle Market, 1844, and the Baltic Warehouse, both at Newport. The most awe-inspiring iron structure, Crumlin Viaduct of 1853–7, which incorporated wrought-ironwork from Blaenavon, succumbed to demolition in 1965 (*see* p. 50).

Collieries

Traces of the earlier form of coalmining, used until the C18, whereby 'hushes' of water were released to scour out surface seams of coal, can be seen on the hilltops above Blaenavon and at Upper Race, Pontypool.

The sinking of coal mines began in earnest in the early C19. A map published in 1843 shows no fewer than forty-seven collieries in the county. But it was in the early C20 that there was the largest concentration of working collieries. Between 1913 and 1921 the county formed part of Britain's largest coalmining area, and part of the largest coal-exporting area in the world. Clearance of sites after the final deep-pit closures in the 1980s and '90s have, however, left remarkably little to see. In many cases it is only unexpectedly placed housing development which provides the clue to the existence of collieries which have otherwise been totally swept away.

Three important complexes of COLLIERY STRUCTURES remain. Historically most significant is Glyn Pits, Pontypool, where are preserved *in situ* two early steam-engine houses, fine masonry structures, one dated 1845, the other of *c.* 1860. The architecturally finest set of colliery buildings in the whole of Wales survives at Crumlin, where the symmetrical group of red and yellow brick buildings erected for the Navigation Colliery 1907–11 is still almost 111
intact, eloquently representing the pride of the Edwardian boom years. Big Pit, Blaenavon, by contrast, retains structures of many 109
dates, from the early C19 to shortly before its closure in 1973. Everything is workaday and unpretentious. However, the whole complex is preserved as it was when in operation, including an outstanding series of underground tunnels and structures, all accessible to the public.

Limeburning

Early ironworks required supplies of limestone to flux their furnaces. This led to the quarrying of limestone where it outcropped round the edge of the Coal Measures. The QUARRY at Trefil, N of Tredegar, dates from that period. At the same time improvements in farming methods created a demand for burnt lime as a fertilizer. Low, rectangular, tapering stone KILNS were constructed to burn the lime. The burning-cone of the kiln required to be charged from the top, and discharged through an arch at the bottom. Kilns were therefore normally built on bank-side sites, typically in this area close to the Brecon and Abergavenny Canal. Groups of kilns thus sited survive at Gilwern, Llanelly, at Govilon and, most evocatively, at Goytre Wharf, Goetre. A fine isolated single kiln is at Llanvaches.

Water Transport

Two RIVERS, though both strongly tidal, provided transport routes. The River Wye was navigable through Hereford as far as Hay, and the industrial development at Tintern and Llandogo depended on it. Warehouses, or traces of them, probably C18 in date, survive close to the river at both places. The River Usk was generally navigable as far as Caerleon, but at Newport extensive riverside quays were built, and here also there survive one or two warehouses, of the early and mid C19.

The canal-mania of the 1790s saw the construction of two linked CANALS in the county. The Monmouthshire Canal, 1792–9, extended from the River Usk at Newport N-wards as far as Pontnewynydd, with a western arm of almost equal length up the

Ebbw Valley to Crumlin. The Brecon and Abergavenny Canal, authorized in 1793, was constructed in three parts: the N-most 1796–1800, engineer *Thomas Dadford jun.*, the parts through Monmouthshire, from Gilwern, Llanelly, to Llanfoist, 1802–5, engineer *Thomas Cartwright*, and from Llanfoist to Llanfihangel Pontymoile, 1809–12, engineer *William Crossley*. The canals came under one ownership in 1865 and today are known as the Monmouthshire and Brecon Canal. Both canals had numerous flights of locks. The longest, fourteen locks mainly arranged in pairs, is at Rogerstone, on the Crumlin arm. Other notable features are Goytre Wharf, Goetre, with a handsome single-arch aqueduct, and the many well-built stone accommodation bridges which take minor roads and trackways over the lower half of the Brecon and Abergavenny Canal.

Railways

Primitive horse-worked railways had appeared in South Wales by the C17. From the 1790s industrial development in Monmouthshire created the greatest concentration of tramroads in Britain or elsewhere. They were essential for the transport of iron products from the works at the Heads of the Valleys to the newly constructed
2 canals, and so to the coast. Above Blaenavon and in the Clydach Gorge, Llanelly, terracing and rock-cut inclined planes allow the lines of several of these early railways to be traced. Some of the most significant monuments can be mentioned. The N portal remains of Pwll-du Tramroad tunnel, Blaenavon, which was, when opened *c.* 1815, the longest railway tunnel in the world, 1½ m. (2.4 kilometres) in length. At Llanfoist and Govilon are several substantial stone warehouses of 1820–2, built for the canal-side storage of iron goods. These are among the earliest railway warehouses anywhere. Finally, the four-arch stone viaduct at Bassaleg, dated 1826, is an exceptionally early railway viaduct built on an impressive scale. Widened in 1863, it remains in railway use.

Modern locomotive railways soon demanded long and high RAILWAY BRIDGES in order to span rivers and river valleys. *I. K. Brunel* from 1850 to 1852 designed and constructed the great tubular suspension bridge at Chepstow to take the South Wales Railway over the River Wye. This partly survives. It was a structure which could cope with the heavy and differential loadings imposed by passing trains, and is closely parallel to Robert Stephenson's two great, and admittedly longer, railway bridges in North Wales: Conwy Bridge and the Britannia Bridge over the Menai Straits. It served as the prototype for Brunel's own Saltash Bridge, Cornwall. Of the most spectacular railway construction in the county, *T. W. Kennard*'s Crumlin Viaduct, 1853–7, only the masonry abutments survive. The elegant, web-like framework of cast-iron tubes, forming a series of tapering piers, the tallest no less than 204 ft (62 metres) high, to support the decking and rails, was unfortunately dismantled in 1965. Later and smaller all-metal viaducts of this sort, however, survive in England, at Meldon, Devon, and Bennerley, Derbyshire. The more normal form of viaduct, consisting of a series of masonry arches, appeared on all the various railway lines which traversed the county. Several have been demolished, but the longest, the twenty-two-arch viaduct of 1861 at Wyesham, survives, though the railway it served closed in 1959.

The greatest challenge to Victorian railway engineers was presented by the need to make a rail link between England and Wales. The Severn Tunnel was constructed between 1873 and 1886, the longest undersea railway tunnel in the world until the 1980s. The celebrated engineer *Sir John Hawkshaw* first acted as consultant, and from 1879 was in complete control. The tunnel remains today intact and in use, and at Sudbrook, Portskewett, much is left of the workers' village, built by the contractor T.A. Walker in the 1880s, and the mighty red brick pumping-engine hall, built *c.* 1886. The six great steam engines of 1885–6, constantly in action to pump out the Great Spring, were replaced by electric pumps in 1962 and unfortunately removed in 1968.

Ports

The other essential component in the successful industrial development of South Wales was the provision of PORTS. The three major ports, which grew in competition with one another throughout the C19, were Swansea and Cardiff in Glamorgan, and Newport in Monmouthshire. Only during the 1820s and '30s did Newport outshine its rivals. Thereafter, it lagged behind Cardiff in dock construction, relying on riverside wharves for storage even into the early C20. The importance of the river for shipping at Newport in this late period is eloquently demonstrated by the transporter 110
bridge, a type of suspension bridge, built over the River Usk 1901–6 to the design of the French engineer *F. Arnodin*, with assistance from the borough engineer *R. H. Haynes*. Tall, lattice-braced steel piers support a high-level deck clear of the tallest masts of passing ships, and from it a small transporter platform is suspended. Three enclosed docks were, however, constructed: the Town Dock, 1835–42, enlarged 1856–8, the Alexandra Dock, completed 1873, and the Alexandra South Dock, built in three stages 1893–1914 at the height of the coal-exporting boom. This eventually covered 96 acres (39 hectares), making it larger than any dock in the coal-exporting ports further W. Today it is the only dock at Newport which has not been filled in.

NINETEENTH- AND EARLY TWENTIETH-CENTURY ARCHITECTURE AND DECORATION

Nonconformist Chapels

NONCONFORMIST CHAPELS include a good many that are early in date, so that the isolated wayside chapel is still quite a characteristic sight. In the 1830s and '40s, when allegiance to a Nonconformist cause, whether Baptist, Methodist, Congregationalist or Independent, had become thoroughly respectable, handsome classical chapels began to appear in the centres of towns. Of these, the county has several impressive examples. The earliest surviving chapel which is thorough-goingly Gothic dates from 1854, and thereafter the style became increasingly popular, to the end of the century and beyond. Yet, if surviving chapels are representative of what was built, the peak of chapel-building had been reached as early as 1870. The 1880s and '90s seem to have been relatively barren, and it was only after the 'Revival' of 1904–5 that there was a sudden last flurry, before the First World War brought more than a century of activity virtually to a standstill.

The oldest surviving Baptist chapel in Wales is at Govilon, constructed in 1695, but, doubled in size, re-windowed and re-roofed, it now reveals nothing of late C17 character. The setting for early dissenting worship is well demonstrated by two purpose-built Quaker meeting houses which probably date to the late C17. Both are attached to farms. That at The Cayo, Llandenny, must once have been handsome and conspicuous, square under a hipped roof, the large windows classically proportioned. At The Pant,
81 Llanfihangel-ystern-llewern, the meeting house is attached to the farmhouse itself, a two-storeyed, square block, again displaying high-quality craftsmanship and some classical detail, here all in brick.

During most of the C18 chapels were located in farmhouses or cottages, or were built to look like such domestic buildings. A good example of a cottage-like chapel, though modernized, is the Baptist chapel at Penygarn, Trevethin, of 1727. Earlswood Chapel, Shirenewton, 1754, must have been similar, but a later addition has obscured its original façade. Here, however, original simple fittings survive. The first Hanover Congregational chapel at Llanover is an appendage to the cottage built by the first minister in 1744 and bequeathed to the congregation.

When, at the end of the C18, typical chapel façade compositions crystallized, they retained the memory of the cottage chapels in being entered in the long side wall, not the short end. A pair of large central windows would light the pulpit, placed so that it backed on to the entrance wall, and flanking doorways gave access underneath the galleries. This was clearly the arrangement at Capel Ed, Goetre, 1807, and at the undated Ebenezer, Pontnewynydd, and it remains the arrangement at Siloh, Pontllanfraith, 1813, the best survivor of the type. Beulah, Newbridge, 1809, though probably lengthened, retains the spirit of this kind of frontage. The well-preserved, though currently disused, Baptist chapel at Penallt, of *c.* 1820, originally had a central doorway in its long wall. The gable-end entry became popular from the early C19. Several of the earliest examples are in urban sites, where space constraints probably encouraged the use of this plan. The chapel in Castle Street, Abergavenny, originating in 1792, has been enlarged. At Usk the Wesleyan Methodists built to this plan in 1817, the Baptists in 1842. So did the Baptists at Abersychan, 1827. But the best early survivor of this type is the remote rural Baptist chapel of 1837 at Ffwthog.

The square plan was also favoured at this time, preferred, it is said, by preachers for acoustic reasons. The Methodist chapel at Abergavenny dated 1829 is of this type, as are the well-built and well-preserved rural chapel dated 1830 at Maesygwartha, Llanelly, and the second Hanover chapel at Llanover, of 1839. The theatrical effect of the interior of this type of chapel when built on a large scale can, perhaps, be best seen at Tabor Baptist Church, Brynmawr, 1836, reconstructed 1857–8.

All these early chapels, in so far as their windows are normally
round-headed, can be categorized as minimally classical. In the
late 1830s, however, the first examples of thorough-going classical
chapel design can be found. The Baptist chapel at Pontrhydyrun,
Cwmbran, 1836, is fully temple-like, even if it does not burgeon
into columns. The Wesleyan Methodist chapel at Monmouth, of 83
1837 by *G. V. Maddox*, is an even more convincing piece of architecture, in which all the familiar elements outside and in cohere
into proper, consistently Ionic, compositions. Also at Monmouth
is the (unfortunately abandoned) Congregational chapel of 1843–4,
by *William Armstrong* of Bristol, its façade composition of two
Corinthian columns between antae a reduced version of the
Brunswick Chapel in Bristol. Most remarkable of all these classical
essays is the Baptist chapel in Crane Street, Pontypool, 1846–7.
This is uniquely temple-like in having originally received light only 101
from above, as Greek temples were believed to have done. The
façade is overpoweringly Greek, its narrow portico supported on
square antae and a pair of baseless, powerfully tapering, fluted 99
Doric columns. The concept of the chapel seems to have been a
certain *Aaron Crossfield*'s, but the design was worked up by *J. H.
Langdon*.

The classicism of later chapels was either loose or formulaic.
Loosest and lushest is *A. O. Watkins*'s ashlar-faced chapel with 100,
Rococo-esque detail, built in 1858–9 for Congregationalists on a 102
spectacularly steep site in Victoria Road, Newport. Its two doorways in the long side wall are as unconventional as the mighty triple arch behind the pulpit inside. The leading purveyor of formulae was the Swansea minister–architect, the Rev. *Thomas Thomas* of Landore. An example of his pilastered temple-front design is Saron, Tredegar, 1858–9. Penuel, Ebbw Vale, 1865, is similar and may also be by him. His other, more memorable, formula features a wide, full-height relieving arch under a pedimental gable. Carmel, Beaufort, of 1865, is a characteristic example. A variant on these ideas is *Samuel Hancorn*'s former Bethcar, Ebbw Vale, of 1860–1. The basic formula, which did not need an architect to produce it, consists of nothing more than two storeys of round-headed windows, the central one in the three-bay façade normally tripartite, and the roof gable approximately pedimental. Berea, Blaina, 1850–3, is one example, Salem, Fleur-de-lis, 1860, another. Variations of one kind or another are, of course, found. Thus Horeb, Blaenavon, 1862–3 by *T. Thomas*, civil engineer, has double-height windows in the façade and a columned porch, and Ebenezer, Blaina, 1860–1 by *D. Morgan*, civil engineer, has a Diocletian window in the pediment. Both these last retain their

galleried interiors largely intact. Another particularly splendid, if conventional, interior survives at the Baptist chapel at Abersychan, remodelled in 1868 by *W. Ardick & Sons* of Warminster.

Round arches could also develop into Romanesque or Lombardic styles. The earliest survivor in this idiom is at Newport, the impressive Romanesque façade of the former Wesleyan Methodist chapel in Commercial Road, designed by *J. Wilson* of Bath and built in 1849. The Newport architect *R. G. Thomas* made the next
98 display of this sort, in the polychromatic Baptist chapel at Castleton, Marshfield, 1858–9, with an enormous wheel window in the centre of the entrance front, and even a stumpy steeple. Back in Newport, *Habershon & Pite* in 1864 built the Lombardic chapel for Presbyterians in Havelock Street. This also has a big wheel window and polychromatic walls. Both these chapels retain their galleried interiors, that at Newport with a dramatic composition of pulpit and organ. *Habershon, Pite & Fawckner* in 1866 used the style in Newport again, with somewhat less panache, at Summerhill Baptist Chapel. The largest and most expensive essay in the style, however, is the mighty Baptist chapel of 1877 at Abergavenny, by *George Morgan* of Carmarthen, an architect widely employed by Baptists throughout South Wales. Here the façade has not only a wheel window but flanking towers crowned by steep slated roofs. The big chapel built for Methodists at Blaenavon *c.* 1885–6 by *John Wills* of Derby is mixed Romanesque and Gothic, with a tower. The one later chapel with a full-blown Lombardic-style façade is the tall and capacious Welsh Baptist chapel of 1893 at Risca. The interior here is spectacular, galleried on all four sides, with a permanently visible baptistery in front of the pulpit and an enormous arch for the organ behind.

By the end of the century, however, round-arched styles for chapels had given way almost entirely to Gothic. The existence of the pointed arch was quite early acknowledged in a couple of rural chapels, which were given windows with pointed heads, at Henllys, 1836, and Llangwm Uchaf, 1840. In the Valleys it makes its first appearance in *Philip Hambleton*'s stylistically confused Wesleyan Methodist chapel of 1849–50 at Pontnewynydd. The earliest example of full-blown Gothic is the roguish little former chapel of 1854 at Castleton, Marshfield, also built for Wesleyans. Conventional Gothic arrived in 1855, in *J. Wilson* of Bath's Methodist chapel at Chepstow. A prominently sited Gothic example of these years is at Usk, *Habershon & Pite*'s former Congregational chapel of 1861–2, in a Geometrical style and with a spirelet over the gallery stair-turret.

The main phase of Gothic chapel-building is introduced by *E. A. Johnson*'s Bethany Baptist Chapel in Abergavenny of 1882, in a well-handled Geometrical style, and then immediately by the first of the large, church-like urban chapels, built in 1882–3 for Methodists on Stow Hill, Newport, by *Habershon & Fawckner*. This stands sideways to the road, showing off its Geometrical traceried upper windows; it has a transeptal arrangement at the pulpit end and, to mark the entrance, a full-scale tower and spire. It was doubtless intended to face down the Catholic church opposite (for which, *see* p. 433). The Baptists built something similarly conspicuous in a fashionable suburb of Newport, at Llanthewy Road, as late as 1912, by *Charles E. Compton*. Another Geometrical-style chapel in a Newport suburb, St Julian's Methodist, 1901–2, has full arcades in the Anglican way, though the piers are of cast iron and the arches of timber. The most interesting example of this type is the large and sombre Mount Pleasant, Pontypool, for Congregationalists, of 1903–4 by *Swash & Bain*. It has fully stone arcades with octagonal piers, a gallery only at the entrance end, and had pulpit and communion table matching one another either side of a choir and organ recess.

For smaller Gothic chapels at the turn of the century Perp was the preferred style. Examples are Zion, Newbridge, 1897 by *Swash & Bain*, Carmel, Abertillery, 1906–7 by *Habershon, Fawckner & Co.*, West End, Ebbw Vale, 1907, and, rather larger, Tabernacle, Newbridge, 1912–13 by *N. Gasenius Lewis*. All these have galleried interiors of traditional type. Beechwood Park Presbyterian chapel, Newport, as late as 1923, keeps to the same style and galleried interior. The largest late chapel in a Perp style is *E.A. Johnson*'s finely detailed Presbyterian chapel at Abergavenny, 1907–10. This has no galleries, but transeptal projections at the pulpit end, and an impressively elaborate hammerbeam roof.

Roman Catholic Churches

Roman Catholic churches are few but unusually interesting. During the penal period, Monmouthshire was a hotbed of Catholicism and produced more than one martyr. Leading landed families adhered to the old religion, most notably the Morgans of Llantarnam and the Joneses of Treowen and Llanarth. At Llanarth Court is an excellent example of the semi-disguised Catholic chapel which by the late C18 the authorities were prepared to wink at. It was built probably in the 1790s, and the row of large round-headed windows down one long side makes it easy to mistake for an orangery. In 1793 Catholics in Monmouth built a church in the middle of the town, but this was discreetly hidden behind cottages. After the passage of the Catholic Emancipation Act in 1829 these subterfuges were no longer necessary, and over the following forty years or so all the main towns in the county gained a prominent Catholic church. Naturally, for such buildings a medieval style was most appropriate. The polemics of A.W.N. Pugin, the leading Catholic architect and propagandist from 1836, ensured that they were almost all Gothic. Thus the first and most ambitious in the county, built in Newport in 1839–40 by the Catholic church specialist *J.J. Scoles*, is E.E. The aisled nave would not have pleased Pugin, as its piers are of cast iron; but the street frontage is dominated by a tower which closely imitates the C13 tower of St Mary, Stamford. *Scoles*'s smaller and less expensive church of 1845–6 at Pontypool, however, is Neo-Norman. The church built on the outskirts of Usk in 1847 to the design of *Charles Hansom*, another architect widely employed by Catholics, is Geometrical in style, as Pugin advocated. The most convincing achievement is that of *Benjamin Bucknall*, the disciple of Viollet-le-Duc, at Abergavenny,

104 whose splendid Dec church of 1858–60, with accompanying presbytery, has a Puginian wholeheartedness. While the church at Usk gained a tower, in 1865, it was perhaps inevitable that the soaring steeple which Bucknall envisaged was never executed. Lastly, in 1871 the church-hiding cottages at Monmouth were demolished, and *Bucknall* added a façade towards the street, with a small but eye-catching porch-tower. Later Catholic churches become large and dull, as at Pillgwenlly, Newport, 1886–9 by *W. B. Gardner*, and at Ebbw Vale, 1905–24. In contrast is the striking clifftop church of 1939–40 at Newbridge, by *P. D. Hepworth*, a gift to the Valley communities made by a member of the family whose chapel at Llanarth Court opened this section.

Anglican Church-building from the 1830s

This began in earnest in the later 1830s, and within a decade was in full flow. Successive waves of activity carried its momentum through to the last years of the century. In part this was the result of the new seriousness of purpose within the Church of England, which had been inspired above all by the Tractarian movement of the mid 1830s. Equally, the newly emancipated Roman Catholics were felt to be a threat, and in South Wales the great increase in population which the development of industry engendered led to a demand for new churches, to establish a presence among all the chapels of the Nonconformists. Finally, it is clear that many rural churches had fallen into a dire state of neglect: by 1880 over twenty of them had been totally or virtually rebuilt. The restoration of churches was sweeping, so that interiors of pre-Victorian character survive only at Llangeview, Llangibby and Nash. Just pre-
84 Victorian is the remarkable Neo-Norman ensemble at St Thomas, Overmonnow, Monmouth, 1830–1 by *Matthew Beasen*.

In the choice of an architect, local connections mattered. The young *T. H. Wyatt*, nephew of the Duke of Beaufort's agent, had a monopoly of work in the first decade. Thereafter *John Prichard* was effectively diocesan architect within the diocese of Llandaff (which until 1921 included Monmouthshire), and for twenty years from 1849 bestrode the field, together with his partner, *J. P. Seddon*. Their partnership lasted from 1852 to 1863, and after that Seddon was for a time the more favoured of the two within the county, or to be more precise, within the archdeaconry of Monmouth. At the end of the century Seddon went into partnership again, this time with the young *J. Coates Carter*. Carter's own churches of the 1920s constitute a remarkable late flowering, and form the culmination of this section.

T. H. Wyatt's churches are normally Gothic. The first, St Paul, Newport, 1835–6, is naively youthful, showing some feeling for drama in its porch-tower, but very little understanding of the style he was struggling to master. In 1838 he took the more scholarly *David Brandon* as partner, an arrangement which lasted until 1851. This, however, was not enough to redeem the Neo-Norman design of the reconstructed transepts and chancel at the former priory church at Chepstow, which they finished off in 1840–1, after the dismissal of the first architect, *William Harris* of Bristol. Their Holy Trinity, Abergavenny, 1840–2, has been so enlarged that it has lost its original character, although the accompanying Tudor Gothic almshouses and parsonage survive. *Wyatt & Brandon*'s restoration of Usk church, 1844, has also been largely eliminated. The chancel which they added to St James, Pontypool, in 1845 is acceptably Dec, but the new church built at Goetre, 1845–6, and the rebuilding of the body of Trevethin church, 1846–7, have Perp details without being convincingly Perp in general form. *Wyatt & Brandon*'s last ecclesiastical essay in the county is the new church at Govilon, 1847–8, which is E.E., with plate-traceried windows. It too has been subsequently much enlarged.

For T.H. Wyatt, Monmouthshire churches formed but one part of a far-reaching and diverse practice. *John Prichard*, who from 1848 took over as first the exclusive and then the principal church-builder and restorer in the county, was an architect of a very different kind. He had trained under T.L. Walker, an associate of Benjamin Ferrey, Pugin's boyhood friend and biographer. Prichard's early church at Merthyr Mawr in Glamorgan was designed in collaboration with Ferrey. For Prichard, as for Pugin, church design was the central and overwhelmingly most important component of his practice. Like Pugin, too, he believed in the universality of Gothic for C19 architecture, and in his partner *J. P. Seddon* he found a like-minded ally. Within the county, with one minor exception, all their work consists of the new-building and restoration of churches, the provision of fittings for them, and the design of parsonages and church schools.

Prichard's first church, however, is exceptional. At Malpas in 1849–50 he rebuilt the rich C12 chapel. The new building seems to have been a faithful copy of the old one, but with further Neo-Norman components, such as the E window and the bell gable. He also added a mighty Neo-Norman lychgate. His next new church, Llanishen, 1852–4, though small and cheap, epitomizes his Gothic vision, with steeply pitched roofs and vestry with prominent chimney, and details in simple Dec. A prominent W spirelet is supported on a wall-shaft. *Prichard & Seddon*'s Llandogo, 1859–61, their best 103
and best-preserved church in the county, elaborates upon this model with considerable verve. It has lean-to aisles, arcades with slender circular piers, and a W porch which forms the foundation for a fantastically elaborated W spirelet. At the same time, however, *Prichard & Seddon* were engaged on two more ambitious churches, both of which survive in a somewhat compromised state. Holy Trinity, Pontnewydd, Cwmbran, 1858–60, is most notable for its polychromy in three different kinds of stone and for its porch-steeple, with timber-framed belfry stage inspired by local medieval models. Only the angular Dec tracery strikes an aggressively High Victorian note. Polychromy and spiky profiles are used on a large scale and to much more dramatic effect at St John, Maindee, Newport, 1859–60. The W front is a display of self-conscious originality in its complex and wilful interlocking of disparate forms.

Later, *Seddon* alone built one completely new church, Wyesham, 1873–5. This is blunt and effective, in a Geometrical style, but without the fertility of imagination shown earlier. The firm rebuilt several churches on old foundations, retaining the medieval towers, thereby clarifying the medieval compositions and homogenizing the style as Geometrical or Dec. Some were in effect new designs. The most successful is *Prichard*'s late re-creation of Llanddewi Skirrid church in 1879. The largest, Caerleon, lacks character (chancel by *Prichard & Seddon c.* 1855, nave and porch by *Seddon*, 1867–8). Others are Rockfield, 1859–60, and two small jobs by *Seddon*, Newchurch and Oldcastle, both of 1863–4. In their restorations of medieval churches they worked according to the principles of their time, replacing what were seen as late and debased features with something in a late C13 or early C14 style, though sound and substantially designed Perp features were allowed to survive. The most important church restored by *Prichard & Seddon* was Llantilio Crossenny, 1856–7, where their intervention was notably tactful. *Seddon*'s subsequent *magnum opus* was the successful underpinning of the crossing tower and steeple at Grosmont, in which he was engaged through much of the 1870s. But here his restoration of the E.E. chancel involved the conjectural reinstatement of missing lancet windows.

During the 1850s and '60s the only other architect who was employed on church work with any regularity was *John Norton*, who had offices in Bristol and London. In 1852–3 he largely rebuilt Shirenewton church, and in 1854 was employed to build two new churches in the Valleys, at Pontllanfraith and Blaina (Aberystruth), both now demolished. His most important work, by far the largest Anglican church in the Monmouthshire Valleys, is
107 Christ Church, Ebbw Vale, 1860–1, in C13 style, with plate tracery and a huge W wheel window, fashionable features at that date. Norton was subsequently entrusted with the restoration of the important medieval churches of Magor, 1861–8, where his renewal of masonry was disappointingly thorough, and Redwick, 1874–5, where he was more restrained. His last work, the new church at Cwm, Ebbw Vale, 1881–2, is small and cheap, but remains faithful to plate tracery.

Church architects with a national reputation made the occasional appearance. *Henry Woodyer* carried out a heavy-handed restoration at Caldicot in 1857–8 and another at Itton in 1869, and largely rebuilt Panteg church 1874–6, introducing several idiosyncratic features. *Charles Buckeridge* designed two churches in 1873, shortly before his premature death. *J. L. Pearson* supervised their execution. The unassuming E.E. church at Pontnewynydd remained incomplete and has now been abandoned. Llanfrechfa is the rebuilding of a medieval church, and reuses some Perp windows. Nevertheless, it is mainly Dec in style, handsome, well-proportioned but lacking in personality. *J. D. Sedding* enlarged Govilon church in 1871–2, and 1873–6 reconstructed the modest rural church of Llanfair Kilgeddin, neither in themselves especially memorable, but at the latter providing the setting for unforgettable later embellishment (*see* below, p. 61). The most celebrated of the London architects was *G.E. Street*, who reconstructed Monmouth church reusing the C18 walls, 1881–3. Such a compromise was not what Street had wanted, but his design for a completely new cruciform church was far too expensive. In the event, by refenestrating the walls with long paired lancets, adding a chancel with an E composition of five stepped lancets, and creating an open hall-church effect internally, he achieved the county's most impressive large-scale interior of the century.

The other new-built and remodelled churches which deserve mention are all by local architects. A curiosity is St Mark, Gold Tops, Newport, 1872–4 by *Habershon, Pite & Fawckner*, aiming to evoke a late medieval Cotswold church. *E.M. Bruce Vaughan* of Cardiff is represented in the Valleys by three typical, indeed routine, works, at Griffithstown, 1887–8, Cwmtillery, Abertillery, 1890–1, and Fleur-de-lis, 1893–4. *E.A. Johnson* of Abergavenny designed a conventional church at Rogerstone, 1887–8, and a livelier one on a magnificent site at Aberbeeg, 1907–9. This remained unfinished, as did the barn-like church of 1899–1900 at Brynmawr by *Nicholson & Hartree* of Hereford. The large church at Abertillery, built by *C.B. Fowler* of Cardiff over the period 1898–1906, has quite a noble interior in the spirit of Bodley. More thoroughly Bodley-like is St John the Baptist, Newport, by *F.R. Kempson* of Llandaff, built 1898–1900. This church forms part of an extensive group, including the vicarage of 1902, the hall of 1903 by *H.J. Griggs* of Newport, and a mission house and children's home, 1907, by *Griggs* with *W. Bucknall* of London. *Kempson* began a similar church at Cwmbran in 1907, left incomplete until the 1950s. Much later, 1926–9, *Griggs* embarked on one final Bodleyesque church, at Newbridge, but got no further than the chancel and transepts.

One further development at the end of the C19 requires mention. All the major ex-monastic churches which had been remodelled earlier in the century were now worked over again to bring them into line with what it was felt a large medieval church should look like. The nave of Abergavenny church was in 1881–2 remodelled by *Thomas Nicholson* of Hereford in a handsome but conventional Dec style. At Usk in 1899–1900 *G.E. Halliday* of Llandaff recast the nave, using medieval evidence. Most ambitious was the reconstruction by *Seddon & Carter* of the E end of Chepstow church, in a campaign which began in 1890 and was abandoned incomplete in 1913. What was achieved impresses nonetheless, crossing, chancel and partially reconstructed transepts, all in a soaring Geometrical design reminiscent of their contemporary new churches in Glamorgan, at Cardiff and Penarth.

Once *Coates Carter* was on his own, his church design developed in a radically different direction. Although he remained faithful to Gothic principles and, in general, to Gothic vocabulary, he simplified his style and gave more self-conscious expression to the inherent qualities of the materials with which he worked, in an Arts and Crafts spirit. His sense of spatial drama ensured that even the simplified designs enforced by cost remain strongly individual. His first church to be begun was St John the Divine, Pontypool, built 1912–13 and 1924–6, on a sloping site over a hall. It combines a lofty exterior when seen from the E with a broad, low interior with quirky late Perp details, in the tradition set by Norman Shaw in his London suburban churches at Latimer Road and Bedford Park of the 1870s. By far the most theatrical of *Coates Carter*'s churches is at Abercarn, 1923–6, its tower soaring high on a hill above the valley-bottom settlement. Its present derelict state only enhances its Piranesian grandeur. But it is the town church of SS Julius and Aaron, Newport, which shows the architect at his most radical. After two more ambitious designs of 1910 and 1917 had been rejected, a scheme of 1923 was executed in slightly reduced form, but never brought to completion. Yet for all these compromises, the design, ruggedly carried out in rough Pennant sandstone and red brick with the minimum of mouldings, has remarkable force. Inside, the arcade piers are of concrete. Similar materials and an even more primitivist style, which avoids the pointed arch altogether, can be seen in the little hall-cum-church of St Philip, Newport, built in 1924. Only *Coates Carter* could have conceived this remarkable little building.

Victorian Church Fittings

No new-built Victorian church nor any scheme of restoration during the period could be considered complete without the provision of worthy fittings. So VICTORIAN CHURCH FITTINGS require their own paragraphs. Most important were the reredos, the pulpit and the font, and architects might lavish great care on their design. But a well-funded scheme could also involve architect-designed choir stalls and pews, lectern, screens, wall decorations and floor tiles. Stained-glass windows might be inserted as part of a scheme, but by no means always so; indeed stained glass largely took over from marble monuments as the preferred medium for commemorating the deceased. *John Prichard* and *J. P. Seddon*, whether in partnership or working independently, regularly supplied specially designed fittings. Llandogo, 1859–61, has the most complete ensemble, though all the elements are simply designed. *Prichard & Seddon*'s restoration at Llansoy, 1858, involved a similarly full set, as did *Seddon*'s at Llanfoist in 1872, in memory of the ironmaster Crawshay Bailey, so particularly well funded. The centrepiece of *Seddon*'s work at Llangwm Uchaf, also in the 1870s, was his spectacular restoration of the medieval rood screen and loft, but the incumbent also commissioned an extensive series of new fittings.

Among *Prichard*'s restorations, the one that led to the fullest refitting was at Mitchel Troy, *c.* 1876, while his rebuilding of Llanddewi Skirrid church, 1879, involved provision of a full set of fittings. Some of the most splendid individual pieces do not belong to ensembles. *Prichard*'s early Neo-Norman rebuilding of Malpas in 1849–50 enabled him to create a rich Neo-Norman font, pulpit and reading desk as well. Later notable fonts are *Prichard & Seddon*'s impressive pieces of solid geometry at St John, Newport, *c.* 1860, and Llanhennock, 1863, and *Prichard*'s, to a highly unusual design, carved with flowers and netted fish, at Mitchel Troy, *c.* 1876. Among pulpits, there is an exceptionally elaborate one at Rockfield, *c.* 1860, as well as two by *Prichard* based on the famous C13 pulpit at Beaulieu Abbey, Hampshire, at Llanbadoc, 1873, and Mitchel Troy, *c.* 1876. The late pulpit by *Prichard* at Mathern, *c.* 1882, is the most handsome example in timber. The pulpit at Rogiet, 1903, by *Seddon & Carter* is Art Nouveau. The other exceptional item is the splendid organ at Usk, made for Llandaff Cathedral to *Seddon*'s design in 1862.

The only impressive ensemble in a church by another architect is at *Buckeridge*'s Llanfrechfa. The reredos, with a large relief carved by *Redfern*, and the tall timber chancel screen, the font and tomb-chest-like immersion font are all of 1874, supplied after Buckeridge's death and so probably to the design of *J. L. Pearson*, who completed the job. Floor tiles by *Godwin* of Lugwardine are used here to telling effect. *John Norton*'s restorations at Magor and Redwick make similar effective use of floor tiles, as does *J. D. Sedding*'s reconstruction of Llanfair Kilgeddin, *c.* 1876. *Sedding*'s rectilinear alabaster reredos here is very much in keeping with them. Some notable reredoses include sculpture. *Redfern*'s at Llanfrechfa, already mentioned, has a relief of the Last Supper. *Sir Gilbert Scott*'s at Brynmawr, 1860, brought in from Richmond, Yorkshire, frames Christ in Majesty and saints under trefoiled arches and gables. At Llangattock-vibon-awel is an alabaster reredos of 1875 by *Earp*. At Llandogo there is a white marble eucharistic relief, part of *Seddon & Carter*'s enrichment of the chancel in 1889. The two most toweringly architectural compositions were both made for Roman Catholics, one at Abergavenny, 1883 to the design of *Edmund Kirby* of Liverpool, the other brought into SS Julius and Aaron, Newport, from the monastic church at Capel-y-ffin, Powys, and made *c.* 1882 to the design of *H. F. Webber*. *Kirby* also designed the reredos in the R.C. domestic chapel at Glen-trothy, Llanvetherine, *c.* 1885. Also of this period is the important font at Monmouth, made by *Farmer & Brindley* to *G. E. Street*'s design *c.* 1883, but now unfortunately moved from its carefully considered setting.

Two important schemes of wall decoration remain. At Llandogo in 1889 the side walls of the chancel were decorated by *Seddon & Carter* with angels and lilies. But far more extensive, varied and
delightful are the sgraffito decorations applied to the entire interior 106
at Llanfair Kilgeddin 1888–90 by *Heywood Sumner*. Artistically they are undoubtedly the most important work mentioned in this section.

Victorian Stained Glass

There is a good deal to admire and enjoy in the stained glass in churches throughout the county. Pugin led the revival of medieval methods of making stained glass and the medievalizing representation of sacred subjects in glass. The earliest signs of the influence of his ideas can be seen at Trevethin, in two windows of 1847 by *Thomas Willement*, with small, strongly coloured scenes in roundels, echoing C13 practice, but painted not stained. Windows at Mathern by *Joseph Bell* of Bristol, one dated 1848 the other *c.* 1854, are similar in composition and colour, as are the windows by *George Rogers* of Worcester of 1850–5 at Malpas and *c.* 1854 at Llanfrechfa. The firm which Pugin himself promoted and encouraged to make windows of a quality and character to satisfy him was *Hardman*. Their singing colours and legible compositions can be seen in windows at three Roman Catholic churches: Usk, 1857 and *c.* 1862, Newport, 1859, and Abergavenny, 1861, particularly intense. Their window at Itton of *c.* 1869 may have been designed by the architect *Woodyer*. The most impressive *Hardman* piece in the county is later, the dramatic Ascension in the E window at Llandogo of *c.* 1879. The most convincing evocation of the hieratic figures and intense greens and reds of early C13 glass is *Alfred Gerente*'s saints of 1857, made for Butterfield's All Saints, Margaret Street, London, but ejected by the architect and now to be found on the staircase at Llanfrechfa Grange, Llanfrechfa. The series of windows in the domestic chapel there, of the 1860s by *Wailes*, a Pugin disciple, pale by comparison.

By the 1860s new firms were coming to the fore, experimenting with a wider range of colours, and more complex compositions, owing less to the Middle Ages and more to contemporary easel painting. The most powerful representatives of the changed approach are *Heaton, Butler & Bayne*'s fine, if idiosyncratic, windows, both of 1866, at St Maughans and Llangattock-vibon-awel. The complexity of their narrative style may be seen in the large window of 1879 attributed to them at Grosmont, and above all in the series of seven crowded scenes of *c.* 1896 at Caerleon. Similar in concept are the two large and colourful windows at St John, Maindee, Newport, one of 1865 by *Chance Brothers & Co.*, the other of *c.* 1873 by *Samuel Evans* of West Smethwick. A much smaller, and unfortunately damaged, piece by *Chance Brothers* is the charming group of music-making angels at Oldcastle, 1864, made under *Seddon*'s instructions. *Seddon* was involved in the design of one other window, at Llangwm Uchaf, of *c.* 1877. This is an Annunciation of Pre-Raphaelite fervour and jewel-like coloration, not to mention superlative technique.

Prichard & Seddon designed the window of 1862 at Dixton made by *Lavers & Barraud*. This was a very variable firm, though from 1860 their principal designer was *Nathaniel Westlake*. There are windows by them at Caerwent, 1865 (brought in), at Raglan, 1868 and 1875, Llangattock-vibon-awel, also of 1875 and particularly good, and at Redwick, 1875 again. Two strongly contrasting windows at Chepstow, 1877 and 1896, both seem to be by this firm.

Powell's was another firm which employed a number of different designers. There are two particularly fine windows by them in the county, at Caldicot, 1870, and Llandevaud, designed by *Henry Holiday*, 1882.

During this period, by contrast, *Clayton & Bell*, like Hardman, consistently maintained the spirit of Pugin in their windows. At Llanfrechfa is a fine series by them of *c.* 1874; a window of *c.* 1867 at Llanwenarth is theirs, and the window of *c.* 1870 at Tintern Parva can be attributed to them, as can the handsome heraldic window of 1872 at Raglan. Similar in character is *Joseph Bell*'s highly effective illustration of the Sacrifice of Isaac at Magor, 1880.

Most instantly recognizable among the stained-glass firms active at the end of the century is *C. E. Kempe*. He modelled his characteristic figures, stocky and heavily robed, sweet-faced and golden-locked, particularly on the C15 windows at Great Malvern Priory, and it is from such late medieval glass that he also derived his preference for subdued colouring and for individual figures, relegating narrative groups to secondary positions. However, in his earliest work Kempe ranged more widely and imaginatively. His window of 1879 at Llangattock-vibon-awel is a delightful composition of angels. Especially remarkable is the great baptistery window of 1883 at Monmouth, in which nude youths of Hellenic beauty 105
pour out the four rivers of Paradise, and four baptismal scenes show what *Kempe* could do as an illustrator. Six other windows at Monmouth, 1882–8, show him establishing his characteristic style. It can be seen again at Llantilio Crossenny, 1887 and 1898, at Wonastow, a fine Adoration of the Shepherds of 1897, at Llantarnam, 1901, 1902, and at Llanfihangel-ystern-llewern, 1906. Position is important, so chancel E windows always have a certain power, as is the case with *Kempe*'s Crucifixion windows of 1904 at Caldicot and 1907 at St John the Baptist, Newport.

The heavy elaboration which is in different ways typical of Heaton, Butler & Bayne's later work and Kempe's mature style can be seen in EARLY C20 STAINED GLASS too. Such makers whose practices flourished particularly in south-east Wales are *John Jennings*, well represented at Llanfair Kilgeddin, 1894 and 1910, and Holy Trinity, Abergavenny, *c.* 1914 and 1920, and *R. J. Newbery*, mainly to be found in Glamorgan, but with a whole churchful of windows at Cwm, Ebbw Vale, *c.* 1902–22.

Already by the turn of the century a younger generation of designers and makers was reacting in favour of a simple, clear style from which shading was largely banished, and there was a renewed emphasis on the pure colours of the stained glass itself. *Ninian Comper* was the leader. Windows by him at St John the Baptist, Newport, of 1901, Wonastow, 1903, and Wyesham, 1906, come like a douche of cold water. The two windows of *c.* 1922 by *F. C. Eden* develop this idiom, freshly at Trevethin, and on a grand scale but with a loss of intensity at Abergavenny. *Arnold Robinson* of *Joseph Bell & Son* was working in a similar spirit in his attractive window of 1930 at Rogiet. This paragraph can close with a list of strongly characterized curiosities: the storybook window of 1910 at Llanbadoc by *Gerald Moira*, two intense pieces by *A. J. Davies* of the *Bromsgrove Guild*, at Bedwellty, *c.* 1925, and Wyesham, 1926, and the spectacularly colourful windows by *Florence Camm* at Wolvesnewton, 1924, and *Theodora Salusbury* at Newchurch, 1931.

Victorian Church Monuments

A few later C19 sculptured memorials deserve mention. At St George's, Tredegar, there are two with portraits (†1851, by *J. E.*

Thomas, and †1868, by *E. W. Wyon*). At Trevethin the bust of Capel Hanbury Leigh (†1861) is unsigned. *J. Milo Griffith*'s monument (†1881) in Crane Street Baptist Church, Pontypool, has a pair of sensitive relief portraits. *J. Forsyth* signs an idiosyncratic bust-length relief portrait at Marshfield, †1887, and the similar piece (†1891) at Lower Machen is clearly by him too. The relief portrait at Llanfihangel Crucorney is dated 1887 and signed *Romanelli*. The only exceptional piece of this period is *H. H. Armstead*'s monument at Llantilio Crossenny, commemorating a judge (†1881) with a relief of blind Justice.

During the C20 monuments erected in churches have dwindled into insignificance. In the county only one remains in the memory, *W. Goscombe John*'s haunting gilt-bronze relief (†1919) at Marshfield of a woman reluctantly leaving life. It is a revealing reversal of emphasis from monuments of a century earlier.

Early Twentieth-century Church Fittings

This account of memorials has run on well into the C20, so it is necessary to provide a parallel account of other EARLY C20 ECCLESIASTICAL WORK. The most interesting designer and architect in the first decade of the century is *Arthur Grove,* son of a vicar of Govilon, whose range and idiom place him squarely in the Arts and Crafts movement. His monument to his father, †1897, in the churchyard at Govilon makes characteristic use of stylized foliage. His chancel screen at Llanvaches Church, 1907–8, employs foliage in more unexpected ways. Also at Llanvaches he introduced a strikingly notched nave roof and abstract stained glass in the church, and designed a wittily detailed parish room, 1908, alongside. Glass, timber and stone sculpture all have a part to play in the remarkably original porch he added to Wonastow Church in 1909. His scheme of 1910 at Tredunnock is less noteworthy, but includes a fine lettered tablet by *Eric Gill*.

In this context there is the Art Nouveau-ish pulpit and screen at Llanvetherine by an unknown designer, also the handsome set of fittings at Bedwellty by *E. P. Warren*, 1910, and three pieces by *J. Coates Carter*: the sumptuous carved and painted reredos now at Chepstow, the Perp rood screen at Abertillery of 1921, and the sacrament house at Wonastow, 1922. *W. D. Caröe* designed the handsome Neo-Baroque war memorial in Abergavenny Church, and 1932–5 extended the chancel of Caerleon Church in his favourite fancy Perp style, and supplied a number of fittings.

Domestic Architecture from the 1830s

COUNTRY HOUSES IN A MEDIEVAL STYLE were slow to appear. James Wyatt's Fonthill had been built and had collapsed (in 1825) before anything significant had happened in Monmouthshire. The earliest datable such house is the prim little castellated shooting box built on the motte of Abergavenny Castle in 1819. The trendsetter, however, seems to have been Llanover House, 1828–37, built by *Thomas Hopper* for Sir Benjamin Hall, M.P. (later Lord

Llanover), and his wife, the celebrated promoter of Welsh language and culture. It was presumably the Halls who selected the Elizabethan style for their new mansion (which was demolished in 1935). It was of three storeys, on an E-plan and crowned by a pierced parapet, not particularly Welsh in character. The eccentrically detailed stables survive, as do gate lodges, of which the principal one does have a Welsh model (at Crickhowell, Powys).

The principal beneficiary of the change of fashion was the well-connected *T. H. Wyatt*. In 1834–5 he reconstructed the large but rather shapeless Elizabethan Llantarnam Abbey, and gave it some
external coherence by means of handsome entrance arches which 112
frame views of the house from the two directions of approach. His gate lodge is a prettier version of Hopper's at Llanover. In 1837 he began to work for his most faithful clients, the Rolls family
of The Hendre. Between then and 1841 he was employed by pp.
J. E. W. Rolls to extend the S front of the shooting box built by his 248
father in the late 1820s, adhering to the Neo-Norman style already established, but indulging in a great deal of grotesque sculpture. Wyatt's later phases at The Hendre, of 1858 and 1870–2, are Tudor Gothic, the domestic style into which he had early settled down. His Malpas Court, 1836–8, and Llandogo Priory, 1838, are in that style, as is his enlargement of Cefntilla, Llandenny, for Lord Raglan in 1858, and Llangattock Manor, Llangattock-vibon-awel, a secondary house of the Rolls family, built as late as 1877–80. There is little to distinguish these buildings, erected over a period of forty years. Only the stepped gables of the gate lodges at The Hendre, 1850, strike a fresh note.

Wyatt was not alone in his preference for Tudor Gothic in the middle decades of the century. *G. V. Maddox* had used it for his own house, Pentwyn, Rockfield, *c.* 1834–7, and in the 1840s the Newport-based architect *J. H. Langdon* made it his own. Langdon built The Friars, Newport, for the antiquary Octavius Morgan *c.* 1844, and Llanfrechfa Grange, *c.* 1848, where his client was a son of Wyatt's client at Malpas Court. Both houses, in scale little more than villas, display elaborate pierced bargeboards on their many gables, placing them still in the tradition of the *cottage orné*. *Langdon*'s parsonages of 1845–6 at Caerwent and Langstone use the same idiom on a smaller scale. A full-blown country house in this style is the extraordinary Nevill Hall, Abergavenny, built as late as the late 1860s by an unknown architect. Dingestow Court, on the other hand, is a substantial country house, reconstructed and enlarged in 1845–6, in a scholarly Elizabethan style. In fact, the S front, at the request of the client Samuel Bosanquet, of the Essex banking family, is a copy in stone of a brick house of the 1590s in south-east England, Franks at Horton Kirby, Kent. The stable court at Dingestow Court is a little later, 1859–60, by the ecclesiastical specialists *Prichard & Seddon*. Here they adhere to an appropriately quiet Tudor idiom.

In several PARSONAGES *Prichard & Seddon* appear in more characteristic colours, as exponents of Puginian Gothic. The parsonages at Llanfrechfa, 1856, and Llanmartin, 1857–8, are sensi- 113
tive but animated essays in polychromy, mixing local stones and

brick. The slightly later one at Caerleon, of 1862, is subdued by comparison. The only other parsonage by an Ecclesiological architect, that at Caldicot by *Henry Woodyer*, is also of 1862. The lively elevation it presents towards the church is an excellent example of the 'true picturesque', explicit of the varied functions of the internal spaces. *Edmund Sedding*'s Govilon Hall, built as the rectory in 1867, is Tudor Gothic in style and on a substantial scale. Finally, in 1886–8, *J. D. Sedding* built the vicarage at Brynmawr in a Norman-Shaw-inspired idiom, with slate-hung upper storey.

To turn from individually designed houses to SPECULATIVE DEVELOPMENT in the mid and late C19, one has to explore the suburbs of Newport and the outskirts of Abergavenny. In Newport,
97 Victoria Place is a short but complete example of stuccoed classicism, of as late as 1844. For the looser Italianate style, with houses still stuccoed but in more varied groupings and breaking out into turrets and window bays, Maindee is the most fruitful of Newport's suburbs. This was being developed from the early 1850s. The best individual example is Cambrian House, St John's Road, dated 1859. Gold Tops was another area under development during the 1850s, and here good Italianate and *cottage orné* examples survive. *R. G. Thomas* was active in both areas, but at Gold Tops the *Habershon* firm seems to have had the lion's share of the work. Clytha Park was developed in the 1860s, still with Italianate villas. By the late 1870s, when *A. O. Watkins* was involved in developing Stow Park, High Victorian Gothic and Norman Shaw's tile-hanging and half-timbered gables held wide appeal; though the later phase of this development, *c.* 1882–5, showed knowledge of the red brick Queen Anne style developed in Kensington a decade earlier. *Watkins*'s Nant Coch, now Rougemont School, of 1879, is an elaborate example of the earlier style.

In Abergavenny suburban expansion began in the 1880s. Here the local architect *E. A. Johnson* was allowed to have his head from 1884 to the turn of the century. His Shaw-inspired style, resourcefully expressed in the local materials of Pennant sandstone and yellow Ebbw Vale brick, gives the town a special flavour.

In order to complete the account of domestic architecture in the county up to 1914, the impact of the ARTS AND CRAFTS MOVEMENT must be assessed. This was felt almost entirely through the activities and patronage of rural landowners, who could draw on connections with the cultural avant garde in London. The first house to mention, Tal-y-coed Court, Llanfihangel-ystern-llewern, was built 1881–3 for J.A. Bradney, the future historian of Monmouthshire, immediately after his coming of age. His architect was not metropolitan, but from Hereford, *F. R. Kempson*, then at the outset of his career as an ecclesiastical Gothicist. Between them they created a most unusual building for its date, an evocation in red brick of a house of the 1660s, crowned by a high hipped roof and bold symmetrical chimneystacks. The first full-blown Arts and Crafts scheme was *Guy Dawber*'s enlargement of Itton Court, 1893–6, in a picturesque late medieval idiom which aimed to integrate the C14 gate-tower and the early C18 range into a

coherent courtyard house. Inside, an early C18 character was allowed to dominate. At the same time J. A. Rolls of The Hendre, soon to be elevated to the peerage as Lord Llangattock, embarked on the last phase of enlargement of his mansion and the enhancement of 114
his extensive estate. For his architect he chose *Aston Webb*, who between 1894 and 1906, while at the height of his career as a fashionable public architect in England, designed a variety of buildings on the Rolls estate, together constituting the outstanding architectural performance of the period in the county. The centrepiece is the library wing added to The Hendre in 1895–6. It is in a mixed late Gothic and Elizabethan style, but with the broad, low proportions characteristic of Arts and Crafts design, and some equally typical sculpture. The library itself is a sumptuous room, with a many-light bay window and two enormous chimneypieces, the larger a complicated inglenook with overlooking closet, challenging Norman Shaw's great chimneypieces at Dawpool and Cragside. Among houses on the estate, the agent's house, Croes Vaen, designed in 1894, is particularly suave, and at Rockfield there are both the pretty little Swiss Lodge of 1905 in the park, and the ingeniously detailed single-storey range of roadside almshouses, 1906.

The buildings put up by *O. P. Milne*, a former assistant of Lutyens, for Viscount Rhondda on his estate at Llanwern, are smaller, quieter and, in a sense, more characteristic of the Arts and Crafts ideal, in that they depend for most of their effect on the sensitive handling of local materials. Between *c.* 1906 and 1913 Milne built at Llanwern the village hall, and various cottages, together with a house at Llanhennock, also of 1909, for Lord Rhondda's daughter and son-in-law. Some of the most attractive and interesting work of this class was by local architects. *Norman Evill*, another Lutyens pupil, but son of Walter Evill, architect of Chepstow, in 1909 added a large, picturesque wing to Shirenewton Hall, a Jacobean-style mansion of 1901. *Arthur Grove*, whose ecclesiastical work has already been mentioned, seems to have designed the interior which most fully displays the Arts and Crafts ethos, the tunnel-vaulted ballroom at Hilston Park, St Maughans, added in 1912. Plasterwork on the vaults, foliage bands and signs of the Zodiac, and an elaborate inglenook fireplace, an abstract composition of polished stone and tile, create a memorable ensemble.

Before introducing the third local architect, one or two other pre-1914 works can be mentioned. *E. P. Warren*, Bodley's pupil, rebuilt Maesruddud (now Maes Manor Hotel), Blackwood, in 1900 and 1907 in an uncomfortably hard Tudor style. *A. T. Bolton*, better known as curator of Sir John Soane's Museum than as an architect, built one of his few houses at Llanhennock, Colomendy Wood, 1913–14. This is reticent externally, but has some spatial panache inside. Finally, Llansantffraed Court, dated 1912, is a handsome essay in Lutyenesque classicism, apparently by *Fairfax B. Wade*.

Eric Francis of Chepstow enjoyed the patronage of H. Avray Tipping, the prolific author of articles for *Country Life*. In 1894 Tipping acquired Mathern Palace, the fragmentary remains of a C15 and early C16 palace of the bishops of Llandaff, which he

converted and somewhat enlarged with a tact William Morris himself would have applauded, incorporating some of the ruined fabric into a romantic garden. A decade later it was Tipping's passion for creating gardens which led him to a much more dramatic site nearby, at Mounton, where between 1911 and 1914 he built
115 Mounton House. This is a full-scale country house, apparently
p. designed by himself, and owing two of its most visually arresting
413 effects to late medieval houses in Yorkshire and Gloucestershire, about which he had recently written for *Country Life*. Its vernacular vocabulary, however, combined with a certain sweeping panache, shows an unmistakeable debt to Lutyens (another favourite of *Country Life*). The interiors are eclectic, with various brought-in pieces. The house is largely built of local limestone, handled with a knowledge of local vernacular building practice – probably the contribution of *Eric Francis*, who seems to have acted as executant architect. Francis had trained under Dawber. His surehanded way with local materials is shown in several smaller houses of the early 1920s. The retirement house he built for Tipping in 1922–3, High Glanau, Cwmcarvan, and its accompanying cottages, are the mature expression of their shared philosophy. Others are Golden Hill and the village hall at St Arvans. His largest post-war house, Wyndcliffe Court, St Arvans, of 1922, with its shaped gables and internal plasterwork, however, shows that he had a taste for the decorative, as does his unusual Neo-Baroque war memorial at Chepstow of the same period.

The swansong of the Arts and Crafts movement in the county dates from the mid 1920s. This is the model village laid out for Lord Treowen at Llanover. His architect, *Alfred H. Powell*, grouped round an irregular green individually designed cottages and pairs, their walls of local stone and stone-slate roofs handled with loving craftsmanship. *Powell*'s, too, are the more formally designed school bearing a Welsh inscription and the war memorial consisting of nothing more than an upright, field-found stone. Here is a real search for the roots of local culture.

GARDEN DESIGN, so important for many of these houses, deserves a few more words. The most exotic garden in the county is at Shirenewton Hall, where from 1901 various Chinese structures of brilliantly coloured glazed tile were set up, and an elaborate Japanese garden laid out. *Thomas H. Mawson*, having laid out Bellevue Park, Newport, in 1892, with formal terraces on the hillside site, gained one other commission, for the grandly conceived garden at Maesruddud, Blackwood, of *c.* 1907.

Nineteenth-century Public Buildings

These may be discussed not through a consideration of the styles which they assumed, nor of the careers of particular architects, but through the authorities, or other bodies which were responsible for their erection.

The county Justices of the Peace looked after BRIDGES, and in Monmouthshire the County Surveyor *John Upton* designed several.
95 His finest is the bridge over the River Usk at Llanfair Kilgeddin, of

1821. The large spandrel voids, which had been used to ensure the stability of William Edwards's celebrated bridge of 1756 at Pontypridd, Glamorgan, are here merely decorative. For the most significant bridge in the county, however, the one which, spanning the River Wye at Chepstow, provided the S-most road crossing 94
from England into Wales, a bridge-designer of national repute was employed. *John Rennie*'s elegant cast-iron bridge of 1814–16 rests its five segmental arches on strong, sheer ashlar piers. It resembles his Southwark Bridge, erected in the same years over the, admittedly much wider, River Thames.

Road improvement, by contrast, although authorized by parliament, was carried out by private turnpike companies, which levied tolls on users for their upkeep, under an Act of 1756. The 1820s and '30s were in Monmouthshire the most active for the construction of turnpike roads. Several of the toll-keepers' cottages survive, at Caerleon, Llanbadoc (dated 1837), Mitchel Troy and elsewhere. They are dressed up in Tudoresque *cottage orné* style.

The Poor Law Amendment Act of 1834 required County Justices to provide for poor relief within groups, or unions, of parishes, for each of which a WORKHOUSE was to be built. Monmouthshire was divided into five unions, but only two workhouses survive, both built in 1837–8. That at Abergavenny, one of the many designed by *George Wilkinson* of Oxford, has a Tudor-style front range that presents quite a friendly face to the outside world. The Newport workhouse (now St Woolos Hospital), by *T. H. Wyatt*, embodies more frankly the spirit of the Act, utilitarian and forbidding, its tall, red brick ranges forming a Greek cross within a square. In this context it is appropriate to mention the pauper lunatic asylum, built under the Lunacy Act of 1845 on the outskirts of Abergavenny to serve Monmouthshire and three other neighbouring counties: Pen-y-fal Hospital. It was designed by *Fulljames & Waller* of Gloucester and built 1849–52. Its extensive frontage, gabled and lancet-windowed, with decorated incinerator chimneys, must have been intended as an enhancement of the prospect from the town, as its further subsequent embellishment would seem to confirm. St Cadoc's Hospital, Caerleon, built as a mental hospital 1903–6, to designs by *A. J. Wood* of London, is a characteristic representative of its time, its great scale minimized by the compact faceted layout of its wards.

The county GAOL built at Monmouth in 1789 (*see* above, p. 44) was replaced by the County Justices in 1841–2 by one more centrally sited in the county, at Usk. *T. H. Wyatt* was the architect, under orders from the Surveyor General of Prisons in London to use the brand-new Pentonville Prison as model. Hence the semi-polygonal plan, within which long, straight cell ranges radiate from a central block. Towards the road an intimidating stretch of sandstone wall with central arched entrance confronts the outside world. The adjoining single-storeyed Italianate Sessions House is also by *Wyatt*, but later, designed probably in 1858 and built 1875–7. It confirms the county's association of classicism with the enforcement of law.

The expression of municipal pride by the building of TOWN HALLS was a slow and patchy process. The remodelling of the

Town Hall at Usk in 1816 and 1835 left it larger, but still quite modest. The Duke of Beaufort financed the building of the miniature Town Hall at Grosmont 1829–32. The Town Hall at Pontypool, built 1854–6 after the manner of an Italian palazzo, was paid for by the local landowners, the Hanbury Leighs – though a competition was held to select the architect, won by the Wolverhampton firm of *Bidlake & Lovatt*. Only Abergavenny and Newport made significant gestures of civic pride. At Abergavenny a modest town hall and market house had been built in 1794–5 to
116 a design by *John Nash*, replaced in 1825. The present building, the most ambitious secular example of High Victorian Gothic in the county, is of 1869–71 by *Wilson & Willcox* of Bath. Utilitarian market hall and corn exchange are fronted by a tall, stone-faced range towards the street with council chamber above shops, and a splendidly upstanding and conspicuous angle tower. Newport's Town Hall, of 1883–5, again designed by an English provincial architect, here *T. M. Lockwood* of Chester, in association with *E. A. Lansdowne*, a local man, has unfortunately not survived. The Market Hall, however, is a not unworthy substitute, 1887–9 by the Town Surveyor *Conyers Kirby*, assisted by the obscure *T. E. Watkins*. Its lofty, steep-roofed frontage centred on a steep-roofed tower maintains the late medieval cloth-hall image so popular for mid-Victorian civic buildings. Otherwise, mention need be made only of the semi-Jacobean Rolls Hall, Monmouth, 1887–8 by *F. A. Powell*, another act of private patronage, as its name suggests. However, this paragraph can end with the Shire Hall, Newport, badly sited and awkwardly designed in a Jacobean style by the County Surveyor *William Tanner*, and built in 1901–2.

EDUCATIONAL BUILDINGS can be categorized in three groups according to their promoters, the Church, the State and private institutions. Grammar schools had been founded here and there by philanthropic individuals since the C16, and some of their buildings have already been mentioned (*see* p. 43). The organized provision of widespread primary education began in the early C19, with the foundation in 1811 of the (Anglican) National Society, and the (non-denominational) British Society in 1814. The former was much more successful than the latter, and over the ensuing three-quarters of a century national schools were built in their hundreds throughout the country, usually designed by architects active in church work. Normally such schools consisted of no more than a schoolroom and the teacher's house, but this gave scope enough for picturesque composition. Gothic, naturally, was the style almost invariably adopted. In Monmouthshire during the mid-century boom in building national schools, *Prichard & Seddon* received many of the commissions. Most memorable is their polychromatic Castleton School at Marshfield, of 1857, but quieter examples by them are at Magor, 1856, and Llanellen, 1861–2. A little later *Seddon* was responsible for two more, those of 1870 at Llangwm Uchaf, and 1873 at Wyesham.

Universal primary education was finally required by law under the Education Act of 1870, which provided for the establishment of school boards for towns and groups of parishes throughout

England and Wales. The earliest surviving board schools in Monmouthshire are small, mostly rural ones of the 1870s, by local architects and builders. Those by *E. H. Lingen Barker* of 1877 at Grosmont and Skenfrith fall into this category, but the earliest to proclaim itself as such is *Lawrence & Goodman*'s of 1875–6 at Tregare. *Walter Evill*'s of 1877 at Chepstow shows the heavy hand of the Duke of Beaufort's patronage. Single-storey board schools on a larger scale survive at Rogerstone, 1888 by *E. A. Lansdowne*, Abertillery, 1898 by *George Rosser*, and Abergavenny, an intermediate school by *E. A. Johnson*, 1897–8. Of the large, two-storeyed board schools – still so numerous in Glamorgan – with accommodation for boys and girls in their hundreds, only a few examples survive. In the Valleys the best is at Aberbeeg, 1901 by *R. L. Roberts*. There is another, of 1901–3 by *Lansdowne & Griggs*, at Pontnewynydd. Of the many built in Newport, only two are left, a plain one of 1892–3 by *Swash & Bain*, and a splendidly large and elaborate one dated 1902, by *Conyers Kirby & Son*, recently sympathetically restored. From after 1902, when local councils took over responsibility for school-building from the boards, a few more survive. At Abersychan is a lively little council school of 1902–3 by *Lansdowne & Griggs*, but by far the most conspicuous, in siting, scale and design is the Baroque example, now St Woolos Primary School, on Stow Hill, Newport, 1904–5 by *H. J. Griggs*. *John Bain*, County Education Architect from 1907, designed in a Neo-Georgian idiom, best seen at Abersychan, 1913, and Bassaleg, completed 1935.

The largest pre-1914 educational buildings erected by local authorities were for further education. The Technical Institute at 118
Newport, designed by the Borough Surveyor *Charles F. Ward* and built in 1909–10, is the best representative of Edwardian classicism in the county. It is a model demonstration of how to combine practical planning with a simple but grand external expression. The entrance at one corner plays with convex and concave forms, and is crowned by a copper dome which is one of the landmarks of Newport. The training college at Caerleon, begun in 1912 to the design of *Alfred Swash & Son*, by contrast squanders its magnificent ridgetop site, with an overstretched façade in an indeterminate Tudor-cum-Baroque style.

The third category, of privately endowed schools, is the most diverse. Usk Grammar School (founded 1621) was modestly rebuilt *c.* 1843 and 1863–4 in Tudor style. Monmouth Free Grammar School (founded 1614–15) was rebuilt also in the mid 1860s in Tudor Gothic. Here the architect was a London man, *William Snooke*, architect to the Haberdashers' Company, which controlled the school. As Monmouth School burgeoned into a flourishing Victorian establishment taking boarding pupils, Snooke's successor, *Henry Stock*, was called in to erect the School House, 1895–6. Its stepped gables and clustered chimneystacks grab attention at the entry into the town over the River Wye. The Haberdashers went on immediately in 1895–7 to build at Monmouth a complete Girls' School on a prominent site overlooking the town, where *Stock*'s trademark gables and huge mullion-and-transom windows make an even more dominating composition. At Pontypool, *Stock* built a third school for the Haberdashers' Company, West Monmouth School, 1896–8, where his style is only slightly more restrained, but the site is disappointingly sequestered. The other old foundation which gained new buildings at this time was King Henry VIII Grammar School, Abergavenny, where on a new, edge-of-town site the local architect *E.A. Johnson* built 1896–8 a many-gabled group which can be distinguished from his board school nearby only by its slightly more elaborate detailing.

Three other types of Victorian and Edwardian building deserve notice, one required by every self-respecting town, the others found largely within the industrial settlements of the Valleys, that is to say banks, workmen's institutes and hotels.

The earliest identifiable purpose-built BANK is at Usk, of 1848 by *R.G. Thomas*. Its stuccoed frontage is still in an early C19 mood, enlivened only by lotus-cap porch columns. *Thomas* – to digress for a moment – was responsible a decade later for a more advanced classical piece in the Masonic Hall, Newport, of 1855–8, which adopts the palazzo style. Also palazzo-style, but stone-faced not stuccoed, is the bank of 1857 in Pontypool by the bank specialist *T.R. Lysaght* of Bristol. The next period of bank-building activity was the 1890s. At Abergavenny in 1892 *E.A. Johnson* felt impelled to adopt an Italianate style, as at Newport did *C.R. Gribble* in 1892 and *A.E. Lloyd-Oswell* in 1895. *Seward & Thomas* of Cardiff employ their normal Mixed Renaissance for Barclays Bank, Pontypool, adapting it adroitly to a sloping corner site. However, *Lloyd-Oswell* in the centre of Abergavenny, at his Lloyds Bank of 1895–7, threw convention to the winds in an orgy of pink stone, red brick and half-timbering, with oriels, gables and an overall Jacobean aura. The more monumental classicism typical for banks in the early C20 is well represented by *T.B. Whinney*'s Midland Bank, Pontypool, of 1910–11.

WORKMEN'S INSTITUTES can be found dating from the late 1860s to the mid 1920s, though the period of their greatest popularity was *c.* 1890–1915. The two earliest, the Working Men's Free Institute at Monmouth, 1867–8 by *Benjamin Lawrence*, and the Mechanics' Institute at Griffithstown, 1871–5 by *Lawrence & Goodman*, are unusual in being Gothic. The end-of-the-century style was Mixed Renaissance. This is the style of the enormous
117 Workmen's Institute at Blaenavon, centrally placed in the town and built in 1893–4 to the design of the prolific Newport architect *E.A. Lansdowne*, as it is of lesser institutes at Blaina, 1892 by *F.R. Bates*, and Tredegar, of 1893. The series continues with institutes at Ebbw Vale, 1907, Fleur-de-Lis, 1911, Risca, 1915 by *R.L. Roberts*, and the undated institutes at Llanhilleth and Newbridge. The Miners' Welfare Institute at Blackwood of 1925 shows, as one would expect by that date, a rather more focused classicism. On the other hand, *Walter Rosser*'s Library & Institute of 1923–4 at Abercarn is still in an Arts and Crafts idiom, similar to his hospital at Aberbeeg, 1920–2.

Eye-catching HOTELS were built in some numbers in the years around 1900, both in Newport and in the Valleys towns and settlements. Few can be precisely dated or the names of their architects identified, but two particularly notable documented examples are the monochromatically grey but ebulliently Baroque hotel at Waun-lwyd, Ebbw Vale, of 1898–9 by *Swalwell & Creighton*, and the carnival display of red and yellow brickwork at Newbridge, 1901 by *F. R. Bates*.

Early Twentieth-century Housing

Housing at the beginning of the C20 shows a marked break with the last decades of the C19, when far-extended terraces had threaded their way along valley bottoms and criss-crossed steep hillsides. Now some colliery companies began to take the initiative in raising housing standards. The Garden City movement initiated by Ebenezer Howard in the earliest years of the new century, and first realized from 1903 by Parker & Unwin at Letchworth, Hertfordshire, conditioned their ideas. The largest new Valleys scheme was Oakdale, intended for the miners in the Tredegar Iron p. 459 and Coal Company's Oakdale Colliery. Designed by *A. F. Webb* of Blackwood in 1910–11, it was planned as a village of 660 houses, with terraces of shops, workmen's institute, hotel and two churches integrated into the layout. Even the choice of site, on a broad, gently sloping shoulder of hillside, was a break with tradition. The planned relationship of housing and community buildings was another. The influence of Letchworth and the early English garden suburbs is noticeable in the mixture of facing materials, red brick and pebbledash, and some pretty details, especially doorhoods. The most memorable feature, the symmetrical overall plan, is also probably derived from Letchworth.

The other extensive development of this period is not in the Valleys but on the outskirts of Chepstow, to house workers in the shipyard there. The first phase, of Hardwick Village, *c.* 1915–19 by *Dunn, Watson & Curtis Green*, responds to a sweeping hillside site with varied groups of terraces and pairs. Concrete blockwork was deliberately chosen for walling as an expression of modernity. The second phase, The Bulwark, 1918–19, designed by the Admiralty architect *Henry Farmer*, with advice from *H. Avray Tipping*, is more rigid and formal. Two small immediately post-war Valleys developments designed by *Walter Rosser* best capture the spirit of Parker & Unwin. In his little garden suburb at Pontywaun, Risca, of *c.* 1918–22, semi-detached houses are enlivened with exceptional variety in the use of materials. His other scheme, also begun in 1918, Victoria garden suburb at Ebbw Vale, makes ingenious use of its site to create the impression of a compact hillside village rather than anything suburban. The Dingle, a little group beside the steelworks at Ebbw Vale, is probably *Rosser*'s too.

Interwar

The interwar years saw both continuity and disruption. After 1918 the economic situation was far less favourable to building than it had been in what now must have seemed the golden years around

1900. In particular, Valleys industries saw a period of deep and sustained depression. What had seemed easy now became draggingly difficult. CHURCH-BUILDING is a case in point. What was achieved in the 1920s has been discussed above (pp. 59–60), but it can be noted here that of the most ambitious churches, that at Newbridge remains unfinished, that at Cwmbran was completed in the 1950s, when the New Town required it, and *Coates Carter*'s SS Julius and Aaron, Newport, was built to a design twice reduced from the original intention. Only *P. D. Hepworth*'s R.C. church at Newbridge of 1939–40 was completed as intended.

The most direct physical consequence of the First World War was the erection of WAR MEMORIALS. The Valleys communities suffered particularly severe losses, as the many columns of names in the memorial at Pontypool most poignantly express. Typical memorials are topped by figures of private soldiers, some weary, some triumphant. Examples are at Ebbw Vale, Monmouth and Tredegar. The most powerfully characterized of these figures is on the memorial at Abergavenny, 1921 by *Gilbert Ledward.* At Chepstow *Eric Francis* made the memorial an abstract, decorative feature at the focal point of the town. The memorial in the centre of Magor includes a bronze relief portrait by *A. G. Wyon* of Viscount Rhondda †1918, who is also commemorated by a lofty cross in Llanwern churchyard. The war memorial at Newport, 1922 by *Cyril F. Bates & Colin L. Jones*, though large, is lacking in imagination, since it follows the lead of Lutyens's Cenotaph in Whitehall, London.

What little PUBLIC AND COMMERCIAL ARCHITECTURE there is of the interwar period can all be seen in Newport. The fussy Mixed Renaissance style of the turn of the century, which dominated the town centre, was firmly set aside. In its place the austere classicism favoured in the 1920s throughout Britain found expression here and there. The largest commercial scheme is Royal Chambers, a fifteen-bay block redeveloped in 1928–9 to designs by *Cyril F. Bates & Colin L. Jones*. Tuscan aedicules break out high up from its sheer Portland stone walls. Smaller but more powerful are the roughly contemporary former offices of the *South Wales Argus* in Market Street, by *J. Bain*, with their Neo-Egyptian overtones. There is nothing more to draw attention to until the later 1930s.
119 The Odeon Cinema in Clarence Place, of 1937–8 by the cinema specialist *Harry Weedon* of Birmingham, is a splendid example of streamlining in Dudok-inspired brickwork. What should be the climax of this paragraph, however, Newport's grandly scaled Civic Centre, is something of a disappointment. A national competition was won by *T. Cecil Howitt* of Nottingham, and the building erected from 1937. Its white Portland stone bulk, symmetrical and centred on a tall tower, commands the town effectively from its hillside site. But the pitched pantiled roofs, the wall-texturing, quilted rather than rusticated, and the generally conventional detailing rob it of dignity close at hand. The best internal space is the central stair
122 hall, embellished 1961–4 by *Hans Feibusch*'s subtle and impressive murals on the upper landing.

POST 1945

The POST-1945 PERIOD has seen as much diverse building with as many heights of achievement as any preceding half-century. First, chronologically, come the CHURCHES. The Church in Wales had two important opportunities. First was the reconstruction after fire of the church at Christchurch. This was carried out 1953–5 by *G. G. Pace* with token respect for the medieval building, but boldly simplifying its forms and relying on unbroken white plaster surfaces to create an atmosphere of repose. The large E-ward extension of St Woolos Church, Newport, after it had been raised to cathedral status, was put in the hands of *A. D. R. Caroe*, 1960–4. This is a much more cautious performance, with clear Gothic allegiance after the manner of Sir Giles Scott. Both buildings come to a powerful climax at the E end, Pace's church in the blazing colours of *Harry Stammers*'s stained glass, the cathedral in *Piper* and *Reyntiens*'s inescapable but puzzling mixed-media reredos. Into numerous other churches commemorative STAINED GLASS continued to be inserted. There is some *Stammers* glass, of 1972, at Llantilio Pertholey. Otherwise, more-or-less local artists were employed, above all *Celtic Studios* of Swansea. Between 1948 (before the firm was formally established), when a window by *Howard Martin* went into St Hilda, Griffithstown, and 1985, no fewer than twenty-three churches in the county were supplied by *Celtic Studios* with their characteristic figural glass. Their windows of 1969 and 1990, at Risca, are thus a surprise, confident abstract pieces. Of the varied work of *John Petts*, there are good examples at Mynyddislwyn, 1970, and Llanddewi Rhydderch, 1988. *Geoffrey Robinson* of *Joseph Bell & Co.* of Bristol supplied windows *c.* 1979–82, at Griffithstown, Llantrisant and Nash. Largely abstract symbolic designs by *Alan Younger* can be found at Bassaleg: three from 1977 to 1990, and at St Arvans, 1994.

Roman Catholics have been much more ready to build Modernist churches, though nothing particularly noteworthy has resulted. A weak echo of Le Corbusier's Ronchamp is sensed at St David, Newport, by *F. R. Bates, Son & Price*, 1963. The chapel for Benedictine nuns at Llantarnam Abbey was built in 1957 by the same firm. The chapel of 1963–4 at Troy House, Mitchel Troy, by *Kenneth W. Smithies*, is in two parts, one for nuns, the other for the girls they taught. Among fittings, there are the stained glass at All Saints, Ebbw Vale, intense figures of 1948 and 1953 by *J. E. Nuttgens*, and ceramic works at St Alban, Pontypool, by *Adam Kossowski*, 1955–6.

The rebuilding of Nonconformist churches here and there has produced little worthy of comment. Most convincing is the polygonal Baptist church at Rogerstone, 1995–6 by *Biscoe Craig Hall*.

Building by Public Authorities

The principal authorities active in architectural design after the Second World War were Newport Borough Council, Cwmbran

New Town Development Corporation from 1949 to 1982 and Monmouthshire (from 1974 Gwent) County Council. The achievements of each can be considered in turn.

Newport Borough Council from the late 1940s embarked on a major building campaign, which produced large new housing estates with their attendant schools and terraces of shops to the NE, N and SW of the town. The Borough Architect *Johnson Blackett* and his team adopted the unemphatic Modernism favoured by their colleagues in local authorities throughout Britain. In some ways this had developed out of the stripped classicism of the 1930s, but now full advantage was taken of the flexibility and airiness possible with a simple vocabulary of brick walls, generally brown or caramel in colour rather than red, lightweight, wide-span metal roof structures, generally flat or gently monopitch roofs, and metal windows allowing unrestricted expanses of glazing. Housing was generally in short terraces or three- or four-storey blocks of flats. Schools, both single-storey primary schools, and the slabs glazed end to end which characterized secondary schools, were the most prominent buildings in these developments. The revival of interest in the Picturesque during these years encouraged informality of layout and attention to the relationship between buildings and their landscape setting. The largest expanse of such development is to the NE of Newport, the St Julians, Alway and Ringland estates. The most Picturesque is at Malpas, to the N, where former parkland was developed. However, the most characterful and thoughtfully detailed is the Gaer–Stelvio estate, to the SW, developed *c.* 1946–51 on quite steeply sloping ground overlooking Tredegar Park. The way the layout of the housing has been made to respond to the contours of the site is particularly remarkable. The largest educational building for which Newport Borough Council was responsible, however, was designed by a private firm. This is Newport Technical College, 1956–8 by *Sir Percy Thomas & Son* of Cardiff. Their cautious Modernism is quite closely in step with Johnson Blackett, and their reluctance to let go of symmetry helps to give order to such a large group.

Much more significant, even in a national context, are the results of Newport Borough Council's two major commissions to non-local architects in the late 1960s and 1970s. *Evans & Shalev*'s
125 Bettws High School, 1969–72, is a virtuoso exercise in exposed reinforced-concrete construction and an example of rigorously compact three-dimensional planning; thus on both counts it can be considered a piece of Brutalism. The great estate of nearly
p. one thousand houses at Duffryn, intended as a largely self-
218 sufficient appendage to the SW of Newport, and built 1976–9 to the designs of *MacCormac & Jamieson*, is even more an expression of theory. The two-storey terraces of monopitch-roofed houses form an almost unbroken, sinuous line contained within the perimeter band of a 96-acre (39-hectare) site. This leaves an extensive central area, part grassed, part wooded, virtually free of development. At Duffryn, then, the theories on 'perimeter planning' developed in the 1960s at the architecture department of Cambridge University, and worked out in fullest detail by

Richard MacCormac, were put into execution on an unprecedented scale.

The development of Cwmbran, unlike the post-war growth of Newport, was set within the framework of a master plan. This was prepared in 1951 by *Minoprio, Spencely & MacFarlane,* and established the overall form of the town, with a central rectangular area where community buildings and most shops were to be concentrated, a series of residential areas loosely arranged around it, and another series of industrial parks. The plan, expanded to cater for a population of 55,000 rather than the 35,000 at first envisaged, was implemented under the guidance of four successive Chief Architects, three of whom left decisive marks on the character of the town, in particular its housing. *J. C. P. West*, 1950–62, worked in an undemonstrative idiom, designing housing similar in spirit to that of Newport Borough Council at the same time, but with pitched roofs. *Gordon Redfern,* whose period as Chief Architect covered most of the 1960s, had to face up to the explosion in car ownership. He adopted the Radburn system of planning, which segregated cars and pedestrians as far as possible, and embraced the ensuing possibilities for designing houses in terraces with communal front spaces and small private gardens behind. Staggered plans, mono-pitch roofs, much greater extremes in glazing, give the housing which he designed a vigorous, sometimes hectic visual interest. He was also responsible for the one high-rise building in the town, a twenty-two-storey block of flats intended as a landmark near the town centre. *J. L. Russell* was exerting his influence even before
he took over as Chief Architect in 1972. His housing takes a middle 124
position between those of his predecessors. Cars were no longer segregated from housing, but pedestrians, and particularly children, were protected by the arrangement of houses in groups round short culs-de-sac with footpath access from group to group, and front-of-house car parking interspersed with shrub planting. House design became quieter again, but with more varied colours and textures than in the 1950s. As a coda, there is the lively, brightly coloured little group of housing at Forgeside by *MacCormac Jamieson Prichard,* completed in 1985.

The town centre was largely designed during *Redfern*'s time. The covered shopping envisaged by West, here much in advance of his time, was not implemented, but a totally pedestrianized area was achieved by an early use of multi-storey car parks with direct foot access. The main town-centre buildings, a theatre and several
office blocks, glory in exposed concrete. The largest, Monmouth 123
House, 1965–7, makes especially effective use of concrete strongly textured in a variety of ways.

SCHOOLS, in Cwmbran as well as throughout the rest of the county except Newport, were the responsibility of Monmouthshire County Council. Early on, the council experimented with commissioning private architects. Langstone Primary School, 1951–2 by *Gollins, Melvin & Partners,* is an excellent little example of what could result, fully in the spirit of the Hertfordshire schools of the period. The council's principal architect was *Colin L. Jones*. He had been active in the county since the 1920s, but was able to establish *c.* 1950 an idiomatic Modern style for both primary and secondary schools. The style respects the general conventions of the period while having enough individuality to enable one to recognize instantly schools designed within the County Architect's Department. Trademarks are the shallow-pitched, normally copper-clad roofs, the brown or caramel brickwork, and the glazing, especially on the three-storey classroom blocks of secondary schools, where broad horizontal bands of classroom windows are interrupted at regular intervals by broad vertical strips of staircase windows. There is a particularly good selection of such schools, both primary and secondary, at Cwmbran, the earliest of all being Llantarnam School, 1950–4. Croesyceiliog Comprehensive School, 1955–9, is an unusually self-conscious group, and illustrates the policy of including accommodation for adult education, thereby increasing the overall budget. Other typical examples elsewhere in the county are at Caldicot, *c.* 1957–8, and Trevethin, both with later additions. The Tertiary College at Cross Keys, Risca, *c.* 1956–61, is another good representative.

During the 1960s, after Jones had been succeeded as County Architect by *Sydney Leyshon*, Monmouthshire schools lost their characteristic identity. Planning of both primary and secondary schools became more compact and often in-turned, with grouping round one or more internal courtyards. Fairwater Comprehensive School, Cwmbran, 1969–71, epitomizes this approach.

From 1974 Gwent County Council's Architect's Department, under *Kenneth P. Jones*, continued to have plenty of school work. From now on there was a much greater variety of approach, assistants were given greater autonomy, and during the 1980s several memorable buildings were produced. The Children's Assessment Centre at Abergavenny, 1975–7 by *Jones* with *Glyn Smith*, a series of grey brick pavilions with monopitch roofs, is very much a product of its date, as are the large red brick, split-pitch-roofed additions to Abersychan Comprehensive School, 1977–80, design architects *John Postill* and *Norman Robson-Smith*.

During the 1980s, however, *Robson-Smith*'s design, fired by Richard Rogers's Inmos factory (*see* below), took off in four highly personal educational buildings. First, 1983–8, came two of four intended phases of the arts range of Gwent College of Further Education at Caerleon. What looks like an extraordinary glass cascade clothes exposed steel-framing, which defines the complex split-level internal spaces. The three primary schools *Robson-Smith* went on to design all exploit steel-framing, in rectilinear and diagonal structures, to create spatial interest internally and a brightly painted external armature. The polychromatic brickwork follows the fashion of the late 1980s. Pentrepoeth, Bassaleg, 1985–6, is the most rigorously composed, employing triangular forms with ingenious variety. Eveswell, Newport, completed 1990, manages a sloping urban site with eye-catching verve. Blaen-y-cwm, Brynmawr, 1988–91, with its sheltering roofslopes and enfolding plan, is most in tune with *Gwent County Architect's Department*'s other schools of the period, from Cwmffrwdoer, Pontnewynydd, *c.* 1982–3, designed by *John Postill,* to that of the early 1990s at Cross Ash,

Skenfrith, 1989–91. Another individualistic effort is the large addition to Overmonnow Primary School, Monmouth, designed by *Charles Parry*. Last comes the unusually formal primary school at Risca, 1991–3, design assistant *Kim Cooper*. Few secondary schools were built by the County Council during this period, but *John Postill*'s Abertillery Comprehensive School of 1984–6 develops the clustering, protective primary school idiom on a larger scale.

Civic Buildings and Sculpture

A wider view of the county's public architecture over the past fifty years reveals buildings for a variety of functions, which chart changing thinking about the relationship between efficient layout and external expression in community provision. In particular one can contrast ideas current in the years around 1970 with those in the air twenty years later. *Sir Percy Thomas*'s Crematorium at Panteg of 1958–60 is early enough to echo interwar or even pre-1914 idioms with its overtones of Voysey and Sir Herbert Baker's South African works. Mature, unquestioning Modernism finds its major expressions in two buildings of a decade later. *Percy Thomas Partnership*'s Nevill Hall Hospital, Abergavenny, 1965–74, is a blunt composition of two linked five-storey blocks, each an H in plan. *Robert Matthew, Johnson Marshall & Partners*' County Hall, Cwmbran, 1969–77, also gives simple expression to its mainly office function, in a seven-storey Y-plan arrangement which allows for completely regular bands of fenestration. The lower, civic section down the slope, linked by a bridge and cantilevered storey by storey, has greater individuality. For their adjoining County Police Headquarters, 1971–7, the architects saw no reason to vary or contrast their style – though it is interesting to recall that in 1970 they were engaged on designing their revolutionary Hillingdon Civic Centre, London, in which an open-plan layout is masked by a cascade of broken forms. At Duffryn, for a national government building, the *Percy Thomas Partnership* developed the straightforward expression and diagonal planning of County Hall, Cwmbran, in their Central Statistical Office, completed in 1973, in plan an X-and-a-half. The inappropriately impregnable-looking little Public Library at Tredegar, of 1974–5 by *Powell, Alport & Partners*, in total disregard of its town-centre setting, is the sort of building which made the public keen for something more friendly and engaging.

The Gwent County Council schools of the 1980s, discussed above, were one response to this desire. Another was the adoption of a 'Neo-vernacular' idiom in housing design. This is well represented by the *Holder Mathias Partnership*'s three infill schemes in the centre of Chepstow, 1982–9. In public architecture *PSA Projects Cardiff*'s two contemporaneous schemes, the Patent Office, Duffryn, 1989–90, and the Crown Court, Newport, 1989–91, demonstrate how respect for context and individual expression can be combined. The Patent Office adjoins the Central Statistical Office and continues its plan of cornerwise courtyards, but not its design. The bands of brown brick and bronzed glazing of the earlier building give way to an altogether more sprightly idiom, the continuous glazing screened by a network of white steel maintenance decks and overhung by projecting pitched roofs. The Crown Courts at Newport boldly but neatly occupy the central space between the wings of the Civic Centre, and find a way to allude to its architecture without imitation. The most recent public building to require mention, the Central Police Station at Newport, opened in 1993, is the last major work of *Gwent County Architect's Department*, before it was disbanded as a result of the local government changes of 1996. This is a more seriously considered building than it looks, dressing up cell block, administration office and sports hall in a wayward but arresting combination of sheer yellow brickwork, full-height areas of glazing and etiolated Neo-Egyptian pilotis.

The most remarkable recent civic work, however, is the series of town-centre sculptures commissioned by Newport Borough Council. The council started by erecting from 1975 a series of mosaic panels of historical subjects by *Kenneth Budd*, and later *Kenneth & Oliver Budd*. At the end of the 1980s their ambitions advanced. The free-standing pieces range from the monumentally Caro-like metal construction set up beside the river by *Peter Fink*, 1990, to the enigmatic commemorative figure groups in Commercial Street, 1989 by *Christopher Kelly* and 1990 by *Paul Bothwell Kincaid*, and to the
127, hyper-realistic animals by *Sebastian Boyesen* of 1994–5. *Andy*
128 *Plant*'s *faux-naïf* automaton clock in John Frost Square was made
for the Ebbw Vale Garden Festival of 1992.

Bridges

In order to complete the story of bridge design in the county, mention should be made of cable-stayed cantilever bridges. The George Street Bridge, Newport, 1962–4 by *Mott, Hay & Anderson*, is the earliest example of this type of bridge structure in Britain. The same firm completed another in 1966: the M4 (now M48) bridge over the River Wye at Chepstow. Subsequently the cable-stayed cantilever system has become very common, and the Second Severn Crossing which reaches Wales at Portskewett, 1992–6 by *Sir William Halcrow & Partners* with *SEEE*, is of this type.

Factories

The concluding paragraphs of this introduction have been reserved for the one type of building in which during the last half-century the county can claim a significant role at national level. Here two buildings stand pre-eminent, but several others also stay in the
120 memory. Brynmawr Rubber Factory, built 1947–53 by the
p. *Architects' Co-operative Partnership*, with *Ove Arup & Partners* making
134 a vital contribution as structural engineers, pioneered large-scale,
thin-shell concrete vaulting in post-war Britain. The nine shallow domes, supported internally on only four clustered reinforced-concrete piers, created a vast, largely unimpeded production area. Reinforced concrete was used in other striking forms in the peripheral structures, which together served a tightly programmed

production process. Sadly, the vision of the client, Lord Forrester, to bring employment to a desperately depressed area of the Valleys, proved too idealistic, and the factory has languished disused since 1982. A concrete structure of the mid 1950s which has survived much better, though also disused, is the 'slimes thickener' at
Hafodyrynys Colliery washery, Crumlin, drum-shaped and saucer- 121
domed, and now eerily isolated in a wooded valley.

The other immediately post-war factory, for British Nylon Spinners at Llanfihangel Pontymoile, 1947–8, is still fully functioning. It was designed by *Sir Percy Thomas & Son* in their characteristic idiom of that period. The soaring rectangular, brick-framed 'spinning tower' on its main-road site in the centre of the county remains a familiar symbol of the clean industry which has since the late 1940s taken over from ironworks and coal mines almost everywhere. The image of the cubic, anonymous factory, as found above all in the USA, is expressed clearly enough in two later factories by the *Percy Thomas Partnership*, Parke-Davis, also at Llanfihangel Pontymoile, where a group of grey brick pavilions built 1971–3 is placed in a landscaped setting, and Alfa-Laval, Cwmbran, 1973, where the factory activities are enclosed in a white cube, linked to a curtain-walled administration block. But there was another way to design factories, one which did not hide the production process but expressed it. This approach has been followed to striking effect in two ambitious factories in the county. Whitbread's brewery, Magor, 1979 by *Frederick Gibberd, Coombes & Partners*, is a spacious grouping, of pavilions and vats linked by high-level pipes, demonstrative of the process of brewing. At the Inmos microchip factory, 126
Duffryn, 1982 by *Richard Rogers & Partners* (structural engineers p.
Anthony Hunt Associates), the sterile production areas are invisible 220
within a rectangular envelope. What are flamboyantly displayed are the structural armature of steel trusses and tension rods, and the service containers, stacked over the central spine and linked to the interior by snaking rooftop ducts. The whole building, for all its visual oddity, is convincing as the neat and inevitable solution to a set of problems, much more so than the quirky gymnastics of its famous predecessor, Piano & Rogers's Pompidou Centre in Paris.

Since the early 1980s industry has continued to flourish and develop around Newport, but there is nothing further to report. Everything seems to take place within anonymous sheds. Largest of all are the vast sheds of the LG Wales complex at Coedkernew, of 1996–8. All very efficient, no doubt, but totally failing in what is one of the primary duties of all architecture, engagement with the outside world.

FURTHER READING

The earliest general sources of information on buildings in the county are Thomas Churchyard's lengthy poem of 1587, 'The Worthines of Wales', and Thomas Dineley's *The Account of the Official Progress of the First Duke of Beaufort through Wales, 1684* (ed. R.W. Banks, 1888), illustrated with Dineley's pen vignettes of buildings. Among early guidebooks, the most useful is H.P. Wyndham, *Tour through Monmouthshire and Wales* (1781). Next comes a classic, *An Historical Tour in Monmouthshire* by William Coxe – Archdeacon Coxe – published in 1801 (facsimile reprint 1995, with introduction by J.K. Knight). This two-volume work combines the vividness of a shrewd and observant tourist's responses with impressively extensive documentary research, numerous engravings – based on drawings by the author's travelling companion, Sir Richard Colt Hoare – and surveyed maps of many earthworks and all the county's towns by Thomas Morrice. Over a century later there followed a full-scale county history, J.A. Bradney's *A History of Monmouthshire,* 4 vols. in 9 (1904–32; reprinted 1991–3, together with vol. 5, on the hundred of Newport, edited from Bradney's notes by M. Gray). Bradney's approach, with its emphasis on genealogies and monumental inscriptions, was out-of-date in its own day, and his understanding of architecture rudimentary; but his pages are full of clues and cannot be ignored. No modern history of the county has yet been written (though one is planned, to be edited by Madeleine Gray and Prys Morgan). Instead, readers are directed to John Davies's magisterial *A History of Wales* (1993). Among guidebooks, the most comprehensive is C.J.O. Evans, *Monmouthshire – Its History and Topography* (*c.* 1953), but the one which first evaluated the county's architecture, and drew attention to what was of interest particularly among Victorian buildings, was P. Howell and E. Beazley, *The Companion Guide to South Wales* (1977). The listing of statutorily protected buildings by Cadw: Welsh Historic Monuments is currently in full swing in the county. The lists which have been issued are important descriptive and evaluative documents, incorporating much primary research.

The two most important periodicals, *Archaeologia Cambrensis* (which covers Wales as a whole) and the *Monmouthshire Antiquary,* contain much of relevance on prehistoric and Roman remains and on medieval buildings. Brief readable accounts of the most significant monuments from the Bronze Age to the late Middle Ages, except for parish churches, are in E. Whittle, *A Guide to Ancient and Historic Wales: Glamorgan and Gwent* (1992). For greater detail, *see* J.A. Taylor (ed.), *Culture and Environment in Prehistoric Wales* (1980), and the Cadw guides to the two main Roman sites: *Caerleon, Roman Fortress,* by J.K. Knight (rev. edn 1994), and *Caerwent, Roman Town,* by R.J. Brewer (2nd edn 1997), both with full bibliographies.

Most medieval castles have been thoroughly investigated and published. Of Chepstow Castle, the primary analysis is by J.C.

Perks, in *Transactions of the Bristol and Gloucester Archaeological Society* (1946–8), largely followed in the Cadw guide by J.K. Knight (rev. edn 1991). On some important points this has recently been revised by further research, presented at a symposium in 1999, but yet to be fully published. Other castles for which Cadw has published guides are the Three Castles (Grosmont, Skenfrith, White), by J.K. Knight (*c.* 1992), and Raglan, by J.R. Kenyon (rev. edn 1994). An alternative theory of the development of Raglan is A. Emery, 'The development of Raglan Castle and Keeps in Late Medieval England', *Archaeological Journal* 132 (1975). The fragmentary remains of the huge, unfinished castle at Llangibby were brilliantly discussed by D.J. Cathcart King and J.C. Perks in *Archaeologia Cambrensis* 105 for 1956. J.K. Knight's analysis of Usk Castle is in *Ancient Monuments and their Interpretation*, M.R. Apted, R. Gilyard-Beer and A.D. Saunders eds. (1977), and of Newport Castle in *Monmouthshire Antiquary* (1991). For the Monnow Bridge and gate there is M.L.J. Rowlands's monograph (1994).

The only major castle that has not yet been subjected to a full archaeological and documentary study is Caldicot. O. Morgan and T. Wakeman, *Notes on the Architecture and History of Caldicot Castle* (1854), remain important, as they antedate the late C19 reconstruction. An overview of castle-building, particularly in its military aspects, which gives full weight to the castles of South Wales is provided by D.J. Cathcart King, *The Castle in England and Wales, An Interpretative History* (1988).

The two major monastic sites are both in the care of Cadw: Welsh Historic Monuments. Tintern Abbey has an excellent Cadw guide by D.M. Robinson (3rd edn 1995). An important subsequent article, reconstructing the pulpitum screen, by S.A. Harrison, R.K. Morris and D. Robinson, in the *Antiquaries Journal* 78 (1998), briefly discusses the architecture of the abbey in relation to the West Country as a whole *c.* 1300. For this and other Cistercian foundations, see D. Robinson (ed.), *The Cistercian Abbeys of Britain* (1999). The place of Llanthony Priory in the same context a century earlier is dealt with by H. Brakspear in 'A West Country School of Masons', *Archaeologia* 81 (1931). Cadw has yet to replace O.E. Craster's official guide (HMSO, 1963). Subsequently, there have been published the excavation report by D.H. Evans and I. Soulsby, *Monmouthshire Antiquary*, vols. IV (1980) and V (1983–4), and a note by J. Rhodes with new evidence to date the construction of the church, *Monmouthshire Antiquary*, vol. VI (1990).

For medieval parish churches, Sir Stephen Glynne's mid-C19 notes, published in *Archaeologia Cambrensis* in 1902, but made when Victorian restorations had barely begun, are full of sharp observation. Otherwise, a useful handbook is M. Salter, *The Old Parish Churches of Gwent, Glamorgan & Gower* (1991), with a number of plans. By far the most thorough and systematic study is E.M. Evans's unpublished report for Cadw, 'Gwent Historic Churches Survey' (Glamorgan–Gwent Archaeological Trust, 1998). This presents an archaeological analysis of every church in the county with claims to preserve medieval fabric.

The farmhouses of the county between *c.* 1500 and *c.* 1700 are the subject of the single most important publication on any aspect of the county's buildings, *Monmouthshire Houses*, 3 vols. (1951–4), by Sir Cyril Fox and Lord Raglan. This is a ground-breaking work, one of the very first attempts to analyse the development of vernacular buildings, a subject subsequently studied with such intensity all over Britain. Indeed, Peter Smith, in his introduction to the reprint edition of 1994, calls it 'this landmark in the history of scholarship, a landmark, in its own field, as significant as Darwin's *Origin of Species*'. For these houses in their Wales-wide context, there is Peter Smith's own authoritative *Houses of the Welsh Countryside* (1975).

Among post-medieval country houses only Tredegar House has a full and thorough guide, by D. Freeman (1989). Otherwise one turns to articles in *Country Life*, e.g. on Clytha by R. Haslam, 8 and 15 December 1977, which also deals with Pontypool Park. Country house parks and gardens are comprehensively surveyed in E. Whittle, *Gwent Register of Landscapes, Parks and Gardens of Special Historic Interest* (Cadw, 1994), and set in their Welsh context in her *The Historic Gardens of Wales* (1992). Among towns, Monmouth has been best served, by K. Kissack's two books, *The Lordship, Parish and Borough of Monmouth* (1996) and *Monmouth, the Making of a County Town* (1975).

For C19 industry and transport, regional surveys must be consulted, such as S.R. Hughes, M. Parry, B. Malaws and A.P. Wakelin, *Collieries of Wales* (RCAHMW, 1994), W.J. Sivewright, *Civil Engineering Heritage: Wales and Western England* (1986) and D.S.M. Barrie, *A Regional History of the Railways of Great Britain*, vol. 12: South Wales (1980). The major early ironworks site, Blaenavon, being in the care of Cadw, has its authoritative guidebook, by J.K. Knight (rev. edn 1992).

For Victorian buildings in general there are few modern surveys. Best are A. Jones, *Welsh Chapels* (1996), and M. Seaborne, *Schools in Wales, 1500–1900, A Social and Architectural History* (1992). The most accessible surveys of Victorian ecclesiastical art and architecture, such as P. Howell and I. Sutton, *The Faber Guide to Victorian Churches* (1989), and M. Harrison, *Victorian Stained Glass* (1980), have disappointingly little on Monmouthshire examples. The only locally active architect whose achievements have been assessed in print is T.H. Wyatt, in J.M. Robinson, *The Wyatts* (1979). The architectural drawings by J.P. Seddon in the Victoria and Albert Museum are the subject of M. Darby's *Catalogue* (1983). Unpublished monographs are T. Blackshaw's on J.P. Seddon (University of London Ph.D., 2000) and S. Smith's on R.G. Thomas (University of Wales College Newport, 1996). Aston Webb's work at The Hendre is documented and discussed in Ian Dungavell's thesis on that architect (University of London Ph.D., 1999).

Early industrial housing, of which tantalizingly little survives, was recorded by J.B. Lowe and D.N. Anderson, *Iron Industry Housing Papers*, 1–3 (1972), and J.B. Lowe, *Welsh Industrial Workers' Housing 1775–1875* (1977). For terraced housing in general there is S. Muthesius, *The English Terraced House* (1982). The influence of the Garden City movement is traced in S. Unwin's unpublished report for Cadw, 'Early Twentieth Century Planned Housing in Wales, an Inventory' (1991). The development of Oakdale Village is thoroughly discussed in G.D. Nash, T.A. Davies and B. Thomas, *Workmen's Halls and Institutes: Oakdale Workmen's Institute* (1995). At the other end of the social scale, articles on H. Avray Tipping's three country houses were published in *Country Life*, 19 November 1910 (Mathern), 13 February 1915 (Mounton), 8 June 1929 (High Glanau, Cwmcarvan), and assessed as a group by R. Haslam in the same periodical, 6 and 13 December 1979.

For the century up to 1914, the riches of local newspapers and building periodicals remain to be tapped. Among the former, the *Monmouthshire Merlin* was the most important, and it has been effectively exploited only by K. Kissack, *Victorian Monmouth* (n.d., *c.* 1985). Among the latter, the *Builder* (from 1843), *Building News* (from 1855) and the *Architect* (founded 1869) are the most important – in that order. For church restoration, the records of the Incorporated Church Building Society in Lambeth Palace Library, though unpublished, are an essential source.

For architecture after 1919, the building periodicals provide a less thorough coverage than before. Developments and buildings of national interest were, of course, widely reported; but here mention need be made of publications on only four. Most substantial is P. Riden's monograph on Cwmbran, *Rebuilding a Valley: A History of Cwmbran Development Corporation* (1988). Most revealing are the record of a seminar on the building of the Brynmawr rubber factory, edited by A. Saint, in *A.A. Files* (autumn 1985) and V. Perry's monograph *Built for a Better Future* (1994). The Inmos factory, in the context of Richard Rogers's other buildings, is fully presented in K. Powell, *Richard Rogers* (1994). The Duffryn housing scheme is appraised in *Architect's Journal*, February 1980.

GWENT

ABERBEEG/ABER-BIG 2000

A scattered settlement at the confluence of the Great and Little Ebbw rivers. The church commands the knoll where the valleys meet.

CHRIST CHURCH. Chancel with landmark SE tower, transepts and the first bay only of an aisled and clerestoried nave. Built 1907–9 by *E.A. Johnson* of Abergavenny. Snecked rock-faced Pennant sandstone with Doulting stone dressings. Perp style. The unbuttressed tower has a square SE stair-turret and traceried belfry windows in deep reveals. Ashlar battlements. The interior is also unhackneyed in its details. Tall chancel arch on triple-shafted responds with branch and foliage caps. Arcades continued across the transepts, the buff Bath stone arches on circular piers and responds of pink Alveley stone. – REREDOS. 1913 by *R. L. Boulton & Sons* of Cheltenham. Of stone with a relief of the Last Supper. Side panels of Jasper marble. Brought in from Llanhilleth church (q.v.). – STAINED GLASS. Chancel S, St Luke, 1967 by *J. Wippell & Co.* – S aisle W, Baptism of Christ, 1966 by the same. – N aisle W, St Illtyd and local industries, 1967 by the same.

The RECTORY, to the W, is also by *Johnson*, 1897–8.

TY'R GRAIG PRIMARY SCHOOL, Commercial Road. Built as a board school in 1901, by *R. L. Roberts* of Abercarn. Unusually large and formal, facing the church across the valley. Rock-faced Pennant sandstone dressed with yellow brick and Portland ashlar. Two-storeyed, the front towards the valley composed symmetrically in five parts, the second and fourth framed by ashlar pilaster strips and crowned by gables. Tripartite windows in the usual board school idiom. The plan is a double pile, with halls at two levels in the rear range and classrooms clustered round them on three sides. No fewer than four handsome stone entrance doorways, girls' at the N end, boys' at the S, and two for infants in the valleyward front. The school and its playground are raised above the road by a massive curved stone wall, through which the three categories of schoolchildren each have their separate approach. Identical wrought-iron gates and overthrow for each.

ABERTILLERY AND DISTRICT HOSPITAL. Behind the church. 1920–2 by *Walter Rosser* of Abercarn. The epitome of the cottage hospital, the main administration range like an opulent Home Counties house. Two-storeyed under a generous red-tiled hipped roof. The symmetrical E entrance front is busily detailed in brick, tile-hanging and tiles set edgeways, both in herringbone panels and to form a broad segmental arch over the central doorway. The substantial white-painted timber windows happily survive. Single-storey ward range at the back, pebble-dashed and given battered buttresses *à la* Voysey where the ground drops at the S end.

GELLI, on the hillside above Trinant, 1¼ m. S. A remarkably well preserved early C17 longhouse, set in the usual way end-on to the slope, the cowbyre at the lower end. The doorway into the cross-passage survives, and so does a pentice, extending the full length of the S side wall of the inhabited part.

2090 ABERCARN

Here the slopes of the Ebbw Valley, steep and heavily wooded, loom over the settlements, Abercarn itself and Cwmcarn, 1 m. S (*see* below). Ironworking began here early, before the end of the C16; coalmining started *c.* 1836. Industry flourished from 1845, when Ebenezer Rogers opened the Abercarn and Gwyddon Collieries, and tinplate works were developed. In 1862 Abercarn's major colliery, the Prince of Wales, was sunk in the valley bottom. Today there is little readily visible of this industrial history.

ST LUKE. Hidden among trees on a hillside platform above the Gwyddon Valley, a pair of formidable cypresses guarding the W doorway. 1853 by *Charles Turner* of Newbridge, built at the expense of Sir Benjamin Hall of Llanover for the conduct of services in Welsh, and thus to be, as the *Builder* reported, 'on the simple model of the ancient British Christian churches of Wales'. Yet there is nothing particularly native about the Perp style, or the rock-faced Pennant sandstone walling, or the plan of nave and lower chancel. Quite a large W bell gable. The W doorway bears the shields of arms of Hall and his wife.*

ST LUKE (former). The church built 1923–6 by *J. Coates Carter* is a disused shell. Only the soaring S tower is seen from afar. Yet to approach it and enter its windowless hulk is a powerful architectural experience. It stands high on a shoulder above the road, from which a long flight of steps wanders up to the towering W front. This is an awesome sight, sheer walls of hammerdressed local sandstone almost devoid of ashlar dressings. Cavernous central entrance, its massive lintel set under a wide, smooth four-centred arch with a concave lip abruptly meeting the rough walling above. A crypt to l. and r. here, so a further, internal flight of steps leads to the level of the church floor. The church consists of a continuous aisled nave and chancel with clerestory and a N porch. Long lancets grouped in twos and threes, with a stepped E group of five. Internally the space is subdivided into

* After a dispute with the Church of England in 1862 the church was handed over to Calvinistic Methodists (Presbyterians). Since the failure of the 1920s church (*see* below) the two denominations have shared the building.

chancel and four-and-a-half-bay nave by chamfered piers continuous with wide four-centred arches. The building was reported in 1958 to be suffering from severe subsidence and structural defects, which the substitution of flat concrete roofs failed to cure. It was closed *c.* 1980.

WAR MEMORIAL, Gwyddon Road. Tall, ashlar-faced Cenotaph supporting a bronze figure blowing a trumpet and holding a wreath. The memorial was designed by a local architect, *J. H. Highley*, and unveiled in 1923.

The centre of Abercarn is marked by the WAR MEMORIAL, but is otherwise a disappointment. Scattered about the various parts of the settlement are the usual late Victorian terraces of workers' houses, many of them quite colourful, their Pennant sandstone fronts enlivened with red and yellow brick and terracotta. Off CEMETERY ROAD, high on the hillside, PERSONDY TERRACE and PENRHIW TERRACE, of the 1920s, belong to the end of a house-building campaign promoted from 1919 by Lord Treowen of Llanover. His architect was *George Davies*. The Pennant sandstone walling and the composition of gables show the hand of an Arts and Crafts disciple.

BLAST FURNACE, ½m. E, on the N slope of the Nant Gwyddon. The remains of a mid-C18 ironworking furnace, the earliest to survive fairly intact in the South Wales coalfield. Visible features are: one of the cast-iron beams supporting the top of the casting-arch; a low wall round the top of the furnace, from which an infilled arch spans to what remains of the charging-house, with a truncated masonry bridge-house. To the S is a feature which may be the top of either a broad charging-bank arch or a vaulted water-powered bellows chamber. Upstream 110 yds (100 metres) to the E is a fairly large pool impounded by a low masonry dam with stepped discharge weir. The original dam presumably powered a water wheel at the furnace, driving large bellows to provide the necessary draught.

CWMCARN

1m. S

A characteristic late C19 valley-bottom mining settlement, extending in a virtually unbroken terrace, of Pennant sandstone with Ebbw Vale brick dressings, for nearly a mile along COMMERCIAL ROAD and NEWPORT ROAD (one section dated 1889), and further S in short terrace-lined cross-streets plunging down the hillside, JAMESVILLE, EDWARDVILLE, and so on. The Baptist chapel takes its place in the street frontage of Commercial Road, but the Anglican church, as so often, sought the higher ground and so achieved less prominence. The centre of the settlement is at the S end. Here the fancifully decorated CWMCARN HOTEL is a vivid reminder of commercial prosperity in the late C19. Also the PRIMARY SCHOOL, built as a board school, single-storeyed and many-gabled, probably *c.* 1890. And, something a little unusual, the LIBRARY & INSTITUTE of 1923–4 by *Walter Rosser*. Nine-bay street front of rich red brick, two-storeyed with tile-hanging between the windows and tripartite brick piers subdividing the bays. Deep, rendered, blind attic. Central recessed porch with wide-spaced Tuscan columns.

St John the Evangelist, Park Street. By *A.F. Webb* of Blackwood, *c.* 1925. Gothic, notable mainly for being painted blue with white dressings. – STAINED GLASS. E and W windows, 1935 by *T. W. Camm & Co.* of Birmingham, emblematic of the Passion.

English Baptist Church, Commercial Road. Quite an imposing front, if minimal in its Gothicism, added in 1882 by *E. A. Lansdowne.* – STAINED GLASS. Abstract patterns in all the roadward windows. The chapel-like Sunday School at r.-angles was added in 1904.

3010 ABERGAVENNY/Y FENNI

The thriving market town owes its existence to its strategic position on the N bank of the River Usk where it exits from the mountains. The contrasted shapes of the surrounding mountains make an unforgettable setting: the smooth cone of the Sugarloaf to the NW, the Blorenge, a hunched shoulder looming from the SW, and the isolated ridge, the Skirrid, away to the NE. The Romans recognized the importance of the site, establishing the fort of Gobannium, but the town is in origin a Norman settlement. Hamelin de Ballon soon after 1087 constructed a motte-and-bailey castle, and before the end of the century founded a Benedictine priory. The present parish church is the much-remodelled church of the priory, and contains the splendid monuments of the Hastings lords of Abergavenny, and then of the Herberts. Their castle, however, did not become an important stronghold. The little town which grew up, or was laid out, between castle and priory and on the rising ground to the NW was walled probably 1295–1319. Nothing of the walls survives today, but Coxe's map of 1801 indicates their line. The heart of the town was to the N, where High Street and Nevill Street enclosed a triangular network of narrow lanes with St John's Church (p. 106) in their midst. Cross Street, the S-ward continuation of High Street, with the market place on its E side, was crossed midway by Monk Street, leading E to the church, and a lane to the W, leading to Castle Street and the castle. The street pattern survives, but the visual centre of gravity has shifted to the market place, where an ambitious Town Hall was built 1869–71. Its copper-capped clock tower dominates the town as much in the distant view as it does close at hand.

After a stagnant C18 Abergavenny's period of expansion was the C19. The growth first of ironworking and then of coalmining only a few miles away in the hills to the W clearly benefited the town. A western suburb centred on Baker Street was developed after leases were granted 1832–5; and another suburb to the SE grew up not long after, clustered round the railway station, opened in

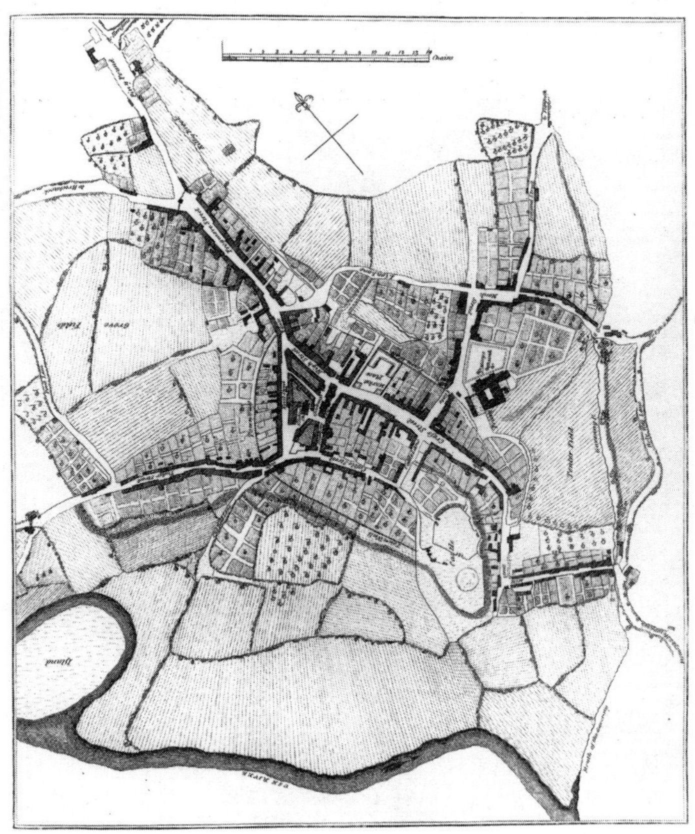

Abergavenny. Plan, 1801

1854. Further, more spaciously laid out suburban housing sprang up from the 1890s, providing many an opportunity for the leading local architect, *E. A. Johnson*. The main contribution of the C20 has been the usual not altogether successful attempt to divert traffic from the town centre, with bypass roads to the S and E and an inner bypass to the W and N.

ROMAN FORT. Although Abergavenny had long been suspected as the site of an early Roman fort, certain proof was lacking until excavations in 1972–3 behind Castle Street located one edge of it. The fort stood on the crest of the bluff immediately N of the castle. The strategic importance of the site is obvious, and it is not surprising that a fort was established here as early as *c.* A.D. 55–60. Evidence was found of two timber-framed barrack blocks and a small timber granary. Traces too of a stone bath-house, built *c.* A.D. 150 to the S. After the closure of the fort, probably in the C3, the site continued as a Roman settlement, the name of which was Gobannium.

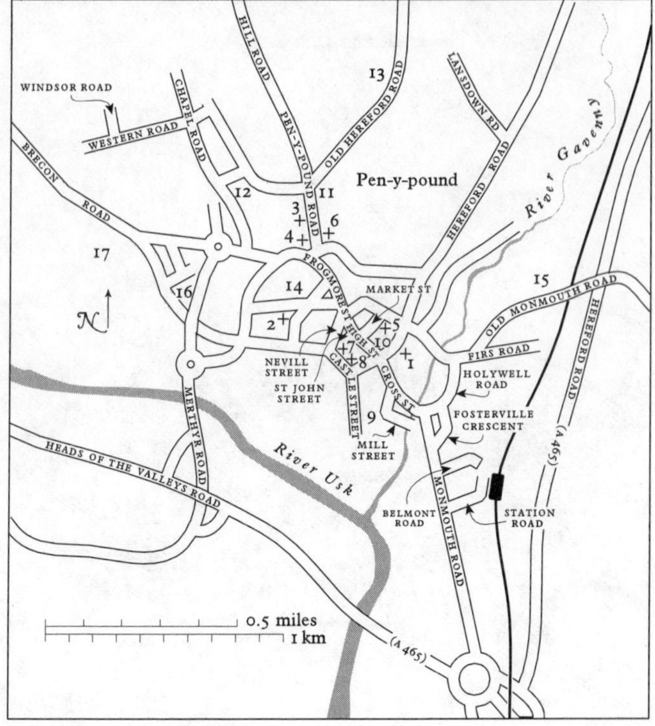

1 St Mary
2 Holy Trinity
3 Our Lady and St Michael (R.C.)
4 Baptist Church
5 Bethany Baptist Church
6 Presbyterian Church
7 Methodist Church
8 United Reformed Church
9 Castle
10 Town Hall
11 King Henry VIII Grammar School (former)
12 Harold Road School
13 King Henry VIII Comprehensive
14 Public Library
15 Pen-y-fal Hospital (former)
16 Workhouse (former)
17 Nevill Hall Hospital

Abergavenny

ST MARY. The church of the Benedictine priory founded after 1087 by Hamelin de Ballon, Lord of Abergavenny, was taken over in its entirety by the townspeople after the suppression of the priory in 1536. They preserved two glorious late medieval fittings, and an array of fine monuments. No Norman fabric is visible in the church, and what remains that is medieval belongs to a rebuilding in the early C14, to a cruciform plan with large, two-bay burial chapels extending E of the transepts to flank the W half of the choir. The medieval nave and N aisle were in 1828–9 converted into a single preaching space, *William Whittington* surveyor, with an 'amphitheatrical' arrangement of galleries. This in its turn was swept away in 1881–2 when *Thomas Nicholson* of

Hereford re-formed the nave and N aisle. Further later alterations, as closer inspection makes clear.

Starting at the E end, the sanctuary bay is lit by huge Perp windows, the E window of 1922, those to N and S probably of *E.A. Johnson*'s restoration of 1896, all reinstating the late medieval forms. The chancel chapels have Dec side windows, of three long, trefoil-headed lights. The NE window of the N chapel is a more elaborate, indeed beautiful, composition. Three lights with intersecting tracery, the lights cinquefoiled, the interstices above filled with delicate trefoils and quatrefoils. Hollow-moulded frame. The huge Perp E window of the N chapel is wholly C19. The N transept N window was reconstructed in 1954. In the S transept there has been less modern interference. Blocked early C14 four-light window in the E wall. It is moulded with two sunk chamfers (cf. the chapel arcade inside). Cusped Y-tracery. High in the chancel wall, above the E bay of the S chapel, part of a blocked Perp three-light clerestory window, evidence of the design of the upper parts of the monastic choir, now otherwise entirely lost. The crossing tower is quite modest, of the C14, with two-light Dec belfry windows, square NW turret and battlements. The N and S walls of the nave and aisle are medieval and have long three-light windows with cinquefoiled lights. Twin-gabled W front with three-bay, projecting, full-width porch, all of 1881–2 by *Nicholson*.

Inside, Nicholson's five-bay arcade between nave and N aisle is conventional: quatrefoil piers with moulded caps carry moulded two-centred arches. The crossing is early C14. The E and W crossing arches have typical Dec forms, an inner order with sunk chamfer, set on big head corbels, those on the E arch representing a bishop and a king, and an outer order with continuous sunk quadrant. The pairs of wide arches which open up the chancel side walls into the side chapels are clearly of the same date, with two sunk quadrants. The N and S crossing arches, however, though similar in date, are treated differently, with chamfer, roll and chamfer, the imposts decorated with ballflower. The ribbed vault of the chancel is of plaster, called 'modern' in 1836.

FURNISHINGS. – CHOIR STALLS. The full complement of the monastic stalls survives, to N and S of the choir, with at the E single seats under towering pierced canopies (that to the N largely restored) and at the W pairs of return stalls. The stalls have elaborate blind tracery on their fronts, and at the tops of their high backs. The N tracery patterns part Dec, part Perp, the S a uniform Perp canopywork design. Coved top tester with crowning foliage trail, with traces of colour and made-up pinnacles at the ends. The stall ends to the N are carved as poppyheads, those to the S carved into animals. The S stalls are dated by the name carved on one end, 'Wynchester', that of the prior 1493–1516. Double, not necessarily Tudor, rose on the soffit of the NE canopy. Crowned rose and Prince of Wales feathers on one of the SE misericords. Dr Charles Tracy points out that the stalls have been made up from several elements not of the same

date, probably for Prior Wynchester. The seats, in particular, of several patterns, must be mid-C15 or earlier. The stalls were conserved and partly restored in 1998 by *Hugh Harrison*. – FIGURE
33 OF JESSE (N transept), probably part of a REREDOS, C15. This wonderful over-life-size reclining figure is of timber, and still retains traces of the gesso and paint, red and blue, with which it was originally covered. A bearded, robed and hatted figure, like some late medieval merchant, holds the stem of the tree which springs from his heart, while an angel applies a cushion to the back of his head. The tree bearing the ancestors of Christ which originally grew from the stem must have been on a mighty scale, a counterpart to the one in stone which forms the tracery of a complete window at Dorchester Abbey, Oxfordshire. Richard Symonds in 1645 saw 'on the boughs divers statues but spoyld'. – FONT. The circular bowl is Norman, incised with a series of radiating arcs round its underside, above a thick rope moulding. Neo-Norman shafted stem and Neo-Norman domical COVER of 1897. – FIRST WORLD WAR MEMORIAL. By *W.D. Caröe*. In a crisply cut white stone frame like an early C18 hanging wall monument, with many fanciful classical details. – CRUCIFIX (N aisle). Of *c.* 1977 by *Frank Roper*. – ALTAR (Herbert Chapel). 1997–8 by *Keith Jameson*. Simple and solemn, of Portland stone. The bold, terse inscription is from Henry Vaughan. – CANOPY FRAGMENT (in the Herbert Chapel). Of stone. C15. What did it come from? It looks too big to have belonged to a monument. – ROYAL ARMS. Of Queen Anne. Large and brightly painted. It bears the date 1709 and was restored *c.* 1995. – STAINED GLASS. Chancel E. Virgin and Child between SS Christopher and Michael in an expansive early Renaissance architectural setting. 1922 by *F. C. Eden*. – S aisle SE. Saints and scenes, 1916 by *John Winbolt*. Kempe style. – N transept N. Nativity with shepherds and kings. Expressionist. 1957 by *Frederick W. Cole*.

MONUMENTS. The church contains one of the outstanding series of medieval monuments in the British Isles. The finest of all is in the N transept. Two are at the entrance to the N (Lewis) chancel chapel with a further important post-medieval effigy in the chapel itself. Five plus two post-medieval are in the Herbert Chapel on the S side of the chancel. They will be described by location in this order.

39 NORTH TRANSEPT. – John, second Lord Hastings †1325. Wood. Exquisitely carved and characterized knight in armour, his legs elegantly crossed, his feet resting on a (sadly headless) lion. Traces only of the coloured and gilt gesso which originally covered the entire figure.* Its close kinship to the stone effigy of Aymer de Valence (†1324) in Westminster Abbey confirms a date *c.* 1325–30. The tomb-chest has been made up with stone panels carved with figures of eight delightfully individualized knights under rich cusped and crocketed shields. Mouldings enriched with blobs like embryonic ballflower. Traces of colour here too. There were in the late C16 fourteen figures in all and

* Conserved by *Carol Galvin*, 1994–5.

the present arrangement cannot quite be the original, as a close look shows. Claude Blair has convincingly argued that the monument once stood, under a canopy, in the N chancel chapel.

NORTH CHAPEL. Eva de Braose †1257. A remarkable and 38
well-preserved mid-C13 sandstone effigy of a recumbent lady wearing a wimple and holding a heart, on a made-up tomb-chest with original plain shields. A large armorial shield covers much of her body. Her dress falls in straight folds, and at her feet lies a hound. Stiff-leaf border. Traces of polychromy. – A Hastings lady. Mid-C14 limestone effigy of a recumbent lady, the most strongly characterized in the church. The figure is unusually small and has long, crimped hair. Her hands are not in an attitude of devotion but held some now lost object. A chain dangling from one hand and disappearing into her pocket suggests that the object may have been a pet animal. (Archdeacon Coxe in 1800 identified it as a squirrel.) Made-up tomb-chest with original shields in quatrefoils. – Dr David Lewis †1584, first Principal of Jesus College, Oxford. Erected by 1587, when Thomas Churchyard noted it. Recumbent stone effigy, in cap and fur-trimmed robe, the head resting on cushion and book. The sides of the tomb-chest are carved with crude classical arcading and foliage. Robed figure in low relief under the r. arch. The monument most remarkably bears the name of the sculptor, *John Gildon*. To see other, much more fantastic, works by Gildon, it is necessary to go to Bosbury, across the border in Herefordshire.

HERBERT CHAPEL. The seven principal monuments in the Herbert Chapel were all dismantled and restored 1994–8, by *Michael Eastham*, and three were re-erected in new positions.* They now stand in three ranks, two under the arches between chancel and chapel, two centrally in the chapel, and three against the S wall. The monuments date from the early C14 to the late C17, and here they will be described in turn chronologically, with a comment on the significance of the siting of each. – Sir Lawrence de Hastings †1348. (Centre W, but moved in 1996 from beneath the W arch between chancel and chapel, to allow visibility from all sides, as there had been before the late medieval choir stalls were set up.) Of Painswick limestone. Tomb-chest with a fine recumbent effigy of a knight in chain-mail armour and surcoat, a close-fitting basinet covering his head. He has straight legs and his feet rest on a bull. Broken helm under his head. The tomb-chest is narrow, with space along the sides for five niches under nodding ogee arches, but only one at the ends. The weepers all gone from the niches, except the one which was carved integrally with its pedestal, a long-haired man in armour, vividly characterful, even though
headless. – Sir William de Hastings †1348 (S wall centre). 40
Recumbent effigy of Painswick limestone, turning slightly outwards, his legs crossed at the ankles and feet resting on a

* I am grateful to Mr Eastham for explaining what has been done and the reasoning behind the alterations. Mr Eastham conserved the monuments in the N transept in the same programme.

greyhound, his hands not in prayer, but one placed on his breast, the other grasping a dagger. (Both arms, sadly, are broken.) The armour and surcoat, however, indicate in their handling that this and the previous effigy are products of the same workshop. Plain tomb-chest, but a pierced backplate behind the effigy, angled to follow the window embrasure. It is a design in which Dec begins to give way to Perp. Square, hollow-moulded frame bearing small, four-petalled flowers. Paired cinquefoiled panels, with central trefoils under ogee arches. Panelled spandrels. At the springing of the arches miniature lion heads with their tongues out. – Sir William ap Thomas †1446, and his wife Gwladys †1454. (Centre E, occupying the focal position in the chapel, to emphasize that a new dynasty was appropriating what had been the Hastings burial chapel. The monument has been re-erected a few feet W of its former position.) Large and rich, the recumbent effigies and tomb-chest with its many figures all of alabaster. In fact the monument is an outstanding product of the celebrated late medieval Midlands alabaster workshops. He wears plate armour and a chaplet on his head, which rests on a helm with moor's-head crest. His legs are long and straight, and rest on a timid-looking lion. She wears a horned headdress, and angels hold a cushion diamond-wise beneath her head. Note traces of bright paint, red sprinkled with black, on the angels' wings. On each side of the tomb-chest no fewer than twelve robed figures, carrying scrolls in one hand and, formerly, attributes in the other. They seem to represent twelve prophets and the twelve apostles, a series regularly found in other contexts in the Middle Ages but extremely rare on a monument. On the short E end a vivid Annunciation, with the half-length figure of God appearing above Gabriel. Large censing angels to l. and r. Effigies and tomb-chest figures alike have the remains of vaulted canopies above their heads. The W end restored blank. – Sir Richard Herbert of Coldbrook †1469, and his wife Margaret. (Under the E arch between chancel and chapel, the second most honorific position.) Also alabaster and of high quality. Recumbent effigies. On a tomb-chest, with large, mutilated canopies over their heads. He wears plate armour, his legs are straight, his feet rest on a lion. His bare head with long trimmed hair rests on his helmet. She wears a webbed chaplet on her head and a dress which falls in long, straight folds, its hem bitten by the pair of lapdogs on which she rests her feet. On the tomb-chest, crocketed arches shelter what is left of nine shield-bearing angels. On the E end a Virgin and Child with SS Margaret and Catherine. – Richard
41 Herbert of Ewyas †1510 (S wall E). A canopied wall monument, with a mutilated and restored inscription giving the date. The canopy arch, of flattened ogee profile, is of limestone, retaining a good deal of rather worn colour, and pitted with dowel holes where gilt lead stars were fixed. The large spandrels, now blank, were filled with armorial beasts, which disappeared during the C19. The finials, however, have been recently rediscovered and replaced. Fine alabaster effigy of a bare-headed, straight-legged knight, his feet on a lion. The little figure of a seated bedesman

beneath one foot, rediscovered when the conservators dismantled the monument and now hidden once more (a replica is on the wall), confirms that the monument was intended to be set under a wider wall arch. The present arch is of limestone. Alabaster tomb-chest with eight seated figures, four of which are shield-bearing angels. Central armorial panel lost. Against the backplate a tall, narrow alabaster panel of the Coronation of the Virgin, with tiny mutilated figures of Sir Richard and his wife kneeling in adoration below. To l. and r. small figures of six kneeling sons and two standing daughters. – Andrew Powell †1631, and wife (S wall W, formerly in the NE corner of the chapel). Gruesomely water-dissolved alabaster effigies, recumbent, he in civilian dress, on a tomb-chest of 1998, to which the original brass inscription plaque is affixed. – William Baker †1648, and wife. (Under the W arch between chancel and chapel, originally butting against the W respond, but in 1996 moved slightly E-wards and its W end made up.) Erected after Charles II's Restoration in 1660. The inscription shows that Baker's widow could remember his age at death but not the year in which he died. Large kneeling figures at a prayer-desk, under a depressed ogee arch supported by an Ionic demi-column which sprouts from the top of the prayer-desk. Altogether a crude performance compared with the medieval monuments. Of limestone, retaining a good deal of original colour.

Finally, the floor of the chapel is largely made up of medieval GRAVESTONES and post-medieval LEDGER SLABS, rediscovered when the raised floor level was lowered again as part of the 1990s restoration. They have been relaid largely in their former positions. – Floor slab dated 1699 (E of N stalls), with relief figures in ruffs and farthingales even cruder than usual for this type of local rustic production.

Nothing recognizable survives of the CONVENTUAL BUILDINGS to the S of the church. The S-ward extension of the S transept must include part of the monastic dormitory and its undercroft. One upper blocked doorway and lancet in its E wall may belong to the dormitory, but the other blocked windows and the truncated corbelled chimney-breasts must relate to its post-Dissolution use. The wall with window embrasures which forms the boundary wall to a car park here is what survives of PRIORY HOUSE, built *c.* 1700. It was of nine bays and two storeys crowned by a heavy hipped roof, and was demolished *c.* 1950.

BARN, SW of the church. Built, probably in the C17, to face the W end of Priory House. Its walls, of Old Red Sandstone, are now waveringly deformed, but originally its E front must have been quite a showpiece. Seven-bay composition, spoilt by the blocking of the three cart-entrances. Between them trios of long ventilation slits, and above, under the eaves, four oval openings formed of moulded brick. Heavy hipped roof. Ten-bay tie-beam and queen-strut roof.

Two-storeyed CHURCH ROOMS S of the church, 1999 by *Morgan & Horowskyi.*

HOLY TRINITY, Baker Street. The church is the centre of a Gothic group built 1840–2 by *T. H. Wyatt* of *Wyatt & Brandon* at the expense of Miss Rachel Herbert. The church is built of squared grey sandstone and had depressed-headed lancets under hood-moulds – see the W end. Single-storey ranges of ALMSHOUSES flank the church to N and S, their porches recessed and prettily bargeboarded, and the gabled PARSONAGE stands in the SE corner beside the road. The internal spaces of this enclave were invaded as the church grew larger. In 1886 *Thomas Nicholson* added the chancel, its E wall and four-light Perp window hard up against the pavement. Cross-gabled aisles were added by *E. A. Johnson*, S aisle 1897, N aisle 1909, leaving little more than passage access to the almshouses. Inside, Wyatt's nave is wide and retains its W gallery. Johnson's five-bay arcades are almost round-arched, on circular piers, and their boarded ceilings exaggerate the impression of width. – PULPIT. Of stone. Early French Gothic, of *c.* 1870. Presumably brought in. – STAINED GLASS. Chancel E, St Michael greeting Christ, with saints in the outer lights and a scene of Christ carrying the cross below. 1920, signed by *John Jennings*. – S aisle. Two windows in powerful narrative style, illustrating three scenes from the life of Elijah (from the W, 1 Kings 19.5, 1 Kings 21.20, 2 Kings 2.11). Also by *Jennings*, before 1914.

104 OUR LADY AND ST MICHAEL (R.C.), Pen-y-pound Road. 1858–60, paid for by a local solicitor, John Baker Gabb. The architect was *Benjamin Bucknall*, fresh from his labours on the great Puginian mansion of Woodchester Park, near Stroud, Gloucestershire. The church shows all the vigour and ambition of a self-confident young architect. Local Old Red Sandstone with Bath stone dressings. Towards the road the steeply gabled E end of the chancel presents a magnificent Dec six-light window, and composes with the spacious Tudor Gothic PRESBYTERY to the l. Note the irregularity with which the presbytery is designed, reflecting the interior disposition of functions, in the way Pugin advocated.

To the S a grand tower and spire were intended. Instead, one sees only the three tightly spaced bays of the chancel, with two-light Dec windows between deep buttresses, and the higher, clerestoried nave of six bays, with two-light windows at both levels and shallow buttresses. To the W, a five-light Dec window over a low, shafted doorway. The interior maintains the aspiring mood, the arch-braced roofs very steep, the arcade arches steeply pointed on quatrefoil piers. Uncarved capitals and corbels above. Chancel arch very high and chancel side windows set in deep ashlar splays. Only here has a little foliage carving been carried out. – REREDOS. 1883, designed by *Edmund Kirby* of Liverpool, carved by *A. B. Wall* of Cheltenham. Dec, of stone, stretching the full width of the chancel. It carries an indescribably complex array of angels, some under arches, others under canopies, yet others perched on pinnacles. Set forward in the centre, the tabernacle containing the host. This is what the angels are adoring. – CHANTRY CHAPEL, off the S aisle. Added 1894.

It commemorates local Catholics of penal times, by means of an oil PAINTING of St David Lewis (alias Father Charles Baker), and a large SCULPTURED ROUNDEL, signed *Battersby*, Roma, for Father Augustine Baker. Note the handsome brass RAIL. – PAINTINGS. Deposition, probably mid-C17 French. – Trinity, late C16, Italian or Spanish. Complex iconography. – Copy after Raphael's St Michael, 1861 by *Kenelm Digby*. Amateurish. – STAINED GLASS. In the chantry chapel, an excellent window with roundel portraits of members of the Baker family and their patron saints, 1861 by *Clayton & Bell*. – Chancel E, Mary, Joseph and saints, under canopies, complementing the reredos. By *Hardman*, the outermost pair of saints added in 1898. – N aisle E, Mary and Joseph, 1860 by *G.B. Maycock* of Clifton. Wailes style. Good quality. – N aisle, saints, 1879, signed by *Swaine Bourne*. Anaemic.

BAPTIST CHURCH, Frogmore Street. 1877 by *George Morgan* of Carmarthen. Large and expensive (cost £4,200), grimly confronting the town from the end of Frogmore Street. In a Romanesque style, of snecked rock-faced Old Red Sandstone with Bath stone dressings. The façade centres on a wheel window over a columned double porch, and is flanked by stair-towers rising to arcaded belfry stages and steep, iron-crested French pavilion roofs. Much carved foliage. Exposed two-storeyed side elevations. Inside, the space has been horizontally subdivided, retaining original pews and gallery seating. Organ in a large arch behind the minister's seat. – STAINED GLASS. In the wheel window. Mainly geometrical patterns. Clearly of *c*. 1877.

BETHANY BAPTIST CHURCH, Market Street (formerly Museum of Childhood). 1882, an early work by *E.A. Johnson*, and a lively showpiece, though not expensive (cost £1,600). Gothic. Red brick with Bath stone dressings, on a foundation of Old Red Sandstone. Façade with paired gabled entrances and a pair of bold, Geometrically traceried windows over. Cross-gabled flanking stair projections. The design is satisfyingly tied together with stone stringcourses and banding.

PRESBYTERIAN CHURCH, Pen-y-pound Road. 1907–10 by *E.A. Johnson*. Rock-faced stone, grey, not the usual red, from Llangattock, with Bath stone dressings. Arts and Crafts Perp, with many witty touches, including the undulating forecourt wall. Central six-light, uncusped window, under a gable with triple finial. Short tower to the l., with short openwork top stage and spike. Contemporary SCHOOLROOMS and HALL at the rear. Ungalleried interior, under an elaborate and well-detailed timber roof employing hammerbeams, tie-beams and crown-posts. Short transepts and wide arch for the organ above the minister's seat.

METHODIST CHURCH, Castle Street. Dated 1829. Simple white-rendered three-bay box under a pyramidal slate roof. Windows in two storeys, round-headed above, square-headed below. Tuscan porch. Interior probably refitted in the mid C19, galleried round three sides on thin iron columns. Railed pulpit at the far end.

UNITED REFORMED CHURCH, Castle Street. Built in 1792, enlarged and remodelled in 1839. Rendered white. Overall pediment. Long, round-headed windows to l. and r. and central Tuscan porch. Galleried interior. The pedimented SUNDAY SCHOOL beside it is almost as big.

CASTLE. Hamelin de Ballon, during the last decade of the C11, consolidated his grip on the lordship of Abergavenny in the usual way by constructing an earthwork castle. His motte remains immediately recognizable, and the outline of the bailey to the N can readily be traced. By the late C12 the lordship and castle had come into the hands of the first of a sequence of powerful families, none of whom treated Abergavenny as a principal residence, even though they regularly used the monastic church as a place of burial. The principal masonry remains of the castle, the outer wall of a large hall, and a complex lodging tower attached to its SW end, probably belonged to a major scheme of improvement made early in the C14 by the first of the Hastings owners, John, first Lord Hastings †1313. The lodging tower, part square, part cylindrical, is one of a group built in the Usk Valley, of which another is at Crickhowell, and a third at Brecon. In the C15 an unimpressive gatehouse was built, extending from the NW of the hall. Thereafter nothing of significance was done until the Civil War. Richard Symonds, who was with Charles I at Raglan in 1645, called Abergavenny Castle 'ruined', but it was only in 1647 that Parliament voted to destroy its defences. What remained was thereafter systematically robbed of cut stonework. By the late C18, however, it was attracting the attention of Picturesque tourists. In the first years of the C19 walks were made within the walls, and in 1819 the Earl of Abergavenny built an uncompromisingly rectangular shooting box (now the town's Museum) on top of the motte. The building stone throughout is mauve local Old Red Sandstone.

The entrance from CASTLE STREET into the castle grounds leads directly to the GATEHOUSE. Only the side walls of the narrow entrance passage survive, rising to an upper storey, where there was a heated room lit by windows on both sides. The defensive apparatus seems to have been minimal. What remains of the entrance arch is surmounted by the worn jambs of a superarch; but there is no sign of there having been a portcullis. Draw-bar slots for the main door. The battered base of the SW wall of the gatehouse was clearly built over the N angle of the adjacent curtain wall. As seen from the inner side, it is clear that this wall formed one of the long sides of a large rectangular hall, of which the short NE and SW end walls also rise to a considerable height. At the N end traces of a spiral stair. A few corbels in the long NW wall for roof timbers, and one spyhole slit window. Also clear evidence that the hall stood over a low undercroft. One double-chamfered lancet at its S end. Unfortunately, the long SE inner wall of the hall has completely disappeared, but it must have contained all the main windows.

The SW TOWER is also very fragmentary, but in part rises almost to its full height. It seems not to have communicated directly with the hall. The W half is square in plan, but converted by spurs, now largely robbed, to a polygon. The S half forms a three-quarter cylinder. Surviving shaped stones where the two parts join make it clear that they were constructed together. At the N end a spiral stair went up, lit by a long slit in the re-entrant angle with the hall. There were lodgings at three levels in the tower, but the only ashlar detail to remain is a nearly round-headed rere-arch to a window embrasure at the highest level. In the circular part, door jambs with pyramid stops of late C13 character. Also well-preserved garderobes at two levels. There was a further garderobe in the section of wall added to the E.

The SW tower must have projected beyond the range enclosing the S side of the courtyard. Of this range, one fragmentary wall remains, with the jamb of a doorway. The range clearly extended as far E as the N end of the service block of the shooting box, and the medieval stonework here, which rises quite high, may have belonged to a corner turret. The walls enclosing the bailey to E and N have been reduced to no more than a few courses, and in places have disappeared altogether. To the E the ground drops precipitously. In MILL STREET below, the base of a tower. (Its cellar door has jambs with pyramidal stops, suggesting that this is further work of *c.* 1300.)

The SHOOTING BOX is an unsympathetically utilitarian structure, enlivened only by thin polygonal shafts at the angles. It is linked to a N service block of similar shape at a lower level. All the windows renewed for the Museum.

TOWN HALL, Cross Street. 1869–71 by *Wilson & Willcox* of Bath, 116
after a competition (replacing a modest Market House by *John Nash* of 1794–5 and Market of 1825). The tall, campanile-like angle tower, strongly corbelled under a green copper pyramid roof and with angle tourelles, is a landmark for miles around. Close-to, the bulk of the building oppresses, five big bays by three, gable-ended over two tall storeys. The style is early French Gothic at its most uncompromising. Polychromy and contrasts of texture play their part, mauve rock-faced walling of Old Red Sandstone set off against buff Bath stone ashlar and radiating voussoirs of mauve, grey and green. Very large two-light upper windows, with flat shouldered heads to the lights, under ashlar tympana pierced with pairs of encircled cinquefoils. A row of shields in the sill-band. The arcade below retains its original glazed arches. Plate-traceried rose in the downhill gable-end. At the other end, facing Market Street, three wide arches with plate tracery in their heads, and three windows above subdivided by shouldered arches with plate-traceried tympana. At the foot of the tower, a doorway with segment-headed arch and much foliage carving opens on to the main stair. The rooms on the first floor have been much altered. The council chamber is lit by the glazed heads of the arcade on the main front. The top storey, fitted out as an assembly room with tie-beam and queenpost roof, was

remodelled in 1906, when the lusciously enriched balcony-front was inserted, and probably at this time converted into a theatre. The theatre was refitted *c.* 1990.

At the rear, the contemporary MARKET HALL, airy and utilitarian. Pitched roof on slender iron posts. Seven graded, arch-headed windows in the gable-end.

KING HENRY VIII GRAMMAR SCHOOL (former), Pen-y-pound Road. 1896–8 by *E. A. Johnson*, extended by him in 1904. A lively performance in a Perp style. Single-storeyed. W (entrance), S and E fronts each a different, near-symmetrical composition of gables with panelled tops, four-centred-headed windows of three, four or five lights, and panelled chimneystacks. To the E the stacks stand on the gables. Snecked, rock-faced Old Red Sandstone, dressed with mustard-coloured ashlar. Extension to the N in matching style with fewer gables. Inside, the hall, to the S, and the classrooms retain their original canted, boarded ceilings.

HAROLD ROAD SCHOOL, Harold Road. Built as an intermediate school for girls in 1897–8 and extended as a county girls' school in 1910. The hand of *E. A. Johnson* is readily discerned. Single-storeyed, gabled, in a Tudor style with pretty Jacobean touches. Yellow brick dressed with Bath stone.

KING HENRY VIII COMPREHENSIVE SCHOOL, Old Hereford Road. Built in two phases by *Monmouthshire County Architect's Department*, *c.* 1956–61, County Architect *Colin Jones*, and *c.* 1968–72, County Architect *Sydney Leyshon*. The concrete-framed Upper School towards the road belongs to the first phase, a long, flat-roofed range of two storeys, the upper on pilotis. The later, larger, more varied, flat-roofed group of two and three storeys further W, used as Lower and Middle school, is unusually convincingly detailed.

PUBLIC LIBRARY, Victoria Street. 1905–6 by *B. J. Francis* of Abergavenny. Rock-faced local sandstone with Bath stone dressings. A big, mullioned bay window and statue-crowned gable take advantage of the acute-angled site.

PEN-Y-FAL HOSPITAL (former), Old Monmouth Road. An early and remarkably complete, if much extended, Victorian asylum, built soon after the Lunacy Act of 1845, which required counties and boroughs to provide accommodation for pauper lunatics. Closed in 1997. It was erected 1849–52 to the designs of *Fulljames & Waller* of Gloucester, for 250 inmates, to serve the counties of Monmouth, Hereford, Brecon and Radnor. The main, three-storeyed SW front, over 600 ft (183 metres) long, of mauve Old Red Sandstone ashlar with buff Bath stone dressings, is Tudor Gothic in style and full of incident, though less imposing than the Jacobean-style asylum the firm had just completed at Denbigh in North Wales. The pavilion-like centre was remodelled *c.* 1883 by *Giles & Gough*, when the three-bay chapel was displaced from its original position over the main entrance in favour of boardroom and committee rooms. Theirs are the semi-classical details, the plain top parapet and clock turret on the roof ridge. To l. and r. the façade largely retains its original forms, with a lively array of gables, projecting chimney-breasts and grouped lancet windows. Set back at the outer ends, the most dramatic original feature, a pair of massive polygonal ventilation shafts, faced with ashlar and decorated with crouching beasts at their bases and crowning gargoyles. The four main gables were reconstructed in 1909–10 by *E. A. Johnson,* when the outer pair were dated 1851 and 1910. Behind, the original plan included five parallel ranges of individual cells and workrooms at r.-angles to the main front, and there were walled 'airing courts' to both front and back, where inmates could take exercise. The infirmary block projecting forward at the r. end is of 1859–61; its larger fellow at the l. end is part of *Giles & Gough*'s big campaign of 1881–3, which included much infilling and extension at the back. Theirs too is the CHAPEL, which stands isolated and prominent near the entrance. It is cruciform in plan, with a canted apse, Geometrical tracery and a crowning spirelet which is prominent in the distant view. – STAINED GLASS. E window, the Annunciation, *c.* 1884, clearly by *Lavers, Barraud & Westlake* (A. Brooks).

Further extensions of 1890–1 by *Alfred Swash.* NURSES' HOME, to the NW, of brown brick, built in the 1920s. The hospital faces extensive landscaped grounds, now dense with mature specimen conifers. These are entered from the road past a substantial Gothic GATE LODGE, probably of *c.* 1851. The large gabled HOUSE across the road was presumably built as the superintendent's residence.

MAINDIFF COURT, 1½ m. NE. The Victorian mansion of Crawshay Bailey jun. has been pulled down. The buildings of the mental hospital erected in the early 1930s are mainly by *John Bain* of Newport, a series of brown brick pavilions in a mild Neo-Georgian style.

WORKHOUSE (The Old Workhouse Studio), Hatherleigh Place. Built as the Abergavenny Union workhouse 1837–8 by *George Wilkinson* of Oxford. Tudor, of Old Red Sandstone rubble with Bath stone dressings. The S, entrance front, is a lively, symmetrical composition of five bays, with four-centred carriage arches, now blocked, in the second and fourth bays and gables over the others. Some idiosyncratic details, e.g. the kneelers for the gables with pendant balls, and, most conspicuous, the elaborately moulded corbels which support the central gable over the broad, polygonal central bay. Large windows in the bay, to survey all who passed through the arches. Behind, fragments remain of the cruciform layout of the workhouse itself.

NEVILL HALL HOSPITAL, Brecon Road. A bulky presence W of the town. Designed by the *Percy Thomas Partnership* and built 1965–70 and 1971–4. The main elements are two identical five-storeyed, flat-roofed WARD BLOCKS. Each is an H in plan and they are set on the same alignment but *en échelon,* so that the S upright of one H and the N of the other form a continuous spine. Yellow brick with windows in broad continuous bands and a windowless stair projection at the ends of each slab. NURSES' HOUSING set apart to the SE, a series of three-storeyed, flat-roofed ranges.

Here, at the back of the site, is something completely different, the former NEVILL HALL (now Conference Centre), a fantastic Tudor Gothic mansion built in the 1860s by James Charles Hill as The Brooks. In 1890 the house and estate were purchased by William Nevill, first Marquess (but nineteenth Lord) of Abergavenny, hence the change of name. Hence, too, the Nevill bull and misleading date 1889 on the SW front. This, then, is the mansion of an heir to the family which developed the Blaenavon Ironworks, later appropriated by the local aristocrat. The name of the architect who indulged in such a recklessly exuberant, and by the 1860s somewhat outmoded, performance is unfortunately not known, nor even the exact date when the house was built.

Before embarking on a description, one can steady one's nerves by noting that the plan is quite conventional, a rectangular main block entered from the NW with a long L-shaped service wing running back from its E corner. Grey-buff rock-faced stone in small courses with Bath stone ashlar dressings. Two storeys and semi-dormers. Heavy mullioned windows and heavy window bays, rectangular and polygonal. Height is emphasized by the tower (now truncated) over the entrance porch, by the steep, pointed relieving arches over the upper windows to the l. and r., and by the shaped and pierced bargeboards over these windows and over gables and semi-dormers on all fronts. The steep roofs, the projecting chimney-breasts and the crowds (now much thinned) of tall, clustered chimneystacks rising clear of the roof ridge reinforce the soaring effect. The SE side of the house is the most artfully composed, as it faces a small lake. Here, in the angle between the high house and the not quite so high service range is an elaborate stone orangery, its central bays projecting and shafted all across, the shafts with lush foliage capitals. The two tiers of contrasted bargeboards constitute a veritable apotheosis of a much-loved feature of mid-C19 houses.

The porch opens into a deep, poorly lit hall, in which the staircase rises awkwardly over the entrance doorway. At the far end double doors open into the conservatory. To the l. the dining room, to the r. morning room and drawing room. The house came into hospital use in 1920, and now is inevitably fringed by utilitarian huts and corridors.

THE LODGE on the Brecon Road, although it bears the Nevill crest, was clearly built by J.C. Hill. It anticipates the materials and many of the motifs of the main house. It also retains an extraordinary feature lost from the main house, roof tiles diagonally striped in red and black.

BRIDGE, ½ m. W, carrying the A4143 over the River Usk. Of stone. Segmental arches. Pointed cutwaters carried up almost to parapet level. The structure is a composite of three dates, the downstream arches and piers surviving from the C15 bridge, those upstream belonging to a tramroad bridge of 1811 by *William Crossley*, and the roadway and parapet formed *c.* 1868, when the two bridges were amalgamated.

TRAMROAD, Springwells Road. A 330-yd (300-metre) length of

the formation of the horse-worked Llanfihangel Tramroad, engineered in 1811 by *William Crossley*, its line heading off N-wards across the meadows.

RAILWAY STATION, Station Road. Built in 1854 for the Newport, Abergavenny and Hereford Railway by *Charles Liddell*. Rock-faced local sandstone. Simple, Italianate.

PERAMBULATION

The Town Hall in CROSS STREET makes the obvious starting point. The row of three houses in MARKET STREET facing its return front is worth a look. C17–C19. The upper storey overhangs the pavement on iron posts. No. 4 Cross Street, opposite the Town Hall, has a pretty, early C19 shopfront. Three doorways subdivide it, framed by slender Gothic shafts with capitals in the form of bunches of grapes (for the shop was a wine shop). Full-width iron veranda over, with delicate Gothic balustrade. Next door, to the E of the Town Hall, KING'S HEAD HOTEL, medieval in origin. Two-centred C15 stone archway wide enough for carts, moulded with continuous hollow, roll and hollow. Cross Street then descends gently towards the SE, where two of the town's most self-confident buildings soon appear, facing each other. On the l., LLOYDS BANK, a Jacobean fantasy of 1895–7 by *A. E. Lloyd-Oswell*. Generously glazed ground storey of pink Alveley stone ashlar. Above, three timber oriels project on fancifully carved stone aprons, against a background of red brick. Two vast, overhanging, half-timbered gables crown the composition. On the r. the ANGEL HOTEL, a splendidly broad frontage of *c.* 1820. Stuccoed and painted white with black dressings. Three storeys under a top parapet, the lowest channelled. Two-plus-one-plus-two bays, the central one a little elaborated over an entrance flanked by fluted Doric columns *in antis*. The taller bay added to the l. has broad, slightly canted groups of sash windows on all three storeys. Further down on the l. Nos. 37–40 form the GUNTER MANSION, where Thomas Gunter in the C17 had an illegal Catholic chapel in the roof space.* Towards the street the rendered front is hardly distinguishable from its neighbours. At the back, however, the whole rubble-built elevation remains, its windows mostly C18 timber sashes, with two gabled projections in its W half. The r. projection contains a timber newel stair which leads to an upper-floor room with a richly decorated plaster ceiling. This is mid-C17. The main beams and subsidiary framing bands are enriched with vine trails. In the rectangular fields thus created, a repeating pattern of four winged heads of cherubim. Is all this meant to have a religious significance too, or would that have been unwisely conspicuous in penal times? Finally, set back on the r. at the corner of MILL STREET, the handsome late C18 TAN HOUSE, of red brick, recently incorporated into PEGASUS COURT, retirement homes in an C18 idiom.

* A painting of the Adoration of the Magi detached from the plastered wall of the chapel is preserved in the town Museum.

Back at the Town Hall, HIGH STREET continues the line of Cross Street. On the r. OLD BANK has a mid-C19 classical façade shorn of its moulded details as part of the restoration of 1977–80 by *Alex Robertson, Peter Francis & Partners.* To the l. first ST JOHN'S STREET, where the MASONIC HALL makes a surprising appearance. Three-stage tower of St John's Church, the medieval parish church of the town. The church was appropriated in 1543 by Henry VIII, after the Dissolution of St Mary's Priory had freed the priory church for the townspeople's use. The body of the church has been absorbed in later buildings, but the W gable with blocked two-centred-headed doorway can be seen in St John's Square. Coxe (1801) says that the tower was taken down and rebuilt 'about fifty years ago', a curious piece of antiquarianism for the mid C18.

To the l. of the tower a simple, two-storey, domestic-looking attachment added or remodelled after 1760, to provide a study above and a writing school below. Small reset medieval head corbel. The freemasons took over in 1898, when the new school buildings in Pen-y-pound Road (p. 102) came into use.

From here the second turning to the l. out of High Street is NEVILL STREET, the only consistent Georgian street in the town. A pleasant variety of stuccoed and colour-washed frontages on both sides but only two individual buildings to note. No. 11, on the r., of five bays and two storeys, is rusticated below, and has a top parapet, above a fluted frieze and dentil cornice. Central doorway with Adamesque fluted pilasters, quasi-Doric entablature and pediment. A date in the 1780s is suggested. Further along on the l., No. 14, with cow-head corbels supporting the cornice. These must date to 1873–80, when the building was in use as the Cow Temperance Inn. The two oriels below, however, are evidence of a much earlier timber-framed building. The windows themselves have been heightened, but the lintels and sills are late C16 or early C17, carved with animals in runs of stylized foliage and the arms of the Vaughan family of Tretower. Inside, a panelled post with moulded cap provides evidence that the front was originally jettied, and perhaps dates back to the early C16.

At this point High Street becomes FROGMORE STREET, which curves gently downhill. Before it straightens out, BARCLAYS BANK on the l., dated 1892. Italianate. Of grey rock-faced Forest stone with generous Bath stone dressings. Pedimented date panels break the skyline over the outer bays. The architect was *E. A. Johnson.**

At the end of Frogmore Street the twin-towered frontage of the Baptist Church (p. 99) and, facing it, the WAR MEMORIAL for the Monmouthshire Regiment. Crowning figure of a soldier in full battle kit resting wearily on his rifle, 1921 by *Gilbert Ledward.*

Beyond the Baptist Church, PEN-Y-POUND ROAD, where the Presbyterian Church (p. 99) and King Henry VIII Grammar

* The architect's name was kindly supplied by the archivist to Barclays Bank, Miss J. Campbell.

School (p. 102) cluster opposite a group of C18 houses. As the hill rises, the R.C. church and school appear on the l., and beyond, a one-storey Gothick TOLL COTTAGE of 1831.

OUTER ABERGAVENNY

Off the MONMOUTH ROAD, to the SE of the town, a high-class Victorian suburb developed, doubtless encouraged by the proximity of the railway station (*see* above, p. 105). In STATION ROAD, two examples of the neat Italianate idiom still current in the 1850s: No. 34, at the junction with the main road, and GREAT WESTERN HOTEL, facing the station. Particularly full-blooded examples of the late C19 idiom are the four villa pairs in FOSTERVILLE CRESCENT, lavishly dressed with caramel-coloured terracotta. Are these the crescent of nine villas in Monmouth Road for which *E. A. Johnson* called for tenders in 1886? In BELMONT ROAD something even more idiosyncratic, FAIRLEA, designed and built by *W. White*, 1887–8, as an advertisement for his patent 'Hygeian Rock' composition. Gabled and bargeboarded extravaganza, of yellow brick with applied half-timbering and double-height timber veranda. The patent rock fills the cavity brick walls. Further N, off FIRS ROAD, a larger villa, COED GLAS, the grounds dominated by the tall, variously angled pavilions of the Children's Assessment Centre, 1975–7 by the County Architect *K. P. Jones* and Assistant County Architect *Glyn Smith*. Grey brick, the top storey clad in black tiles. Monopitch tiled roofs. Quite a memorable group.

In PEN-Y-POUND, on the hillside N of the town centre, some more late C19 villas. HAVERANG HOUSE, in LANSDOWN ROAD (now Saxonbury Nursing Home), is of 1884–5 by *E. A. Johnson*. Yellow brick. Lively grouping of gables. Other, only slightly less imposing late Victorian houses by *E. A. Johnson*, *c.* 1894–5, are in the spaciously laid-out roads of STANHOPE PARK on the NW edge of the town, e.g. THE ROWANS, at the N end of CHAPEL ROAD, and THE HALL, at the top of WINDSOR ROAD, the latter making specially idiosyncratic use of Johnson's favourite yellow brick in combination with grey stone.

THE PENTRE, Brecon Road, 1 m. NW. Uncompromising white block, five bays wide, three storeys high, said to have been built in 1817. Full-width veranda on thin iron posts. A canopy for every window. Large iron-framed HOTHOUSE with convex roof detached from the house to the W.

LLWYNDU COURT, 1 m. NW. White Italianate villa with a pair of pedimental gables and a polygonal bay. Built *c.* 1830 for Richard Baker Gabb.

THE HILL, Hill Road, Pen-y-pound. 'Rebuilt in 1904', wrote Bradney two years later. But in 1903 *E. A. Johnson* advertised tenders only for alterations and extensions to the house. The rectangular, three-storeyed main range under a shallow, hipped roof with lower, irregular wings could well be early C19. But the crisply detailed five-bay façade of the main range, faced with Bath stone ashlar, is presumably Johnson's, though unusually formal for him. The way the projecting central bay is developed, with porch on slender square piers, canted bay above, and armorial top balustrade, is impressively adroit.

PARC LODGE FARM, 2 m. N. A delightful, textbook group of C17 farmhouse and barns stepping down the slope above the Afon Cibi stream. It stands at the centre of the medieval deer-park enclosed in the valley below Sugarloaf Mountain by the monks of Abergavenny Priory. The BANK AND DITCH which surrounded the park can be traced for much of its length, to the W, where pastureland meets the bracken-covered moor, and to the E through ancient oak woodland.

COLDBROOK PARK, $1\frac{1}{2}$ m. SE. The mansion was pulled down in 1954. It was in origin medieval, enlarged in a somewhat gauche Palladian style for Sir Charles Hanbury Williams, the diplomat and wit, *c.* 1746–53. It stood near the head of the little valley. Immediately to the SW the C17 STABLES survive, but were drastically converted into a house in 1985. The swags below the eaves on the NW front copy plaster decoration which was on the stables. The low rubble-stone walled enclosure adjoining to the W, with horizontal slit windows at the wallhead, was built as KENNELS. On the N side of the main lake, the partly surviving WALLS of a large C18 kitchen garden, stone without, brick within. Further lakes, higher up, have been formed, as part of a new landscaping of the grounds by *Richard Herbert* and *Elizabeth Banks*, begun in 1994. A winding yew avenue leads up to the little Jacobean Gothic CHAPEL built after 1906 at the E-most extremity of the grounds.

2000

ABERSYCHAN

The steep, straight High Street is well provided with chapels, but the church of the Establishment stands typically isolated on the hilltop. The ironworks, founded 1826 and expanded 1850, lay in the valley to S and E.

ST THOMAS, Varteg Hill (disused). 1831–2 by *Edward Haycock*, of local sandstone. High-sided five-bay nave intended for galleries, box-like chancel. Lancets, thin buttresses. – STAINED GLASS (removed in 1995 to the church-cum-hall in BLUETTS ROAD). Christ between saints, 1937 by *F. W. Cole* for *William Morris & Co.* of Westminster.

BIBLE CHRISTIAN CHAPEL, High Street (disused). Rendered front dated 1850. Long, round-headed windows flank the central door and the trio of round-headed windows above it. Pedimental gable, its cornice arched up just enough to accommodate the central windows.

HIGH STREET BAPTIST CHURCH, High Street. Another rendered three-bay front, its pedimental gable decorated with pierced bargeboards and enclosing a tablet dated 1827. That is an unusually early date for a full-blown two-storey façade like this. *W. Ardick & Sons* of Warminster remodelled the chapel in

1868, though the exterior was said to have been 'barely altered'. While the pedimented central doorway, round-headed flanking windows, and central round-headed window may belong to the first build, the rendered enrichment, including the projection of the central bay and the fluted angle pilaster strips, must be of 1868.

The interior is entirely of 1868, and excellently preserved. Exposed tie-beam and kingpost roof. The galleries on all four sides, supported on slender iron posts, have two-part fronts, boarded below and of pierced, bowed ironwork in a handsome classical pattern above. Simple oriel pulpit. Above the gallery at this end a high, wide arch provides raked seating for the choir, and the organ is set far back behind. Original pews throughout. Behind the chapel a symmetrical layout of elders' room, hall and flanking classrooms, with continuous half-glazed panelling and doors.

NODDFA WELSH BAPTIST CHURCH, Varteg Hill. 1846. The contractor, and probably the architect, was *Philip Hambleton* of Pontnewynydd. Pedimental gable on angle pilaster strips. Long, round-headed windows flank the segment-headed central doorway and triplet window. The interior is galleried on three sides on thin iron supports.

TRINITY METHODIST CHURCH, High Street. 1869–70 by *E. A. Lansdowne* of Newport. Broad front of snecked, squared stone, the bargeboarded gable supported by Doric pilasters at two different heights. Round-headed windows, the central twin sharing an E.E. shaft. Axial doorway of 1953. The interior has arch-braced roof trusses pierced with foiled patterns. Galleries on all four sides, the choir gallery of 1885, the ORGAN on it of 1904. The handsome PULPIT on foliage brackets is presumably of 1870.

PRIMARY SCHOOL, Lower Harpers Road. 1902–3 by *Lansdowne & Griggs*. Single-storeyed but a lively design. Red Cattybrook brick with white Portland stone dressings, on a podium of rock-faced Pennant sandstone. Central hall between classrooms, symmetrical under three gables, that over the hall open on pilaster strips and penetrated by a big, round-headed window with brick mullions and stone voussoirs. Almost the same composition at the back. Irregular S wing.

COMPREHENSIVE SCHOOL, Manor Road. Built in 1913 by *John Bain* of Newport as a higher elementary school. Classical, symmetrical. Red brick, the clerestory of the central hall banded with stone. Hipped roof and domeleted bellcote. This is somewhat obscured by large additions of 1977–80, also of red brick, but entirely different in idiom. Split-pitch roofs. Contrasts between fully glazed and virtually unglazed elevations. The long, irregularly rectangular block takes advantage of the steeply sloping site, with classrooms arranged on four half-levels. By *Gwent County Architect's Department*: design architects *John Postill* and *Norman Robson-Smith*.

BRITISH IRONWORKS, ¾ m. W. The fragmentary remains of the ironworks built for the British Iron Company in 1826–7 to the design of the fashionable young London architect *Decimus Burton*. Enlarged in the 1840s and again after the works were taken over by the Ebbw Vale Company in 1852. The works closed in 1883.

The approach from the B4246 is through the BIG ARCH. The arch was constructed in 1879, to give access to the ironworks site under the newly constructed Monmouthshire Railway, which joined the London and North Western Railway branch immediately to the N. The main surviving buildings of the ironworks form a single-storey quadrangle, with walls of Pennant sandstone and shallow roofs originally slated. Most recognizably Burton's are the two angle pavilions of the front range, built as offices, the r.-hand one retaining its ashlar quoins and window and door surrounds (and internally a mighty kingpost roof truss), the other altered and heightened. The rest of the quadrangle was built as a series of workshops in the 1840s. Within it, against the SW range, are the remains of a REVERBATORY FURNACE, for puddling and remelting the iron, a unique survivor of a type of structure which once stood in serried ranks in the major ironworks.

BRITISH IRONWORKS COLLIERY (immediately to the N of the Ironworks). The most important survival is the PUMPING-ENGINE HOUSE of 1845, one of the best-preserved beam engine houses remaining in Wales. Built of squared Pennant sandstone and reinforced, appropriately, with a good deal of cast iron. The beam of the pumping engine pivoted on the sill of the large round-headed opening in the upper S gable. Its function was to pump out coal workings immediately beneath the rolling mills of the ironworks. A little further N is the massive square base of a mid-C19 CHIMNEYSTACK of rock-faced Pennant sandstone, also with much cast-iron reinforcement.

ELIZABETH ROW, on the hillside W of the ironworks. The survivor of sixteen terraces of workers' houses largely built *c.* 1825, for the opening of the ironworks. Two-storeyed, rendered, the segment-headed windows with cast-iron frames. A second, shorter terrace may have been for foremen, and the overgrown enclosure to the W must have been the site of the manager's house and garden.

CWMBYRGWM WATER-BALANCE PIT, on the hillside to the SW (at SO 251 034). Mid-C19 brick-lined oval colliery shaft, blocked 10 ft (3 metres) down, its head divided by a heavy timber beam. Strewn round the site are fragments of the cast-iron and timber mechanism which enabled loaded wagons to be raised up the shaft, counter-balanced by water-filled iron basins. Sadly, the intention to restore the machinery has not been implemented. This is the sole survivor of a type of equipment of which there were over sixty examples in operation in Monmouthshire alone in the early C19.

CWMBYRGWM RED ASH COLLIERY ENGINE HALL. Of red brick, *c.* 1900.

LOWER NAVIGATION COLLIERY ENGINE HALL, ½ m. SW of Talywain at SO 254 040. Built *c.* 1900–10 of red brick and concrete, with a bit of panache typical of the collieries of the Edwardian steam-coal boom. Two by four bays under a hipped roof. Angle pilasters. Tall, segment-headed windows light the main engine storey. Thc base of the Waddle ventilating fan outside against the W wall is a rarity.

GARNDIFFAITH

1 m. N

ST JOHN, Stanley Road. 1932 by *A.F. Webb* of Blackwood. Gothic. Pebble-dashed walls and dressings of grey artificial Portland stone. Not surprisingly, the Incorporated Church Building Society objected to its design. – STAINED GLASS. Nave S, St Francis and Clothing the Poor. 1963 by *Celtic Studios*.

VIADUCT, Garndiffaith. Built in 1876–7, to the design of the engineer *John Gardiner*, to carry the London and North Western Railway on the Merthyr-to-Abergavenny line. Nine tall round-headed spans. Rock-faced masonry with arch-rings and soffits of brick. Two corbelled-out safety recesses on each side.

CWMAVON

2 m. NE

CWMAVON HOUSE. White. Two-storeyed, of four bays by five under a hipped roof. Built for the forge-master of Varteg Forge *c.* 1830. FORGE ROW, built for workers at the forge on the hill alongside to the S, is a little earlier, *c.* 1804–6. A two-storey terrace of twelve tiny houses, just a doorway and a window wide, but with shared stacks and alternating plans, so that they read as six. Excellently restored as six in 1987–8 by *Ferguson Mann*, the stone walls whitened, doors and window frames painted in earth colours.

BREWERY (now plastics factory), immediately S of Forge Row. Built in 1900 to the design of *George Adlam & Son* for Westlake's Brewery of Blaenavon. Sited on the bank of the Afon Lwyd, where it could take advantage of the reliable water flow. Yet this is no mere practical building, but makes a magnificent show towards the approach from the N. At the entrance the substantial MANAGER'S HOUSE of five bays, two-storeyed under a hipped roof. Rendered, with Baroque colonnetted doorway and gabled dormer above. The BREWERY itself rises majestically through five tall storeys behind the busy little two-storeyed, hipped-roofed OFFICE. Pennant sandstone, the office lavishly dressed with Bath stone ashlar, the brewery with red brick. The office sports an angle tourelle and other artfully disposed fenestration, but its stacks and shaped porch gable have been lost. The brewery displays its top three storeys and a roof gable. Three wide bays, but where the third and fourth storeys have widely spaced segment-headed windows, the top storey has six rectangular ones in pairs. Small but telling semicircular window within the gable. Round the side the fenestration pattern is repeated for four of the six bays.

2000 ABERTILLERY/ABERTYLERI

The town developed on the hillside above the tinplate works which had been established in 1846, and grew as collieries sprang up above and below it in the Little Ebbw Valley. CHURCH STREET, wide enough for a weekly market, is the heart of the town. The parish church stands here. The few remaining chapels occur unobtrusively in the tight grid of streets to the W of HIGH STREET. Perhaps the most characterful building in the town is the Bush Hotel, at the bottom of High Street, for public buildings are almost entirely lacking.

ST MICHAEL THE ARCHANGEL, Church Street. The first church on the site was by *John Norton*, 1853–4. The present building was designed by *C. B. Fowler* of Cardiff, the nave and lean-to aisles built in 1898–9, the chancel in 1905–6, six bays in all. Snecked, rock-faced Pennant sandstone and Bath stone dressings. The chancel rises as high as the nave, the sanctuary bay alone breaking free of the aisles. Flèche over the chancel arch. In the chancel windows Geometrical tracery, grouped trefoiled lancets in the aisles. Large and idiosyncratic four-light S (ritual W) window with a transom, flattened mullions and a little plate tracery. Inside, one realizes that this is one of Fowler's finest churches, in the Bodley spirit. High, wide nave, wide aisles. Canted boarded roof running through unbroken into the chancel. Octagonal piers, of brick, now unfortunately painted over, with deep moulded caps and double-chamfered arches. Gabled piscina and sedilia in chancel and E (ritual S) chapel. – PULPIT. Of stone, polygonal, with the symbols of the Evangelists under arcading. A conventional piece, *c.* 1903. – ROOD SCREEN and ROOD. 1921 by *J. Coates Carter*. Lavish Perp, now moved incongruously to enclose the sanctuary bay. – STAINED GLASS. Grisaille glass in the nave, 1898 by *A. Savell*. – Chancel N (ritual E), Ascension, brought in from St Luke, Pontnewynydd. By *Mayer & Co.*, *c.* 1891. – W (ritual N) aisle), Transfiguration. A strongly coloured, arrestingly hieratic visualization of the subject. Signed by *M. & A. O'Connor*, 1854.* Lady Chapel, Virgin and Child between SS Anne and Elizabeth. 1940 by *Bristow Wadley & Co.* of Cardiff.

BAPTIST CHURCH, King Street. Dated 1855. Rendered. Round-headed openings in rusticated surrounds. The entrance doorway is flanked by two long windows now blocked. Two tiers of windows towards the street. The interior was remodelled in 1892 and has galleries on three sides with bowed, pierced metal fronts. Iron supports decorated with curious relief crosses. The PULPIT stands, in typical mid-C19 fashion, between two long, round-headed windows.

CARMEL WESLEYAN METHODIST CHURCH, Carmel Street (disused). 1906–7 by *Habershon, Fawckner & Co.* Arts and Crafts Perp. The porch with five-light Perp window over and the emphatic square tower to the r. form a tight group close up to the road. Built of dour grey Forest stone. (Interior galleried

* The window was made for *John Norton*'s church.

all round, the roof supported by columns on the gallery fronts.)

TABERNACLE CONGREGATIONAL CHURCH, Chapel Street. Dated 1875. Rock-faced façade with pointed windows, long at the sides, a short pair above the pointed central doorway. Also buttresses. The interior is galleried on all four sides, the wainscoted front curved at the angles. The iron supports are more substantial than normal, with scroll and foliage caps. Ceiling with two central roses ringed with vines. – STAINED GLASS. Of *c.* 1900. A repeated pattern in each window, of wheat sheaves below and vine stems rising to support bunches of grapes at the top.

MARKET HALL, Market Street. 1892–3 by *Alfred Swash* of Newport. A tall rendered front, in a minimal style called 'English Renaissance' at the time of opening. Interior completely remodelled.

COMPREHENSIVE SCHOOL, Alma Street. 1984–6 by *Gwent County Architect's Department*: design architect *John Postill.* Huddled in the valley bottom, one-storey and two-storey pavilions round a courtyard, with buff brick and blockwork walls and broad, black-tiled roofslopes carried forward as canopies, like a crowd sheltering under umbrellas. Scarlet gutters, downpipes and brackets. Ingeniously planned with much stress on diagonals, the buildings prolonged by low walls, and dense planting, which emphasize the sense of enclosure and protection.

PRIMARY SCHOOL, Princess Street. Built as a board school for girls in 1898 by *George Rosser* of Abercarn. Pennant sandstone. Single storeyed, with the usual symmetrical arrangement of gables. Addition of 1909.

WAR MEMORIAL, Somerset Street. Bronze figure of a soldier waving his tin hat in the air, on a tall granite pedestal. By *George Thomas*, unveiled in 1926.

BUSH HOTEL, High Street. Red brick with stone dressings. Jacobean. Symmetrical three-storey main front crowned by a pair of straight-sided gables balancing tiny segmental pediments. This is probably the hotel for which *Swash & Bain* of Newport called for tenders in 1895.

CWMTILLERY

$1\frac{1}{2}$ m. N

At the head of a side valley of the Little Ebbw, overlooked by unexpectedly verdant and wooded hills. A reservoir lies yet higher.

ST PAUL. 1890–1 by *E. M. Bruce Vaughan* of Cardiff. Nave and lower chancel up against the hillside. N porch towards the valley view. Characteristic composition of the W gable, a pair of two-light plate-traceried windows and a bell gablet above. Snecked, rock-faced Pennant sandstone. Hammerbeam nave roof. – PULPIT and CHOIR STALLS. Of timber. Perp, the latter unusually substantial. – STAINED GLASS. Chancel E, Christ in Majesty between SS Paul and David. 1957. – Nave W, Annunciation and Noli me Tangere, 1960–1, signed by *A. E.*

Buss of *Goddard & Gibbs*. – Nave S, Jesus and his parents: 'I must be about my father's business'. An unusual subject. Presumably by *Celtic Studios*, *c*. 1970.

GWRHYD-MAWR, on the mountainside ½ m. N. of the settlement. Two small, white, single-storey farmhouses, probably of the mid C17, set close-up at r.-angles to one another (cf. Upper Hafodarthen, Llanhilleth). The main house, set end-on to the slope, is of hearth-passage plan, with a cowshed dated 1816 added prominently at its lower end.

2080 BASSALEG/MAESALEG

ST BASIL. The church was almost certainly of Celtic origin. A priory was founded here in the first decade of the C12 by Robert de la Haye as a cell of Glastonbury Abbey, but was abandoned in 1235. From the beginning of the C19 the Morgans of Tredegar Park had their mausoleum here, on the N side of the chancel, and this has profoundly affected the fabric and fittings of the whole church. An early nave arcade with 'heavy square pillars and low arches' was replaced in 1878, but there is late medieval evidence in chancel, tower and S porch. Perp outer entrance to the S porch, two-centred multi-moulded arch on paired shafts. Inside the porch a pair of demi-angel corbels bearing shields and two head corbels, all presumably reset. The tower looks Tudor, of three stages, unbuttressed. Battlements. Segment-headed W doorway with above it a square-headed window of three trefoil-cusped lights. Pointed tower arch formed of undressed stones. In the chancel the panel-traceried E window is Perp, the square-headed S window Tudor, of four arched lights under a hood-mould. Finally, before leaving the exterior of the church, mention must be made of the free-standing late C14 or C15 chapel which stood on the S side of the S aisle, described in Sir Stephen Glynne's notes (1836) and depicted in a drawing of *c*. 1846, but subsequently removed without trace.

Inside, the chancel arch, fairly small, of two chamfered orders dying into the imposts, could be of the C14 or C15. The nave arcade was rebuilt in 1878–9 by *Habershon, Fawckner & Co.*, the Morgan family's retained architects. Five bays. Slender, alternately round and octagonal piers and double-chamfered arches. The Dec windows probably theirs too. In 1902–3 *C. B. Fowler* restored the chancel, added the organ chamber at the E end of the S aisle, and probably renewed the Tudor wagon ceilings throughout. Finally, *W. D. Caröe* in 1916 enlarged and converted the Morgan mausoleum on the N side of the chancel into a chapel, with a two-bay entrance arcade to the S, in a showy Perp style. – REREDOS. In the N chapel, part of Caröe's refitting, with a relief of the Adoration of the Kings. – CHANDELIERS. A pair, of brass, with two tiers of branches, dated 1822. Said to have come from St Woolos, Newport. – HATCHMENTS. A splendid series of eleven of the Morgan family, displayed all round the nave. – STAINED GLASS. Chancel E, the Four

Evangelists, by *Cox & Son*, probably *c.* 1850. Strong colours, strongly characterized heads. In the tracery lights a dozen C17 German grisaille panels. – N chapel E, SS David, Basil and Dyfrig. 1917 by *Kempe & Co.* – N chapel N, Crucifixion, part abstract. 1977 by *Alan Younger*. Also Baptism of Christ *c.* 1990. – N antechapel N, Virgin and Child and a saint flanking the arms of Lord Tredegar, a presumptuous conceit. – Nave N, theological virtues. 1904 by *A. Savell & Co.* – Nave NE, military saints, for a war memorial. The primary colours well judged in relation to the flanking brass name plaques. Probably by *Martin Travers* (A. Brooks). – S aisle S, Christ Raising Jairus's Daughter below saints. 1910 by *Kempe & Co.* – S aisle E, Empty Tomb. 1964 by *G. Maile Studios*. – S aisle W, the four elements. 1988 by *Alan Younger*. – MONUMENTS. Among the Morgan monuments in the N chapel three stand out. – Sir Charles Morgan †1806. Standing wall monument, by *Coade & Sealy*. Reclining female in the pose of the antique statue known as the Cleopatra, high upon a large sarcophagus. The intention of the concept is not easy to grasp. – Mary Margaret Morgan †1808. Standing wall 87
monument. Signed by *Sir Richard Westmacott* and one of his most impressive works, in which Grecian restraint holds Romantic emotionalism in check. Mourning family of seven children grouped below a draped sarcophagus. – Sir Charles Morgan †1846, by *J. Evan Thomas*. White marble hanging wall monument, with twenty-one tinctured shields of arms superimposed on its frame. – Attached to the exterior of the S wall of the chancel, relic of an earlier era, inscription slab to Hugh Jones †1719, bailiff at Tredegar.

In the CHURCHYARD E of the chancel the post-1916 extension to the burial ground of the Morgans of Tredegar. – Gwyneth Morgan †1924. A strange conception, by *Cecil Thomas*. The triangular stem decorated with Celtic interlace bears a crucifix and heads of sleeping females with interlace hoods. Above this a figure of a pensive woman holding an inscribed shell.

LYCHGATE. Erected as a war memorial in 1926. Oak, with a bronze figure of St George standing against a red and gold mosaic background, signed by the sculptor *Gilbert Bayes*.

VIADUCT, E of Pye Corner (ST 288 872). The largest surviving early railway viaduct in South Wales, and one of the largest built anywhere before the era of the locomotive railway. A plaque dates it: Rumney Railway Co. 1826. The company's surveyor, *George Overton*, presumably designed the viaduct, which is of ashlar stonework and consists of four round-headed arches 26 ft (7.9 metres) in span, set on short piers with pointed breakwaters. Widened in 1863 for use by the Brecon and Merthyr Railway.

COMPREHENSIVE SCHOOL, Caerphilly Road. Of two dates, the parts kept wide apart from each other, representing two different philosophies of design. The earlier was completed in 1935 to the design of *John Bain*. It faces E towards the road across a broad expanse of playing field, a unified and symmetrical nineteen-bay composition. Brown brick of two storeys under a steep hipped roof. The centre three bays are modestly ceremonial with widely spaced sash windows, the central stone doorcase framed by Corinthian pilasters carrying an open segmental pediment, the window above pedimented. Ridgetop chimneystacks further mark this part out. To l. and r. extend the classroom ranges, with large rectangular windows.

The later half of the school lies at the back towards the W and is entered from The Griffin. It was built *c.* 1957–8, and is a loose picturesque composition, with all the hallmarks of the quietly Modernist idiom of *Colin Jones*, Monmouthshire County Architect. Caramel brick, shallow pitched roofs on all the various parts. The central accent is a tall rectangular brick tower, beside which to the r. is the hall, extended at r.-angles at the back by a two-storeyed classroom range. The main classroom range to the l. is three-storeyed, and has typical metal-framed windows in continuous bands, alternating with dark bands of boarding.

PENTREPOETH PRIMARY SCHOOL, Bryn Hedydd. 1985–6 by *Gwent County Architect's Department*: design architect *Norman Robson-Smith*. Long, low and symmetrical on its hilltop site. Broad, shallowly pitched roofs clad with metal sheeting define the plan and stress the lowness. There are three pavilions, the central one, for the hall, rising a little with a band of clerestory windows, that to the E for junior classrooms, that to the W for infants. Spine corridor from end to end. A full-height V-plan window in each pavilion projects towards the view. Also the occasional child-height porthole. Lively colour scheme, the cladding white fibrous cement panels and black timber boards. Red metalwork. The building is steel-framed, and internally the frame and roofslopes are visible, the classrooms grouped in polygonal clusters.

At RHIWDERIN, 1¼ m. W, a varied group. The COMMUNITY CENTRE in PENTRE TAI ROAD was probably built as a church school *c.* 1860. Gothic. Rock-faced Pennant sandstone with dressings of buff brick and Bath stone at key points. EBENEZER CONGREGATIONAL CHAPEL, at r.-angles to the E, off HARLECH DRIVE, is dated 1864. Old-fashioned gabled front of Pennant sandstone with long, round-headed windows flanking the central doorway. Yellow brick oculus in the gable above. GLOCHWEN FARM lies away to the E, beyond CHAPEL TERRACE. The earliest part of the whitewashed farmhouse is the E range, of the later C16. The corbelled stack against the upper (N) gable-end shows that it had a heated upper chamber. (Inside, post-and-panel partitions separating the hall from two unheated rooms. Stairs in the normal position, beside the hall fireplace.)

Amongst the new houses at Rhiwderin there is a small square ENCLOSURE (ST 264 877) rather similar to that at Y Gaer, Trellech (q.v.). The clay bank survives well only on the SE corner, and no ditch can be seen.

At PEN Y LAN (ST 259 849) a small bi-vallate enclosure may be seen behind the houses.

BEAUFORT 1010

The settlement, at the head of Ebbw Vale, takes its name from the Duke of Beaufort, who did no more than lease land here in 1780 to Edward Kendall for an ironworks. Between 1785 and 1833 five forges were built for the Beaufort Ironworks, but no trace of them remains today. A modest church and two chapels in a hollow establish the identity of the place.

ST DAVID. 1890–4 by *Halliday & Anderson* of Llandaff, for no more than £1,100. E.E. Nave and lower chancel, N porch. Rock-faced Pennant sandstone and dressings of yellow Ebbw Vale brick outside, red brick inside, including the moulded chancel arch. – STAINED GLASS. Chancel E, Good Shepherd between SS David and John, 1891 by *W. G. Taylor*. – Chancel N, Good Samaritan, by *Geoffrey Robinson c.* 1976.

ENGLISH CONGREGATIONAL CHAPEL, 1857. Pebble-dashed, the dressings painted buff. The front is a basic classical arrangement: long, round-headed side windows flank a round-headed doorway. Large oculus in the gable.

CARMEL INDEPENDENT CHAPEL, 1865. A similarly arranged façade, but pulled into a coherent architectural composition. Central triple-arched window in a segmental frame. The central bay is set in a wide and high, round-headed recess which penetrates up into the pedimental gable. Rock-faced Pennant sandstone, with grey granitic ashlar for the rustication which enriches every opening and angle. The architect was the Rev. *Thomas Thomas* of Landore, who repeated this design in several chapels in the Swansea area. The interior is equally memorable, galleried on three sides on thin iron posts. Flat boarded ceiling centred on a large and elaborate plaster rose. An unusual feature is the marbling as well as graining of the panelled gallery fronts. Posts marbled to match.

Large GRAVEYARD in front of the chapel, packed with memorials.

BEDWELLTY/BEDWELLTE 1000

ST SANNAN. One of the medieval ridgetop churches characteristic of upland south-east Wales but an exceptionally large one and unique in plan. It consists of two naves of equal size, a wide chancel that straddles them both, a tower standing W of the S nave, and a S porch. *W. G. & E. Habershon* restored the naves in 1858–9, the chancel was reconstructed by *G. E. Halliday* 1903–5 and a N vestry added 1909–10 by *E. P. Warren*. Externally there is Dec evidence in both naves, a pair of three-light, square-headed S windows (restored, presumably accurately, by the Habershons) and the three-light NW window with reticulated tracery. Otherwise everything is minimally Perp or Tudor. The tower is battlemented, of two stages with a rectangular NE stair-turret. Inside, however, the tower arch is clearly Dec, showing that the present tower had a predecessor. Two wave-moulded orders dying into the imposts. Small Tudor doorway to the turret r. of it.

The arcade between the two naves is the oldest part of the church. It must be of the early C13. Four short, stout, circular piers, with shallowly moulded caps, carry quite sharply pointed, double-chamfered arches. The E pier of the arcade consists of three semicircular responds forming a trefoil plan. Identical double-chamfered arches N and S open into the chancel and link to matching N and S responds. So the original plan seems to have been a double nave with chancel and chancel aisles of equal width, divided by a now-lost arcade probably of two bays. Late medieval wagon roof in the N nave. – FITTINGS. Mostly of 1910 by *Warren*, including the PULPIT, READING DESK, CHOIR STALLS and bow-centred ALTAR RAILS, also the WAINSCOT in the chancel. Note the wreathed oval PLAQUE in the chancel E gable, commemorating this scheme, 1911, designed by *Warren*. – CUPBOARD (in the sanctuary). Late medieval, the W end carved with emblems of the Passion, the front decorated with dense blank panel tracery l. and r. of the central door. A remarkable piece, perhaps intended as a cope chest. It should be compared with the Easter Sepulchre at Coity, Glamorgan. – STAINED GLASS. Chancel E, Crucifixion, 1910 perhaps by *Herbert W. Bryans* (A. Brooks). – Chancel S, Dorcas. By *A. J. Davies*, *c.* 1925. – N aisle NW, St Michael between SS David and Senan, 1896 by *Kempe*. – N aisle NE, theological virtues. 1917, signed by *Wippell & Co.* – N aisle centre, commemorating a First World War death. Also by *Wippell*, 1920.

In the CHURCHYARD three steps and the base of a CROSS. The LYCHGATE is probably late medieval, much restored.

TWYN Y BLEIDDIAID (SO 186 026). Only an inconspicuous ring of small stones survives from what was originally a large Bronze Age cairn.

2010

BETTWS

Just a hamlet, a chapel and two farms, in the hills N of Abergavenny.

CHAPEL. Built as a chapel of ease in Llantilio Pertholey parish, and virtually rebuilt in 1829, *John Pratt* surveyor. The most convincing medieval feature the S doorway, with crude four-centred head, blocked in 1893. Of the same date, the E triple lancet made up of reused lengths of medieval keeled roll moulding. – STAINED GLASS. Christ as a modern Good Shepherd. 1977 by *Celtic Studios*, designer *John Edwards*.

GREAT BETTWS FARM. Later C19, looking somehow French with its big hipped slate roofs, its particoloured brick chimneystacks, and the setting of gatepiers, yard and barns.

BETTWS 2090

2 m. NW of Newport

ST DAVID. A small, simple, but heavily restored medieval church, originally a single-cell building, to which the nave with W bell gable was added. W porch and lean-to S vestry of 1974. The windows belong to a mid-C19 restoration; the grey rubble-stone walling has obtrusive recessed pointing of 1974. The jambs and arch voussoirs of the medieval E window can just be made out, but the most telling survival is the windowless N wall. The chancel arch is quite wide, two-centred, cut through the original W wall.

BETTWS HIGH SCHOOL, Bettws Lane. A beehive of a compre- 125
hensive school, for 1,760 children, the first major work of *Evans & Shalev*, who won a competition run by Newport Education Authority in 1967, and built 1969–72. The compact, rigidly rectilinear building on a sloping site is a brilliant exposition of concrete construction (structural engineers *Anthony Hunt Associates*), modular design and orderly planning. One is astonished to learn that the building consists of no fewer than ten teaching units (miniature schools within the school), each arranged round its own open courtyard, workshops, laboratories and specialist teaching rooms, as well as an assembly hall, a sports hall and even a swimming pool.

The view from the N is austere. A straight drive passes the blocky little CARETAKER'S HOUSE (1968) and runs beside a running track to the flat N wall of the school. The facing material of the school is small concrete blocks of 2:1 proportion, which provide the module for the design of the whole building. To the N the upper storey boldly overhangs the fully glazed ground floor. Only the green wall-top trim lightens the austerity a little. When one comes round to the E to enter the building, its full character becomes apparent. It is laid out down the slope in three storeys, each projecting almost completely beyond the one above. S-facing walls are fully glazed under deep overhangs. At the lowest level a rectangular pool extending the full width of the building.

The internal circulation pattern consists of three E–W uncovered walkways, one at each level, and five N–S walkways, communicating under cover from level to level. Here coffered concrete soffits loom overpoweringly. But the internal courtyards and rooftop play areas, together with many internal changes of level, create extraordinarily diversified spatial experiences. And everywhere there is the S-ward view, across the school's playing fields to wood and hillside beyond.

BETTWS NEWYDD 3000

CHURCH (dedication unknown). A little grey stone building, Perp, nave and chancel in one, with W double bell gable (remodelled in the C19) and W porch, clearly a medieval addition. N vestry and

organ chamber of 1894 by *H. Prothero*. There is no preparation
37 for the spectacular survival inside of ROOD SCREEN, LOFT and TYMPANUM, perhaps the most complete rood arrangement remaining in any church in England or Wales. The rood stair and doorway also intact. Only the rood itself – the figures of the crucified Christ, of Mary and John – has gone, destroyed over 450 years ago. The screen is quite simple, of five narrow openings with Perp panel tracery each side of the four-centred-headed arch into the chancel. The loft has the characteristically richly decorated front, if a bit coarser than that at Llangwm Uchaf. Two convex foliage bands, of vine and oak, mark the bressumer. Pierced vertical panels of tracery above, under ogee canopies with outsize crockets. Another foliage band below the rail. The tympanum has stout cross timbers in the centre, presumably structural, rather than the cross for the figure of Christ. Pierced panels l. and r., to allow people on the loft to see into the chancel. Contemporary ribbed wagon roof, boarded in the chancel, plastered in the nave, on moulded wall-plates. – FONT. Norman, unusually fine.* The underside incised with concentric semicircles and resting on a rope moulding. C15 octagonal shaft and base.

In the CHURCHYARD three steps and square base, decorated with crosses and quatrefoils, for a CROSS.

BETTWS LODGE, on the slope below the church. Simple mid-C19 classical house (built before 1845) of three bays and three storeys flanked by lower one-bay wings. Narrow staircase bow at the back.

BETTWS, 2 m. NE. The remotely situated farmhouse has been much restored since Fox and Raglan saw it. It stands on a steep slope, and is of two parts. The E range along the slope is late C16. The main range at r.-angles down the slope was added in the early C17, retaining the earlier house for service uses. It is of two full storeys, with a full-height W porch of the sort that encloses both the entry and the stair (cf. Trevela, Llangwm Uchaf, 1601; Nant-y-banw, Llantrisant, 1625). Entry was into a hall, with unheated service room to the r., and to the l. the back-to-back hearths of hall and parlour. This unusual arrangement is signalled outside by a pair of lozenge-plan stacks, and inside made possible a parlour lit on three sides. Underneath the parlour, a cider-cellar, entered from the road through a door with typical early C17 shaped head. Fox and Raglan saw one or two timber windows with sunk chamfer mouldings, but most of the present windows are late C20 reconstructions.

COED Y BWNYDD (SO 366 068). The hill-fort is covered in beautiful National Trust woodland but the defences are clearly visible since there is little undergrowth. The camp is in a naturally strong position, and on the N side there is only a low inner bank. On the S and E, on either side of the straight entrance passage, the defences are multiplied with a series of three banks and ditches.

* The fabric of the church itself may well be Norman too. The foundations of an earlier E wall were found in 1952 20 ft (6 metres) E of the present one, and the inner face of the W wall shows traces of an earlier, steeper roof.

The outer end of the entrance passage is barred by a long low mound, now just visible in the field to the E, outside the field gate. Small-scale excavations in the interior and across the ramparts have shown that they were built in two stages and may have remained unfinished. On the S of the entrance they were designed on the *glacis* principle with a continuous slope from bottom of ditch to top of bank. On the N side the inner bank was revetted at the back with timber and on the front with turf, but was subsequently deliberately levelled. There was evidence for several round houses on the interior but there were no datable finds; however, radiocarbon dates suggested occupation from the early Iron Age.

BISHTON *3080*

ST CADWALADR. A small Dec church, with Perp remodelling, damaged in 1760 when part of the tower fell into the nave, and restored (though surely not rebuilt as Bradney states) in 1887. Built of grey limestone for the walls, purple Old Red Sandstone for quoins. Trefoil-headed lancets of *c.* 1300 in the chancel N and S, and another nave N. The three-stage W tower with NE stair-turret has belfry windows which also look Dec, or early Perp. They have two ogee cusped lights with an ogee quatrefoil under a pointed head. The W doorway of the tower, however, is Perp, two-centred, with continuous hollow, wave and hollow mouldings under a big hoodmould. The three-light Perp window over it is all of the C19. The plate-traceried E window and two S windows in the nave are C19 insertions. Medieval N doorway, with continuous wave, but C19 N porch. The church seems always to have been entered from the N, though it was only the routing of the main railway line a few yards S of the church that rendered this arrangement imperative. Inside, the tower arch has tall jambs and the arch itself is of two sharply pointed orders, all plainly chamfered. It is hard to know what to make of the chancel arch. Most of it must be C19, but it incorporates rustic head corbels at impost level, and the ogee-headed niche built integrally with its S jamb has hacked-back crockets, and so must be medieval. Stoup inside the N doorway. – FONT. Apparently late medieval. Irregular octagonal bowl on a chamfered stem. – STAINED GLASS. Chancel E, Christ as Good Shepherd and as Light of the World, *c.* 1915.

BLACKWOOD/COED DUON *1090*

ST MARGARET. By the little known *Bowes A. Paice* of London. Nave and S porch of 1875–6. Lower chancel, added in 1890–1, presenting a broad, canted apse towards the road. Deep S vestry and organ chamber. Snecked Pennant sandstone quarried on the site and Bath stone dressings. Geometrical tracery in the undersized windows of the apse, plate tracery in the nave.

Scissor-braced nave roof. For the later phase *Maurice B. Adams* was executant architect. He had worked with Shaw at Bedford Park, London, and here introduced a Norman Shaw-style colour scheme: roof with green-stained timbers and cream plaster, walls of salmon red with Persian red dado. None of it survives. – ORGAN. 1995 by *Frank Bradley*. Classical-style case brightly decorated. – STAINED GLASS. Several windows by *Herbert Davis*, most of them signed. – Apse, *c.* 1891, Empty Tomb between the Four Evangelists, against a background of orange trees. – Nave W, Christ preaching, 1896. – Nave NE, Works of Mercy, 1896. – Nave SE, Feed my Sheep, 1899. – Nave S central, Entry into Jerusalem, 1897. – Others by *Jones & Willis*, *c.* 1917: S vestry E, St Margaret of Antioch. – Nave N central, Faith, Hope and Charity.

CENTRAL METHODIST CHURCH, Cefn Road. 1898 by *Rosser & Roberts* of Abercarn. Gothic, faced with purple glazed brick. Cuspless tracery and twin, segment-headed doorways of pale ashlar stone. The interior has been horizontally subdivided, but there remain the handsome ribbed segmental ceiling and STAINED GLASS in a typical repeating Art Nouveau pattern.

MOUNT PLEASANT ENGLISH BAPTIST CHURCH, Cefn Road. 1890–1 by *W. L. Griffiths* of Newport. Gothic. Rock-faced Pennant sandstone dressed with red brick. The broadly gabled entrance front quite a composition of lancets. The interior has galleries on three sides carried on iron shafts with foliage caps. Meagre queenpost roof trusses.

THE LITTLE THEATRE, Highland Terrace. Built in 1904 by *R. L. Roberts* of Abercarn as a Primitive Methodist Church. Gothic front of Pennant sandstone well seen on the hillside site.

COMPREHENSIVE SCHOOL, Tŷ-Isha Terrace. Built in 1956–7 by *Monmouthshire County Architect's Department*, County Architect *Colin Jones*. The department's familiar idiom is present, the ranges under shallowly pitched green metal roofs, the walls of caramel brick, the generous glazing. But, since the site was reclaimed land liable to subsidence, the layout has an unusual profligacy: hall, gymnasium, and single-storeyed trios of classrooms all stand isolated from one another, linked only by minimal covered walkways. Flat-roofed two-storeyed teaching block added in 1974–5.

PERAMBULATION

The HIGH STREET follows the line of the Sirhowy Tramroad, laid down in 1805. This makes the street unusually long and broad. St Margaret's Church stands just beyond its N end. Starting here, the first major accent, on the r., is the MINERS' WELFARE INSTITUTE (now theatre and cinema), dated 1925. Rendered classical front with Frenchy details, rather tentatively handled. Next on the l. the tall, classical front of BARCLAYS BANK, *c.* 1922–3, notable mainly for being entirely faced in Portland stone ashlar. Then CEFN ROAD slants up to the r., with its chapels. After that the MARKET PLACE, just a cottagey

L-shaped side street, *c.* 1986–9 by *Hoggett, Lock-Necrews*. Finally, a good way farther along on the r. a big Art Deco CINEMA (now bingo hall) with vertical fins and upper bank of windows.

GELLI-DYWYLL, $\frac{2}{3}$ m. N. A forlorn-looking group beside the road. The house, of *c.* 1600, is rendered grey, of one-and-a-half storeys, with a single-storey porch, and at the back a large pillar stair and a kitchen wing. Behind, two large rubble-stone BARNS set at r.-angles to one another.

MAES MANOR HOTEL (formerly Maesruddud), 1 m. N. The house, of local rock-faced stone, was built for the colliery owner Edmund Williams, by *E. P. Warren*, Bodley's pupil, in a gabled and bay-windowed Tudor style. It is an L in plan and was constructed in two stages, the NE wing being dated 1900 on the handsome rainwater-heads, the SW wing 1907, replacing an earlier house. The next owner, L. Brewer Williams, had a grander vision. From 1907 he employed the garden designer *Thomas Mawson*, working with *Warren*, to lay out an ample and stately garden and form a setting for a much larger intended house.

The straight drive approaches from the E through tall GATEPIERS carrying ball finials and past twin LODGES by *Warren* dated 1912. It leads to a large entrance court to the E of the house, partly enclosed by a Pennant sandstone wall with further gatepiers. To the S, where the ground drops to a wide view, a semicircular garden opens out. A design for a house which would have been in scale with all this was published by Warren in 1914. The only executed building of that date, however, is the rendered COACH-HOUSE to the W.

The INTERIOR of the house is much altered, but retains two handsome classical chimneypieces of *c.* 1907. In a courtyard to the W, now roofed over, an ashlar niche dated 1900.

BLAENAVON/BLAENAFON *2000*

Of all the industrial settlements in the Valleys, Blaenavon remains the most eloquent, in its isolation, in its buildings and in their spatial relationships to one another. The driving energies of the C19, the paternalism of the ironmasters in the early part of the century, and the workers' independence and self-help at its end, are all apparent.

EARLY IRONWORKS

Iron was being extracted from the SW flank of the Blorenge from the late C16. The Hanburys of Pontypool held a lease of Lord Abergavenny's Hills, as they were known, for this purpose.

BLAENAVON IRONWORKS, North Street. In 1788 the Earl of 108
Abergavenny granted a renewal of this lease, on 12,000 acres (4,860 hectares) of mountain-top moorland, to a group of Staffordshire entrepreneurs, led by Thomas Hill. The attraction of the area for ironworking was that coal and ironstone both

outcropped up here, and limestone could be quarried nearby, providing all the materials requisite for the smelting of iron. An ironworks of exceptional size, fired by coke and blown by steam power, was quickly constructed, with two blast furnaces, and a third added before 1798. The works illustrated in Coxe's *Tour* (1801) can still be recognized today, though it takes a strong imagination to see the Ironworks as Coxe saw them: 'having the appearance of a small town, surrounded with heaps of ore, coal, and limestone, and enlivened with all the bustle and activity

Blaenavon, Ironworks. Engraving, 1801

of an opulent and increasing establishment. The view of the buildings . . . is extremely picturesque, and heightened by the volumes of black smoke emitted by the furnaces.'

Two further blast furnaces were added *c.* 1810, to cater for the expansion in production necessitated by the Napoleonic Wars. By 1815 in South Wales only the ironworks at Cyfarthfa and Dowlais, Merthyr Tydfil, were larger than Blaenavon. Stack Square, which faces the ironworks to the S, was built in the earliest years, 1789–92, probably to house key workers brought in from the Midlands. Other scattered terraces of housing to the SE and SW, visible on a plan of 1814, have all been swept away, leaving the works more isolated than they were originally. There is only one major surviving structure built after the change of ownership in 1836, when Thomas Hill III sold to the newly formed Blaenavon Iron & Coal Company. This is the water-balance tower constructed in 1839. In 1861, when Forgeside Ironworks, across the valley to the SW, came into service, the original works were no longer needed. A single furnace continued to operate until 1904, and some of the buildings remained in other uses until as late as the 1960s. In 1974 Blaenavon Urban District Council passed the site and buildings into the hands of the Secretary of State for Wales. They are now cared for by Cadw: Welsh Historic Monuments, which has carried out much consolidation, in order to make them accessible to the public.

A detailed description of the site should proceed from the rear (N) to the front of the site, to enable the buildings to be considered in relation to the process of iron production. The works occupy an artificially levelled area formed by quarrying away the hillside. The quarry-face thus created supports the CHARGING-BANK, stone-revetted on its N face, from which the furnaces were charged. Also at the back of the site are the remains of low CALCINING KILNS in which impurities in the iron ore were burnt off. Towards the W are what is left of eleven ovoloid burning cones related to the furnaces of 1788–90. To the E are two further, more prominent, kilns of *c.* 1810. At the foot of the quarry-face stand the principal remains, the BLAST FURNACES. One of the pair of 1788–9 survives, and both the pair of *c.* 1810, these standing almost to full height. Square tapering towers of Pennant sandstone house the cone-shaped furnace shafts constructed of firebricks. These cones can be well seen in the later pair of furnaces, from which much of the stone casing has been stripped (in 1911 to build the nearby church of St James, now disused). The base of each furnace is opened up with tuyère arches in the sides, through which air was blasted to heat them, and arched openings in front through which the molten iron was tapped. At the back the remains of a stone gallery can be seen, on a series of arches, added in 1853 for blowing-engines which further increased the heat in the furnaces.

Of the CAST-HOUSES, built in front of the blast furnaces, only one and part of another survive, relating to the earlier furnaces. Here, the molten iron ran out on to sand beds in which channels had been marked out, and hardened into pigs, the end product of the whole process. The cast-houses have arcaded openings in their end walls and a pattern of oculi and round-headed openings in their gables, all to assist the cooling process. The large pointed-headed opening in the l. cast-house is part of a mid-C19 remodelling which converted it into a foundry, to enable trucks on a railway to enter.

The coal required to feed the furnaces could at first be extracted on or near the ironworks site. The masonry ARCHES which led into two early mining tunnels survive, one in the charging-bank, the other at the foot of the water-balance tower. The WATER-BALANCE TOWER, at the NE corner of the site, was intended for the movement of materials on site, between the upper and lower levels. It was built in 1839, and is much the largest structure on the site. The sloping face towards the furnace yard is a fine piece of masonry, of Pennant sandstone rubble with profuse ashlar dressings. Deep, flared buttresses and arched openings brace the side walls. Large projecting arch at the back. The cast-iron framework for the brake wheel at the top of the tower survives, and inside it five of the six Tuscan columns which carried the wheel frame.

STACK SQUARE is a rare survival of late C18 industrial workers' housing. Three two-storeyed terraces form a square open towards the ironworks. In the centre of the square the base survives of the mighty chimneystack erected in 1853 to serve a new blast-engine house, now demolished. The houses consist of a single living-room-cum-kitchen, lit by windows (with cast-iron frames) flanking the entrance doorway and heated by a large hearth in the rear wall between a pantry and a spiral stair to two little bedrooms above.

Other structures on the site include cast-iron COLUMNS in the centre which supported the blast mains of the 1850s blast-engine house; at the entrance from North Street, the former PAY OFFICE and a fragment of another 1850s blast house; SW of the foundry the BASE of a chimneystack; SE of the water-balance tower two early C19 vaulted STOREHOUSES; to the S the large COMPANY SHOP, where the workers could buy food and other goods on credit.

To the N of the ironworks, the B4246 leads over the hilltop to several other important early sites. First there is evidence of the earliest form of mining in the area, employed from the late C16 to the late C18. The hillside to the SE of PEN-FFORDD-GOCH (Forge Pond) is covered in water-scoured gullies created by releasing 'hushes' of water from small reservoirs and thus exposing coal seams and deposits of iron ore.

Traces of INCLINED PLANES can also be found on the hillside, for example E of the face of Pwll-du Quarry (SO 251 115). The importance of these early transport systems was appreciated by Coxe, who commented on their great expense and on their visual attraction: 'the road, sometimes conveyed in a strait line, sometimes winding round the sides of precipices, is a picturesque object, and the cars filled with coals or iron, and gliding along occasionally without horses, impress the traveller, who is unaccustomed to such spectacles, with pleasing astonishment.'

PWLL-DU TRAMROAD TUNNEL, 1½ m. N (SO 245 117). The stone-built N portal survives of the railway tunnel opened *c.* 1815 from Blaenavon Ironworks. Almost 1½ m. long, it was then the longest such structure in the world. Hill's Tramroad, named after Thomas Hill II, ran through the tunnel and then for 3 m. (4.8 kilometres) to the NE round the shoulder of the Blorenge to Llanfoist Wharf on the Brecon and Abergavenny Canal. Traces of the line of the tramroad S of Pwll-du Quarry face, and of a mid-C19, double-track, powered railway inclined plane (SO 238 111).

GARNDDYRYS FORGE, ½ m. further NE, was opened in 1816, with puddling furnaces and rolling mill to produce wrought iron from Blaenavon's pig iron. The forge closed in 1860 and only earthworks remain, together with two dried-out reservoirs, the ruin of the manager's house to the S and platforms to the N on which terraces of workers' houses stood.

THE TOWN

ST PETER. A substantial, no-nonsense building erected in 1805 at the expense of Thomas Hill and the ironworks manager, Samuel

Hopkins. Of buff local ironstone, squared and carefully coursed. Three-stage W tower, unbuttressed, six-bay nave, chancel later lengthened to two bays. Pointed-headed windows with timber Y-tracery. Simple N and S doorways. The chancel arch, wide and of four-centred profile, is set on Doric caps and has a classically panelled soffit, so even the minimal stylistic references are not entirely consistent. The galleries round three sides of the nave were introduced in 1888. The boarded nave ceiling with ventilators, as if for a Nonconformist chapel, presumably at the same date. – FONT. 1805. Of cast iron but elegant. Circular bowl on 79
slender baluster stem. – STAINED GLASS. Chancel E, Christ as Sower and Shepherd. 1887 by *Swaine Bourne* (A. Brooks). – Chancel S, patron saints of four local churches indicated by their names and semi-abstract designs. 1967 by *Frank Roper* of Penarth. – MONUMENTS. Samuel Hopkins †1815. Simple tablet signed by *W. Hollins* of Birmingham. – Samuel Elmes Steel †1867. Relief portrait above a Gothic inscription panel. Angels l. and r. Signed *Tyley's* of Bristol.

In the CHURCHYARD four tomb-chests S of the church with cast-iron tops. One is dated 1809.

ST PAUL, Coedcae. 1893 by *E. A. Lansdowne* of Newport. Lancets.

HOREB BAPTIST CHURCH, Church Street. 1862–3 by *Thomas Thomas*, civil engineer of Blaenavon. Long round-headed windows flank the central pedimented porch on Ionic columns. The shorter, central round-headed window edges up into the open pedimental gable. Rendered. The interior has been little altered. Galleries on three sides, on well-proportioned iron columns. Coved ceiling with swirling plaster rose in the central roundel.

PARK STREET METHODIST CHURCH, Park Street. Built for Wesleyans, and a confident statement, of *c.* 1885–6, by *John Wills* of Derby. Of grey-green Pennant stone. Bold, if coarse, Romanesque-cum-Gothic façade, with a central rose over triple lancet, and to the r. a rectangular tower. Two-storeyed flank towards High Street.

SCHOOL, Church Road. One of the most significant buildings in Blaenavon, the earliest known ironworks school in Wales. The school closed in 1982, and at the time of writing the building stands sadly derelict. Built in 1816 at the expense of Sarah Hopkins, sister of Samuel, who had died the previous year – a 'ludus literarius', as it is called in the Latin inscription reset on the later central porch. Three-bay, single-storeyed schoolroom ranges to l. and r., ending in two-storey pavilions barely rising higher, but extending back in three bays, for teachers' houses. So a Palladian composition, in spite of the pointed windows. Walls of squared Pennant sandstone, slated roofs of shallow pitch.

PRIMARY SCHOOL, Coedcae Road. Built as a council school in 1905–6 by *B. J. Francis* of Abergavenny. Typical of its date. Red pressed brick with grey Forest of Dean ashlar dressings. Single-storeyed, with gables given a few scrolly details.

WORKMEN'S INSTITUTE, High Street (Torfaen council offices). 117
A gargantuan affair of 1893–4 by *E. A. Lansdowne* of Newport, expressing the self-confidence of the community in no uncertain

terms. Grey rock-faced Pennant sandstone from Newbridge dressed with buff Ebbw Vale brick and buff stamped terracotta panels. I-plan, of two tall storeys, the skyline crowned on three sides by curvaceous pedimented gables of various scales and forms. The entrance front centres on three generous doorways, a central stone one with rusticated spandrels and swan-neck pediment, and flanking ones of brick. Lanky pilaster strips above communicate with the roof gables. The interior contained an upper hall seating over 1,500 which could be used for theatricals. It was reached up a 'double grand stair', and on the ground floor were a newspaper room, a magazine room and a recreation room.

WAR MEMORIAL, at the corner of Church Road and High Street. Of Portland stone, and echoing the form of Lutyens's Cenotaph in Whitehall, though incorporating a louvred belfry and clock-stage within it. Unveiled as late as 1931. Designed by *R. L. Edmunds* of Blaenavon.

POST OFFICE, Church Road. Cultured Neo-Georgian, dated 1937. Of five bays and two storeys under a hipped roof laid with Westmorland slates. Sash windows. The architectural emphasis is on the central pedimented stone doorcase with Gibbs surround.

PERAMBULATION

A walk downhill from the site of the Blaenavon Ironworks along Church Road to St Peter's Church is instructive. First on the l., behind a long, high stone wall is TŶ MAWR (The Beeches Nursing Home), built for Samuel Hopkins *c.* 1800. Colour-washed buff. Hugely scaled range towards the road, of three high storeys and three very broad bays, framed by raised angle pilasters and deep flat strings. Many later, irregularly spaced windows. Shallow hipped roof.

Nothing more until Sarah Hopkins's school on the r., with St Peter's Church beyond. Church, Workmen's Institute and Horeb Baptist Church cluster together, expressing vividly the three forces, Established church, Nonconformist religion and communal secularism, which together drove Valleys culture in the C19. From here PARK STREET and HIGH STREET run straight and parallel up the hill, lined by continuous terraces of two-storey stone-faced cottages.

LATER INDUSTRY

FORGESIDE, ½ m. SW. Of the ironworks which the Blaenavon Iron & Coal Company began to construct in 1838, and eventually brought into service in 1861, little survives. In the line of industrial sheds, however, where large-scale metalworking continues, is one nine-bay stone range with segmental brick arches of the late C19 or early C20.

At the approach to Forgeside from the E, the four-square, stone FORGESIDE INN, then the simple (former) SCHOOL, extended in 1910 by *J. Bain* of Newport, and, beside it, ZION ENGLISH BAPTIST CHAPEL, dated 1874. Rubble Pennant sandstone front with yellow brick dressings. Round-headed openings. The settlement itself retains several of the close-set streets of HOUSING erected for the labourers in the ironworks, two-storeyed stone and rendered terraces.

BIG PIT, ½ m. NW of Forgeside. A once typical South Wales colliery, 109
developed from early C19 workings of the Blaenavon Ironworks Company, with a haulage shaft sunk in 1860 when the Forgeside Ironworks began to be developed, and enlarged and developed piecemeal, with many C20 structures, until closure in 1973. What makes Big Pit special is its complete state of preservation both above ground and underground. Everything is accessible to the public, since the pit became a colliery museum in 1983.

The cluster of pithead buildings is dominated by the HEADFRAME with the winding gear which hauled the cages up and down the shaft. It was constructed, of steel joists, in 1921, replacing successive timber predecessors. Beside it, part of the original WINDING-ENGINE HOUSE, though the present structure is C20, of red brick. The complete TRAM CIRCUIT of rails survives, a great rarity now, though by the end of the C19 nearly all collieries had one, to carry the trams full of coal from the pithead to the fans of railway tracks downhill. Other buildings, of whitewashed stone, near the pithead include the FITTING SHOP, BLACKSMITH'S SHOP, STABLES and ELECTRICAL SHOP (now teashop), all simple, practical buildings of *c.* 1900.

To the NE is the OFFICE, whitewashed stone below, brick above. At r.-angles to it, the two-storey ELECTRICAL WORKSHOPS of polychrome brickwork, built before 1920. Behind, the single-storey DRIFT-MINE HAULAGE ENGINE HOUSE is single storeyed, also of red and yellow brick. Also part of this group is the four-bay, single-storey DEPUTIES' LODGE, in which the under manager had his office. The FITTING SHOPS, stone of four bays and of five, were built in 1910 and 1917. Wide end doorways gave access to a narrow-gauge railway. SAW MILL to the E, also served by a railway. To the SE stand the MINERS' BATHS and CANTEEN, *c.* 1930. Concrete, in a Modern style, with flat roofs and metal-frame windows, as was typical for the colliery baths built throughout Britain at that time. Inside, the fittings remain largely intact. Finally, high on the hillside to the SW, sited over the top of the colliery upcast shaft, the brick FAN and COMPRESSOR HOUSE, of 1909–10.

The extensive UNDERGROUND STRUCTURES accessible to the public include a barrel-vaulted stone CHAMBER, to house a steam-powered haulage engine, dating back perhaps to the 1840s. There are great lengths of ROADWAY, the roofs in the earlier parts barrel-vaulted in Pennant sandstone rubble, the later roofed with supports of steel hoops and intermediate timbering. Also two sets of STABLES, the larger in two rows of whitewashed brick stalls, two WORKSHOPS and two brick CHAMBERS housing electrically powered haulage engines.

1000 BLAINA/BLAENAU

The medieval church of Aberystruth, rebuilt by *John Norton* 1854–6, was demolished soon after 1966. The settlement developed after the opening of Cwm Celyn Ironworks in 1840–1. It extends downhill for about a mile from the BLAINA INN to the Workmen's Institute.

BEREA UNITED REFORMED CHURCH. Built 1850–3 for Welsh Congregationalists on a steep hillside site below the Blaina Inn. A typically robust-looking façade, with round-headed openings in two storeys and a shallow pitched roof-line. Raised angle strips the only embellishment. Randomly laid ironstone. The prominent iron discs belong to structural bracing of 1878–80. The interior is galleried on three sides, the boarded fronts on a plaster cove. Flat boarded ceiling probably of 1892. The ground-floor seating and the balustraded pulpit and stairs look like original furnishings.

EBENEZER PRESBYTERIAN CHURCH, West Side. 1860–1 to the design of *D. Morgan*, civil engineer. The façade is crowned by a pedimental gable enclosing a Diocletian window. Wide round-headed doorway between round-headed windows l. and r. Hoodmoulds. Alternating stone quoins, buff for the openings, grey at the angles. Ochre rendered walls. Galleries on three sides, supported on slim fluted columns with leaf capitals. Pierced metal gallery fronts. Later pulpit before a generous blind arch. – STAINED GLASS. Of *c.* 1900, with Art Nouveau patterns in blood red and green in all windows.

The chapel stands at the N end of WEST SIDE, an isolated, tight-knit group of late C19 cottage terraces.

PRIMITIVE METHODIST CHAPEL, Gladstone Street. 1865, in the style of the Rev. Thomas Thomas of Landore. Pennant sandstone rubble façade with brick dressings. Central bay enclosed by a superarch which rises into a pedimental gable. Interior galleried at the entrance end only (R. Scourfield).

SALEM BAPTIST CHAPEL, High Street. 1848. Memorable for the mighty letters which proclaim its name. Rendered buff and brown. Three-bay façade with round-headed windows in two tiers. At the back the two long windows which originally flanked the pulpit have been blocked. Narrow interior crowded by galleries on three sides, resting on thin clustered iron piers, part of a late C19 remodelling.

UNITED REFORMED CHURCH, High Street. 1886. Of coursed rubble. Minimal Gothic. (Typical interior, galleried on three sides.) The rendered hall set astride the rear is dated 1900.

INSTITUTE AND LIBRARY, High Street. 1892 by *F. R. Bates*. A confused composition of gables and canted window bays towards the road, made chaotic by the random use of grey Pennant sandstone and red and yellow brick.

CHAPEL FARM, Coldbrook Vale, ¾ m. NW. The most complete and comprehensible survivor of the few cruck-constructed houses in the Valleys, probably built in the mid C16. The two central trusses of a three-bay house survive intact, together with a magnificent stone fireplace at the downhill end. This is formed of monolithic chamfered jambs with a massively deep chamfered monolith for the lintel. The walls are all of stone, replacing the original timber framing, but earlier than the remodelling of the interior, which floored it over to create a habitable roof space. Gable-end entrance doorway in a heavy timber frame S of the fireplace, spiral stair to the N of it, cut into the thickness of the wall. Stop-chamfered ceiling beams and joists, and post-and-panel screen, forming an unheated inner room. No original windows, but the chamfered sill of a three-light window with mortices for stout diamond mullions has been preserved.

BRYNGWYN 3000

ST PETER. Of local sandstone rubble. The earliest evidence is inside the W tower, the C13 simply chamfered nave W doorway and lancet above. The tower itself, of two stages with battlements on a moulded stringcourse must be an addition but shows pre-Perp features; a two-centred-headed S doorway and trefoil-headed belfry lancets. The S wall of the nave has typical late medieval fenestration, two storeys of square-headed two-lighters at the E end, and a large, square-headed three-lighter further W, all conditioned by the need to light the rood, its loft and stair. Timber-framed S porch, with arch-braced and wind-braced roof, awkwardly overlapping the four-centred-headed S doorway. The chancel, a little lower and narrower than the nave, is apparently all Perp, its three-light, pointed-headed E window with panel tracery. N aisle and vestry added in 1871 by *John Prichard.* Chancel arch reinstated after 1854 (see the Latin inscription). – FONT. Hexagonal on panelled shaft and base, a local late medieval type, here enriched with shields. – ALTAR RAILS. Late C17. Thick turned balusters. – PULPIT. Timber. Probably by *Prichard.* – REREDOS. Timber, with shutters, and a relief of the Crucifixion and saints. 1923 by *Creed & Heal.* – MONUMENTS (in the vestry). Two rustic tablets: Frances Frampton †1665. – Thomas Jenkins †1779.

In the CHURCHYARD one step, the broached base and much of the shaft of the medieval CROSS.

MOTTE, at WERN-Y-CWRT, ½m. S. A small, low mound under trees, in the middle of the hamlet.

BRYNGWYN MANOR, 1 m. S. Late C17 stone house, rectangular under a hipped roof, much reconstructed after 1901. Rear stair projection. Chiefly interesting for having ruddled, i.e. red limewashed, walls.

PLAS HENDY, ¼m. N. Dated 1903. Unaltered small country house, stone below, roughcast above, with a little decorative timberwork in the gables and dormers. The architect was *Richard Creed.*

1010

BRYNMAWR

The town developed from the 1830s largely as a dormitory for the workers in the Nantyglo Ironworks. The earliest streets, Alma Street, Bailey Street, Clydach Street, are said to follow the tramways which contoured across the hillside. Grid street plan superimposed *c.* 1840 by *John Thomas*, a public health inspector. The church, a latecomer, occupies a site at the top of the town, the chapels, survivors of the sixteen extant in 1950, dot the streets lower down. Architecturally, Brynmawr is best known for the rubber factory, a structural and social experiment on a grand scale, the first post-war Modern Movement industrial building in Britain, built 1947–53 by the *Architects' Co-operative Partnership* on the SW edge of the town. Sadly, the factory closed in 1982, and, although the first post-war building in Britain to be listed, was condemned to demolition by the Secretary of State for Wales in 1996. At the time of writing only inertia and the inherent strength of the buildings keep them standing.

ST MARY, Dumfries Place. Designed in 1895 by *Nicholson & Hartree* of Hereford, and built 1899–1900, to replace a church of 1872. Nave and lean-to aisles, and chancel of equal height, providing a vast slope of slate roof under a continuous ridge. Temporary W wall, in place of the W bay intended. Dec style. Rock-faced walls of Gilwern stone, purple in the chancel, brown in the nave, the dressings throughout of red Hollington sandstone. Rock-faced interior walls as well. Arcades with double-chamfered arches on octagonal piers. Trefoil corbel shafts, with foliage caps for the chancel arch. – REREDOS. Of stone. Triple-gabled, with figures of Christ in Majesty and saints under trefoiled arches. By *Sir Gilbert Scott*, 1860, brought in from Richmond Parish Church, Yorkshire. – PULPIT. Of stone, worthy of William Burges. Massive, cylindrical, displaying reliefs of Evangelist symbols and set on a short, stout red marble stem and a huge stiff-leaf wreath in which lurk winged hounds. Made for Sutton Parish Church, Surrey. – FONT. By *Jones & Willis*. – STAINED GLASS. Filling almost all the windows. Signed *J. Jennings*, 1920, and one N 1932. – One N aisle window *c.* 1942, probably by *A. K. Nicholson Studios*.

VICARAGE, SW of the church. 1886–8 by *J. D. Sedding*. Stone below hung with black slates above, the windows groups of sashes, one or two slightly bracketed out. One gabled projection to the front, with porch tucked in beside, and one to the back. One of the slab-like chimneystacks remains. A deft design, though its origins in the Home Counties style of Norman Shaw have not been wholly disguised.

ST MARY (R.C.), Catholic Road. Of rubble-stone. Round-headed side windows. Said to date from 1863.

BETHESDA INDEPENDENT CHAPEL, Alma Street. Dated 1850. Round-headed windows in the façade, the long side ones cut across by galleries.

PRESBYTERIAN CHURCH, Bailey Street. Gothic. Rock-faced stone walls. Quite small.

REHOBOTH CONGREGATIONAL CHURCH, King Street. Dated 1827, but probably reconstructed *c.* 1850. Square-headed windows. Full-width lean-to porch. Altered and renovated in 1904 by *Habershon & Fawckner.*

TABOR BAPTIST CHURCH, Davies Street. Dated 1836, but reconstructed in 1857–8. The most imposing chapel in the town. Rendered façade framed by pilaster strips under a pedimental gable. Two storeys of windows, all round-headed at the sides. On the façade, the lower are square-headed under floating architraves, the upper round-headed, a triplet in the middle over the wide round-headed doorway. All have architrave surrounds with imposts. Inside, the impressive early arrangements partly survive. The modern pulpit is set between two long, blocked windows, indicating a typical early lighting arrangement. Galleries on three sides on thin iron posts, their seating steeply raked. The boarded ceiling with splendid plaster ceiling rose must be a late C19 embellishment.

BRYNMAWR COMPREHENSIVE SCHOOL, Intermediate Road. Presumably by *Monmouthshire County Architect's Department.* Conspicuous beyond the edge of the town. Opened 1970, a little old-fashioned for that date. Three-storeyed slab, the full-width window bands remodelled. To the l. a taller brown brick entrance pavilion, to the r. a short return wing ending in a sheer brick wall. Shallow pitched roofs.

BLAEN-Y-CWM COUNTY PRIMARY SCHOOL, Barley Field Way. 1988–91, by *Gwent County Architect's Department*: design architects *Norman Robson-Smith* and *Martin Lougher.* A vivid building, canted protectively along three sides of an octagon. Single-storeyed, the clerestoried hall in the centre slightly higher than the rest. Striped walls of brown and buff brick. Some porthole windows. Shallow pitched slate roofs, carried on down as a continuous glazed veranda. All metalwork painted scarlet.

RUBBER FACTORY, Blaina Road. The wreck of the most inventive industrial building of its time and still, for all its dereliction, an impressive sight. The factory was the brain-child of Lord Forrester, director of Brimsdown Rubber Company, subsidiary of Enfield Cables. His vision was to provide large-scale post-war employment in the Valleys, which had suffered catastrophically from the Depression of the 1930s. But he determined to do this by erecting a factory which would provide a high-quality and unhierarchical working environment and be precisely tailored to the needs of the production process, which was the conversion of raw rubber into a variety of manufactured goods. To realize his vision he chose a young, democratic architectural team, the *Architects' Co-operative Partnership*, and the brilliant structural engineers *Ove Arup & Partners.* What resulted, built 1947–53, was a factory extending over 6 acres (2.4 hectares), almost entirely covered by a variety of thin-shell concrete vaults. The greatest feat, structurally and aesthetically, is the creation of the
enormous central production area, covered by nine rectangular 120
handkerchief domes, a mere 3 in. (7.5 centimetres) thick, set three by three and supported on their corners by deep horizontal

beams, which themselves rest on just four groups of clustered, slightly raking pillars. The shallow curvature of each dome creates segmental clerestory windows in all four directions. Rows of shell-concrete tunnel vaults fringe the factory on two sides. To the N small-scale vaults covered loading and storage areas; under the larger vaults to the W lay the mill room where the rubber was processed. To the S, overlooking an expanse of water, a more conventional office range crowned with box-like concrete projections, for cloakrooms and lavatories. The entrance ramp along the E side flanking the road has gone, and in its place is a standard office block added after 1956, when Dunlop Semtex took over.

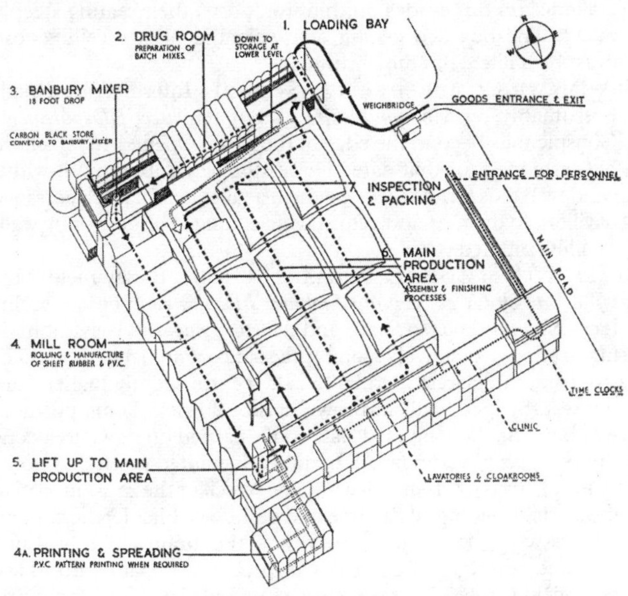

Brynmawr, rubber factory. Axonometric

Across the road to the E, the BOILER HOUSE, under an inverted paraboloid concrete roof, housing a spiral stair supported only at the top and bottom, a *tour de force* of engineering skill.

In POND ROAD, across the water to the S, a circular, stone-clad PUMP HOUSE under a concrete saucer dome. This was part of the rubber factory provision too.

In HEOL ISAF and HEOL GANOL, N of the road to Beaufort, HOUSING of 1949–50 by *Yorke, Rosenberg & Mardall* for workers in the rubber factory. A three-storeyed pitched-roof block and short flat-roofed terraces, all with end walls of random-laid Pennant sandstone.

BUCKHOLT 5010

2 m. N of Monmouth

A straggle of houses along the A466 on the Herefordshire border.

ST JOHN. Just a stone tabernacle of 1889. – FONT. The octagonal bowl is dated 1663 and incised with the names of churchwardens, its sides carved in relief with rosettes. Said to have come from Dixton Church.

BWLCH TREWYN 3020

TREWYN. Said to have borne the date 1692 on the E front. The view from the E is indeed of a late C17 ensemble. The symmetrical façade of the house is of seven bays and two storeys, of local stone under a hipped, stone-slated roof. The house is raised ceremoniously on a double terrace with central steps, above a railed forecourt entered through emphatic gatepiers. Only the ungainly dormers, cement-rendered and gabled, their windows pointed, strike a false note, though the heavy casement windows below, with their mullion-and-transom crosses, are also C19.

The building history is obscure and complicated. There are extensive vaulted cellars, where the head of a four-centred doorway, plainly chamfered, demonstrates the late medieval origin of the house. What appears to be a second such doorway is reused on the N front. During the C17 the estate was acquired by the Delahays of Allt-yr-ynys, 1 m. away to the NE across the Herefordshire border, and the front of 1692 faces in that direction. The C19 owners were the Rosher family,* who first encased the E front in Bath stone ashlar and added the dormers, then re-exposed the Old Red Sandstone walling and inserted the heavy casement windows. This seems to have been part of *E. H. Lingen Barker*'s activities in 1877. Finally, in 1990, the C17 character was re-emphasized. The dentilled cornice of the E front is of this date, copied from the cornice of the dovecote (*see* below). The five-bay S front was also regularized and sash windows substituted for casements. One square stone window, of indeterminate date, remains to hint at complexities tidied away. Towards the W the house is completely irregular, yet most of the windows, casements here, are of 1990. The square, two-storeyed structure beside the back entrance was probably a game larder. Timber-framed upper storey and pyramid roof. The N side appears all mid-C19, cement-rendered.

The interior has undergone its own several drastic reorderings. A three-bay entrance hall occupies the centre of the E front, with a wainscoted room of late C17 character in the SE corner. Upstairs, two S rooms have Rococo overmantels said to be of papier mâché. The trail-work which extends from one of them, looping across walls and under beams, must surely be early C20. The NE room has a mid-C19 white marble chimneypiece on

* Promoters of Rosherville, the Thames-side resort at Northfleet, Kent.

which groups of putti play with bunches of grapes. Since this was clearly meant for a dining room it cannot be in its original place.

The forecourt GATEPIERS look mid-C18. They are rusticated, and carry splendid vases, with gadrooning, foliage and masks. Across the road to the NE, an exceptionally fine DOVECOTE of *c.* 1700. It is of red brick, octagonal, with a large, round-headed panel recessed in each face. Dentilled timber cornice and open arcaded crowning lantern.

THE MANOR HOUSE, immediately to the N, was a service range or stable until the early C20, when it was dressed up in late C17 style to go with its new name.

DAN-Y-BWLCH, $\frac{3}{4}$ m. SW. The C17 longhouse seen by Fox and Raglan survives, but entirely sacrificed to farm uses. Cowhouse with sleeping chamber over occupied the downhill end, with entrance cross-passage behind the chimneystack. The residential upper part of the range is of one-and-a-half storeys.

4 PENTWYN HILL-FORT (SO 321 230). The hill-fort crowns the S end of Hatherall Ridge, just across the valley from the fort on Twyn y Gaer, Ffwthog. There, excavation has taken place. Although Pentwyn remains unexcavated, surface indications suggest that this, too, is a multi-period site. The rectangular enclosure at the N end may be the earlier section. It has a huge rampart 20 ft (6 metres) high in places on the N side, and a southern ditch and bank which now cuts across the centre of the fort. The defences of the S half are multivallate, with an impressive entrance track winding beneath the SE ramparts (followed by the current Offa's Dyke path). The E side is so steep that little extra defence was needed. On the W there is a low bank with a ditch mutilated by a modern track.

3090

CAERLEON/CAERLLION

THE ROMAN FORTRESS

Caerleon (the Roman Isca) was the base of the Second Augustan Legion and the military headquarters for South Wales from *c.* A.D. 75 until the end of the C3. Its position on slightly raised ground by the tidal estuary of the River Usk gave it security from flooding while making it accessible to sea-going vessels. In both respects it was superior to Usk (q.v.) which had preceded it as a legionary centre. The greater part of the fortress, which covered around 50 acres (20.25 hectares), lies under the modern village, and only the amphitheatre, part of the fortress baths, four barrack-blocks and parts of the south-western defences are visible today. Excavations and chance discoveries have made it clear that the fortress itself was surrounded by a considerable settlement, with cemeteries beyond, and with substantial docks by the river, which then flowed rather closer to the fortress than it does today.

Excavation and comparison with similar fortresses elsewhere in the Roman world have allowed much of the plan of Isca to be

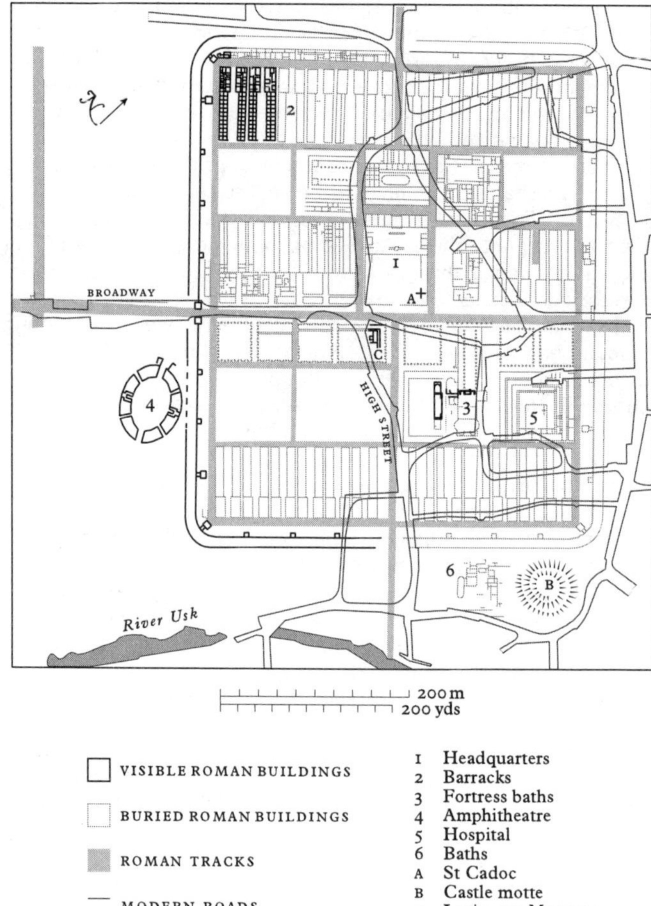

Caerleon. Plan of Roman fortress

reconstructed. In the main it appears to follow the standard design for such installations, having a rectangular outline with four gates, one in the centre of each side. At the centre of the site, where the parish church now stands, was the headquarters building (*principia*), facing the road to the SE gate, with the road linking the SW and NE gates running in front of it. Behind the headquarters building was the palace of the legionary commander, built around an oval courtyard, with a large building, which may have been a covered exercise hall or parade ground, on its SW side. To the NE was the legionary workshop. To the SW of the headquarters building were five sets of barracks for the first cohort, and to the NE a large block, which may have been stables, with barracks beyond.

On the opposite side of the main road will have been houses for the senior officers of the legion, although they are assumed to be here by analogy with other sites rather than on the evidence of excavation. Behind them, in the E quarter of the fortress, lay two major buildings, the great baths and the legionary hospital. This last, although known only from a very fragmentary plan, appears to have followed the customary design for such buildings, with rows of wards opening off wide corridors, the whole arranged about an internal courtyard with a large central hall, probably the operating theatre. The baths are among the most spectacular examples known in Britain. They cover an area of around 5½ acres (2.25 hectares), the parts on public display extending to no more than one-sixth of the whole. Baths of this type formed the social centre for the legion, and the complex included not only the customary suite of Turkish baths, but also a large colonnaded courtyard with a swimming bath, and a vast exercise hall, some 210 ft (65 metres) long. Fragments of another extensive bath building were found in the C19 outside the fortress walls to the SE, close to the castle motte, whilst a third, smaller set lay near the amphitheatre.

The greater part of the remainder of the fortress was devoted to barrack blocks for the 5,000 legionaries, although somewhere there must have been one or two groups of large granaries.

The fortress was originally built almost entirely of timber, with defences consisting of an earthen bank and ditch. Rebuilding, in the local Old Red Sandstone, apparently began at the end of the C1, and a fine marble inscription of A.D. 100 referring to the Emperor Trajan, which is in the site museum, probably marks the beginning of the process which continued intermittently for a century or more. As we know it today, the plan of Caerleon is that of the stone fortress, and although we may presume the general plan of its timber predecessor to have been similar, absolute proof is lacking. Excavation has made it clear that some of the major buildings, including the headquarters building, the baths and the hospital, were demolished at the end of the C3, and it is now generally accepted that the Second Legion was moved from the area and the fortress closed at about that date. Thereafter, the military headquarters for South Wales may have been in the newly constructed fort at Cardiff.

FORTRESS BATHS, NE of High Street. Within the L-shaped cover building of 1984–5 is displayed part of the enormous fortress baths. In front is the long, narrow rectangle of the swimming pool, originally open-air. The pool within the display area, 84 ft (25.6 metres) long, represents an early C2 shortening at both ends of the original pool which was as much as 135 ft (41 metres). Under the decking at the entrance end is what remains of an apsidal fountain house (*nymphaeum*), a decorative feature demolished when the pool was shortened.

The rear half of the display area includes on the l., part of a heated changing room, with remains of the brick pillars of the heated underfloor space, and on the r. part of a cold plunge bath. The main drain of the bath runs between them. Beyond is the NW end wall of the cold bath hall (*frigidarium*), the first of the three great vaulted bathing halls. Here can be seen the foundations of a rectangular bath recess flanked by two apsidal alcoves. Doorways at the outer ends of the wall led to the basilical exercise hall to the NW. Part of a MOSAIC PAVEMENT, displayed on the SE end wall, was found on the site of a second heated changing room, to the NE. The sites of the other two main bathing halls, the *tepidarium* (warm) and *caldarium* (hot), to the SE, have been located under houses and gardens in Backhall Street.

The other remains which are now visible all lie on the SW side of the fortress and are approached along the BROADWAY, which crosses the line of the defences on the site of the SW gate. A fine length of the FORTRESS WALL can be seen on the S side of the lane, whilst to the N the bank which preceded it is clearly visible with the ditch in front of it.

The AMPHITHEATRE, which was excavated in 1926–7 by T.V. 5
and R.E.M. Wheeler, is one of the most striking structures to have survived from the Roman period in Britain. Until relatively recently it was known locally as King Arthur's Round Table, reflecting the widely held belief that Caerleon was the site of Camelot. When visiting the amphitheatre it must be remembered that it was part of a military establishment, and that one of its prime functions will have been for military displays and ceremonies. This is reflected in the arrangements for access into the arena from the seating, a feature not normally thought necessary in an amphitheatre. Nonetheless, the provision of dens for beasts or gladiators opening off the arena indicates that its architect had the entertainment function firmly in view.

It was constructed *c.* A.D. 80 on a site so close to the fortress defences that the ditch had to be partially refilled. Few things in Roman Britain show the confidence of the Roman army at this date as clearly as the decision to place this enormous structure almost on top of the fortress rampart, a position which breaks every rule in the military textbook. The basic plan is an ellipse, with the seating raised on banks of earth derived from digging out the arena. At back and front these banks are revetted in masonry, with external buttresses where the slope of the ground necessitated additional support for the outer wall; elsewhere the symmetry of the design was maintained by the use of pilasters. The main entrances to the arena were on the long axis, and the remains of their vaulted tunnels are a striking feature of the building. Access to the seating was by six symmetrically placed entrances, the pair on the short axis being more elaborate than the others. The other four consisted of short, downward-sloping tunnels ending in steps, which led first up to the seating and then down into the arena. Those on the shorter axis, however, opened into small rooms giving on to the arena, with stairs to the seating on each side of them. Above these rooms, which were for animals or contestants, will have been boxes for important spectators, such as the commander of the legion.

Evidence from the excavations and from Trajan's Column suggests that the seating itself was carried on a massive timber superstructure with its main posts embedded in the bank and outer wall. It was probably the strain resulting from this arrangement which led to the construction of additional buttresses on the outer wall in the C3. Other changes included raising the floor levels in the entrance passage, probably to overcome the problem of water accumulating at the foot of the stairs, and this in turn necessitated the demolition of their vaults to give sufficient headroom. At the same time the door from the tunnel into the room on the E side of the arena was blocked off, leaving it accessible only from the arena.

The excavated LEGIONARY BARRACKS lie in the W corner of the fortress, the only group to be seen in Britain. They are four in number, arranged in facing pairs, but only the foundations of the W-most are original; the others, which are at a higher level, are modern replicas of those originally excavated. Each barrack held a 'century' and consisted of twelve pairs of rooms, opening on to a veranda, with a 'flat' and 'office' for the centurion at one end. The apparent complexity of the centurion's quarters in the W-most barrack is the result of later modifications to the original plan. Each pair of rooms will have held eight men, the inner room serving as the sleeping quarters, the outer being a storeroom for equipment. The fact that a century contained only eighty men meant that two sets of rooms must have had other uses, possibly as N.C.O.s' quarters.

Behind the fortress bank are the remains of two turrets, cooking ovens, kitchens, a latrine (see the drain) and a fragment of the stores building which ran along the NW sector of the fortress wall.

Within a couple of miles of the fortress, villas or suburban houses seem to have been built. Across the River Usk 1¼ m. NE (ST 356 912) there are said to have been found in the C18 parts of a massive Roman building, including fragments of sculpture. Parts of a tessellated floor were found in the C19 1¼ m. W, at ST 322 908. Fragments of building remains and coins discovered at St Julians, Newport, 1½ m. SW (ST 323 900), late in the C18 may indicate the existence of a Roman building there.

Simple stone buildings found at Great Bulmore (ST 359 915; ST 361 914) in 1815 and in recent excavations were probably part of an extensive ROMAN SETTLEMENT alongside the road from Caerleon to Usk. The site is notable for having produced a series of important Roman tombstones reused as flooring slabs within buildings, but almost certainly originally coming from one of the cemeteries outside Caerleon.

THE TOWN

The history of modern Caerleon begins in the late C11, when the Norman invasion of South Wales caused the erection of an exceptionally large motte to the SE of the long-deserted Roman fortress, close to the River Usk. Caerleon became the centre of a lordship, had borough status by the later C12, and was a port, since the river was navigable. Yet it has never grown into a proper town, blocked by the development of Newport barely 3 m. (5 kilometres) downstream.

Even today much of the W half of the legionary fortress remains under meadows. Modern housing development is largely out of sight, overspreading the hillsides to the NW, above the Hospital and behind the College of Further Education.

ST CADOC, High Street. The church is large and has a complicated history. An aisled Norman nave, to which a SW tower was added in the late C13, underwent a Perp rebuilding. The chancel was rebuilt by *Prichard & Seddon c.* 1855, the nave and aisle walls reconstructed and S porch added by *Seddon* in 1867–8. Finally, 1932–5 *W. D. Caröe* extended the chancel and added a S chapel and N vestries. Old Red Sandstone walls throughout. The tower is unbuttressed, with lancets at three levels, the lowest originally cusped, and a battlemented Perp top stage. The four-light Perp windows in the nave relate to their medieval predecessors. Caröe's parts are also Perp, but have the fanciful details in which he tended to indulge, see especially the chancel E window.

Inside, the W bay-and-a-half of the Norman S arcade survives, built into the N wall of the tower. It is crude work, much restored. Rectangular pier, plain imposts, arches of two unmoulded orders. The Perp arcades, of four full bays on the N side, are also much restored. They have the standard pattern of four shafts in the cardinal directions with moulded caps and bases, carrying wave mouldings round the arches, and continuous double waves on the diagonals. Does the chancel arch, high and wide, with continuous hollow and double wave, belong to the chancel of 1855? In Caröe's chancel more fancy details in the square-headed piscina and sedilia. Two arches with continuous mouldings open into the S chapel. Boarded wagon roofs throughout, that in the chancel with moulded principals. – REREDOS, ALTAR RAILS and CHOIR STALLS, all of timber, by Caröe *c.* 1935, also the ALTAR RAILS in the S chapel. – REREDOS in the S chapel. Alabaster, with a deep relief of the Last Supper. Late C19, displaced from the chancel. – ORGAN CASE. Part of the chancel ensemble, 1952, designed by *Alban Caroe.* – STAINED GLASS. An impressive series of nine windows, inserted *c.* 1896 in memory of Charles Williams †1720 (*see* Williams Charity School below), extends clockwise from the S chapel E to the N aisle NE, to narrate the life of Christ from the Annunciation to the Resurrection, two scenes per window. Seven are by *Heaton, Butler & Bayne*, but the first and fourth (nave W) are by *Gibbs & Howard*, the latter signed. The style in general is Netherlandish mid-C16, and great relish is taken in the vivid, if crowded, narration of the episodes. The series is interrupted by two windows moved from the chancel into the S chapel on its completion in 1935. These are SS Thomas and John, 1873, possibly by *Joseph Bell & Son*, and Ruth and Boaz, 1898, probably by *Heaton, Butler & Bayne*, but more strongly coloured than their Williams windows. – Theirs too, very late, the S aisle SW window of 1931. – Chancel E, Christ the King and saints, 1952–3 by *Celtic Studios.*

LYCHGATE, and flanking piers crowned by obelisks, by *W. D. Caröe*, 1919.

The VICARAGE, NW of the church, is by *J. P. Seddon*, 1862. Quite big, of Pennant sandstone with Bath stone dressings. A sober design, without exaggerated Gothicisms, but typical of the ecclesiologically approved parsonage of the period.

SS JULIAN, AARON AND DAVID (R.C.), High Street. 1884–5 by *Graham, Son & Hitchcox*. Small. Geometrical Gothic.

CASTLE. Little enough is readily visible of what must have been a strong castle, erected close to the N bank of the River Usk. The massive MOTTE, 200 ft (61 metres) in diameter at the base, comparable with the motte at Cardiff, is completely hidden by the high, embattled stone wall of the 1840s, which forms a continuous enclosure along CASTLE STREET and CASTLE LANE. It is known to have been in existence by 1086 and was presumably thrown up immediately after the Norman Conquest by the newly created Lord of Caerleon, Caradoc ap Gruffydd, or his son. Excavation has shown that it was raised over the standing remains of a Roman bath building. Two Roman column bases stand in the garden nearby. A stone structure on top of the motte, which is said to have disintegrated in the great frost of 1739, is conjectured to have been a C12 shell keep. At the foot of the motte the base of a twin-towered gatehouse has been identified.

In 1217 Caerleon Castle came into the possession of William Marshal the Elder. The most easily visible part of the castle, the stump of a circular stone TOWER attached to the SW corner of the Hanbury Arms, 200 yds (180 metres) SW of the motte, was built by him. It has three finely preserved arrow slits, identical in form to slits in his Garrison Tower at Usk Castle. Note that the slits were begun in Dundry limestone, but finished off in robbed Roman sandstone. Since Marshal died in 1219, this tower is precisely datable. It must have been one of a series protecting the outer ward of the castle. The blocked arch low down on the riverside was cut through in the C17 or later, so that cider barrels could be rolled in.

BRIDGE, carrying the road to Newport over the River Usk. Built 1806–12 by *David Edwards*, similar in design to the bridge at Tredunnock, but spoilt by later road widening. Ashlar piers with pointed cutwaters taken up to form refuges at road level. Three arches formed with single rings of voussoir stones, their shape steeper than segmental. (The datestone of 1800 was brought from the demolished bridge at Newport.)

GWENT COLLEGE OF HIGHER EDUCATION, College Crescent (now part of University of Wales College, Newport). The enormously extended ridgetop range, thirty-one bays long, three storeys high with central clock tower, was begun in 1912, as a training college for 100 students, to the designs of *Alfred Swash & Son* of Newport. Mauve Old Red Sandstone, and Bath stone dressings for the various rather pinched accents, some Baroque, some Tudor. Tall, thin clock tower with sheer rectangular shapes. The l. third of the range completed to a simplified design which upsets the symmetry of the whole. Flanking the approach from the town, a pair of pavilions, one intended as the principal's house, the other a caretaker's and power house.

To the S, for the FACULTY OF EDUCATION, several unexciting blocks of the 1960s. To the N, for the FACULTY OF ART AND DESIGN, a spectacular cascade of steel and glass down the steep hillside. This is the two W-most units of a four-unit scheme prepared in 1982 by *Gwent County Architect's Department*, County Architect *Ken Jones*, principal design architect *Norman Robson-Smith*. One must admire the daring which enabled a local authority to commission and carry through such a radical and individualistic scheme, even though only half of what was intended has materialized. For the steel and glass structure, Richard Rogers's newly finished Inmos factory at Duffryn (*see* p. 219) gave inspiration. The E half, the SCHOOL OF FINE ART, was built 1983–5, the rest, the SCHOOL OF 3D DESIGN, 1986–8.

From the entrance court of the College, in front of the 1912 range, there is nothing to see but a single-storey glazed entrance pavilion under a slated roofslope. In order to appreciate the extent and drama of the building it is necessary to follow the service road round at a lower level to the N (or catch a glimpse from a train on the Newport to Abergavenny line). From here one can see how overwhelmingly the need for N-lit studios has been satisfied. The lowest of the three storeys has a brick wall, and a sloping glazed roof, behind which the upper two storeys step in and out and up and back, each with glazed walls and glazed roofslopes. At intervals there are narrow, fully glazed projections, stepping back under gables in rhythm with the main roofslopes. Contrasting metal trim heightens the formal contrasts, black for the main glazing, red for the gabled projections and for the balustrades of viewing platforms. A glazed canopy spans the service road across to the boiler house and store. The shiny steel triple STACK at the W end of the boiler house is an important vertical feature. To the S, and visible only beyond the entrance pavilion, are three storeys of offices and seminar rooms, with deep slated roofslopes. Inside, these are separated from the studios and workshops by irregular longitudinal corridors at all three levels. The gabled N projections cover cross-corridors giving access to the studios.

The RATHMELL BUILDING, 1995–7, based on the design of *W. Davies* of *Bowen, Dann, Davies Partnership*, replaces the unexecuted E half of the 1980s scheme. It also houses departments of the Faculty of Art and Design, but quite differently. The roof is a huge, metal-clad asymmetrical curve, on which one looks down from the main forecourt, butted up against what had been intended as the temporary end of the School of Fine Art. Brown brick walls, punctuated by a variety of windows. Entrance under the top end of a colonnade all along the E side of the building.

STUDENT HOUSING, to E and N, also of 1995–6. In three-storey blocks, brown brick below, white cement panel cladding above, from which vertical timber struts project to carry the eaves, a clear echo of Richard MacCormac's housing at Duffryn (*see* p. 217).

WILLIAMS CHARITY SCHOOL (now primary school), High Street. 'Erected and Endow'd by ye Bounty of CHARLES WILLIAMS Esq. A Native of this Town', in 1724, as the prominent tablet records. This is educational bounty on an exceptional scale for the C18, and the rustically classical building became, in its layout, a model for later Welsh schools in the C18 and early C19 (cf. Blaenavon, p. 127). Half-H plan, with classrooms in the centre, the lofty main one for boys, the dormer-lit roof space above, it seems, for girls. In the wings, houses for the master (l.) and mistress (r.). The projecting central porch opened directly into the boys' schoolroom. Three-light mullion-and-transom window with voussoired lintel over it, and large flanking round-headed windows. Round-headed windows in two storeys light the wings. The iron window frames with lattice glazing bars are early C19. Overall hipped roof with dormers. At the rear, large C19 and C20 additions, so that it is not now clear how the girls reached their schoolroom or the teachers entered their houses. The single-storey projection to the left contained the master's kitchen.

LEGIONARY MUSEUM, High Street. Another remarkable educational initiative, this time a Victorian one. The Caerleon Antiquarian Association was founded in 1847 and its museum was opened in 1850. The handsome and scholarly four-column Greek Doric portico of Bath stone ashlar is of that date, by *H. F. Lockwood* of Hull. The museum as originally built was temple-like, even to the extent of being lit from above, as Greek temples were in the mid C19 thought to have been (cf. Pontypool Baptist Church, p. 477). The present museum, of 1987, has windowless walls of Bath stone ashlar, chamfered at the top, the clerestory windows hidden in the recessed chamfered attic.

ST CADOC'S HOSPITAL, Lodge Road. 1903–6 by *A. J. Wood* of London. Built as the Newport Borough Lunatic Asylum and laid out on the approved pattern of the time, a central administrative block set between a pair of ward ranges. Similar ward ranges behind, three l. and three r. forming two faceted quadrants. Red brick dressed with Bath stone and sparsely banded with yellow brick. A few touches of Baroque decoration round the entrance and a copper clock turret above, on a steep pyramidal roof. To the E a red brick Gothic CHAPEL (disused).

ORCHARD HOUSE, Norman Street. Built 1907–8 by *E. J. May* as an orphanage. Home Counties homely. Red brick, gabled.

PERAMBULATION

A walk down the HIGH STREET from the church to the river takes in almost everything. The most evocative group comes at once, where the lychgate, the Williams Charity School and the portico of the Legionary Museum stand obliquely to one another at the junction with the road to the Roman amphitheatre. Next on the r., one of Caerleon's characteristic high stone walls, interrupted only by little, white SALMONS COTTAGE. Beyond, the PRIORY HOTEL, almost entirely built *c.* 1800 for a member of the Morgan family, which had possessed the site since the C15. Old Red Sandstone rubble walling. Two-storey ashlar porch. Windows with arched lights towards the road and at the back. One single-lighter only is pre-C19. How far, if at all, the present building reflects its predecessor is not clear. Inside, C19 stone-vaulted corridor round three sides of an internal court.

To the S, at the junction with CROSS STREET, the space opens out triangularly. Here on the l., YE OLDE BULL INN, C16 in origin with three three-light and two-light upper windows, square-headed under hoodmoulds and with arched lights, similar to those in the Priory Hotel. These appear to be genuinely of the C16, but not, perhaps, in their original positions. The applied half-timbering is, of course, early C20 make-believe. Otherwise simple, rendered, sash-windowed frontages and one early C19 shopfront with bowed display windows.

Beyond this the High Street narrows and the enclosure wall of the castle grounds begins on the l. At the far end the Roman Catholic church on the l., and, free-standing beyond the end of the street, the HANBURY ARMS, L-plan, rendered, hipped-roofed, looking superficially of the C18. But the E range has a three-light timber mullioned upper window on the N side, and to the S three Tudor upper windows like those in the Bull Inn. They confirm a C16 date for the E two-thirds of the range, which was extended in the C17 to link to the C13 SW tower of the castle (*see* above). With that the Usk River bridge and open country are in sight. Across the bridge an early C19 TOLL-HOUSE, polygonal towards the road, with Tudor Gothic detail.

LODGE FARM (ST 322 913). The hill-fort overlooking the town is particularly interesting because the two phases of development can be clearly distinguished. The original fort was fairly small, a single low bank without a ditch surrounding the western end of the hill. Later the enclosure was more than doubled in size and greatly strengthened, with three new banks and ditches on the N side and three merging to two on the S side. The entrance track at the W end runs straight in through the banks, which are very high at this point. The later inner rampart clearly over-rides the original bank here. The E end where the farmhouse stands has been rather disturbed, but there seems to have been a second inturned entrance at this end.

CAERWENT

4090

THE ROMAN TOWN

Caerwent (Venta Silurum) was the capital of the tribe of the Silures in the Roman period. It was founded late in the C1 A.D., possibly on the site of a Roman fort, although the walls, which are its most striking remains, were not built until the C4. The site is relatively free from later buildings; a fact which allowed extensive excavation to take place in the years before the First World War. As a result we have detailed plans of the buildings for somewhat over half of the site. By the standards of the period these excavations were competent, but when studying the plan of the town which they produced it must be appreciated that they rarely elucidated the problems of alterations to the buildings, and in particular, hardly ever defined the date of their construction. As a result, the plan is a palimpsest recording features of varying dates, not all of which will have been in existence simultaneously. It is also probable that there were more timber buildings than the excavators located. Excavations more limited in scope, but to a modern scientific standard, 1981–95, uncovered the forum-basilica and temple in the centre of the town, and a courtyard house to the NW.

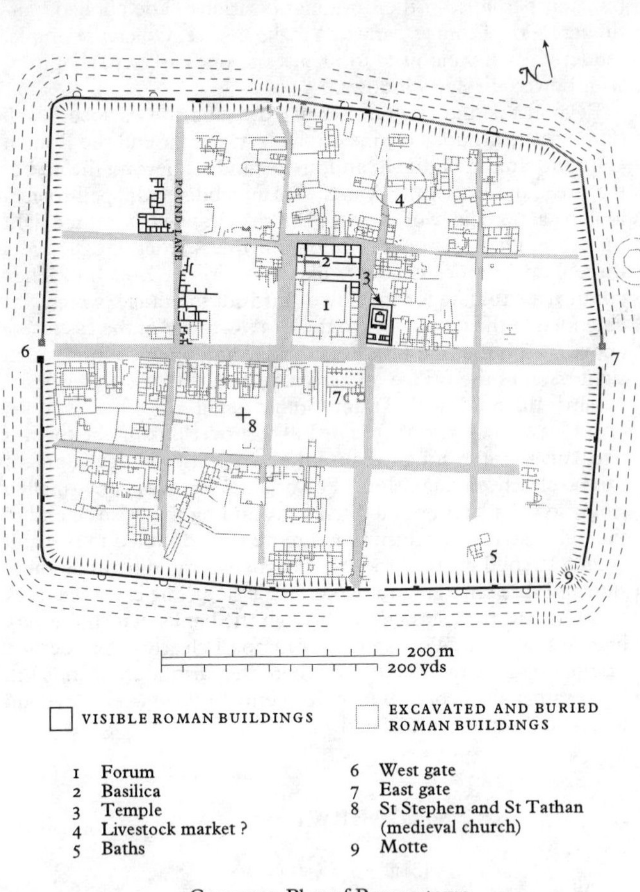

Caerwent. Plan of Roman town

Four groups of buildings are now visible, parts of a pair of houses and shops on the corner of Pound Lane, the courtyard house also accessible from Pound Lane, the temple which faces the main street, and the forum-basilica; the war memorial, in the centre of the village, is also built on a Roman foundation. The present road through the village largely follows the line of the main E–W Roman street, but other roads ignore the Roman grid plan. The forum and basilica lay at the centre of the Roman town, opposite the modern churchyard. They consisted of the customary large courtyard surrounded by shops and offices, with the great basilican hall on its N side. To the E stood the temple, whose foundations remain uncovered and which is described below. Facing the forum were the public baths, of which only the front hall and part of the cold baths could be excavated. The remainder of the main street was found to be fronted by shops and workshops of the normal long, narrow form which enabled the maximum commercial use to be made of this important road. Examples of these shops can be seen at Pound Lane (*see* below).

The majority of the buildings which lay on the side streets were private houses, some of considerable size, with two notable exceptions. By the S gate lay an unusually large building which, from its position and plan, was identified, perhaps correctly, as a *mansio* or inn for people travelling on public business. The second is the elliptical structure lying in the NE quarter of the town which was identified as an amphitheatre. This identification creates more problems than it solves, and it is now thought more likely to have been a livestock market.

TEMPLE. Built in the C4 and set at the back of an enclosure, which was entered through an apsidal enclosure on its S side. Only the foundations survive, formed of two rectangles, one within the other. At the front two short projecting walls mark the position of steps into the building, whilst a small apse at the back of the inner room indicates the presence of a statue niche. It may be reconstructed as a temple of the normal Romano-Celtic type, with the inner shrine (*cella*) rising above a surrounding colonnade. (Another temple, of octagonal plan, stood just outside the W wall of the town.)

FORUM and BASILICA. These occupied the central space in town, immediately NW of the temple. The forum, a square paved courtyard, lay to the S. Its NE corner has been excavated, together with the N-most of a series of small rectangular shops or offices which extended along its E side. The foundations of the basilica can be seen beyond, lying E–W the full width of the N side of the forum. Its total length was 182 ft (55 metres), and it was aisled in the normal way. The E two-thirds of the basilica has been excavated. Traces of the wide, shallow flight of steps survive, up which access could be had through a low colonnade into the S aisle. Inside, the aisles were separated from the nave by Corinthian columns of local sandstone *c.* 30 ft (9 metres) high. This has been deduced from fragments found in excavation, for only the sleeper walls on which the columns stood remain in place. The rectangular extension of the nave to the E served as a law court, or tribunal. The rectangular recess in the centre of the N side was a shrine. It was flanked by a series of rooms, the largest of which, immediately to the W of the shrine, has been identified as the council chamber. It has a partly mosaic floor, and a plaster wall-covering was found on the S wall painted with an architectural perspective.

The POUND LANE SITE, which lies on the N side of the main road half-way between the forum and the W gate, was excavated in 1947–8, and as conserved, presents a plan of bewildering complexity with walls of all periods combining to create an almost meaningless structure. In essence, the sequence began *c.* A.D. 100 with a pair of narrow shops with living quarters behind them. Later the eastern shop was demolished and the site used for the construction of two new wings for the other house, creating a U-shaped building with a central courtyard opening through a colonnade on to the street, into which it projected slightly. Later subdivision of the original rooms has added still further to the complicated sequence of foundations. A second house to the N was a simpler structure with ranges of rooms around a central courtyard.

A second COURTYARD HOUSE, further NW off Pound Lane, was excavated 1981–4 and awaits full display. This is datable to the early C4. The exposed walls show that it consisted of suites of rooms arranged round two rectangular courtyards. The main living rooms opened off the N courtyard, which was enclosed on three sides by a corridor. The handsome and well-preserved geometric mosaic pavement in the corridor was covered up again after excavation to preserve it from the weather. Two rooms here had underfloor heating. The S courtyard seems to have been primarily for farm use.

6 The outstanding monument of Venta Silurum is the wall of the *civitas* – easily the most impressive town defence to survive from Roman Britain, and in its freedom from later rebuilding one of the most perfectly preserved in Northern Europe. As is normal with the city defences of Roman Britain, the stone wall was preceded by an earthen rampart and ditch, probably built late in the C2, the wall being added a century and a half later. The bastions which strengthen the N and S walls were added 349–50, as a walled-in coin hoard indicates. The date of the second, outer ditch is uncertain. The area enclosed was *c.* 44 acres (18 hectares), placing Caerwent among the smaller Roman towns of Britain. In places, particularly on the S side of the town, this wall still stands over 17 ft (5 metres) high and retains large areas of its original facing. The upper part of the wall is narrower than the base, but at intervals it continues at its full width to the top, producing rectangular platforms (counterforts), whose function is uncertain, although they may have been for mounting artillery.

There are four gates, one in each side. Of these the most important were the E and W gates, but the continued use of the main road through them means that little is known of their plans, save that they were flanked by projecting towers. The N and S gates were clearly of secondary importance, a fact which is reflected in their having been walled up in the late Roman period. Both are exceptionally well preserved. They have single arches, with superstructures which probably rose above the level of the wall as towers. The S gate originally projected slightly in front of the wall, but it was cut back when the gate was sealed. A drain ran through the gate below the road, and a second one was constructed when the arch was blocked. The arch is particularly well preserved on its inner side. The N gate lies by the North Gate public house. It is essentially similar to the other, save that it never projected in front of the wall and its façade was therefore not demolished when it was blocked. The masonry of the blocking wall is less regular than in the S gate and may be later in date; it was also less complete, for a bolt hole was left through it.

The towers or bastions which are such a striking feature of the S wall were added in the mid C4, probably as part of a general refurbishing of the defences which can be paralleled in many other Romano-British towns. For reasons which are not apparent, they were only built on the N and S sides. The W-most tower on the S side is unusual in having the remains of a blocked door in its E face; presumably it was intended as a sally port.

For the two inscriptions preserved in the porch of St Stephen and St Tathan's Church and other finds, *see* below. Many other finds from the excavations are in Newport Museum.

Two mosaic pavements discovered in the C19 $1\frac{1}{4}$ m. (2 kilometres) to the W of the Roman town (ST 446 910) probably mark the site of a Roman villa or suburban house. At Whitehall Brake (ST 475 911), extensive structural remains, including well-preserved walls and a mosaic pavement, indicate the existence of a substantial Roman building. Although generally referred to as a villa, its proximity to Caerwent suggests that it is more likely to have been a suburban house.

ST STEPHEN AND ST TATHAN. Caerwent is documented as the site of a monastery by the C10. Solid evidence was provided by the discovery in 1992 of a pre-Norman disc cross-head to the SE of the church. However, the chancel, the oldest part of the present building, is of the C13. There are known to have been chancel aisles, long demolished. Perp nave and N porch, Perp W tower, probably an addition. Medieval S arcade, but the S aisle and S vestry are of 1910–12 by *G. E. Halliday*, who had restored the chancel in 1893–4. The church is built of limestone, partly local, partly imported from Somerset.

The E end of the chancel is a handsome E.E. composition. Two long and quite broad lancets, trefoil-headed and hollow-moulded. Ashlar pilaster buttresses at the angles rise almost to the eaves. N wall reconstructed in the 1840s and given matching lancets. The nave has a N wall of squared stonework heightened with a few rubble courses. Three-light pointed-headed window with two tiers of cinquefoiled tracery lights, three-light square-headed window with cinquefoiled lights and a hoodmould. The porch which stands between them is a fine, tall Perp piece. Ashlar face, rubble sides. Bold base-moulding carried round to include the E stair projection. Diagonal buttresses with panelled faces. The entrance arch must originally have been handsome, two-centred-headed, with three continuous hollows separated by slender rolls with tiny moulded caps. In the major hollow, undercut square flowers, mostly broken off. Similarly shaped nave

N doorway with four close-set hollows and a big hood. Trefoiled statue niche over, for which a two-light window over the porch arch provided light. E stair, reached through a doorway with double-wave moulding, clearly leading merely to a gallery from which the statue in the niche could be dressed (cf. Caldicot). Small stoup. The tower is simpler, of two stages on a battered ashlar base and roll moulding. Top moulding, angle gargoyles and battlements. Polygonal SE stair-turret with external doorway. The W doorway of the tower is four-centred, moulded with wave, hollow, wave, and has a three-light window over. The belfry windows are no more than square-headed two-lighters, the lights with cusped ogee heads. Stone cusped-lattice bell-louvres.

Inside, the tower arch has two steeply pointed wave-moulded orders dying into the imposts, and beside it a stair doorway matching that outside. Several other internal features deserve explanation. A second stoup, E of the N doorway, this one broadly chamfered under an ogee arch, must be a reset C14 piece. The chancel arch is C13, but has been tampered with – it was reported to be in pieces in 1851 – and its components do not fit one another. The responds are chamfered, their caps lobed and the wide two-centred arch elaborately roll-moulded. The E lancets have a small, continuous inner roll. That leaves the three blocked arches in the chancel S wall, segmental on square imposts. They are presumably late medieval and originally opened into a chapel. – SANCTUARY FITTINGS and ALTAR RAILS. 1965 by *G. G. Pace*. Of blackened iron. Their typical busy forms effective against the scraped and
74 whitened walls of the chancel. – PULPIT. Dated 1632, with the churchwardens' initials. On each face a cartouche set within an arch, and a jewelled panel below. One cartouche is carved with a naive representation of Llandaff Cathedral. Inscription from I Corinthians round the top: Woe is unto me if I preach not the Gospel. – FONT. Possibly a C12 tub, remodelled in the C18. Of stone. Big, hexagonal bowl trimmed into a circle, on a boldly profiled stem. The foot, however, with simplified leaves, may be late medieval. – ROMAN REMAINS. In the N porch a finely lettered and historically important STATUE BASE, datable shortly before A.D. 220. The statue was of Tiberius Claudius Paulinus, commander-in-chief of the Second Augustan Legion (*see* Caerleon, p. 136) A.D. 211–17. Also a small ALTAR. – In the S aisle a section of mosaic PAVEMENT, and on the W window-sill various cut stones and a CINERARY URN. – CROSS-HEAD. In the S aisle. Carved with a Crucifixion on the front and a figure of a bishop on the back. Presumably from a C15 churchyard cross. – STAINED GLASS. Chancel E, Good Shepherd and St Stephen, *c.* 1884. No doubt by *Burlison & Grylls*. – Nave N. Three Passion scenes of 1865 by *Lavers & Barraud*, brought in from Angersleigh, Somerset. – Tower W, SS Nicholas, Michael and George. 1948 by *Arnold W. Robinson* of *Joseph Bell & Son*. – MONUMENT. Elizabeth Ann Stell †1852. Large tablet signed *Tyley* and still using their willow weeping over an urn of fifty years earlier.

LYCHGATE. 1902–3 by *G.E. Halliday*. The timber superstructure is quite lavishly carved.

The former VICARAGE, in Caerwent Gardens to the E of the town wall, was built in 1845–6 by *J. H. Langdon*. Typical of the architect, Tudor style, symmetrical with flamboyant pierced barge-boards. Rock-faced brown local stone with Bath stone dressings.

MOTTE. Straddling the SE angle of the Roman walls. Probably datable to the late C11. Tiny in comparison with the Roman enclosure, which must have served in part as its bailey.

WAR MEMORIAL, N of the church. An unhackneyed design. A square base carries a thick-set obelisk, on which a bronze lamp is set. Relief wreath on each face of the obelisk.

BURTON HOMES, Green Lane. Almshouses dated 1913, probably by *Alan H. Davies* of Newport (*see* Newport, p. 446). Single-storeyed, of rock-faced Old Red Sandstone with Bath stone dressings. Tudor style with Arts and Crafts detail. The shallow U-plan provides for twelve residents, each with a mullion-and-transom window under a gable, a timber porch and an iron rose pergola. Taller central gabled projection with a squat Venetian window over a round-headed doorway and scroll-topped angle buttresses.

ROYAL NAVAL PROPELLANT FACTORY, 1 m. N. The many flat-roofed brick buildings scattered across the hillside belonged to one of the two cordite explosives factories operated by the Royal Navy during the Second World War. For safety reasons earth-work blast-mounds surround many of the buildings.

At CRICK, 1½ m. E, CRICK MANOR is a badly compromised manorial group beside the A48. The late C13 CHAPEL which stands at the W end of the group was built for Sir William Deneford or his son. Its E gable-end remains intact, with two large, widely spaced lancets dressed with purple Old Red Sandstone. Attached to the S a former barn, to the N a recent extension, making the chapel the central component of a house.

The MANOR HOUSE, built for the Moore family, descendants of the Denefords, consists of two parts. The W half, still quite impressive, is a late medieval stone hall on a low undercroft. Coursed, squared local stone with yellow Triassic sandstone quoins. One S window lights the undercroft, square-headed with two pointed lights. The hall itself is provided with three large doorways, chamfered and segment-headed, one in each of its three external walls, and there does not seem to have been a normal screens passage arrangement. Also one late C16 four-light mullion-and-transom window per side. Hoodmoulds. Sunk chamfer mouldings, and the refinement of a sunk fillet down the centre of each mullion and transom. The interior of the hall is open to its tie-beam and crown-post roof. The cross wing to the E, gabled and rendered, is C16 in origin, but has been drastically remodelled and was in the C18 doubled in depth to provide a regular sash-windowed E front. At the back the stump of a stone porch remains adjoining the hall, and further E a two-storeyed projecting wing. Two blocked C16 mullioned windows here.

BROOK COTTAGE, across the A48 to the SW, is a fragment of a second substantial stone house. What survives is a mid-C17 parlour wing, its end towards the road lit by a tier of three stone windows centred under the gable, the lower two of three lights under hoodmoulds, the mullions sunk-chamfered. The square stone structure a few yards away to the E is a detached KITCHEN, dated by Fox and Raglan as late as *c.* 1690. Well-preserved hearth arrangement in the E wall.

MOUNT BALLAN, 2 m. SE. Compact and roughly symmetrical rendered house in a Tudor style, with bargeboarded gables and dated 1837 on the l. gable of the N front. The dated gable composes with its twin and the porch between them. Single-storey window bays to N and E, double-height ones to the S. A large rambling wing to the W, the product of great additions made after 1880 for Thomas Andrew Walker, contractor for the Severn Tunnel, was demolished in 1998.

PENHEIN. *See* Llanvair Discoed, p. 362.

4080

CALDICOT

ST MARY. Quite a large and handsome church, its walling of local limestone rubble, built in three main phases. Norman central tower. Dec chancel and nave. Perp N aisle, S porch and upper stage of the tower. Heavily restored in 1857–8 by *Henry Woodyer*, who rebuilt the N aisle and added a N vestry, put a pyramidal cap on the tower and renewed much of the cut stonework. Vestry of 1911 extended E-wards in 1928 by *Griggs & Vaughan*.

The early date of the tower is confirmed by one small S window. Its quoins have been concealed by buttresses added, no doubt, when it was doubled in height. Perp two-light, pointed-headed belfry openings. The Dec rebuilding of chancel and nave must originally have been quite spectacular. There survive two two-light chancel S windows (their stonework renewed) and the three-light W window of the nave, of yellow Triassic sandstone. Cusped ogee reticulated tracery and a wavy outline to their heads dictated by the reticulation pattern, a local idiosyncrasy (cf. Redwick, Rogiet). The nave SW window is quite different, but also unusual, early Perp in character. Two-light, square-headed, with a two-centred arched head inscribed within it. The apex of each cusped ogee light is carried up as a mullion, framing an irregular lobe within the arched head. A sweeping Perp remodelling gave the chancel a three-light E window and a S priest's doorway, and the nave two large, three-light S windows. Panel tracery, deep concave reveals and hoodmoulds on spurred stops. W doorway with panelled soffit (cf. Redwick, Undy). The S porch is the showpiece of this period, tall and ashlar-faced, its S face and battlements in oolitic limestone, the sides of Triassic sandstone blocks. Slender paired angle buttresses. Plinth and basemoulding. The two-centred-headed entrance archway, moulded with two continuous waves, triple shaft and double wave, is set under a bold ogee crocketed hood. Triangular panel of foliage between arch and hood. Inside the porch, the four-centred-headed S doorway is simple and renewed, with a mutilated stoup beside it under an ogee arch, and image niche above it. Statue of the Virgin and Child, 1906 by *Boulton & Sons* of Cheltenham. Also a narrow E doorway at ground level and matching upper N doorway, leading not to an upper room within the porch, but probably to a timber gallery used to dress the statue in the niche. Close-set head corbels to support the roof timbers. The N aisle, as rebuilt by *Woodyer*, has buttresses, plinth and basemould matching those of the porch.

The interior has been scraped. So in the nave S wall the jambs are visible of two of the original C14 windows, one at the E end, the other W of the porch. The N aisle arcade, of five bays, was reconstructed by Woodyer, presumably on the old lines. It is a typical West Country Perp design, the lozenge-plan piers formed of four angle shafts with embattled caps carrying filleted arch mouldings, and continuous intermediate hollows. Labels on leaf corbels of Victorian naturalism. In the S wall of the nave, at its E end, a renewed piscina, and a drain-hole in the window-sill alongside. The tower arches, enlarged when chancel and nave were rebuilt, are of typical early C14 form, quite steeply pointed, the outer order chamfered, the inner, dying into the imposts, with a slight roll. The traces of green and blue stencilled flowers here are remnants of a mid-C19 decorative scheme. In the chancel, evidence of the original N fenestration, a trefoil-headed lancet and the jambs of a sanctuary window. Black and white marble sanctuary steps, 1906 by *Prothero & Phillot*. – ALTAR RAILS. By *Woodyer*. Turned timber balusters alternate with iron crosses. – FONT. By *Woodyer*, 1858. Square bowl on an octagonal stem. – SCREEN. Reusing a low screen by *Woodyer*. – PULPIT. By *Woodyer*, 1858. Of timber, circular, with thin applied decoration. – PAINTING. Vision of St Agnes, by *F. Hamilton Jackson*. – STAINED GLASS. Chancel E, Crucifixion. 1904 by *Kempe*. – Nave W, 1870 by *Powell's*, designed by *Henry Holiday*. Martha and Mary, Good Samaritan, education of Timothy. The outstanding window in the church. – N aisle W, SS Gabriel, Michael and Raphael, 1923 by *Kempe & Co*. – N aisle N windows. Outer lights grisaille patterns, by *Powell's*, centre lights replaced by later designs: E, *c.* 1912 by *Heaton, Butler & Bayne*; centre, Suffer the Little Children, *c.* 1956 by *E. J. Dilworth*; W, Annunciation, 1981 by *Geoffrey Robinson*. – MONUMENT. Mutilated medieval figure of a cleric, set most strangely into the thickness of the wall in the SE angle of the porch.

In the CHURCHYARD, SE of the church, the MONUMENT to Elizabeth Turberville Williams, the vicar's wife, †1861. Like a medieval churchyard cross, but idiosyncratically detailed. Clearly by *Woodyer*.

VICARAGE (The Manor Nursing Home), W of the church. Substantial and characteristic High Victorian Gothic. By *Henry Woodyer*, after completing the restoration of the church, for the Rev. Edmund Turberville Williams, a house fit for a vicar whom Bradney calls 'a clergyman of distinction and an ornament to the church'. The date 1862 is on the S front. Grey local limestone with Bath stone dressings. Steep, red-tiled roofs. The W entrance front is long and flat, two-storeyed with lancet-headed mullioned windows, the lower ones transomed, the upper interrupting the eaves line under a variety of gablets. Two slab-like chimney-stacks rise off the wall-head above the single-storey porch. Window bay at the r. end, and another round the corner to the S. The E front, facing the church, is altogether livelier. Here, close-packed together, a two-light canted window bay under a big gable, a circular stair-turret capped by a conical roof, and a cusped gable which indicates where Mr Williams had his private oratory – see the traceried ground-floor window below. Inside, the main space is a narrow, double-height hall. The principal stair, winding up in the turret at the back, leads to a balcony overlooking it. (Some good chimneypieces.)

Woodyer's SCHOOL of *c.* 1858 has been demolished.

CASTLE. After Chepstow and Raglan, Caldicot is the largest and best-preserved castle in the county. Its keep and its gatehouse are among the county's finest medieval structures. Yet Caldicot is not a name to conjure with, the castle's history has been little studied and the dates of even its finest parts remain to be conclusively established. There are several reasons for this curious neglect. First, perhaps, is its inconspicuous and apparently unstrategic position, in the water-meadows beside the Nedern Brook. Even today, shielded by tall and spreading trees, it is hardly visible in any distant view. Second, there is a dearth of documentation, broken only in the late C14 by a sudden glut of evidence, much of it hard to relate to the surviving building. Finally, the modern ownership has doubtless played a part. The castle was acquired in 1885 by J. R. Cobb, the castle fancier who also owned Manorbier and Pembroke castles further W in Wales. It remained in the hands of his descendants until 1963, when it came into the care of Chepstow Rural District Council. Today the castle belongs to Monmouthshire County Council, which opens it to the public but without the publicity which Cadw can generate for its sites. Plans are in hand to undertake the documentary research and structural analysis which the castle deserves, but in the meantime the account that follows can only be provisional.

After the Norman conquest of South Wales Caldicot came within the lordship of Caerwent. Some time after 1087 it was in the possession of Walter Fitzroger, who died in 1127. The first earthen castle is likely to have been constructed during this period. By the mid C12 Caldicot had come by marriage to the de Bohuns. The masonry castle was probably begun by Henry de Bohun †1220, and continued by his son Humphrey †1275. The circular keep, all the drum or bow-fronted towers, and much of the curtain walls must belong to this campaign. The next period of building activity seems to have extended from the late C13 to the second quarter of the C14, when a suite of handsome apartments was formed in the SE quarter of the castle, and a splendid new S gatehouse was constructed. The documented works of the 1380s, during the ownership of Thomas Woodstock, Edward III's youngest son, who had married a de Bohun heiress, include the N postern tower, which bears his name. Other important but less easily identified works were carried out 1385–9.

In 1521, after the attainder of the third Duke of Buckingham, Woodstock's last descendant, Caldicot became part of the Duchy of Lancaster, fell out of use and gradually decayed into ruin. The estate was leased in turn to the Somersets, Earls of Worcester and Dukes of Beaufort, the Hanburys of Pontypool and others, until its sale by the Duchy in 1857 to a local landowner, Charles Lewis of St Pierre, from whom, nearly thirty years later, Mr Cobb acquired it. Cobb converted the gatehouse into a residence and made habitable no fewer than three of the towers.

The castle is built on a site underlain by Old Red Sandstone, as the reddish earth reveals. But its walls are almost entirely of Triassic sandstone quarried at Sudbrook, 1½ m. SE. The stone varies in colour from grey to a strong yellow and even to pink in the keep, and in character from large, squared, finely jointed blocks to rubble more or less regularly coursed. Similarities and contrasts in the character of the masonry from part to part help to clarify the sequence of construction. The castle can best be examined in detail by walking the entire circuit outside the curtain walls, then going through the gatehouse into the ward, and finally investigating the interiors of the gatehouse itself and several of the towers.

The earthen MOTTE of *c.* 1100 is conspicuous at the NW angle of the enclosure. Its height and pronounced conical form contrast

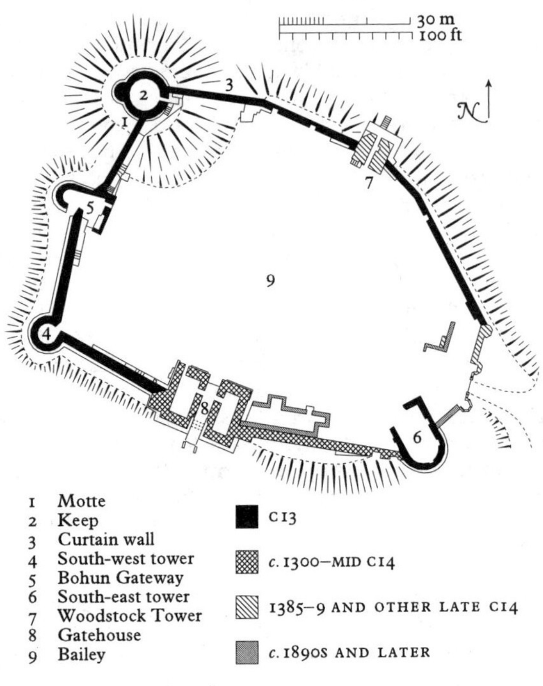

Caldicot Castle. Plan

with the shallowness and defensive weakness of the ditch which surrounds the rest of the castle. The motte is crowned by a magnificent circular KEEP, which must have been inspired by the circular towers built by William Marshal, above all the great free-standing keep at Pembroke, but also nearby at Chepstow and Usk, shortly before his death in 1219. It is broad for its height and constructed of extremely finely jointed sandstone ashlar. Above a short, slightly battered basement topped by a chamfered stringcourse rises the principal storey. This occupies two-thirds of the full height of the keep. A mere set-off separates it from the short top stage. From the W side projects a boldly bowed turret internally solid almost to the top. Arrow loops in three directions in the main stage of the keep. Paired square slots in the top stage may have been intended to provide seating for a timber hoard, or fighting gallery. The battlements were partly remade by Cobb. But the blocking and heightening which he allowed to remain suggest that the whole keep was heightened not long after construction.

The CURTAIN WALLS that enclose the bailey and butt up against the keep to E and S are constructed of smaller, roughly coursed Triassic sandstone blocks, and were clearly constructed later than it. Doubtless they replaced a timber palisade, and may well have begun to do so as soon as the keep had been completed. The W curtain wall runs almost straight to the SW TOWER, interrupted midway by the Bohun Gateway. All this is early to mid-C13 work and is understandable as a coherent composition, forming a defended western flank to the castle. It was, however, constructed in at least four phases. Adjoining the keep is a completely plain stretch of curtain wall. The first break comes where there is a slight change of direction. One cruciform arrow loop here. S of this the wall rises from a chamfered moulding over a battered apron. Apron and moulding continue round the BOHUN GATEWAY. This is a D-plan tower projecting so far forward of the curtain that there is room for a broad arched entrance in its S face, another similarity to Pembroke (Horseshoe Gate). Inner and outer segmental arches, both slightly chamfered, with portcullis groove between them and two 'murder-holes' above. The threshold of the entrance is up at the top of the batter, with a small, square-headed opening cut through at ground level below. This indicates that it was approached across a bridge, spanning the ditch at a sharp angle, though no trace of such a structure survives. The only other defensive provisions in the tower are three arrow loops uniform with that in the curtain wall, but giving no further protection to the entrance. At the top, projecting corbels with holes for a hoard. All this is highly unusual, more like a large, defended postern than a principal entrance.

The curtain wall to the S of the Bohun Gateway was clearly built concurrently with it, as the moulding which tops its battered apron continues into the jamb of the arched entrance. The SW TOWER, on the other hand, is not bonded into the curtain, and its apron has no crowning moulding. In this, in its fat cylindrical form, with a slight set-off two-thirds of the way up, and in its fabric of squared blocks, it is comparable with the keep. Traces of arrow loops.

Similar masonry can be seen in the SE TOWER. This also projects from the curtain wall as a stout drum, has a battered apron with top moulding, cross-slits for arrows at two levels, and a crown of corbels and hoard slots, and battlements with arrow slits. The squared masonry of the lower third, however, gives way to coursed rubble higher up, suggesting a break in construction. The back of the tower is extended as a rectangular projection within the curtain, clearly to provide spacious residential accommodation.

The S curtain wall runs straight from the SW tower to the SE tower, interrupted in the centre by the bulk of the C14 gatehouse. The curtain wall E of the gatehouse clearly pre-dates it, and equally clearly is of two builds. The lower part of the wall, where large, squared blocks predominate, goes with the lower part of the SE tower. Two blind recesses down here, with pointed arched heads, of uncertain function. Higher up, the walling is more irregular, extending upwards to battlements pierced with arrow slits, which may belong to a third campaign. The curtain at this point clearly acted as the outer wall of a residential range. Two pairs of small rectangular lights must have served an undercroft. Above, in a different spacing, one plus three, are two-light traceried windows, with an ogee-headed lancet between them. This and the tracery patterns, encircled quatrefoils over cinquefoiled lights, and in one case a leaf-like pair of mouchettes, suggest a date in the first half of the C14. The three grouped windows which adjoin the SE tower are quite long, and two of them are transomed. They must have lit an important upper room.

Chronologically, the gatehouse clearly comes next; but in order to examine its exterior and interior together, it will be best to come back to it having first completed the circuit of the curtain wall. The S-most stretch of the E CURTAIN WALL is of the Cobb period or later, not following the medieval line – see the fragments of the original curtain on the SE tower. The three thin, polygonal turrets immediately to the N cannot be earlier than the late C14. The S-most two have rectangular slits low down, and in the wall between the N-most two is a two-light transomed window with cusped ogee heads to the lights. This all relates to some other internal structure with a room over an undercroft.

The N CURTAIN WALL continues, with a series of slight changes of direction, all the way to the keep. It is virtually featureless, but is interrupted midway by the WOODSTOCK TOWER, 28
which served as a defensible postern gate. The tower is both the best-preserved feature of the castle and the only closely datable one. For it bears a highly unusual form of identification: the lowest stone in the r. jamb of the postern gateway is carved with the word 'Thomas' in a quatrefoil. This shows that the tower was built during the period in which Thomas Woodstock owned Caldicot, 1383–97. The tower is indeed called 'new' in the surviving accounts for 1385. It is polygonal, rising from a square base by

means of bold pyramidal spurs. The gateway has a chamfered two-centred head, and a broadly chamfered inner arch, between which is the slot for a portcullis. In the N face ogee-headed lancets at two levels. Machicolated battlements with arrow slits. Further W a probably contemporary square, corbelled projection. The fabric of the N curtain wall suggests that much of it may date from Woodstock's time, in a thorough-going strengthening of this side of the castle. There are payments in 1385 for making what must be this wall, described as being between the 'great tower' and the 'dovecote', a tower which Woodstock was then replacing.

It is time to return to the S side of the castle, and examine the GATEHOUSE. This must originally have been a splendid piece, idiosyncratic in design but undoubtedly a work of the mid C14, so almost certainly built by the Humphrey de Bohun who inherited in 1335 and died in 1361. It is faced with finely jointed Triassic sandstone ashlar, doubtless a good deal restored by J. R. Cobb. The main body of the gatehouse is a broad, severe rectangle on a battered base. Square flanking towers, set back to l. and r., descend sheer to the bottom of the dry moat, and rise to corbelled battlements decisively higher than the battlements of the gatehouse. Symmetrically arranged single-light windows at ground level and principal level show that the gatehouse and the towers were primarily envisaged as a residence, and considerations of defence were secondary. The lower windows have ogee trefoiled heads in square frames, but the upper ones must originally have made quite a show. The lights are quite large, with cusped ogee segmental heads, and are set in projecting frames, originally on head corbels – one survives in the W tower – and under shallow pinnacled canopies – traces of their outlines survive in the wall face. Two rows of big putlog holes at this level. The battlements and top of the E tower are all restored, but at the top of the W tower the corbel table on a row of heads is original.

The central entrance is both handsome and well-protected. Segmental outer arch moulded with two waves, and set high up on plain vertical jambs. Similarly moulded transverse ribs for the two-bay barrel vault within. Porter's spyhole in the wall here, and in the vault square 'murder-holes', and slot for a portcullis. Beyond this protective barrier is an inner arch, of two-centred profile, outlined with a filleted roll, and a passage in two bays with octopartite rib vaults. The ribs are filleted and rest on head corbels, a woman wearing a wimple, a man with scrolly curls and another in a hat. In the side walls, central seat recesses, and beyond them two-centred-headed doorways with angle roll moulding. These open into porters' lodges. Note the deep stepped internal sills of the N windows of the lodges.

On entering the castle BAILEY one can see the back of the gatehouse. The entrance passage is framed on this side by a segmental arch on tall jambs identical to that on the outer face, and a two-centred arch within it. The wall on this side was clearly considerably ruined and drastically restored by Cobb. The four upper windows are basically original, but the larger ground-storey windows must be to a new design by Cobb. He constructed his own residence above and around it, with a substantial wing abutting the curtain wall to the E. This is all half-timbered with brick-nogging and red-tiled roofslopes, so is easy to discount. The INTERIOR of the gatehouse, despite Cobb's conversion, has a good deal more to show. An inconspicuous doorway at the W end of the N front, largely renewed, opens to a straight flight of steps, clearly original, under a fragmentary ribbed vault. One head corbel for a vault rib survives. The stairhead turns under an octopartite rib vault and enters the W end of the great chamber. This is now subdivided, but must originally have been a magnificently spacious room. The four N and two of the S windows are internally moulded with hollow and wave, have seats in the embrasures and chamfered segmental rere-arches. The central S window, over the portcullis, which must always have been in a separate space, is more simply treated. Plain rectangular fireplace in the N wall. In the SE and SW angles small doorways, presumably to garderobes. Loose stone medallion here inscribed with an A, supposedly for Alianore, wife of Thomas Woodstock; this may have come from some now demolished late C14 building in the bailey.

Within the BAILEY there is something to see in four of the five towers. The KEEP, in spite of the interventions of J.R. Cobb, retains its original arrangement with rooms on three levels, reached by an E newel stair within the thickness of the wall. The lowest room is a basement excavated within the motte. It is provided with a small W window high up, on an enormously deep splayed sill, and a garderobe with drainage sump. So this could be used as a prison. The room above, at entrance level, retains the rere-arches for four windows, the windows themselves remade by Cobb. Continuous corbel moulding to carry roof timbers. The fireplace hood is entirely Cobb's. The well-appointed top room has N and S pointed-headed window reveals with seats (and arrow slits, now hidden, below the remade windows). Garderobe reached through the reveal of the N window. Of the C13 fireplace hood one corbel remains. At the present roof level there is clear evidence of a further chamber up here. The back of the turret is hollowed out in a wide vaulted recess, the corbels l. and r. of it presumably to support roof beams, the crease-line of the roof clearly marked. A passage in the wall-thickness has a rebated window with segmental head.

The BOHUN GATEWAY is clearly seen from the bailey side to have been fitted up as a principal well-defended entrance. Portcullis chamber over the gateway, accessible through a doorway from the wall-walk to the S, and lit by a slit window in the front wall. W recess in the thickness of the wall, with three arrow slits. In the end wall of the gateway at this level, traces of a fireplace hood on corbels. Within the threshold, a large rectangular hole in the ground, aligned with the ditch-level doorway noted outside. Was this some sort of booby-trap? The rear wall of the Bohun Gateway is largely destroyed, and it is not clear how it was entered from the bailey.

The SE TOWER with its large rectangular rear projection provided a spacious and impressive upper chamber. Here, in the bowed front of the tower, three small rectangular windows with seats in the embrasures, the central one immediately above an arrow slit, suggest that the tower was originally conceived for defence but was later converted for residential use. That the conversion took place late in the C13 is suggested by the plate-traceried E window in the rectangular rear part, with roll-moulded rere-arch, and by the remains of a handsome hooded chimneypiece in the W wall opposite. A side shaft with moulded cap carries a multi-moulded corbel. Tantalizingly, that is all. There are, however, traces of original plaster here, painted with false masonry joints. Parts, too, of segment-headed doorways at the inner end of the chamber. To the S of the fireplace a passage and doorway cut through, clearly to give access to the suite of first-floor rooms created immediately to the W of the tower in the early C14 and lit by the windows noted outside. These windows have uniform hollow-chamfered rere-arches, suggesting that they are all of one date, in spite of their contrasting tracery patterns.

The WOODSTOCK TOWER retains its internal arrangements complete. The postern gate on this side is a two-centred arch of two chamfered orders, leading to the rubble-vaulted postern passage. Above are three storeys of accommodation, consisting at each level of a room and a passage with a garderobe at the end of it, reached through a two-centred doorway off a newel stair. Access from the stair also to the wall-walk of the curtain. All this corresponds to the 'new tower' itemized in the building account for 1385: '50 ft. high with battlements 6 ft. high with a portcullis and vault for drawing the portcullis, with 3 chambers and stone windows, 3 fireplaces and 3 latrines to be made in the same chamber'.

Finally, there are traces of buildings erected against the inner face of the curtain wall. See in particular the robbed fireplace E of the Woodstock Tower. To l. and r. of it corbelled flights of steps ascend to the wall-walk. Many of the features itemized in the accounts of the 1380s may refer to such structures, which have been subsequently demolished.

ROMAN REMAINS. Excavations at ST 473 893 have revealed the existence of a small and undistinguished Iron Age and Roman SETTLEMENT.

A group of Roman pottery KILNS were excavated at ST 475 875 in 1966. A short distance away (at ST 483 874) aerial photographs have revealed a rectangular, ditched enclosure which may be connected with the kiln site.

COMPREHENSIVE SCHOOL, Mill Lane. In two contrasted halves, the N of *c.* 1957–8, the S of 1966–7, all by *Monmouthshire County Architect's Department*. The earlier half is a typical product of *Colin Jones*. The later, built when *Sydney Leyshon* was County Architect, is less typical, its main component a four-storey block with exposed concrete frame taken up a further storey to enclose rooftop apparatus.

LLANTHONY SECUNDA MANOR, Church Road, ¼m. N. The name, a modern adoption, refers to Llanthony Secunda Priory,

Gloucester, which acquired lands in Caldicot shortly after its foundation in the C12. It is possible that the priory had a grange here. The house, of local limestone, is an L in plan, built in two parts, a two-bay E-facing range of three storeys, and behind it a S-facing range of four storeys, with in the S wall a full-height straight joint between them. Medieval evidence in both parts. Projection for a spiral stair in the angle between the two ranges, probably a C17 improvement. The two-centred-headed doorway at first-floor level, very near the S end of the E front, can hardly be in its original position. Furthermore the chamfer moulding returns at the bottom, as if the stonework originally belonged to a window. The large, square windows in this front, with timber frames and relieving arches in the stonework above, tell of a thorough remodelling in the late C17. Round the corner to the N, however, there is medieval evidence, a projecting chimney-breast corbelled out for fireplaces at both upper levels. Inside this range, several plain C17 fireplaces. The SW range, which is clearly added to the E range, has at all three upper levels virtually complete medieval rooms, all on an oddly miniature scale. Each has to N and S pairs of single-light, segment-headed windows, provided with seats in the embrasures. In the W wall each has a fireplace with stone lintel and flanking recesses lit by slit windows in two directions. There must have been a mural stair in the S recess. All this is hard to date – one can only call it late medieval. It is also hard to parallel, the closest comparison being with some of the houses for small communities of chantry priests studied by W.A. Pantin.*

To the E of the house beside the road, a stone BARN of *c.* 1800. The setting on the other three sides has been drastically compromised by late C20 housing.

For MITEL TELECOM *see* Portskewett, p. 485.

DEWSTOW HOUSE, 1½m. W. Simple early C19 three-bay villa fronted by an over-emphatic single-storey Tuscan loggia. (In the grounds an early C20 underground FERNERY, a network of underground passages and toplit chambers with artificial rock-work and stalactites.)

CHAPEL HILL/LLANANDRAS 5000

The village for Tintern Abbey, so mainly catering for the needs of tourists.

ST MARY. On the hillside above the houses, approached up a steep stone-paved roadway. Unroofed in 1973. Medieval in origin, but virtually rebuilt by *John Prichard* 1866–8. Do the elegant three-light E and W windows with two different Dec tracery patterns represent early C14 work, or are they Prichard's homage to Tintern Abbey below? Saddleback N tower, perhaps reusing a single-light Dec window over the doorway. Nave and chancel in one. S vestry and burial chapel.

* *Medieval Archaeology*, vol. 3 (1959).

In the CHURCHYARD, N of the church, two unusually splendid TOMB-CHESTS, one, under a big pyramid, commemorating Richard White †1765, the other bearing a sarcophagus with gadrooned top and four bold side scrolls, for Charles Richards †1722. The inscriptions, entirely worn away, are given by Bradney.

METHODIST CHURCH (Wesleyan). In the village. 1861–2 by *Samuel Hancorn*. Dec. Just a gabled rectangle. Multicoloured walls of local sandstone. Gable window a spurred hexfoil in a flat-bottomed spherical triangle.

5090 CHEPSTOW/CAS-GWENT

Chepstow was founded as a frontier town, planted in the later C11 at the lowest defensible point on the River Wye, the border between England and Wales. The reuse of Roman material in the C11 keep of the castle, and scattered finds of coins and pottery, some of the late C1 A.D., some of the C3–C4, suggest Roman activity here, near where the Gloucester–Caerwent road must have crossed the River Wye. No specific site, however, has been identified of a fort or a settlement. William the Conqueror, immediately after 1066, granted the Welsh kingdom of Gwent, what became the Marcher lordship of Striguil,* to one of his principal Norman lieutenants, William fitz Osbern. The great stone keep which fitz Osbern had erected by the time of his death in 1071 was the first masonry castle in Britain, earlier even than the Conqueror's White Tower at the Tower of London. It still dominates the greatly extended castle which crouches along the crest of the limestone cliff above the swirling waters of the Wye, presenting an appearance of utter impregnability from the English side of the river.

Fitz Osbern also founded a Benedictine priory, on a site *c.* 300 yds (275 metres) to the SE. All that remains is the nave of the priory church, shorn of its aisles, taken over by the town for its parish church after the Dissolution.

The town itself extends as a single, straightish street, High Street, then Middle Street, then Bridge Street, down the slope from SW to NE between castle and priory, to the river bridge. The town wall (Port Wall), which was constructed probably 1272–8 across the high ground to protect castle, priory and town on their peninsula, largely survives.

Chepstow's post-medieval importance was first as a port and centre of ship-building and repair. A graving dock was constructed in 1759. Secondly the town became a tourist centre, as in the second half of the C18 the Wye Valley became one of the most fashionable haunts of the Picturesque traveller. On this the enterprise of Valentine Morris of Piercefield Park, immediately N of the town (*see* p. 470), had a considerable bearing. None of this activity, however, did much to increase the size of the town. In 1801 the population was 2,080, and a century later it had risen only to 3,067. The first important suburban development,

* From the Ystraigyl – the bend in the river.

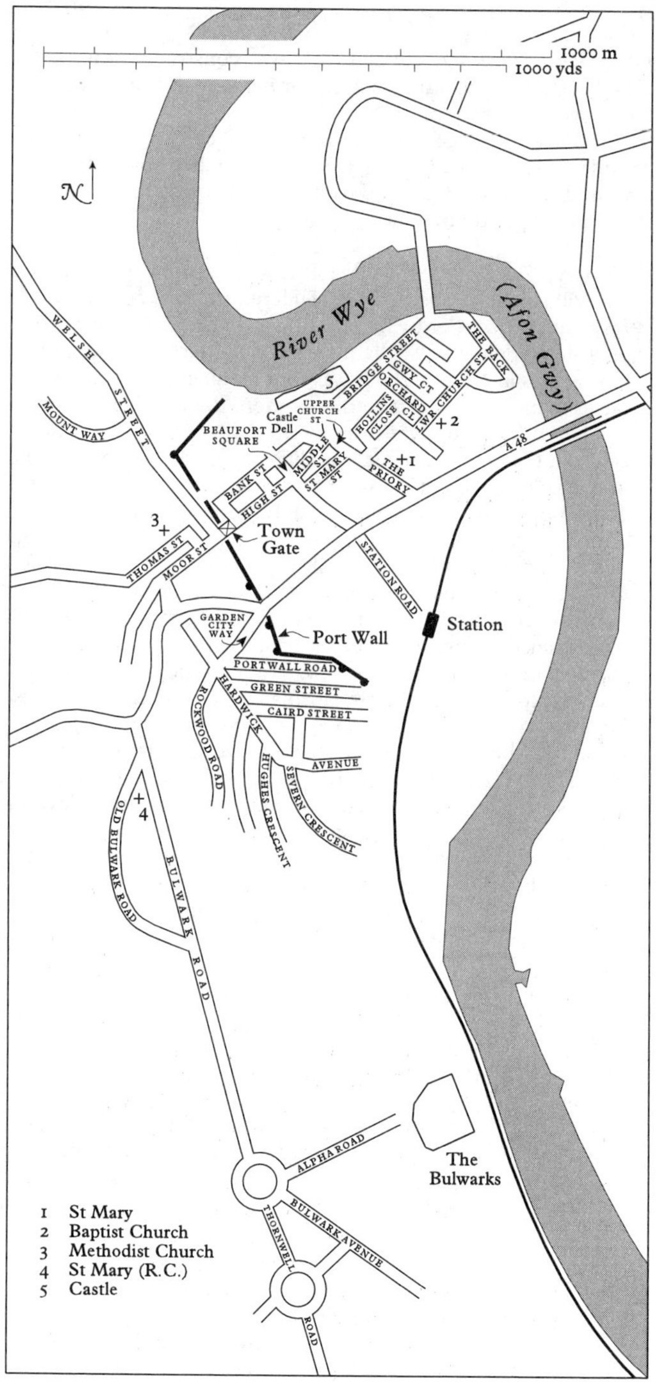
1000 m
1000 yds
N
River Wye
(Afon Gwy)
WELSH STREET
MOUNT WAY
BRIDGE STREET
GWY CT
ORCHARD
HOLLINS CLOSE
CL
LWR CHURCH ST
THE BACK
UPPER CHURCH ST
Castle Dell
BEAUFORT SQUARE
MIDDLE ST
ST MARY ST
THE PRIORY
BANK ST
HIGH ST
A 48
Town Gate
THOMAS ST
MOOR ST
STATION ROAD
Station
GARDEN CITY WAY
Port Wall
PORTWALL ROAD
GREEN STREET
CAIRD STREET
HARDWICK
AVENUE
ROCKWOOD ROAD
HUGHES CRESCENT
SEVERN CRESCENT
OLD BULWARK ROAD
BULWARK ROAD
ALPHA ROAD
The Bulwarks
BULWARK AVENUE
THORNWELL ROAD
1 St Mary
2 Baptist Church
3 Methodist Church
4 St Mary (R.C.)
5 Castle

Chepstow

Hardwick Village and the Bulwark, was constructed during the First World War, for workers in the armaments factory which had taken over the dock area.

The Severn Bridge and M4 motorway, constructed 1964–6, and the inner ring road, 1971–3, have made Chepstow both accessible and sequestered. A good deal of new housing has sprung up, much of it of better than usual quality.

ST MARY, The Priory. St Mary's Priory, Chepstow, was founded by William fitz Osbern, Earl of Hereford, between 1067 and his death in 1071, or by his son Roger de Breteuil, before 1075, as a dependency of William's earlier monastic foundation at Cormeilles in Normandy. It was thus an alien priory and seems never to have had a community of more than twelve monks.

The church, however, was a different matter. The founder saw to it that a monumental building was erected on a scale and in a style to match the austere grandeur of the keep which was going up in the same years a few hundred yards away. What remains of the early Norman church is a tantalizing torso, the five W bays of what was originally a six-bay nave rising their full three storeys but shorn of their aisles. The choir was pulled down immediately after the suppression of the priory in 1536. As will be explained below, the nave was almost certainly vaulted, which strongly implies that the choir was vaulted too, and must have been exceptional as an early Norman great church. The crossing tower fell in 1701, destroying the transepts. In 1705–6 a new E wall was built at the E end of the nave, and its W end built up to form a new W tower. Between 1838 and 1841 came the third destruction. A new Neo-Norman E end was devised with a short chancel and new transepts, a design which involved the demolition of the E bay of the nave. The rest of the nave was filled with galleries, enabling the aisles to be pulled down. *William Harris* of Bristol seems to have initiated the scheme, though *Blore*'s name is also mentioned, and it was finished off in 1840–1 by *T. H. Wyatt & Brandon*. This in its turn soon seemed intolerable. *Seddon & Carter*'s (i.e. principally *J. Coates Carter*'s) design of 1890 to restore the nave to its Norman completeness and to build entirely new transepts and chancel in a rich Geometrical style was partly executed (nave restoration and crossing 1890–1, chancel 1896–7, S transept 1904–5) but was abandoned unfinished in 1913. This history has left an extraordinarily disjointed building, unified only by the extreme height which the three-storey elevation of the monastic nave dictated. The original building stone was yellow Triassic sandstone quarried not far away at Sudbrook, but the Norman builders transferred to a finer quality oolitic limestone before their work was done. In both the C19 works a purplish grey Forest sandstone was used.

8 Detailed inspection naturally begins at the W front. It must be the last part of the primary phase of building, and is in a festive style. The lower two stages are of the early C12, constituting the W wall of the nave. Rich central doorway shafted in five orders, the shaft caps decorated with plain, spear-shaped leaves, the

arch mouldings richly carved, with two kinds of zigzag, with a lozenge pattern and with Xs in boxes (cf. the late C11 doorway in the keep of the castle), the central order a plain roll and hollow. Narrow blind arches to l. and r., with zigzag decoration and shafts *en suite* with the doorway. Above, a trio of windows under a billet-decorated label. Rich zigzag here, too, but of a more advanced character, outward-pointing and overlapping the roll moulding of the arches. The top two stages constitute the early C18 tower. This was designed by the port surveyor, *Stephen Harvey*, in an amusingly rustic classical idiom. Its W face has lower windows with triangular pediments, an upper, belfry window with a segmental pediment, and angle buttresses, much diminished from the breadth of the Norman ones below, also crowned by miniature pediments. On the other sides the tower is plain, with round-headed, almost Neo-Norman belfry windows.

To turn the corner to the N is a shock. Five bays of the Norman nave minus its aisle, leaving a sheer wall, with blocked nave arches below blind triforium openings and a glazed clerestory. Unmoulded, round-headed forms at each level. The Neo-Norman N transept of 1838–41 is worse, since the full height is encompassed in a single storey, necessitating excruciatingly long windows. N doorway with zigzag squashed flat. The Neo-Norman NE vestry, 1880 by *John Prichard*, is a much more convincing affair. *Seddon & Carter*'s three-bay chancel has Geometrical windows, three-light to N and S with bullseyes over, five-light to the E, all handsome and scholarly, though unrelated to the previous history of the church. S transept of 1838–41 transformed by *Seddon & Carter*, who gave it lancets and Dec windows. On this side the first bay of a reinstated aisle has been left jaggedly discontinued.

The visitor entering by the N doorway in the W bay of the nave is at once confronted by a substructure of the inserted W tower. It is best to emerge into the nave itself before looking around. The four unencumbered bays seem overwhelmingly high and narrow, in a style of characteristic early Norman austerity. The main arcade has rectangular piers, which carry arches of two unmoulded orders on simple abaci, the imposts of the inner order cut away. At triforium level the two elevations differ. To the N there are single, plain, round-headed openings, but on the S side the composition is considerably more complex, paired shafted arches with shafted sub-arches. Clerestory windows on both sides plain and deeply set. It is clear that the elevations have suffered further mutilation, for a full-height plastered scar in each bay marks where an impost of some form has been cut away. The outline of the plaster patching high on the S side strongly suggests that the nave was originally vaulted.*

Examination of the W bay of the nave yields further evidence. Here the arcade arches have not been mutilated, so that the

* G. Ormerod, *Strigulensia* (1861), describing the church as it was before 1838, states that both nave and aisles had vaults of tufa with oolite stone ribs, and refers to 'vaulting shafts ascending from the first string course in front of every pier'.

inner order retains its supporting imposts, a pilaster strip to the E and a half-round respond to the W, with simple cushion capital. The tower supports set into the W bay of the nave are also Norman but are also clearly an insertion. They must have been constructed in 1705–6 reusing masonry salvaged from the demolished crossing and transepts. The main tower arch is majestically tall, enriched with nook-shafts, their caps and bases both reusing moulded Romanesque shaft bases, and roll mouldings. Half-round responds with mutilated leaf capitals. The imposts above the capitals, however, moulded like classical cornices, are clearly new work of 1705–6. Low N and S arches, for access into the then still surviving side aisles. These also have nook-shafts and roll mouldings. Altogether this reused material suggests that the interior of the Norman church was originally a good deal more richly treated than now appears. Within the ringing chamber, the upper triplet of the W front is seen to have free-standing colonnettes, with embryonic leaf capitals and billet-moulded abaci, new motifs which go with the elaboration of the W front outside. However, the segmental arches which they carry were clearly reconstructed in the early C18.

In the eastern half of the church there is one more relic of the original structure, the base of the NW crossing pier. This is complex in plan and suggests a yet further elaboration which is hard to grasp. It is of Triassic sandstone, confirming that it dates to the earliest phase. Rectangular in plan with chamfered corners, and applied half-round shafts, three S, two E, N and W, and one in each diagonal direction. Attic base mouldings.

Seddon & Carter's oblong crossing and two-bay transepts create a hall-church effect. Moulded arches on tall quatrefoil piers. Boarded roofs, trefoil-section on fan vaults in the crossing, pointed tunnel vaults in the S transept, set on stone corbels carved by *Frith* of Cheltenham. N transept left bald and incomplete, in strong contrast to *Seddon & Carter*'s noble chancel. This has its sanctuary side windows under moulded rere-arches which rest on filleted triple shafts with stiff-leaf capitals. Simpler treatment of the E window, but the sanctuary up five steps. The N and S walls of the windowless W bay are treated with an asymmetrical arrangement of two arches, as if indicating a change of mind. N aumbry set in a genuine late C13 arch, trefoiled under a stilted superarch and label, the side shafts with fine undercurled stiff-leaf capitals. Where did it come from? – FITTINGS. – FONTS. One (S aisle) is Norman, plain but well-proportioned. Cylindrical bowl with rim moulding, cylindrical stem and moulded base. – The other (under the tower) is a splendid Perp piece, though sadly worn. Octagonal bowl, boldly moulded top and bottom, with paired quatrefoils on the faces. Slender octagonal stem linked to free-standing angle buttresses by means of miniature fliers, a perverse idea. – REREDOS. A sumptuous affair of painted wood, clearly by *Coates Carter*. Christ blessing between roundels of the Annunciation, Baptism of Christ, Crucifixion and Empty Tomb. Made in 1922, and brought here in 1985 from St Luke, Newport. – CHOIR STALLS. Elaborate but conventional, of 1902, to *Seddon & Carter*'s design. – PULPIT. Of stone, Geometrical. 1891, by *Coates Carter*. Donated by Freemasons, see their emblem in the top foliage band. – ORGAN (chancel S). With an unusually elaborate and pretty Gothick case of *c*. 1800. – ROYAL ARMS (W end of the nave). Painted on canvas and dated 1841. – STAINED GLASS. Chancel E, 1896. Ascension, boldly designed across all five lights. Brown and gold tonality. Clearly by *Lavers & Westlake* (A. Brooks). – S aisle S and nave SE, 1877 by *Lavers, Barraud & Westlake*, illustrating miracles of Christ, the figures under early Renaissance canopies. – Nave SW. Dramatic striding figure in front of an obelisk and the vine-clad columns of Solomon's Temple. Probably the window *Samuel Evans* of West Smethwick inserted in the church in 1896. – MONUMENTS. Second Earl of Worcester †1549 (nave W). Probably mid-Elizabethan in date. Recumbent effigies under a flat canopy supported on arches and Corinthian half-columns and crested with strapwork and fancy angle obelisks. – Margaret Cleyton and her two husbands and twelve children (S transept). Dated 1620, so erected before her death in 1627, yet she is shown recumbent, her husbands kneeling behind. Children small-scale against the dado below, in the normal way. Recently garishly repainted, the figure of Time and skeleton of Death which stand behind the husbands entirely redone, by *H. Crowther*, then in 1980–4 by *Keith Underwood*. – Mary Harvey (tower ringing chamber). 1712. Rustic tablet. Corinthian pilasters carry a swan-neck pediment. – Richard Vaughan †1713 (tower ringing chamber). Handsome large cartouche, typical of the date. Cherubs above, cherub heads below, all in a drapery surround. – Francis Davis (chancel N). Hanging wall monument, 1766 by *James Paty jun.* of Bristol. Typical of that date, the inscription panel surmounted by an open pediment, an urn and a pyramid. – Susanna Higfoot (S transept). Tablet, 1779 by *William Paty* of Bristol. – Sophia Price †1787 (under the tower). Pretty tablet with cherubim at the top, naturalistic swags and drops of foliage, and Rococo scrollwork below. – James Jenkins †1847 (under the tower). Plain Grecian hanging wall monument, topped with a draped urn. Signed *T. Tyley*, Bristol. – John Kirby †1827 and wife †1851. Tablet with draped urn and inscribed scroll, erected after her death, old-fashioned by that date. Signed *Tyley*, Bristol.

No trace of the Priory's CONVENTUAL BUILDING remains above ground. Excavation in 1973–4 on the S side of the church revealed the footings of three sides of a C12–C13 cloister not aligned with the church and on a surprisingly meagre scale.

ST MARY (R.C.), Old Bulwark Road. 1975. The church is a dramatic response to the liturgical movement. In plan a quarter circle. Concrete flying buttresses against the bowed W wall connect with internal concrete roof beams which radiate from a cross-filled oculus at the highest point over the altar. What a pity that the detailing is all crude and off-the-peg.

BAPTIST CHURCH, Lower Church Street. Debased Gothic frontage of 1869 under three overlapping pedimental gables.

Polychromy of big voussoirs in buff Bath stone and brown Old Red Sandstone against pinkish-grey local limestone walling. Inside the form of the chapel of 1816 is discernible. A typical pair of round-headed windows at the inner end, to light the pulpit. – MONUMENT. Rev. Thomas Jones †1873. Gothic tablet, an open bible within the shafted arch surround.

METHODIST CHURCH, Thomas Street. Dated 1855 and built to the design of *James Wilson* of Bath. Ornate, bepinnacled Dec façade. Return side with two-light windows, so the building was clearly not intended for side galleries. Altogether an unusually church-like chapel for its date (but cf. Charles Street Chapel and Tredegarville Baptist Church, Cardiff).

THE CASTLE

The clifftop situation, the stern fortification of the earliest parts and the sumptuous enrichment of later ones, combined with the exceptional completeness of so much, make Chepstow Castle one of the most exhilarating and instructive castles in the whole of Britain. It can be interpreted in broad terms as the product of four major campaigns, within a period of little over two centuries, from immediately after the Norman Conquest to the last quarter of the C13. Tudor remodelling for domestic purposes, and remodelling during the Commonwealth to strengthen the fortification for the use of cannon, have not seriously compromised its medieval character. The first builder was, so Domesday Book records, William fitz Osbern, whom William the Conqueror created Earl of Hereford shortly after the Battle of Hastings in 1066. He chose the site, on the rocky spur which forms the last cliff on the Welsh side of the River Wye as it flows towards the Severn. Here he erected the long, narrow rectangular hall-keep, with probably stone-walled baileys to E and W, an unscalable cliff to the N, and a readily controlled valley (now The Dingle) to the S. Chepstow, then, has claim to be the first stone castle in England, though by this time they were normal enough in Normandy. Fitz Osbern's intention was to control the main route from England into South Wales, and to form a bridgehead from which to advance his power westwards into the Welsh kingdom of Gwent. Though the rocky site encouraged the use of stone for the castle, fitz Osbern did not quarry stone locally. Instead he chose the yellow Triassic sandstone which could be quarried at Caldicot and Portskewett 5 m. to the SW and transported by water. The advantage of this stone was that it yielded large square blocks, far more impressive and regular than Chepstow's indigenous limestone. There is also plenty of reused Roman material, smaller squared stones and thin courses of red brick. Fitz Osbern died in 1071, and his son, Roger of Breteuil, forfeited his lands to the king four years later, so this first castle seems to have been constructed within the eight years 1067–75.

The next builder was almost certainly William Marshal, who came to possess the castle in 1189 on his marriage to the Clare heiress Isabella. It was Marshal who introduced the drum tower, a feature of contemporary French fortification, into the castle

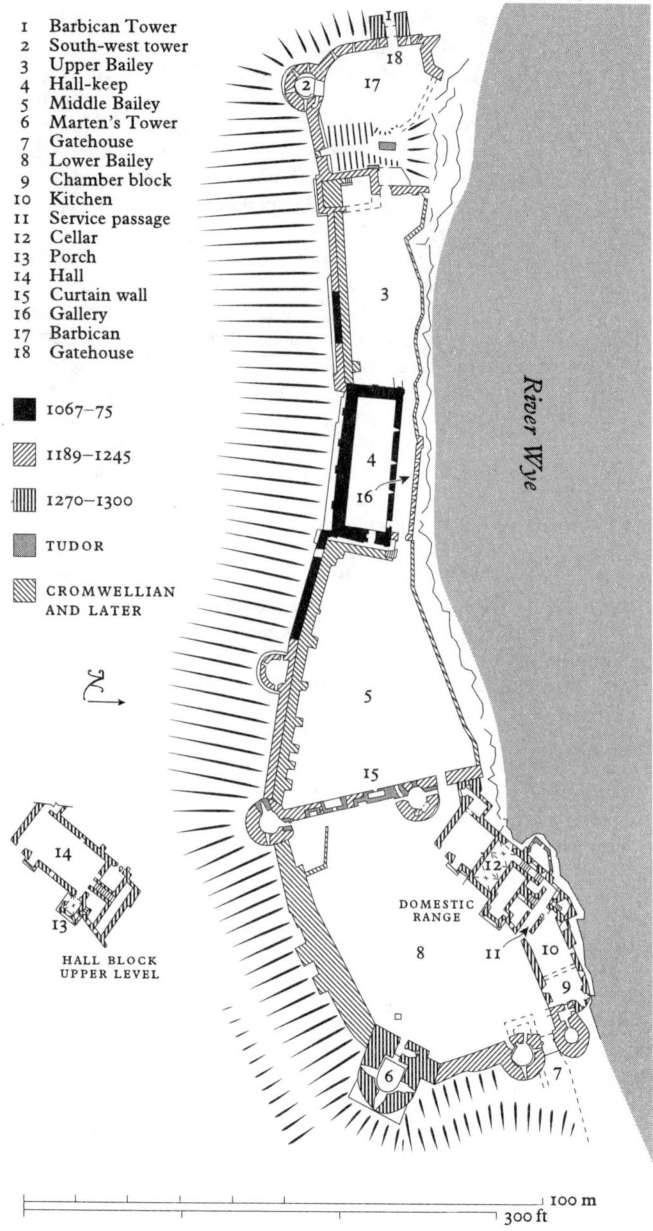

Chepstow Castle. Plan

architecture of South Wales. At Chepstow he built at least four such towers. Those in the straight wall, which greatly strengthened the lower, E, end of the eastern bailey, have long been recognized as his. But powerful evidence has recently demonstrated that the outer gatehouse with its two round towers was almost certainly built not later than *c.* 1189, and so was Marshal's too.* He began the use of the local grey limestone for walling, with fine oolitic limestone imported from Dundry across the Bristol Channel for ashlar dressings. Its buff colour and excellent state of preservation make it easy to recognize.

William Marshal died in 1219 and was succeeded in turn by his five sons, the last of whom died in 1245. During much of this period further new building was in hand, not only to extend its defences but also to provide elegant accommodation. Two gifts by the king of oak trees are documented for these building campaigns, the first to the eldest brother, William, in 1228 for work on the 'turris', presumably the hall-keep, the second to the third brother, Gilbert, in 1234. Style also dates several elements of the castle to this period. It seems that at first imported Dundry stone continued to be used for dressings, but in later years it was eked out by much more local, and less durable, Old Red Sandstone, of a strong purple hue. With all this in mind it is possible to suggest that the younger William Marshal, followed by Gilbert, raised the W third of the keep, to provide a private chamber above the hall, and the remodelled Upper Bailey, in particular building there the rectangular tower with a beautifully finished chamber over a basement. The chamber is perhaps to be identified as the 'camera comitisse' and thus the state apartment of William's mother, Isabella. The Barbican, protecting the Upper Bailey where the ground rises towards the W, may also be of his time. The last work of this phase, where Old Red Sandstone is most prominent, is the SW tower of the Barbican.

The final major phase of construction was that of Roger Bigod III, Earl of Norfolk, who inherited the Marcher lordship of Striguil in 1270. A series of receivers' accounts for the lordship indicate that *c.* 1271–2 he added the tower in front of the W gateway of the Barbican; that 1278–87 (after a break to construct the town walls – *see* The Port Wall, p. 182) he built a sumptuous hall and kitchen range immediately within the gatehouse of the Lower Bailey, his director of works being the mason Master *Ralf* (died 1293); and 1286–93 he further embellished and strengthened the Lower Bailey by constructing Marten's Tower at its lowermost, SE, corner, thus providing a self-contained residence which could be isolated from the rest of the castle. Finally, 1293–1300, it seems, the E two-thirds of the keep were heightened.

To the Tudor work no firm dates can be attached. During the

* Tree-ring analysis of the timber doors of the lower gatehouse in 1998 showed that they are not C16, as had been supposed, but several centuries older. The trees from which the doors are made were felled some time between 1159 and 1189, and evidence of shrinkage indicates that they were used unseasoned. The doors give every sign of having been made to fit the archway. They hung there until 1964, but are now on display elsewhere in the castle.

C16 the castle belonged to the Somersets, Earls of Worcester. During the Civil War the fifth Earl held it for the king, and in 1645 and 1648 it twice fell to Parliamentary forces, the S curtain wall being badly breached. After the war Cromwell himself obtained the castle, and the S wall was reconstructed much thicker, with embrasures for cannon all along the top. Such precautions, however, proved otiose, and the castle, though garrisoned until 1690, became a superior prison, Marten's Tower taking its name, somewhat incongruously, from the regicide Henry Marten, who was imprisoned there for twenty years by Charles II. The castle remained the property of the Dukes of Beaufort until the early C20, and in 1953 was conveyed as a guardianship monument to the Ministry of Public Building and Works. It is now in the care of Cadw: Welsh Historic Monuments.

The castle extends in a W–E axis, where the River Wye describes the last of its violent loops on its way to the Bristol Channel. The underlying rock slopes down quite sharply from W to E, so the main entrance is at the lowest level, and even the addition of the Barbican at the W end left the castle overtopped by rocky outcrops in that direction. Today a footpath descends gently along the bottom of THE DINGLE from the upper car park to the lower car park, allowing a full-length view of the S side of the castle, as it faces across to the backs of the houses in Bridge Street and Hocker Hill and their gardens. This must from the beginning have been the physical relationship of the castle and its dependent town.

Exterior from the South

As an introduction to the castle, it is worth following the footpath down The Dingle, and examining in turn the exterior of its five sharply demarcated parts: Barbican, Upper Bailey, Hall-keep, Middle Bailey, Lower Bailey.

The rectangular BARBICAN TOWER, added in front of the W gateway of the Barbican by Roger Bigod, perhaps *c.* 1271–2, provided the protection considered in the later C13 to be necessary for an entrance. Three portcullis slots within the pointed tunnel vault. Three large, cruciform arrow slits set symmetrically at the top of the outer face of the tower, and a corbel table for battlements, now gone. The outer entrance arch and front wall of the portcullis chamber above have been torn away, and the tall arch which replaces them is of the C20. The sides of the tower are battered for three-quarters of their height. In the S side two more arrow slits to cover the flanking wall.

The earlier C13 W wall of the Barbican, which this tower was intended to strengthen, is towards the N, where it meets the clifftop, irregular and fragmentary. To the S, however, it remains virtually intact, pierced only by an impressive array of arrow slits, three long ones low down, and two more in the merlons of the battlements. At its S end it curves and joins the boldly projecting drum of the SW TOWER. This is completely plain, of local grey limestone, against which the purple Old Red Sandstone of the Latin cross-shaped arrow slits contrasts starkly. The slits occur at three levels, in an array which could cover all points of the compass towards the field. The tower is clearly an addition built near the end of the younger Marshals' ownership.

The S enclosure wall of the Barbican is featureless, except for the round-arched head low down of a postern gate. Immediately S of this there slightly projects the short end of a rectangular tower, built at the SW angle of the UPPER BAILEY, of grey limestone with finely cut Dundry stone dressings. This is the tower thought to have been built for the Countess Isabella after 1219. It was clearly not intended exclusively for defence, since at mid-height are two round-headed windows, not large, but elegantly detailed with two orders of chamfers. The l. one frames a square-headed light, the r. one a round-headed light. Top battlements, coped, and the centre two provided with Latin cross arrow slits with oeillets.

Next comes the straight wall of the Upper Bailey itself. This has clearly been much reconstructed, but the E half has in its lower half extensive areas faced with yellow Triassic blocks. So this would appear to be part of William fitz Osbern's late C11 enclosure wall. All along the top a row of mid-C17 cannon loops, externally splayed to increase their field of fire. The rectangular projection where the wall joins the keep has quoins of Dundry stone, so must be a contribution by one of the Marshals.

7 This brings us to the HALL-KEEP, William fitz Osbern's Great Tower. It is a most impressive masonry structure, all the more so given its pioneering status in Britain. Presumably it was built by masons from Normandy. The flank wall of the keep is of five bays, the E-most bay slightly narrower than the others. The yellow Triassic stone is used in large, squared blocks to form a projecting plinth, in smaller, regularly coursed blocks for the main walling and as ashlar for the pilaster buttresses. A continuous band of reused Roman bricks runs across unbroken at the level of the principal floor inside. Otherwise there is no indication of the interior arrangement, for the S side was designed without windows. The single lancet which breaks through one of the pilasters is a C13 insertion. The C13 heightening of the keep has disappeared from the S side, so from this direction it displays almost its original height and mass, rectangular not square, and not particularly lofty.

The curtain wall of the MIDDLE BAILEY extends E-wards slightly proud of the S wall of the keep. It has been so much reconstructed that only the eye of faith can discern C11 masonry here. Close to the keep the head of a blocked postern. More cannon loops crown the wall-head. Half-way along, a D-plan tower, its battered base much robbed, its grey stone walls pierced by arrow slits at two levels. It is contemporary with the adjoining stretch of curtain wall to the E as far as the next tower. This tower is circular and a characteristic work of the elder William Marshal *c.* 1200. (Compare particularly the Garrison Tower at Usk Castle, p. 592.) It has a battered base and then rises in three storeys firmly divided from one another by chamfered ashlar set-offs of Dundry stone. Long arrow slits of dressed stone terminating in circular oeillets. The tiny SW-facing lancet low down may be contemporary, but the larger one above is clearly a Tudor insertion.

The remaining stretch of S curtain wall is very irregular, and probably mostly of the mid C17, i.e. contemporary with the cannon slots along the top. MARTEN'S TOWER comes next. 23
Built by Roger Bigod III 1286–93, it is both the most complete and the most architecturally satisfying part of Chepstow Castle, conceived on a grander scale than any of the earlier C13 works. It is a D in plan and projects from the SE corner of the curtain with truly dramatic effect. Its defensive capacity is reinforced by the two sharply pointed spurs, which project from the curved face of the tower and slope down to form a rectangular skirt at ground level. Purple Old Red Sandstone down here, looking like a great wine mark below the grey limestone of the main walling. A particularly elaborate arrow slit centred between the spurs, and two more at this level to l. and r. Above spur level, four more arrow slits are arrayed. At the top, two trefoil-headed lancet windows, with sockets for iron bars, and, above a string-course, deep coped battlements pierced by arrow slits and crowned by much eroded half-length figures. At the rear of the tower to l. and r. rectangular projections rise higher. They are also battlemented, and that to the r. has a large E-facing window with two-centred head, serving a chapel. One two-light Tudor window pierces the tower to the NE.

So at last we can approach the E, entrance, front of the castle. Marten's Tower at its S extremity is in piquant contrast to the twin drum towers of the GATEHOUSE at its N end. The gatehouse, now seemingly datable to *c.* 1189, is typical of the Marshals' work, of grey limestone with Dundry stone dressings. Several Tudor windows, of two and three lights, however, puncture its severity. The towers have strongly projecting battered bases and long arrow slits at three levels, plain below, the lowest in the batter itself, cross-shaped above. The holes in a row all across near the wall-head were probably intended for timber beams to support a timber hoard, or fighting platform. No battlements, but a parapet with C17 gunloops. The entrance between the towers is strongly fortified. Originally there was a low, projecting barbican, as a jagged stump of wall on the l. tower indicates. Upper segmental arch with a slot behind, through which missiles could be dropped. Lower segmental arch over the passageway, with in its underside two 'murder-holes' for more missiles. To the l. an arrow slit for close-range shooting. Then come the slots for a portcullis. Great double doors (the present ones are replicas of the late C12 doors on display elsewhere in the castle) are set in a round-headed arch. Finally there are the slots for a second portcullis.

Within the Castle Walls

The rear walls of the gatehouse towers, visible from within the LOWER BAILEY, start slightly bowed, but their upper parts are straight, and there were rectangular rear projections. Within the S tower at ground level was a guardroom, its rear projection all gone, revealing that in the upper levels of the tower were several heated chambers. The basement of the N tower formed a windowless prison. The lower storey of its rear projection survives, providing a lobby to the prison. In the S wall of the projection the springer of an arch which would have linked to the rear wall of its now demolished fellow.

The DOMESTIC RANGE, built by Roger Bigod III 1278–87, extends from the back of the gatehouse all along the N side of the Lower Bailey. The fact that he sited his suite of entertaining rooms here suggests that the gatehouse, built with such obsessive attention to defence nearly a century earlier, was no longer required to fulfil this function. (Having just built the Barbican gatehouse and the Port Wall as the town's defences, Bigod clearly saw the W, uphill end of the castle as the one requiring protection.) The range consists of a great hall, private chambers at its upper and lower ends, the latter above service rooms, and at a lower level, further extremely elaborately arranged service and storage rooms. The sheer ingenuity with which everything has been woven together on the irregularly sloping clifftop leaves one full of admiration for those who planned it. It is built of mauve Old Red Sandstone from Tintern, with dressings of the same.

In order to understand the essentials of the layout it is best to pass through the ticket office and come out into the Lower Bailey. From here the S wall of the range is seen to be largely intact as far as the hall porch, but the hall itself is very ruinous. At the bottom, adjoining the back of the outer gatehouse is a chamber block of two bays, two-storeyed over a basement, and linked to the outer gatehouse chambers. Each storey has a two-light window to the r. of a doorway. Numerous corbels projecting from the walls suggest that timber stairs and galleries must have been constructed against the wall face to give access to the doorways, and to the chambers which they and the windows serve. The upper window retains its step-and-hollow moulded tracery, forming a quatrefoil over two trefoil-headed lights. Its hoodmould, idiosyncratically, follows the trefoil outline of the window head. Further W, isolated in a stretch of wall, is a similar, but much larger and longer window, with a transom. This lit and ventilated the kitchen and seems remarkably grand for this purpose. Next comes a two-centred doorway into the cross-passage, with C20 windows of twin pointed-headed lights at two levels above. Note here also a blocked, round-headed upper window of Dundry stone, evidence that a Marshal-period structure is incorporated in Bigod's range. All this stretch is crowned by uniform battlements with arrow slits in the merlons.

Inside the range, the very ruined interior of the CHAMBER BLOCK can be seen rising confusedly above the roof of the ticket office. Several two-light, quatrefoil-headed windows, and even a doorway, open towards the river. The block was separated from the kitchen by a wall, of which only the jagged stumps remain to N and S. The KITCHEN has no original hearths. Either they were in the destroyed E wall, or there never were any and cooking was done on a central open hearth. There was clearly a gabled roof in five bays running W–E, as is shown by the sockets for its timber wall-posts and the stone corbels which supported them. A central hearth would have required a large smoke louvre in the middle of this roof. In the N wall a large window matching that on the S, but with traces of a circular oven on its sill, and a doorway apparently opening over the cliff-face. It must have led to a timber platform and stair climbing up the face of the cliff to the chamber doorway further E. Further W in the N wall an inserted fireplace blocking a window, itself later blocked. In the W wall the rebated N and S jambs of a serving hatch opening into the passage beyond, the wall above it reinforced by two relieving arches. The masonry infill below the lower arch has fallen out. At the top of the wall here a corbelled-out chimney-breast, serving the private chamber described below (p. 176).

The SERVICE PASSAGE is the working heart of Bigod's domestic range. It is unified architecturally by the two-centred heads and continuous hollow chamfers to all openings. From the kitchen it is entered near its S end. On the W side of the passage two doorways open further N. The first gives access to a storeroom with two sets of stone cupboards. The second is at the foot of the straight flight of steps up to the hall. Note the rebated doorway near the foot of the flight. Immediately N in the passage itself was another doorway, of which only the jambs and an arch springer survive, separating the preparation areas from the storage areas down below. Beyond this doorway, on the E, first a short passage to a spacious double garderobe corbelled out over the cliff-face and provided with a pair of windows, then a double cupboard rebated for doors. Opposite, a steeply pointed arch of Dundry stone stands at the head of a flight of stone steps cut into the cliff-face. They descend to the storage area under a pointed tunnel vault, at first well lit by a N window, and reach a mid-landing. This is set under an elegant quadripartite vault with broad, filleted ribs. The landing gives on to a polygonal stone balcony, clearly an addition, butting against buttresses attached to the outer wall face. The balcony originally had a W doorway and windows to N and E. Stores brought to the castle by water could be hauled up the cliff-face to the balcony. In the wall above, windows for two upper chambers E of the hall. The flight of steps continues down from the landing under a pointed tunnel vault with transverse ribs. At the foot, a pointed-headed doorway with bull-nose moulding opens into the N end of a splendidly proportioned storage CELLAR, which runs back transversely under the hall. This too has a quadripartite rib vault, of three bays, the ribs plainly chamfered, but resting on quite elaborately detailed circular corbels. Light is admitted through a once barred window in the N wall. This was originally longer, probably a doorway, again related to hauling stores up from river level. The whole room is almost perfectly preserved, making it all the more eloquent of the panache and magnificence of Bigod's manner of living and entertaining.

With that it is necessary to return, and go out along the service passage into the Lower Bailey again, in order to enter Bigod's HALL. The two-storeyed, battlemented PORCH is the most completely surviving part of the hall. It is a curious structure, with a lanky look, as the angle pilaster buttresses die back at half height. Because of the sloping ground, the entrance doorway is in the W side of the porch, not at the front. Here, facing S, is another long two-light window with a transom and quatrefoil head. Inside, the entrance arch is richly moulded with a hollow and three filleted rolls. There is a two-bay quadripartite rib vault, the ribs also filleted, and the corbels fluted and conical. NE doorway to the newel stair which leads to the porch chamber above. The doorway into what was originally the screens passage of the hall, quite plain, is off-centre to the porch. On the wall above, remarkable survival, a large area of original plaster painted in outline with two shields of arms as if hung on the wall, the r. one emblazoned with the red chevron of the Clares. The painting is known to have been paid for in 1292–3. The HALL itself is roofless and its walls are much reduced in height. The side wall towards the bailey was heavily buttressed. The two windows here are sadly fragmentary, but enough remains to show that they had rere-arches with hollow-chamfered jambs, and arch heads decorated with a slender filleted roll between two bands of four-petal flowers, differing in design from window to window. All four walls of the hall were divided at mid-height by a continuous undercut stringcourse, which jumps up over apertures. At the N end of the E wall it takes account of an upper doorway, the position of which indicates that there was originally the normal arrangement of a screen at the service end with a gallery over it. In the E gable a finely moulded window of two trefoiled lights with an encircled quatrefoil above, under a conventionally pointed head. This would have admitted light from above the roof of the range E of the hall. A symmetrical group of three service doorways opens into this range. They are quite small, and their hoods on emphatic corbels are largely worn away. The central doorway stands at the head of the flight of stairs down to the service passage (*see* p. 175 above). The side ones lead into buttery and pantry, now devoted to exhibition space. From the pantry there was direct access into the porch stair-turret. Extending above these rooms and above the service passage is what must have been a large, handsome private chamber, now part of the exhibition space, but originally accessible only from the stair-turret in the porch. It has two-light N and S windows, and in the centre of the E wall a fireplace with an unusually fine and well-preserved monolithic hood, steep and smooth, and corbelled out on filleted jamb shafts. So the principal chamber was sited above the service rooms at the lower end of the hall. This was the inevitable consequence of lack of space beyond its upper end, where the entrance into the Middle Bailey had to remain clear. At that end all that could be contrived was a small, originally two-storey chamber block projecting towards the cliff edge, served by a stair-turret built against the Middle Bailey curtain wall. Trefoil-headed N lancets. Remodelled in the early C16 with two-light windows.

The remaining building which opens off the Lower Bailey is MARTEN'S TOWER. Here there was no need for ingenuity in adapting to an awkward site, and Bigod's architect could plan with single-minded logic. His purpose was to provide a second residence of some splendour, which could, unlike the domestic range, be sealed off and defended, or otherwise made private. So its three small doorways, one opening from the Lower Bailey and two, high up to l. and r., opening on to the wall-walk of the curtain wall, are each provided with a slot for a small portcullis. The walls of the tower are immensely thick, the flat face of its D-plan providing a full-height newel stair within the depth of the wall to the l. and garderobes to the r., both lit by nothing more than long slits. Set back to l. and r., rectangular projections for the wall-walk doorways, the l. projection slightly enlarged and provided with trefoil-headed lancet windows at two levels, the upper lighting the chapel sited at the top here. The deep crowning battlements, above a moulded stringcourse, remain entire, with moulded coping. Arrow slits only in the two central merlons. The l. and r. projections are carried up as turrets, with battlements at a higher level, aligned with those on the external face of the tower. The central entrance doorway is low, segment-headed and quite insignificant, though its five chamfered orders cut far into the depth of the wall. Aligned above it are two later insertions: large, matching, four-light transomed windows. The upper one has a hoodmould and cinquefoiled lights above and below the transom, and must be late C15. The lower is of timber.

The interior of Marten's Tower is equally intact, lacking only its timber floors and roof (which survived until the early C19). It is four-storeyed and the walls are set back storey by storey to provide seating for the floor timbers. At the upper two levels, however, there are also continuous stone corbel tables of convex profile, identical to that in the private chamber in the domestic range. The lowest level is unlit and must have been for storage. Above that, in all three storeys, the widely splayed rere-arches of arrow slits and lancet windows leave surprisingly little uninterrupted wall surface. The storey at the level of the Lower Bailey was for defence, with three arrow slits. From here the stair leads up to a vestibule lit by the timber mullion-and-transom window. The deep ashlar rere-arch, with bold moulded ribs traversing its shallow segmental soffit, must be a C15 improvement; the timber window doubtless had a stone predecessor. The principal room at this level is lit by three slit-like lancets. Mighty fireplace with chamfered monolith lintel and sunk-chamfered, trefoil-topped jambs. Beside it, blocking a fourth window, is a smaller, Tudor fireplace with delicate mouldings. Note the garderobe doorway here. The top level has an almost identical ashlar rere-arch to the late medieval mullion-and-transom window lighting the vestibule. The main room is internally hexagonal, not circular. The splays to the lancet windows are fitted with seats, and there is a large fireplace with monolith lintel. At this level on the stair, pointed rere-arches for lancets in three directions and a triple-chamfered arch to the wall-walk.

Immediately above, there is a narrow doorway and beyond it a chamfered arch into the CHAPEL. The chapel, though small, is richly decorated. One N and one S trefoil-headed lancet, their rere-arches enriched with continuous roll and hood, the sill of the N lancet provided with a seat, the S lancet accompanied by a trefoil-headed piscina. The glory of the chapel was clearly its large E window, though nothing of its tracery remains. Undercut hood, originally on carved corbels, broad hollow surround enriched with multi-petal flowers, close-set round the arch, more widely spaced down the jambs. Continuous convex corbel table for the roof. Finally, the roof space of the tower must have been heated, for there is a fireplace at wall-walk level. Up here the demi-figures on the merlons can be well seen, in their tantalizing decay.

The Lower Bailey is firmly separated from the Middle Bailey by William Marshal's straight CURTAIN WALL of *c.* 1200, ending in a drum tower at the S end, already noted from the exterior. Near its N end is a second drum tower, immediately next to and clearly intended to protect the main entrance into the Middle Bailey. Both towers have a single bold, chamfered set-off above the lowest storey, and at three levels long arrow slits of primitive form but sited so that archers could cover all directions. The entrance arch itself, in contrast to the round-headed arch of the Outer Bailey gateway, has a two-centred pointed head of two square orders and chamfered jambs top and bottom. The timber doors have been dated to the early C16. The jamb of a doorway immediately to the N, perhaps for a guardroom. All the other openings which riddle the wall and towers are later medieval insertions, a variety of windows and fireplaces, indicating that timber buildings were erected against the wall and that the N tower was pressed into use as a kitchen. The S tower was also affected by the post-Civil War thickening of the S curtain wall to enable cannon to be set on top of it. This thickened curtain wall extends along the S side of the Middle Bailey, and a spur from it is constructed beneath the E end wall of the keep.

The HALL-KEEP, the earliest part of the castle, built in the late C11, still stands high above the rest. The early Norman walls survive intact, but of the top storey added in the C13 only the N and W walls remain. It is a rectangle two bays by five, the bays defined by thin pilaster buttresses. Its long, windowless S wall has already been noted (p. 172). Entry, presumably up a flight of timber steps, at its short E end, is through a handsome square-headed doorway in the r. (N) bay. The lintel, semicircular tympanum and two outer orders of voussoirs of the doorway are all chip-carved with what came to be a standard early Norman pattern of Xs in boxes. The only other surviving decoration is the band of Roman bricks, which is carried across the buttresses and arches up over the doorway voussoirs. A tiny round-headed opening in the l. bay, just above the tile band, lights the mural stair which rises from the jamb of the doorway to an internal upper doorway in the SE corner (*see* below). The two lancets, externally chamfered, much higher up in the upper storey, belong to the C13 remodelling. Originally, for the sake of security, there were no windows except in the N wall, overlooking the cliff. This wall is also much thinner than the others.

In order to inspect the N wall it is necessary to pass into the GALLERY, which extends along it between the keep and the brink of the cliff. For the present the gallery itself should be ignored, and attention directed to the complicated evidence on the N wall of the keep. Here there is no tile band, but C12 windows or traces of windows at two levels. Those in the basement are centred on the bays, but those above, lighting the hall, seem to have been grouped in widely spaced pairs, and so were off-centre to the bays. There is also a narrow doorway towards the W end. The hall was refenestrated, probably in the second quarter of the C13, with much larger windows, which ignore the early Norman design altogether. There are three to the E and one much larger near the W end, lighting the dais end of the hall. The three are plate-traceried, with a quatrefoil over two trefoil-headed lights, double-chamfered externally and all set under keeled hoodmoulds on stiff-leaf whorls. The lights are long enough to be transomed. The NW window develops these ideas on a larger scale, though damage to the tracery does not make it immediately easy to grasp the pattern. Two pairs of chamfered trefoil-headed lights are set under two roll-moulded trefoil-headed hoods, their top lobes enclosing quatrefoils. In the apex above, a quatrefoil encircled by a roll and set under a two-centred chamfered superarch with hood on leaf whorls. One wonders at all this care and subtlety lavished on the exterior of a window which can only be viewed by craning one's neck.

The top storey of the Hall-keep is not all of one build. The two W bays of the N face are clearly contemporary with the mid-C13 windows below. There are two two-light windows up here, and W of them a two-centred-headed doorway, which must have been reached by a timber external stair. The E bays, added in the late C13, are set above a stringcourse. The broad central section is lit by one two-light window, and in the narrower E section, marked off by the continuation upwards of an C11 pilaster buttress, there is another. The W face of the keep is windowless, except for two enigmatic loopholes high up and two cross-shaped arrow slits in the C13 top stage.

The interior of the Hall-keep is entered through a doorway forced through at the E end of the N wall. Inside, the first impression is of a narrow space enclosed by soaring walls. The ground, much of it exposed rock, slopes quite sharply, and at this end the floor of the basement was above head height, as a series of joist holes indicates. Above, the unmoulded embrasures of the N windows of the basement are almost intact, and above the level of their heads along the N and S walls run rows of much more substantial joist holes, indicating the level of the hall floor. Much bigger square sockets central to the E and W walls mark the position of a central floor beam, which must have been supported on a row of posts the length of the basement. There survive from the C11 hall traces of the N windows, one complete (NE) and the jambs of others, and towards the W a decorative scheme which suggests that at this end there was a separate chamber, served by the N doorway (doubtless at the head of a flight of timber steps). The scheme consists of four round-headed recesses, originally painted with a white trellis pattern on red plaster, across the W wall, and four others, now blocked, at the W end of the S wall. The pointed superarch in the W wall presumably related to the original roof gable, but what was the purpose of the two deeply splayed circular loops off-centre within it?

The C13 remodelling of the hall made it into something far more spectacular. The greatly enlarged windows have already been noted externally. Towards the hall they are handsomely treated. The three transomed two-lighters have hoods formerly on heads and are outlined by a continuous filleted roll. Within that are three roll mouldings, the middle one filleted, on stiff-leaf capitals. The jamb shafts are lost. Seats within the embrasures. Immediately W of the W-most of these windows is the
22 springing of a sumptuously treated transverse two-bay arcade, with its fellow in the S wall opposite. The arcade must have taken the place of the C11 partition between hall and chamber, in order to frame the views towards the dais end of the enlarged hall. It also supported the E wall of the new upper chamber, constructed at the same time above the dais end. The springers show that the richly, not to say excessively elaborated arches were set under hoods and moulded with two small outer rolls and two inner rolls, separated by a hollow filled with lavishly sculptured dogtooth. Below all these are five filleted rolls set on two trios of lush stiff-leaf capitals one below the other, and a short shaft, carried doubtless on a figure corbel, now mouldered away to an indecipherable lump. The NW dais window also boasts a hood on head corbels, a continuous filleted roll and one remaining stiff-leaf capital for the shafted inner order. Evidence here, too, for window seats, and rebates for shutters. The two W lancets, their splays cut through a much thicker wall, have steeply sloping sills. They too are decorated with hoods on leaf whorls and continuous filleted roll. A moulded upper string runs round the W, N, and doubtless originally the S walls, but to the E is interrupted by the gable arch.

The top storey is, as we have seen, of two dates: the W third for the new chamber built above the dais end of the hall, the rest constructed by Bigod in the 1290s. The two windows in the earlier part of the N wall, with tracery identical to that of the hall windows below, are simply treated internally, their rere-arches merely chamfered. The doorway too is plain. To the E, first a moulded relieving arch curves across the wall face. This accommodates a mural stair which provided access to the wall-walk. The doorway into it is in the jamb of the first of two windows further E. The doorway and the windows all have the shouldered 'Caernarfon' arch form typical of the end of the C13, and are thus the clearest indication that this is all Bigod's work. Once again the windows are provided with seats. In the NE corner a large and splendid, if damaged, corbel, carved as a bearded head with scrolling locks equally typical of this date.

Outside, to the N of the keep, the narrow, passage-like GALLERY ascends, its floor the living rock. Its outer clifftop wall is without any frills. Built and dressed with Tintern Old Red Sandstone, it may be mid-C13, one of the last works of William Marshal's sons, or more probably was another of Bigod's contributions. Its purpose was to make the N side of the keep defensible and thereby segregate the Middle Bailey from the Upper Bailey. Its lower, E, wall survives intact, the pointed entrance arch continuously double-chamfered, the battlements above provided with cross-shaped arrow slits. In the N wall, poised above the cliff-face, six pointed, chamfered arches, originally open down to the rock, and thus probably giving access to a wooden lookout balcony of which no trace remains. The return wall at the upper, W, end has been entirely removed.

The gallery leads into the UPPER BAILEY at its NE corner. This bailey is quite small and narrow. The keep looms over its E end. In the SW corner of the bailey stands the rectangular tower, with its finely cut Doulting dressings, which has been identified as the one where the Countess Isabella de Clare, William Marshal's widow, had her private chamber. Everything about it proclaims that this is a work of the early C13. The S and W walls and part of the N wall survive, enough to show that the chamber was a loftily proportioned and beautifully detailed room over a low basement. The windows are little more than slits, but their rere-arches are finely moulded with pointed heads and keeled rolls. Two, however, for no apparent reason, are round-headed, and their rolls are not keeled. Most were provided with seats in the splays. On the walls extensive patches of plaster survive, and in the head of the SE window, excitingly, the plaster is still lined out in red to imitate finely jointed stonework. So one can visualize the walls of the whole chamber treated in this way. The position of the chamber doorway is not clear. The ragged hole at the S end of the W wall was made in the C17, when the curtain wall was strengthened for cannon. Jamb for a N doorway into the basement. The coped battlements of the S and W walls remain intact. Surprisingly, they have no arrow slits (though C17 gunloops have been cut through the S battlements). The exposed, W end of the Upper Bailey is altogether lacking in substantial defences. The gateway, immediately N of the Countess's chamber, is nothing more than a tall, pointed, double-chamfered arch secured by a pair of (early C16) doors swinging back under a segmental rere-arch. To the N a flight of steps, now much ruined, rose straight over the top of the gateway to give access to the roof and battlements of the Countess's chamber.

The BARBICAN, though clearly built subsequently to the formation of the Upper Bailey, must have been envisaged all along, for it provides the strong defence which the Upper Bailey patently needs. The outward appearance and reality of strength of the Barbican has already been appreciated (*see* above, pp. 171–2). From inside, its functioning can be more fully understood. A rock-cut ditch protects the W side of the Countess's chamber tower, with a bridge spanning from the gateway of the Upper Bailey into the Barbican. The present bridge is modern, on a C16 pier. At the S end of the ditch the blocked postern gateway, the Old Red Sandstone head of which was noted outside. Internally, it has a semicircular head rebated for a door. The defences towards the W were progressively strengthened, first by the SW tower, then by Bigod's rectangular gatehouse. At first reliance was placed on archers. Their arrow slits low in the curtain wall, and in the merlons of the battlements, have segmental rere-arches formed without cut stone. The SW tower provided more of the same. It has a flat back, and slit windows at the E end show where a newel stair ascends in the NE angle. The central section of the tower back, now a full-height, straight-sided gap, must originally have been of timber. Note the horizontal slots high up for the rear beam of the top floor. Inside the towers, the rere-arches of the widely splayed arrow slits at all three levels have neatly formed semicircular heads. Between the SW tower and the gatehouse there is an unusually well-protected wall-walk, with internal battlements on a projecting corbel table. These must have been added to the curtain wall when the SW tower was built, for the only way on to the wall-walk was up the newel stair in the SW tower.

Finally, the GATEHOUSE. As first built in the second quarter of the C13, there was nothing here but a pointed-headed gateway with segmental rere-arch. This was a much weaker arrangement than William Marshal's Middle Bailey gateway, which has the adjacent protection of a drum tower with covering arrow slit. Yet it was left to Roger Bigod in 1272, nearly half a century later, to provide the Barbican gateway with adequate protection. This has been largely described already (*see* p. 171). A few of its features, however, can only be seen from inside. The two rooms over the portcullis passage are lit from windows in the inner face. The portcullis chamber has no more than a slit. The upper room, however, has a window of two round-headed lights, a peculiarly old-fashioned form, and slit windows in other directions. The access to these two rooms was only along the wall-walk from the S. The pointed-headed doorway from the wall-walk into the top room survives intact.

THE PORT WALL. Roger Bigod III, as part of his late C13 strengthening of the castle, probably 1272–8, constructed a stone wall over two-thirds of a mile long across the neck of the promontory. It extended from the W end of the castle in an arc across the high ground S-wards, then plunged down the hillside to the SE and met the River Wye near where the railway station now is. It thus enclosed a much greater area than was occupied by the castle, town street and priory precinct. A single gateway, the Town Gate, provided an exit from the town to the W. Until the C20 the Wall survived virtually intact, breached only for the railway, in 1850. But during the First World War, extension of the shipyard required the removal of the eastern third. In the 1960s a substantial gap was made W of the Town Gate to give access to the town's upper car park, and in 1971 an even larger one E of it to allow the inner relief road to swoop through. Between the two the wall is largely hidden within houses in Welsh Street to the W of the Town Gate.

In spite of all this, substantial stretches of the Port Wall survive. They can be described from NW to SE. The NW-most stretch of the wall, extending to the SW from the castle across CASTLE DELL, has been reduced to a few stones hidden in the hedge bottom. The first impressive stretch starts at a square turret overlooking Castle Dell and extends S-wards, standing almost to full height. From the car park the wall-walk is clearly visible, but the battlements which protected men patrolling the wall have been lost. Small doorway with four-centred head, clearly a C16 intrusion. Then, before the car park entrance, the first of the surviving late C13 bastions, projecting boldly forward on an elongated D-plan. It is quite plain, without arrow slits, and open at the back. One must imagine that it originally had timber staging at the level of the wall-walk, to enable patrollers to monitor the exterior face of the wall. To the S of the entry to the car park a further stretch of wall is visible, much reduced in height, and the base of a second bastion.

Next comes the TOWN GATE itself, spanning the High Street in a widened pointed N arch, and to the S by the original arrangement of carriage arch and pedestrian arch beside it. It is not clear how much, if any, of the fabric of the gate goes back to the C13. It is said to have been rebuilt by the Earl of Worcester in 1524. A simple square in plan, the gate is crowned by a corbel table and reconstructed battlements. High on the outer face, two worn and illegible heraldic panels supported by angels, presumably of 1524. Below them, two lancets restored in the C20. At this level on the inner face two C19 brick oculi. Houses hem the gate in on either side.

Immediately to the SE, behind the George Hotel, is an isolated but well-preserved bastion. Next comes the interruption of the inner relief road, GARDEN CITY WAY. But beyond that is the best-surviving stretch of wall, complete with two bastions and intact up to the, now somewhat ragged, battlements. Some original coping stones. Here the absence of an external defensive ditch is noticeable. Nor were defenders on the wall-walk or in the bastions provided with arrow slits to shoot through. The only openings in the walls, a row of square slots high up, served merely to drain rainwater from the wall-walk. Beyond, after a further break, the hillside drops steeply down. Here a final stretch of wall and two more bastions survive behind the houses in PORTWALL ROAD and GREEN STREET, best seen from below by the railway station.

POLICE STATION, Moor Street. 1912 by *William Tanner*, the County Surveyor. Heavy-handed Arts and Crafts Tudor. Off-centre porch bay with a curvaceous gable.

94 ROAD BRIDGE. The cast-iron replacement for the historic timber bridge carrying the road between England and Wales across the River Wye. 1814–16 to the designs of *John Rennie*, made by *J. U. Rastrick* and *William Hazeldine*. A supremely elegant composition of five shallow segmental lattice arches carrying the gently curved roadway. The arches nearly alike in profile, though widely different in span: central 112 ft (34 metres), intermediate 70 ft (21 metres) and outer 34 ft (10 metres). This superstructure rests on reassuringly strong tapering piers of squared ashlar, their bull-nosed cutwaters barely pointed. The finishing touch is the delicate iron balustrade to the footway, enlivened with the bold date 1816, occasional scrollwork panels and lamps at the centre and ends raised on scrolled shafts.

RAILWAY BRIDGE. Only the substructure survives of the extraordinary tubular suspension bridge built 1850–2 to *I. K. Brunel*'s design. Tall cast-iron Tuscan columns in trios, now filled with concrete, and a massive rock-faced stone abutment on the Welsh side, with responding ashlar pilasters. All this carries the present railway bridge superstructure of 1962.

RAILWAY STATION, Station Road. 1850 for *I. K. Brunel*'s South Wales Railway, designed by *N. Lancaster Owen*. Single-storeyed, of stone with Italianate detail. Deep bracketed eaves carried round three sides.

To the NE of the station, the contemporary former CORN MILL (now Fairfield-Mabey Engineering Yard offices). This was built in 1851 by Robert Sharpe, one of the contractors for Brunel's railway bridge. Handsomely proportioned three-bay, five-storey block under a shallow hipped roof. It is set below the level of the railway to provide rail access to its middle storey. The mill was powered by steam. In the early 1890s it was converted into a maltings, and two MALTING-KILNS were erected at the lower riverward level. These had characteristic steep pyramidal roofs.

To the SW is preserved a section of one of the TUBES of Brunel's railway bridge.

SHIPYARD, beside the River Wye to the SE of the town centre. The extensive remains of National Shipyard No. 1, built during the First World War and in operation 1918–25. There survive some of the steel-clad ship-framing SHEDS, and the eight concrete SLIPS on which ships were built and from which they were launched.

WYE VIADUCT, 2 m. S. The M4 (now M48) motorway enters Wales not by the great bridge which spans the River Severn, but over the viaduct crossing the estuary of the River Wye immediately to the W. Both were constructed 1961–6 to the design of *Freeman, Fox & Partners* with *Mott, Hay & Anderson*, using the cable-stayed cantilever construction which the latter had pioneered at George Street Bridge, Newport (*see* p. 448). Masts heightened and stays reinforced in 1982.

PERAMBULATION

Investigation of the town should begin at the historic crossing over the River Wye from England into Wales, where the raw limestone cliffs loom over the fast-flowing river and Rennie's iron bridge contrasts sweetly in its artifice against them. At the foot of BRIDGE STREET, where THE BACK swings away to the l., a variety of houses, of the late C18 in appearance, group irregularly. Several have their pebble-dashed walls lined out in imitation of masonry blocks, a speciality of the town. The first serious piece of architecture, the MUSEUM, soon appears on the l. Built as Gwy House in 1796 for an apothecary, Warren Jane jun. Five bays, two storeys, pebble-dashed and coloured a dark red, so that the semicircular single-storey porch of Bath stone, with coupled Doric columns (surely imitated from Bonomi's at Piercefield Park, p. 472), stands out more boldly perhaps than intended. Pediment over the slightly projecting centre three bays. Windows here in sunk vertical panels. So this is all quite a subtle performance. Single-storey bow round the corner to the r., probably added c. 1830. Large C20 additions at the back. The interior also shows some subtlety. On the central axis a sequence of contrasted spaces, bow-sided outer vestibule, rectangular inner vestibule and bow-backed stairwell, separated from one another by a sequence of segmental arches. Cantilevered stone stair with simple iron balustrade, rising under a small oval dome to an upper landing with another segmental arch. Reticent plasterwork, largely confined to Greek key borders and friezes of upright leaves to some of the ceilings. GWY COURT, behind, is subtly detailed and spatially varied infill housing, partly rendered, partly brick. 1982–3 by the *Holder Mathias Partnership*. ORCHARD CLOSE, entered along Orchard Gardens from LOWER CHURCH STREET, is more of the same, completed in 1989. Next in Bridge Street is the CASTLE VIEW HOTEL. Five unequally spaced bays and a central pediment unrelated to the fenestration below. Clearly an older house was refronted in the C18. The view of the castle from this point is spectacular, and shows how the town developed inland well clear of its walls and ditches. The car park, however well landscaped, inevitably detracts somewhat. Modest TOURIST INFORMATION CENTRE, *c.* 1992 by the *Percy Thomas Partnership*. Next on the l. an interruption, the former CHEPSTOW BOARD SCHOOL, small, single-storeyed but early, 1877, by the local architect *Walter Evill*. Pinkish-grey local limestone with Bath stone dressings. Simple Gothic. The surprising detail is the carved relief with the coronet of the Dukes of Beaufort at the apex of the central gable. Next door, gable-end to the street, CROMWELL HOUSE, perhaps of C16 origin. (Roof with wind-braces, a Chepstow speciality.) Then, Hollins Close Gardens, leading to HOLLINS CLOSE, a further scheme of the 1980s by the *Holder Mathias Partnership*. Quite an extensive housing development dovetailed into the town centre, full of interest in its intricate layout and interplay of materials.

At this point interest transfers to the W side of Bridge Street. First the austere Georgian front of ASHBURNE HOUSE, five bays wide, three storeys high, painted white with black trim. Ionic pilasters frame the central door. Then a charming row of three-storey cottages, Nos. 33A–47, climbs the hill. They must be early

C19, to judge by their single-storey segmental bow windows. These create quite a ripple, as each two-bay cottage has a bow – a few are missing at the upper end. No. 48 is late C18 and much grander, in fact one of the finest fronts in the town. Two storeys, three broad bays. Sashed and pebble-dashed. The lower windows, tripartite under blank semicircular tympana, flank a round-headed doorway crowned by an open pediment on brackets. Narrower upper windows, the central one also under a semicircular tympanum. ST ANNE'S comes next, medieval in origin, of squared limestone blocks, the main part gabled towards the road. Coupled sash windows of the early C19 under C16 hoodmoulds. But the tiny trefoiled window in the gable suggests a pre-C16 origin. This is confirmed by the two-light window in the side wall to the S, the trefoiled lights and flat-topped surround both hollow-chamfered. The building deserves further investigation.

The THOMAS POWIS ALMSHOUSES command the crest at this point, and the view down Bridge Street. A delightfully artless and unspoilt ensemble of 1716, built of roughly squared local limestone. L-plan, one arm of eight bays by two, the other of five bays by two. Uniform, evenly spaced mullion-and-transom cross-windows on both storeys, the heads of the lower ones linked to a continuous cyma-profiled stringcourse. A similar string crowns the façades. Three doorways under triangular pediments on brackets give access to the ranges, where six poor men and six poor women were to be housed, according to the will of Thomas Powis, vintner, late of Enfield, but of course a native of Chepstow. This information is conveyed by an inscription panel set over the doorway in the five-bay range and under a sundial attached rather precariously to the parapet.

In UPPER CHURCH STREET opposite, which leads to St Mary's Church, another set of almshouses, the SIR WALTER MONTAGUE ALMSHOUSES, founded in 1614. Just a low, two-storey range hard up against the street. Early C17 in origin, but the heavy bargeboards to the gables and the heavy labels over the windows present an early C19 appearance.

The main street continues uphill under the name of MIDDLE STREET, but more attractive is the lane beside it, HOCKER HILL STREET, too narrow for vehicles and paved with setts. At its foot on the r. a three-storey C18 house of red brick, lying back coyly so that its full width is impossible to determine. At the top ST MAUR, another regular three-storeyed house, where Nelson stayed in 1802, but surely modernized later in the C19.

So we have reached BEAUFORT SQUARE, the heart of the town, though not a square in the formal sense. On its S side, at the head of ST MARY STREET, is the BEAUFORT ARMS, with a three-storeyed C18 front of five bays plus one with an off-centre entrance. Attached to its r. the stuccoed ASSEMBLY ROOMS (now TSB Bank) of 1807. Symmetrical three-bay front, its upper windows round-headed, the lower openings altered, though the central doorway retains its pairs of Tuscan columns. Narrower three-bay return.

The pivotal feature of Beaufort Square, set on a steep flight of steps, is the FIRST WORLD WAR MEMORIAL, of 1921 by *Eric Francis* of Chepstow. In an C18 idiom, of two tall stages contrasting in design, and crowned by a gadrooned urn. BARCLAYS BANK is its backdrop, looming boxy and overscaled on its island site. 1968–70 by *Merton Jones & Richards* of Abergavenny. In BANK STREET, NW of the war memorial, the ROYAL BRITISH LEGION HEADQUARTERS, a narrow Regency front with segmentally bowed windows on three storeys, a metal canopy over the entrance and a top balcony almost as if it were in Brighton. Behind the bow at the lowest level, parts of two bays of a stone ribbed vault, perhaps of the C14. Higher up in Bank Street, the stone end wall of No. 13, corbelled out at mid-height, may have belonged to a C16 timber-framed front with a jetty. Next door, OLD BELL CHAMBERS has another austere C18 brick front, the brickwork painted over. In HIGH STREET, which climbs the hill beside Bank Street, nothing of special note until at the top the two streets come together to form a small open space in front of the Town Gate (for which *see* p. 183). The GATE HOUSE (Citizens' Advice Bureau) to the l. of the Town Gate, with an anonymous-looking three-storeyed front, rendered and sash-windowed, was built in 1609 by Margaret Cleyton (see her monument in the church, p. 167). The date and Mrs Cleyton's initials are on the lintel of the square-headed entrance doorway. The door surround has ovolo and wave mouldings and part of a framing of linked squares and circles, a typical Jacobean motif.

Through the Town Gate, immediately to the l., the stark Neo-Tudor frontage of the GEORGE HOTEL, 1898 by *Veall & Sant* of Cardiff. Further up, in MOOR STREET, only the Police Station (p. 183) and Methodist Church (p. 168). It is more profitable to turn sharply r. into WELSH STREET. Here are livelier examples of the eclecticism of *c.* 1900. On the l. the KING'S HEAD, its sweepingly arched doorhood flanked by broad, segment-headed windows in concave surrounds. Beyond on the r. CASTLE COURT, presenting a heavily glazed Jacobean-style front towards the road. Three-storey porch between two-storey window bows. At the end of the street on the l., on the corner of MOUNT WAY, comes THE LODGE, datable between 1902 and 1908. This was built as a gate lodge to The Mount, and is a witty, if rather belated, essay in the Norman Shaw style. Stone, tile-hanging and half-timbered gables. THE MOUNT itself stands back above the road, beyond a pair of fine wrought-iron GATES with overthrow. The house, quite plain and faced with Bath stone ashlar, must date from c. 1850. Three bays by three, three storeys crowned by a simple parapet. The entrance front has a projecting single-storey porch between single-storey canted bays.

Thereafter, a string of 1930s houses fringes the E side of the road. The flat-roofed WHITE HOUSE, of *c.* 1935 by *F. R. Bates* of Newport, is a typical but not particularly distinguished representative of Modernity of that moment. Lastly, mention may be made of ST TEWDRIG, Mathern Road, SW of the edge of the town in open country W of the A466. Built in 1849 for a local solicitor, W.E. Toye. Small Italianate country house faced in ashlar stone, with a pyramid-roofed belvedere tower, and characteristic shallow-pitched gables on deep bracketed eaves.

Back at the Town Gate, GARDEN CITY WAY leads beside the Port Wall to the extensive garden suburb, HARDWICK VILLAGE. This was built *c.* 1915–19 for workers in the nearby shipyards by *Dunn, Watson & Curtis Green* in a style stated by Dunn as 'meant to be unaffected of our time', and clearly much indebted to the Parker & Unwin garden suburb model. The closest comparison is with the contemporary LCC estates, for instance at Eltham, designed by Sir Frank Baines. The site is a valley, steeper to the N than the S, and the road layout takes advantage of it. There is a valley-bottom spine, HARDWICK AVENUE, off which rib-like side roads extend, straight and close-set on the steeper side, gently curved on the other. The houses all have concrete block walls, many now rendered over, tiled roofs and stocky red brick ridge-top chimneystacks. They are grouped in terraces of four, with pairs in specially favoured situations, as along PORT WALL ROAD, the topmost of the N roads, and forming open-ended courts along Hardwick Avenue. Each group is symmetrical, but play is made with pairs of gables set close together or far apart, catslide roofs and end projections, to provide constant variety. Originally all this was enhanced by substantial but elegantly detailed timberwork, in window frames and doorway canopies, but all too much has given way to metal or PVC replacement.

Further S, off BULWARK ROAD, is THE BULWARK, more planned housing, centred on THE OCTAGON, at the intersection of Bulwark Avenue and Victoria Road. This, built in 1918–19, was the small beginning of what would have been a veritable garden city, intended for workers in the Chepstow shipyard after it had been taken over by the Admiralty. The architect was an Admiralty employee, *Henry Farmer*, but *H. Avray Tipping* gave aesthetic advice. At THE OCTAGON, the houses have Neo-Georgian overtones, with sash windows and angle pilasters. Elsewhere, as in ALPHA ROAD, which runs straight towards The Bulwarks prehistoric fort (bounding the development at the N), there is less formality.

THE BULWARKS (ST 538 927) is a strong promontory fort on the cliffs above the Wye S of the town. The enclosed area has been eroded, but even so it seems small, considering the strength of the defences around it. These defences consist of a double rampart with an impressively deep ditch between them. The stony ramparts are overgrown, but their scale can be well appreciated on the northern side. The entrance is on the W, and can be approached from the caravan park on the cliff edge.

Beneath a tree in the middle of the Thornwell Farm estate 1½ m. S (ST 539 916) are the remains of a newly recognized COTSWOLD-SEVERN TOMB. A rectangular chamber and antechamber similar to Gaer Llwyd, Newchurch (q.v.), can be seen in the centre of the oval mound. Trial excavation revealed a length of characteristic dry stone walling near its S edge.

CHRISTCHURCH/EGLWYS Y DRINDOD 3080

Barely beyond Newport's suburban sprawl, but the size and the siting of the church on a ridgetop, with a wide view N-wards over the River Usk and Caerleon, suggest its early significance.

HOLY TRINITY. The history of the church is complex and dramatic, and its plan is complicated. Five-bay aisled nave with N and S porches and a grand tower at the W end of the S aisle, chancel with N and S chapels and SE vestry. The walls, of Old Red Sandstone, are all medieval, but after a fire in 1877 *J. P. Seddon* restored the building and after a second fire in 1949 the interior was rebuilt 1953–5 by *G. G. Pace* on the old plan but to a completely new design.

The earliest feature is Norman, the large and handsome S doorway. It has nook-shafts with scallop capitals and beaded imposts. The main order round the arch is decorated with outward-pointing zigzag. In the sanctuary N wall a large lancet and in the E wall the sills of a triplet. So there must have been quite a grand E.E. chancel. The S doorway may have been moved, so is not necessarily evidence that the nave was aisled by the C12. The tower is massive, tall, but unbuttressed. Blocked lancets at the top of the lower stage show that it was started in the C13, and implies an aisled nave by that date. Perp upper stage, of Old Red Sandstone rubble rather than grey local limestone. Small two-light belfry windows with cusped, arched lights. Top corbel table and reconstructed parapet. In an upper chamber of the tower, a fireplace, and from this chamber a squint window into the church. The only Dec contribution is the two-light window, with hood on leaf stops, W of the S porch. Of a Perp remodelling little now remains, other than the N rood stair projection and the porches. Note the ashlar front to the N porch and its blocked two-centred outer arch moulded with continuous wave, hollow and wave. (Original barrel-vaulted porch ceiling.) Pace faithfully reconstructed the five-light E and four-light W window, but simplified those in the aisles and chapels.

Pace's interior uses uniformly white-rendered piers rising without a break into steeply pointed arches. Plastered segmental ceilings, pink in the nave, brown in the aisles. The S chapel, by contrast, has a white transverse plaster ceiling, a barrel framed by two half-barrels, forerunner of the extraordinary plaster vault in Pace's St David's Chapel at Llandaff Cathedral. The only medieval survivals are the stoup by the S doorway and in the S chapel a mutilated piscina with a pretty vault. – FITTINGS. A complete set by *Pace*, 1955–8, illustrating the range of his design in stone, timber and metal. – STAINED GLASS. The triumphant climax of the rebuilt interior is *Harry J. Stammers*'s great E window of 1958, with its sweeps of singing colours. Enthroned Christ among a praising multitude, i.e. a visualization of the Te Deum. – N chapel E, Adoration of the Kings and Shepherds. 1961 by *H. W. Harvey*. – MONUMENT. John and Isabella Colmer †1376

(S chapel). Incised floor slab with worn figures of a civilian and a lady, and a bold inscription round the border.

CHURCH HOUSE. Late medieval L-plan house of two storeys, backing on to the S boundary of the churchyard. The E–W range is largely built of grey local limestone, the cross range largely of mauve Old Red Sandstone. Square-headed windows, the lights arched, some given hoodmoulds with square stops. Many have been restored, or may be C19 insertions. The upper hoodmoulded windows in the S wing, set on a stringcourse, are so close under the eaves as to suggest that the wall-head has been trimmed here. The W and N gable-ends remain largely unaltered. In the W gable two unrestored windows to the l. of the chimney flue and two small blocked lights in the gable, flanking it. In the NE gable-end a small four-centred-headed doorway. This is said to have been for the benefit of the parson, who had the use of a room in the house. Broad, projecting chimney-breast beside it.

THE GREYHOUND HOTEL, opposite Church House. By *E.A. Lansdowne* of Newport, *c.* 1900.

3000

CLYTHA

CLYTHA PARK. Clytha can boast the two outstanding examples of late C18 fanciful Gothic in the county and the finest early C19 Greek Revival house. Gothic was the choice of William Jones of Llanarth (†1805), Greek of his great-nephew and heir, also William Jones (later Herbert). The elder Jones was satisfied with an early C18 house, but after the death of his wife in 1787 set his mind to improving the park with a showy entrance archway and built a huge eye-catcher-cum-banqueting house, Clytha Castle, on the hillside to the S. The old house remained until the younger Jones came of age in 1820, when its successor was begun on a new site. Finishing touches were being put to it in 1828.

The GATEWAY, on the old Abergavenny to Raglan road, under construction in 1797, is the epitome of the C18 idea of Gothic as an airy and unconstrained idiom. Four tall and slender ashlar piers with nook-shafts support pyramidal crocketed pinnacles. Central arch wide and steeply pointed, with crocketed hoodmould soaring up to carry a big foliage finial. Narrower side arches of flattened four-centred profile, under a horizontal cresting of trefoils. Sir Richard Colt Hoare, who saw it when brand new, was led to believe that John Nash had designed the gateway. Prettily detailed Gothic LODGE behind, probably not much later.

The PARK was laid out in 1790 by the Shropshire architect and landscape gardener *John Davenport*. The present drive sweeps through it (not on its original line), presenting as was surely
92 intended a diagonal view of the four-square HOUSE, standing on its low artificial mound. The younger William Jones's architect was *Edward Haycock* of Shrewsbury. His concept was of a completely consistent Greek Doric house, as a preliminary design makes clear; but his client did not concur in such austerity. So

the two show façades, both two-storeyed, of exquisitely cut Bath stone ashlar with sandstone (Grinshill?) dressings, are more strongly contrasted than the architect had intended. A giant four-column Ionic portico with a pediment projects boldly from the centre of the SE, entrance, front. The columns have Erechtheum capitals. One broad bay to l. and to r. Note the slightly later cast-iron and glass storm porch under the portico. The SW front is of seven bays, the centre three set forward slightly. Single-storey Greek Doric columns surround a bow, which rises two-storeyed under a balustrade. The two fronts are unified by the continuation of the plain frieze and cornice of the giant portico, supported at the angles by pilaster-like antae. Plain parapet too, a higher section in the centre of each front. The windows have simple architrave surrounds, except the tripartite ground-floor windows flanking the portico, which are pedimented. Seven-bay NE front, faced with buff render, not ashlar. The NW front was formed after the unfortunate removal in 1957 of the low service wing with conservatory, which formed a counterpoint to the main block of the house.

The interior is entirely Doric, yet spatially varied and lively. Circular ENTRANCE VESTIBULE, ringed with unfluted, baseless 93
Doric columns, of yellow scagliola. They carry a grey marbled entablature, from which springs a very shallow dome. Central plaster rose and radiating ribs, echoing the pattern in the pavement. In the walls, niches alternate with three doors and a fireplace. The extravagantly spacious STAIRCASE HALL, in the centre of the house, is toplit. Conventional cantilevered stone stair rising in straight flights in the square well. Exquisite balustrade, one slender baluster and a pair of bars framing palmettes to each step. Full-blown Greek Doric columns on the upper landings, and matching antae against the solid walls, supporting an entablature with charming palmette cresting. Square lantern with tiny plaster vault, and vertical windows framed by miniature Greek Doric columns. The principal ground-floor rooms all have restrained plasterwork, just ceiling rosettes and borders, of varied acanthus and palmette designs. In the DINING ROOM, in the E angle, there is a full-height servery recess framed by antae. The present LIBRARY, in the S angle, has a white marble chimneypiece with Greek Doric columns and a row of upright acanthus leaves on the lintel. The DRAWING ROOM, which incorporates the bow in the centre of the SW front, has the most elaborate chimneypiece, white marble, its flanking caryatids bearing lamps in their hands and cushions on their heads. Early C18 BACK STAIRS, of timber, brought in from the old house and cut down, so that there are two, not three turned balusters per step. (Upstairs a Rococo plasterwork overdoor depicting a pastoral scene brought in from the demolished Coldbrook Park, Abergavenny.)

In the grounds N of the house a small lake, and an enormous D-plan walled KITCHEN GARDEN. Beyond that a stone GATEWAY, incorporating a depressed-headed arch from a demolished farmhouse, Perthir. The large foliate cross on top must be of the C19.

89 Clytha Castle. On the hillside ½m. sw of the house, William Jones in 1790 built this stupendous folly, Gothic and Geometrical, thereby obtaining magnificently unimpeded views of the shapely mountains to the nw, Skirrid and Sugar Loaf. A tablet on the building, however, records his reason for its erection: 'It was undertaken for the purpose of relieving a mind sincerely afflicted by the loss of a most excellent Wife'.* The plan is an L, the central square two-storeyed block with higher circular stair-turret being the only habitable part. From it screen walls angle back, their parapets swooping up and down in two big concave curves. Drum towers close the composition. Castellation, lancet windows, arrow slits and other happily pre-archaeological Gothic details. Everything big and simple, to read from a distance. Rendered walls and Bath stone dressings. Although long attributed to John Nash, the recently rediscovered building accounts show that it was designed by *John Davenport*.

Capel Aeddan, ⅓m. ne of the house. Just a few heaps of stone in a field. Fragments of Perp windows and doorways have been found, suggesting that the chapel was a simple late medieval building like such nearby churches as Trostre and Kemeys Commander.

Chapel Farm, ⅓m. ne. At first sight the tall mullioned windows, some with transoms, and the shaped bargeboards to the gables suggest an early c19 date. But these are merely improvements to an unusually well-preserved c16 and c17 farmhouse, of two parts, set obliquely to one another. Entry is from the sw through a c17 two-storey porch with inner arch of four-centred form. The range into which this leads is historically of great interest, as it retains a complete cruck truss set into stone side walls at such a height that a semi-attic upper storey is formed. It represents the intermediate stage in the transition from the cruck-trussed open hall to the storeyed house. There was a stair to this upper room in the w gable-end wall. Original c16 timber windows at both levels in the n wall, with diamond mullions. The e range has another such upper window, but otherwise is of the c17, its e wall a c19 reconstruction. Here post-and-panel partitions survive in plenty, creating two rooms and a passage downstairs, three rooms and a lobby upstairs, a layout of unusual privacy.

Great House, ¾m. sw. Late c16 two-unit farmhouse, enlarged in the early c17 by extending the range to make a parlour and room over, and a stair-turret behind backing into the hillside.

At Cwm Farm, ¾m. s of Great House, a fine farmyard complex, with a long barn on the n side, built of Old Red Sandstone rubble.

Whitehouse Farm, ¾m. se. Stone, rendered white, of course. Of two dates. The earlier, s, range was built as a small independent c16 house, to which *c.* 1600 was added at its n end a cross range projecting to the w, and both higher and wider than the original building. This later range retains its original square-headed e doorway and above it the frame of a contemporary

* But, as a contemporary observer noted, she was also 'the female heir of the House of Tredegar, who bestowed on the proprietor a splendid fortune'. D. Williams, *History of Monmouthshire* (1796).

window. In the N wall a six-light upper window with thick diamond mullions survives, and in the W wall a lower four-light window.

Internally much has been lost, but in the earlier part there survive the original N gable-end entrance doorway with arched timber head, and beside it the blocked stone fireplace with chamfered lintel. In the *c.* 1600 range the hearth in the W wall has gone, but the spiral stair in the SW corner beside it rises to the most remarkable feature of the house, a square post-and-panel lined lobby, from which open no fewer than four arch-headed doorways, two to the two stair-flights, two to the two bedchambers.

COEDKERNEW/COEDCERNYW 2080

The little parish church of ALL SAINTS, rebuilt in 1853–4 by *W. G. & E. Habershon*, has been converted into a house.

LG WALES COMPLEX, S of the A48. This enormous industrial estate, developed 1996–8, is mainly remarkable as representing the largest overseas investment (Japanese in this case) ever made in Wales. Unlike its neighbour at Duffryn (*see* p. 219), there is nothing here of architectural consequence.

CRUMLIN/CRYMLYN 2090

Crumlin was celebrated for the unique iron VIADUCT which carried the Newport, Abergavenny and Herefordshire Railway for one-third of a mile at a height of 204 ft (62 metres) across the valley, but was, sadly, demolished in 1965. It consisted of seven spans each 150 ft (46 metres) long, and was built 1853–7, at a cost of £62,000, to the design of the London engineer *T. W. Kennard.* The two masonry piers from which the viaduct sprang, high on the sides of the valley above the modern crossroads, still indicate its breathtaking height and length. Two further piers on the sides of the minor valley to the W for a subsidiary three-arch span.

NAVIGATION COLLIERY, N of Kendon Road. The colliery build- 111
ings, conspicuous in the valley bottom immediately N of the main road junction, were built 1907–11 for Partridge, Jones & Co. Although the colliery closed in 1967, the buildings remain almost intact, the finest group in Wales and an outstanding example of the proud showpieces which Edwardian colliery owners could erect at a time when the South Wales coalfield was being developed into the largest coal-exporting area in the world.

The buildings form a nearly symmetrical group on two terraces along the valley bottom, all of red brick with yellow brick pilaster strips and eaves bands, and further unified by the consistent use of round heads for the windows and other openings. On the lower terrace are two eleven-bay, single-storey buildings at the outer ends of the group. That to the N housed the OFFICES, with oculi in the gable-ends. That to the S was the VENTILATION FAN HOUSE, with gable-end vents. At its N end the Pennant sandstone AIRWAY with yellow brick tunnel vault extracted stale air from the upcast shaft.

On the upper terrace the tall central CHIMNEY dominates. It is of red brick, strongly tapering and of square section, and is flanked by two almost identical WINDING-ENGINE HOUSES, of five bays by three with ventilation clerestories. The steel HEADFRAMES that originally stood beside them, over the tops of the shafts, have unfortunately been demolished, depriving the colliery of its most eloquent features. Other original buildings are the long, narrow WORKSHOPS and STORES, with tall smithy chimneys, and, S of the S engine house, the now roofless LAMP-ROOM. The latter is set on a substantial seven-bay red brick podium with segment-headed windows. Also a POWDER STORE, and at the S end a WATER TOWER. The PITHEAD BATHS, at the N end, are of course later. Red brick, but in the distinctive functional style favoured by the Baths Welfare Committee in the 1930s.

121 HAFODYRYNYS COLLIERY, 1 m. E. The WASHERY building, strictly a 'slimes thickener', is an arresting sight beside the A472. Just a giant concrete cylinder set on short stilts and covered by a shallowly domical concrete cap. The structure is all that survives of a complete Modernist colliery constructed *c.* 1954–8. There were various concrete-framed buildings with brick and glass panels as infill, in an idiom inspired partly by the interwar collieries in Germany of Peter Behrens and others, partly by the Festival of Britain. Washery plants were key elements in post-war efficiency improvements. In the thickener, water was drawn off from the waste slurry, and what remained was concentrated for drying and tipping.

Within a decade, in 1966, the colliery closed, and in 1985 the site was cleared. The thickener remains because the Pontypool Park Estate planned to convert it into a restaurant.*

BETHEL BAPTIST CHURCH, Hafodyrynys Road. Built in 1905. The long entrance side divided into four bays by pilaster strips, with a vestry projecting from the first and a porch from the fourth. Paired round-headed lower windows, and, unusually, bullseyes above.

2090

CWMBRAN/CWMBRÂN

Cwmbran is the only major town established in Wales under the New Towns Act of 1946.‡ The site included the C19 settlements which had sprung up around the tinplate works established at Pontnewydd in 1802 and Pontrhydyrun in 1806, the forges of the Cwmbran Iron Company, and the other later C19 works,

* This entry is based on notes kindly supplied by Dr Peter Wakelin of Cadw.

‡ The expansion of Newtown, Powys, authorized under the Act in 1967, was on a much smaller scale.

including the coalmine at Pontnewydd, wireworks at Oakfield and vitriol works near the site of the present town centre. The site was designated and Cwmbran Development Corporation set up in 1949. A master plan prepared by *Minoprio, Spencely & MacFarlane* was adopted in March 1951 and approved by the Government the following August. The population of the designated area was already 13,000 but was planned to rise to 35,000. There was to be a town centre surrounded by seven residential neighbourhoods, together with schools and a college, the latter never built. House-building started at once and continued steadily until the early 1980s, the target population being successively revised upwards to 45,000, and eventually 55,000. Cwmbran is now the sixth largest town in Wales. Construction of the town centre did not begin in earnest until the 1960s, and was completed in 1977. Wider acceptance of the town was symbolized by the decision in 1963 to site Monmouthshire (subsequently Gwent) County Hall here. The Corporation's Chief Architects were *J. C. P. West*, 1950–62, *Gordon Redfern*, 1962–9, *J. L. Berbiers*, 1969–72, and from 1972 to 1982 *J. L. Russell*, who had been Deputy Chief Architect from 1964. They were responsible for the design of nearly all the new town's buildings. Exceptions are the schools, which were designed by *Monmouthshire County Architect's Department*, several, unfortunately rather insignificant, religious buildings by independent architects, and the County Hall, by *Robert Matthew, Johnson Marshall & Partners*. From 1982 the Corporation disposed of its assets, selling the town centre in 1985. It was finally wound up in 1988.

PRE NEW TOWN BUILDINGS

Old Cwmbran

ST GABRIEL, Commercial Street. A large Dec church, the chancel as high as the nave. Lean-to aisles, W porch. Rock-faced grey Pennant sandstone, and Bath stone dressings. Designed by *F. R. Kempson*. The chancel with S chapel was built in 1907–8, the first two bays of the nave in 1914–15, and the remaining two in the 1950s, when the development of the New Town at last justified the ambition of the original concept. The interior is spacious and stately, under Bodley's inspiration. The effect is achieved by the width of the aisles and the wide spacing of the octagonal nave piers. Chancel vaulted with transverse arches. – CHANCEL SCREEN. Of the 1950s. Full width, with a cove, but greatly simplified from its medieval Devonian models. – FONT. Neo-Norman.

ELIM UNITED CHAPEL, Commercial Street. 1844. Rendered. Modest, with but a single storey of round-headed windows.

Llanyrafon

LLANYRAFON FARM. The principal survivor from the pre-industrial landscape preserved in a grassed enclosure beside the

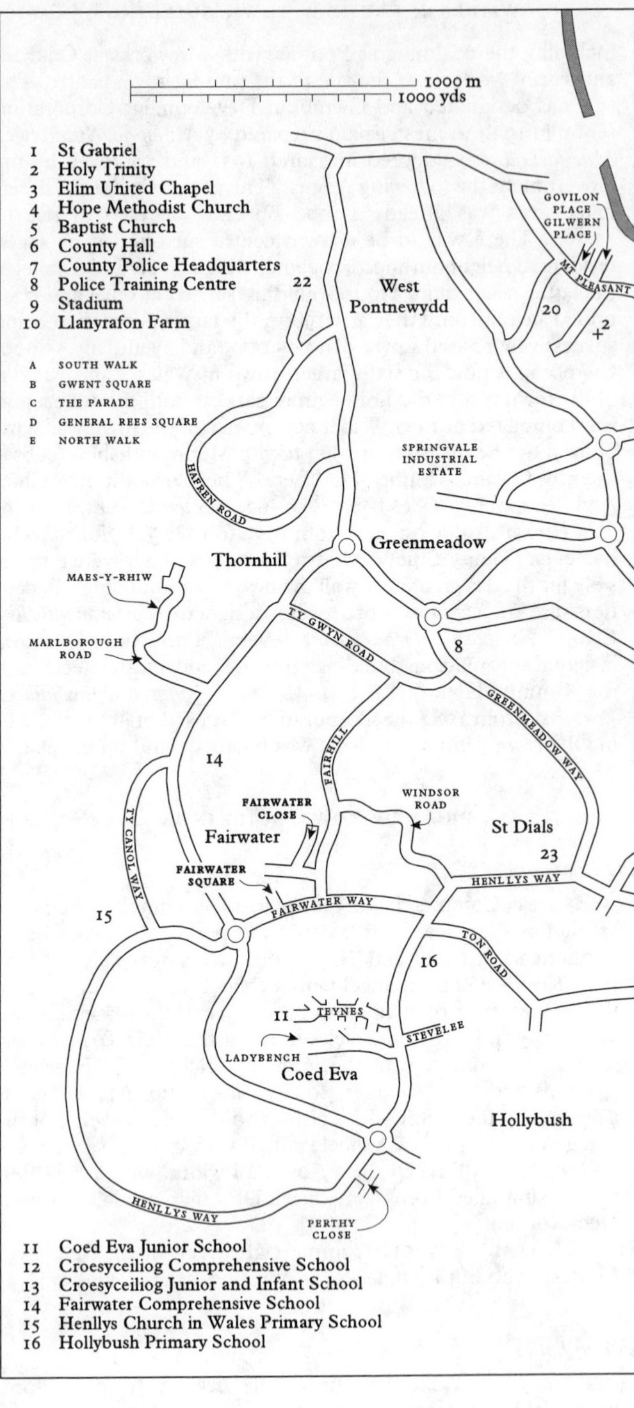
1000 m
1000 yds
1 St Gabriel
2 Holy Trinity
3 Elim United Chapel
4 Hope Methodist Church
5 Baptist Church
6 County Hall
7 County Police Headquarters
8 Police Training Centre
9 Stadium
10 Llanyrafon Farm
A SOUTH WALK
B GWENT SQUARE
C THE PARADE
D GENERAL REES SQUARE
E NORTH WALK
GOVILON PLACE
GILWERN PLACE
MT PLEASANT
22
West Pontnewydd
20
2
SPRINGVALE INDUSTRIAL ESTATE
HAFREN ROAD
Greenmeadow
Thornhill
MAES-Y-RHIW
MARLBOROUGH ROAD
TY GWYN ROAD
8
GREENMEADOW WAY
14
FAIRHILL
WINDSOR ROAD
FAIRWATER CLOSE
TY CANOL WAY
Fairwater
St Dials
23
FAIRWATER SQUARE
HENLLYS WAY
FAIRWATER WAY
15
TON ROAD
16
11
TEYNES
STEVELEE
LADYBENCH
Coed Eva
Hollybush
HENLLYS WAY
PERTHY CLOSE
11 Coed Eva Junior School
12 Croesyceiliog Comprehensive School
13 Croesyceiliog Junior and Infant School
14 Fairwater Comprehensive School
15 Henllys Church in Wales Primary School
16 Hollybush Primary School

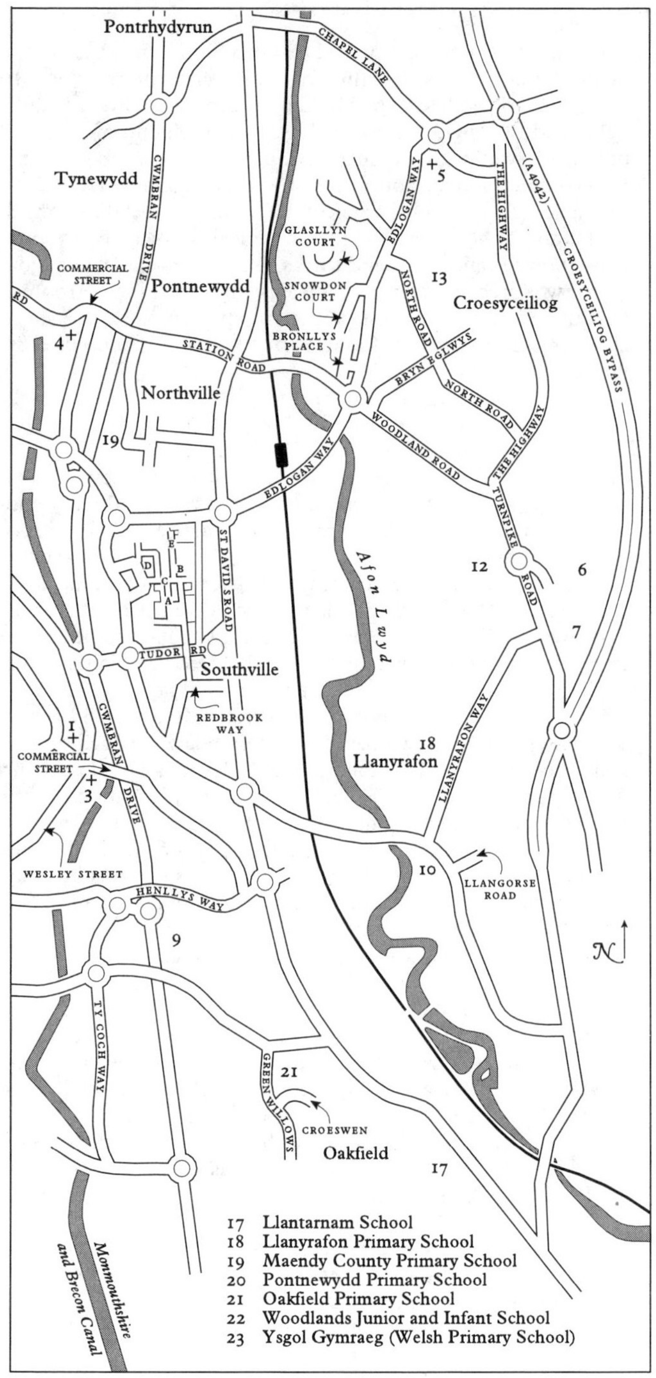

Pontrhydyrun
CHAPEL LANE
Tynewydd
CWMBRAN DRIVE
(A 4042)
EDLOGAN WAY
5
THE HIGHWAY
GLASLLYN COURT
COMMERCIAL STREET
Pontnewydd
SNOWDON COURT
NORTH ROAD
13
Croesyceiliog
CROESYCEILIOG BYPASS
RD
4
STATION ROAD
BRONLLYS PLACE
BRYN EGLWYS
Northville
NORTH ROAD
WOODLAND ROAD
THE HIGHWAY
19
EDLOGAN WAY
ST DAVID'S ROAD
TURNPIKE ROAD
Afon Lwyd
12
6
7
TUDOR RD
Southville
REDBROOK WAY
1
COMMERCIAL STREET
3
CWMBRAN DRIVE
18
Llanyrafon
LLANYRAFON WAY
WESLEY STREET
10
LLANGORSE ROAD
HENLLYS WAY
9
N
TY COCH WAY
GREEN WILLOWS
21
CROESWEN
Oakfield
17
Monmouthshire and Brecon Canal
17 Llantarnam School
18 Llanyrafon Primary School
19 Maendy County Primary School
20 Pontnewydd Primary School
21 Oakfield Primary School
22 Woodlands Junior and Infant School
23 Ysgol Gymraeg (Welsh Primary School)

Cwmbran

Afon Lwyd. The three-storeyed entrance porch near the centre of the S front shows that this was more than a farmhouse. It must date to the late C16. Mullioned stone windows, of three lights and two, light the room above the porch entrance. Inner porch doorway with chamfered, square-headed timber frame. Hall chimneypiece of stone, depressed-headed and double-wave-moulded. (Another similar one in the room above.) The E third of the house, however, is earlier, a typical mid-C16 two-room, two-storeyed range with end stacks. A post-and-panel partition with two arched doorways divides the two lower rooms. Chamfered beams and joists in both rooms. The early C18 staircase was removed to the COMMODORE HOTEL, 200 yds (183 metres) W, *c.* 1892.

Pontnewydd

HOLY TRINITY, Mount Pleasant Road. Built 1858–60 by *Prichard & Seddon*, a characteristic mixture of quirky individuality and scholarly reference to local medieval practice. Nave with S porch and steeple, lower chancel. N aisle added in 1889 by *E.M. Bruce Vaughan*. Polychromy of pale brown local limestone laid in squared and roughly tooled courses, diversified with bands of mauve Old Red Sandstone between strips of Bath stone ashlar. Prominent batter to the base of the walls. Dec detailing, the big E window of three lights, a spurred quatrefoil at its head. Two-light side windows with pointed quatrefoils. The porch bears a slated hipped roof in two tiers with intermediate arcaded timber belfry stage, inspired by medieval steeples as at Rockfield, or Kentchurch, Herefordshire, even if, typically, it is much more steeply profiled than the models. Bruce Vaughan's N aisle, built to match, is not so subtly textured. In the reconstruction of the W wall in 1984 the original window design was lost. Inside, only the wide and steep chancel arch, with continuous wave moulding, speaks strongly. Bruce Vaughan's arcade has clustered piers. The nave roof, with notched scissor braces, seems to be a replacement by *E.A. Lansdowne*, 1870. – CHANCEL SCREEN. Displaced to the W end. An elegant High Victorian piece, the timber arcading filled with a delicate brass armature. – STAINED GLASS. None, unfortunately, contemporary with the church. – Chancel S, St Cecilia, *c.* 1878. Signed by *J. Jennings*. – Chancel E. Crucifixion, 1956 by *G. Maile & Co.* – In the N aisle a miscellany of saints of different dates, the best perhaps the central pair, SS George and Nicholas, 1916, designed by *James Hogan* for *Powell*'s. Also Suffer the Little Children, *c.* 1889, clearly by *Heaton, Butler & Bayne*.

The church was the centrepiece of a group by *Prichard & Seddon*. But the SCHOOL to the NW, with wings added in 1859, has been pulled down, and the VICARAGE of 1860, W of the church, built to a much simpler design than the original richly polychromatic one, has been drastically altered.

HOPE METHODIST CHURCH, Commercial Street. Built for Primitive Methodists in 1866, as an inconspicuous tablet in the gable records. Pennant sandstone dressed with yellow brick, the brickwork renewed in a pinkish grey at the front. Round-headed openings, the central upper pair gathered together with an oculus under a relieving arch.

KING'S HEAD HOTEL, Station Road. 1905 by *Swalwell & Havard* of Newport. Rendered, roughly C17 style front. Strapwork cartouche under the gable enclosing a king's head.

Pontrhydyrun

BAPTIST CHURCH, Chapel Lane. Exceptionally large and noble for its date, 1836. A tall pedimented rectangle, the pediment carried on coupled pilasters (strictly, antae) of Bath stone ashlar. Single pilasters down the sides. Open entrance porch on short Ionic columns. Long, round-headed windows. Interior modernized. At the back a later SABBATH SCHOOL. In the BURIAL GROUND a group of prominent, obelisk-crowned monuments.

Industrial Remains

Little trace remains visible of the industrial past of the area covered by the present town.

The site of PONT-RHYD-Y-RUN TINPLATE WORKS, founded in 1802, lies N of the town on the E bank of the Afon Lwyd (ST 299 973). Some small buildings, early to mid-C19, related to the water-powered forge, surrounded by modern industrial sheds. Also the somewhat altered FORGE BRIDGE, C19, segmental stone-arched span carrying a road over the Afon Lwyd.

CWMBRAN IRONWORKS. The high Pennant sandstone wall W of Forge Hammer Retail Park was built partly to retain the charging-bank of the ironworks and partly as a revetment wall. The works were established in the 1840s by R.J. Blewitt of Llantarnam Abbey.

LLANYRAFON MILL, 1 m. SE of the town centre, where Llanyrafon Way crosses the Afon Lwyd. Of three storeys, rubble-stone, probably largely of the early C19. Low overshot water wheel with curved wrought-iron buckets. Also some internal machinery, in spite of a serious fire in 1971.

The MONMOUTHSHIRE CANAL, constructed 1792–9, runs for 4 m. (6.4 kilometres) through the W side of the town, though some stretches have been in-filled. Three of the arched sandstone OVERBRIDGES also remain, two of them beyond the N edge of the town, where there is also a short canal TUNNEL. Several flights of LOCKS form the most impressive survival. A flight of five, PONTNEWYDD LOCKS, with side ponds, is N of Five Locks Road. CWMBRAN LOCKS, $\frac{1}{4}$ m. S, are ten now gateless chambers, partly altered and in-filled in the 1960s as features in a public park. As the canal passes into open country S of the town, the TY COCH LOCK FLIGHT consists of seven locks, the lowest four with side ponds, with $\frac{1}{4}$ m. further S, LLANTARNAM LOCKS, a further flight of three.

THE NEW TOWN

The town centre stands at the heart of the designated area, to the S of Pontnewydd and to the NE of Old Cwmbran, between the parallel courses of the Afon Lwyd on the E and the Monmouthshire and Brecon Canal on the W. It is entirely pedestrianized, bypassed on the E by St David's Road and on the W by Cwmbran Drive (A4051). Industrial estates extend to the N (Avondale), W (Springvale) and SE (Grange and Court Road) with more (Ty-coch and Llantarnam Park) away to the S. Towards the W the moorland ridges of Mynydd Maen and Mynydd Henllys close the view. The originally intended seven housing neighbourhoods encircling the town centre increased to over a dozen, mainly by extending the built-up area W-wards to the lower slopes of the ridges. However, the principle of keeping housing separate from through roads has been maintained, so that in many places grassy landscaped slopes and patches of woodland enclose the housing. The larger neighbourhoods have their own schools and local shopping and community centres. There are just two major vertical accents. One is the twenty-two-storey tower block immediately S of the town centre, which *Gordon Redfern* conceived as 'a campanile or cathedral spire to serve as a landmark to travellers'. The other is less central and beckoning, the County Hall, rising no higher than seven storeys, and sited on the eastern periphery at Croesyceiliog.

A perambulation of the new town is hardly practical, nor even a guided tour. So, the public buildings of interest will be dealt with first, then the town centre and finally housing and industry.

Principal Public Buildings

COUNTY HALL, Turnpike Road, Croesyceiliog. *Robert Matthew, Johnson Marshall & Partners*' complex, commissioned in 1963, was built 1969–77, so untouched by the new ideas which made the firm's Civic Centre at Hillingdon, London, designed in 1970, so revolutionary. It is in fact typical Modernism of the 1960s, well-proportioned, straightforward, but not particularly memorable. Y-plan administration block. The seven-storey arms of the Y have windows of bronzed glass in broad continuous bands between dark aggregate panels. The second storey is carried across the access road as a bridge, and then becomes the topmost of a three-storey polygonal civic block, where the council chamber is set at a lower level. This latter is stepped towards the S to form a series of creeper-hung balconies.

COUNTY POLICE HEADQUARTERS, alongside. Similar in style, but only of two and three storeys. 1971–7, also by *Robert Matthew, Johnson Marshall & Partners*.

POLICE TRAINING CENTRE, Greenmeadow Way. 1974 by *J. L. Russell*. For cadet training throughout Wales and the West of England. Quite a large U-plan building, varied and informal. Two-storeyed, of purplish-brown brick, the walls articulated by close-set, full-height piers. Monopitch roofs clad with silver corrugated metal. The dining room to the l. has a prominent clerestory and bowed end window. Over the central entrance the roof comes down low like a policeman's helmet.

STADIUM and SPORTS CENTRE, Henllys Way. The stadium, with the only running-track of international standard in Wales, and the long, high GRANDSTAND on its W side were opened in 1967. The boxy, metal-clad SPORTS CENTRE backing on to the latter is of 1972–3, by the *Percy Thomas Partnership*, design partner *Dale Owen*.

SCHOOLS. Schools were the only type of new building within the New Town for which the Development Corporation was not responsible. As elsewhere in the county, they were designed and built by Monmouthshire County Council, one primary school for each neighbourhood and three secondary schools for the town as a whole. All of them stand in spacious playing fields and many are prominently sited, so they represent effectively the County's achievement in post-war school building, and most are mentioned here. Normally the County used its own Architect's Department, but a few were commissioned from private architects.

COED EVA JUNIOR AND INFANT SCHOOL, Teynes. Built *c.* 1964–7 and designed by *Stephen Thomas* of Newport. The central feature is the windowless, grey brick boiler house. Juniors and infants each have a two-storeyed, flat-roofed range with external steel frame. Curtain walling and boarded eaves.

CROESYCEILIOG COMPREHENSIVE SCHOOL, Woodland Road. 1955–9 by *Monmouthshire County Architect's Department*, County Architect *Colin Jones*, job architect *T. E. Moore*. The idiom is typical, caramel brick walling, windows in long bands, and at the rear full-height vertical windows for staircases. Shallow, copper-clad roofs. The grouping, on the other hand, is unusually coherent and eventful. The entrance, marked by a miniature copper spirelet, is into a loose single-storey courtyard, with the wing for adult education on the l., and hall and gymnasium in a range to the r. Beyond are the main elements: a tall, plain, brick clock tower and two long, four-storey classroom ranges running back parallel to one another behind. They are steel-framed. The W range, with brown boarding between the windows, opened in 1957 as the secondary modern school, the E range, with blue panels in curtain walling, in 1959 as the grammar school.

CROESYCEILIOG JUNIOR AND INFANT SCHOOL, North Road. *c.* 1953–6 by *Monmouthshire County Architect's Department*, County Architect *Colin Jones*. A typical group, a series of single-storey classrooms stepping forwards from r. to l., their angles marked by copper-green posts, and a taller hall in the centre at the back. It is best appreciated from above in Brynhyfryd, where the characteristic shallow-pitched green roofs define the layout.

FAIRWATER COMPREHENSIVE SCHOOL, Ty Gwyn Way. 1969–71 by *Monmouthshire County Architect's Department*, County Architect *Sydney Leyshon*. In two parts. To the NE an uncompromisingly rectangular, two-storeyed hall and leisure-centre block, clad in metal sheeting, to the SW a complex of classrooms, mainly single-storeyed and arranged round a series of courts. Something more expansive and outward-looking would have better suited the splendid, high-lying site.

HENLLYS CHURCH IN WALES PRIMARY SCHOOL, Ty Canol Way. By *J. H. Evans & Partners* (design partner *A. Sully*), opened 1991, imitating the 1980s style of *Gwent County Architect's Department*. Deep, pantiled roofs dominate the low brick walls, and rise in the centre pyramidally over the hall. The classrooms clustering on either side form a symmetrical group. Blotched buff brick, with a black mid-height band and dark red window frames.

HOLLYBUSH PRIMARY SCHOOL, Ton Road. Built in 1961 as a secondary modern school, but converted to a primary school in 1972. It has all the hallmarks of *Colin Jones*'s idiom as head of *Monmouthshire County Architect's Department*. Brick tower at one end of the hall block, and three-storeyed classroom range attached at r.-angles.

LLANTARNAM SCHOOL, Llantarnam Road. 1950–4 by *Monmouthshire County Architect's Department*, County Architect *Colin Jones*. The Department's first secondary school, showing their house style crystallizing. On the entrance side, the hall near the centre of the group, the tall, brown brick clock tower at the r. end. At the rear two long classroom blocks in line, one of three storeys, the other of two. Windows in continuous bands. Shallow pitched roofs, their deep eaves carried on brick piers which project at the ends of the blocks. Areas of decorative header bond at significant points. Later additions, after the school had become comprehensive, of 1971, 1973 and 1975 (sports hall).

LLANYRAFON PRIMARY SCHOOL, Llanyrafon Way. Opened in 1957. Another typical example of the work of *Monmouthshire County Architect's Department*, County Architect *Colin Jones*, in the mid 1950s. A long, symmetrical, single-storey range, and a two-storey range in parallel behind.

MAENDY COUNTY PRIMARY SCHOOL, Wayfield Crescent, Northville. 1960–1 by *Richards & Trollope*. In two parts, one single-storeyed in the normal County Council style, the other two-storeyed, curtain-walled.

OAKFIELD PRIMARY SCHOOL, Green Willows. 1955–7 by *Monmouthshire County Architect's Department*, County Architect *Colin Jones*. Grey metal-clad, unlike the Department's normal idiom.

PONTNEWYDD (formerly Mount Pleasant) PRIMARY SCHOOL, Bryn Celyn Road. Opened in 1955, the first primary school in the town. An unusually formal example of the work of the *Monmouthshire County Architect's Department*, County Architect *Colin Jones*, with two-storey ranges forming a double-T plan. Tower at one end. Windows in long bands alternate with vertical boarding. Green, shallow-pitched roofs. Caramel brick.

WOODLANDS JUNIOR AND INFANT SCHOOL, Thornhill Road. Single-storeyed and in-turned round a series of courtyards, so that it ignores the far-stretching view over the town. Buff brick, metal roofs, including several monopitch outcrops. Built *c.* 1975–7, designed by *Gwent County Architect's Department.*

Ysgol Gymraeg (Welsh Primary School), Henllys Way, St Dials. 1960–1 by *Monmouthshire County Architect's Department*, County Architect *Colin Jones*. Small, single-storeyed but evolved beyond the Department's normal early style. So the roofs are flat and the lighting includes clerestory windows. But the short, brown brick tower is familiar, and the way the eaves come forward on end piers.

Town Centre

J. C. P. West made a design for a covered, pedestrianized shopping centre in 1953, an advanced concept for its time. But by the time work was ready to begin *Gordon Redfern* had taken over as Chief Architect, and as built 1963–77 the town centre embodies his ideas. He retained the principle that the centre should be accessible only on foot, with multi-storey car parks tucked in at the side, where the sloping site allowed them. But he did not provide covered walkways. Coverings were belatedly added in 1986 by *Hildebrand & Glicker*. So there is a sharp contrast between their brightly coloured metal canopies and the many-textured concrete of Redfern's buildings.

The town centre can be explored from s to n. At the s-most extremity, across Tudor Road, all that was built of a proposed Civic Centre, the Magistrates' Court, by *F. R. Bates, Son & Price*, and Police Station, by *Monmouthshire County Architect's Department*, two uncommunicative cubic blocks. The town centre proper has as its major accent at the s end Monmouth House, a seven-storey block built 1965–7. 123
Powerfully projecting s stair-tower, its end wall boldly textured with striation, disc and nailhead. The large sunken water garden to the s, with board-marked concrete retaining walls, is quite a period piece, though the landscaping is somewhat overgrown thirty years on. Monmouth Walk is covered by a yellow and blue segmental space-frame roof. Here is a bronze fountain, Mother and Child, with horizontally streaming hair. By *Theo Crosby* and *Polly Hope*, erected in 1982, a copy of their fountain in Hyde Park.

From here South Walk extends n-wards under a sloping glazed roof. It leads to the central space, Gwent Square. The e side of the square is occupied by Gwent House, 1969–73, an eight-storey slab by *Richard Sheppard, Robson & Partners*, with corrugated concrete panels between the window bands. The projecting lift shaft interrupts them. The centrepiece of the n side is the Congress Theatre, opened 1972, a windowless concrete box against which a gilt clock face and polychrome relief of a Welsh shepherd and his wife are set effectively. Simple upstairs theatre with raked seating for 315. To the w, David Evans's store, 1964. Mosaic-clad columns form a covered walk with above an upper storey faced with close-set metal fins. The way the building projects into the corner of the square is a deliberate piece of picturesque asymmetry. Beside it, THE PARADE, lined with shops in two storeys, the upper galleried, and more space-frame roofs. At the far end a spiral concrete ramp enclosing an abstract sculpture painted black, Family Group, by *David Horn*, set up in 1965. At this point vehicles can gain access, in GENERAL REES SQUARE, where the alien presence of GENERAL REES HOUSE is all too prominent. Virulent green glass-reinforced plastic and green tinted glass. Misshapen pedimental feature over the central porch. All a recladding by *Robertson Francis Partnership* in 1990 of a four-storey Electricity Board block of 1959. THE STRAND, N of General Rees Square, is another covered passage with shops. Large blue and white tile mural of wildlife 'designed and executed' by *Polly Hope*, 1983–4. Further E, the N end of the town centre has, in NORTH WALK, undemonstrative terraces of shops, the only part of *West*'s scheme to be carried out, 1956–9, and a later roof of glazed pyramids.

Housing

The housing that is interesting in architectural and planning terms was all built for the Development Corporation, setting standards for elsewhere in Wales, as indeed for the private housing increasingly permitted at Cwmbran itself. The most instructive way to explore it is not topographically but chronologically.

Minoprio, Spencely & MacFarlane built TYNEWYDD, N of Pontnewydd, 1950–2, a small, simple layout of white-rendered terraces still reminiscent of interwar garden villages. *J. C. P. West*, the Development Corporation's first architect, assisted by *Miall Rhys-Davies*, worked in six areas, in all of which building began during the period 1951–3. In those early years, when cars were still something of a luxury, it was possible to lay out neighbourhoods with little provision for off-street parking. Subsequent addition of car-parking spaces destroyed a good deal of the originally generous landscaping. West favoured spine roads with culs-de-sac opening off them. NORTHVILLE, N of the town centre, is his densest layout, where the plain, brown brick terraces with shallow pitched roofs seem uncomfortably closely stacked. SOUTHVILLE, S of the town centre, is similar but a little less dense. The first of the larger, outlying neighbourhoods to be started was WEST PONTNEWYDD, to the NW. The houses, in informal terraces, are set back behind generous verges and front gardens. The only slightly later OAKFIELD to the SE shows increasing variety of design. Note the porches with unobtrusive brick patterns. Oakfield has the earliest neighbourhood shops, opened in 1954, a staggered, single-storey row off CROESWEN.

To the E of the Afon Lwyd *West* laid out LLANYRAFON and, on the more pronouncedly sloping ground to the N, CROESYCEILIOG. Both are built up of short, two-storeyed terraces, in a mixture of pink, caramel and chocolate brick and pebbledash. Croesyceiliog is the more visually interesting, as many of the terraces are staggered and there are other attempts at variety, such as the canted pairs along NORTH ROAD and BRYN EGLWYS. Both have local shopping centres, Croesyceiliog off THE HIGHWAY, Llanyrafon in LLANGORSE ROAD. West insisted that they should be confined to single and two-storeyed units, for the sake of 'the intimate and cosy atmosphere we are trying to create'.

By the time *Gordon Redfern* took over in 1962 car ownership had to be taken seriously. He favoured the segregation of traffic from pedestrians, by making the housing accessible only from footpaths, and providing separate courts for garages and parking spaces, in accordance with the Radburn system developed in the United States. This system is most thoroughly pursued to the SW of the town, above all in FAIRWATER, 1963–6, N and S of FAIRWATER WAY. The housing off WINDSOR ROAD shows it at its most rigid. *Redfern*'s houses are built with monopitch roofs, loadbearing cross walls of buff or mushroom-coloured brick, some with weatherboarding front and back, but large windows only at the back. The model for this idiom must be Eric Lyons's South London estates for Span. To the W of FAIRHILL, in TON ROAD and FAIRWATER CLOSE, terraces under continuous roofslopes, after the tradition of terraces in the mining valleys. In COED EVA, further SW, several smaller groups in the Span idiom, less dogmatically planned, TEYNES and LADYBENCH, for example, W of HENLLYS WAY, and STEVELEE, E of it. The flat-roofed terraces further N, to the E of FAIRHILL, built in the mid 1960s, were designed not by Redfern but by *Alex Gordon & Partners*. The Fairwater SHOPPING CENTRE, in FAIRWATER SQUARE, is *Redfern*'s most flamboyant gesture in this area. Pink brick party walls are carried up far above the shop roofs. THE TOWER, 1965–7, his twenty-two-storey tower block of flats in REDBROOK WAY, Southville, is in a class of its own. It not only acts as a marker for the town centre but masks the chimney of the central boiler house, which heats the town centre and discharges its fumes 220 ft (67 metres) above the ground.

During *J. L. Berbiers*'s time the only major neighbourhood to be begun was HOLLYBUSH, on the southern perimeter of the town. This, designed by *J. L. Russell* as Deputy Chief Architect, was under construction from 1971 for over a decade. Here the housing is more varied, in terraces straight, staggered and canted, pairs and even a few detached houses. In the brickwork subtle effects of colour and texture are achieved, and tile-hanging makes an appearance. Most important is a new rapprochement with the car. Garages in isolated courts are abandoned in favour of parking spaces, at a ratio of up to two per house, in front of, or close to houses. Houses are grouped in loose, open-ended, landscaped courts, each with its own sense of identity, but allowing pedestrians to walk through to adjacent courts. These ideas are expressed with particular clarity in *J. L.* 124
Russell's little redevelopment scheme of GILWERN PLACE and GOVILON PLACE off MOUNT PLEASANT, Pontnewydd, of *c.* 1976–7. The largest and most free-flowing group is PERTHY

CLOSE, Hollybush. An equally clear exposition of *Russell*'s philosophy is provided in Croesyceiliog, where SNOWDON COURT and GLASLLYN COURT off EDLOGAN WAY combine Corporation housing with old people's accommodation funded by the Local Authority, and in every group a house designed for a disabled occupant. The more demonstrative and sculptural style gaining general popularity in the 1970s is represented by the little development at BRONLLYS PLACE in Croesyceiliog, by *J. L. Russell*, intended as student housing when the University of Wales Institute of Science and Technology was expected to move from Cardiff to Cwmbran, and completed in 1977. Here two-storey and three-storey staggered terraces of flats have full-height polygonal stair-turrets in front and balconies at the rear, all faced in a strongly coloured brownish-red brick.

From 1975 onwards the main direction for further expansion lay to the W, at THORNHILL, where the ground rises much more steeply. A particularly successful group here is MAES-Y-RHIW, at the top of MARLBOROUGH ROAD, 1974–7 by *Diamond, Redfern & Partners*. The white-rendered, staggered terraces make continually varied play with steeply pitched roofs, projecting monopitch porches, and garages in single-storey links, or projecting from house-fronts. Further N, the culs-de-sac off HAFREN ROAD play similar games, but with less conviction. Brown brick, and some tile-hanging.

TALIESIN, Forgeside. By *MacCormac Jamieson Prichard*, completed in 1985. A lively footnote to their great scheme at Duffryn, but quite unlike anything else at Cwmbran. Fifty-seven flatlets and a warden's house, tucked in between two major roads, are arranged in three open-ended courts giving glimpses of the hills to the W. Varied materials; russet brick and white render for the walls, grey metal cladding of the external staircases and blue, black-trimmed sheeting on the top storeys and monopitch roofs. The courts start single-storeyed at their open ends and rise by whole and half steps to crowning pavilions four storeys up. Eccentric runs of white-framed windows. A sequence of square-headed openings gives access through the ranges for pedestrians. At the back, car parking under blue canopies like circumflex accents. Altogether a brilliant and memorable little scheme, a miniature reworking of ideas from Ralph Erskine's Byker Wall, Newcastle.

Industry

Until 1958 no new industry was allowed within Cwmbran, and throughout the 1960s it was discouraged, on the grounds that there were plenty of jobs available in existing factories in the town, or nearby at British Nylon Spinners and Llanwern steelworks, and that new industry should be directed further up the Valleys, where the need for employment was much more acute.

From *c.* 1970, when the Corporation at last obtained freedom to develop its own policy, it began to build factory and workshop units speculatively for rent. The first group of these ADVANCE FACTORIES was built in 1971 in SPRINGVALE INDUSTRIAL ESTATE, to *J. L. Russell*'s design. They wear a uniform of dark green corrugated steel cladding. Sawtooth N roof lighting. A second group is in LLANTARNAM INDUSTRIAL ESTATE, 1981, also by *Russell*. Buff brick and brown steel cladding. Here a few curves and quirks lighten the mood, as do grassy mounding and trees.

More substantial, purpose-built factories are sited along TY COCH WAY. Two in particular impress. ALFA-LAVAL, W of the road, is of 1973 by the *Percy Thomas Partnership*, design partner *Keith Mainstone*. It adopts the international idiom of technological industry, smooth, tidy and enigmatic. Large, rectangular, white-clad factory, and at r.-angles to it a curtain-walled administration range. GEC–MARCONI, E of the road, was completed in 1983 for Ferranti, to the design of *J. L. Russell*, newly retired from the Corporation. As one would expect, this is much more in keeping with the town's architecture. Red brick range subdivided by full-height piers, alternately single and doubled. Glazed, convex centre to the N end. The building is only one-third of what was originally intended.

CWMCARVAN/CWMCARFAN *4000*

ST CATWG. Apparently a Perp church, situated on a hillock looking across to higher wooded ridges to S and E. The austerely impressive W tower lives up to its site. Of grey ashlar, unbuttressed, plinth and three stages demarcated by boldly projecting strings. Two-light, pointed-headed belfry windows. Tapering NE stair-turret. Battlements. Datable *c.* 1525 by the evidence of a will. Nave, N and S porches and small lower chancel all of Old Red Sandstone rubble. The nave has two square-headed S windows with cinquefoiled lights, the S porch a two-centred arch with shafted imposts and deep hollow moulding. Four-centred S doorway. Chancel windows all small and debased two-lighters, reinstated by *Prichard*, who rebuilt the chancel in 1872. Three-light nave N window of 1879. But in origin the church is pre-Perp, as the trefoil-headed lancet in the nave N wall shows. Its late C13 or early C14 date is confirmed inside by the tower arch, of two orders with sunk waves, the inner one dying into the imposts, and the chancel arch, similar in form but plainly chamfered. Furthermore, the internal batter of the nave walls is an early sign. And what is one to make of the blocked S doorway in the nave? Renewed, but possibly evidence of Norman beginnings. Nave roof of typical late medieval form, a ribbed barrel vault, on moulded wall-plates. Plaster between the ribs painted blue. – FONT. Octagonal, with unusual stepped profile. Of the C15? – TOWER SCREEN. Made up of Jacobean arcaded panels. – ALTAR RAILS, CHOIR STALLS and stone PULPIT. All must belong to *Prichard*'s restoration.

In the CHURCHYARD the unusually impressive substructure for a CROSS, five steps and a base converted by bulbous stops from octagonal to square.

PENTRE WHEELER, 1 m. SW. Small and naively symmetrical farmhouse front, of historical value for the boldly centralized date, 1683, a time when symmetry for a complete façade was not yet taken for granted by the farmers of Monmouthshire. Three bays, two storeys under a pitched roof, with chimney-breasts projecting from the gable-ends. Small timber mullioned windows, of three lights below, two above. (Inside, a post-and-panel partition and full-height staircase with turned newels and balusters.)

HIGH GLANAU, 2 m. E. The house was built in 1922–3 by *Eric Francis* for H. Avray Tipping to retire to from Mounton House (*see* p. 412). As at Mounton, Tipping had already begun on the garden, clearing glades within the hillside woodland and exposing boulders. The house is set above stone-walled terraces and axially sited octagonal pond, and has its own formality. On the upper, entrance side a broad slated roof slopes down, punctuated by a pair of gabled turrets, one slate-hung for the porch, the other of random stone for the stairs. Towards the garden and the view, the two-storeyed front is centred on a trio of slate-hung gables, framed by a pair of chimneystacks. Inside, as Tipping noted, there is 'A cottage plan, but considerable amplitude'. So the porch provides the traditional vernacular 'lobby entry', and the spacious central living room is set between parlour and kitchen. (The living room has walls of exposed Hollington stone, and a massively beamed ceiling with ribbed plasterwork in the fields. Plaster ceiling in a contrasting, lozengy pattern in the parlour.)

To the NE, GLANAU LODGE, also by *Francis*, built as the gardener's cottage, also with slate-hung upper walls. Further SE, GLANAU COTTAGES, built by *Francis* for Tipping's 'farmery'. Orange pantiled roofs, triple gables and twin framing stacks. Older barn and farmyard behind.

2020

CWMYOY/CWM-IAU

The parish of the Vale of Ewyas and its steep enclosing scarps. Llanthony Priory (*see* p. 340) occupies the valley floor, while the parish church and isolated farmsteads cling to the hillsides here and there. For outlying parts of the parish towards the W, *see* Bwlch Trewyn (p. 135) and Ffwthog (p. 227).

ST MARTIN. On a steep slope, the tower tipping towards the hill, the chancel tipping away from it, the nave between roughly upright. The church was the victim many centuries ago of movement in the Old Red Sandstone and marl on which it stands, as the two stiffly vertical C18 farmhouses close by suggest. *J. James Spencer*'s restoration of 1889 did not try to set the church straight. The earliest evidence is in the nave, one round-headed N window of the C12. Lancets in the chancel, plain S, trefoil-headed N, and an ogee-headed cusped E pair, of the C13 and C14. In the nave S wall a pair of trefoil-headed lancets and a square-headed C16 window of three arched lights. S porch, presumably medieval, without dressed stone. The tower is also impossible to date, its windows no more than single rectangular lights, open to the nave by an arch little bigger than a doorway. The happily unself-conscious interior is dominated by the nave roof, dated by the Royal Commission to the late C13 or early C14. Single-framed rafter roof in five cants, continued down with wall-posts built into the thickness of the walls. Massive tie-beams moulded with hollow, step and ovolo. Chancel up four steps. Pointed chancel arch constructed without dressed stones. All the windows here rebated for shutters. – COMMUNION RAIL. Late C17. Finely turned balusters. Ball finials. – FONT. Norman tub, egg-shaped with roll lip. – SCULPTURE. Medieval stone cross bearing the crucified Christ. Poignant, if quite crudely carved and thus hard to date. – In the porch inset plaster panels, C17. One large square one bearing a scrolly cross among a miscellany of cast motifs, and four smaller discs with stylized flowers. – MONUMENTS. Late C17 to early C19 tablets, a display of rustic zest. The earliest (chancel), dated 1682, bears the following verse (written as prose): Thomas Price he takes his nap in our common mother lap waiting to heare the bridegroome say awake my dear and come a way. – There are tablets signed by all three generations of the *Brutes* of Llanbedr, Powys. The most enjoyable are in the sanctuary: William Griffits †1774, signed *Aaron Brute*. – James Prosser †1775, signed *J. Brute*, an exceptionally colourful Rococo piece with angels in flight, flower drops and scrolls. – *A. Duke* and *John Prichard* of Clodoch sign other tablets. – Elizabeth Williams †1822. Signed *Thomas Roberts*. More sombre than the others, in the early C19 mood, with a relief of a sarcophagus, bones threaded through its ring handles.

The typical CHURCHYARD CROSS: four steps, base with big broaches and part of the shaft.

At HENLLAN, 2 m. NW, a simple little BAPTIST CHAPEL of 1865, built at the corner of a farmyard.

LLWYNCELYN, at Stanton, 1½ m. SE. A fine farm group as seen 55
from the S, the gable-end of a barn below, the farmhouse above. But the house is something quite exceptional, a complete late medieval hall house, with parlour wing, all of stone. The two gable-ended ranges form an L, the hall range extending downhill, the parlour set across its upper end. (Inside, smoke blackening of the roofs shows that both hall and parlour were originally open full height. Both roofs of arch-braced collar beam type, with wind-braces. At the lower end of the hall the screen to the passage was originally an aisle-truss, a feature more characteristic of North Wales. Two ogee-arched, tracery-headed doorways open into a pair of service rooms beyond. At the upper end of the hall traces of the high-table bench and doorways into the parlour and another service room. The hall and parlour fireplaces are later insertions, as is the floor creating two storeys throughout.)

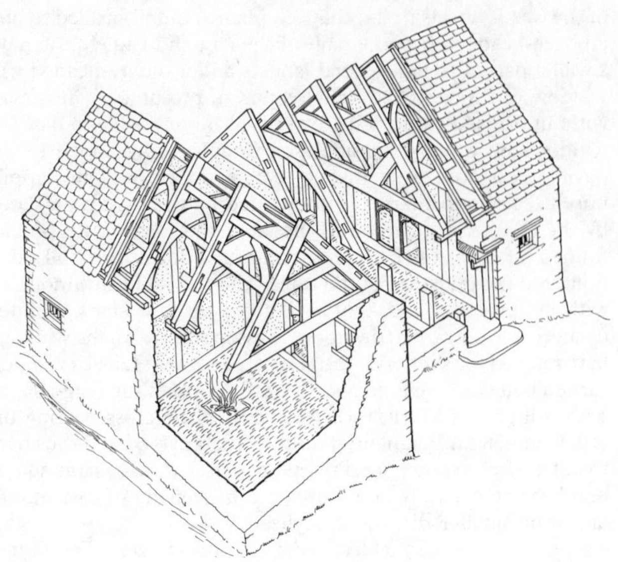

Cwmyoy, Llwyncelyn. Cutaway

LITTLE LLWYGY, 1¾ m. SE. High up and lonely on the hillside. The house consists of two disparate parts, the earlier a one-room, stone-walled, early C16 dwelling, now converted to an outhouse, the later an early C17 addition at the uphill (SE) end, of one-room plan but two-storeyed with habitable roof space. The early house was entered by a doorway (later masked by an oven) in the downhill (NW) end wall, lit by a long, low timber window with diamond mullions in each long wall. Both windows survive, the NE one altered. Splendid stone fireplace against the SW wall, its crudely rectangular opening hollow-chamfered. Later in the C16 a half-loft seems to have been constructed across the NW half of the room, and the partly surviving cruck trusses of the room seem to belong with it. Later doorway in the NE side wall.

The uphill part, of two and a half storeys, is gabled in all four directions, so that the NW gable faces over the original house. The SE gable is dislocated to provide room for a chimneystack and full-height spiral stair. Characteristic NE elevation, windows at three levels, four-light, two-light, one-light, off-centre to the gable, chimneystack at the gable apex. Inside, the stair has a shaped door-head at the top of the first flight. Contemporary three-bay BARN across the yard.

TREFEDW, 2½ m. SE. The C16 and C17 farmhouse and outbuildings have been much altered, but a fine, unaltered BARN, probably of the C17, stands by the roadside. Five bays. Two further uphill bays for cartsheds with a hay loft above reached by an external flight of stone steps. Magnificent, if decayed, original door to the threshing bay, with enormous, fleur-de-lys-ended iron straps. Queenpost roof. Only the corrugated iron roof covering spoils the effect.

TY-HWNT-Y-BWLCH, ¾ m. NE. A lonely farmstead on a hillside which one would think too steep to make a practical site for building. The farmhouse is C16 and C17, of longhouse plan. The little stable beside it is probably C19, the four-bay barn with queenpost roof is dated 1720. The neat calligraphy of the datestone suggests a pride of possession which could be felt even up here in mountainside isolation. Inside the house, the hall partitions survive at the dais end and to the cross-passage, where a doorway is carved with animals, leaves etc., another sign of joy in life up here.

CWM BWCHEL, 3½ m. NW. Another inaccessible farmstead, tucked into a wooded combe overlooking Llanthony Abbey. Fox and Raglan found part of a cruck truss, but the farmhouse consists of a range built in two stages, the second consisting of cross-passage and parlour block added behind the hall fireplace gable in the normal way. Detached kitchen opposite the parlour end. The timber entrance doorway into the house is quite a showpiece. Square-headed, architrave-moulded frame, surmounted by a beam carved to look like voussoir blocks, side brackets. Shaped door-head of unusually lively profile providing space p. 38
for the owner's initials and the date 1694.

GARN WEN (SO 280 255). A prehistoric cairn much tampered with in recent centuries. The high, narrow upper part is modern, but it has been built on the remains of a much larger Bronze Age cairn. SW of this conspicuous monument there are a number of small set stones which may form a pattern of circles or cairn kerbs and alignments. However, the naturally stony nature of the ground makes it difficult to identify artificial structures with complete confidence.

DEVAUDEN

4090

ST JAMES. Built in 1815 as a school. The low, polygonal chancel was added in 1838.*

TREDEAN, ½ m. W. A large and ambitious house in a loose, Voyseyesque style, of 1902–4 by *A. Jessop Hardwick* of Kingston-on-Thames for H. J. Simpson. White, roughcast walls and a good deal of half-timbering. The house, built as a shooting lodge, is hidden deep in woodland, but its existence is signalled on the main road by a pert half-timbered LODGE.

DINGESTOW/LLANDDINGAD

4010

ST DINGAT. Tower of 1846 by *T. H. Wyatt*. Nave with timber S porch and lower chancel all drastically restored and N transept added in 1887–8 by *Richard Creed* on the basis of plans by *Ewan*

* Information from Alan Brooks.

Christian. The S wall was rebuilt, but the late medieval arrangements for lighting the rood loft were replicated. New N windows were inserted in the nave, and inside, the chancel arch was renewed. The three-light N window of the transept is a fine Geometrical design presumably Christian's. – STAINED GLASS. Chancel E probably *c*. 1860. Roundels of the Lamb surrounded by symbols of the Four Evangelists. – MONUMENTS. Sir John Bernard Bosanquet †1847. Ambitious standing wall monument set under a shafted Gothic arch. A seated figure of Faith comforts a grieving woman who has collapsed across her lap. Signed by *Joseph Edwards* and dated 1853. – The inscription dilating on the virtues of Sir John's father, Samuel Bosanquet †1806, on the wall opposite, is worth reading.

In the CHURCHYARD three steps and the broached base for a CROSS.

CASTLE, NW of the church. Substantial convex grassy platform, roughly square, and traces of a bailey. The timber buildings here were burnt by the Welsh in 1182. Perhaps subsequently rebuilt in stone, though no trace of stonework is visible now.

MOTTE-AND-BAILEY, ¼m. E. On steep ground in Mill Wood, accessible from the bridleway.

DINGESTOW COURT. One of the county's major houses, with an unusually complicated building history. The gatehouse range contains the most readily recognizable elements of a house of the Jones family built *c*. 1600. The house itself was rebuilt by James Duberley in the later C18, and acquired in 1801 by Samuel Bosanquet of Epping, Essex, as a summer residence. His grandson, also Samuel, in the mid C19 entertained ambitious schemes for rebuilding on a grander scale, but they were only partly realized. In 1845–6 *Lewis Vulliamy* added a new Elizabethan-style S front. In 1859 *Prichard & Seddon* prepared designs for a much more rhetorical Elizabethan N front with soaring porch tower. They managed to build only a small SW extension to the house and the charming stable court. All that came of their abortive N front design was a two-storey N porch added *c*. 1870 by *Lawrence & Goodman* of Newport. Also by *Lawrence & Goodman* the single-storeyed Perp E wing of 1877. Interior remodelling of 1888 by *Richard Creed*. Utilitarian NE kitchen wing of 1927.

The first view of the house from the N reveals all too clearly the incompleteness of the C19 schemes. The C18 three-storeyed, white-rendered N front remains, of seven bays, the first and seventh breaking slightly forward. Segment-headed sash windows. In stark contrast the mid-Victorian central porch, of rock-faced stone, with three-light Perp upper window and overscaled top balustrade. To the W the GATEHOUSE RANGE comes forward at r.-angles. This is also a composite of several dates, rendered, the archway signalled by the late C19 stepped gable of stone above it. The W side of the range is much more eloquent, in fact the complete gatehouse of *c*. 1600 survives. Wide and high segmental arch, four-light mullion-and-transom window over, and three-light window in the gable. Sunk chamfer mouldings throughout, suggesting the date. Moulded strings demarcate the storeys. Traces of further early C17 fabric at the W end of the house, suggesting that the relationship of gatehouse and house, at r.-angles to one another, is now as it has always been. (For the stable court, *see* below.)

Vulliamy's S front must be considered next. Though of local stone, it is a close copy of an Elizabethan brick house, Franks at Horton Kirby in Kent. This was Samuel Bosanquet's idea; a sketchbook survives in which he drew the façades of several Elizabethan houses in south-east England which took his fancy. Sober gabled composition with large mullion-and-transom windows, those in the outer bays in two-storeyed canted projections, the columned and pedimented entrance unemphasized as it is off-centre. Recessed middle bay without a gable. Tall chimneystacks in strikingly asymmetrical groups, and a central pair of singletons, not copied from Franks. Short W extension by *Prichard & Seddon*, 1859, and lying back further W a fragment of the *c.* 1600 house, much altered.

The interior retains four significant C19 rooms. The HALL in the centre of the N front looks like a characteristic, spatially varied, late C19 hall-cum-dining room as popularized by Norman Shaw; it was given its present form by *Creed* in 1888. Heavily beamed ceiling, handsome C18 staircase, with twisted balusters and ramped handrail, rising from the W end under a decorated skylight far above. The chimneypiece is an extraordinary mélange of disparate woodwork, twisted side columns, top frieze dated 1593, the tracery of a Perp rood screen, and a good deal else. However, in Samuel Bosanquet's sketchbook of *c.* 1845 an idea for such a chimneypiece with twisted columns is drawn out, and the staircase was in its present position by 1859, so Creed did not start from scratch. The DRAWING ROOM in the SE corner is a period piece of the 1840s. Fitted as a library with pilastered bookcases all round, but made decorative by the Frenchy red mottled marble chimneypiece and the Jacobean-style ceiling. Moulded timber beams form squares, each enclosing a deep central plaster pendant and corner fleurs-de-lys. Next door, the ANTE-ROOM, also of *c.* 1845–6. Curvaceous white marble chimneypiece, and remarkably well preserved original wallpaper, with fretwork borders and naturalistic flower sprays. The third room in the S range is the DINING ROOM, enlarged by *Prichard & Seddon* and provided by them with a thin-ribbed plaster ceiling, said to be copied from a C17 ceiling in an inn at Monmouth.

The STABLE COURT, 1859–60, is *Prichard & Seddon*'s most significant contribution to Dingestow. Towards the stable court the gatehouse range is extended N-wards with a pair of coach-houses and a pretty external timber stair carried on a flying buttress. Closing the court to the N is a charming single-storey range with stone dormers, symmetrical except for the assertively off-centre stone chimneystack on the roof ridge, imitated from the famous C14 stack at Grosmont Castle (q.v.). At its W end, another low stable range comes forward, ending in a broad, half-timbered hay-loft gable.

The farmhouses of Dingestow are of exceptional interest, and include four which retain the earliest form of timber-framing in the county, cruck-truss construction, of the late C15 or C16.

LOWER LLANTROTHY, 1 m. N. The long, low, storey-and-a-half farmhouse range, though much altered, contains in the roof space the upper parts of three readily visible cruck trusses. There may originally have been as many as six. The barn across the yard to the S reuses two other crucks in an otherwise box-frame construction, of which the E end wall survives. The fragment of a cruck-framed building set cornerwise to the SE of the house, which Fox and Raglan interpreted as the remains of a detached kitchen, has been pulled down. So the whole, probably C16, farmstead was originally of cruck construction.

LOWER TAL-Y-FAN, 1¼ m. SW. A zany-looking group from the N, kinking obliquely part-way along. The earliest part, however, is the S half, single-storeyed with dormers low in the roof. Fox and Raglan found parts of three cruck trusses of what was probably a three-unit timber-framed hall house of the late C15 or early C16. The stone encasing walls are probably a century or so later, about the time the house was aggrandized and extended N-wards. Several timber windows, of four and three lights with sunk chamfers in the encasement and the extension belong to this period. The most impressive feature, however, is the two-storey porch projecting from the W side of the addition. S doorway here, chamfered with four-centred head. (Inside, the doorway to the upper room in the porch has a shaped head identical to those dated 1599 at Allt-y-bela, Llangwm Uchaf, q.v.) The N-most component is a three-storeyed, limewashed block twisted at an angle, and identified as a granary. This also has sunk-chamfer windows in its N wall, six-light above and four-light below. The reason for the alignment of the granary is that it was built across the SE end of an obliquely positioned, late C16 half-timbered BARN NW of the house. Originally these two farm buildings were detached from the house, but subsequently an awkwardly designed link section joined them to it.

UPPER TAL-Y-FAN, 1⅜ m. SW. This too is in origin a late medieval house of cruck construction. One-bay N addition of two full storeys built perhaps in the early C17. Within the roof space of the early house the top of one cruck truss is visible. What is most impressive is the internal evidence of the late C16 remodelling of the house, to form two heated rooms with a ventilated dairy between them. The S room has at the gable-end a massive stone fireplace constructed of three monoliths, and a ceiling with transverse chamfered beam and chamfered joists with diagonally cut stops. Two of the timber partitions which enclosed the dairy survive, the N one of the normal post-and-panel construction, the E one retaining its top ventilation panel of zigzag slats. The N room has another fireplace of monolithic structure, a stone winding stair beside it to the l. and a door to the r.; this is now formed in C18 panelling and leads to the extension, but is presumably on the site of the original entrance doorway.

PARLOUR FARM, 1¾ m. NW. The farmhouse, datable to the later

C16, contains one of the county's handsomest arrays of enriched carpentry. Externally it is unprepossessing enough, thanks to drastic modernization since Fox and Raglan recorded it. The hall is to the N, the higher, thick-walled parlour wing gabled E and W, which gives the appearance of a T-plan. Fox and Raglan saw evidence that the hall was subdivided, to give an unheated inner room, suggesting that the parlour wing beyond it was an addition. However the carpentry details recorded by them were similar throughout the house, ceiling beams and window mullions alike moulded with shallow hollows and angle rolls. Now all the interest is concentrated in the parlour wing. It is entered in its NE corner through a handsome four-centred-headed door in a double-chamfered frame (with draw-bar slot). From there one's eye is drawn to the SW angle of the room, where an L-shaped settee with a panelled back is tucked in below a seven-light mullioned W window and a six-light mullioned S window. The ceiling has massive moulded beams and moulded joists. The p. 37 room above the parlour, originally reached by a mural stair in the SE corner, must have been the best bedroom, for it has equally splendidly moulded ceiling beams. The soffit of the central one is carved with a leaf trail, an embellishment unique in Monmouthshire farmhouses. Original S and W windows here too.

Across the farmyard to the NW, a probably contemporary BARN, timber-framed and weatherboarded over Old Red Sandstone dwarf walls.

TY MAWR, 1¼m. W. An unusually complete C17 farm complex, p. 33 the farmhouse dated 1640. Most remarkable is the little GATEHOUSE beside the road, of red brick laid in English bond. This is gabled in all four directions, the gables given small bargeboards and finials, over a wide segmental arch on vertical jambs. The red brick BARN to the r. is by contrast in Flemish bond, so a little later. Across the road to the S, a second, five-bay threshing BARN, probably the earliest structure in the group. This one is partly of local Old Red Sandstone, but the gable-ends and the upper part of the side wall facing the road, and thus facing towards the farmhouse, are timber-framed and weatherboarded. Crucks flank the central opening on the timber-framed side, creating a curiously asymmetrical roof structure.

The FARMHOUSE, of stone, stands end-on N of the gatehouse but not on axis with it. Two-storeyed, gable-ended, of three units, providing on the ground floor a hall (S) and parlour (N), with an unheated pantry between them. The S gable-end wall, with the entrance in it, was rebuilt in the C19. Reset high in it the datestone (Hec domus facta fuit per W.W. Anno Domini 1640). That date goes well with the regularity of design of the whole house: three evenly spaced four-light windows above and below on the long walls, and two two-lighters above and below in the N gable-end. Pigeon loft in the gable itself. The windows retain their stone-slab hoodmoulds and several their ovolo-moulded timber mullions. Inside, ovolo mouldings on the parlour fireplace lintel and on ceiling beams, but plain chamfers upstairs. The low free-standing range at r.-angles to the S gable, part timber-framed, part of stone, seems to have included a kitchen at the houseward end, now much altered. Pigeon loft in the gable here too.

5010 DIXTON/LLANDIDWG

ST PETER. Between the tranquillity of the River Wye and the thunder of the traffic on the A40. There was a Celtic monastery at Dixton, and the first reference to the church is of the C8. The strangest feature of the church is the length of the nave, about twice as long as the stocky tower and conventionally proportioned chancel would lead one to expect. Herringbone masonry exposed inside low down in the middle of the nave N wall is probably of the late C11. Perhaps there was lengthening in both directions when tower and chancel were built, maybe in the late C13. The tower, rendered below, with one W lancet, has a short belfry stage of stone and a short stone spire, octagonal on broaches. In the nave, also rendered, the SW window is medieval, early C14, as the two long trefoil-headed lights with quatrefoil over suggest. In 1397 the church was called 'intolerably dark'. The two much bigger S windows belong to *Prichard & Seddon*'s restoration of 1861–2, as does the S porch. N porch and vestry opening off it, both of 1824. Reset early C14 window in the vestry. The chancel walling of Old Red Sandstone is exposed, its C14 N and S walls in their original condition, with a two-light sanctuary window each side, a S priest's door and rectangular low-side window, and N trefoiled lancet. A special feature is the stone bench along the S wall outside. E window of 1861. Inside, the walls and wagon-vaulted ceilings all retain their white plaster render. Small tower arch. Chancel arch of 1861. – COMMUNION RAIL. Turned balusters. – FONT. Tapered octagonal bowl on a massive broached base. Recut in 1861 – or new-made? – SCULPTURE (N porch). Relief of the martyrdom of St Peter. – ROYAL ARMS. Dated 1711. Painted on boards. – STAINED GLASS. Nave S, Christ Raising Jairus's Daughter and Healing the Son of the Widow of Nain. 1862. Designed by *Seddon*, made by *Lavers & Barraud*. – Nave S, Blessed are the Pure in Heart, *c.* 1871, probably by *Ward & Hughes* (A. Brooks). – Chancel E. Lamb worshipped by saints. 1953–4 by *Francis Stephens*.

In the CHURCHYARD the broached base of a CROSS, and part of the shaft, on a single step. Modern cross-head.

(MOTTE, $\frac{1}{4}$ m. NW. Low, worn down, of the late C11 or C12.)

85 NEWTON COURT, $\frac{3}{4}$ m. N. A handsome Neoclassical house, dramatically elevated on the hillside, its three full-height bows making the most of the site. It was built for George Griffin, *c.* 1799–1802, and remains virtually unaltered, the only blemish being the substitution of casements for sash windows on the entrance front. The play made with bows makes it tempting to suggest that the design may have been supplied before his death in 1797 by *Anthony Keck* of King's Stanley, Gloucestershire.

The facing material is purplish Old Red Sandstone, used, in a *tour de force* of mason craft, as ashlar on the SW, entrance, front, in brick-like blocks on the SE, garden, front, and rubble on the other two faces. The raised angle quoins and emphatic window voussoirs are of grey ashlar. Now for the design. The SW front has two three-bay bows framing a slightly pinched single central bay, where a porch on Tuscan columns stands at the head of a little curving perron with a decorated metal handrail. The SE front is of five spacious bays, the first with blind windows, the central three in a bow. A continuous, unemphatic cornice crowns both façades.

The front door opens into a groin-vaulted corridor through the depth of the house. To the l. of its first three bays the drawing room, to the r. the library, both with bowed ends and very reticent Neoclassical enrichments. The fourth bay of the corridor opens to the r. into the dining room, also with a bow, where the decoration is slightly richer. The fifth and final bay opens to the l. to the staircase. This goes up and back to an upper landing under a segmental arch. Balustrade of alternate ironwork panels and groups of plain timber balusters. A round-headed window of great length floods it with light. The same plan is repeated on the upper floors, with flat-ceilinged corridors.

To the l. of the entrance front a WALL, intended as the back wall of an orangery, of the same purple stone, decorated with a three-bay blind arcade. Behind this a small service court and a three-bay SERVICE RANGE, the central bay with two storeys of windows under a giant relieving arch and crowning pedimental gable. Coach-house to l. and r. The forecourt to the house is entered through a substantial pair of rusticated GATEPIERS carrying spherical gadrooned urns. Wrought-iron GATES of Neoclassical design.

DUFFRYN 2080

Duffryn is a suburb of Newport, developed since 1974 in the parkland of Tredegar House, but so firmly segregated by the A48 from the southern outskirts of the town that it feels like a separate place, and a highly unusual one. It consists principally of Newport Borough Council's last major housing estate, but there are also the celebrated Inmos microchip factory and other business and government buildings, which add up to the most remarkable concentration of late C20 architecture in the whole of Wales.

HOUSING. The largest experiment in 'perimeter planning' ever attempted. Low rise is combined with high density by ingeniously packing wriggling terraces of two-storey housing into a perimeter band which encloses open ground, including a triangular wood, almost as large in ground area as the band which surrounds it.

In 1974 Newport Borough Council held a limited competition for the design of what was intended to be the first, but eventually

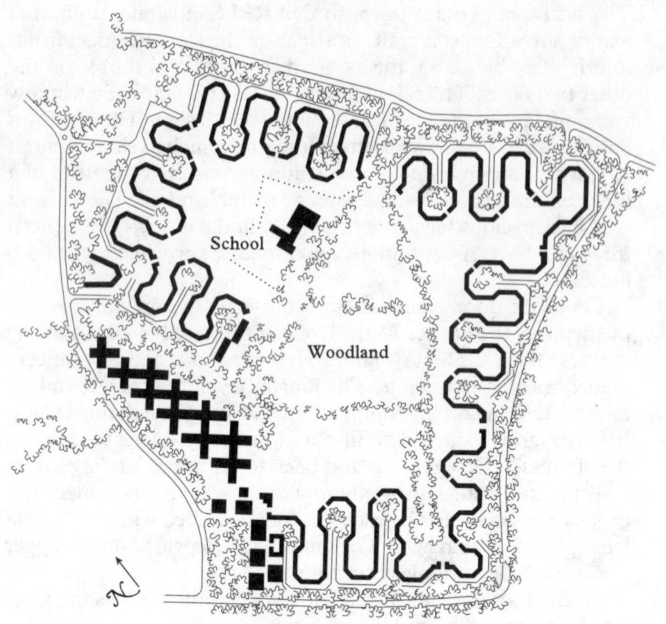

Duffryn, housing. Plan as designed.
South-west corner not built

became the only phase of a scheme to build 4,000 new houses. The consortium which won the competition was led by the engineers *L. G. Mouchel & Partners*, with the architects and planners *MacCormac & Jamieson* and *Wales & West Design Group*, and three firms responsible for design detail, *H. D. Watkins & Associates*, *J. H. Evans & Partners* and *Powell, Alport & Partners*. The key name among all these was that of Richard MacCormac, the chief exponent of the theoretical ideas developed at Cambridge University architecture department in the 1960s by Sir Leslie Martin and Lionel March. MacCormac had already masterminded a development which implemented the theory, at Pollards Hill, Mitcham, for the London borough of Merton, 1968–71. Duffryn, with 977 houses on 96 acres (39 hectares), was more than twice as big as Pollards Hill, but was built to a lower density. The construction period was three years, 1976–9.

The layout is easy to comprehend. Two-storeyed terraces continue round the entire perimeter of the site, interrupted only by footpaths which lead to back gardens and the open ground beyond. The terraces come forwards and recede to form irregular octagonal courtyards built up on seven of their eight sides (a softening of the rectilinear plan-form of Pollards Hill, already anticipated at Watermeads, Mitcham, begun 1974). There are no garages, but the house frontages are wide enough to provide hard standing for cars as well as approach paths and small gardens.

By contrast with this lively layout, the house-fronts are relentlessly uniform. The ground storey is faced with brick, in one of three shades, reddish-brown to mushroom. Then comes a band of smooth, cream-coloured asbestos cement in which the upper windows are set, and above that sombre brown tile-hanging. At the back things are livelier. The houses are of timber-framed structure, and here the framing is allowed to show, and even to form upper-level trellises, though the creepers which were intended to dangle from them are nowhere to be seem. Monopitch roofs on deep eaves.

The OLD PEOPLE'S HOUSING at WOODSIDE on the W segment of the circuit is differently planned, though part of *MacCormac & Jamieson*'s scheme. A grid of small courtyards, open-sided or open-cornered.

Within the peripheral housing the open ground is occupied by just a single building, the PRIMARY SCHOOL of 1976–7, reached down PARTRIDGE WAY. This is by *Gwent County Architect's Department*, design architects *Glyn Smith* and *Alan Poulter*. Irregular plan, buff brick walls, small windows and pyramidal roof-lights, so it ignores the idiom of the surrounding housing.

The DISTRICT AMENITIES CENTRE, intended for the SW corner, was unfortunately never built, so one of the principal planning aims at Duffryn, to create a largely self-sufficient development, was not achieved. There were, however, two comprehensive schools already close at hand.

DUFFRYN COMPREHENSIVE SCHOOL, Lighthouse Road. By *Johnson Blackett*, Newport borough architect. Four independent blocks, each with its own hall and three-storey classroom range, the first completed in 1959. Typical vocabulary of curtain walling, restrained patterning on the brick end walls and flat roofs.

ST JOSEPH'S R.C. COMPREHENSIVE SCHOOL, Tredegar House Drive. 1967 by *F. R. Bates, Son & Price*. Flat-roofed, three-storeyed curtain-wall ranges with windows in long bands.

TREDEGAR BUSINESS PARK lies NW of Duffryn housing, approached from a roundabout on the A48. Immediately encountered on entry is the celebrated Inmos factory.

INMOS MICROCHIP FACTORY (Newport Wafer-Fab Ltd). 1982 126
by *Richard Rogers & Partners*. (Structural engineers, *Anthony Hunt Associates*.) Here Rogers's principle that structure and services should be exposed on the outsides of buildings coincided with his client's need for a virtually sterile environment for the manufacture of microchips. The result is an unforgettable image as well as a structure as logical as it is flamboyant. The plan is a rectangle, eight bays deep (a further twelve were planned but never built), the structure a series of nine mighty H-plan trusses of tubular steel painted sky blue. Each truss consists of a tall, boldly cross-braced spine, from which, one third of the way up, spread far-extending arms. The arms are braced by the thinnest

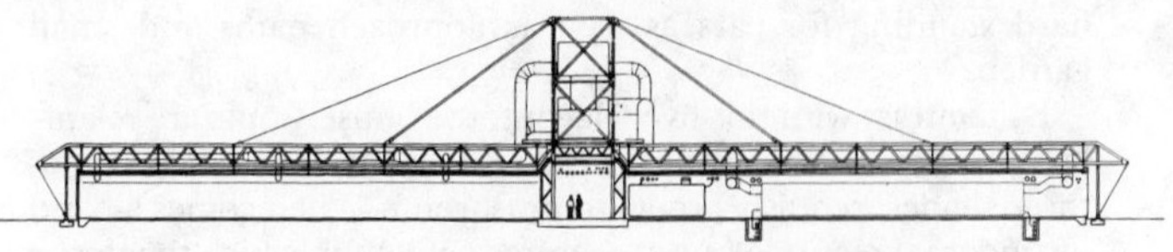

Duffryn, Inmos microchip factory. Section

of steel rods slanting down from the spine-tops, and their pointed outer ends are supported by straddling tubular posts and rods. From the arms, the curtain-walled offices are suspended, while the complex services and ducting are put on display, stacked at two levels on a central deck spanning from truss to truss, and snaking over the office roofs. The box-like service containers and the ducts are painted silver, except for acid-bearing ducts which are buttercup yellow. Inside, a broad, straight central corridor occupies the space formed by the legs of the principal trusses. To the N is the sterile space where the microchips are produced, to the S everything else: offices, machine rooms, canteen, even an internal courtyard. The contrast in function is made clear in the curtain walling, to the N patterned with an undifferentiated grid, to the S spotted with windows and louvred panels within the grid.

To the W a lunar landscape of white gas canisters serving the factory. To the S, the long-awaited extension, in a completely different idiom, three-storeyed, clad in white steel sheeting with windows in long bands, and self-conscious bowed ends. 1996–7 by *M. + W. Pearce* of Bristol on a design and manage contract.

Further W, two linked government offices stand close to the A48 within the mature trees bordering the landscaped park.

CENTRAL STATISTICAL OFFICE, by the *Percy Thomas Partnership*, completed in 1973. Five-storeyed. Brown brick walls and central tower, bronzed windows in broad continuous bands. Built round one complete square courtyard and a half courtyard, which are set anglewise to one another. (SCULPTURE. – Untitled, 1972 by *Hubert Dalwood*. Metal, in angular sheets and bars, on a multiple stem. – Abacus, 1974 by *Peter W. Nicholas*. Stone. Smoothly modelled forms and wired aperture, in the manner of Barbara Hepworth.)

PATENT OFFICE. 1989–90 by *PSA Projects Cardiff*, design directors *John Roberts* and *Tony Stevens*. Adjoining the former to the W and continuing the plan of interlinked courts and the division into five storeys. In structure and appearance, however, there is a sharp contrast. Steel frame, continuously glazed walls protected by a strongly overhanging pitched roof, and a second overhang below it. Against the three main storeys slender steel posts support steel maintenance decks, all painted white.

At Cleppa Park, a MEGALITHIC TOMB (ST 277 850), which has been badly damaged. The six remaining stones do not give any clear indication of the original shape or size of the burial chamber.

EBBW VALE/GLYN EBWY 1000

Everyone has a mental picture of Ebbw Vale, of grimy steelworks, of coal tips and close-set Victorian terraces, and everyone knows the outline of its history over the past two hundred years, of ever-accelerating industrial expansion throughout the C19, followed by devastating decline as heavy industry faltered and foundered. The reality has been more diverse than that caricature, and at the end of the C20 retains a strong continuity with the industrial past, even as the valley has been reshaped for a post-industrial future.

The Ebbw Vale Ironworks were established in 1790 by Walter Watkins, Charles Cracroft and Jeremiah Homfray, who built a blast furnace and casting shop at Pen-y-cae. Another ironworks had already been established at the head of the valley, at Beaufort (*see* p. 117), and a third came into action a mile or so downstream at Victoria in 1838. Already by 1841 the population of the valley was 9,000. No housing of this period survives, but the great scale of Christ Church, Briery Hill, begun in 1860, demonstrates clearly enough the dynamic growth of the mid C19. By 1870, in Ebbw Vale and Beaufort together, there were no fewer than twenty-one chapels. In 1864 the first steelworks was constructed. A proper town centre began to develop only from *c.* 1870, with the laying out of Market Street and the growth of Briery Hill immediately to the S. In spite of so much redevelopment in the 1960s, Market Street, now pedestrianized, remains the hub of the town, extending S-wards on the hillside above the bypass road and the tinplate works to Briery Hill.

The settlements further S down the valley, Victoria, Waun-lwyd and Cwm, were products of coalmining at the end of the century. The Marine Colliery was sunk at Cwm in 1895. By 1901 the population of the valley had passed 20,000.

The decline of the early C20 was arrested when in 1935 Richard Thomas & Co. bought the site of Ebbw Vale Iron- and Steelworks and built new steelworks there. By the 1960s the Ebbw Vale Steelworks was the most advanced in Britain. Also in the 1960s Market Street was largely redeveloped and a sort of civic centre built at its N end, and there was sweeping rebuilding of C19 terrace housing. However, the valley bottom still presents a sight unseen elsewhere in South Wales, an extent of roofs many hundreds of yards long, under which the tinplate works are still in full production.

Further down the valley the story is different. Coalmining has died here since the mid 1980s, as almost everywhere else in South Wales. But Victoria was in 1991 made the site for a spectacular Welsh Garden Festival, which from 1992 was consolidated as a permanent park over 60 acres (24 hectares) in extent, and the nucleus of a new, firmly post-industrial housing and shopping development, though without any strong architectural character.

EBBW VALE IRONWORKS

What remains of the works lies to the N of, and is partly utilized by, its successor British Steel Tinplate. Everything can be seen along

Steelworks Road, which runs N–S in the valley bottom, parallel to the town but at a lower level. At the N end the road passes under BIG ARCH (Newtown Bridge), built by the Ebbw Vale Ironworks Company and dated 1813. Monumental round-headed arch for a horse-railway conveying iron ore to the company's blast furnaces to the SE (*see* below). Crowning the N side of the bridge are pairs of tall, narrow reverberatory-brick arches which carry the modern roadway. To the W the road is carried on a rock-faced stone ARCH of 1859.

To the NW of Big Arch, the much-altered IRONWORKS SCHOOL 1844–5, with three tall, round-headed windows in its pedimental front gable. Also WESLEYAN ROW, a terrace of ten two-storeyed, early C19 workers' cottages. To the S of Big Arch THE DINGLE, a pretty group of houses in garden suburb idiom, probably of *c.* 1920 by *Walter Rosser*. For Ebenezer Chapel *see* below, p. 224.

Further to the SE a massive, Pennant sandstone retaining WALL is built against the side of the valley, one section strengthened by a series of buttresses. The wall incorporates at its foot a very large bank of early C19 BLAST FURNACES, retained to form the lower two-thirds of the charging-bank for late C19 furnaces, now removed. The earliest furnace had been constructed in 1790, a second by 1805 and a third by 1823. They are probably incorporated within the N end of the wall. Parts of blocked FURNACE CASTING-ARCHES can be seen low down, the second of which may belong to a blast furnace constructed in 1839. Much of the ring of the semicircular brick casting-arch can be seen. The remaining arches are largely obscured by tree-grown mounds of dumped earth. Next to the S, however, is the head of a brick casting-arch dated 18[5]8 on the sandstone keystone. Then come another dated 1862, an incomplete arch of finely laid Pennant sandstone, and finally a small brick arch, perhaps too small to have belonged to a blast furnace. So there are visible remains of four fairly complete furnaces, a truncated fifth and a doubtful sixth. Records indicate that only four furnaces were active at one time. Nevertheless only the six-furnace bank at Cyfarthfa, Merthyr Tydfil, is a larger survival of early C19 ironworks furnaces in Britain. The only other features of the retaining wall to note are, at the N end, the round-arched opening of polychrome brickwork to a stairway up to the charging-bank, and the outlets of three high-level coal shutes, with cast-iron lintels over the bottom shute openings.

Across Steelworks Road are various administrative buildings. At the N end THE CROFT, mid-C19 rendered house of three by three bays and three storeys, the top one oddly squeezed into full-width gables in each direction. Next to the S comes EBBW VALE HOUSE, formerly the ironmaster's residence, three-storeyed and rendered white but modernized and of no architectural character. Beside it to the W, LEVER HALL, opened 1955 as a concert hall and theatre, a typical early 1950s flat-roofed group. Brown brick, concrete window frames, even pilotis. By *Sir Percy Thomas & Son*. But the most spectacular demonstration of industrial self-confidence is yet further S, the GENERAL OFFICES of 1913–15. The architect was *F. J. Veall* of Cardiff. The strung-out composition towards the road has to be seen to be believed. The materials are shiny red brick and generous buff ashlar dressings, with polished pink granite for the bowed three-bay Tuscan porch. This forms the centrepiece of the two-storeyed central block, which has tripartite end bays crowned by elaborate shaped gables. Round-headed lower windows, gross mullion-and-transom upper ones. Single-storey extensions, to the r., ending in a gable over a big mullion-and-transom bow window, and to the l., ending in a short but fantastically detailed clock tower. The ashlar top stage of the tower is twisted through 45 degrees and topped by a little copper dome. Beyond, like an afterthought, the shaped gable of a substantial cross range. (Astonishingly, much more was intended at this end, making the tower the central feature.) Inside, a central vestibule opens to an imperial staircase, and the manager's office at the N end has a barrel ceiling.

Immediately to the S, the far-extending steel sheds of BRITISH STEEL TINPLATE WORKS.

CHRIST CHURCH, Church Street, Briery Hill. The mighty building 107
rears up from the steep hillside, commanding the industry which spreads across the valley floor below. It was erected in 1860–1 for the Ebbw Vale Ironworks Company, to the design of *John Norton.* E.E. Spire completed 1891 by *Kempson & Fowler.* Mauve Old Red Sandstone dressed with grey Forest stone and, for the window heads, Bath stone. The company's plan to build the floors, roof and spire entirely of iron had to be abandoned. Nave and lean-to aisles, W porch and soaring SW porch-steeple, producing an intimidating W front towards the street. Large central wheel window above long two-light windows with spurred quatrefoil tracery. Plate-traceried windows in the aisles. The porch has a steep ashlar gable carried on pairs of black colonnettes. The steeple rises broad and high to the r.; the belfry stage is an original composition, the two-light belfry openings with richly moulded heads set in canted walls carrying gabled clock faces. Bold cylindrical angle turrets on spurred bases, and with conical caps ringing the base of the octagonal slated spire. Five-bay nave, its clerestory windows in the form of encircled cinquefoils. The chancel, stepping slightly down from the nave, nevertheless seems enormously high on the steeply falling ground. Hall below, forming a two-storeyed, polygonal E end, vertically united by full-height buttresses. Long two-light chancel windows with Geometrical tracery.

The interior is quite straightforward, the nave piers circular and coloured black,* the steep arches double-chamfered. Moulded chancel arch on triple corbel shafts. Exposed timber roofs in nave and aisles, chancel roof boarded. – REREDOS, 1931, and flanking blind-traceried panels, 1917, belong to a scheme designed in 1914 by *Harold Brakspear.* – ROOD SCREEN. Part of the same scheme. – LECTERNS. Two fine brass lecterns,

* The limestone shafts were rolled in pitch and then polished. Information from R. Scourfield.

late C19, one with an eagle, the other an angel. – FONT and PULPIT. Of stone, polygonal with sunk enrichment of the angles. Are these by Norton? – (IMMERSION FONT. Under the floorboards at the W end. Contemporary with the building of the church.) – STAINED GLASS. Chancel E. Three windows depicting the twelve apostles, *c.* 1861. No doubt by *O'Connor* (A. Brooks). – Nave W. Wheel window, patternwork by *Powell*'s to *Moberly*'s design, 1861. Main lights, saints and scenes by *Celtic Studios*, 1953. – S aisle E, Resurrection and Good Shepherd. 1898 by *Jones & Willis*. – N aisle NE, music makers. 1968 by *Celtic Studios*, designer *John Edwards*. – Several other signed windows with dates in the C20, of no special interest.

ST JOHN, Libanus Road (disused). 1908–9 by *G. E. Halliday*. Red Ebbw Vale brick and Forest of Dean stone dressings. Perp.

ALL SAINTS (R.C.), Tredegar Road. 1905–24. Enormous, but architecturally null. Lancets. – STAINED GLASS. Two windows by *J. E. Nuttgens*, in arresting contrast with their setting. N aisle W, Baptism of Christ. 1948. – S aisle W, SS Peter and Paul. 1953. Notable development in technique and in intensity of effect between the two windows.

EBENEZER CALVINISTIC METHODIST CHAPEL, Station Road. 1850, remodelled in 1911. Three-bay rubble-stone front, with round-headed windows in yellow brick, part of the remodelling no doubt. Domestic encroachment of various dates, the two-storey stone-fronted Vestry House nudging in from the r., the similar Chapel House set back at the l., and New Cottage built into the side of the chapel itself.

PENUEL CALVINISTIC METHODIST CHAPEL, Church Street, Briery Hill (now scout hall). Dated 1865 and a typical classical chapel front of that date. Tuscan pilasters carry a deep, plain entablature, arched up in the centre for the name tablet, and a pedimental gable. Round-headed windows, long in the outer bays, a short triplet in the centre over the doorway. Snecked Pennant sandstone, the dressings rendered and painted. Attributed to the Rev. *Thomas Thomas* of Landore (S. Hughes).

WEST END CONGREGATIONAL CHURCH, Tredegar Road. 1907. Lively Perp façade of mauve Old Red Sandstone dressed with buff terracotta. Interior galleried on three sides, the supports fluted iron columns with Corinthian caps. Fussily detailed woodwork. – STAINED GLASS. In Art Nouveau patterns.

MUNICIPAL OFFICES, Civic Centre. By *J. L. Thomas*, opened 1965. Straightforward and typical of their date. Two-storey entrance and council-chamber range, and five-storey offices at r.-angles at a higher level behind. Both parts are flat-roofed, with rectangular windows in continuous bands. Dark brown brick, pale green render, and grey-brown corrugated cladding.

WAR MEMORIAL, between Steelworks Road and Libanus Road. In an unusually elaborate setting, a tall granite plinth carries a bronze statue of a soldier triumphantly waving his tin hat. By the *Craftsmen's Guild*, London, unveiled 1924.

COUNTY LIBRARY, Market Street. Formerly Bethcar English Wesleyan Chapel, built 1860–1 by *Samuel Hancorn* of Newport.

Three-bay façade under a pedimental gable. Giant Ionic pilasters frame long windows in the outer bays and support pieces of entablature, from which a central arch rises into the gable. The centre bay of the façade altered, so that Hancorn's semicircular portico is lost, and the interior remodelled for library use, in 1958–9.

LITERARY AND SCIENTIFIC INSTITUTION, Church Street, Briery Hill. 1853. Eleven-bay stone front, symmetrical, with a pair of bargeboarded gables.

WORKMEN'S HALL, Eureka Place. Dated 1907. Not large but busily Baroque. Bowed three-storeyed, four-bay façade, under a straight, recessed attic. The figure of a miner standing within a broken pediment has gone from the skyline. Much play with blocked columns, cartouches and foliage carving. Rock-faced Pennant sandstone, and ashlar dressings painted over. The architect's name seems not to be recorded.

HEALTH CENTRE (YSBYTY'R TRI CHWM), College Road. 1994–5, by *Tony Adams*. Quite extensive, planned round two and a half courtyards, but single-storeyed. Pantiled roofs, from which large monopitch dormers shoot up at intervals. Entrances under reversed monopitch canopies. White rendered walls framed in brown brick. Small red-trimmed windows. Plenty of restless incident in the courtyards too.

COLLEGE OF FURTHER EDUCATION, Cemetery Road. Built *c.* 1957–8 by *Monmouthshire County Architect's Department* in their typical idiom. Three-storeyed ranges with continuous bands of windows under shallow pitched roofs. Y-plan, to take advantage of the triangular site.

WILLOWTOWN PRIMARY SCHOOL, Mount Pleasant. The Junior School at the back is of 1903–4 by *David Morgan* of *James & Morgan* of Cardiff. Brown Pennant sandstone with dressings of Forest ashlar and red brick. Typical single-storey council school, the central hall reconstructed, the flanking classrooms with shaped gables. The two-storey range down the hill, inscribed Manual Instruction and Domestic Science Centre, must be part of the council school built in 1909 by *Henry Waters* of Ebbw Vale.

GARDEN CITY, ¾m. S of Briery Hill. A grand name for this little garden suburb development isolated on the hillside. The houses are rendered and gabled and have dormers and semi-dormers pushing in to red-tiled roofslopes. Some reticent Arts and Crafts detail. Canted group at the central T-junction. Two straight-ridged terraces at the highest level. Altogether quite an artful performance. Designed, as Victoria garden suburb, by the local architect *Walter Rosser* in 1918, for Ebbw Vale Steel, Iron & Coal Company. Originally it was not so lonely, but stood immediately above Prince of Wales Colliery.

VICTORIA

2m. S

Of the Victorian settlement, the only significant survivor is the former ST MARY'S CHURCH, Glan Ebbw Terrace, 1897 by

E. M. Bruce Vaughan of Cardiff. Small. Lancets. From 1986 the sites of steelworks and colliery and most of the late Victorian housing were cleared and the celebrated GARDEN FESTIVAL laid out here in 1991–2. Lavishly planted trees continue to flourish, but most of the festival structures of interest have been removed (*see* Newport, p. 453). The master plan for the new village was made in 1992 by *Nealon Tanner* of Bristol. At the N end VICTORIA BUSINESS PARK, where GWENT COURT consists of a series of self-consciously overdesigned pavilions, their red brick walls banded with Pennant sandstone. Full-length clerestory lighting as well as glazed canted ends. Further S much conventional housing of the mid 1990s. At the S end a Japanese GARDEN designed round two small artificial lakes, and, prominent on the hillside above, the Wild West style FREE EVANGELICAL NON-DENOMINATIONAL CHURCH. Highest and furthest S, the SHOPPING CENTRE, 1996–8. Laid out across the hillside as a square between two covered passages, terminating at the S end in two circular tent-like pavilions and a segmentally roofed hall. Single-storey shops throughout. Rugged, untouched hillside rises immediately to the W.

Across the valley to the E, at WAUN-LWYD, the PARK HOTEL stands up prominently. 1898–9 by *Swalwell & Creighton* of Newport. Of grey stone, but a showy Baroque design. Symmetrical front, with Venetian windows crammed into the gables and a heavily scrolled and rusticated porch. Handsome chimneystacks.

CWM

3 m. S

A characteristic late C19 valley-bottom settlement, built to house the miners of Marine Colliery. The spine street, MARINE STREET, is extremely long and unwaveringly straight, built up with continuous two-storeyed rendered terraces all along, their ridgetop stacks and red chimneypots serried against the sky. The polychromatic façade of TALLISTOWN CONGREGATIONAL CHURCH is almost the only interruption.

ST PAUL. The church stands typically isolated beyond the N end of the settlement. 1881–2 by *John Norton*. Small and cheap, rock-faced Pennant sandstone with yellow brick dressings, principally the plate-traceried W window facing the road. N aisle 1909–10 by *E. M. Bruce Vaughan*, who also extended the chancel. – STAINED GLASS. An important collection by *R. J. Newbery*. – Chancel E, *c.* 1902, Crucifixion between SS Peter and Paul, and small scenes of Nativity and Empty Tomb below. – Nave W. Piecemeal subject matter. Dove of the Holy Spirit in the top quatrefoil, and in the main light Suffer the Little Children, Ascension and the first two in a series of scenes from the life of St Paul. – N aisle, Pauline subjects, 1911–14, and war memorial, 1922. – Chancel S, Revelation vision of the woman clothed with the sun. 1963 by *Celtic Studios*.

METHODIST CHURCH, Mill Terrace. *c.* 1900, Gothic, snecked

Pennant sandstone with liberal Bath stone ashlar dressings on the entrance front.

COLLIERY VENTILATION FURNACE (SO 188 037). Squat circular brick ventilation chimney and shaft, constructed in the mid C19 and disused by 1876. This is the only known survivor in Wales of a once common pre-fan type of shaft ventilation.

FFWTHOG/FFWDDOG

2020

The valley W of the Vale of Ewyas has no church.

TWYN Y GAER HILL-FORT (SO 294 220). The hill-fort was partially excavated in the 1960s when work on the entrances showed that the sequence of enlargement, reduction and change is not in fact that which a study of the surface remains might have suggested. The defences follow the long narrow summit of the hill and consist for most of the circuit of two close-set ramparts with an entrance at the E end. The interior is divided into three sections by cross banks. A postulated sequence might have made the W-most section the earliest, with a subsequent expansion of the fort to its full extent and a final reduction to half size marked by the straight cross bank in the centre. However, excavation has shown that this bank was part of the original enclosure of the hill, to the E of which was a fenced area, perhaps for stock. Later the fenced area, which had been gradually extended E-wards, was also surrounded by a permanent bank and ditch with an elaborate and often modified entrance passage. The banks marking off the W section have been shown to belong to the final period of occupation. All these changes seem to have taken place during the Iron Age, for there is no evidence of either late Bronze Age or Roman material. Both the pottery and details of the design of the gates show that in its early stages this fort belongs with the Marcher hill-forts, but later comes under influences from the S.

TABERNACLE BAPTIST CHAPEL, in a lonely spot 1 m. up the valley. Simple gable-ended building, dated 1837 on a tablet which also records the initials of the builders, *S. T.* and *J. T.* Two sash windows at the front, two at the back. Contemporary interior galleried on three sides. Long rows of hat-pegs at both levels. The pulpit between the back windows. Baptisms must have taken place in the stream close by. Note the walled forecourt with continuous stone bench. – MONUMENTS. Several signed gravestones in the burial ground, including two small ones to babies, attached to the chapel wall, signed *J. Edwards* of Abergavenny.

The adjoining MINISTER'S HOUSE is clearly an addition.

At the entrance to the valley, beside the little bridge over the Grwyne Fawr, PONTESGOB COTTAGE, its walls limewashed red in traditional fashion. This is an unusually well preserved example of the small two-unit house of the early C17. Originally of one storey only with habitable roof space. The entrance doorway is in the gable-end, opening into the hall beside the hearth, and a turning stair to the roof space adjoins the hearth on the other side. Post-and-panel partition, with evidence of doors at both ends, originally opening into two small, unheated rooms.

Across the field to the S, PONTYSPIG FARM, also partly of the C17. Two-storeyed, with stairs in a gabled projection. (Ovolo-moulded windows.)

Two farmhouses on the hillside further up the valley deserve mention, ½m. N. of the chapel. First comes TY MAWR. This consists of three parts. To the S is a mid-C17 single-unit range of two full storeys. This has four-light and five-light timber windows at both levels with roll-moulded lozenge-plan mullions, carefully restored in 1995–6. The E gable-end is crowned by a stack, and the irregularity of the window arrangement shows that the stairs rise, in the usual way, beside the hearths. The wing projecting to the N is of two main parts. The kitchen on the downhill (W) side is of the late C18 or early C19, but the E half is much older and more surprising, largely composed of the two-storey porch of a C16 house. The C16 house itself has been abandoned and is reduced to wall-stumps. So the house, having first been extended in the C17 into an H-plan in this curious manner, was in the late C18 curtailed and made more compact. The porch survived because it was pressed into service as a dairy beside the newly built kitchen.

Inside there is more to see. In the kitchen two formerly outer doors at r.-angles to one another, one to the S range, the other to the porch-link. Fragments of the pentice which sheltered them are visible above the kitchen ceiling. So two households could have co-existed independently during the H-plan phase. The porch has a wide, four-centred entrance arch with a broad, continuous chamfer, and a similar narrower, off-centre inner arch. Stone side benches. In the upper storey a fireplace with chamfered jambs. The C17 range is identically treated at both levels, the ceiling beams chamfered, the joists with angle rolls like the window mullions. The spiral stair which connects them is spacious and well lit, and continues up to the roof space. At the first-floor landing three timber doorways, two arch-headed, the third with a shaped head in a stepped design.

The impressive seven-bay BARN S of the house is further evidence of farming prosperity here in the C17. At the upper end it dies into the hillside. The middle bay is stone-flagged as a threshing floor between opposing doorways, from which a flight of steps leads down to a stable in the lower half. The lower gable-end originally had a symmetrical arrangement of windows on three levels, and flanking ground-floor doorways. Further stables and pigsty added later to l. and r.

UPPER HOUSE FARM, 300 yds (275 metres) further along the hillside, is less ambitious, but also an interesting group. The house is set E–W in the usual way, down the slope of the hill, which is fairly steep up here. The upper half is a two-unit C17 range, with a post-and-panel partition forming an unheated chamber at the upper end. A cross-passage and storage room (rather than a byre) added soon after, at the S end, behind the hearth and covering the original entrance doorway. Lean-to kitchen and dairy added to the N, the former with a big, bowed oven projection. A separate range to the N, later converted for use as malt-house and stable, with cart-house attached, has a fireplace in its upper end wall, which suggests that it was at first intended as a domestic annexe. The four-bay BARN to the S is neatly dated 1828 on a tie-beam.

FLEUR-DE-LIS 1090

ST DAVID. 1893–4 by *E.M. Bruce Vaughan* of Cardiff, an architect whose churches are frequently found in the Valleys over the border in Glamorgan. This is a typical work. Rock-faced grey Pennant sandstone with Bath stone dressings. Nave with E double bell gable and lower chancel. Perp E and W windows, two-light Geometrical side windows. – STAINED GLASS. Chancel E, Adoration of the Kings and Shepherds. 1894. Probably by *Heaton, Butler & Bayne* (A. Brooks).

SALEM INDEPENDENT CHAPEL, High Street. Broad, uncompromising front of Pennant sandstone under a big pedimental gable, dated 1860. Five upper round-headed windows, the central three in a group. Square-headed windows flank the doorway.

PENGAM AND FLEUR-DE-LIS WORKMEN'S LIBRARY AND INSTITUTE, High Street. Dated 1911. A towering block, the two lower storeys faced with Pennant sandstone, under an ashlar frieze for the name and a series of disc metopes, the top storey faced with red brick. At the uphill end, surprisingly, a two-storeyed bow under a half-timbered gable.

GLASCOED 3000

ST MICHAEL. Simple lancet box, with heavy tie-beam roof inside. 1848–9, officially by *T.H. Wyatt* of *Wyatt & Brandon*, though he claimed to have taken barely any interest in the project, leaving it to a pupil. *J.H. Evins* of Abergavenny signed the completion certificate. – STAINED GLASS. Chancel E. Opalescent glass, sprays of clematis top and bottom, a cross in the middle. 1987 by *Bryn Young*.

GOETRE 3000

The main hamlets in the parish are Penperlleni to the S and Nantyderry to the E. Church and Church Farm stand by themselves W of Nantyderry.

ST PETER. 1845–6 by *Wyatt & Brandon*, replacing a medieval building. Nave with W double bell gable and S porch, lower chancel. Snecked Old Red Sandstone and Bath stone dressings. Middle Pointed proportions, but Perp details, intended as an echo of the old church. – FONT. Norman, of the local type with concentric circles incised above a rope moulding. – STAINED GLASS. Chancel E, Christ as Good Shepherd between SS John and Peter. 1903 by *Heaton, Butler & Bayne*. Clogged with modelling. – Nave NE, SS Michael and Gabriel. Sugary angels on lavender clouds. 1921 by *Joseph Bell & Son* of Bristol. – Nave SW, baptismal window. 1985 by *Celtic Studios*. – Nave NW, Annunciation. 1986 by *Celtic Studios*.

CHAPEL, Capel Ed Lane, ½m. SW. Dated 1807, so one of the earliest formalized chapels in the county. White rendered front of the long-wall type under a hipped slate roof. Two large, round-headed windows between two doorways, one blocked, the other hidden by a later porch. The chapel was built for Calvinistic Methodists. Interior stripped out. Large addition of the 1980s to the rear.

SARON BAPTIST CHURCH, Saron Lane, ¾m. W. 1826, rebuilt 1875, says a tablet over the entrance. Whitewashed rubble-stone, three bays by two, entered at the short end. Round-headed windows. This is all typical of the earlier date, so the tablet must record no more than enlargement and refitting. Simple interior, with gallery at the entrance end, on thin iron posts. Minister's seat and 'big seat' beneath. – WAR MEMORIAL, for the 1914–18 war. White marble tablet with a mourning woman by a sarcophagus, exactly as it might have been a century earlier.

NATIONAL SCHOOL (now two houses), N of the church. 1869, by *T.H. Wyatt*. Of stone, quite simple.

CHURCH FARM, NW of the church. A good group, the three-bay C17 house unusually formal, with central three-storeyed gable and windows under hoodmoulds symmetrically disposed below it. Original central doorway and door, protected by a delightfully rustic C18 columned porch. The windows themselves are C18 casements.

Unaltered BARN adjoining to the r., with central porch and pentice roofs.

GOYTRE HALL, ¾m. NW. A C17 T-plan farmhouse remodelled in an antiquarian spirit and enlarged for the Rev. Thomas Evans, after 1870. The SE range retains the chamfered jambs of a C17 stone fireplace (with fireback dated 1699 – an importation?), and spiral stair beside it rising through two storeys to the roof space. A pair of arched door-heads at the first-floor landing look C17. The NW range was clearly an addition – see the roof levels. It has chamfered ceiling beams in the main ground-floor room. Mr Evans built a two-storeyed polygonal entrance porch in the angle between the ranges (inscribed with a date, 1447, relating to Herbert history), and probably contrived the group of four lozenge-plan stacks which crown the house. The large ovolo-moulded mullion-and-transom windows of timber are another scholarly modernization. The front doorway has the first of several shaped heads in the house, all, it seems, put in for Evans. Several genuine brought-in pieces, including six small overmantel reliefs of *c.* 1600 carved with Old Testament subjects. The music room, a late C19 addition to the W, has an enormously spreading S window bay and a W inglenook. The present ceiling with genuine

C17 ovolo-moulded beams is said to have been brought in from a house in Abergavenny in the early C20. The original music-room roof, with chamfered queen-trusses and boarded ceiling, was jacked up a storey higher when the C17 timbers were inserted, and now overpowers a pair of bedrooms.

To the W, a single-storey STABLE COURT dated 1868.

NANTYDERRY HOUSE, ¼ m. E. Built *c.* 1830 for Robert Farquhar, owner of Blaendare Ironworks, Pontypool. Two-storeyed, of one-plus-three-plus-one bays, the windows in the outer bays tripartite and set within pseudo-pedimented projections. Sadly, the mouldings have been trimmed off. Symmetrically placed, slab-like chimneystacks. Later enlargement in two stages, the first attributed to *T.H. Wyatt* (Kelly), the second of 1898 by *E.G.C. Down* of Cardiff.

TY-COOKE, 1½ m. SW. The approach is inviting, past a long, straight stone wall, and through a gateway crowned by a gabled pigeon loft, into a cobbled yard. Two houses face the yard. That on the N side is the earlier, of the early C17, and long converted to farm uses. It has a shaped timber door-head, and one surviving four-light timber window with sunk-chamfered mullions. The central gabled dormer has been dismantled. Upper-cruck roof structure. On the S side of the yard, its formidable-looking successor, built at the beginning of the C18 for Thomas Cooke, chief manager of the Hanburys' ironworks at Pontypool. The front to the yard is completely regular, three storeys high and four bays wide. In the two main storeys large timber windows of three lights with a transom. Unfortunately, C19 pebbledash and the refashioning of the roof have deprived the front and two-bay E side of their original character. Round the back, however, the Old Red Sandstone rubble walling is exposed, with deep projecting stair-turret and full-height chimney-breast. Originally the traditional tower-like character of the house must have contrasted oddly with the regular fenestration of the entrance front. The only original internal feature is the stair, rising in short, straight flights up a square core. And there is one surprise, the hall chimneypiece, a lusciously carved white marble object of the late C19, brought in from Maindiff Court, Abergavenny, the house built by Crawshay Bailey jun. *c.* 1875.

GOYTRE WHARF, 1 m. NW. On the Brecon and Abergavenny Canal and approached from the NW through a fir wood. The site is one of the most complete and eloquent expressions of the impact on agriculture at the end of the C18 of the new developments in industry and transport. It has been excellently restored by British Waterways. This part of the canal was constructed 1809–12 by the engineer *William Crossley*. All the structures by the wharf are presumably of that date.

As seen from the W, the canal is carried on a low embankment at the far side of a bowl-like depression. Set into the r. bank of the depression are three LIMEKILNS. One of the three circular burning-cones survives, its open top level with the canal, readily accessible for the supply of limestone from barges. Its sides are lined with firebricks. The face of the kilns is a finely constructed retaining wall of squared limestone blocks, with three pairs of round-headed arches which open into the vaulted kilns. At the back of the r. pair of arches can be seen the surprisingly small iron grates, which intercommunicate with the foot of the surviving cone. Beyond the kilns the canal passes over a segmental AQUEDUCT of similar fine limestone masonry. Note its elegant curved wing walls. The aqueduct provided access to the kilns for farm carts collecting burnt lime for fields E of the canal. Diminutive AQUEDUCT COTTAGE beside it, one room up, one down, was built for the operator of the weighbridge on which the burnt lime was weighed. The narrow outer portion of the cottage served as the operator's office. The much larger HOUSE facing the kilns at a higher level to the N (now interpretation centre and shop) was for the limekiln manager. Converted STABLES attached to its E end.

MONMOUTHSHIRE AND BRECON CANAL. The canal winds picturesquely through woods and pastures, crossed by seven segmental-arched bridges, not to mention the aqueduct at Goytre Wharf (*see* above), all part of *William Crossley*'s work in extending the Brecon and Abergavenny Canal 1809–12.

3080

GOLDCLIFF

The Benedictine priory was founded in 1113 by Robert de Chandos, lord of Caerleon, for a prior and twelve monks, and given to the monastery of Bec in Normandy. The last monks left in 1467. Its site was on the high point of the so-called 'gold cliff', on the shore of the Severn Estuary. No trace is visible today.

ST MARY MAGDALENE. Small, single-cell church built inland, 1 m. NW, after 1424 when Goldcliff Priory was partly destroyed by a flood. Its S and W walls are constructed of squared limestone blocks, perhaps salvaged from the priory. They include two fragments of C12 fret decoration inserted in the S wall *c.* 1850. Windowless N wall. S porch. Low, battlemented W tower, apparently of the C18 or early C19, see the broad lancets. The S and E windows belong to the restoration of *c.* 1880. Inside, continuous plaster barrel vault on C18 moulded wall-plates, cut across by the Victorian chancel arch. Evidence that there was a W gallery. – FONT. Medieval. Roughly cut octagonal bowl on a thick roll and shapeless stem. C18 COVER, flat, with a turned finial. – PULPIT. Timber. Dated 1913. A pretty piece. – CURIOSUM. Brass plate on the chancel N wall, recording another flood, of 1606.

In the CHURCHYARD the broached base and shaft stump of a CROSS.

ROMAN REMAINS. Near the site of Goldcliff Priory, a Roman boundary stone was found in 1878. It probably relates to the construction of a sea wall by the Second Legion, and suggests that the land held by that legion extended as far as the River Severn at Goldcliff, some 3 m. (5 kilometres) from Caerleon.

GOVILON 2010

Govilon grew up during the early C19 in the parish of Llanwenarth, at a distribution point on the Brecon and Abergavenny Canal (constructed 1796–1812), which served the nearby ironworks to the W. The population quadrupled during the first twenty years of the century, and by 1831 had almost reached 2,000. The canal weaves through and above the length of the village as it contours along the hillside.

The Baptist Church, which must have stood in isolation for the first century of its existence, is the focal building at the centre of the village, immediately N of the canal. Housing is mostly of the 1950s and later. The most evocative survivors of Govilon's industrial housing are Nos. 1–3 CHAPEL COTTAGES, backing on to the burial ground of the Baptist Church.

BAPTIST CHURCH, Station Road. The oldest Baptist chapel in Wales, though of early C19 appearance. Built 1695, doubled in depth S-wards in the C18, and remodelled 1869–70. White-rendered on three sides, slate-hung to the W. Domestic-looking S, entrance, front. To the N two large round-headed windows. Inside, these flank the pulpit in the characteristic C19 arrangement. Handsome balustraded C18 gallery on the other three sides. It is partly supported by two full-height timber piers, which mark the line of the wall removed when the chapel was doubled. – PULPIT. Bearing five dates, from 1696 to 1955, which relate to the building and remodelling of the chapel.

In the BURIAL GROUND a confident array of monuments, including many pink polished granite obelisks.

ST CATHERINE. Built in 1847–8 as a chapel of ease by *Wyatt & Brandon*. Simple rectangle with S porch, of snecked local sandstone with Bath stone dressings. Plate tracery. In 1871–2 *J. D. Sedding* added a lean-to N aisle, and, more significantly, a lofty one-bay chancel, its big windows with Geometrical bar tracery. On the N side of the chancel he built a vestry as the base of an intended tower.

Inside, Sedding's N aisle has a conventional E.E. arcade. Plain, wide chancel arch. More personal, the broad sedile and piscina in the chancel. – FONT. A heavy piece, late C12 in style but presumably all of *c.* 1871. Square bowl with trefoiled underside, on five shafts. – STAINED GLASS. Chancel E, Noli me Tangere, Resurrection and Empty Tomb, with Last Supper below. Of *c.* 1871, no doubt by *Lavers, Barraud & Westlake* (A. Brooks). – Nave SW, Jesus and a disciple. 1860, surely by *Hardman*. Small, but of high quality. – N aisle N, chalice and wafers before a stylized landscape, cf. Psalm 23. 1990 by *John Petts*.

In the CHURCHYARD, E of the church, MONUMENT to the rector, the Rev. George Grove †1897, by his son *Arthur Grove*. Octagonal shaft crowned with idiosyncratic cross-head and ringed by an undercut band of stylized leaves. A typical Arts and Crafts piece.

CHURCH HALL, down the hill E of the church. Paid for by the Rev. Mr Grove and built *c.* 1889. Probably designed by *Arthur Grove*, then aged nineteen. Gable-ended stone rectangle with a few personal touches.

WAR MEMORIAL, 1¼ m. NW, beside the B4246. Designed as the entrance to the recreation ground by *Arthur Grove, c.* 1920. Pennant sandstone walls and decorative piers. All the cresting has been removed. Later roadside piers with carved heraldic panels commemorating King George V.

GOVILON HALL. Built as the rectory, and dated 1867. The architect was *Edmund Sedding*, brother of J.D. Sedding. Sober and substantial Tudor Gothic house of rock-faced grey Forest stone with Bath dressings. Two unexpected details, a half-timbered gable bearing the date and the word WELCOME, and a glazed ridgetop lantern.

LLANWENARTH HOUSE, ½ m. W. A remarkable mid-C16 house, tall and compact, built by the Morgan family, but much altered in the early C19. The closest comparison is with the, admittedly larger, Llancaeach-fawr, Gelligaer, a few miles across the border in Glamorgan. The house is constructed of carefully laid slabby Old Red Sandstone with well-made angle quoins. Pronounced batter to the walls. Three-bay E entrance front of three storeys. The broad, deep, not quite central porch projects strongly. Small gable to the l., and larger one to the r., the top windows rising into them. One-bay gabled returns, and a second N gable over a C16 extension. The only dressed feature in its original position is the four-centred porch doorway, with fine continuous hollow, quadrant, hollow moulding. The positions of the windows have not changed, see the voussoired relieving arches and the finely moulded stone hoodmoulds; but the timber windows beneath them are C19, much deeper and slightly wider than their predecessors. Several of the original four-light stone windows, with hollow chamfered mullions, are reset in the early C19 extension at the back of the house. Of the chimneystacks, a row of six and another of four, only the bases remain. To the S projects a low, stone-vaulted segmental undercroft, with the jambs of a stone doorway which linked it to the house. Inside, there remain the splendid C16 upper-cruck roof trusses of the main range and the NW addition. Otherwise the interior was entirely remodelled in the early C19. Central stair with timber handrail and simple banisters rising under an octagonal top light.

BAILEY'S IRON WAREHOUSE (now British Waterways regional office). Built on the canal wharf *c.* 1821 for the benefit of the railway opened that year from the Bailey brothers' Nantyglo iron furnaces. Coursed rubble-stone. Three-storey front towards the canal with central doorway and segment-headed windows. The E and W ends, to which the railways ran, are blind, but on the former the cast-iron mountings for a loading platform and a crane.

In a garden S of the wharf, the monumental masonry wall of a set of early C19 LIMEKILNS, with drawing arches built into the side of the canal bank.

GRACE DIEU PRIORY

4010

$3\frac{1}{2}$ m. W of Monmouth

A Cistercian foundation, first attempted in 1217, colonized from Abbey Dore in 1226, but moved to a new site in 1236. No trace of either site remains. At its suppression in 1536 there were two monks, and it was valued at less than any other Cistercian house in England or Wales. Thereafter the Herberts of Wonastow acquired the site, and Sir Thomas Herbert (†1588) is said to have built a lodge in his deerpark at PARC GRACE DIEU, about half a mile (0.8 kilometre) SW of the supposed monastic site. Nothing, it seems, is left of that either.

GRIFFITHSTOWN

2090

$1\frac{1}{2}$ m. SE of Pontypool

A dense grid of streets lined with cottage terraces extends on the hillside above the Monmouthshire and Brecon Canal. HIGH STREET, PICTON STREET and BROAD STREET, at the N end, were laid out by engineers of the Great Western Railway on a farm acquired for the purpose by a GWR supervisor, Henry Griffiths, hence the name of the settlement. The S-ward extension came after the opening of the Panteg Steelworks in 1873. In SUNNYBANK ROAD, which runs along the top, middle-class villas of the turn of the century.

ST HILDA, Sunnybank Road. 1887–8 by *E. M. Bruce Vaughan* of Cardiff. E.E. Of grey Pennant sandstone with grey Forest dressings. Quite a large church, but cautious in its design. Five-bay nave and lean-to aisles. S porch. Clerestory of encircled quatrefoils in pairs. Lancets elsewhere, those on the W front shafted. Lower chancel and S transept. Flèche meagrely remade in 1934 by *H. J. Griggs*. No surprises inside either, circular piers with moulded caps and bases, wide and high chancel arch. – PULPIT. Of stone, octagonal, carved to the architect's design by *William Clarke* of Llandaff. – STAINED GLASS. Chancel E, Crucifixion. 1888 by *Samuel Evans* of West Smethwick. – Nave W. 1912 by *Jones & Willis*. Queen Victoria between Edward VII and Alexandra, the Queen Mother, with New Testament parables beneath their feet. – Other windows by the same at the W end of the S aisle, *c.* 1919. – N aisle NE, Virgin and Child, and St Hilda. 1948, signed by *Celtic Studios*, but designed by *Howard Martin* before the firm was officially set up. – Next in the N aisle, SS Michael and Gabriel. – S aisle SE, Christ in the carpenter's shop. Signed by *Hardman*, *c.* 1954, apparently aping Celtic Studio's style. – Next in the S aisle, Good Samaritan and Mary Magdalene anointing Christ's feet. 1958 by *Celtic Studios*. – N aisle W, St Hilda, *c.* 1979, and Noli me Tangere, *c.* 1982, by *Geoffrey Robinson* of *Joseph Bell & Son*. Clear, bright colours and confident, if wayward, patterns.

BAPTIST CHURCH, Commercial Street. 1877 by *George Morgan* of Carmarthen. Pennant sandstone front with (painted) brick dressings. Long, round-headed windows in quite a thoughtful composition. Typical interior, with galleries of 1906 on three sides, the gallery fronts bowed, of pierced ironwork mixing Greek and Romanesque foliage forms. Above the pulpit a full-width segmental arch for an organ.

CONGREGATIONAL CHAPEL, Kemeys Street. 1885–6. The contractor was *John Burgoyne*. Rendered. Round-headed windows in two storeys. (The interior was refitted in 1907.)

MECHANICS' INSTITUTE, Commercial Street. Built 1871–5, by *Lawrence & Goodman* of Newport. Single-storeyed, yet in an early French Gothic style, with massive foliage-capped columns at the entrance, and an apse.

COUNTY HOSPITAL, Coed-y-gric Road. Built as a workhouse, 1895 by *E.A. Lansdowne*. Tall range with meagre details. Dark grey Pennant sandstone with buff Ebbw Vale bricks forming full-height pilaster strips.

4020

GROSMONT

A close-knit, intricate village climbing up the hill. But the Town Hall, which encroaches on the road half-way up, tells that Grosmont is more than a village. Up a lane to the NE the castle stands higher than the houses but hidden from them. The borough laid out when the castle was built in the C12 and C13 gained municipal status but never grew beyond village scale. Ambitions for it in the C13 are best indicated by the grand cruciform church set back downhill behind trees to the S.

ST NICHOLAS. A noble E.E. building, crowned by an octagonal Dec crossing tower and spire, rescued from near collapse and partly rebuilt by *J.P. Seddon*. In 1869–70 he took the chancel and S chancel chapel down to the ground and reconstructed them. The tower arches and piers he underpinned and largely rebuilt 1873–5 (N) and 1879. The transepts were partly rebuilt in 1878 by *James, Seward & Thomas* of Cardiff. The aisled nave, however, was merely repaired. The church is constructed of the local Old Red Sandstone, and retains on the exterior of the W wall and tower traces of the whitewash which was regularly applied even as late as *c.* 1800.

The E wall of chancel and chapel is a new design by *Seddon*, with two three-light Geometrical windows, obscuring the fact that the two parts were not originally of the same date, and improving the medieval design of the chancel, which had an E window 'curiously inferior to the side ones'. The serried array of N chancel lancets, a group of three and a group of four, replicates the C13 design. Irregular Geometrical windows in the S chapel, roughly corresponding to what had been there. The transepts both have a lean-to W aisle, but their C13 character has been compromised. The grouped S lancets in the S transept are of 1878. In the N transept the quirky five-light E window looks like a C19 design, but the long three-light N window, the mullions carried up to the arched window head and only the outer lights arch-headed, is of the late C13, its idiosyncratic design corresponding to the N aisle windows at Skenfrith (q.v.). The crossing steeple is a neat piece of geometry. The low octagonal tower rises above angle projections on the diagonal faces. Two-light belfry window in each face with simple Dec tracery. Plain parapet. Tall octagonal stone spire unbroken except by tiny lucarnes near the apex.

Nave and lean-to aisles under continuous roofslopes. NE gabled window inserted to light the rood loft. Dec N porch with square-headed side windows, two-light E and one-light W, covering a fine E.E. N doorway. This has continuous mouldings, a quadrant and a hollow framing a filleted roll, under a filleted hood. Otherwise the N wall is blind. Two windows in the S aisle by *Seddon*, 1888, replacing square-headed ones. The W front makes no attempt to create a show. Plain pilaster buttresses mark off the aisles, which are lit by small lancets. Simple chamfered nave doorway, and over it a Dec insertion, an undersized four-light window with reticulated tracery.

The interior is a shock. The nave is unfurnished, the floor 16
paved with stone ledger slabs. So the plain, strong early C13 arcades can be appreciated to the full. They are of five bays, their E and W responds set against stub walls. Short, stout circular piers stand on round bases and plinths and square sub-plinths. The circular capitals are finely moulded, the arches double-chamfered, under continuous moulded hoods. Tie-beam and kingpost roof structure, the rafters forming a profile in five cants. In the transepts things become more complicated. In the N transept, a wide, double-chamfered blocked arch separates the main space from the W aisle. In the S transept, what appear to be the jambs of two roll-moulded arches which are incompatible with each other. Does all this indicate an intention to extend the transept W aisles W-wards, forming nave aisles as wide as the transepts? To the E a glazed screen of 1888 by *Seddon* separates the unused nave from the functioning parts of the church.

Beyond the glazed screen, the crossing first requires consideration. The stonework here is virtually all Seddon's, following the medieval design as faithfully as possible, even if the irregular interplay of white and mauve ashlar blocks is his idea. The vocabulary here is much richer than in the nave arcades, though the broad, generous proportions are similar. The piers consist of octagonal responds carrying stiff-leaf caps of early C13 type, flanked by bull-nosed imposts carrying upright leaves at capital level. The arches have bull-nosed soffits with angle rolls and filleted hoods. (Above the ceiling, squinches and reinforcing arches to support the tower.) In the N transept N wall, piscina under a cinquefoiled arch, a reduced version of the C13 piscina in the chancel (*see* below). In the S transept E wall, a wide, low blocked arch, barely pointed, its mouldings suggesting an early C14 date, presumably a tomb recess.

The chancel is mature E.E., later in style than nave and crossing, though, as has already been mentioned, all reconstructed

by Seddon. Side lancets grouped four in the chancel plus three in the sanctuary. Each group has its own hoodmould over undercut multimoulded rere-arches on tall, slender shafts with large caps. The N lancets copy what Seddon found; the S lancets are his insertions where there had been a windowless wall.*
15 Reset at the E end of the S wall a splendid mid-C13 double piscina. Shafts carry an order of undercut dogtooth which runs up the sides of the arch. Within the arch, moulded and spurred cusping on moulded corbels. The ambitious E window, as already noted, is Seddon's invention. Doorway to the S chapel, replicating the medieval arrangement. The chapel itself entirely rebuilt by Seddon. The medieval function of such a large structure, the full length of the chancel, but communicating with it only by a door, is not at all clear. – FONT. A strange piece, an octagonal bowl, a sunk disc on each face, set on a roll and a thick circular stem. Probably Norman, the bowl remodelled in the C15. – CHOIR STALLS and READING DESKS. 1870 by *Seddon*. – PULPIT. Grey ashlar and Penarth alabaster. 1878 by *James, Seward & Thomas*. – STAINED GLASS. Chancel E, 1879, commemorating the funding of the restoration by J. E. W. Rolls of The Hendre (q.v.), and dominating the chancel. The subject is Feeding the Five Thousand, a curious one. The centre light is more strongly coloured than the outer lights, and other slighter discrepancies suggest that the composition has been made up from disparate parts. The outer lights look like the work of *Heaton, Butler & Bayne*. – SCULPTURE. Virgin and Child (nave S window-sill). Of stone, late medieval, small and fairly crude. What was its original context? The sill itself is a medieval grave-slab, and there are fragments here of two others, one with encircled cross, the other with four-petal motif, hammer and arrow. – MONUMENTS. Knight (S transept). Unfinished recumbent figure of the late C13 or early C14, apparently intended to be shown in chainmail holding a shield. A rare survival of great technical interest. – Charles William and his wife Joan (S transept). Stone grave-slab carved in relief with naive praying figures, she with far-spreading ruff, beneath a now illegible inscription, and a row of three crowned angels above. Dated 1636 and signed *I. B.* (The date 1708 is an irrelevant addition.)

In the CHURCHYARD part of the shaft and the big spurred base of a CROSS (*see* also Town Hall below).

CASTLE. Grosmont is the most compact of the Three Castles, the strongly defended residence of a great lord rather than a fortress which could be garrisoned. The site is imposing, though this is hard to appreciate today, when the approach leads up a lane from the quiet village street, and trees screen the panoramic view to the S. The present castle, built on the site of a C12 ringwork, is the work of Hubert de Burgh, who was Lord of the Three Castles 1201–4 and again 1219–32, with C14 modifications by the Earls of Lancaster, either Henry of Lancaster, lord 1296–1333, or his son Henry of Grosmont †1361. During Hubert's first period as

* See the plan published by Seddon in the *Civil Engineer and Architect's Journal*, 1 January 1864, p. 6.

lord he built the great rectangular hall block on the NE side of the inner ward and protected it with the deep but narrow ditch which encloses the D-shaped ward. The gatehouse and walls with three circular towers which follow the curved line of the D (doubtless replacing an earlier timber enclosure) belong to a second, slightly later campaign. Hubert must have embarked on this after 1219 at a time when his military experiences in France and England had given him fresh ideas on fortification. In 1227 the king granted him fifty oaks for his new buildings at Grosmont. The C14 work strengthened the gatehouse but, more importantly, made the domestic accommodation more spacious and comfortable, so it is appropriate that the only perfectly preserved feature is a tall and decorative C14 chimneystack which surmounts 26
the castle with memorable incongruity.

The later history of the castle follows familiar lines. In 1405 it saw action when it was unsuccessfully attacked by the Welsh during Owain Glyndŵr's uprising. Thereafter, it was redundant and by the early C16 had been abandoned. A survey of 1563 reported its ruin and decay: 'Tymber, iron and lead is rotten or taken away'. The Duchy of Lancaster in 1825 sold the Three Castles to the Duke of Beaufort, and in 1902 Grosmont Castle was sold to Sir Joseph Bradney, the antiquary and county historian. In 1923 the castle passed into the care of the Ministry of Public Building and Works, after which its walls were consolidated and excavations carried out. Today it is in the care of Cadw: Welsh Historic Monuments.

The approach is from the S, across the OUTER WARD. Traces of the enclosing ditch, partly in cottage gardens. Stone foundations of a rectangular two-room building, a storehouse or stables, which presumably had timber-framed walls.

The CASTLE is constructed of local Old Red Sandstone, fairly regularly coursed but varying in colour from mauve to grey. Virtually all the accessible ashlar dressings have been robbed. The way into the INNER WARD across the present bridge follows the line of the medieval bridge and drawbridge. The much-ruined S-facing GATEHOUSE consists of two parts. In front, extending to the bottom of the dry moat, a rectangular, angle-buttressed projection within which the drawbridge was raised and lowered. This overlaps the battered base of the main part of the gatehouse, so is an addition. The C13 gatehouse had a slightly bowed outer wall, rather than the two drum towers which were soon to become so popular. In the surviving SW wall, beam sockets for the floor of the guard chamber above the entrance passage. Jambs of two doorways from the passage, one to the l., one to the r., the former stop-chamfered like other openings in Hubert de Burgh's work. Straight joints between the NE corner of the gatehouse and the S and W walls of the hall demonstrate that the hall was there before the gatehouse.

The HALL BLOCK, even in its ruined state, seems overpoweringly large for the inner ward, even though set back as far as it will go against the NE escarpment of the ditch. It is a rectangle twice as broad as deep, set on a prominent battered plinth, and, as

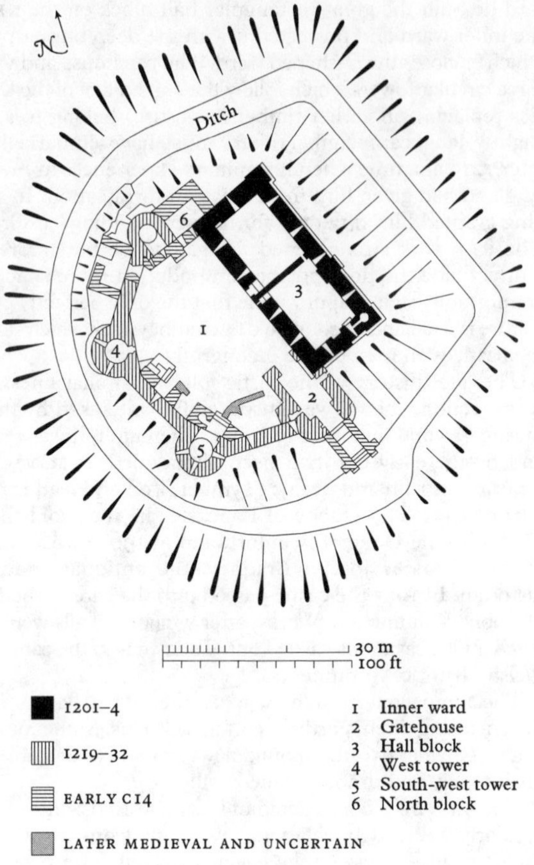

Grosmont Castle. Plan

can be seen at the NE corner, had pilaster buttresses clasping the angles. Evidence of windows and hearths at two levels, so the undercroft was habitable as well as the upper-floor hall. Twin doorways in the centre of the SW wall give access to the two halves of the undercroft. Central dividing wall, with a narrow, chamfered doorway in its far NE end, linking the two rooms. Long slit windows in all outer walls, with, unusually, stepped sills. At the E angle of the r.-hand room a spiral stair ran up from the embrasure of the adjoining window to give access to the hall above. The main approach to the hall, however, was probably by an external timber stair from the inner ward. The upper parts of the walls are very ruined, but it is possible to deduce from the spacing of windows and the siting of fireplaces that the hall occupied the southern two-thirds of the upper floor. The hall fireplace was in the NE wall, central between two windows. The N third formed a private chamber, heated from a fireplace in the NW end wall.

The CURTAIN WALL and two of the three circular MURAL TOWERS, added by Hubert de Burgh to his hall block at the same time as he built the gatehouse, survive largely intact, with some C14 modification to the towers. Embrasures for arrow slits in the curtain wall and in the towers. The W TOWER remains a purely military structure, as designed by Hubert de Burgh. Arrow-slit embrasures at three levels. Chamfered jambs of the doorway into it from the inner ward. The cylindrical basement has been filled in. The SW TOWER retains its C13 basement, but in other ways has been greatly altered. The flat front facing the inner ward is all of the C14. Wide and high pointed arch springing from ground level, and windows above it lighting rooms formed in the top two storeys of the tower. Spiral stair inside the arch to the r., to give access to the upper rooms. In the rooms arrow slits have been widened to form windows, and fireplaces have been inserted, that in the upper room retaining its ashlar jambs and a corbel for its hood. Outside, two of the small rectangular windows of the topmost room survive intact, and the top of a polygonal stair-turret. Wall-head moulding taken round the turret, and remains of battlements with part of a cross-slit. The two stone piers added against the curtain wall between the SW and W towers must have supported some high-level timber walkway or gallery.

The C14 N BLOCK eliminated the third of the C13 mural towers. Only the circular basement survives, filled in when the block was constructed, but now, rather confusingly, re-excavated. The block itself was constructed astride the line of the C13 curtain wall. Part of its S wall facing the inner ward survives. Traces of windows at two levels, to the l. of the chimney-breast. Flues for two hearths, served by the famous chimneystack. This stack rises from an ashlar skirt and has a moulded foot to its octagonal shaft. Trefoil-headed smoke outlet under a gablet at the top of each face, and delicate coronet-like top. This evidence of the elegant sumptuousness of the Lancaster work is tantalizing indeed. To the r. of the stack little survives, just the jambs of a doorway and the embrasure of a window with internal seats. Outside the curtain wall to the NW, and diagonally joining the N block is a second rectangular C14 block. This is hard to see except from the field beyond. It had rooms at three levels, but only the SW half still stands, with evidence of windows in the SW wall. The Lancaster apartments, extending from the SW tower to the N block, must have been spacious as well as elegant, but it is impossible now to understand how their various remaining fragments contributed to coherent suites of rooms.

Half-way up the STREET stands the little stone TOWN HALL, rebuilt 1829–32 at the expense of the Duke of Beaufort (who relinquished all his rights in Grosmont in 1902 – see the inscription). On the traditional plan, open arcaded market space below, council chamber above reached by an external stone stair. In quite an up-to-date Tudor style, though the wide supporting arches are segmental. The large octagonal top step of the late medieval CHURCHYARD CROSS, ornamented with rows of encircled quatrefoils, is loose underneath the arcade.

Uphill of the Town Hall, GLANDŴR, a well-proportioned
but formulaic mid-C18 house of five bays and two storeys under
a hipped roof with dormers. Rendered walls with raised angle
quoins. Sash windows. Under the eaves the date 1742. Only one
other house in the street deserves mention, HOWELL'S HOUSE
(formerly The Shop), for its heavy timber door-frame with step-
p. 38 shaped head dated 1611. In front of this and several other houses,
early C19 and later garden RAILINGS in a variety of patterns. At
the top of the street the former SCHOOL, 1877 by *E. H. Lingen
Barker*. Simple Gothic.

TOWN FARM, SW of the Town Hall. The date cut in the lintel of
the front door is 1673, and that dates the building, though the
59 door itself, central in the three-bay frontage, seems to have been
inserted here under the lintel of a window, of which one light
survives. Otherwise the house, of rubble-stone whitened, is
remarkably little altered. The two-storeyed front has a complete,
symmetrically arranged display of four-light timber windows,
with ovolo-moulded mullions and slate hoodmoulds. The original entrance was in the upper gable-end, into the hall, with fireplace and timber mural stair alongside it. Doorways with shaped
p. 38 heads in hall and parlour, and also in the central unheated service
room, which is enclosed by the usual post-and-panel partitions.
Ovolo-moulded ceiling beams.

Across the lane, BARN dated 1671 on the door lintel. Renewed seven-light timber mullioned window.

GREAT TRESENNY, ¼m. SW. A fine unmodernized farmstead. The farmhouse forms the l.-hand half of the long W-facing range towards the road, with beyond to the r. stabling and the gable-end of a five-bay barn lying back at r.-angles. The farmhouse is larger than Town Farm, but similar in plan: two-storeyed with heated hall and room over to the N, added heated parlour and room over to the S, and unheated service rooms in the middle. The doorway near the centre of the W front is not original. Some timber mullioned windows survive, especially a four-lighter at the rear of the hall, in a broad chamfered frame. Upper four-light W window with sunk chamfers. This detail suggests that Great Tresenny may be early C17, half a century or more earlier than Town Farm. The doorway leads to a paved through-passage flanked by post-and-panel partitions. Only that to the r., with four-centred-headed doorway, is in its original position. That to the l. has been brought from elsewhere in the house. Originally the passage must have been part of the space of the hall to the l. The hall has a fireplace opening in the N wall with monolith lintel, and beside it quite a spacious stone stair leads up to the show room of the house. This has ceiling beams moulded with hollow, ovolo and hollow, and decoratively chamfered joists. The lobby and unheated pantry in the centre of the house remain, but the post-and-panel partitions seen by Fox and Raglan are not now visible. The parlour end retains the upper part of a post-and-panel partition and C13 stones with filleted angle rolls, clearly reused from the castle, in a door jamb and the upper part of the chimney-breast.

LOWER TRESENNY, $\frac{1}{4}$m. SW. The house is of four phases. The centre range came first. The W cross wing was added in the later C16 to provide two handsome private rooms below and another above. The service accommodation, to the E, an L in plan, was developed, probably in two phases, during the C17. Externally, the white rendered walls and altered windows give little away. Diamond-mullion windows survive at the service end, an upper eight-lighter in the E gable, a N six-lighter and another in the S wall. Inside there is much more to see. In the service end the kitchen fireplace remains, backing on to the NE wing, which is therefore presumably an addition, though its stack has been removed. The earliest part is entered from the service addition through a doorway in what was originally the gable-end wall, with the plain but massive hall fireplace beside it. In the room above, part of a cruck truss, so this is a cruck-framed hall house with inserted floor. A post-and-panel partition to the W divides the early house from the late C16 W cross wing. Here there is an array of moulded ceiling beams as rich and varied as any in the county. In the lower N room and upper S they have alternating ovolos and hollows with intervening quirks, the latter with the mouldings drawn together into spear-like stops. The lower S room, quite small and now a store, has broadly chamfered beams and joists with angle rolls, so this must have been a rich little study or closet.

To the SW a small stone GRANARY and beyond it a large BARN, now much mutilated. Its gable-ends are of stone, its side walls half-timbered. Its most remarkable feature is the great cruck truss which stands N of the site of the threshing floor. Its pair to the S has been replaced by a gimcrack modern truss.

HEOLD ALBERT, 1 m. SW. The skeletal timber HAY BARN towards the road is the most remarkable feature of the farmstead. It backs on to the end of a five-bay stone BARN. Flanking the barn, to enclose the farmyard, to the l. a CIDER HOUSE (the horse-powered cider mill still in the uphill part) and to the r. a long STABLE range, the loft with three blocked, pointed-headed openings. The barn is probably of the C18, the rest early C19.

The FARMHOUSE, at the bottom of the group, is a compact two-storeyed C17 range. In the N gable-end the upper two of three original timber, ovolo-moulded windows survive, a four-lighter for the roof space, a six-lighter at first-floor level. Inside, one elaborately moulded beam is the only eloquent survivor.

UPPER DYFFRYN, $1\frac{1}{2}$m. SE. Tall, compact early C17 farmhouse, 58
almost certainly built for John Gainsford, sheriff of Monmouth- p. 35
shire 1604, †1635. Two-storey E porch, originally entered axially through a door framed by two massive stone slabs. The main body of the house is rectangular, two-storeyed of three bays by one, its timber windows largely original, of between two and five lights, with ovolo-moulded mullions. Those under the N and S gables align centrally and diminish in width from storey to storey with three-lighters for the roof space. On the E, entrance side, by contrast, the symmetry is not exact, the porch slightly off-centre, the window l. of it a two-lighter, that to the r. of four

lights. In the centre of the W front a stair-turret boldly projects, the windows here of the more old-fashioned type, with diamond mullions. Beside the stair-turret, a broad chimney-breast carries three diamond stacks. The interior plan was simple, and can be readily understood in spite of later partitions. Each of the two main storeys is separated into a larger and a smaller room running from front to back of the house, hall (l.) and parlour (r.) below, chambers above. Typical post-and-panel partitions below and above. The stairs rise in short flights round a hollow rectangular core, the lowest flight of stone, down to the cellar, the others of timber, all the way up to the attic space. Chamfered ceiling beams in the main rooms, but no decorative fancies anywhere in the house. To the NW a contemporary DAIRY with granary over, see the timber mullioned window, and above to the S beside the road, a four-bay BARN, probably of the C18.

LOWER DYFFRYN, 2½m. SE. Low-lying, and extraordinarily remote, an E-plan mansion built, it seems, *c.* 1600 for a branch of the Cecil family. Its present state is melancholy. There was a remodelling in 1846 (see the date on the E side), when a spurious date of 1506 was added to a W chimneystack, but from *c.* 1870 it seems to have been reduced to its present status as a farm. In 1902 most of its internal woodwork was removed to Hilston Park, St Maughans (*see* p. 524). So many windows remain blocked and others are ungainly sashes. The gables all bear skimped timber bargeboards, and the original chimneystacks have gone or been replaced with inadequate brick substitutes. Yet the remaining C17 evidence suggests that the house had a vernacular character from the start. The entrance front faces E and was apparently symmetrical. The large medieval lancet with cusped ogee head on the inner face of the N wing must be *ex situ.* Central two-storeyed porch, with entrance arch of depressed four-centred form, hollow-chamfered. The doorway within has a moulded timber head, of the type found in C17 farmhouses in the county. Two-light hoodmoulded window above. One original four-light mullion-and-transom window in the S wing, and another round the corner of three lights under a stone-slab hoodmould. The windows are of timber, moulded with a form of sunk chamfer. These too, then, relate to local vernacular practice. The W front is the least altered, and is nearly, but not quite, flat, of five bays crowned by large gables over the end bays and a small one in the middle. Two big projecting chimney-breasts which flank the small gable maintain the near symmetry. Here many of the windows, though much renewed in the C19, are of timber, mullioned, those under the end gables transomed as well. Ovolo mouldings, and stone-slab hoodmoulds. In the N front a large timber mullion-and-transom staircase window survives.

Inside, the plan is difficult to unravel. The porch enters into what was presumably the lower end of a single-storey hall. The thin-ribbed plaster ceiling looks C19. Remnants of the principal staircase to the N, with flat balusters, vertically symmetrical and elaborately profiled.

The setting of the house is still quite evocative. The enclosing walls remain of a rectangular GARDEN on the W side. The N wall, which survives almost to full height, bows out in the centre to form a sort of gazebo, with a two-light window in it giving a glimpse across the valley into Herefordshire. Square turret at the W end, where the wall ramps up.

To the S of the house a two-storey GRANARY, and further away, up the hill to the SE, quite a grand BARN.

KINGSFIELD, ¾ m. N. A fine early C17 farmhouse all of one build, its stone walls whitened, but deprived of some features since Fox and Raglan saw it. The entrance front, of two-and-a-half storeys facing E, was a deliberate composition, but its nearly central porch is now reduced from two storeys to one, and the central of the three attic gables has been removed. The windows here and in the S gable-end, with wide segmental heads of cut stone with keyblocks, must be a late C17 modernization. The rear elevation forms an impressive group, for the square stair projection is set between a pair of chimney-breasts. One original three-light window low down to the l., with ovolo-moulded mullions. The porch doorway has a shaped timber head and leads into the hall. This is separated from the parlour to the l. and two unheated service rooms to the r. by post-and-panel partitions with roll-moulded angles. Ovolo-moulded ceiling beams. The doorway from hall to stair also has a shaped timber head. The stair rises in short straight flights of massive timber treads round a hollow boxed-in core, as at Upper Dyffryn (*see* above). One upstairs post-and-panel partition.

The OUTBUILDING which stood NE of the house, dated 1638 on its shaped door-head, has been demolished. The date must p. 38 correspond closely with that of the house.

GREAT MARLBOROUGH, 2½ m. W. A handsome late C17 house, not large but with some pretension to classical rigour. It is a five-by-one-bay block, of two storeys under a hipped roof. Straight joints in the rear wall probably indicate where a stair projection has been removed. The two chimneystacks are set side by side here. The walls are of small shaley slabs packed neatly to create a fine-grained texture. Angle quoins. Vertically proportioned timber cross-windows with flat voussoired heads and segmental relieving arches are evenly spaced across the main, NE front. The SE upper window, however, has an elaborately notched frame, the detailing similar to that on the porch dated 1675 at High House, Penrhos (q.v.). If all the window frames were originally like this the house would have worn quite a festive air. In the NW porch a stone doorway made up with lengths of C13 filleted moulding, like those at Great Tresenny (*see* above).

BLAENTROTHY, 3½ m. SW. Isolated mid-C17 house, square, of brown Old Red Sandstone with a central doorway, and a projecting chimney-breast in the middle of each side wall. The stair-tower at the back, now rebuilt, was, however, off-centre. The seven-bay BARN which stands close on the S side quite overwhelms the house.

3000 GWEHELOG

2 m. N of Usk

There is no church, as Gwehelog was part of the parish of Usk. Much of it was formerly common land.

LLANCAYO HOUSE. Built by Edward Berry after he had completed Court St Lawrence, Llangovan (*see* p. 316), and before his death in 1818. Quite a sizeable three-storeyed double-pile block, the S front of five regular bays with angle quoins. The three-bay E (entrance) front, clearly built at the same time, is by contrast an eccentric composition. Glazed windows in the centre bay only, and a small timber porch on Doric columns carrying an elegant iron balcony. In the outer bays recesses, probably originally filled with false glazing, round-headed in the lower two storeys, square at the top. Bracketed cornice taken round both fronts, but above it the E front sprouts two pedimental gables over the outer bays. The pediments enclose blind lunettes. From their tops rise chimneystacks. So it is the presence of chimney-breasts lower down that requires the outer bays to be blind.

On axis to the N of the house, and presumably contemporary with it, a large and exceptionally well ventilated threshing BARN. Three pairs of opposing doors, and two tiers of long ventilation slits. This is part of an early C19 MODEL FARM, as is the three-storey MILL to the W.

WINDMILL, N of Llancayo House and barn. The tall tapering tower, of coursed rubble-stone, is a conspicuous object in the flat floodplain of the River Usk. Round-headed openings in five storeys. It was constructed before 1813 and burnt out before 1830. Cap, sails and machinery have all gone.

UPPER LLANCAYO. A tall, stone, single-range house, of two storeys, gable-ended, late C16 or early C17. It has been much altered, but enough survives to give an idea of its original character. Most impressive is the full-height porch in the centre of the W entrance front. The doorway here is square-headed and chamfered and has a row of short, square-headed lights over it. Battered plinth to porch and house. No original window survives on the main front, just the relieving arch for one upper one. The gabled S end is heavily restored. Are its tiered stone mullioned windows, diminishing in width storey by storey, faithful copies of what was there?

CAMPSWOOD CAMP (SO 379 038). An interesting hill-fort, surrounded by woodland, but with a clear interior. It is best to approach it from the S, entering the wood opposite a stone barn, for one can then appreciate the complex and impressive entrance through the annexe. The camp is in two parts, a large oval enclosure on the very top of the hill and an annexe to the S. The main enclosure has two banks and ditches on the vulnerable S side, where they can be well seen on either side of the simple entrance; for the rest of the circuit only the inner rampart is recognizable. In front of the entrance there is an annexe half the size of the main enclosure, and probably a later addition. This has a fine entrance causeway through double banks and ditches, the side banks sweeping in to curve round on either side behind the inner ditch. On the E the annexe is bounded by a single bank and ditch; the arrangement on the W is difficult to make out because of the steep slope and the trees. There has been some disturbance in the annexe due to C18 or C19 pottery manufacture.

GWERNESNEY/GWERNESNI

4000

ST MICHAEL. A small C13 or early C14 church, its rubble walling and dressed stonework all of mauve Old Red Sandstone. Nave with S porch, and lower chancel. The W wall and double bell gable largely by *J. P. Seddon* of *Prichard & Seddon*, who restored the church in 1853–4. The lancet window here is partly old, and so is another in the nave N wall, with restored trefoiled head. The S doorway, two-centred with a broad chamfer, may also be of *c.* 1300. The E window, of two trefoil-headed lights, establishes a similar date for the chancel. Miscellaneous later windows, Perp, Tudor and of 1853–4. Two mutilated stoups, one in the porch, the other in the nave. The chancel arch is wide, sharply pointed and polygonal in section, but formed without dressed stones. It may well have been reconstructed like this when the rood loft was inserted in the C15. Late medieval wagon roof in the nave, plastered between moulded ribs. The barn-like chancel roof must be post-medieval. – ROOD LOFT. The rood beam survives, resting on three stone corbels. It retains some of its decoration, a pierced, cusped trail (cf. Llangattock Lingoed). – CHANCEL SCREEN. Simple Perp. Is the stencilled repeating pattern of the C16 or the C19? – ALTAR RAILS. Late C17. Turned balusters. – FONT. C19 octagonal bowl on a medieval circular stem and moulded foot. – FONT ENCLOSURE. Made up of two simple late medieval screens. Note the slots for traceried spandrels. – PULPIT, CHOIR STALLS and PEWS. Simple, clearly by *Prichard & Seddon.*

CHURCH FARM. Small, later C16 hall house, gable-end on to the churchyard. Corbelled-out upper chimney-breast in the gable.

RECTORY. 1817 by *Walter Gwatkin* of Chepstow, builder. Plain, of three bays, with a simple classical door-case.

THE HENDRE

4010

The only full-scale Victorian country house in the county, the seat of the Rolls family, whose local power reached its zenith in the person of John Allan Rolls, first Baron Llangattock (created 1892), but whose name has been immortalized by the baron's third son, the Hon. Charles Stewart Rolls, engineer, pioneer aviator and co-founder in 1904 of Rolls-Royce Ltd. The family's fortunes rested on the strategic marriage in the later C18 of John Rolls of The Hendre to Sarah Coysh, sole heiress to three family fortunes,

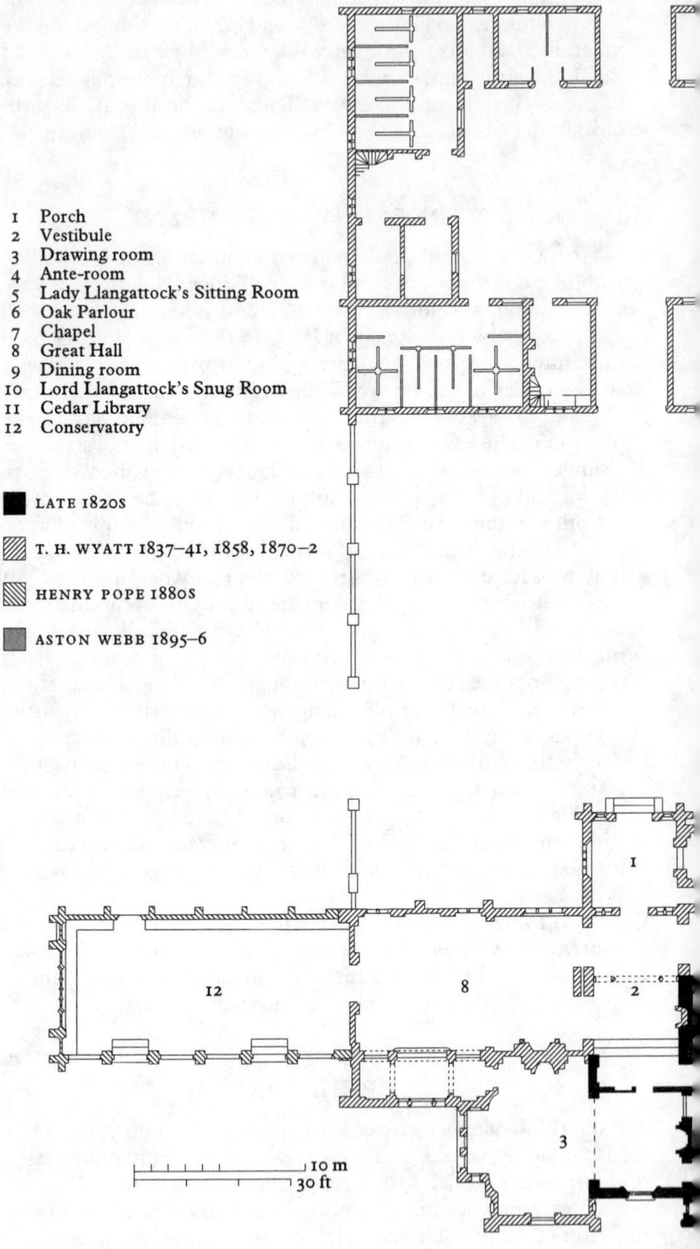

1 Porch
2 Vestibule
3 Drawing room
4 Ante-room
5 Lady Llangattock's Sitting Room
6 Oak Parlour
7 Chapel
8 Great Hall
9 Dining room
10 Lord Llangattock's Snug Room
11 Cedar Library
12 Conservatory

LATE 1820S

T. H. WYATT 1837–41, 1858, 1870–2

HENRY POPE 1880S

ASTON WEBB 1895–6

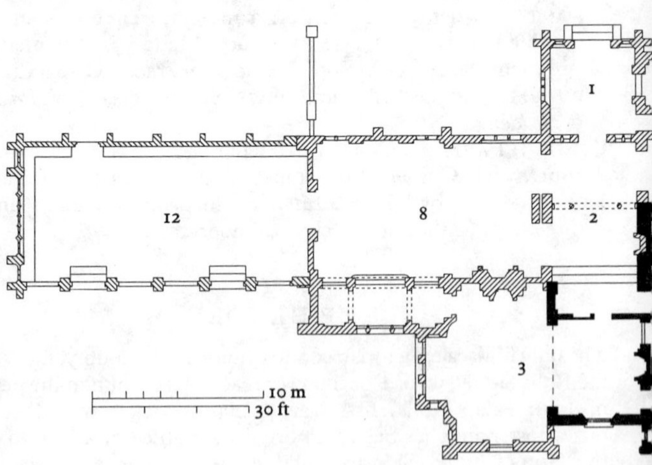

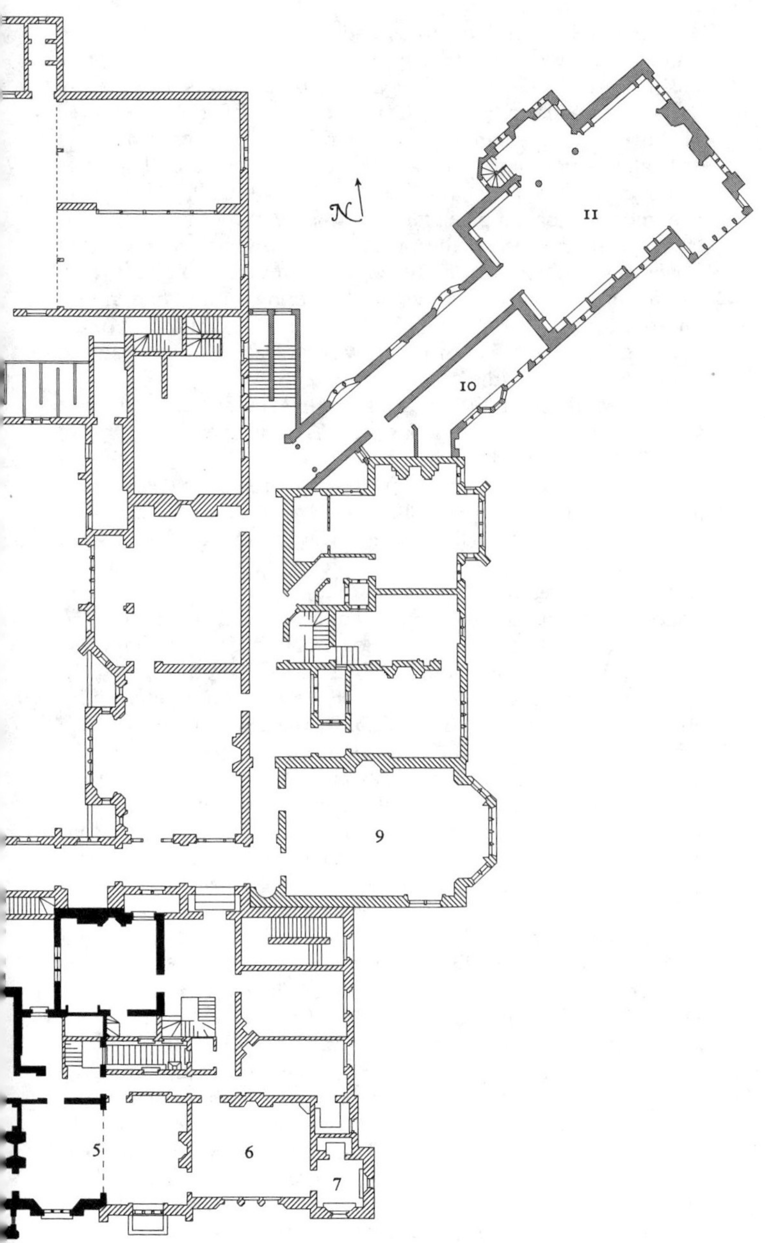

The Hendre. Principal floor plan

including land in South London which became ever more valuable over the ensuing century and a half.

In the late 1820s John Rolls's son, also John (*c.* 1776–1837), built, to the design of an unknown architect, the compact shooting box in a bizarre Neo-Norman style which remains as the kernel of the present mansion. During the period 1827–30 his agent scoured old houses in Monmouthshire and Herefordshire for early wainscot and other fittings for it. Already by 1829–30, however, Rolls was planning enlargement. In November 1829 *G. V. Maddox* of Monmouth supplied plans for 'the additional rooms', but a year later, September 1830, the fashionable London architect *P. F. Robinson* submitted a rival scheme for expansion on a grand scale. In the event John Rolls achieved nothing more than minor improvements to the hall and the addition of service rooms to the old farmhouse, which at this stage was allowed to survive, carried out under *Maddox*'s direction in 1833–4.

John Etherington Welch Rolls, on his inheritance, at once switched architects to the rising star, *T. H. Wyatt*. From 1837 to 1841 Wyatt extended the house, still in Neo-Norman, and laid out the garden, all at a cost of over £10,000. From 1850 the park was improved and gate lodges built. In 1858, in response to changing fashion, Wyatt added to the house a great hall in Neo-Tudor style. But it was his son, J. A. Rolls, inherited 1870, who brought The Hendre to its present gargantuan extent. This he did in three main stages, by adding 1870–2 a Neo-Tudor entrance court to *T. H. Wyatt*'s design, then in the mid 1880s a massive dining-room wing, designed by *Henry Pope*, formerly Wyatt's clerk-of-works, and finally, yet grander and much more swagger, the Arts and Crafts Tudor library wing, 1895–6 by *Aston Webb*. By the time this had all been achieved the length of the corridor from the front door to the library was no less than 240 ft (73 metres). Many of the rooms were panelled with miscellaneous Jacobean and later overmantels, door surrounds and wainscot, collected, as noted above, by John Rolls from local C16 and C17 houses. Finally, one should not forget that, as a correspondent in the *Connoisseur* ambivalently noted in 1907, 'From end to end the house is now full of objects of all sorts and kinds, most of which are of more or less interest, on account of their great variety and antiquity'.

Meanwhile, the family's landholdings surrounding the house were increased, until in 1892 the newly created Lord Llangattock was able to enclose a thousand-acre (400-hectare) deerpark, and create a 2-m. (3-kilometre)-long picturesque carriage drive from the E entrance lodge at Rockfield (*see* p. 516). But such panache could not last. Lord Llangattock died in 1912 (two years after C. S. Rolls had lost his life in a plane crash) and his heir was a victim of the First World War. Today the deerpark has become a golf-course, and the mansion its club house. At the time of writing a major, most commendable programme of fabric repairs is in progress.

The drive, which leaves the B4233 and enters the park from the N, soon swings away to the r. and then curves back to approach the entrance courtyard of the house from the W. The first surprise is that the house is built of red brick, dressed with Bath stone. Why such an apparently alien material should have been chosen is not clear, though in the decades around 1700 many substantial farmhouses in this NE corner of the county were constructed of it, so perhaps the pre-existing house suggested a material in which no other Victorian country-house builder in Monmouthshire showed the slightest interest.

The courtyard is bounded to the W by a low ornamental wall, and on the other three sides by Tudor-style ranges. The only peculiarity is the siting of what is clearly an open-roofed, medievalizing hall not centrally, but at the W end of the S range. Its diapered brickwork and the junction with the porch show that it antedates the rest, the only part of J. E. W. Rolls's house to face the courtyard. Almost all the rest was put up by his son, J. A. Rolls, 1870–2: the porch, the corridor, the staircase tower at the SE corner (later heightened) and the two-storeyed, gabled E range. The r. half of this last part was occupied by billiard and smoking rooms, the l. half, with its three gabled semi-dormers, formed the start of the service quarters, fronted by a slightly later addition. The entrance range of the stable court, closing the entrance courtyard on the N, is also of 1870–2.

To go into more detail, the hall has buttresses and large mullion-and-transom windows. The main windows elsewhere are mullion-and-transom with arched upper lights. An oriel window above the porch arch. Also on the porch the family motto and a welcoming tag, Open House Open Hearth, as beloved by the Victorians. The parapets on the E range, with bands of quatrefoils, are a post-1872 embellishment. Groups of heavy octagonal brick chimneystacks crown the steep roofslopes. Finally, one cannot avoid noticing the riot of gargoyles.

Above and behind the porch the gables of the earlier entrance front peep up. To find more of this house one must skirt round the W end of the hall, and past the further-projecting, plainly pinnacled CONSERVATORY, by *Pope*, 1885 (the date 1924 refers to the blocking of its W windows), in order to reach the S front. The style here, and this is the second shock, is recklessly Neo-Norman. Gargoyles and grotesque animal corbels break out wherever one looks. The front is largely two-storeyed and has seven components. The centre three project slightly under gables, the outermost are carried up as towers. Within this scheme, symmetrical in principle, nothing balances with anything else. Bays two, three and four belong to the 1820s house. Here the lower windows, in spite of being Neo-Norman, are of timber, one in a projecting bay, others within cut and rubbed brick surrounds. Also, inconsistently, an upper Gothic oriel, also of timber. The SE tower was clearly intended by Wyatt as the major accent, set on a sloping stone base and crowned by a two-stage ogee cap. A very long and thin window extends through the height of the two main storeys, and above it a small, thin window pushes up under a gablet through a lower roof stage. Clock face in a strap-work surround between the two roof stages. The SW tower bears J. E. W. Rolls's initials in raised brickwork. Its top stage, however, was added by his son. A Neo-Norman corridor runs across the back of the hall. The E front starts Neo-Norman but more restrained. Beyond the SE tower a symmetrical block, the four windows of the top storey syncopated against the three in the storey below. Underneath are three wider arched openings where the ground drops. In 1872 this was the E-ward limit of the house. What comes next, the dining-room range of the 1880s, dramatically demonstrates J.A. Rolls's escalating ambitions. The style is Tudor. The three full storeys are occupied by large mullion-and-transom windows, and as a climax a gable over a three-storey, polygonal projection windowed all round at all levels. Quatrefoil parapet beyond, and then a lower, gabled section, marking the next pause in construction.

114 The last component is the wing added in 1896 by *Aston Webb*. This extends diagonally from the NE, and at last shows the hand of an architect who can achieve his effects with deftness and subtlety. Now for the first time the fact is acknowledged that the principal floor, carried across from the ground floor of the S range without a change of level, has, because of the fall in the ground, been continued in the E wing at first-floor level. So the wing has its lower windows set under wide segmental arches spanning from buttress to buttress, which encourages one to read the lower storey as a bridge, carrying the lofty principal storey. This is in two parts. The corridor link from the body of the house is lit by high-set mullioned windows and a generous oriel breaking out half-way along. The main part, enclosing the Cedar Library, is of three bays, the first two lit by tall two-light windows with two transoms, the third by a huge six-light oriel with three transoms. Top parapet tweaked up to form low gablets alternating with merlons. Note the string-course just below it, decorated with rectangular panels carved into animals and birds, the sculpture now integrated into the architecture. The end elevation brings sculpture into play to even greater effect. It is crowned by a gable, through which a short panelled chimneystack rises, a 'pelican in her piety' carved at its foot. The chimney-breast below projects slightly and is topped by a triangular panel carved with the Tree of Knowledge and the date 1896. Mullion-and-transom windows to l. and r. at library level, and small segment-headed windows below. The whole composition is tautly framed by full-height buttresses. The other, NW-facing length of the wing, though fronting the stable court, also has plenty of incident. Broad projecting chimney-breast, with little inglenook windows at three levels, hinting at high jinks inside. Further along, two two-storeyed window bows, partly obscured by later additions.

In order to investigate the INTERIOR it is necessary to begin again at the porch in the entrance courtyard. From here exploration in three directions reveals the family's increasing ambitions, first to the S to the suite of quite small but overpoweringly fitted rooms of the 1820s house; then to the W into the great hall of 1858; and finally to the NE along the far-extending corridor which leads with many twists and turns to the great dining room and eventually the Cedar Library. The room names given here are those of 1907.

The PORCH is fitted with fireplace and mirror overmantel. It opens into a VESTIBULE with at its inner end big fluted Doric columns and a triglyph frieze. Beyond, extending to the S front, lies a DRAWING ROOM, originally two rooms subdivided by a double arch. Here is a Jacobean timber chimneypiece and overmantel, the first of many collected by John Rolls, and in the further half of the room niches with fretwork tops and decorated ceiling paper typical of *c.* 1840. From here the suite of rooms extends E-wards across the S front. First comes the ANTE-ROOM, brightly lit by the Neo-Norman timber bay window. Ceiling with shallow strapwork bands. Early-Renaissance-style door panels with profile heads. The central room in the suite was LADY LLANGATTOCK'S SITTING ROOM. It has two chimneypieces, one made up with timber twisted columns and a cartouche dated 1650, the other, probably a new design of the 1830s, incorporating music-playing putti with baskets on their heads. More putti above the door jambs. The abundance of carved woodwork increases yet further in the next room, in spite of its small size. This, called the OAK PARLOUR in 1907, was originally the dining room. Jacobean-style wainscot with arcaded top frieze, chimneypiece incorporating Jacobean terms and overmantel with three armed men, one Hercules, between gadrooned arcaded panels. More Jacobean terms flank the two doors, which are most exotic with their pierced acanthus panels. These, of course, require secondary doors, to keep out the draughts. Finally, in the SE tower, a tiny cabinet fitted up as a chapel. More Jacobean timberwork, but also a slate reredos decorated with religious symbols, and a timber balustraded grille opposite. The room may have been meant as a – somewhat tasteless – joke. In 1907 it was referred to as the 'chamber of horrors' and visitors were not allowed to see inside.

Back at the porch, there is only one room to see towards the W, *Wyatt*'s GREAT HALL of 1858. It is overhung by a coarse timber roof, of hammerbeam and collar-beam construction with acorn pendants. Armorial corbels. Above the entrance an organ, by *Bevington*, between two segmental balcony arches.

In the opposite direction, from the inner vestibule a square, single-storeyed space opens up. It has a top light at the centre of a rib vault, and bears the date 1872 and the initials of J. A. Rolls in the grisaille glass window which occupies one side. Beside it, one last element of the earlier house. This is the principal staircase, quite small, the stair with thick turned balusters ascending in a square, open well. Large, three-light stained-glass N window here by *Willement*, dated 1838 and bearing the name of J. E. W. Rolls. At the foot of the stair a door into one of the S rooms. Early-Renaissance-style heads on the door itself, elaborate framing pilasters and strapwork at the top enclosing the unexpected date 1682.

Upstairs, two further rooms are fitted out with brought-in timberwork. One has wainscoting and a chimneypiece awkwardly made up with big Corinthian columns. The other has an overmantel with crude terms at two levels, a door-case framed by Ionic balusters and an arcaded frieze enriched with caryatids.

The corridor which extends beyond the foot of the principal stair under a series of segmental arches leads to the rooms at first-floor level in the E range. The major one is the gigantic DINING ROOM. The chimneypiece here consists of an alabaster mantelshelf set with red marble jewels and paired supporting columns, their caps and bases of white marble, their twisted shafts of mottled mauve Devonshire marble. The top lights of the great mullion-and-transom bay window are filled with STAINED GLASS (designer not recorded) illustrating eleven of Aesop's fables. Opposite, between the pair of doorways, an inlaid armorial panel and niches to display plate. The next room, lined with embossed Cordova leather, was MR ROLLS'S ROOM, i.e. the domain of Lord Llangattock's eldest son and heir. Here, appropriately, the STAINED GLASS depicts four knights. Chimneypiece and overmantel in early Renaissance style. Decorated plaster ceiling.

The final section of the corridor is *Aston Webb*'s. At once a tautening of the architectural effect is felt. A Doric timber Serliana arch frames the entrance to it, and its ceiling is segmentally vaulted with geometrical plaster decoration. Half-way down on the l. an oculus with STAINED GLASS of fishermen in a Romanesque style. On the r. the door to LORD LLANGATTOCK'S SNUG ROOM, its oriel window overlooking the garden and park. At the end of the corridor comes the CEDAR LIBRARY. This is a fitting climax and a *tour de force* of design, if dependent on Norman Shaw's showpiece rooms at Dawpool and Cragside. Beamed ceiling of cedar, with inlaid soffits to the beams. Enriched plaster frieze. Two motto-laden chimneypieces, one, at the far end, of timber and crowned by a swan-neck pediment, the other, in the centre of the long NW side of the room, a gigantic inglenook composition dominating the room. Fireplace surround of stone carved with fruit, flanked by the recesses of the inglenook and by two thick-set columns of black and white African marble with bronze volute capitals. These carry not a mere overmantel but a complete upper room, reached by twin spiral stairs, and fitted with doors between the upper Composite columns, so that anyone in this eyrie can open them and peep down into the library. The STAINED GLASS in the inglenook windows represents buildings and scenes significant for the family, and in the largest of the SE windows gives an imposing heraldic display.

The ghost of the Victorian GARDEN LAYOUT can be readily made out, its various levels relating to the drop from the S to the E front of the house. To the SE a cast-iron fountain and the traces of formal beds around it. To the E, in axis with the end of the Cedar Library wing, a square, single-storey PAVILION, clearly by *Aston Webb*. Red brick with a rusticated arched opening to the S. Square-plan cap of ogee profile with a step, echoing the top of the clock tower of the house.

The SERVICE BUILDINGS were much extended *c.* 1900 to the

E and NE of Wyatt's stable court. They include GARAGES and WORKSHOPS, where C.S. Rolls carried on his experiments, and, further away to the E of the drive, a GAS-MAKING HOUSE and ELECTRICITY-GENERATING HOUSE, to power the mechanisms which made The Hendre in Lord Llangattock's time a thoroughly forward-looking estate. Yet, for all their modernity of function, they are all dressed up in an Old English style, red brick below, half-timbered above.

The ESTATE VILLAGE is a picturesquely accidental group on the B4233, clustered at the main entry to the park. On the S side of the road the single-storey GATE LODGE, *c.* 1850 by *T. H. Wyatt*. It is of rock-faced Old Red Sandstone with stepped gables and a window bow under a semi-conical roof. Opposite, on the N side of the road, *Aston Webb*'s DRINKING FOUNTAIN, bearing the date 1894 and the perhaps admonitory text 'Pure life Pure water'. LYCHGATE beside it, for a pair of COTTAGES dated 1893, the l. one presumably built as the village shop. The sequence continues W-wards. First comes an L-plan COTTAGE, stone below, diapered red brick above, incorporating the initials of J. E. W. Rolls and the date 1866. The VILLAGE HALL beyond is also L-plan, of 1904, not certainly by Aston Webb. Ground-hugging proportions. Stone below, half-timbered above. The wings end in tall oriel windows under overhanging half-timbered gables, and a lean-to timber gallery extends all along the inner face of the L. A little further on, at the crest of the hill, OAK HOUSE, a symmetrical gabled pair, the outer gables of stone, the inner half-timbered. This is not dated, but must be by *Aston Webb*, built, it is said, in 1906 for the head coachman and head gamekeeper. Over the next crest a conspicuous cottage, SUNNYSIDE, not in Webb's style, white-rendered above mauve sandstone, with a heraldic display in one gable and the date 1903 on the other. Finally, on the S side of the road, the HOME FARM, probably early C19. Trim late Georgian white farmhouse. Long stone ranges come forward to the road at r.-angles, with large lancet openings in the gable-ends. To the S, on a side road, RAGLAN LODGE, which looks like a further contribution by *Aston Webb*. Single-storey. Half-timbered under a sweeping roof. Datable shortly before 1900.

Turning E from the gate lodge and drinking fountain, there is one larger house on the hillside N of the road, set a little apart. This, CROES VAEN, built for Lord Llangattock's land agent, is by *Aston Webb*, 1894,* in a suave Arts and Crafts Tudor style. Rock-faced sandstone. The two-storeyed composition towards the road is firmly controlled, the l. bay treated as a low tower, the r. under a broad gable. Long, low-seeming central section, the doorway pushed over to the r. within a bold semi-circular recess. Low, wide, mullioned windows. The interior is a miniature compendium of contemporary motifs, the main stair spilling out into the entrance hall, the back stairs clerestory-lit, the dining room provided with an inglenook.

* The architect's design drawing survives in the house.

Further E two more cottages dated 1893, and a two-storeyed LODGE clearly by *Wyatt*. For the third lodge and other estate buildings, *see* Rockfield (p. 516).

2090 HENLLYS

ST PETER. A simple medieval church alone in open hill country. The chancel may have been built first and the nave added to it, see the crudely pierced chancel arch. The tall, slim W tower with a battlemented NE stair-turret rising well clear of the tower parapet was a further addition, Perp of two dates. Three-light window with panel tracery over the blocked W doorway. Tower arch of the typical Perp form, with chamfered arch and sub-arch, the latter dying into vertical imposts. The heavily rendered nave has charmingly ignorant tracery in the S windows, presumably of the early C19. S porch with small, depressed outer arch. Chancel E window Perp, a twin of the tower W window. Inside, the chancel has a late medieval plastered, ribbed wagon roof on plain wall-plates, with bold, if quite crude, square foliage bosses. The boarded nave roof is of 1871, part of *E.A. Lansdowne*'s restoration. – FONT. Of red granite. Roughly cut octagonal bowl on a cylindrical stem. Of what date? – (WALL PAINTINGS. Medieval traces in the chancel.)

In the CHURCHYARD the base and stump of a CROSS shaft on four modern steps.

ZOAR CHAPEL, Castell-y-bŵch, 1½ m. NE. At a lonely upland crossroads, set back from the road behind a small burial ground. Dated 1836. The simple little rendered building has three pointed windows with timber Y-tracery in its long, roadward wall, and is entered at one of the short ends, through a modern porch. Simple, unspoilt interior, the minister having no more than a railed platform opposite the entrance, the congregation open-backed benches. Central stove. No galleries. Disused at the time of writing.

CWRT HENLLYS, 1 m. NW. The little farmhouse with its three-bay barn alone on the hillside contains unexpected late medieval features. In the long S wall a two-centred, roughly chamfered stone doorway, and immediately inside two more at r.-angles opposite one another.

5090 HOWICK/YR HYWIG FACH

The smallest parish in the county and lacking a church.

HOWICK FARM. A fine group set on a mound above the road, two three-bay BARNS in the foreground. The creeper-clad FARMHOUSE behind, on the N side of the yard, consists mainly of a small mid-C16 house. It is built entirely of stone with stone details, the most completely surviving example of the few such buildings in the county. Across the nearby Gloucestershire border, however, there is plenty to compare with it. Two full storeys. Hoodmoulded windows with arched lights, and step and chamfer mouldings, two reset in the C19 dormers. Two-room plan, with fireplace in the E gable wall, between an unusually well built mural stair and the original entrance doorway, now blocked. N garderobe projection. Two four-centred-headed stone doorways open into the smaller, W room, one in the S wall, the other in the W wall. Is either in its original position? C17 timber doorway beside the latter. C17 extension to the W, constructed in much inferior masonry, with, at the back, a pair of reconstructed lozenge-plan chimneystacks.

ITTON/LLANDDINOL 4090

The grouping of church and manor house, so familiar in England, is not often found in Wales. Itton is one of a small number of such manorial groups in the SE of the county (cf. Penhow, St Pierre), though visually not especially evocative.

ST DEINIOL. Nave and lower chancel. W tower with octagonal NE stair-turret. Broad and deep S porch. Grey local limestone, used in large squared blocks in the tower. The only recognizable medieval features are the simple early C14 tower arch and chancel arch, of purple sandstone, with two hollow-chamfered orders, the inner carried on crude head corbels; also the porch arch, probably Tudor, almost round-headed with a roll and a chamfer. Otherwise everything is owed to *Henry Woodyer*'s restoration of 1869. Plate-traceried windows. His boldest stroke was to pierce arches through l. and r. of the chancel arch. – ALTAR RAIL. A handsome design, of quatrefoils in latticework, by *Woodyer*. – FONT. Bowl with cusped underside, corbelled down to the octagonal stem. Also by *Woodyer*. – STAINED GLASS. By *Hardman*. Chancel E, Crucifixion, the mourners in roundels, set against a background of stiff-leaf in blue and red. Legible and arresting. Is this the window which *Woodyer* is said to have designed? – Chancel S, Resurrection, 1872. – MONUMENTS. John Curre †1726. A splendid ledger slab, immediately inside the S door. – Rebecca Curre †1827. Signed by *Tyley* of Bristol. Such tablets with a willow weeping over an urn were his stock-in-trade. – Matthew Curre. 1914 by *Guy Dawber*. Bow-fronted marble tablet in an C18 style. – W.E.C. Curre †1930. White and green marble, also C18 in style, also designed by *Dawber*.

In the CHURCHYARD, part of a SHAFT of Forest stone, quatrefoil in plan. Not like normal cross shafts. The LYCHGATE, dated 1892, its timber gable enclosing open arcading, is a conventional piece, also by *Dawber*.

ITTON COURT. A courtyard house consisting of a medieval W gate-tower, an early C18 E range, and extensive additions for the Curre family by *Guy Dawber*, 1893–6, which knitted everything lovingly together. Subsequent subdivision and alteration have compromised Dawber's internal effects, but the exterior is virtually as he left it.

The approach rises gently from the S, past a long range on the r. into an irregular W-facing outer court, somewhat collegiate in character. Several minor earlier buildings are absorbed into Dawber's ranges, which are of grey rubble limestone with buff Bath stone dressings. Ashlar battlements. Mullioned windows of every shape and size, some transomed, some breaking out into bays and oriels. The focal point, rising well clear of the rest, is the medieval gate-tower. This is of Old Red Sandstone, with a double-chamfered two-centred arch front and back. Battlementing on small corbels, one or two in the form of crude heads. Higher stair-turret with similarly corbelled battlements. All this may be of the C14. The grey limestone S front is almost entirely by Dawber, but the two pre-existing E bays, with upright cross-windows, gave him the fenestration pattern which he continued regularly all across. This provides a transition to the classical formality of the E front.

The E front is one of the most distinguished, if conventional, early C18 compositions in the county. It must have been built for John Jeffreys, who acquired Itton in 1701 and sold it to the Curres in 1749. Two storeys and seven bays, the centre three brought forward under a pediment, hipped roof and dormers. Bath stone dressings and rendered, colour-washed walling. Enrichment consists, predictably enough, of raised angle quoins and window surrounds with block corbels and keystones. Wave-moulded door surround, however, supporting a triangular pediment. The only oddity is the central window, formed of two arched lights. The N front, mainly of the early C19, is minimally classical but uncomposed.

The house is entered under the gate-tower to the r. A wainscoted lobby leads abruptly into the great hall contrived by Dawber, a vastly long, low, wainscoted room, its main chimneypiece on the short W end, with timber overmantel projecting on black, fossily columns. A big aperture at the E end of the N wall, now blocked, gave a dramatic view of the staircase in the E range. This is of the early C18, with two turned and one twisted baluster per step and shaped tread-ends. It may have been introduced by Dawber, or at least rearranged. In the C18 range a square S room, panelled, with a full-height, shell-headed niche in the S wall, and the drawing room, which originally occupied the rest of the range, but has been subdivided. The only other room recognizably of Dawber's arrangement is the billiard room, at the S end of the S range, now thrown into one with the E and W appendages added by him as an afterthought. – STABLE, 200 yds (183 metres) S. Stark red brick courtyard, to satisfy Mr Curre's fox-hunting needs. Surprisingly, this is also by *Dawber*, designed in 1893.

HOWICK LODGE, ¾ m. NE. By *Dawber*. T-plan, pebble-dashed with slated roofs and trimly bargeboarded gables in all three directions.

VILLAGE HALL, ½ m. N. Of 1914–19 by *Dawber*, in his Arts and

Crafts Cotswold style, employing random local limestone and stone slates. L-plan, with a big chimney-breast in the crook of the L, to heat both the hall and the billiard room.

In the group of COTTAGES 100 yds (90 metres) E of the Village Hall, Nos. 2 and 3 are a symmetrical pair by *Dawber* of the same date and similar in style.

KEMEYS COMMANDER 3000

ALL SAINTS. In a farm group embraced by a bow of the River Usk. Perp, of grey-brown local limestone. Tiny nave and chancel in one, with oversized W double bell gable and a W porch which is, unusually, timber-framed. Square-headed S windows with cinquefoiled lights, the three-lighter in the nave with ogee heads to the lights, the two-lighter in the chancel without. Three-light E window under a pointed head. Deep hollow reveals for them all. Priest's door with four-centred head and small high window for the rood loft. Windowless N wall. Inside, the wagon roof runs through unbroken, ribbed and plastered in the usual way. Walls scraped, at the restoration by *Richard Creed* in 1897. – SCREEN. Much renewed, with simple Perp panel tracery, similar to the screens at Mamhilad and Bettws Newydd (qq.v). Nothing of the rood loft remains, except the bressumer beam, which is so firmly built into the N and S walls as to suggest that church, rood screen and loft were all constructed together.

CHURCH HOUSE, SW of the church. Built as the parsonage, of cruck construction, but according to Fox and Raglan, without an open hall. The stone walls encased it, probably in the C17, but retained the original single-storey height. (Post-and-panel screen with painted figures and texts, now much faded.) The BARN in line to the r. is a later addition.

CHURCH COTTAGES, opposite, incorporate in Nos. 2 and 3 a C17 three-unit house with cross-passage behind the hearth, a characteristic plan.

CHAIN BRIDGE, ½ m. NW. Rebuilt in 1906 without chains but with curved iron girders.

KEMEYS INFERIOR/KEMEYS ISHA 3090

The little medieval church of All Saints stood between the River Usk and the manor house on the hillside above, until 1960–2, when the church, doomed by road proposals, was dismantled and the stone reused in the new choir of St Woolos Cathedral, Newport. (For the windows, *see* below.) Its site is now separated from the house by the two carriageways of the A449 and their rushing traffic.

KEMEYS MANOR (formerly Kemeys House). There was a lordship of Kemeys in the Middle Ages, and a family of this name was active in south-east Wales by the early C13. Kemeys followed

Kemeys for generations until George Kemeys, having served as sheriff in 1699, sold the estate shortly afterwards. The fabric of the L-plan house reflects this history. It is built of an unusual greenish stone, presumably quarried locally. The N third of the main range is a square C13 tower, to which in the C16 a two-storeyed, four-bay range of identical depth was neatly added, with a full-height gabled W porch at the junction. In the late C17 a short wing was pushed out E of the S end of the C16 range. Probably this had a hipped roof from the start. A hipped roof consistent with it was clamped on the entire main range either then or after the end of the Kemeys ownership, reducing the height of the medieval tower, and requiring the eaves line of the C16 W front to be slightly built up. Lower lean-to N service range, also under a hipped roof.

To go into further detail. The angles of the medieval tower all remain visible, the SW one as a step in the wall plane of the W front, the SE as a straight joint. The NW angle stands free and is visible right down to its steeply battered base. The only original opening is the head of a blocked W lancet quite high up. Inside there is more to see. In the E wall at an upper level part of a mural stair, leading to a doorway with two-centred head, beyond which rises a circular stone newel stair, soon curtailed by the later roof. The upper levels of the tower were integrated into the C16 house by means of a straight flight of stone stairs in a lean-to annexe to the porch. A four-centred-headed doorway in the N wall of the porch opens on to the foot of this stair, and at its head there are similar stone doorways in three directions. Tudor two-light windows under hoodmoulds in the W face of the tower, in the porch and in the stair annexe. Entrance arch to the porch, with depressed head and ovolo moulding. Much larger W windows in the C16 range, all but one C20 Tudor-style. The lone original, immediately S of the porch, is of four lights, the mullions moulded with a step and chamfer, the hoodmould given square, outlined stops. Similar hoodmoulds survive over the other lower windows and voussoired relieving arches, so the C20 work must copy fairly faithfully what had been there. Round the corner to the S, a tier of similarly detailed windows on three levels, and a straight joint beyond, suggesting that the windows were originally centred under a gable-end. Fine groups of lozenge-plan chimneystacks. The remaining E bay of the S front belongs to the late C17 addition. The mullioned windows with arched lights here were inserted in the 1960s from the demolished church. The three-light Perp window with panel tracery set in the garden wall beyond came from the church too. The timber C17-style E and N windows in the wings were reinstated or inserted in the 1960s. (An elaborately carved stone panel, formerly set over the rear entrance, dated 1623 and bearing a relief of a man carrying a scroll and an hourglass, as well as a Welsh inscription, was brought into the house in the 1960s, and has subsequently disappeared.)

The rest of the interior can be taken together. The inner doorway of the porch has plain chamfered jambs, and a timber

lintel which must be an alteration. The similar E doorway at the opposite end of what was the screens passage remains intact. The single-storey hall opens out to the r. It has a fireplace at each end, the chimneypiece to the N original, of stone, quite plain, that to the S made up of old bits. Parlour to the S with a wide C16 chimneypiece, its depressed-headed opening plainly chamfered. The best sights are in the SE wing. The small ground-floor room has a late C17 plaster ceiling of quite good quality. Oval high-relief wreath of fruit, a rose and bunch of grapes within it, rosettes in the spandrels. The rest of the wing is occupied by a spacious open-well staircase which opens from the SE corner of the hall. Some of the original flat balusters survive. But the real surprise is the plasterwork here. On the string of 63
the stair intermittent plaster vine trails, which in one place mutate into a cherub. Much more spectacular is the sight which greets one on the first-floor landing. Here three doorways in a row are embraced by a composition of twisted vine-clad columns crowned by demi-angels holding armorial shields. Roundels to l. and r. above the doorways, and naive heads with pendant doilies.

The bones of the C17 GARDEN survive, in particular long, grassed terrace walks at two levels where the ground drops in front of the house to the W. Aligned on these towards the N, and clearly meant to be seen in conjunction with them, a handsome stone BARN. It has a full-height projecting porch near the centre of the long side towards the terraces, with segmentally arched entrance, small mullioned windows above, and between them a tablet bearing the date 1597.

OLD KEMEYS, $\frac{3}{4}$ m. NE. Three-unit early C17 farmhouse of two storeys set end-on to the hillside. Entrance is, as it must always have been, into the hall at the W, downhill, end. This is a splendid little room, with a characteristically overwhelming display of enriched timbers. Massive, ovolo-moulded ceiling beams, close-set joists with scratched moulding. Timber partition not of the usual post-and-panel type, but with small fielded panels, framed so as to correspond with the spacing of the joists. Even the N window has a timber lintel with broad ovolo and fancy stops. Mullions removed. The wide fireplace opening beside the entrance has stone jambs and a deep timber lintel. The stairs, in a square projection at the lower end of the S wall, rise in short, straight flights up a square core. This seems to be a slightly later C17 improvement.

KEMEYS FOLLY, on the ridgetop $\frac{1}{2}$ m. E, but approachable only from Cat's Ash. Square, battlemented prospect tower, with at one corner a tall, octagonal turret, also battlemented. Probably first built in the C17. Called 'ruined' by Dr Pococke in 1756, praised by Archdeacon Coxe in 1801 for its 'grand and sublime' views, and reconstructed as a house in 1911–12 (with Neo-Jacobean plasterwork and woodwork).

4090 KILGWRRWG/CILGWRRWG

HOLY CROSS. The lonely little building in its walled churchyard on the crown of a grassy knoll is a touching sight. Its undulating walls indicate the rescue campaigns it has required, one by *John Prichard* in 1871, another in 1989–90. Nave and lower chancel, of Old Red Sandstone, the N, S and E walls internally battered, a sign of pre-Perp date. S porch and W bellcote added by *Prichard*. The most impressive medieval feature is the nave S window, Perp, of three cinquefoiled ogee lights with glazed spandrels under a square head. Four-centred head to the S doorway, two-centred to the blocked W doorway. C19 N and E windows. No chancel arch, just a solid roof truss. – STAINED GLASS. War memorial E window, angels emblematic of peace and victory. By *R. J. Newbery c.* 1920.

In the CHURCHYARD a monolithic CROSS, shaft and head, completely unmoulded. Medieval, but of what century?

LOWER KILGWRRWG. Nearest neighbour to the church. The central bar of the little H-plan building is single-storeyed, clear sign of an early date, in spite of drastic modernization. Two early S window openings. Fox and Raglan found evidence inside of an early C16 cruck-framed house. Was the stone building at r.-angles downhill to the E built as a detached kitchen? A substantial four-bay threshing BARN uphill to the S completes the group.

3080 LANGSTONE

CHURCH (dedication unknown). Alone, S of the modern village. A small church, nave with S porch and lower chancel, of coursed grey and mauve stone. Its most intriguing feature is the W-ward extension of the nave, with a timber W doorway, its segmental lintel inscribed with the date 1622 and names of the churchwardens and the bishop of Llandaff of the time. Was its purpose to provide room for a W gallery? Trefoiled N lancet of the C14, probably reset. Perhaps of the same date the simply chamfered S doorway, and similar outer arch to the wagon-roofed S porch, which is clearly an addition. So the body of the building must be of the C14. The typical Perp improvements to the lighting are unusually regular, square-headed cusped two-lighters with hoodmoulds, N and S in the sanctuary and N and S lighting the E end of the nave. In the C19 the Perp square-headed E window was replaced, and the cusped heads of its three lights were set into the apex of the E gable. C19 N chancel chapel and S vestry. Further details of the Victorian restoration are unknown. – FONT. C18. Moulded octagonal bowl on a square stem. – STAINED GLASS. Chancel E, Baptism and Ascension of Christ, *c.* 1901. – W lancet, Virgin and Child. 1964 by *G. Cooper Abbs* for *Wippell & Co.*

The former RECTORY, 1845–6 by *J. H. Langdon*, stands 1½ m. NE of the church, in Cat's Ash Road, Llanbedr. The window hoodmoulds and the extravagant bargeboards proclaim the typical cottage Tudor style of its architect. Rendered walls. Somewhat altered and encroached on by late C20 housing.

EARTHWORKS. In a field close to the road at COED Y CAERAU (ST 378 915) are three overlapping earthworks, the earliest of which (the N one) has been identified as a small Roman fort with an outer ditch, perhaps an outpost to Caerleon. The middle site, a double circular enclosure, overlaps the outer defence and is in turn overlaid on the S by a single enclosure with a stone bank. The relationship of these enclosures makes the site one of great interest in any study of native and Roman interaction, but it must be admitted that the banks are now badly eroded, and relationships can be only provisionally disentangled from air photographs. The supposed Roman enclosure is fairly easy to see and the central site can be viewed best from the gate.

MOTTE, at Langstone Court, ¼ m. N, beside the motorway. In the trees N of the house a large, low motte within which traces of a square tower have been found.

LANGSTONE COURT. Not large, but of three different dates. The central part has a large, rectangular, two-light window of stone in its W wall, now internal. To the W is an addition of the late C17, as is shown by its substantial timber staircase, rising to the attics in a pinched open well. Elaborately turned balusters, and big turned pendants.

CAT'S ASH FARM, 1 m. N. The gabled stone barn towards the road is clearly a medieval chapel in origin, see the blocked two-centred window with hoodmould in the E gable. It can be identified as the chapel of St Curig, first founded in the early C12 by Robert de Chandos and granted to his priory at Goldcliff (q.v.).

The altered C17 farmhouse at r.-angles behind bears a datestone of 1604.

PRIMARY SCHOOL, Cat's Ash Road, Llanbedr. 1951–2, an early work by *Gollins, Melvin & Partners*. Two staggered single-storey ranges of dull red brick, fully glazed towards the S, clerestory-lit to the N.

INMOS MICROCHIP FACTORY NO. 2, Coldra, ½ m. NW, by the motorway interchange. 1984–5 by *Powell Alport Partnership*, without the resources or the flair of Richard Rogers's factory at Duffryn (*see* p. 219). The architects were indeed instructed not to expose the services as Rogers had done. But the blue steel spars projecting from the silver shed make this a poverty-stricken parody of its predecessor.

LLANARTH

3010

ST TEILO. The plain but substantial three-stage W tower with NE stair-turret is almost a twin to the tower at Llandenny (q.v.) and probably mid-C16 in date. No buttresses, but walls of squared Old Red Sandstone blocks, and strong defining stringcourses and moulded plinth. The battlements and pinnacles of Ham Hill stone are of 1884–5 by *Richard Creed*. Wide nave and lower chancel, of rubble sandstone, basically Dec, see the foiled lancets in the nave (S) and chancel (N and S). S doorway and S porch with two-centred arches. Elaborate Perp alterations at the E end of the nave when the rood loft was installed. Two internal N doorways to the rood-loft stair, the lower with panelled jamb. Three nave windows by *Prichard*, 1847, apparently inserted into old rere-arches. Chancel arch 1884–5 by *Creed*. Is the E window, an awkward lancet triplet, of the C20? – FONT. Perp. Hexagonal bowl on panelled stem and concave panelled foot, typical of this part of the county. – STAINED GLASS. Chancel E, Christ and four archangels. 1969 by *Celtic Studios*, in their Expressionist idiom. – MONUMENT. Elizabeth Jones †1787. White marble obelisk and tablet, entirely covered with her husband William's expressions of woe, in prose and verse. For his other expressions *see* Clytha, p. 190.

In the CHURCHYARD, three steps and the broached base for a CROSS.

The church is at the S end of the VILLAGE. Near the centre, TYRNANT, an engagingly Janus-faced house. The front towards the road is of *c.* 1830, of three bays and two storeys, rendered white. The outer bays are bold full-height bows. Tuscan eaves with paired brackets. Towards the garden the façade is also of three bays and two storeys, but a century or so earlier. Brick, unfortunately painted white. Windows with small keystones. Porch hood on scrolly side corbels and central guttae. Nos. 1–2, BRYNTEG make a prominent mark here, a pair of High Victorian cottages in red brick. At the N end of the village, early C20 ESTATE HOUSING, and the former R.C. village SCHOOL (converted to a house in 1990). This is of stone, gabled, with timber mullion-and-transom windows. Towards the road cross-windows in the gable-end and a step-topped gateway. Built to the plans of *D. Roberts* in 1858.

LLANARTH COURT (now hospital), ½m. SE. A monster Neo-classical house, built for John Jones of Llanarth and Treowen, Wonastow, probably shortly before 1793. Early engravings show its bulk as now, a three-storey double pile thirteen bays long. The S front, facing the park, retains its original massing, the end three bays in full-height bows, the centre three bays brought slightly forward under a pediment. But the single-storey central porch, bearing 'a resemblance in its proportions to that of the celebrated Temple of Paestum' (J.P. Neale, *Seats*), has disappeared. In 1849–50 *W. G. & E. Habershon* altered and extended the house, and they must be responsible for the present rendering of the walls, the moulded architrave surrounds to the windows, and in particular for converting the park front from Doric to Ionic. In the bows single-storey coupled Ionic columns carry an entablature with heavy block cornice over the ground-floor windows. In the centre four Ionic columns set on channelled piers rise through the upper two storeys to carry a pediment with another heavy block cornice. Both cornices are carried right round the house. The mid-C19 work doubtless included the projecting three-bay entrance porch on the N side, channelled, and carrying a scrolly metal balcony balustrade. Pedimented E service wing also of this date.

The interior retains little of either the late C18 or the mid C19. In the CENTRAL S ROOM an C18 chimneypiece with Greek key pattern frieze of yellow marble. The two SW ROOMS thrown together and subdivided by a screen of two marble Ionic columns. Mid-C19 marble chimneypiece here, with reliefs of putti and scrolling foliage in an early Renaissance idiom. The STAIRCASE, in a spacious square well, has a mid-C19 cast-iron balustrade. In the ENTRANCE HALL, however, there is something special, the timber hall screen from Treowen (brought here in 1898, and in 1999 likely to be returned thither). In the frieze the date 1627 and the flowery initials W.I. for William Jones. Quite a handsome composition of two depressed-headed arches flanked by banded Tuscan columns on high pedestals. Circular panels with demi-baluster enrichment, similar to that on overmantels still *in situ* at Treowen. The timber chimneypiece in the hall may be another early C17 importation from Treowen, much modified.

The PARK to the S of the house was laid out in 1792 by *Samuel Lapidge* in Capability Brown style, a semi-formalized river traversing the foreground. In 1805 *J. C. Loudon* elaborated the planting and naturalized the river, which he considered had been 'much injured by art'. Its present form, a long, thin lake, was established by further work in 1849.

The main entrance to the park from the SW passes under a demonstrative GATEHOUSE dated 1863. By that date all concern for Neoclassicism had been abandoned. Multicoloured local stone laid in alternating bands of tile-like slabs and crazy-paving. Big pointed arch and three storeys of windows under a precipitous slated roof with iron cresting. In spite of the contrast with the mansion one suspects that *Habershon* was responsible.

ST MARY AND ST MICHAEL (R.C.). At r.-angles to the N front of the house and also built in the late C18. So this is a rare case of a Catholic family building themselves a chapel in the park several decades before Emancipation (cf. e.g. Lulworth Castle, Dorset, and Ugbrooke, Devon). The long, white-rendered building, with six large round-headed windows to the W, and even angle quoins, could easily be mistaken for an orangery, as was doubtless intended. The N (ritual E) apse is an addition of *c.* 1930. Internally it is screened off by two slender Doric columns. The gallery at the S (ritual W) end, carried on Doric columns, must also be a later insertion. – The interior is enlivened by STAINED GLASS. Five of the six W windows are filled with impressive Continental glass set in naively colourful early C19 borders. The half-figures in three windows, Salvator Mundi, St John the Evangelist and St James, clearly belong to a single series. The finest piece is a mid-C16 Circumcision scene. All four are considered the products of a Cologne workshop *c.* 1520.* The N-most window contains typical Swiss or German C17 grisaille

* I am grateful to Professor Rüdiger Becksmann of the Corpus Vitrearum Deutschland for his opinion.

panels, one dated 1650. The S-most, St Theresa of Lisieux, *c.* 1929 by *Hardman*. Pallid. – Apse windows, SS Francis and Bernard, *c.* 1939 by *Margaret Rope*.

Outside, in front of the apse, a tall CROSS, crowned by a rare late medieval cross-head carved with the Virgin and Child on one face and a Crucifixion on the other.

57 LITTLE PIT COTTAGE, $\frac{3}{4}$m. SW. The most completely surviving
p. 33 cruck-truss hall house in the county, of three bays, probably datable to the mid C16. On the W and N walls almost all the timbers are exposed, the cruck blades and framing in rectangular panels on the W gable-end, and on the N side widely spaced uprights. Timber sole-plate. The S and E walls, however, were later enclosed in stone. Original doorways in line with each other in the N and S walls, their lintels shaped into four-centred heads. They opened into the E end of the hall. (Framed internal partitions.) Stone hearth and chimneystack inserted in the hall to make the usual 'chimney backing on the entry' plan. Unheated inner room at the W end, service rooms E of the entrance doorways.

COED-Y-GELLI, $\frac{1}{2}$m. NW. The whitened stone range lying E–W at the rear is a typical two-unit house of the later C16. The entrance doorway near the centre of the S wall is masked by the later brick range, also whitened, set at r.-angles to the S. The doorway leads into a corner of the hall, a post-and-panel partition immediately to the l., with an ogee-headed doorway into the parlour. (Traces of painted floral decoration on the partition.) The hall fireplace in the E gable has gone, but a mural stair to the upper storey survives in the SE corner. Upstairs the partition is timber-framed, with two blocked, four-centred-headed doorways. (Painted decoration is reported to be under the whitewash on the E wall up here.)

To the W of the house a fine five-bay, red-brick BARN of *c.* 1700. Porch to the central threshing bay.

3000

LLANBADOC

ST MADOC. Set on falling ground between the road and the River Usk. Medieval nave, S porch and lower chancel. The earliest datable features are Dec, the trefoil-headed lancets N and S in the chancel, and perhaps the porch arch, two-centred and enriched with a hollow moulding between rolls, with a coarse ogee-headed label. Various Perp windows, the chancel E window of three lights, given a four-centred head in 1872 and reused hood on demi-angels. Square-headed S windows. Thin, probably C16 W tower, crowned by corbelled battlements. Small rectangular belfry openings. The tower blocks the C14 W doorway of the nave and trefoiled lancet above. Lean-to N aisle and N vestry, added by *John Prichard* in 1872–3. The interior is dominated by *Prichard*. E.E. chancel arch on overscaled shafted responds, low stone chancel screen. In the chancel, outsize twin-arched stone screen to the vestry and organ chamber, its central shaft with stiff-leaf cap. Nave arcade not so characterful. – FONT. Medieval. Square bowl with chamfered corners. – PULPIT. Stone. Typical of *Prichard* in its lobed plan, its stiff-leaf decoration and the tapering corbel which supports it, inspired by the famous reading desk in the refectory at Beaulieu Abbey, Hampshire. Carved by *Crisp* of Leamington. – REREDOS. Of stone. The outer recesses, cinquefoil-headed, flanked by narrow blind panels, appear to be medieval. The main part is of 1905 by *Veall & Sant* of Cardiff, the statues carved by *Wormleighton* of Cardiff. – STAINED GLASS. Chancel N, Christ carrying a child, 1872. Finely preserved. – Chancel E, Crucifixion and emblems of the Four Evangelists. C13 style. Of 1872 or earlier? Glass contemporary with Prichard's restoration was reported to be mostly by *Holland & Holt* of Warwick. – Nave S, Suffer the Little Children, 1910 by *Gerald Moira*. A period piece.

The parish includes the outskirts of Usk on the W bank of the river. At the W end of Usk Bridge a TOLL-HOUSE, dated 1837. Canted towards the road and bridge. Like a Tudoresque *cottage orné*. GLAN YR AVON HOUSE HOTEL, 200 yds (183 metres) N of the bridge, consists of two parts. The N third is a rendered villa in French Gothic style dated 1868, the rest, in an approximation to a matching style, is of 1992 by *Peter Williams* of Newport, expanding the villa into a full-blown hotel.

GWENT TERTIARY COLLEGE, The Rhadyr, ¾ m. N of the bridge. Established in 1913 as Monmouthshire Institute of Agriculture with funding from the Haberdashers' Company (*see* Monmouth, Pontypool), but in 1923 taken over by Monmouthshire County Council. Farm complex centred on a red brick BARN dated 1917, on the W side of the road. The MAIN BUILDINGS, on the E side, quietly Neo-Georgian with hipped roofs predominating, were constructed in several phases: 1923–5 by *J. Bain* of Newport (men's hostel, laboratory block), 1934 by *Bain* (women's hostel), 1939–40 (dining hall and kitchen block), and 1959–62 by *K. L. Davies & W. E. Hole* of Newport (assembly hall and staff houses).

TWYN BELL. A partial ringwork overlooking the church from the crest of the escarpment. It has been incorporated into the garden of a Victorian house, its sides terraced, its top planted with yew, turkey oak and monkey puzzle.

HENRHIW, 2¼ m. NW. A fine farm group facing the A472. Two-storeyed late C17 farmhouse, of four bays, the entrance doorway in the second bay (with original studded door). This stands back in the centre, a square GRANARY set forward towards the road to the l., a large BARN, with long ventilation slits to the r. A second BARN, with rows of ventilation holes, further to the r. of the group.

CEFN ILA, 1 m. NW. The clump of wellingtonias on the hillside tells of a Victorian garden. The house, enlarged by *Alfred Waterhouse* for Edward Lister 1862–4, was burnt down *c.* 1970. The large colour-washed brick COTTAGE above, much modernized, may be Waterhouse's bailiff's house.

CILFEIGAN, 1¼ m. W. Three-bay, three-storeyed, grey rendered and regularly fenestrated E front, so entirely early C19 in appearance.

However, the entrance doorway, four-centred-headed and chamfered, indicates that the structure is much earlier. Single-light stone window of the C16 lighting the spacious spiral S staircase. Behind looms a mighty stone BARN, of nine bays.

PRIORESS MILL, 1½ m. NW. A mill on the River Usk here is documented from the C16. The limewashed stone house and mill buildings probably originated in the C17. The MILL is of two parallel ranges, with a wide, cast-iron water wheel down by the river. The HOUSE is single-storeyed with habitable roof space, and has a large gable-end hearth and spiral stone stair beside it.

3090 LLANDDEWI FACH

ST DAVID. Reconstructed in 1856–7 by *J. P. Seddon* of *Prichard & Seddon*. Small Perp nave and lower chancel, with round-headed blocked W doorway and W double bell gable. Here, in rebuilding a late medieval church, the architect resisted the temptation to translate it into a purer style. In fact, while the walling and dressed stonework are virtually all new, Seddon argued that he was retaining the square-headed windows as part of the history of the building. Sadly, disused at the time of writing, the interior stripped out.

LLANDDEWI COURT, 1¾ m. NW. L-plan C16 farmhouse, interpreted by Fox and Raglan as two originally non-intercommunicating houses of two storeys, both of the later C16. The only surviving feature is a blocked three-light timber window with diamond mullions in the gable-end of the smaller, one-bay house. Several others recorded by Fox and Raglan have subsequently been modernized. Attached to the SE corner of the larger house, a later C16 stone ox-house, and beyond, set at an obtuse angle a little down the hillside, a four-bay BARN of similar date. Both have diamond mullion windows like that in the house. The three buildings thus embraced a spacious, sloping farmyard.

3010 LLANDDEWI RHYDDERCH

The church stands in a little valley at the W end of a compact village almost entirely built in the second half of the C20.

ST DAVID. A small church of Old Red Sandstone in a steeply sloping churchyard. The most arresting feature is the low, unbuttressed W tower. Its top stages are of timber construction, in a typical Border design. Vertically boarded below, set-back belfry stage of exposed studs, and pyramidal cap. The main part of the tower seems early. It has what appear to be small Norman windows, mid-height N and S, and another low down on the N side. The body of the church is conventional in plan, nave with S porch, and lower chancel. The chancel has early C14 evidence: the E triplet of cusped lancets, and the very wide, segmental chancel arch, chamfered and jacked up high on chamfered imposts. Perp nave, as is shown by one S window partly old, and the S porch, with a typical combination of two-centred outer arch and four-centred inner doorway, both similarly moulded. Earlier cusped lancets reset in its side walls. In 1862–3 *J. P. Seddon* of *Prichard & Seddon* rebuilt the entire N wall and renewed the roofs. – FONT. Medieval. Of mottled Old Red Sandstone on a base carved with bold foliated spurs. – ALTAR RAILS and TOWER SCREEN. Both clearly by *Prichard & Seddon*. – STAINED GLASS. Chancel E. Tree of Life, by *John Petts*, 1988. Dominating the interior of the church. – MONUMENTS. Several typical rustic tablets, the earliest Seth Powell †1785, signed *John Lewis*, Abergavenny.

In the CHURCHYARD, the usual lower part of a medieval CROSS, three steps, a well-preserved broached base and the stump of a shaft, on to which a Crucifix was set in 1923.

BAPTIST CHAPEL, ½m. SW. Small rendered chapel set in a walled burial ground. Built in 1826 for Particular Baptists.

SCHOOL, ¼m. S. 1867. Small, Gothic and typical of its date. The steep-roofed schoolroom is lit by long lancets, and beside the porch a bold chimney-breast projects. Now converted to a house.

CEFN GWYN, 1 m. NE. An unusually eloquent farmstead, sited on a S-facing slope with a panoramic view across the Vale of Usk. The approach from the N was, until the way was barred by a big metal barn, under a brick-gabled entry spanning between two BARNS, that to the W a standard three-bay threshing barn. The two-storeyed FARMHOUSE, across the yard to the S, is a single range of two dates, see the straight joint, and the slight change of level in the roof ridge. The W half is a two-unit house of the later C16, its entrance to the E, the hall with its fireplace to the W. The E half is a parlour of 1637 added beyond the unheated storeroom, not behind the hall fireplace, which would have been more normal. Two S wings of 1637 or later, that to the W for a kitchen. One timber four-light upper window with ovolo mouldings survives at the E end of the S front, with two short rows of nesting holes for doves in the wall beside it.

Inside, the early part has in its W wall the usual line-up of mural stair, of stone to the first floor, of timber on up to the roof space, wide hearth with mighty timber lintel, and deep cupboard lit by a tiny N window. Upstairs the post-and-panel partition survives, but below only the mortice trench in a beam shows its former position. Here, structural timbers are simply chamfered.

The parlour addition of 1637 is, typically, more displayful, all timber members being moulded with stopped ovolos or, on door-frames, double ovolos. In the C16, house doorways of this sort were inserted in the S end of the E wall (now internal) and the E end of the S wall, and a shaped door-head at the entry into the SW wing. The extension of 1637 has a N doorway, with double-ovolo frame, which opens into a passage separated from a large parlour by means of a post-and-panel partition, in which is a doorway bearing the date. Ovolo moulding of the planks on the room side only, and of the ceiling beams.

MYNACHDY FARM, 1 m. NW. The large but workaday farmhouse, gabled and cement-rendered, conspicuous on the hillside S of the B4233, was built in 1890 by *William Graham, Son & Hitchcox* of Newport.

3010 LLANDDEWI SKIRRID/ LLANDDEWI SCYRRID

Church and Court stand alone beneath the flank of the Skirrid Mountain.

ST DAVID. Thin medieval W tower, built of Old Red Sandstone with massive quoins. Lancets. The body of the church, nave and lower chancel, gabled N vestry, S porch, was rebuilt in 1879 by *John Prichard*, at the expense of Crawshay Bailey jun. It is an unusually homogeneous building for this architect, in its materials, pinkish-purple rock-faced Old Red Sandstone and pink Forest of Dean dressings, and in its Dec style. Windows with intersecting tracery and pointed trefoils occupying the interstices. Typical bull-nosed jambs to the porch arch. The interior is a complete ensemble, presumably all by *Prichard*. Recent injudicious colouring, however, of reredos and pulpit. Nave roof of moulded arch-brace and collar purlin type, familiar to the architect from many examples in Glamorgan. Floors tiled throughout, in the usual increasing elaboration from W to E. – REREDOS. Of stone, the full width of the sanctuary, carved with significant flowers and birds. – ALTAR RAIL. Of brass. – PULPIT. Of stone, with more naturalistic carving. – CANDLESTANDS. Of brass. – PEWS. Typical of *Prichard*. – S DOOR. Also typical. – There are two pre-1879 furnishings. – FONT. C12 tub incised with zigzag on the rim, set on C15 moulded base and shaft reassembled in the wrong order. – ROYAL ARMS. Small, carved. Datable after 1837. – STAINED GLASS. Chancel E, Crucifixion with saints, *c.* 1887, no doubt by *Hardman* (A. Brooks). – Nave S, Good Shepherd between Nativity and Baptism of Christ, *c.* 1879 by *Cox & Sons*. – MONUMENT. Jessie Partridge †1883. Small hanging monument, of stone, carved in high relief with angels hovering over a lily. (Signed by *Evans* of Abergavenny.)

In the CHURCHYARD, fragment of a medieval CROSS, just a broached base and part of the shaft.

LLANDDEWI COURT. Of the C15 in origin, a hall house much enlarged, altered and modernized. A stone doorway with two-centred head at either end of the cross-passage.

PARISH HALL, ¼ m. SE. Of *c.* 1885. Corrugated iron on a timber frame. The cruciform plan and pointed windows show that it was intended for use as a church. A rare survival, which has doubtless long outlasted its intended life span.

LLANDEGVETH/LLANDEGFEDD

3090

ST TEGFETH. Small, just a nave and lower chancel, and a W porch with timber spandrels. All except the chancel E wall was reconstructed for John James (*see* Lan-sor below) in 1875–6 by *E. A. Lansdowne*, who reinstated the miscellaneous old windows in regularized walls. One Norman N window in the nave, and a second made to match. On the S side the nave windows are the simplest Tudor, square-headed with a mullion, the outer two genuine, the central window a copy. Chancel N lancet and E window of three arched lights under a square head and hood, the latter dated perhaps by a will of 1541 leaving money to glaze the chancel windows. Inside, chancel arch of 1875–6, round-headed and constructed of Forest ashlar. Inscriptions on it record parish benefactions and explain the rationale behind the reconstruction of the building.* – PULPIT. C18. Completely plain, timber, polygonal. – BOX PEWS. In the N half of the nave. A rare survival in this part of the world. – STAINED GLASS. Chancel E, St David between knights, *c.* 1919, brought in from Llanddewi Fach. – MONUMENTS. David Williams †1729. Wreathed oval tablet. Drapery and cherubs' heads below, naturalistic flowers in the upper spandrels. – Rustic tablets, C18 and early C19, several signed.

The little VILLAGE largely consists of colour-washed council houses of *c.* 1950. Nothing came of a scheme of 1939 by the Subsistence Production Society to house out-of-work miners in sixty prefabricated timber-framed houses of Swedish design, by *Cyril Sjöstrom* (later Mardall of Yorke, Rosenberg, Mardall). They were to have been built at Cwrt Perrot W of the church.

LAN-SOR, 1 m. SE. L-plan stone house of one-and-a-half storeys, given its present character by John James (†1883), who clearly had antiquarian interests. It started as a modest late C16 or early C17 farmhouse and a service range running downhill at r.-angles. Much-altered sunk-chamfer windows in the former. The latter made picturesque by two castellated turrets at the back, to hide water tanks. Various brought-in pieces inside, and in the dining room a suitable text in Welsh from the Book of Proverbs.

RESERVOIR and DAM. The largest reservoir in the county, planned in the 1950s and completed in 1966, to supply Cwmbran with 40 million gallons of water per day. All but 3 per cent of its contents is derived from the mountains to the N, piped along a 3½-m. (5.6 kilometre) pipeline from the River Usk. The public road runs over an earthen dam. Upstream of it, a simple, circular, concrete outlet-valve tower, capped by a low copper dome and reached from the W bank by a five-span concrete-beam viaduct.

LLANDENNY

4000

The church stands at the centre of the little village, enticingly glimpsed through the medieval lychgate. VILLAGE FARM, across

* See J. A. Bradney, *A History of Monmouthshire*, vol. 3, p. 279.

the road lower down the slope, is of stone colour-washed pink. The chimney-breast projecting from the front wall suggests an origin not later than the early C17.

ST JOHN. Built of coursed Old Red Sandstone. Blunt and dominant, probably post-medieval W tower, unbuttressed, its three stages defined by stringcourses. Battlements. NE stair-turret. Belfry windows of the plainest. The narrow nave is apparently C12 in origin: see the very small round-headed N window and the S doorway with solid semicircular tympanum. Perp S porch and fenestration of the nave. The chancel is lower, and Dec, its S and E windows single and paired trefoil-headed lancets. Lean-to N vestry, 1860 by *J. P. Seddon* of *Prichard & Seddon*. Inside, the small, plainly chamfered arches to tower and chancel do not provide further dating evidence. Pretty Perp S doorway to the rood-loft stair. The wagon roof of the nave looks C19, the overwhelming tie-beam and queen-strut chancel roof may be of the C17. *G. E. Halliday* stripped and reconstructed the walls internally in 1900–1. – FONT. Dated 1661 on the lip. A charming
75 piece, the curved octagonal sides of the bowl decorated with cartouches, the bowl and stem incised with floral patterns. Clearly by the same craftsman as the celebrated sundial at Trellech (q.v.). – STAINED GLASS. Chancel E. Christ Prophesying the Raising of Lazarus. 1881, no doubt by *Clayton & Bell* (A. Brooks). – Nave N. Faith and Hope. Of *c.* 1880, perhaps by *Samuel Evans* (A. Brooks). – Nave S. All three theological virtues. 1918 by *Daniells & Fricker*. – Window over the pulpit.
76 Angel, signed by the same. 1919. – MONUMENTS. Roger Otes †1706 and son †1710. White marble cartouche of metropolitan quality. Putti at the top. Palm-fronds and garlands of flowers. – David Lewis and family, after 1732. Tablet with palm-fronds at the sides.

In the CHURCHYARD, three steps and the small broached base for a CROSS.

The LYCHGATE retains its late medieval side walls, but the oak lintel and roof were renewed in 1900.

CEFNTILLA. The manor house of the Oates family, dated 1616, greatly enlarged by *T. H. Wyatt* for the second Lord Raglan. The house and estate had, as an inscription over the front door records, been bought by 1,623 of the 'friends, admirers and comrades' of Raglan's father, the Field Marshal, and presented to the family in 1858 as a mark of gratitude and to enable them to maintain the port of the ennobled. The Jacobean house was a rectangular single pile with a two-storey window bay, serving hall and great chamber, near the E end of the N front. The bay remains, with much enlarged windows, to the l. of Wyatt's Neo-Jacobean entrance porch. Wyatt engulfed the rest, using similar Old Red Sandstone rubble walling, but Bath stone dressings. The style is Tudor, the composition asymmetrical from every direction, but not memorably grouped. The timber gallery across the centre of the S front represents a C17 feature. To the W a complex service court, and small stable court beyond.

Inside, the Jacobean hall is recognizable and retains a chimneypiece with guilloche-decorated frieze and plaster overmantel. This, which bears the date 1616, consists of a many-quartered shield of arms of the Herberts, whom the Oateses must have served or otherwise owed allegiance to, flanked by gawky figures of soldiers holding banners. The hall frieze, of 48 timber, is something much more unusual, early Renaissance decorative carving of shields, some armorial, some with emblems of the Passion, in grotesquework foliate scrolls. The frieze came from Usk Priory, and if the initials E W on one shield refer to Ellen Williams, the last prioress, it is datable to shortly before 1535. Frieze and chimneypiece coloured in the 1930s with artistry and scholarship by the fourth Lord Raglan (of Fox and Raglan fame) and his wife.

THE CAYO, ¾m. NW. An intriguingly varied farm group, though uniformly whitewashed. The most unusual component is the steeply hipped-roofed, late C17 QUAKER MEETING HOUSE standing at the foot of the group. It is of three bays by three, built of well-squared and coursed stone, the large, upright windows to the front and r. side constructed with voussoired heads and keystones. The deep eaves brackets have been sawn off. The meeting house occupied the roof space and was approached up a once handsome timber stair. The newel post at its foot, with gadrooned top, survives in battered state. The fittings have all gone from the meeting house itself.

A seven-bay BARN is set at a higher level behind. The FARMHOUSE itself stands at r.-angles on the crown of the slope. It is of two parts, both two-storeyed and of two bays. The r. half, lower and of stone, is of *c.* 1600, the l. half, of brick and set on a half-basement, must be a century later.

COLDBROOK, 1¼m. NW. A substantial farmhouse containing one of the county's most overwhelming displays of enriched timberwork, of the mid or later C16. The house is of two storeys plus gables, extended to the W in the C17. As to the plan, the hall was originally entered in the E gable-end, beside the hall fireplace, with spiral stair beyond. Evidence of two small inner rooms at both levels. That is all typical of later C16 local house-planning. The oddity is the inclusion of the two-storey parlour wing at r.-angles to the N. The remarkably lofty single-storey hall has massive ceiling beams moulded with a series of five p. 37 ovolos alternating with five steps, converging into spear-shaped stops. Joists also moulded and spear-stopped. Post-and-panel screen across the inner end of the hall with ogee-moulded chamfers. Within the screen, a doorway with two-centred arched head, set between upright timbers which seem to have supported a canopy over a bench against the partition. At r.-angles to this a far more showy doorway, its four-centred head and jambs moulded with three ovolos and steps, converging at the bottom in the usual way. Outer square-headed frame with a second, identical suite of mouldings. The doorway gives entry into a small square parlour, its window, opposite the doorway, set in a richly moulded frame.

TREWORGAN, 1¼ m. NE. The house, its component parts of three different dates, stands uncomfortably close to the A449. The earliest part, of stone, faces W towards the road. It was the stair wing added to a yet earlier house, replaced in the early C18 by the handsome brick E-facing block. This is of two storeys and five bays, the centre three slightly grouped together. Flat window heads of rubbed brick. A raised platband divides the storeys. On its S end wall, a reset datestone 160[5], probably displaced from the stair wing. The three-bay brick wing at r.-angles to the N must have been built not much later in the C18.

4090 LLANDEVAUD/LLANDIFOG

1 m. N of Llanmartin

ST PETER. 1843 by *Edward Haycock*. Small, minimally Gothic box with miniature chancel, stigmatized when built as 'a modern vandalism on the ruins of an old chapel'. – REREDOS. Of timber, *c.* 1900. Reliefs of passion flower, vine and lily. – STAINED GLASS. An unexpectedly varied and interesting collection. – Nave W, Christ in the House of Martha and Mary, and Suffer the Little Children. 1882 by *Henry Holiday* for *James Powell & Son*. Fine, and characteristic of this partnership. – Chancel E, emblems of the Passion, 1897, probably by *R. J. Newbery*. – Nave NE. Good Samaritan. Newbery-like, but by *John Hall & Sons Ltd*, 1927–8. The Samaritan quite a heroic figure. – Nave NW. Risen Christ. *Celtic Studios*, 1961. A towering figure rising above Golgotha and the mushroom cloud of a nuclear bomb.

5000 LLANDOGO

The village is scattered up the hillside to the W under hanging woods. To the SE the River Wye describes one of its many loops. The church stands on flat ground close to the river.

103 ST OUDOCEUS. 1859–61 by *J. P. Seddon* of *Prichard & Seddon*, one of the firm's most high-spirited small churches. Polychromatic interplay inside and out between local mauve Old Red Sandstone and ochre Bath stone. Stiff-leaf foliage in expected and unexpected places. Geometrical style. Nave under a steeply pitched roof with lean-to aisles, chancel nearly as high and just as steeply roofed, with lean-to N organ-chamber of 1889, by *Seddon & Carter*. S porch. The W front is the showpiece. The central gabled (and stone-vaulted) porch supports a thick polygonal shaft with foliage cap, from which springs a triple colonnette, also foliage-capped. On this rests an extraordinarily elaborate belfry, consisting of a sort of pulpit in the sky, polygonal, carrying shafts with stiff-leaf caps and trefoiled arches. These, assisted by buttresses to N and S, support the crowning octagonal spirelet with its single telling circle of crockets. A pair of long,

subtly moulded two-light windows* and flanking buttresses complete the composition. Plenty of other details to enjoy and puzzle over, such as the fat corner colonnettes supporting the ends of the gutters, and the treatment of the base of the whole building, a roll moulding over a flush band of mauve sandstone on a battered plinth. Note how the roll moulding when it reaches the S porch steps up boldly and arches over as a hood-mould to the entrance arch.

The interior is calmer, the banding of mauve and ochre quite restrained. Arcades with slender circular piers, moulded caps and double-wave moulded arches. Hoodmoulds on head corbels. Chancel arch high, wide, but steeply pointed, as the chancel it opens into is narrow. Continuous sunk quadrant moulding interrupted by stiff-leaf sprigs up the arch. Cusped arch-braced roofs in nave and chancel, the former on angel hammerbeams. – The chancel WALL PAINTINGS, including large angels and rows of lilies on the side walls, are by *Seddon & Carter*, 1889. – REREDOS. Alabaster, with a white marble relief. Also of 1889 by *Seddon & Carter*, carved by *William Clarke* of Llandaff. Doves in foliage scrolls, between wheatsheaf and vine branch. Above, flanking figures of Moses and Aaron, mosaics by *Powell*'s. Below, sanctuary TILES, with a repetitive design of kings casting down their crowns. – Other fittings are by *Prichard & Seddon*, typical but quite subdued, FONT and PULPIT of stone, CHOIR STALLS, LECTERN and PEWS of timber. – STAINED GLASS. Chancel E. Ascension. Very fine. By *Hardman, c.* 1879. – A miscellany of later windows, of which the most unusual is that at the W end of the N aisle, 1908 by *Heaton, Butler & Bayne*. The Good Wife: Proverbs 31. 27–8. – One S window by *Kempe & Co.*, 1929. – MONUMENT. Anna Gallenga †1897. With a profile portrait in a roundel.

HOLY TRINITY, Whitebrook, 2 m. N. Built by subscription in 1835. Almost a square in plan, of local sandstone rubble, heavily buttressed on the valley side. Pointed timber windows with Y-tracery. Tiny timber-clad bell-turret. The interior is dominated by a fantastically carved SCREEN, the work of the *Rev. Joshua Stansfield* in 1892.

LLANDOGO PRIORY, ½ m. SW. A courtesy title for a gabled and bargeboarded villa standing prominently on the hillside. Built in 1838 for John Gough by *Wyatt & Brandon*. Local mauve sandstone. Recessed centre with two-storeyed timber veranda between symmetrical gables, an oriel window under the r. gable.

PILSTONE, 1½ m. E of N. A symmetrical *cottage orné* built shortly after 1830 for a bachelor, Captain George Rooke, who, having built it, preferred to live in a house on the opposite side of the River Wye. The walls are of squared blocks reused from the late C17 predecessor house. Two-storeyed, three-bay S front with strongly projecting full-height porch. Gables wherever possible, now deprived of their main ornament, boldly cusped bargeboards.

* Copied from the clerestory windows in the transepts at Tintern Abbey (T. Blackshaw).

The front corners of the house are chamfered, the angles of the roof eaves carried on moulded corbels. This detail is repeated on a larger scale in the diagonal alignment of the service range to the NW and the octagonal plan of the coachman's house, which closes the composition beyond a gabled arch into the stable court.

BIGSWEIR BRIDGE, 1¼ m. NE. Built in 1825 to carry the new turnpike road from Chepstow to Monmouth over the River Wye. An elegant design of cast iron, by *C. Hollis*. A single segmental arch and a nearly horizontal road beam, linked by zigzag sub-members. The masonry flood arches were added in the mid C19. Single-storey TOLL-HOUSE.

COED ITHEL BLAST FURNACE, 1¼ m. S, on the W side of the A466 at SO 527 026. Two sides of the early C17 square rubble-masonry furnace stand almost to full height, with part of its inner lining, fused by the heat when the furnace was in use. Also fragments of the blowing-house and part of the blast-water-wheel pit.

WHITEBROOK INDUSTRIAL REMAINS, 1½ m. N. The now beautifully wooded valley of the Whitebrook, from its confluence with the River Wye, up to New Mills, 2 m. W, was from at least the early C17 until the late C19 a centre of intensive water-powered industry. The Society of Mineral and Battery Works established here *c.* 1606 a branch of Tintern Wireworks. Wireworking continued for a century, but by 1720 had died out. From *c.* 1760 papermaking took over. By 1841 about fifty people were employed in paper mills in the valley, and much of the present housing was built for millworkers. By about 1880, however, papermaking had ceased, and the valley lapsed into its present rural tranquillity. Apart from housing, the main survivals are waterworks in the form of dams, ponds and leats, mills – ruined or converted – and the ruins of warehouses and other works buildings. The identifiable sites are too fragmentary to be described at length here, but they can be briefly mentioned, from E to W.

Where the Whitebrook joins the Wye (SO 538 068), traces of a QUAY, and ruins and footings of WAREHOUSES, related to papermaking. The ruined MILL and mill pond downhill from Tump Farm (SO 537 067) may mark an early wireworks site.

The group near Whitebrook Farm (SO 537 066), including a roofless mill and long, low masonry dam, seem to have belonged to GLYNN PAPER MILL, in operation *c.* 1800–50. Whitebrook Farmhouse was probably the manager's house. Next upstream are the more extensive remains of BRIDGET'S (Wye Valley) MILLS (SO 535 066). Various ruined buildings of Old Red Sandstone, partly with brick dressings, evidence of later C19 construction. Also the manager's house, and masonry mill-pond dam and leat, 400 ft (120 metres) upstream.

Next come the sites of two C17 WIREWORKS MILLS. One, high on the valley side to the S (SO 536 065), has a distinctly different arrangement for water supply from the valley-floor mills, with a leat 700 yds (640 metres) long. The other, where Manor Brook joins the main stream at SO 531 064, can be identified by various ruined walls. Upstream again are the ruins of the large CLEARWATER PAPER MILLS (SO 531 067). These were the first paper mills in the valley, constructed in 1760, possibly on the site of a C17 wireworks. Some 200 ft (60 metres) NW of the C18 mill are the remains of a water system, dam, pond and leat, with masonry walls, now ruined. On the hillside to the SE, the high masonry walls of a C19 MILL BUILDING, with tall round-headed windows, and a lofty octagonal stone CHIMNEY. This indicates a higher level of mechanization than at the early paper mills. (Clearwater Mill is known to have been fitted with a steam engine by 1863.)

Nothing more for about a mile, then, at SO 519 071, the foundations of SUNNYSIDE MILL. Also here, the much-altered MANAGER'S HOUSE (now Traligael), and at some distance uphill a large stone CHIMNEY, dated 1870, from which a stone-lined flue extends under the road down to the mill site.

FERNSIDE MILL, 400 ft (120 metres) W at SO 515 072. The only mill in the valley to remain largely intact. It was a paper mill of the pre-steam-engine era. Four-storey, seven-bay MILL BUILDING of coursed Old Red Sandstone rubble. Segment-headed windows. The upper two storeys were used as drying lofts and had in the long walls two tiers of vertical, open-slatted louvres. Also a STABLE for ten horses, and the two-storeyed, sash-windowed MANAGER'S HOUSE, with a dominating mid-C19 addition, gabled and bargeboarded. Finally, a short way upstream (SO 513 073), NEW MILLS CORN MILL, a roofless shell, but retaining some milling machinery and a wheel pit.

LLANELLEN/LLANELEN

3010

ST HELEN. A small Perp church, much rebuilt by *John Prichard* in 1850–1. The most memorable feature is the little corbelled-out W spirelet, crocketed and pinnacled, not at all like Prichard's later idiom. It stands over a one-bay W extension of the nave. Lower chancel, rebuilt by *Prichard*, and N vestry added by him, reusing the medieval priest's door and a window. That leaves the nave, with four-centred S doorway and typical Perp square-headed windows of three cinquefoiled lights. S porch, its outer arch rebuilt, S rood-stair projection, its window an insertion. Medieval details in purplish-pink Old Red Sandstone, Prichard's in buff Bath stone. Inside, the nave roof seems largely late medieval, of the normal ribbed and plastered wagon type on moulded wall-plates. – FONT. Copying the local Perp type, hexagonal on panelled stem and foot. A second, disused, FONT, a tub converted for use as a sundial, hence the digits cut in its rim. – STAINED GLASS. Nave W, Raising of Jairus's Daughter. 1884 by *Hardman*.

PRIMARY SCHOOL, on the main road N of the church. 1861–2 by *Prichard & Seddon*. Local mauve sandstone with buff dressings of Bath stone. Tall, gabled schoolroom towards the road, with long triplet lancets in the end walls and low shouldered side windows. Teacher's house at r.-angles behind.

BRIDGE, ¼m. NE, taking the Abergavenny to Pontypool road over the River Usk. Three segmental arches under a rather hump-backed roadway. Designed and built by *John Upton* of Gloucester, engineer, in 1821, as an inscription records.

ORCHARD FARM, ½m. SE. Apparently a modern bungalow with dormers, but in reality a late C16 stone hall house, with unheated inner room, the hall entered away from the hearth. (Fireplace in the end gable, as usual, with spiral stair beside it up to the roof space.)

GLAN USK, ¾m. SE. Apparently a late Georgian sash-windowed farmhouse, but originating in the early to mid C17 as a rectangular S-facing range with projecting stair-tower at the rear. The range was made deeper *c.* 1708 (dated sundial noted by Bradney), almost absorbing the stair-tower. The stairs rise in short flights up a square core and are unusually well illuminated by two-light windows at four levels. The top two windows unaltered, with ovolo mouldings. Of *c.* 1708 the panelled NE closet with angle fireplace, a charming, unaltered period piece. Across the yard to the N a two-storey stone SERVICE RANGE retaining original timber openings. One upper window with diamond mullions.

CWM MAWR, 1½m. SW. In its own deep combe high on the wooded flank of the Blorenge, the house appearing above a couple of barns, all of whitened rubble-stone. The house itself is obviously of two parts. The earlier lies back, end-on to the hillside. Its age is revealed only inside, where two upper-cruck trusses survive, in a standard late-C16 two-unit plan, with a hearth in each gable-end and a mural stair, now removed, beside each. In the early C17 the house was extended on the downhill side. The new part, having two full storeys and a habitable roof space, is dramatically taller than the old. Also an oddly jagged S projection, containing entrance porch and stair-tower. The only original window, a four-lighter at the upper level of the N wall, is old-fashioned, with hood, arched lights and sunk chamfer moulding. The porch opens into what was clearly a cross-passage, and the original entry to the stair opens from the hall. Stairs in short flights up a square core. Doorways with shaped heads at two levels, and another in a timber-framed partition in the roof space. The top flight of the stairs looks like an expedient, taken across the top of the porch, and lit by a tiny slit window.

CARN Y DEFAID (SO 271 099) and its neighbouring cairn are conspicuous landmarks on the summit of the ridge, clearly visible from the lower ground to the E. Such siting is more typical of the Bronze Age monuments of the Glamorgan uplands than of Gwent, where the barrows often stand in the valley bottoms.

MONMOUTHSHIRE AND BRECON CANAL. The canal runs along the lower slope of the Blorenge. Along its route six of the typical hump-backed, segmental-arched stone BRIDGES constructed by *William Crossley* as part of the canal works 1809–12.

LLANELLY/LLANELLI 2010

The large parish, until 1974 in Breconshire, includes the settlements in the Clydach Gorge and at Gilwern. These grew up in connection with the Clydach Ironworks, owned by the Hanburys of Pontypool Park and in operation from the 1690s to the 1860s. The high ground to the NW remains rural and remote. Here, typically, stands the medieval church, facing a panorama of peaks to the N and E.

ST ELLI. The W tower is what one will remember. Broad and squat (reduced in height in 1868), unbuttressed and devoid of mouldings, it carries a slated spire, of 1897 by *Baldwin* of Brecon, which starts pyramidal but turns octagonal one-third of the way up. The rectangular SW stair-turret crowned by a half-timbered gablet adds to the peculiar geometry of the whole. Nave, S porch and lower chancel. Gabled N aisle in one with full-length N chapel. Slabby Old Red Sandstone throughout. Various Perp windows, all of *Joseph Nevill*'s restoration of 1867–8, except two N two-lighters of red sandstone. The S porch has a medieval entrance arch, two-centred with a double chamfer. The interior is also heavily restored. The chancel arch and the roofs of nave and chancel belong to the restoration of 1910–11 by *J. Vaughan Richards* of Crickhowell. The arcades, with continuous chamfers and insubstantial piers, also look suspiciously like early C20 work. The pointed tower arch is undatable. That leaves just one important late medieval component, the continuous barrel vault of the N aisle and chapel, plastered between moulded ribs, on deep moulded wall-plates. The piscina in the S wall of the aisle also confirms that its fabric is medieval. – FONT. Globular bowl. Of the C12? – ALTAR TABLE. An exceptional Jacobean piece. Bulbous gadrooned legs. Marquetry frieze. – STAINED GLASS. Chancel E. Christ the Good Shepherd in a sheep-filled meadow. Inserted in 1909 by *Powell*'s, though dated 1901. – N aisle N, St Elli received into the Church, *c.* 1911 by the same. – N aisle E, Christ Blessing with ironworks and colliery scenes, 1968 by *Celtic Studios*. – MONUMENTS. Two stone slabs in the sanctuary with crudely cut figures in shallow relief, one dated 163[?], the other 1646. – Edward Lewis †1713. Large, rustic, hanging wall monument, with baying hound heads at the top, framing an incongruously elegant brass inscription plate. – Catherine Williams †1844. Gothic wall monument signed by *J. Thomas* of Newport. – John Maund †1850. Heavy Gothic wall monument signed by *W. Meredith Thomas*.

In the CHURCHYARD, four steps and the base of a CROSS.

BETHLEHEM BAPTIST CHAPEL, Maesygwartha. Dated 25 December 1830. Alone with its MANSE and caretaker's COTTAGE. Built of rubble ironstone with dressings of the same. The entrance front is a handsome two-storeyed composition, round-headed windows above flanking an oval one, segment-headed windows below flanking a round-headed doorway. The interior is largely unaltered, the galleries on three sides carried on slender iron columns, the preacher's platform and pair of stairs to it with slim turned balusters. Two tall, segment-headed windows flank the pedimented backboard to the preacher's seat.

TY UCHAF, ½m. NW. The upper half of the main range is a two-storeyed stone farmhouse of *c.* 1600. Hall with fireplace at the downhill end, and the entrance doorway beside it. Post-and-panel partition with end doorway opening to storerooms. Large blocked window in the upper gable-end. The hipped-roofed S addition has a corbelled stack, so there was a heated upper room here.

NEUADD, ½m. S. The story here is similar. The partition has chamfered planks stopped low down, indicating that a bench ran across the hall opposite the fireplace.

PANTYBEILIAU, ½m. SW. Early C19 villa of three bays and two storeys. Porch on Ionic columns.

DAN-Y-GRAIG, ¾m. N, beside the A4077. Another early C19 three-bay villa, but a much more characterful one. The outer windows, the upper ones segment-headed, are set in generous, full-height bows. The straight eaves cornice oversailing the bows must have been an afterthought.

CLYDACH HOUSE, ¾m. S. Symmetrical, double-pile, white-rendered house dated 1693 on an armorial panel over the front door. Original timber mullion-and-transom casement windows at the back. The front sashed and the third storey added in the early C19. (Central open-well stair with twisted balusters, of 1693.)

At GILWERN two modest late C19 chapels. HOPE BAPTIST, dated 1876, is the standard gable-ended rectangle built of rock-faced Old Red Sandstone with long, round-headed windows and no frills. It cost £500, and the contractor was Mr *Burgoine* of Blaenavon. The UNITED REFORMED CHURCH is dated 1885. Pennant sandstone with yellow brick dressings. Timber Gothic tracery.

INDUSTRIAL REMAINS

The CLYDACH GORGE is a remarkable relict landscape of the
2 Industrial Revolution in a setting of great natural beauty. Fragments of several ironworks remain. But the gorge, 3½m. (5.6 kilometres) long, also funnelled transport routes from the ironworks on the uplands to the W, down to the Brecon and Abergavenny Canal, the deep ravine providing a challenge to C19 civil engineers. As a result there were as many as four roughly parallel horse-worked railways dating from the late C18 and early C19; considerable lengths of their formations remain as roads or hillside terraces. A turnpike road was laid through the gorge in 1812–13 and a public locomotive railway in 1862, not to mention the Head of the Valleys road (A465) in the 1960s.

Ironworks

LLANELLY BLAST FURNACE, 100 yds (90 metres) SW of Clydach House (*see* above). What is left of an early ironworks, perhaps that which Capel Hanbury set up in 1684, consists of three elements: a CHARGING-BANK, at Sale Yard, faced with rubblestone; the stub of the CHARGING-BRIDGE behind to the NW; and higher up a substantial bank of LIMEKILNS.

LLANELLY FORGE, a little further down the valley, at SO 236 140. In operation from 1697 to 1878, initially to convert the iron cast at Llanelly Blast Furnace into wrought iron. No industrial structures survive, but NE of Clydach House the outline of the now dry water-power pool can be traced, and its long, low masonry DAM to the NE. Also some HOUSING. FORGE ROW, for twenty workers and their families, is partly of *c.* 1800, and partly probably early C18, see the steep roof-pitch. Very little of such early iron-workers' housing survives in Wales. Also single-storey STABLES. FORGE HOUSE, E of the road junction, was built as, or became, a tin-house, and by 1878 held the tinning bays added to the rolling mills.

CLYDACH IRONWORKS (SO 229 132). The site was excavated in 1986, revealing comprehensible remnants of the ironworks founded in the boom years 1793–5, and expanding by 1841 to employ over 1,350 people. The works went out of production in 1877. SMART'S BRIDGE, which provides access to the site, bears the date 1824. It is constructed of cast iron and carried a railway linking with the Clydach Railroad across the River Clydach. Simple lancet tracery in the spandrels of the arch. To the W of the bridge, a three-storeyed terrace of WORKERS' HOUSING, *c.* 1800.

The ironworks originally had two blast furnaces (constructed in 1793 and 1797); a third was added *c.* 1826 (not excavated), and a fourth 1842–4. After excavation, the circular refractory-brick linings of the furnace stacks can be seen, surviving up to the 'boshes' where they bellied out to their greatest width. The dressed stone casing, which originally stood 44 ft (13.4 metres) high, has all been robbed away. In front, on a riverside terrace, remains of the cast-house in which the iron pigs were formed. At a higher level is the WATER-WHEEL PIT, which housed a huge cast-iron wheel 42 ft (12.8 metres) in diameter, which drove the blowing-cylinders. See the wear marks where the wheel rubbed against the sides of the pit. At the top of the site were the charging-houses. The high gable wall of the CHARGING-HOUSE of the 1793 furnace still dominates the site. The coking-ovens to the SE, and the aqueduct which brought in water at the highest level of all to drive the water wheel, have all disappeared.

To the S of the blast furnaces the formation of a counter-balanced RAILWAY INCLINED PLANE, constructed before 1811, can be seen. This enabled pig iron to be lifted to the higher-level ROLLING MILLS constructed in 1805, *c.* 200 yds (180 metres) up to the SW. Reused buildings stand on their site.

Transport Lines

The Clydach Railroad was constructed in 1794 by *John Dadford* as a horse-worked edge-railway formation linking Wain Dew

Colliery, Beaufort, with Glangrwyne Forge on the River Usk. The single-arch BRIDGE of coursed rubble-stone at Maes-ygwartha (SO 230 138) belonged to this railway. The bridge is spectacularly set above a waterfall.

The road uphill from Clydach Ironworks to Cwm Llan-march follows the line of the LLAN-MARCH RAILROAD, also engineered by *Dadford* in 1794, to link with the coal and iron-ore mines. The terraced formation beyond to Pwll-du indicates the line of the BLAENAVON STONEROAD, opened in 1799. The construction of the lower half of the Brecon and Abergavenny Canal in 1809–12 led to the extension of the railway NE-wards, as what became known as the LLAN-MARCH TRAMROAD. A single-arched stone BRIDGE (SO 233 137) carried this tramroad. Another early single-arch stone bridge, of *c.* 1811, is the LLAN-MARCH TRAMROAD AND AQUEDUCT BRIDGE (SO 225 176). The bridge deck is extra deep to accommodate below the railway a leat from the River Clydach to the Clydach Ironworks rolling mill. The track ascending from immediately S of the bridge is the formation of a second counterbalanced RAILWAY INCLINED PLANE, constructed in 1811 at the steep gradient of 1:4 or 1:5.

High on the SE slope of Clydach Gorge can be traced the circuitous terraced formation of the GOVILON TRAMROAD, constructed in the early C19 to connect the Bailey brothers' Nantyglo Ironworks with the Monmouthshire Canal. The engineer was *Thomas Hill* of Blaenavon.

On the N crest of Clydach Gorge can be seen the near-horizontal terrace which is part of the BAILEYS' LLANGATTOCK TRAMROAD, of 1831, the third of Joseph and Crawshay Bailey's early railways through the gorge from Nantyglo Ironworks. This had something of the experimental railway about it, partly flat, partly of inclined planes.

The MERTHYR, TREDEGAR AND ABERGAVENNY RAILWAY was in 1862 carried along the upper SE slopes of the gorge. Two viaducts, two tunnels, and high retaining walls, all of the same rock-faced masonry, remain, though the line closed in 1958. NANT DYAR VIADUCT is of nine arches built on a curve. Immediately S of it is what remains of Clydach RAILWAY STATION, with to its SW the TUNNEL PORTALS of the tunnel under Clydach Camp (Twyn-y-dinas).

Limeworks

At LLANELLY QUARRY (SO 222 124) a later C19 double limekiln, stone-built with brick-lined charging-bowl and discharging arches. Further E a second pair dated 1892.

CLYDACH LIMEWORKS (SO 233 127), alongside Nant Dyar Viaduct, has a pair of limekilns and other remains, perhaps of *c.* 1862, when the building of the railway required large quantities of lime mortar. To the NE, at a higher level, two more masonry limekilns, perhaps built *c.* 1877, when the railway line was doubled. At BLACK ROCK LIMEWORKS, on the N side of the gorge at Cheltenham, ½ m. W of Clydach, another pair of masonry limekilns. These works were in operation from 1794 to 1908. *See* also below, under Auckland House.

Canals

At GILWERN are important remains relating to the Brecon and Abergavenny Canal, constructed from Gilwern to Govilon 1802–5 by the engineer *Thomas Dadford jun.* The EMBANKMENT at SO 244 144 is one of the largest canal earthworks in Wales. It blocks the lower mouth of the Clydach Gorge, and a long round-arched TUNNEL takes the River Clydach through the base of the huge bank. A similar, smaller TUNNEL, high up at the N end of the bank, allowed the Clydach Tramroad through to Glangrwyne Forge. On the SW side of the bank an overflow channel and weir release a torrent into the river far below. The canal is now cased in a concrete channel at this point.

AUCKLAND HOUSE, N of the embankment (SO 242 146), was built in at least four stages as the Baileys' and Brewers' iron-warehouses, in 1819 and 1820 to store iron brought down from the ironworks at Nantyglo, Coalbrookvale and Beaufort. Wide blocked arches in the long, rectangular, coursed-rubble building show where railway sidings originally ran in. This was one of the very first purpose-built railway warehouses anywhere.

A block of LIMEKILNS survives NE of Auckland House. They were probably constructed soon after the opening of Llanelly Wharf in 1817. The small size of the drawing holes in their rubble front walls is a sign of early date.

Downstream from Gilwern Aqueduct is the single-span segmental-arched BRIDGE which was built in the early C19 to carry the Usk Valley road over the River Clydach. On the NW side of the bridge, DAN-Y-BONT WOOLLEN MILL. This is also early C19, a long, narrow three-storey structure of white-painted rubblestone. Of six bays, extended by a further three at the S end.

LLANFAIR CILGOED *3010*

$2\frac{3}{4}$ m. N of Llantilio Crossenny

ST MARY. 1842–3 by *R. H. Evins*, surveyor of Abergavenny, with corrections by *T. H. Wyatt* at the request of the bishop of Llandaff. Lancets. Four-bay nave with W bellcote and small W porch. One-bay chancel much lower. Roughly coursed Old Red Sandstone. Thin tie-beam and kingpost roof in the nave. – STAINED GLASS. Chancel E, Virgin and Child. 1982 by *Geoffrey Robinson* of *Joseph Bell & Son* of Bristol.

The site of the medieval chapel, which belonged to a grange of Dore Abbey, Herefordshire, is in a grassy hollow to the E.

LLANFAIR DISCOED *see* LLANVAIR DISCOED

3000 LLANFAIR KILGEDDIN/ LLANFAIR CILGEDIN

ST MARY THE VIRGIN. The church stands in isolation to the NE of the scattered village, in the meadows beside the River Usk. Nave with W double bell gable and S porch, lower chancel with N vestry. Yet this is no longer just a humble little late medieval building, but also an expression of Victorian wealth, taste and piety unique in the county. The Rev. W. J. Coussmaker Lindsay, who became rector in 1872, commissioned *J. D. Sedding* to reconstruct the church, 1873–6, incorporating some medieval pieces, and to provide it with handsome fittings. Then, after the death of his wife, he commissioned, as a memorial to her and
106 on Sedding's recommendation, a complete scheme of sgraffito wall decoration by *Heywood Sumner*. This was carried out 1888–90, the artist's first major essay in the medium. It is this decoration which should make Llanfair Kilgeddin a place of pilgrimage for disciples of the Arts and Crafts movement. Thanks to the Friends of Friendless Churches, building and decorations survive in excellent condition. After the church was reported in 1982 to be in danger of settlement, it was closed for worship and would have been demolished had not the Victorian Society persuaded Cadw to fund its repair and the diocese to vest it in the Friends. The structural engineer *Brian Morton* supervised repairs 1986–8.

Closer examination from the outside reveals Sedding's approach to his task. In the chancel medieval Old Red Sandstone walling, with a blocked S priest's doorway which may be C19, and one genuine plate-traceried N window. The Dec E window is obviously C19. In the nave the S wall and S porch are reconstructions, though the windows, including one for the rood loft, are meant to convey an authentic impression. Two original N windows in the nave, Perp with square heads and cinquefoiled lights. A third in imitation, in Sedding's W extension. W double bell gable, entirely to *Sedding*'s design, capped by a gablet pierced with trefoiled oculi. The W doorway has medieval jambs.

Inside, the width of the nave is very apparent, the chancel arch wide and simply chamfered. Chancel roof largely medieval. It is not surprising that the need was felt for WALL DECORATIONS. Their subject is the Benedicite, the hymn of praise to God by his creation, illustrated verse by verse and scene by scene all round nave and chancel. *Sumner* veers wittily from Neo-antique idealization to contemporary realism, but the sgraffito technique, which requires the top layer of plaster to be cut back line by line to reveal coloured plaster underneath, enforces simplicity and clarity, so that, as a contemporary critic noted, he 'tells a story which an inmate of the nursery can read as it runs'. Only the figure of Christ in Majesty over the chancel arch lacks conviction. The scheme is signed and dated 1888 on the nave SE window-sill. – FONT. Late medieval. Hexagonal on a panelled foot with shields. Also a remarkable late medieval COVER, flat and covered in blind tracery patterns. – The circular bowl of a second FONT, possibly Norman. – PULPIT. 1875. Of timber, polygonal, carved with reliefs of the Four Evangelists under crocketed arches. – CHANCEL SCREEN. Dense Dec tracery in the lights. Brought in and heavily restored by *Sedding*. – ALTAR RAILS. Clearly by *Sedding*. Of iron and brass. – REREDOS. By *Sedding*, 1875. Alabaster, the full width of the E wall. A restrained and elegant design of rectilinear panelling enclosing a band of quatrefoils at the top. Tiny gilt rosettes and square leaf bosses decorate the green marble framing. – TILE PAVEMENTS. Throughout. Handsome pattern in the chancel. An integral part of *Sedding*'s scheme. – STAINED GLASS. Chancel N, an enjoyable jumble of medieval fragments. – Chancel E, Adoration of the Shepherds, 1894. – Chancel S, Visitation with Simeon and Anna, *c.* 1910. Both are by *John Jennings*, though only the latter is signed. Their overworked Germanic style, with heavy canopywork, is completely at odds with the wall decoration. Yet they went in during the later years of Mr Lindsay's incumbency.

In the CHURCHYARD, a CROSS on four restored steps with a broached base, and a new shaft and head by *Sedding* with reliefs of the Virgin and Child and the Crucifixion. On the model of such medieval crosses as those at St Donats and Llangan, Glamorgan. Restored in 1912, see the inscription on the steps.

SCHOOL, in the main hamlet beside the B4598. Of 1871. Red brick with black brick trim. School and schoolhouse form a varied group, a rustic version of what Butterfield might have done.

MOTTE, opposite the school. Just a low mound close beside the River Usk. 95

BRIDGE, 1¼ m. N of the hamlet, carrying the Usk to Abergavenny road (B4598) over the River Usk. Constructed *c.* 1821 by *John Upton* of Gloucester, to an unusual and handsome design. Three elliptical arches, their stonework laid as voussoirs all the way up to the parapet. Circular spandrel voids, singletons at the ends and trios over the cutwaters, their value decorative rather than structural.

LLANFAIR COURT, at the W end of the hamlet. Built as the rectory. An attractive, irregular group of several periods, rendered white. The S front is a symmetrical composition, thanks first to *James Maddox* 'surveyor and carpenter', who in 1815 built the E two-thirds. His was an eccentric design, with three windows above, the centre one round-headed, to the two expansive French windows below. In 1955–6 *Alex Gordon* extended the façade W-wards in an identical idiom, so that the upper windows alternate A–B–A–B–A.

PANTYGOITRE, 1 m. N of the village. The main block is square, white, three-storeyed, of five bays by six. Built after 1776 as an addition to the N of a modest, two-storeyed house of 1726. Both parts were of red brick. The colour change was made before 1832, and so was the addition of thin, unfluted Greek Doric columns formed of sandstone monoliths, which carry a veranda across the E and N fronts. Also plain stone frieze and cornice, and an attic panel, to indicate that the E is the entrance front. An elegant timber ORANGERY curves out from the NW corner, with wafer-thin Tuscan pilasters.

The house stands in a small PARK adorned with specimen trees.

PANTYGOITRE FARM, E of the B4598. Trim white C18 farmhouse of three storeys, and two contemporary BARNS. That to the S is of stone and red brick, that to the NE of brick, five bays with a tall porch. Further E, along CHURCH LANE, a stone C17 BARN with a porch, extended in red brick. The gable of the extension treated as a dovecote.

LLANVAIR GRANGE, 1¼ m. W of the village. Handsomely set on a rise between groups of lofty conifers. The formidable and rather urban-looking stuccoed front block, of three storeys, five bays wide and one bay deep, was, according to Bradney, added to an earlier house for John Shaw before *c.* 1830. The façade has recessed corners, and the central bay projects slightly under a very small pediment. The high ground storey is channelled. Otherwise the austere spirit of the Greek Revival reigns. Plain sash windows. Plain top cornice and blocking course, to mask the shallow pitched roof. The chimneystacks have been removed and the columned porch is of the C20.

LLANFIHANGEL CRUCORNEY/
3020
LLANFIHANGEL CRUGCORNEL

The church stands in the middle of what was until the 1960s a highroad village. Skirrid Mountain Inn conspicuous to the E, to the W a pair of BARNS, timber-framed and weatherboarded above stone. The Hereford–Abergavenny traffic now speeds past on the modern A465 a stone's throw to the SE.

ST MICHAEL. The victim of unsympathetic reconstructions. Built of slabby Old Red Sandstone, with dressings to match. The tall, unbuttressed C15 W tower forms quite a landmark. Low battlements on a stringcourse with gargoyles crudely carved into human heads. Two-light belfry lancets with cusped tympanum. Five-bay nave and lower chancel, both with angle buttresses. Other medieval evidence suggests the origin of both parts in the late C13 or C14. In the chancel, several features reset by *Richard Creed* when he rebuilt the walls 1884–6. One N lancet and one S, and a pair under a cusped tympanum on the N side of the sanctuary. Priest's door with two-centred head and continuous chamfer. In the nave only a lancet high in the W wall, looking into the tower, and two-centred doorway below. Otherwise the nave, with its egregious paired lancets, was rebuilt in 1835, probably by *T. H. Wyatt.* The tall S porch, however, is late medieval, the outer arch nearly round-headed, moulded with an ovolo between two hollows, the S doorway with four-centred head and similar mouldings drawn together into a stop low down. In 1976–7 *E. A. Roiser* unroofed the three W bays of the nave and built up a utilitarian wall to enclose the two E bays. – STAINED GLASS. Chancel E, Virgin and Child between St John the Divine and St Elizabeth of Hungary, 1888 by *C. E. Kempe.* –

MONUMENTS. Worn Old Red Sandstone tomb slab carved in 73
relief with life-size praying man and woman in late C16 dress. They kneel in twisting poses on the steps of a cross, which bears three small kneeling figures (of children?) at its head. An altogether extraordinary object. Richard Scudamore †1695 (sanctuary N). Hanging wall monument typical of the period. The oval inscription panel framed by a wreath and flanked by black twisted Ionic columns. These carry a broken pediment with putti on its sloping sides and armorial display between. Skulls and crossbones in the lower spandrels. – Imogen Hall. Hanging wall monument dated 1887. White marble relief portrait bust with posies of flowers below. Signed *Prof. Romanelli*, Florence.

SKIRRID MOUNTAIN INN. A remarkably complete mid- to late C17 building, constructed of the local shaley Old Red Sandstone. Large timber mullion-and-transom windows, ovolo-moulded, some two-light, some four-light and some of eight lights, not altogether regularly disposed. Central square-headed doorway and original door. However, the pattern of relieving arches, two plus three plus two, over the lower windows suggests that the fenestration may have been drastically altered, and that originally there was an arrangement of symmetrical upright windows. The most advanced feature is the plan, a double pile. Hipped roof over the two-storeyed front half, single-storeyed rear, the catslide roof-slope interrupted by the staircase gable. Inside, large heated rooms to l. and r. with plain but massive stone chimneypieces, and the rear pile at a slightly lower level. The l. room has stop-chamfered beams and joists. The staircase, with flat pierced and shaped balusters, rises in short flights round a square open well in the centre of the rear pile.

LLANVIHANGEL COURT, $\frac{1}{3}$m. SE. The most impressive and internally the most richly decorated country house of the decades around 1600 in Monmouthshire, but the product of a complicated and puzzling building history. What seems to have happened is this. The E range was built by Rhys Morgan in the mid C16, in 1559 it is said, as a two-storeyed, single-pile house (like, for example, Flemingston Court, Glamorgan). Half a century later this became the parlour range of a much larger, roughly H-plan house, built either by Morgan's son, Anthony, before 1608, or by Nicholas Arnold (M.P. for the county 1626, High Sheriff 1633). The new, N-facing entrance front, a self- 52
conscious composition poised above terraces and a grand central flight of steps, survives essentially in its original form, even if windows and doorway have been altered. Inside, a series of plaster ceilings, datable to any time between the 1590s and 1630s, decorate the principal rooms. In the later C17 Arnold's son John (inherited 1665, High Sheriff 1669, M.P. 1681–98) remodelled the N front and the main stair, and greatly enlarged the service accommodation. Several dates occur about the house, yet none of them unarguably dates a building phase. They are: 1627 on a sundial on the E range, 1635 on a fireback in the kitchen, 1673 on a lead cistern, 1679 on a charcoal stove in the kitchen, and 1694 on a fireback in the hall.

John Arnold built the handsome stable block and planted two broad, straight avenues, one of pines aligned on the N front, the other of sweet chestnuts, partly surviving, S-wards towards the flank of the Skirrid Mountain. Today there is no formal approach to the house, which is first seen from above, from the SW, as a picturesque agglomeration tucked into the hillside, beyond a heavily buttressed stone retaining wall, a timber-framed barn and the brick-fronted stable. Slabby Old Red Sandstone rubble is the main constructional material for the house itself.

Close inspection must begin at the SE corner of the house. Here the off-centre upper window in the S gable-end provides the clearest evidence of the first phase. Roll-moulded frame and mullions forming three arched lights, hood on square stops, typical of the early to mid C16. Further C16 evidence inside (*see* below). The sundial above the window, dated 1627 and bearing the initials of Nicholas Arnold, was clearly fixed to a pre-existing wall. The walling and window below, however, are a careful reconstruction of c. 1925, after the removal of a strange Egyptian-style room which had been added as recently as 1905.

The E front was also greatly reconstructed at the same time. Here, two huge, two-storey window bays had been added *c.* 1905. In removing them, the regular C17 design was re-created, two-storeyed, five bays under three triangular gables, the windows mullion-and-transom crosses, with the one exception that the central bay was reconstructed blank. The C17 stonework remains in the gables; below, it is largely of 1925.

The N front is a careful, two-storeyed, six-bay composition, the outer pairs of bays projecting as short wings. Gables here, too, plain and triangular, wide ones over the outermost bays, narrow ones over their neighbours, but the two recessed centre bays are gable-less. Complete symmetry is maintained by the central doorway. But this is a later C17 alteration. A flush relieving arch in the inner side of the W projection shows the site of the original doorway. This masking of the doorway from the frontal view was a typical device *c.* 1600 (cf. Chastleton, Oxfordshire; Burton Agnes, Yorkshire), in order to reconcile the demand for an external appearance of symmetry with the traditional entry through a porch (here completely absorbed into the W projection) into the screens passage at the lower end of the hall. That leaves the windows. They are C17 mullion-and-transom crosses. It is probable that these too are a modification (contrast the window in the S wall of the hall visible inside, *see* below). Their consistently upright, classicizing proportions suggest a date after 1665, contemporary with the resiting of the entrance doorway, rather than one in the early C17. The unusual mouldings, hollow-chamfered sides to mullions and transoms, and a central sunk ovolo, do not clarify the dating.

The W side of the house is a wonderfully confusing jumble, with mullioned and mullion-and-transom windows of various patterns and dates, some clearly of the C17, others quite modern. The short, narrow wing which projects near the N end must be an addition, see the way it overlaps a three-light window high up. The stepped arrangement of windows S of this wing indicates a back stair, the ovolo-moulded top windows typical of the mid C17. Immediately S again, the massive kitchen chimney-breast breaks forward, bearing two heavy C19 stacks. Brick service porch on the N side of the transverse S range. The S range extends beyond the kitchen to the W and to the E, where the hillside is cut back for it, and it almost encloses a picturesque service court-yard on the S side of the house. In this direction the S range has a bold hipped roof, and its windows and those lighting the kitchen have timber mullion-and-transom crosses, all of which can hardly be earlier than the 1670s. Confirmation that this great expansion of the service end of the house goes with the remodelling of the N front is in the window mouldings: the timber kitchen windows are detailed in the same way as the stone ones on the N front. The S side of the hall range is masked partly by a two-storey C19 corridor, partly by a big roughcast hipped-roofed staircase projection in the angle with the E range. This is probably early C17, but neither the hipped roof nor the large timber windows can be original, the former later C17, the latter probably C19. Note the way the stair projection overlaps a mullioned ground-floor window in the E range.

Examination of the interior should begin in the HALL. It is a single-storey room. In its S wall one original window, of three lights with a transom and sunk chamfer mouldings, important evidence of the *c.* 1600 fenestration, and so (as noted above) a clue to the original appearance of the N front. Beside it, a contemporary chimneypiece, the depressed-headed fireplace arch with a hollow moulding, within a rectangular, roll-moulded frame. To the l. of the window a big, broad, stone doorway, four-centred-headed, with a bold, continuous chamfer. Original hinged and studded door. This was the S exit from the screens passage, opposite the N porch. No sign of the screens. The N porch is internally clearly defined and has a decorated plaster ceiling, in a square pattern of thin moulded ribs centred on a pendant. The hall itself has a similar thin-ribbed ceiling, in a continuous pattern of linked stars within quatrefoils, with rosettes and fleurs-de-lys in the fields. All this is consistent enough. It is the upper end of the hall that puzzles. Here, where the dais should be, is a large timber-framed enclosure with a doorway in its N end to steps down to a wine cellar. (The panelling which covered it is now upstairs in the King's Room.) The ceiling decoration is finished off against the top of what must be late C19 timber-framing, and does not extend into the N dais bay.*

* Mr Peter Smith, formerly Secretary of RCAHMW, has pointed out that the construction of the partition shows that it is no older than the C19. This means that the plasterwork, which fits the partition, cannot be Jacobean. He also contrasts the refinement of the ceilings here with the much coarser treatment of similar designs in the genuine ceilings at Plas-mawr, Conwy, Gwynedd. He concludes that the Llanvihangel ceilings are modified re-creations of the original plasterwork. Dr Claire Gapper has kindly pointed out that T. Garner and A. Stratton, *Domestic Architecture of England during the Tudor Period* (1911), illustrates details of the ceilings but does not include Llanvihangel in their list of plaster ceilings of the period. It is tempting to suggest that the reworking conjectured by Mr Smith was indeed carried out in the late C19, under the supervision of Garner's firm, *Bodley & Garner*.

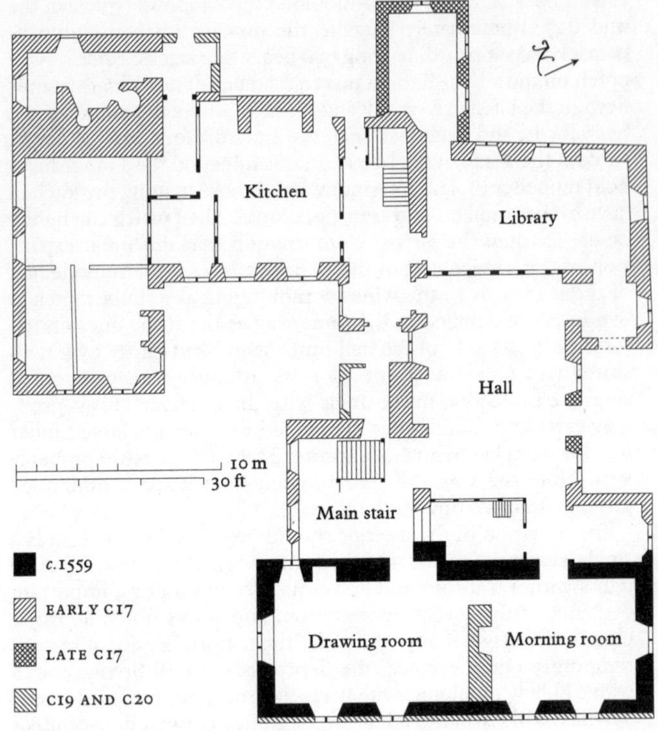

Llanfihangel Crucorney, Llanvihangel Court. Plan

The bay is indeed reduced to a sort of closet. Panelling here brought in from Coldbrook Park, Abergavenny (*see* p. 108). The MORNING ROOM, E of the hall dais in the C16 range, was the parlour in the early C17. It has a thin-ribbed plaster ceiling very similar to that in the hall, but with a different set of interlocking geometrical patterns, and small-fielded panelling crowned by an inlaid frieze patterned in a rhythm that relates to the plasterwork. The room was shortened in the early C20 by means of an inserted S wall, see the curtailed ceiling design. The DRAWING ROOM, which lies beyond the inserted wall within the mid-C16 range, is reached from the hall via the foot of the main stair. Here, where the stone walls are exposed, is more visible evidence of the mid-C16 house. The doorway from the stair-foot has been cut through a fireplace. One ogee-moulded jamb survives, as does the chimney-breast for it projecting back into the dais enclosure. To the l. of this a smaller, complete, fireplace, with depressed chamfered head, and a two-light mullioned window. So the drawing room is formed from the hall and an inner heated room of the mid-C16 house. In the E wall a stop-chamfered jamb, clearly reused material.

The MAIN STAIR is a fine piece of late C17 timberwork. It

rises in broad, straight flights in a square open well. Moulded closed strings, vigorously twisted balusters, plain newels with turned, vase-like finials and pendants. (Traces of an earlier C17 stair underneath the landings.) STAINED GLASS of *c.* 1905 signed by *J. Dudley Forsyth* in two windows, one referring to a supposed visit paid by Charles I to Llanvihangel Court in 1645. Upstairs there is more plasterwork. The QUEEN'S ROOM, above the hall, was presumably the original great chamber. It is entered through an early C18 pedimented door-case, but the room itself is largely in its early C17 state. The stone fireplace surround matches that in the hall below, the small-fielded panelling has a frieze similar to that in the morning room, but without the inlay. Thin-ribbed plaster ceiling in a slightly less dense geometrical pattern than those downstairs. The pattern is interrupted at the W end by a partition and continues over the passage beyond, which was obviously part of the Queen's Room originally. At the N end of the passage, above the porch, a CLOSET with an individually patterned plaster ceiling. Back in the upper storey of the E range two further large rooms. The MASTER BEDROOM, just like the parlour (morning room) below it, has a richly patterned, ribbed plaster ceiling curtailed at its S end by a modern wall. The KING'S ROOM, to the S, has lost its plaster ceiling, leaving the criss-cross of supporting beams exposed. It is possible that in the C17 these two rooms were one, forming a gallery the full length of the E range. The stripped walls of the King's Room show further C16 evidence, a simple stone chimneypiece in the W wall and a blocked window l. of it. In the S wall the mid-C16 window noted outside.

In the W half of the house there is less to note. Description can begin again in the hall. Its W wall is timber-framed, dividing it from what is now the library. This LIBRARY must originally have been two rooms. Note the position of the fireplace, close to the N end of the W wall, its chimneypiece a small version of that in the hall and clearly proportioned for a room half as big as the present one. The later C17 projection at its SW corner forms a sizeable closet at this level. A doorway, with C17 door, at the S end of the library opens into a C17 passage. The back stairs rise at the W end of the passage, with at the top a doorway shaped into a double ogee-headed opening into the attics. The KITCHEN, now dining room, is divided from the back stairs by a timber partition, and further such partitions enclose a pantry and passage further S. At the W end of the S range a bakehouse with massive brick ovens.

SUMMER-HOUSE, some way E of the house, late C17, of brick, circular, with stone-slated conical roof and stone buttresses. It is the lonely survivor of three which stood at the corners of a large walled garden. To the S of the house the C17 STABLE and BARN are set at r.-angles to one another. The contrast between them is piquant. The stable has a delightful N front, typical of the 1670s. Red brick, laid in somewhat irregular Flemish bond. Large timber mullion-and-transom windows, classically proportioned and grouped three and three about a central doorway with timber

architrave-moulded frame. A moulded timber cornice carries the
61 roofslope. Inside, splendid contemporary turned timber stall posts, two extended up to support the floor of the loft above. The barn is timber-framed, at the time of writing an unclad skeleton, after the removal of the brick nogging which filled the square panels within the timber framework. Of five bays, the central threshing bay slightly narrower than the others. There is one last archaeological puzzle to unravel. The footings of the barn at its N end stand on the battered stone base of the stable, suggesting that the stable was constructed first. Close investigation shows that the stable's end and rear walls are of stone, not brick, and its roof reuses upper-cruck trusses, so the brick façade and internal fittings of the stable belong to a remodelling which may well postdate the construction of the barn.

At the NE end of the village street, TŴR MIHANGEL, a two-storey stone house ending in an octagonal battlemented tower, intended as an eye-catcher from the Court.

Beside the River Honddu, ¼ m. N of the village, an instructive vernacular group, including a much-altered MILL. BRIDGE COTTAGE, hard up against the road, single-storeyed plus a habitable roof space, was dated by Fox and Raglan to the early C17. It was completely altered in the mid-1990s. MILLBROOK, across the road, forms an L in plan, the lower range which comes forward to the road apparently the earlier – see the straight joint in the W wall. The main, two-storeyed range is a classic two-unit house, perhaps of the late C16, missing only its entrance doorway. Original window openings, indicated by their timber lintels, with restored timber frames of 1988, based on a single survivor in the E gable wall, showing that the mullions were of the normal lozenge-plan form. Unaltered interior. The hall has ceiling joists stop-chamfered with a torus bar and broach. Post-and-panel screen with sockets for a bench, and ogee-headed doorways into the pair of inner rooms. Spiral mural stair beside the hall hearth in the E gable wall, with stone steps to the upper floor and timber steps to the roof space.

STANTON MANOR FARM, 1 m. NW. A cowshed N of the farmhouse incorporates part of a CHAPEL, built by Llanthony Priory, probably in the early C14, for the tenants of their manor at Stanton. One small ogee-headed S lancet is readily visible. (Another in the N wall and the blocked E window.)

PANDY, 1¼ m. NE, is a hamlet of late C19 grey stone houses and two grey stone chapels, dumpy, hipped-roofed ZOAR BAPTIST of 1837, lanky, gable-ended HOPE CALVINISTIC METHODIST of 1866.

TY DERLWYN, 1¾ m. NE. Crazily gabled and bargeboarded house of *c.* 1878, built for Jeremiah Rosher of Trewyn, Bwlch Trewyn. Additions of 1890 by *E. A. Johnson*.

PENISHAPLWYDD, 2¼ m. NE. The symmetrical N front of the late C17 range retains a set of four uniquely decorative timber windows. Three lights with a transom, arching segmentally in the centre light and supporting a central upper mullion carved in relief. It is a version of a form found in eastern England from early in the century, and most famously at Sparrowe's House, Ipswich. The central doorway was eliminated by the addition of a gabled scullery in 1886, when a new farmhouse was added crosswise to the W, designed by *Edwin Foster* of Abergavenny. Half-timbered BARN across a yard to the N.

LLANFIHANGEL GOBION 3000

ST MICHAEL. A small Perp church, chancel and nave in one, S porch with open timber gable, lean-to N aisle and short, simple W tower with pyramid roof. The rubble walls, large quoins and dressed work are all of local grey stone, lightly restored in 1925. Two-light pointed-headed E window with simple tracery. N and S windows square-headed, of one, two or three cinquefoiled lights and glazed spandrels, a characteristic local detail. Deep, hollow window surrounds. The N and S rood-loft stair projections, both lit by small windows, must have been built at the same time as chancel and nave. Only the S doorway, which has a two-centred head and continuous sunk chamfer moulding, looks as if it could be pre-Perp. Most notable inside are the timber aisle-posts, polygonal and moulded, carrying the wall-plate. Arch-braced roofs in nave and chancel. – FONT. Perp. An unusual design, the bowl circular and enriched with rope-like arcading and IHS. The panelled octagonal stem is more run-of-the-mill. – SCULPTURE. Outside, at the W end of the S wall, a small, crude, late medieval stone panel carved with two angels holding a cloth in which stands a praying figure, doubtless intended for a human soul.

In the CHURCHYARD the remains of a late medieval CROSS, three steps, the broached base and the lowest stone of the shaft.

MOZERAH PRESBYTERIAN CHURCH, $\frac{1}{3}$m. NE. Built in 1839. White-rendered box with two timber porches. The small graveyard is full of showy Victorian monuments.

MANOR HOUSE, $\frac{1}{4}$m. NE. Two-storeyed late C16 stone house of two bays, to which a central two-storeyed porch with four-centred arch was later added. Inside, ceiling beams survive in both rooms above and below. To the r. they are richly moulded and have moulded joists, to the l. they are merely chamfered.

LLANFIHANGEL PONTYMOILE/ LLANFIHANGEL PONTYMOEL 3000

The little church and the thatched Horse and Jockey pub form an isolated pair beside the former turnpike road to Usk. The roundabout on the Pontypool bypass, 100 yds (90 metres) NE, breaks the spell.

ST MICHAEL. Nave and lower chancel. S porch. The primrose colour-wash, the shallow-pitched roofs on deep eaves, and the coarsely cut stonework of the windows and doorways all make one suspect the whole building to be post-medieval. Rebuilding in 1736 is reported, and a restoration by *D.J. Lougher* in 1904. Yet inside there is unmistakeable medieval evidence, the internal batter on the nave S wall, the doorway for a rood stair and the nave W doorway. Most obviously, chancel and nave both have plastered, ribbed wagon roofs of typical late medieval character. The oddest feature is the square stone double bellcote on the W gable, carried internally on three pointed arches. – FONT. Medieval. Shallow circular bowl with nailhead decorating the lower rim, perhaps a C12 tub reshaped in the C13. Octagonal stem on a spreading panelled foot, a local type. – STAINED GLASS. Chancel E, Jesus as Resurrection, Raising of Lazarus, Jesus Wept. Crowded scenes in pale colours. 1889. – (Two nave windows, 1901, clearly by *Joseph Bell & Son*. A. Brooks.)

TY-MAWR, ¾m. NE. A characterful farmhouse, largely of Pennant sandstone rubble, late C16 and early C17. The two parts are unusually sharply differentiated from one another. The low N half is a small hall house of one storey and a habitable roof space. The high S half, of two tall storeys and habitable roof space, is a very grand parlour wing, almost a new house. The most instructive view is from the E, where a massive, almost windowless, gabled projection encloses a staircase, originally lit by two small windows, and a chimney-breast. To the r. of this, under a pentice, a massive rectangular timber doorway, with sunk chamfered frame, its head of the shaped profile so popular from the beginning of the C17. The doorway opens, not into the normal through passage, but into a passage with doors in four directions, N into the earlier hall, E to the stairs, S to the parlour and W to a spacious square pantry enclosed by post-and-panel partitions on two sides. The doorway to the parlour has a simple arched head, and the fireplace opening there is chamfered with stone jambs and cambered timber lintel. The stairs, much renewed, rise in short, straight flights round a square core. The chamber above the parlour was clearly not a mere bedroom but a major living room in gentry fashion. Its stone fireplace has an angle roll, and on the lintel the initials of the builder and his wife, but not, tantalizingly, a date. Stop-chamfered beams throughout the house. Clearly high, spacious rooms were preferred to rich decoration. A second moulded door-head, however, reset in the doorway from the stair into the roof space over the hall, certainly not its original position.

MONMOUTHSHIRE AND BRECON CANAL. The canal, extended 1809–12 by *William Crossley*, winds at the foot of the escarpment down to Pontypool. Seven segmental-arched bridges carry minor roads and field paths over it.

PARKE-DAVIS PHARMACEUTICAL RESEARCH CENTRE, ½m. NE, beside the A4042. 1971–3 by the *Percy Thomas Partnership*. One-storey and two-storey pavilions, the manufacturing units steel-framed, the research and administration blocks of reinforced concrete. All are unified by the grey facing bricks, the windows in unbroken bands, and the cornices of vertically corrugated cladding. Well landscaped toward the road.

DUPONT FACTORY, 1 m. NE, beside the A4042. Built for British Nylon Spinners in 1947–8 by *Sir Percy Thomas & Son*, for the production of nylon yarn. One of the firm's first essays in a Modern idiom. Steel-framed blocks clad in brown brick. Windows in horizontal bands. But the dominant element, the massive rectangular 'spinning tower', also of brown brick, is given on its N face a great central panel with vertical concrete fins, serving a similar function to that provided by a portico on a classical building. In MAMHILAD PARK INDUSTRIAL ESTATE, immediately to the N, five more factory units built as part of the same development.

LLANFIHANGEL ROGIET *4080*

ST MICHAEL. The church, disused at the time of writing, is surrounded by a farmhouse, its barns and outbuildings, a mere couple of fields W of Rogiet Church. So profligate was church-building round here in the Middle Ages, each small manor requiring its own place of worship, that there was a third one, at Ifton, ¾ m. E of Rogiet (q.v.), pulled down *c.* 1755. As it is, the two Rogiet churches, with their landmark towers, stay in the memory, even when glimpsed from the railway or the M4. The tower is late medieval and seems on a larger scale than the rest of the church, of two tall storeys, with diagonal buttresses dying away below half-height (as at Rogiet). Small, two-light, rectangular belfry windows, deep corbelled battlements and angle pinnacles. Blocked two-centred W doorway, double-chamfered. The body of the church, nave, lower chancel and N aisle, is in origin older than the tower, although that is not apparent outside. Cusped ogee-headed S and E lancets in the heavily Victorianized chancel. Nave and S porch have Perp or later details. The lean-to aisle is a rebuilding of 1904 by *Henry Prothero* of Cheltenham. Inside, however, the chancel arch is unequivocally Dec, as is demonstrated by the (sadly hacked) corbel heads with scrolling locks, which support the inner steeply pointed, double-chamfered arch order, and the ogee-headed recesses l. and r. The two W bays of the N arcade may be contemporary, see the arches, on octagonal piers with simply moulded caps. Part of a third bay to a different, later, design, the arch four-centred with chamfer and hollow chamfer mouldings, possibly for an unusually elaborate rood-stair door. Plain, unmoulded tower arch. – FONT. Low square bowl on a tapering, crudely panelled stem. Presumably late medieval or later. – MONUMENTS. Two once-fine early C14 effigies. – Anne Martel. Recumbent lady, her feet on a greyhound. An inscription in French runs round the rim of the slab below, promising forty days' pardon to anyone who will say a *paternoster* and an *Ave Maria* for her. C15, i.e. later, tomb-chest with shields within quatrefoils on its sides. – Mutilated recumbent knight in chainmail and surcoat, cross-legged and drawing his sword. – Sarah Temperance Williams †1849. Ogee-topped tablet crested with heavy foliage crockets and a grape-bunch finial.

In the CHURCHYARD three steps and the broached base of a CROSS.

4000 LLANFIHANGEL-TOR-Y-MYNYDD

The church in its tree-fringed churchyard is the lowest component in a remote rural group. A barn stands beside the lane, and between the two CHURCH FARM, two-storeyed of *c.* 1600.

ST MICHAEL. Medieval nave and lower chancel of Old Red Sandstone rubble. W double bellcote typical of *Prichard & Seddon*, who restored the church in 1853–4. Deep S porch. This has a four-centred entrance arch moulded with a double wave. Basket-arched S doorway. Tudor mullioned S window. Other S windows and the E window are of the restoration. The wide chancel arch is undatable. – ALTAR RAILS. Late C17. Turned balusters. – FONT. Surely by *Prichard & Seddon*. Octagonal bowl with stepped faces. Spurred base.

LLANGUNNOG FARM, ¾m. SW. The site of a medieval parish church, the last remains of which, noted by Bradney in 1904, had disappeared by 1939.

TY-MAWR, ¾m. SE. An isolated group, low farmhouse and tall barn set side by side, end-on to the hillside. The large hall window of the house is C17, of four lights with a transom. Sunk chamfer moulding. Fox and Raglan found earlier evidence inside, of cruck construction.

4010 LLANFIHANGEL-YSTERN-LLEWERN/ LLANFIHANGEL-YSTUM-LLYWERN

ST MICHAEL. Small and sequestered, but retaining little of its medieval fabric. Built of all-too-friable local Old Red Sandstone rubble. *T. H. Wyatt* rebuilt much of the chancel in 1874. The nave was restored, and the square timber bellcote and the timber S porch added in 1895. E window of the C14 with cusped Y-tracery, early C16 nave S window, square-headed with three cinquefoiled lights but no hoodmould. The nave roof is also largely late medieval, having tie-beams as well as a ribbed and plastered wagon vault on moulded wall-plates. Simple medieval PISCINA in the chancel and mutilated STOUP inside the S doorway. – FONT. Medieval. Hemispherical bowl on an octagonal stem. – STAINED GLASS. Chancel E, SS Michael and George. 1906 by *Kempe*. – MONUMENTS. William Hopkins, rector, †1698. Exceedingly rustic wall monument. Tasselled rope surround to the inscription panel. Miniature figures above of a naked angel blowing a trumpet at a minister in coat and breeches.

– Sarah Loyd †1774. Small marble scroll-framed cartouche. – Sir Joseph Bradney, the historian of Monmouthshire, †1933. Brass plaque with very long Latin inscription. – Other plaques in a cluster, for his widow, †1946, and sons, †1918 and 1948.

OLD RECTORY, 200 yds (183 metres) E. 1845 by *Wyatt & Brandon*. Of stone, gabled.

THE PANT, ¾ m. W. A delightful group, as seen from the N. Low, 56
timber-framed range, and, downhill of it, a red brick, gable-ended cross range of two bays and two tall storeys. The timber-framed wall, so like that at nearby Little Pit Cottage, Llanarth, belonged, it seems, to a hall house of three-room plan of perhaps the mid C16. Cruck-truss end walls rebuilt in brick. The low-set diamond-mullioned window relates to a later inserted floor. Inserted timber-framed hearth, with the initials I.B., for John Beadles, and date 1687 cut in a beam. The brick range incorporated a Quaker meeting house. Its formality with 81
studiedly symmetrical cross-windows to the E and finely shaped brick stringcourses to E and S, is quite surprising. Wide E basement doorway to a cider cellar. It is possible that the date 1687 refers also to the erection of the meeting house. A Quaker burial ground was laid out here shortly before 1661, and the last active Quaker owner, Jenkinson Beadles, died in 1695 aged twenty-seven.

UPPER RED HOUSE, ¾ m. SW. Also of red brick, late C17, the brickwork now, as formerly, limewashed red. Just a farmhouse, but completely formalized. Three bays, two storeys, under a hipped roof. Two-storeyed hipped-roofed porch with segmental entrance arch. Mid-height platband continuous round house and porch. The chimneys, brought together into a cruciform central stack, were unfortunately reduced in bulk in the C19. Broadly proportioned windows under recessed segmental relieving arches, the timber frames ogee-moulded internally. Lobby-entry plan, with the timber stair twisting up behind the central back-to-back hearths, an old-fashioned feature which shows up the experimental nature of the design. The sloping site, however, has been adroitly used, to provide in the basement two full-height rooms entered from the downhill end, and a segmentally barrel-vaulted cider cellar at the uphill end. A second, similar cellar under the single-storey service wing, also of brick, built only a short time after the main house.

THE MAERDY, 1 m. N. A third red brick house of *c.* 1700. An L in plan, of two storeys, gable-ended. Entrance is in the angle between the ranges. Plain platbands. Vertical mullion-and-transom cross-windows regularly spaced, suggesting that this is the latest of the three. Two contemporary brick BARNS alongside.

TAL-Y-COED COURT, 1½ m. NW. Built 1881–3 for the twenty-two-year-old Joseph Bradney, the future historian of Monmouthshire, and dated 1882. His architect was *F. R. Kempson* of Hereford, normally a Gothicist, but here working in what was called at the time 'Queen Anne'. Red brick with stone dressings. A convincing evocation of a mid-C17 Artisan Mannerist house, not at all what one would expect in South Wales at that date. Five-bay W entrance front. Big hipped roof with lofty dormer windows and high, symmetrical panelled chimneystacks. Timber arcaded veranda across the S front. A generous stone bow window projects off-centre from the E front. Lower range added to the N in 1884, for library and kitchen. Stable block at r.-angles beyond. Inside, a good deal of panelling, but nothing of special note. – The little square LODGE by the road gives a foretaste of what is to come. The gadrooned stone HORSE TROUGH across the road clearly belongs too.

2010 LLANFOIST/LLANFFWYST

The village is almost a suburb of Abergavenny, beneath the wooded slope of the Blorenge.

ST FFWYST. A simple medieval church built of local sandstone rubble, just a nave and lower chancel. Characteristic Perp square-headed window of three cinquefoiled lights in the nave N wall, also the rood-stair projection. Added S porch, stone side walls and a timber roof, and a two-light window probably of the C16. In 1872 the church was restored in memory of Crawshay Bailey, the ironmaster. The gawky Dec E window is of that date, and the gabled N vestry and organ-chamber. *J. P. Seddon* must have been the architect. W window and double bell gable by *H. V. Ashley*, 1906, also the ridgetop louvre. Inside, the lofty chancel arch and matching arch to the organ-chamber are of 1872. – FURNISHINGS. These appear to be by *Seddon*. – Typical circular stone PULPIT and octagonal FONT, both set on stout shafts with stiff-leaf caps. – The timber CHOIR STALLS and PEWS with enriched ends, not to mention the S DOOR, also suggest *Seddon*'s hand. – BRASS LECTERN and SANCTUARY LAMPS. – FLOOR TILES. Highly decorative throughout, surely also of 1872. – ROYAL ARMS. Of Queen Victoria. Carved wood. Quite small, but handsome. – STAINED GLASS. Much inserted at the restoration of 1872, mostly by *Charles A. Gibbs*. – Chancel E, Crucifixion between Adoration of the Shepherds and Baptism of Christ. – Chancel S lancets, Parables of the Talents and Sower, appropriate for the self-made industrialist. – Nave SE, Faith, Hope and Charity. – Nave S, Ruth and Boaz, and Sacrifice of Isaac. Purple, mauve and turquoise coloration. – Nave NW, Suffer the Little Children, also *c.* 1872, but by *Clayton & Bell*. – Nave W, Faith between angels, 1906 by *J. Jennings*.

In the CHURCHYARD an unusually complete medieval CROSS, four steps, broached base and most of the shaft, but no head.

Immediately beyond the church and the end of the village to the NW, a cluster of early C19 villas in their own grounds. All are smartly rendered, two-storeyed, with three-bay fronts. SOUTH LODGE, closest to the church, has round-headed windows. It was built before 1834 for James Jones, brewer of Abergavenny.

DAN-Y-BLORENGE, beyond, a square three bays by three, has tripartite windows below on the front towards the road. GLAN NANT-Y-LLAN, N of the road, built before 1829 for John Price, solicitor of Abergavenny, is a double pile with pointed-headed sash windows to front and back.

LLANFOIST HOUSE, ¼ m. W, is on a grander scale and beautifully situated under the wooded slope of the Blorenge. Austere, three-storey, five-bay C18 façade under a hipped roof. No decoration except alternating angle quoins and broad plain strings between the storeys. Sash windows, diminishing in height as the storeys rise, a slight but welcome subtlety. Said to have been built, incorporating parts of an earlier house, for John Chambre (†1777), and shown in its present form in an engraving of 1793.

GROVE FARM, Gypsy Lane, ½ m. SW. Rescued from dilapidation in 1994–5 and carefully restored preserving much instructive evidence of its earlier history. The earliest part of the house is the two-storey E range datable inside to the late C16. The projecting chimney-breast on the long E side heated the parlour, that on the W side the hall. N service addition, of two storeys over a cellar, a C17 three-light ovolo-moulded timber window in its N wall. In the C18 the body of the house was doubled in depth towards the W. Sash windows. Two S window bays of timber form the typical Victorian contribution. Inside, the only late C16 features are in the upper SE room. Cambered timber fireplace lintel in the E wall, with to the l. the timber cambered head and jambs of a narrow arch to a stair, and to the r., part of a curious diagonal passage through the depth of the wall, painted with extraordinarily fresh, presumably C17, floral patterns. Otherwise, the interior features are mostly concentrated in the C18 part. In the centre a staircase with slender turned balusters. In the SW corner at ground level a boarded, not panelled, room with two arched recesses and a small Neoclassical timber chimneypiece with an oval relief of Ceres. Above this, the most unusual room in the house, its plaster walls modelled to look like fielded panelling, painted yellow picked out with sea-green borders to the fields. Normal fielded panelling in the upper NW room. That leaves the service addition. This is entered at two levels from the original hall/kitchen. Lower doorway wide enough to roll cider barrels into the segmentally vaulted cellar. Upper doorway to a large larder which retains its fittings of timber storage cupboards with slatted ventilation panels, its shelving and even its pig-killing slab, with pork-curing compartments opposite.

CEMETERY, ½ m. NE. Laid out in 1892. The architect was *E. A. Johnson*. CHAPEL, in an E.E. style, overwhelmed by an octagonal SE turret, its ashlar candle-snuffer cap appearing above the trees beyond the S outskirts of Abergavenny.

BRECON AND ABERGAVENNY CANAL. The canal, extended 1809–12 by *William Crossley*, contours along the side of the Blorenge through majestically mature woodland. In a small side valley in the hillside high above the village, a cluster of early industrial structures. In 1822 Thomas Hill opened a TRAMROAD from his

Blaenavon Ironworks to the canal at this point. The formation of three steep railway inclined planes along the NW bank of the valley streamlet can easily be seen. Also higher up, the ruins of the incline's DRUM AND BRAKEHOUSE and STABLES.

Beside the canal, in line with the bottom of the incline, the long, tall, white-rendered building which faces on to the loading dock is the WHARFINGER'S HOUSE, built by Thomas Hill *c.* 1822. Original ground-level openings, a doorway flanked by broad segment-headed windows. Those above have been altered.

On the N side of the dock, the WAREHOUSE (now boathouse) is one of the earliest railway warehouses anywhere. Built by Hill *c.* 1822 to store the iron products from Blaenavon. One-by-five-bay canalside building of squared, coursed Old Red Sandstone with ashlar dressings, under a hipped roof. The lowest storey towards the canal and at the ends is open, with square stone pillars supporting long timber lintels. The upper storey has been converted for residential use, and the central loading doors and crane have been removed.

Finally, to the S of the Wharfinger's House, a stone revetted TERRACE, which carried the horse-worked railway to Thomas Hill's iron TRAMROAD BRIDGE, also constructed in 1822. The bridge, which survives, is a simple affair of cast-iron plates laid on cast-iron T-section girders.

To the NE a further RAILWAY INCLINE drops down towards the village, but the limekilns towards which it led have disappeared.

3090 LLANFRECHFA

ALL SAINTS. Of the medieval church there remain the W tower, part of the W end of the nave and the S porch, which are all of a single build. In 1873–4 the rest of the nave and chancel were rebuilt much larger, with N aisle and outsize N vestry, by *Charles Buckeridge*, *J. L. Pearson* taking over after Buckeridge's death. The unbuttressed tower is late medieval, substantially built of squared grey sandstone blocks. Basemould, and strong strings to define three stages. Battlements. Square NE stair-turret. Handsome two-centred W doorway with continuous hollow chamfer, but just a small window of two cinquefoiled lights over it. Similar belfry windows but with ogee heads to the lights. The porch is small, of rubble-stone, and retains its open wagon roof on moulded wall-plates.

Buckeridge's church looks incongruously urban and regular, built of snecked, tooled Old Red Sandstone of an even mauve hue, with buff Bath stone ashlar dressings. Battered base to the walls. Perp E window high up, Dec S windows, pointed-headed in the nave, square-headed in the chancel, as in the vestry. Lean-to N aisle with simple Perp windows, reused from the old church. Inside, one more piece of medieval evidence, the crease-line of the nave gable against the tower. Buckeridge's arcade has straightforward octagonal piers, with moulded caps and double-chamfered arches. Matching chancel arch and responds. The unusual length of the chancel is emphasized by the stately E-wards ascent of tiled steps. TILES by *Godwin* of Lugwardine. Rich Dec triple sedilia and piscina. – REREDOS. Of 1874, with an impressively large-scale relief of the Last Supper by *Redfern*. CHANCEL SCREEN. Of 1874, timber, tall and transparent. – FONT and IMMERSION FONT. Both of 1874. The former conventional, its octagonal bowl with elaborated quatrefoils on the faces. The latter unusually conspicuous, like a tomb-chest with quatrefoil panels on the sides, but covered by a wooden lid. – The sumptuous effect of the chancel is completed by STAINED GLASS. – Chancel S and E, an outstanding set by *Clayton & Bell*, 1874, seven scenes to be read in sequence from W to E. Resurrection of Christ and his post-Resurrection appearances, culminating in the E window with a celestial vision of Christ in Glory.* – Chancel N, Suffer the Little Children and Noli me Tangere, *c.* 1854, retained from the old church and clearly by *George Rogers* of Worcester (compare his windows at Malpas, q.v.) – Nave S, Crucifixion and Healing the Lame, *c.* 1884, and Good Shepherd and Sower, *c.* 1891, both by *Lavers & Westlake*. – N aisle W, Christ with a child, *c.* 1895 by the same. – N aisle centre, commemorating a death in war, *c.* 1915, signed by *William Pearce Ltd.* – N aisle E, St Elizabeth between SS Francis and David. 1914 by *Kempe & Co.* – Nave SW, the Boy Christ between his parents. 1916 signed by *Daniells & Fricker*. – MONUMENT. William Griffith †1831. Tablet signed by *Cooke* of Gloucester.

VICARAGE, ¼ m. SW, on the B4236. 1856 by *Prichard & Seddon*. A 113
vigorous example of their way with Ruskinian polychromy. Buff local stone with red and yellow brick for bands and voussoirs and for the striped chimneystacks. Bath stone ashlar dressings. Even the original roof slates survive, in broad bands of green and purple. By contrast, the Gothic detail is restrained. The main architectural accent is on the garden side, a full-height polygonal bay projecting at the r. end under a steep candle-snuffer roof. Note the emphasis on the upper storey, with pointed window lights here and flat, shouldered ones below. Inside, the original timber staircase survives.

LLANFRECHFA GRANGE HOSPITAL, 1 m. NW. The small mansion standing among the various wards and recreational blocks of the hospital was built *c.* 1848 by the local architect *J. H. Langdon* for Charles Prothero in what was described at the time as an Elizabethan style. It is two-storeyed, of red brick, generously dressed with Bath stone, and flaunts on its gables an array of bargeboards, pierced and cusped and painted ox-blood red, which belong firmly in the *cottage orné* tradition. Equally flamboyant is the cusped trellis balustrading that crests the two-storey polygonal window bays projecting under most of the gables. Except in the projections, windows are mullion-and-transom crosses under hoodmoulds. The porch starts square,

* The account of the opening of the church in 1874 in the *Monmouthshire Merlin* makes it clear that all the windows were already in place. So the later dates in inscriptions below the S windows are misleading.

turns polygonal, and is flanked by full-height polygonal shafts bearing scaly ogee finials. In plan the house seems at first to have been straightforward enough, but later additions have complicated matters. The entrance, W, front was flat except for the porch, with a lower service wing extending to the l. The garden front remains in its original form, symmetrical, a single central bay framed by slight projections where the window bays and bargeboards match one another. The E front had a bargeboarded gable over a square projecting bay at the l. end, a large staircase window beside it and then a flat three-bay front. Service extension to the r.

In 1860 the estate was bought by F.J. Mitchell, who over the next thirty years made additions in most directions. First, to the E, came a CHAPEL, low and rendered, with Dec traceried windows, and a canted E end under three sharp gables. After that he took care to match his additions to the pre-existing house, and only close examination establishes what he did. Flanking the entrance porch he added to the l. a one-storey bay window to light the library and to the r. a conservatory (now demolished). The service range grew in various ways, and here, on a W addition, he attached his initials and the date 1892.

The interior contains some treats. The entrance hall, and the room to the r., now thrown into one, both have Tudor stone chimneypieces and thin ribbed plaster ceilings of no particular character. Similar chimneypiece in the library. The large SE room, however, presumably the original drawing room, has a spectacular plaster ceiling of *c.* 1848 in full-blown Jacobean style, encrusted with openwork pendants. The walls here are decorated with full-height pilasters carved with strapwork. The timber overmantel of the chimneypiece is a genuine early C17 piece, with typical arcading and grotesque caryatids. The staircase, with slender twisted balusters and strapwork on the closed string, is presumably of *c.* 1848. But the most remarkable feature of the interior is the STAINED GLASS. In the chapel all ten lights are filled with glass of the early 1860s by *William Wailes*. The scenes illustrate the major events from the Nativity to the Last Judgement. The staircase window is filled with brought-in glass, of outstanding quality but not in its original arrangement. Large, hieratic figures of SS Athanasius, Catharine and Alban, signed and dated *A. Gerente*, Paris, 1857. The artist's name, the date and the strong colours, in particular the resonant greens, make one suspect that this is part of the glazing scheme Alfred Gerente supplied for the windows of the Tractarian model church, All Saints, Margaret Street, in London, but which the architect William Butterfield ordered to be taken out because its colours, particularly the greens, were incompatible with the polychromy of his interior.*

At CAERAU (ST 330 934) is a small prehistoric ENCLOSURE with a single large rampart and traces of an outer bank. The bank seems to be made of clay, and the ditch is scarcely visible. The entrance is on the E side.

* Michael Kerney points out that the saints correspond with those in the S aisle windows at All Saints, Margaret Street, which would seem to clinch the matter.

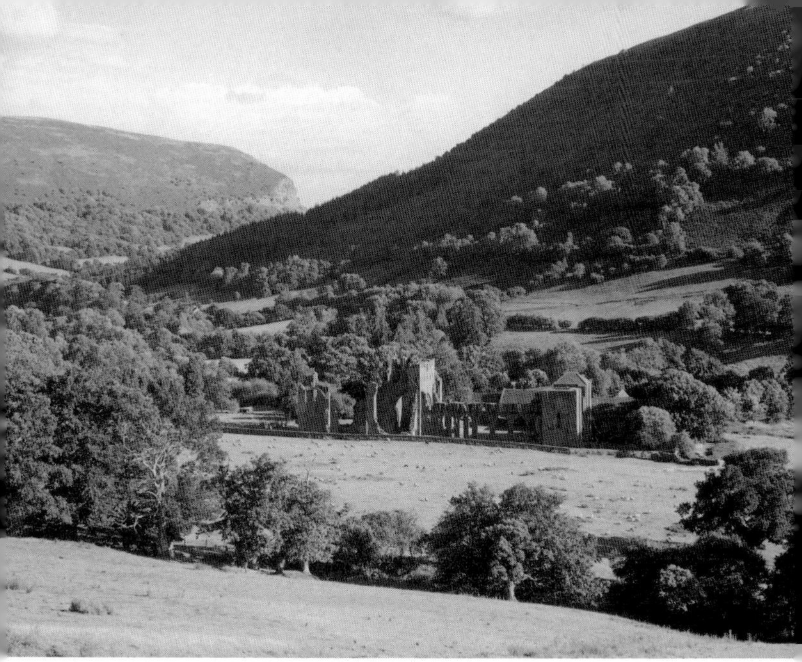

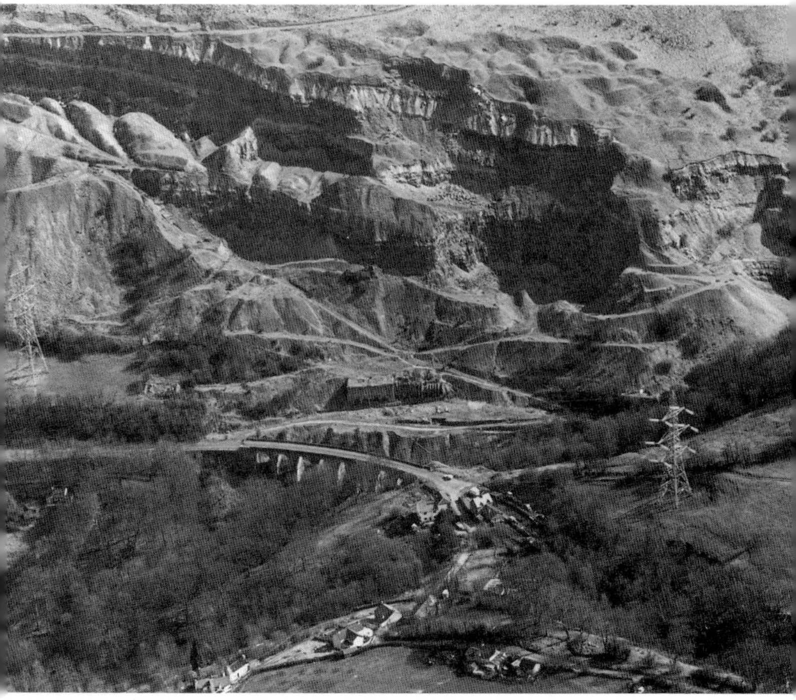

1. Landscape: Vale of Ewyas with Llanthony Priory
2. Landscape: Llanelly, Clydach Gorge

3. Trellech, Harold's Stones, Bronze Age alignment
4. Bwlch Trewyn, Pentwyn, Iron Age hill-fort
5. Caerleon, amphitheatre, *c.* A.D. 80
6. Caerwent, south wall of the Roman town, fourth century A.D.

3 | 5
4 | 6

7. Chepstow Castle, Hall-keep, *c.* 1067–71
8. Chepstow, St Mary, west front, early twelfth century
9. Newport, St Woolos Cathedral, west doorway and nave, 1140s
10. Newport, St Woolos Cathedral, west doorway, capital

7 | 9
8 | 10

11. Llanthony Priory, nave arcade from crossing tower, *c.* 1200
12. Tintern Abbey, refectory, mid thirteenth century
13. Llanthony Priory, west front, early thirteenth century

11 | 12
13

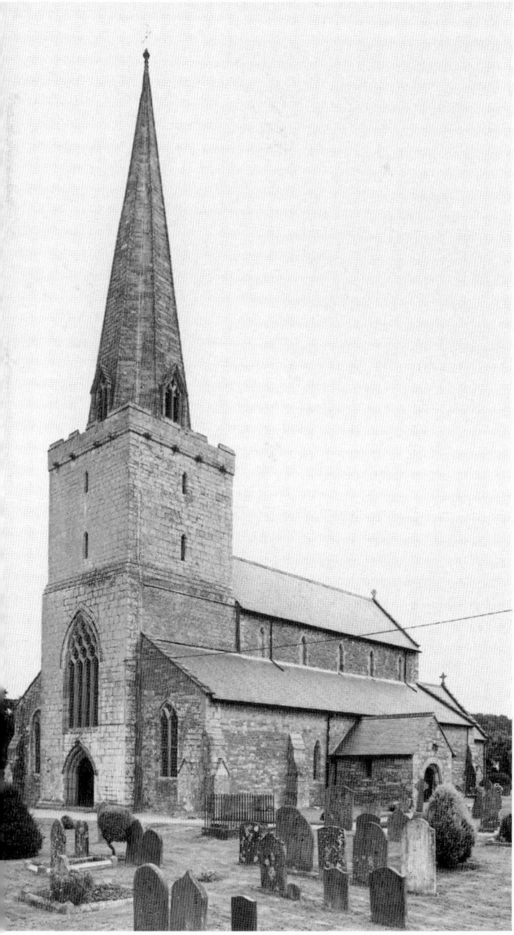

14. Marshfield, St Mary, south doorway, early thirteenth century
15. Grosmont, St Nicholas, double piscina, thirteenth century
16. Grosmont, St Nicholas, nave interior, thirteenth century
17. Trellech, St Nicholas, early fourteenth century

14 | 16
15 | 17

18. Tintern Abbey, north transept, corbel, late thirteenth century
19. Tintern Abbey, crossing, after 1269
20. Tintern Abbey, west front, late thirteenth century
21. Tintern Abbey, processional doorway from cloister, *c.* 1300

18 | 20
19 | 21

22. Chepstow Castle, keep, corbel and arch springer, mid thirteenth century
23. Chepstow Castle, Marten's Tower, 1286–93
24. Skenfrith Castle, keep, 1220–2
25. Monmouth, Monnow Bridge, 1272, and Gate, 1297/*c.* 1315

22 | 24
23 | 25

26. Grosmont Castle, chimney, fourteenth century
27. Llangibby Castle, garderobe chutes, early fourteenth century
28. Caldicot Castle, Woodstock Tower, 1385–9

26 | 28
27

29. Peterstone, St Peter, from the north-west, fifteenth century
30. Peterstone, St Peter, nave, fifteenth century
31. Usk, St Mary, north porch, 1460s
32. Mathern, St Tewdric, north aisle and west tower, 1478–96

29 | 31
30 | 32

33. Abergavenny, St Mary, Jesse, late medieval
34. Mitchel Troy, St Michael, churchyard cross, fourteenth century
35. Llangwm Uchaf, St Jerome, head corbel, early fourteenth century
36. Llantilio Crossenny, St Teilo, head corbel, early fourteenth century
37. Bettws Newydd, church, rood screen and loft, fifteenth century

33 | 35
34 | 36
 | 37

38. Abergavenny, St Mary, monument to Eva de Braose †1257
39. Abergavenny, St Mary, monument to John, 2nd Lord Hastings †1325
40. Abergavenny, St Mary, monument to Sir William de Hastings †1348
41. Abergavenny, St Mary, monument to Richard Herbert of Ewyas †1510, detail

38 | 40
39 | 41

42. Raglan Castle, Great Tower and South Gate, mid fifteenth century
43. Raglan Castle, main gatehouse, 1461–9
44. Raglan Castle, window in apartment range, 1461–9, from without
45. Raglan Castle, window in apartment range, 1461–9, from within
46. Raglan Castle, state apartment, 1461–9, bay window

42 | 44 45
43 | 46

47. Llanmartin, Pencoed Castle, gatehouse and main range, sixteenth century
48. Llandenny, Cefntilla, frieze from Usk Priory, early 1530s
49. Raglan Castle from the north
50. Raglan Castle, chimneypiece in long gallery, late sixteenth century

47 | 49
48 | 50

51. Mathern, Moynes Court, 1608–10
52. Llanfihangel Crucorney, Llanvihangel Court, north front, early seventeenth century
53. Wonastow, Treowen, *c.* 1627
54. Wonastow, Treowen, staircase

51	53
52	54

55. Cwmyoy, Llwyncelyn, late fifteenth-century house and later barns
56. Llanfihangel-ystern-llewern, The Pant, mid sixteenth century
57. Llanarth, Little Pit Cottage, mid sixteenth century

55 | 56
57

58. Grosmont, Upper Dyffryn, early seventeenth century
59. Grosmont, Town Farm, 1673
60. Mamhilad, Persondy, interior, late sixteenth century
61. Llanfihangel Crucorney, Llanvihangel Court, stable, later seventeenth century

58	60
59	61

62. Mitchel Troy, Troy House, plaster ceiling, probably *c.* 1611
63. Kemeys Inferior, Kemeys Manor, plasterwork on stair, probably 1670s
64. Monmouth, Great Castle House, ceiling, *c.* 1673, detail
65. Tredegar House, north-west front, probably by Roger and William Hurlbutt, *c.* 1664–74

62 | 64
63 | 65

66. Tredegar House, gilt room, mid 1670s
67. Tredegar House, entrance doorway in north-west front
68. Tredegar House, stable, probably by Roger and William Hurlbutt, 1685–8
69. Tredegar House, forecourt gates, by William and Simon Edney, 1714–18

66 | 68
67 | 69

70. Monmouth, Great Castle House, 1673
71. Mitchel Troy, Troy House, 1681–4
72. Monmouth, Shire Hall, by Fisher of Bristol, 1724

70 | 71
72

73. Llanfihangel Crucorney, St Michael, monument, early seventeenth century
74. Caerwent, St Stephen and St Tathan, pulpit, 1632
75. Llandenny, St John, font, 1661
76. Llandenny, St John, monument to Roger Otes †1706 and his son †1710

73 | 75
74 | 76

Erected This Monument as y^e last Token
of a moſt Dutiful Daughter
and of
An Affectionate & truly Mournful Siſter.

Here lies the Body of JOHN HANBURY Esq.
of Pont-poole in the County of Monmouth
Who by his great Understanding and Humanity
made the People of this Place and Neighbourhood Rich and Happy:
And They will tell their Children to latest Posterity
That He was a Wise and Honest Man.
He was Chosen in eight Parliaments.
And was Knight of the Shire for the County of Monmouth
He was appointed by the Great Duke of Marlborough
One of his Executors to his last Will.
He married Bridget Daughter of Sr. Edward Ayscough of Kelsey in the County of Lincoln
By whom he left five Sons, John, Capel, Charles, George and Thomas.
He died the 14th day of June 1734, in the 76th Year of his Age

77. Trevethin, St Cadoc, monument to John Hanbury †1734, probably designed by James Gibbs and carved by J. M. Rysbrack
78. Pontypool, Pontypool Park, overmantel, 1730s
79. Blaenavon, St Peter, font, 1805
80. Llanover, St Bartholomew, royal arms, 1816/37

77 | 79
78 | 80

81. Llanfihangel-ystern-llewern, The Pant, Quaker meeting house, late seventeenth century
82. Nash, St Mary, nave, fittings probably *c.* 1792
83. Monmouth, Wesleyan Methodist Church, by G.V. Maddox, 1837
84. Monmouth, St Thomas, Overmonnow, nave, by Matthew Beasen, 1830–1

81 | 83
82 | 84

85. Dixton, Newton Court, *c.*1799–1802
86. Piercefield Park, by Sir John Soane, 1792–3
87. Bassaleg, St Basil, monument to Mary Margaret Morgan †1808, by Sir Richard Westmacott
88. Piercefield Park, staircase landing bracket, by Joseph Bonomi, late 1790s

85 | 87
86 | 88

MARIA MARGARETA MORGAN

89. Clytha Castle, by John Davenport, 1790
90. Wyesham, The Kymin, Naval Temple, 1800
91. Pontypool, Pontypool Park, Shell Hermitage, by G. S. Tit, 1830–44
92. Clytha House, by Edward Haycock, *c.* 1820–8, exterior
93. Clytha House, vestibule

89	92
90 91	93

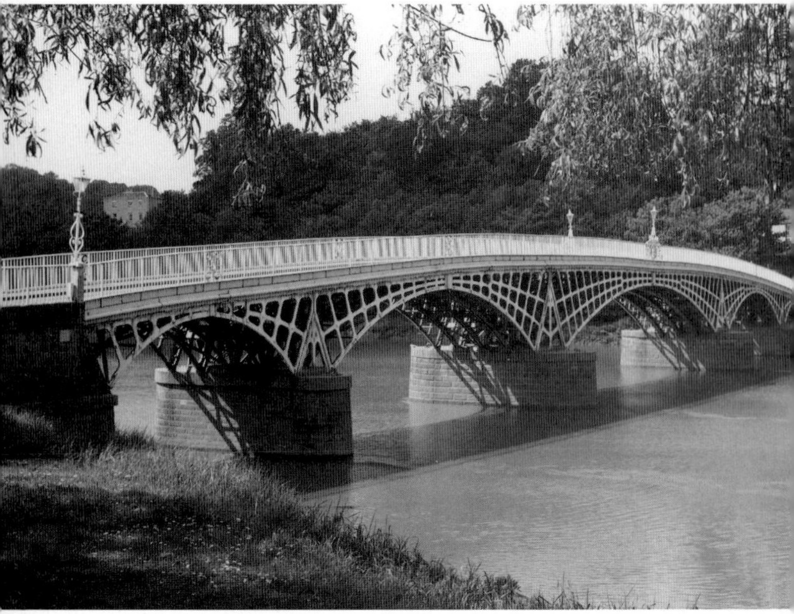

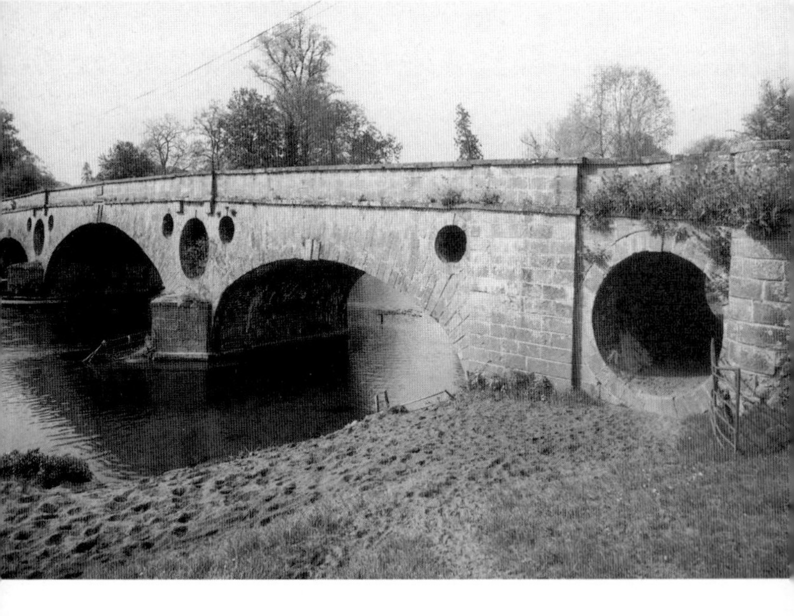

94. Chepstow, bridge, by John Rennie, 1814–16
95. Llanfair Kilgeddin, bridge, by John Upton, *c.* 1821
96. Monmouth, Shambles, by G.V. Maddox, 1837
97. Newport, Victoria Place, 1844

94	96
95	97

98. Marshfield, Castleton Baptist Church, by R. G. Thomas, 1857–8
99. Pontypool, Crane Street Baptist Church, by Aaron Crossfield and J. H. Langdon, 1847
100. Newport, United Reformed Church, Victoria Road, by A. O. Watkins, 1858–9
101. Pontypool, Crane Street Baptist Church, interior
102. Newport, United Reformed Church, Victoria Road, interior

98 | 100
99 | 101
| 102

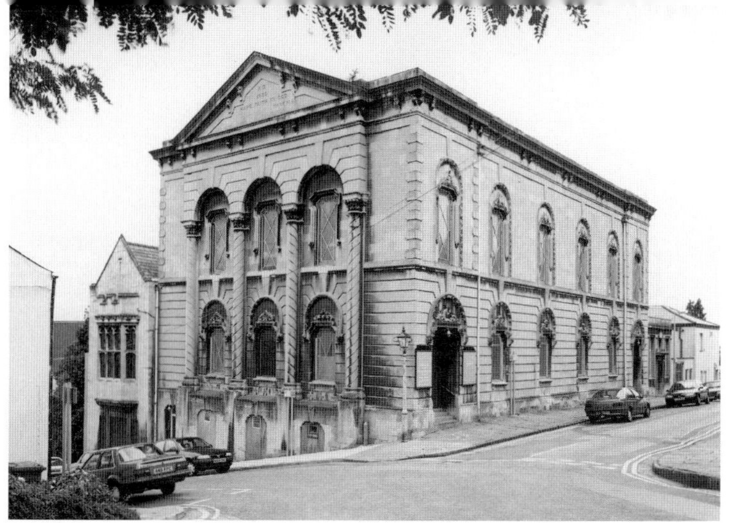

103. Llandogo, St Oedoceus, by Prichard & Seddon, 1859–61
104. Abergavenny, Our Lady and St Michael, R.C., church and presbytery, by Benjamin Bucknall, 1858–60, exterior from the east
105. Monmouth, St Mary, stained glass by C. E. Kempe, 1883, detail
106. Llanfair Kilgeddin, St Mary, sgraffito panel by Heywood Sumner, 1888–90
107. Ebbw Vale, Christ Church, by John Norton, 1860–1

103 | 105 106
104 | 107

domus Domini

O·YE·WINTER·&·SUMMER·BLESS·YE·THE·LORD
PRAISE·HIM·&·MAGNIFY·HIM·FOR·EVER
O·YE·WINDS·OF·GOD·BLESS·YE·THE·LORD
PRAISE·HIM·&·MAGNIFY·HIM·FOR·EVER

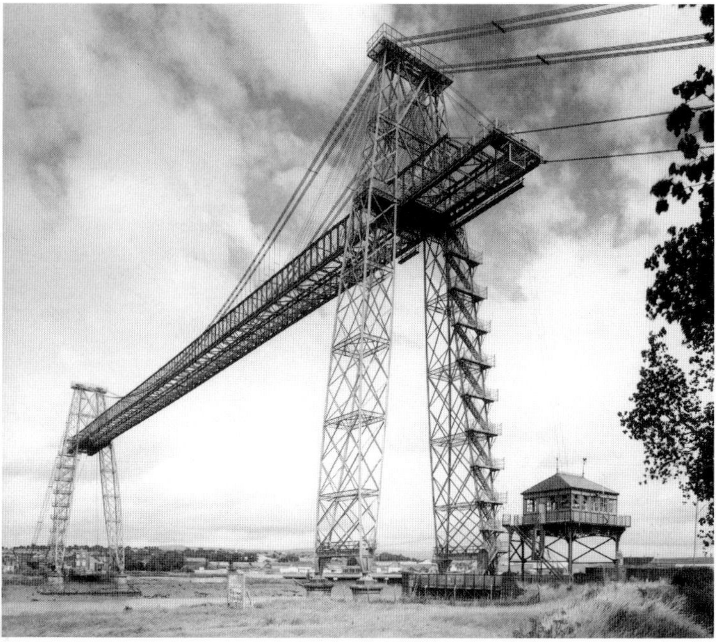

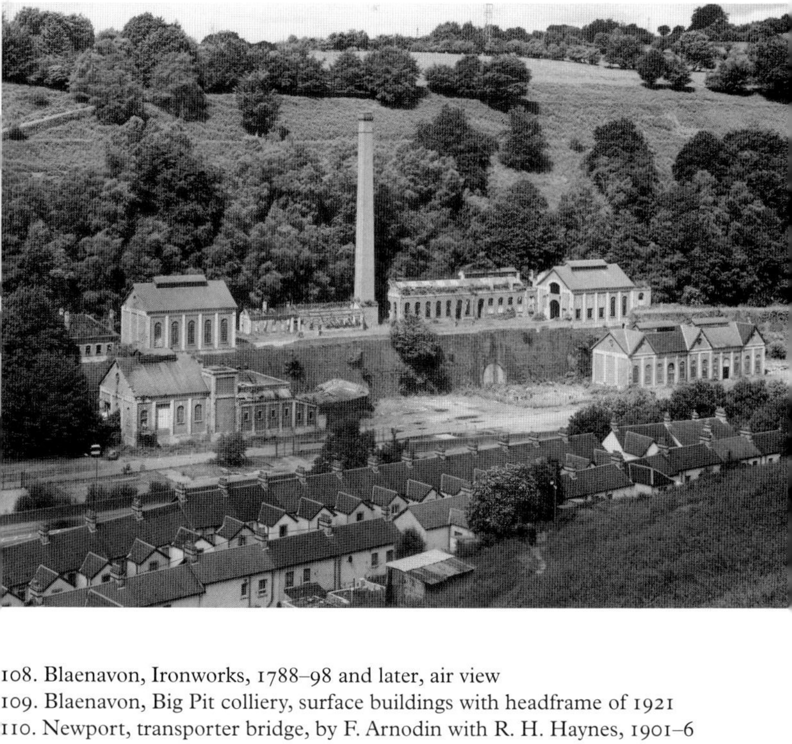

108. Blaenavon, Ironworks, 1788–98 and later, air view
109. Blaenavon, Big Pit colliery, surface buildings with headframe of 1921
110. Newport, transporter bridge, by F. Arnodin with R. H. Haynes, 1901–6
111. Crumlin, Navigation Colliery, 1907–11

112. Llantarnam, Llantarnam Abbey, reconstructed by T. H. Wyatt, 1834–5
113. Llanfrechfa, vicarage, by Prichard & Seddon, 1856
114. The Hendre, library wing by Aston Webb, 1895–6, from the north-east, with earlier parts by T. H. Wyatt beyond
115. Mounton, Mounton House, by H. Avray Tipping and Eric Francis, 1912–14

112	114
113	115

116. Abergavenny, Town Hall, by Wilson & Willcox, 1869–71
117. Blaenavon, Workmen's Institute, by E. A. Lansdowne, 1893–4
118. Newport, Technical Institute, by Charles F. Ward, 1909–10

116 | 117
118

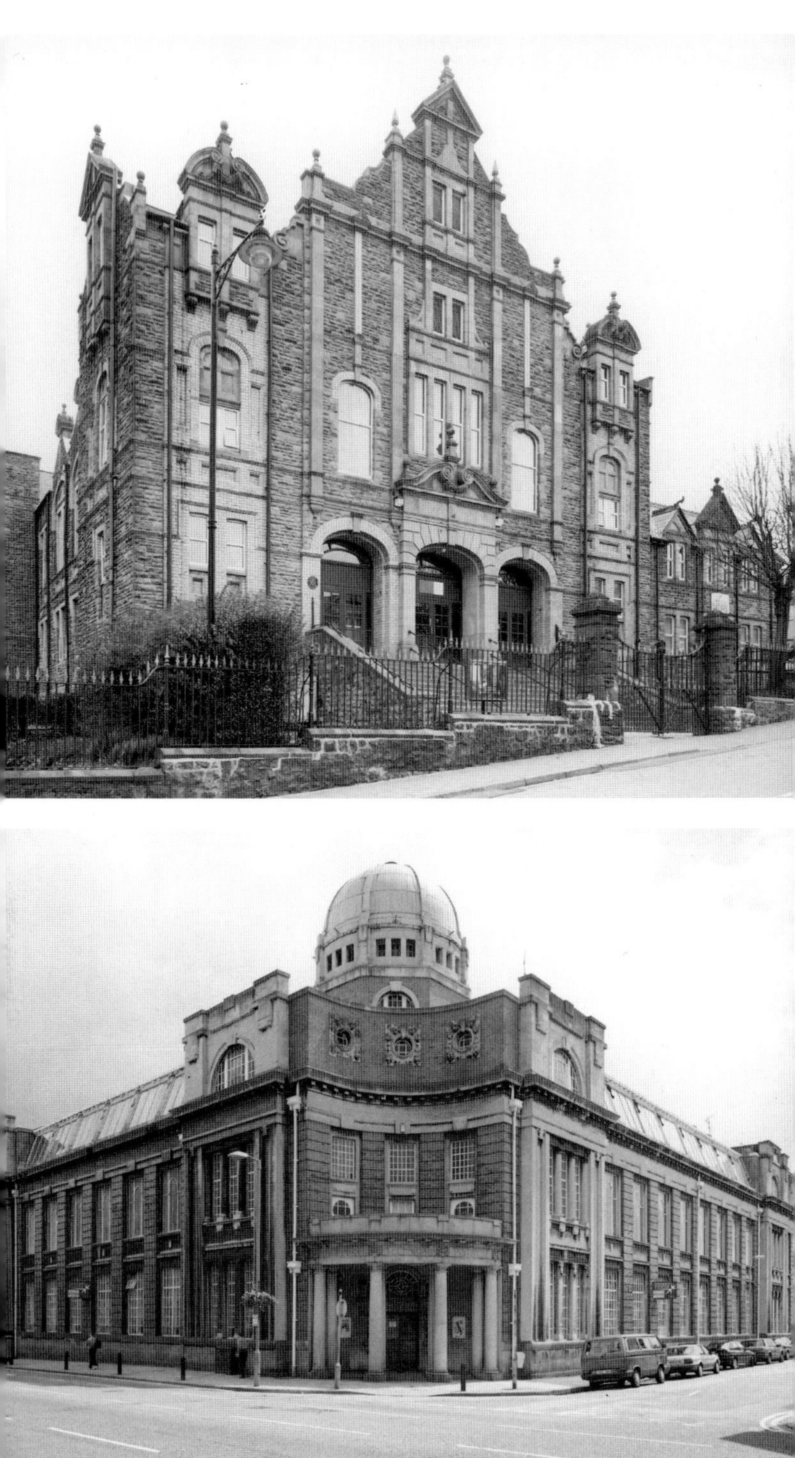

119. Newport, Odeon Cinema, by Harry Weedon, 1937–8
120. Brynmawr, rubber factory, by the Architects' Co-operative Partnership, 1947–53, production hall (photo *c.* 1953)
121. Crumlin, Hafodyrynys colliery washery, mid 1950s
122. Newport, Civic Centre, stair hall showing murals by Hans Feibusch, 1961–4

119 | 121
120 | 122

123. Cwmbran, town centre, Monmouth House, by Gordon Redfern, 1965–7
124. Cwmbran, housing at Mount Pleasant, by J. L. Russell, *c.* 1976–7
125. Bettws, High School, by Evans & Shalev, 1969–72
126. Duffryn, Inmos microchip factory, by Richard Rogers & Partners, 1982

123 | 125
124 | 126

127. Newport, 'In the Nick of Time', by Andy Plant, 1992
128. Newport, 'Vision of St Gwynllyw', by Sebastian Boyesen, 1995

LLANGATTOCK-JUXTA-USK/ LLANGATWG DYFFRYN WYSG 3000

(The Bryn)

ST CADOC. Nave and chancel were amalgamated into one in 1827 when *John Upton* re-roofed them, but the crease-line of the original nave roof remains on the E face of the tower. The tower itself is unbuttressed and has no projecting stair-turret. Slit windows at four levels to N, S and W. Top stage rebuilt without quoins under a pyramid cap added perhaps also in 1827. The body of the church has Perp square-headed N and S windows with straight heads, cinquefoiled lights and glazed spandrels, of two lights and of four. They are much patched. Two of the S windows are set in shallow projections. One clearly lit the rood loft, but why was the sanctuary window treated like this too? Four-light C19 E window with early Perp tracery, presumably part of *John Prichard*'s restoration in 1865–6. In the E wall two small recesses, clearly medieval. The S one has a four-centred head and is rebated for a door. What was their function? The interior, entered through the added S porch, has a pleasing rustic brightness, the sturdy struts of Upton's roof trusses stark against the whitewashed ceiling and walls. Lower and upper rood-loft doorways. – PEWS by *Prichard.* – Is the aggressive timber PULPIT by him too? – FONT. Medieval, and surely not all of one date. The egg-shaped bowl, the roll moulding below, and the circular stem may be C13. The hexagonal base with sloping sides looks of the C15. – TILES. Set in the W wall. Mid C15. One is even dated 1456. Eight different patterns, most of them constituting parts of designs which ran over several tiles. They resemble tiles made at Great Malvern Priory, but have recently been shown to be contemporary, locally made copies. Others have been found at the local priory churches of Monmouth, Tintern and Llanthony (qq.v.). Why a group of them is in this modest parish church has not been explained. – MONUMENTS. Worn medieval grave-slab (by the font) with reliefs of a floriated cross and what has been interpreted as a battleaxe. – Zirophaeniza Powell †1625 (chancel S). Brass plate engraved with a representation of a lady kneeling at a prayer desk in ruff and hood. A cock, presumably heraldic, in a frame top l. – Rev. Herbert Jones †1644. In the centre of the sanctuary, a worn relief of a praying man in surprisingly courtly dress. The inscription, long lost, is recorded by Bradney. – Robert Lucas †1750 and his wife †1770 (sanctuary N wall). Mutilated hanging wall monument of white and yellow mottled marbles.

In the CHURCHYARD the shaft of a late medieval CROSS, on four hexagonal steps.

The church stands, overlooking the water-meadows of the River Usk, at the S end of THE BRYN, a compact and intricate village with much mid-C20 council housing. The little red-brick PRIMARY SCHOOL was built as an early, and very small, board school, in 1875–6 by Messrs *Haddon Brothers.*

LLANGATTOCK HOUSE, ½ m. NW. Built in the C17 for the Wroth family. Of brown local stone. The tall, flat-fronted two-storeyed range facing the road seems wholly unplanned, though the two-centred porch is roughly central. This has a four-centred stone entrance doorway. At the l. the nearly blind gable-end of a cross wing. At the back, a stair projection with small ovolo-moulded windows low down. Otherwise the fenestration is all of the C18 and C19. (Inside, Fox and Raglan report, the hall has a monumental fireplace surround.)

GREAT HOUSE, Penpergwm, 1½ m. N. The tall, grey-rendered block which rears up so unexpectedly among the remote meadows appears to be of mid-C18 date. The builder must have been Robert Lucas, who was buying land here aggressively in the 1730s and died in 1750, or his son Richard, who served as sheriff in 1768. E façade of three storeys, the top storey blind, and six bays, the sash windows arranged two-plus-two-plus-two, but with the centre pair in the middle storey replaced by a single Venetian window. The galumphing porch below it is obviously a Victorian addition, but so is the deep hipped roof, which *c.* 1890 replaced a roof hidden behind a parapet. The house is a double pile, but the sides and back are irregular and suggest earlier origins. Two-light timber window with sunk chamfer moulding in the three-storey N porch.

Inside, there is a great deal more to see and to puzzle over. To take the plan first. The Victorian porch leads into a smallish square hall in the centre of the main range. A room to the l. and another to the r. complete a balanced layout in the front range. Behind the hall, a stair rises, in typical C18 fashion, leading to a spine corridor extending the full width of the house. Similar arrangement of three E upper rooms. However, the decoration of these rooms tells a different story of an elaborate fitting out in the early and mid C17, as well as C18 work. Bradney suggested that the wainscot and chimneypieces had all been brought in. But their completeness and coherence make one loath to believe that. And such an array would have been worthy of the early C17 owner, Judge Andrew Powell †1631. Can the C18 remodelling have involved a drastic enlargement and reshaping of the house, while preserving many interiors intact? When render was recently removed from the walls, a full-height straight joint was revealed to the l. of the porch, and masonry clearly of two dates, the earlier, to the N, of C16 character.

The entrance hall is wainscoted to full height with small-fielded panelling below a deep arcaded frieze, with a naive repeating plant pattern under each arch. This looks all of *c.* 1600. The chimneypiece and overmantel certainly are made up reusing a set of carved scrolls at both levels. Arcading in two tiers. The room to the N of the hall is decorated in a style of joinery a generation later, with a surer grasp of classical conventions. The small-fielded panelling rises to a dentilled entablature. The chimneypiece and overmantel are both flanked by Doric pilasters, broad, rather crudely tapering and fluted, set on tall rusticated pedestals. The overmantel centrepiece is an extraordinarily elaborate composition, centred on a perspective arch flanked by paired colonnettes and cut-out side scrolls, and crowned by an extravagant broken pediment. To see what is upstairs one must return to the entrance hall, and pass through a wainscoted archway of typical C18 depressed form, to the staircase in a rear W projection. The stair is a remarkable piece of mid-C18 chinoiserie with obliquely criss-crossing timber balustrading and openwork newels. It rises in three flights up the walls of a square well, lit by a large round-headed W window, which is set under the l. arch of a two-bay plaster arcade. On the S wall, a large rectangular plasterwork frame with eared corners and scrolls top and bottom. The top landing forms the central section of the end-to-end corridor, which has a plaster cornice and coved ceiling. At this level there are no fewer than three more rooms, central, NE and NW, with panelling and chimneypieces clearly by the same joiner as the NE room below, though the chimneypieces are slightly less elaborate.

Finally, there is more C17 work at ground level to the SW: three timber moulded doorways, one built integrally with a timber stud partition, and all clearly associated with a paved E–W passage. This just adds to one's sense that the early house must have been of considerable size, but on a baffling plan.

LLANGATTOCK LINGOED

3020

ST CADOC. Well seen from the road above to the N, built of Old Red Sandstone, slabby rubble walls and dressed ashlar blocks. Stone slate roofs. Quite a long nave, and slightly lower chancel, almost windowless on this side. Emphatic Perp tower on a moulded plinth, with NE turret bound to the tower by a mid-height stringcourse. Top battlements to both. Perp three-light E window in the chancel and other Perp S windows in chancel and nave. S porch with two-centred entrance arch and doorway, both plainly double-chamfered. Porch roof of ribbed wagon form. Angle stoup. The SW window, of Bath stone, was inserted by *Prichard* in 1876. Inside, two-centred chamfered arches to tower and chancel are perhaps evidence of a C13 or C14 origin for the church. Arched recess and piscina S of the chancel arch, for a side altar. Perp wagon roofs, boarded, on embattled moulded wall-plates. – FONT. Plain circular bowl on a circular shaft and foot. Of the C13? – ROOD LOFT. Only the bressumer survives, richly carved with two undercut vine trails, and fragments of the mouchette band above and cresting below. – PEWS. Two sets of high-backed pews in the chancel, decorated with a variety of incised guilloche patterns. The S set dated 1634. A rare survival. – TOWER SCREEN. Made up of nondescript pieces with two date panels of 1593 and 1617 that do not belong. – PULPIT, ALTAR RAILS, REREDOS. Simple, of timber, by *Prichard*, 1876. – WALL PAINTING. Faded royal arms over the chancel arch. – STAINED GLASS. Medieval fragments in the tracery of the E and one S window, a rarity in the county. – MONUMENTS. Several local tablets, all quite simple, but signed by no fewer than four different makers: *Thomas Brute*, †1660 (but made in the mid C18), †1731 and †1765; *J. Prosser*, †1796; *Lewis*, †1804; *John Prichard* of Clodoch, †1816, †1818.

In the CHURCHYARD, base of a CROSS on four steps.

HENDRE, ¾ m. NW. The farmhouse is approached through a dramatic gatehouse arrangement created by roofing over between two outbuildings. This provides cover for the loading of hay into the loft in the lower one. The farmhouse beyond, with shaly Old Red Sandstone walls, looks C17, with its gables and central two-storey porch facing into the hillside. But, as Fox and Raglan found, the walls encase a cruck-trussed timber house.

OLD COURT, 1 m. E. The N range is part of a C15 hall house with stone details of unusual sophistication. In the N wall, close to its E end, the transomed hall window, with two trefoil-headed lights in a rectangular hollow-moulded frame. To the W of it, the hall chimney-breast, and further W a smaller, unenframed window with two trefoiled lights which must have lit an upstairs parlour. The straight joint beyond it marks the end of the C15 house. In the S wall, a C15 stone doorway with two-centred head, chamfered on pyramid stops. Inside, the similarly chamfered jambs of the hall fireplace survive. Also a four-centred-headed stone doorway in the original, W, wall, now internal. In the early C17, when the property belonged to Lewis Morgan, a cadet of the Morgans of Tredegar, the medieval house was drastically remodelled. The screens passage and whatever lay beyond it were removed. Thus the E gable-end is a typical composition of that date, with ovolo-moulded timber windows set axially under the gable, five-light below four-light below three-light. The hall itself was floored over and its walls were heightened, while the chimney-breast was given typical lozenge-plan stacks. To the S a cross range was added, gabled to S and W and entered from the W through a splendid studded door. This has trident-ended hinges and is set in a chamfered frame with cambered head. The rooms at both levels in this range remain largely in their C17 state, the lower retaining its four-light ovolo-moulded S window. The ceiling beams below are moulded with a double ovolo but upstairs are merely chamfered, the plaster ceilings in both rooms with typical dragged lines framing the beams.

Quite long, two-storeyed extension of the main range to the W, and lower SE addition, both with stone flights of steps to upper granaries.

GREAT HOUSE, 1¼ m. E. Not so great now, but there is tantalizing evidence that this was once quite a grand and decorative building, more than a farmhouse in scale and ambition. Of two storeys, but Bradney says that a third was removed in the late C19. L-plan, the main range consisting of hall between parlour (W) and service end (E), the latter extended backwards with a kitchen. The S, entrance, front is dourly rendered, the three richly moulded original windows seen by Fox and Raglan now gone. The front doorway, however, is a fine piece of carpentry, its four-centred head, square frame and lintel all roll-moulded. Similarly shaped head to the N kitchen doorway, and original door.

Inside, the ground-floor rooms are notably high, and the ceiling beams moulded with ovolo and wave. Most unusual are the fireplaces of hall and parlour. Each has a deep timber lintel decorated with a band of fluting, and even the stonework of the parlour fireback is made decorative with a trellis pattern. Beside the hall fireplace, in the N wall, a doorway which must originally have opened into a stair projection, now removed.

UPPER KATHLEA/CELLI, 1¼m. NE. C17 stone house of three units, with two-storey porch. (Within the porch, a chamfered timber door-frame with a strange depressed-ogee lintel.)

(LOWER KATHLEA/CELLI, 1¼m. NE. Disused and inaccessible at the time of writing. The main range contains parts of two cruck trusses. It was remodelled and extended in the early C17, when a large parlour bay was added. Shortly afterwards came a much more unusual addition, a free-standing block containing a handsome ground-floor chamber, set at r.-angles, linked only by a porch and lobby with shaped-headed doorways in three directions, the stepped shape identical to that at Howell's House, Grosmont, dated 1611.)

LLANGATTOCK-VIBON-AWEL/ LLANGATTOCK-FEIBIAN-AFEL

4010

The Rolls family was all-powerful in Llangattock during the C19. Their seat was The Hendre (*see* p. 247), but on the higher ground to the N they rebuilt the church and erected a secondary house, a school and other estate buildings.

ST CADOC. Only the S porch tower of the medieval church survives. It is impressively tall, unbuttressed, the entrance doorway of the design popular from *c.* 1300, with two chamfered arches dying into the imposts. Three-light Tudor window over. Minimal belfry opening. Battlements capped by a shallow tiled roof, doubtless added in the late C19. The church, nave and lower chancel with S family chapel, was drastically restored and enlarged by *T. H. Wyatt*, who renewed the W window and added the vestry in 1852–3, and in 1875 extended the chancel and added the organ-chamber and entrance porch to the family chapel, and the N aisle with handsome, if conventional, four-bay arcade. Mixed Dec and Perp style. In 1866, before the second enlargement, *Cox & Son* lavishly decorated the interior. Their painted decoration of walls and chancel ceiling has disappeared, but there survive the tiled floor, with three steps up into the chancel and three more into the sanctuary, and the biblical texts in encaustic tiles on the sanctuary steps and all along the wall-head of chancel and nave. – REREDOS. Alabaster, 1875 by *Thomas Earp*. – CHANCEL SCREEN. Low, of alabaster. 1875. – COMMANDMENT BOARDS. Of zinc. Part of *Cox & Son*'s reredos of 1866. – STAINED GLASS. Three leading Victorian makers are here seen at their best. – Chancel E, Crucifixion. 1875 by *Lavers & Barraud*. – Chancel SE and NE, Four Evangelists. 1866, by *Heaton, Butler & Bayne*. – Nave W, tiers of music-making angels, each playing a different instrument. A fresh early work of *C. E. Kempe*, 1879. – Also by *Kempe,* saints in the S chapel, 1884, and (*Kempe & Co.*) N aisle W, 1918. – Nave S, Virgin and Child enthroned, and Kings bearing gifts, 1914 by *Powell*'s. – MONUMENTS. Memorials of pre-Rolls parishioners, touchingly rustic tablets on the nave S wall, including a brass plate for Thomas Evans †1629, and headstones attached to the inner walls of the porch.

In the CHURCHYARD, the base of a medieval CROSS incorporated into one of 1860 by *T. H. Wyatt.* To the SE a group of TOMBS of members of the Rolls family, Charles Stewart Rolls, the famous aviator, †1910, and others to 1923, marked by tall Celtic crosses.

LLANGATTOCK MANOR. Virtually a new house, built for J. A. Rolls, 1877–80 by *T. H. Wyatt*, replacing the C17 manor house of the Evans family. Quite large and varied, in a Tudor Gothic style, of local mauve sandstone with Bath stone dressings.

Also doubtless by *Wyatt*, the LODGE at the top of the drive and the FARMHOUSE part-way down.

SCHOOL, $\frac{1}{4}$m. N (now Monmouth Montessori School). Undated. A companion to the manor in materials and style. Presumably by *Wyatt.* Two schoolrooms in the N wing, the teacher's house to the S, provided with an array of half-hipped gables and a diagonal bay window across the SW angle.

KELDA, $\frac{1}{2}$m. NW. Formerly the parsonage. But can this, with its regular three-bay front, be the parsonage erected by *Prichard & Seddon* in 1856–7? The finely laid sandstone walling is worthy of them.

At NEWCASTLE, 1$\frac{1}{2}$m. NW, a low MOTTE among the houses, commanding a wide view to the W. Also POOL FARM, one of the most completely surviving cruck-trussed hall houses in the county, though the front towards the road hardly gives a hint of that. Timber-framed rear (N) wall. Inside, part of the truss which formed the original W gable and most of the central truss dividing the internal space into two nearly equal halves, a post-and-panel partition integrated with it. The planks are chamfered to the W, i.e. towards what was the hall, plain towards the E room. Standard later C16 insertions, an intermediate floor, and an enclosed hearth in the W wall, between entrance doorway and spiral staircase, mutilating the cruck blade. Subsequent extension to the E and rebuilding of the E wall.

3000 LLANGEVIEW/LLANGIFIW

ST DAVID. A typical small Perp church, nave and lower chancel, but one which has largely escaped the Victorian restorer. Rubbly walls of Old Red Sandstone, dressings of the same. The only unusual feature is the siting of the porch, at the W end, not the S side. Three-light E and S windows of the usual sort, square-headed with cinquefoiled lights, some with ogee heads to the lights, some not, some with hoodmoulds, some not. The largest window, of Bath stone, must be a C19 insertion. Windowless N wall. C19 W bellcote. Wide, pointed chancel arch, formed without cut stone.

Whitewashed interior, retaining its C18 furnishings, unlike any other in the county. – FONT. Medieval, but of what date? Low, square bowl chamfered at the angles. – PULPIT. Octagonal, with reading desk below. – BOX PEWS. Note the squire's pew in the chancel, and the MONUMENT, to William Jones †1829 and others, like a gravestone set in the wall above. – ALTAR RAILS. Of *c.* 1700. Twisted balusters. – ROOD LOFT. This is the important medieval survival. Moulded and embattled bressumer. Open-fronted loft. Sadly, all the applied decoration has been lost. In 1999 the church passed into the care of the Friends of Friendless Churches.

MAERDY, ½m. NE. An unspoilt farm group, C18 house and clustering barns. Will it remain evocative after the conversion of the barns, proposed at the time of writing?

At COED-CWNWR, 1½m. SE, the ROGER EDWARDS CHARITY ALMSHOUSES, 1825–6 by *Edward Haycock*. Single-storeyed, of Old Red Sandstone under a severe slate roof. The building is an L in plan and turns its back on the road. Small pointed windows, and three larger ones at the angle, where a chapel was sited. Behind, the roof comes down on iron posts to form a protective loggia, under which are the doors and big windows.

NEW COURT, 1½m. S. A handsome farm group, improbably sited on a steep slope at the head of Llewelyn's Dingle. Three-storeyed, three-bay farmhouse colour-washed buff. Farm buildings step down the hillside in line.

LLANGIBBY/LLANGYBI 3090

The compact village has been tactfully enlarged to N and W, allowing church, inn and a couple of handsome outlying houses space in which to make their effect.

ST CYBI. The church is one of the most interesting in the Usk Valley. Nave and chancel of nearly equal width set at the foot of the slope down to the floodplain of the River Usk. Perp W tower, providing entrance to the church but presumably an addition. The tower is unbuttressed, of two stages rising from a battered base. Square-headed belfry windows, of two cinquefoiled ogee lights. Wide W outer doorway double-chamfered with two-centred head. Similar single-chamfered inner doorway and damaged STOUP. Blocked window, or perhaps an image niche, above. In nave and chancel all the datable features are Perp. Blocked four-centred S doorway. A variety of handsome three-light windows, N and S in the nave, and chancel E. Rood-stair projections both N and S. The S vestry and heavy patching of the S wall belong to *W. H. Dashwood Caple*'s restoration of 1909–10; he also largely restored the SE window.

The interior is a delight, bright and airy with its limewashed plaster, wall paintings and remarkable C17 fittings. Doubtless the late date of the restoration helped, and its basis on a report by *W. D. Caröe*. The chancel arch, of cut Old Red Sandstone, is extremely wide, four-centred in form and elaborately moulded with three rolls separated by hollows. Its width was dictated by the rood-loft arrangement, for the doorway to the stairs was clearly built integrally with it. Simple image niche W of the S doorway. – WALL PAINTINGS. Two schemes partly superimposed on one another, late medieval figure scenes and C17 inscriptions. On the nave N wall, two monumental standing figures, identified as the Virgin weighing down the scales of St Michael in favour of the blessed. On the N wall of the chancel, 'Christ of the Trades', i.e. Christ wounded by the tools of people who worked on a Sunday. – Nave S, the Apostles' Creed in a strapwork surround. Nave N, the Ten Commandments. – ALTAR RAILS. Of *c.* 1700. Twisted balusters. – PULPIT. Mid C17. A mighty object, rectangular, under a small square tester. Two faces are decorated with arcaded panels in deep relief flanked by Doric colonnettes and set in emphatically eared frames. – FONT. The date 1662 and names of the churchwardens are deeply incised on the lip of the octagonal bowl. Shields in strapwork on the faces. Shafted stem. Clearly by the same craftsman as the font at Llandenny and the sundial at Trellech (qq.v.). – MONUMENTS. Lady Elizabeth and Mrs Ann Williams. 1685. White marble cartouche of excellent quality. Drapery, cherub heads and naturalistic flowers surround the inscription. Winged skull below. – John Francklyn, rector, †1707. Convex black oval panel lined out for gilt lettering now perished. Set in a stone cartouche. – Sir John Williams †1738. Grey veined marble tablet topped by a piece of yellow marble and a white urn. – John Morgan †1805. Hackneyed Neoclassical sentiment. Veiled woman mourning by an urn overspread by a luxuriant weeping willow. Signed *Tyley* of Bristol. – Donald Arthur Addams Williams †1915. Black wall tablet set with a white cross on which hangs a sword. Signed *Maile & Son* of London.

In the CHURCHYARD, SE of the church, a HOLY WELL is reported.

The STANDING STONE on the flat lands close to the river is traditionally associated with the arrival of St Cybi from Cornwall. It might, however, be an older stone, dating from the Bronze Age, since the Tredunnock barrow stood not far away on the same floodplain.

CHRISTCHURCH, Coed-y-paen. By *Sir Matthew Digby Wyatt*, begun 1848, delayed for legal reasons and completed in 1860–1. E.E. Dignified and coherent, but pre-Ecclesiological, built of sombre grey-green Forest stone. Dominant three-stage W tower, with set-back angle buttresses dying in below the belfry stage where ashlar angle strips replace them. Lancets in the lower stages, plate-traceried belfry openings. Trefoiled corbel table and battlements. Boxy three-bay nave, with lancets and full-height buttresses. One-bay chancel. Plain, whitewashed interior, enriched only by an exuberant outbreak of stiff-leaf carving on the chancel arch imposts.

BETHEL BAPTIST CHAPEL, Ton Road. On the hillside above the village. Dated 1837. White, two bays by two, under a nearly pyramidal roof. Round-headed windows. Converted into a house.

WHITE HART INN. Conspicuous at the centre of the village. The nucleus of the building is early C17, a two-bay range facing W with cross-passage and service extension to the S and a one-bay wing added to the NE angle. Fine array of timber mullioned windows to W and N, mostly ovolo-moulded, all of three lights, except for a four-lighter upstairs in the later range. This lights a parlour naively decorated with sunflowers and fleurs-de-lys in the plaster ceiling and above the fireplace.

NEW HOUSE, at the N end of the village. A handsome example of a substantial farmhouse of *c.* 1700, in which a completely symmetrical front is achieved. Walls of limewashed local stone. Five bays, two storeys, under quite a steep hipped roof. The windows are timber casements of classical proportions with mullion-and-transom crosses. The eaves rise pedimentally over the centre bay to accommodate one more such window at roof level.

PENARTH HOUSE, ¼m. S. Early C19 villa of three bays and two storeys. Tripartite lower windows. Glazed lunette over the doorway.

CASTLE, ¾m. NW. There is much more here than meets the eye, though the drive, running straight from the modest C19 GATEHOUSE uphill to the W, and the straight and very wide AVENUE of Scots pine trees which continues the line E-wards as far as the River Usk indicate the presence of a historic estate. The story starts with a C12 motte sited on the hillside overlooking the river. In 1245 the estate came to the de Clares. In the early C14 a huge, luxurious and heavily fortified castle was begun, either by the last of their line, Gilbert de Clare III, who was killed aged twenty-four at the Battle of Bannockburn in 1314, or by Hugh le Despencer, Edward II's favourite, who held the estate briefly 1322–6. Eventually, Llangibby came into the possession of the Crown, and in 1554 it was sold to the Williams family of Usk, whose late C17 house survived until 1951. Today, the avenue, originally planted *c.* 1707, the drive and a pair of grandly scaled service ranges preserve the axis which reached its conclusion in the Williams mansion.

MOTTE. The earthwork is easily made out under a clump of trees to the S of the drive.

SERVICE BUILDINGS. Big, rendered white, and very characterful with their bold oval upper openings. The S range was a stable and coach-house, the N range the kennels of the celebrated Llangibby foxhounds. The latter incorporates a dovecote at the W end.

MEDIEVAL CASTLE. In the dense woodland which covers wide stretches of the hilltop, there lurk, to the N of the public footpath, ruins of the enormous, forgotten early C14 castle of

Tregrug.* It consists of a huge, roughly rectangular, walled enclosure, aligned E–W, from which the ground drops in all directions. To the W the natural defences were reinforced by a formidably complex system of artificial rock-cut ditches. Access from the E is along a tractor track through a breach in the enclosure wall. Traces here of a circular tower, and to the S of it a straight stretch of wall up to *c.* 20 ft (6 metres) high. Close to the SE angle, at the E end of the S wall, the footings have been found of a twin-towered gatehouse. The most impressive part of the enclosure wall is on the N side, where it survives almost to full height, on the brink of a sheer cliff. A gap half-way along, flanked by thickened walling, must mark the site of a tower.

The really strong fortifications were reserved for the W end. The NW corner, the highest point, was developed as a massive residential tower, the SW corner covered by a W-facing keep-gatehouse. Though neither stands much above undercroft level, and great chunks of the tower walls lie tumbled in the ditch to the W, both clearly belong to the tradition of fortification initiated by Gilbert de Clare at Caerphilly Castle from 1268, and developed in the Edwardian castles of North Wales until the mid 1290s. The gatehouse and tower at Llangibby seem in design to have been more elaborate and sophisticated than those elsewhere, as might be expected at this, the latest castle in the series. They were constructed of local rubble-stone, like the enclosure walls, but faced with squared blocks of Old Red Sandstone.

The NW LORD'S TOWER (as Cathcart King and Perks call it) was a deep, strongly bow-fronted rectangle in plan, with to the N a rectangular garderobe turret. The building seems to have provided a single large, well-appointed room on at least two levels. The back (E) is the most accessible part. Here bold circular turrets, project diagonally from the angles. In the N turret, one corbel and the chamfered springers of a hexagonal rib vault. In the S turret, traces of a stair. Against the S wall of the tower, a flight of steps and part of a chamfered jamb with handsome carved stop. Projecting from the S wall further W, a two-bay chamber, its vault largely intact. The vault ribs are brought down on finely moulded circular caps which rest on fragmentary stiff-leaf corbels. To the W of this, a tunnel-vaulted recess, related to a garderobe above. Remains of a stone basin here.

The GATEHOUSE, at a lower level at the SW corner of the enclosure, is the least difficult part of the castle to comprehend, for all the ivy growth and tumbled stones. The two circular stair-turrets projecting from the E-ward corners survive for 15 ft (4–6 metres) or so in height. Between them, the straight back wall and central entrance way are still partly flanked by straight walls. Jambs of two doorways here and grooves for a centrally placed portcullis. Towards the W, where the ground drops steeply, the bases of the great twin round towers which formed

* Brilliant documentary and archaeological detective work by D.J. Cathcart King and J.C. Perks has established the castle's significance and explained why it 'never made its mark in history' (*Archaeologia Cambrensis*, vol. 105, 1956). Their interpretation is followed here.

the front of the gatehouse. What clearly demonstrates that the gatehouse was intended as a well-appointed residence, on the model of the Constable's Tower at Caerphilly Castle, is the extraordinarily generous provision of garderobes. On the N side of the N tower a triple chute. On the S side of the S tower a much larger, dramatically projecting chute. To look up into it, and see 27
the four differently sized chutes and the bold corbelling back of the outer wall by means of four chamfered arches, is to appreciate a little of the mastery and confidence of the builders of the castle. To the E of the gatehouse a further continuous stretch of enclosure wall, standing up to 20 ft (6 metres) high, with at its E end a fragment of a D-shaped tower. Nothing more as far as the SE angle of the enclosure.

Finally, the question arises why such a large and patently ambitious castle has been forgotten. Cathcart King and Perks conclude that it was abandoned unfinished. They point out that no trace has ever been found of masonry structures within the vast enclosure, though there may have been timber ones (*see* Tregrug below). The castle is documented as having been inhabited only in the mid C17, when Sir Trevor Williams in 1645 occupied it with a garrison of sixty men, and in 1647 held it against the forces of Oliver Cromwell. It must have been after capture by the Parliamentary force that the Lord's Tower was slighted – its fallen masses of masonry show all too clearly the effect of dynamite.

TREGRUG, ½ m. N. The neat, white, three-bay farmhouse is smaller brother to New House (*see* above). More notable is the C17 threshing BARN, close beside the road to the S. This is of five bays, substantially built of mauve Old Red Sandstone, with long ventilation slits. Inside are the remains of a late medieval arch-braced roof, ten trusses in all, though only two at the N end and one at the S remain intact. This must have been made for a residential building, and tradition has it that it came from Llangibby Castle. But if Cathcart King and Perks are right (*see* above) there never was a free-standing roofed structure within the walls of the castle.

LITTLE CWM-DOWLAIS, 2 m. N. Reconstructed *c.* 1700 from earlier material. Flat two-storeyed front of three not quite regular bays, systematized by the three emphatic dormer windows. Cream washed walls. Timber casement windows. (Rear wing for stair and pantry.)

CWM FARM, 2¼ m. NW. The small stone building illustrates the typical practice of adding to a house and later rebuilding it to harmonize with the addition. Here the S half is a typical C17 parlour wing, of two storeys, with the hearth in the S end wall, between a spiral stair and windowless closet on each floor, entered through a four-centred-headed doorway. Boldly chamfered joists. The timber mullioned windows with sunk chamfers, seen by Fox and Raglan, have given way to 1960s plate glass. The N half (see the straight joint in the E wall) mirrors the S, with adjacent hearth and stair, but is less substantially built. It must replace a pre-C17 structure, and creates the familiar two-unit plan-form.

GRAIGWITH, 2$\frac{1}{4}$ m. W. Remote and forlorn-looking in its overall of grey render. A typical two-room, two-storeyed, late C16 farmhouse, improved in the early C17 by means of an E stair-tower rising to give access to the roof space, and extended by a further bay later in the century. (Post-and-panel partition, and flat, decorative stair balustrade.)

TON, $\frac{3}{4}$ m. SW. A perfect Monmouthshire farmhouse, tall, white and gabled, tucked down in the fold of a green side valley. Dated 1663. The full-height porch, the parlour wing to the r. of it, and the pantry wing rear l. belong to that date, but the bay l. of the porch was a pre-existing single-unit hall block, with hearth and stair in its r. gable-end. Thus the additions achieved the preferred arrangement with the entry into a passage behind the hall hearth, but produced an almost symmetrical frontage. Porch entrance arch formed without dressed stone. Date on the
p. 38 shaped timber door-head within. The small original window openings largely survive. Inside, chamfered beams in the older part, but ogee-moulded beams in the parlour and chamber over. The timber fireplace lintels in both these latter rooms are even further decorated, with incised flowers and scrolls.

LLWYN-CELYN, 2 m. SW. Two-storey cottage remodelled and enlarged *c.* 1835 by means of a stout, three-storey tower-like SW addition, for the rector, the Rev. Charles Addams-Williams. Cream rendered. Tripartite sash windows typical of the date.

4000

LLANGOVAN/LLANGOFEN

ST GOVAN. An unusual composition, as seen from the W. Late medieval, turret-like gabled double bellcote with cinquefoiled lights (supported internally on huge piers). W doorway under a flattened four-centred head, with a presumably earlier ogee-headed stoup to the r. So the entrance to the church was from the W. The S porch seems to have been built in the early C17 (bequest of 1625), reusing sections of moulding in its crudely fashioned outer arch. Chancel lower than the nave, both with lancets, of the C13. Restored 1888–90 by *A. W. Probyn & J. P. Moore* of Gloucester. – (FONT. Medieval. – SCREEN and PULPIT, 1908–9 by *Moore*, carved by *Frith*. – MONUMENT. John Ayleworth †168[?]. Slab signed *W.H.*, carver.)

In the CHURCHYARD, close to the S porch, the broached base and the shaft of a late medieval CROSS, on five high steps. Carved head of 1902.

CHURCH FARM, below to the E, is an evocative group of the early and mid C17. Entrance from the road is between the short end of the three-unit farmhouse and its detached kitchen. A low barn and cart-house close the yard to the S.

TRECASTLE, 1 m. N. An unusually well preserved motte-and-bailey complex, the motte under a dense covering of trees, a farmstead built on the inner bailey, and the outline traceable of a big outer bailey down the slope.

The farmhouse, OLD TRECASTLE FARM, is full of interest.

T-plan. The stem, extending to the N, of one-and-a-half storeys, is the kitchen wing and is of two builds, see the straight joint in the E wall. C17 cross range of two full storeys with chimney-stacks and mural stairs in the gable-ends, and even a latrine for the upper SE room. Massive timber doorway at the S end of the E wall of the lower range, the lintel shaped into a four-centred head. Immediately inside, at r.-angles, a second similar doorway, retaining its original studded door. This opens into the hall in the S range, a richly appointed room. Ceiling beams moulded with hollow, roll and hollow, post-and-panel partition, p. 37 the posts with moulded, not merely chamfered, angles. In the parlour beyond, the beams are also moulded, but the partition is more simply treated. Late C17 plaster embellishment of the ceiling with encircled rosettes and olive fronds all in rectangular borders. The stair from the parlour goes right up to the roof, with a pair of four-centred-headed doorways at first-floor level. The first-floor rooms are divided by a second post-and-panel partition, the doorway in it given a shaped head of the type so popular in C17 farmhouses in the county.

Fine contemporary BARN to the N, with hay loft and stables at either end.

OLD HOUSE, 1 m. NW. Three-unit late C16 house of two full storeys, on a steeply sloping site, the downhill service unit cross-gabled. Entry at this end into a cross-passage backing on to the hall hearth. Rendered grey and modernized externally. Only one original timber window, with close-set diamond mullions, survives, high in the lower end wall. (Fox and Raglan record the rich mouldings of the hall ceiling beams and partition.) p. 37

COURT ST LAWRENCE, ½ m. NW. Built for Edward Berry, a Spitalfields silk merchant, some time between 1802 and 1818. The small, white Regency villa was originally approached obliquely from the W, so that its siting above a little wooded valley made an effect. Three-bay W front, two-storeyed under a shallow slated roof on bracketed eaves. Full-width veranda, its entablature originally carried on rough tree trunks. Canted SE angle treated as the side of a bay projecting from the S front. To the N, a Victorian two-bay extension. The long range extending to the E is dated 1876 on a rainhead, but incorporates an earlier five-bay BARN at its further end. Much notched woodwork here on gables, eaves and two porches. The principal porch, set diagonally between the two ranges, has above it a heavily timbered window set across the re-entrant angle. The architect for this part was *Henry Crisp* of Bristol (who had been in partnership with E.W. Godwin). Inside, it is clear that the Regency house was originally entered in the l. bay under the loggia. Narrow entrance passage and, axially beyond, a simple curved Regency staircase. Crisp's diagonal E window creates a spacious and well-lit upper landing. Curious two-bay stone colonnades at both levels. Their short, stout columns have capitals carved with naturalistic foliage clearly inspired by the leaf capitals in the courtyard of the University Museum at Oxford.

3020 LLANGUA/LLANGIWA

St James. Alone in a meadow beside the River Monnow, reached down a grassy drive from the A465. The simple little medieval building is constructed of massive blocks of Old Red Sandstone. Nave and lower chancel of equal width – but see the straight joint between them. Various square-headed windows with arched lights, all piecemeal insertions. Only the S slit window in the nave may be original. Is the simple S porch of the C18? W tower unbuttressed, with timber-framed top (remade 1954) of two short stages, the upper verticals baluster-shaped. Pyramid cap. The interior is dominated by the wagon roofs of nave and chancel, of flattened profile, awkwardly fusing with each other where the chancel arch should be. The usual grid of ribs, black against the white plaster. Some small octagonal bosses. The church was restored in 1889, by *Thomas Nicholson* of Hereford, and in 1954 by *E.A. Roiser*. – FONT. C12 tub on circular shaft and small tripartite, broach-like feet. – ROYAL ARMS. Small, finely carved, in a frame. Not dated, but late C17.

4000 LLANGWM ISAF

St John. The ruined little medieval church was rebuilt 1849–51 by *John Prichard*. Of local Old Red Sandstone. Nave and chancel in one, with inserted chancel arch, like its predecessor. The bell gable over the chancel arch is Prichard's addition. Most of the windows are Perp, not what Prichard would have chosen left to himself. W porch probably retained from the old building, its arch moulded with continuous wave, hollow and wave, a local late medieval form. Inside, the walls are hammerdressed. – PULPIT. 1965, designed and built by the churchwarden, *W. G. Stephens*. Bow-fronted, of ashlar and hammerdressed stone.

Ringwork, ½ m. NW. The late C11 or early C12 earthwork fortification is clearly visible on the hillside, though overgrown with trees.

4090 LLANGWM UCHAF

St Jerome. The church, built of slabby Old Red Sandstone, stands in a little valley, a siting which seems to magnify its size. Its plan-form is unusual, a long nave, with S porch and short, lower chancel, and a tower set to the N of the latter. Nave and porch were largely rebuilt 1863–9 by *J. P. Seddon*, implementing a scheme first made in 1858. Tower restored by *Seddon*, chancel restored by *Ewan Christian*, where a rainwater head is dated 1869. The W doorway in the nave, and the two-light window above, represent what was there before, while the four-light Perp window with square head at the E end of the nave S wall is a genuine medieval survival, clearly intended to light the rood. Otherwise Seddon found 'remarkably few windows, only lancets', suggesting a C13 or even a C12 origin for the building. (Both churches at Llangwm are mentioned in 1128.) Seddon inserted several entirely new ones, including the two-light chancel E window. The tower is unbuttressed, of two tall storeys with crowning battlements. Polygonal SW stair-turret. The belfry windows are of the simplest, but the lowest stage is lit from three directions by cinquefoiled ogee lights under square heads, suggesting a C15 date. Inside, this is confirmed by the form of the tower arch, of two wave-moulded orders, the lower dying into the imposts of the upper, and the small, four-centred-headed doorway to the stair. A squint beside the arch, so the lower storey of the tower may have provided space for a side altar. Since access to the rood loft is up the tower stair, it looks as if the two may have been constructed at the same time.

The glory of the interior is the rood screen and loft. It almost totally obscures the one other surviving element of medieval fabric, the chancel arch. This is an unusual C14 piece, high and wide, outlined by a continuous broad chamfer, with to the E a quadruple-chamfered arch on green-man corbels. – ROOD 35
SCREEN and LOFT. A breathtaking sight, rising almost to the roof, screen with central doors, coving, bressumer and loft. The inexhaustibly varied horizontal foliage trails which mask the bressumer and other structural beams are mainly of *c.* 1500, the rest a sympathetic reconstruction by *J. P. Seddon*, 1876–8. He took the screen and loft at Patrishow, Breconshire (Powys) as his principal guide. The discreet colouring in red and blue behind some of the undercut bands he introduced on the evidence of traces of medieval paintwork. – CURIOSUM. Hourglass-shaped stone object found reused in the wall during the C19 reconstruction. The hollow upper section and central band are decorated with a relief trellis pattern, suggesting a late C11 or early C12 date. Cut down at top and bottom. In form, it seems most like a pillar piscina. – The OTHER FITTINGS are by *Seddon* at his most imaginative. – Octagonal stone FONT on short black shafts with foliage caps and cylindrical upper drums which almost consume the bowl. Four-petal flowers round the lip. – PULPIT. Of stone, circular, subtly modelled, on dark green and brown shafts. – LECTERN. Timber. Crested book rest on a buttressed and panelled shaft and octagonal base. – CHOIR STALLS and PEWS also to Seddon's design. – FLOOR TILES. Of *c.* 1866–8. Nave and chancel tiled throughout in a handsome and coherent pattern, also designed by *Seddon*, made by *Godwin* (figures) and *Maw* (patterns), and deserving close examination. – STAINED GLASS. Chancel E, Annunciation. *Seddon* designed this too, *c.* 1877, the cartoon by *H. A. Kennedy*, the window executed in Rust's 'antique' glass by *S. Belham & Co.* (T. Blackshaw). The nervous intensity of the figures, their Pre-Raphaelite style and the unusual colouring in turquoise and brown make this an exceptional creation. – A few early C16 fragments in the Perp S window in the nave.

BAPTIST CHAPEL, $\frac{3}{4}$m. SW. Characteristic rural chapel, small and white and dated 1840. The only unexpected feature at that date is the pointed heads to the windows.

THE OLD SCHOOL HOUSE, $\frac{1}{2}$m. SW, on the B4235. The modest national school built by *J. P. Seddon* in 1870 has been converted into a house.

PWLL FARM, ½m. SE. Sadly modernized. The S gable-end towards the road bears the date 1671. The N upper room has two timber windows with sunk chamfers, one of five lights, the other of three. Typical shaped door-head into the room they light.

ALLT-Y-BELA, 1½m. W. Alone and deserted in the bottom of a remote little valley. The towering three-storey parlour block of p. 38 1599 and its crown of lozenge-plan stacks is in the last stages of collapse. What makes their dereliction all the more poignant is that it is known who built the block, Roger Edwards, founder of Usk Grammar School. The lower range to the NE, which is better preserved, consists of a two-unit C16 house, originally single-storeyed with an attic, extended in the C18 or C19.

p. 35 TREVELA, 2m. S. Historically important as the earliest dated farmhouse in the county of the tall, compact type popular throughout the first half of the C17, here three full storeys high. The date, 1601, is on the SE entrance projection. But extensions of 1984 to the SW and of 1987 to the NE, overall smooth white render on the walls, pantiles on the roofs, and a black hood-mould to every window, combine to annul the house's historic character. What is left externally is the syncopated fenestration of the SE gable-end, where the three-storey porch and the full-height stair are combined under a single gable, and the stop-chamfered stone surround of the depressed-headed entrance doorway. Also the stumps of three lozenge-plan stacks on the NE gable. Inside, the stair remains impressive, its timber steps radiating from a mighty timber newel, truly a 'mast', as Fox and Raglan dubbed it. Doorways with shaped timber heads at three levels, partly reinstated. The shape, a matching duplication of lobe, swooping upward curve and knob, is the same as that at Allt-y-bela (*see* above). The two lofty ground-floor rooms also survive, the hall to the l., with a fireplace opening topped by a massive monolith, the parlour to the r. with a wider fireplace opening bridged by a deep timber lintel. To the l. of this, twin timber doorways with four-centred heads, one to the stone stair which twists down to the cellar, the other to the timber stair which twists up to the floor above.

Rectangular stone OUTBUILDING with a dovecote across the full width of its upper storey. Its datestone of 1648 is now reset on the house.

TY LLWYD, 1m. N. A two-storeyed, two-unit house of the late C16 which must once have been among the most displayful examples of the carpenter's craft in the county. The exterior, however, is completely modernized. The windows recorded by Fox and Raglan have all disappeared, leaving only the entrance doorway in the N gable-end, with simplified four-centred head. But inside there is still enough to impress. The ceiling beams of hall and parlour are five-sided with angle rolls, and what remains of the upstairs post-and-panel screen is elaborately moulded with quadruple wave. Also one E upstairs window lintel with angle rolls and an arched door-head with incised leaf carving, now loose.

GAER FAWR (ST 441 988) is the largest prehistoric HILL-FORT in Gwent and commands fine views in all directions. The modern entrance is at the SE corner but the original one may have been on the W side. At the S end the two ramparts are close together, the inner one being remarkably well preserved with a drop of about 40 ft (13 metres) from the top of the bank to the bottom of the ditch. On the E side the defences are overgrown. At the N end the banks diverge, which has led to the suggestion that the defences are of two periods.

LLANHENNOCK/LLANHENOG

3090

ST JOHN. The slender tower is of the C15, unbuttressed with a rectangular NE turret and battlements. Belfry stage defined by stringcourses. Here there are twin square-headed openings in deep hollow reveals. Cinquefoiled lights. The very short nave all rebuilt (except the S doorway) and lean-to N aisle and vestry added in 1862–3 by *Prichard & Seddon*. Lower chancel, the walling old, with a blocked S priest's door. The three-light E window, with Perp tracery under a two-centred head, is medieval. Inside, tower arch and chancel arch probably of 1862–3. – FONT. Dated 1863, so by *Prichard & Seddon*. A memorable, if monochrome, piece of High Victorian geometry. Octagonal bowl with crocketed gables against the faces and ballflower on the underside. A complex moulding leads down to the thick, pyramidal stem and moulded base. – STAINED GLASS. Chancel E. St John the Baptist preaching, 1901 by *Heaton, Butler & Bayne*. – Nave S. SS Michael and George, *c.* 1919 by *Jones & Willis*. – N aisle W, 1952, by *Celtic Studios*.

In the CHURCHYARD, broached base and shaft stump of a CROSS, on modern steps.

BERLLAN-DEG, 1½ m. N. A substantial and little altered house that p. 33 shows the native tradition at its fullest development, datable probably to the second quarter of the C17. A single range. Two-storeyed throughout, but the E end containing hall and parlour slightly higher than the cross-passage and service end. Most of the original timber windows survive, quite large, with ovolo-moulded mullions and stone slab hoodmoulds. Four-lighters front and back for hall and parlour, three-lighters for the chambers above. Smaller windows at the SE corner, for closets off parlour and chamber above. Stout square-topped timber doorway displaced from the S end of the cross-passage to give S access to the service end. There may originally have been a detached kitchen, of which no trace survives. Within the cross-passage, a stone doorway with chamfered four-centred head opens into the hall, between hearth and mural stair. At the stairhead a pair of timber doorways with characteristic early C17 shaped heads, one opening into the chamber over the hall, the other into the roof space over cross-passage and service end. They confirm that the whole house was built as one. Between hall and parlour the usual post-and-panel partition with arched door-head. On the parlour side a section of the screen is painted with a crude lattice pattern enclosing leaves alternating red and green, a rare survival of contemporary decoration. The parlour, as Fox and Raglan noted, is significantly larger than the hall. In its end wall, a wide hearth between the closet already noted and a twisting timber stair which gives access to chamber and roof space.

GLEN USK, ¾m. E. An exquisite white-rendered Neoclassical villa tucked into a nook in the hillside with a view over the windings of the River Usk. Built for Sir Digby Mackworth, Bart, *c.* 1820. His architect is unknown. The S front is three-storeyed, the roof invisible behind the shallowest of blocking courses. Two very shallow full-height bows flank a broad, flat central bay. Tripartite sash windows at all levels, the lowest carried right down to the ground behind an elegant iron arcaded veranda. The N, entrance, front was brought forward *c.* 1840. Here a central single-storey hall is fronted by a stone screen of Doric columns carrying an entablature with a peculiar variant on a triglyph and metope frieze. Forward-projecting full-height wings, their fenestration fussily varied, arcaded on the ground storey, Venetian above. All this is in the looser style typical of the early Victorian years.

Inside, the entrance hall has niches in the side walls, and an inner screen of two Ionic columns of yellow scagliola. Both bow-windowed ground-floor rooms have reticent plaster ceiling friezes with palmette patterns. In the E room twin white marble chimneypieces with thin fluted Doric columns.

Free-standing Ionic TEMPLE immediately W of the house, erected before *c.* 1865 as a toplit picture gallery, converted *c.* 1900 into a billiard room with inner library. Its projecting S portico has uncomfortably stout fluted columns. Attached half-columns along the sides.

STABLE COURT to the NE of the house, informal, roughcast and whitened, in a simple classical idiom. Clock tower with top dovecote.

OAKLANDS, ½m. S. Built by Lord Rhondda as a wedding present for his daughter, Margaret Haig Thomas, and son-in-law, Sir Humphrey Mackworth of Glen Usk. By *Oswald P. Milne*, who exhibited his design at the Royal Academy in 1909. Single range under a pantiled hipped roof. The entrance front is of stone below, black-boarded above, with an off-centre white bay window. The garden front, all stone, has an off-centre, gabled, full-height bay.

COLOMENDY WOOD, ¾m. N. An exceptionally interesting Arts and Crafts house of 1913–14 by *A. T. Bolton*, later Curator of the Soane Museum, for R. C. Talbot Leybourne, a railway locomotives engineer, who must have delighted in the ingenuity of the house. Happily it remains virtually unaltered, together with its terraced and compartmented hillside garden, also laid out by *Bolton*. As built, the house is in effect two-thirds of what Bolton had originally designed, so what had been intended as a symmetrical, strongly Jacobean E garden front became an irregular composition. The only tight group is the two-storey polygonal W entrance porch with soaring chimney-breast beside it. The exterior is largely defined by its facing materials, mauve Old Red Sandstone rubble for the family part, matched by Red Wilderness ashlar, emphasizing doorways; grey pebbledash for the N service end and stable court; iron-stained slates to cover the steeply sloping roofs. Timber mullioned windows, all painted black. Flat arches to the windows formed of tile voussoirs. Embossed lead bands cap the two double-height window bays towards the garden.

Inside one realizes that the external grouping is largely dictated by the principle that major rooms downstairs and up should have windows in two adjacent walls, normally centrally placed. The only exception is the hall, which faces E and rises two-storeyed at the heart of the house. This is the *pièce de résistance*. One enters it at one corner and sees it from the W through the open timberwork of the staircase, which rises straight and free-flying to a first-floor corridor. The corridor has a balustrade of shaped cut-out balusters, which is doubled above the stair for no practical reason but to add to the spatial complication. All this faces the two-storey, mullion-and-transom bay window, with the fireplace at r.-angles to it, and up above, a half-timbered overhang from which an internal oriel window projects, to give a high-level peep down into the hall. The elements in this room clearly derive from Norman Shaw (e.g. Adcote) and Philip Webb (Forthampton Court), but here in this small space they have an intoxicating intensity. The other main rooms downstairs are the drawing room (S) with pseudo inglenook, and dining room (NE). Above them no more than two bedrooms with their dressing rooms, one of which is provided with the oriel overlooking the hall.

The only other detail of accommodation to note is that the stable court has stabling for three horses and, sign of the times, a motor house.

CAE CAMP (ST 359 938). A small hilltop camp with two ramparts and a ditch between them. On the E side the outer rampart is cut by the road and the interior has been damaged by quarrying. The entrance is protected by an overlapping of the banks.

LLANHILLETH/LLANHILEDD

2000

Llanhilleth consists of three elements: the medieval church remote on its hilltop, long terraces of cottages contouring round the hillside, and the valley-bottom housing and Workmen's Institute for the colliers in Llanhilleth Colliery.

THE HILLTOP

ST ILLTYD (closed in 1957, restored by Blaenau Gwent Borough Council after 1984 and now in occasional use as a hall). Battened-down appearance. Short saddleback W tower, its W doorway pointed and simply chamfered. Belfry slits without cut stone. Nave lit only by two square-headed S windows, Perp of three cinquefoiled lights. Lower chancel, lit only by a Perp basket-arched E window of three cinquefoiled lights, with restored cork-like knobs on the cusps. (Inside, the chancel arch is crudely pointed. Wagon roofs in nave and chancel. – FONT. Medieval. Plain, square.)

CASTELL TALIORUM, N of St Illtyd's Church. The foundations, excavated 1924–5, of a circular medieval tower and a keep-like structure of irregular Greek cross plan.

MOTTE, SW of the church. Mound of uncertain age with eroded sides.

UPPER HAFODARTHEN, ¼ m. SE. The farmstead high on the hillside has a breathtakingly wide and distant view to the S. From the road above, its layout is apparent, two small houses set close together at r.-angles to one another and subsequently joined. This is an example of the not uncommon siting of two houses in a single farmyard dubbed the 'unit-system'. Fox and Raglan dated both houses *c.* 1600. (The W house, end-on to the slope, is of three-unit, longhouse type with small unheated inner room, but the E house is of two units, hall and parlour of equal size. Spiral stair beside the hall fireplace, and doorways with arched heads in both. Also post-and-panel partitions with unusual stop-chamfers, suggesting that the same craftsman built both houses.)

(LLANHILLETH FARM, 1½ m. SE. An even remoter high-lying farm. The house, disused at the time of writing, started as a longhouse of *c.* 1600, and incorporates a pair of cruck blades. It is unusually planned, with a corridor lit by an internal window. Early C17 three-storey cross wing, its spiral stair having twin arched first-floor doorways. P. Davis.)

THE VALLEY

ST MARK, Commercial Road. 1898–9 by *C. Telford Evans* of Cardiff. Lancets.

PRIMARY SCHOOL, above Commercial Road. Early C20. Pennant sandstone with Bath stone dressings. Twin gables crowned by fancy finials face the valley, and a third marks the boys' entrance at the S end. Two-storeyed. The windows in their usual groups of three but unusually classical in shape and mouldings. The plan is irregular, on the awkward hillside site. Note the vast retaining walls below and behind.

HOTEL, Commercial Road. Of *c.* 1900. Typically showy and disorganized front, with its three unequal gables and its mix of rock-faced Pennant sandstone, harsh red brick and fake half-timbering. Probably the hotel for which *C. Telford Evans* called for tenders in 1898.

LLANHILLETH COLLIERY WORKMEN'S INSTITUTE, sited opposite the E end of MEADOW STREET, the central of three long, straight terraced streets in the valley bottom. Institute and terraces are both faced with grey Pennant stone and red brick.

The Institute has a lively façade, of two tall storeys over a basement. An intricate network of pilaster strips and stringcourses frames the round-headed windows. Fancy gable crowned with balls and acroteria. The lofty red brick porch looks like an afterthought. The date must be *c.* 1900.

LLANISHEN 4000

A scattered ridgetop village looking W over the Vale of Usk. The church is tucked in above a wooded glen.

ST DENIS. 1852–4, an early church by *Prichard & Seddon* (designed by Prichard, supervised by Seddon), and a cheap one, costing £650. Their idiom is readily recognizable. Nave and S porch, lower chancel and lean-to N vestry given a stone chimney with pierced smoke vents. Steeply pitched roofs and precisely laid walling of snecked, squared Old Red Sandstone. Bath stone dressings, but no emphasis on polychromy. Simple Dec windows. The W end has been carefully considered. The gable is crowned by an octagonal spirelet on a box-like bellcote, anchored to the wall by a long shaft on a head corbel. Paired windows and trefoil-headed W doorway are separated from one another by a stepped stringcourse. Diagonal buttresses. The interior is less characterful. Steeply pointed chancel arch on corbel shafts. Arch-braced roofs. – ALTAR RAIL. On floriated metal supports. – PULPIT. Timber, polygonal. – FONT. Stone, octagonal, on a four-shafted stem. Presumably all are by *Prichard & Seddon.* – STAINED GLASS. Chancel E, a crowded Crucifixion scene, 1901 by *Joseph Bell & Son.* – MONUMENT. Stephen Prosser †1865. A disembodied hand holds an inscription scroll. Signed by *J. Davies* of Pontypool.

(In the CHURCHYARD three steps and part of the shaft of a CROSS.)

LLANVAIR, $1\frac{1}{4}$ m. NW. The farmhouse, close up to the road, is of two parts of *c.* 1600. The full-height S stair projection served the lower, earlier, W half. Here three-light upper windows with hoodmoulds survive. Sunk-chamfered mullions. Lozenge-plan chimneystacks. The square addition to the W produced a cross-passage behind the hall stack, and a kitchen below extra bedchambers. The whole building has been pebble-dashed, which is a pity.

TREGEIRIOG, $1\frac{3}{4}$ m. NW. The earliest component is the timber-framed cross wing at the back, dated by Cadw no earlier than the late C17. The main range pulled together to give a symmetrical five-bay front of two storeys under a central one-bay pedimental gable, a typical C18 manoeuvre. A datestone of 1758 reset inside presumably records when this was done. The agent of the Duke of Beaufort's local estates lived in the house at the time.

3090 LLANLLOWELL/LLANLLYWEL

ST LLYWEL. Small single-cell building of Old Red Sandstone rubble. In the W wall a tiny Norman window, and an equally small lancet in the N wall. S porch and S rood-loft stair projection, and between them a square-headed Perp window with two ogee lights, glazed spandrels and a hood on square stops. The S doorway has a flat stone lintel in which geometrical patterns are scratched. Of what medieval date is this? N wall largely rebuilt by *John Prichard* in 1871–2. Heavily restored E window, of three trefoiled lights, datable *c.* 1300. – FONT. C12, a circular bowl with incised rim, set on a modern stem. – STAINED GLASS. Chancel E, Adoration of the Lamb. By *A. L. Moore*, *c.* 1897.

The late C19 OLD RECTORY, and GREAT HOUSE FARM, late C16 in origin, make a good group across the road from the church.

PENTWYN, ½ m. N. The farmstead is conspicuously sited on a hillock overlooking the River Usk. Only the W wall of the farmhouse remains largely in its original late C16 state. Two upper mullioned windows, one a three-lighter, the other two-light. What is of special interest is that they are of stone, with arched lights, hollow mouldings and hoods.

3080 LLANMARTIN

ST MARTIN. The W tower is Perp, unbuttressed, of two stages with simple plinth moulding and stringcourses. Polygonal NE stair-turret and battlements. The body of the church, short nave with S porch, and slightly lower chancel with N vestry, was rebuilt in 1857–8 by *Prichard & Seddon*, to *Seddon*'s design, incorporating some medieval features inside. In order to acknowledge this conservatism, Seddon uses harmonizing materials, grey limestone and purple Old Red Sandstone, and Perp window tracery. A typical personal touch is the strong slope on the wall-bases, and the band of purple masonry above it. Inside, the tower arch is tall and narrow, the imposts rendered, the two chamfered orders two-centred-headed. The wide and high chancel arch may incorporate medieval stonework. Two continuous chamfers, the inner one very broad. Reset Perp vestry doorway, moulded with a deep, narrow hollow between two waves. The wagon roof in the nave, plastered, with moulded ribs, and gilt bosses at the intersections, imitates the local late medieval idiom. Chancel roof stencilled, the only surviving part of a scheme of 1880 by *Joseph Bell & Son*, to the design of *Edward Honey* of Bristol. – STAINED GLASS. Almost all the windows are filled with bright geometrical patterns made up from reused glass, giving a festive air to the interior. – Chancel E, also made up with scenes, probably of the 1850s, from a much larger window. – Nave N, work of mercy. Signed by *E. R. Suffling*, *c.* 1900. – MONUMENT. Parts of an important early C16 monument reset in the chancel N wall, identified by the heraldry as commemorating Sir Thomas

Morgan of Pencoed †1510. Various fragments, in particular small kneeling figures in the angles l. and r. The front of the tomb-chest is carved with a central shield-bearing angel flanked by jostling groups of frontal kneeling sons and daughters. The four-centred arch under which all this is set belonged to a burial chapel built under the will of Sir William Morgan, 1541, but derelict by the late C18.

OLD VICARAGE, 300 yds E. Also by *Seddon*, 1857–8. Full-blooded High Victorian polychromy, buff Bath stone and red brick against grey stone walling. Pointed relieving arches above the sash windows are given special emphasis. Timber-framed entrance porch. The garden front is crowned by three small gables, and a larger one over the canted window bay at the r. end.

In PENCOED LANE, opposite the Old Vicarage, early C20 Arts and Crafts cottages probably by *Oswald P. Milne* (*see* Llanwern). First ARNSIDE, presenting three black slate-hung gables towards the main road. Then, further down on the l., WOODSIDE and ROSELEA, a symmetrical pair, with two broad, slate-hung central gables. Slab-like stone chimneystacks.

PENCOED CASTLE, 1¼ m. E. The large and imposing early Tudor 47
mansion languishes as an unconsolidated ruin in a farmyard. To come upon it at the end of an inconsequential lane is quite a shock. The drum tower standing forward to the SW is clearly medieval and the free-standing gatehouse beyond it to the N is Tudor, but the main building behind, on the E side of the courtyard, has smooth ashlar masonry and crisp dressings which even raise the doubt that this may be no more than some late Victorian magnate's abandoned folly-mansion. So it is necessary to rehearse the list of owners from the C13 to the C20, together with what little is known about their building activities.

Sir Richard de la More had a house at Pencoed in 1270. By the late C15 the estate had come to a branch of the Morgan family of Tredegar. Sir Thomas, owner from *c.* 1480 to 1510, his son, Sir William, knighted 1513, †1542, his grandson Sir Thomas, knighted 1544, sheriff 1548 and 1559, †1565, and great-grandson, Sir William, †1584, all had the local power and distinction to justify the construction of a substantial mansion. Leland's description of Pencoed in 1538 as 'a fair maner place' is not much help, so to attribute the building to one or other Morgan depends on issues of style. Long-gone heraldic glass in the gatehouse included the arms of the first Sir William and his son. The last descendant of the Morgans sold up in 1701, after which a succession of owners farmed the estate but let the house sink into ruin. Finally, in 1914 Lord Rhondda bought the estate and before his death four years later made great strides in restoring the centre of the main building, with *G. H. Kitchin* as his architect. His widow employed *Eric Francis* in 1922–3 to build a free-standing house immediately to the N, but sold up in 1931. Thereafter Francis's house became the farmhouse, a bungalow was built *c.* 1960 to the SW, but the Tudor mansion reverted to its previous mouldering state.

The drum TOWER is clearly the earliest feature at the SW angle of a walled enclosure, perhaps of the later C13. It survives largely intact up to its corbelled crown. It is built of local Old Red Sandstone, but the yellow Triassic sandstone dressings are all Tudor insertions. Sundry small square windows, and two doorways with four-centred heads, one at ground level, the other at the head of a spiral stair, giving access to a walkway along the top of a now much reduced wall which links the tower to the gatehouse further N.

The GATEHOUSE is wholly Tudor and on a much grander scale, though constructed of similar materials. Rectangular in plan, of three storeys, with full-height, forward-facing turrets, also square, their corners chamfered. In the turrets, single-light windows with arched lights and hoodmoulds at irregular intervals, to light a SW newel stair and NW garderobes. The central archway is high and wide but almost segment-headed. Continuous sunk chamfer moulding between small rolls. Rubble segmental vault within, formed of rubble masonry (cf. the gatehouse at St Pierre, p. 526). Above the vault were large rooms at two levels, lit by three-light windows front and back, the stonework of all but one now robbed away. The intact, upper W, window, and a blocked S two-lighter, have arched lights and hoods on square stops. Against the N wall of the gatehouse, the crease-line of a two-storeyed gabled building, now demolished. Archdeacon Coxe's plan of 1800 shows that the courtyard into which the gatehouse opens was originally closed to the N by continuous buildings which linked in an irregular L with the gatehouse. All that survives of this range is the E end of the front wall. A solitary fragmentary upper window, of three ogee-headed cinquefoiled lights, suggests that this range was late C15 and of high quality.

The MAIN RANGE, adjoining this fragment and extending S-wards as a backdrop to the courtyard, is largely intact, though in turn ruined, restored and then abandoned once more. Coxe's engraved view of 1800 provides a check on the accuracy of the restoration of the W front. The central feature is a three-storeyed porch rising the full height of the range and topped by a deep, plain parapet. Coxe shows similar parapets elsewhere. The battlements which continue right round the range were all added for Lord Rhondda. To the N of the porch the range is three-storeyed, to the S two-storeyed, where the hall lies below the great chamber. At the S end, a tower-like, slightly projecting parlour wing, also three-storeyed, but of two different heights, for the main room at each level and for its closet. What unifies these disparate parts is the grey-green ashlar stone facing. This is clearly original, a piece of swagger that imitates the ashlar masonry of Raglan Castle (q.v.). The parlour wing, as the coursing of its ashlar shows, was an afterthought. Its almost windowless W end wall, however, is of sandstone rubble, as are the S, E and N fronts of the range itself, where greater privacy sanctioned a less expensive treatment. The porch arch has a slightly pointed head, and above it a segment-headed recess with moulded surround, from which a heraldic achievement has no doubt been robbed. Enclosing, slightly chamfered superarch. The porch entry is rubble-vaulted on later plaster cornices. A service doorway also survives at the N end of this front, with a draw-bar socket in the jamb. The only original window is low down to the l. of the porch, of two arched lights under a hood. Hollow mouldings. All the others, similar in form if of various sizes, reflect what Coxe's engraving shows, except the two large, transomed hall windows, which are modern inventions, larger than those indicated by Coxe. The E front has in the centre a double-chamfered doorway, opening into the screens passage, with a transomed window S of it, to light the hall. Immediately beyond rises the strongly projecting hall chimney-breast, and a stair-tower serving the parlour wing. The N end of the E front also terminates in a projection, broader and less deep. The kitchen is here. The big square stacks crowning the kitchen and parlour wings were all added by *Kitchin*.

The interior of the building is in a ruinous state at the time of writing, and can only be entered gingerly. The most notable features can be mentioned in order from the N. The KITCHEN has a N fireplace about 15 ft (4.6 metres) wide, with a massive oak lintel. In the S wall, a blocked doorway with a two-centred chamfered head, presumably an indication of pre-Tudor fabric here. W of the kitchen a stone stair rises in short, straight flights up a rectangular core, to give access to the two upper storeys in the N half of the range. The ground-floor room N of the hall, much restored for Lord Rhondda, has a piscina in the N wall, so must have been the CHAPEL. The HALL, to the S of the screens passage, is single-storeyed and retains its original stone fireplace opening, wide but plain, with flattened four-centred head and small hollow, roll, hollow mouldings. At the S end of the hall a doorway opens into the parlour, lit by a four-light S window, and with its own closet and windowless storeroom to the W. A second doorway beside the first leads to a cellar, and a third, at the S end of the E wall, gives on to the foot of a remarkably spacious staircase. Short, straight flights of stone steps, central square core, and segmental vault of rubble-stone. It provides access to the great chamber over the hall, and to the rooms at two levels over the parlour. The fireplace opening in the great chamber is moulded with a wave and hollow. In the W wall opposite, the embrasures of the two five-light windows have not been restored. The heavily beamed ceiling, however, is all of *c.* 1914. In the parlour wing the main room at each level is lit by windows on three sides, with a fireplace in the W wall beside a doorway into a large closet.

So, finally, to summarize. The fragment of the N range may well have belonged to a house built by Sir Thomas Morgan (†1510), and so, in part, may the kitchen. This may have been the 'fair maner place' to which Leland refers. The main range and the gatehouse make sense as the product of a single mid-C16 campaign, by the second Sir Thomas between 1542 and 1565. The arched window lights one can accept as being as late as the mid C16. Features which would fit this and not an earlier date are the arrangement of single-storey hall with great chamber over and the spacious stairs with straight flights. The emphasis on height is also characteristic of the second half of the century rather than the first. Nor had the free-standing showpiece gatehouse lost its fascination by mid-century. But the complete absence of symmetry in plan and elevation shows that the self-consciousness of Elizabethan prodigy houses has yet to be reached.

DOVECOTE. In a field to the NE. Of rubble-stone. Large, square and gabled, but roofless. Fitted throughout inside with nesting boxes. Datable to the late C16.

BARNS. In a continuous range, forming an L to the N of the house, built of stone and impressive in scale and completeness. Probably of the C16 and C17. At the S end, a seven-bay storage barn set E–W. This is two-storeyed, the upper level reached by an external stone stair against the W gable, and lit by three timber windows in the long S wall. The threshing barn which runs N from its W end must be the earliest of the three. It is also of seven bays, with the usual opposed full-height doorways and long ventilation slits. Two-storeyed eighth bay at the S end entered by a four-centred-headed doorway with small square flanking windows. The N-most barn is also for threshing, five-bay, and built in line with, though slightly narrower than, its predecessor.

HOUSE, immediately N of the castle. 1922–3 by *Eric Francis* for Lady Rhondda. Cottage style, with stone walls, timber casement windows and pantiled roofs.

3000 LLANOVER/LLANOFOR

Llanover is an estate village, but unusually open-textured and picturesquely grouped. It is largely a creation of the early C20, but its inspiration comes from Lady Llanover's campaigns of a half-century earlier to promote the revival of Welsh culture, as the careful explorer will discover. The village extends along the W side of the A4042; the park wall of Llanover House runs beside it to the E. The parish church is by itself a mile away to the NE.

ST BARTHOLOMEW. Beside the River Usk, accompanied only by a white cottage and a grey mill. Handsome Perp W tower built of pale brown squared blocks. Three storeys defined by moulded plinth and stringcourses. Top battlements. Rectangular NE stair-turret. Two-centred W doorway of Old Red Sandstone, moulded with wave, hollow, wave. Twin belfry openings, with cinquefoiled ogees under a square head. Longish nave and S porch, longish lower chancel stepping down the slope. The nave, heavily rendered, has renewed Perp N and S windows, square-headed of three cinquefoiled lights. The broad, low S porch is an addition by the churchwardens in 1750 (preserving a stoup from its predecessor). S rood-stair projection. The chancel has the earliest evidence, of the early C14, if the renewed trefoil-headed lancet in the N wall is anything to go by. The E window is unrestored, Perp, of three lights, traceried under a four-centred head.

Inside, more indisputable Dec evidence, ogee-headed PISCINAS in nave and chancel. Tower arch and chancel arch of a form found from the C14 to the early C16, an outer arch on tall imposts and an inner arch dying into them. Wave mouldings on the tower arch, a chamfer and a quadrant on the chancel arch. The roofs throughout are of the typical late medieval form, plaster wagon vaults criss-crossed by moulded ribs and set on embattled wall-plates. – FONT. Round bowl on a rope moulding, ringed by crude six-petal flowers. Is this of the C12, with later embellishment? – ALTAR RAILS. Dated 1700. Turned balusters and finials. – ROYAL ARMS. Of the type datable between 1816 80
and 1837. Painted with much panache, the heraldic shield leaning rakishly between an excitable lion and unicorn. – STAINED GLASS. Chancel E, Christ and saints. By *Wippell & Co. c.* 1939. – Above the rood stair, 1988 by *John Petts*. – MONUMENT. William and Mathew Prichard, the latter †1610. Brass inscription plate with small armoured figures either side of a mantled shield of arms.

In the CHURCHYARD, the exceptionally impressive remains of the medieval CROSS, a broached base and spurred shaft on four steps. – Also the massive stone SARCOPHAGUS for Sir Benjamin Hall, Lord Llanover, his father-in-law Benjamin Waddington and their descendants *(see* Llanover House below). It is covered in heraldry, biblical texts and genealogical inscriptions in Welsh and in English, and bears the date of Hall's death as 27 April 1868. – The tall rusticated SEAT within the railed enclosure was added *c.* 1912.

WELSH CHURCH, SW of Rhyd-y-meirch. Built in 1898 by *B.J. Francis* of Abergavenny, under a bequest of Lady Llanover, for the benefit of Welsh-speaking Calvinistic Methodists on the Llanover estate. Rock-faced local stone with Bath stone dressings. Nave with off-centre W bellcote and lower chancel. E.E. and Dec windows.

HANOVER UNITED REFORMED (formerly Congregational) CHURCH, SE of Rhyd-y-meirch. The white-painted T-plan stone cottage-cum-chapel bears a plaque inscribed with the name Hanover, the date 1744 and the initials of the founder of the congregation, Rees Davies, and his wife Mary.

The CHAPEL built for an expanded congregation to the W of Rees Davies's chapel and the burial ground is dated 1839. It is square in plan, pyramid-roofed, with lower SCHOOLROOM at r.-angles, added in 1868. The walls are of well-laid brown rubble-stone, slate-hung on the weather side. Round-headed windows on all four sides, two wide apart flanking the entrance, two closer together lighting the pulpit, and one on each flank. The original galleries remain, on three sides, supported by thin iron shafts. Pulpit, 'big seat' and pews of 1892–3 by *Edwin Foster* of Abergavenny. – TABLETS. Indenture transferred from the old chapel, and dated 1767, recording the donation by Rees and Mary Davies in 1747 of 'this Room . . . for a Pious meeting place' and the 'Dwelling House, Barnstable, Lands & Orchards Belonging to it for ye use & support of ye Dissenting Prot. Ministers for Ever.' – Evan Lewis, minister, †1773.

In the BURIAL GROUND a cluster of tall, later C19 memorials, some of stone, some of pink polished granite, crowd towards the chapel door.

LLANOVER HOUSE. The high stone wall which borders the E side of the A4042 indicates the extent of the park created by Sir Benjamin Hall. He bought the Llanover Court estate in 1826 and married the heiress of adjoining Tŷ Uchaf (*see* below), thus amalgamating the two estates. He soon began a political career, was M.P. for Monmouth from 1832, and from 1837 for Marylebone. He became First Commissioner of Works, which explains why the bell in the clock tower of Barry's Houses of Parliament is called after him, Big Ben. Raised to the peerage as Lord Llanover, he died in 1867. Lady Llanover was a celebrated promoter of Welsh speaking and playing the Welsh harp. Within the park stand, at the S end, the late C18 mansion of Hall's father-in-law, Benjamin Waddington, known as Tŷ Uchaf, and in the centre the scanty remains of Hall's own mansion, built 1828–37 to the design of *Thomas Hopper* and demolished in 1935.

TŶ UCHAF. Benjamin Waddington of Nottinghamshire bought the estate *c.* 1792 and added to the house a three-storeyed, red brick block towards the NE. This is an exercise in Neoclassical elegance and restraint. Five-bay NE front, the ground-floor windows set within blind arcading of rubbed brick arches set on slight stone impost mouldings. Semicircular porch on two slender columns with Adamesque composite capitals. Exquisitely detailed fanlight and glazed door panel. The central window above given a sparing stone surround with elegant brackets. At r.-angles to the NW, a second five-bay front, this one with the three l. bays in a broad, shallow, full-height bow. Fenestration and crowning cornice and blocking course unite the two façades, which were presumably intended to be appreciated together from the diagonal view. The two-bay brick continuation to the SW provides a link to the much lower, older house. This bears a plaque recording its 'repear' in 1742, but has been thoroughly remodelled in the C20. Inside the Neoclassical house the two main ground-floor rooms have simple but exquisite marble chimneypieces. The staircase, with slender turned balusters, is set in the centre of the two-bay link.

The circular GARDEN to the SE, also created for Waddington, is enclosed by a red brick wall round its N half, in the centre of which stands an earlier circular DOVECOTE. Round and beyond the garden to the S flow miniature watercourses.

Sir Benjamin Hall's Elizabethan-style mansion stood ¼ m. N of Tŷ Uchaf. The STABLES, by *Hopper*, to the N of the site of the mansion, still stand in a derelict condition. Exuberant show front, of yellow ashlar. The entrance arch is set in a Tudoresque turreted gateway. The side turrets diminish as they rise, after the fashion of bottles, and are crowned by ogee stone caps and large metal weathervanes. In the N return wall, also of ashlar, two large stone windows with one mullion and one transom. All this show was for the benefit of visitors arriving down the drive from the main, NW, lodge. Behind, there is a simple single-storey stable courtyard.

The NORTH LODGE (Porth-mawr), at the NW corner of the park, was more in the way of a ceremonial entrance. It must be by *Hopper*. Four-square, ashlar-faced and battlemented, with a higher battlemented turret, spanning the drive by means of a pointed arch. Welsh inscriptions over the arch within and without, which addressed the arriving and departing guest, have worn away. The lodge is modelled on a gateway which is all that survives of a mansion of the Herberts at Crickhowell, Powys.

RHYD-Y-MEIRCH, W of the A4042, opposite the main park gate. A group of whitewashed cottages standing apparently at random just below the level of the main road and reached by a network of paths. The POST OFFICE, facing the road, is in a terrace of four. Also the MILL HOUSE, and, at the S end, TY NANT, dated 1795, and WELL COTTAGE, with at the bottom of its garden a circular PIGSTY with restored conical, stone-slate roof.

Next to the N is a group of 1950s cottage pairs, red brick below, the upper storey in a tiled mansard roof. They are evenly spaced facing a small and featureless rectangular green.

The N-most third of the village goes by the name of TRE ELIDYR. It is the touching and, in a way, inspiring realization of the dream of a hamlet, built for Lord Treowen in the mid 1920s to the Arts and Crafts ideal by *Alfred H. Powell*, colleague, fellow spirit and biographer of Ernest Gimson. The village incorporates a war memorial and a Welsh school, consists of a dozen cottages and cottage pairs set with artful irregularity round a rectangular green, and is held together by a narrow, tree-lined perimeter road. The SCHOOL, dated 1925, is single-storeyed, the centre three bays brought slightly forward under a rustically detailed pediment. Rendered walls, stone-slate roofs. It stands on the axis of the green, slightly elevated, and bears the words, in letters large enough to be read from a distance, Ysgol Harddwch Gwlad (Schooling, Beauty, Country). The GREEN is bounded by a stone wall, bowed on one of the long sides, where a semicircle of pleached limes encloses the WAR MEMORIAL, unveiled in 1922, a field-found, shaft-like stone set on three steps and bearing an iron cross. The COTTAGES, one (Nos. 12–13) dated 1925, are substantially constructed of local brown rubble-stone with stone-slate roofs and a little weatherboarding and slate-hanging for variety's sake. Stone slab porches and gabled dormers add to the diversity, as, most idiosyncratic of all, do the plans of one or two which are angled obtusely. Their apparently random siting and generous gardens make it hard to grasp the group as a whole. One or two later interlopers, faced with artificial stone. They are dated 1965. *Powell* clearly also designed the SOUTH LODGE to the park, and two COTTAGES within the park wall on the E side of the A4042.

COURT FARM, E of North Lodge. The long and imposing N front was constructed in three stages, as the straight joints relating to the gabled end sections clearly indicate. Two small early houses aligned N–S parallel to one another were joined together in the C17 by means of an E–W hall range, entered by a broad but low stone N porch. The entrance arch of the porch, of depressed outline, is moulded with hollow, roll and hollow. Small, similarly shaped window above, to light a tiny room under the porch gable. Sunk-chamfered mullioned windows, to the l. a three-lighter above a two-lighter, to the r. a four-lighter above an exceptionally wide window, of six lights. The only other original window is one of three lights in the NW gable. Restored four-light parlour window below. The S side of the house has a complicated array of chimneys, some with lozenge stacks, some rectangular. In the centre they rise through the roofslope, showing that the cross range has been made slightly deeper S-wards. (In the SW gable-end, traces of an original entrance doorway.) Modernized E and W fronts.

Inside, the history of the house can be read in more detail. The E wing was originally cruck-trussed and timber-framed, probably early C16. The upper parts of three trusses are readily visible, but the timber-framing has been replaced by stone walls. Fine stone fireplace at the S end, with stone jambs and timber lintel, and stone winding stair in the wall thickness close by. In the C17 this house became the service end of the new, much larger building. So the N porch opens into a cross-passage, with a typical post-and-panel partition on the l., i.e. towards the service end. The partition on the r. is of a later type, with a mid-height rail and widely spaced uprights. The depressed-headed doorway in it opens into a splendid C17 hall. The six-light N window, sunk-chamfer moulded, illuminates the upper end of the hall, where there are remains of a dais canopy. Contemporary S fireplace opening, the square surround of timber elegantly moulded. An area of small-fielded panelling over it. The parlour to the W occupies the entire lower storey of the W range. Its original arrangement when a free-standing house cannot be understood, but as a parlour it is both spacious and well fitted, with small-fielded panelling and window-seats, probably late C17, and a stone S chimneypiece with monolith lintel surviving from the C16 house. From the SW corner of the hall a late C17 dog-leg stair with elegant turned balusters leads up to a similarly panelled great chamber over the hall. In the modern passage E of the stair, a large timber upper doorway, originally external, and a square window with moulded stone surround. Their significance is not clear.

To the S of the house, continuous SERVICE RANGES enclose a courtyard.

TY MAWR, 1 m. SE. The regular upright windows with mid-C19 raised surrounds and keyblocks disguise a well-preserved two-unit house of the late C16 almost doubled in length towards the S a generation or so later. The fireplaces of the original hall and parlour have similar chamfered stone jambs and timber lintels. The front door, at the N end of the addition, opens into a passage behind the hall fireplace, from which the added parlour is divided by a post-and-panel partition. Its central doorway has a typical early C17 shaped head. The stair which rises at the far end of the passage round a stout octagonal timber newel is presumably contemporary. Upstairs a second, similar partition. On the E side of the addition, a closet wing raised over a cellar which is fitted with stone side benches, presumably for storing cider barrels.

MONMOUTHSHIRE AND BRECON CANAL. Constructed 1809–12 by *William Crossley*. The part that meanders N–S through the parish is crossed by seven of his humped, single-arch BRIDGES.

LLANSANTFFRAED/LLANSANTFFRAID 3010

ST BRIDGET. A tiny church, built of local Old Red Sandstone blocks, having panoramic views towards the uplands to S and W. Nave and lower chancel. Oversize W double bell gable. The W porch with its surprising stone vault was added by *Prichard & Seddon* in 1856–7. Theirs, too, are the nave windows and chancel arch. In the chancel, Perp square-headed windows with cinquefoiled lights, and simple piscina. – FONT. C12. Round bowl, its underside decorated with radiating semicircles and rope moulding. – REREDOS. Two very fine alabaster panels set in the E wall. They are typical productions of the C15 Midlands alabasterers, and represent the Entombment and the Resurrection. They have been in the church since before 1790. – PULPIT. Plain C18 wainscot. – SCREEN. Made up, rather gauchely, incorporating medieval scraps, in 1931. – MONUMENTS. These are what makes the church unforgettable, a series of C17 gravestones let into the walls, recently painted and made legible. What one reads, however, is spelled with amazing creativity. In the chancel, the ancestors of William Jones, back to 1438, set up in 1624. Note the knowledge of St Paul's Cathedral in London indicated by the couplet: Your worthy bones deserve of me in bras A rarer tombe then stately Hatton has. – In the nave, undated and unattributed, topped by a large hexfoil motif, an inscription concluding: Crisht alon is my redimer. – Jones family, up to 1684. – Markret Valont †1692.

In the CHURCHYARD, the ivy-clad remains of a CROSS, three steps, base and part of the shaft.

LLANSANTFFRAED COURT HOTEL. Dated 1912, and built for J.H[erbert] by *Fairfax B. Wade* and *C. Frankis* (R. Haslam). Quite a surprise, as if strayed from Sussex or Berkshire. In fact, Lutyens's Monkton House, Sussex, is probably its model. Red brick with vitrified headers and decoratively used tiles. In a later C17 style, with raised angle quoins and big hipped roof with dormers. Seven bays by four, the N and S fronts subtly differentiated from one another, the W end overwhelmed by a balustraded double perron stair descending from the upper storey. Inside, vaulted spine corridor, and in the central drawing room, a late C18 marble chimneypiece reused from the predecessor house.

4000 LLANSOY/LLAN-SOE

ST TYSOI. A complete small Perp church unusually handsomely detailed, nave with S porch and lower chancel. Slabby Old Red Sandstone walling, the cut stonework both purple and grey. The plain, unbuttressed W tower, devoid of cut stone, may be no earlier than the early C19. Lightly restored in 1858 by *J. P. Seddon* of *Prichard & Seddon*, whose only significant contributions are the E and two N windows (their proposed belfry stage to the tower not executed). The Perp work presents instructive combinations. The S porch arch, for instance, is wide and two-centred, moulded with wave, hollow, wave and an angle roll on a moulded base; but the S doorway, with a similar combination of mouldings, has a four-centred head. Polygonal STOUP in the porch. Square-headed S windows, of paired, cinquefoiled, ogee-headed lights in deep concave reveals. S rood-loft stair projection. The chancel arch, though probably built with a rood in mind, is the most old-fashioned feature, with a flattened super-arch and two-centred inner arch dying into the tall imposts. Wave-moulded throughout. – ALTAR RAILS. C18. Handsomely bulbous turned balusters. – PULPIT. Of timber, integral with the low timber chancel SCREEN. By *Seddon*, as are the PEWS and CHOIR STALLS, and also the FONT. – STAINED GLASS. Chancel E and nave N, *c.* 1914, signed by *Jones & Willis*. – Nave S, *c.* 1956 by *Geoffrey Robinson*. Brilliantly coloured evocation of the text Genesis 8. 22. Fine lettering.

CWRT-Y-BRYCHAN, 1 m. SE. C16 cruck-trussed BARN of five bays. At the lower end, an added stable and granary range, with one ovolo-moulded timber window. The HOUSE has been drastically modernized but retains in the gable-end of the rear wing the head of a stone Tudor upper window of two arched lights.

The HILL-FORT adjacent to Great House, 1 m. NW, has been rather badly damaged, but the multivallate defences can be well seen in the wood just E of the house. On the SE side there are four banks with two deep ditches and an intermediate shallower one; on the E side, beyond a modern mutilation near the road entrance, the sequence is more normal, with a counterscarp bank and two large ramparts and ditches. The original entrance may have been at the NE corner. On the N and W sides the natural slope of the hill is steeper, and the defences have been eroded by agriculture, but two banks or scarps can still be made out. The area enclosed is about 5 acres (2 hectares), a fairly standard size for hill-forts in the county.

LLANTARNAM 3090

St Michael and All Angels. A complex building of several periods. The first thing seen from the road is the uncompromising Tudor W tower. It is built of squared blocks of local stone, of two tall, unbuttressed stages with a square NE stair-turret. The depressed-headed W doorway has two continuous ovolo mouldings, and the two-light window above has arched lights and a hoodmould. Similar belfry windows. The nave is the earliest element, see one small blocked N window of the C12 or C13. The nave and slightly lower chancel mainly show Perp evidence, particularly two S windows, one in the nave to light the rood, the other in the sanctuary, square-headed three-lighters, the ogee-headed lights cinquefoiled. The Perp E window is C19, presumably part of *E.A. Lansdowne*'s restoration of 1869–70. The large N chapel is a surprise, much wider than the chancel. It underwent a Tudor remodelling, but the expansive E window, now blocked, and continuous moulded stringcourses, cut by the later N windows, are tantalizing evidence of its original handsome, perhaps C13 design. Note the jambs of a tall blocked opening at the S end of the W wall.

Inside, the tower arch is Tudor, with emphatic convex quadrant mouldings. The obtusely pointed chancel arch, wide but not high, with two broad chamfers dying into the imposts, may be pre-Perp. N stair to the rood loft. The two-bay arcade to the N chapel looks late C16. Depressed, four-centred arches, double-chamfered, set on a central octagonal pier with sub-classical capital, fluted and rope-moulded. Above, a reset stiff-leaf corbel. Does this confirm the origin of the chapel in the C13? The barn-like chapel roof is probably Lansdowne's. The unfortunate scraping of the walls took place in 1921. – FONT. Medieval, but of what century? Is it made up? The two-stage square bowl passes by means of spurs and ribbing down to an octagonal stem on a circular base. – STAINED GLASS. Nave S, Virgin between SS James and John. 1901 by *Kempe*. – Nave N, SS Ambrose and Augustine of Hippo. 1902 by *Kempe*. – Chancel E, Christ the King between SS Michael and Peter. 1916 by *Kempe & Co.* – Chancel S, Good Shepherd between SS Stephen and Lawrence. 1905 by *Heaton, Butler & Bayne*. – MONUMENTS. Nothing survives of the monuments for which the N chapel was built. Even the ambitious Elizabethan monument for which it may have been remodelled is a wretched fragment. Side panels decorated with drops of fruit, shields and tablets, shield of arms of Morgan at the top and a text from Philippians. – Martin Kuyck van Meirop †1775 (N chapel). Neoclassical hanging wall monument. Black pyramid between urns, in a heavy stone frame. – Mary Kemeys †1798 (N chapel). Circular inscription panel below a draped urn.

In the CHURCHYARD, part of the octagonal shaft of a medieval CROSS, on a spurred base and four renewed steps.

Llantarnam is a main-road village which has not quite been absorbed into Cwmbran. THE GREEN HOUSE INN, facing the road S of the church, is a handsome three-bay, early C18 house, dated 1719. The upper windows, timber casements, are original, the wider lower windows under hoodmoulds were clearly enlarged in the early C19.

LLANTARNAM ABBEY, ½m. SE. A Cistercian abbey was founded in 1179 by Hywel ap Iorwerth, Welsh lord of Caerleon. Early references are to Caerleon Abbey, and the community may not have settled at Llantarnam until the late C13. All that remains of that period is the great eleven-bay stone BARN, *c.* 200 yds (183 metres) NW of the present house. It is roofless and ivy-clad, but its walls survive almost intact. Central threshing bay framed by stub walls. All the other bays are ventilated by long slits reaching almost to the present ground level. These are formed with carefully cut stone and have bold inward splays. The W gable-end is pierced by slits at three levels, the E one opened up by a wide, four-centred, presumably early C19 arch. Three flying buttresses barely restrain the E end of the N wall from collapse.

The abbey was dissolved in 1536. Its lands were purchased in 1554 by William Morgan of Caerleon, who constructed a house, presumably making use of some of the monastic buildings. Archdeacon Coxe, who visited in 1799, found a 'large antiquated mansion, damp, dreary [which] having been long untenanted exhibits an appearance of gloom and decay', and noted the date 1588 on the porch. The eventual heir of the Morgan estates was Reginald James Blewitt, who in 1834–5 reconstructed the mansion largely to the Elizabethan design (see the sketch in Bradney, vol. III, pt 2, p. 238). His architect was the young *T. H. Wyatt*, who was thus introduced to Monmouthshire, where he would be almost continuously active for the next forty years.

The estate was bought in 1895 by Sir Clifford Cory, of the Cardiff coal-shipping family, and in 1946 came into the possession of the Sisters of St Joseph, who returned it to monastic use, and for whom various additions, including a large chapel, have been made between 1952 and 1984.

The park is entered from the A4042 through *T. H. Wyatt*'s PORTH MAWR (main gate), dated 1836. Two four-centred-headed archways, large for carriages, small for pedestrians, faced with Bath stone ashlar, an impressive extravagance. Internal stone rib vault on head corbels. Well-carved central leaf boss. To the r. a polygonal buttress with spy slit and crowning eagle, to the l. a diminutive gate lodge, provided with a canted window bay to the front and an oriel at the back.

The handsome wooded park was bisected in 1994–5 by the Cwmbran bypass, under which the drive to the house makes its ignominious way. So the picture presented by the entrance front
112 of the HOUSE and its FORECOURT is all the more delightful, apparently unaltered since 1836. Two step-topped ARCHWAYS of Bath stone span the drive, one in the N forecourt wall, the other in the W. Both retain their cast-iron gates, scrolly cresting and crowning polygonal lamp-holders. The strongly off-centre placing of the archways ensures that the visitor first sees the

mass of the house obliquely, for the architect must have been anxious to mitigate the sheer, artless bulk of the reconstructed Elizabethan house. The house is an L in plan, a long arm enclosing the E side of the court, a short, canted-ended arm the S side. Both are three-storeyed, battlemented and faced with exceedingly smooth Bath stone ashlar. Wyatt added a rendered polygonal turret, rising barely higher than the rest, to terminate each range. The N turret is capped by a lead-covered ogee dome set within a fringe of pinnacles and semicircular battlements. Off-centre, pinnacled porch of three storeys in the W front, and to the r. of it, two double-height mullion-and-transom windows of three wide lights, clearly to illuminate the hall. Otherwise the windows are monotonously mullioned, of four arched lights under hoodmoulds. The only rogue (a Wyatt embellishment) is an oriel top l., set on heavy corbels and under a shaped gable. Over the secondary doorway in the S range, a handsome cartouche of arms with strapwork detail in the surround and the date 1637, re-cut in the C19. On it, a metal knocker, with pierced Gothic decoration and a small central relief of the Virgin and Child. This bears the date 1516 in Roman numerals, and has been taken to be a relic of the Cistercian abbey. The suspicious, however, will consider it an early C19 confection.

The S front of the house is rendered. In the centre, the only element of Wyatt's house visible on this side is a two-storey canted window bay, very fully glazed, and above it a shaped gable bearing a squirrel, emblem of the Cistercian abbey. The lower gabled bay to the r. was added for a dining room. To the r. of that, replacing a conservatory, a large CHAPEL, 1957 by *F. R. Bates, Son & Price*. This makes no attempt to ape the style of the house, though the firm's Modernism has been restrained in deference to it. Random polychrome local stone and brown brick. (Concrete parabolic arches span the interior.) The three-storey RESIDENTIAL BLOCK extending S-wards from the SW corner of the house, 1966 by the same architects, is of no particular interest. The rear (E) of the main range is gabled, and attached to it is *Wyatt*'s single-storey SERVICE COURT. A second storey was tactfully added in 1952. Notice how the approach to the service court snakes between high, rubble-stone walls and under another ashlar four-centred arch.

Inside the house Mr Blewitt's taste wavered. The HALL, originally double-height, but its ceiling lowered for the Sisters of St Joseph, has a Jacobean-style chimneypiece and overmantel. The DRAWING ROOM, which opens from its S end and is lit by the S window bay, is clumsily Rococo. The style is maintained by the buff marble chimneypiece, the wall panels, the double doors to the hall, even the monogrammed window pelmet, but is transgressed by the strapwork ceiling with central openwork pendant. At the W end of the range another, smaller room with a strapwork ceiling, and S of it, the awkwardly placed principal stair. This is of C17 type, rising in an open well, the balusters turned, the square newels decorated with strapwork. It probably incorporates C17 elements.

Finally, the GARDEN. The low stone enclosure walls of Wyatt's garden remain, with moulded coping and one or two cast-iron gates into the park beyond. Angle bastions to the SE and SW, in which life-size STATUES are set, one a pilgrim, the other a musketeer in a plumed helmet. Are they C17 in origin? (In the KITCHEN GARDEN to the E, a C19 life-size figure of a monk, kneeling in prayer. It came from a grotto constructed *c.* 1905 by Sir Clifford Cory W of the house, where he brought together all the fragments he could find of the medieval abbey. They are now dispersed again.)

PENTREBACH FARM, 2 m. SW. Pentrebach belonged to the Morgans of Llantarnam Abbey, who seem to have built here on quite a large scale. What survives is of two parts, both unusual. The long, two-storeyed W range, of stone, is of the mid C16, as its three lower and two upper stone mullioned windows, with arched lights, suggest. (Three-storeyed N porch.) The E cross range, much taller and originally of three storeys, with narrow gabled projections to N and S, is of red brick, with corbelled upper chimney-breasts suggesting a date certainly not later than the mid C17. It is in fact probably a good deal earlier. Its builder is likely to have been Edward Morgan (1548–1633),* whose intransigent recusancy led to his paying no less than £7,900 in fines between 1606 and his death. If he built before the fines began to be imposed this would be an exceptionally early use of brick in the county (the C15 brickwork at Raglan Castle alone being earlier). Subsequently, the large, presumably mullion-and-transom windows were blocked, floors were removed and the entire range converted into a mighty barn. The building and its history deserve detailed investigation.

MOTTE, 1 m. SE. Beside the by-road and grazed close, so the typical form of the C12 earthwork is readily comprehended. Conical mound surrounded by ditch and bank.

LLANTHONY/LLAN HONDDU

The Vale of Ewyas, enfolded in the Black Mountains, retains a remoteness which makes it easy to understand why it was attractive 900 years ago to the founders of a religious community. The broad, green valley bottom proclaims fertility, and the steep-sided enclosing ridges confirm seclusion. The founders of the priory were two high-ranking hermits. Shortly before 1100, William de Lacy, a relative of Hugh de Lacy, Lord of Ewyas, while out hunting, came upon a ruined chapel of St David, where he was inspired to abandon courtly life and devote himself to a life of solitary prayer and study. In 1103 Ersinius, a former chaplain to Queen Matilda, wife of Henry I, joined him. They soon gathered a band of disciples, and built a church dedicated to St John the Baptist, which was consecrated in 1108. A decade later, probably with the Queen's

* The only other possible builders, Edward's grandsons William †1641 and Henry †1662, were 'of Pentrebach', but, being styled merely 'gent.', could hardly have had the social standing to justify construction of such an ambitious house.

encouragement, a group of canons from newly founded Augustinian houses in south-east England were invited to assist in the foundation of Llanthony as a priory of Augustinian canons, the first in Wales. With the death of Henry I in 1135, the priory, an outpost of Norman influence, became a target for the native Welsh, and the canons retreated across the Severn to Gloucester, where a cell, Llanthony Secunda, was established. It was only the loyalty of a few to the mother house, and its endowment with Irish estates by a second member of the de Lacy family, Hugh, the fifth baron (†1186), which saved the first Llanthony from being abandoned. The Irish revenues were devoted to rebuilding the priory church on a splendid scale, though work may not have begun until after the death in 1189 of prior Roger of Norwich, the third of the three priors who, according to Gerald of Wales, despoiled the church. It was still far from finished in 1205, when the revenues from the church of Duleek in County Meath were allocated to building the priory church over the following twelve years. Even in its ruined state, it is a remarkable example of the Transitional style from Norman into early Gothic. Whether there was a break in construction midway through the building programme and a change of design, as has been long asserted, can only be established on close examination of the church. The remains of the claustral buildings show that they were completed later in a mature E.E. style.

The subsequent fortunes of the priory ebbed and flowed. The early C14 seems to have been a period of prosperity, its early rights being confirmed in 1324–5. Renewed building seems to have taken place around that time, most notably the construction of a new gatehouse in the SW corner of the precinct. But by the mid C15 the priory seems barely to have been functioning, and in 1481 it was formally merged with its daughter house in Gloucester. Both houses were suppressed in 1538.

Welsh Llanthony and its estates were acquired by Nicholas Arnold of Llanfihangel Crucorney, and in the early C18 passed, along with Llanfihangel, to the Harley family, earls of Oxford. Part of the medieval infirmary was during this period converted into a parish church, St David's. Nothing, of course, was done to arrest the gradual dilapidation of the monastic buildings, though at least its remoteness preserved the church itself from systematic robbing. The process of decay can be followed in a series of prints and drawings, starting with the Bucks' views of 1732. The E window fell out after 1777, the W lancets collapsed in 1803, and in 1808 the top stage of the crossing tower was taken down. By then, however, Llanthony had been acquired by a more interventionist owner. Colonel Sir Mark Wood, who bought the estate in 1799, converted the SW tower into a shooting box, and the W range into a house for his steward. The present hotel is their successor. He sold the estate in 1807 to Walter Savage Landor, better known as a poet than as a landowner. Landor's attempts to transform Llanthony into a Picturesque feature in a landscaped park with a new mansion house were a failure, and were abandoned in 1813, yet they still make their mark on the landscape (*see* below, p. 350). The final collapse in the church took place in 1837, when four piers of the nave S

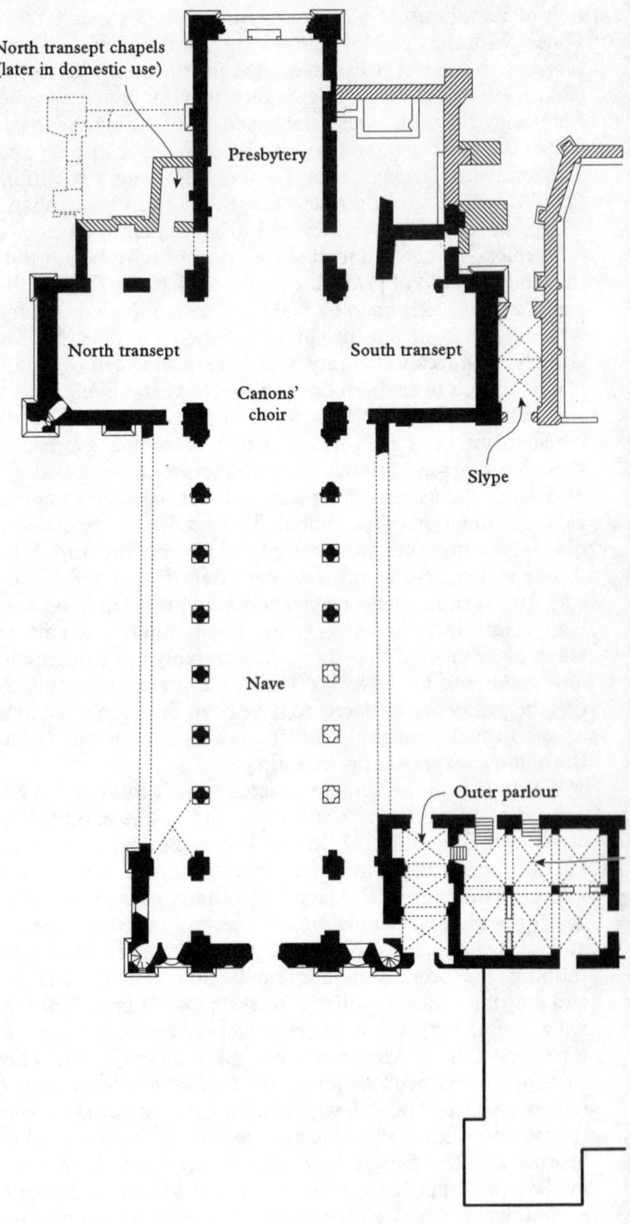
North transept chapels
(later in domestic use)
Presbytery
North transept
South transept
Canons'
choir
Slype
Nave
Outer parlour

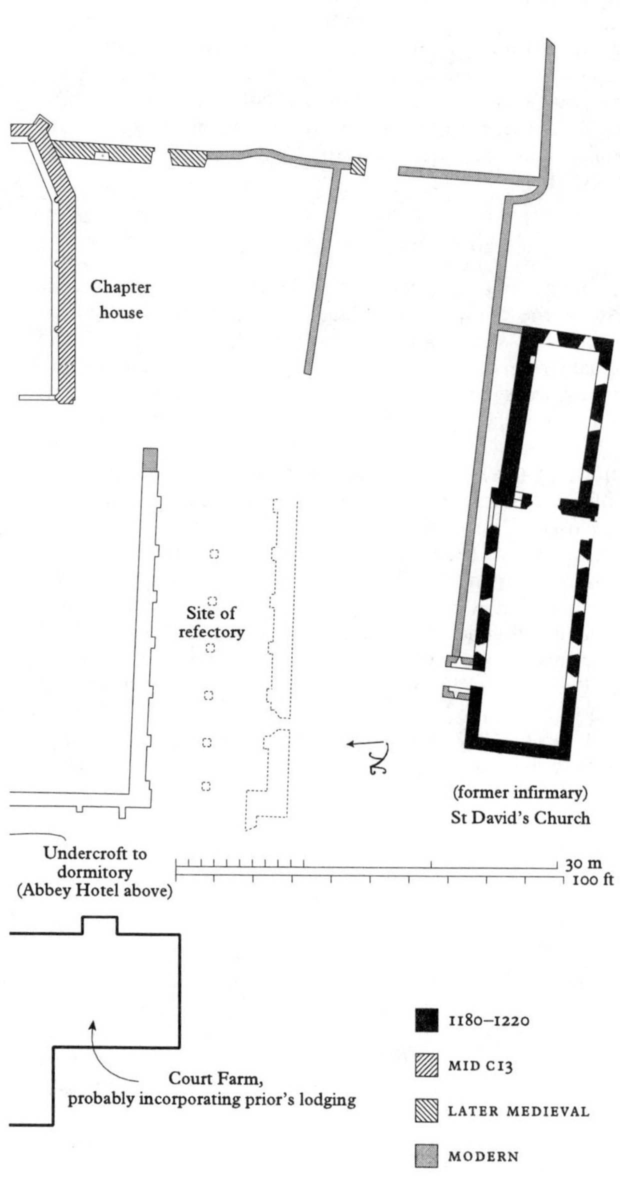

Llanthony Priory. Plan

arcade fell down. Thereafter the building was first propped and then reinforced. The crossing tower was strengthened in 1936–7. In 1951 the ruins were placed in the guardianship of the state, and a programme of consolidation and excavation began. Today, a happy equilibrium is maintained between Cadw's guardianship of the ruins, the Abbey Hotel's tactful occupation of the range converted by Colonel Wood, and the agricultural activities which emanate from Court Farm to the SW. Except at weekends and bank holidays, the remoteness of the Vale of Ewyas can still be powerfully felt.

THE MONASTIC CHURCH

Enough remains of the church to enable a fairly full mental reconstruction of the complete building. The three-bay presbytery survives in its NE corner almost to eaves level, enough to indicate the original fenestration. Of the crossing, the S and W arches stand and carry the walls of the crossing tower above them to half-height. The S transept is largely intact, though the N transept, except for its crag-like NE angle, has been largely reduced to its footings. In the N transept the original arrangement of paired E chapels is shown on the ground, although it was altered later both here and in the S transept. The seven-bay nave N arcade is complete, part of the triforium above it and a trace of the clerestory. The whole composition is known from Wyndham's engraving of 1777. Of the S arcade, there is now much less, but enough to show that it was virtually identical. The W bay of the N aisle keeps its vault. Only of the nave aisle walls is there nothing left. The W towers, set in the W bay of each aisle, have lost a top stage, and the trio of lancets in the W wall of the nave is known only from C18 views. The inner faces of the W bays preserve the profile of the nave vault. The W front remains a fairly coherent design, in spite of the yawning gap in the middle. The total internal length is 210 ft (64 metres).

E.W. Lovegrove, in his detailed analysis of 1943, emphasized a break in construction which he observed one bay W of the crossing, and a change of style at that point. The Ministry of Public Building and Works (Department of the Environment) guidebook has followed this interpretation; but the recent rethinking of the documentary evidence for the building (*see* above) makes a long break midway through construction unlikely, and a walk through the building with an eye on the forms of its architecture, rather than on the constructional details, gives the impression that the church of Llanthony Priory was built to a single, unified design. The exceptional detailing of the crossing and the E bay of the nave must have a functional explanation, rather than relating to a change in design. Whoever worked out the design was doubtless familiar with the great West Country churches of the last quarter of the C12, in particular the W bays of the nave of Worcester Cathedral (1175–80), Wells Cathedral transepts and nave (from about 1180) and Glastonbury Abbey (begun 1184). The trumpet-scallop capitals of Worcester, the continuous roll moulding to outline arches, such a memorable feature of Wells, and the insouciant inclusion of round arches in a generally pointed-arched design, familiar from Glastonbury, all occur throughout the church at Llanthony, as does the use of triple shafts, the central one keeled, and capitals with square or polygonal abaci, leitmotifs of all the great West Country models. At Llanthony, however, small and remote by comparison, everything is subjected to a systematic and appropriate simplification. So, having established what to look out for, one can embark on detailed examination, beginning at the E end. The church is built of Old Red Sandstone, partly ashlar-faced and partly of rubble, with a certain amount of tufa. The lime mortar render which would have brought the latter to a smooth finish is all gone.

Description

The outer E wall of the presbytery was ashlar-faced, its strongly battered plinth crowned by a roll moulding. Broad pilaster buttresses clasp the angles. The full width between them above the plinth was originally occupied by a grand composition of lancets. Only the N jamb of the N-most survives, double-chamfered outside, and with two internal orders of shafts, the inner shaft keeled, the outer with a shaft-ring. What was the original composition is unknown, for in the early C14, as Herne's engraving of 1788 shows, the lancets were replaced by a single traceried window. The N tip of its hoodmould survives, and the reset trumpet-scallop capital and abacus below it must belong to an adjustment at the same time. In the NE angle a single shaft with trumpet-scallop capital carries the chamfered springer of the E-most bay of the presbytery vault, which clearly had a steeply pointed profile. The side walls of the presbytery are of rubble outside and in, with ashlar pilaster buttresses and an internal dado moulding in the form of an undercut roll continuing round all three sides. Of the lancets which stood on the roll, one in each bay, only the N lancet in the E bay survives, long and narrow, with reconstructed semicircular head. The vault shafts against the N and S walls are the standard trios, the centre shaft keeled, the capitals emphatic trumpet-scallops with chamfered polygonal abaci. The circular, waterholding bases, however, have been shown to be later C13 insertions, when the floor level was raised. The only other surviving feature in the presbytery is the S doorway in the W bay, giving access to the S transept chapel. This is round-headed under a hoodmould, with a continuous chamfer and an inner square order resting on short corbel shafts with trumpet-scallop capitals.

TRANSEPTS. The S TRANSEPT is the only part of the priory church where the walls survive virtually to their full height and provide a real sense of enclosure. They are internally rubble-faced, and divided at mid-height by an undercut string, partly surviving on the E wall, but hacked back on the S wall, where it formed a sill to the two great round-headed lancets. The lancets are double-chamfered inside and out. The oculus in the gable above is double-chamfered only outside, since it was originally invisible from the interior of the transept but lit the roof space above the vault. The transept was vaulted in two bays, as can be seen by the slender angle shafts with trumpet-scallop capitals from which the vaults sprang. Externally, the transept has broad, ashlar pilaster buttresses with broad set-offs. The E wall of the transept is opened up by a high and wide round-headed arch under a hoodmould. It is chamfered and has a square, corbelled inner order, exactly like the SW doorway in the presbytery. Yet it cannot be an original feature, since it cuts through the mid-height stringcourse. The stonework of its N springing point from the SE crossing pier also shows disturbed masonry where the arch was inserted. It seems that twin arches into what were originally two transept chapels were later in the C13 cleverly reconstructed as one. Round-headed recess S of the arch, of uncertain purpose. The enlarged chapel itself seems to have been of three bays, of which the W bay largely survives. Large blocked S lancet here, and the r. jamb of the central S lancet. The best evidence for the mid-C13 date of this work is in the vault supports. On both the N and S walls vault springers survive. They have hollow-moulded ribs and rest on round, moulded caps on filleted triple shafts. In the SW angle, however, a reset corbel shaft with trumpet-scallop cap. A second trumpet-scallop cap below it, carrying a plain chamfered springer which must have belonged to the vault of the original chapel. The line of the two-bay vault of this chapel can be seen against the N wall. At the E end, footings of the later C13 altar, and a hole in the N wall where there was a cupboard.

The remains of the N TRANSEPT, though scanty, can nevertheless tell us a little more. Here the lowest courses of the chamfered jambs remain of the paired entrances into the two chapels which originally opened from the E wall of the transept. A C13 GRAVE SLAB, tapered and carved with a foliated St Andrew's cross-head, is laid in the SW angle of the outer chapel. In the N wall of the outer chapel, remains of a cupboard. The N transept and its chapels were excavated in 1978–9 and the footings of the original early C12 church found underlying the present structure. The footings have been left partly exposed. They show that the earlier church was on a similar scale to the present one, but not quite on the same alignment. The excavations also revealed the surprising later history of this part of the church. In the mid C13 a start was made in reconstructing the two chapels as one larger one, in the same way as in the S transept. Remains of the new E wall, further E than the original, built up against the buttress of the choir wall. However, this project seems to have been abandoned, and from the mid C14 the transept and its chapels were apparently put to domestic uses, the transept converted into a kitchen, and the chapels into a series of small rooms.

CROSSING. Turning now to the CROSSING, one can look up first to the tower. Only the lower half of the W and S sides survives, but that is enough to convey something of the treatment here, sober but clearly of decorative intent. Originally there were three tiers of three openings on each side. The lowest, originally visible only inside, is of plainly chamfered, round-headed openings. Wall passage at this level. Against the outer W face a larger, pointed-headed opening, in the apex of the roof gable. The next stage has openings which outside are double-chamfered and alternate with single-chamfered blind recesses. Inside, the openings are single-chamfered with intermediate paired shafts, an unexpected departure from the trios in which shafts are used elsewhere. Wall passage at this level too. C18 engravings show that the openings had round heads. They also record a top stage with paired, pointed openings. The tower rests on bold, wide, pointed arches, those to the S (and formerly N) slightly but significantly differentiated from those to the W (and formerly E). The S arch and the W springer of the N arch have three orders of chamfers, the outer two carried right round uninterrupted, the innermost resting on corbels with the now familiar triple corbel shafts with trumpet-scallop caps and polygonal abaci. The only unfamiliar feature about them is that the shafts rest on cautiously carved foliage sprigs. The W arch, and the S springer of the E arch, by contrast, have a square outer order which dies into the wall, a chamfered middle order supported on a boldly modelled horizontal bracket, and an inner order resting on a shafted corbel just like those to S and N, and set at the same height, that is to say higher than the horizontal sections. The faces of the piers below all this are of plain ashlar. The explanation of this arrangement must be that the canons' stalls stood here, under the tower, a perfectly normal position in monastic churches, the tops of the stalls fitting neatly under the horizontal brackets. The outbreak of foliage at the bases of the corbels may also be explained by their ready visibility from the stalls.

NAVE. Passing into the NAVE we find many of the same motifs, but in different relationships, and one important new one. The nave is of eight bays, with narrow aisles flanking seven of them, and a longer W-most bay set between the W towers. The arcade 11
of sharply pointed arches is ashlar-faced, but the triforium above has rubble walls. The E-most bay of the arcade repeats the system of the S and N crossing arches, having no fewer than four chamfered orders, the outermost treated like a hoodmould, the middle two continuous and the inner one carried on single-shafted corbels with enriched trumpet-scallop caps and embryonic parsley-like foliage, comparable to that in the crossing. This suggests that the choir stalls were intended to extend across this E bay of the nave. The doorways instead of arches at the E end of both aisles indicate that the canons' area could be closed off from the nave; and the return stalls and a timber screen could have provided an equally effective barrier across the nave, but one bay further W.

The remaining bays of the nave arcade shift unobtrusively to a different design, in which two continuous chamfers frame a continuous roll set in the re-entrant angle between them. Each roll comes down on to a circular moulded base of flat waterholding type, below which the Greek cross plan of the pier is deftly resolved into a square. Towards the aisles triple-shafted corbels with trumpet-scallop caps and polygonal abaci support the chamfered springers of the aisle vault ribs. Over the seventh bay of the N aisle the stone vault itself with chamfered ribs largely survives. Above, the triforium was expressed with twin pointed openings outlined by continuous rolls, and framed between vertical chamfers, as is fully shown by one surviving example near the E end on the N side and another at the W end on the S. The similarity with the treatment of the transept triforium at Wells is suggestive. The round-headed outer arches of the triforium were originally hidden within the roof space of the aisles, as the crease-line of the aisle roof on the E face of the NW tower makes clear. The clerestory has virtually disappeared, but the E faces of both towers provide some clues as to the way it was arranged. There was a wall passage at this level, and the vertical chamfers noted at triforium level rose to encompass the clerestory openings, which, as Wyndham's engraving shows, were round-headed. The pointed profile of the vaults above is indicated by the wall-mouldings which survive against the inner faces of the W towers. Here the vaults are supported on full-height triple wall-shafts with trumpet-scallop capitals. No trace of the vaults themselves, which suggests that the high vaults, unlike those in the aisles, were of timber or tufa and have disappeared without trace. In all the bays further E, instead of wall-shafts, triple-shafted corbels at triforium level, stopped just below the continuous string which runs across, clasping them, and marks the break between ashlar and rubble walling. Again there are echoes of Wells, in the way the clerestory wall-shafts are handled. The unification of triforium and clerestory, on the other hand, looks to Glastonbury, or even Worcester, as does the continuing preference for trumpet-scallop caps in favour of further experiments with their development as foliage.

13 WEST FRONT. The WEST FRONT brings together all the familiar motifs in a strong and coherent composition which must have made a splendidly self-confident statement when it was intact. It is wholly ashlar-faced, and enough plain, smooth stonework is left to set off the blind arcading which is the main form of decoration. Sculpture is nowhere admitted, so that the continuous roll mouldings which outline almost every element gain remarkable force. The façade is virtually flat and divided into three almost equal parts, the W front of the nave set between N and S towers which project only by the depth of their angle pilaster buttresses. These buttresses are extremely broad, so the tower faces are also divided into three almost equal parts. They rise from battered bases, undiminished in width through three stages, and originally continued on for at least one further stage, now entirely lost. Angle nook-shafts spring from above the lowest stage and continue right up. The outer buttress of each tower is plain except for a succession of slit windows for newel stairs. The inner buttresses have a plain lowest stage, but the shallow middle stage and the tall top stage are both decorated with pairs of blind

roll-moulded lancets, the upper ones exceedingly elongated. Horizontal roll mouldings define the various stages, integrating the buttresses with the intermediate wall face. Here, at the lowest stage, pairs of pointed niches outlined with a single inner and a pair of outer rolls. The stage above is occupied by the aisle W windows. These are round-headed, as also is the window on the return face of the N tower at this level. The W windows, but not the N, are again roll-moulded beyond deep chamfered splays, and have hoodmoulds, the S one on crude headstops. Above, in the tall top stage, blind arcading, triple shafts carrying trumpet-scallop caps, polygonal abaci and small, pointed, roll-moulded arches. One anomalous capital on the S tower sprouts into leaves and has a square abacus.

Between the towers only the bottom stage survives. In the centre, a broad, pointed-headed doorway outlined by three orders of rolls, the central one keeled, but all now hacked away. A fourth, outermost roll survives, and fuses with the outermost rolls of the blind arches which flank the doorway. These arches are idiosyncratically designed, with shallowly curved backs, continuous rolls, and a broad, plain outer band with radiating voussoirs. The spandrel area above this composition is completely plain below the roll which forms the sill of the next stage. Sadly, there is now no next stage, just a yawning rectangular gap, from which the great triple lancets toppled in 1803. What remains are the outer jambs of the outer lancets, embellished with two-plus-one shafts set *en échelon*. The mid-height roll continues over them to form shaft-rings. They have the inevitable trumpet-scallop capitals. The lancet jamb itself is, by contrast, a plain, continuous chamfer. This is just enough to show that these lancets were extremely lofty, and that they were set back deeply, giving the centre of the W front a modelled character in contrast to the surrounding flat surfaces. Internally, the lancets have two shafts *en échelon*.

THE MONASTIC BUILDINGS

The canons' cloister lay in the normal arrangement on the S side of the nave of the priory church. Nothing of the cloister itself survives, but the remains of the ranges sited on its W, S and E sides indicate its scale, commensurate with the church, and further evidence of the considerable size of the community in the early C13. The roof-height of the E range is indicated by the corbels for its wall-plate and the drip-mould above.

Part of the WEST RANGE is incorporated in the Abbey Hotel, successor to the 'shooting box' fitted up *c.* 1800 by Mark Wood here and in the SW tower of the church. The crease-line of the original roof is visible on the S side of the SW tower, at a much higher level than the present roof. So the upper storey of the range, presumably occupied by the canons' dormitory, has entirely disappeared. However, a narrow ground-floor room next to the tower does survive from the early C13 structure. It was probably the OUTER PARLOUR, which had a W doorway, now blocked and converted into a window. The doorway is trefoil-headed, and its outer face is quite elaborately treated with two continuous keeled rolls, a round-headed superarch and stiff-leaf sprigs in the spandrels thus formed. Semicircular hood-mould. These are motifs not found in the church, suggesting that the W range belonged to a slightly later phase. The outer parlour is groin-vaulted internally in three bays running E–W. To the S of this, at a lower level, is a groin-vaulted UNDERCROFT, three bays long and two wide, the exposed rubble vaults carried on square piers, their angle chamfers carried up to bold spear stops, their bases hidden below the present floor. The range above is largely a reconstruction *c.* 1800. Next to the W doorway of the outer parlour is a window of two pointed lights outlined with shallow continuous rolls.

Springers of the vault of the REFECTORY UNDERCROFT survive against the S side of the S wall of the cloister garth. The site of the S wall of the undercroft is known, suggesting that it was two bays deep and probably seven bays long.

The remains of the buildings which opened from the E cloister range are much more eloquent. The SLYPE, a two-bay vaulted passage S of the end wall of the S transept, survives almost intact. It is clearly an addition to the transept, and in style partly matches the church, but is partly more developed. The E arch is lost except for its lowest courses, but was merely decorated with a poorly defined roll moulding. The handsome rib vault rests on shafted corbels with the familiar trumpet-scallop caps and polygonal abaci, but the vault ribs have paired filleted ribs. Small bosses of quite developed stiff-leaf foliage. The W entrance arch to the slype is in a fully mature E.E. style. The strongly pointed arch is moulded with a broad chamfer and a small roll and hood. It was supported on jambs round which clustered trios of detached shafts with shaft-rings, spare but fully developed stiff-leaf capitals and polygonal moulded abaci.

The CHAPTER HOUSE immediately adjoins to the S. The triple arches at its entrance are sadly reduced to their lowest courses, but what remains of the outermost jambs indicates a rich design of five detached shafts, set *en échelon* on each jamb two-plus-one-plus-two, standing on circular, waterholding bases. Much-worn limestone blocks of Dundry type are all that remain of what must have been their stiff-leaf capitals. The walls of the chapter house itself survive to a considerable height. It was a large and handsome rectangular room vaulted in three bays, with an unusual half-hexagonal fourth bay to the E. Internally, the walls are divided into a high dado and a main wall set back above with a high-set lancet in each bay. Part of one lancet survives to indicate this. The bays are internally demarcated by triple wall-shafts, the central one filleted, on circular, water-holding bases. The dado sill moulding is taken across the shafts to form shaft-rings. Above dado level, detached shafts, now gone, framed each bay.

The exterior treatment of the chapter house can be deduced from what survives of its SE facet. Here there is part of a buttress decorated with a heavy, undercut sill. The chamfered sill of the lancet window and a keeled string below also remain. The jambs of the surviving lancet are plainly chamfered.

Back at the entrance to the chapter house there is one further feature to trace. Immediately to the S was another wide and richly decorated doorway. Its N jamb has very worn limestone stiff-leaf caps, aligned with the caps of the chapter house arches. Circular base and abacus, and the springing of a multimoulded arch. What this doorway gave access to is not clear.

COURT FARM, W of the W cloister range (Abbey Hotel), may have been built as the PRIOR'S LODGING. T-plan. The two storeys of sash windows in its W wall make the S range look entirely Victorian, but there is clearly older walling between the windows, and the continuous base moulding looks medieval. The shorter cross range to the N is clearly of a different build. Its W gable-end has a central projecting chimney-breast with small rectangular windows set symmetrically at the three levels to l. and r. (lowest r. converted in the C19 into a doorway for a granary). Trace of an upper blocked window at the E end of the N wall. The most telling survival is inside the roof of this range. A boldly moulded wall-plate crowns the wall-heads and runs across the top of a post-and-panel partition, which once divided the space below into a larger (W) and smaller (E) room. A tie-beam in the larger room, triply hollow-moulded on its soffit, with a moulded socket for a cross-beam, shows that this room had a flat ceiling with interlocking moulded beams. There must have been here a handsome late C15 chamber.

ST DAVID. The church stands across the road S of the cloister. It was fitted up as a church after the Dissolution, using part of the late C12 infirmary as its nave, and the infirmary chapel as its chancel. The round heads to the windows must all be post-medieval. Inside it is clear that the windows in the nave, all three N and the two W-most S, were originally carried up above the present eaves line. Blocked doorways in the nave, two S and one C14 one at the E end of the N wall. C19 N porch and doorway. The internal recesses in the W wall of the nave have been interpreted as fireplaces related to the infirmary use. The large C14 chancel arch, with bold continuous hollow and chamfer, is rebated on its E side for doors. The church was restored by *J. James Spencer* of Bath in 1886–7, when the arch-braced nave roof was constructed. – FONT. Medieval. Plain octagonal bowl. – ALTAR RAILS. C18. Turned balusters. – STAINED GLASS. Nave N window by *Celtic Studios*, 1985. Dove of the Holy Spirit. – MONUMENTS. A wonderful array of rustic wall tablets in the chancel, ranging in date from 1723 to 1854. Some of the later ones are signed, by *Thomas Roberts* and by *Joseph Prichard* of Longtown. Also one by *J. Brute*, †1816.

To the S of the infirmary lay a square walled enclosure, identified by excavation. Footings exposed SE of St David's Church. Further S, part of a ruined circular DOVECOTE, in the SW angle of the enclosure. It is lined with nesting boxes right down to ground level.

GATEHOUSE, 150 yds (137 metres) W of the priory church, beside the road. Clearly part of a complex of buildings. The gatehouse was built in the early C14, but extended and brutally adapted after the Dissolution for use as a barn. In the gable-end towards the road, a full-width arch with two-centred head, plainly chamfered, and above it a handsome group of three lancets, the outer ones trefoil-headed with sunk quadrant moulding, the central one taller and given a hoodmould. Internally, the gatehouse consisted of a narrow front bay, and a deeper rear bay, but the cross wall between them, with double-chamfered cart arch and foot arch, has been crudely hacked away. Both bays were prepared for vaulting, the corbels in the front bay intended to be carved. At the inner end, a second full-width arch, double-chamfered. Over it, evidence of a heated room, the flue for a large central fireplace, and trefoiled rebated windows to l. and r. Further evidence in the W side wall near the entrance of upper-level accommodation. Part of a doorway, and on the outer face a skewed arch to support it, and lancet window adjoining. The ruined building attached to the SW has similar evidence. Further W, beside the road, a long unpierced wall ending in a square turret-like projection. To the E of the gatehouse there must have been further structures in the Outer Court – see the E wall-stub in the gatehouse itself and bumps in the grass further E.

Y SIÂRPAL, ½ m. E. Walter Savage Landor, between acquiring the estate in 1807 and being declared bankrupt in 1813, was intermittently at work building himself a house on the hillside above the priory. Substantial walls remain in the undergrowth, but not enough to trace with any certainty the drawing room, library, dining room and twelve bedrooms which the house was said to comprise in 1811. More significant is Landor's contribution to the landscape. He planted trees on a grand scale, and many of the mature beeches and chestnuts, and particularly the broad avenue to the ruins of his house, still stand.

LLANTILIO CROSSENNY/
3010 LLANDEILO GRESYNNI

In the Middle Ages Llantilio Crossenny was a manor belonging to the bishops of Llandaff. *See* Hen Gwrt below. Furthermore, White Castle (q.v.) stands in the parish. Both these facts must help to explain the exceptional scale of the church.

ST TEILO. An unusually grand cruciform church, built of roughly coursed Old Red Sandstone and crowned by a landmark shingled spire. The crossing tower is of the C13, the aisled nave of *c.* 1300, both E.E. in character. The chancel is decisively Dec, clearly rebuilt in the early C14, at the same time as the N transept was incorporated into a spacious N chancel chapel. The S transept has a S window with Y-tracery and tiny rectangular lights high to the E, evidence of an upper chamber. Later high-level additions: a clerestory to the nave in the late Middle Ages, the spire in 1708–9. *Prichard & Seddon*'s restoration of 1856–7, initiated by Col. H.M. Clifford in memory of his son (*see* churchyard below), introduced two-light E.E. windows into the S aisle, small square-headed ones in the N aisle and a new W doorway. Gabled W porch.

Inside, the nave is limewashed white, high and uniform. Handsome four-bay arcades, octagonal piers with shapely moulded caps incorporating S-curved forms, two-centred arches with two broad chamfers. Narrow aisles, each retaining its original W lancet. The crossing tower stands on wide but low, two-centred arches with two continuous chamfers, one broad, one narrow. The rood-loft stair above the W crossing arch provided an approach to the rood which led not upwards but precipitously downwards. Within the tower the floor of the ringing chamber is of 1708–9, supported on four massive corner-posts.

The chancel walls, scraped internally, give evidence of a complicated history. Many typical early C14 details in chancel and N chapel and on the three low arches between them, presumably for monuments. Intersecting tracery in the three-light SE window and the three-light chancel E window, the latter cusped. Internal sunk chamfers on both, and also on the E arch between chancel and chapel. The rere-arch of the chapel E window further enriched, with ballflower in the sunk chamfer. Unfortunately, the tracery here is a Perp replacement. Other Dec features are the handsome cinquefoiled PISCINA in the chancel, and in the N chapel the two corbel heads below the E window and the three-light N and W windows, with trefoils balanced on the ogee heads of the lights. The central arch between chancel and chapel is the most highly enriched feature. Low triple shafts with polygonal caps carry an arch moulded with hollows and quadrants and a broad central fillet. NW corbel head vividly carved as a Green Man with lolling tongue. 36

Finally, the S wall of the chancel shows traces of an internal upper room, perhaps a watching chamber to enable a priest or hermit who had his cell in the S transept to see mass at the main altar. See two blocked doorways at the junction of transept and chancel, a blocked upper doorway and in particular the corbels to support a floor at an upper level. Big, square-headed S chancel window, perhaps inserted at the same time to provide improved lighting. – FONT. Plain C12 tub. – PEWS. 1857 by *Seddon*, arranged in uninterrupted rows across the nave, to maximize visibility E-wards through the tower arches. – STAINED GLASS. Chancel E, Christ the King between St Luke and the Sower. 1960 by *Celtic Studios*. – One window in the N aisle by the same, 1958. – N chapel, three windows by *Kempe*: 1887, Gethsemane, 1898, Noli me Tangere, and 1909 (*Kempe & Co.*). – MONUMENTS. John Walderne, wife and three sons. Floor slab at the W end of the chancel. Crude, low-relief figures. Said to have been dated 1620. – Charles Prosser. A similar, bushily bearded figure, and wife, dated 1621. – Hon. Thomas Medlycott †1738 (N chapel).

Hanging wall monument. Fluted Corinthian side pilasters carry lamps. – Jane Hughes †1815 (chancel). Oval tablet signed by *Reeves* of Bath, with Adamesque urn and two weeping willows. A typical provincial piece. – Mary Ann Bosanquet †1819 (chancel). Wall monument, a high-quality London work, signed by *Flaxman*. Typical of the fervid emotionalism of the early C19. Five distraught mourners at the deathbed, and Mrs Bosanquet's long-dead infant son descending as a cherub on rays of light. – Sir Henry Mather Jackson Bart, Q.C. †1881 (N chapel). Wall tablet by *H. H. Armstead* (Bradney). Roundel of blind Justice. Thick foliage surround. – Many small marble tablets of the early C19 scattered around the aisle walls, and one of local stone (†1791) signed by *James Jones* of Abergavenny.

In the CHURCHYARD four steps and the broached base for a medieval CROSS. Elaborate shaft and crucifix added as a First World War memorial. – MONUMENT. Henry S.M. Clifford †1856. Coped tomb-chest on which is laid a copper foliate cross. Finely lettered inscriptions. Surely by *Seddon* (T. Blackshaw).

LLANFAIR CILGOED CHAPEL. *See* p. 283.

WHITE CASTLE. *See* p. 596.

LLANTILIO COURT. Built in 1775 for John Lewis, but demolished in 1922. The park wall W of the churchyard and the specimen trees in the fields beyond are still potent reminders of it. (Traces of terraced gardens.) Farm range of *c.* 1800 with clock tower S of the church.

HEN GWRT, ¼m. NW. The well-preserved moated site of the manor house of the bishops of Llandaff. The grassy platform *c.* 165 ft (50 metres) square was excavated after 1941, when the site was taken into the guardianship of the Ministry of Public Building and Works. Traces were found of the timber-framed episcopal manor house and of the substantial C15–C16 stone hunting lodge of the Herberts which replaced it. One beam survives of a timber BRIDGE across the E arm of the moat.

At BRYNDERI, 1¾m. N, the former POWELL'S FREE GRAMMAR SCHOOL, built in 1820. A severe little Neoclassical design. Red brick. Five round-headed windows recessed under rubbed-brick arcading. Extension to the r. in a similar style, 1901 by *B. J. Francis* of Abergavenny.

TAL-Y-COED, 1¼m. E. The small, rendered farmhouse stands prettily against a wooded hillside. The l. half was identified by Fox and Raglan as in origin a one-bay, early C16, timber-framed house. The rest is of the first half of the C17, with two three-light upper windows to the front and the stairs in a square tower at the back.

GREAT CIL-LWCH, 1¼ SW. A full-scale late medieval open hall is a rarity in the county. Here most of the characteristic elements are present. To the W, a single-storey porch, its outer and inner arches both four-centred, with continuous sunk quadrant moulding. Half-timbered porch gable, a typical local touch. Matching E doorway in line, at the far end of the screens passage. The screens themselves have gone, but it is clear they supported a gallery over the passage, as is shown by the timber-framed wall above, with mortises for the joists of the gallery floor and a pair of blocked, four-centred-headed doorways, which originally gave access to it. The hall itself, opening to the N, is of four bays and retains the arch-braces and collar-beams of three roof trusses. C17 chimney-breast added against the N end wall, the fireplace opening with timber lintel and stone ovolo-moulded jambs. The hall windows are mostly of 1964–5, but see the original square-headed windows of one and two lights in the E wall. – STAINED GLASS. A fine, small figure of St George, late C15.

The gabled three-storey N and S cross ranges were added in the C17. In the W wall of the S range, the blocked depressed-headed doorway with simple chamfer may be contemporary with the hall. Adjoining the N range, an E stair projection. Both ranges have massive stacks with typical lozenge-set chimneys. Fenestration of these parts also of 1964–5. In the N range the ground-floor room has a late C17 decorated plaster ceiling of basic design, a circle between two rectangles with central rosette and diagonal sprigs. In the roof space of the S range fragments of a more ambitious, and probably earlier, plaster vault. Randomly disposed vine scrolls and small leopard and pelican in her piety.

TREADAM, 1¼ m. NW. The cluster of three houses, all of which display C17 timberwork inside, is the successor to a sizeable medieval hamlet. THE OLD COTTAGE, closest to the road, is the smallest but the best-preserved of the three. Built probably *c.* 1600. Old Red Sandstone walls and stone-slate roof. Two-room layout, both rooms with fireplaces, but not the usual gable-end entry. The r. doorway in the S side wall is original. The l. one replaces an eight-light timber mullioned window, which has been displaced upwards into a central gable. Originally there was no upper storey, only a habitable roof space. Post-and-panel partitions. The upper one must be brought in.

TREADAM FARM, behind, is a substantial house of two distinct phases, two-storeyed throughout. Reconstruction of most of the external walls in the 1990s has obscured the building history. Inside the E half, however, there remain four-centred-headed doorways, post-and-panel partitions and five-sided ceiling beams decorated with angle rolls. From these Fox and Raglan deduced that this half was built in the late C16 as an unconventionally planned cross wing to an earlier, perhaps late medieval, house, which in the late C17 was almost entirely replaced by the present W half. The massive stone fireplace in the W wall of this latter half, with a candle-bracket projecting above its r. jamb, probably survives from the early house.

Timber-framed BARN to the S, also of the C17, though much reconstructed, and converted 1998–9 into a concert room. Reused in it, part of a cruck, probably another tell-tale trace of the early house.

GREAT TREADAM, a little further to the S, presents a rendered, three-bay front of two storeys towards the road. This is early C19. Plain parapet. Doric timber porch. Inside, however, moulded timber ceiling beams show that the house itself was built probably in the first half of the C17 and had some pretensions.

GREAT TRE-RHIW, 2½ m. NW. One of the most completely surviving farmsteads in the county. The grey-rendered house is an L in plan, the W range originally a complete early to mid-C17 house. Near the l. end of the front, a heavy stone door-case with chamfered four-centred arch. Two original upper timber windows, four-lighters with ovolo mouldings.

But it is the farm buildings which really impress. They stand immediately to the E of the house, and are constructed of Old Red Sandstone rubble with slate roof coverings. The C17 BARN is of eight bays, its two N trusses of kingpost construction. At r.-angles to its W side, a pair of two-storeyed, gabled additions, the S one retaining its working cider mill and press, the N one a cattleshed and hay loft, said to have been dated 1696. Cattle stalls and chaff-bin in here. Adjoining to the N, a yard enclosed by cattle pens, their pent roofs carried on stout stone piers. Between this and the house, a GRANARY, with the usual flight of external steps to the upper storey.

At THE CROFT, two fields further E, another, even more remarkable C16 BARN, originally belonging to Great Tre-rhiw. It is of four bays, three open, the W one floored at mid-height. The trusses alternate between crucks and framed construction. The N wall even retains its weatherboarding below, and its upper ventilation panels of wattle interlace.

UPPER TRE-RHIW, 2½ m. NW. Here is the largest surviving C16 cruck-truss barn in the county, six bays long. The decaying corrugated iron cladding is unworthy of such an important structure.

CWMERAU, 3 m. NW. The tops of cruck trusses survive in the roof. The stone-walled house which incorporates them must be an early C17 reconstruction of the original timber-framed house. The N half, as far as the central chimney with lozenge stack, is a completely preserved two-unit structure of hall and inner parlour, with four-light sunk-chamfer windows front and back. The constraint in height imposed by the cruck trusses was overcome by raising a gable for a full upper storey over the hall. The S half, with cross-passage and service rooms, had an ovolo-moulded window, so its reconstruction must have come a little later. The second gable here is a recent addition. Inside, the S half was replanned in 1996–7, but the N half survives largely intact. From a cross-passage, the entrance through the thickness of the wall is so deep as to have outer and inner door-frames, the latter with simple shaped head. The mural stair twists up over it. Half the post-and-panel partition separating the hall from an unheated NE room survives, as does the cross-partition separating this room from the heated NW parlour, now thrown into one with the hall. Double-roll angle mouldings on the partitions and a shaped-headed doorway.

The flanking BARN and OUTBUILDING towards the road were sweepingly altered for new uses *c.* 1995. The former is dated on the roadward gable-end 1627.

LLANTILIO PERTHOLEY/ LLANDEILO BERTHOLAU

3010

The parish is unusually large and varied, extending to the slopes of four mountains, Bryn Arw to the N, Deri to the W, and Great and Little Skirrid to the E and S, respectively. The church, in the valley, stands secluded beneath the railway line, beyond the northern edge of Abergavenny's suburbs.

ST TEILO. Also unusually large and varied, of local Old Red Sandstone. Nave with aisles stopped short of the W end, and W of them, S porch and N tower. Chancel flanked to the N by an aisle and two chapels and to the S by a transeptal chapel. SW lean-to meeting room of 1981 by *R. Merton Jones*. Good Dec three-light E window in the N chancel aisle. Tower belfry windows pointed-headed with two cusped lights. S aisle wall and windows 1709, nave W window 1719, chancel E window 1872. Tower parapet 1890–1 by *Kempson & Fowler*.

Inside, the history of medieval growth is easier to read. The earliest part must be the aisleless W end of the nave. The pointed arch cut crudely through the wall E of the tower belongs to the beginning of a N aisle pushed out in the C13. The tower itself belongs to the early C14. Its large E arch into the aisle and smaller S arch into the nave are uniformly treated. The pattern is of ovolo-moulded imposts carried up high to support a flattened pointed arch and an inner arch, steeper and moulded with a sunk wave, dying into the imposts. A similar arch of the N arcade further E and the NE window already noted outside, even if they are a little later, show that the N aisle soon extended almost to the E wall of the chancel. The S arcade is Perp, of two bays plus one, the unequal arches chamfered and set on crude octagonal supports. No chancel arch.

The three late Perp chantry chapels which cluster round the chancel N and S are the most memorable parts of the church. Two-bay N (Triley) chapel with fancifully detailed timber arcade. Tall octagonal pier and responds carved on alternate faces with vertical cable moulding and rows of sunk encircled quatrefoils, flattened segmental arches trimmed with cusps terminating in flowers. The single-bay S (Wernddu) chapel has similar timber responds and arches even more elaborately carved. Finally, the tiny Nevill chapel on the N side of the sanctuary has a rib vault of stone. Late Perp ribbed wagon roofs throughout the rest of the church, partly reconstructed by *George Pace* in 1974 after a fire. – FONT. Perp. Octagonal bowl sloped down to the square base. Trefoil leaves in the angles of the base. – PEWS. A fine early C16 pair, of Somerset type, brought in. Poppyheads, and ribbonwork below. – PULPIT. Apparently Jacobean, but of 1893. Incised patterns. – LIGHT FITTINGS. *c.* 1974. – WALL PAINTINGS. Early C18 texts on the splays of the W window. – STAINED GLASS. Chancel E, Christ in Majesty, 1896 by *A. L. Moore*. – Nave W, Ascension, 1972 by *Harry Stammers*. – N aisle E. St Teilo rides a reindeer among flowers. Appealing to children.

1991 by *John Petts*. – MONUMENTS. There are no medieval monuments, in spite of the named chapels, but only rustic C18 tablets, of the kind typical in this area, attached to the walls inside and out. – Georgiana Ellis †1807 (s transept). Signed *Millard & Cooke*, Gloucester. Neoclassical hanging wall monument. A small willow weeps over an urn. This indicates the taste of the gentry.

ST TEILO'S HOUSE, ¼m. W. Built as the vicarage by *David Vaughan* of Cardiff and dated 1860. Prominent pierced bargeboards to the main gables, Pennant rubble walls with Bath stone quoins and window mullions. Tudor Gothic details and irregular plan.

PENYCLAWDD COURT, 2½m. N. The house, the long barn beside it to the s and the well-preserved motte behind to the W, below the steep flank of Bryn Arw, make up one of the most evocative manorial groups in the county.

The grassy MOTTE, of typical C12 conical form, remains well-defined if low. It is partly encircled by two ditches. The HOUSE, little more than a large farmhouse, is crowned by a fine array of lozenge-wise chimneystacks. It was constructed in three stages, probably between the later C16 and the early C18. It is two-storeyed, of stone, with stone-slated roofs, and was sympathetically restored 1984–7 by *Graham Frecknall* of Monmouth. The timber windows in particular were then returned to their original low, broad shapes, so that internally, one can comprehend the original ambience of the house, in terms of space and light (or lack of it), to an unusual degree.

The approach is from the NE, that is to say to the rear of the house. The short, low kitchen wing projecting to the NE is the latest part. From the SE end of the main range the massive hall chimney-breast projects, with a corbelled addition for a later upper fireplace. The main entrance doorway, in the middle of the SW front, leads into a cross-passage. All this belongs to the earliest part. To the l. of the doorway the roof ridge steps up to a higher level, where a T-plan addition was made in the early C17 to the NW, the parlour end of the original house. Timber-framed gable where the change in roof height occurs, and, almost at the junction of the T, a splendid multiple stack, the four chimneys forming a saltire cross. The stack, not the timber-framed gable, marks the end wall of the original house. One single-light stone lower window here. The cross wing is gabled at both ends and has stone mullioned windows of two, three and four lights under hoodmoulds, the mullions hollow-chamfered. Deep NW stair projection, now under a sloping roof, but originally gabled.

Inside, the original post-and-panel partition between cross-passage and hall survives, and the hall chimneypiece with mighty monolithic lintel. To the N of the latter, a mural stair, doubtless the only means of access to the upper storey when the house was first built. The window in the NE wall is blocked by the added kitchen wing. The parlour cross wing, at the other end of the house, is restrainedly handsome. The ground-floor room has a square-headed stone chimneypiece enriched with hollow and roll mouldings and fleur-de-lys stops, and is lit by windows on three sides. The staircase has stone steps rising in three shallow flights to a doorway with shaped timber head. This is the impressive approach to what seems to have been the manorial courtroom. The inner side of the doorway has a double wave-moulded frame. The stone chimneypiece here is a twin to the one below, if slightly smaller. Plain, stop-chamfered ceiling beams, the plaster fields between them enriched with finger-dragged outlining of the beams. Similar enrichment of the plaster window reveals here and in the adjoining room. The stairs originally continued on up beyond the courtroom door, to give access to the roof space, but the top flight has been curtailed now that the staircase gable has been removed. One further feature upstairs remains to be noticed. The length of the main range is subdivided by a timber-framed partition which forms a corridor. This improvement in circulation is probably contemporary with the parlour wing. Its C17 date seems to be proved by the remodelling of the space over the hall, where a new stone fireplace with the corbelled chimney-breast noted outside clearly relates to a room reduced in width by the corridor.

To the NE of the house, C17 GARDEN WALLS have been reconstructed and a charming C17-style garden created.

The stone BARN, across the yard from the kitchen wing, is of six bays, with the usual ventilation slits.

BLAENGAVENNY, 2¼ m. N. The big C16 or C17 BARN towards the road has a cowhouse at semi-basement level and timber-framed storage area above. The HOUSE which lies inconspicuously behind is largely single-storeyed, consisting of two parts. The hall of three narrow bays has a most unusual roof structure, with collar-beams and segmental arch-braces, probably of the mid C16. Two-light stone window for the W inner room, and the outer jambs of wider stone windows for the hall. The single-storey porch dated 1621, and shaped doorway into the cross-passage within, go with the parlour addition to the E.

TRILEY COURT, 1 m. NW. Well seen on the wooded slope of the Deri. The long, low, red brick house was built between *c.* 1820 and 1837 by a London merchant, F. S. Secretan-James-Woodhouse of The Paragon, Blackheath, who named it Arcadia. Two storeys, eleven bays, the centre five brought forward, with a pinched Venetian window, under a peculiar plaster pedimental feature. The Tuscan stone surround to the entrance doorway must date from *c.* 1900.

WERNDDU, 1 m. SE. Late C17 house of semi-double-pile plan (cf. Skirrid Mountain Inn, Llanfihangel Crucorney). The N front regularized in the C18. To the S the staircase bay rises above catslide roofs. The staircase itself is a fine piece, its short straight flights in a square open well. Big moulded newel caps and pendants. Flat shaped and pierced balusters.

3090 LLANTRISANT

ST PETER, ST PAUL AND ST JOHN. A handsome church, W tower, nave and lower chancel, all on a big scale and with slightly battered wall-facing, which gives the building a stern appearance. Built of Old Red Sandstone rubble, the dressed stonework of the windows a fine limestone. Restored in 1880–1 by *E.A. Lansdowne*. Cusped S lancet of *c.* 1300 in the chancel. Nothing else is datable earlier than the late C15 or even early C16. The unbuttressed tower and rectangular SE stair-turret have a bold base moulding of beak-like profile. Tudor W doorway, almost round-headed, and plain, rectangular, two-light belfry openings. Tudor S porch, but the S doorway is two-centred-headed with two broad chamfers. Handsome, if conventional, three-light Perp windows with two-centred heads N and S in the nave (one N by *Lansdowne*). Big S rood-stair projection, of squared masonry blocks, clearly an addition. In the chancel a pair of four-centred-headed Perp windows, one E, one S. Ogee-headed lights and hoods on demi-angel stops.

Inside, the width of the nave is remarkable. Wide and high chancel arch, moulded with continuous wave and two hollows. Tower arch not large, of the long-lasting form with chamfered inner order dying into the imposts, and above it a tablet dated 1593. To what does that relate? – FONT. Octagonal. Bold, childish inscription on the bowl: Iohn Iones 1673. – STAINED GLASS. Chancel E, Christ the Good Shepherd. Hieratic figure, singing colours. By *Geoffrey Robinson*, 1981. – MONUMENTS. Susanna Gardner Kemeys †1804. Hanging wall monument. Hope leaning on an urn looks up towards the descending dove of the Holy Spirit. Signed by *Reeves & Son* of Bath. – John Kemeys Gardner Kemeys †1830. Hanging wall monument signed by *R. Walker*, Bristol. A sarcophagus carries a fractured Ionic column and branch of weeping willow.

In the CHURCHYARD two steps and the broached base for a cross.

NATIONAL SCHOOL, $\frac{1}{2}$m. NE. Mid-C19. Small, Tudor-style, now tactfully converted into a house. By *J. H. Evins* of Abergavenny.

THE CWM, $\frac{1}{3}$m. NE. The T-plan house is of two dates. The main range has a little C18 panelling *in situ*, but nothing else to date it closely. To the N, a square block, datable to the late C16, clearly built to provide a private upstairs chamber as an addition to the house which the present main range has replaced. Note the way in which the SW angle of the C16 block is chamfered back, to clear a window in the re-entrant angle between it and the main range. The C16 block has, most unusually, windows of stone, with arched lights having sunk spandrels. One low down in the N gable-end is almost intact, of two lights under a hoodmould and voussoired relieving arch. There must have been something similar in the storey above. The W window at this level is of four lights, and has been restored. There was clearly a matching window to the E. Internally, the rooms at both levels have been subdivided. The lower had the character of an undercroft. The upper was enriched with ovolo-moulded ceiling beams, and plaster bands outlining them and the window embrasures. In the S wall one corner of the stone, chamfered, square-headed fireplace opening has been exposed. The wide stone doorway at the S end of the E wall, four-centred-headed and broadly chamfered, has been blocked. It is rebated on its outer face, so must originally have stood at the head of a stair which occupied a projection later trimmed back to form an externally flush wall.

NANT-Y-BANW, 1½ m. E. The diminutive-looking farmhouse stands behind and below later outbuildings on a sloping shelf above a stream. It bears the date 1625 above the SW window of the hall, and its cruciform plan, responding to the differing levels of the site, shows the ingenuity of vernacular house-planners of the early C17. The house was restored and thoughtfully modernized in the late 1980s. The main gable-ended range lies SW–NE, with a single-storey kitchen wing (recently slightly heightened) projecting forward to the SE. Gable in the main range above, to light the roof space with windows at two levels. Original timber mullioned windows with sunk chamfers, here and to the NE. Fox and Raglan deduced that the entrance was round the back in the NW wing, which also accommodated a spacious staircase. This interpretation has been the basis of the restoration in the 1980s. The entrance door, at semi-basement level, is C17, but has been brought in from the demolished Graig Olway, Llangeview, and the staircase, rising in short, straight flights round a square core, has been designed, doubtless correctly, in imitation of the type found at e.g. Upper Dyffryn, Grosmont. Some C17 windows show how the staircase was originally planned.

Inside there are typical but not especially rich timber fittings. Shaped door-head, and matching modern one to the r. beside it p. 38 opening into the hall. Post-and-panel partition between the hall and the present dining room, which has been formed by removing the partition between two unheated service rooms, of which one opened into the hall, the other into the kitchen. On the chamber storey above, another post-and-panel partition and a shaped door-head in it.

LLWYNAU, 1¼ m. S. The mid-C17 farmhouse underwent a radical but intelligent restoration in the mid 1990s. The main, two-unit house is largely intact. The original entrance at the N end of the E gable-end retains its chamfered timber door-frame. The hall fireplace beside it is spanned by a long chamfered lintel, and its lozenge-plan stacks have been reconstructed. A spiral stair twists up in the SE corner. One original N window in the hall, of four lights, ovolo-moulded. The post-and-panel partition, plainly chamfered, divided hall from parlour. A loose wooden panel carved with the date 1652, seen by Fox and Raglan but now lost, may indicate when the house was constructed. Outside the E wall ran a covered passage, the broad N door-frame of which survives, and a further two-storeyed bay. This can be interpreted as an entry shared by people and cattle on the long-house principle, cowhouse and loft. All this has been successfully converted to modern needs, with glazed front wall to the passage, stairs in the passage, and the hay loft turned into a brightly lit living room.

Diagonally to the SE 20 ft (6 metres) away, in a position incompatible with the longhouse use of the main building, is a two-storey detached KITCHEN, retaining its hearth, spiral internal stair, and probably later external flight of steps to the upper storey.

BERTHOLEY HOUSE, 1¾ m. S. The dramatically ruined shell of an important early C19 mansion, gutted by fire in 1905, stands on the hilltop behind majestic trees. Had it survived intact it would have been one of the outstanding Neoclassical buildings in the county. The last of the Kemeys family, John Kemeys Gardner Kemeys, is said to have begun work *c.* 1795, but the main builder was his son-in-law, Colthurst Bateman, *c.* 1830. His architect is unknown. Much stands to the full three-storeyed height, including the end bays of the rendered W entrance front. These were set slightly forward and have ground-floor windows under round-headed relieving arches. Five-bay N front, the l. three bays in a broad full-height bow. Top entablature carried round both fronts. In the centre at the back was an elliptical toplit stair, of which half the brick-lined well remains. (Reconstruction began in 1999.)

Behind the mansion, a detached, two-storey SERVICE RANGE, probably incorporating part of Edward Kemeys's house of 1616 (detached datestone). Also, an early C19 STABLE BLOCK and a rectangular, gable-ended stone DOVECOTE.

4090 LLANVACHES/LLANFACHES

ST DYFRIG. The church has the usual plan, W tower, nave with S porch, and lower chancel, and is built of local stone, grey, pink and buff. The tower is quite large, and is presumably late medieval, with flattened two-centred, chamfered W doorway. Its lower half is constructed with finely squared blocks and massive quoins, but the upper walling is more rubbly, and the minimal belfry window and obtuse saddleback roof further indicate that the original ambitions were not followed through. Square SE stair-turret with chamfered angles, part of the ambitious scheme. Wide, pointed tower arch with two chamfered orders dying into the imposts. Of the nave, at least the S wall pre-dates the tower, see the join with the stair-turret. The long SW lancet, with ogee cinquefoiled head, dates it to the C14. The crudely formed S doorway may well be early C17, the date of the door, with characteristic fan-decorated head. The blocked, round-headed N doorway with simple chamfer must be late medieval. Of similar date the rood-loft stair window. In the S porch a mortar does duty as a stoup. The chancel was rebuilt in 1850 by *R. H. Evins*, the nave restored and tower W window inserted by *Prichard & Seddon* in 1862–3. The chancel arch is presumably theirs too. In 1907–8 *Arthur Grove* restored the church again. (At the expense of Viscount Tredegar, see the TABLET lettered by *Eric Gill*.) His is the embellishment of the nave roof with strong arch-brace and tie-beam trusses painted black with a pattern of white-painted notching. His too is the abstract glazing, with pink and olive teardrops and lozenges. – FONT. A good plain C15 piece, an octagonal bowl, its underside curved, on an octagonal stem with moulded base and spurs to the square plinth. – PULPIT. Timber. Typical of *Prichard & Seddon*. – CHANCEL SCREEN. Timber. 1908 by *Arthur Grove*. Art Nouveau foliage and flowers take the place of conventional cusps and cresting. – STAINED GLASS. Chancel E, Crucified Christ alone, possibly by *Morris & Co.* (T. Blackshaw), between grisaille lancets, 1863. – Nave SE. Feeding the poor, 1897, signed by *R. J. Newbery*. The glazing enlarged below by *Grove*, with an abstract plaited pattern in aggressive contrast to Newbery's earnest naturalism. – MONUMENTS. Grave-slab fragment (S porch). Medieval. Carved with reliefs of cock, woodcock and other creatures. – Matthew and William Waters †1807 (tower). Rustic tablet with cherub heads at the top and drops of flowers at the sides in the idiom of a century earlier.

PARISH ROOM, W of the church. 1908 by *Arthur Grove*. Small but deftly detailed in an Arts and Crafts spirit. Of local grey rubble-stone. Canted end towards the road, with a decorative full-height chimneystack in the centre and semicircular windows l. and r. The entrance gable encloses a plaster semidome in a dark, discreetly notched frame.

TABERNACLE UNITED REFORMED CHURCH, ½ m. SE, beside the A48. The early C20 chapel and hall, the latter dated 1924, stand on the site of the first dissenting meeting in Wales, convened in 1639 by William Wroth, who had resigned as rector of Llanvaches the previous year.

LIMEKILN, ¼ m. NE beside the by-road to Wentwood Reservoir. Early C19. The twin segmentally vaulted stone outlets and the conical charging-funnel above survive virtually intact.

WENTWOOD RESERVOIR, 1 m. N. Constructed in the 1840s, to supply water to Newport. The castellated valve tower with corbelled walkway must be late C19. It is reached by a multi-span wrought-iron viaduct.

LLANVAIR DISCOED/LLANFAIR DISCOED 4090

ST MARY. 1882–3 by *Ewan Christian*, retaining no more than the outer jambs of the S porch and the depressed-headed S doorway from the medieval church, which had been largely rebuilt in 1746. Nave and lower chancel with simple Dec details. The tall and elegant W bell gable is by *Prichard & Seddon* of 1854. – FONT. Hexagonal bowl on a matching hexagonal foot. Possibly C18. – CURIOSUM. Recut stone inscription panel, in the porch, originally fixed on a stile into the churchyard. It reads:

Who Ever hear on Sonday
Will Practis Playing At Ball
it May be before Monday
The Devil Will Have you All.

This must be a Puritan response to James I's Book of Sports, reissued by Charles I in 1633, which allowed 'lawful recreation', including archery and dancing, after divine service. This was the issue which is said to have driven the rector of neighbouring Llanvaches to gather together the first dissenting congregation in Wales (*see* p. 361). – STAINED GLASS. Chancel E, Christ as Good Shepherd, Light of the World and Bread of Life. 1937 by *J. Wippell & Co.* – Nave N, posies of flowers on swirls of blue. What does it mean? 1986 by *Geoffrey Robinson*. – MONUMENTS. Thomas Pride †1787 and James Pride †1825. Quaint hanging wall monument probably of the latter date, in spite of the Baroque idiom. At the top a putto flies before clouds, swags of flowers drop to l. and r., and a starry crown is set below the inscription. – Edward Williams †1808. Large hanging wall monument of similar character. An upward-pointing putto sits on the oval inscription panel, with emblems below of Time and Resurrection. – Elizabeth Williams †1811. Also an oval inscription panel, and crudely carved figures, but here the imagery is more up-to-date. A reclining woman holds a child and looks up at a winged cherub's head. Neoclassical urn on top.

CASTLE, W of the church. The ruins of the small but well-defended castle of the lords of Llanvair Discoed stand in some parts as high as 20 ft (6 metres) and more, but in a state of disgraceful neglect. Gnarled trees sprout from the wall-tops in several places. Roughly coursed local brown stone walling. No cut stonework survives. The cylindrical towers suggest a date in the C13, when the FitzPayn family held the lordship, followed by the Monthermers by the end of the century. The best-preserved tower is at the SE angle, and the stretch of straight wall joining it to the W has robbed openings which suggest that a first-floor hall or chamber was sited here, protected by a ditch and bank to the S. Further W, a smaller tower on a flared base, from which a solid wall runs N-wards. This probably connected with the remains of the apparently free-standing tower immediately to the W, and formed part of a twin-towered gateway. The flat inner court to the N is further defined only by a high, featureless chunk of wall on its E side.

The VILLAGE clusters into quite a well-defined street, castle and church at the top, and at the bottom a BARN and a roofless DOVECOTE, with the peculiarity that its nesting holes and perching ledges are external. Also here, COURT HOUSE dated 1635. The date is carved on an inscription tablet in Welsh set into the one-storey gabled porch, above its segmental chamfered stone arch. The house itself, symmetrical, of five bays and two tall storeys, its eaves tweaked up into a gablet in the centre for one more window, must be a good deal later, *c.* 1700. Wood-framed mullion-and-transom casement windows under slightly segmental heads.

(DINHAM CASTLE, 3 m. E. The ruins of a small, square keep, similar to that at Penhow Castle, and other walls, assigned to the C13, within a wood.)

PENHEIN, ¾ m. N. A grey rendered villa built soon after 1813 for

Samuel Brookes and standing in a beautifully mature park. Nash's Picturesque Italianate villa style, first used at Cronkhill, Shropshire, in 1802, was Mr Brookes's inspiration. So a full-height polygonal tower stands at an angle towards the view. Tuscan bracketed eaves. But the full-height rectangular porch and the general boxiness of the five-by-three-bay house betray a less skilful hand than Nash's. The house was, according to Bradney, partly rebuilt and enlarged in 1876.

TREWEN, 1½ m. SE. An isolated group of ten little whitewashed houses drawn up formally to face each other at the far end of a poplar avenue. 1937 by *T. Alwyn Lloyd* for the Welsh Land Settlement Society. Built in conjunction with a co-operative farm where the occupants of the houses, out-of-work miners, were given employment.

The HILL-FORT in LLANMELIN WOODS, 1 m. E (ST 461 926), is well-known due to its excavation in the 1930s, when it was cleared of trees. THE OUTPOST (ST 463 927) remains obscured and overgrown. The main multivallate enclosure occupies the point of the hill with steep slopes on the W and S; the entrance is on the SE, approached by a track from the E. A series of rectangular annexes were later constructed above this track, probably part of the final remodelling of the site. In the C13 A.D. two stone huts were built within these annexes. Excavation, though extensive, was very limited, and evidence for the development of the site is not very firmly based. Postholes beneath the inner rampart at the entrance hint at an early timber phase; the stone-revetted inner rampart differs from the dump construction outer banks, suggesting a different date. A sequence is more clearly seen in the alterations to the entrance. Evidence for occupation from the C3 B.C. or even earlier, to about 75 A.D., was found in the interior and beneath the annexe banks, but no house plans were defined.

On the flat summit of GRAY HILL, 1 m. NW (ST 437 935), is an interesting group of Bronze Age ritual and burial monuments. Unfortunately, all of them are damaged and there is no record of any finds. There are three burial cairns on the hill, two standing stones and a kerb circle. This last is the most interesting monument, lying close to the smaller of the two standing stones. It consists of a ring of contiguous stones about 2 ft 6 in. (0.8 metre) high and approximately 30 ft (9 metres) in diameter. Two arcs of this kerb survive to N and S, and inside the circle there are two fallen stones. That on the W looks like a misplaced kerbstone, but the E one is longer and may have been part of some upright central feature. Some 50 yds (46 metres) further N there is another tall standing stone which does not appear to be associated with a cairn or ring. The N side of the hill is pitted with small quarries for walling stone. The sites are difficult to find on the bracken-covered hill a little way off the track from the car park near the reservoir.

FIVE LANES BARROWS, 1¼ m. S (ST 450 909 and 449 910), can still be recognized, though badly damaged by agriculture. A tree stands on one in the centre of the field.

3010 LLANVAPLEY/LLANFABLE

A linear village, of white C19 and C20 cottages, church and pub on the brow of the hill at the E end.

ST MABLE. Built of Old Red Sandstone in a variety of pink and grey hues, without heavy C19 restoration. The chancel is E.E. with an exceptional composition for its E window, two large lancets and an encircled cinquefoil above, all enclosed internally within a rere-arch. Dec evidence in the unbuttressed W tower, a Y-traceried window above the W doorway. Later belfry windows of paired uncusped lights. Corbelled battlements. The nave underwent a Perp remodelling. Crease-line on the tower E wall of an earlier, steeper roof. Large square-headed windows, one N and one S, of the common local design, the cinquefoiled arched heads linked by vertical bars to the lintel, forming glazed spandrels. Inside, the chancel arch and tower arch match, both two-centred with continuous chamfer, of the C13 or C14. Roofs in chancel and nave of the standard late medieval type, ribbed wagon vaults on moulded wall-plates. Bosses missing from the rib intersections. – FONT. C12 bowl, with unmoulded zigzag round the rim. – DOUBLE PISCINA in the chancel and two AUMBRIES in the E wall. – ALTAR RAILS. Dated 1724. Thin, widely spaced, turned balusters. – PULPIT. C18. Octagonal. Cut down. – MONUMENTS. Several tablets by local makers, one signed by *J. Brute*, †1769, another by *James Jones*, †1780.

In the CHURCHYARD four steps and broached base for the late medieval CROSS.

OLD RECTORY. Standard early C19 two-storeyed, three-bay sashed box under a shallow slate roof. By *Adolphus Fairchild* of Abergavenny, and built for £573 19s. in 1831–2.

LITTLE TON, ¼m. S. The L-plan stone house, reconstructed 1996–8, encapsulates two solid trusses of a mid-C16 timber-framed house, both now impressively exposed to full height. That to the N, of cruck construction, was the original end gable. That to the S, entirely box-framed, incorporates a post-and-panel partition. So this was a late cruck house, in which the two types of framing were used together.

3010 LLANVETHERINE/LLANWYTHERIN

ST JAMES THE ELDER. In a churchyard sloping down to the River Trothy. Built of slabby local Old Red Sandstone. The tower is memorable, the battlemented belfry stage overhanging on a corbel table. Rectangular windows of three arched lights suggest a C16 date for it. The Perp nave has a windowless N wall with rood-stair projection, and large four-light S window with cinquefoiled lights. Lancet dated 1703. Perp S porch, with typical two-centred arch moulded with ovolo, hollow, ovolo, and ribbed wagon roof. Stoup. The chancel is Dec, see the matching two-light S and three-light E windows with steep-headed cusped lights. Inside, trefoil-headed PISCINA in the chancel. The interior provides one further structural feature to ponder, the chamfered tower arch, of two-centred form on plain vertical imposts. This could be contemporary with the chancel: so nave and tower may have been only remodelled, not new-built, in the C15 and C16. Chancel arch dated 1872, apparently not part of *Charles Buckeridge*'s restoration of 1870. Wagon roofs in nave and chancel heavily renewed by *Buckeridge*. – FONT. By *Buckeridge*. Octagonal bowl. – ALTAR RAILS. C18. A dainty design. Twisted balusters, ball finials and miniature gates. – PULPIT. Of timber. An exquisite Arts and Crafts piece of *c*. 1900, with panels of leafy branches and typical lettering. – CHANCEL SCREEN. Low, of timber. Also of *c*. 1900. – STAINED GLASS. Chancel E, Nativity scene of 1905. (– Nave N, 1976 by *Geoffrey Robinson*.) – MONUMENTS. Worn figure of a priest, life-size, in low relief (sanctuary N). – Floor slab with big foliate cross, dated as late as 1601. – David Powell †1621 (chancel), rector and former fellow of All Souls College, Oxford. Floor slab (now set vertically) with life-size relief of a bearded man in academic robes holding a book. Roughly carved but vigorously characterized. – Similar slab (also vertical) carved with a woman in a tall hat and ruff, Powell's wife. The date 12 April 1715 is a subsequent addition. – Several tablets signed by *Thomas Brute*, †1724, 1729 and 1741. Another outside on the E wall of the chancel, signed by *Brute*, commemorating the rector's wife †1734.

In the CHURCHYARD, four steps and the broached base for a CROSS.

NEWHOUSE FARM, ½m. S. Much-altered, late C16, two-unit range running E–W, of two full storeys and gable-ended roof. Evidence of a post-and-panel partition which divided the lower storey into two roughly equal halves. Square-headed, hollow-moulded fireplace opening in the N wall of the E room. The spiral stair beside it belongs to a one-room block of three low storeys added in the early C17. This is exceptionally completely preserved. Doorways with shaped heads open from the stairs into the two upper rooms. Ovolo-moulded fireplace surround, and ovolo-moulded timber window frames of four, three and two lights. Later S range, perhaps replacing an early hall.

Across the yard, a C16 OUTHOUSE with two upper-cruck trusses and intermediate floor.

GREAT POOL HALL, 1½m. NE. Much-altered but still impressive gentry house, compact and originally very tall. It is dated 1619, and its builder was John Powell (hence, it is thought, the name of the house). Most remarkable is the use of timber-framing, for most of the E front, and for internal walls. The local stone used externally is a greenish shale, and dressings are of stone slates for window hoods, and timber for door and window frames. The house is an L in plan, the two ranges not properly integrated with one another, and it stands across the slope of the site, so that the main range is entered at two levels, a storey lower to the E than to the W. Originally the E front was four-storeyed, and there were gables to W and N, but these and the dormered roof to the E were all removed in the early C20. So now it is the three great slab-topped chimney-breasts, projecting to N, S and W, which dominate. They too must originally have risen higher, by means of grouped stacks.

Detailed examination can begin with the E front. It is symmetrical. The ground storey is of stone, strongly battered for its full height. Here is a central single-storey porch, timber-framed over dwarf walls, with square-framed inner door. Three-light window to the l. under a stone-slate hood. This lit the kitchen, as the oven projecting from the S end gable shows. The two timber-framed upper storeys, heavily plastered and painted pink, are set within stone gable-end walls and jettied on broad, shallow, completely plain brackets. The top row of brackets is now immediately below the roof, showing that a further storey has been lost. Two widely spaced five-light windows at each level, the lower two original, with sunk chamfer moulding. The S front of the SW range is much altered. The foundations of a central canted bay have been found, and two straight joints show that it rose two storeys high. Blocked windows to l. and r. The windows at three levels in the centre postdate the removal of the bay. To the W the chimney-breast is flanked by two-light windows at both upper levels. Round on the N return of this wing a full-height straight joint close to the gable suggests that on this side the wing was intended to be timber-framed. Two three-light windows here are overlapped by the W front of the main range, which would suggest that this front has been brought forward. The W front is of three bays and is entirely of the early C20. The central doorway is oddly recessed, and the original door is set behind a modern door. This arrangement also implies the bringing forward of the W front, as does the off-centre placement of the chimney-breast in the return wall to the N. The reason why this was done will become clear inside, but there is a hint in the placement of the windows to the r. of the W doorway, out of alignment with the rest. They must light the half-landings of a staircase.

Inside, the staircase is a splendid object indeed, though it cannot be indigenous to the house. It bears the date 1665 and is of the then fashionable type which rises flight by flight on a dog-leg plan from the bottom to the top of the house. Portly turned balusters, emphatically moulded strings and stout newel posts with ball finials and pendants. Tentative sunk patterns on strings and posts. The great width of the flights and the awkward narrowness of the half-landings suggest that the staircase was designed for a larger building. The clearest evidence that, in order to fit it in, the W wall of the N range had to be moved forward several feet is on the first floor, where a fragment of timber-framed wall with an inset window frame indicates the original position of the W wall. It also shows that the main range was originally timber-framed front and back. The rest of the
p. 38 interior has been largely stripped of its original decoration. One naively ambitious plaster ceiling survives in the first-floor S room. Thin, flat bands make a design of quatrefoils within

quatrefoils. Fleur-de-lys finials and free-floating rosettes. Bradney reports that there were other plaster ceilings in the house, and the digits of the date 1619 survive from one of them. A carved overmantel has found its way to Glen-trothy (*see* below).

So the final word can be on the plan. In the centre at the lowest level is the kitchen, entered from the E, with to the N two unheated rooms (see the mortises for a partition), and to the SW a second heated room. The hall is on the floor above, entered from ground level on the W side. Because of the thickening of the range to take the staircase, the hall is now an L in plan. A stout post-and-panel partition divides it from the parlour, beyond which, in the SW range, is the room with the decorated plaster ceiling. This last room also has the peculiar feature of the chimney-breast projecting deeply into the room, forming deep recesses l. and r., which are lit by two-light windows. A similar arrangement is in the chamber above. The two E-facing chambers in the main range are divided by a post-and-panel partition.

A fine C17 seven-bay BARN stands above the house to the NW. It has a tall central porch, and lean-to stables and cart-houses mask the stone front wall l. and r. The rear of the barn has a good deal of timber-framing.

WINSTON COURT, ½m. NW. Small and simple late C16 or early C17 farmhouse with many typical features, shaped entrance door-head, moulded ceiling beams in the hall, post-and-panel partition. Also one rare survival, decorated plasterwork in the hall ceiling. The decoration forms a quincunx of squares with roses and ballflowers in the fields.

GLEN-TROTHY, 1¾m. NE. Built on a new site by Col. John Francis Vaughan in the mid C19 and rebuilt 1883–5 by his son Reginald Vaughan. The Vaughans were Catholics – Cardinal Vaughan was Reginald's brother – and a Catholic architect was employed, *Edmund Kirby* of Liverpool. The house Kirby designed would grace a Scottish glen. Tudor-Gothic, crowned by steep, slated roofs and thick red brick chimneystacks. At the SW angle, under a candlesnuffer cap, a well-windowed polygonal projection gives views down the valley. Lower, gabled service range, continuing the house E-wards, and ending in a pyramid-roofed NE turret.

The most remarkable feature of the house is the FAMILY CHAPEL at the E end of the S front. Outside no great show is made of it, just a cross-enclosing oculus high in its E wall. The interior, tall and narrow, is by contrast extraordinarily well appointed and lavish in its decoration. Red plastered walls. Compartmented wagon ceiling, painted somewhat amateurishly with a multitude of religious subjects and emblems. The recessed sanctuary filled with an elaborately arcaded stone REREDOS, sacrament house and life-size Crucifixion scene. In niches to l. and r. life-size statues of the Virgin and Child and St Joseph. Raised at the W end, the family pew, and in the wall behind it an inconspicuous squint, providing a view of the altar from the master bedroom. – STAINED GLASS of 1887 and 1904. – N sacristy.

Otherwise, all that need be noted is that the N entrance hall has a heavy timber chimneypiece and the heavily timbered principal stair opening off it to the E. The drawing room, to the W, has an overmantel partly made up with bits from Great Pool Hall (*see* above). These must include the well-carved caryatids, but presumably not the cartouches between them, carved with Catholic subjects, though these look C17 too.

2010 LLANWENARTH

ST PETER. Quite a large church, isolated in the meadows beside the River Usk, just beyond the edge of Abergavenny housing. Built of Old Red Sandstone. The earliest part is the lower stage of the tower and the lean-to S addition, which is lit from a cusped lancet, and entered from the tower internally through a chamfered doorway with two-centred head. Dec nave and lower chancel built in line with the tower and lean-to, so off-axis with the tower itself. Late medieval S porch. In the nave, two large Dec N windows of different patterns, and two equally large S ones, inserted either in 1853 or as part of *John Prichard*'s restoration in 1877. The chancel displays a charming miscellany of openings employing ogee forms. Reticulated three-light E window. Inside, a handsome PISCINA under an ogee arch. Otherwise the interior adds nothing more, as the chancel arch is of the C19, and the small, pointed tower arch is formed without dressed stone. In the nave, ribbed and plastered wagon roof on plain wall-plates. – FONT. A very basic Norman tub. – REREDOS. Dated 1878, of timber. Cusped panels and heavy pinnacles. Apparently by *Prichard*, but a routine piece. – ALTAR RAILS, PULPIT and READING DESK, all of timber, clearly to *Prichard*'s design. – STAINED GLASS. Chancel S, Baptism of Christ, *c.* 1867 by *Clayton & Bell*. – Chancel E, Christ Blessing between SS Peter and John, *c.* 1872. Mundane figures, probably by *Wailes* (A. Brooks). – Chancel S lancet, St Cecilia, 1911 by *Powell*'s.

In the CHURCHYARD the WAR MEMORIAL incorporates the finely moulded broached base from the medieval cross.

3080 LLANWERN

The name Llanwern is known today for the mighty SPENCER STEELWORKS established by the Government in 1958 and opened in 1962. Its site extends for 3 m. S of the railway line. The two steel-clad mill ranges occupy half the length. *Sir Percy Thomas & Partners* were employed to give some architectural coherence to the bulkiest elements. Cladding in contrasting colours was used for the various functionally different components. Thick belts of trees further mitigate its visual impact.

Church and village, N of the railway line, belong to a different world. Llanwern Park, the seat of Lord Rhondda, a large, four-square, mid-C18 mansion, has been demolished, but evidence of his paternalistic influence can be seen in the village.

ST MARY. Small and isolated, E of the village. Perp. Nave and chancel in one, the N wall entirely windowless, S porch, and a W tower, squat but unusually showy. The walls of the church are of grey local limestone, the dressings largely of purple Old Red Sandstone. The plain plinth shows that the body of the church and the porch were built together. Diagonal E buttresses. The three-light chancel E window is of early Perp form, two-centred-headed, the tracery of cusped hexagons. Two-light S windows, that for the sanctuary a single light, square-headed, with large ogee cusped lights. Two-centred-headed S doorways to porch and nave. The tower, on a moulded plinth, is divided into three stages by strings. Diagonal buttresses with many set-offs, the SE one resting awkwardly on the nave eaves. NE polygonal stair-turret. Battlements and prominent water spouts. The belfry openings, two-centred-headed under hoods with stops in the form of heads, contain, unfortunately, C19 plate tracery.

Inside, the tower arch is impressive, narrow but tall, with a broad chamfer to the imposts and superarch and also to the sub-arch. (C14 piscina.) – CROSS-HEAD. Apparently pre-Conquest. – PEWS. Prichard's typical design. – STAINED GLASS. Sanctuary S, five painted panels, Christ blessing the Elements and other more enigmatic subjects. Executed *c.* 1840 by *Sarah Salusbury* of Llanwern House. – Chancel E, Adoration of the Shepherds and Kings, 1957. – Nave S, Christ the Good Shepherd, 1958. Both by *Celtic Studios*.

In the CHURCHYARD, the broached base and part of the spurred shaft of a CROSS. – MONUMENT. Viscount Rhondda †1918. A second cross, tall and of crisply idiosyncratic outline.

The VILLAGE lies ½ m. to the W. The VILLAGE INSTITUTE is by *Oswald P. Milne*, whom Lord Rhondda employed on Llanwern Park from *c.* 1906. Simple, deftly proportioned gable-end to the street, with out-swept eaves, a typical Arts and Crafts image. Two cottage pairs also by *Milne*, one to the N, WISTARIA and its fellow, the other at the corner of BISHTON ROAD to the S, MYRTLE COTTAGE and BAY TREE COTTAGE, built in 1913. This is the most worked-up design, centred on a clustered brick chimneystack. Twin rendered gables oversail canted bay windows.

GREAT MILTON, Milton Hill, W of the village. Substantial L-plan farmhouse of two storeys with habitable roof space. Local limestone rubble walls. The NW range is interpreted by Cadw as of the mid C16, refenestrated with ovolo-moulded mullioned windows in the early C17, when the taller cross range was added to its N end. Some C17 timber windows survive. (Inside, in the earlier range, the ground-floor S room retains its fireplace and chamfered ceiling beams. In the later, a broad timber newel stair up to the attic.)

THE THATCHED COTTAGE, ½ m. N of the village. Also by *Milne*, designed for 'a maiden lady with one servant' for a contract price no more than £650, and built in 1909. Local rubble limestone walls, thatched roof. T-plan, with gable-ends, appearing informal in its rural situation. The prominent chimney-breast set in the angle beside the front door is a telling touch.

2080 LOWER MACHEN

ST MICHAEL. A small and simple medieval church, built of Old Red Sandstone rubble. Nave with S porch, lower chancel and W tower. The church was used from the early C18 as their place of burial by various branches of the Morgan family, and their mausoleum on the N side of the chancel is the most remarkable part. The rest of the church was drastically restored in 1900–1 by *C. B. Fowler* of Cardiff. The tower is of the simplest, on a battered base, the battlements on a corbel table. The W doorway with chamfered two-centred arch may well be C16, the square belfry openings later still. The S porch has a depressed four-centred outer arch with a chamfer, late medieval. All the other openings are of the C19. Inside, however, there is further medieval evidence. Clearly the tower was added to an earlier nave, see the chamfered W doorway and lancet window over. The pointed chancel arch of undressed stone is impossible to date. Flanking recesses, probably for altars beneath the rood loft. Rood-loft doorways to the N. Piscina in the chancel. The mausoleum (*see* below) is square and was probably built *c.* 1716. It boasts a handsome, classically moulded entrance arch closed by wrought-iron gates, and within, a coved plaster ceiling on a classical cornice. – FONT. Tiny bowl on a circular stem. Of the C18? – ROYAL ARMS. Small gilt relief over the chancel arch, of George IV or William IV. The crouching lion and unicorn are typical of early C19 royal arms. – HATCHMENTS. Eleven, a notable series, extending from 1767 to 1867. – MONUMENTS (all in the mausoleum). – John Morgan of Ruperra †1715. Hanging wall monument with three veiled cherub heads under an architrave which bows up for them. Fluted side pilasters and palm-fronds at the sides and foot. 'Mr Stanton', i.e. *Edward Stanton*, was paid for it in 1717. – John and Martha Morgan †1719 and 1720, and Sir William Morgan †1731. Noble standing wall monument, the twin inscription panels under a triangular pediment carried on well-carved Composite columns. At the top flaming lamps flank an achievement of arms supported by a pair of huntsmen with hunting horns wrapped round their waists. – Charles and John Morgan †1787 and 1792. The inscriptions are on the front of a sarcophagus on Gothic panelled corbels. Weeping cherub and veiled urn on top. – Charlotte Ann Morgan †1891. Vesica-shaped inscription panel framed with cherubs' heads, lilies and stars. Clearly by *J. Forsyth* (*see* Marshfield). – Hon. Frederic Courtenay Morgan. 1906. Scrolly cartouche surrounded by four cornucopias of flowers.

In the CHURCHYARD two steps, the base and part of the shaft of a medieval CROSS.

The village is small and compact, and largely consists of substantial C19 houses.

MACHEN HOUSE, W of the church. Enlarged from an earlier house in 1831 for the Rev. Charles Augustus Morgan, a younger son of Sir Charles Morgan of Tredegar House. White, with a full-height canted bay at the W end of the S front, and Gothic touches round the entrance to the E. This front was symmetrical under three gables, until the r. bay was pulled down in the 1950s. The front door opens on a spectacular sight, a white-painted cast-iron screen of three etiolated Gothic arches which spans in front of a spacious, free-standing spiral staircase of the sparest joinery possible. Cusped pierced spandrel under each wafer-thin tread. The circular newel post, however, round which the stair rises, is of reassuringly substantial girth. The stair, it must be admitted, is a little too broad for the space available; indeed, the wall behind is hollowed out to take it. Small top lantern. Three spacious S rooms, each with a brought-in late C18 chimneypiece, all of timber and in an Adam style. Two came from Ruperra Castle, Glamorgan, that in the SW drawing room from Tamworth, Staffordshire.

Much remains of the Rev. Mr Morgan's elaborate GROUNDS. Two lakes, one fed by a stream which emerges from a rocky cascade, the other spanned by a three-arch 'Willow Pattern' bridge. Single-storey BOTHY with pointed windows and a low, castellated tower. Elaborate BEE BOLE with three pointed arches. Enclosing castellated WALL, from which belvedere turrets project towards the road to the S.

In the village centre THE COTTAGE, *c.* 1840, symmetrical with bargeboarded gables and hoodmoulded windows.

PLAS MACHEN, ½ m. SE. This was the seat of the Morgan family before the move to Tredegar House in the 1660s. By 1801 it was a farmhouse 'hastening to decay'. The house was reduced in size, and the remaining L-plan building was restored and improved, perhaps *c.* 1869 by *Habershon & Pite*. The approach is past a fine group of BARNS to the E front. The house wears a picturesque crown of C19 red brick chimneystacks and lozenge-plan shafts of yellow brick. Walls of Old Red Sandstone rubble partly rendered. Early C16 two-storeyed porch, the entrance arch four-centred, moulded with a double wave under a hood. Four-light window over, hollow-chamfered, the lights arched, under a hood on square stops. Corbelled chimney-breast round to the r., showing that the porch room was heated. To the r. of the porch, a stair projection, and then a two-storeyed range with three-light windows matching that in the porch, quite irregularly disposed, and some of them probably C19 insertions. To the l. of the porch a three-storeyed gabled bay comes forward slightly. Three-light windows here with straight-headed lights, the top two with hollow-moulded mullions, the lowest ovolo-moulded. The wing coming further forward at the l. is C19, replacing a much larger, forward-projecting Elizabethan range.

The S garden front is in three parts. To the r. the return face of the C19 wing, with large three-light windows. A straight joint

Lower Machen, Plas Machen. Engraving, 1801

separates it from the gabled centre section, where two grand, six-light transomed windows are set in line under the gable. Their stonework is C19. The l. section of the S front is set back from the rest, with a chimney-breast serving the rooms lit by the big windows. This is the least altered part and has C17 hood-moulded mullioned windows of Old Red Sandstone at two levels, with a third in a small gable. To the W, this range stands on the edge of a steep drop. To the N, a lower gabled range in the re-entrant of the L-plan. A few one-light and two-light windows face this way.

Inside, there is nothing to note except a four-centred stone arch and stone newel stair beyond it. No trace remains of the 'circular apartment, called the hunting room' seen by Archdeacon Coxe, which was decorated with a 'rich stuccoed ceiling, representing the figure of Diana in the middle, with seats, churches, and hunting parties, in twelve surrounding compartments'.

CASTELL MEREDYDD, ½m. N. A rocky outcrop commanding the valley of the River Rhymney, first fortified in the late C12 by the Welsh lord Meredydd Gethin, but captured by Gilbert de Clare in 1236. Excavation in 1975 identified a round tower as having stood to the E, and traces of the curtain wall of a bailey with SW entrance gate-tower, all presumed to be of the early C13.

Fragments of ROMAN BUILDINGS found at various times within the village make it clear that there was a relatively extensive settlement here from early in the Roman period. The discovery of both coins and Roman pottery in the nearby old lead workings makes it certain that these were being exploited in the Roman period, and there can be little doubt that the settlement was linked with these mines.

BEGWNS (ST 224 900) and TWYN PANT TEG (ST 240 888), the

two grass-grown cairns on the E end of Machen ridge, are examples of Bronze Age monuments designed to be seen for many miles around.

MAGOR/MAGWYR 4080

ST MARY. One of the most ambitious churches in the county, though the ambitions were not all realized. The earliest part is the central tower, of C13 date. The chancel, quite long, is Dec. Three-bay Perp nave with aisles continued E-wards to clasp the tower, and two-storeyed N porch, all built in a single campaign (though the porch must be on the site of a predecessor – see the way the N aisle narrows). Walls mostly of local brown rubble-stone. *John Norton*, in a heavy restoration of 1861–8, renewed almost all the external cut stonework, but only the E window of the chancel is to his design.

The tower is unbuttressed, with a square NW stair-turret, parapet on a corbel table, and belfry openings in the form of paired lancets. In the chancel the S window with a quatrefoil over two cusped ogee lights suggests an early C14 date. A stone incised with zigzag is built into the wall near the SE angle, a trace presumably of the preceding C12 chancel. Blind chancel N wall. In the Perp rebuilding of the nave, however, the N side became the more important. The ashlar battlements to the N aisle are panelled, but to the S are plain. More importantly, the porch on the N side is a showpiece, ashlar-faced and given delicate diagonal buttresses which rise full-height to carry ferocious gargoyles and pinnacles. Most arresting is the entrance arch-way, with paired shaftlets in a broad, concave reveal overlapped by big cusps. Three-light window over. The porch is rib-vaulted in stone with a central pendant. Two-centred inner doorway moulded with continuous wave, double wave, hollow and double wave. Image niche above with ogee head and side pinnacles. The aisles have diagonal and intermediate buttresses and three-light windows with panel tracery. Handsomely fenestrated W wall, having a three-light window for the N aisle and four-lighters for nave and S aisle.

Further signs of Perp ambitions inside, stone corbels in the aisles and in the pseudo-transepts, heads and a few grotesque figures supporting springers, as if there was to have been vault-ing throughout. Handsome if rather low three-bay arcade, the capitals carved as demi-angels holding scrolls. Here, too, there has been much restoration. The contrast between the schematic, somewhat grim heads of the unrestored angels on the N side and their sweet-faced Victorian counterparts on the S is instruc-tive. The piers have the typical West Country form, of four shafts and four hollows, with slim extra shafts in the hollows, as if to support the angels' wings. Keeled rolls, large and small, on the arches. Note the Green-Man corbel over the SW pier, and the vaulted image niche on the SE pier, set on a knobbly leaf corbel and canopied in two directions.

To the E the tower intervenes abruptly, its low, pointed but unmoulded W and E arches retaining their E.E. form. Perp arches cut through the N and S walls of the tower have a broad, continuous wave moulding, plain ashlar imposts and broad panelling on the arch soffits. Similar arch between N aisle and pseudo-transept. The corresponding arch on the S side is differently handled, its shafting more in keeping with the arcades. – FONT. Perp. A handsome piece, somewhat out of the ordinary. Octagonal bowl, the faces hollow-chamfered above double-cusped arcading. Octagonal shaft with roll mouldings. Flared base. – SCULPTURE. Big foliage boss beside the font. From a vault? – TILES. Clearly part of *Norton*'s restoration. They extend in handsome patterns across four long, shallow steps forming an ascent the full length of the chancel. – STAINED GLASS. Chancel E, 1880 by *Joseph Bell & Son* of Bristol. Sacrifice of Isaac, an unusual subject for the C19 (but foreshadowing the Crucifixion, hence its suitability here), arrestingly narrated. – Chancel S, Annunciation. 1988 by *Geoffrey Robinson*. – Nave S, Good Shepherd between saints. 1930–1 by *Kempe & Co.*, and war memorial *c.* 1920, no doubt by *Clayton & Bell* (A. Brooks).

In the CHURCHYARD two crumbling steps and the square, moulded base of a churchyard CROSS, and the octagonal base of a WAYSIDE CROSS.

CHURCH HALL (S of the church). Built as a national school in 1856 by *Prichard & Seddon*. Unassuming. Single-storeyed and gabled, built of local limestone rubble. The surprising thing is that the S-facing three-light schoolroom windows have four-centred heads and Perp panel tracery. To the N, grouped lancets, in the architects' usual idiom. Addition of *c.* 1900 to the E.

EBENEZER BAPTIST CHURCH. The original chapel of 1816 still stands, its datestone displaced on to an addition of 1906. Simple, of three bays by two, the windows round-headed. Interior stripped out.

PROCURATOR'S HOUSE, W of the churchyard. A cliff-like ruin of Old Red Sandstone with dressings of local yellow Triassic sandstone. The name suggests a greater antiquity than the building can boast. Between 1238 and 1385 the tithes of Magor were indeed collected by a procurator on behalf of the Italian abbey of Anagni. But what remains, the full-height E wall and part of the N wall of a building of two full storeys over a cellar, cannot be as early as that. The square-headed windows were clearly mullioned, and a doorway with four-centred head at the S end of the E wall is typical of the C16. This must be the 'mansion house belonging to the vicarage of Magor' mentioned in 1585 as standing by the wall of the churchyard. It is likely to have been built early in the C16, when the vicar of Magor was a secular priest appointed by the abbot of Tintern. The vicarage was subdivided into three rooms at main floor level, a kitchen with its fireplace in the N wall, and the other two heated from fireplaces backing on to the churchyard. Spiral stair to the top storey in the SE corner. The plan is typical of late medieval priests' houses.

The isolated gable-end a little further N belonged to a separate building.

The VILLAGE grows out to the N of the large churchyard. The main space, THE SQUARE, is irregularly squarish, its most imposing house, MAGOR HOUSE, on the NW side. This is of the later C18, and straightforward enough, two storeys, three bays, rendered. Round-headed door-case under a broken triangular pediment. The WAR MEMORIAL, in the centre of the space, is a little out of the ordinary. Of stone. Four pedimental gables enclosing shields are set on four corner piers. The central pillar thus sheltered bears lists of names of the fallen, and on one side, a circular bronze relief portrait of Viscount Rhondda (1856–1918), signed by *Allan G. Wyon* and inscribed 'for he too died serving the nation as food controller'.

THE LAWNS, West End, 200 yds NW. Old people's flats of c. 1975 by *Powell, Alport & Partners*, characteristic of the date. A close-knit group, in short staggered terraces. Two-storeyed, of grey brick, under monopitch roofs. Metal covered walkways, not integrated with the design of the houses.

CHESTNUT CLOSE, 200 yds NE. A second, more extrovert, cluster of local authority housing of the 1970s. Toy-like single-storey detached houses with split-pitch roofs, their brickwork painted yellow.

To the N of Chestnut Close, the WHEATSHEAF INN, C18. Adjoining the inn to the N, towards NEWPORT ROAD, is a C16 range, part of MANOR FARM. Though very fragmentary, it retains the two-centred arch of a large stone doorway and small stone windows on two storeys, single-lighters with cusped arched heads and hoodmoulds, and a two-lighter with uncusped arched lights and no hood.

VICARAGE, ¾m. NW. 1861 by *John Norton*. Tudor Gothic, of stone. Typical of the date.

WHITBREAD BREWERY, 1 m. NW. 1979 by *Frederick Gibberd, Coombes & Partners*. A complex of rectangular pavilions interspersed with groups of cylindrical vats and, as the boldest accent, a tall steel chimneystack. High-level piping links many of these elements. In front of all this, an enormous breadth of greensward, so that one sees both a demonstration of the process of brewing and a consciously arranged composition.

MOTORWAY SERVICE STATION, ¾m. NW. 1990–1 by *Scott Brownrigg & Turner*.

MALPAS 3090

ST MARY. The small but richly decorated Neo-Norman church, built in 1849–50 by *John Prichard*, is an elaborated copy on the old site* of the C12 chapel which had belonged to a cell founded here, probably between 1107 and *c.* 1110, by the Cluniac abbey

* Thomas Prothero had wanted to build on a new site, adjacent to his house, Malpas Court (*see* below). When he could not get his way, he halved his contribution to the rebuilding fund.

Malpas, St Mary. Engraving, 1801

of Montacute, Somerset. The intention to reuse the decorated components of the old building seems to have proved impractical. (One C12 head corbel is preserved in the vestry.)

The churchyard is entered from the W, on the axis of the W doorway of the church, through an arched Neo-Norman LYCHGATE. The church itself is built of mauve and grey Old Red Sandstone. The shafted W doorway, its arch enriched with three sorts of zigzag and a dogtooth hoodmould on animal heads, and the single-light window over, both follow the C12 composition, but the overloaded double bell gable is Prichard's invention. The four-bay nave and lower, two-bay chancel have shafted windows set on a continuous stringcourse. Deep buttresses, not really of a C12 form. The triple E window, almost the full width of the chancel, with oculus over, is a new composition of Prichard's. The interior is dominated by the chancel arch, splendidly large and elaborately enriched. Triple-shafted imposts, and scallop and leaf capitals, all different, just as in the medieval predecessor, as described by Sir Stephen Glynne. – FONT, PULPIT and READING DESK. All of Caen stone, to *Prichard*'s design, and taking Neo-Norman enrichment to further lengths. – STAINED GLASS. Chancel E, scenes from the life of Christ, in roundels, 1850 by *George Rogers* of Worcester, and typical of the date. – Chancel S, Christ taking two girls to heaven. 1855, clearly also by *Rogers*. – Nave S central, Crucifixion, in memory of Thomas Prothero †1853. Probably by *Rogers*. – Nave W, Call of Peter, 1864, and nave SE, Christ in Majesty, *c.* 1867, both clearly by *Hardman* (A. Brooks). – Nave SW, St George, *c.* 1900 by *Heaton, Butler & Bayne*. Breaking the consistency of style at last. – MONUMENT. Henry Jones †1837. Neoclassical hanging wall monument. A woman stands beside a pedestal on which is set a big urn draped with a swag of oak leaves.

In the CHURCHYARD, the prominently sited MONUMENT to Thomas Prothero. A large cross, now lacking its head, set on a sloping inscribed base, in a railed enclosure.

VICARAGE, S of the church. Large, gabled, of stone. 1887 by *Middleton, Prothero & Phillot* of Cheltenham.

MALPAS COURT PRIMARY SCHOOL, Whittle Drive. Opened 1953, by *Johnson Blackett*, Newport Borough Architect. A characteristic and well-preserved example of the local primary school style of the 1950s. Largely single-storeyed, the wide, regularly spaced, metal-framed windows reaching up to the eaves, which project on tapered fins. Brown brick.

MALPAS COURT, Whittle Drive. Built 1836–8, the first completely new mansion designed by *T. H. Wyatt*, who would subsequently go on to do so much in the county. His client was Thomas Prothero of Newport, agent to the Morgan family of Tredegar House. The house is not large, but full of incident, in a gabled Tudor style. It is faced with distractingly rugged rock-faced Pennant sandstone, sparingly dressed with Bath stone, and stands, two-storeyed, on a level platform beyond which the ground drops to the S and W towards the Monmouthshire and Brecon Canal. The E, entrance, and S fronts group together in self-conscious asymmetry, developing on either side of a three-storey polygonal tower set back in the re-entrant SE angle. To the E a two-storeyed porch projects, with an oriel above the four-centred entrance arch and polygonal clasping buttresses crowned by lattice-patterned pinnacles. Gable with a step, and a bird on the top pinnacle. Beyond the porch, one gabled bay and, lying back, the gabled service range. The S front is symmetrical, of three bays, the outer bays with huge mullion-and-transom lower windows, the central bay behind an open three-sided porch with ornamental spandrels and pierced parapet. The W front, overlooking the valley, has two broad, single-storey bay windows, and a two-storey window bay.

LODGE. Beside the main road N of Whittle Drive. Single-storeyed, of rock-faced Pennant sandstone, its gables bearing large, wavy bargeboards.

WOODLANDS, on the A4051 facing the entrance to Whittle Drive. Probably also of the 1830s, but quite different in character. Two-storeyed, rendered white, with a shallow slated roof and shallow pediments over shallowly projecting symmetrical bays.

BRYNGLAS HOUSE (Community Centre), ½ m. E, but reached from the S up Brynglas Road. Hidden from clustering suburbia by magnificent mature conifers. Mid-Victorian classical mansion of two storeys, entirely rendered, built for Thomas Cordes, M.P. for Newport, *c.* 1870, it is said. Although there is a Regency reticence in the spare detailing, the awkward composition gives away the later date, when architects were losing their sense of proportion. The S entrance front is a mere three bays wide. From its central canted bay projects a one-storey porch on Ionic columns. The E front facing the garden (and originally a distant view) is four times as long. The six-bay central section has a flat-faced upper storey, but below breaks out into a pair of canted window bays with windows in all three directions, leaving space between them only for a small and inadequate central niche. Beyond all this to l. and r., very broad and shallow three-bay full-height bows. The fronts share a plain top entablature. Shallow pitched roof over the central section of the E front, and a single surviving central chimneystack.

The HOUSING ESTATE S of Whittle Drive was developed in the early 1950s by Newport Borough Council, Borough Architect *Johnson Blackett*. Three-storey blocks of flats are dotted about the parkland of Malpas Court. Also flat-roofed terraces on the slope to the S, off WESTFIELD DRIVE, and a characteristic row of SHOPS in RUSSELL DRIVE. The primary school belongs to the scheme, and Malpas Court itself has become the community's social club.

3000

MAMHILAD

ST ILLTYD. A small Perp church, but more elaborately developed than most in this area. Of local Old Red Sandstone. Nave with separately gabled chancel stepping down the hill. W double bell gable. S porch and also W porch. Windows and doorways all Perp, but differing in details from one another. An earlier building must have been gradually but comprehensively modernized. The nave N wall and lower parts of the chancel N and S walls, of slabby, slate-like stones, rather than blocks, must belong to a building which pre-dated any of the existing openings. The date 1482 was found in plasterwork in the S porch at the restoration. The W porch is clearly an addition. NW and SW nave windows and quatrefoil in the W gable by *Prichard & Seddon*, 1864–5. Round-headed chancel arch, its moulding confirming that it is Perp, not Norman. – FONT. Medieval. Circular bowl, perhaps originally a C12 tub, reshaped and tapered down to the panelled base. – SCREEN. Perp. Much renewed. W GALLERY, incorporating the bressumer and front of the rood loft. Bold pierced tracery panels, with foliage trails above and below, and an embattled beam. Compare the loft at Bettws Newydd. – STAINED GLASS. Chancel E, Crucifixion. Mid-C19, reusing some medieval glass. – MONUMENT. William Morgan, wife and son, *c.* 1823. Hanging wall monument with inscription panel shaped like a Grecian sarcophagus. Signed by *T. Tyley* of Bristol.

The CHURCHYARD is full of table tombs, jostling for place among the yew trees. The spurred base is all that remains of the medieval CROSS.

RECTORY (former), $\frac{1}{4}$m. S. 1855 by *R. G. Thomas* of Newport. Red brick with stone dressings painted over. Tudor style. The main front was originally symmetrical, and tall chimneystacks have been truncated.

NATIONAL SCHOOL, $\frac{1}{2}$m. S. Dated 1856. Mauve local stone and red brick dressings.

PERSONDY, $\frac{1}{2}$m. SW. That is to say, the parsonage, though so far from the church. A completely preserved demonstration of C16

Mamhilad, Persondy. Cutaway

joy in oaken carpentry. Small, two-storeyed, of stone unattractively rendered outside. The plan is of the normal two-unit type, with entrance doorway, hearth and spiral stair in line in the S wall. The hall with chamber over occupies the S two-thirds of the space, the rest is subdivided for parlour and service room below, and two inner rooms above. The timber frames survive of several original windows, all low but of various widths. The hall windows of five lights E and W, other rooms with three or two lights. Internal post-and-panel partitions, with four-centred door-heads, the posts moulded, chamfered or plain according
to the importance of the room each section enclosed. Ceiling p. 37
beams and joists enriched on the same principle, but here the mouldings are of ebullient richness, multiple quadrants drawn
together at the ends into leaf-shaped stops. In the hall the 60
rippling effect this creates is overwhelming. Yet a simple chimney-piece here, stone jambs and massive timber lintel.

The little house was intelligently modernized in the 1940s by the addition of a single-storey, enclosed, lean-to veranda along the S and E walls, maintaining the integrity of the interior while making the house practical for modern living.

The parson's BARN at r.-angles to the SE has fared less well in conversion to a house.

MONMOUTHSHIRE AND BRECON CANAL. The canal winds NE–SW through the parish towards the foot of the mountain ridge.

It was engineered by *William Crossley* 1809–12, and within these 2 m. (3.2 kilometres) is crossed by no fewer than ten of his typical single-arched accommodation BRIDGES.

MAMHILAD PARK INDUSTRIAL ESTATE. *See* Llanfihangel Pontymoile.

2080 MARSHFIELD/MEIRYN

ST MARY. In the C12 the advowson of Marshfield was granted to St Augustine's Abbey, Bristol. Enough remains of the early C13 church to show what a splendid building it must have been, unique among the parish churches of south-east Wales, and clearly by the masons who built the nave of Llandaff Cathedral. The nave walls, the S doorway, the reset W doorway and the chancel arch all survive. This is not at first apparent, since the W tower, S porch and chancel are all Perp, as are all the nave windows. The nave was restored and N vestry added by *Habershon & Pite* in 1866, and the chancel was restored in 1867. A second restoration took place in 1908–9 under *E.M. Bruce Vaughan*, but, remarkably, the damaged E.E. details were not made whole. The church is of Old Red Sandstone.

The quality of the E.E. work is at once indicated by the doorway reset in the W tower. It has a pointed head and two continuous filleted rolls, each shadowed by smaller rolls. The tower itself is plain, unbuttressed, crowned by corbelled battlements, its battered plinth modern, its W window of 1908–9. The battered plinth of the nave, on the other hand, is clearly early C13, and was topped by a moulded string, which has been
14 hacked off. The early C13 S doorway, within the porch, is round-headed, its moulded arch overlapped by close-set undercut chevrons, most of them sadly snapped. Filleted side shafts carry tall stiff-leaf capitals. Perp image niche. To see the grandest C13 feature it is necessary to enter, but the other Perp features of the exterior can briefly be described first. The S porch is more impressive than the rest, because of its outer arch, two-centred, the continuous mouldings consisting of a double wave, a hollow decorated with square flowers, a wave and a hollow. Side shafts have small caps and the stumps of pinnacles. The three-light E window has panel tracery under a two-centred head and a hood on square, outlined stops. Nave N projection for the rood-loft stair. The rood-loft windows noted by Glynne in 1858 have been restored away.

So to the interior. The chancel arch extends further the decorative range of the early C13 work. Pairs of detached shafts carry fine stiff-leaf capitals, fully comparable with those at Llandaff Cathedral. The arch itself is pointed, but its two orders are merely chamfered, as in the nave arcade at Llandaff. The tower arch by contrast is Perp, but also impressive, tall and narrow, and continuously moulded with wave and double wave. Nave roof of 1908–9, chancel roof of 1923. – FONT. Octagonal bowl on black marble shafts with leaf capitals, *c.* 1863. –

IMMERSION FONT. At the W end of the nave, 1908. – PULPIT. Neo-Jacobean. By *Bruce Vaughan*, 1908. – REREDOS. 1883. With crocketed gables, pinnacles and figures of saints. By *Harry Hems* of Exeter to *Habershon & Fawckner*'s design. – SCULPTURE. The small figure in the niche in the S porch is by *W. Goscombe John*, *c.* 1909. – STAINED GLASS. Chancel E, Salvator Mundi between SS Paul and John. 1883 by *Edwin Horwood*. – Sanctuary, Virtues: N, 1887 by *Cox Sons Buckley & Co.*; S, 1888, probably by *Heaton, Butler & Bayne*. – Chancel NW and SW, more Virtues. – Nave NE, 'And a little child shall lead them'. 1912 by *Powell*'s. – Nave N centre, Nativity and Empty Tomb. By *A. Savell*, *c.* 1892. – Nave SE, Holy Family and Mary and Martha. 1911–12 by *Powell*'s. – Nave S centre, Nunc Dimittis. By *Burlison & Grylls* (A. Brooks), *c.* 1910. Charming. – Tower W, Charity and female saints. By *William Morris & Co.* of Westminster, *c.* 1921. – MONUMENTS. Fanny Henriette Walker †1887. White marble vesica-shaped bust-length relief of a woman in prayer. Cherubs, lilies and stars in the frame. Signed by *J. Forsyth*. – Lady Ellen Webb †1919. Gilt-bronze relief by *W. Goscombe John* of a woman glancing back as an angel welcomes her into the afterlife. The sculptor exhibited the relief in 1921 as Mors Janua Vitae. (– Basil Webb. Small bronze bust by *W. Goscombe John*. P. Howell.)

BAPTIST CHURCH, Castleton, facing the A48. 1857–8 by *R. G.* 98
Thomas of Newport. An astonishing sight in its Neo-Norman polychromy. Rock-faced Old Red Sandstone lavishly dressed with yellow, purple and even glazed lapis-lazuli-coloured bricks. Three-bay front, the doorways in the side bays, the broad, slightly projecting centre dominated by a huge wheel window, with an arcade of four small lights below, and a crowning gable given Lombardic corbelling. Over the r. bay rises an octagonal turret carrying a flared spirelet covered with fish-scale tiles. The sides of the building are given full architectural treatment, blind below, with four arched windows above. Conventional interior, however, the galleries on three sides supported by thin iron columns with plain caps. Pierced metal gallery fronts. Open timber roof with tie-beams and double queenposts.

WESLEYAN METHODIST CHAPEL (now Masonic Hall), Castleton, facing the A48. Dated 1854 on a gatepier. So this is what the Baptists next door were competing with. Exaggeratedly Gothic. Rock-faced Old Red Sandstone and Bath stone for dressings. Big, coarse, four-light Dec window in the gable-end towards the road, and to the r. an elaborate, presumably truncated porch steeple. The doorway, its arch formed of three radiating ogees, looks positively Arabic.

SCHOOL (now Old School House), Castleton. Gothic. Contemporary with the chapels, and just as high-spirited, but infinitely more sophisticated. Designed by *Prichard & Seddon* in 1857. It is a pity that conversion to a house has disfigured some of the windows. Old Red Sandstone with Bath stone for dressings, and red brick in two narrow bands and in the patterned, pointed relieving arches over the major windows. Some blue brick too. The building is divided into two steeply gabled pavilions (one for boys, one for girls), linked by a single-storey veranda, its roofslope carried on shafted stone corbels. It is fascinating to observe in how many ways the two pavilions are differentiated from one another while clearly remaining a pair.

MARSHFIELD PRIMARY SCHOOL, immediately to the S, is stylistically a world away, with its flat roof and full-height glazing. 1965–6 by *Powell & Alport*, and in itself nothing special.

5090

MATHERN/MERTHYR TEWDRIG

A memorable group created by bishops of Llandaff: church, gabled palace to the SW and Moynes Court, an eccentric silhouette away to the W across a miniature valley.

ST TEWDRIC. Grandiosely enlarged by John Marshall, bishop of Llandaff 1478–96. He widened the nave aisles and added the S porch. In a separate campaign he built the noble W tower, which is identified as his by shields bearing the eagle of St John the Evangelist, and the arms of the see of Llandaff impaling an M. Much of the pre-existing church survives, almost all of the C13: the long chancel, the chancel arch and the four-bay nave arcades. The W pier and arch of the N arcade, however, belong to a yet earlier, probably C12 church.

The approach is from the E. The chancel, of local rubble limestone and sandstone, grey, buff and a little pink, is unified by a continuous sill-level roll. Chancel E window a tall triple lancet, single N lancet between square-headed Perp windows. The matching Perp S windows, however, were described in 1852 as 'nearly new'. Restoration of the chancel in 1881 by *Ewan Christian* (which accounts for the dislocation of the sill roll in the SE corner). S organ chamber dated 1889.

Marshall's nave aisles are both of generous width, gabled and given large two-centred-headed three-light windows through-
32 out. The N aisle is the more perfect composition. It is of three wide bays (so ignoring the four-bay arcade spacing inside), the N windows spaced apart by the highly unusual and effective device of coupling the buttresses between them. Diagonal angle buttresses too. All have scroll-capped set-offs. The composition is firmly tied together by a cyma basemould, and by the continuation of the window hoodmoulds as a string, which appears to pass behind the buttresses. The windows themselves are set in deep concave reveals and have cusped elongated hexfoils above ogee-headed lights. The fabric of the walling round the windows suggests that they were a later – but surely not much later – insertion.

The S aisle deploys many of the same components, but with less consistency and deftness. Here the porch, part of the composition, forces a four-bay arrangement, so the buttresses are not coupled. Slight irregularities in the way the window pattern is interpreted, and no continuity in the hoodmoulds. Contemporary porch roof, of the typical late C15 form with arched braces, collar purlin and square leaf bosses at the intersections. Handsomely moulded porch arch and S doorway.

The tower, unlike the rest of the church, is built of squared ashlar blocks. Though tall and handsomely proportioned, it is more austere than the aisles. Moulded base, square-cut string-courses dividing its height into three stages. Diagonal buttresses, over-riding the lower string but not the upper. Small battlements and angle pinnacles. The W doorway is enriched by no more than two broad hollow chamfers; the three-light window above it has tracery based on that of the aisles, but without ogees. Single-light windows in the middle stage with the Marshall heraldry. Belfry windows of two cusped ogee-headed lights under a blind-traceried head. Polygonal NE stair-turret. On the S face, a sundial, painted, with an iron gnomon. Of the C18?

The interior is dominated by work of the C13. The chancel E triplet stands within a superarch outlined by a roll moulding. Double PISCINA under a handsome splayed arch on imposts. The moulding here consists of a filleted roll flanked by similar smaller rolls. The chancel arch is wide, of two-centred form, but merely chamfered. The squints l. and r. low down and high up must belong to the late medieval rood arrangements, see the door to the rood loft built integrally with the lower S squint. The C13 arcades are quite ambitious in form, though different from one another in detail and proportion. Piers of lozenge plan with four slender circular shafts added in the cardinal directions. Moulded bases and caps echo their roundness. In the N arcade the piers are low, the arches pointed and double-chamfered. The S piers are taller, but carry single-chamfered, nearly round-headed arches which look as if they may be a C15 replacement. The tower arch, very high and narrow, has two extremely broad and deep hollow chamfers, a magnification of those on the W doorway.

Finally, the earliest component. The W pier of the N arcade, square and stout with chamfered angles and a plain impost, must be of the C12. Single-chamfered W arch, probably C15. The base of a similar pier was reported to have been uncovered in 1881, 12 ft (3.7 metres) to the N. This might indicate a Norman aisled nave on the site of the present N aisle. The discovery was made during *John Prichard*'s restoration of 1880–2.

FITTINGS. – FONTS. The disused font in the N aisle, a plain octagonal bowl on an octagonal shaft, bears the scratched date 1705 on one face. – Late C19 Perp font, also octagonal, but large, and the faces decorated with blind tracery. – REREDOS. Timber. Elaborate, *c.* 1914. – PULPIT. Timber. A handsome piece clearly by *Prichard.* Octagonal, with blind-traceried faces on an enriched tapering stem. – PEWS. In the nave. Also typical of *Prichard.* – STAINED GLASS. In the W window of the S aisle late C15 fragments have been collected together. Many armorial panels, some related to Bishop Marshall. The grisaille glass patterned with flaming stars throughout the aisle windows, perhaps of 1881, takes up the medieval coloration. – Sanctuary N. Crucifixion between the Virgin and Child, and the Resurrected Christ. Signed and dated by *Joseph Bell* of Bristol, 1848. An early example of the Pugin-inspired revival of medievalizing stained glass. – Sanctuary S. Faith, Hope and Charity, a dour trio. Erected in connection with a death in 1854, also by *Joseph Bell*. – N aisle E, Ascended Christ and saints, signed by *W. G. Dixon* and dated 1882. – Chancel E, Crucifixion. By *Horace Wilkinson*, 1914. *En suite* with the reredos? – MONUMENTS. Tomb slab (nave) bearing a staff in relief. Medieval, but of what century? – INCISED SLAB (in the centre of the chancel floor). Illegible, but said to mark the place where the heart and bowels of Miles Salley, bishop of Llandaff, †1516, are buried. (– BRASS. Philip Williams †1562 and Alice Williams †1567. Engraved plaque showing small kneeling figures.) – Thomas Hughes †1667 (S aisle). Black touch tablet in a strapwork surround incorporating skull and hourglass. – Catherine Rosser †1806 and Samuel Rosser †1818 (N aisle). Black and white marble double wall tablet. Shield-shaped inscription panels. Her half signed *Greenways*, Bristol, his signed *I. Wood*, Bristol. The latter must have been responsible for the ingenious doubling. – Sir Edward Keynton Williams †1830 (S aisle). Shield-shaped inscription panel backed by sword and flag. – Elizabeth Smith †1837 (S aisle). Small Gothic eight-pointed tablet. Angels supporting the inscription panel alternate with triangles of foliage. Ballflower border. – James Justice Hayes Williams †1838 (N aisle). Grecian tablet signed by *J. M. Payton* of Bristol. – Rev. James Williams †1846 (N aisle). Long inscription in a pointed-topped vine-scroll border.

In the CHURCHYARD, N of the church, a medieval arch, two-centred with a broad chamfer, set in a fragment of walling. What did it belong to?

PALACE, SW of the church. Mathern was one of three medieval palaces of the bishops of Llandaff, and after Owain Glyndŵr's rebellion in the early C15, the only one kept habitable. Its position in the SE corner of the diocese, close to the Severn Estuary and the English border, recommended it to successive bishops for 300 years. In the early C18, however, it fell out of use and became a farm. In the 1770s large parts were demolished, and by 1801, when Archdeacon Coxe visited, the remainder was 'in a sad state of dilapidation'. At last, in 1889, the Ecclesiastical Commissioners sold to a lay owner. Five years later the palace was acquired by *H. Avray Tipping*, the garden designer and future architectural correspondent of *Country Life*. By 1899 he had restored and enlarged what remained of the former episcopal palace as a modest but romantic country house set in a delectable garden. Since 1957 the palace has been used as a guest house by Richard Thomas & Baldwins Ltd, and subsequently by the British Steel Corporation.

John de la Zouche, bishop 1408–23, is said to have built the present palace, and a loose datestone of 1419 is reported. The N range appears of that date. All other medieval features suggest an early C16 date, and indeed Bishop Godwin, writing a century later, attributed hall, refectory, kitchen and chapel to Bishop Miles Salley (1500–16). But there was an outer gate-tower to the NE, demolished in the C18, and this was probably part of Zouche's work. It must have led into an outer court. The main surviving range formed the E, entrance, range of an inner quadrangle, most of which has been demolished. Tipping wove in his own contributions with such tact and restraint that the whole can be described together. Local grey limestone.

The approach from the E passes between the gable-ends of a pair of close-set COTTAGES, which Tipping sited so as to withhold the full view of the palace from the visitor until the last moment. One then sees that the main range has a chapel in a wing coming forward to the l., and a gate-tower to the r. All this in its undemonstrative irregularity suggests perhaps that late medieval bishops of Llandaff had little power or splendour to boast of. Most impressive is the E window of the chapel, of four lights under a four-centred head with a hoodmould on head-stops. Yet the tracery is simple, cuspless. What is more, the mid-height band of masonry that subdivides the windows must be a very early alteration, as the lower half has been converted into a set of arched lights. A two-light upper window round the corner to the N, with a hood on square stops, and similar S windows at two levels, also show that the range had become two-storeyed by the middle of the C16.

The external flight of steps up the N flank of the chapel wing must be of the C18, when the palace was in farm use. It masks a four-centred-headed doorway at the S end of the main range. The S half of this range is two-storeyed, and has one two-light and one four-light window at each level without vertical alignment. Arched lights and deep, plain reveals. To the r. of this the range steps up abruptly to three storeys, forming the gatehouse and a set-back section beyond, all under a later continuous roofslope. Plain, irregularly polygonal SE stair-turret rising well clear of the rest. The entrance arch of the gatehouse is of flattened four-centred form, double-chamfered. Two-storeyed canted oriel above, its windows of one-plus-two-plus-one arched lights. The oriel is faced with ashlar, but devoid of decoration. Slit windows to the r. indicate that garderobes were sited in the NE angle of the gatehouse (cf. Pencoed Castle, Llanmartin).

Set back obliquely beyond the gatehouse is the gable-end of the N range of the inner courtyard. This is clearly earlier, and, as already noted, must belong to Zouche's building of *c.* 1419. Long, central two-light window with transom and pointed head, the lights trefoil-headed, and trefoil cusping below the transom. Single-light window to the l. of equal height, trefoil-headed and with cusped transom. In the gable, a pair of small trefoiled lancets with pierced circle over. All these must have lit a lofty hall open to the roof. The W end of this range is marked by two tall, shallow buttresses against the N wall. C17 extension with a three-light N window, its mullions ovolo-moulded, and a square-headed stone doorway under a flat bracketed hood. C20 weather-boarded upper storey here.

The W side of the main range corresponds with the E front,

the inner entrance arch of the gatehouse double-chamfered, the windows of two or four arched lights. The S range of the courtyard is in ruins, and featureless except for a four-centred-headed doorway and window over it. Tipping absorbed it into his garden, and shrubs still tumble over it. The single-storeyed lean-to addition to the main range, under a steep pantiled roof, must be an C18 creation, though the tall three-light window in the N end of the addition, with a transom and arched lights, belongs to the early C16 range whose ruins have just been noted. Tipping extended the lean-to to wrap round the SW angle of the house, inserting simple timber windows below the pantiled roofslope. He also added the S-facing open timber porch, and the low but extensive service court on the S side of the chapel wing.

The interior is hard to interpret, now that much even of Tipping's work has been swept away and all internal stonework is covered in emulsion paint. Early C16 doorways to the gatehouse stair-turret at ground and first-floor level, four-centred-headed with continuous hollow and wave. On the second floor, square-headed stone doorways, one with elegant cusped pointed outline in relief on the lintel, presumably of the C17. In the so-called long parlour at ground level N of the gatehouse, a stone chimneypiece, the most notable early C16 feature. Flanking shafts with oak-leaf caps support a concave shelf decorated with rosettes. Between this and the four-centred fireplace arch, a deep band decorated with trios of blind trefoil-headed panels. Not skilfully carved. The N range is conventionally two-storeyed inside, retaining nothing of the C15 hall. The lower ceiling is carried on heavy beams on stone corbels carved with episcopal shields of arms. This conversion of the hall probably dates to the C16.

Tipping's SW extension provided two of his main reception rooms, both bipartite. An arch divides the dining room into a barrel-vaulted half and a half that is flat-ceiled. In the latter, a brought-in C18 chimneypiece of white and yellow marble. The drawing room, further S, is an L in plan. Here the brought-in chimneypiece is of timber, c. 1740, with swags and drops of fruit and leaves, Rococo scrolls and, in the centre, two birds standing on flaming torches.

The VILLAGE is little more than a loose-textured group of substantial houses. THE CHANTRY, SE of the church, is perhaps of *c.* 1880. Stone, two-storeyed under a hipped roof framed by red brick chimneystacks. But mullion-and-transom windows, that for the stair in the centre. Double-gabled side elevations. MATHERN LODGE, further E, is a Tudor-Gothic *cottage orné*.

THE INNAGE, beyond the end of the village to the E. A small, two-storeyed C16 manor house in many ways untypical of Monmouthshire. It is built of local stone, an irregular H in plan, and presents its main front towards the SW. Here the gabled l. wing comes forward as far as the adjoining two-storeyed porch. The windows of both are stone-mullioned, moulded with a hollow chamfer. Similar four-light hall window in the recessed centre. These cannot be earlier than the late C16.* In the r. wing, which projects forward further, there are four-light windows at both levels in the gable-end, and these have the earlier form, arched lights, but also a hollow chamfer. Projecting chimney-breasts to the NE and NW. These both serve fireplaces with timber lintels and stone jambs, those of the hall fireplace chamfered. At the SE end of the hall, however, an early C16 doorway, four-centred-headed and double-wave-moulded. At r.-angles to it, opening into the lower room in the S wing, a similar shaped doorway, plainly chamfered. The chimneypiece here is entirely of stone, its depressed arched head moulded with a continuous sunk wave. So all the earliest evidence is in the S, parlour, wing, and the hall range must replace a yet earlier hall. The remains of a timber screen at the N end of the hall, dated by Fox and Raglan to the late C15, have disappeared.

The house is accompanied by unusually many stone farm buildings, with pantiled roofs.

MOYNES COURT, ¼ m. W. The delightfully trim and regular house 51
built by Francis Godwin, bishop of Llandaff, 1608–10, stands between a medieval gatehouse to the NE and a roughly rectangular earthwork to the SW, presumably the site of the medieval house. In relation to the palace, then, Bishop Godwin built himself what would at the time have been called a lodge, a compact but well-appointed occasional residence for privacy and recreation.

The GATEHOUSE is a C14 structure, square in plan, with two square, eccentrically placed stair-turrets, one front r., the other back l. Inner and outer carriage arches are of depressed two-centred outline, plainly chamfered, and the vault is divided into three bays by chamfered transverse ribs. One trefoiled lancet high on the NW side wall. Otherwise the upper parts were remodelled by Godwin. Windows with ovolo mouldings. Small back gable and another at the front, not aligned with each other.

Bishop Godwin's HOUSE, aligned on the gatehouse and framed between contemporary forecourt walls, is dated 1609 on the armorial panel over the central doorway and 1610 in nailheads on the door itself. It is built of local pinkish-grey limestone and presents an appearance of absolute symmetry. Five bays, two storeys with a third in the three gables. Steep, gable-ended roof and, appearing above its ridge, groups of chimneystacks, a square of four in the centre and trios set lozenge-wise to l. and r. The mullioned stone windows are ovolo-moulded, under unobtrusive hoodmoulds, the lowest of four lights and tall enough to have transoms, those above of three lights. The flush relieving arches over all windows would originally have been hidden by overall rendering of the walls. Central projecting full-height porch with four-centred-headed doorway in a square surround, its incised decoration like minimalist triglyphs. Jumped-up hoodmould. The inner door is displaced to the r., no doubt to lead into the screens passage at the lower end of the hall. In

* The armorial panel dated 1618, set over the porch arch, is a recent misleading insertion.

plan the house is a double pile, but the rear range was not constructed all at once. Straight joints suggest that originally the plan was rather a T, with two central full-height gables. The fenestration can never have been regular here and has been much altered. Internally, only the staircase is original. It stands behind the r. rear gable and rises in short straight flights up a solid square core.

Contemporary ten-bay BARN to the E of the house. Ventilated by typical slits and small triangular apertures. Converted for domestic use 1995–6.

At NEWTON GREEN, ½m. N, there is a little more to see. Small stone SCHOOL (now day nursery) of Ecclesiological character, built probably c. 1860. Late C19 ESTATE HOUSING for the Vaughan-Hughes family of Wyelands (*see* below), including an E-plan range, presumably an almshouse, with verandas, dated 1891. Stone below, half-timbered above.

WYELANDS, ¾m. N. An exquisite ashlar-faced classical villa, by *Robert Lugar*, who was better known as a Picturesque, Nash-inspired designer. His client was George Buckle, who was sheriff of Monmouthshire in 1819 and died in 1824. N front of three wide bays, the centre slightly recessed, the outer bays crowned by pedimental gables. Deep Tuscan bracketed eaves. Single-storey porch, an entablature brought forward on pairs of handsome Ionic columns. Sash windows, the lower ones with architraves on deep, slender consoles. The S front is almost identical, the lower windows tripartite, the porch absent. Instead of a central doorway there is a window, a false one, as the chimney-stack above indicates. By contrast the W front is deliberately non-symmetrical, with a broad, canted window bay towards the r. To the E extends a slightly lower service wing, rendered and lined out to look like ashlar. The front door leads into a rectangular hall subdivided by two Ionic columns. The stair rises to the l. from the inner hall. Balustrade with slender handrail but cast-iron balusters, every other one moulded and entwined with scrolling foliage. The painted-glass window on the upper landing, depicting hops and roses in pink, green, red and orange, must be original. Greek key ceiling borders in these public spaces. The main rooms, to W, SW and SE, have palmette ceiling borders in three different patterns. Restrained mid-C19 marble chimneypieces. Drawing room (SW) and dining room (SE) have chamfered corners, the latter with a servery beyond a segmental arch. But most noteworthy is the way the interior disposition of walls and fireplaces is unrelated to the design of the exterior, necessitating not one but several false windows.

In the mid C19 a stone CONSERVATORY was added to the S of the service wing, and the garden formalized, with arcaded balustrading, and a square SUMMER-HOUSE to the SE. This has shaped gables in each direction, a hint of strapwork, and a Frenchy square dome. To the NE, a square, stone-walled KITCHEN GARDEN, and beyond that the HOME FARM. The park is full of mature specimen trees. NORTH LODGE, single-storeyed, with canted ends and Tuscan eaves, clearly also by

Lugar, provides a foretaste of the house. So the ensemble is remarkably complete and beautifully preserved. Only the covered SWIMMING POOL, E of the service wing, reveals the activities of the 1990s.

MICHAELSTON-Y-FEDW/ LLANFIHANGEL Y FEDW

2080

ST MICHAEL. Quite a large C13 church, nave and lower chancel, with a plain, late medieval W tower, S porch and S transept. Restored 1894–6 by *Seddon & Carter*. Local Old Red Sandstone is the walling material throughout, with yellow Triassic stone for the 1894 dressed work. The chancel E wall makes the most impressive show, its three large lancets set under a continuous hoodmould and above four short buttresses, the outer ones gabled. Two S lancets, one N, largely a re-creation of 1894. Blocked N doorway. Lancets in the nave too, one N one recognizably medieval. Otherwise, they and the large three-light Dec windows are all of 1894, as is the S doorway. The tower, on a battered base, has a small but handsome Perp W doorway, moulded with a continuous double wave, deep hollow and wave under a hoodmould. Everything above is plain and rather meagre, the top battlements corbelled out. Small crocketed angle pinnacles. Inside, the tower arch has the typical form of two chamfered orders dying into the imposts. Identical chancel arch, presumably a later medieval replacement for the C13 arch. In the chancel, double E aumbry and evidence of two blocked N doorways. Are the latter C12 in origin? The S transept, which served as pew and burial chapel for the Kemeys, later Kemeys-Tynte, family of Cefn Mabli, must be post-Reformation. Typical mid-C16 windows, square-headed with arched lights. The transept oddly straddles the chancel arch, to give a view into both chancel and nave. The nave roof may be partly old. It is of the usual ribbed wagon form, but the enriched ceilure at the E end is most unusual, so may be Seddon & Carter's idea. – FONT. A rare and idiosyncratic C18 piece. The bowl is encased in upright leaves, and the stem carved in the form of a tree, round which a serpent is entwined. But there are no accompanying figures of Adam and Eve, as in Grinling Gibbons's font in St James Piccadilly. (– WALL PAINTING. Medieval traces in the reveal of the chancel N window.) – STAINED GLASS. Chancel E, Ascension with saints, *c.* 1891. Probably by *George Parlby* for *Powell*'s (A. Brooks). – Nave N, Virgin and Child, *c.* 1942. Signed *J.B.* and *W.A.* – MONUMENTS, in the S transept. – Unidentified early C17 wall monument commemorating 'uncle wife brother and daughter'. Ionic side columns. Strapwork surround to the back panel. – Mary and Anne Kemeys †1708. Draped oval tablet with cherub heads in the drapery.

DRUIDSTONE. A large sandstone block standing in the stable yard of Druidstone House, 1 m. S. It is 9 ft (2.7 metres) high and 3–4 ft (0.9–1.2 metres) wide, and there is a record that it originally stood in the centre of a ring of smaller stones, one of which survived until recently in a field about 100 yds (90 metres) away. If this is true it must have been an impressive Bronze Age circle.

4010 MITCHEL TROY/LLANFIHANGEL TRODDI

ST MICHAEL. A small but impressive Dec church, built of Old Red Sandstone, the dressings both purple and grey. Partly reconstructed by *John Prichard* 1873–6. The W tower is strangely undersized, its W face just one broad buttress. Note the worn inscription on a SW quoin, doubtless referring to a benefaction to building the tower: ORATE PRO GODEFRIDO ET IOHANNE. The top stage is of 1909 by *Ernest G. Davies,* replacing a spire which had fallen in the C18, destroying the N aisle. Nave with lean-to aisles, the N aisle rebuilt by *Prichard.* Medieval S porch, its entrance arch two-centred and moulded with one large and two small hollows. S doorway with two crude double waves. The E window of the S aisle is a memorable oddity, of three lights with cusped ogee heads of diminishing size under a straight top which slopes down parallel with the roof-line. Chancel rebuilt by *Prichard* using the old N and S trefoil-headed lancets and supplying a rather fanciful E window, made up using some old fragments. The most handsome parts of the church are the C14 three-bay nave arcades, moulded with two sunk quadrants running unbroken up piers and arches. The chancel arch has a continuous hollow and wave dying into the imposts low down, a form Prichard frequently used, but which is here apparently largely medieval. Handsome stone organ chamber contrived by *Prichard* at the W end of the N aisle. – FONT. A C12 tub. – Many FITTINGS by *Prichard.* Most memorable is the second FONT, with a circular bowl, waterlilies and passion flowers carved on its rim and netted fish underneath, and a stem surrounded by red and green marble shafts. – PULPIT. Of red, green and buff stone, carved with stiff-leaf and ballflower, the broad, foliage-covered corbel imitated from the famous lectern at Beaulieu Abbey refectory, Hampshire. – CHANCEL SCREEN. Low, of stone, with cinquefoils enclosing red polished marble balls. – CHOIR STALLS. Of timber, their angel finials missing. – S DOOR. Typical *Prichard*-designed carpentry. – FLOOR TILES. By *Godwin* of Lugwardine throughout. – STAINED GLASS. A good deal, but most of it disappointingly unimpressive and decayed. – Chancel E, Ascension. 1873 by *Ward & Hughes.* – S aisle E, a soldier in medievalizing armour tramples on a snake while the light of the Holy Ghost streams down on him, *c.* 1875. It provides an interesting insight into mid-Victorian popular theology. This too is by *Ward & Hughes*, as is the N aisle E, Christ and the Centurion, also *c.* 1875. – N aisle N, Good Shepherd. 1886 by the same. – S aisle W, Christ Blessing. Also of *c.* 1886, but probably by *Clayton & Bell* (A. Brooks). – S aisle S, Empty Tomb. 1960 by *Celtic Studios.*

In the CHURCHYARD a highly unusual C14 CROSS SHAFT, 34
slender, rectangular, tapering and carved on the angles with alternating shields and ballflower. On three steps. – LYCHGATE. Medieval. Of the standard simple but satisfying pattern, a pitched stone-clad roof on wall slabs.

TROY HOUSE, 1½ m. NE. On low ground, beside the River Trothy, and little more than a mile across the Monnow from Monmouth. A puzzling house in many ways. First there is the archaeological puzzle, to discern the early C17 house, built for Sir Charles Somerset, in the various projecting blocks to N and E of the building. Then there is the historical puzzle, to explain why the first Duke of Beaufort, having built Great Castle House in the centre of Monmouth town in 1673, should within a decade, 1681–4, have built what is virtually a new house close by at Troy. Thirdly, and most stunning, if not puzzling, is the ducal scale of the new work. A memorandum by the Duchess, preserved at Badminton, however, resolves some of these problems, by recording that the new range was built for the son and heir, the Marquess of Worcester, on his marriage, to be 'suitable to his quality'. The shell cost the Duke £3,000, but the Marquess paid for 'finishing the house to his mind'.

Description must begin with the first Duke's N-facing range. 71
It is in what was in the 1680s the approved modern pattern of a hipped roof over a regularly fenestrated block, the central section brought slightly forward under a pediment. Yet it is a single pile, three bays deep but no less than thirteen bays wide, the centre five under the pediment, and is of three very tall storeys, not just of two. Old Red Sandstone walling, originally harled. Thin ashlar dressings, the raised window surrounds red, the raised quoins grey. No further enrichment, beyond a wave-moulded plinth and wave moulding to the pediment. Grandeur is achieved only in the flight of steps to the entrance doorway in the piano nobile. They rise in two parallel flights to a half-landing and then bridge across in a long flight at r.-angles to the house. At the E end, on a much smaller scale, a four-bay, four-storey block with segment-headed sash windows of C18 type and facing of grey ashlar blocks. This masks an early C17 wing, the remains of Sir Charles Somerset's house. A second wing projecting S has a four-centred stone entrance arch, also doubtless early C17.

Inside the early C17 house are three good-quality, typically
Jacobean decorated plaster ceilings. In the ground storey one 62
ceiling has thick ribs with elaborate sprigs in vases sprouting from them, and an openwork central pendant. Frieze of sphinxes flanking shields. A second ceiling at this level has thin ribs making star patterns, and relief sprigs of a different design. Central solid pendant and frieze of roses and oak leaves. Above, the third ceiling is somewhat simpler, the thin ribs bearing sprigs of roses. Leaf bosses. Reset in the 1680s range, a Jacobean chimneypiece (from Raglan?) with terms bearing Ionic caps. Lion masks over. The single surviving interior feature of the Duke of Beaufort's building is the magnificently spacious open-well

staircase, projecting from the back of the range in its own pavilion. The stair goes up from ground level through two storeys, has thick twisted balusters, which are formed into newels in groups of four, and a ramped handrail.

To the W of the house, a rectangular WALLED GARDEN, entered through a rusticated sandstone doorway with strapwork, a heraldic shield, the initials of Elizabeth and Charles Somerset – son of the fourth Earl of Worcester and his wife – and, formerly, the date 1611. (Stone-lined bee boles in the garden walls.)

To the S, at TROY HOUSE FARM, a row of cottages clearly formed out of an early, possibly medieval building, and at r.-angles beyond, a seven-bay BARN, probably of the C18. Closer to the W and S of the house, a miscellany of (now disused) buildings erected in the 1950s and '60s for the Good Shepherd Order of nuns which ran a school here. These are uncompromisingly modern in style, in particular the CHAPEL, 1963–4 by *Kenneth W. Smithies* of Bristol. This is rectangular with a rectangular, flat-roofed clerestory, and windows at two levels filled with abstract STAINED GLASS, by *Whitefriars Stained Glass Studios*. Internally, the chapel was planned as two independent spaces, for the Sisters and for the girls, with the sanctuary separating them from one another.

TROY LODGE, to the N beside the road. Early C19. Single-storeyed with pointed windows in its canted end.

TOLLGATE HOUSE, ¼ m. further SW towards the village, has three diagonal full-height bays, to supervise the fork in the road. Built *c.* 1810, when the turnpike road between Monmouth and Raglan was constructed.

LYDART HOUSE, 1 m. SE of the village. Handsomely proportioned white C18 façade, of six bays and two storeys, under a flared hipped roof with semicircular dormers like those of the 1820s at Tredegar House (q.v.).

On the hillside above, a grey-rendered STABLE, a proper little classical composition, its centre bay brought slightly forward under a pediment, the windows round-headed with emphasized keystones and impost blocks.

LYDART FARM. Dourly rendered. The three-bay front shows its early date only in the corbelled chimney-breast at the N end. At the back a long wing extends downhill. Here the stone hoodmould of one S upper window remains, evidence that the range was built in the later C16 with stone detail, a rarity in the county.

MONKSWOOD

3000

The name refers to the monks of Tintern Abbey, whose estate of Estavarney here was the largest of their outlying farms, or granges.

ST MATTHEW. 1882–4 by *E. H. Lingen Barker*. Small and undistinguished, nave and lower chancel, with double W bell gable.

Greenish local stone and Bath stone dressings. Dec. Arch-braced nave roof on naturalistic flower corbels.

Nos. 1–19 West Road, ¼ m. sw of the church. Unusually formal housing, dated 1939 and built for workers at the Royal Ordnance Depot at Glascoed. Cream pebble-dashed walls, hipped roofs. Symmetry is asserted by the regular spacing of the gabled projections and by the cubic chimneystacks.

MONMOUTH/TREFYNWY 5010

The architectural highlights of Monmouth are classical: Stuart, Georgian and early Victorian. Its Roman antecedents are obscure. It is generally accepted as being on the site of Blestium, mentioned in the Antonine Itinerary. It is now known that there was an early fort here, and an important late Roman centre of ironworking. But the origins of the town lie in the years immediately after the

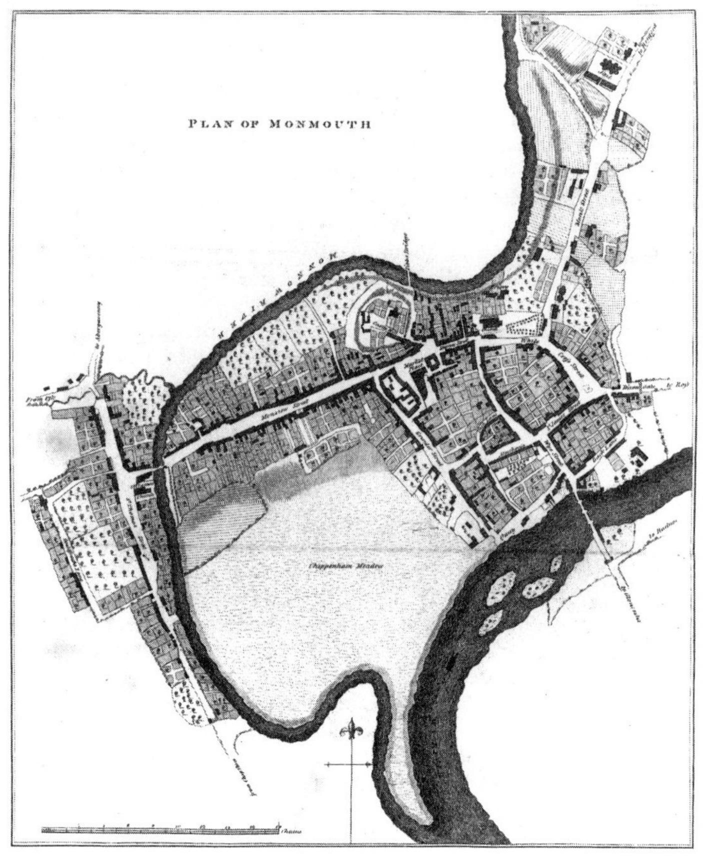

Monmouth. Plan, 1801

Norman Conquest, when William fitz Osbern, Earl of Hereford, constructed a castle near the confluence of the Rivers Wye and Monnow, and shortly afterwards a Benedictine priory was founded alongside. The castle occupied the highest point, overlooking the Monnow where it begins to describe a great bow before flowing into the Wye. In due course the outer bailey of the castle became the site of the town's market, known today as Agincourt Square, and an informal grid of streets (Whitecross, Wyebridge, St Mary, Greindor – now Glendower, and Weirhead – now under the A40) occupied the neck of land between the castle and the River Wye. Town walls were built 1297–*c.* 1320, together with the remarkably surviving fortified bridge over the Monnow at the far end of the 'great causeway' (now Monnow Street), leading to the suburb of Overmonnow.

At the Acts of Union, 1536–43, which absorbed Wales into the English legal and local governmental systems, Monmouth was designated a county town and gave its name to Monmouthshire. Hence the cuckoo-in-the-nest effect which the Shire Hall gives in the town's little market square. The many handsome C18 houses dotted about the town also partake of the county town cachet. Of commercial activity during this period, when Monmouth was a busy river port with quays and warehouses along the River Wye, all trace has been obliterated by the A40 bypass.

After the dissolution of the priory in 1536, few of its buildings survived. The parochial nave of its church was rebuilt 1736–7. Nor did the castle fare better. Its hall remained in use for a time as the courtroom for the county assizes, but in 1647 its great circular tower, which must have dominated the town since its construction in the mid C13, was pulled down. On its site, less than thirty years later, the first Duke of Beaufort built a swagger town house out of the materials. This, Great Castle House, appears prominently in distant views of the town, but is easy to overlook when in the town centre.

What gives Monmouth its particular architectural flavour is the contribution of the local architect *George Vaughan Maddox*. For two decades from the mid 1820s he put up a sequence of public buildings and private houses in the town, in a style deft, cultured, and only occasionally unresolved. His greatest work is Priory Street, a remarkably early inner bypass, where his magnum opus, the Market House and Shambles, is located. It is most unfortunate that a fire in 1963 deprived the Market House of its crowning clerestory and upper portico. The most conspicuous later Victorian buildings belong to the two schools of the Haberdashers' Company, in particular those erected in the 1890s by the Company's surveyor, *Henry Stock:* the School House of the boys' school, facing the Wye Bridge, and the new girls' school on the hillside above the town. Since then, there have been no new buildings of special note, but one crucial modification to the road pattern, when in 1965–6 the A40 was re-routed to bypass the town. Such traffic relief was essential, but the new road unfortunately cuts the town off from the River Wye, its economic lifeblood in previous centuries.

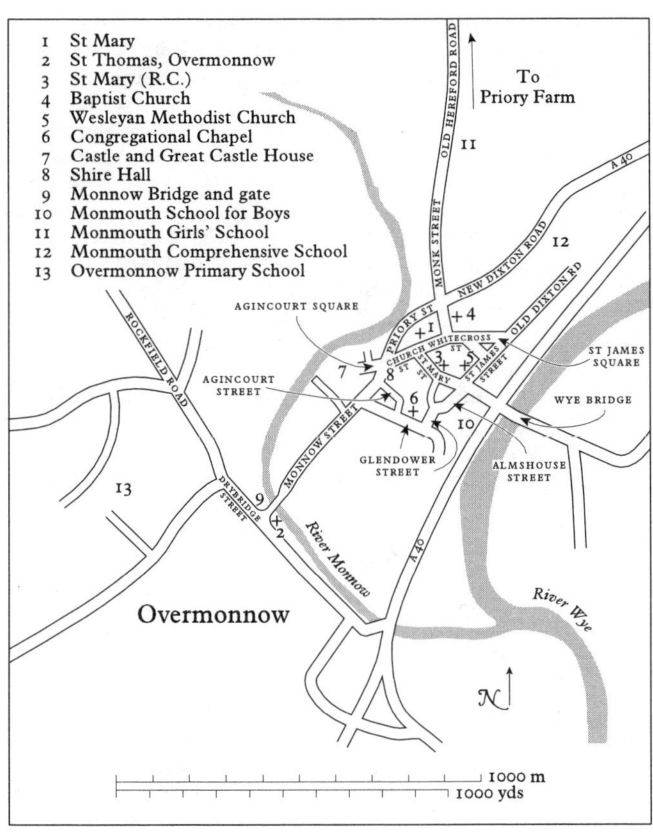

Monmouth

St Mary. The Benedictine priory of St Mary, Monmouth, was founded *c.* 1075 and the priory church consecrated in 1101. A fragment of the W end of this church survives. The W steeple is an addition of the late C14. After the Dissolution the monastic choir fell into ruin, and the nave became the parish church of the town. In 1732 *Francis Smith* of Warwick demolished the medieval nave and in 1736–7 built a new aisled church slightly further S, so that the W tower opened not into the nave but into the N aisle. Lord Torrington (1781) thought it 'very elegant' and Coxe (1801) 'extremely light and well proportioned'. By the mid C19 taste had inevitably changed: for E.A. Freeman (1854), it was 'a most unsightly modern church', and G.E. Street delivered the *coup de grâce* in his structural report of 1879: 'it might be said to have no style at all; at any rate it was extremely unattractive and uninteresting'. Street would have swept the Georgian church away entirely, and produced a design for a new, cruciform building, to cost £22,000. That was too ambitious, so Smith's N and S walls were retained and remodelled, and a new E end added, 1881–3, the tender price coming down to £6,172. After Street's death in 1882, his son *A. E. Street* took over, with *Richard Creed* continuing as clerk-of-works.

The approach is from the SW, revealing the steeple to advantage. This, built of Old Red Sandstone, is of three tall stages, with slender diagonal buttresses reaching by way of five set-offs almost to the top parapet. Low W doorway with two continuous sunk waves, splendid four-light W window with cusped reticulated tracery, the middle band of reticulation enclosing stretched ogee quatrefoils. The needle-like steeple is to the design of *Nathaniel Wilkinson* of Worcester, replacing, shortly before 1743, a stouter medieval predecessor. Crowning Corinthian capital removed by Street. On the E wall of the tower note the crease-line of the medieval roof, indicating that the nave was clerestoried. On the slab of wall to the S, a section of Norman stringcourse, with downward-pointing zigzag. Street's shafted doorway at the W end of the S aisle is set under a simple gable. Externally, Street's church disguises the Georgian predecessor but is constrained by its proportions. Five bays faced with squared grey-pink blocks of local Buckholt stone, plus a new sixth bay and a one-bay sanctuary of pink Old Red Sandstone. Long paired lancets and to the E five stepped lancets, full-height pilaster buttresses, plain parapet, all with Bath stone dressings. N vestry with prominent chimneystack.

Inside, the stout, semi-cylindrical W respond with plain moulded cap survives of the S arcade of the late C11 nave. Its base is below the present floor level, but what is visible implies that there was an arcade with substantial circular piers of West Country type. Soaring C14 tower arch beside it, the mouldings no more than two pairs of chamfers, the imposts plain. Street's interior aims for openness and maximum visibility. Six-bay arcades, the slender piers clustered, a cylindrical core surrounded by shafts with shaft-rings, the shafts of Purbeck marble in the E bay, of Bath stone in the nave. Moulded caps. There is no chancel arch, but the tie-beam at the point where it should be rests on stone corbels. All windows have rere-arches supported on Purbeck shafts. – REREDOS. Large, dark oil painting of the Adoration of the Kings, austere and unusual. 1888 by *Watney Wilson*. – CHANCEL SCREEN. Timber, the five cusped arches designed for maximum transparency. Reset at the W end of the nave. Similar, simpler screens remain *in situ* N and S of the chancel. – PARCLOSE SCREENS to N chapel. 1928 by *W. D. Caröe*. – S (LADY) CHAPEL SCREEN AND GATES. Of *c.* 1885. Richly Dec. Executed by Cheltenham craftsmen, *H. H. Martyn* (woodwork) and *W. Letheren* (ironwork). – FONT. A fine piece, carved by *Farmer & Brindley* to *Street*'s design. Concave-sided octagonal bowl bearing shields with emblems of the Passion and Germanic-looking foliage, set on eight shafts of black veined marble. Moved in 1982 from its proper position beneath the tower. – FLOOR TILES. A miscellany of well-preserved medieval tiles, set in the wall and floor of the S aisle. A few are clearly of the C13,

most of the C15, one dated 1465. The later ones are of Malvern type, but made locally (the kiln has been excavated in Monk Street). – SCULPTURE. Romanesque capital, recently found reused in C18 walling. – STAINED GLASS. By *C. E. Kempe* or his firm in almost every window. The windows at the W and E ends 105
form a coherent programme of seven windows, inserted 1882–8 and probably masterminded by the vicar, the Rev. Wentworth Watson. – S aisle W, 1882, archangels. – Tower W, 1883, for the baptistery. A vigorously designed and splendidly coloured composition. The Four Rivers of Paradise, poured out by golden-haired nude youths, flow down behind busily peopled biblical scenes of baptism, to reappear at the bottom of the composition. – Chancel E, 1884. Christ in Majesty and the Twelve Apostles. Here Kempe's familiar style begins to assert itself. – Chancel N and S, 1888. Scenes of the Resurrected Christ: Empty Tomb and Noli me Tangere (N), Supper at Emmaus and Breakfast by the Lake (S). – S aisle SE and E, 1885, Passion scenes and Crucifixion. – S aisle, 1904 and 1911, *Kempe & Co.*, saints, and 1923, the same, war memorial saints. – N aisle 1905 and 1911, *Kempe & Co.*, saints in the former, royal Edwards in the latter. – S aisle SW, 1938 by *C. C. Powell*, to the design of *B. F. L. Clarke*, curate of the church of the time, but better known as an architectural historian of C18 and C19 churches. So the subject of the window is appropriate, the founder and architects of St Mary's. – MONUMENTS. Three fine hanging wall monuments in the N aisle. – Henry Allen, 1767 by *James Paty jun.* of Bristol. Bulgy sarcophagus outlined in yellow marble, bearing a plain white urn and a black obelisk. – Joseph Price †1796. An early work by *Sir Richard Westmacott*. Large relief showing Mercury on an anchor, and a putto rigging a mast. Inconspicuous Grecian detail. The fact that Price was marine paymaster and naval storekeeper to the East India Company explains the imagery. – Robert Bevan †1837. Signed by *Thomas Smith* of 5 Savoy, Strand. Tall pedimented stele against which stands a figure of Hope between seated Faith and Charity. Medallion portrait above. – In the S aisle, various tablets. The prettiest is to Elizabeth Mynors †1707, in an oval. The finest is to John Hoskyns †1715 (Bradney), with drapery surround, spoilt by the additional inscription panel beneath. – John Allan Rolls, first Lord Llangattock (nave W), 1914. Half-length relief portrait in a self-consciously naive columned frame.

The CHURCHYARD is entered through fine wrought-iron gates of 1759, hung on rusticated stone piers with side arches, probably of the 1830s.

MONASTIC BUILDINGS. These lay on the N side of the church. Traces of the infirmary were discovered in 1906 when the site was prepared for the Baptist Church in Monk Street to the E. In PRIORY STREET, the remains of the PRIOR'S LODGING, extended when in use as ST MARY'S NATIONAL SCHOOL by *Prichard & Seddon*, 1856, by *Seddon*, 1870 and 1884, and by *G. E. Halliday*, 1896; now in parish community use. What one sees from the road largely retains the medieval shape, with new windows and chimneystacks. The only recognizably medieval feature is the sumptuous mid-C15 oriel window and a blocked arch below which suggests that this was originally the gatehouse range. The oriel is of one-plus-four-plus-one lights, the upper tier cinquefoiled, the lower arched. In the hollow top moulding, a row of square flowers. Hoodmould on square stops. Panelling below the window, and big head corbels, an angel between a civilian (r.) and what may be a bedesman.

ST THOMAS, Overmonnow. A small C12 church on the W bank of the River Monnow, drastically Neo-Normanized. Of Old Red
84 Sandstone throughout. The nave was virtually rebuilt in 1830–1 by *Matthew Beasen*, surveyor, under the eye of Arthur Wyatt, the Duke of Beaufort's agent. W doorway, 1880 by *F. Mew*. The chancel is largely medieval, restored by *Prichard*, 1873, and its E wall rebuilt and vestries added 1888-90 by *F. A. Powell*.

The most impressive C12 survival is the chancel arch. High and wide, moulded with a roll and outward-pointing zigzag, under a hoodmould. Impost shafts renewed. In the chancel, two C12 N windows and two S, largely original internally, roll-moulded. Their steeply sloping sills rest on a continuous string. Large doorway with zigzag in the chancel N wall, believed by Prichard to be in its original position. – FONTS. Two. One is small but highly enriched. The bowl is carved with crude faces, a serpent and birds pecking grapes, all in the style of the C12 Herefordshire school, the stem with bold interlace. Conical timber cover clearly of the 1830s. The font itself appears to be a pastiche of the same date. – The second font has a plain octagonal bowl with ribbed underside. Probably of the C15. – SEATING. The complete arrangement of 1831 in the nave, a remarkable survival. Enclosed pews towards the front, open benches at the back and against the N and S walls. – GALLERIES at the W end and extending along much of the N and S walls. Obtrusive Neo-Norman detailing, especially the alarming pendants below the gallery fronts. – STAINED GLASS. Chancel E, Christ between saints, 1957 by *Celtic Studios*. Quite powerful.

ST MARY (R.C.), St Mary Street. The E end survives of the church built as early as 1793, inconspicuously set back behind a row of cottages. Pointed-headed sash windows. Early C19 staircase to an upper room behind the present sanctuary, which dates from a remodelling of 1837. Triple sanctuary arch. In 1871 the cottages were demolished and the church extended by *Benjamin Bucknall* towards the street-line. Quite a show front towards the street. Rock-faced Old Red Sandstone, against which cream ashlar dressings contrast piquantly. E.E. Narrow central projection with the shafted entrance doorway in it. Above this, twin lancets set under corbelling which echoes their outline. Double bellcote crowned by a precipitously steep slated roof. The nave, thus extended, forms a long, narrow, rectangular body, with plate-traceried side windows. – FONT. Very strange. The serpent of Eden twines round the stem and grasps the apple attached to the bowl. Presumably of 1888, the date on the baptistery floor. – STAINED GLASS. Sanctuary N, Virgin and Child, and nave S, cherubim in a royal blue sky. In a Regency taste.* – Nave N, *c.* 1900, attributable to *Hardman* (A. Brooks).

BAPTIST CHURCH, Monk Street. Built in 1906–7 by *Benjamin Lawrence* of Newport, as a match for his Working Men's Free Institute (*see* p. 406) next door. Rock-faced Old Red Sandstone with Bath stone dressings. Dec to Perp style. It faces St Mary's Church with a big five-light traceried window. Octagonal stair-turret to the l., crowned with an ashlar bell-stage and snuffer cap. Projecting gabled porch. The interior is dominated by the thin hammerbeam roof. Gallery to the W only. – STAINED GLASS (porch). Salvator Mundi. 1964 by *G. Maile & Son.* – MONUMENT. Rev. Reynold Rogers †1824. Tablet with draped urn against an obelisk.

WESLEYAN METHODIST CHURCH, St James Street. 1837, by 83
G. V. Maddox, and a most satisfying work, though lying discreetly back from the street-line. Three-bay pedimented façade, stuccoed, its design enhanced by the recent white, lemon and dark blue colour scheme. Greek Ionic upper pilasters support the pediment. Round-headed upper windows recessed within shallow arcading. Rectangular, pedimented windows below, and a projecting porch of paired, fluted Ionic columns carrying an entablature. They must originally have had moulded bases. The interior, quite exceptionally for an early C19 chapel, is a coherent piece of considered architecture. Three-bay plaster groin vault over the inner entrance vestibule. Typical fenestration: a pair of long windows to flank the pulpit, and sashed side windows, round-headed above, square-headed below. Well-proportioned Ionic columns carry the galleries round three sides. Large plaster roses decorate the gallery soffits. Flat plaster ceiling on a cove. The bow-fronted pulpit is reached by contemporary stairs to l. and r. with shaped tread ends and slender turned balusters. The dominance of the pulpit was reduced in 1885 when it was lowered and the whole floor raised by 2 ft (0.6 metre), burying the column bases in the process.

CONGREGATIONAL CHAPEL, Glendower Street, 1843-4, by *William Armstrong* of Bristol. Quite a noble classical façade, the channelled central bay flanked by giant Corinthian columns *in antis*, the angles defined by giant antae. Top entablature and balustraded parapet. Round-headed upper windows, square-headed lower. The design is a reduced version of the Brunswick Chapel, Bristol, where Armstrong had been contractor. Long derelict, the building is due to be redeveloped behind the façade.

CASTLE. All that remains of what must have been the strategically important stronghold of the lords of Monmouth are two ruined rectangular buildings interlocking obliquely with one another, entirely built of Old Red Sandstone. Of an early C13 circular tower of great height and strength on the site of Great Castle House and an early C15 gatehouse spanning Castle Hill, nothing remains to be seen. The larger, lower building, the GREAT HALL, which lies forward to the l. as one approaches from the

*Brought in from the R.C. chapel of Coedanghred, Skenfrith, built *c.* 1840 and demolished in 1924 (P. Howell).

E, was clearly open to the roof. The NE entrance doorway retains a late C13 moulded shaft-base. This is enough to suggest that it was built soon after 1267 for Edmund Crouchback, who held the lordship from that date. High plinth, cut through in the E wall by a five-light mullioned window. Inside, blocked openings at the E end may indicate a screens passage. There was a fireplace in the centre of the N wall, and there were two large windows in the S wall, each with one mullion and one transom, under a segmental rere-arch. By the C16 the Monmouthshire county assizes were held in the Great Hall, and it may originally have been built for a similar purpose, as a courtroom for the Marcher lordship.

The Great Hall links at its NW corner with the GREAT TOWER. This is part of the original masonry castle, a two-storeyed, rectangular keep of the C12, a small version of the great keep at Chepstow Castle. Pilaster buttresses clasp the angles. Three original, round-headed E windows, to light an undercroft, and similar windows higher up to light a mural stair leading to the first-floor hall, which retains one C12 S window. As remodelled in the mid C14, perhaps for Henry, Duke of Lancaster (lord of Monmouth 1345–61), this hall must have been a splendid room. The finest surviving feature is the long two-light E window, with remains of a traceried head, continuous internal sunk wave mouldings and embrasure seats. Similarly moulded doorways in the centre of the S wall and in the corner leading to the Great Hall.

70 GREAT CASTLE HOUSE. Built for Henry Somerset, third Marquess of Worcester and later first Duke of Beaufort, within the castle precinct and dated 1673. A house of splendid swagger outside and in, and presumably intended primarily for official and ceremonial purposes by the Marquess, who in 1672 had become Lord President of the Council of Wales and the Marches. Constructed of square blocks of mottled pink and grey Old Red Sandstone, probably much of it reused from the demolished castle gatehouse. The cut stone has recently been much renewed. The house is three-storeyed above a high basement and crowned by a hipped roof boldly projecting on a coved plaster cornice. Flanking slab-like brick chimneystacks. All this sounds quite up-to-date, but the plan is of a recessed three-bay centre between broad one-bay wings, and the windows are of stone, mullioned, two-light in the centre, three-light in the wings, those on the two tall middle storeys given a transom. Stringcourses between the storeys. The ornamental composition applied to the centre bay consists of belted Doric pilasters to flank the door, Ionic pilasters to flank an Italianate timber casement window, and at the level of the top storey, a semicircular stone fan with side sills, for three bulbous vases stuck with crude flowers. Long, low additions of *c.* 1900 to l. and r., keeping in keeping, for the Monmouthshire Royal Engineers and their museum, which remain in occupation today.

The interior is astonishing. Square central entrance hall dominated by a painted stone chimneypiece with flowers and fruit carved on imposts and frieze, and an overmantel dominated by two huge swags and a central pendant raspberry. The pair of thin Greek Doric columns in the centre of the room are, of course, early C19 supports to the floor above. To the right, a small, square, overpoweringly decorated room. Panelling with many small fields vigorously lugged at every corner. Massive crowning architrave. Looming plaster ceiling, a rosette within a fat circular wreath, the end panels enclosing figures in scrolling foliage. Behind the hall the principal stair reaches from the bottom to the top of the house. Dog-leg plan, but the carpentry clearly intended for a plan of greater spaciousness. Newel posts and ball finials awkwardly jostle each other. Close-set balusters, twisting above bulbs.

On the first floor all five rooms have been thrown together into one. This happened as early as *c.* 1700, when the County Assizes were transferred here from the medieval Great Hall of the castle. Heavily detailed panelling of uniform design all round the room, and central marble fireplace surround, typical of *c.* 1700. The ceiling plasterwork, however, goes back to 1673, each of the five original rooms having had its own appropriate design. Over the centre room, the full width of the three middle bays, a large, tight-packed, oval wreath, flanked by small round ones and naively designed flower vases. To the front on the r. the ceiling is a virtuoso display of the plasterer's craft. Dangling
from the centre is a circle of swags built up on a leather armature. 64
The ceiling beams are encrusted with serried rows of plaster leaves, and the coves are embossed with designs of flowers and foliage, part taken from pattern-books, part surely the plasterer's own invention. The matching room to the l. is more subdued, a cross of heavy plastered beams, and Jacobean-looking foliage sprigs embossed on the flats between. Two small rooms at the rear had plain flat ceilings.

SHIRE HALL, Agincourt Square. A mighty affair, still in a Wren- 72
inspired Baroque style, though built as late as 1724, by an otherwise unknown architect, *Fisher* of Bristol. Bath stone ashlar. Five bays by two, the centre bay of double width, crowned somewhat awkwardly by a pediment. Giant Ionic pilasters all across, their capitals with finely profiled volutes, support chunks of architrave and bulging frieze, below the continuous, but stepped, cornice. Ground floor with broad open arches of flattened segmental outline. Paired upper windows, long and thin with semicircular heads. Each pair has a plain raised panel linking the sill to the arch below. Small keystones and impost blocks further enliven the façade. In the central double bay, an incongruous statue of Henry V, who was born at Monmouth. This is of 1792 by *Charles Peart*. The open lower stage is internally subdivided by Tuscan columns, baseless no doubt to avoid interference with cart traffic, and cross walls.

In 1828 *Edward Haycock* remodelled the courtrooms and built a new rear stair-tower. The stair is of stone with a heavy metal balustrade. It rises in one flight and returns, and then repeats the process, a piece of spatial gymnastics which does not wholly succeed, as the flights are quite short. At the top, however, is a further surprise, a pair of mighty unfluted Greek Doric columns, helping to carry the glazed lantern which lights the stair. The lantern is square below, and turns octagonal by means of fluted spandrels. Vertical glazing up here and a miniature ribbed plaster vault centred on a feathered rose. The COURTROOM on the first floor is also by *Haycock*. It retains its complete set of fittings. Magistrate's seat under a pedimental canopy. The opposite wall opened out by means of two massive square piers carrying an architrave and wreathed frieze. Modern blocking here.

STATUE. Charles Stewart Rolls, the pioneer of aviation, killed in 1910. Bronze, a lively figure scrutinizing a model of a biplane. Dated 1911, signed by *W. Goscombe John*. Reliefs on the pedestal of balloon, biplane and racing car. Base designed by *Aston Webb*.

25 MONNOW BRIDGE AND GATE. The sole survival in Britain of a gate-tower on a bridge at the entry to a town, a form of medieval fortification once common throughout Europe. The bridge, built largely of Old Red Sandstone, has three segmental arches on hexagonal piers forming pointed cutwaters, and was built in the late C13 – 1272 is the traditional but undocumented date.* Broad reinforcing ribs on the undersides of the arches. Arch faces rebuilt further out to provide footways *c.* 1827–30. The gate-tower was constructed on top of the townward pier as part of a system of defensive walls and gates erected between 1297 and *c.* 1315. It is quite shallow, spanning the roadway front and back with reconstructed round-headed arches between pilaster buttresses. Portcullis grooves l. and r. of the outer (SW) arch, and a cross-shaped arrow loop in the l. pilaster (and traces of another lower down in the r. pilaster). The bowed ends of the gate-tower are brought neatly down on to the tops of the cutwaters, the upstream bow originally containing a circular newel stair. The pedestrian arches are C19, the upstream arch of 1819, the downstream arch of 1845. Higher up, more of the original defences can be made out. The two arrow slits over the outer arch served the portcullis chamber, as did the corbelled garderobe projection to the l. The machicolation here, three buff sandstone arches on bold corbels, and relieving arch above, is a medieval modification. The wall-head and hipped, stone-tiled roof, however, are early C18, replacing the original battlements, when the gatehouse accommodation was made two-storeyed. Roof reconstructed 1832.

WYE BRIDGE. The important medieval bridge was rebuilt in 1615 and widened in 1878–80 by *Edwin Seward* of Cardiff. Five segmental arches, pointed cutwaters and corbelled parapet. The earlier, more steeply pointed arches remain just visible within the C19 ones.

MONMOUTH SCHOOL FOR BOYS, Almshouse Street. The Free Grammar School endowed by William Jones, haberdasher, and built in 1614–15 was rebuilt, to provide a schoolroom, two classrooms and a chapel, in 1864-5 by *William Snooke* of London for

*In 1988 part of an earlier, timber bridge was found in the river bed beneath, datable by tree-ring analysis to the 1170s.

the Haberdashers' Company. *Snooke* added three more classrooms in 1870, a library in 1875, and in 1877-8 formed boarding houses by converting the houses of headmaster and lecturer in Wyebridge Street. School House, however, which faces the River Wye with its dramatic grouping of stepped gables, clustered chimneystacks and angle turret, is by *Henry Stock*, 1895–6. Rock-faced Old Red Sandstone and Forest dressings throughout. More recent buildings will be noted below.

In Almshouse Street, Snooke's original buildings seem to have been symmetrical. A big inscription panel, flanked by four-centred archways, is set in front of the gable-end and bellcôte of the original chapel (now library), the central feature a broad arched window of five uncusped lights. To the l., the gable-end, with five-light Perp window, of the later chapel. To the r., a buttressed and stepped-gabled range by *Stock*, and then the much lowlier frontage of the JONES ALMSHOUSES, 1842–3 by *J. B. Bunning*, now incorporated in the school, their six gabled porches blocked. Conspicuous groups of yellow brick chimneystacks. Across the road the semi-modern HALL of 1961 by *J. L. Caldwell*.

Here is the entrance to the main quadrangle, which is loosely surrounded by a miscellany of buildings. On the r., attached to the hall, the RED LION BLOCK, a more convincingly 1960s range, generously glazed. To the l., past the back of the almshouses, the way leads through to an inner quadrangle. This is equally informal, with the many bays and gables of Snooke's various buildings. Stock's SCHOOL HOUSE, at the far NE corner, was also clearly designed for outward not inward show. The interior of the CHAPEL is wide and quite low, under an arched-brace and kingpost roof. – STAINED GLASS in the E window, by *Ward & Hughes*. Not all of one date. The central light, Blessed are the Pure in Heart, is dated 1879, the rest added up to 1890. Biblical stories of which boys were the heroes. – WAR MEMORIAL SHRINE, 1950 by *Francis W. Stephens*.

In GLENDOWER STREET, the rectangular stone building with large mullion-and-transom windows, now GLOVER MUSIC SCHOOL, was built as an arts and science block, 1908 by *Stock, Page & Stock*. The most recent contribution is the three-storeyed SCIENCE BLOCK in the SE corner, 1981–4 by *W. F. Johnson & Partners*. As seen from the A40, its pink sandstone walls and its gables are clearly meant as a counterpoint to School House. The windows in vertical strips, even across angles, associate it with the late C20.

MONMOUTH GIRLS' SCHOOL, Old Hereford Road. A second foundation by the Haberdashers' Company, designed by *Henry Stock* and built 1895–7. On a splendid site overlooking the town, to which Stock responded with his soaring, step-gabled, nearly symmetrical block, a large heraldic relief proudly displayed high in the centre. Rock-faced Old Red Sandstone and Bath stone dressings, including the clustered chimneystacks. In complete contrast, the HALL and GYMNASIUM to the r., of 1964. Flat-roofed, walling of buff brick and great expanses of glazing. In fact the gymnasium is transparent, hardly impeding the view of the hills beyond. The School now makes use of the much-altered buildings of the former UNION WORKHOUSE, on the opposite side of the road. This was built 1868–71 to the designs of *G.C. Haddon* of Hereford. Red brick and purple Old Red Sandstone with quirky Bath stone details.

MONMOUTH COMPREHENSIVE SCHOOL, Old Dixton Road. The three main parts relate to the three successive schools which have occupied the site. In the W corner the former William Jones Elementary School, built in 1903 for the Haberdashers' Company, and so doubtless designed by *Henry Stock*. Simple, gabled, single-storeyed, in pink rock-faced sandstone. The buildings erected in 1964–5 for the Secondary Modern School are by *Monmouthshire County Architect's Department*, County Architect *Sydney Leyshon*. They are typical of the Department's undemonstrative Modernism, though sited with some formality. GYMNASIUM, with exposed metal frame, and HALL, both glazed full-height towards the road, form a pair of pavilions. Behind them rises the three-storeyed CLASSROOM RANGE. All have slightly pitched roofs. Gable-end walls of caramel brick. The less orderly two-storeyed and single-storeyed classroom blocks extending to the NE date from *c.* 1976–7, built to cater for expansion when the school became comprehensive in 1977. Dark brown brick and a variety of black-tiled monopitch roofs. By *Gwent County Architect's Department*, County Architect *K.P. Jones*, job architect *N. Robson-Smith*. Other late C20 contributions, the cubic LEISURE CENTRE in particular.

OVERMONNOW PRIMARY SCHOOL, Gibraltar Drive, off Rockfield Road. Approached through parkland trees. There are two parts, both low, of buff brick, the earlier opened 1977, by *Owen Luder Partnership*, flat-roofed, the later gabled, 1989–90 by *Gwent County Architect's Department*, design architect *Charles Parry*. This latter part wittily exploits two ideas. Three of the gables are brought forward so that an exposed, green-painted truss protects the end of a sheltered enclosure. The diagonal of the gable profile is repeated in sloping wall-ends, V-windows and other unexpected motifs, with a red brick coping for emphasis. A building like this must surely rouse a child's visual awareness.

PERAMBULATION

The great period of prosperity and fashion for Monmouth was the second half of the C18 and the early C19, if its street architecture is an accurate guide. To appreciate this one should start in front of the Shire Hall in Agincourt Square and make short forays in three directions, to E, N and SW.

AGINCOURT SQUARE is little more than the triangular forecourt to the Shire Hall. Here the town's principal inns are clustered together. The KING'S HEAD, on the S side, consists of two parts. Five-bay, three-storeyed C18 main front, crowned by two later C19 half-timbered gables. The building is earlier behind.

Witness to this is a small room on the ground floor. It has a late C17 decorated plaster ceiling, in which is a large rose surrounded by a large wreath with four small ones in the corners. Even more significant is the plaster overmantel with frontal demi-figure in painted plaster of a crowned and robed Charles II, flanked by his initials, C R, and two pots of droopy roses. To the l. a narrower four-storey section, of three bays, the lowest storey treated as a strongly rusticated four-bay arcade. This looks of *c.* 1740, and was originally a bank. The third half-timbered gable to the r. crowns *T. H. Wyatt*'s imitative COUNTY CLUB of 1877.

On the N side of the Square, the PUNCH HOUSE is straightforward enough, early C19, of two-and-a-half storeys and three wide bays, the sash windows tripartite on the ground storey. The third, and handsomest, the former BEAUFORT ARMS, lies back to the l. of the Shire Hall. It could be a work of G.V. Maddox of the 1830s. Three-and-a-half storeys. Five bays, the centre three slightly projecting and framed by Ionic pilasters extending through two storeys, over a ground storey of gently segmental arches framing the windows. Through the carriage arch to the r. the rear of the building is accessible. Here more early C19 elements, on the r. a single-storey bow with broad metal balcony over, and on the l. a whole symmetrical three-bay façade squeezed in, the ground-storey again with segmental arcading over tripartite windows. Doorway with elegant brackets. The building was converted to shops and flats *c.* 1989 by *Graham Frecknall.*

1. To the North

One should first leave Agincourt Square at its upper, narrower end. No. 1, AGINCOURT HOUSE, on the r. is a fine, if heavily restored, early C17 half-timbered building, the walls rendered over. The renewed pierced bargeboard of the gable towards the Square is dated 1624. Two-storeyed oriel below. Two similar oriels in the flank wall. From here PRIORY STREET curves away. This was laid out by *G. V. Maddox* in 1837 to bypass the town centre. On the l. is what remains of *Maddox*'s MARKET HALL of 1837–9, a grandiose and scholarly Greek Doric composition, executed in golden-hued Bath stone. Pairs of columns *in antis* flank the windows in the end bays and the doorway in the centre. Three-bay intermediate screen walls, demarcated by antae. Continuous entablature. The pedimented Ionic temple front above in the centre, with cupola and clerestory running back, has unfortunately all disappeared, destroyed by fire in 1963 and not reinstated. Instead, in 1968–9 *Donald Insall & Associates*, for the Post Office, Nelson Museum and Local History Centre, added a pitched roof above the entablature, breaking the Grecian spell. At the back, overlooking the River Monnow, a frankly Modern display of metal-framed oriels. On this side, however, there is more to see of *Maddox*'s construction. Below the road level, served by a causeway embanked over the

96 river, he formed a SHAMBLES, which survives virtually complete. Down here the material is mauve Old Red Sandstone. Arcade of twenty-four arches on piers which are not vertical but inclined for extra strength. Within each arch, a rectangular doorway and semicircular window above for ventilation. These open into deep storage rooms barrel-vaulted in brick. In one or two rooms timbers stuck with rows of meat-hooks still survive.

The long, convex, stuccoed frontage on the E side of Priory Street seems also to have been built to Maddox's design. Nos. 1–6 form a symmetrical, three-storeyed frontage nineteen bays long. The centre three bays are crowned by an attic lit by a Diocletian window under a pediment. Giant pilasters on the three bays to l. and three to r., their capitals a sort of Greek Composite. The outer reaches of the composition are lower. Nos. 7–9 are lower still, but form their own symmetrical composition. Ionic pilasters with fluted necking carry a pediment across No. 8. Next come the railings of St Mary's churchyard. Past the former prior's lodging (*see* p. 397), Monk Street runs across. Here to the S, the Baptist Church (*see* p. 399) and the almost equally ecclesiastical-looking WORKING MEN'S FREE INSTITUTE (now Arts Centre), 1867–8 by *Benjamin Lawrence*. Coursed Old Red Sandstone with dressings of Bath stone. Tall, narrow gabled frontage, dominated by a shafted three-light window with stiff-leaf caps, surmounted by a diapered tympanum bearing an armorial roundel. The *Builder* called it 'Italian Gothic'. Also on the E side No. 5, the Royal George, one of the town's finest C18 houses. Three-storeyed under a flared hipped roof, of seven bays, the centre three tightly spaced and set back a little, everything emphasized with raised quoins. Central round-headed window. Porch with Adamesque Corinthian capitals and Adamesque Doric frieze – a combination Adam himself would not have disallowed. Frieze continued to l. and r., carried on slices of pilaster in the corners. Built probably in the 1730s, the Adamesque modernization a half-century later. Opposite, OAK HOUSE, built 1846, in instructive contrast, a white, two-storeyed villa, the detailing Grecian. Porch with Ionic columns *in antis*. Tripartite lower windows.

Where MONK STREET continues to the N of Priory Street the houses come more densely, with interestingly varied groups on both sides. First on the W side a semi-detached pair, Nos. 8 and 10, of five bays and two-and-a-half storeys, made into a unified composition by the upper-level Ionic pilasters in the centre three bays. Windows under round-headed relieving arches. 1839 by *G. V. Maddox*, No. 8 for himself. Next, set back, the FREEMASONS' HALL, built as a theatre in 1797, converted in 1837 by *Maddox* for its present use and refronted by him in 1846. A miniature temple façade, the central three-bay pediment on baseless Tuscan pilasters, raised up on a ground stage with wide segment-headed entrance. Non-matching side bays. Then CADOGAN HOUSE, also early C19, of two-and-a-half storeys. Doorway with open pediment on fluted Greek Doric three-quarter columns provided, uncanonically, with bases. The group opposite, on the E side of the road, is similar in date but not quite so impressive. No. 9 has tripartite sash windows on all three storeys. No. 11 is irregular but boasts a doorway fronted by large and correct Greek Doric columns *in antis*. The W side continues with Nos. 16 and 18, two-and-a-half-storeyed, channelled below, pebble-dashed above but lined out like masonry. It is a semi-detached pair, as the Doric, portico-like double porch shows. Called 'new built' in 1831. No. 20 is a reticent but elegant member of the group, also early C19, also of two-and-a-half storeys. Three generous bays wide. The lower windows set under semicircular tympana, the central upper one within a generous round-headed relieving arch. Trellis porch.

Then, two houses set back independently. First, on the E side, PARADE HOUSE presents a normal Georgian format, three-storeyed under a hipped roof, but the windows, in pairs, all have four-centred heads. Is this Tudor hint an alteration, or does the house date from the 1840s? Then on the W side, the best house in the entire street, CHAPEL HOUSE. This is mid-C18 or earlier, of seven bays, the central three with narrow windows, under a flared hipped roof. Later C18 door-case, its open pediment on fluted half-columns with fluted caps. The house stands handsomely back between symmetrical stretches of contemporary red brick wall, giving access to service yard and garden. Inside, the central square hall has a wreathed plaster ceiling, and beyond a pair of rectangular openings in its back wall rises the staircase in a square well. Three twisted balusters per step, and groups of four as newels – a modest imitation of the Duke of Beaufort's staircase at Troy House, Mitchel Troy. Plasterwork wreath in the ceiling here too. So the plasterwork echoes that in the Duke's other, even more local, residence, Great Castle House (*see* above, p. 400). Finally, just before the hill steepens, there is something on both sides of the road. On the r., NORTH PARADE HOUSE, with another rendered frontage of *c.* 1800. Three bays and three storeys, linked to a warehouse to the l. by a continuous cornice and parapet. The usual sub-Adam timber door-case (cf. Chapel House above), flanked by canted timber bays also enriched with sub-Adam details. Upper windows with keystones. Raised angle quoins and broad flat strings mark out the composition. Humble but symmetrical rendered terraced cottages to l. and r., their paired doorhoods on shaped brackets. Opposite, THE OLD GAOL, a square, boldly detailed house of Old Red Sandstone under a shallow pyramidal roof. This is all that survives of *William Blackburn*'s County Gaol of 1788–90, and seems to have belonged to its gatehouse. (Inside, a representation in coloured glass of the complete original buildings).

2. *To the East*

From a new start in Agincourt Square one can strike out into CHURCH STREET. This is narrow, pedestrianized and largely of the early C19, with continuous three-storeyed, stuccoed terraces on both sides. (No. 24 was refronted by *Maddox c.* 1840 and has a good contemporary shopfront.) On the l. one stronger accent, a three-storeyed composition with four-bay recessed centre, arcaded over a wide archway, and slightly projecting side bays under a continuous dentilled top cornice. The heavy architrave surrounds suggest a date in the 1840s. It gives access to WHITE SWAN COURT, the triangular space left on the formation of Priory Street.

Church Street is continued E-wards by WHITECROSS STREET. On the r., sited to command the vista up Monk Street, WHITECROSS HOUSE, a mid-C18 house of five bays and three storeys under a hipped roof, but rendered and painted white with black dressings. THE HOLLIES, a three-storey red brick house at the back at r.-angles, looks contemporary. The dominant building in Whitecross Street is ROLLS HALL (now Public Library), 1887–8 by *F.A. Powell*, Golden Jubilee gift to the town by J.A. Rolls of The Hendre, the future Lord Llangattock. In a Jacobean style, of rock-faced Old Red Sandstone and grey Forest ashlar. The hall is spanned by a pedimental gable enclosing strapwork. Unequal flanking turrets, that to the l. enclosing the balcony stairs and sporting a lead-covered flèche. Inside, a large hall with giant banded Ionic pilasters and a proscenium arch at the far end, well converted as the Public Library in 1992, with minimalist metal stairs. Just beyond, ST JAMES HOUSE has a fine mid-C18, two-and-a-half-storey front of red brick. Shallow flared hipped roof. The raised stone angle quoins and keys and the central windows, round-headed below and lugged and scrolled at the top level, suggest the date. Early C19 porch on Greek Doric columns. (A little C17 plasterwork inside.)

Whitecross Street comes to an end in the modest triangular ST JAMES SQUARE. Here a catalpa tree overspreads the WAR MEMORIAL of 1921, the figure of a soldier sculpted by *W. Clarke* of Llandaff. There is just one substantial C18 house, CARTREF, of the usual proportions, five bays wide, three storeys high. In OLD DIXTON ROAD, beyond, on the r. the OLD NAG'S HEAD. This has been built up against a stone drum tower of the EAST GATE, part of the town defences constructed between 1297 and *c.* 1315. No. 16, on the l., with its canted end towards the road, was clearly built as a toll cottage, a further reminder that the present cul-de-sac was originally one of the main thoroughfares out of the town.

ST JAMES STREET leads out of St James Square to the SW. On both sides a continuous sequence of C18 and early C19 houses, those on the l. mostly with bracketed doorhoods, those on the r. a little posher, with pedimented doorways on columns. No. 18, on the r., is something out of the ordinary, though not quite symmetrical. Paired sash windows with central bracket on all three storeys. Doorway with Ionic columns, the caps given diagonal volutes. Pedimented window over. Is this all of a piece, of *c.* 1830? Next comes the Wesleyan Methodist Church of 1837 (*see* p. 399) behind its railed forecourt. Then THE GRANGE, another late C18 or early C19 façade of five bays and three storeys.

Pedimented Doric porch with Adamesque metope frieze. Its pretty red brick STABLE complex, of similar date, survives to the l. So much for the N side of St James Street. The last building on the S side, the QUEEN'S HEAD INN, looks like a C17 timber-framed house. The date 1630 is reported to appear on it, and there is a thin ribbed early C17 plaster ceiling inside. But the half-timbering is all of 1922, by *Harry A. Dancey* of Gloucester. Only the seven-light oriel window represents what was there before.

ST MARY STREET opens up to the r. at this point. Nothing of note except the Roman Catholic Church (*see* p. 398), and the return is soon made to Church Street and Agincourt Square.

3. To the South-west

This is mainly a long, straight, downhill walk along MONNOW STREET to the Monnow Bridge. Pleasingly continuous array of C18 and early C19 shops and houses, in the main modestly two-storeyed, with several Victorian interventions. But before the descent a turn to the l. should be made into AGINCOURT STREET, for two small pedimented houses, No. 9, its pediment botched, and No. 6, its pediment bottomless. The latter stands free at the end of the street behind a tiny railed forecourt, and bears a date 1578, which can refer to nothing visible. Pretty five-bay composition, a delicate metal balcony serving the central three upper windows. GLENDOWER STREET joins in to the l. For the two individually notable buildings, the Glover Music School and the former Congregational Chapel *see* above, p. 399. Otherwise there are more three-storey terrace houses, not uniform, but mostly probably of *c.* 1800. From some of them render has been removed, revealing finely pointed red brickwork.

Back in Monnow Street, first on the l. comes No. 18, LLOYDS BANK. This also is of red brick, of three bays and two-and-a-half storeys under a top parapet. Quite handsomely trimmed. Blind ground-floor arcade of moulded arches on imposts. Upper windows with bold architrave surrounds. In the garden at the back is a remarkable timber SUMMER-HOUSE. The painted inscription 'Lord Nelson's seat', with the date of the admiral's visit, 19 August 1802, is an addition of 1956. Four Doric columns carry in a most eccentric arrangement twin entablatures, one on top of the other, each with a fluted frieze and dentilled cornice. Top parapet. Within, a coved plaster vault over a continuous bench with central elegant iron seat. The ensemble is completed by a wrought-iron balustrade, and gentle ramps to l. and r. (For more serious Nelson-worship *see* The Kymin, Wyesham.) A little lower down the street on the l., No. 58, CORNWALL HOUSE, the most imposing house in the street and more complicated than it looks. The front range is set back behind a railed forecourt with overthrow and lamp-holder, and has side doorways in single-bay, single-storey wings, the doorways not quite matching. The house itself, late C18, rendered, of five bays and three storeys under a cornice, has raised angle quoins, and a slightly later pedimented porch on thin Greek Doric columns. To the rear, facing a walled garden, is a wider façade of completely different character. This is mid-C18, said to have been built in 1752. Red brick with plenty of white trim. Two tall storeys, two-plus-three-plus-two bays, the centre trio under a pediment enclosing a Diocletian window. Flared hipped, slated roof. Keystones to the windows and rusticated surround to the segment-headed central doorway. The interior has a simple early C19 staircase, and in one rear room an Adamesque chimneypiece of timber carved with exquisite delicacy.

Further down Monnow Street, on the r., No. 85, the tallest house in the street, four full storeys, but a completely plain sashed façade. On the l., No. 102, a much more elegant late Georgian frontage. Brick, painted. Three-storeyed, of three wide bays. Windows diminishing in width storey by storey. On the ground storey they are tripartite, have semicircular fanlights and are set under relieving arches linked to the central door-case with its Greek Doric half-columns. Finally, on the l., the ROBIN HOOD PUBLIC HOUSE, a late medieval relic. Of stone, the main surviving feature the wide, four-centred doorway, its arch moulded with a hollow and step and the spandrels filled with mouchettes.

So to the Monnow Bridge (*see* p. 402). Across it the suburb of OVERMONNOW, its church, St Thomas (*see* p. 398), on the river bank. In front of the church, in the centre of a roundabout, a CROSS, heavily restored in 1888 by *F.A. Powell.* Opposite, OVER MONNOW HOUSE faces the W end of the church. This is yet another late Georgian house of five bays and three storeys. Very wide central bay, with a round-headed window over a round-headed door, its pediment open to give room for the arched head. (Large central hall and fine staircase behind.)

DRYBRIDGE HOUSE, Overmonnow, at the far end of Drybridge Street, dated 1671 and built for William Roberts. He gained a minor post in the Office of Works when in 1672 he was appointed Receiver and Paymaster of the Works at Windsor Castle, and was in post during Hugh May's great remodelling there. Whether Roberts's contacts with the most advanced architectural thinking in the country had any effect on the design of his house is hard to judge, for almost every detail was vamped up in 1867 for C.H. Crompton-Roberts. The house is an I in plan, presenting towards the road a short E front of five bays and two storeys under a hipped roof on a timber bracketed cornice. The slightly projecting porch of 1867 masks a datestone of 1671 under a swan-neck pediment. The grey Old Red Sandstone rubble walling must be of the earlier date, and so must be the walling of the N front, both its projecting wings and its re-entrant centre. In the latter, a stone doorway of this period, chamfered and with a depressed four-centred head, a decidedly provincial feature. The projecting W chimney-breast also looks part of the primary construction. The Victorian details where classical are wilfully impure, the semi-dormers on the E front in particular defying description. To the W cross range, two large mullion-and-transom bays were added, one-storeyed to the N, more than two-storeyed to the W. Plenty of small-scale carved enrichments, panels and bosses, some heraldic, some figural. Crompton-Roberts's initials also occur here and there.

Inside, there is much panelling and other heavy woodwork, none of it easy to accept as pre-1867. Drops of flowers and fruit in a Gibbons style flanking the chimneypiece in the back lobby may be C17. In the dining room, l. of the entrance vestibule, the gilt and black timber chimneypiece is of *c.* 1790, Neoclassical, with small dancing and music-making figures in the frieze. Otherwise everything reflects the heavy-handed mid-Victorian taste so apparent outside. Dining-room ceiling beams set on stone corbels carved with birds and monkeys. At the rear, occupying almost all the W range, a huge ballroom lit by the bay windows. Wall decoration of bulbous Tuscan half-columns over a panelled dado. Coarse Jacobean-style chimneypiece and overmantel. Rich Jacobean-style plaster ceiling. In the top lights of the windows grisaille glass roundels of Arthurian subjects, attributed to *T. W. Camm*.

The SERVICE COURT to the S includes C18 red brick buildings encrusted with notched timberwork of *c.* 1867.

PRIORY FARM, Priory Lane, off Old Hereford Road, 1 m. N. The farmhouse, released from a coat of render in 1996, has been revealed as a high quality building of the late C17, which is said to have borne the date 1672 on the central datestone, now unfortunately worn away. The house consists of a single-pile range of five bays and two storeys under a steeply pitched roof. The end gable walls, crowned by chimneystacks, are windowless and constructed of squared limestone blocks. The E front is by contrast of a rich purplish-red brick, symmetrical and enriched with fine limestone details. Alternating quoins at the angles of the façade and up the jambs of the central doorway. Monolithic door-head. Vertically proportioned windows, the lower longer than those above, all with neat stone voussoirs. Dormer windows added in 1997. At the back the wall is of brick above stone, partly masked by service additions. Nothing of significance inside. Footings of an earlier building adjoining to the N.

To the SE, a tall five-bay BARN with central projecting porch, and a stone STABLE for two horses. Also an enigmatic building of Old Red Sandstone rubble, partly of three storeys, partly of two. Probably C17. At both upper levels two-light timber windows with diamond mullions and iron stanchions survive. In the lower part, remains of a cider mill.

CROFT-Y-BWLA, 1¼ m. NW. A refined classical villa built probably *c.* 1830 to the design of *G. V. Maddox* for Thomas Dyke, grocer of Monmouth, and mayor in 1832. Sited on a spur so as to gain a distant view of the town. The house is a square in plan, three bays by three, of two storeys under a shallow hipped roof on bracketed eaves. Sash windows. The walls are smoothly rendered and delicately lined out to look like ashlar. The single-storey NE porch, of greenish Forest stone, has a pair of Greek Doric columns between antae. Round the corner to the SE there is a full-height canted central bay and an exquisite wrought-iron veranda (much decayed at the time of writing) extending across the entire front. (Inside, a small groin-vaulted vestibule opens into a rectangular, toplit staircase.)

To the NW, large, plain mid-C19 STABLES of red brick, on three sides of a rectangular court.

The single-storey LODGE beside the road, rendered, with broad pilaster strips and a rustic timber porch, must also be by *Maddox*.

FORGE AND POWER STATION, ¾m. NW, beside the River Monnow. The first forge on the River Monnow was built in 1628. The earliest surviving structures are the two-storeyed, late C18 WORKERS' HOUSES. In the row of six, the outer pairs had single ground-floor rooms, and the two larger central ones were clearly for workmen of higher status. The central arch gave access to a communal bakehouse at the rear.

The brick GENERATING STATION, its turbines powered by the flow of the river, was built in 1899.

5090

MOUNTON

ST ANDOENUS. In a tiny churchyard squeezed between the lane and the wooded cliff. One-bay chancel and two-bay nave, medieval in origin but reconstructed in 1880 by *Walter Evill* of Chepstow. Ashlar bell gablet. – STAINED GLASS. Chancel E, Deposition and Resurrection. Presumably of the 1860s, reset. – Nave S, Virgin and Child with St John. 1933 by *Reginald Bell*. Charming. – Nave N, St Francis and Works of Mercy. 1962 by *M. F. Farrar Bell*. – Nave S, musical instruments. 1979 by *Celtic Studios*. – MONUMENT. William Hollis †1799. Oval tablet topped by an elegant Neoclassical urn. Signed by *Drewett & Co.*, Bristol.

In the CHURCHYARD, by the vestry door, a remarkably early GRAVESTONE, for Christopher Cooper †1680.

115 MOUNTON HOUSE SCHOOL, ¼m. NE, but approached from Pwllmeyric. The last full-blown country house built in the county, dated 1912 on rainwater heads and completed in 1914. H. Avray Tipping, garden designer and architectural correspondent of *Country Life*, having in the late 1890s restored Mathern Palace (*see* p. 384), in 1907 turned his eyes 2 m. (3 kilometres) N to Mounton, where first he cultivated a garden in the gorge by the church. On inheriting a life interest in the family fortune in 1911, he at once set about building a completely new house on the clifftop plateau above. The house is the fruit of collaboration between *Tipping*, who was referred to in 1915 as 'the designer' who 'has built what he pleased for himself', and the young Chepstow architect *Eric Francis*, trained under Dawber. It shows all the skill in handling local materials which such an Arts and Crafts training could develop, combined

with self-conscious reminiscences of specific medieval houses with which Tipping was familiar. But the panache with which the house and its setting are contrived owes not a little to the example of Lutyens. The principal materials are locally quarried, grey, pink-stained limestone used in square hammerdressed blocks, and stone slates for the roofs. Half-timbering and slate-hanging are reserved for special effects. Timber-framed windows.

The approach across the park from the E is managed with great care. The drive, straight and wide, passes a double-gabled pair of COTTAGES, and is then flanked by stretches of buttressed wall, as at Markenfield Hall, Yorkshire, a late medieval house which Tipping wrote about for *Country Life* in 1912. Matching service and stable courts to l. and r. Their single-storey gable-ends and flanking walls with central gatepiers prolong the enclosure. To the W, at the end of the vista, nothing but a loggia of stone piers framing a view over the cliff to the church and Tipping's garden below.

The house lies back to the S, invisible until the last moment, its expansive forecourt bounded on the l. by a range of the

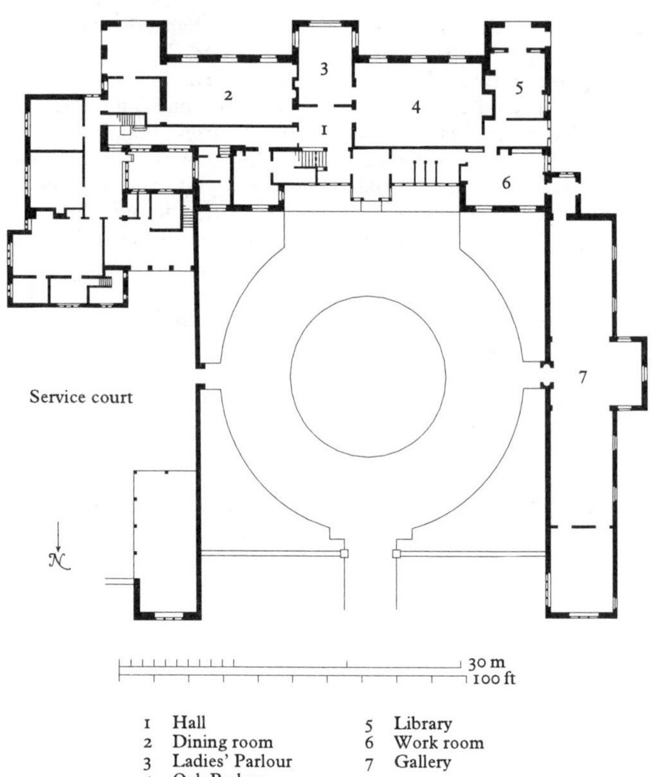

Mounton, Mounton House. Plan

service court and on the r. by a long-gallery wing one storey high. Beyond them the house seems exaggeratedly large. It is nearly symmetrical, two-storeyed, and the continuous bands of windows across the centre emphasize its breadth. A huge hipped roof rides above. Here is surely an echo of Lutyens's Marsh Court, Hampshire. The most dramatic feature of the entrance front is the contrast of the stonework of the slightly projecting ends with the close-spaced half-timbering of the walls and central porch between. This abrupt juxtaposition of materials was something else suggested by a late medieval house, this time Brinsop Court, Herefordshire, on the restoration of which Tipping had recently advised. In the stone parts large timber-framed windows are set under segmental relieving arches. For this the model was near at hand, Moynes Court, Mathern (*see* p. 387).*

It is hardly practical to walk round the outside of the house, nor did Tipping intend one to do so. To the W the cliff drops away in a yard or two. To the E the wing at the far end of the service court bars the way. So the interior will be described next, the garden front and garden last. The front door opens into a small lobby, beyond which to the l. is the square HALL. From its E end the main staircase rises in a framed timber cage. Jacobean detail. From the SE corner of the hall a doorway leads into the NW corner of the DINING ROOM. This is extremely large and decorated in an C18 style. The cue for the change of style is provided by the door-cases and the white and grey mottled marble chimneypiece brought from *Adam*'s Brasted Place, Kent, which had been the Tipping family home. Plaster wreaths on ceiling and walls. Black and white marble floor, an odd piece of pretension. To the W of the dining room, the LADIES' PARLOUR (now staff room), in the centre of the garden front. This is quite small and has a brought-in C18 timber chimneypiece. Beyond that, in another change of gear, the heavily Jacobean OAK PARLOUR. This is undeniably a handsome room. The composition of full-height Doric columns and pilasters which incorporate the great fireplace on the far wall have their counterparts forming a pseudo-screen on the entrance wall. Plaster ceiling with broad enriched relief bands forming complex patterns. The Prince of Wales feathers and initials P.H. give away the fact that it has been made from a cast of the ceiling of 1610–11 in Prince Henry's Room over the Inner Temple Gateway, London. Beyond, in the SW angle of the house, Tipping had his LIBRARY (now headmaster's study), opening directly through a columned loggia into the garden. (His former WORK ROOM in the NW angle has a bizarre chimneypiece and overmantel in exposed brickwork, into which are let casts of Quattrocento relief panels. Upstairs, Tipping's bedroom also has a decorated plaster ceiling.)

The GARDEN FRONT is extremely long, gabled over centre and end projections, the latter forming loggias, that to the W columned, that to the E with round-headed French windows.

* Also Llanthony Secunda, Caldicot (p. 160), not far away. Francis subsequently used the motif again and again.

The upper storey between the projections is hung with green Westmorland slates. A paved terrace extends the full width of the front, and beyond that a broad grass terrace of even greater length. In the bowed ends, backed with clipped yew hedges, a pair of enormous Neoclassical stone URNS, also brought from Brasted. Their design is curious, with monkey heads and tails, and is not documented as by Adam.

In the walled courts S of the drive, LIVING UNITS for the School, 1988, sympathetically designed by *Gwent County Architect's Department*, job architect *Martin Lougher*.

BIGWOOD, ½m. E, overlooking the drive to Mounton House. Little more than a cottage, in Arts and Crafts mode, by *Norman Evill*.

ST LAWRENCE, ¾m. NE. Three-bay, two-storey, late C18 house, the S front handsome if simple. Rendered and colour-washed. Top parapet, the centre bay under a pediment.

MYNYDDISLWYN 1090

ST TUDOR. One of Gwent's ridgetop medieval churches, accompanied only by a pub and a scatter of mid-C20 bungalows. It was rebuilt *c.* 1819 'on a larger scale' than its predecessor, leaving only the W tower untouched. This has a Perp W doorway, two-centred with continuous wave, hollow and wave mouldings. The other openings are formed without dressed stone. The tower is of three stages, demarcated by stringcourses. Battlements. Rectangular NE stair-turret rising boldly higher. The tower arch has tall chamfered imposts, and a chamfered sub-arch dying into them. The early C19 church is indeed large, nave and chancel in one, and wide, gabled N aisle reaching almost to the E wall. Big, pointed-headed N and S windows with iron glazing bars. Quite a convincing four-bay arcade, if somewhat crudely detailed. Octagonal piers with moulded caps and wide arches, pointed and chamfered. In 1907 *E. M. Bruce Vaughan* of Cardiff began an improving restoration. His must be the two Perp E windows. The toothed stonework at the SE angle reveals his intention to extend the chancel. – FONT. Presumably of *c.* 1819. Square bowl with ogee underside, on a classically shaped pedestal, all the mouldings over-emphatic. – STAINED GLASS. Chancel E, Jesus appearing to the Maries at the empty tomb. By *Heaton, Butler & Bayne*, *c.* 1911. – Chancel S, a text from Ecclesiasticus boldly integrated into abstract patterns. 1970 by *John Petts*. – MONUMENT. John Jones of Abercarn †1865. Large Grecian tablet signed by *A. H. James* of Newport.

NEW BETHEL UNITED REFORMED CHURCH, 1 m. N. An isolated chapel 'Built 1765', rebuilt 1855, but modernized in the early C20 with fussy rock-faced stone dressings. The late C19 interior has galleries on three sides and a pulpit in the traditional arrangement, flanked by two round-headed windows.

But what one will remember about New Bethel is the crowd of monuments in the BURIAL GROUND, and in particular the presumptuous memorial to James Thomas †1901, bearing a statue which overtops the chapel roof.

TWYN TUDUR, immediately S of the church. A finely preserved C12 domical motte and surrounding ditch, completely bare of trees or shrubs.

PONT BREN GWYN, 2 m. SW (ST 167 920). One of the most interesting of the Bronze Age cairns on Machen ridge, since the burial cist can be seen in the centre. The small cairn nearby is all that remains of a group of cairns – a cairnfield – though they may be simply field clearance heaps.

BRONZE AGE CAIRNS. On the summit of Machen ridge, $2\frac{1}{2}$ m. SW, there is a group similar to the concentrations to be found on the Glamorgan ridges. Twyn Cae Hugh (ST 174 915) stands at the edge of the forestry plantation and was originally surrounded by a ditch. The two cairns on Twyn yr Oerfel (ST 181 907 and 183 906) are good examples of the type but both have been disturbed. There is a low stone ring attached to the eastern cairn.

1010

NANTYGLO

Ironworks were first established here in the early 1790s, as an offshoot from Blaenavon. They did not prosper until after 1811, when they were leased by Joseph Bailey, nephew of Richard Crawshay of the Cyfarthfa Ironworks at Merthyr Tydfil, and Matthew Wayne. In 1820 Joseph was joined by his brother Crawshay Bailey. Though booming by the 1840s, the business was harshly and meanly run. The early workers' houses, built on the E side of the valley *c.* 1813–30, were tiny, two-roomed terraced cottages, notoriously small and cramped. One terrace, Bayliss Row, had windows facing only into the hillside, so that they should not overlook the ironmaster's house.

The most evocative survivors of this regime, however, can be found on the gentler W slope. Of TŶ MAWR, built for Joseph Bailey to overlook the ironworks, only the laid-out footings of walls remain. At ROUNDHOUSES FARM, higher up the slope, a rectangular walled enclosure within which stand two stout cylindrical TOWERS of rubble-stone, one partly ruined. Also three stone-built ranges of farm buildings forming a rectangle open towards the E. The towers are said to have been built as a place of refuge for trusted workers at the ironworks in case of unrest. This may have been in 1816, prompted by the Merthyr Riots of three years earlier, or at the time of the Chartist Risings, *c.* 1838.

The SW tower, originally one storey higher than the other, although lit only by slit windows, could house four families. Part of one of the long ranges was also intended to be habitable. Structurally, all the buildings exploited iron products, in their roof trusses, lattice beams and floor joists as well as window frames. The fittings from the SW tower have unfortunately all been removed, and some from the NE tower were sold for scrap *c.* 1942.

WESLEY CHURCH, ½ m. N. Built as an English Wesleyan chapel in 1825. House-like. Interior remodelled. Gallery over the entrance with pierced metal front.

NANTYGLO COMPREHENSIVE SCHOOL, Pond Road. Built c. 1970–1 by *Monmouthshire County Architect's Department*. Two flat-roofed ranges, one three-storey and one two-storey, faced with grey panels. Upright rectangular windows in continuous rows.

NASH 3080

ST MARY. A large church and an extraordinary surprise, standing alone but for a scatter of council houses in the flat meadows 2 m. (3 kilometres) S of the outskirts of Newport. Tall Perp N steeple, built by Eton College, holders of the rectory of Nash since 1450, mighty four-bay Georgian nave with S porch, chancel of 1861 by *J. P. Seddon* of *Prichard & Seddon*. The three parts are unified only by their thin-coursed grey limestone walling. The late C15 steeple is unique in SE Wales. It consists of a tall three-stage tower, with diagonal buttresses dying in half-way up. Square SE stair-turret. Small trefoil-headed belfry windows, parapet pierced with similar trefoil-headed openings. Lofty stone spire, octagonal and completely plain except for a band of trefoils in relief half-way up. The tower does not intercommunicate with the church and seems never to have done so. Small E doorway, two-centred-headed with a wave moulding. Note the putlog holes all the way up the E, N and W faces of the tower. Restored by *Seddon & Carter* in 1897. There are some clues as to the form of the medieval church. At the NW corner of the nave, a broad buttress with set-offs establishes that the present nave is the same length as its predecessor. A former N aisle has left the crease-line of its gable in the W wall of the tower. The parishioners petitioned to demolish it in 1792. So that must date the simply detailed N wall of the nave. The rest of the nave must belong to the 1730s or '40s. The Baroque details of the S porch especially suggest that, the outer arch of flattened segmental form, on chunks of triglyph entablature and gadrooned capitals, the inner arch a flattened ogee with scrolly keystone and concave-sided capitals to the imposts. Varied but less vigorous details elsewhere. Broad, pointed S windows with architrave surrounds and keystones like open books. Round-headed W window in a similar surround, over a round-headed doorway. Compared with all that, the chancel is straightforward enough, steeply gabled with a three-light, Geometrical E window, typical of its date and designer.

The interior has a further surprise in store, a complete
Georgian ensemble of W GALLERY, BOX PEWS and three-decker 82
PULPIT, presumably installed shortly after 1792. The barrel-shaped boarded ceiling is presumably of this date too. – STAINED GLASS. Chancel E, SS John Baptist and Evangelist. 1972 by *Celtic Studios*, in their Expressionist style. – Chancel S, Nunc Dimittis. By *Geoffrey Robinson*, 1982.

EAST USK LIGHT, 1 m. SW. Cylindrical white tower 44 ft (13 metres) high, erected in 1893 to mark the E bank of the River Usk.

POWER STATION, Uskmouth, 1½ m. W. By *Johnson Blackett*.

2090 NEWBRIDGE/CEFN BYCHAN

The winding HIGH STREET is lined by a sequence of ambitious or at least conspicuous buildings: church, chapels, workmen's institute and hotel.

ST PAUL, High Street. 1926–9 by *H.J. Griggs* of *Griggs & Vaughan*. A belated essay in the Bodley manner, nobly lofty, its elaborately traceried Dec windows set high up, but a torso. Chancel and two-bay transepts only. The intended nave, mighty SW tower and SE Lady Chapel not built. The facing material is rough, heavily iron-stained Pennant sandstone inside and out. Ashlar mainly reserved for internal dressings, especially the tall octagonal piers and sharply moulded arches of the two-bay arcades which screen the transepts. – REREDOS. By *J. Wippell & Co.* – STAINED GLASS. Much in a mildly Expressionist idiom. – Chancel E, Christ in Glory, 1960 by *George Cooper-Abbs* for *Wippell & Co.* – Transept upper windows, with complex iconography, 1970–6 by *Wippell Mowbray*.

OUR LADY OF PEACE (R.C.), Ashfield Road. Built 1939–40 by *P.D. Hepworth* at the expense of Mrs Fflorens Roch of Llanover. The white-rendered walls, pantiled roofs and the N tower, crowned by balconies in all four directions, make a conspicuous group rising out of trees above a quarried cliff, like a white reminiscence of San Francesco at Assisi. Close-to, the group is complex, with polygonal W baptistery, lean-to S aisle and E ambulatory arrangement. White Neo-Georgian PRESBYTERY immediately to the W. The interior of the church is little altered and has much character. High, narrow nave lit only by the long clerestory windows. White walls, no mouldings. Against this neutral background the roof, its deep tie-beams painted in geometric patterns, seems barbarically bright. Even more dramatic is the painted ironwork, the SCREEN to the narthex, and the extraordinary Mexican-style ELECTROLIERS with their dangling red tassels. – FONT. Of travertine, the tall, angular form typical of the 1930s.

BEULAH WELSH BAPTIST CHAPEL, North Road. The broad, rendered front has an unusual, syncopated array of round-headed openings, four upper windows and three lower between a pair of doorways. The inscription panel gives dates, of building 1809, of enlargement 1818 and 1823, and of repair 1884. The façade is probably of the middle two dates, the rendered embellishments of the last. The interior retains its substantial fittings of 1884. Galleries round three sides set on slim iron posts with leaf capitals. Against the rear wall, the railed preaching rostrum, between two windows. So the early C19 layout was retained at the refitting. Segmental boarded ceiling.

The large BURIAL GROUND contains an unusually regular array of headstones.

TABERNACLE BAPTIST CHURCH, High Street. 1912–13, by *N. Gasenius Lewis* of Abertillery. Quite a lofty façade. Snecked Pennant sandstone with dressed stonework painted over. Five-light Perp window above the central pair of pointed entrances. Those to the galleries in slightly projecting side-turrets. The interior has been floored across at gallery level, but retains surprisingly much of its original character. Arch-braced and hammerbeam roof, and ceiling boarded in three cants. Spreading organ set in a wide arch above the pulpit.

ZION UNITED REFORMED CHURCH, High Street. 1897 by *Swash & Bain* of Newport. Broad, low façade in an Arts and Crafts Perp style. Pennant sandstone with Bath stone dressings. Plain galleried interior under a hammerbeam roof. – STAINED GLASS. By *W. H. Perks* of Birmingham.

COMPREHENSIVE SCHOOL, Bridge Street. Of *c.* 1930, doubtless by *John Bain* of Newport, architect to Monmouth Education Committee between the Wars. Somewhat lamely Neo-Georgian, of grey, rock-faced Pennant sandstone. The central six bays, of two tall storeys, have a hipped roof. Open segmental pediment above the central pair of bays and domed ridgetop turret. Lower wings in line.

CELYNEN COLLIERIES WORKMEN'S INSTITUTE, High Street. Domestic-looking, of red brick and yellow painted stonework. Inconspicuous Jacobean details. Huge rectangular MEMORIAL HALL behind, dated 1924.

THE NEWBRIDGE, High Street. Hotel of 1901 by *F. R. Bates* of Newport. Red and yellow brick disposed not in the normal way for walling and for details, but in broad, contrasting areas, like a jester's tunic.

CWMDOWS, beside the B4472, ⅓ m. NW. The best-preserved early farmhouse in the uplands of the county, datable to the late C16, although in a disconcertingly suburbanized setting. A single range squeezed between the road and the cut-back hillside. Almost all the original openings survive, including five diamond-mullion timber windows. So it is possible to understand the internal arrangements from outside. The S, roadward end was the cowhouse, entered through its own doorway, with a loft above. The main door, immediately to the l, opens into a cross-passage, which was also boarded over, and the three-light upper window here suggests that the area above the passage was habitable, as the cowherd's bed-space. The hall, to the l. of the cross-passage, is entered from it, has its hearth backing on to the passage, and a mural stair winding up on the W side of the hearth (see the tiny W window lighting the stair). The five-light mullioned E window of the hall survives, and so does the E window of one of the two unheated inner rooms beyond the hall. Over the hall, an unheated bedroom, lit from the E and rising into the roof space. A narrow second one beyond, lit from a three-light window in the N gable. The house has been well conserved, its stone walls and mullioned windows whitened in the traditional way.

(TREOWEN, on the hilltop W of the R.C. church, is housing

developed from 1925 on land belonging to Lord Treowen of Llanover. His architect was *George Davies*. The earliest houses are stone-faced and have an Arts and Crafts flavour.)

4090 NEWCHURCH/EGLWYS NEWYDD

The parish, in two parts, E and W, is extensive and heavily wooded, with much of Chepstow Park Wood in the E half, and much of Wentwood in the W. The church stands on a ridge at the junction of the two parts.

ST PETER. Nave and lower chancel, with lean-to S vestry, rebuilt by *J. P. Seddon* in 1863–4 in simple Dec style. E window a disc above two trefoiled lancets. Medieval W tower and N porch heavily restored by him. The tower is short, with a square SE turret, top stringcourse and battlements. Double-chamfered W doorway and blocked trefoiled lancet above. Inner doorway instead of a tower arch. The porch has a characteristic Perp outer arch, moulded with wave, hollow and wave. – FONTS. An early, disused tub, and a Victorian font with flat cover, presumably by *Seddon*. Stepped octagonal bowl on a square base. – STAINED GLASS. Chancel E, 1931 by *Theodora Salusbury*. An arresting conception vividly executed. The Virgin and Child look down from a starry night sky on adoring kings and shepherds.

GAER LLWYD, 1 m. SW. The Megalithic tomb (ST 447 968) stands in a field close to the road but nearly all trace of the long cairn stretching to the NW behind it has disappeared. The backstone and two portal stones of the chamber remain upright, and a side stone has fallen beneath the tilted capstone. In front of the chamber are two lower upright stones defining a wide antechamber, a characteristic feature of many Cotswold-Severn tombs. Three fallen blocks of uncertain status lie in front of the antechamber. This is the best-preserved and most characteristic of the Neolithic tombs in Gwent, a group linking the Cotswold area and Breconshire, where there is a concentration of such monuments.

BRONZE AGE BARROWS. Two barrows stand on the summit of the ridge now covered by Wentwood Forest (ST 417 946). They are ditchless and built of turves or earth, classic examples of the standard 'Bowl Barrow'. They survive to a height of at least 6 ft (1.8 metres) and until recently were the finest barrows to be seen in Gwent. Sadly, the surrounding woodland has been roughly felled, and the monuments look dishevelled. Up to the last century many others must have rivalled them in size, but have now been reduced by ploughing and other disturbances to a scarcely recognizable swelling.

CAS TROGGY, 3 m. SW. A substantial fragment of a stone castle virtually invisible in a thicket below the edge of Wentwood Forest. It seems to have been begun by Roger Bigod shortly before his death in 1307. A stretch of straight wall survives bearing the embrasures of two pointed-headed recesses, presumably for windows. To the E, part of an angle tower of indeterminate shape, and adjoining it to the NE, better preserved than the rest, a rectangular projection supported on arches in two directions and pierced by what appear to be garderobe chutes. Scarping for a moat all along the S side of the structure.

NEWPORT/CASNEWYDD 3080

INTRODUCTION

Newport is by far the largest town in the county, with a population in 1996 of 136,800. Although Newport, or 'Novus Burgus', had by the early Middle Ages replaced Caerleon as the port on the tidal River Usk, and had gained borough status by *c.* 1120, its period of greatest growth as a port and thus as a population centre was the early C19. The Monmouthshire Canal, opened in 1799, linked it with the iron-producing areas between Pontypool and Abergavenny, and shortly afterwards a network of tramroads connected the port with the other Monmouthshire valleys to the W. The developing export of coal at first benefited Newport in particular, but by the mid C19 Cardiff had gained the supremacy which it has never subsequently lost. The first of Newport's docks, at Pillgwenlly, was opened in 1842, its extension in 1858. Other larger docks, further downstream, opened in 1875 (Alexandra Dock) and 1893 (South Dock). Major improvements to the port facilities continued to be made until 1914. Today the overwhelming impression of Newport is of a sprawling Victorian town, even though its riverside centre was savagely recast in the 1970s for the benefit of the car and the lorry, and its edges continue to expand. Further dynamic expansion seems likely, as the M4 continues to make Newport the best-connected town in Wales.

The topography of medieval Newport was peculiar, torn between the hilltop and the river crossing over half a mile away to the NE. The original nucleus, on the hill, was the church dedicated to, and said to have been founded by, the local C6 saint, St Gwynllyw (Woolos). An earthwork castle was erected nearby in the late C11 or early C12 – and swept away in 1846 by excavations for the railway. The importance of the crossing over the River Usk to the NE was reinforced by the building of a second castle beside it in the C14. This was the work of the new lord of Gwynllŵg (Wentlooge in English), created after the death of the last de Clare lord of Glamorgan in 1314. The town grew up as a long street between church and crossing, with its East Gate beside the crossing and its West Gate at the W end of the High Street. The present Stow Hill, which climbs up to the church, must originally have been quasi-suburban, though Leland (*c.* 1539) writes of the West Gate as being in the middle of the town, and mentions a third gate up by the church. There is no evidence that the medieval town was ever walled, but that it was succeeding as a town is suggested by the fact that an Augustinian friary was established here, close to the bridge over the River Usk, in 1377. The bridge itself, first mentioned *c.* 1100, was rebuilt at least twice during the Middle Ages and remained a timber bridge until its reconstruction in stone in 1800. Thereafter, development of the town on the E bank of the river became more attractive. So what Leland had called 'al yn one streate' and Archdeacon Coxe in 1801 could still describe as a 'long, narrow and straggling town', was by the mid C19 experiencing a new prosperity and burgeoning expansion on to the surrounding hills on both sides of the river.

Thus was established the scale and character of the Newport of today. Of pre-C19 Newport little enough has survived, just the terminal markers, to the SW the church, enlarged into St Woolos Cathedral, and to the NE the ruins of the castle, together with one single C17 merchant's house in the High Street. The C19 architecture of Newport, it must be admitted, cannot match that of its South Wales rivals, Cardiff and Swansea. The dominant architectural practice, the *Habershons*, responsible for buildings of every type from the 1850s until after 1900, meekly followed changing fashion over the half-century without much individuality. They owed their employment principally to the fact that they were retained architects to the Morgans of Tredegar. The buildings of other local architects of greater character, *R. G. Thomas* and *J. H. Langdon*, have had a poor survival rate, but the work of *A. O. Watkins* is worth looking out for. Among Victorian buildings there have been two significant losses, the Town Hall (1883–5 by *T. M. Lockwood* of Chester with the local architect *E. A. Lansdowne*) and the Corn Exchange of 1875–8 by *Lawrence & Goodman*. The major work of the interwar period, the Civic Centre, is in its turn no match for Swansea Guildhall. After 1945 Newport grew greatly, spreading estates of council housing over the surrounding hills. The most remarkable of these is at Duffryn, *see* p. 217. Over the past decade or more the Borough Council's efforts have turned back to the centre of town, creating extensive pedestrianized areas, streets, squares, underpasses and riverside quays, enlivened and diversified by sculpture and murals. The sculpture in particular is notably diverse and powerful, as will be further explained below.

ST WOOLOS CATHEDRAL

When the diocese of Monmouth was carved out of Llandaff in 1921 at the disestablishment of the Church in Wales, St Woolos, the medieval parish church of Newport, was declared its pro-cathedral. Only in 1949, after the former monastic churches of Abergavenny, Chepstow and Monmouth, and even Tintern Abbey itself, had been considered and rejected for raising to cathedral status, as had the construction of a completely new building, was St Woolos confirmed as the cathedral of the diocese. The church dedicated to St Gwynllyw was a Saxon foundation. By the late C11 it was the premier church in the Cantref of Gwynllŵg and in 1093 was granted by William Rufus to Gloucester Abbey. The present building consists of a Perp W tower, an aisleless narthex, known as St Mary's chapel, adjoining the tower to the E, and E of that a five-bay Norman nave with aisles and clerestory, probably datable to the 1140s.* This last is the finest Norman parochial structure in the county, though completely masked externally by heightened and widened Perp aisles. Three restorations have left their mark: in 1818 the windows of St Mary's Chapel were enlarged; in 1853–4 *W. G. & E. Habershon* drastically restored the aisle windows, rebuilt the S porch to a new design and receiled the roofs; in 1913 further roof renewal took place and the windows in St Mary's Chapel were re-formed again, as lancets. The architect this time was *William Davies*, with advice from *Harold Brakspear*. Finally, the choir which was needed for the new cathedral was built 1960–4 by *A. D. R. Caroe*, replacing a chancel largely of the 1850s by the *Habershons*.

As a prelude to detailed examination, the site must be appreciated. It is at the E end of a ridge which drops sharply in three directions, providing a commanding view over the estuary of the River Usk, and was chosen, according to a tradition which goes back at least to the C13, by the local chieftain, St Gwynllyw, in the late C6 as the site for a timber church. For the present, successively enlarged, church there is all too little space. Access is practical only from the W, so description must start there too.

The Perp W tower, much restored, is quite tall, of three storeys, the walls of mauve Old Red Sandstone rubble, the full-height angle buttresses and polygonal NE stair-turret faced with Bath stone ashlar. Double plinth moulding, undercut strings, top battlements. The two-centred-headed W doorway has continuous wave and hollow, and a hoodmould with outlined stops. Three-light window above, with standard panel tracery. Meagre upper windows, of two uncusped lights under hoodmoulds. Headless statue in a niche on the S face of the top storey. The shield with double Tudor rose on the upper S stringcourse probably refers to Jasper Tudor, lord of Newport 1485–95. The statue may also have represented him. They presumably date the tower to the late C15. The rest of the exterior can be more summarily dealt with.

St Mary's Chapel is of three bays, the lancet windows, as already noted, re-formed in 1913. Of the same date, the Perp door-frame at the SW corner, set in an early doorway. The octofoil

* The evidence for the date is an indulgence granted by Theobald, Archbishop of Canterbury 1139–46, to all 'qui devotionis intuitu ecclesiam Sancti Gundlei de Novo Burgo requisierint'.

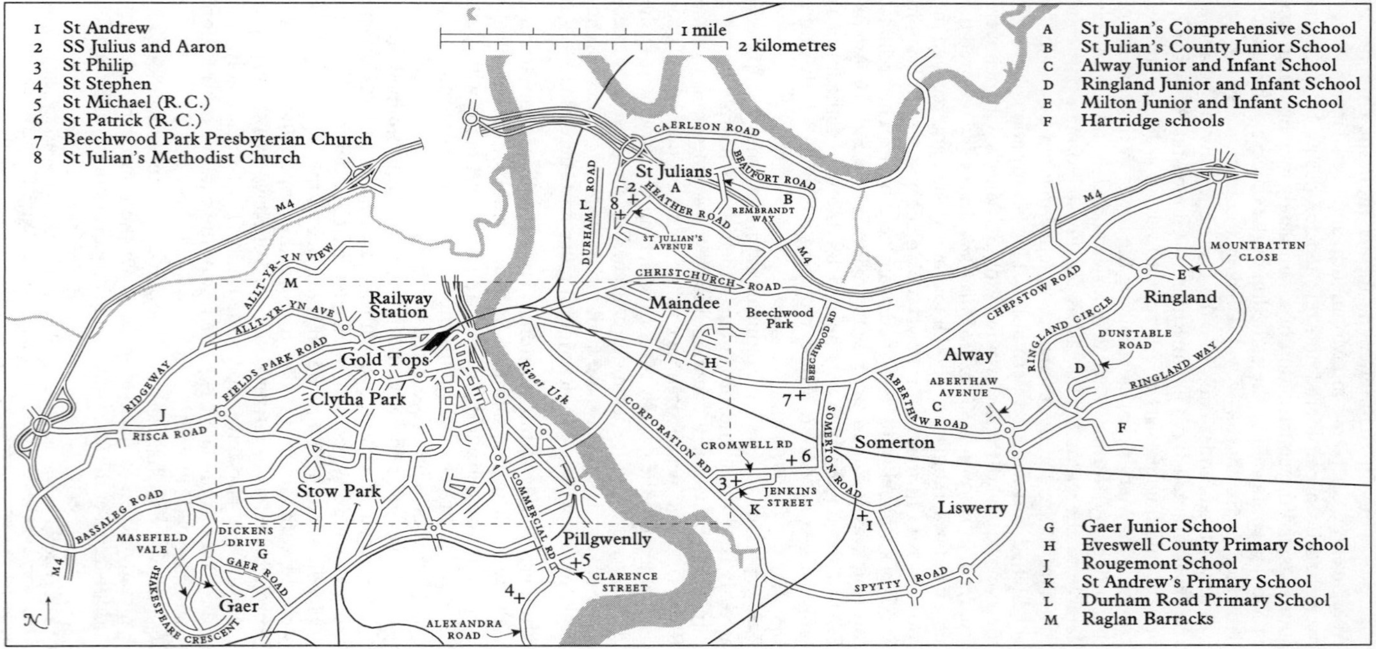

1 St Andrew
2 SS Julius and Aaron
3 St Philip
4 St Stephen
5 St Michael (R.C.)
6 St Patrick (R.C.)
7 Beechwood Park Presbyterian Church
8 St Julian's Methodist Church
1 mile
2 kilometres
A St Julian's Comprehensive School
B St Julian's County Junior School
C Alway Junior and Infant School
D Ringland Junior and Infant School
E Milton Junior and Infant School
F Hartridge schools
G Gaer Junior School
H Eveswell County Primary School
J Rougemont School
K St Andrew's Primary School
L Durham Road Primary School
M Raglan Barracks
CAERLEON ROAD
BEAUFORT ROAD
St Julians
HEATHER ROAD
REMBRANDT WAY
DURHAM ROAD
ST JULIAN'S AVENUE
M4
ALLT-YR-YN VIEW
ALLT-YR-YN AVE
CHRISTCHURCH ROAD
Maindee
Beechwood Park
BEECHWOOD RD
CHEPSTOW ROAD
Ringland
MOUNTBATTEN CLOSE
RINGLAND CIRCLE
DUNSTABLE ROAD
RINGLAND WAY
Alway
ABERTHAW AVENUE
ABERTHAW ROAD
Railway Station
Gold Tops
FIELDS PARK ROAD
Clytha Park
RIDGEWAY
RISCA ROAD
River Usk
CORPORATION RD
CROMWELL RD
JENKINS STREET
SOMERTON ROAD
Somerton
Liswerry
SPYTTY ROAD
Stow Park
BASSALEG ROAD
MASEFIELD VALE
DICKENS DRIVE
GAER ROAD
SHAKESPEARE CRESCENT
Gaer
COMMERCIAL RD
Pillgwenlly
CLARENCE STREET
ALEXANDRA ROAD
N

Newport, general

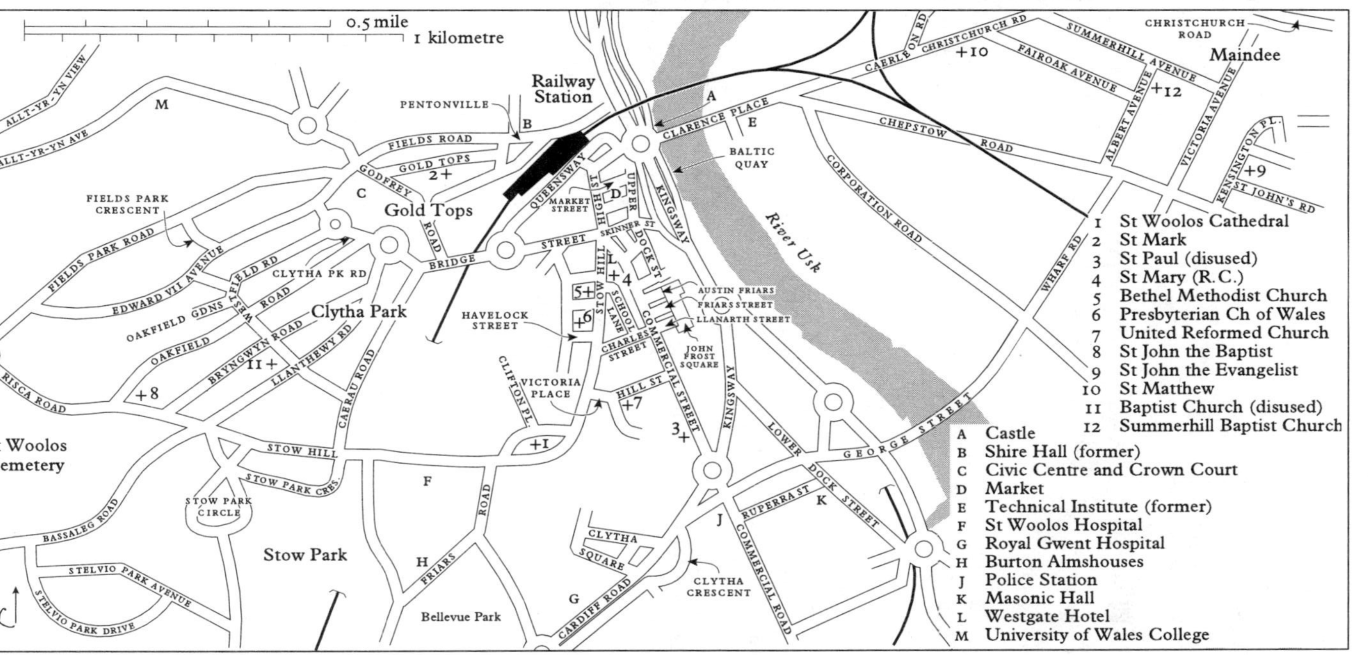

Newport, city centre

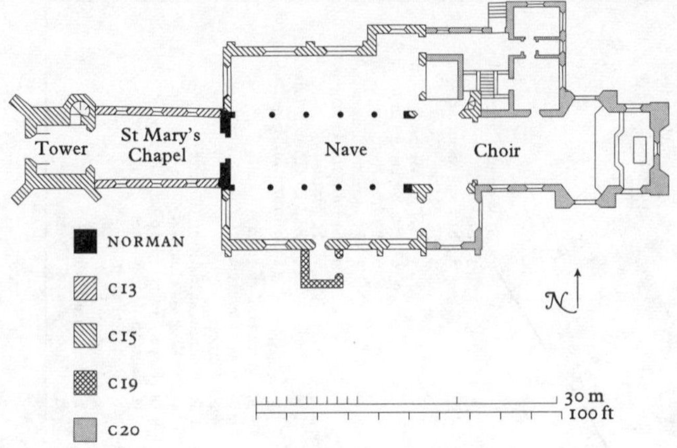

Newport, St Woolos Cathedral. Plan

window at the E end of the S wall is medieval, originally in the upper storey of the S porch and inserted here in 1913. The nave aisles, heavily restored by the Habershons, have four-light Perp windows and thin buttresses. The window tracery, which is probably trustworthy, is of a design based on elongated, cusped hexagons. It suggests that the aisles were widened several decades before the building of the tower. The E bay on the N side projects to form a short transept. Caroe's CHOIR is in the tradition of Sir Giles Scott, unequivocally Gothic but understated. The W bay widens into a S chapel, and N organ-recess. Pseudo-transepts further E, with simplified window tracery and clasping buttresses. In the E wall a large oculus high up, with tracery in the form of a cross. Deep, canted reveals between the buttresses and the wall. Shallow top gable. The drop in the ground gives room for a hall below. Transverse N vestries, extended 1990–1, to form a second hall, by *A. J. Beer*.

Inside, there is much more to see and ponder. The tower arch is unexpectedly impressive, high, wide and steeply pointed, with rich continuous mouldings, including wave and double wave. St Mary's Chapel, by contrast, is only a little more communicative. Its walls were thoroughly scraped in 1913, revealing that there was never a N or S doorway. Irregular, pointed recesses in the N and S walls, doubtless intended for monuments. At the
9 E end, a splendid Norman doorway, the outer arch decorated with downward-pointing and outward-pointing zigzag and a billet-moulded hood. The nook-shafts which support the arch to l. and r. are stout monoliths and have attic bases and wave-moulded imposts, which look like reused Roman pieces. The
10 richly carved capitals have outward-curving leaves and angle volutes, like classical Composite capitals, but small figures and birds appear at random among the leaves in a way that guarantees their C12 date. The doorway forms the grand entry to the

Norman nave, but its relationship to St Mary's Chapel must also be considered. Its exceptional state of preservation and the absence of any evidence that it was ever fitted with doors show that it was never external. So St Mary's Chapel, even if in essence a C13 structure, must have had a Celtic predecessor. A comparable plan is seen at Llantwit Major, Glamorgan. From the doorway three steps descend to the nave.

The five-bay nave is a textbook Norman design. Round piers, round moulded bases, and scallop capitals with square abaci. Semicircular arches of two unmoulded orders. The W and E responds, however, are square, not round, their angles chamfered, the E chamfers delicately outlined. The aisles must originally have been narrow, their roof-line immediately above the heads of the arches, for the clerestory windows, aligned over the arch heads, barely leave room for it. Similar W window over the entrance doorway. Over the E arch of the S arcade the Norman window has been replaced by a pair of cusped ogee-headed lights, and three two-light Tudor windows, much renewed, all clearly intended to admit light on to a late medieval rood. The medieval wagon roof of the nave is unboarded, allowing its structure to be well seen. At the E end of the N aisle a complex arrangement of arches and a half-arch, where the transept meets what is left of the pre-cathedral chancel. Caroe's choir conveys the same impression inside as out, lofty but bland. The pseudo-transepts help to make the sanctuary very light. Low down in the N transept, a reset medieval squint window, with miniaturized Perp tracery in a rectangular frame. – REREDOS. The focal point of the cathedral, 1964 by *John Piper* and *Patrick Reyntiens*. It is abstract, multimedia and hard to interpret, indeed hard to come to terms with. Patchy gold and brown stained glass fills the E, cross-enclosing oculus, around and below which a canvas extends down to the floor, painted to look like marbling or like a turbulent, muddy river flecked with red. The whole is framed by a broad, mauve band painted direct on to the plaster of the E wall. – FONT. In St Mary's Chapel. Apparently a magnificent C12 piece, but largely of 1854. The circular shaft and base with trefoiled angle leaves are said to be old, and the square bowl, with open-mouthed heads from which issue long curling stems, contains an old fragment, inserted in 1913. – RELIEF. Star of David, 1983 by *Arthur Giardelli*. Of cork and mirror-glass. – STAINED GLASS. The Victorian glass has been severely pruned, leaving figure scenes in several windows without their backgrounds. – S chapel E, by *Hardman*, *c.* 1890. Presentation in the Temple, reduced to four isolated figures. – S aisle SE, the story of the Good Samaritan. 1875 by *Hardman*. – S aisle central and SW, saints. 1915 by *William Pearce Ltd*. – N aisle W, Christ and little children. By *Hardman*. – In St Mary's Chapel, two N windows, abstract, are clearly by *Frank Roper*, *c.* 1970. Brought in from the demolished St Luke, Bridge Street. – MONUMENTS. The medieval monuments in St Mary's Chapel are a sorry sight, the battered remains of large and fine effigies. – Under the SW arch, cross-legged knight in chainmail and surcoat, of *c.* 1300, headless, handless and footless. – Under the NW arch, a fairly well preserved early C14 figure of a lady in a dress which falls in elegant folds at her feet. – Panel of four well-preserved weepers (N central arch). They bear the arms of Sir John Morgan of Tredegar †1493. It is not clear whether this belongs with the torso of a knight or the headless alabaster figure of a woman which occupy the same arch. – Sir Walter Herbert of St Julian's †1568 (S aisle W). The recumbent figure of a knight is a mere fragment, but the tomb-chest and canopy, of oolitic limestone, are well-preserved. Two bays by one, arcaded canopy over the tomb-chest, with fluted Ionic columns against the piers, supporting a well-proportioned entablature, and Ionic half-columns within, supporting a ceiling decorated with flat geometric patterns. Against the tomb-chest, oval armorial panels with gadrooned surrounds. So this is an assured classical design, at quite an early date. It can be closely compared with several monuments in Gloucestershire, and was doubtless imported ready-made across the River Severn. – In the aisles, several standard Neoclassical tablets: the earliest Mary James †1792 (N), signed *E. Morgan*, Canton, the largest Rev. Matthew Monkhouse †1822 (N), signed *H. Wood*, Bristol, the latest Thomas Hughes †1846.

CHURCHES AND CHAPELS

Between the 1830s and the 1920s Newport was abundantly furnished with places of worship. The ancient parish of St Woolos was first subdivided in 1836 on the completion of St Paul's Church. Three more Anglican churches appeared in the 1850s, including the town's most conspicuous suburban landmark, St John Maindee, begun in 1859. The next burst, of six churches, came 1872–86, with a further seven at intervals between 1891 and 1925.

The Roman Catholics were content with two large churches, one in the town centre built as early as 1838, the other in the dock area of 1886. Nonconformist chapels, by contrast, proliferated. By 1830 Baptists, Congregationalists, Independents and Methodists, both Calvinistic and Wesleyan, had all opened chapels in the town. Thereafter, at least a further thirty were built during the period. A new one opened virtually every other year between 1856 and 1883, reflecting the town's dynamic growth during the mid-Victorian decades. The most sought-after position was on Stow Hill, on the way up to St Woolos. The Roman Catholics built handsomely there in 1838, the Baptists in 1862 and the Wesleyan Methodists in 1882, while the show chapel of the Congregationalists, of 1858, was only just off it.

Early commissions went to architects with a wide reputation, T.H. Wyatt, J.J. Scoles, James Wilson of Bath, Prichard and Seddon. But from the mid-century local architects established a virtual stranglehold. The Habershon firm in particular, having restored St Woolos 1853–4, was constantly in work. Between 1857 and 1907 they built three Anglican churches, and at least fourteen chapels for six denominations.

In the second half of the C20 a few insignificant Anglican churches have been built, and two substantial Roman Catholic ones, together with a small but impressive Baptist church. Otherwise, the story is of destruction: nearly two-thirds of the Nonconformist chapels have been demolished or are in other uses, and five of the Anglican churches have gone.

ST ANDREW, Somerton Road, Liswerry. 1882 by *E. A. Lansdowne*. An inexpensive little cruciform church. Lancets. – STAINED GLASS. Chancel E, Christ the King between the Call of Peter and Andrew and steelworkers. By *Wippell & Co.*, *c.* 1964. – Nave NW, the Virgin teaching Jesus to read. 1975 by *Celtic Studios*.

ST JOHN THE BAPTIST, Risca Road. 1898–1900 by *F. R. Kempson* of Llandaff. A hall church in a Dec style. Varied window patterns, well seen from the road. The gabled aisles, continued as chapels, are stopped short of the sanctuary bay. S porch open by means of large arches to E and W. W tower prepared for but not built. The materials are mauve Old Red Sandstone from Risca and Bath stone dressings. Spacious interior, predictable but satisfying. Five-bay nave, the piers with four shafts and four hollows, the arches double-wave-moulded. Three wave mouldings on the high and wide, shafted chancel arch. Niches flank the E window, with figures of the Annunciation. – FONT. 1900 by *Kempson*. Rich Perp. – ROOD SCREEN with ROOD, and PULPIT. 1910–11, made by *Harry Hems* of Exeter, to *Kempson*'s design. Lavish Perp. – PAINTINGS. Lamentation. Late C15 panel, perhaps North Italian. – Beheading of St John the Baptist. C17, Neapolitan. – STAINED GLASS. S aisle SE, Christ between SS George and Michael, 1901, an early work by *Ninian Comper*. – Chancel E, Crucifixion with angels and saints. 1907 by *Kempe*. – S chapel E, Virgin and Child with saints, 1910. – S aisle centre, Adoration of the Crucified Christ, 1920, and Christ between SS Mary and Thomas, *c.* 1930, both by *Kempe & Co.* – N aisle windows by the same, SS Paul, Stephen and John, 1924, Adoration of the Shepherds, 1916. – S aisle SW, Christ and the Woman with the Issue of Blood. 1945 by *Comper*, a late work to compare with the early one at the other end of the aisle.

The church is at the centre of an unusually extensive group. To the N of the church, CHURCH HALL, in Bryngwyn Road, modest but well-designed, the walls of Old Red Sandstone mixed with red brick. 1903 by *H. J. Griggs*. To the NW, in Oakfield Road, red brick, Gothic VICARAGE, built in 1902, and probably designed by Kempson. Beyond this, CLEWER COURT, which was built as a mission house and children's home for a sisterhood from the House of Mercy, Clewer, Berkshire. 1907 by *H. J. Griggs* with *W. Bucknall* of London. Tudor Gothic, of Old Red Sandstone with Bath stone dressings under a steep, tiled roof. A roughly symmetrical composition, concluded by an upper-storey chapel to the l., and to the r. by a diagonal bay under a steep pyramidal cap. The building has been sympathetically converted into flats.

ST JOHN THE EVANGELIST, Kensington Place, Maindee. A large

and confident church built in 1859–60 by *Prichard & Seddon*, but compromised by the inexpensive completion of the steeple in 1911 by *J. Coates Carter*, and internally by an inept reconstruction in 1951–2 after a fire. The plan consists of a four-bay nave with aisles (N aisle added in 1911) extended as chapels, so that the chancel projects to the E by one bay, a W porch and SW porch steeple. The style is Geometrical, with plenty of quirks, especially the use of spurred tracery in many varieties. The beloved polychromy is obtained from mauve Old Red Sandstone walling, dressed and narrowly banded with Bath stone ashlar, and enlivened with relieving arches where smooth Bath and rough Pennant voussoirs alternate. The W front has the most arresting composition. The alternating voussoirs of two two-light windows and a rose in the spandrel between them are set under a trefoiled superarch. All this is to enframe a niche for a statue of the patron saint, now no longer in position. The steep central porch gable protrudes into the composition from below. Identical gabled S porch at the base of the SW steeple, beyond a massively battered, polygonal SW stair-turret. In the second stage of the steeple, paired lancets, angle buttresses and an increase in the density of banding. Above this, not the intended belfry and spire rising to 180 ft (55 metres), but the feeble square-topped tower of 1911. The only further point worth noting outside is the great size of the three-light S windows. Five-light chancel E window.

The interior is a ghost of its former self, the arcades and chancel arch reinstated after the fire to the original design, but without understanding. Thus the unfinished pier capitals, prepared to receive rich foliage carving by *Earp*, are reproduced as giant white dumplings. Foliage carving was also intended round the chancel arch. Simplified roofs. The one magnificent survival is stained glass in two of the enormous windows.* – STAINED GLASS. Chancel E. 1865 by *Chance Brothers & Co.*, surely designed under the supervision of the architects. Richly varied coloration, and elaborate iconography. Ascension flanked by large standing figures of the Four Evangelists. Below, small scenes of the Nativity, Crucifixion and Resurrection. In the tracery, Opening of the Seven Seals. – S chapel E. Signed by *Samuel Evans*, *c.* 1873. Similar in style and concept. Scenes from the life of St John the Evangelist, in the centre the Healing of the Lame Man at the Beautiful Gate. – FONT. Designed by *J. P. Seddon* and only slightly fire-damaged. It exemplifies the love of complex geometry felt by High Victorian Gothicists. A pyramidal shaft bears short shafts on its slopes. Their abaci fuse into a single spurred trefoil, on which rests the hexagonal bowl.

SS JULIUS AND AARON, St Julian's Avenue. An important work by *J. Coates Carter*, 1925–6, though incomplete and reduced in height and width from the design of 1923. Earlier schemes by Coates Carter, for a brick church in 1910, and for a grand Perp

* Preserved, ironically, because at the time of the fire it had been removed for repair after wartime damage.

basilical one in 1917, came to nothing.* The three-bay chancel rides high towards the road, with a row of three lancets under the gable. S chapel not built. Three bays of the slightly higher nave, with E double bell gable and lean-to aisles under continuous pantiled roofslopes. Walls of irregular Old Red Sandstone, dressings of red brick. Internally, the blunt simplicity is much more powerful. Concrete piers in the nave, tall and slender cylinders with slight octagonal caps on fins. Wide, four-centred arches of dull red brick, the E one narrowed for upper openings to a rood loft never installed. Similar brick chancel arch, very high and wide, on rectangular imposts. In the chancel, blocked four-centred arches on square piers, high to the S, low to the N, for the unbuilt chapels. All this contrasts starkly against the exposed rubble side walls. Barn-like roofs with tie-beams and wind-braces, that in the chancel a substitute for the intended concrete vault. – REREDOS. A towering Gothic piece of 1882, installed in 1932 from the church built at Capel y Ffin, Powys, by *Charles Buckeridge* and *J. L. Pearson*, 1872–82, for the monastic community founded by Father Ignatius. Designed by *H. F. Webber* and made in Munich. – FONT. Big square bowl on five circular shafts of black Caldey Island marble. Insignificant relief panels on each face. – CARVED STONE. Relief of a wyvern, supporter of the arms of Sir William Herbert, brought from his demolished C16 mansion of St Julian's.

ST MARK, Gold Tops. 1872–4 by *Habershon, Pite & Fawckner*. A large and conventional Perp church for a prosperous suburb, of mauve Old Red Sandstone with Bath stone dressings. The intention was to imitate a C15 Cotswold wool church, and the three-stage W tower, with its paired belfry windows and eight pinnacles, provides one of Newport's landmarks. The aisled and clerestoried nave, with N and S porches, and the lower chancel, are battlemented throughout. Ambitious N vestry *en suite*, 1902 by *Graham, Hitchcox & Co*. Inside, the five-bay arcades are supported on thin, octagonal piers with over-large moulded caps and double-chamfered arches. Triple-shafted chancel arch. Conspicuous roof trusses of two different designs in nave and chancel. W gallery. – ROOD SCREEN with LOFT, and REREDOS. 1902–5. Perp. Timber. Designed by *Graham, Hitchcox & Co.*, and made by *William Clarke* of Llandaff. – STAINED GLASS. A great deal, none of it memorable. Only documented windows are listed here. Chancel E, Ascension. 1891 by *A. Savell*. – Chancel N, Noli me Tangere. 1909 by *Jones & Willis*. – Chancel SE, Angel at the Empty Tomb, also by *Savell*. – Chancel SW, saints. By *John Hall & Sons*, *c*. 1918. – S aisle E, Faith, Hope and Charity. 1876. – S aisle SE. St Mark in three guises. 1913 by *Savell*. – Others in the S aisle, *c*. 1920–1 by *John Hall & Sons*. – Nave NW, Suffer the Little Children. 1949 by *William Morris & Co*. of Westminster, designer no doubt *F. W. Cole* (A. Brooks).

VICARAGE W of the church. 1877 by *Habershon, Pite & Fawckner*.

* For the former, *see Building News*, 18 February 1910, for the latter, drawings preserved in the vestry and in the National Library of Wales.

ST MATTHEW, Christchurch Road. 1891–2 by *Graham & Hitchcox* of Newport. Rock-faced Pennant sandstone and Bath stone dressings. E.E. The plan, a canted E apse, short transepts and wide, low nave, shows that the church was designed for preaching rather than ritualistic worship. Prominent NW polygonal belfry turret. Over the central space looms a roof structure of big arched braces rising to a flat, boarded polygon. The nave has been partitioned off to form a hall. – REREDOS. Painted figure scenes. 1928 by *A. R. Henderson*, who also stencilled the roof. – STAINED GLASS. Sanctuary, saints *c.* 1919. – Nave N, David, *c.* 1919, and Solomon, 1931, by *Samuel Evans & Co.* of Birmingham.

ST PAUL, Commercial Street (disused). 1835–6 by the young, and clearly enthusiastic but inexperienced, *T. H. Wyatt*. Gothic, but without comprehension of its roots in the Middle Ages, nor with a grasp of conventional proportions. Squared and coursed rock-faced Pennant sandstone with Forest dressings. The E front faces the street and is reached up a broad flight of steps. It is centred on an open octagonal vaulted porch formed by the buttressed arches which support an octagonal spire. A Y-traceried window in the wall to l. and r. and acutely pointed terminal cross gables. The N and S side elevations are even odder. Symmetrical, of nine bays, the central seven with tall, thin paired lancets between insubstantial buttresses. In the end bays, acutely pointed gables over projecting porches or vestries. Tiny polygonal W organ apse with another pinched gable over it. The interior was designed with the altar backing on to the E porch and galleries on the other three sides.

ST PHILIP, Jenkins Street. Dated 1924 on the foundation stone, and surely designed by *J. Coates Carter*. Built on a T-plan for dual use as church and hall, without any architectural distinction between the two uses. The materials used are uncoursed, irregular pieces of ironstone for the walling, pantiles on the steeply sloping roofs, and red brick and tile, with a few blocks of stone, to form the windows. These are chevron-headed, in close-set groups of three, those on the S side towards the road under and between a pair of gables, those to the N in a more developed group of five. Leading in the window heads elaborates the pattern further. Inside, the roof trusses of the church part have collar-beams and kingposts unmistakably forming crosses above the tie-beams. The whole building demonstrates how the resourceful use of materials can of itself create interest and beauty – the true Arts and Crafts objective. – FONT. Tiny alabaster bowl hidden within a polygonal timber stem and cover. – PAINTING. An illustration of 2 Kings 18.19. 1927 by *William H. Dudley*.

ST STEPHEN, Alexandra Road, Pillgwenlly. 1883–4 by *E. A. Lansdowne* of Newport. The church's low, spreading form hardly takes advantage of its site, on a grass plot visible from all sides. The materials, predictably, are snecked, rock-faced Pennant sandstone and Bath stone dressings, with a bell gable of yellow brick. Five-bay clerestoried nave and lean-to aisles, widening into transepts in the E bay, lower chancel. The style is resolutely early Gothic, especially in the emphatic arcades. Circular piers with small shaft-rings carry mighty, early French foliage capitals with square abaci. – STAINED GLASS. Chancel E, Ascension. Signed by *A. Savell*, *c.* 1898. A compelling focus for the interior with its dramatic colours. Yet the figures are completely lacking in expression. – Other glass brought in from the demolished Holy Trinity Church: nave W, Four Evangelists, and transept N, Call of Peter.

ST TEILO, Aberthaw Avenue, Alway. 1975–6. Temporary-looking, yet the interior, under its segmental ceiling and lit by slit windows to N and S, is a seemly space.

ST DAVID (R.C.), Park Crescent, Maesglas. 1963 by *F. R. Bates, Son & Price* under the influence of Le Corbusier's Ronchamp Chapel. The windowless apsidal E end with roof rising to a peak above it, and the outbreaks of miniature windows, square in the S wall, triangular to N and W, indicate the source. Walls rendered smooth and white.

ST MARY (R.C.), Stow Hill. 1839–40 by *J. J. Scoles*. A confident and conspicuous statement just a decade after Emancipation. The broad, five-stage, E.E. tower occupies most of the street frontage. The design, with three arcaded stages below the belfry, is based on the tower of St Mary, Stamford. The intended spire was not built, so in 1869 the top parapet and pinnacles were added. The interior is more typical of its time, aisled in seven narrow bays, the arcades of etiolated cast-iron piers, circular with big stiff-leaf foliage caps, carrying double-chamfered arches. One-bay sanctuary dominated by the three great E lancets, and three-bay side chapels separated from the aisles by further, slightly lower cast-iron columns. – ALTARS in the side chapels. 1913 (N) and 1921 (S), by *F. R. Bates*. Figural reliefs, and handsome lettering. – STAINED GLASS. Chancel E. Assumption of the Virgin, by *Hardman c.* 1890. – N and S aisles E, St John and St Edward, by *Hardman*, 1859. – N aisle NW. 1951 by *Charles Blakeman*. Christ saving St Peter from drowning in the Sea of Tiberias. Opalescent glass in bright colours, vivid Expressionist style.

The meagre Tudor-style INFANTS' SCHOOL to the l. of the church is of 1857, by *Charles Hansom*, the substantial Tudor-style PRESBYTERY to the r., of 1905 by *F. R. Bates*.

ST MICHAEL (R.C.), Clarence Street, Pillgwenlly. A lofty, austere church of rock-faced Pennant sandstone with Bath stone dressings, 1886–9 by *W. B. Gardner*. The fussy ashlar SW belfry and spirelet were added by *Gardner* in 1893. Unified clerestoried nave and chancel. Cusped Y-tracery. (– STAINED GLASS. E and W windows by *Hardman*, *c.* 1894. – Aisle windows, eleven in all, by *Mayer & Co.*, *c.* 1890.)

ST PATRICK (R.C.), Cromwell Road. 1962–3 by *F. R. Bates, Son & Price*. Caramel brick, with a prominent tower. Concrete structure and window tracery. In a straightened-up Gothic, less adventurous than this firm's usual style. The interior has passage aisles, but is dominated by the BALDACCHINO over the free-standing altar. – STAINED GLASS. Nave W, mitred bishop in an expanse of mosaic-like greens, purples and red. 1962 by *Jonah Jones*.

BAPTIST CHURCH, Llanthewy Road (disused). 1912 by *Charles E. Compton* of Newport. Prominently sited and ambitious, in an outdated Geometrical style. Rock-faced Pennant sandstone with Bath stone dressings. The tall tower with clasping buttresses encroaches on the composition of the entrance front. This has a six-light traceried window above a lean-to porch in which is set a double-shafted doorway under a gable. Another double-shafted doorway in the tower. (– STAINED GLASS. A set by *William Pearce Ltd.*, contemporary with the building.)

The HALL to the l., similar in style and materials, was built in 1904 as school-cum-chapel by *Habershon, Fawckner & Co.*

BAPTIST CHAPEL, Stow Hill (now a nightclub). 1862–3 by *Habershon & Pite*, though quite untypical of the firm's output. A straightforward but boldly scaled classical façade, its three bays defined by giant Vignolesque Doric pilasters carrying a deep triglyph frieze and big pediment with textbook details. Central doorway under a triangular pediment. Upper windows treated as an arcade. Paint now covers the smooth Forest stone and Bath stone dressings.

BEECHWOOD PARK PRESBYTERIAN CHURCH, Chepstow Road. Dated 1923, but like a chapel of thirty years earlier. Large, Perp-style, of coursed Pennant sandstone with Bath stone dressings. Galleried interior with bowed metal gallery fronts in a standard palmette pattern.

BETHEL METHODIST CHURCH, Stow Hill. 1882–3, by *Habershon & Fawckner*. In a Geometrical Gothic style. Set, most unusually, sideways-on to the street, the entrance at the upper end under a tower and lofty spire. The side windows, shouldered below, traceried above, show by their arrangement that the interior is galleried. Transeptal projection to the r. The interior has been ceiled at gallery level, so the framed roof and the iron columns which support it are not visible at the time of writing.

EMMANUEL EVANGELICAL BAPTIST CHURCH, Rutland Place. 1976–7 by *Iain Freeman* of *Barton, Willmore* of Bristol. An imaginative, coherent and well-detailed group. Church and hall are both of square plan and crowned by steep, partly glazed pyramid roofs. They and the two-storeyed office-cum-flat added by *Freeman* in 1994–5 group round a tiny paved court. Windowless outer walls of mottled pinkish-buff brick. The rounding of all corners unites the various components.

MOUNT SION WELSH CONGREGATIONAL CHURCH, Hill Street. Small, simple and rendered, such details as there are indiscriminately classical and Gothic. Dated 1873, when *A. O. Watkins* altered and extended the building. The interior has a gallery carried round all four sides, pierced metal gallery fronts and an organ above the pulpit.

NEW TESTAMENT CHURCH OF GOD, Commercial Road. Rock-faced Pennant sandstone with poor quality Bath stone dressings. Lombardic style. This may be the chapel built in 1882–3 for Bible Christians by *Habershon & Fawckner*.

PRESBYTERIAN CHURCH OF WALES, Havelock Street. 1864 by *Habershon & Pite*. Memorable outside for its salt-and-pepper random stone walling. Lombardic-style entrance front, a bold wheel window over the porch. Red and yellow brick add to the polychromy here. The interior is unaltered and cheerfully painted in white, pink and pale blue, the pews grained. Galleries on three sides, the fourth a dramatic composition, the organ set above the pulpit and under a large semicircular arch.

Slightly later HALL alongside, in matching materials and style.

ST JULIAN'S METHODIST CHURCH, St Julian's Avenue. Of 1901–2 by an unknown architect. Red brick and sparse Bath stone dressings. Geometrical Gothic style. The transeptal plan and the design of the entrance front are both neatly adapted to the triangular site between two roads. Inside there are no galleries, and slender cast-iron piers carry pointed timber arches high up. Modernized *c.* 1991–2.

SUMMERHILL BAPTIST CHURCH, Albert Avenue. 1866 by *Habershon, Pite & Fawckner*, extended at the front in 1908 with an elaborated porch arrangement. The original centrepiece of the façade, a big wheel window, survives. The INTERIOR of 1866 largely remains. Galleries on all four sides, supported on iron posts with Romanesque foliage caps. – PULPIT. Substantial, of timber, in a Romanesque style. – ORGAN. Above and behind the pulpit, under a segmental arch. – STAINED GLASS. Early C20. A set with repeated Art Nouveau pattern in lavender, olive, buff and forget-me-not blue.

UNITED REFORMED CHURCH, Victoria Road. The showpiece 100
chapel of Newport, set obliquely to Victoria Place, so that both its temple-front end and its richly decorated flank can be admired from a distance. Built for Congregationalists in 1858–9 by *A. O. Watkins* of Newport, with carving by *Mageston* of Bristol. The first peculiarity is that the chapel, because of the steeply sloping site, was designed to be entered at both ends of its six-bay flank. The first and sixth bays are accordingly brought slightly forward, with quoins in the upper storey shaped as clasps over fluted strips. The lower storey is channelled, and the doorways and windows at this level are treated to extraordinary enrichment, their tops shouldered and set under round-topped tympana filled with reliefs of foliage and vine scrolls. The upper windows have fanciful ears and side scrolls. Where all this came from is not easy to say. The contemporary description was 'modern French', and there is undoubtedly something of the Rococo here. But Austrian Baroque models may also have been called into play. The treatment of the window openings in the short end is the same, but here the upper ones are set within a three-bay attached Composite portico, its columns not quite Salomonic, that is to say with shafts not spiralling but merely spirally grooved. On the downhill side, a later Gothic HALL, and attached to the r. end of the flank, a later classical VESTRY.

The interior is if anything even more splendid. Though
Watkins's fittings have been replaced, the original layout survives, 102

with galleries on three sides and the pulpit at the further short end. His is the ceiling, enriched with rope mouldings and carved bosses, flat at the sides, but segmentally raised in the centre, to give space for shallow, presumably cast-iron trusses enriched with prickly foliage. The extraordinary triple arch rising full-height at the pulpit end is probably also his. The arches bear rope and vine mouldings, and are carried on square piers with ovolo-chamfered angles and rich foliage capitals. The fittings, however, are a sumptuous array of high-quality carpentry of *c.* 1900. There is evidence that they were installed between 1896 and 1907, and that *Swash & Bain* were involved as architects. Galleries on three sides carried on substantial timber piers, pews and even choir stalls, all with reticent Baroque detail. The pulpit and organ form a unified composition masking much of the arcade shafts behind. – STAINED GLASS, in all the lower windows, also of *c.* 1895–1906. Mainly New Testament subjects. In a pictorial style, but probably not all by the same maker. One of *c.* 1906 is signed by *Swaine, Bourne & Son* of Birmingham.

WESLEYAN METHODIST CHAPEL, Commercial Road. Secularized. The Romanesque façade of Bath stone remains of the chapel built in 1849 by *J. Wilson* of Bath. The full-height, quadruply shafted arch which frames the upper central windows is a really impressive sight. Rebuilt behind the façade in 1899 by *Habershon, Fawckner & Groves.*

CASTLE

Built in the C14 and presenting an E show front towards the River Usk, its walls indeed rising abruptly from the tidal mudbanks. The E range remains impressive and dramatic even today, in spite of the cruel pinching of the railway bridge on the N and the road bridge to the S. The scanty remains of the other three ranges and enclosing moat were finally eliminated by the inner ring road in 1970.

This is Newport's second castle. The first, naturally enough, was on the high ground close to St Woolos Church. The earthen motte of the castle, constructed probably *c.* 1075 by William Rufus, survived until buried in spoil from the railway tunnel dug in 1846. The need for a second castle arose when the de Clare estates were divided after the death in 1314 of the third Gilbert de Clare at the Battle of Bannockburn. The new lordship of Gwynllŵg, carved out of the lordship of Glamorgan, was granted to Hugh d'Audele, husband of Gilbert's sister Margaret. He was from 1327 in a position to build a new stone castle to control the river crossing, but the style of the surviving range suggests a later C14 date for its construction, and that its builder was Hugh's son-in-law, Ralph, Earl of Stafford (inherited 1347), or Ralph's son, Hugh (inherited 1372, †1386). The castle is first documented in 1405, when urgent repairs were put in hand after damage by Owain Glyndŵr's followers. Major works were carried out *c.* 1435–47 for Humphrey Stafford (created Duke of Buckingham 1444, †1460), which produced a sumptuous and unusual apartment within the E range. The plan published by Coxe in 1801 shows the extent of the walled enclosure to the W. It is known that there was a N gatehouse, but otherwise there can only have been enclosing walls with timber-framed buildings backing on to the N wall. Presumably an ambitious quadrangular plan was intended but left incomplete. Newport never became an important residence for any of its high-ranking owners.

In 1522 the castle was reported to be in disrepair, and during the next 300 years it passed to leading local families, Herberts, then Morgans, who did little to arrest decay. Buck's engraving of 1743 shows the E range in a ruined state not much different from today. In the C19 it was used first as a tannery, then as a brewery, during which time the traceried windows of the hall, shown by Buck, were destroyed. In 1891 the Corporation acquired the S tower, in 1899 Lord Tredegar bought the rest, and 1930–5 the whole castle came into the guardianship of the Office of Works, which in the 1950s carried out quite extensive consolidation and renewal of stonework.

The E front of the castle can be examined only somewhat distantly from the road bridge. It is built of irregularly coursed grey local limestone and purple Old Red Sandstone rubble, creating a piebald effect, presumably intended originally to be rendered over. Some dressings of Doulting-type limestone, some of Triassic sandstone. What first impresses is its symmetry. The composition is simple, three towers linked by straight walls. The central tower is the largest and most strongly projecting. Short spurs convert the E angles into polygonal turrets with, in the recessed wall face between, a broad, depressed-pointed arch for a watergate,

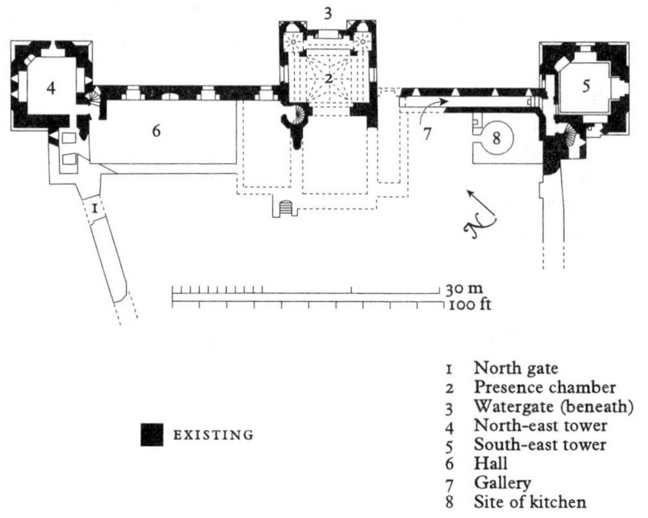

Newport Castle. Plan

and above it a large, two-centred-headed window clearly lighting an important room. The arch is triple-chamfered, and within it there are traces of a groove for a portcullis. So there was a secure dock down here. The evidence for the portcullis, however, suggests that there must have been a room above it for the winding gear required to work it. So the large window cannot be a primary feature.

The NE and SE towers are converted from square to polygonal by means of bold spurs reaching far up the wall faces, in a way reminiscent of the late C13 towers which strengthen the North Dam at Caerphilly Castle. The SE tower rises almost to its full height, with windows at three levels. One at the middle level is of two lights under a hollow-moulded basket arch, and had a transom and trefoiled heads to the lights. The others are trefoil-headed single-lighters, also hollow-moulded, under hoods. All these details suggest that the windows belong to the mid-C15 remodelling. One, at the SW angle, even cuts into the top of the spur. The ragged hole in the E wall shows where a projecting garderobe has been torn away. The NE tower, by contrast, has only a four-light, late C16 mullioned window, evidence of use at a time when much of the castle is known to have been abandoned.

The straight stretches of walling between the towers do not match one another. In the N stretch are restored fragments of three large, transomed, two-light windows, in the S stretch four robbed openings which Buck's engraving shows to have included a lancet window and two arrow loops.

From the W it is possible to examine the remains of the INTERIOR of the range, and to understand to some extent how it was converted for the Duke of Buckingham into an impressive suite of rooms. These were intended, it has been suggested, not so much for splendid entertainment as for the official survey of the duke's properties in South Wales. Most remarkable is the room in the central tower over the watergate. It is a T in plan, the main square space crowned by a tierceron rib vault. The ribs have a central fillet flanked by hollows, and there are carved bosses at the intersections, the central boss a double rose, much larger than the rest. To N and S short arms extend, lit by one N and one S window under restored tunnel vaults, each with a ridge rib and close-set transverse ribs. The E window is of the 1950s restoration. It is flanked by tall, cusped-headed recesses, also much restored, and by recesses in the angles of the room lit by single-light E windows and crowned by miniature octopartite rib vaults. The whole ensemble must have provided a remarkable ceremonial setting. To the W the room clearly extended further, for here there is a wide, double-wave-moulded arch, originally with shafted responds, hollow-and-wave-moulded. The central tower originally rose for a further storey, which may have accommodated a chapel. The spiral stair which gave access to it partly survives, attached to the NW corner of the tower. The doorway to the stair opened to the W, where there must have been a small chamber lit by one of the three large restored windows in the E wall further N. The other two windows clearly lit a hall, and must have formed a symmetrical composition with a fireplace between them. The windows were provided with seats l. and r., and the fireplace had a tall hood, now robbed away. Under the hall is a plain, tunnel-vaulted undercroft for storage. The N tower has the remains of two squarish heated rooms one above the other, reached by a newel stair projecting into the NE corner of the hall. A second doorway in the room beside the stair gave access to a garderobe, the last traces of which were swept away in 1970. It has been suggested that the plain but well-appointed accommodation here was for the lord's steward or treasurer.

The lord himself had his private rooms in the S tower. They were reached from the central tower by a narrow gallery in the thickness of the intermediate wall. The springing of the gallery vault can be seen on the present W (original inner) face of the wall, above the robbed lancet and loops which lit the gallery. (Evidence that a kitchen lay to the W of the gallery.) From the W face of the tower a stair-turret projects, lit by small hood-moulded windows. Attached to the W face of the turret is the stump of the S curtain wall of the castle. The rooms within the tower must originally have been handsome, each with access to a garderobe as well as to the stair. The lowest, at basement level, is square, with squinches in the S angles. This enables the middle room to be octagonal. It is lit by the originally two-light transomed E window, and has a corner fireplace with splayed panelled jambs detailed like the recesses in the presence chamber. The top room, also octagonal and with a fireplace, has eight polygonal corbels which must have carried an elaborately designed timber roof.

PUBLIC BUILDINGS

SHIRE HALL (former), Pentonville. 1901–2 by *William Tanner*, Monmouthshire County Surveyor. Extended 1913. Unimpressively sited on a slope, hard up against the street. Four-storeyed frontage originally of seven bays, the walls of squared limestone rubble dressed with Grinshill ashlar. The matching two-bay addition at the uphill end upsets the symmetry and rhythm of the design. Jacobean style with Baroque touches. Inside, the entrance hall is shallow, dominated by a pair of mighty Ionic columns, their shafts of purple mottled marble. At the back, a free-standing octagonal council chamber, stripped of its panelling and furniture.

CIVIC CENTRE, Godfrey Road. A white presence which dominates distant views of the town from its hillside site. The impulse to build, when the town already contained a town hall and a shire hall, came from the decision in 1936 to move the County Assizes from Monmouth to Newport. The competition to design the new building held in that year was won by *T. Cecil Howitt* of Nottingham. The SW wing, containing the courts, was built 1937–9, but Howitt's design was fully executed only in 1964, with the completion of the central entrance hall, stair and tower.

The style is the ghostly classicism thought appropriate for public architecture of the period, influenced no doubt by Percy Thomas's Swansea Guildhall, but entirely lacking in the panache which infuses that building. The plan consists of a central ceremonial block of two storeys, with a recessed third storey, and a tall, tapering, axial clock tower. To l. and r., stepping down the hillside, administration blocks, also two-storeyed. The principal entrance is through a high, plain, round-headed arch on the SW, uphill, side. Similar arches penetrate the downhill ends of the side blocks. All walls are faced with Portland stone. Channelling is introduced on the lower storey of the downhill side of the central block, above which rise the five tall, rectangular windows of the council chamber; their imposts are formed of curious convex fluted panels, the nearest approach to columns anywhere in the building. Elsewhere, the walls are given an equally curious quilted texture. But what goes furthest to undermine the monumentality of the building is the use of shallow pitched roofs everywhere, covered in brown pantiles. Even the pyramidal cap of the clock tower is given this treatment.

The main entrance leads into a square STAIR HALL, lit artificially from a central, square ceiling panel painted pale blue, which is raised above three stepped tiers of coffering.* The stair
122 rises in two easy, straight flights to a broad, glazed balcony on all four sides of the hall. The walls here were painted 1961–4 with a series of eleven rectangular murals by *Hans Feibusch*, illustrating the history of the county from the first Celtic settlement to the building of the George Street Bridge, opened in 1964. A broadly treated figure style and semi-naturalistic colouring unite the disparate subjects. As a scheme of municipal decoration, it is perhaps unsurpassed in C20 Britain – the murals by Frank Brangwyn in the Guildhall, Swansea, being a special case. (*Feibusch*'s preliminary studies are displayed downstairs, some of them different in composition from the paintings.) – SCULPTURE. Labour, 1929 by *David Evans*. Small bronze group of two straining miners.

The COUNCIL CHAMBER, at the head of the stair and looking over the town, is flooded by light from its five tall windows. Flat ceiling decorated with large, shallow coffers painted red.

The hillside below the centre block is terraced and planted in a large semicircle.

CROWN COURT, Faulkner Road. 1989–91, by *PSA Projects Cardiff*, design director *John Roberts*. Set at the foot of the slope between the arms of the Civic Centre, and effectively harmonizing with it without compromising its own Modern style. Portland stone facing, of course. Seven-by-five-bay pavilion, of two storeys, the upper recessed above a loggia formed by a deep, rectangular lintel carried on slender rectangular piers, placed to set up a rhythm of alternating wide and narrow bays. Note how the piers are set back, not at the angles of the building. In the centre the lintel is brought forward polygonally over a projecting porch.

* It had been intended to use natural lighting.

UNIVERSITY OF WALES COLLEGE, NEWPORT, Allt-yr-yn Avenue. Built as Newport Technical College 1956–8 by *Sir Percy Thomas & Son*. Typical of the unaggressive Modernism adopted for educational buildings in the 1950s, but on an exceptional scale. Three blocks in line, faced in brown brick. That to the l. contains classrooms, so has three storeys of windows in long bands enclosed within a rectangular concrete frame. That to the r. has an upper hall. The middle block runs back a long way, its entrance front forming a tower-like centrepiece, glazed high and wide to reveal the stair rising through three storeys, the landings cutting across the window at each level and displaying their wiry balustrades.

TECHNICAL INSTITUTE (former), Clarence Place. 1909–10. A 118
confident piece of Edwardian classicism and the masterpiece of the borough architect *Charles F. Ward*. Square in plan, presenting identical eight-bay façades N to Clarence Place and W to Rodney Road, with the entrance at the NW angle between them. Three storeys, the top one an attic for studios lit by large square windows tilted in the roofslope. The main elevations have strongly emphasized end bays, entirely of Bath stone. Tripartite windows, the upper ones divided by Tuscan colonnettes. Heavy top attics framing Diocletian windows. The intermediate bays are demarcated by banded red brick pilaster strips, between which the large rectangular windows are set in slightly recessed Bath stone frames. But the heaviest emphasis is reserved for the entrance. The NW corner is cut back in a full-height concave quadrant crowned by a deep brick attic set with three garlanded oculi. Behind is a small but lofty dome, its octagonal drum of red brick below, Bath stone above, the copper-covered dome itself a vivid green. At ground level the concave quadrant is spanned by a convex porch on Doric columns, granite monoliths coupled in depth. The whole composition is tied strongly together by a deep, plain, granite plinth, and a deep, plain, Bath stone entablature. (Inside, an octagonal inner vestibule under the dome leads to a barrel-vaulted toplit assembly room. Behind the two main frontages classrooms are arranged.)

Schools

The Education Act of 1870 established the principle of compulsory primary school education for all children and set up school boards to implement it. Of the numerous board schools built in the town between the mid 1870s and 1902, only a few survive. In 1903 the borough council took over the responsibility for school provision. However, it was only after 1945 that the second great wave of school-building occurred, both to replace outmoded Victorian board schools and to provide for the needs of the great new housing estates. The design of these schools, as also of the estates, was the responsibility of *Newport Borough Architect's Department*, Chief Architect *Johnson Blackett*. For the sake of clarity, the schools described below are arranged in two alphabetical groups, first those up to 1905, then those from 1939 onwards.

CLYTHA PRIMARY SCHOOL, Bryngwyn Road. 1900–1 by *Habershon, Fawckner & Groves*. Single-storeyed, gabled, of red brick with Bath stone in bands and for the large mullion-and-transom windows.

DURHAM ROAD PRIMARY SCHOOL, Durham Road. 1892–3 by *Alfred Swash*, who took *John Bain* into partnership on the strength of this commission. Red brick with sparse yellow brick dressings. The single-storey infants' school presents three equal gables to the side street. The two-storey boys' and girls' block stands back in its playground, and in plan is laid out on the corridor system, without a hall. Towards the playground, a large inscription: KNOWLEDGE IS POWER. Later additions, the first as early as 1896 by *Charles J. Fox*. The well-proportioned brick range of *c.* 1930 backing on to Durham Road is doubtless by *Bain*, who was by then Monmouthshire schools' architect.

ST ANDREW'S PRIMARY SCHOOL, Corporation Road. Dated 1902, the last grand gesture of Newport School Board before the Education Act of 1902 transferred responsibility for education to local councils. The architects were *Conyers Kirby & Son*. The roadward façade makes an overwhelmingly flamboyant impression. The walls are of red brick broadly banded with Bath stone ashlar. The tall, rectangular windows, of white painted timber, are integrated with the design of the banding. Slightly recessed five-bay centre with shallow full-height buttresses. In the broad wings the windows are grouped in threes under pairs of large scrolled gables enclosing scroll-framed oculi. Each of the long return elevations bears another such gable, and here are the main entrance doorways for girls (W) and boys (E), under bracketed capping. The single-storey infants' school at the back is a T in plan, as the broad, simpler gables emphasize. Pleasingly, the buildings were restored and sympathetically modernized in 1997–8.

ST WOOLOS COUNTY PRIMARY SCHOOL, Stow Hill. Built as a council school on a grand scale and sited toweringly on the slope. 1904–5 by *H.J. Griggs*. Symmetrical front of no fewer than three storeys, a rarity in Wales (though common enough for board schools in London). The five central bays are treated like a pavilion, the end bays given large tripartite windows. Boys' and girls' entrances in the one-bay re-entrants between centre and ends. Lavish Baroque details, especially the three big aedicules high up, with open segmental pediments carried on blocked Ionic pilasters, or columns in the case of the central aedicule. The facing materials are rock-faced Pennant sandstone below, red brick and Portland stone for the two principal storeys.

ALWAY JUNIOR AND INFANT SCHOOL, Aberthaw Road. Built 1949–52. Large brown brick group, typical of the early 1950s.

EVESWELL COUNTY PRIMARY SCHOOL, St John's Road. By *Gwent County Architect's Department*, County Architect *K.P. Jones*, design architect *Norman Robson-Smith*. Lively and eye-catching on the slope, especially as seen from the Chepstow Road below. What catch the eye are the colourful materials, yellow veranda posts and diagonal tension rods, and the brickwork, buff with two thin, red mid-height bands, and red outlining to the bullseye windows. The central hall, set back into the hillside, shares a ridge-line with the single-storey range of classrooms to the E and the two-storey block of classrooms to the W, where the ground sinks. Hall roofslope partly glazed to the S, continuous with the glazed ridge over the spine corridor to E and W. In the walls, many small V projections and recessions. Internally, this emphasis on diagonals is taken further, where the classrooms are in clusters of four opening off the canted sides of octagonal vestibules.

GAER JUNIOR SCHOOL, Gaer Road. Built *c.* 1950–1, and perhaps the best of *Johnson Blackett*'s schools. Single-storey S front of three parts, each sharply distinguished from the others. Brown brick central entrance pavilion, taken up slightly higher to the l. to provide room for a clock face. Long, fully glazed classroom range to the r. Slim overhanging concrete eaves on all three parts.

HARTRIDGE HIGH SCHOOL, Ringland Way. Opened 1964, the first purpose-built comprehensive school in Newport. Two-storey and three-storey blocks with flat roofs. Windows in continuous bands. Caramel-coloured brickwork. The three principal blocks, widely spaced apart, are for lower, upper and senior schools.

MILTON JUNIOR AND INFANT SCHOOL, Mountbatten Close. Similar quiet 1960s idiom, against which the single-storey polygonal pavilion with red skylight and overhanging eaves on turquoise struts makes a piquant contrast.

NEWPORT HARTRIDGE COMPREHENSIVE SCHOOL, Ringland Way. Blocks stepping elegantly down the hillside. Brown brick end walls, glazed long sides.

RINGLAND JUNIOR AND INFANT SCHOOL, Dunstable Road. 1956–9. Two-storeyed ranges continuously glazed under eaves.

ST JULIAN'S COMPREHENSIVE SCHOOL, Heather Road. By *Harold Rowe*, built 1938–9, occupied from 1941, but officially opened in 1946. A stolid, symmetrical and extremely long frontage, with undersized accents. Full-height metal windows and brown brick walls. Behind this façade lie three symmetrical courtyards, reflecting the fact that the buildings were erected for two schools, boys' grammar and girls' grammar. The schools amalgamated in 1966 and became comprehensive in 1967.

ST JULIAN'S COUNTY JUNIOR SCHOOL, Beaufort Road. Built *c.* 1952–3. A long, two-storeyed block from which shorter blocks project at r.-angles on the downhill side. In the former a band of clerestory windows extends from end to end; the latter have fully glazed sides. Brown brick walling.

Other Public Buildings

CARNEGIE LIBRARY, Corporation Road. 1906–7 by *C. F. Ward*. Just a little branch library, almost overshadowed by the mighty board school of 1902 (*see* p. 442 above), but architecturally fully able to hold its own, and perfectly preserved. Red brick with generous Bath stone dressings. The style one might call Baroque, but with a typically Edwardian mix of motifs. Single-storeyed. The plan is a T, presenting a bold three-bay front W-wards towards the road, and a more reticent one, also of three bays, towards the N. Channelled stone podium to both. The central entrance doorway, set back under a segmental arch, is framed by even quoins carrying a pediment on plain block brackets. The windows in the side bays are in canted projections, with ashlar aprons. Brick top parapet. Tapered and domed rooftop louvre. Round the side, each of the three bays has a trio of sash windows under a wide segmental relieving arch. Ashlar aprons here too. Shapely, generous rainwater heads on both fronts. Inside, the reading room in the N range has a segmental plaster ceiling and outsize semicircular S window.

MARKET, Upper Dock Street. 1887–9 by *Conyers Kirby*, the Town Surveyor, and *T. E. Watkins*. Since the demolition of the Town Hall, the Market has become the most conspicuous sign of Newport's late Victorian civic pride. The main, two-storeyed, E-facing range of nine wide bays is symmetrical, composed in the manner of a Flemish cloth hall, the central tower soaring up for a further three storeys to be crowned by a steep, lead-covered pyramidal roof. French pavilion roofs over the outermost bays. Otherwise the main front is in an Elizabethan style. Mauve Old Red Sandstone, and generous Bath stone dressings. Large mullion-and-transom windows, some in canted bays. The wide, high central arch leads into the market hall. This is spanned by its original glass and steel arched roof. The two-level timber market stalls were restored in 1988.

POLICE STATION, Cardiff Road. Very large, the headquarters of the Newport division of Gwent Constabulary. Opened in 1993, the last major work of *Gwent County Architect's Department*, and quite an extraordinary Postmodern performance for the Department to sign off with. Two blocks face Cardiff Road, linked by a bridge, the larger (W) for administration, the smaller (E) for recreation. Lemon-yellow brick walls, the top several courses corbelled out to hide the gutters of the mighty black-slated hipped roofs. There are three storeys. In the top storey, brick predominates, pierced by a steady row of small square windows. Below, the fenestration is random, with some very large, dark-blue-framed windows rising through two storeys under overhanging brickwork. To help at these points etiolated steel posts appear. These are fluted, stand on small crimson cubes and are topped by capitals which consist of a crimson disc between crimson triangles. The main entrance, symmetrical in itself but far over to one end, uses all these motifs under a glazed triangular crown. Everything, then, is perverse, designed, it seems, to insinuate that what appears so substantial is really mere cladding on a hidden frame.

NEWPORT CENTRE (leisure centre), Dock Road. 1983–5 by *Newport Borough Council Architect's Department*. In two parts: a polygonal swimming pool, and a rectangular block for squash courts etc. Both halves have windows low down, overborne by deep stretches of corbelled-out walling. Buff brick throughout.

ST WOOLOS HOSPITAL, Stow Hill. There are two principal elements. To the E stand various plain, red brick ranges three storeys high, what remains of *T. H. Wyatt*'s union workhouse of 1837–8. It was built on the plan of a Greek cross within a square, one of the standard workhouse plans, thought to be easy to supervise and good for the inmates' health. Equally tall, of Old Red Sandstone with buff brick dressings, is the long, narrow range to the W, built as the workhouse infirmary in 1867 by *A. O. Watkins*. Further meagre additions towards the road, 1901–2 by *B. Lawrence & Son*.

Also part of the present hospital complex, in FRIARS ROAD to the SE, is something much more comprehensible and interesting. This is THE FRIARS, a large Tudor-style house built shortly before 1844 by *J. H. Langdon* for the leading local antiquary, Octavius Morgan, M.P., and brother of the first Lord Tredegar. The name refers to a supposed Dominican friary here. No trace of medieval buildings remains, nor of the post-Dissolution 'Fryours Howse', mentioned in 1570. It is not clear whether Octavius Morgan's house was built on a new site or incorporates older walling. The main body is faced with Bath stone ashlar, the N (entrance) front symmetrical, two-storeyed under a big hipped roof. Only three wide bays, the central bay brought forward a little under a broad gable. Heavy decorative bargeboards trim the gable, the dormer windows and the single-storey porch. Large three-light, mullion-and-transom windows with emphatic hoodmoulds. Towards the S the vocabulary is similar, but the façade further extended and rambling irregularly. Here the labels of the hoodmoulds bear shields, and on one are Morgan's initials and the fragmentary date 184[?]. The service rooms extend in a rendered range towards the E, accompanied by a low, cant-ended CHAPEL.

Inside, several rooms retain the carved woodwork brought in by Morgan, some probably local, some Continental. In the HALL the fireback is dated 1854, and the overmantel looks early C17, carved with a village street scene. In the former DINING ROOM an arcaded overmantel of similar date, with a small central figure of Charity. Buffets to l. and r. made up with arcaded woodwork. In another room, relief panels in the window reveals. The DRAWING ROOM, S of the hall, has another made-up chimneypiece. Corinthian columns flank the fireplace, and Corinthian half-columns in the overmantel frame subject medallions. This room has a fretwork timber frieze and a plaster ceiling decorated with thin ribs, clearly mid-C19. The STAIRCASE is probably all mid-C19 too. Note the pulpit-like projection in the landing balustrade, providing a vantage point over the stair.

ROYAL GWENT HOSPITAL, Cardiff Road. Nothing seems to remain of the hospital built 1898–1901 to the design of *Richard J. Lovell* of London. The classical range projecting towards the road, of red brick with Bath stone dressings, must be the new wing by *H. J. Griggs*, opened in 1916. What dominate today are two much more recent slabs. That to the W is a no-nonsense affair of the 1970s, faced with brown brick. That to the E, opened in 1991, is seven storeys high. Here the red brick is enlivened by buff brick stripes. Fancifully treated stair-towers at the short ends, each with a tier of bullseye windows and green corrugated cap.

BURTON ALMSHOUSES, Friars Road. Two identical single-storey terraces built in 1907–8 and 1908–9 for Colonel Henry Burton and his sister, Sarah Eliza. Cottage style, but with large mullion-and-transom windows. Generous timber porches. Half-timbered gables break up into the sweeping tiled roofslopes. The architect was *Alan H. Davies* of Newport.

MASONIC HALL, Lower Dock Street and Ruperra Street. 1855–8, the most important surviving building in the town by *R. G. Thomas* of Newport, whose career later burgeoned in Australia. Italian palazzo style adapted for the corner site, with the entrance in a tight recessed bow on the angle. Stucco, smartly painted. Fussy details typical of the date, such as windows with stilted segmental heads, and pilaster strips of alternately smooth and snail-crept blocks. Three-storeyed façade to Dock Street, two-storeyed to Ruperra Street, where the upper-level hall has three large windows, blind as Masonic secrecy requires, their arched heads linked by an impost moulding. Bullseye windows to l. and r., Masonic insignia in the spandrels.

CATTLE MARKET, Ruperra Street. Created in 1844. The large, open quadrangle was originally surrounded by single-storey sheds and offices. They survive in the SW quadrant. In the centre of the S front, a pedimented ashlar block with to its W part of an open range with sections of cast-iron frame and roof trusses. The date 1844 and the name of the Tredegar Ironworks are cast into some of the trusses. The truss design is an A, its feet linked by a segmental tie and a circular casting within its head.

RAGLAN BARRACKS, Allt-yr-yn View. 1843–5. Three long, severe ranges at the top of the site, built of purple Old Red Sandstone with Bath stone dressings. Two-storeyed throughout. Each range has pedimented returns and five-bay central pedimented projections. The central range is no less than thirty-nine bays long.

ST WOOLOS CEMETERY, Bassaleg Road. Opened in 1855. The Gothic stone entrance arch, lodge, and two chapels are of 1854–5 by *Johnson & Purdue* of London. The normal convention of the day held, so the E chapel, for Anglicans, is Gothic, the W chapel, for Nonconformists, is in a round-arched style. The W chapel is cruciform, with a short cylindrical crossing tower and conical roof. Both chapels have covered coach entrances. – Large MONUMENTS cluster in front of the chapels, the most ambitious being surprisingly late. – Charles Henry Bailey †1907, etc., in front of the W chapel, yet, in a stylistic crossover, showily Gothic. Marble enclosure with traceried back panel and copper railings. – Mary Ann Studt †1918, etc., in front of the E chapel. Large marble angel on a tall pedestal.

BELLEVUE PARK, Cardiff Road. Laid out on a 25-acre (10-hectare) hillside site to the design of *Thomas H. Mawson*, who won a competition in 1892 – in spite of having made his design for the wrong site! N and S LODGES, of purple rock-faced Old Red Sandstone (quarried on site) with half-timbered upper storeys. Presumably designed by *Mawson*, or by *Dan Gibson*, the architect who often worked with him (P. Howell). In the middle of the park, a ceremonious complex of TERRACES, constructed in 1910. Old Red Sandstone with red terracotta dressings. At the top an elaborate two-storeyed TEA PAVILION, with fancifully shaped gable-ends, and a recessed balcony under the gable towards the terraces. Elaborate GREENHOUSES to l. and r., and a substantial timber SHELTER with latticework walls. BANDSTAND at a lower level, and, below the lowest terrace, an artificial rocky glen.

MONMOUTHSHIRE CANAL. The canal was engineered 1792–9 by *Thomas Dadford jun.*, enabling the ironmasters to transport their products with ease from the Valleys to the Severn Estuary and the sea at Newport. The S-most section of the canal has long been infilled. The lowest watered stretch starts from BARRACK HILL TUNNEL, part of the original canal construction. Between the NW edge of the town and the M4 motorway the canal splits into the Pontypool (later Brecon) branch, flowing to the N, and the Crumlin branch to the W. CRINDAU BRIDGE, S of the motorway bridge, spans the branches immediately E of their junction. It is exceptional among the many canal overbridges in being constructed of red brick, with stone only for the arch-ring and imposts. Its profile is also unusual, five-centred, giving the bridge exceptional strength. The ROVING BRIDGE at the junction of the two branches was rebuilt in concrete when the M4 was constructed, but a small aqueduct remains to the N. Further W, on the Crumlin branch, the ALLT-YR-YN flight of five locks, and two of the typical little segmentally arched BRIDGES taking farm tracks over the canal.

WAREHOUSE, Canal Parade. This early warehouse stood on the E side of the Monmouthshire Canal, opened in 1799. Mauve Old Red Sandstone rubble below, white local limestone above. Upper loading door towards the canal, wide segmental brick arch at its S end, through which boats may have entered.

TOWN DOCK, 1 m. S of the town centre. Constructed 1835–42. The dock has largely been infilled, but the seaward two-thirds of the large entrance lock remain on the bank of the River Usk. The huge upper walls of snecked, squared Pennant sandstone, partly coped in granite, appear above the silted interior of the lock.

BALTIC WAREHOUSE. Three-storeyed, five-bay stone block on the W side of the Town Dock. Cast-iron roof structure, similar to that at the Cattle Market, and cast-iron window lintels. Probably of the 1840s.

The adjoining three-storeyed, red brick MALTINGS was built *c.* 1896. In the roof, at its S end, the conical caps of the two malting kilns, and two rows of dormer windows set over the malting floors.

RAILWAY STATION, Queensway. The original High Street Station was built *c.* 1846 to *I. K. Brunel*'s design (cf. Chepstow). Its single-storey structure may survive as part of the late C19 two-storey platform buildings, faced in rock-faced Pennant sandstone. Outside the main station entrance, one of Newport's first pieces of street sculpture, Arch Form, of riveted metal, 1981 by *Harvey Hood*.

To the SW, the former RAILWAY ENGINE SHED, probably of the 1840s. Ten-bay shed of white local limestone, wide enough to span four railway lines.

TUNNEL, ¼ m. W. *Brunel*'s monumental round-arched portal of *c.* 1846 is formed of huge rock-faced blocks, in a rock-faced retaining wall. To the N, a second portal, constructed when the tracks were doubled in 1912. Conventional arch of blue engineering brick.

110 TRANSPORTER BRIDGE, the lowest crossing of the River Usk, allowing vehicles and pedestrians to cross from Brunel Street, Pillgwenlly, to Stephenson Street on the E side of the river. Probably the loftiest and by far the most elegant structure in Newport, constructed entirely of steel: 1901–6, to a design evolved in France, by the French engineer *F. Arnodin*, who had already built similar bridges at Rouen and Marseilles, assisted in this case by the Newport borough engineer *R. H. Haynes*. Two exceedingly tall, tapering, lattice-braced piers support a high-level deck, from which is suspended a platform, with octagonal timber control cabin. It was on the platform that people and vehicles could cross the river, but the superstructure was elevated so high in order to give uninterrupted navigation with clearance for the tallest shipping.

GEORGE STREET BRIDGE. 1962–4 by *Mott, Hay & Anderson*, with the borough engineer *D. P. Cartwright*. This was the earliest cable-stayed cantilever bridge in Britain, and had many successors (e.g. the Second Severn Crossing – *see* Portskewett). Pairs of tall concrete masts through which are threaded the three sets of four cable stays.

PERAMBULATION

The heart of Newport is neither the cathedral high on the hill, nor the castle on the bank of the river, but at the site of the town's medieval Westgate, marked by the Westgate Hotel. In the late Victorian period this was the hub of the commercial and business quarter, but since the 1970s it has become a haven of pedestrianization. Here five streets meet. Each can be explored in turn.

Bridge Street

BRIDGE STREET, to the W, can be quickly despatched. The NATIONAL WESTMINSTER BANK, 1892 by *C. R. Gribble*, is a handsome classical essay. Bath stone ashlar. Only two storeys high, nine bays by four, the bays demarcated by Tuscan half-columns. Top foliate frieze and balustrade. The entrance, in the curved corner, opens into a lofty square banking hall, its walls lined by Ionic pilasters of Devonshire marble, the flat coffered ceilings supported on four iron columns cased in faience, their shafts wreathed with spiralling olive trails. All in all a handsome period piece. The building was extended by *H. J. Griggs* before 1914. In front of the bank, the over-life-size seated bronze STATUE of Sir Charles Morgan of Tredegar, 1848 by *J. Evan Thomas*, resited here in 1992.

Commercial Street

Next a walk straight down COMMERCIAL STREET. Immediately on the r., the WESTGATE HOTEL, site of the fatal confrontation in 1839 between the Chartists, led by John Frost, and the authorities. The present tall and busy building is of 1884–6 by *E. A. Lansdowne*. Mixed Renaissance style, Pennant sandstone with lavish Beer stone dressings. Projecting metal entrance porch. In the street in front, an elaborate BRONZE SCULPTURE, entitled Unity, Prudence, Energy. 1989 by *Christopher Kelly*. The title is taken from the motto of the Chartist Union. Three complex figure groups, entitled The Ideal City, Still Life and Apotheosis, are intended, somewhat enigmatically, to symbolize the three Chartist ideals. It says something for the confidence of the Borough Council, which commissioned the sculpture, in both the piety and the intelligence of the people of Newport that they have placed such an elliptical work at the heart of the town.

Next past the Westgate Hotel is WESTGATE BUILDINGS, dated 1897. Similar in style, though entirely of ashlar. Four storeys plus fancy gabled dormers. Opposite all this runs Nos. 1–13 COMMERCIAL STREET, an equally impure Gothic affair, probably of *c.* 1880, with steep French pavilion roofs over the centre and ends of what was a symmetrical composition. Broad oriel windows with notched brackets and pointed lights. The composition is now incomplete, as in the 1930s Nos. 9–12 were rebuilt in an Art Deco style for Marks and Spencer. On the N corner of AUSTIN FRIARS, Nos. 22–24, more Mixed Renaissance in Bath stone, are of 1892 by *E. A. Lansdowne*. Then Nos. 25–26, the HALIFAX BUILDING SOCIETY (former Midland Bank), 1893–4, with coupled Tuscan columns fronting the banking hall. Almost opposite, Nos. 160–164, crowned by strapwork gables, are probably contemporary, by *Habershon & Fawckner*. No. 165 is certainly by *Habershon & Fawckner*, 1886. Nos. 31–34, running as far as the corner of FRIARS STREET, are also by *Habershon & Fawckner*, 1889. Further along on the same side, No. 42, LLOYDS BANK, 1895 by *A. E. Lloyd-Oswell*, manages a more monumental motif, Ionic pilasters through the upper two storeys. Domed turret over the angle entrance. A little further along on the same side, No. 144 (now Thomas Cook), dated 1900, an exceptionally fancy front in red brick and stone, with a broad two-storeyed oriel between two-storeyed tourelles and plenty of relief carving. Nos. 142–143, dated 1895 on a rainwater head, are similar but less exuberant, by *F. R. Bates*. Then No. 137, with a long return to HILL STREET, something a bit grander and earlier, probably of 1876 by *A. O. Watkins*.

Yellow brick, with raised pilaster strips and eaves projecting on big brackets. Note the spiral decoration of the drainpipe recessed at the angle, and its decorative clasps. Built for L & Co. At this point there is another arresting piece of BRONZE SCULPTURE in the centre of the street, commissioned by the Borough Council, 1990 by *Paul Bothwell Kincaid*. It commemorates the super-tramp poet W. H. Davies, a native of Newport and author of the couplet 'What is this life if, full of care, We have no time to stand and stare?' A standing, shrouded figure, apparently with hands on hips, is set between a pair of abstracted branches on which doves perch.

After this nothing more until KINGSWAY and GEORGE STREET interrupt. Here, on the l. the garlanded KING WILLIAM IV public house of *c.* 1900, and on an island in the busy road, another recent sculptural assemblage, the MERCHANT NAVY MEMORIAL, 1991, by *Sebastian Boyesen*, with a seated figure of Navigation on a tall columnar construction.

High Street

Now back to the Westgate Hotel for a fresh start. HIGH STREET begins, on the opposite corner from the National Westminster Bank, with the tall Mixed Renaissance block of the PRINCIPALITY BUILDING SOCIETY. The building was erected in 1891 by *Benjamin Lawrence* of Newport as bank chambers for the County of Gloucester Bank. Three-storeyed red brick and red terracotta, piquantly different from anything else in the town centre, and making its mark with a polygonal balconied turret over the corner and a high, fancy gable on the High Street frontage. No. 35, beyond the National Westminster Bank, introduces the architects who dominate the High Street, *Habershon & Fawckner*. It is of 1886–7, four-storeyed under a steep French pavilion roof. Grey Pennant sandstone with Forest and Bath stone dressings. The next block on the r., four-storeyed and also in a Mixed Renaissance style, but entirely faced with Bath stone, looks like their work too. Note the small sculptured panels and medallion heads. NEWPORT ARCADE, further along on the l., with a long frontage of Bath stone to High Street crowned by eight gables, is also by *Habershon & Fawckner*, the central component, the arcade itself, begun in 1893. ROYAL CHAMBERS, the fifteen-bay block opposite, however, represents interwar Neoclassicism. 1928–9 by *C. F. Bates & Colin L. Jones* of Newport. Portland stone. Four storeys. Tuscan aedicules project high up at centre and ends. Continuous shopfronts with heavy concrete canopies.

In MARKET STREET a small but remarkably powerful essay in a similar idiom, formerly the offices of the *South Wales Argus* and designed by the local architect *J. Bain*. Severe Bath stone ashlar façade of five bays over three, framed by Neo-Egyptian pylons. For Newport Market, *see* p. 444.

At the top of the pedestrianized stretch of High Street YE OLDE MURENGER HOUSE, a most unexpected survival of an early C17 timber-framed house. The two middle storeys of the gabled front retain their central canted oriel window, somewhat altered. Close-set studs all across below, and blocked mullion-and-transom windows to l. and r. The first-floor front room retains contemporary plasterwork. Beams divide the ceiling into four compartments, each of which is filled with a concave-sided lozenge, with rose and pineapple finials and elaborate flower sprigs in the corners.

Next door No. 55, Neo-Grec in Bath stone ashlar, rounds the corner into Queensway. 1926 by *Griggs & Vaughan* with *Percy R. Fry*. LLOYDS BANK, built as the Tredegar Arms Hotel, is part of the same composition. Opposite, on the E side of High Street, the twin, red brick gables of RUMOURS CAFE catch the eye. They are stepped and bear scrolls in the manner of the Dutch early C17. The date must be *c.* 1900. MARKET ARCADE, beyond, is dated 1905, and the KING'S HOTEL beyond that, 1900. The view from the end of High Street is blocked by the towering façade of the former POST OFFICE. The building was erected 1905–7 to the design of the Office of Works architect *J. Rutherford*. Red Ruabon brick lavishly dressed with white Portland stone. Crowded Baroque style. In 1998–9 the façade was incorporated into an even larger OFFICE BLOCK, by *Boyd Rees*.

Stow Hill and Beyond

The fourth route from the Westgate Hotel should be to the SW, up STOW HILL. The street climbs quite steeply on its way towards St Woolos Cathedral. At the foot of the hill facing the flank of the Westgate Hotel, MIDLAND BANK, built in 1896–7 by an unknown architect. Bath stone ashlar. The usual busy sub-classical style of that moment, the entrance, on the chamfered corner, surmounted by a two-storeyed oriel, and a polygonal clock turret with miniature tempietto top. Then comes an ecclesiastical group, St Mary's R.C. Church on the E side, and on the W the classical former Baptist Chapel, followed immediately by the Gothic Methodist Church. (For these, *see* p. 434.) Beyond SCHOOL LANE on the E side, the former HIGHER ELEMENTARY SCHOOL, 1909–10 by *Charles F. Ward*, the Borough Architect, was demolished in 1998. A little further along, CHARLES STREET plunges down to the E. Here the COMMUNITY EDUCATION CENTRE displays a François Premier style typical of the 1890s. Basket arches to the windows, fancy gables, much small-scale carving. From here Stow Hill climbs more steeply, overshadowed from the W by the towering St Woolos County Primary School (*see* p. 442).

Across the road to the E, VICTORIA PLACE opens up. This is 97
a delightful surprise. The short, this time level street was cut through by Rennie Logan & Company, contractor for the Town Dock, to give access to Stow Hill from the dock area below to the SE. Continuous terraces of six identical stuccoed houses flank the street on either side. They were built by the Company

in 1844. Three-storeyed, the ground storey channelled. The front doors are handsomely framed by Ionic three-quarter columns carrying pieces of entablature. The first-floor windows, with moulded surrounds and bracketed architraves, share cast-iron balconies in pairs. Plain top storey and parapet. This handsome ensemble has been excellently restored, 1977 by *Graham J. Hardy*, and enhanced by a uniform colour scheme. The extraordinary United Reformed Church of 1858–9, set obliquely across the end of the street, completes the picture (*see* p. 435). In PARK SQUARE beyond, a cylindrical cast-iron TRANSFORMER, the only survivor of a distinctive early type of 1895. It reduced the voltage of the electricity from Llanarth Street Power Station for the well-to-do households of Park Square.

Back in Stow Hill, No. 81, at once on the E side, is a handsome stuccoed three-bay box, probably of the 1830s, with a porch on Greek Doric columns. Almost opposite on the W side, another well-tended haven, the WILLIAMS ALMSHOUSES, rebuilt in 1901–2 as the QUEEN VICTORIA MEMORIAL, to a design by *Habershon, Fawckner & Groves*. Single-storeyed, red brick ranges form a courtyard open towards and above the road. Large waywardly scrolly lettering in the gable-ends.

With that the road turns sharply W-wards, and divides to encircle St Woolos Cathedral and its tightly circumscribed graveyard. On the S side of the cathedral, the former VICARAGE, symmetrical Tudor. 1844–5 by *Thomas Fulljames* of Gloucester. On the N side of the cathedral, CLIFTON PLACE, a three-storeyed stuccoed terrace, steps down the hill. Simple, not quite uniform classical detail. In 1847 it was described as 'a commanding terrace' newly built. However, Nos. 7–8, embedded in the middle of the terrace, must be a little earlier. They form a pair, faced with hammerdressed Pennant sandstone and dressed with Bath stone. The style is Gothic, the design unusual and rather successful. To l. and r., four-centred-headed doorways in recessed bays. In the centre a broad bay rising under a gable. Tripartite windows here above and below, linked by blind panelling. CATHEDRAL COURT, facing the lower end of the terrace, is typical of *c.* 1970, aggressively distinguished from its early Victorian neighbours. Blocks of three and four storeys under monopitch roofs. Grey brick and green concrete fish-scale tile-hanging. ST WOOLOS COURT, facing the top of the terrace, is dated 1990, and is equally typical of that date, in being a weak pastiche of the stuccoed frontage opposite. To the W of the cathedral, a faience WATER FOUNTAIN was re-erected in 1996. It had been first put up in Belle Vue Park in the name of the British Women's Temperance Association. (For St Woolos Hospital and The Friars, to the S of Stow Hill where it flattens out W of the cathedral, *see* p. 445.)

Further W, in BASSALEG ROAD, St Woolos Cemetery (*see* p. 446), and, opposite, on the S side of the road, STELVIO, or what remains of it after partial demolition in 1996. This was the haphazard but rumbustiously decorated mansion of C. H. Bailey, proprietor of marine engineering works in Newport and Barry.

The house was built over a twenty-year period, 1893–1912 by *Alfred Swash & Son.* Red brick with lavish Bath stone decoration, in a French classical idiom, enriched with naturalistic details at every opportunity. Much of this sculpture was wantonly broken up during the demolition. Considerably further on, in Risca Road, ROUGEMONT SCHOOL. Newly built, as Nant Coch, in 1879 by *A. O. Watkins* of Newport for a Mr T. Colborne. Greatly extended to the E in a matching style in 1914. Rock-faced Pennant sandstone with Bath stone dressings, under steep red-tiled roofs from which red and buff brick ribbed chimney-stacks rear up. Patches of half-timbering painted ox-blood. The style is typical of the modified domestic Gothic of the 1870s. The original main, downhill front consisted of the tall, projecting bay to the l. under a half-timbered gable, the broad, canted bay to the r., and the many-mullioned, many-transomed staircase window between. Note the rich foliage carving below the window.

John Frost Square and the Riverside

The fifth and final sally from the Westgate Hotel is largely an exploration of the redeveloped riverside – the product of the reorganized road pattern of the mid 1970s. This drove a new N–S dual carriageway beside the River Usk, and linked it to the E to the pre-existing road bridge over the river, and to a new W-wards road, QUEENSWAY, serving the railway station and, circuitously, the town centre. This walk can conclude by crossing the bridge over the river into the first space in eastern Newport.

In order to discover the unexpectedly numerous pleasures of this area it is best to turn S-wards down COMMERCIAL STREET once more, and take the fifth turning on the l., LLANARTH STREET. This leads at once into the SE corner of the main new space, JOHN FROST SQUARE. The mid-1970s buildings which surround it are the anonymous and unmemorable work of *Newport Borough Council Architect's Department.* Stretches of grey, caramel and brown facing brick. The LIBRARY, ART GALLERY AND MUSEUM, set across the S end of the square, has been given a face-lift with PVC panels, and three mosaics of 1994–5 by *Sebastian Boyesen*, emblematic of the three functions of the building. But what arrests attention at this end of the square is the AUTOMATON CLOCK. Designed by *Andy Plant* and made 127
in 1992 as Newport's contribution to the Ebbw Vale Garden Festival. It is a parody in polished steel of the Euston Arch. Two thick, square, strongly tapering Doric piers, with massive moulded bases and ridged fluting of the shafts, carry a massive, deliberately crudely detailed pediment in which the clock face is set. On the hour, the structure starts to collapse, revealing first the devil, then skeletons holding hourglasses, and finally the clock mechanism and mannikins mending it. So the whole thing is a modern *memento mori*, as is suggested by its name, In the Nick of Time.

The brick paving of the square in a pattern of overlapping circles is a further element of the 1990s enlivening, with trees planted at the centres of some of the circles. The exit from the N end, however, is in its original condition. Here one wall is lined by an expansive tile MOSAIC, by *Kenneth Budd*, 1978. It depicts the episode, which has acquired almost mythic significance in South Wales, when in 1839 a column of Chartists, with John Frost at their head, marched to the Westgate Hotel to present their demands, and were fired upon by the authorities.

The subordinate space to the N is dominated by *Sebastian*
128 *Boyesen*'s life-size BRONZE BULL, bearing a bell in a bell-frame on its back. The inscription round the bell gives the sculptor's name and the date 1995. The myth which is illustrated in this hallucinatory manner relates to the vision of the early medieval St Gwynllyw, which indicated the site for Newport's parish church (now St Woolos Cathedral).

Continuing N-wards in UPPER DOCK STREET, one passes more 1970s redevelopment, most conspicuously CHARTIST TOWER, a twelve-storey slab. Then, beyond SKINNER STREET, the Market (*see* p. 444) raises its tower aloft. Here, in the pavement, another hyper-realistic, temptingly pattable BRONZE ANIMAL by *Sebastian Boyesen*, 1994, the 'little piggy' that went to market, a basket of fruit and vegetables strapped to its back.

Finally, Upper Dock Street leads to the UNDERPASS which pedestrians must use in order to reach the castle (*see* p. 436), Newport Bridge or the riverside at Baltic Quay. For once in these circumstances the pedestrian is not wholly at a disadvantage, since the underpass crosses the luxuriantly planted sunken space within the roundabout, at the intersection of the roads, blissfully clear of the roaring traffic. The E side of the space is enclosed by a broad, curved, concrete wall decorated with a tile and concrete mosaic by *Kenneth Budd*, 1975, celebrating the transport of iron and coal from the Valleys to the docks at Newport down the Monmouthshire and Brecon Canal. Strictly speaking, the panel commemorates the Monmouthshire Railway & Canal Company, in existence from 1848 to 1880. Other later, smaller mosaics by *Kenneth & Oliver Budd*, 1990, 1991. On BALTIC QUAY, the one and only abstract sculpture erected by the Borough Council's recent efforts. *Peter Fink*'s STEEL WAVE, 1990, is a huge and truly iconic piece, which is already showing signs of becoming the town's symbol. Two scarlet vaulting braces converge to suspend a scarlet hoop, from which hangs a triangle of triangles, each painted in a primary colour. Its significance, as a tribute to Newport steelmakers and seafarers, is easily understood, and it can as readily be enjoyed as a lithe virile form, worthy of Anthony Caro, the inspirer of this genre of sculpture.

The Eastern Suburbs

In conclusion, one can cross the River Usk into the eastern suburbs, by the road BRIDGE, 1927 by *Mott, Hay & Anderson*. Five steel

arches spring between full-height stone piers. This leads to CLARENCE PLACE, a short, wide, straight street terminating in the WAR MEMORIAL. First, on the l., incorporating a deck overlooking the river, CLARENCE HOUSE, 1976 by *H. D. Watkins & Associates*. This is the best building of Newport's redevelopment decade. It consists of three parts, a single-storey curtain-wall W range (now Magistrates' Court), a central ten-storey, curtain-wall tower block, and a multi-storey car park to the E. Shops at street level and a continuous concrete balcony over them bind the parts together. The domed former TECHNICAL INSTITUTE (*see* p. 441), opposite on the S side of the road, is another major statement. The rest of the S side of Clarence Place is the most coherent stretch of commercial architecture in the town. Red brick with decoration in Bath stone. Nos. 10–18, dated 1909, form a five-unit composition, with Ionic pilasters. Next is a four-storey range, Nos. 20–34, similar in composition but with Gibbs surrounds to the windows. Finally, CLARENCE QUADRANT, dated 1901. Three-storeyed with Baroque detail. Here, where the road splits, the WAR MEMORIAL, a tall Portland stone slab inspired by Lutyens's Cenotaph in Whitehall. Designed by *Cyril F. Bates & Colin L. Jones*, who won the competition in 1922. N of the war memorial stands the finest, that is to say the showiest, Art Deco CINEMA in South Wales. Built in 1937–8, 119
by the leading cinema specialist *Harry Weedon* of Birmingham, as the Odeon Cinema, but at the time of writing Al Capone's Pool Hall and Bar. The exterior does all it can to grab the attention of the passer-by. It is faced with black tiles below, buff tiles above, where small windows are outlined in black. Upper outgrowths of reddish-brown brick. The curved entrance is in the re-entrant angle, and above it there are three oculi in a big bow-ended projection. Bold horizontally ribbed fins to the l. and in the slab-like superstructure provide the streamlining thought to symbolize modern art and entertainment. Weedon had built versions of the design before, at Harrogate and Sutton Coldfield. The interior has largely failed to survive the change of use. There is just the bottom flight of the stair sweeping up at the far end of the foyer.

SUBURBAN HOUSING

Newport can boast a range of characterful areas of housing laid out on predetermined plans and built up more or less in accordance with them, some over a period of a few years, others over several decades. The earliest are mid C19, the latest mid-C20. Each naturally caters for a particular economic and social class. Most exploit a steeply sloping site, such as Newport abounds in. The housing areas are located here by approximate distance as the crow flies from the town centre crossroads.

CLYTHA SQUARE and CRESCENT, ½m. S. A small, unusually formal development, presumably of the 1850s. The trapezoidal Clytha Square, on the hillside above the Cardiff Road, is lined with three-storeyed, stuccoed Italianate terraces. Gabled projections negotiate the slope. Nos. 13–14 facing down from the top, Gothic and of yellow brick, must be a decade or so later. Big three-storeyed, pavilion-like houses, part of the original scheme, face the Cardiff Road. The Crescent is aligned on the Square across the road. It is similarly Italianate, but of two storeys only. Immediately E of the Crescent, Nos. 11 and 13 CARDIFF ROAD, a stuccoed Grecian villa and a stuccoed Gothic villa, much altered, both of *c.* 1840.

GOLD TOPS, ¼m. NW. The primary development is the row of seven tall, widely spaced villas on the N side of the road, looking down on the railway line in the valley below, and across to St Woolos on the hill beyond. They were mostly built in the mid 1850s. Nos. 11–12, at the top end, form an ingeniously interlocking pair dated 1856. Here all the decorative frills survive. Cottage-style, so there are pierced bargeboards on every gable and dormer, and bands of fish-scale slates on the steep roofs. Nos. 13–14, by contrast, are a symmetrical pair, with Gothic windows. *R. G. Thomas*'s design of 1855 survives, and shows that here too there were decorative bargeboards and other trimmings now lost. Further down an Italianate idiom takes over, but there is nothing more of special note. *W. G. & E. Habershon* called for tenders for villas here in 1856, so probably designed one or more of what survives. No. 20, not rendered like the rest, but of pepper-and-salt random stonework with red brick bands, must be a little later, of the 1870s. *Habershon, Pite & Fawckner* were still active in Gold Tops at that time.

This is the place to mention the TREDEGAR ESTATE OFFICE, at the foot of Fields Road. 1905 by *J. T. Groves*, i.e. one of the last works of the Habershon firm which benefited from employment by the Tredegar Estate for so many decades. Of stone, symmetrical under a big hipped roof, like a little late C17 country house. A suitable image in the circumstances.

MAINDEE, ¾m. E. The Fairoak Estate was laid out from 1852 on the wedge-shaped, S-facing hillside between CHRISTCHURCH ROAD and CHEPSTOW ROAD. The plan was *R. G. Thomas*'s. The only houses identifiable as to his design are Nos. 31–41 SUMMERHILL AVENUE, three Italianate villa pairs, built in 1853–4, but mostly derelict at the time of writing. The best-surviving housing of the 1850s lies a little to the E. Up the W side of KENSINGTON PLACE extends a long Italianate stucco terrace, only two-storeyed, but enlivened at regular intervals by one-bay pyramid-roofed houses rising a storey higher. At the bottom, facing Chepstow Road, ST JOHN'S NURSING HOME, a substantial stuccoed Italianate villa with much quoining, built shortly before 1852. But by far the most splendid villa hereabouts is CAMBRIAN HOUSE, No. 46 St John's Road, dated 1859. This is in a rustic Italian mode, irregular in plan and centring on a turret with pyramid roof. Cast-iron balconies on all sides at the top of the turret and a splendidly lush cast-iron veranda wrapped round the l. half of the house.

Further E again BEECHWOOD PARK, not part of a speculative layout, but a small mansion built for George Fothergill in its own steeply sloping grounds. These are now a densely wooded public park, laid out in 1900–1 by Mr *Davey* of the Borough Engineer's Department. The house itself is at the time of writing disused. It is of 1877–8 by *Habershon, Pite & Fawckner*, a solemn classical affair of Bath stone ashlar. The S front is two-storeyed, symmetrical, having a porch of paired Corinthian columns set between two-storeyed channelled window bays. Shallow hipped roof on white-painted bracketed eaves. Prominent, non-symmetrical chimneystacks.

CLYTHA PARK, ½m. W. The SE-facing slope S of the present Civic Centre was laid out as a high-class estate probably *c.* 1860. In WESTFIELD ROAD there remain a dozen rendered Italianate villas in large gardens. They must date from the 1860s. The development clearly moved from E to W. OAKFIELD in Oakfield Gardens bears the date 1875 on the gatepier. This house is also Italianate, but faced in Bath stone, and very irregular in plan. No. 5 Westfield Road, of buff brick, with notched mullions and notched heads to the window bays, is obviously later still. It was built in 1886.

STOW PARK, ¾m. SW. A S-facing site at the top of Stow Hill was under development from 1870 with villas to the design of *A. O. Watkins*. Nothing as early as that can be identified. In STOW PARK CRESCENT, No. 6, of yellow brick with black brick and Bath stone dressings and Gothic details, must be of the early 1870s. No. 3, 1878–9 by *A. O. Watkins & Son*, is in a more advanced, Norman-Shaw-inspired style, though still High Victorian in its steep proportions. Mauve Old Red Sandstone banded in red brick. Patches of half-timbering in various places, not all of them original. VILLETTA, a little further W, is a variant of the 'lodge' designed by *A. O. Watkins & Son* in 1880. Stone below, the overhanging upper storey tile-hung.

STOW PARK CIRCLE, on the steeper slope to the SW, was developed in the early 1880s. Many of the original houses survive, in a variety of styles and materials, all of them showing the undisciplined fondness for over-elaboration of the decade. Presumably they are all by the *Watkins* firm. No. 1 is dated 1880, No. 7 1882. ROTHBURY HOUSE has a full-blown symmetrical Jacobean façade of stone, with a full-height bow between full-height canted bays and three shaped gables. No. 15, of Bath stone ashlar, is dated 1885. No. 17 is the most elegant of all, red brick with white timber, small-paned windows, that is to say the Queen Anne vocabulary invented in Kensington in the early 1870s by Shaw and J.J. Stevenson.

FIELDS PARK ESTATE, ½m. W. The estate lies on the rising ground between Gold Tops and Ridgeway (*see* below). A competition in 1892 for laying out an 11-acre (4.5-hectare) site was won by the local architect *Alfred Swash*. The following year *Swash & Bain* were calling for tenders to build substantial villas here, and *Alfred Swash & Son* were still busy on the estate up to 1914. The result is the epitome of the middle-class suburb of the period. An astringent interruption is provided by the well-detailed group of three-storey and four-storey flats, of *c.* 1962 by *Powell & Alport,* at the corner of FIELDS PARK CRESCENT.

SOMERTON, 1 m. E. An interwar attempt at the garden-suburb style, for which SOMERTON CRESCENT forms the entry and HAWTHORNE AVENUE the spine. Pebble-dashed, hipped-roofed pairs and terraces of four set back behind privet hedges and front gardens.

GAER-STELVIO NEIGHBOURHOOD, ¾ m.–1½ m. SW. Extensive and remarkably self-confident and convincing Modernist housing built for Newport Borough Council to the designs of the Borough Architect *Johnson Blackett,* job architect *Alfred Williams, c.* 1946–51. The houses, built on one side only of the subsidiary culs-de-sac, contour round the hillsides in pairs and terraces of various lengths, some two-storeyed, some three-, some faced with brown brick, some rendered, but all with slightly tilted and strongly overhanging flat roofs. In DICKENS DRIVE, near the bottom of the slope, exceptionally long two-storeyed terraces swing this way and that. Most artfully designed are the three-storey flats further up the hill, off SHAKESPEARE CRESCENT, where full-height stair window, and flanking balconies, concrete-slab porch roof and single-storey brick storage block with concave back are linked together in a sculptural composition. HILLVIEW, an eleven-storey tower block by *Harry Fairweather* on the high ground to the NE, was not begun until twenty years later, in 1971. Of the various community buildings envisaged in the original scheme, the only ones to note are the terrace of SHOPS in Gaer Road, and Gaer Junior School, for which *see* p. 443.

ST JULIANS, 1½ m. NE. Two more areas of late 1940s housing for Newport Borough Council by *Johnson Blackett.* The larger lies E of BEAUFORT ROAD, on the crest of the hill, in the typical layout of roads close-set like a ribcage; the smaller is further W, off REMBRANDT WAY. *Harry Fairweather*'s eleven-storey tower block at the highest point of Beaufort Way, a landmark for miles around, arrived *c.* 1971–2.

PREFABS. Newport Borough Council has maintained and kept in use a remarkably large number of prefabs, built in 1946–7 to provide emergency housing after the Second World War, and intended to have a life span of no more than a decade. Newport's prefabs are of the Arcon type, designed in 1944 by *Edric Neel* and *Rodney Thomas* of *Arcon.* The most memorable concentration is at RIDGEWAY, to the NW, where they stand close-set and diminutive in regimented ranks, their corrugated walls painted cream, their corrugated roofs red. Only a few, privately owned, have broken out in other colour schemes, or tiled roofs. There are smaller groups further S, off STELVIO PARK DRIVE, and in MASEFIELD VALE and DRINKWATER GARDENS. To the E of the town are the most extensive concentrations, the BISHPOOL and TREBERTH ESTATES, extending S of the CHEPSTOW ROAD, nearly 300 prefabs in all.

OAKDALE 1090

A model village, built for the miners working in Oakdale Colliery by the Tredegar Iron and Coal Company. The colliery opened in 1907, and a competition was held in 1910–11 to design a village of 660 houses, by far the most ambitious attempt by any mining company in South Wales to provide planned housing for its work-force. In the event, the result of the competition was set aside, and the Company appointed as architect *A.F. Webb* of Blackwood, brother-in-law of its managing director. Nevertheless, the radical departure made by the expansive and highly formalized plan of Oakdale Village from the traditional ribbons of valley-bottom terraces is obvious even on the map. The layout, a broad, straight spine road, intersected by curved and straight transverse streets, is reminiscent of the centre of Letchworth, Hertfordshire, the first

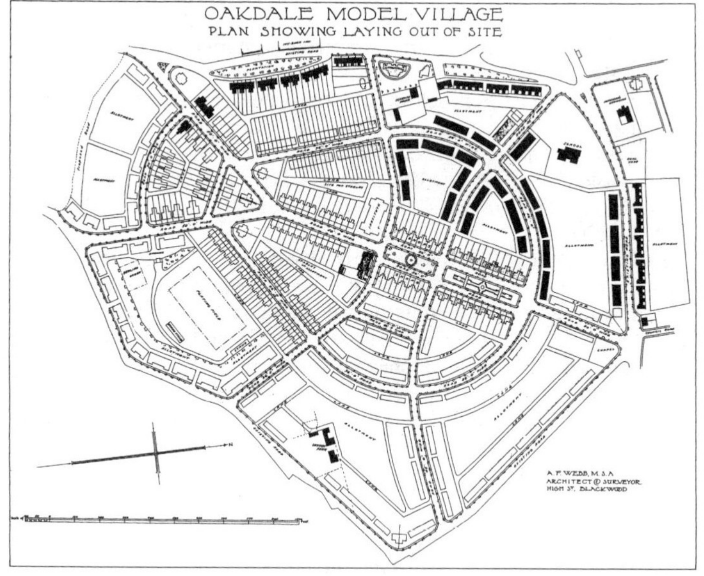

Oakdale. Original layout of model village

garden city, begun in 1903. Architecturally, a watered-down garden-city idiom also prevails, though the housing shows considerable variety of design and resource in the use of materials.

The site slopes gently towards the SW. A straight axial road runs NE–SW. Its middle third is doubled to provide a grassy central public space, where the two largest buildings were sited, a workmen's institute and a hotel – a telling Valleys emphasis. Further down, the road bifurcates obliquely. Crossing it are a peripheral road which describes the form of a tennis racquet, and two central transverse roads, straight in the centre, but angled away from one another in their outer stretches.

The major buildings are all located on the axial road. The PRESBYTERIAN CHURCH, Penmaen Avenue, at the NE end, is dated 1916. Quite small, hall-like, with a broad porch. Rendered white with red brick dressings. Classical detail. The CHRISTIAN CENTRE, at the SW end looking up Central Avenue, is dated 1914. Red brick with stone dressings painted over. Gothic, with cuspless tracery. ST DAVID'S CHURCH, in the lowest, diagonal stretch of Central Avenue, is an afterthought, dated 1955, the architect *R. L. Edwards* of Monmouth. Semi-traditional, of brown brick. Pleasant plastered interior. – STAINED GLASS. Chancel E, 1957 and 1961 by *Celtic Studios*. Christ between SS David and Gwynllyw.

THE OAKDALE, at the SW end of the central green, originally faced the Workmen's Institute, but the latter has unfortunately been demolished and re-erected at the Welsh Folk Museum, St Fagans, Glamorgan. The Oakdale, in the hotel tradition, is a loose composition, its gables half-timbered, tile-hung and pargeted. Red brick and Pennant sandstone, and overpainted stone dressings.

The HOUSING is mostly in short terraces, stepped to take account of the slope. Paired, half-timbered gables at the centre of each terrace. Red brick below, whitened pebbledash above. Deep, flat doorhoods on brackets. In the outer roads the idiom is simpler, but the doorhoods remain a leitmotif.

COMPREHENSIVE SCHOOL, on the B4251. Built *c.* 1965–8, by *Blackett & Partners*. Close-set, flat-roofed ranges tiered down the hillside.

INFANT SCHOOL, Maes-y-garn Road. 1988–9. In the Neo-vernacular style of the *Gwent County Architect's Department* at that time. Pantiled roofs pulled down over low caramel brick walls. Purple trim, especially for the big angle window of the hall. Several glazed porches on yellow posts. A less disciplined group than usual for primary schools of the period.

CYNCOED COTTAGE, ½ m. SE. On the side of a little valley. One-and-a-half-storey C17 farmhouse and outbuildings step down the hillside in line. Rubble-stone walls.

3020 OLDCASTLE/HEN-GASTELL

ST JOHN THE BAPTIST. Derelict at the time of writing. Nave and lower chancel, and S porch, all rebuilt on old foundations in 1863–4 by *J. P. Seddon*. Old Red Sandstone. On the N side Seddon reused Norman lancets, one in the chancel, two in the nave. Strikingly composed W wall, with a big plate-traceried window below a double bell gable. Handsome timber roof to the nave, arch-braced, on wall-plates faced with quatrefoil-pierced panels. – STAINED GLASS. Nave W, 1864 by *Chance Brothers* to *Seddon*'s instructions. Roundels of music-playing angels related to the tracery pattern.

OLDCASTLE COURT. The long range of farm buildings, of Old Red Sandstone, includes at its N end a fine five-bay BARN, with unusual, externally splayed ventilation slits.

PANTEG 3090

The church lies in a dell among the open hills, $\frac{3}{4}$m. SW of New Inn, the settlement which serves the valley-bottom industry.

ST MARY. Built of local limestone and sandstone rubble, a mixture of colours. Only the W tower is medieval, Perp, small and unbuttressed, battlemented with a rectangular NE stair-turret. The W doorway is unusually large, two-centred, with two continuous chamfers. Two-light belfry windows, square-headed, with cinquefoiled ogee-headed lights. The nave was reconstructed in 1849, with Perp windows and a S porch. The chancel, N vestry and lean-to N aisle are by *Henry Woodyer*, 1874–6, site architect *W.H. Cousmaker*. Ogee-headed lancets and even a Perp E window. Idiosyncratic interior. Instead of a chancel arch, a trio of pointed arches on circular piers, and instead of an aisle arcade, a continuous beam incised with a text, supported on octagonal stone piers with brattished capitals. The barn-like nave roof is also of 1874. – FONT. Surely by *Woodyer*. Deep circular bowl encircled by an ivy wreath. Arcaded underside and supporting colonnettes. – REREDOS. 1922 by *Harold King*. Painted with subjects similar to those in the glass above. – CHANCEL SCREEN. Also by *King*, 1935. – STAINED GLASS. Chancel E, Nativity, Crucifixion and Ascension. 1875 by *O'Connor & Taylor*. Bright, uncoordinated colours. – N aisle, two windows by *Celtic Studios*, music-making angels, 1979, and steelworks between disciples fishing and Good Shepherd, 1982.

MOTTE. A C12 motte, called 'low, small and feeble' by Cathcart King, hidden in trees NE of the church.

GWENT CREMATORIUM, $1\frac{1}{2}$m. S. By *Sir Percy Thomas*, 1958–60. Rendered white. Steeply gabled chapel flanked by stark round-headed arcades. Mullioned clerestory windows. TY-GWYN, to the W, which echoes the outline of the chapel, must have been built as the caretaker's lodge.

STEELWORKS, $1\frac{1}{4}$m. SE on the E side of the railway and the A4051. Alongside the road remain the buildings erected in 1870 to make open-hearth steel and rolled steel sheet. Long, curve-roofed range covered in corrugated steel sheet. On its W side, an early COOLING TOWER, timber-framed and metal-braced, a rare survival. The buildings remain in use as part of the present-day stainless steelworks.

PENYRHEOL. *See* Pontypool, p. 483.

PENALLT 5000

OLD CHURCH (dedication unknown). Alone on the hillside overlooking the Wye Valley, approached through a LYCHGATE of the local type, just a pitched roof set on slab-like side walls, and down an avenue of lime trees. The church is built of Old Red Sandstone, used for dressed work as well as rubble walling. Saddleback W tower with Dec details. The two-light W window has ogee forms, as has the lancet above. Paired rectangular belfry openings. Late Perp S aisle and porch, perhaps of 1539, the date on the S door. Three-light, square-headed S window with cinquefoiled lights and an odd, stepped label. The porch arch, though of two-centred form, must be contemporary, as is the depressed-headed S doorway. In the chancel, similar square-headed late Perp windows, perhaps inserted into earlier fabric – the chancel is not aligned with the nave. The windows in the N wall of the nave are of 1885. Inside, late Perp four-bay arcade, with thick lozenge-plan piers, shafted in the cardinal directions, hollow-moulded on the diagonals. Plain tapered caps, and arches with two broad waves which do not relate to their supports. Altogether a typical if rather crude West Country performance. Chancel arch continuously chamfered with broach stops. Late Perp chancel ceiling, a ribbed wagon vault, with square bosses at the intersections of the ribs. Two lengthways ribs are thickened and moulded, and the wall-plates extraordinarily deep and multi-moulded. The rood stair partly survives N of the chancel arch, also a strange diagonal passage arch cut through from aisle to chancel, and small rectangular windows in the chancel arch gable to light the rood. – ALTAR RAIL. Turned balusters. Dated 1743. – PULPIT. Early C17. (The date 1634 on a tablet behind it.) With the usual arcading, guilloche band and frieze of relief strapwork. – FONT. Octagonal. Tapering panelled bowl on a panelled stem. Of the C17? – ROYAL ARMS. Of Queen Anne, dated 1709.

In the CHURCHYARD, S of the nave, remains of a CROSS. Three tall steps, an octagonal base with broaches and part of the octagonal shaft.

PENTWYN, 1½ m. S, is the modern village. The new church is at its S end, the chapel at its N end, and in between, much late C20 suburban-looking housing.

ST MARY. Simple C19 church, of nave and lower chancel. – STAINED GLASS. Chancel E, 1902 by *Joseph Bell & Son*. Until recently the church was attached to the NATIONAL SCHOOL of 1834. This has sash windows and bargeboarded gablets, and has been converted into a house.

BAPTIST CHAPEL (disused). Small, early C19, not later than *c.* 1820, the period of the earliest tombstones in the burial ground. Originally entered in the centre of the long side, between the two broad, round-headed windows. (Simple interior, with immersion font in one corner.)

THE ARGOED, ½ m. SE of Pentwyn. Quite a large, two-storeyed stone house, but a tantalizing one. From the mid C17 it was the seat of the Probert family. A cast-iron fireback with the date 1644 and the initials of Sir George Probert placed over the E porch was noted by Bradney (1913), but has since disappeared. In 1865 Richard Potter, chairman of the Great Western Railway (and father of Beatrice Webb, the socialist thinker), acquired the estate and enlarged the house at both ends. The centre of the house is quite irregular, its windows all C18 sashes. Strapwork cresting over the E porch may be of the early C17, but cannot be *in situ*. The 1860s extensions consist of a taller S block canted full-height to the S, and a service range to the N. Inside there is just enough to confirm the C17 origin of the central section, though not necessarily its double-pile plan. In the hall, entered from the W, part of a ceiling beam moulded with an ovolo and a hollow, and a little plaster decoration: a fleur-de-lys, emblem of the Proberts, and a vine trail on a sloping soffit. The latter indicates where the staircase originally rose. The present stair, though almost in the same position, seems largely a C20 reconstruction. In the dining room E of the hall, a square-headed, chamfered, stone chimneypiece with the Probert arms on the lintel.

The stone STABLE, at r.-angles to the house towards the NW, is also of the C17, and much more satisfying, as it is remarkably unaltered. The interior contains four-plus-four stalls, demarcated by stout turned and moulded posts which support the roof of the hay loft above. The stall-heads are embellished by means of semicircular timber arches with turned pendants, one or two of which survive. The entrance at the W end is wide, four-centred-headed with a sunk chamfer. In the S wall, two quite large stone mullioned windows of three lights, with ovolo mouldings, which have probably been brought in from the house, and a third opening filled with flat timber balusters, which must have belonged to a stair or internal gallery. N bell gable, clearly for farm use.

To the NE a large square GARDEN enclosed with stone walls. The arched openings in the walls may date the whole enclosure to the C17.

PENHOW/PENHW 4090

Castle and church appear exhilaratingly on a grassy, stone-strewn knoll above the A48, and are reached by a lane which curls up from the W past the barns and sheds of Castle Farm. The group as seen from the S suggests the origins of the manorial layout in the C12. The castle stands on the highest extremity of the ridge, the irregular mounds and banks in the field to the SE, between castle and church, clearly indicating defensive enclosures. To the S of the church, the sites of medieval peasant houses have been excavated. Penhow belonged to William Seymour in the 1230s, and it was probably his forebears, the St Maurs, who built the original castle within the lordship of Chepstow. In the late C14 the estate passed away from the Seymours to the Bowles family, and from the late C15 the castle was tenanted, and inhabited by estate stewards or farmers. This resulted in late C17 modernization, and neglect thereafter. In 1973 the castle was purchased by Stephen Weeks, who has restored it for display to the public.

ST JOHN THE BAPTIST. The church has a very odd plan, conditioned by the site, close to a steep drop to the N. Nave and lower chancel, pyramid-roofed S tower rising from the middle of the S aisle, S porch leading into the tower. The tower clearly pre-dates the aisle and porch. N vestry added in 1913 by *H.J. Griggs* of Newport, who also re-roofed the church and reconstructed the tower. All windows are C19 or early C20 replacements. Inside, it is clear that the aisle was formed in the C13, so the walls of nave, chancel and tower may all be Norman. Unmoulded two-centred arches have been cut through the tower walls. The aisle is of two bays E of the tower and two more W of it, the arcades cut through the pre-existing nave S wall. Pointed, slightly chamfered arches on thin piers, the W pier octagonal with oversized square cap on cushion and angle broaches, the E pier circular and banded in two coloured stones, its big square cap carved with C19 foliage. Semi-cylindrical E respond. The only other medieval features are in the chancel, a double piscina under a plain pointed arch, and a C14 tomb recess in the N wall, covered by a cusped ogee arch with foliage finial. The chancel arch with three-bay stone screen may belong to *Griggs*'s restoration. – STAINED GLASS. S aisle E, 1865 by *Powell*'s, designed by *Grieve*, commemorating a rector. Last Supper, Pentecost, Philip and the Eunuch, and Paul Preaching, small scenes crowded with figures. – Chancel E, Good Shepherd and Light of the World, 1925 by *William Glasby*. – S aisle SE, and nave and aisle W, single figures also by *Glasby*, 1927.

In the CHURCHYARD, the steps of a medieval CROSS, a yew tree growing out of them.

CASTLE. The castle, built of local limestone, is small, nor does it appear convincingly defensive, though it huddles on the crown of the knoll, where the ground falls steeply to the N, E and W. Earliest is the rectangular tower to the W, probably C12 in its fabric. An earth-banked enclosure accompanied it to the N and E, later strengthened by a faceted enclosing wall of stone. This is a pattern found in the first phase of White Castle (q.v.), and in several castles in Glamorgan – Coity, Ogmore, Penlline – though none is as small as Penhow. In the C14 the hall range was constructed against the S enclosure wall, and considerably remodelled in the later C15. In the post-Seymour period a new rectangular house was formed within the N enclosure wall. This was handsomely remodelled in the early C18 with a symmetrical N front of three bays and three storeys, which hid the castle's history from travellers on the main road below. Rendered, ochre-washed walls. Shell hood over the central doorway on carved brackets. The sash windows are early C19, replacing mullion-and-transom crosses.

The approach to the castle is from the S, between a pair of stout, rusticated stone gatepiers carrying ball finials, brought here after 1976 from Spring Park, Gloucestershire. It leads to the exceedingly modest SW gatehouse, tucked into the re-entrant angle between keep and hall range. The segmental entrance arch is slightly chamfered and set in a rectangular recess for some simple sort of drawbridge. Armorial panel above, and traces of a large blocked window.

The hall range to the r. is two-storeyed; the chamber at the upper level is lit by a large three-light window, with cinquefoiled lights and glazed spandrels, and the square stops of its hoodmould carved with the emblems of Sir Thomas Bowles (knighted 1482, †1511) and his Morgan wife. The projecting chimney-breast to the r., serving hearths on two levels, and the deep, gabled stair projection, confirm the importance of the upper chamber. Note the tiny single-light windows at both levels in the W return wall, giving sneaking views of the gatehouse entrance, the lower one from a room W of the hall, the upper one from the upper chamber.

From the gatehouse, two successive chamfered, depressed two-centred-headed archways, perhaps early C14, open into the SW corner of the diminutive, irregular courtyard. The C12 keep is attached to the N, the C14–C15 hall range is attached to the E, and the C17–C18 house stands across on the N side of the courtyard. It will be best to continue examination of the HALL RANGE first. The ground-floor hall is entered at its W end through a late C15, four-centred-headed doorway. It is lit by a large three-light N window, closely similar to the S upper window already noted, but without armorial enrichment of the hoodmould stops. Plain, square-headed fireplace opening. There is evidence that the ceiling of this room was originally lower, and that all the late C15 features so far noted outside and in are part of a drastic remodelling of the range, converting it from a first-floor hall over an undercroft into a ground-floor hall with great chamber over. As part of this new arrangement, the two rooms were linked by a spacious winding stone stair in the projecting SE turret. Four-centred-headed doorways at both levels. The upper room was re-created in 1976–7, misleadingly, as a hall, with a new screen and new, steeply pitched open roof. Plain rectangular, chamfered fireplace opening here too. The service rooms E of the hall range partly survive. In the SE room, a late C15 fireplace opening with four-centred head. Against the E curtain wall, traces of further rooms, and reconstructed steps to the wall-walk.

Now back to the KEEP. This is three-storeyed, with an undercroft below a hall with parlour above. The doorway from the courtyard, two-centred-headed with bull-nose moulding, is typical of *c.* 1300. Single-light windows at all three levels. The corbelled battlements belong to a C13 or early C14 strengthening of the top storey. The interior of the upper two storeys is reached from the great chamber through the upper part of the gatehouse by means of a two-centred, chamfered doorway.

Finally, the C17–C18 house. On the courtyard side it is irregularly fenestrated and includes not only the rectangular range on the N side of the courtyard but a return wing to the W extending to the keep. In the return is a handsome late C17 open-well staircase rising through two full storeys. It has square newels with turned pendants, and twisted balusters. In the N range there are two equally handsome rooms. The rectangular dining room has large-fielded, bolection-moulded panelling rising into a multi-moulded cornice. Mighty door-cases with broken pediments. Bolection-moulded fireplace surround and drops of leaves flanking the overmantel. The square parlour, which opens off the dining room to the E, is more restrained. C19 plaster ceilings in both. The colour schemes are of *c.* 1978.

FARM BUILDINGS, SW of the castle. There are two groups. That at the higher level is dominated by a seven-bay C17 BARN, that down below is all early C19, of three components: a five-bay barn with cartshed addition, a stable range, and a byre range, all set parallel to one another.

Fragments of ROMAN BUILDING MATERIAL from the area of the castle and rectory suggest the existence of a Roman building in the area.

4010 PENRHOS

ST CADOC. Unbuttressed W tower, probably of the C16, the embattled top stage on corbels. Nave, with lean-to N aisle of 1878 by *John Prichard*, lower chancel. Local Old Red Sandstone. The S porch, just stone side walls carrying timber arches and roof, is surely also by *Prichard*. The medieval parts are hard to date. Typical Perp windows of three cinquefoiled lights under square heads in nave and chancel, and others reused in the E and W walls of Prichard's aisle. Inside, matching tower arch and chancel arch of the characteristic C14 and C15 form, with chamfered inner arch dying into tall imposts. Perp roofs over nave and chancel of the usual ribbed wagon form on moulded wall-plates. Plastered. Square bosses. – FONT. Octagonal bowl on quatrefoil stem. Presumably by *Prichard*. – STAINED GLASS. Chancel E, small Crucifixion against quarries and diagonal texts. Of *c.* 1848, probably by *Powell*'s (A. Brooks). – Nave S. Nativity with shepherds and kings adoring. 1930, no doubt by *Burlison & Grylls* (A. Brooks).

In the CHURCHYARD, a medieval cross base with decorated broaches. The rest of the CROSS and steps of 1868 by *Prichard*.

OLD RECTORY, N of the church. 1867 by *George J. J. Mair*. Quite large. Tudor Gothic, of red brick with Bath stone dressings.

SCHOOL (now a house), opposite the church. Also by *Mair*, 1867. Small, of red brick.

PENTWYN, ½ m. N. Substantial house of *c.* 1905, clearly by the same architect as Plas Hendy, Bryngwyn. STABLE en suite.

MOTTE, 1 m. N. Typical, but exceptionally well preserved and well seen early C12 motte, ditch and bank.

THE WALKS, ½ m. NW. Nothing much to look at outside. At the back of the N half, however, the wall is timber-framed, and part of a timber upper oriel window survives. Inside, further evidence of a two-storey late C16 timber house: a framed partition wall towards the S downstairs, and above, a complete hammerbeam truss for what must have been a splendid upper room lit by the oriel. The gabled cross range is a C17 replacement of the original S half of the house.

HIGH HOUSE, ⅔ m. NW. The farmhouse, its barns and outbuildings encircle a spacious gravelled yard. How far was this unusual arrangement deliberately planned? The house itself is a bizarre hybrid, of unforgettable silhouette. The date 1675 is on the porch, and on the stair inside. This seems to date the construction of the whole house, but its upper half was skimpily finished off, and much timberwork is older material reused. Heavy overall render makes it difficult to realize that the walls are of stone below but slightly timber-framed above. Such penny-pinching compromises combine oddly with the elaborate decoration of porch and stair. The plan too is forward-looking, four rooms arranged as a double pile, and in the central cross wall, two pairs of hearths back to back. The two pairs of lozenge stacks which thrust up above the roofs reflect this plan. The roofs themselves cannot be what was originally intended, rising at the front as a broad hip, but converted half-way up into a gable. At the back, a single full-width gable. Symmetrically arranged windows towards the front, three-light below, two-light above, but oddly short and small. Their sunk-chamfer mouldings, however, suggest that they must be reused from an early C17 building. The projecting timber porch, by contrast, shows off decorative carpentry skills of the mid 1670s. The broad imposts have sunk relief patterns. Shaped corbels support the many-moulded cornice with fancy crenellation, which is carried up the slopes of the gable. Apex pendant carved with the date. The front door bears bold geometrical patterns, and is set in a double-wave-moulded frame on fluted stops. Inside, the front r. room is entered through a doorway with battlemented surround, and has a complete set of reused ceiling timbers. The mouldings – leaf-stopped rolls and hollows on beams and joists – are typical of the early C17. More such timbers randomly incorporated into the roof. The staircase, by contrast, set in the centre of the rear range on axis with the front door, and dated 1675, is perfectly up-to-date. Dog-leg plan, shaped cut-out balusters, close strings decorated with a pattern of interlocking Cs. At the foot, an original dog-gate with decorative iron hinges. The stone chimneypiece upstairs, with flattened, ovolo-moulded arch, must be another reused item.

Among the farm buildings are two stone threshing BARNS, one of five bays, the other of four.

PENRHOS FARM, 1½m. N. Of *c.* 1700. Five bays, two storeys, under a completely competent hipped roof on coved eaves. Stairs at the rear in a projection rising into the roof. In the centre of the façade, shield of arms of the Dukes of Beaufort, who owned 1,000 acres in the parish and whose chief steward, Thomas Burgh, lived here in the early C18. To the l., a fine group of BARNS and other farm buildings, constructed of mauve Old Red Sandstone.

PENTERRY

5090

ST MARY. Alone in a field above the Wye Valley. Small, nave and chancel in one. Grey rubble-stone. A C12 date is established by the small round-headed window in the N wall. E window probably C15, square-headed, of two cusped ogee lights. Everything else is of the restoration by *Prichard & Seddon*, under way 1853–61, in particular the conspicuous ashlar W bell gable. S doorway moved to the W, and given a timber porch. Tie-beam and queenpost roof.

In the CHURCHYARD, the base and part of the shaft of a CROSS.

EARTHWORKS on Gaer Hill (ST 517 979). Concentric, but only the inner, sub-rectangular enclosure can be easily seen. This is defined by an unusual arrangement of two banks with a median ditch; it has a wide entrance on the southern side. The outer enclosure was very much larger, roughly corresponding with the size of the modern field. On the W side the hedge runs along the outer lip of the ditch, but on the S they diverge, and in the SE sector the double bank with median ditch can be seen crossing the field towards the wood, where it is well-preserved. On the W there are traces of an intermediate bank and ditch which turn towards the entrance on the S. Unfortunately it cannot be seen on the E, although for the most part the earthworks are better preserved on that side because of the presence of a small wood. It has been suggested that this may be a post-Roman site.

4000 PEN-Y-CLAWDD

ST MARTIN. Small, simple and heavily restored. Unbuttressed W tower under a pyramid cap, nave and lower chancel. Restored in 1885 by *H. Prothero & G.H. Phillot*, who added the timber-framed S porch and raised the tower by 8 ft (2.4 metres). The only medieval detail to remain is the cusped ogee-headed S lancet in the chancel, indicating a C14 origin. The chancel arch, with two big chamfers, copied at the restoration, suggests the same. – FONT. C12 tub. – STAINED GLASS. Chancel E, SS Martin and Mary, God blessing from the tracery above. 1885 by *Burlison & Grylls*. – MONUMENT. Worn and mutilated late C13 tomb slab with relief figure of a priest recumbent under a foliate cross, which sprouts lush stiff-leaf sprigs all the way up its stem. This must once have been a fine thing.

PENYCLAWDD FARM, Lower Penyclawdd, 1 m. NW. A well-preserved C16 and C17 farmhouse, demonstrating the typical improvements made by a family going up in the world. Many original timber mullioned windows survive, of three, four, and even one of five lights. Some are ovolo-moulded, some have sunk chamfers, but there seems no clear rationale, either historical or functional, behind the employment of the two forms. The E range must be the oldest part, two-storeyed, end-gabled. The lower room at the E end clearly functioned as hall and kitchen. It has a handsome stone chimneypiece with four-centred head and double hollow mouldings, and beside it a wall-cupboard and an oven, prominently projecting externally. The parlour at the W end has a fireplace lintel of timber, moulded with a double ovolo. Chamfered ceiling beams. Unheated central room. The present entrance is from the S into what is now the kitchen, but the site of the original entrance doorway is not clear, nor has the stair to the upper storey survived. Both may have been eliminated when the parlour end of the house was greatly extended, by means of a three-storeyed W addition, gabled in three directions, and a two-storeyed SW wing. At the NE end of the former, a stair, rising in short, straight flights round a hollow, rectangular newel. Beside it are the major rooms, lit by a tier of mullioned windows not quite aligned under the W gable. The ground-floor room, lit by the five-light window, is lined with handsome early C18 panelling, doubtless made to impress when the owner of the house, Edmund Bradbury, acted as sheriff of Monmouthshire in 1732. In the chamber above, the fireplace cheeks are lined with glazed tiles naively illustrating biblical stories, from the Old Testament on the l., from the New Testament on the r.

Late C17 BARN to the NW, built of red brick. The long side towards the house (and farmyard) has a half-timbered and weatherboarded upper half.

PEN-Y-CLAWDD COURT, $\frac{1}{3}$ m. SE. Notable only for the plain but nobly scaled red brick arch, dated May 1861, close up to the road. High carriage entrance between arched footways.

PETERSTONE/LLANBEDR GWYNLLŴG 2080

ST PETER. The queen of the churches on the flat Levels beside the Severn Estuary, and indeed the noblest and most beautiful Perp church in the whole county. The fact that it belonged to St Augustine's Abbey, Bristol, must have something to do with its ambitious West Country character. Tall, strong W tower and four-bay aisled nave, balanced with one another in scale and unified in detail. The chancel, quite low and short, is attributed by Kelly to *Bodley & Garner*, part of a restoration 1889–91, which also tactfully rectified distortions in the fabric of the nave.* Tower restored 1910. The church is built of coursed grey limestone, with oolitic limestone dressings. Some tentative banding with mauve Old Red Sandstone in the S aisle.

In detail, the chancel is straightforward. Perp, not imitative of the medieval work. It requires no further comment. The nave
has lean-to aisles, their roofs hidden by plain parapets. Diagonal 29
angle buttresses. Three-light windows throughout, the tracery formed of cinquefoil-headed hexagons. Hoodmoulds on square stops. The nave walls rise higher than the aisle parapets but do not provide clerestory lighting. The tall S porch, plain except for an ashlar parapet with angle heads and pinnacles, must be an afterthought, as the banding of the S wall continues within it. The porch arch and doorway have similar combinations of continuous mouldings, so the afterthought must have come quickly. Close-set stone head corbels for the porch roof, the roof itself C19. Plain image niche over the S doorway.

The tower is of three stages demarcated by boldly modelled stringcourses, and has diagonal buttresses rising almost to full height in all four directions, even towards the NE, where the

* Sir Stephen Glynne in 1858 had found the S arcade 'frightfully out of the perpendicular'.

polygonal stair-turret projects. The way the middle stringcourse on the S side continues on the S wall above the aisle parapet shows that nave and tower belong to a single campaign. Three-light W window identical in its tracery pattern with the aisle windows, but embellished with vine stem and leaves in the hollow reveals. Similarly enriched W doorway, with continuous mouldings, the broadest of the hollows containing vine leaves round the arch. The upper openings are small and simple by comparison, single-lighters at two levels in the middle stage, and two-light belfry openings, with cusped ogee lights under two-centred heads. Enrichment returns at the crown of the tower: ashlar panelling of the parapet, angle pinnacles, and in the centre of the faces, niches containing statues representing the Virgin and the three major apostles.

The interior is beautifully calm and spacious, the aisles quite wide, the arcades finely proportioned. But the plastered, white-washed walls and the absence of stained glass also contribute to the effect. The lofty tower arch has bold continuous mouldings, a hollow, a double wave, a hollow and a wave. An identical sequence on the chancel arch, though here part has been hacked away for the rood loft. Lower and upper rood-loft doorways on the N side. Four-bay arcade, linked to the tower by short stretches of solid wall. The piers have filleted shafts and shaftlets on the diagonals. Capitals decorated with sparse leaves, and arches moulded to match the piers. Small, canopied, SW-facing image niche on the SW pier. In the S aisle, a PISCINA under a cusped head. The nave roof is late medieval, a remarkable survival completely unlike the standard wagon roof of SE Wales. Fine stone head corbels support shafted wall-posts and small hammer-beams, from which spring arch-brace and collar trusses. – FONT. Perp. Plain octagonal bowl with roughly shaped concave under-side. Octagonal panelled pedestal, and very broad stone podium. Presumably its position in the W bay of the S aisle is original, so the image for which the niche in the SW pier was provided related to the font. – REREDOS. Alabaster, gabled, with four white statues. Typical of *c.* 1890.

5090

PIERCEFIELD PARK

Between Chepstow and St Arvans

Few of the thousands who throng Chepstow Racecourse on a race day realize what romantic and poignant sights there are to be seen to the E, between the racecourse and the River Wye. The park ends abruptly at the wooded limestone cliffs through which the river has here forced its way in an extravagant double-S loop. From the 1750s the views obtainable from the clifftops became one of the most celebrated sights for those in search of native landscape scenery. The Piercefield estate had been bought in 1740 by Valentine Morris, a wealthy West Indies planter. His son, also Valentine, took over the estate *c.* 1752, at a time when tourism by boat down the Wye from Ross to Chepstow was beginning to become popular, and when the Duke of Beaufort was about to make the first attempt to tidy up Tintern Abbey, 3 m. (5 kilometres) or so upstream, for the benefit of visitors. During the following twenty years the younger Morris, open-hearted and open-handed, landscaped the park with the help of *Richard Owen Cambridge*, created a clifftop walk with seats and platforms at strategic spots, and allowed visitors to perambulate and savour the views every day of the week. As early as 1755, Lord Lyttelton admired its 'wild beauties', and in 1756 Dr Richard Pococke was guided along the walk, and noted a protective iron rail over a perpendicular rock, seats commanding the various prospects and a Druid temple under construction. By 1772, when Arthur Young visited, a 'small neat' temple had been erected, a grotto constructed, and down by the river a cold bath fitted up in a bathing house. He was entranced, declaring that one viewpoint 'the united talents of a Claude and a Poussin would scarcely be able to sketch'. But it was left to William Gilpin, who had visited in 1770 and published his *Observations on the River Wye* in 1782, to analyse the scene aesthetically: 'We cannot . . . call these views picturesque. They are either presented from too high a point; or they have little to mark them as characteristic; or they do not fall into such composition, as would appear to advantage on canvas.' But if Gilpin refused to call Piercefield picturesque, others readily recognized it as sublime. Only the 'dirty' river and its muddy banks impaired the scene.

By 1772 Morris's financial embarrassment forced him to return to the West Indies, and in 1784 he sold the estate to George Smith of Burn Hall in County Durham. Smith continued to open the walks daily, but straightened some of them, so that the more sensitive visitors thought that he had made them too neat. But Smith focused his attention mainly on the house. In 1785 he commissioned *John Soane*, who had already worked for him at Burn Hall, to prepare designs for enlargement. Nothing came of these, but in May 1792 Soane made new designs for a virtual rebuilding, as an exquisite Neoclassical villa. Work went ahead at once, and by January 1793 the roof was ready for slating. The following month, however, Smith in his turn had to admit bankruptcy. Colonel Mark Wood, the next owner, reduced public access to the walks to two days a week, and completed work on the house. For architect, he turned to *Joseph Bonomi*, whose first design for adding colonnades and pavilions was made in 1795, and who had by the time of Archdeacon Coxe's visit in 1799 dazzlingly fitted up the interior of the house.

In 1850 the walks were closed to the public. The Clay family owned the estate from the mid C19, and it was they who in 1923 sold it to the Chepstow Racecourse Company. Thereafter the house was abandoned, stripped of its fittings, and over the subsequent three-quarters of a century has gently but inexorably decayed to its present pathetic, though still recoverable, state.* In the park much majestic planting remains, but the clifftop walks have lost their picturesque and romantic purpose now that Morris's features are lost or overgrown and his carefully managed views largely obscured.

* The story that it was used for target-practice by American troops during the Second World War seems to be apocryphal.

Nevertheless, the Wye Valley Walk largely follows the line of his walks, and the sharp-eyed and well-prepared can still spot traces of his activities.

86 HOUSE. The rectangular central block, three-storeyed and of five bays by three, is all that *Soane* designed. The composition of the SE entrance façade is subtle, a variant of the design the architect had already used at Shotesham Park, Norfolk, 1785–8. In spite of the localized collapses, the crisp precision of its execution in Bath stone ashlar can still be appreciated. An order of Ionic pilasters with enriched capitals runs through the ground and first storeys, to carry a plain frieze and sharply profiled cornice which are stopped short of the outer angles of the façade. Between them, the upper storey is regular, five rectangular window openings, but below there are only three, wide openings, tripartite windows under semicircular relieving arches originally flanking the central doorway. The other two bays below are occupied by niches. So one realizes that the pilasters are not evenly spaced, but in an alternating rhythm. A further detail easy to miss is the slight projection of the centre three bays. These counter-rhythms are resolved in the tall attic storey, where the five rectangular windows match those below, and here, above the level of the pilasters, are seen to be evenly spaced. Plain top entablature and blocking course, an austere rim to the façade. Round the sides, pairs of chimneystacks are corbelled out on unexpected bands of carved foliage. Inside, among the bushes and heaps of rubble, it is possible to make out the simple plan, three rooms wide, two deep. Most cross walls are of brick construction, but some are partly of rubble-stone, and it is clear that earlier masonry is incorporated. The central rear staircase well is rectangular and readily recognizable, the snapped-off stone treads of the stair showing how it ascended up three sides to reach a balcony across the SE end. Here one splendidly
88 scrolly, wrought-iron supporting bracket survives in place, the one surviving trace of *Bonomi*'s interiors.*

Bonomi added a semicircular porch on Tuscan columns to shelter the front door, but that has been entirely robbed away. To l. and r. he added straight, single-storey corridors in five bays faced with Tuscan pilasters, but these too are almost gone. The twin pavilions to which they led have fared somewhat better. They are of three bays. Each is fronted by Doric three-quarter columns carrying an entablature with triglyph and metope frieze and a pediment. The trios of statues which stood on the pediments and gave them a strongly Palladian character have inevitably disappeared. Enough remains of the figured relief panels, set above the doorways and their flanking niches, to show their high quality. They appear to be made of Coade stone.

At a distance behind the house to the W is a derelict SERVICE COURT. It probably dates from the early C19, but is of local workmanship. The front range, two-storeyed, of nine bays with

* Two chimneypieces have been identified, one at 20 Portman Square, London, the other, which bears the signature of the cabinet-maker *George Brookshaw*, in the Philadelphia Museum of Art.

two-bay end wings projecting, incorporates a STABLE. Iron stall-work survives in the l. half. Coach-houses are in the wings. A central passage gave access to a yard, where in the centre of the far side is a handsome five-bay BARN. The very large rectangular KITCHEN GARDEN to the N was in existence by 1793.

To the W, the high stone PARK WALL which borders the A466 for 1½ m. was constructed *c.* 1802 for Colonel Wood. The LION GATE at its S end, now the principal entrance to the racecourse, seems to be contemporary. If so, it must have been designed by *Bonomi.* Handsome composition in Bath stone. Big rusticated piers carrying Coade stone lions flank the carriage entrance; plain stone door-frames mark the pedestrian entries. The composition is framed by square, two-storey lodges with bold alternating quoins and pyramid roofs.

WALK. Access to the N end of the walk from the A466 is through a pair of gatepiers on the S side of the road ½ m. NE of St Arvans village. From the walk there are views across to corrugated white cliffs which rise above the wooded slopes: the Wynd Cliff to the N, the Apostles Rocks and Piercefield Cliffs to the S. Between them the river describes a great loop enfolding the almost circular Lancaut peninsula far below, its green meadows dotted with cottages and cattle. The views of these scenes contrived by Valentine Morris are almost all now obscured by tree growth, but traces remain of some of the viewing platforms and follies which he constructed. The first that can be identified is LOVERS' LEAP, a projecting platform with fragments of protective iron railing. Next is the GIANT'S CAVE, a tunnel through a mass of rock. (A stone giant at one entrance, holding a boulder above his head, was already crumbling away in 1793.) From this the Wye Valley Walk follows the line of the original path down to the COLD BATH beside the river, now a roofless ruin. At the high level the path continues S-wards close below the mansion, though invisible from it. An upright stone or two close to the path is what remains of the DRUIDS' CIRCLE. Next comes the GROTTO, its brick-vaulted shell largely intact, built into the side of the smaller of the two Iron Age hill-forts (*see* below). From this point the path leaves the clifftop as the river describes a second great loop, and continues S-wards across the wooded peninsula. THE PLATFORM survives here a little way off the path. Finally, as the path rejoins the clifftop, THE ALCOVE, a ruined stone bench from which a panorama opens towards the S, with Chepstow Castle part of the composition.

PREHISTORIC REMAINS. In Piercefield Wood (ST 536 960) is the only Monmouthshire HILL-FORT with a stone rampart. It encloses a D-shaped area abutting the cliff edge. The in-turned entrance on the S seems to have been unusually strong, with guard posts overlooked by a bastion. On the W side there is an extra defence in the form of an earthen bank outside the ditch. The general style of the enclosure is similar to The Bulwarks, Chepstow, further down the river, but the nearest parallel to the stone rampart is at Worlebury, across the Severn in Gloucestershire.

A small, univallate camp (ST 532 957) lies on the Wye Valley Walk. In the C18 a grotto (*see* above) was built into the inner side of the bank, and there is a rectangular building of unknown date in the interior.

1090 PONTLLANFRAITH

SILOH PRESBYTERIAN CHAPEL, Gelligroes. Dated 1813. One of the best-preserved early chapels in the county, set back behind a small, railed burial ground. A pair of tall, round-headed windows in the centre of the façade are flanked by a pair of doorways. This is the pattern that goes with the early plan, whereby the doorways give access under the side galleries and the pulpit backs against the middle of the façade. The interior does indeed conform to this scheme. Galleries on three sides carried on thin iron supports. Box pews below. Pulpit between the long windows. Later in the C19 single-storey annexes were added under continuous roofslopes to l. and r., and the whole front was re-rendered with moulded surrounds to the windows, rusticated door-frames and eaves decoration like the fringe of a doily.

GELLIGROES still retains some of its character as a hamlet. Below the chapel, on the E side of the River Sirhowy, a working water-driven CORN MILL, with external overshot water wheel. T-plan structure of two storeys and of one. Whitewashed, coursed rubblestone with dressed quoins. The mill was first constructed *c.* 1625, but it is not clear how much belongs to that early date. PONT GAM, $\frac{1}{4}$m. SW, an early C19 stone arched bridge over the river, carried the Penllwyn Tramroad from Blackwood to Nine Mile Point.

COUNCIL OFFICES, Bryn Road. Dated 1913, and a satisfying representative of the architecture of that moment. Built as the Mynyddislwyn Urban District Council Offices. Trim Baroque façade of five bays and two storeys under a parapet arching up in the centre to display the date. Rock-faced Pennant sandstone with generous dressings of Forest ashlar. Even quoins frame the façade and define its central bay. Here the entrance doorway has a segmental head, and an upper doorway opens on to a curvaceous metal balcony. But character is given particularly by the windows, broad below with segmental heads from which voussoirs radiate, rectangular above in richly moulded surrounds. The architect of this confident piece has not been identified.

CAERPHILLY COUNCIL OFFICES, Blackwood Road. By *David Preece Associates* for Islwyn Borough Council and completed in 1977. Large and severely rectangular, of three storeys, the continuous bands of windows recessed between continuous bands of boxed-out metal cladding. Recessed drainpipes provide the only vertical stresses. Flat, off-centre entrance canopy.

PENLLWYN. The housing was laid out on a roughly radiating pattern of roads, by *A. F. Webb* of Blackwood from 1927. Neither the planning nor the design of the houses has the conviction of Oakdale (q.v.), his major scheme. Embedded in the middle, the

PENLLWYN ARMS, a large stone manor house of a branch of the Morgans of Machen. It has been greatly reconstructed, but the composition of the two-and-a-half-storey S front, with its four gables and mullioned windows, goes back to the early C17. Deep, full-height gabled central porch, its entrance arch constructed without dressed stone. At the back, a projection for a pillar stair. All the windows are C19, many much enlarged from their original size.

WYLLIE VILLAGE, 1 m. S of Penllwyn. Also by *A. F. Webb* of Blackwood, *c.* 1928–9. Long series of terraces contour along the hillside, the upper slightly more ambitious than the lower.

At BRYN, ½ m. SW of Penllwyn, SHANGRI-LA, Forest Hill, is a little period piece of 1930s streamlining. Flat roof. Two storeys, rendered above, brick below. Metal window frames bowed at the ends and painted scarlet.

PONTNEWYNYDD 2000

A valley-bottom settlement, extending virtually without a break from the N end of Pontypool. School, hospital and several substantial villas look down from the hillside to the NE.

ST LUKE, St Luke's Road. Beside the main road and disused at the time of writing. Designed by *Charles Buckeridge* shortly before his death and built 1873–4 and 1876–9, largely under *J. L. Pearson*'s supervision. E.E. Nave and lean-to aisles, producing a simple, well-proportioned W elevation. Lower chancel. The lowest storey only of a NW porch tower. (Tall and spacious interior. P. Howell.)

ALL SAINTS, Hanbury Road, Cwmffrwdoer. Iron-stained Pennant sandstone with red brick and terracotta dressings. Nave and lower chancel, S porch. Lancets. 1905–6 by *D. J. Lougher* of Pontypool. – STAINED GLASS. Indigenous to the church, the four S lancets by *Celtic Studios*, from E to W Annunciation *c.* 1962, Nativity 1956, Mary and the child Christ 1958, Baptism of Christ 1963. – N lancet, St Luke, 1989 by *John Petts*. – The various windows of *c.* 1900 brought in from St Luke's Church look feeble by comparison. They include: Chancel E, Empty Tomb, 1912 by *Heaton, Butler & Bayne*. – Nave NW, Good Shepherd, 1898 by *E. R. Suffling*. – Nave W, two war memorials, 1924 by *J. Newton Whitley* of Bristol and 1948 by *E. G. Croney* of Bristol.

EBENEZER UNITED REFORMED CHURCH, Chapel Road, Cwmffrwdoer. First built in 1741–2 as an Independent chapel for the Rev. Edmund Jones, the locally celebrated preacher and writer. The present building, rendered and colourwashed green, must be early C19. Enlarged in 1848 by the Rev. *Thomas Thomas*, his first dated work. Gable-end entrance through an off-centre porch. The decorated semicircular window below the gable, and the quoins, date from after 1907. The long sides show the typical early C19 lighting arrangements: high-level windows at the angles to light the galleries, a pair of long central windows on the downhill side to light the pulpit. Remodelling in 1911 by *R. Price* converted the interior into vestries, caretaker's house and a long, thin chapel, all within the original space.

Extensive GRAVEYARD full of headstones and some more elaborate memorials.

MERCHANTS HILL BAPTIST CHURCH, on the A4043. 1888 by *George Morgan* of Carmarthen, but a very simple, cheap example of his Romanesque style. Rubble-stone front with a rose window. (The interior has galleries of *c.* 1908, with pierced metal fronts, on all four sides.)

WESLEYAN METHODIST CHURCH, Hanbury Road, at the foot of Zion Hill. 1849–50 by *Philip Hambleton* of Pontnewynydd. Rendered. Lancets, that in the centre of the façade rusticated. Buttressed sides. Other touches of eccentric decoration. Interior completely altered in 1992.

PRIMARY SCHOOL, Leigh Road. By *Lansdowne & Griggs*, 1901–3. Typical upstanding board-school front, well seen on the hillside. Red brick, of two tall storeys. Five broad bays with the usual tripartite windows form a symmetrical façade. Gables over the first, third and fifth, the central gable shaped and pedimented above a meagre Ionic aedicule of Portland stone. Mezzanines make the rear range four-storeyed. The boys' and girls' entrances must have been at the sides but are obscured.

CWMFFRWDOER PRIMARY SCHOOL, Waunddu. This is by *Gwent County Architect's Department*, design architect *John Postill*, *c.* 1982–3. Typically low and spreading under broad slopes of slated roof, but arranged round a tiny internal courtyard. Quiet contrasts in the brickwork.

PONTYPOOL AND DISTRICT HOSPITAL, Hospital Road. (Disused at the time of writing.) Elaborate Gothic group, of pale local limestone with buff brick and stone dressings and Old Red Sandstone bands. 1902–3 by *Robert Williams*. The free-standing range in a similar idiom lower down the hill is dated 1927.

2000 PONTYPOOL/PONTYPŴL

The town lies on the S slope of the narrow valley where the Afon Lwyd debouches from the hill country, before flowing S to join the River Usk at Caerleon. Ironworking forges were in operation in the area as early as the C15, but in 1577 Richard Hanbury made a new start. By the early C18 the family had diversified into tinplating, while under John Hanbury (†1734) the ironworks became one of the most important in Europe. Japanning was another offshoot, developed by Thomas Allgood, a foreman in the Hanbury ironworks, and his son Edward. Successive generations of Hanburys acted as both ironmasters and squires, their mansion house, Pontypool Park, standing in the valley bottom immediately below the centre of the town. In 1730 a market hall was built, and in

1756 the traveller Dr Richard Pococke found 'a little compact town' lying in 'a very romantic situation between the hills'. Half a century later Archdeacon Coxe called it 'a large straggling place containing 250 houses and 1500 souls', and referred to the 'dusky aspect of the town occasioned by the adjacent forges'. The construction of the Monmouthshire Canal 1792–9 boosted trade. Capel Hanbury Leigh *c.* 1807 went into partnership with the celebrated engineers Watkin George and Robert Smith. They remodelled the works and doubled output, but by the 1850s the initiative had been ceded to Ebbw Vale. Today the town centre is still compact, though largely of the mid and late C19, occupying the upper slopes above the parkland of Pontypool Park. Along Hanbury Road, to the S, church, town hall, public library and a large chapel are spaced out. The Hanbury house is a school, a museum occupies the stables, and a stadium and ski-slope have found their places in the park. Various inner ring roads cut off the suburbs, Pontymoel and Cwm-Fields to the S and Waunfelin to the W.

ST JAMES, Hanbury Road. The five-bay nave stands side-on to the street, its sharply pointed windows with pointed quatrefoils over twin cusped lights. This constitutes the church built in 1820 to *Watkin George*'s design. The Dec chancel was added by *Wyatt & Brandon* in 1845, the nave roof heightened in 1875 by a local architect, *Ernest Deacon*, who added the S aisle in 1876–7. Internally, Deacon's arcade and roofs are coarsely detailed. – STAINED GLASS. Chancel E, *c.* 1854. Heavily patterned. – Chancel N and S and nave N, a miscellany of standard subjects, by *J. Wippell & Co.*, mostly of 1922.

ST JOHN THE DIVINE, Penywain Road, Waunfelin. By *J. Coates Carter*, 1912–13, the two W bays of the nave completed 1924–6. In Carter's minimalist later style. Perp going Tudor. Random buff sandstone with generous ashlar dressings. Tall chancel towards the road revealed at the sides to be two-storeyed with a hall underneath. Four-bay nave and gabled aisles. The interior of the church is naturally, yet unexpectedly, broad and low. Fat cylindrical piers with idiosyncratic leaf capitals that manage the transition to the square section of the arcade arches. The arches have wide, four-centred spans. No chancel arch, just a change in roof form, from the arch-braced and wind-braced roof of the nave to the boarded wagon roof of the chancel. Chancel windows deep-set under broad, segmental relieving arches. No fittings of note.

ST ALBAN (R.C.), George Street. 1844–6 by *J. J. Scoles*. Of Pennant sandstone. Neo-Norman, with apsidal chancel. Nave lengthened 1891. (– CRUCIFIX and STATIONS OF THE CROSS. Glazed terracotta. By *Adam Kossowski*, 1955–6.) Forbidding PRESBYTERY to the S, of *c.* 1870–1.

BAPTIST CHURCH, Crane Street. Dated 1847. Greek. Small but 99
monumental, of Bath stone ashlar. Three narrow bays, the central one formed of a boldly projecting portico, two Greek Doric columns between square antae carrying a pediment. This scholarly performance was a joint effort, the design by *Aaron*

Crossfield being 'improved and perfected' by *J. H. Langdon*. The disconcerting Perp windows in the side bays were introduced in 1908. The reason for these windows becomes clear on entering
102 the chapel. As built, it was lit only from the large rectangular opening in the ceiling, in accordance with what was then thought to be the method of lighting ancient Greek temples. The present engraved glass panels set in it must be of the late C19. In 1868–9 the chapel was enlarged by *A. O. Watkins* of Newport, by setting the pulpit end one bay further out. So the slender, square piers which carry the original wall-plate and cove across the void thus created must be his. They maintain the Grecian idiom, with palmette caps, but have Soanean incised decoration up their faces. Matching pilasters against the walls all round. The present galleries, surrounding the interior on all four sides, were inserted probably in 1881, when a pipe organ was installed. They have typical late C19 bowed metal fronts pierced with a dense repeating pattern. The rectangular windows above the galleries may belong to this phase, their tracery and STAINED GLASS in an Art Nouveau design inserted in 1908. – PULPIT. Mahogany. Surrounded by Greek Doric colonnettes, so an original fitting of *c.* 1847. – MONUMENTS. William Williams Phillips †1860. Tablet with cusped corners, anticipating the Gothicism of the windows. Signed *Tyleys*' of Bristol. – Rev. Thomas Thomas †1881. Grecian tablet with sensitive profile busts of Thomas and his wife in a roundel. Inconspicuously signed by *J. Milo Griffith*.

MOUNT PLEASANT CONGREGATIONAL CHURCH, Hanbury Road. 1903–4 by *Swash & Bain* of Newport. Gothic, imitating an Anglican church. The entrance front centres on a four-light Geometrical window, a three-stage tower with diagonal buttresses stands on the r., and behind are a clerestoried nave and aisles. Snecked, rock-faced Pennant sandstone with Bath stone dressings. The interior also has Anglican overtones. It is galleried at the entrance end only. Five-bay arcades, with octagonal piers carrying moulded caps and arches. Hammerbeam roof. Narrow choir recess with large four-light window, the organ set back into one side and choir stalls occupying the rest of the space. In front of the choir arch to the l., the PULPIT, of stone, polygonal, bearing reliefs of Moses, the Good Shepherd and the Good Samaritan. To the r., the site for the communion table, which has been moved to a central position, upsetting the intended equality of Word and Sacrament. – STAINED GLASS. Chancel, *c.* 1904. Christ in the House of Martha and Mary, and Suffer the Little Children. – Aisle, Education of Jesus, *c.* 1936 by *John Hall & Sons*, and Good Shepherd and Light of the World, signed by *T. W. Camm*.

TOWN HALL, Hanbury Road. 1854–6 by *Bidlake & Lovatt* of Wolverhampton, after a competition. Paid for by the Hanbury Leighs, and opened by the head of the family, as the full-width inscription declares. Italianate. Five bays and two tall storeys, rusticated below, smooth above but with rusticated quoins. Small clock tower over the l. bay. Skyline armorial display in the centre. Behind looms a six-storey brown brick extension of *c.* 1989–90, civic offices for Torfaen Borough Council.

MARKET, Commercial Street. Parts of two market halls flank the street. On the E side, the rendered gableted front of the original Market House of 1730, or rather its upper half, as a shopfront has destroyed the lower. Above, three sash windows and, between them, a pair of handsome inscription panels crowned by broken pediments enclosing shells. The inscriptions record in English and in Welsh the erection of the Market House by Mrs Frances Bray, lady of the manor of Llantarnam, and the date. Across the street, the upper half of a handsome stuccoed Neoclassical building, apparently the row of shops built by *G. V. Maddox* of Monmouth in 1840. Here too the ground storey is lost, but the upper storey-and-a-half of an eight-bay frontage remain, bays one and eight set slightly forward. Sash windows, the main ones within shallow arcading. Bay one also contains the modest Tudor doorway, dated 1894, to the present market hall, designed by *Robert Williams* of London and *D. J. Lougher* of Pontypool, who won a competition in 1893. Spacious but utilitarian hall, its partly glazed roof supported on plain iron posts. Utilitarian frontage to MARKET STREET, of grey local Pennant stone with Doulting stone dressings. In CRANE STREET, another low entrance archway of 1894 and, higher up the street, a much more showy entrance dated 1897, a gesture by the newly formed Urban District Council to commemorate Queen Victoria's Diamond Jubilee. Three-bay arcade of four-centred arches on polygonal piers with leaf capitals. Mullion-and-transom windows above with arched lights, and a polygonal, two-storeyed oriel on the downhill corner.

PUBLIC LIBRARY, Hanbury Road. 1907–8 by *Speir & Beavan* of Cardiff. A charming little building in a Baroque style probably influenced by H. T. Hare. Plum-coloured glazed brick and white Portland stone. Broad pilaster strips divide the façade into three bays. Round-headed central doorway flanked by big, round-headed mullion-and-transom windows. Upper windows in an artfully inflected band under the eaves, flanking a central pedimented cartouche. Hipped roof. Plain brick central gablet, as if the money had suddenly run out. Inside, the two main reading rooms are divided from the central corridor by Tuscan piers carrying segmental arches. Tuscan pilasters and panelled roof in the reading room to the l. In the upper rooms, delicate Art Nouveau STAINED GLASS.

HOSPITAL. *See* Pontnewynydd, p. 476.

WEST MONMOUTH SCHOOL, Blaendare Road, Cwm-Fields. 1896–8 by *Henry Stock* for the Haberdashers' Company of London, and unmistakably related to his schools at Monmouth (q.v.). Red brick with Bath stone dressings. Very tall, symmetrical front towards the road, of three storeys over a basement and crowned by gables. Central projection framed by polygonal shafts, with an elaborate heraldic display over the pierced, trefoiled doorway arch, and blind tracery far above in the gable. Further incident is provided by the polygonal turrets with candlesnuffer spirelets which mark the start of wings running back at r.-angles. The free-standing block at the back, containing a gymnasium above a swimming pool, is part of the original scheme.

GWENT TERTIARY COLLEGE, Blaendare Road, Cwm-Fields. Built as East Monmouthshire College of Further Education in 1957 and 1964 by *Monmouthshire County Architect's Department*, County Architect *Colin Jones*. An attractive group of two-storeyed ranges, set on three sides of an open-ended court. Windows in continuous bands. Brown brick. What one sees from the road, however, closing the square, is of 1981–2 by *Gwent County Architect's Department*, County Architect *K. P. Jones*, red brick below, black boarding above, the windows no longer in bands but in grouped pairs. Shallow pitched roof. Hall to the l. with full-height glazing.

GEORGE STREET COUNTY PRIMARY SCHOOL, George Street. 1986–9 by *Powell Alport*. In its busily red and yellow banded brickwork, and its internal spine corridor, where a white tubular frame is exposed, the building reflects the idiom of the County Architect's Department at that time.

WAR MEMORIAL, Hanbury Road. Unveiled in 1924. Wrought-iron gates, designed by *T. P. Francis*, with flaming torches incorporated in the ironwork. The piers carry bronze plaques which record the names of the horrifyingly many local men who fell in the First World War.

PONTYPOOL PARK. The seat of the Hanburys (now St Alban's R.C. High School). Given that this was one of the major mansions of Monmouthshire, its building history seems remarkably mysterious. The first builder was John Hanbury, soon after 1689. His son, Capel Hanbury, who inherited in 1734, seems also to have worked on the house, which at that stage faced E. Archdeacon Coxe reported in 1801 that it was soon to be 'much improved and beautified by the present proprietor [Capel Hanbury Leigh], in conformity with a judicious plan which is now carrying into execution'. It was at this time that the present S entrance was formed. Soon after 1872 John Capel Hanbury greatly extended the house to the W. All this has produced a somewhat sprawling and incoherent outline. The house is mostly two-storeyed, the walls uniformly rendered and painted cream. The symmetrical E front, a recessed three-bay centre and three-bay wings, formed the entrance façade of the original house. The E and S fronts are unified, no doubt as part of Capel Hanbury Leigh's works. Bath stone details, architrave surrounds to all windows. A single-storey projection with Tuscan Doric pilasters is set across the re-entrant centre of the E front. A single-storey projecting portico of four Tuscan Doric columns carrying an entablature is set as centrally as possible in the eight-bay E half of the S front. However, the full-height canted bay immediately to the W was already in existence by 1765. The nine-bay range beyond is of 1872, with the extensive service court behind it.

Internally, one is confronted by an extraordinary array of

& Havard of Newport. Beyond the Market House, in sharp contrast, the small but monumental Bath stone front of the MIDLAND BANK, 1910–11 by *T. B. Whinney*. This vies with the Baptist Church as the most consequential classical building in the town. Four bays, two storeys. Giant Ionic three-quarter columns carry a deep, plain entablature and top balustraded parapet. Finally into Crane Street, which ascends to the l., for the Baptist Church and the Jubilee entrance to the market.

High up, beyond the edges of the town, several farmhouses survive from the pre-industrial era. Two in particular deserve a mention.

At PENYRHEOL, 1½ m. S, MOUNT PLEASANT, a one-and-a-half-storeyed C17 house, its rubble-stone walls greyly rendered. From the long side towards the road protrude the sawn-off ends of beams which carried a full-length pentice. (In the rear wall, a window with diamond mullions. Inside, massive stone hall fireplace with mural stair beside it in the end wall. Post-and-panel partition with flattened-arched doorways into two unheated rooms.)

GELLI-PISTYLL, Tranch Road, 1 m. W. In two parts set in line. The uphill part is a one-and-a-half-storey, two-unit house of typical late C16 character. The position of the stack shows that the living room was at the lower end and the other room unheated. The downhill part is an equally typical early C17 addition. Two-and-a-half storeys. Passage and heated room below, another heated room above, creating a normal three-unit, hearth-passage plan. As seen from the E, the C17 part makes an eloquent little composition. A heavy timber doorway with arched head shelters beneath one end of a full-width pentice. Windows vertically aligned, the middle one sheltered by a second, miniature pentice, that in the attic set in a gablet.

(GLYN PITS, 2 m. SW. The remarkable remains of a colliery, isolated and difficult of access, on the N flank of the Golynos Mountain. In the early C19 Capel Hanbury Leigh sank a colliery here to supply fuel for his Pontypool Iron and Tinplate Works. There survive a pair of masonry-lined shafts between two large and finely constructed engine houses of the mid C19, and almost uniquely, the steam-pumping and winding engines they were built to house.

The ENGINE HOUSES are both constructed of fine ashlar masonry and survive substantially intact to eaves level. Square-headed windows with keystones and cast-iron internal lintels provided light to the interiors. The various round-headed apertures accommodated the winding gear and supports for the machinery. But the engine houses differ in date and mode of construction. The earlier (W) is rectangular in plan, and bears the date 1845 and Leigh's initials. Its E 'bob' wall is almost twice as thick as the others, to enable it to bear the weight of the beam engine. What survives of this is the huge bi-convex cast-iron engine beam pivoted on the cast-iron sill-plate of the 'bob' opening. Inside the engine house is much more ironwork. Framing at two levels, with an air pump below the lower, its driving-rod still passing through the cast-iron lattice. The cast-iron beams and iron-plate floor on which the beam-engine cylinders were seated only partly survives. Two upper timber-beamed floors have largely gone. Outside, between the 'bob' wall and the shaft are low walls and pits on which are the impressive cast-iron crankshaft, flywheel and gears with the winding-sheaves and chains, as well as the pump-rods.

The E engine house is square in plan under a hipped roof and houses an engine constructed between 1859 and 1865. It reflects the development in technology after *c.* 1850, whereby it is sited vertically, no longer requiring the pivot arrangement with thick 'bob' wall. This is the only engine of this type to remain *in situ* in Wales, and one of the earliest surviving in Britain. Inside, there is a thick spine wall aligned with the coal-shaft and reinforced with iron. The external W wall has tall arched openings, those below to provide visibility for anyone operating the winding gear, that at the top to provide access for the winding cables. There is much internal cast iron in this engine house too, in particular the 'cross-head slide', an elegant structure of four Doric columns and entablature which kept the piston-rod of the winding-sheaves vertical.)

At UPPER RACE, 1½ m. SW, can be seen a rare example of a 'hush', a primitive form of coalmining in use up to the C18. Stored water released to race over shallow coal-measures would expose seams of coal. A quarry-like cutting is the main feature, running for 550 yds (500 metres) NW–SE, created by a series of successive channels cut into the mountainside. There are also the earthworks of a feeder watercourse stretching for a mile to the SW. This was intended to tap water from Afon Bran and feed a pond below White House, which could be used to scour the ground E of the main cutting. Also a later artificial pond, now dry, with a massive earthen and masonry dam on its downhill side.

4080 PORTSKEWETT

ST MARY. A small Norman church, of local rubble limestone. Nave and square-ended lower chancel. One N window in the chancel and doorways N and S in the nave establish the date. Both doorways have flat monolithic lintels, that to the N much the deeper. It is decorated with an embossed Greek cross, its arms concave-sided, under a doubly outlined semicircular arch. Quite a variety of later windows. In the chancel, a small Dec S window with Y-tracery and C19 E window. Prettiest is the S window in the nave, square-headed, of two ogee cinquefoiled lights, with double-wave mouldings and stylized leaves carved in the spandrels. Unbuttressed W tower, of two tall stages. The single-light windows in the upper stage, under hoodmoulds with square tops, are typical of the early C16. The blocked W doorway and large two-light window over are contemporary. Square NE stair-turret. Plain S porch. Inside, white rendered walls and a W gallery of 1818, lit by a high N window, suggest that no thorough C19 restoration took place. The most important survival is the C12 chancel arch, round-headed, formed without cut stone. Big plain imposts. The reordering in 1925 by *Griggs & Vaughan* included resiting the gallery stair. – FONT. Perp. Octagonal bowl, its faces carved with quatrefoils, simple blind arcading and one four-petal flower. Plain octagonal stem. – STAINED GLASS. Chancel S. Noli me Tangere. 1870. The drawing has perished. Probably by *Heaton, Butler & Bayne* (A. Brooks). – MONUMENT. Rev. Henry Williams †1819. Black and white tablet, repainted. Reversed torches to l. and r.

In the CHURCHYARD, the five wonderfully worn steps, broached base and stump of a CROSS.

MANOR FARMHOUSE, ¼m. NW. An impressive C16 house, a three-unit, single-pile range of two storeys lying S–N, with hollow-chamfered stone mullioned windows below and above, mostly of three lights. The short, higher wing coming forwards to the road at the N end is a parlour addition, probably also C16, with chamfered as well as hollow-chamfered, three-light mullioned windows. On the N wall curious, apparently C17, shaped lead insets in the plaster. The interior is much altered. Entry is into a cross-passage, with a thick stone cross wall on its N side. This suggests that the S room and passage may be an early addition. Centrally placed in the wall is a depressed-headed stone doorway, chamfered on its S face. The doorway leads into what was the hall. The hall fireplace, in the cross wall W of the doorway, has a mighty monolith lintel of basket-arch profile. E of the doorway a spiral stone stair leads from the hall to the upper storey. The parlour was in the mid C17 given a handsome plaster ceiling, with unusually lavish cornice mouldings, central concave-sided lozenges sprouting fleurs-de-lys and sprigs of flowers, and angle motifs to match.

OLD VICARAGE, a little further along the Crick road. Rendered house of the C18, painted white with pale blue dressings. The S front is of five bays and two storeys, with an apology for a central pediment enclosing a circular window. The other windows are segment-headed in rendered surrounds with keystones. The casement window frames must be late C19. A round-headed central doorway and end stacks complete the symmetrical composition.

ROMAN REMAINS, ½m. N (ST 498 887). Fragments of walling and building debris on Portskewett Hill indicate the remains of a Roman building, probably a small villa.

MITEL TELECOM, ¾m. W. 1982–4 by *Teron*. A low, far-stretching rectangle, for the manufacture of telephone systems and microchips. Its single-storey walls are of bronzed glass, over which the roof cladding forms a chamfered band. Entrance in a central, double-height, fully glazed pavilion. The entrance hall is a hall of mirrors. The clean but enigmatic image suits such a high-tech industry, and makes an interesting contrast to the Inmos factory, Duffryn, at Newport (*see* p. 219), designed at the same time for a similar function.

HESTON BRAKE MEGALITHIC TOMB, ½m. NE (ST 506 887). Visible on the summit of a prominent hill above the estuary.

The remains of a long rectangular chamber are set at the S end of a denuded cairn which stretches for some 60 ft (18 metres) behind it. The chamber has high portals at the entrance and seems to have been divided into two by a projecting jamb. Although the design of the chamber is not a very typical one, it may be classed as a terminally chambered Cotswold-Severn tomb, dating from the early or middle Neolithic period.

At SUDBROOK, ¾ m. SE, overlooking the Aust/Portskewett river crossing, is the strong coastal Iron Age HILL-FORT (ST 505 874), so close to the sea that much of the interior has been washed away. The huge inner rampart survives around the NW and NE sides, but the two outer banks and ditches are preserved only on the NW side; on the E they were levelled during medieval occupation and have been encroached upon by the C19 industrial settlement. Excavations 1934–6 revealed that the inner rampart had been built up in several stages, its final extent covering an occupation dating from the C2 B.C. Settlement debris of the same date was incorporated in the body of the rampart, suggesting that the material for its construction had been scraped from the interior, where evidence only of later, C1 A.D., occupation was found *in situ*. This later material is comparable to that from Lydney (Gloucestershire) and Llanmelin (*see* Llanvair Discoed, p. 363) nearby. When the Roman army arrived, they took the hill-fort over as a convenient coastal base.

Recent reassessment of the material from the pre-war excavations suggests that the fort was held for a relatively short time by the Roman army during the conquest of Wales. Although it is unusual for a Roman army to utilize an Iron Age fort, it can be explained here by Sudbrook's importance as a bridgehead on one of the main crossings of the Severn Estuary. The evidence of the *Antonine Itinerary* shows that it remained a major route into South Wales throughout the Roman period.

Immediately E of the fort, the remains of a medieval CHAPEL. The footings are traceable of a square nave and quite a long, square-ended chancel. The chancel arch is double-chamfered. This and other evidence, now lost, suggested that the chancel was C14. Norman nave window noted in 1895. Cinquefoil-headed W window. Of the S porch, only the cut stonework of the hollow-chamfered entrance arch survives.

SUDBROOK VILLAGE. The Severn Tunnel, built 1873–86 by the Great Western Railway Company, was the longest undersea tunnel in the world, and remained so for a century, until the Hokkaido Tunnel, Japan, and the Channel Tunnel were built in the late C20. At Sudbrook there survive the pumping-engine houses vital for the construction of the tunnel and its maintenance, and much of the village built to house the workforce. The engineer for the tunnel was *Charles Richardson*, with *Sir John Hawkshaw* as consultant, though from 1879 *Hawkshaw* took over fully. T. A. Walker acted as contractor.

As approached from the W, the VILLAGE comes first. Nine two-storeyed terraces of housing survive, built 1880–9. Their walls are mostly of brick or rubble-stone, but in SEA VIEW a terrace of ten constructed 1882–4 are of concrete blocks. This is an exceptionally early example of the revival of concrete as a building material. Opposite STONE ROW at the E end, THE VILLAS, six semi-detached pairs for managers. The original communal buildings which remain are the SCHOOL of 1884, rubble-stone with brick dressings, and two buildings already erected by 1882, the single-storey gabled POST OFFICE, and, just beyond, the INFIRMARY, with a long ward block stretching back behind the street frontage.

But it is the five red brick engine houses, to the E, which dominate. The largest is the four-storeyed, hipped-roofed ENGINE HALL. This was built after the completion of the tunnel in 1886 to pump out 20 million gallons a day from the Great Spring, which had in 1879 flooded the workings, almost causing a catastrophe. Until 1968 it housed six great steam engines, but since 1962 steam power has been replaced by electricity. Externally the engine hall is severe, of seven bays by three, with round-headed windows in three storeys and a blind top storey. The tall opening in the centre of the N side allowed a railway line to enter the building. Internally the hall was subdivided into three, with in the centre a shaft nearly 30 ft (9 metres) wide for the six large cast-iron pumping mains sited above the vaulted cap which seals the Great Spring. On either side of the shaft-head stood the huge and cumbersome beam engines which operated the pumps. The engine cylinders, cast by *Harvey & Co.* of Hayle, Cornwall, in 1885–6, have been removed. Wrought-iron galleries gave access to the engines, and the lower two storeys of windows provided lighting. The top windows lit the beam-loft. The massive riveted wrought-iron frame of its floor survives in the W chamber. The windowless top level houses two travelling cranes, dated 1886 and running on tracks on the long side wall-heads.

NOS. 2–3 ENGINE HOUSES, immediately to the E, are earlier, but smaller and less well preserved. They housed three vertical engines which pumped water from the main drainage culvert of the railway tunnel.*

To the S of No. 2 engine house are two more red brick buildings of two storeys, both erected in 1924, the BOILER HOUSE and the VENTILATION-FAN ENGINE HOUSE. The TOWER between them, clad in corrugated asbestos, formed the air-tight casing over a second shaft, 15 ft (4–5 metres) in diameter. The oblong brick TOWER to the S formed the outlet for the fan. The large-diameter fan (still extant) continued in use until 1995, when it was replaced by smaller ones underground.

SECOND SEVERN CROSSING. The first road link between England and Wales over the estuary of the River Severn, the Severn Bridge, was built 1961–6 (*see Gloucestershire: the Vale and Forest of Dean*). It is a suspension bridge of daring length and innovative structure – so much so, that it required major strengthening 1985–91.

* The two Bull engines in No. 2 engine house, in constant use until 1954, are now preserved in museums, one in the Welsh Industrial and Maritime Museum, Cardiff, the other in the Science Museum, London.

The second crossing was designed and constructed 1992–6 by *Sir William Halcrow & Partners* and the French firm of civil engineers *SEEE*. It carries the six-lane M4 motorway across the estuary a couple of miles further S, where it has widened significantly. Only the central section is a bridge, spanning the deep-water channel. Most of the length of 3$\frac{1}{4}$ m. (5.2 kilometres) consists of approach viaducts supported on reassuringly close-set concrete piers, their feet visible at low tide. The span of the central bridge, 1,495 ft (456 metres) long, is less than two-thirds the span of the Severn Bridge. On the other hand, the two H-shaped pylons from which it is suspended by fans of taut steel stays are, at 450 ft (137 metres), taller than those of its predecessor. A visual comparison between Bridge and Crossing, so easy to make from every direction, tempts one to contrast the almost reckless elegance of the former with the cautious substance of the latter.

4000 RAGLAN/RHAGLAN

It is the magnificent late medieval castle that makes Raglan famous. Church and village occupy a significantly lower position $\frac{1}{2}$ m. to the S.

ST CADOC. The most conspicuous part is the fine, tall C15 W tower; but the story begins in the chancel, where there are two early C14 S windows with cusped Y-tracery, moulded internally with a sunk chamfer. The nave, though Perp, also antedates the tower. One original N window, of three cinquefoiled lights under a square head and typical glazed spandrels. The rere-arches of the two large pointed-headed S windows are also old. S rood-stair projection. The S porch must be contemporary. It has a shafted, two-centred entrance arch, the outer order a deep continuous hollow, but the S doorway is by contrast of flattened four-centred profile, moulded with wave, hollow, wave. The tower is of four stages, set on a moulded plinth and crowned by moulded battlements and crocketed pinnacles. The W doorway and window over and two-light belfry openings are all to standard Perp designs. What make the tower unusual in this part of the world are its buttresses, diagonal where they stand free, dying back to become no more than raised strips up the top third of the tower, decorated with cusped panels. This last feature is most unusual, but closely resembles a feature in the castle: the decorated jambs of the windows at the rear of the gatehouse. They are thus datable to the 1460s, which may therefore be the date of the tower. Inside, the tower arch is tall and narrow, its two orders enriched with a sunk ovolo, the inner dying into the imposts high up.

The N chapel, the burial place of the lords of Raglan, can hardly be earlier than the second quarter of the C16, after the Somersets had inherited from the Herberts. The four-light, square-headed N (formerly E) window has merely arched lights, and the two-bay arcade is a debased version of the late medieval pattern, the central pier with four shafts and four hollows, carrying flattened four-centred arches moulded with wave, hollow and wave.

Everything else is of *T. H. Wyatt*'s restoration of 1867–8, the Dec E windows of chancel and chapel, the two-bay W-ward continuation of the chapel, the chancel arch, the wagon roofs and doubtless the internal scraping of the walls. – PULPIT. 1868, making use of the rood-loft stair and incorporating three medieval panels of blind tracery. – FONT. 1868 by *Wyatt*. Also a fragment of the C15 font, enough to show that it was a handsome piece, octagonal, with a shield-bearing demi-angel on each face and a top frieze of shields on quatrefoils. – STAINED GLASS. N chapel N. Heraldic, commemorating the military exploits of the first Lord Raglan. 1858 by *Mark Bowden & Co.* of Bristol. – N chapel E. With Beaufort heraldry, 1872. A rich amalgam of tinctured and mantled shields, grisaille quarries and patterned borders. Perhaps by *Clayton & Bell* (A. Brooks). – Chancel E. Adoration of the Shepherds, Crucifixion and Empty Tomb, with Ascension in the tracery. 1868 by *Lavers & Barraud*. – Tower W. SS Peter, John and Paul. 1875, also by *Lavers & Barraud*. – MONUMENTS. All that remain of the once imposing monuments of the Somerset Earls of Worcester after Parliamentarian vandalism in 1646 are three mutilated alabaster effigies huddled together under a fragment of alabaster cornice. They can be recognized as an armoured knight, a peer in garter robes and a woman, representing respectively the third Earl †1589, the fourth Earl †1628 and his wife.

In the CHURCHYARD, the three steps, the base and the stump of the shaft of a CROSS. The base is unusually fine, square turning octagonal by means of spurs, the N face ornamented with an elaborate blind niche, the other cardinal faces with encircled quatrefoils. Top chamfer dotted with flowers.

Until the realigned A40 bypassed it, Raglan was an important main-road village, midway between Monmouth and Abergavenny. Hence the group of inns in the village centre. The BEAUFORT ARMS, diagonally opposite the church, has a Tudoresque façade of *c.* 1840 and typical C17 rear centred on a projecting chimney-breast carrying lozenge stacks. Adjoining to the W, the SHIP INN, L-plan and also C17 in origin. Further W, the CROWN INN, its main three-bay front of C18 formality. CASTLE STREET, flanked by ranges of low white cottages, aims straight towards the castle, the intervening bypass and traffic hidden from view.

CASTLE

Raglan is the most spectacular blossom in the late flowering of castle construction in England and Wales during the C15, when flamboyant display was at least as important as practical considerations of defence. There may be tall, defensive residential towers of equal impressiveness at Tattershall, Caister or Ashby-de-la-Zouch, and gatehouses at least as splendid at Herstmonceux or Kirby Muxloe, but Raglan was unique in the C15 in having both these imposing features.

This makes it all the more tantalizing that virtually nothing is known about the building history of the castle. There is no licence to crenellate, nor even the most fragmentary building account. According to family tradition expressed in the C17 family chronicle, the *Herbertorum Prosapia*, the Great Tower was built by Sir William ap Thomas. He married the Raglan heiress, Elizabeth Bloet, in 1406, in 1432 acquired the freehold of the manor, with its fortified manor house, and died in 1445. This would seem to be confirmed by the poem in praise of ap Thomas by the Welsh bard Guto'r Glyn, where the tower standing above all other buildings is mentioned. William ap Thomas had fought in France under Henry V and subsequently held various official positions in South Wales, culminating in the chief stewardship of the Duke of York's Welsh estates in 1442–3.

There is no doubt that the great expansion of the castle, including the gatehouse, was the work of ap Thomas's son, Sir William Herbert. He too saw military service in France. He spent the 1450s building up his wealth in land and trade, and, supporting the Yorkist cause, was from 1461 one of Edward IV's closest lieutenants and enormously powerful throughout Wales. In 1465 the lordship of Raglan was created for him, and in 1468 he was raised to the peerage as Earl of Pembroke, only to be captured the following year at the Battle of Edgecote by Warwick 'the Kingmaker', and executed.

Tradition has, however, been challenged by Anthony Emery,* who has argued that the Great Tower was too grandiloquent a structure to have been erected by someone such as ap Thomas, of only local power, and that Herbert must have been responsible for both phases. This theory, flying in the face of family tradition, can be related to the two phases in William Herbert's later career, the 1450s and the 1460s. Until some new facts come to light it is impossible to adjudicate between tradition and counter-theory. Tradition is supported by the radical nature of the transformation of the castle's defences wrought in the second, 'gatehouse', phase of construction; but Emery's theory gains plausibility from the close similarity in style exhibited by all the C15 buildings, as will be pointed out in detail below.

In the later C16 the castle was sumptuously converted into a grandiose mansion by William Somerset, third Earl of Worcester, whose family had acquired Raglan by marriage at the beginning of the century. The third Earl inherited in 1549 and seems still to have been engaged in improvements shortly before his death in 1589, since Thomas Churchyard, writing in 1587, refers to 'Earle Worster living nowe, who buildeth up, the house of Raggland throwe'. Improvements undoubtedly continued under the fourth Earl (†1628) and the fifth Earl (created first Marquess).

It was the first Marquess, however, whose loyalty to Charles I and determination to resist the Parliamentary forces under Sir Thomas Fairfax led to the final tragic chapter, in which the castle proved unequal to the devices of C17 warfare. After its capture,

* *Archaeological Journal*, 1975.

Fairfax ordered the castle to be 'slighted', that is to say rendered unusable. In particular the Great Tower was undermined until one-third of it collapsed, and the gatehouse entrance was battered down.

Though confiscated by Cromwell, Raglan was recovered by the Somersets before the Restoration. Thereafter, the family, Dukes of Beaufort from 1682, established a new seat, at Badminton in Gloucestershire. What remained at Raglan of the roofs, stairs and other fittings was gradually removed, and there was clearly much further demolition and robbing of stonework. The fifth Duke, however, who succeeded in 1756, in an early recognition of the historic and aesthetic value of medieval ruins, forbade further pilfering, and efforts were made to stabilize what remained. Though still to this day the property of the Dukes of Beaufort, the castle has been since 1938 a monument in guardianship, and is now maintained and opened to the public by Cadw: Welsh Historic Monuments.

The BUILDING MATERIALS of Raglan Castle demand a paragraph to themselves. The facing stone used in all the C15 works is largely an extremely fine yellowish-grey sandstone, quarried at Redbrook in the Wye Valley about 8 m. (13 kilometres) away to the NE. It could be cut into close-jointed ashlar blocks, and its qualities gave the Great Tower its name of the Yellow Tower of Gwent. The Elizabethan building material was, by contrast, the locally abundant but far inferior mauve Old Red Sandstone, used as more or less coursed rubble for walling, but also occurring in blocks which could be cut to a smooth face, and even used for tracery (see the hall bay window). Red brick occurs earlier at Raglan than anywhere else in the county. It was used in the 1460s for remodelling the Great Tower and in a few other places, and it seems to have been used systematically as a lining material by the Earls of Worcester. The long-demolished Red Gate, still under construction in the 1640s, must have made a show of red brick.

The SITE of the castle is not naturally a strong one, but the ground drops away on all sides except the N, giving panoramic views. This is characteristic of the sites chosen for the earthen castles, mottes and ringworks thrown up at the end of the C11 or soon after, by or in response to the first Norman invaders of South Wales. There is every reason to believe that Raglan Castle originated as such an earthwork. The irregular plan of the present building must reflect not merely its two-stage development in the C15, but also constraints imposed by pre-existing structures. It is tempting to believe that the Great Tower stands on the site of a motte, and that the irregular rectangle enclosed by the other ranges perpetuates the shape of the bailey that went with it.

Raglan was granted to the Bloet family *c.* 1174, being then within the lordship of Usk. Slight references to their house here survive in documents of the C14, in particular accounts of 1375 which list repairs to the hall, the lord's chamber, and its garderobe. Fragments of late C13 tiles found on site and identical to tiles found at Tintern Abbey suggest that the Bloets had long had a chapel too. It is reasonable to suppose that the Bloet house consisted of a hall range set between two courts, and that it conditioned the layout of the residential nucleus throughout all the subsequent aggrandizement.

THE FIRST PHASE OF WORKS IN THE C15 (whether by ap Thomas *c.* 1435–45, or by Herbert after 1450), consisted of the construction of the rectangular SOUTH GATE, a fortifiable entry
42 into the S corner of the SW courtyard of the Bloet house, and, *c.* 70 ft (21 metres) away to the SW, the huge, free-standing hexagonal GREAT TOWER, fitted as a residence five storeys high and surrounded by a broad moat, so that it could be reached from the house only over a drawbridge. This combination of moderate house and mighty keep-like residential tower is comparable to Ralph, Lord Cromwell's Tattershall Castle, Lincolnshire, of *c.* 1430–50, though the Great Tower at Raglan is much the more genuinely defensible of the two, as one would expect in the border region of South Wales. It clearly betrays familiarity with the local tradition of free-standing keep towers (though circular not hexagonal) built in the C13, of which Tretower and Bronllys, in Powys, and probably the long-gone tower at Monmouth, provided suitable models. The hall was probably built or reconstructed in this phase.

THE SECOND C15 PHASE, that of Sir William Herbert at the pinnacle of his wealth and influence, *c.* 1461–9, involved a comprehensive improvement and enlargement which rendered the recent works largely useless or embarrassing. The South Gate was replaced as the entrance to the castle by a new, much stronger and more
43 displayful GATEHOUSE to the NE. This gave access to the hall range from the opposite side and thus involved a major reorientation of the castle. A range of sumptuously decorated state apartments was constructed to the SW of the new gatehouse, between the upper end of the hall and the moat of the Great Tower. A new fixed bridge was constructed to link them with the apartments in the Great Tower, and the Great Tower itself was surrounded by a platform with lobed angle projections on which cannon could be mounted. Further APARTMENT RANGES were built round the SW court, incorporating the South Gate. The two main sets of apartments to the SW were approached by means of an exceptionally impressive central staircase. At the angles of the NE courtyard two further, very strongly constructed hexagonal towers were sited, that to the E, the CLOSET TOWER, providing residential accommodation adjoining the gatehouse, that to the N fitted up as a mighty KITCHEN TOWER. The office range between them was subsequently rebuilt, and only the lines of its foundations are known. But to the W of the Kitchen Tower Herbert's works came to a sudden stop, dramatically visible in a change in walling here. Of the rooms in the hall range, all that can confidently be attributed to Herbert is the reconstruction of the CHAPEL.

THE THIRD EARL OF WORCESTER'S ELIZABETHAN RECONSTRUCTION transformed the castle into a mansion where hordes of retainers still had their place, enabling the Earl to entertain on a lavish scale, but defensibility gave way to enjoyment of the site and the views. Thus the hall was thoroughly remodelled in traditional form, and all the service rooms, except the kitchen in its tower, were rebuilt to match. The chapel range alongside the hall was heightened and extended towards the NW, so that a long gallery of 126 ft (38.4 metres) formed its top storey, ending in a great polygonal bay glazed with lofty windows on all sides, looking towards the shapely mountains of north Monmouthshire. Far below, the sloping ground was formed into two long, broad terraces, with an elaborate water garden in the valley bottom.

Further embellishment in the early C17 was on a more modest scale. The moat was made pleasurable by means of a walk round its outer edge and a series of shell-lined niches sunk into the retaining wall. Two ornamental outer gateways were added, one the White Gate, stone-faced, the other, the Red Gate, of brick and still under construction at the time of the siege and slighting of the castle. This has now entirely disappeared.

Other long-lost features of Raglan Castle are recorded in a memorandum of 1674, written by someone who had known the castle before the Civil War. He recalls the 'artificial Water Work' in the moat, which 'spouted up water to ye height of ye Castle', and in the middle of the SW court the 'pleasant marble fountain ... called ye White horse, continually running with clear water.' The South Gate led to a bowling green 260 ft (80 metres) long and thence to the gardens (*see* below, p. 510).

PERAMBULATION

Exterior

The present approach to the castle from the SE corresponds with the direction of approach ever since the 1460s. By walking round the perimeter of the castle it is possible to understand the three main phases of construction and the ways in which first the orientation and then the function of the castle were rethought. On entering through the gatehouse, however, and exploring the courtyards and the ranges which surround them, one will be most aware of the Elizabethan mansion and the way in which the Earls of Worcester incorporated the Herbert castle into it.

Entry into the castle enclosure is through the WHITE GATE, where the roadway spans a shallow ditch revetted with a wall on its inner side. The gate was a typical late C16 or early C17 ornamental structure, though sadly little survives of it, just one jamb and springer of the four-centred entrance arch, a shell-headed niche to the r. of it, and the lower storey of a half-hexagonal turret. Though trifling in comparison with what is to come, the gate self-consciously anticipates the gatehouse beyond, in its use of a hexagonal plan and in its greenish ashlar. Note the thinness of the facing slabs, suggesting that such stone was by then hard to come by, and the internal lining of red brick, typical of the last phase of building.

The White Gate is aligned on the gatehouse, but this is a work of the second C15 phase, so instead of examining it next, one should concentrate first on the GREAT TOWER. As explained above, the exact date of the Great Tower in the mid C15 is controversial, but whatever the date, it was the Great Tower which

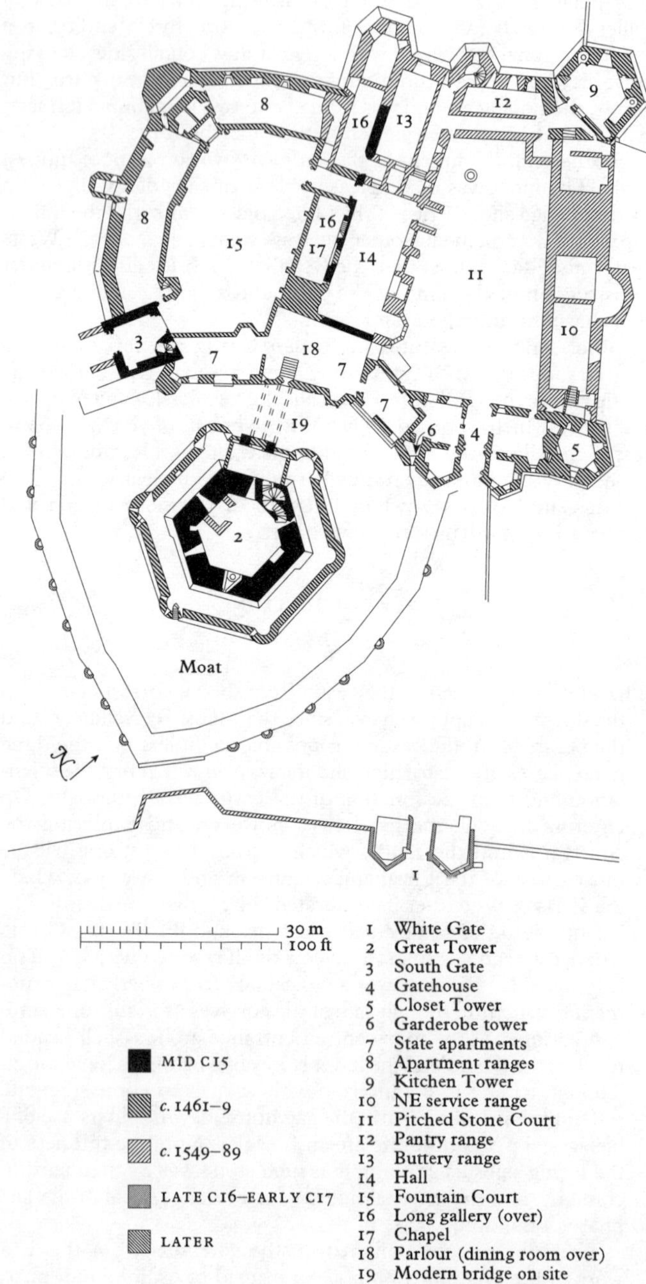

Raglan Castle. Plan

established the architectural character of the castle. In plan it is hexagonal, in height it is four-storeyed, though the C17 description says it had a fifth. The ragged top to the tower and the great rent which has entirely removed two of its sides are the result of deliberate destruction in 1646. However, one is still impressed by the beautiful fabric of the smooth, close-jointed ashlar with which the tower is faced. Only the battered base is constructed of random masonry. The lowest storey is made defensible with a lobed cross-slit in the centre of each face, with a gunloop immediately below (except on the E face). One more cross-slit, higher up on the W face. Otherwise, the walls are irregularly pierced with small windows, one-lighters and, in the upper half, the occasional two-lighter, their rectangular frames moulded with recessed wave and chamfer, the lights cinquefoiled.

The traces on the NW face of the remarkable double drawbridge, which was originally the only link between the Great Tower and the rest of the castle, are best examined close up from within the castle (*see* below, p. 508). But it should be noted now that these drawbridges were of bascule, or counterpoise, type, regularly used in France, but uncommon on this side of the Channel. Whoever built the Great Tower, Sir William ap Thomas or Sir William Herbert, would have seen such bridges while campaigning in France. Herbert even went so far as to adopt, in or before 1451, a stylized representation of a bascule bridge as a personal badge, as can be seen elsewhere on the castle (*see* below, p. 498) and on the parochial aisle at Usk priory church.

The interior of the Great Tower can be glimpsed through the great gap caused by the collapse of the N and NE facets of its wall. Though details cannot be made out from a distance, it is clear that each storey consisted of one large, well-appointed room. The tier of doorways to a garderobe at each level in the S angle is particularly clearly visible. (*See* further below, p. 509.)

Surrounding the Great Tower, and covering much of its battered base, is a hexagonal platform with a circular turret projecting from each angle. Its use of squared ashlar blocks of yellowish-grey sandstone – see a single course remaining in places at the top of the turrets, and a larger area as the NW wall face – relates it to parts of the castle built by Sir William Herbert in the 1460s. He must have decided that the gunloops in the tower were ineffective, and constructed the platform in order to replace them. The walls of the platform and its turrets, when complete, would have blocked the line of fire of the gunloops. The turrets have cross-slits but no gunloops, so it is probable, as Arnold Taylor has suggested, that the platform was intended to support cannon, which could thus be used more freely and efficiently than when mounted within the walls of the Great Tower. The SW turret is provided with a garderobe, and the S turret with steps and an externally rebated doorway, for access to the moat.

The outer wall surrounding the moat to the E and S was probably constructed in the early C17, in connection with a moatside promenade. The brick-backed niches in the wall are undoubtedly of that date. The C17 eyewitness tells us that they were originally lined with shell-work and occupied by figures of Roman emperors. Traces of the shell-work in the niches can still be seen.

The SOUTH GATE must be examined next. It was built in the first campaign, contemporary with the Great Tower, as its masonry and window details show. Externally it is plain and utilitarian, a mere rectangle in plan. The entrance arch is two-centred with a simple chamfer, and has a superarch with tall, vertical imposts which would have accommodated a drawbridge when raised. Evidence for a portcullis too. The entrance is off-centre, and a single-light window above to the r. lights an upper room. Inside, the reason for this displacement is clear. The entrance passage gave an immediate impression of splendour; it was fan-vaulted in two bays, as the surviving springers show. But its E wall was opened up by a chamfered arch, a bay-and-a-half wide, its head trickily related to the vault springer. A fireplace in the SE angle suggests that a porter was stationed here. In the NE corner a newel stair ascends to the upper room, and enough of its upper flight survives to show that it continued to the roof. But nothing more remains of the top of the South Gate, except the jamb of what must have been a large window lighting the upper room at its inner end.

So much for the mid-C15 work. In order to examine Sir William Herbert's great remodelling in the 1460s, it is necessary to return past the Great Tower and approach the GATEHOUSE. This, with the CLOSET TOWER close beside to the r., and the sumptuous STATE APARTMENT range angling away behind the Great Tower to the l., must when intact have given an extraordinary impression, menacing and luxurious together. The ashlar walls of yellow-grey sandstone are constructed with at least as much precision as in the Great Tower phase. There is even one improvement in quality, for the battered base is now not rubble-faced, but of squared blocks, in narrower courses than in the walling above. The single-light windows in gatehouse and Closet Tower imitate those of the earlier work, but have merely a sunk hollow moulding, making their modelling within the wall more abrupt.

The GATEHOUSE is of the twin-tower variety, and is consciously related to the design of the Great Tower, in that the towers are hexagonal in plan, and so present not a flat face but a sharp angle to the front. In the centre of each forward face, single-light windows at three levels. For defence low down, gunloops are arrayed, one in every face within the batter at basement level, and another at ground level. For defence high up, the towers have elaborate machicolated battlements. Deep, arcaded corbelling sets the battlements boldly proud of the tower tops. Heads, human or animal, project at every angle above the corbelling (every other one forming a drainage gargoyle). Enough remains of the battlements to show that they were all pierced with cross-slits. Such heavily crowned towers were typical of French late medieval castle-building. The most damaged part of the gatehouse is the entrance bay itself. Enough remains, however, for the defensive arrangements to be understood, the full panoply of conventional devices. Outermost is what survives of the rectangular recess for the drawbridge when drawn up, completely covering the entrance. Of the outer entrance arch, only the jambs survive, shafted with polygonal caps, and the springing of a four-centred arch. Behind the jambs come the grooves down which a portcullis could be lowered, and more gunloops, cut through the portcullis grooves. Note the spyholes l. and r. The inner entrance arch is intact, four-centred and moulded with a hollow and two waves. Above, part of the vault of the portcullis chamber can be seen, but the front wall at this level has been wrenched away, so that one can only study the stumps still remaining against the towers in order to deduce what was there. It seems as if the portcullis chamber was lit by a row of windows matching the one-lighters in the towers. Above must have run a deeply corbelled walkway with machicolated battlements, matching those crowning the towers.

The CLOSET TOWER, one bay to the r. of the gatehouse, was built at the same time. Its gunloops, single-light windows, and great corbelled crown all match those of the gatehouse towers, but the structure itself is broader and slightly lower, forming a strong termination to the castle at its eastern corner.

Round the E corner, the C15 service range has been completely reconstructed, so one should turn back to the gatehouse and examine the range of STATE APARTMENTS beyond it. These too are identical in build to the gatehouse, but since they extend round behind the Great Tower, their walls rising direct from the waters of the moat, it was clearly felt that they needed no further defensive protection. In particular, their windows could open into expansive bays, even if the view from them was curtailed a mere 30 ft (9 metres) away by the mass of the Great Tower.

The polygonal addition to the l. of the gatehouse is a GARDEROBE TOWER, as the chute at water level shows. It is two-storeyed, and its windows are uniform with those in the gatehouse. It even has gunloops below the lower windows, so the desire to disguise its function went to considerable lengths.

The STATE APARTMENT RANGE, originally two-storeyed throughout, has been either demolished or sadly damaged, so that not one of its exotic windows remains intact, and much has to be deduced from the merest fragments. There were two two-bay ranges, the bridge to the Great Tower spanning from the further bay of the second, and beyond that a third, also of two bays, ending in a second, much smaller garderobe turret butted up against the South Gate. From end to end the walls rose sheer from the moat, and it is down at this level, the only level where the masonry is intact, that the design can be most clearly understood. The windows were arranged in shallow projections, as their masonry supports at moat level indicate. The outer wall of the E third stands largely intact for its full two storeys, and there is even one battlement, pierced with a cross-slit. Of the windows, however, only the upper ones retain cut stonework. They were tall, transomed, with square heads and cusped upper lights.

The r. window is of two lights, set on a compartmented dado and flanked by flat, pinnacled shafts. The l. window was of four
46 lights, brought slightly forward as a shallow bay, with similar pinnacled side shafts. In four deep compartments in a band above the window are carved alternately the Herbert emblem of the bascule bridge and a curvaceous ribbed shield, presumably once tinctured with the Herbert arms. In a second band above, at battlement level, the same motifs are repeated on a smaller scale. These windows seem to have lit bedrooms. The principal parlour and great chamber above were in the adjoining range, next to the bridge to the Great Tower. Here all that remains is a full-height stump of the E end of the outer wall. It includes the moulded and shafted jamb of an even more elaborate two-storey window arrangement. The window lighting the great chamber had two transoms, and above it ran an elaborate moulding decorated with a crumpled ribbon. Sir William Herbert's bridge to the Great Tower, replacing the bascule bridges of the first build, was fixed and of stone and brick (*see* p. 508, below). The present elegant stone bridge was constructed in 1957.

Beyond the South Gate extends the faceted outer wall of the APARTMENT RANGES which enclosed the SW court (Fountain Court). The fabric and the details proclaim that all this was further work carried out in the 1460s for Sir William Herbert. Immediately W of the South Gate little survives above basement level. Then comes a deep, semi-octagonal garderobe turret, furnished with arrow slits and gunloops to cover the flanking walls. After this the outer walls survive almost to full height, on either side of a big, semi-hexagonal tower, in which the great stair rises (*see* below, p. 506). Single-light windows at both levels for the apartments. The tower walls are unpierced except for functional arrow slits and gunloops covering the flanking walls, and, at a slightly higher level in the two outermost faces, cross-slits which can have had no more than a symbolic function.

49 Next, on the NW side of the castle, above the great grassed terraces, there is a sudden change. Yellow-grey sandstone ashlar gives way abruptly to purplish Old Red Sandstone rubble. This, then, is the third Earl of Worcester's later C16 work taking over from Sir William Herbert's. Two mighty polygonal projections push forward, the lower half of their walls extravagantly flared, with between them a short stretch of straight wall. This is a dramatic and, one feels, somewhat extempore device to increase the extent of the service accommodation. Single-light and two-light cusped-headed windows at two levels in the flare and one above it to light various service rooms. Drain outlets at the foot of the straight wall. The E projection houses a full-height newel stair, with single-light windows at four levels in its outer face. The tops of the W projection and the intermediate wall are, by contrast, opened up with a glorious expanse of mullion-and-transom windows. These are constructed of Bath stone, contrasting in colour with the walling, and are delicately moulded with a hollow and roll outlining each light. Originally the windows in the W projection, which lit the end of the long gallery, were of

four lights and so tall that they required two transoms. In the straight wall beyond, a matching six-light window, but less tall, so it has only one transom. All the lights, as in the gallery windows, are straight-headed, unlike the cusped heads elsewhere. This window must have lit another important chamber in the topmost range. Below it, quite large mullioned windows at two levels, a five-lighter over a three-lighter, with trefoiled lights.

Part-way along the straight wall further N the Old Red Sandstone of the Earl of Worcester's work gives way again to the ochre ashlar of Herbert. Single-light windows in both parts. Then at once Herbert's great hexagonal KITCHEN TOWER, retained by Worcester. Here the facing ashlar of the battered base has been largely robbed away. Above, single-light windows and gunloops at two levels, in the storey above slightly larger single-light windows, and in the top stage windows of two and three lights, suggesting that there were living rooms at the top of the Kitchen Tower. The furthest, E, face of the tower is extensively patched in brick, either an original feature, to absorb the heat from the great hearth within, or evidence of post-Civil War industrial activity in this part of the castle.

The NE RANGE, joining the Kitchen Tower in a straight line to the Closet Tower, was entirely rebuilt in the C16, in Old Red Sandstone, ashlar in the battered base, rubble above. Gaping holes show where the dressed stonework of windows has been robbed. In the centre, a half-hexagonal projection, also of C16 construction, but reusing parts of gunloops half-way up. Square-headed single-light windows at two upper levels.

Interior of the Gatehouse Range

One should enter the castle through the GATEHOUSE. So far only its outer entrance arch has been examined. This opens into a rectangular space, originally vaulted on corner shafts with polygonal capitals. The vault supported the portcullis room. On the inner side, a further pair of finely moulded four-centred arches, with portcullis groove between and rebate for doors, making an identical repetition of the external system of defences. Within the range which backs on to the gatehouse there remains evidence of two more vaulted bays of similar design. The central vault support on the E side cuts across a wide depressed arch, the head of which was clearly adapted to take it. The back of the arch, however, is rebated for double doors, which must have closed on to the vault shaft. Pentagonal porter's lodges in the gatehouse towers, one provided with a fireplace. The lodges open into large, much-altered, rectangular rooms l. and r. of the vaulted entrance passage. The E room gives access to the interior of the CLOSET TOWER. Here, uniquely for Raglan, the doorways have bull-nosed mouldings. The jambs of the doorway to the tunnel-vaulted cellar have been gouged out to allow the passage of barrels. Outer and inner doorways to the ground-floor room. This is lit by four single-light windows and has a fireplace and garderobe. Similarly fitted upper room. So this was a fully habitable tower, which may have been intended for the use of Sir William Herbert's resident steward.

The room W of the entrance passage has been much altered, but was originally an important one. From its SW corner a newel stair ascends to a three-room apartment on the first floor overlooking the courtyard. The three rooms were lit by the row of six large, close-set windows which will shortly be examined from outside, the first room by three windows, the second by two, the third by one.

Buildings around the Pitched Stone Court

It is time, then, to emerge from the gatehouse range into the NE courtyard, commonly called the PITCHED STONE COURT. The court takes it name from its strongly convex cobbled surface, which allows rainwater to drain off into channels. This is the C16 surface, and C15 cobbling has been found underneath. The court is trapezoidal in shape and long for its breadth. Before the C16 rebuilding of the office range which enclosed it on the NW it was even narrower. The site of Sir William Herbert's office range can be easily seen from the traces it has left against the inner faces of the Closet Tower and the wall to its r.

The most impressive survival of Sir William Herbert's work of the 1460s in the Pitched Stone Court is the rear of the gatehouse range, ashlar-faced and set on a moulded plinth. The archway at the inner end of the entrance passage matches those in the gatehouse itself. In the wall to the W of it, two windows, both very damaged, but once handsome. They were clearly flanked by shafts which terminated in pinnacles, and must have been similar to windows in the state apartment facing the moat. Across the centre of the upper storey of the range is the sequence of six large and well-preserved windows mentioned above. They are closely set, rectangular, of vertical proportions. The tops and bottoms of their frames are formed by the moulded stringcourses which run right across the façade. The faces of the narrow jambs which divide them are decorated with sunk, trefoil-ended panels, a pretty motif. The low top storey of the range, of Old Red Sandstone, and with windows of two or three square-headed lights, is clearly an addition by the third Earl of Worcester, who must also have reconstructed the battlements. Patching at the SW end of the range, to arrest structural movement, has made it difficult to understand the original arrangement here. The three head corbels may have been reset.

The other three ranges of the Pitched Stone Court all belong to the third Earl of Worcester's thorough remodelling. On the l. is the hall, occupying two-thirds of the SW range, but the rest of that range, the short NW end, and the NE range were all devoted to the extensive service rooms required by the Earl's numerous household and lavish entertaining. The service arrangements can be examined first, and then the hall.

The NE SERVICE RANGE is very ruined, its inner wall demolished all the way along. The stretch of outer wall adjoining the

Closet Tower is also down to foundation level, but a drain in the floor and outlet in the thickness of the outer wall show that the ground-floor room was devoted to some wet function, perhaps the brewery – adjoining the cellar where, as noted above, barrels were stored. The rest of the range preserves its outer wall almost to full height, first as a half-hexagonal projection, then running straight to the Kitchen Tower. The projection must have accommodated the bakehouse, as there is a very large bow-backed hearth here flanked by ovens. The hearth has three draught-holes, formed partly from the reused gunloops noted outside. Square-headed upper windows show that there were two storeys of servants' lodgings above. The rest of the range was subdivided into three rooms at ground level, the middle one provided with a fireplace flanked by ovens, the furthest with a wide cooking hearth. Evidence of further servants' lodgings above. Note the use here of brick to line hearths and in the reveals of windows.

Next comes Sir William Herbert's KITCHEN TOWER, set back from the angle of the court and originally visible from it only above the courtyard ranges. Much remains here that demonstrates the scale of lordly cooking. But first the entrances in the outer wall must be noted, and the fact that the walling, because originally internal, is of Old Red Sandstone rubble. There are three entrances, all with chamfered four-centred heads. The very prominent one at an upper level linked upper rooms in the now demolished Herbert office range with the rooms in the upper half of the Kitchen Tower. The doorway in line below opens on to a flight of steps to the wet larder in the basement. The basement has a rubble vault, cupboards in its inner walls and, in its two outer walls, trefoil-headed lancets with gunloops below.

The third entrance, a low, four-centred, chamfered arch rather than a doorway, links the kitchen itself with the passage to the hall. Within the arch is a triangular servery area. From it a doorway, quite richly moulded with wave and hollow, though low and narrow, opens into the kitchen. Beside the doorway, a wide serving hatch, broadly hollow-moulded. The KITCHEN itself is pentagonal, and had mighty hearths to W and E, each provided with an oven. The cut stonework of the W fireplace has been robbed, but there remains the gunloop, at the back of the hearth, the most glaringly useless of all these gunloops of dubious usefulness. To the l., a drain and single-light window. The E fireplace, however, remains intact. The opening is about 12 ft (3.7 metres) wide, its segmental lintel formed of two great stones. Drains on both sides here. The two N walls of the kitchen are pierced with wide four-centred-headed lancets and gunloops below. The kitchen was groin-vaulted – see the rubble-stone springing of the vault. The vault is not high, so that the kitchen when in use must have been a hot, uncomfortable place.

The upper storey of the Kitchen Tower was divided into two well-appointed chambers. Twin two-centred-headed doorways in the SW corner. The S room has lost its fireplace, but retains its windows, a three-lighter with cinquefoiled lights oddly placed over a single-lighter, and a garderobe. In the N room the moulded jambs of the fireplace remain, flanked by two-light cinquefoiled windows with seats, to take advantage of the glorious view.

The PANTRY RANGE running SW from the Kitchen Tower has the beginning of its outer wall with one single-light window in a stub of C15 work. Otherwise the range is entirely the Earl of Worcester's, part of what must have been an enormous expansion and upgrading of the areas for storing food and drink. Only the external wall survives, nearly to its full height. The range has a now inaccessible basement lit by one N window, and three storeys above it, with a passage in the thickness of the wall at the top level. Newel stair at its SW end, for access to the upper storeys. The footings of the inner walls of the range show that the pantry was flanked by a fairly narrow passage, which formed the vital route of access from the kitchen to the hall.

The BUTTERY RANGE, at r.-angles to the pantry range and extending as far as the screens passage of the hall, is much larger and more completely preserved. Some of the Earl of Worcester's private and state rooms lay in two storeys above it, so the range requires examination storey by storey. The wall towards the Pitched Stone Court largely survives, with external moulded plinth and, at ground-floor level to light the passage, three single-light windows with cusped, depressed heads. The passage extended not only towards the hall, but also a short way in the other direction to the foot of the spiral stair in the pantry range. Only the lowest flight of the stair survives, down to a cellar under the buttery. The buttery itself occupied the full length of the centre of the range at ground level. The surviving barred window at its NW end, of three trefoiled lights, must have been its only direct source of illumination. At the SE end of the range are three wide doorways with depressed segmental heads, one at the end of the passage, two opening from the buttery. Steps up within them lead to small square vestibule areas, their dividing walls now gone, from which there was direct access to the screens passage. Service passage and buttery each has its doorway into the screens passage, and in the middle is the buttery serving hatch.

Above the buttery there were two storeys of apartments. At first-floor level were two rooms belonging to the private apartment. One was lit by two large windows facing the Pitched Stone Court, their cut stonework now largely robbed away. The other room was lit by the four-light window with cusped lights in the NW wall overlooking the garden. The doorway into the former room, four-centred and double-wave-moulded, survives, and so does its chimneypiece with flattened arched head and continuous hollow and roll on moulded bases. The latter room has a simpler fireplace, with chamfer and wave moulding. As these descriptions suggest, the third Earl of Worcester continued to use a late Perp idiom in his new work, as we shall see again, more strikingly, in the hall.

In the state apartment on the top storey, however, the third Earl employed an up-to-date classicizing style. This change of style coincides with a change of material, from local Old Red Sandstone to imported Bath stone. The many-light windows overlooking the garden have already been noted. Within the buttery range, the two state rooms both retain intact Bath stone chimneypieces, their sunk-chamfered frames incised with repeated pairs of dashes, their moulded cornices set, one over a fluted frieze, the other over a frieze decorated with interlocking spurred circles. The room overlooking the Pitched Stone Court also retains its ovolo-moulded window of two-plus-two square-headed lights with a transom. (For the long gallery to their SW, *see* below, p. 504.)

The Hall

To complete the circuit of the Pitched Stone Court, it remains to look at the HALL. This must first be examined from the court itself, where its outer wall remains virtually intact. Its traditional character is remarkable, late medieval in almost every respect. The moulded plinth is carried on from the buttery range, but here is ashlar-faced. The porch which gives entry to the screens passage has an entrance arch of flattened profile, decidedly Tudor in character, moulded with a small wave. Porch rooms in two storeys above, both lit by three-light windows with flattened cusped lights. The fenestration of the hall itself is oddly complicated. First come two (renewed) four-light windows with two transoms and cusped top lights, separated from one another by a full-height buttress. Then there is a deep projection for the fireplace, and a large window above it. Finally there is the great polygonal dais window, of three-plus-two-plus-three lights and no fewer than four transoms. Here too the topmost heads are cusped.

The interior reveals more. The inner porch arch is bolder than the outer, of four-centred profile, double-wave-moulded. The same shape and moulding on a smaller scale is used for the passage arch and buttery hatch where they open into the screens passage. Of the timber screen there is, of course, no trace. Doorway in the wall above, giving access to the gallery over the screen, and two-light spy window into the hall above that. The hall fireplace is simple enough, its jambs moulded with wave and hollow, but the segmental lintel is formed of plain voussoir stones, just like the rere-arches of the windows. Doubtless all this was originally hidden by a decorative timber chimneypiece. It is worth looking into the hearth, to see the way the chimney flue splits and goes up on either side of the window above. The dais wall is faced with ashlar. Set into it is a large square panel of Bath stone bearing in relief the arms of the third Earl as a Knight of the Garter, an honour he received in 1570. Above, in the gable, the frame of a four-light, transomed window, and the profile of the former timber roof, which was clearly of hammerbeam construction. Stone corbels projecting from high in the side walls show where the wall-posts of the roof trusses rested.

The other (SW) long wall of the hall clearly antedates the Earl of Worcester's construction and was incorporated into it. Blocked, segment-headed rere-arches of two large windows. The SW doorway of the screens passage, which led to an outer porch, is large, of two-centred profile, and is plainly chamfered. It must surely belong to the first phase of C15 work. Furthermore, its rere-arch voussoirs match those of the blocked windows, so the entire SW wall of the hall must be mid-C15, if not earlier. The great scale of the pre-Worcester hall is further indicated at the dais end. Here, in the SE end wall at the back of the ashlar facing, and thus invisible from the dais itself, is a blocked doorway opening towards the parlour. That seems to establish that the hall had reached its full length before the third Earl of Worcester reconstructed it.

The part-surviving recess and doorway at the SW end of the dais are best left for consideration a little later (*see* below, p. 505).

Buildings around the Fountain Court

The FOUNTAIN COURT (named from a marble fountain called 'The White Horse', mentioned in 1587) is reached through the SW doorway in the screens passage. The court itself was constructed by Sir William Herbert in the 1460s, but from it one can see the rest of the third Earl of Worcester's private and state apartments. On passing from the screens passage through the SW doorway, one finds oneself on the site of a second hall porch. In its NW wall was a doorway opening into an entry running alongside the building. At its far end survives a four-centred chamfered arch at the foot of a newel stair. This stair, with its lining of Old Red Sandstone shale, was either new-built or drastically reconstructed by the third Earl of Worcester. It provided access to his private apartments at first-floor level of the three-storey range, which ran parallel with the Buttery Range to end in the great polygonal projection noted from outside. The interior of this range, now that much of its SW side wall has gone, can be seen from Fountain Court. At ground level was a room lit by a two-light N window. In the private apartment above there remains a fireplace and a three-light N window. The details of all these features are typical of the third Earl of Worcester's traditionalist work. The top storey, however, has more classicizing detail in Bath stone. Here was the LONG GALLERY. The interior of its canted, multi-light window was provided with a stone seat supported on scroll-shaped corbels, several of which remain. The other special feature of this room
50 was the chimneypiece. Only one end of it survives, but it is enough to show that the fireplace opening was square-headed within a gadrooned frame, and that paired full-length flanking figures, one male, one female, carried a deep entablature. The two surviving figures, hung with chains of flowers, are copied

from a plate in Hugues Sambin's *La Diversité des termes*, published in Dijon in 1572.* Geometrical decoration on the frieze and on the blocking course above. Doubtless the chimneypiece once supported an elaborate timber overmantel. The original length of the long gallery is recorded to have been 126 ft (38.4 metres).

Underneath the S end of the long gallery lay the CHAPEL. This must have been built in the 1460s, as it blocks the two hall windows which are suggested to be mid-C15. The chapel was quite small, as the footings of its buttressed outer wall make clear. All that survives of it above ground level is visible in and against the SW wall of the hall, against which it was built. The springing of the two E bays of a four-centred rib vault is readily recognizable as of C15 date, the wall ribs brought down on to handsome, well-preserved bearded heads. The shallow recess in the wall face below the l. bay has been interpreted as housing for high-backed stalls. Further W the wall is more drastically cut back to accommodate a flight of steps rising from E to W. They must have gone up to a pew or closet at the W end of the chapel. In order to fit in this stair and closet, the rest of the stone vault must have been removed, which suggests that they were a work of the Earl of Worcester, related to the construction of the long gallery immediately above. In the NE corner of the chapel is a small barred window looking into the hall. Immediately beside it, the stub of the E wall of the chapel, stone below, brick above, and preserving at the top the jamb of the doorway into the end of the long gallery.

Beyond the SE end of the chapel is the rubble foundation of a large rectangular structure, through which a modern flight of steps has been constructed to the C15 doorway, which gives access to a cellar under the parlour. The rubble foundation, which must originally have sealed off access to the cellar, is most likely to have supported a new great stair, constructed by the third Earl of Worcester, rising from the dais end of the hall to give access to the Herbert state apartments, and also to the new long gallery. The way from the hall to the foot of the stair must have been through the unexpectedly lowly, four-centred-headed doorway which partly survives in a recess at the SW end of the dais (as noted above, p. 504).

That exhausts the C16 works, and it is time to survey what remains of the C15 FOUNTAIN COURT. This was one of Sir William Herbert's finest creations, yet it is one of the most tantalizing parts of the castle. Just enough survives to show that the ranges of apartments here were sumptuously decorated, yet their inner walls have almost all been demolished virtually to ground level. The original splendour must be deduced from the few surviving fragments. First of all, one should look at the meagre traces of the porch which covered the SW doorway of the screens passage, and from which there must have been entry into the chapel. The bottom of one of its outer jambs shows that

*As demonstrated in his collected essays (1999) by Sir Howard Colvin, who owns the third Earl of Worcester's marked-up copy of this book.

it was framed by a composition including a major and a minor shaft. The GREAT STAIR, which originally faced the S porch across the Fountain Court, had a similar arch to the porch, which is now only slightly less ruined. Here the hexagonal bases of the major shafts both survive, but nothing more. Between them, however, the wide, four-centred-headed arch is intact, moulded with hollow, roll, hollow, and originally having decorated spandrels. A broad horizontal frieze above is carved with a curling scroll, its upper moulding defining the sill of an extremely large upper window, now no more than a gaping socket. All this, then, formed a two-storey porch, intended to give access and illumination to an imposing stair within. The stair, its steps much broken, starts to rise in a wide, straight flight of five steps. Then come two four-centred doorways, to l. and r., which opened into the ground-floor apartments. Beyond the doorways, dwarf walls providing handrails narrowed the rest of the flight somewhat. At the top, a further pair of doorways into the upper apartments, and in the centre of the canted ashlar back wall, a narrow, triple-chamfered doorway. This opened only into the windowless top storey of the tower behind. The entire back wall is spanned by a giant, chamfered relieving arch, which must have supported the rear end of the staircase roof. Although straight flights of stairs in lodging ranges are not unknown in other late medieval houses (e.g. Haddon Hall, Eltham Palace), the staircase here must have had a spaciousness and grandeur hard to parallel in C15 England. Once again inspiration may have come from France, where staircases were given ceremonial importance, and designed accordingly.

The layout of the two-storeyed APARTMENT RANGES can be deduced in some detail. They were distributed, as has already been noted, on both sides of the great stair, which provided access to them. Of their inner walls virtually nothing survives above the (robbed) plinth. Near the centre of each range was a slightly projecting window bay. To judge by the one surviving upper-window jamb, hollow-moulded and shafted, S of the staircase, the inward-facing windows were tall, broad and handsome. The outer wall of the NE apartment range, however, is almost intact. It had two rooms at each level, each provided with a single-light window and a fireplace. The lower apartments were, as normal, the less elaborately treated. Chamfered rere-arches to the windows, and double-wave-moulded fireplace jambs. Above, the window rere-arches are wave-moulded, the four-centred fireplace surrounds outlined with a roll on moulded bases within a rectangular wave-moulded frame. The third Earl of Worcester's remodelling of the newel stair at the NE end has encroached on the window of the upper apartment. Underneath the great stair there is space for storage rooms entered from the apartments, and in the tower behind, garderobes, also entered from the apartments. The turret to the S (as noted above, p. 497) provided further such facilities.

At the S end, adjoining the South Gate, is the fragmentary polygonal stair-turret which served the southern apartments.

Next to it, at the end of the upper S apartment is a precious survival, an intact single-light window which provides further 44–
evidence for the design of the fenestration towards the Fountain 45
Court. It is square-headed, with panel tracery in the head. Its outer face is framed by a hollow chamfer and a roll moulding, and is set under a hood resting on a miniature figure in an elegant pose. The interior of this little window is equally exquisite, its rere-arch shafted, its four-centred head moulded with a fillet and leaf spandrels. Of the stair-turret enough survives to show that it gave access to both storeys of the apartment range from an external doorway at the back of the South Gate. Here are the springers of three close-set ribs, handsomely moulded with hollow, roll, deep hollow and wave. They rest on the sadly indecipherable remains of carved limestone corbels. What the ribs supported must have been an arch – see the remains of its rubble core – supporting an external balcony across the back of the pre-existing South Gate, directly linking at first-floor level the apartment ranges that have just been examined with the state apartment facing the Great Tower. The doorway from the upper apartment in the Fountain Court on to the balcony survives.

The STATE APARTMENT RANGE is, as has already been noted, a ghost of its former splendour. Enough remains to show how its SW end was built up against the NE corner of the South Gate, with a doorway cut through to link with the newel stair within the gate. The polygonal garderobe turret added against the gate has also been noted. Of the two-storeyed range which occupied the SE end of the Fountain Court, all too little remains. Moulded plinth robbed out. The lower room not only had access to the garderobe turret and the newel stair in the South Gate, but footings show that the room was splendidly illuminated from a bay window facing Fountain Court and a wide, deep-set window towards the moat. The fireplace opposite the former and beside the latter survives, of red ashlar, its rectangular frame double-wave-moulded. Beyond lay the room identified in the C17 description as the PARLOUR, with the DINING ROOM (i.e. great chamber) above. The main upstanding feature in the parlour is the approach to the bridge to the Great Tower. This will be considered below (p. 508). Of the two-storey window bay overlooking the moat, which lit both rooms from near the NE corner, there is nothing left to see from inside except the panelled embrasure and stumps of two transoms of the upper window. The C17 description records the rich decoration of the parlour with 'fair Inlayd WAINSCOTTE, and curious carved figures'. Beyond the parlour the Herbert state apartments extended further along the moat, with one lower and one upper room. The remains of their externally splendid windows have been described above (p. 497). Inside, the lower room retains its handsome chimneypiece with cusp-ended panels on the jambs. Originally, it is clear, there was no access from this room into the gatehouse range beyond, so the state apartment ended here.

The Great Tower

That leaves one further area to explore, the INTERIOR OF THE GREAT TOWER, the exterior of which was discussed right at the beginning. The justification for this procedure is that the interior of the Great Tower remained in use by the Earls of Worcester, and the bridge to it opened out of the parlour. Before embarking on description, it is worth recalling that the Great Tower itself was constructed in the first mid-C15 phase, but that its timber bascule bridges were replaced by Sir William Herbert in the 1460s with a fixed stone bridge. So it was already at that time acknowledged that the Great Tower was to be seen no longer as a stronghold that could be isolated from the rest of the castle, but as a great, self-contained extension of the lord's residence, accessible directly from the state apartment. The Earls of Worcester continued to use the Great Tower in the way Sir William Herbert had envisaged.

In the parlour a modern flight of steps leads up to the doorway to Sir William Herbert's fixed bridge. The doorway has a depressed four-centred head and is decorated with a wave mould. A second, largely robbed aperture in line above it, and to the r., the remains of a newel stair lit at two levels by square-headed cinquefoiled lights, typical of the 1460s work. This arrangement has been interpreted as the approach to a two-storeyed bridge, but it seems more likely that the upper opening was a window, and the stair provided access to this vantage point over the end of a bridge of normal design.

The present bridge of 1957 utilizes the springers of the 1460s bridge, and towards the Great Tower masks a substructure of two dates. Down at moat level are the twin masonry piers on which rested the fixed part of the original timber bridge. They are embedded in the base of a forebuilding which was constructed in the 1460s, in connection with the replacement stone bridge, but which has otherwise disappeared. On the face of the Great Tower above the bridge is an at first sight bewildering palimpsest of grooves and apertures. Close inspection, however, can make sense of them. First, there are the sockets for the timber bascule bridges (*see* above, p. 495) when in the raised position. Most conspicuous are the long vertical slots which housed the beams extending from the bridge platforms. The central pair was for the main bridge, the braced singleton to the r. for the pedestrian bridge. When the bascule bridges were removed, the sockets were filled with brick blocking, most of which has since fallen out. The socket for the pedestrian bridge itself has been much cut through by later apertures, but its shape is easily discerned. The socket for the main bridge platform, on the other hand, is still partly filled in, but it is possible to trace its complete outline, and also part of the arch through which the platform pivoted when being raised or lowered. The row of corbels above the arch presumably supported the end of the bridge. The rectangular aperture between the beam sockets for the main bridge must belong to this first period, but has been enlarged. It is cut through by a narrow horizontal groove extending almost the full width of the wall face. This is the crease-line of the roof of the forebuilding added in the 1460s. The forebuilding was altogether three storeys high, the lowest at the level of the springing of the bridge. Its middle storey opened into the Great Tower through the perfectly preserved central doorway inserted into the lower half of the main platform socket. This has the depressed four-centred head and generous mouldings, two broad waves in this case, typical of the 1460s campaign. A pair of plain doorways were cut through from the Great Tower into the top storey of the forebuilding. The l. one is intact, the r. one, which was set into the socket of the pedestrian platform, has lost all its cut stonework.

The INTERIOR of the GREAT TOWER is arranged as a sequence of large hexagonal rooms stacked one above another, and reached from a broad newel stair beyond a two-centred doorway immediately to the l. of the entrance from the bridge. The area immediately opposite the bridge was originally a lobby into which the bascule bridges pivoted, and its subsequent rearrangement, with brick-lined recesses, may be of the 1460s, after the fixed bridge freed this space for other uses.

The newel stair can be descended and ascended to all levels. The bottom flight was modified to give access to a doorway, cut through the wall in the 1460s when the platform was constructed round the base of the Great Tower. The brick lining of the door jambs is particularly clear evidence that brick was being freely used in the 1460s. Outside, from the platform, the stone piers supporting the NW end of the bascule bridges can be seen, and brick infill and vault springing of the 1460s, incorporating them into the structure of the fixed bridge.

Inside the Great Tower there remains evidence that the cellar was fitted up as a kitchen. The chamfered jambs of its fireplace survive, and a well in the embrasure of a gunloop. No windows down here, but the cross-slits and gunloops will have provided a fair amount of light. The cobbled floor is modern. Stone corbels for the beams of the timber floor above. The remains of a large stone-walled enclosure may be what is left of the third Earl of Worcester's strong room, which he is said to have had in the Great Tower. The room at entrance level has single-light windows in two faces, provided with seats in their broadly splayed embrasures. The square-headed fireplace opening is plainly chamfered, and there is a garderobe. The chamber above is a little more richly treated. The fireplace opening is moulded with a deep hollow and has shafted jambs. One of the windows is of two lights, so at this level internal comfort was considered as important as defensibility. Evidence that the Earls of Worcester still continued to use this room for pleasure is in the pair of brick-backed niches inserted above the seats in the embrasure of a S-facing window. The top surviving storey is much damaged. A two-light window up here too. This no doubt was a bedchamber.

The Gardens

The bowling green, 260 ft (80 metres) long, lay SW of the South Gate. Charles I, who visited Raglan in 1645, is said to have much appreciated it, not least for its wide view, from Abergavenny to Chepstow. The terraces no less long at three levels to the NW of the castle are now of mown grass from end to end. (Slight traces of stone revetment walls with central projecting bay, and footings of a brick summer-house.) In the valley bottom to the N a marshy area is all that remains of the Great Pool. Traces of a geometrical water garden at its NE end.

CIVIL WAR EARTHWORKS. When in the summer of 1646 the first Marquess and his garrison of 800 men were besieged by a Parliamentary force under Sir Thomas Fairfax, both sides naturally threw up earthworks. Mounding in the fields on both sides of the present car park is what remains of the bastions constructed on the orders of the Marquess to protect the vulnerable SE and W approaches to the castle. The Parliamentarians' pentagonal gun emplacement, 340 yds (310 metres) ENE of the castle, can also be made out. It was from here that their guns shot at and destroyed the cannon mounted on the tops of the castle towers.

CASTLE FARM, 100 yds E of the castle. A most remarkable front of red brick with stone dressings, seven bays long, the seventh cut through by a segment-headed cart arch. It must be the sole survivor of the 'stables, & barns lately built, like unto a small Town' before the Civil War, as recalled in the memorandum of 1674. The probable date then is the 1630s, and the use of exposed brick here is only the logical extension of the use of so much internal brickwork in the castle over the preceding two centuries. The brick is laid in an indeterminate bond, but has its decorative use in the serrated upper stringcourse, where the bricks are laid at an angle. Stone lower stringcourse. Two-light, chamfered, mullioned stone windows, those above intact, those below much altered and enlarged. Two stone door-cases. That in bay two has a four-centred head in a square surround and roll and wave mouldings which suggest that it is a reused C15 piece from the castle. That in bay five has a simple depressed arch and wave moulding. Central ridgetop chimneystack, its shafts unfortunately rebuilt in reduced form. Inside nothing to see except one plain massive fireplace, imposts and lintel just three monoliths. Brick wall and relieving arch over.

THE WARRAGE, 1¼ m. NE. Fine farmyard range at the roadside, of pink and brown Old Red Sandstone rubble, consisting of a five-bay barn, probably of the C17, with flanking byre and cider mill. Early C19 red brick cartsheds to the N.

CEFN MAEN, 2½ m. SW. Typical later C16 two-unit house of two storeys, later extended by one bay at the E entrance end, the typical development. Outside, two upper sunk-chamfered N windows remain. Inside, the original entrance doorway has a plain arched timber head, the hall fireplace is set beside it, and beyond that, a twisting mural stair with timber treads. The hall ceiling has chamfered beams and chamfered joists with diagonal stops. The post-and-panel partition between hall and inner unheated room has been removed, but its fellow upstairs still remains. The posts are chamfered only towards the major room. Plain arch-headed doorway.

The Pant, 1¾ m. sw. Modernized stone cottage. But inside the w half Fox and Raglan found two intact cruck trusses. Extended to the E in the late C16, with the usual addition of an entry and third room behind the hall hearth.

REDWICK *4080*

St Thomas. One of the finest among the churches of the Levels. It is largely built of local pinkish-grey limestone with ochre Triassic sandstone dressings. The plan is unusual (but cf. Magor), a central tower between Dec chancel and nave with Perp clerestory, lean-to aisles and lofty S porch. Restored by *John Norton* in 1874–5. The lowest stage of the tower is clearly the earliest part of the church, as its SE and NE quoins descending below the line of the chancel eaves make clear. The top two stages are Perp, faced with Triassic sandstone ashlar, each having one two-light window in each direction, traceried under a pointed head, those in the middle stage blind. Top battlements and angle pinnacles.

The chancel E window is a most extraordinary feature (but *see* Caldicot, Rogiet), expressive of Dec fantasy. Of three lights, the reticulated ogee tracery dictating the wavy profile of the arched head. The snake-like hoodmould emphasizes the eccentric outline. Run-of-the-mill Dec N window, but square-headed Perp windows on the S side, the SE one very large, of three lights in a deep hollow reveal. Minuscule priest's doorway.

The nave, of three bays, is quite low, the windows of the aisles and clerestory square-headed, of two lights, except the three-light E window of the N aisle, with cinquefoiled hexagons in the tracery and a pointed head trimmed by the eaves, as if a parapet has been removed. N doorway with plain chamfer. The W wall of nave and aisles rebuilt by *Norton*, resetting a worn sandstone doorway in the centre. This was once a handsome piece, its two hollow mouldings enriched with square flowers. Springers above, apparently crouching beasts to carry a canopy. Showpiece S porch, clearly an addition, its ashlar outer face restored in 1875. Bold base moulding, diagonal buttresses dying in below the panelled and battlemented parapet (cf. the tower parapet at Peterstone). The entrance archway, two-centred-headed, has a hood on big worn heads, is continuously moulded with step, hollow, wave, and has a panelled soffit. Inside, the S doorway is of the same shape, with continuous quadrant and hollow. Defaced image niche above and defaced head corbels to carry the roof trusses.

The interior shows that the nave was built and the tower remodelled in the early C14, probably contemporary with the chancel. Three-bay arcades on octagonal piers with moulded caps and double-chamfered arches. The clerestory to N and S rests on a corbel table, confirming that it is an addition. Unusually many C14 and C15 recesses in various places. Stoup by the S door under a shaped head. In the S wall of the S aisle, a trefoil-headed piscina which must have gone out of use when the stair and doorway were inserted beside it for a rood screen the full width of nave and aisles. Also an image niche in the E wall here, with multicusped head, and another, mutilated, on the E respond of the S arcade. On the E respond of the N arcade, a piscina, and in the N aisle E wall quite a fine C14 niche, cusped with leaf crockets and ill-defined finial. The W and E tower arches were enlarged in the early C14, though they are still quite low. Splayed arches of two chamfered orders, the inner dying into the imposts of the outer. Note the big, badly worn head corbel where the SE impost had for some reason to be cut back. The chancel is whitewashed and brightly lit by the windows on three sides of the sanctuary. A piscina here too, under a trefoil head. The roofs are by *Norton*, that in the nave quite elaborate, with tie-beams and pseudo wall-plates decorated with pierced quatrefoils. His, too, the tiled floors throughout, two full-width, widely spaced steps forming a gentle ascent through tower and chancel. – FONT. C13. Square bowl with scalloped underside on four octagonal shafts and circular central pier. Broad, waterholding foot. Heavily retooled in the C19. – IMMERSION FONT. Screened off at the W end of the S aisle, clearly part of *Norton*'s remodelling. – PULPIT and CHOIR STALLS. Also by *Norton*, but nothing special. – ROOD LOFT. The loft itself is a reconstruction of 1948, the standards and rail original, but the bressumer a steel replacement. The diagonally set corner posts and cusped spandrels which support it, however, are late medieval. The posts are enriched with deep multi-layered panels with cusped heads and crocketed finials. Loose length of vine trail on a window-sill in the N aisle. One can only imagine the magnificence of the screen and loft which these tantalizing fragments indicate. – STAINED GLASS. Chancel E, Nativity, Crucifixion and Empty Tomb, scenes forming a band with C13-style grisaille-work above and below. 1875 by *Lavers, Barraud & Westlake*.

In the SE corner of the CHURCHYARD, the worn base and part of the shaft of a WAYSIDE CROSS, originally standing *c.* 200 yds (183 metres) away on the road to Whitson.

The church stands at the centre of the loosely clustered village. At the churchyard gate, a cottagey SCHOOL of 1846, extended 1886, and an Arts and Crafts style CIDER PRESS AND BUS SHELTER, built of stone and concrete, to the design of *Hubert Jones* of Redwick, as late as *c.* 1975. Mill wheels and other objects of local historical significance are sheltered here. Also, not under cover, the village STOCKS.

BRICK HOUSE FARM, ¼m. NW. Big, bald early C19 farmhouse, built of pink brick. Of seven slightly uneven bays and three storeys, framed by massive rectangular chimneystacks. Segment-headed sash windows, with keystones. Entrance doorway in bay five.

RISCA 2090

Risca, with its suburbs Pontymister to the SE and Cross Keys and Pontywaun to the NW, spreads along the bottom of the lower Ebbw Valley for over 3 m. (5 kilometres). First collieries, from the late C18, then brickworks from the mid 1830s and tinplate works from 1843, all contributed to its growth. After 1880 Captain P. S. Phillips took over the tinplate works and converted it to steel-making. This was combined in 1897 with the Britannia Foundry at Pontymister to form the Monmouthshire Steel and Tinplate Works. Today traces of heavy industry are hard to find. Though later C20 housing has colonized the steep lower slopes of the enclosing hills, their rounded tops remain green, planted with sweeping conifer woods.

ST MARY, Church Road. The dominant building in the town, erected 1851–3 by *W. G. & E. Habershon* to replace the medieval church. The demolition of the medieval church in 1852 revealed part of a circular wall of *c.* 12 ft (3.7 metres) radius with a tile and concrete floor, which may have been part of a Roman building. In a self-confident, if somewhat heavy-handed Dec style. Nave and lean-to aisles, S porch, and chancel with emphatically buttressed S tower and spire. Flowing tracery throughout, in the paired aisle windows, in the four-light E window, and in the five-light W window, where cusped mouchettes seem to be leaping about like salmon. The interior is quite stately, with arch-braced roofs on stone corbels, three-bay nave arcades with steeply pointed arches on circular piers, and a dramatically lofty chancel arch. – REREDOS. Of *c.* 1883, to commemorate a medical man, hence the relief of the Good Samaritan. – PULPIT. Polygonal, of stone, with red marble shafting, stiff-leaf foliage and figures of the four Doctors of the Church. Probably of the 1890s. – STAINED GLASS. In the chancel arresting abstract designs by *Celtic Studios*, the S and two N windows of 1969, the E window of 1990. Quite outside their normal scope. – S aisle SW, Ruth and Boaz, Christ Walking on the Water. A pair *c.* 1890, probably by *Joseph Bell & Son* (A. Brooks). – S aisle W. Miracles of Christ. The only survivor of the original glass of *c.* 1852. Not of good quality, if typical of the date.

ST MARGARET, Pontymister. 1910–11 by *S. H. Hutchings*. Nave and lower chancel. Fantastic Geometrical E and W tracery patterns of encircled, multicusped quatrefoils.

BETHANY ENGLISH BAPTIST CHURCH, Tredegar Street. Built 1857–8 by *W. G. & E. Habershon*, given a new façade in 1875 and greatly extended backwards. The façade is of grey Pennant sandstone with dressings of buff Ebbw Vale brick. Polygonal stair projections, dying back below the gable, flank a porch with paired arched doorways. A pair of arched windows above. Within, the lower half of the Habershons' rendered façade survives. The interior is unusually long for its width and height, the result of the extension of the original three bays by a further four. Galleries on all four sides, supported on thin iron piers with foliage caps.

The SCHOOLROOMS behind remain remarkably unaltered.

The main hall is surrounded on three sides by rooms with sliding partition fronts. Further rooms at an upper level are separated from the hall merely by curtains.

MORIAH WELSH BAPTIST CHURCH, St Mary's Street. Dated 1893. Large. The entrance front is an ambitious Lombardic design, executed in snecked, hammerdressed local brown stone and caramel ashlar. Shafted triple window over the gabled porch in a central bay defined by panel-topped strips. Two-storeyed, polygonally ended stair-turrets project sideways to l. and r. The interior is spectacular, short but high. The galleries have bowed and richly pierced metal fronts carried round all four sides and canted at the entrance end. Fluted shafts with floral caps. The ceiling has a boarded central flat on a deep plaster cove. Permanently exposed baptistery below the pulpit. Yawning arch above and behind for an organ. Extensions of the 1980s at the back.

GWENT TERTIARY COLLEGE, Cross Keys, 1 m. NW. The successor to the Crumlin School of Mines. By *Monmouthshire County Architect's Department*, c. 1956–61, when *Colin Jones* was County Architect. This is one of the department's rare commissions for tertiary education buildings, so a more emphatic gesture than usual has been attempted. The entrance block has a symmetrical end towards the road, with copper-clad pedimental gable, and brown vertically boarded walls, in the centre of which an enormous window frames the entrance doorway. To the r., the brown boarded hall, with a single large window front and back and an asymmetrically curved roof. At the back, two more characteristic classroom ranges, three-storeyed under shallow pitched roofs, with windows in continuous bands.

COUNTY PRIMARY SCHOOL, Danygraig Road. 1991–3, by *Gwent County Architect's Department*, design architect *Kim Cooper*. Quite out of the normal run of late C20 primary schools, in its formality and in its vocabulary. The small rectangular site visible on all sides must have dictated the compact plan. Towards Danygraig Road the high, convex-roofed hall pushes forward its pale rendered bulk, flanked by low brown brick ranges under monopitch roofs. The inconspicuous main entrance is in one of these. Further back, flanking two-storey classroom ranges, festooned with sea-green metal porch-pergolas. At the rear the high central element reappears, here rendered pink, with a two-storey metal balcony from which the playground can be surveyed. Windows of three sizes regularly disposed complete the sense that this is a building where nothing has been left to chance.

POLICE STATION, Tredegar Street. 1892 by *William Tanner*, the County Surveyor. Red brick striped with yellow, more eye-catching than normal for the police.

COLLIERS WORKMEN'S INSTITUTE, Tredegar Street. 1915 by *R. L. Roberts* of Abercarn. Red brick and grey Forest stone. Porch tower.

GARDEN SUBURB, Pontywaun, 1½ m. NW. About sixty semi-detached houses, built c. 1918–22 to the designs of *Walter Rosser*, at the expense of the Ebbw Vale Steel, Iron and Coal Company for the managers and officials of the Abercarn, Cwmcarn and Prince of Wales collieries. A convincing demonstration of the Parker & Unwin garden suburb style, ringing the changes resourcefully on exposed sandstone and rendered walls, grey slated and red tiled roofs, gables and hips, canted bays and bows. Simple hillside layout of two straight culs-de-sac opening from THE CIRCLE in the centre, where the houses are set in four canted groups.

TWMBARLWM, $1\frac{1}{2}$m. N (ST 243 925). The medieval MOTTE, visible for miles around, stands on the rampart of a large PREHISTORIC ENCLOSURE. The single bank and ditch ringing the top of the hill is probably unfinished since there is a wide gap at the W end.

VIADUCT, $\frac{1}{4}$m. S of St Mary's Church. Sadly, only part of the E abutment survives of the thirty-two-arch viaduct constructed 1802–5 by *John Hodgkinson* to carry a horse-worked railway across the floodplain of the Ebbw River. Squared Pennant sandstone masonry of fine quality.

NANT CARN CANAL AQUEDUCT, Pontywaun (ST 220 930). Built in the mid 1790s to take the Crumlin arm of the Monmouthshire Canal. The canal engineer was *Thomas Dadford jun.*

ROCKFIELD *4010*

ST CENEDLON. A good group as seen from the E, chancel with N vestry under a catslide roof, higher nave and N aisle under a longer catslide roof, and square, timber-topped tower behind. S porch. Only the tower is medieval, a Border type. Unbuttressed, the windows mere slits. C19 Perp W window. The top stage has close-set uprights under a slated roofslope supporting the belfry. Timber louvres and slated pyramid cap. The rest is of 1859–60 by *Prichard & Seddon*, replacing a Perp church with a Dec one. The interior has several typical touches. N arcade piers with Early French stiff-leaf caps. Nave roof with principal rafters carried on naturalistic flower corbels. Wind-braces. Characteristic chancel arch and tower arch, the chamfers dying into the imposts. Many painted inscriptions of 1860. – FITTINGS mainly by *Prichard & Seddon*. – FONT. Simple. Octagonal, with spurred quatrefoils on the faces. – PULPIT. Elaborate. Of stone, carved with a dove and naturalistic flowers and foliage, waterlily, ivy, oak, on a cusped and shafted base. – ALTAR RAILS and CHANCEL SCREEN. Of iron, presumably by *Prichard & Seddon*. – SCREEN FRAGMENTS, in the vestry. Small sections of vine-trail frieze and traceried panels from a late medieval rood screen. – ROYAL ARMS. Of William III, dated 1700. Painted on panel. – STAINED GLASS. Two chancel S windows, a pair of *c.* 1868. One is typological, Crucifixion and its Old Testament prefiguration Moses and the Brazen Serpent; the other eucharistic, with wheat, grapes and chalice. – Chancel E, *c.* 1900. Resurrection, the terrified soldiers in a Germanic, early C16 style. Coloration typical of *Burlison & Grylls*. – Tower W, Suffer the Little Children,

1889, clearly by *Hardman* (A. Brooks). – N aisle, three by *Powell's*, 1930.

In the CHURCHYARD, a CROSS of 1865 on three medieval steps. – LYCHGATE. By *Seddon*, 1877, a display of simple carpentry structure.

Former SCHOOL, on the brow of the hill SE of the church. Small, single-storeyed, of local stone, built in 1845. The front elevation, with a projecting window towards the road, under a white, coved cornice, is probably a remodelling by *Aston Webb c.* 1900.

PENTWYN, above the church to the N. Much-altered Tudoresque villa, of three dates, largely by *G. V. Maddox* of Monmouth, *c.* 1834–7 for himself, an addition to an earlier house, and partly after 1864 for the parson, the Rev. John Harding.

ALMSHOUSES, ½ m. SE, beside the B4233. 1906 by *Aston Webb* for Lord Llangattock of The Hendre. Pretty, symmetrical, single-storey range, of local Old Red Sandstone, part mauve part grey, and black-and-white half-timbering. Tudor detail, but ball-topped, shaped gables at the centre and ends. Note the rail-back seats for the four inmates and their visitors.

The dark grey stone GATE LODGE, immediately to the N, guards the entrance to the 2-m. (3-kilometre) drive to The Hendre (*see* p. 247). Stepped gables, and single-storey bow windows in three directions. It is by *T. H. Wyatt c.* 1850. GATEPIERS and arcade-topped wall clearly later, probably by *Aston Webb*.

SWISS LODGE, ¼ m. into the park, is by *Aston Webb*, 1905. A sweet little thing, single-storeyed, but not particularly Swiss.

The VICARAGE and the TERRACE at the crossroads at the centre of the village, brick below and half-timbered above, are presumably Rolls estate housing *c.* 1900, though not, it seems, by Webb.

ROCKFIELD PARK, ¾ m. NE. Early C19 white villa, of three bays and two storeys under a high and steep hipped roof with dormers. The lower windows are tripartite sashes of inordinate size, the porch between them Ionic, with four attached columns, the central pair carrying a pediment.

2080 ROGERSTONE/TŶ-DU

ST JOHN THE BAPTIST, St John's Crescent. 1887–8 by *E. A. Johnson* of Abergavenny. Dec. Nave and lower chancel, the W end towards the road made into something of a composition. SW porch, N vestry. Rock-faced grey Pennant sandstone with Bath stone dressings, on a plinth of mauve Old Red Sandstone. Inside, the wide nave is covered by an elaborate arch-braced roof, formed so that major and minor semicircular trusses carry kingposts. – STAINED GLASS. Chancel E, Christ appearing to the Magdalen. By *Heaton, Butler & Bayne*, the date 1935, astonishingly late for such highly elaborated sentimentality. – Nave S, St John the Baptist and Virgin and Child, 1952 by *Celtic Studios*. – Nave W, scenes from the life of Christ. 1965 by *R. W. Coomber* for *Wippell & Co.* Another elaborate piece, this one typical of its date. – Chancel S, Good Shepherd. 1950. Chancel N, Christ the King surrounded by flames and holding a miner's lamp. 1964. These also by *Wippell & Co.*, the former signed by *A. F. Erridge*.

ST BASIL AND ST GWLADYS (R.C.), Tregwilym Road. 1892 by *W. B. Gardner*. Small and unfinished, of coursed rubble Pennant sandstone with Bath stone bands and dressings. Lancets and trefoiled lancets. The memorable feature is the composition towards the road of the transept-cum-vestry with image niche and bell gable.

BETHESDA BAPTIST CHURCH, Bethesda Place. 1995–6 by *Biscoe Craig Hall*, design partner *Martin Heijne*. The mauve brick polygon under a black-slated pyramid roof with glazed apex looks at first sight a conventional essay in participatory worship space. But there is subtlety here, in the masked full-height slit windows so set as to convert the essentially square plan into a pentagon. Inside, beyond the glazed porch and low foyer, a pure, lofty, light-filled space opens up. The plan here is a square rotated through 45 degrees, under a steep, irregularly octagonal roof, its alternatingly wide and narrow faces clad in pale boarding. Exposed buff brick walls. Panelled timber composition behind the minister's seat.

WESLEYAN METHODIST CHAPEL, Tregwilym Road. Secularized. 1906 by *W. H. Scott* of Cardiff. Pennant sandstone. Flat, steeply gabled front towards the road. Lancets.

PRIMARY SCHOOL, Tregwilym Road. Disused. Built for the Rogerstone and Henllys School Board in 1888 by *E. A. Lansdowne*. Single-storeyed with a lively array of stepped gables. Rock-faced Pennant sandstone with red brick dressings.

PUBLIC LIBRARY, Tregwilym Road. 1905 by *Swash & Bain*. A neat little classical front, a bullseye in the gable. Rock-faced Pennant sandstone with Bath stone dressings. Appended to the l., a single-storey porch with another bullseye.

HOUSING, Oak Road. By *Powell, Alport & Partners*, *c.* 1970–1. The staggered lines of the terraces, monopitch roofs and areas of boarding are typical of the date. Also three-storeyed blocks for old people. Brown and buff bricks.

ALUMINIUM WORKS, Tregwilym Road. Offices for the Northern Aluminium Company, designed in 1949 by *Richard Sheppard & Partners*. The long, rectangular administration block faces the road, the doorway central, the three storeys of windows in continuous bands. So a piece of no-nonsense Modernism, but nothing special.

THE FOURTEEN LOCKS, ¾ m. E. All the valley canals of South Wales had flights of locks, but none so spectacular as this one. It gives a rise of 168 ft (51 metres) in half a mile, on the Crumlin arm of the Monmouthshire Canal. The flight was constructed as part of the canal dug 1792–9, to the design of *Thomas Dadford jun.* It has been re-watered, but the locks are now gateless. They, their extensive side-ponds and a broad sheet of water on the canal line at the top level have been laid out for public display. The locks are not true staircase locks, but are grouped in pairs with short intervening pounds. They also have long picturesque sheets of water at the side. These open through segmental arches in the aprons of the upper of each pair of locks, the top three to the NE, the bottom three to the SW. They consist of unusually deep masonry chambers, as can be seen in one lock which has been cleaned down to its masonry invert arch, a common form of floor-strengthening but one not normally visible.

Half-way down on the E side, a single rubble-built LIMEKILN of the normal Monmouthshire type.

YNYSFRO RESERVOIRS, ½ m. N of the Fourteen Locks. Two small C19 water-supply reservoirs for Newport, the upper (Old Pool) earlier than the lower (New Pool).

BRONZE AGE CAIRN, 2 m. NW. A small cairn 30–40 ft (10–13 metres) across and almost 3 ft (1 metre) high, survives in the centre of a field (ST 255 906) at Ty-sign, just above the housing. From here the contemporary cairns of Machen ridge (*see* Lower Machen) can be seen outlined against the sky.

4080 ROGIET

The church stands in a farm group away from modern housing development. A few feet to the W, the large stone FARMHOUSE, and across the yard to the N an outbuilding with timber-mullioned windows and a large C17 or C18 BARN with ventilation slits.

ST MARY. The tall W tower, very short nave with S porch, and longer, lower chancel create a memorable profile. The chancel is Dec, a minor member of the local group (cf. Redwick, Caldicot) which have cusped reticulated tracery forming a wavy outline to the window head, as here in the three-light E window. Ogee-headed S and N lancets. Local yellow Triassic stone dressings, as for the other buildings in the group. The tower is dressed with Triassic stone too, but is not so easy to date. The nobly high but narrow arch which opens into the nave has square imposts and two chamfered orders dying in far up. That looks C14. External details however are Perp in character. Diagonal buttresses dying in very low down. Depressed-headed W doorway with continuous wave, hollow and wave. Simple mid-height stringcourse, corbelled battlements and pinnacles. Small belfry windows of two square-headed trefoiled lights without hood-mould. The tower's appearance of height is emphasized by the sheer, square SE stair-turret crowned by an odd octagonal, conical-topped cap. The nave is Perp, its shortness due to rebuilding of an early nave after the construction of chancel and tower. Square-headed S window of two trefoiled lights under a hood-mould. Two-centred S doorway with continuous hollow and wave. The round-headed outer arch of the S porch, with small continuous mouldings, is also characteristic of local late medieval work. Discreet lean-to N aisle and vestry added in 1903 by *Seddon & Carter*.

Inside, the arcade of 1903 is unexpectedly decorative. The

heavy arch-braced roofs in chancel and nave are also of that date. Plain chamfered chancel arch, perhaps of the C14. Ogee-headed stoup. C15 doorway to the rood-loft stair. – FONT. Probably of the C12. Circular bowl on a thick circular stem. – PULPIT. Of timber. 1903 by *Seddon & Carter*. With Art Nouveau overtones. The relief figure of a Pre-Raphaelite woman represents the Virgin Mary. – STAINED GLASS. Chancel E, Virgin and Child between Sower and Good Shepherd. 1930 by *Arnold Robinson* of *Joseph Bell & Son*. An attractive piece. – N aisle N, Adoration of the Shepherds, 1961, and Feed my Sheep, 1966, both by *Celtic Studios*. – Nave S, Suffer the Little Children, 1966 by the same. – N aisle W, Annunciation. 1981 by *Geoffrey Robinson*. – MONUMENT. Brass plaque to commemorate the Severn Tunnel railway works. 1987, designed by *R. Earnshaw*.

WINDMILL, ½m. N. Just a circular stone tower. A date as early as the C16 has been suggested.

The HOUSING ½m. NE, on the B4245 and in IFTON ROAD, short red brick terraces with gables sweeping out at their feet, was built for Chepstow Rural District Council 1920–2 by *Eric Francis*. Many minor alterations have compromised its character.

ST ARVANS

5090

ST ARVAN. The S wall of the chancel is Norman, as the narrow priest's door indicates. Slab lintel on imposts, the l. one decorated all over with Xs in boxes and blobs in the spaces. Paired lancets further E. All this is of Old Red Sandstone. Small W tower, square with chamfered angles, called 'modern' in 1840. Chancel E and N walls, N vestry and three-bay aisled nave all of 1883–4 by *John Prichard*. Dec with eccentricities. Wide, low aisles, extra lighting from prominent timber dormers, and strange rhomboidal three-light W windows, their form echoing the roof-line. Prichard had medieval authority for these at Mitchel Troy, a church he had restored a decade before. Quite a spacious interior, the arcade piers with continuous mouldings, a wave and a broad chamfer. Chancel arch on short wall-shafts with leaf sprig corbels. Prichard's wagon roof in the chancel and celure over the sanctuary have been recently brightly repainted. – FONT. Octagonal stone bowl on red mottled marble shafts. By *Prichard*? – STAINED GLASS. Chancel E, Crucifixion, 1932 by *Horace Wilkinson*. – S aisle W. Nunc Dimittis. 1947, signed by *A. L. Wilkinson*. – N aisle, two N windows signed by *Alan Younger*, one dated 1994. Their ambiguous, near-abstract colourism is in thought-provoking contrast to the Comper-inspired clarity and narrative obviousness of the earlier windows. – MONUMENTS. Cross shaft (N aisle W window-sill). The regularly disposed interlace suggests a C10 date. Part of the encircled cross-head survives. – Figure of a lady or civilian (S aisle W window-sill). Worn and headless. Of the C14 or C15. – John Bainbridge †1844. Grecian tablet, signed by *T. Tyley* of Bristol.

The village has been much enlarged in recent decades.

MEMORIAL HALL, ¼m. SE, beside the A466. By *Eric Francis* of Chepstow, 1923–4. Neat and simple with one witty twist, still in Arts and Crafts mood. Big gabled roof, walls of grey local stone with slate details. Mullion-and-transom timber windows. Symmetrical front towards the road, centred on a large, square window. The symmetry is upset by the gabled entrance porch pushed across to the r. as far as it will go. Doorway in its side wall, giving place to a run of blind balustrading under the timber-boarded gable. Down the side, regularly spaced windows. Later extension at the back.

Also at the S end of the village the TURNPIKE COTTAGE of *c.* 1822, two-storeyed, canted towards the road to give the keeper a good view both ways. Sash windows under hoodmoulds. The eye-catching little FOUNTAIN of 1893 at the road junction is of cast iron. Dolphins twisted round the central stem and water-pouring boys. Cast at the Sun Foundry, Glasgow, and supplied to the County Council by The Iron Stores Co. Chepstow, as can be read on its base.

WYNDCLIFFE COURT, ½m. NE. Dated 1922 on rainwater heads. The architect was *Eric Francis* of Chepstow. Cotswold Tudor style, relaxed and sophisticated, as the architect, still under the spell of his master, Guy Dawber, exploited his experience working for H. Avray Tipping (*see* Mounton). Built of snecked squared local stone, the mullion-and-transom windows of timber with leaded lights. The N entrance front is low, broad and not quite symmetrical, the hooded doorway the only decoration. To the S the ground drops, and here, above a terraced garden, the façade is taller and tauter, the symmetry of the forward-projecting centre emphasized by pedimented gablet, ball finials and other touches of decoration. Lying back to the l., a short gable-ended wing with an oriel window facing W. To the r., a two-bay Doric loggia and service wing behind. Axially below the house, a pool under a hemispherical ashlar niche with dolphin keystone. Sunk garden aligned on the W front, with stone summer-house at the SW angle. The interior is less coherent, dominated by a huge panelled drawing room occupying two-thirds of the centre of the house. Plaster ceiling with high-relief vine and hop trails, designed by the client, *Charles Lee Clay*.

GOLDEN HILL, 1½m. S. Also by *Eric Francis*, built in 1924 for Miss Edith Clay. Little more than a cottage, though graced with a two-storey porch. Another exemplary essay in the Arts and Crafts use of stone and timber, with a touch of red brick in the soffit of the porch arch.

On axis to the S, HUNTING STABLES and groom's COTTAGE, the latter, completed by 1919, given quirky, ogee-topped semi-dormers.

ROMAN REMAINS. Building debris at Wyndcliffe (ST 528 975) suggests the probable site of a Roman building.

ST BRIDES NETHERWENT 4080

ST BRIDGET. Alone in its walled churchyard, approached across a field. The low saddleback-roofed W tower is medieval, originating in the C13 or early C14, as is shown by the N lancets, a pair below and a singleton above. Small, worn head corbel in the W wall. The aisleless, lancet-lit nave and N porch are entirely of the mid C19 (1848 says Bradney), replacing an aisled predecessor, of which the N aisle collapsed in 1790, the S aisle in 1812. The walling of the chancel is medieval, its blind N wall typical, but the E and S windows and oversized priest's door are of the mid-C19 reconstruction. Internally there is nothing pre-C19 left in the fabric. – FONT. C12. Large, goblet-like bowl on a later moulded stem. – STAINED GLASS. – Chancel E, Crucifixion and Ascension *c.* 1874, subsequently cut down, and SE, Suffer the Little Children, all by *Cox & Son*. – Chancel SW. Good Shepherd. 1938 by *F. S. Baldwin* of *John Hall & Sons*. Stuck in a style of *c.* 1900. – Nave SE and NE, saints. Clearly a pair, of *c.* 1954.

Excavation has revealed the sites of about ten houses clustered round the church. The village seems to have been abandoned in the C18, hence the subsequent collapse of the church.

BARROW, ½ m. NE (ST 433 903). Reduced to a slight swelling in the ground. In the last century this mound was 9 ft (2.7 metres) high and was found to cover a cremation burial with a fine bronze dagger. More recent excavation has shown that the barrow was built in two stages and was surrounded by a shallow ditch.

ST BRIDES WENTLOOGE/ LLANSANFFRAID GWYNLLŴG 2080

ST BRIDGET. The church is Perp of more than one date, and has been a victim of its site, on the flat 'moors' beside the Severn Estuary, having sunk appreciably into the marshy ground, the grand tower leaning rakishly. An early C17 tablet in the porch indicates the height to which the great flood rose in 1606. Repairs have been half-hearted. *Seddon & Carter* in 1899 replaced some window stonework, and partly reordered the furnishings. By 1993 the church was under threat of demolition. Happily, conservative stabilization and repair were carried out 1995–7 by *Alan Miles & Partners*. Blocking of tower arch and N arcade have been removed, but much churchwardens' whitewash has been allowed to remain.

The Perp W tower looms over the body of the church, nave with simple S porch, lower chancel, and short, separately gabled N aisle. In its division into three stages, its diagonal buttresses, fenestration and panelled top parapet, the tower is closely similar to that at Peterstone. Its W doorway and window over are smaller, but it has an image in a niche half-way up the S face, as well as the crowning images (Trinity E, Virgin and Child S), and especially elaborate panelling at the top of the stair-turret. Part of the tower top has crumbled, with the loss of the other two images and the angle pinnacles. As at Peterstone, the tower is finely constructed of grey limestone with buff dressings. The body of the church is clearly later than the tower.

The walls of nave and chancel are of coursed squared limestone low down, but higher up mixed rubble-stone takes over. So it looks as if there may have been damage and reconstruction in the late Middle Ages. The nave windows, three S, one N, are three-light, their tracery pattern similar to Peterstone's, with elongated hexagons. The E-most window on the S side is elaborately moulded, the mullions with wave and hollow, the whole set in a hollow reveal. The rest are simpler, and their stonework has been considerably renewed. S doorway with four-centred head, complex continuous mouldings, and four-petal flowers in the largest hollow. Hoodmould on headstops. Vaulted niche above with pinnacled side shafts. Also traces of a stoup. The chancel has standard late Perp details. The N aisle postdates the nave – see the straight joint at its E end. Its windows are by *Seddon & Carter* copying those in the nave, though their hoodmoulds on headstops are old.

Inside, the piecemeal growth of the building is apparent. The tall tower arch has continuous sunk ovolo and double-wave mouldings. The chancel arch is quite different, with roll, hollow, roll, the rolls set on small polygonal caps and slender round shafts. The two-bay N arcade is different again. Widely splayed, double-hollow chamfered arches rest on crudely moulded lozenge caps and piers of four shafts and four hollows. Leaf sprigs nestle at the foot of the inner arch hollows. The medieval reddening of the outer hollow is visible beneath the whitewash. Canopies for images on the E respond and central pier. N rood stair, and corbels for the loft at the E end of the nave. The roofs of nave and aisle are late medieval, of boarded wagon form, that in the nave with both principal rafters and purlins moulded, also stone head and demi-angel corbels, an odd combination. Note the awkward way in which the nave roof at the W end joins the tower. – FONT. Perp. Small and awkwardly proportioned. – PULPIT and PEWS. C19, timber. Brought in from St Mary, Swansea, in 1899.

WEST USK LIGHTHOUSE, $1\frac{1}{4}$m. E. Tapering brick-built light-tower of 1821 by *James Walker*, the first of twenty-nine lighthouses which he designed for Trinity House around the coast of Britain. At the top the cast-iron railings of the lantern survive, but the lantern itself was removed in 1922; a replica has now been put in place. Surrounding the base are two dwellings forming a drum, probably added in 1867. White-painted ashlar on a rock-faced plinth. Their interiors partly survive, wedge-shaped upper rooms with fire-proof brick-arched ceilings on cast-iron beams.

4010 ST MAUGHANS/LLANFOCHA

ST MEUGAN. Alone with a farmhouse and barns, surveying a panoramic view to the N. At first sight a complete Perp church, of Old Red Sandstone, on the unusual plan of nave and chancel in one, flanked by a matching full-length S aisle. However, a straight joint in the S wall shows that the aisle was built in two stages. Lancets in the N wall of nave and chancel and Y-traceried chancel E window indicate they had been built by *c.* 1300. Unbuttressed W tower with two-storeyed timber top stage, like those at Rockfield and Skenfrith nearby, its wind-vane, dated 1865, recording the addition of the upper stage by *J. P. Seddon.* The S aisle E window is obviously his too, and the S doorway. Simplest S porch (dated 1732 on the keystone). Inside, one pre-Perp feature remains, the short, half-round W respond, showing that the nave had a S aisle from the beginning. Everything else is of the late medieval reconstruction. Most startling, the massive octagonal timber posts of the arcade. Arch-braces renewed. The posts are said to have been encased in plaster. Late medieval wagon roofs throughout, plastered between lengthways and cross-ways ribs. Heavily moulded wall-plates. Small bosses added in 1865. – FONT. A C12 tub. – PULPIT. Timber, presumably by *Seddon.* – STAINED GLASS. Chancel E, Adoration of the Shepherds, 1866. Intense, Pre-Raphaelite, with vivid red, turquoise and purple. Characteristic of the work of *Heaton, Butler & Bayne* at that period. – S aisle S, another Adoration of the Shepherds, cut down and brought in from Llangattock-vibon-awel Church in 1914. This too is strongly coloured, but the Titianesque pictorialism suggests a date *c.* 1840.

In the CHURCHYARD, N of the church, a tall, needle-like polished granite obelisk, commemorating John Hamilton †1868 and facing his seat, Hilston Park, across the valley.

TRIVOR, ¾m. NE. A tall and handsome farmhouse built *c.* 1630, left unfinished and completed only near the end of the C17. The mauve Old Red Sandstone walling remains unrendered, the original windows are of timber, with ovolo-moulded mullions, and above the roofs rise two stately chimney-breasts, each bearing no fewer than six brick lozenge-plan stacks. The E, entrance, front is the best preserved. The entrance doorway, with its original timber frame, is in the projecting stair-tower. Two-light windows at three levels to light the stair, and gabled top. The principal rooms lie to the S of this. The three-light mullion-and-transom hall window must have been reset slightly to the r. of its original position – see the straight joint and the relieving arch of brick, clearly an insertion. Five-light mullioned window above, for the principal chamber. Lower extension, further S, for a kitchen with granary over. To the N of the stair-tower the windows are late C17 casements squeezed into three storeys. This is the parlour wing, extending backwards towards the W. On the W side little more to note, only the doorways at r.-angles to each other, into hall and parlour wing, and the later doubling of the kitchen wing.

Inside, the hall is separated from the parlour by a post-and-panel partition, rather mutilated. The hall ceiling beams are moulded with two ovolos chamfer-stopped, and so are those in the chamber above. The staircase, in the porch-tower but entered from the hall, has short, straight flights round a hollow, rectangular newel. Two doors off the first-floor landing and a third into the NW chamber have shaped heads, all variants of a pattern of which several examples occur in other houses dated between 1599 and 1638. One disappointment of the house is its lack of substantial fireplaces. Fox and Raglan also draw attention to the flimsy roof timbers and suggest that the house was temporarily finished off when first constructed, hence the late C17 NE windows.

Contemporary stone BARN to the NE, its S front partly timber-framed and weatherboarded. At the time of writing, regrettably, there are plans to convert it into a house.

HILSTON PARK, $2\frac{1}{2}$ m. NE. A major early Victorian stuccoed classical mansion, about which little is known. It was built soon after 1838 for a Bristol banker, George Cave, and completed for John Hamilton (*see* churchyard above). The two-storeyed N front is dominated by the mighty pedimented *porte cochère* of four giant Greek Ionic columns. The front is of nine bays, the outer pairs slightly recessed, which further emphasizes the portico. Coupled antae demarcate angles. Uniform entablature all across. The S front, by contrast, has two full-height polygonal bays flanking a narrow centre with niches. Later full-width, single-storeyed colonnade, its entablature and fluted Ionic columns entirely of cast iron. Large early C20 additions towards the E. They consist of a N-facing service block, two-storeyed and pedimented on paired pilaster strips, and a S-facing single-storey ballroom with round-headed windows in its polygonal S end. A decorated rainwater head here is dated 1912. The architect of the ballroom at least seems to have been *Arthur Grove*.*

To the S, semicircular LAWN as wide as the house. From it a magnificent panoramic view of the Monnow Valley opens out.

Internally, the plan of the ground storey, completely symmetrical, is probably of the 1830s, but the house was redecorated throughout for James Graham in the first years of the C20. The front door leads into a hall, heated from a heavy stone chimneypiece to the l., with big consoles. Wainscot reported by Bradney to have been brought in from Lower Dyffryn, Grosmont, in 1902. Beyond, the toplit staircase rises on axis. It is on the imperial plan, rising in one flight and returning in two. Two balusters per tread, one turned, the other twisted. Large round-headed openings above on all four sides, some glazed, some blind. The square top light over the stair, linked by spandrels to a glazed oculus, looks like a survivor from the 1830s house, similar to that over the stair at the Shire Hall, Monmouth, by Edward Haycock.

The main downstairs rooms are all decorated in a handsome early C18 Baroque style, with marble chimneypieces, large-fielded panelling and enriched plaster ceilings. The BALLROOM of 1912, for Mr Graham's son, Douglas William Graham, is quite different in style and much more idiosyncratic. In fact it is a full-blown display of Arts and Crafts decoration and spatial

* 'Hulston Park' occurs in a manuscript list of Grove's works.

manipulation. Plasterwork takes pride of place, broad bands of oak leaves traversing the broad span of the coved ceiling. Signs of the Zodiac follow the line of the cove on the tympanum which closes the ceiling at the S end. W arcade of three semicircular arches on square, wainscoted piers, forming an aisle or vestibule towards the adjoining conservatory within the E end of the cast-iron colonnade. At the N end, an elaborate inglenook centred on a chimneypiece with polished fossily stone slabs radiating above a hearth flanked by cheeks of brown mottled tiles.

Upstairs, a NURSERY, clearly by the same designer. Plaster ceiling decorated with animals, fruit and leaves. The fireplace here is lined with metal cheeks embossed with a poem about the four elements. Shallow bow window and a seat all round it. Nothing else upstairs deserves a mention except another early C20 feature, twin marble-lined bathrooms, one each side of the staircase well.

Two early C20 stuccoed LODGES, one at the N end of the front drive, the other ½m. S, on the B4347, clearly by the architect of the service wing of the house. They are a pair and unusually elaborate, two-storeyed on a Greek cross plan. Full-height paired pilaster strips frame sash windows. Complicated hipped roofs.

(FOLLY TOWER, 1¼m. NE of the house, in the middle of a wood. Circular, of three storeys, but now without floors, stairs or roof.)

ST PIERRE *5090*

St Pierre was owned by the Lewis family from *c.* 1500 to the early C20. Church and mansion stand cheek by jowl, the E wall of the church a mere 5 ft (1.5 metres) from the W turret of the gatehouse, in an exaggeration of manorial grouping. Since 1970 this impression has been heavily compromised, as the mansion has undergone such drastic conversion and extension as a luxury hotel, that its historic character has been almost overwhelmed.

ST PETER. Nave and chancel in one, though a straight joint in the N wall shows that the chancel has been enlarged. The earliest evidence is in the nave. In the W wall, a Norman slit window and a blocked round-headed doorway, confirmed as also Norman by the fully visible internal jambs and head. The Norman N window is also best appreciated internally. Herringbone masonry here, another early sign. N porch and doorway plainly pointed and chamfered, the image niche above the doorway with a border of square flowers, of Perp date. Perp also the central S window, square-headed, of two cusped lights under a hoodmould. In the chancel, a trefoil-headed N lancet, suggesting a late C13 date. The wide, cusped, single-light SE window was probably inserted *c.* 1843 (see the stained glass). Was the egregious Neo-Norman priest's doorway inserted at the same time? Otherwise all the various windows and the W bell gable belong to *A. W. Maberly*'s restoration of 1874. Internally he improved the SE window by means of a rere-arch with Geometrical tracery. His, too, the roofs, differentiating chancel from nave. – FONT. Perp bowl, shallow, octagonal, concave below. The shafted stem is C19. – SCREEN. Perp. Traceried over close-set mullions. Embattled top. The central arch is two-centred, with blind, panel-traceried spandrels and thin side shafts. – PULPIT. Of timber. A handsome High Victorian piece, designed by *Maberly*. – STAINED GLASS. Chancel SE, memorial to Fanny Susan Williams †1843, depicting her holding her infant son as a Neo-medieval effigy on a tomb-chest. – Nave S, Ascension and Nativity, *c.* 1859. Small scenes on a background of lilies. Perhaps by *Joseph Bell* of Bristol (A. Brooks). – MONUMENTS. Two C13 coffin slabs. One, said to commemorate William Benet, priest, †1240, has in relief a floriated cross held by a hand, and birds and dragons disposed up its shaft. The other bears an incised marginal inscription in Norman French, which indicates that it covered the tomb of V[rien] de St Pierre, who was living in 1273. In the centre, a floriated cross and a sword in relief. – Many C18 and C19 monuments to members of the Lewis family, including in the sanctuary ledger slabs of marble, an unusual extravagance. – Thomas Lewis †1732. Large hanging wall monument of grey mottled marble. Fluted Doric pilasters at the sides, armorial display and flaming urns at the top.

MANSION (now hotel). The gatehouse, built presumably by Henry Lewis, who inherited in 1508 and died in 1571, is the most impressive feature and the least compromised by the hotel extensions of the 1970s. It is of three storeys, of local limestone, its outer face flanked by sheer, handsomely battlemented turrets formed of five sides of an octagon. Two-centred entrance arch with continuous double wave. Three-light window above, with chamfer mouldings and arched lights, under a hoodmould. Similar two-light top window. All is consistent with an early C16 date. The armorial panel is a C19 insertion. Within, segmental tunnel vault of uncut stone, and a small four-centred-headed doorway to the stair-turret. The range which extends E-wards from the gatehouse has one original upper window at the W end, but all the rest belong to a heightening in the C19 to provide more extensive service accommodation. The L-plan N range, which encloses an outer court, is wholly C19 (see the engraving in Coxe's *Tour*, 1801).

The inner court S of the gatehouse has been entirely roofed over to create a foyer for the hotel. So the entrance front of the Lewis house has become virtually invisible. Its upper parts can be glimpsed from within the gatehouse range, revealing a symmetrical skyline, crenellated between end gables. A rainwater head dated 1765 relates to work by Morgan Lewis, perhaps formalizing this front. Only from the SE can the rest of the house be appreciated. It is of local limestone. A three-by-one-bay gabled range facing E, which forms an L with the entrance range, is probably of the early C17. It must originally have been symmetrical to the E, but added chimneystacks and window bays, and the wholesale Tudorizing of the fenestration, make this hard to determine. The splendid trio of lead rainwater heads with embossed achievements of arms also look early C17. (The arms are of medieval Welsh heroes claimed as Lewis ancestors, and so do not provide a closer date.) A parallel W range fills in the angle of the L. It projects further S, and terminates in a two-storey window bay beneath a gable. The ensemble is a convincing mid-Victorian Picturesque composition. The date of this remodelling and enlargement seems not to be recorded, though it was most likely carried out by Charles Edward Lewis, who succeeded to the estate in 1872, and is described by Bradney as 'a prominent man in all that went on in his native county'.

Inside, the hall, with stone chimneypiece and ribbed plaster ceiling, seems wholly Victorian. The dining room to the l. has a plaster ceiling of thin ribs forming interlocking stars and lozenges, which may be early C17, and an armorial frieze which is certainly earlier than 1801. (To the r. of the hall, a blocked early doorway, identified by Sir Cyril Fox as leading to the buttery.)

PARKWALL LODGE, ½ m. W. Simple Gothic cottage of *c.* 1840. Canted bay towards the drive, with a lancet in each face. The rusticated GATEPIERS are presumably late C18.

RUNSTON, 1½ m. NW. The site of a deserted hilltop village. The only building to remain is the church of ST KEYNA, now a stabilized ruin. It was built, of local grey limestone, in the C12, and its walls remain almost to full height. Small rectangular nave, squarish lower chancel. Full-height W slab of masonry to support a bellcote, but also the foundations of a tower built against the W wall, predecessor to the bellcote. A tiny, deeply splayed N window in the nave, and the round-headed chancel arch, well turned in ashlar blocks, on plain imposts, survive intact. Otherwise, robbed gaps show the positions of N and S nave doorways, S nave window, and N and S chancel windows. Solid E wall without trace of a window. Since the body of the church was never remodelled to improve its illumination, it gives, even in its ruined state, an excellent idea of the neat symmetry which has been distorted in all other C12 churches in the county.

Bumpy ground and loose stones to the N of the church, and down the slope to the E and SE for over 200 yds (183 metres), show where the village houses stood. Sites of twenty-five have been traced. The village was in serious decline by the mid C16: six houses were inhabited in 1571, the last burial in the church took place in 1770, and the last two houses were abandoned soon after 1785.

SHIRENEWTON 4090

The village retains its dense, intricate centre, though a good deal enlarged recently. The church is the focal building, the hall to the NE is only glimpsed behind a formidably high stone wall.

ST THOMAS A BECKET. Medieval central tower, the chancel and nave with S porch rebuilt, the gabled N aisle added, in a Dec style, by *John Norton*, 1852–3. The tower rises unbuttressed to a heavy crown of battlements on a corbel table, out-topped by its rectangular NW stair-turret. Cinquefoiled S window low down. Belfry slits. The E and W tower arches, of two chamfered orders, the lower dying into vertical imposts, suggest a C13 or C14 date. – STAINED GLASS. The stamped quarries in E, S and W windows belong to Norton's rebuilding, 1852 by *Powell's*. – Chancel S, scenes from the life of Christ, *c.* 1867. This must be by *Hardman* (A. Brooks).

GAERLLWYD BAPTIST CHAPEL, 3 m. NW. Small and whitewashed, in a walled burial ground overshadowed by a yew tree. Two large, round-headed N windows provide the only light. Altered interior. The chapel was built *c.* 1841 for Welsh Calvinistic Methodists, and acquired for Particular Baptists.*

EARLSWOOD CHAPEL, 2 m. NW. The humble T-plan stone building is of two dates. The rear range, with a pointed-headed window in each gable-end, is of 1754, which means that it is one of the earliest purpose-built chapels to survive in the county. The forward-projecting entrance range was added in 1908. Evocative interior, low under roofslopes, the seating the simplest of bench pews.

SHIRENEWTON HALL.‡ An Italianate house of *c.* 1830 was completely encased and transformed in a Jacobean style for Charles Liddell, a shipper in the Far Eastern trade, who acquired it in 1900. The date 1901 occurs on the S gable-end. Who his architect was seems not to be known. In 1909 he employed *Norman Evill* to add a wing extending the S return towards the E, for a billiard room, loggia and belvedere tower, and to remodel the N, service end. The materials in the first phase are mauve Old Red Sandstone with yellow Bath stone dressings. Evill used the same yellow stone for his loggia, but a cooler Forest ashlar elsewhere. The W, entrance front and the S front towards the garden are both two-storeyed, roughly symmetrical compositions with gables of various shapes over the end bays and large mullion-and-transom windows, some of them slightly projecting. The main evidence that this is a remodelling, not a completely new house, is the gabled but inelegantly windowless r. bay of the entrance front. Evill's addition is much more zestful. The loggia is triple-arched on columns, with niched ashlar back wall and strapwork balustrade. Hard up against it, the semi-fortified-looking tower, its top stage corbelled out and given a saddleback roof and crenellated stair-turret.

Inside, there is one great dramatic coup. This is the handling of the hall. From the narrow entrance vestibule it rises two-storeyed, the staircase on the l. leading from it to an upper balcony. The main space of the hall is toplit, and an organ is placed here high up. At the far r. end a second balcony creates a lower, cosier space, where the fireplace overmantel bears the favourite Victorian motto 'East West Home's Best', and a full-height mullion-and-transom window gives a view of the garden

* Mrs S. Williams kindly provided the documentary evidence.

‡ I am grateful to Mr Graham Knight for showing me original drawings for the house and garden buildings.

to the S. Much Jacobean-style woodwork here and in other windows. Chinese detail in the billiard-room ceiling, and a little Japanese room N of the hall, created after 1909.

The GARDENS were largely laid out and planted with specimen trees 1880–1900 by E.B. Lowe, the horticulturalist and botanical author. Here Liddell set up further, much more powerful, reminders of the Far East. To the E of the house, three Chinese structures. First, a massive open PAVILION of red sandstone, within which an enormous bell stands under a roof covered with elaborate yellow and green glazed tiles. Beyond is a similar, smaller SUMMER-HOUSE, with in front a marble sundial set on a stone crouching monster. And beyond again, another open PAVILION, its domed copper roof carried on four columns.

To the SW of the house, 400 yds (366 metres) away down the hill, a complete JAPANESE GARDEN survives in a remarkable state of preservation. Below a tea-house, six ponds are laid out at various levels. A red painted timber archway, and two bridges, one painted red, the other of stone, mark the routes of winding paths around and between the ponds. Trees, some evergreen some deciduous, some tall some bonsai, add to the effect of intricacy and surprise.

The simple classical STABLES, N of the house, are a survival from the 1830s.

Beside the road, W of the house, a Tudor LODGE, probably by *Evill*, and rusticated gatepiers supporting a set of elaborate wrought-iron gates.

Several idiosyncratic early C19 houses face the churchyard from various directions. On the N side, close to the gates of Shirenewton Hall, THE OLD RECTORY, of 1839–41 by *J. Daniels* of Crickhowell. This has a wide, white, symmetrical front of five bays, the centre three grouped together, with (later) timber bay windows flanking the central doorway under a sloping pentice. The doorway and all the other windows have cambered heads, the windows set under incongruous hood-moulds, a nod in a Tudor direction. To the SE of the churchyard, CAEPWCELLA, another Tudoresque design of perhaps a decade earlier. Of stone, three bays, with decorative barge-boards to the gabled ends and in the centre of the front. Paired octagonal chimneystacks ride prominently above the roof. The central mullion-and-transom bay window, and the recessed doorway to the r., must be part of a late C19 remodelling. THE CHANTRY, next door, to the W of the church, is notable only for its pretty cast-iron veranda.

HOME FARM, ¼ m. SW (now a golf clubhouse). Early C19. Grey stone farmhouse backed by a large quadrangle of farm buildings. This is entered, in the centre of a symmetrical composition, through an imposing pedimented arch, above which rides an elegant little octagonal cupola.

LLWYN-Y-CELYN, 1 m. NW. The house at the centre of the compact farmstead is said to have the date 1705 scratched on the cellar vault. (The datestone bearing that date and the initials

G T must be modern.) It represents an early application of classical principles in Monmouthshire farmhouse design. Two-storeyed S front of three wide bays, a big pedimental feature over the central bay. Later single-storey central porch. End stacks. The plan is up-to-date too, the spacious open-well staircase, with acorn finials and delicate turned balusters, rising full-height in the centre of the building opposite the front door, the hall opening to the r., the parlour to the l. Fox and Raglan point to a telling sign of the unfamiliarity of such a scheme: in order to preserve the symmetry of the front while making the hall the largest room, its fireplace is pushed out to the E into a deeply projecting chimney-breast. The windows have been altered, and the central service wing projecting beyond the stair at the rear has been adapted.

Across the farmyard, a pair of pantiled, three-bay BARNS, end-on to one another.

THE GRONDRA, 1 m. E. A small country house of *c.* 1800, re-roofed probably in the 1860s, and with puzzling additions. The main front faces E and is of three bays and three storeys. It has a simple central doorway and tripartite sash windows diminishing in size storey by storey. They are provided with architrave surrounds on brackets. Rendered, colour-washed walls. Bold angle quoins of Old Red Sandstone ashlar. The remodelled roof rests on timber brackets and is flanked by pairs of Bath stone chimneystacks. Also of the later date, the heavy stone first-floor balcony. All this, however, is not what one first sees, but a single-storey S range from which projects a four-column Ionic entrance portico with Bath stone columns. Can this be of the 1860s too? A matching N range, and, to the W, a cottage incorporating C16 or C17 timbers enclose a tiny rectangular court. So it is possible that the portico was added to what originally served as one of a pair of service ranges. Inside, aligned on the E doorway, a tight, open-well staircase of *c.* 1800 rising the full height of the house. Two slender turned balusters per tread.

To the SW of the house, a large, tunnel-vaulted ICE-HOUSE.

On the road below, LOWER GRONDRA FARM, the former home farm. 1877 by *Henry Crisp* of Bristol. Stone, with red brick chimneystacks and red brick semi-dormers. Crisp had been in partnership with E. W. Godwin, which might explain this unconventional treatment.

4020 SKENFRITH/YNYSGYNWRAIDD

Hardly more than a hamlet, clustered beside the walls and drum towers of the castle. The most modern contributions, at the S end, are of the early and mid C19. Stone BRIDGE over the River Monnow of 1824 and white-painted BELL INN beside it, relics of coaching days. Opposite, a neat twin-gabled WATER MILL dated 1867. Three storeys plus attic, external breast-shot water wheel of cast iron. In the street facing the castle, a TERRACE of cottages, of local stone with red brick dressings, its central gable raised up to display an inscription, now worn to illegibility. The church, though large, stands low and inconspicuous to the N.

ST BRIDGET. A C13 church of some ambition, with aisled nave and W tower. Aisles widened and given large windows, and chancel reconstructed, in the early C14. The usual late medieval improvements, S porch, rood loft with its access and lighting, and also a lean-to vestry on the S side of the chancel. The church happily escaped any more Victorian restoration than the renewal of nave and chancel roofs, 1896 by *E. G. Davies*. Repairs in 1909–10 by *William Weir* on SPAB principles retained virtually all the medieval Old Red Sandstone dressings, and even today the stonework of only one window, S aisle W, has been replaced.

The W tower is broad and low, presumably intended to go higher, but curtailed by the instability of the foundations – see the massive propping buttress. Handsome W doorway with typical E.E. mouldings, two continuous rolls and a roll-moulded hood. Filleted stringcourse above. Chamfered lancets. Typical late medieval timber belfry, in two stages, the upper inset, under a pyramid roof. To see the rest of the E.E. work it is necessary to go inside. Tower arch of three broad, stop-chamfered orders, the inner two springing from polygonal imposts with rather meagre moulded caps. Four-bay nave arcades of the normal kind, the piers circular with simply moulded bases and moulded caps not entirely uniform in their proportions. Double-chamfered arches. Similar chancel arch, but on semi-octagonal responds, the moulded caps only slightly projecting, the S cap decorated with an inconspicuous row of dogtooth.

The later work is best appreciated outside. The gabled N aisle is especially handsome, its walls of squared blocks, its three N windows grandly scaled. They are of three lights, the outer lights arch-headed, the centre merely framed by vertical mullions. Such angular tracery experiments seem to date from *c.* 1300. The W window is perhaps contemporary, of four cusped lights, with a big central Y providing space for two pointed trefoils and a pointed cinquefoil at the apex. The E window of the aisle, with cusped reticulated tracery, should be a little later. However, the chancel N window corresponds with this, while its E window matches the N aisle N windows, an odd reversal. Chancel S window Perp, square-headed with ogee cinquefoiled lights. The vestry must be a C16 addition, its square-headed window with uncusped lights. The gabled S aisle is set on an S-profiled base moulding, and has late C14 E and W windows, their tracery in transition from cusped reticulation to Perp panel tracery. The S porch is a post-Reformation addition, overlapping the image niche over the S doorway. Big four-light Perp S window, square-headed with ogee cinquefoiled lights forming a row of shield-shaped apertures above, the prototype perhaps for the standard multi-light Perp window found in so many churches in the N and E of the county.

Inside there is little more to note in the fabric. Debased Perp vestry arches towards the chancel and S aisle, the latter incorporating part of the stair to the rood loft. Tie-beam roofs in nave and aisles, combined with ribbed and plastered wagon vaults, those in nave and chancel of 1896. N aisle wall-plate dated 1663. – FONT. Plain, octagonal, dated 1661. – ALTAR RAILS. Late C17 or C18. Thick turned balusters. – PULPIT. Of stone. Plain, polygonal, certainly pre-C19, but of what date? Stair balustrade uniform with the altar rails. – HOURGLASS BRACKET. Of wrought iron, fixed to the chancel N wall. – READING DESK. Incorporating what appear to be panels from the rood screen. – LECTERN. By *George Jack*, *c.* 1909. Of timber. On an elegant stem. A small seated figure of St Bridget supports the shelf. – BOX PEWS. N aisle W end and S aisle E end. Jacobean, decorated with two different patterns of arcading. – OPEN PEWS. Several early ones in the N aisle, with embryonic poppyheads. – COPE. Early C15. Fine and unmutilated, embroidered with the Virgin, angels etc., on crimson velvet. – WALL PAINTINGS. Traces of C16 or C17 inscriptions in several places, most notably on the chancel E wall, the Ten Commandments and Creed in foliage borders (see the copies in the N aisle). – STAINED GLASS. Chancel E. Many medieval fragments, C14–C16, mostly quarries and borders, and a much-repeated crown motif. – MONUMENT. John Morgan †1557 (N aisle). Tomb-chest with incised figures of a bearded man in cap and robe, and his wife. On the sides, low relief kneeling figures of four sons and four daughters. Armorial achievements on the short ends. A piece of provincial carving to commemorate the Steward of the Duchy of Lancaster and last Governor of the Three Castles.

CASTLE. Skenfrith was one of the Three Castles which were brought together into a single lordship by King Stephen in 1138. They remained in common ownership for nearly eight centuries, until 1902. Skenfrith Castle was subsequently acquired by the National Trust, and is now cared for by Cadw: Welsh Historic Monuments.

Evidence of a C12 castle has been found by excavation, including traces of a substantial stone building. The castle we see today, however, belongs to the early C13, erected by Hubert de Burgh, almost certainly during the years 1220–2. It reflects the latest ideas on castle design at that moment, in particular the use of circular towers. Most memorable is the circular keep, of a type pioneered in France by Philip Augustus in the decades around 1200. But Skenfrith's is not the largest or the first round keep in Wales, those titles go to the keep at Pembroke Castle in the far SW. The low-lying site beside the River Monnow hardly seems suitable for a strongly defensible castle, but originally a stone-revetted water-filled moat, fed from the river, enclosed it on three sides. The present grassed area outside the walls relates fairly closely to the extent of the moat. The curtain wall with circular angle towers encloses a trapezoid inner ward, from the centre of which rises the keep. Most walls survive nearly to their full height, with sockets in some places for the timbers of the 'hoards', enclosed timber platforms from which bowmen could
24 operate. The keep overtops the curtain walls, in an embryonic

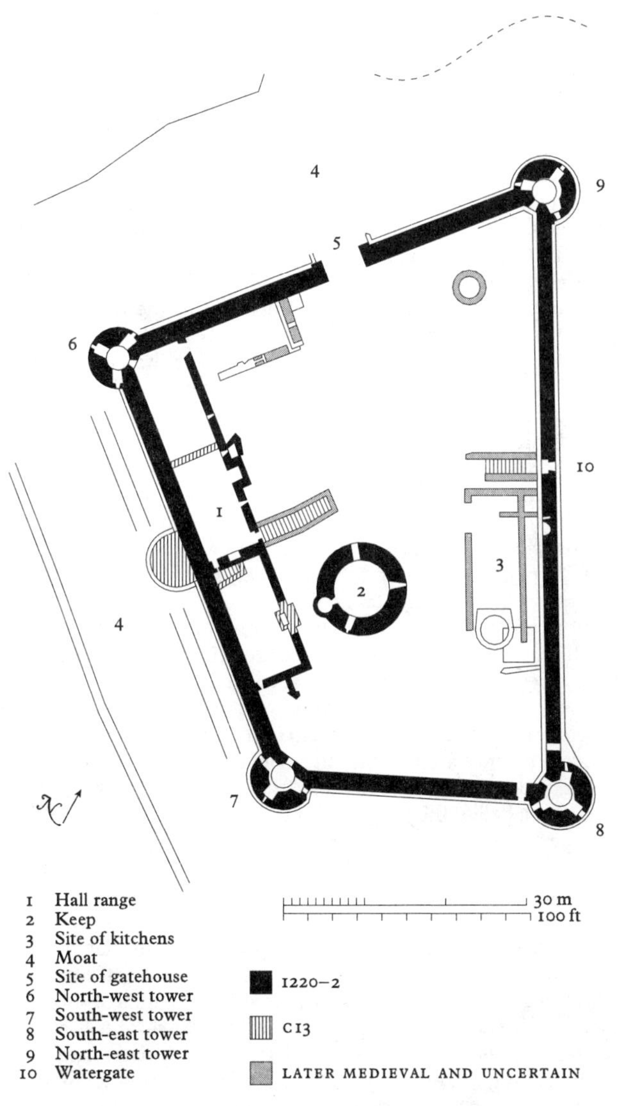

Skenfrith Castle. Plan

system of concentric defences, a system vastly developed in the last quarter of the C13, first by Gilbert de Clare at Caerphilly Castle, Glamorgan, and then in Edward I's castles in North Wales.

The castle is built of Old Red Sandstone roughly coursed. The curtain walls have an external sloping batter for almost half their height, but the cylindrical angle towers rise vertical from the ground up. Yet both were built together. E curtain towards the river with no batter, the main arched watergate midway along it. Only the extra tower in the centre of the W curtain wall is an addition. This is solid up to wall-walk level. Arrow slits in the angle towers at two levels. The lower tier, sited just above the level of the batter of the curtain walls, is arranged in threes, one facing forward, the other two raking the adjacent curtains. The cut stonework of all these slits has been robbed away, but gaping holes indicate where they were. One perfectly preserved upper slit, however, in the NE tower, and another, cross-shaped and thus later, in the SE tower.

Entry into the castle is from the N. Now the way leads through a wide rent in the curtain wall, but the Bucks' engraving of 1732 shows its original form, a large arch, without flanking turrets or any indication of portcullis or drawbridge to give the entry protection. Within the walls there are three things to examine: the interiors of the angle towers, the domestic quarters built in the NW angle of the courtyard, and the keep.

The angle towers are all identical in design. Windowless storage basement, accessible presumably through a trap door in the floor of the room above. Here wide, arched embrasures for the three arrow slits at this level, and evidence of a doorway in the solid back wall. Sockets for the beams of an upper floor, and the embrasures of the upper arrow slits.

The walls of the hall and other rooms built against the W curtain wall are set several feet below the present ground level and were only discovered by excavation in 1954. These rooms were filled in very early, since regular flooding made them unusable, and reconstructed at a higher level. Hence even cut stone detail has survived down here, while the upper rooms have almost completely disappeared. Originally there were only two rooms, a very long hall to the N and a more normally proportioned S room. A later cross wall subdivides the hall. Typical C13 detail, a stop-chamfered, segment-headed doorway at the N end, S of it a barred single-light window, also chamfered, and, further S and more impressive, a complete fireplace opening. This was blocked in even before the rooms were infilled, but its flat head and chamfered jambs, topped by embryonic sprigs of stiff-leaf foliage, have been revealed. To l. and r., the sills and jambs of single-light windows. A doorway with external steps down to it is at the SE corner of the hall. In its S wall traces of two doorways, one superseding the other. In the S room, the chamfered jambs of a fireplace in its E wall. Pyramidal stops, different from those in the hall, suggesting a later date in the C13. Small doorway in the S wall, its chamfered jambs on broach stops of yet another kind.

The kitchen and other service rooms were on the E side of the courtyard, as excavation has shown, but only the base of a circular oven is exposed.

The circular KEEP looks splendidly sheer. Low battered base topped by a bold roll moulding. The chamfered jambs of two single-light windows set on the roll. Original round-headed entrance doorway at first-floor level, above the rent in the wall which provides access now. Sockets flanking the head of the doorway were probably for beams for a porch, and access to it must have been by a timber stair. Convex W projection for an internal spiral stair to the topmost level. The room up here was lit by large windows; see the robbed holes high up. Internally, the rooms at three levels are easily made out, and remains of the spiral stair in the W projection, from first to top floor and so to roof level. The top room was provided with fireplace and garderobe as well as large windows. So here was a fully habitable pair of rooms.

At NORTON, $\frac{3}{4}$m. W, a handsome early C18 farmhouse, two-storeyed under a big hipped roof on coved eaves, the end bay brought forward slightly. Cross-windows of classical proportions. Massive chimneystack at the S end.

PRIMARY SCHOOL, Norton's Cross. Built as a little rural board school in 1877 by *E. H. Lingen Barker*. Of local sandstone, single-storeyed, gabled, Gothic.

LLANTELLEN, 2$\frac{1}{2}$m. W. A small stone manor house, late medieval in origin, reconstructed as a fully two-storeyed building in the early C17, partly rebuilt in the C19, remodelled and extended *c.* 1990. Yet the medieval plan remains easy to read, a hall range between parlour cross wing to the S and service cross wing to the N. The stone doorway into the lower end of the hall remains in place in the E wall. Two-centred head, chamfer on pyramid stops. Sockets for a draw-bar. Timber mullion-and-transom windows in the wings, the E window to the parlour of as many as six lights, upper NW window of four. Details recently renewed and simplified. Inside a splendid display of C17 carpentry survives. p. 37 The parlour ceiling is almost intact, the beam and joist mouldings large hollows and small ovolos in an interplay of unusual elegance, gathered into spear-like stops. The parlour has been shortened to the W, losing its original fireplace. Hall ceiling beams of mighty scale, more elaborately moulded, but shortened at both ends in the C19 reconstruction. It is not clear whether the half-beam at the N end relates to the site of a C17 partition.

DOVECOTE to the W, beyond a wing of *c.* 1990 and embedded in a C19 stable range. This must be of C17 date, square, of stone, two-storeyed under four-way gables. Timber openings in the gables with diamond mullions. Inside, nesting boxes from top to bottom, 800 or so in all.

BLACKBROOK HOUSE, 1$\frac{3}{4}$m. NW. The house stands tall and white, on the hillside among trees, an uncompromising and unexpected classical statement in this deeply rural corner of the county. It was built, it seems, 1797–1800 for Colonel the Hon. John Lindsay. His architect is unknown. Nor is it known what alterations took place during the C19, though the house cannot be entirely in its original state. Its overall shape has not been altered, a three-storeyed rectangle with sash windows under a dentilled top cornice, with shallow roofslopes just visible. Since at least the 1860s (see the glazed porch) it has been entered from the W, hillward side. But here there is just one window, a large Serliana under a relieving arch, the glazing carried down to the ground behind the porch. The three-bay S front is the easiest of access, and is an imposing composition. Three equal semicircular windows in the top storey. Below, the outer windows predominate in both storeys, tripartite under segment heads. But in the centre of the ground floor there is no door, but a niche. Five-bay, regularly sashed E front, the centre three bays recessed slightly behind a single-storey loggia of four slender, fluted Greek Doric columns. Such an order before *c.* 1800 was an exceeding rarity, yet the dentilled entablature which the columns carry is clearly designed to echo the profile of the top cornice. So is the colonnade an original feature? The N front repeats the design of the S, but with a blind centre bay, an oddly pompous treatment to face the service yard.

Inside, the staircase rises dramatically in a bow towards the W Serliana window up to a first-floor landing. From here a back stair continues up to an extraordinary bowed gallery. This must have been intended as a servants' lookout, but was enlarged in the later C19 when a billiard room was installed in the top storey. Simple vertical banisters and slender handrail, so there is no distraction from the spatial gymnastics. The staircase also clinches the supposition that the present W entrance is not original, as its lowest flight almost blocks the way in. The fall in the ground makes an E entrance virtually unworkable, yet that is what the logic of the plan requires. Did Mr Lindsay's architect prepare his design without visiting the site (B. Cherry)?

Further up the hill to the NE, a stone-walled KITCHEN GARDEN, with farm buildings beyond, crowned by a long weatherboarded BARN.

At CROSS ASH, 3½ m. W, COUNTY PRIMARY SCHOOL, 1989–91. By *Gwent County Architect's Department*, design architect *John Postill*. The usual low, spreading group under black slate roof-slopes. In front, the hall roof rises to a pyramidal skylight. At the rear, a straight, unusually formal run of classrooms. Brown brick, with upright caramel bricks for dressings, and green gutters and window frames.

5000 TINTERN ABBEY/ABATY TYNDYRN

Tintern is one of the most evocative monastic sites in Britain. The so-nearly complete state in which the church appears to have survived stimulates the visitor's imagination, and so does its siting, almost recklessly close to the brown waters of the River Wye on a stretch of meadowland framed by the steep, tree-clad slopes of the river valley.

The founder of Tintern Abbey was Walter de Clare, lord of Chepstow (†1138), who in 1131 established here a colony of Cistercian monks from L'Aumône in northern France. This was the first Cistercian foundation in Wales, and in the whole of Britain later only than Waverley in Surrey, founded 1128. Of the stone church and monastic buildings, almost certainly of timber, erected when the community was first established almost nothing survives, so the austere C12 Cistercian ideal, strictly following the rule of St Benedict, is not represented in the architecture at Tintern. What we see today are the remains of a rebuilding on a much greater scale and largely uninhibited by scruples. Work on this great project seems to have been in progress from the early C13 to the mid C14, made possible by a series of generous land grants by successive lords of Chepstow, in particular the younger William Marshal in 1223–4 and Roger Bigod III in 1301–2. Reconstruction of the church is known from contemporary annals to have started in 1269. The first mass in the nearly completed presbytery was recorded by William Worcestre in the 1470s as having taken place in 1288. The whole building was finished by Roger Bigod and consecrated at his request, according to an extract from a lost chronicle, in 1301. Work on the church must have continued for a good many more years. The dismembered pulpitum is datable stylistically to the 1320s. Even as late as 1340 reference was made to 'the Keeper of the Work of the church of Tintern'. The buildings are almost entirely constructed of local Old Red Sandstone, both the coursed and squared stonework of the walls and the generous ashlar dressings, where the characteristic colour range, from purple through mauve and buff to grey, can be readily seen.

At the time of its dissolution in 1536 Tintern was the wealthiest abbey in Wales. The buildings and most of the estates were granted to the then lord of Chepstow, Henry Somerset, second Earl of Worcester. Between 1541 and 1546 the lead was stripped from the roofs and sold, but the Earl and his successors never felt the need to convert the buildings into a residence. Nevertheless, the abbot's lodging and the infirmary were levelled to the ground, and the rest of the monastic buildings gravely despoiled. Only the church itself was too dauntingly big to dismantle. Ironworking in the adjacent Angidy Valley caused the ruins to be colonized by workers' tenements.

It was not until the 1750s that the site came to be valued once again, now for its aesthetic qualities rather than for any monetary value. As the tour down the Wye Valley began to become popular, the Duke of Beaufort cleared, levelled and turfed the interior of the church, but allowed ivy to continue tumbling picturesquely over the walls. Even so, in the eyes of the aesthetic pundit William Gilpin, the abbey church was not picturesque enough. In his *Observations on the River Wye*, which appeared in 1783, he passed the notorious judgement: '. . . though the parts are beautiful, the whole is ill-shaped. No ruins of the tower are left, which might give form, and contrast to the walls, and buttresses, and other inferior parts. Instead of this a number of gable-ends hurt the eye with their regularity; and disgust it by the vulgarity of their shape. A mallet judiciously used (but who durst use it?) might be of service in fracturing some of them; particularly those of the cross isles, which are not only disagreeable in themselves, but confound the perspective.' The most admired effect was that of the interior of the church viewed from the W door. As Sir Richard Colt Hoare expressed it in 1798: 'No ruin I have seen in England has so striking effect on the mind and sense as that of Tinterne when the door first opens and presents the whole extent of this most beautiful Gothic aisle, overhung with ivy in the most picturesque manner, and terminated by the magnificent eastern window through which is seen a distant hill covered with copse wood, on which fortunately there are no buildings or breaks to disturb the repose and tranquillity of the scene.' The late C18 and early C19 saw an uneasy mixture of tourist activity and rural poverty, and in 1821–2 the new turnpike road (now A466) was driven unfeelingly through the abbey precinct.

The modern era dawned in 1901, when the ruins were purchased by the Crown from the Duke of Beaufort. Thereafter the site was gradually cleared, the ivy removed and the tottering walls repaired.

Tintern Abbey church. View of the east end, 1848

At first repairs were carried out by *F. W. Waller* of Gloucester, but after the Office of Works took over responsibility in 1913–14 much more ambitious works were undertaken, supervised by Charles Peers and completed by 1928. Few visitors realize that the S aisle roof rests on steel lattice girders, or that the piers of the S aisle have all been taken down and reconstructed with steel stanchions embedded in them. Today visitors to Tintern come in their thousands, and the seclusion and tranquillity found here by the Cistercian monks can rarely be captured. The approach road passes uncomfortably close to the W front of the church, and the VISITOR CENTRE of the 1970s, to the N, is all too stolid and unsympathetic. Once among the abbey ruins, however, the visitor can even on the busiest day find space enough for contemplation and undisturbed scrutiny.

In examining the buildings, it is best to make one's way first across the site to the S, where the church stands, then to study the cloister N of the nave, and the accommodation for the monks and lay brothers grouped round it. The infirmary to the E and the abbot's lodging to the NE can be studied next. Finally, it is necessary to leave the present enclosure, to find the accommodation for guests, now no more than excavated footings W of the church, the inner gatehouse and traces of the precinct wall S of the A466, and the watergate by the river bank to the NW.

THE TWELFTH-CENTURY ABBEY

In the years after the foundation of the abbey in 1131, the church and monastic buildings necessary for the new community to function were erected. Nothing visible today is immediately recognizable as of the C12, but the siting of the church and a good deal of its plan-form were deduced when the site was systematically cleared in the early C20. Certain upstanding walls of the cloister and its adjoining buildings can be shown to be of C12 date. The plan of the C12 CHURCH can be seen laid out in the crossing and N aisle of the nave of the present church. A square-ended presbytery is indicated, transepts with twin E square-ended chapels and a long, narrow, aisleless nave. However, no thorough excavation has taken place, and the form of choir and transepts is not firmly established. The only genuine C12 fabric is the base of the pilaster buttress at the SW angle of the nave, visible through a grille in the grass.

The MONASTIC BUILDINGS were sited, not as usual on the S side of the nave but to the N, to take maximum advantage of the limited flat ground and to facilitate drainage into the river. The W wall of the present CLOISTER must be essentially of the C12, since the C13 parlour is built up against its W face. Similarly, to the E of the cloister, the entry to the bookroom on the N side is clearly set against an earlier wall, originally built as the N wall of the C12 N transept and its outer chapel. Further N, the side walls of the MONKS' DAY ROOM (the lower storey of the dormitory range) contain C12 masonry, retained when the room was first lengthened and then remodelled (*see* below, p. 551).

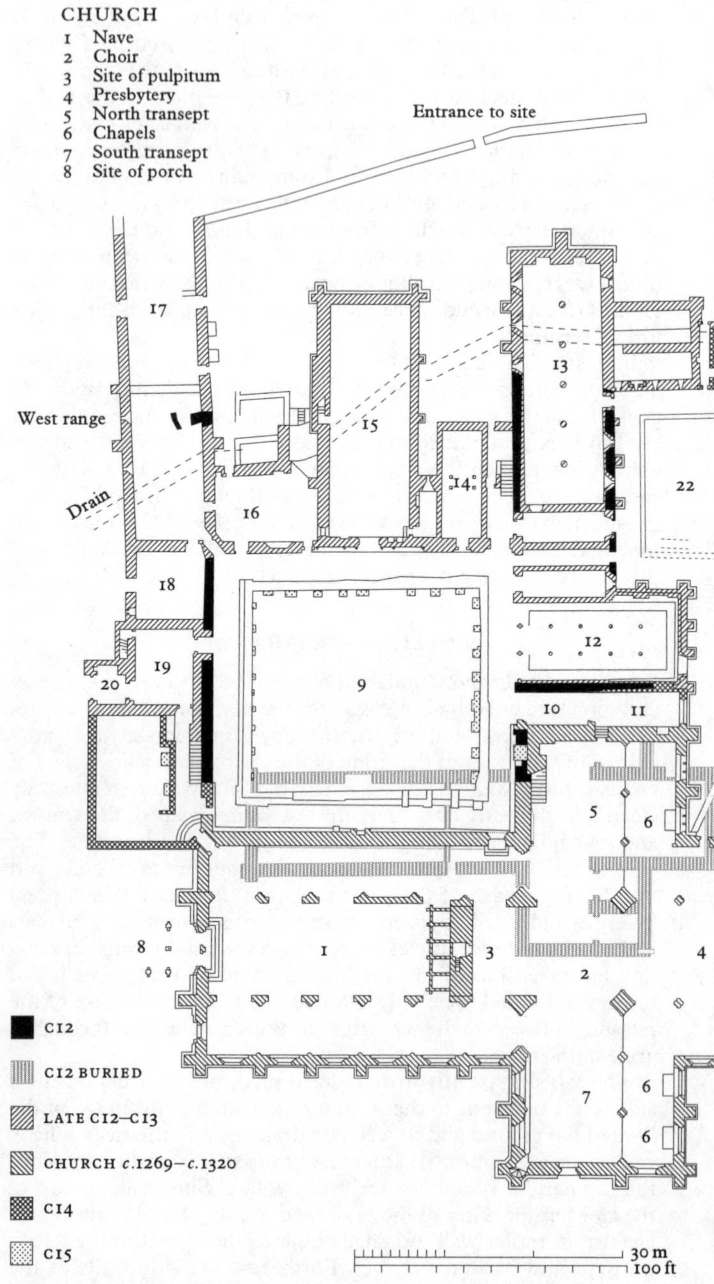

Tintern Abbey. Plan

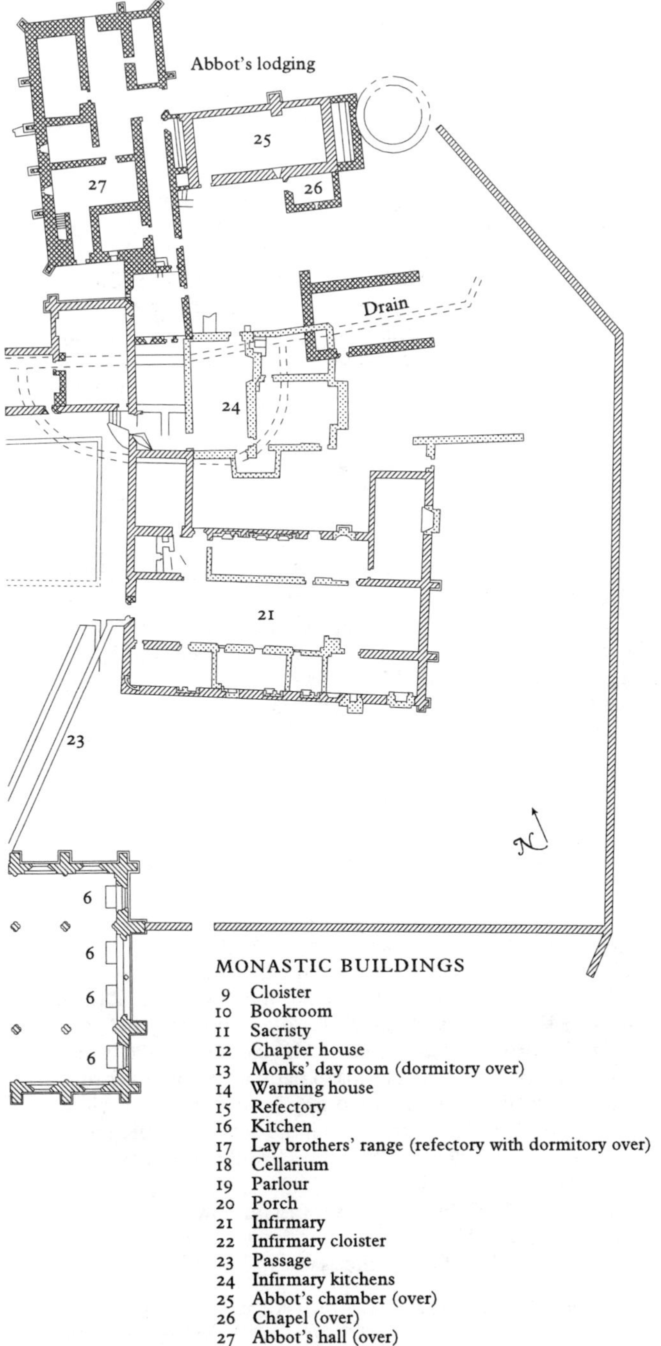
Abbot's lodging
25
26
27
Drain
24
21
23
6
6
6
6
N
MONASTIC BUILDINGS
9 Cloister
10 Bookroom
11 Sacristy
12 Chapter house
13 Monks' day room (dormitory over)
14 Warming house
15 Refectory
16 Kitchen
17 Lay brothers' range (refectory with dormitory over)
18 Cellarium
19 Parlour
20 Porch
21 Infirmary
22 Infirmary cloister
23 Passage
24 Infirmary kitchens
25 Abbot's chamber (over)
26 Chapel (over)
27 Abbot's hall (over)

THE LATE THIRTEENTH-CENTURY CHURCH

The new church begun in 1269 was laid out to the SE and S of the C12 church. It was constructed in phases, in such a way as to enable the existing building to be kept in use as long as possible, so that the monks' offices need never be interrupted, although the old building had to be destroyed before the N aisle and N transept of the new one could take its place. The present building is 236 ft (72 metres) long, a third as long again as its predecessor, and double its width, with aisled four-bay presbytery and aisled six-bay nave. The transepts have twin E chapels, as before. But of course it is the great increase in height and in the brightness of its illumination which will have made the new church so dramatically different from the old. Even today, now that the roofs have gone, and with them the effect of lighting in the interior, it is the huge size of the major windows which amazes, particularly as enough of their tracery survives – the nave W window almost in its entirety – to convey something of their original effect. Yet in other respects the church is not excessive, but rather, in its proportions and in its decoration, expresses the happy mean. In style, it is clear that its designer, or rather designers, were aware of recent metropolitan developments.* The W front was intended as a grand statement to the outside world, and it is easy and natural to admire it first. But a detailed examination should begin at the E end and move W-wards, first outside, then internally, following as far as possible the sequence in which the building was constructed, so that the significance of developments in the design can be understood within the unity of the whole.

Exterior

PRESBYTERY AND SOUTH TRANSEPT. The cruciform plan is especially well seen from the SE. A clerestory of moderate height rises above lean-to aisles. Although the roofs are all gone, the gable-ends indicate their moderate, approximately 45-degree, pitch. There was clearly never a crossing tower. Unifying features throughout are the moulded plinth at the base of the walls, and the shallow buttresses which demarcate the bays and, as they rise, step back by means of gabled set-offs, until they become mere pilaster strips. Pilaster strips in the clerestory. The wall-heads, which look so even, have lost a parapet or battlementing all round. Only the simple supporting corbel tables survive, enough to show that the buttresses all die away into them and were not carried up higher. So the church will always have had a severe outline.

The windows of presbytery and S transept, however, must be examined in detail. They are set low down on a continuous chamfered string, both the enormous ones which light the main

* However, as Dr Richard Morris has recently suggested, the church should probably be considered as the work not of master masons brought down from London, but of talented masons employed elsewhere in the West Country during the late C13 and early C14.

vessels and the quite modest aisle windows. All, of course, have two-centred heads, of moderate steepness. The presbytery E window, originally of eight lights, extends virtually the full width between the angle pilasters, and its apex almost reaches the gable set-off. What remains of its tracery is a mere skeleton, just the central mullion (reconstructed by *Waller*) and the upper part of the composition of three great circles, together with a few stubs of the foiled patterns which they enclosed. Examination of the stubs 150 years ago, when there was a little more to see, enabled the reconstruction of the whole design, a classic Geometrical composition. Externally the window is enriched with no more than a single order of slender shafts with moulded base and cap, and a hollow arch-mould and hood. There is a deep, sloping sill. Below, at ground level, a blocked arch under a flattened, voussoired head, the blocking crudely interrupting the plinth mould. It has been suggested that it gave a way to the workmen to barrow in materials during construction. The three-light E aisle windows and the similar window in the gable, which lit the roof space, have all lost their tracery. The pattern seems to have been a rather austere one, each light trefoiled, but the side trefoils set well below the plain pointed heads of the lights. The windows are externally double-chamfered and have small hoods. Small lancets above to light the aisle roof spaces. The N and S windows of the presbytery aisles and clerestory were of two trefoil-headed lights with encircled hexfoils in the heads. Those in the clerestory have survived better than those in the aisles. The former have voussoirs above their heads, the latter hoodmoulds. The N transept will be discussed as part of the interior. Its only feature that must be acknowledged outside is the pair of dramatic E flying buttresses, a structural precaution much at odds with the concept of the rest of the building.

The S transept employs the same vocabulary as the eastern arm. The two chapels have three-light E windows which matched those at the E end of the presbytery aisles. The clerestory windows match those of the presbytery. In the sheer W wall, windows of this pattern occur at both levels and are unusually well preserved. They have voussoirs as well as hoodmoulds. The sills of the lower windows are set just above the string, not on it. The S wall of the S transept is largely opened up by another enormous window, framed with side shafts exactly as the presbytery E window. Unfortunately its tracery has completely gone, but the stumps of the mullions show that it was of six lights. The stumps are set on the boldly coped, triangular gable of a handsome doorway. The doorway preserves the circular moulded caps and bases of three orders of detached shafts, and the slender shafts of an attached inner order which originally nestled behind. Arch-moulding of three rolls and three hollows. Within all this a continuous chamfer frames the doorway. The monks would have used this doorway when processing to the W front on Sundays, and for access to their cemetery (D. Robinson). To the r., the two-light S window of the SE chapel, of the usual pattern. To the l., a polygonal projection, with seven slit windows, to light an internal newel stair to the roof. The gable window is broader and lower than its E counterpart, but its tracery pattern is lost.

NAVE. The S side of the nave continues the now familiar design for four bays. Two-light windows above and below with encircled hexfoils. At both levels they have hoodmoulds and no voussoirs. In the two W-most bays, however, there is a striking change in the aisle windows. They are much shorter, and have unencircled quatrefoils in their heads. Simplified jamb-moulding too. The stringcourse steps up to meet their higher sills. It is tempting to think that this change was caused by the addition of an attached structure, yet the buttresses have fully moulded plinths, as if they were intended to remain visible. The change is in fact the first sign of a new building phase which includes the W front. At the SW corner the two angle buttresses are, uniquely, taken up above the parapet to end in pinnacles. One survives (but was replaced in replica in 1996). Octagonal, the faces gabled and decorated with blind tracery, top finial.

The WEST FRONT is unmistakeably the design of a second master. This is most obvious in the form of the great seven-light window, happily almost intact, which lights the nave, but all the other elements are also subtly reconceived. Besides that, however, the W front is treated with an elaboration of mouldings not found elsewhere on the exterior of the church, in order to impress the approaching traveller. The basic composition echoes that at the E end, though the main window is slightly less wide, and the framing buttresses have only two, not three, gabled set-offs (the S buttress was inaccurately restored in the Waller period). The gable window is very large, and was of five lights. Its tracery is completely gone. The main window has its seven lights grouped two–three–two, so that they rise between mullions with small shaft-rings into four steeply pointed arches, the centre two overlapping, within which are a row of pointed trefoils under lobed daggers. In the window head are three large circles, the outer two enclosing a pattern of four trefoils. The composition can be closely paralleled in the E window of St Etheldreda, Holborn, London, of *c.* 1284, and in the Lady Chapel at Exeter Cathedral, under construction in the 1280s. All owe their inspiration to the late C13 rebuilding of the choir of St Paul's Cathedral. The deeply sunk frame of the window has three orders of slender attached shafts, with moulded caps and one row of shaft-rings, carrying the multimoulded arch surround. Below are the twin W doorways. These are pointed, trefoil-headed and set within an elaborate composition of blind pointed arches. The central arch framing the doorways is quite broad. Pointed sub-arches over the doorways contain encircled hexfoils in their heads, and between them is a sharply pointed vesica, which originally contained a statue. Its broken pedestal survives, together with a foliage corbel with stiff-leaf turning naturalistic. Traces remain of a subtle background diaper pattern. Many of the mouldings are keeled. The detached supporting shafts have all disappeared. To l. and r. are blind pointed arches rising to the same height, but occupying narrower spaces, so much more steeply proportioned. The arches enclose three encircled quatrefoils. The bases on which the detached shafts stood have concave faces. One cap remains with miniature dogtooth. The aisle windows are of three lights, quite short, with trefoiled heads. In detail they are not a pair, and the S one, which has shafted mullions, does not extend right up to its voussoired relieving arch, so must be a very early replacement. Beneath it, a secondary doorway into the S aisle. This is quite handsomely treated. The caps of its now lost detached shafts carry a big arch roll. Continuous inner hollow. Above the aisle window on each side a lozenge-shaped opening, originally cusped, to light the aisle roof space. In front of the W doorway there remains the foundation of a C14 porch, the bases of three of the original four complex lozenge-plan piers, which may have carried a small chapel for a revered statue of the Virgin.

Much of the N side of the church cannot easily be seen externally, where monastic buildings adjoin, so it can best be examined with the rest of the interior.

Interior

The first impression, today as for Colt Hoare, is of the unimpeded vista from end to end, with the great E window providing a distant view of wooded hillside. But that is misleading, for originally the internal space was subdivided by various screens, so that it could not have been comprehended in a single glance as it is now. For all that, the architecture is remarkable for its uniformity, and here, inside, even more powerfully than outside, the harmony and moderation of the proportions make themselves felt. Rich mouldings are applied to piers, arches and windows, but carved ornament is rarely to be found.

The E window, which rose to fill the space below the high vault, was provided with an elaborately moulded rere-arch carried on no fewer than four orders of shafts. The outer shafts, which die away above the arcade arches, were coursed and partly survive, but the rest were detached, held in place by shaft-rings, and have disappeared. The aisle windows are also internally shafted and have multimoulded arches, and, what is more, have moulded rere-arches which were set on detached shafts, now gone. Detached shafts for the clerestory windows too, some of which survive on the S side, very worn and of sandstone rather than the Purbeck marble one might have expected. The clerestory rises above a completely plain, solid triforium level (a characteristically Cistercian piece of austerity), demarcated at top and bottom by an undercut roll. The four-bay presbytery arcade has arches with many roll mouldings, some filleted. The arches rest on piers of moderate height, quatrefoil in plan, consisting of four major shafts in the cardinal directions. The four minor, detached shafts have disappeared. The moulded caps and bases take account of all eight shafts. Lozenge-plan plinths with chamfered angles. There is evidence that solid walls about one-third the height of the piers originally closed off the aisles from the presbytery. They have been neatly cut back, presumably in pre-Dissolution times, leaving against the E and W faces of the piers flat, coped stubs. Finally, the vaults. Only the springers are in place, but they are enough to show that the vaults were of simple quadripartite form, the ribs filleted. Triple wall-shafts, those carrying the high vault brought down on small leaf corbels where they meet the arcade arches. Loose on the ground, several

Tintern Abbey church.
Reconstruction of the east wall, 1848

big bosses from the high vault, carved with foliage, some stiff-leaf, some naturalistic horse chestnut leaves in a mixture characteristic of the transitional period at the end of the C13.

In the S transept the arcade to the E chapels matches that in the presbytery, as does the clerestory over it. But the W clerestory, where the wall rises perpendicularly for its full height, is treated differently, the triforium level recessed to provide a wall passage. Doorways here with shouldered lintels, the so-called Caernarfon arch associated with Edward I's castle-building in the 1280s.

The crossing piers introduce a variation. The system of major 19
and minor circular shafts is repeated, but all are filleted, and all are built integrally with the pier. The minor shafts, however, have no necking and so seem to die into the underside of the pier capitals. Oddly, these details are used not only on the full-height shafts towards the crossing but also on the arcade responds backing on to the crossing piers, so that the responds do not match the arcade piers in choir and transept. In the nave, however, this discrepancy is rectified, as the outer responds in the nave aisles match their fellows on the backs of the W crossing piers. The crossing arches have simplified mouldings, consisting merely of a bold filleted roll between broad hollows. The springers and toothing remain for the crossing vault (except over the E arch, where *Waller*'s reconstruction has eliminated the toothing).

So to the NAVE. The N arcade is largely gone, reduced to the stumps of the piers. The S arcade, however, shows that the design of the nave, though superficially the same as in the eastern arm, is subtly differentiated from it. Here the minor shafts of the arcade piers are integral, not detached, and so, of course, survive. The arcade arches have simple mouldings like those in the crossing, two broad hollows framing a filleted roll. The S aisle vault is supported on single, not triple, shafts against the outer wall. But in the N aisle, where the outer wall backs on to the S walk of the cloister, there are merely short wall-shafts on moulded corbels. Higher up, the nave elevation at first matches that of the presbytery. But after two bays there was a change of mind, and the shafts of the clerestory rere-arches, which start as the detached sort, are in the four W bays built integrally. This minor, and originally almost invisible, change in the design has been shown to relate to a full-height break in the masonry, and goes with the change in aisle window design two bays further W already noted above. The break represents the pause in construction during which the entire design was reviewed, and a new composition devised for the W front, as already discussed. The tri-lobed wall-shafts for the high vault and the vault springers match those further E, but in the two W bays they are somewhat enlarged, and one contains a pair of beasts fighting within foliage. The inner face of the great W window is less lavishly framed than the exterior, with a single order of shafts, and arch mouldings which integrate it with the profile of the high vault. The inner face of the W doorway shows a change of mind, since it has three moulded shaft-bases but no room for shafts above them. In the

N aisle the two-light windows have unencircled quatrefoils in their heads, that is the new design adopted in the two W bays of the S aisle. Their length is of course curtailed by the solid wall of the cloister walk outside.

Before leaving the nave, there is one further, very conspicuous, item to consider. This is the remaining sections of walls built into the bottom half of each nave pier and into the W crossing piers. The latter clearly formed a backing for the timber choir stalls which were sited under the crossing in the normal way. The choir extended across the E bay of the nave, and the next bay was occupied by a deep pulpitum, many fragments of which survive (*see* below, p. 556). There is evidence in this bay of doorways in the side walls, giving access to the altars under the pulpitum. The handsome head corbel high above the S arcade in this bay may also have been related to the pulpitum. The walls further W enclosed the area where the lay brothers sat. They gained access to their seating through a doorway set diagonally across the NW corner of the N aisle, and then through the W bay of the N arcade, where there seems to have been no wall.

It remains to examine the NORTH TRANSEPT, which must have been the last part of the church to be built, presumably in the 1290s, after the choir of the C12 church had finally been removed. The E bay of the N aisle, with the processional doorway from the cloister, must belong to this final phase too, but will be described below (p. 549). The design of the N transept seems to have followed the principle that all parts readily visible from the choir should match the presbytery and S transept, but elsewhere something more up-to-date was permissible. Thus the arcade piers had detached shafts, the arches have keeled mouldings, and the clerestory window design includes encircled hexfoils. Vault springers, and wall-shafts on finely carved leaf
18 corbels. More importantly, the great six-light N window, though partly blocked by the gable-end of the dormitory range, and so given a transom with trefoil-headed lights below, is of a pure Geometrical design. At the top is a large circle enclosing four cinquefoils, and below to l. and r., under steeply pointed superarches, are single encircled quatrefoils. It is possible, indeed likely, that this repeats the design, now lost, of the S transept S window. The gable window, originally intended to light the roof space, is a simple affair, of three trefoil-headed lancets under a superarch. The most conspicuous newly designed details of the N transept are the E windows of the two E chapels. One includes an unencircled hexfoil, the other had a composition of alternating pointed and lobed forms. Otherwise, one need only note the wall passages to both E and W, their doorways not shouldered but straight-headed. Linking N passage running behind the lower mullions of the N window. The night stair, against the W wall of the transept, was reinstated in the *Waller* period, leading to a broad, finely moulded doorway at its head into the dormitory. The smaller doorway to the E at ground level leads into the sacristy. It seems to have been enriched with cusping within its two-centred head.

MONASTIC BUILDINGS

The living quarters of the monks and lay brothers, though laid out on the N rather than the more usual S side of the church, otherwise conform to Cistercian practice. A comprehensive programme of rebuilding took place in stages during the C13 before work started on the new church. The monks' refectory, dormitory and chapter house, as well as the lay brothers' quarters, were all rebuilt substantially larger than they had been before, doubtless to accommodate increasing numbers. To the E a grandly scaled infirmary was built. Nor did the rebuilding shun fine decoration; in many ways the C13 monastic quarters seem to have been more sumptuous, even showy, than the new church. During the C14 and C15 further works were put in hand, most notably a grand enlargement of the abbot's lodging to the NE. The monastic buildings have survived much less well than the church, the infirmary and abbot's lodging having been reduced to little more than footings. Nevertheless, many telling features survive in whole or part, and a detailed scrutiny of the whole site is rewarding. It is natural to begin in the cloister, then to examine in turn the rooms that opened off its E, its N and its W walks, and finally to look at what is left of the infirmary and abbot's lodging.

The CLOISTER retains its C12 width E–W, but with the resiting of the church further S, its N–S dimension was increased, so that the garth became nearly square. In the S walk there is a good
deal to see. Most eye-catching is the processional doorway at its 21
E end, opening into the church. This must have been one of the last elements of the church to be completed, *c.* 1300, and in a decidedly more advanced style. It dispenses with shafts, and has three orders of continuous mouldings. The innermost is cusped round the arched head (cf. the door in the N transept to the sacristy), the middle order consists of a broad band of undercut floriated dogtooth, unfortunately vandalized, and two outer hollows complete the composition. The doorway is set under a blind gable decorated with a large pointed trefoil. The window above must be contemporary with the doorway, with alternating pointed and lobed elements in the tracery (cf. N transept chapel E window). To l. and r. of the doorway are broad panelled imposts, part of a scheme which is carried on in the S end of the E cloister walk, against the wall of the transept. It is clearly Perp in character, and must relate to a scheme for reconstructing the cloister for which funds were being raised in 1469. Less conspicuous features of the S cloister walk include the continuous bench against the wall, with in the centre traces of a canopied seat. This has been identified as the 'collation' seat, where the abbot sat to hear a reading before the procession into the church for compline. In the wall above, sockets for supports for roofs at two different levels. Of the arcades on which the roof rested, no trace remains *in situ*, but fragments in the lapidary collection (*see* p. 556) have been pieced together to reveal the C13 design, a remarkable one with two syncopated arcades of trefoiled arches.

In the E cloister walk the bench continues, against the wall of the transept. A pair of round-headed, rebated recesses here, one blocked by the C15 remodelling of the cloister, are thought to have been cupboards for books. They are probably C12 in origin. The narrow space immediately beyond the end of the transept was, after the completion of the new church, converted into two rooms: a sacristy to the E (entered from within the N transept, *see* p. 548), and to the W a bookroom. There remains, almost intact, the beautiful arched double doorway opening into the bookroom from the cloister. The deep frame of continuous mouldings, the cinquefoiled heads to the doorways and the pointed trefoils above them, are all new, further developed motifs suggesting an early C14 date. Circle at the apex, presumably enclosing a foiled feature, in typical Tintern fashion. Slender filleted rolls enrich every bar in the pattern.

Beyond the bookroom is the SACRISTY – the dividing wall between them has gone. Here there is a quadripartite vault with handsome ovolo-moulded ribs with central fillet, resting against the S wall on moulded half-round corbels, the W one enriched with a small band of dogtooth. Part of the E window remains, of five stepped trefoil-headed lights under a segmental head, all hollow-moulded. Immediately to the N lay the CHAPTER HOUSE. It must have been a splendid, vaulted room in an elegant E.E. style, but sadly little remains. It was rectangular, five bays long and three wide. From the cloister it was entered through a full-width arcade of three wide arches. Only the lowest courses of the piers and responds survive, filleted attached shafts and lobed bases showing that the piers also included no fewer than eight detached shafts. The entrance arcade was clearly not fitted with doors but opened directly into a vestibule. This must have extended through the three W bays (where the dormitory ran across overhead – see the crease-line of the dormitory roof against the N wall of the N transept). The two E bays, beyond the line of the dormitory, could rise higher, and they probably formed the chapter house proper. Only here is there a wall bench. The moulded pier bases are circular throughout, though differing in detail. (Some small, plain floor tiles remain.) In the NE and SE angles, where the wall masonry survives to a higher level, sockets for clusters of short, detached respond shafts and the vault springers with filleted ribs. Also here the sills of three-light windows, and, outside to the E, the bases of quite strongly projecting buttresses.

At the N end of the E cloister walk the lowest courses remain of a doorway with detached shafts leading into a narrow room immediately N of the chapter house. This has been identified as the monks' parlour. To the N again, a passage, its W doorway opening not off the cloister walk but N of its NE corner. This passage led through into the infirmary cloister to the E. A doorway at the W end of its N wall opened into a six-bay, vaulted room lying N–S, the monks' day room. Above this lay the monks' dormitory, running S-wards to link with the N transept, a total length of *c.* 170 ft (52 metres). But of this great upper room nothing survives, except the outline of its roof against the N transept already noted. Of the MONKS' DAY ROOM, on the other hand, a good deal remains. First of all, a straight joint in the W wall shows that the three N bays are an addition, made when, probably *c.* 1200, the room, and the dormitory above, required to be greatly enlarged for an increased number of monks. One complete round-headed lancet at the N end of the E wall, with external chamfer and hoodmould, suggests the date. Deep external buttresses, added to the E wall of the S half, integral in the N half. Plain, C13 lancet windows, or parts of them, survive between the buttresses. Internally, remains of the C13 vault system. Of the central row of piers, the octagonal chamfered plinths, water-holding bases and several courses of the octagonal shafts survive. At the S end of the E wall, two inserted C13 corbels, semicircular moulded caps on corbel shafts, carrying the springers of chamfered ribs. The profile of the inserted vault is visible along much of the E wall. Also a doorway with segment-headed rere-arch and a later fireplace. One particularly interesting feature visible near the N end of the room is part of the monastic drainage system, its stone covering slabs partly removed to expose slots for a vertical lock-stone, which could control the flow of water, and access steps. The drain runs under the adjoining rectangular building to the E. This was originally two-storeyed, and divided into two halves. The N half, over the drain, was the monks' necessarium, or latrine, opening off the dormitory. The S half included a ground-floor room entered by a door and lit by lancet windows in its S wall. It has been suggested that this may have provided a day room for the novices.

The range which opens off the N walk of the cloister is of the early to mid C13 and better preserved than any other part of the monastic buildings. The E half is of two storeys, with traces of a third. The W half was largely occupied by the refectory, the most glorious room in the abbey.

The E-most doorway, wide, two-centred-headed with a continuous chamfer, opens into a square space covered by a quadripartite vault, its chamfered ribs resting on moulded half-round caps (like those in the monks' day room but a little richer) and plain corbels. N of this is a second bay under a pointed tunnel vault, under which one can see that a flight of steps began to rise, the day stair to the monks' dormitory. Two-centred, double-chamfered arch, and beyond that a chamfered segmental arch, at a higher level, to accommodate the stair as it rose. A second, lower and narrower segmental arch to the W, rebated for a door. This gave access to a yard to the N. The next doorway in the cloister walk was much richer, but has been robbed of its arch mouldings and jamb shafts. A filleted roll moulding survives. This opened into the WARMING HOUSE, originally vaulted in two bays. The S bay survives, with chamfered ribs forming a quadripartite vault, and moulded round caps on short shafts or leaf sprigs, all very similar to the adjacent passage vault. Between the two bays was a remarkable covered hearth, of which only tantalizing fragments survive. Narrow passages to E and W were spanned by steeply pointed chamfered arches, of which the E arch remains. But of the great hood which covered the hearth, so that the fire gave out its heat in all four directions, only one pier, and the massive corbel which supported the N lintel, are in place. Traces of a later, conventional fireplace in the footings of the N wall of the room. The upper storey which extends above the warming house and day-stair entry is lit by three S and two N double-chamfered lancets, with to the W on the cloister side a small, square window fitted for bars. (Inside there are two rooms, the small inner one, which is lit by the barred window, provided with a stone vault – it was clearly a strong room.) The third storey is much ruined, but C16 two-light N and S windows with arched lights suggest that this block may have been modernized and occupied after the Dissolution by some functionary of the Earl of Worcester.

The significance of the REFECTORY was signalled by the treatment of its entrance wall in the cloister walk. The sadly depleted remains indicate that there was a central many-shafted doorway, flanked by narrow recesses and wide outer recesses, for basins, all separated from one another by groups of shafts. Circular shaft-bases with waterholding mouldings, and attached filleted roll mouldings originally set back between the detached shafts, are just enough to indicate the richness of the jambs. The arch mouldings have all been wrenched away. Inside, the S double bay was windowless, flanked by a kitchen to the W and a pantry to the E. Rectangular serving hatch from the kitchen, under a blind chamfered arch. Beside it in the S wall, a rectangular recess, interpreted as the seating for a flap table when raised and not in use. On the other side of the entrance doorway, twin trefoil-headed, chamfered recesses, the r. one a cupboard, rebated for a door, the l. one provided with a shelf and sink-hole, so for washing dishes. A doorway at the S end of the E bay opens into the long, narrow pantry, which is lit by a small N lancet. Above the pantry doorway, remnants of rich blind arcading, shafts and mouldings of traceried arches, partly recently renewed. This E wall of the refectory extends N-wards almost to full height for
12 two more double bays, these provided with large windows set on a shelf above a high, blind dado. The windows retain almost intact their external plate tracery. Each bay has two pairs of long, trefoil-headed lancets, and a disc pierced in the tympanum above. A further, larger disc in the arched head which unites each pair. This composition is repeated four times in the two double bays where it survives, though the top discs in the S double bay have been filled in. Towards the refectory the composition was repeated in linear form. Slender shafts with shaft-rings remain, attached to the wall face, with bold circular caps and bases, and there are stubs which show where there were free-standing shafts. The composition in the arch heads has to be deduced from what survives in the solid double bay at the S end. The N-most double bay of the refectory has been reduced to the level of its solid dado. Nor does the W wall survive any higher. In the middle it is thickened to accommodate a mural

stair leading to the pulpit, and the pointed-headed doorway to the stair. The KITCHEN to the W is very ruined. Its main fireplace is thought to have been in a cross wall which has completely disappeared. In the NW corner, a cupboard with a shelf. The hatch to the refectory is set under a broad, chamfered relieving arch on this side too.

The WEST RANGE consists of two parts. To the N is what remains of the lay brothers' accommodation, while to the S are the rather better-preserved arrangements related to the entry for visitors into the monastic precinct. The LAY BROTHERS' RANGE extended N from the NW corner of the cloister, but originally had no direct access to it. Their dormitory must have occupied the full length of the upper storey, but this has completely disappeared. The S half of the lower storey was their refectory, directly communicating with the kitchen by means of a doorway. It must have been quite a handsome room, groin-vaulted. The two surviving trefoil-headed W lancets have hollow-chamfered rere-arches and are treated externally with two hollow chamfers, detailing similar to that used in the serving end of the monks' refectory. The vault has been completely robbed away, so that only its profile is visible on the W wall above the lancets. Below floor level, the base of a doorway out of alignment with the room. This, with its angle roll, is clearly a survivor from a C12 building, presumably part of the original lay brothers' accommodation. Just N of this both a change of masonry, showing that the room was lengthened, and the footings of a cross wall, where it was subsequently reduced in length again. These must reflect a great increase in the numbers of lay brothers in the C13, and a dwindling in the C14.

To the S of the lay brothers' refectory, and backing on to the W cloister walk, is what remains of a square room identified as the cellarer's, with to the W traces of a doorway and a complete lancet externally chamfered and internally rebated, which provided direct contact with the world outside the precinct. To the S again, not communicating with the cellarium, is the PARLOUR, and projecting W-wards from it, the PORCH. From the parlour a doorway opens into the W cloister walk. The upper storeys of porch and parlour both survive – the former is roofed and a good deal reconstructed. They belong to the great C13 improvements, but were themselves subsequently improved to make the approach to the precinct a little more impressive. The outer arch of the porch retains its C13 form at the bottom, with four thin roll mouldings taken down to meet a chamfered plinth. Inside, the vault and inner doorway, with two hollow chamfers on the arched head dying into broad chamfered imposts, are of the C15. The room over the parlour has a C13 S window, within which in the early C14 was inserted a smaller, more richly designed two-light window, with spurred 'Kentish' tracery in its head. Access to this room from the parlour was through a doorway in its NW corner, up a straight flight of steps, now external but originally enclosed, to an ante-room in the upper storey of the porch. The two upper rooms, it is suggested, were occupied by the cellarer, who thus could supervise access to the precinct.

INFIRMARY. The monks' infirmary lay, in the normal siting, E of the other monastic buildings, beyond a second cloister E of the monks' dormitory range. Footings only of the cloister are now visible, and of the infirmary there is not much more. But even so there is enough to indicate the scale and grandeur of the provision for the sick and aged. The infirmary was built in the mid to late C13 and remodelled in the C15. It is a long rectangle aligned W–E, with square N projections at both ends, and E and SE angle buttresses on a chamfered plinth. Internally the space was subdivided in the usual way into three aisles, separated from one another at their W and E ends by solid walls. The main central area clearly had arcades, probably of five bays, separating the side aisles, where the beds will have stood. Enough of the NW and SE responds survives to show that they were triangular, with circular shafts on moulded circular bases attached to each angle. So the free-standing arcade piers must have been lozenge-shaped, with attached shafts at the angles. Traces of two N doorways (probably for access to the kitchen to the N) and a third into the NW room, which was clearly the necessarium, or latrine, as a drain runs under its N end. The W doorway must have been a C14 modification, for its surviving S jamb is moulded with an outer double wave and an inner single wave. It seems to relate to the traces of a narrow diagonal passage which linked the infirmary (and the abbot's lodging) under cover to the N aisle of the presbytery. The main body of the infirmary underwent a major remodelling in the late Middle Ages. The open aisles were transformed piecemeal into a series of small rooms, so the arcades were replaced with solid walls, while fireplaces, many with cupboards beside them, were inserted into the outer N and S walls. The SE room was even given its own garderobe – see the pit and seat over it. The NE room was also provided with a wide hearth and chimney-breast in its E wall.

The INFIRMARY KITCHENS were rebuilt at the same time. Their remains, though little more than footings, give the best indication of the comfortable lives led by those who occupied the infirmary, probably senior monks and semi-permanent guests – corrodians – rather than invalids, during the last century or so of the abbey's existence. There were two kitchens, both rectangular, both entered at the SE corner, and both provided with wide hearths set in chimney-breasts projecting from their E walls. A curious U-shaped S passage linked the two. To the N of the E kitchen, a slate-floored room, which must have been a scullery. The memorable feature is the great monolithic, double-wave-moulded lintel of the W hearth, now cracked and grounded, but in its completeness a particularly vivid reminder of how much magnificence has been lost. Its splendour is perhaps best explained by the assumption that this W kitchen was also intended to serve the abbot's lodging adjoining to the N.

ABBOT'S LODGING. This great complex to the NE of the monastic precinct is of three main parts and two dates, early C13 and mid to late C14, reflecting an earlier and a later concept of the way in which abbots should be housed. Only in two places do more than the lowest few courses of its walls survive.

In order to identify the C13 parts one should first look at what is left of the L-shaped block E of the monks' reredorter. Its N plinth and NW angle buttresses with ashlar chamfer are typical C13 details. It is suggested that this, originally two-storeyed, block formed the earliest abbot's lodging, at a time when the abbot no longer slept with the monks in the dormitory, but occupied lodgings intercommunicating with it, in this case via the reredorter block. In the C14, however, the lodging was converted, after the abbot had left it for more segregated accommodation. There is C14 evidence of a passage against the reredorter block, entered from the S by a doorway with wave-and-hollow-moulded jambs. The cross wall dividing the lower storey into two, with fireplace flanked by doorways, must also have belonged to this remodelling. Original stone paving in the W half.

Further to the NE are traces of an originally free-standing, rectangular two-storeyed block, identified as the nucleus of the second ABBOT'S LODGING. Parts of the S wall remain as high as the upper storey, but of the other three, little is left above ground level. Chamfered jambs of two upper openings, and part of the chamfered plinth of a N buttress indicate its C13 date. The block is thought to have been first built for visiting abbots, in particular from the mother house of L'Aumône, who were expected to make periodic visitations. However, its C14 improvements, a small rectangular chapel opening off the S side of the upper storey, and a latrine extension at the E end, seem to have been for the abbot of Tintern himself, when his accommodation was absorbed into a much enlarged abbatial lodging. The chapel extension is the best-preserved structure in this part of the precinct. It is built of local grey limestone with purple Old Red Sandstone dressings. A ground-level room has a W doorway and S lancet. In the chapel above, part of a two-light E window remains, and the jambs of a piscina, shafted with circular caps and bases.

The great rectangular ABBOT'S HALL lay N–S between the two C13 structures, and linked to the second lodging midway along its E wall. This must have been a magnificent building, but its walls are tantalizingly reduced to no more than their lowest few courses. Angle buttresses and buttresses dividing the W wall into five bays, the outermost bays slightly wider than the rest. Bold plinth mouldings to the buttresses. One can only guess at the splendour of the grandly scaled hall which must have occupied the upper storey. At ground level there was a complex of passages and storage rooms. Entry was through a handsome internal porch to the E, facing away from the abbey and towards the river, the direction from which visitors would have arrived. Here the jambs of the outer doorway and two inner doorways display handsome combinations of wave and chamfer mouldings on pyramid stops. From here a passage runs S-wards within the building, with the stumps of further fine doorways at its S end, and comes out into a square room, the W wall of which (partly of C13 date, as noted above) survives to a considerable height. Slit windows here at two levels. The S wall of this room retains the splay of a single-light window and the jambs of a double doorway, internally rebated, and externally chamfered. The doorway opened into a small yard W of the infirmary kitchen, which, as has already been suggested, probably also served the abbot's hall.

The INNER COURT WALL survives largely intact to the E and S of the infirmary, and was probably built at the same time. To the N it is angled NW-wards, but dies away beyond the abbot's lodging. The foundations of a circular dovecote have been excavated at this point, across the line of the wall. The S wall links to one of the E buttresses of the church. How the wall ran on SE of the church is not known, though the row of farm buildings here probably indicates its line.

LAPIDARY COLLECTION

Tintern has an unusually large collection of loose carved stones. The most interesting are displayed close to the modern entrance to the precinct. From them the design of two important lost features has been reconstructed: that of the C13 cloister arcade (*see* p. 549, above), and the early C14 nave pulpitum. So much of the pulpitum remains that its complex and highly ornamented form has been reconstructed on paper and its date in the 1320s established on stylistic grounds.*

OUTER COURT

Foundations have been excavated to the W of the modern approach road and car park, and one or two pieces of wall stand to some height. These must belong to the GUEST ACCOMMODATION which the abbey will have required, and were probably part of the great programme of improvement undertaken in the C13. To the W was a long, narrow range, the blind E end wall of which stands quite high. Two courses of the sloping ashlar base of the thick side walls, and the bases of a central row of octagonal piers, show that the building was six bays long and had a handsome vaulted undercroft, above which there was presumably a dormitory. Nearer the road a four-bay aisled hall has been excavated. Only the sites of the aisle piers are marked. The N bay was walled off at some later date. S of this, a smaller rectangular building, partly destroyed by the construction of the A466. The N end of its E wall, however, stands quite high and retains parts of chamfered rectangular windows in two storeys, the upper one barred.

ST ANNE'S HOUSE, at the foot of the hillside to the S, incorporates what remains of the principal GATEHOUSE and its

* See S. Harrison, R. Morris and D. Robinson in *Antiquaries Journal*, vol. 78 for 1998.

CHAPEL. This was clearly a handsome early C13 structure. The present house is formed out of the chapel and its undercroft, and retains its E window of three long lancets and plate tracery of three quatrefoils. Two C13 head corbels reset under the eaves. In the N wall, C19 grouped lancets and one genuine one. Also two springers of the two-bay vault of the entrance gateway, with circular moulded caps and chamfered ribs. The undercroft below the E end of the chapel seems to have been occupied by the porter. C13 chamfered doorway and two-light window with trefoiled head.

Inside, there is more to see of the C13 chapel. The inner side of the E window is exquisitely treated, with shafts having capitals to which trefoiled stiff-leaf foliage is naively applied, and the quatrefoils set within moulded circles. Beside the window, a post-Dissolution chimneypiece, its jambs made up from a pair of many-moulded shafts on many-moulded bases from the pulpitum of the abbey church. In front of both window and fireplace are laid several rows of finely preserved TILES, also from the church.

The other entrance to the precinct which still survives is the WATERGATE. This can be found NW of the car park, a wide, double-chamfered, segmental arch, beside the Anchor Hotel. This was probably for everyday use. If there was a more impressive watergate for the use of the abbot and his guests further E near his lodging, it has disappeared.

Short stretches of the OUTER COURT WALL have been identified W of the watergate, and continuing for considerable distances NW and SE of St Anne's House on the hillside S of the A466.

INDUSTRIAL REMAINS

Tintern developed from the late C16 as an industrial centre, exploiting the water power of the Angidy Brook and transport available on the River Wye. In the 2-m.(3-kilometre)-long Angidy Valley, remains of no fewer than thirteen water-powered works have been identified, with eleven water-supply ponds and dams, and numerous houses built for workers and managers. In 1717 there were already four fineries, two chaferies and a wire mill. By 1821 twenty water wheels were in operation, only one of which survives today. Identifiable sites and structures can be described from E to W, starting at the River Wye, and proceeding up the brook.

VIADUCT, at the N end of the village. Of *c.* 1865. Three steel-truss spans on two high rock-faced piers, built to carry a branch of the Wye Valley Railway across the river, to serve the Tintern Wireworks. The steelwork was designed by *S. H. Yockney*.

ANGIDY RIVER DOCK. The Old Red Sandstone ashlar walls, rebated for lock gates, survive from a dock at the mouth of the Angidy Brook. In the N wall, remains of a very large waterwheel pit. The so-called CIDER WAREHOUSE to the SE may have served as a warehouse for the nearby forge and wireworks.

ABBEY MILL, beside the Royal George Hotel in the centre of the village. Two-storeyed with an attic, of Old Red Sandstone rubble. Cast-iron water wheel on its SE side. SW loading door accessible from the top of the masonry dam, which now carries the A466. Patched masonry in the mill wall indicates the site of the Abbey Forge which was in action here until the early C19. The HOTEL originated as the ironmaster's house.

ABBEY WIREWORKS, 300 yds (275 metres) upstream (SO 526 001). The works were probably in operation from 1567, but the last trace of early building was removed in 1990. The arches in the boundary wall which supports the Angidy Valley road may have been constructed as water-power intakes. To the E, a sunken chamber in which is a water turbine used for the tinplate works which occupied the site from *c.* 1880. To the S, a mid-C19 works pond, now dry, and above it, retaining walls on the site of Block and Hammer Mills. The white-rendered, two-storeyed HOUSE here bears the initials of Edward Foley, of the C17 ironmaster family, and the date 16[?].

MIDDLE WIREWORKS, 600 yds (550 metres) higher up, retains a substantial masonry dam, forming a large pond, and foundations in the river below of a tilt-hammer mill. CHAPEL HOUSE, to the SW, must incorporate a building of the Chapel Wire Mill.

ABBEY TINTERN BLAST FURNACE, 100 yds (90 metres) upstream again. The furnace was operated by the Foley family from 1669 or earlier. The site was excavated in 1979–80, and the extensive remains of rubble-stone buildings belonging to the charcoal-fuelled C17 blast furnace laid out for display. What can be seen are the masonry furnace stack, built into the hillside in the characteristic way, and partly surviving to full height; the foundations of the casting-house alongside; the bases of square piers for an aqueduct, which conveyed water in a timber trough to feed the furnace blast water wheel; the water wheel's masonry-lined pit; and the foundations of the 'blowing-house', where first bellows, then cast-iron cylinders provided a blast for the furnace. Behind the stack are the charging-bank with foundations of the charcoal store above, and remains of a clerk's office.

Further upstream still are the fragmentary remains of PONT-Y-SAESON FORGE (SO 508 003), with rows of former workers' HOUSES on the hillside to the W. Also, further E (SO 509 003), the ruins of the UPPER WIREWORKS (New Tongs Mill). Here high stone retaining walls terrace the site. A wheel pit survives, and the remains of a long feeder watercourse beside the Angidy Fawr, with a ruinous aqueduct which took it across the Angidy Fechan.

5000

TINTERN PARVA

ST MICHAEL. Only the S porch is medieval, of the C15. Impressively, it has a stone vault on angle shafts. Nave and lower chancel largely rebuilt in 1846. However, a restoration of 1889 by *J. Coates Carter* is reported, and it is tempting to think that the windows, plate-traceried in the nave s wall, and in particular the w bell gable, are of his doing. Arch-braced roofs. – FONT of the C14 or C15, unusual and impressive. Quite small. Octagonal bowl on an octagonal shaft taken down to a square base by emphatic pyramidal spurs. Butterfield would have admired it. – STAINED GLASS. Chancel E. Crucifixion between Christ blessing children and Good Shepherd. Datable *c.* 1870, no doubt by *Clayton & Bell* (A. Brooks). – MONUMENT. Julia Roberts †1839. Hanging wall monument with relief of a deathbed scene, the bed of elegant Grecian form. A large palm-bearing angel hovers above. Signed *Woolcott*, Bristol.

At the centre of the main-road village, WYE VALLEY HOTEL of the 1920s catches the eye. The plan is three-eighths of an irregular octagon open towards the road. Resourceful play is made with white render, red brick on porches and central entrance arch, and tile voussoirs.

CAIRNS, 1 m. W. Round cairns, stone-built Bronze Age burial monuments, are rare in Gwent but a good, though damaged, example may be seen in the forest at Barbados Green (SO 520 009).

TREDEGAR *1000*

The town takes its name from Tredegar House, near Newport, seat of the Morgan family, the principal landowners here at the head of the Sirhowy Valley. The Tredegar Ironworks were formed in 1799 after land had been leased for mineral working from Sir Charles Morgan. Coalmining started in 1806. Housing, a market house, chapels and a church were all in existence by 1840.

ST GEORGE, Church Street. 1835–6 by *John Jenkins* of London. Plain, classical, one would say, in spite of Neo-Norman details towards the street on the w porch-tower and flanking windows of the nave. The nave is of seven bays, the side windows round-headed, very closely set and linked by a continuous hoodmould. Short, lower chancel. Wide and high Neo-Norman chancel arch, elaborately and quite convincingly decorated. Galleries with more cursory decoration, surviving to N and S, curtailed at the W end. – STAINED GLASS. Chancel E, Ascended Christ. By *G. Maile & Son*, *c.* 1967. Routine. – MONUMENTS. Alfred Homfray †1851, surgeon to Tredegar Ironworks (chancel N). Grecian wall monument. Three-quarter-face relief portrait of a bearded man encircled by a snake of eternity and resting on a spray of poppies. Signed *John Evan Thomas*. – Mary Elizabeth David, 1860, wife of the Ironworks manager (chancel S). Large hanging wall monument. A kneeling woman mourns and comforts children under a draped urn. Signed by *Joseph Edwards*. – William Bevan †1868, principal agent of the Tredegar Iron Company (nave W). Tablet, signed by *E. W. Wyon*, with relief portrait of a bearded man flanked by seated mourning clerk and miner. – Horace Shepard †1888, solicitor (nave W). Gothic wall tabernacle.

ST JAMES, Georgetown. 1889–90 by *James & Morgan* of Cardiff. Conventional. Four-bay clerestoried nave and lean-to aisles, lower chancel. Lean-to W porch and double bell gable. Lancets throughout, except the Perp chancel E window. Rock-faced Pennant sandstone with Forest dressings. The arcades have circular piers with moulded caps, chamfered arches and brick outer mouldings, now painted over. The architects got into difficulties at the chancel arch, which has two tiers of shafted responds. Scissor-brace roofs. – STAINED GLASS. In most windows. Many major New Testament subjects treated with utter banality. The only ones to note are two of 1959 by *Celtic Studios*. In the N aisle, Entry into Jerusalem. In the S aisle, Flight into Egypt and Presentation in the Temple.

METHODIST CHURCH, Harcourt Terrace. Memorable for its early C20 gallery front. This runs in a continuous bow round three sides of the interior and is enriched with lush vine festoons in high-relief plasterwork. The chapel was first built in 1825 and enlarged in 1839, but must have been enlarged again subsequently. Façade of coursed grey Pennant sandstone, mutilated by the removal of the central porch. The Lombardic gable and Neo-Norman triple window under it suggest a date *c.* 1880.

SARON INDEPENDENT CHURCH, Oakfield Road. 1858–9 by the Rev. *Thomas Thomas* of Landore. Rendered but confidently classical façade. Three bays demarcated by giant Ionic pilasters which carry a full entablature and a pedimental gable. Double-height side windows, and a central triplet over the doorway. All are round-headed and have architrave mouldings and vermiculated rustication on the keystones.

Tredegar is the only Valleys town with a strongly formalized central space, THE CIRCLE. By *c.* 1850 a square had developed in front of the market house. In 1858 this was transformed when the CLOCK TOWER was erected there. The cast-iron tower, made by *Charles Jordan*, ironfounder of Newport, is in the form of a gigantic Tuscan column. Its cylindrical form so mesmerized later builders that the space around eventually became circular. From it CASTLE STREET ascends to the NW and descends to the SE. In the northern half the CASTLE HOTEL has a broad, rendered front of the 1840s. Heavy classical detail, in particular first-floor windows alternately with Gibbs surrounds and projecting as timber oriels. The cast-iron porch spanning the pavement may be a little later.

PUBLIC LIBRARY, The Circle. Of 1974–5 by *Powell, Alport & Partners*. Small, but holding its own by its Brutalist idiom. Grey brick, however, not exposed concrete, on a sloping red brick plinth. Unbroken front wall curved to the space of The Circle. Side elevation glazed below alarmingly overhanging upper sections of solid wall.

WORKING MEN'S CLUB AND INSTITUTE, The Circle. 1893. Dominant façade of tooled grey Pennant sandstone with Forest ashlar dressings. Mixed Tudor and early French Gothic. Large upper windows break through the eaves line under three gables.

MARKET HALL, Castle Street. Next door to the above, now a carpet warehouse. 1892 by *Hitchcox* of Newport.

MASONIC HALL, Morgan Street. 1893 by *James & Morgan* of Cardiff. The fancy red brick and terracotta front has been painted brown and cream.

BEDWELLTY HOUSE, now council offices. Plas Bedwellty, a minor house of the Morgans of Tredegar Park, was bought in 1800 by the Merthyr ironmaster Samuel Homfray of Penydarren. He rebuilt the house in plain but elegant Regency style in 1825 (date on a column in the basement). Two-storeyed, sash-windowed, under a shallow slated roof on paired bracketed eaves. Rendered walls lined out to look like ashlar. Eight-bay E entrance front with projecting porches in bays three and six. Five-bay S front, the centre three bays in a well-proportioned bow, the lower windows here enlarged. One other subtlety of design is the placing of the stringcourse between the storeys at upper sill level, to make the ground storey look as high as possible. The house and its grounds were given to the town in 1901. The interior of the house was remodelled as council offices, with a good deal of Art Nouveau glazing, at that time.

The GARDENS became a public park, crowded with specimen trees. To the NW of the house, a ROCK GARDEN. The stalactitic entrance arch and rockwork surrounds to beds and pond are of artificial 'Pulhamite' rock. The square building with a bellcote, just beyond, stands over an ICE-HOUSE. Pretty cast-iron BANDSTAND to the SW.

FIRST WORLD WAR MEMORIAL, facing the road SE of the house. A lofty pedestal bears a tall cross against which a bronze figure of a fully kitted soldier stands and presents arms. The figure is signed by *N.A. Trent* and the *Morris Art Foundry*, which cast it.

SIRHOWY IRONWORKS, 1 m. N. The first ironworks in Monmouthshire to be fuelled by coke rather than charcoal. The first blast furnace was erected in 1778, a second in 1797 and a third in 1801. In 1818 the concern was taken over by the Harford family, operators of the Ebbw Vale Works, and in 1832 a 1½-m. (2.5-kilometre) tunnel was constructed through the mountain to take pig-iron from the Sirhowy Works to the rolling mills there.

What remains to be seen is near the E bank of the Sirhowy River, N of the A4047. An elegant, single-arch stone BRIDGE over the river marks the N end of the great Sirhowy Tramroad, built in 1805 for 20 m. (32 kilometres) to the wharves at Pillgwenlly, Newport. The splayed deck and side arches on the E side of the bridge allowed the tramroad tracks to fan out on to the ironworks site. Reset datestones here of 1797 and 1818 (and a boundary stone of the latter date, 100 yds (90 metres) S, outside the Railway Tavern).

One street E of the bridge is a high-arched masonry RETAINING WALL against the valley-side. This seems to have belonged to the late C19 furnaces. Three high, narrow arches of yellow reverberatory brick punctuate the Pennant sandstone wall and extend back into the hillside as brick barrel vaults. The central vault is pierced by a circular opening, and nearby is the cast-iron residue of the base of a metal-clad furnace. To the SE, first the inverted conical reverberatory-brick base of a furnace smelting shaft, and beyond it the top of a second smelting-cone base.

NINE ARCHES VIADUCT, Dukestown. Handsome disused viaduct, built in 1864 to the design of the engineer *John Gardiner* for the Merthyr, Tredegar & Abergavenny Railway. Rock-faced masonry, with brick for arch-rings, soffits and parapets.

2080

TREDEGAR HOUSE

65 Tredegar House is the grandest and most exuberant country house in the county, and one of the outstanding houses of the Restoration period in the whole of Britain. The Morgans of Tredegar were the senior branch of a widely ramified Welsh family which established its dominance in south-east Wales in the late C15, not least by supporting Henry Tudor's bid for the English crown in 1485. By 1540 the family had built here what Leland, writing at the time, called 'a very faire place of stone'. An early C17 sketch plan shows that the house was in three ranges round a rectangular courtyard open to the NW. The SW range of this house survives, incorporated into the magnificent brick house built by William Morgan, who inherited in 1664 and died in 1680. He constructed a new NW range, thus enclosing the fourth side of the courtyard, and rebuilt the NE range to match. It was clearly his intention to rebuild the remaining two ranges, but this proved over-ambitious, so the late medieval SW and SE ranges were retained for service use. William's son Thomas turned his attention to building the stables, which match the house in scale and splendour, on the W side of the spacious forecourt. The ensemble was finally completed when the forecourt was enclosed by a wrought-iron screen with sumptuous wrought-iron gates, made 1714–18. Thus a spectacular view of the house was presented to passers-by on the main road into South Wales, and a view from the house was opened up to the NW with radiating avenues of trees, including a double one aligned on the Iron Age hill-fort 1 m. NE. Today, in spite of a greatly expanded Newport absorbing much of the park, and the duplication of the main road by the M4, the late Stuart effect remains, and house, forecourt, stables, transparent screen and central avenue still read together as one great statement of dynastic wealth and self-confidence.

The enormous increase in the family's wealth during the C19, which resulted from the extraction of minerals from their lands in the Valleys and the development of the port at Newport, did not have a corresponding effect on the house. The roof was reconstructed in the early C19, but Sir Charles Morgan does not seem to have embarked on any significant building to mark his elevation to the peerage as Baron Tredegar in 1859. His son, who inherited in 1875, replanned the internal circulation of the house, constructing 1877–9 a new entrance porch and reconstructing the SE service range. This was all done in careful imitation of the late C17 style, doubtless under the guidance of the first Baron's younger brother, the noted antiquary Octavius Morgan. The second Baron, a great philanthropist and benefactor of Newport, became first Viscount in 1905 and died in 1913. Thereafter the high living of his successors and heavy death duties fast depleted the estate. In 1951 the third Viscount's heir sold the house and grounds to the Sisters of St Joseph, who ran a Catholic girls' school in the house. In 1972 a new purpose-built school was erected in the park, and in 1974 the house was vacated and the estate bought by Newport County Borough Council. Since then the grounds have been largely developed for housing and offices (*see* Duffryn, p. 217), but Tredegar House and its immediate surroundings have been restored and imaginatively enhanced.

Before the house is examined in detail, it will be helpful to set out the evidence as to the date of its construction. Unfortunately no firm answers can be given. The only surviving date on the house is 1672, on a sundial painted on a glass panel in the Cedar Closet – i.e. a movable object not necessarily *in situ*. Octavius Morgan copied estimates, now lost, for the stone enrichments of the house, putting them under the date bracket 1664–74, and he recorded an inscription 'Roger Lewis Butler. 1674', cut on a cellar door, now in store, without specifying whether the door was in the old or the new part of the house. A now lost inventory of 1674 mentions decorative paintings already fixed in place. The monogram 'W. M' incorporated in the chimneypiece of the Gilt Room confirms that the fitting up of the house was well under way or even complete before William Morgan's death in 1680. The house was largely but not fully furnished by 1688, when the first of the surviving inventories was taken. Finishing touches were put to internal painting in the same year. The stables were clearly built a little later than the house. Their brickwork is in Flemish bond, as against the more old-fashioned English bond of the house. Nor do they appear in Thomas Dineley's sketch of the house and forecourt from the NW, made in 1684. However, they must have been started shortly thereafter, as painting and gilding of the 'dial and figure over the stable' were paid for in 1688. It is probable, then, that 1688 was the year in which both house and stables were completed; but when the house was started remains an enigma.

The identity of the architect of Tredegar House, on the other hand, has recently become clearer. The taste for luxuriant decoration, particularly for twisted columns, so conspicuous outside and in, may be the taste of William Morgan himself. But Sir Howard Colvin has made a strong case for saying that he employed the brothers *Roger* and *William Hurlbutt*, master carpenters of Warwick, architects of Ragley Hall *c.* 1679, the only other country house built on the pavilion plan before the 1680s, and whose Maiden Bradley, Wiltshire, of *c.* 1683, used very similar façade enrichments to those at Tredegar. The Hurlbutts' first big job was fitting up the state apartment at Warwick Castle 1669–78, a scheme which could well have recommended them to William Morgan. Colvin's suggestion has been given greater credence by Giles Worsley, who has pointed out that the idiosyncratic design of the stables at Tredegar is in its main motifs identical to the stables built at Warwick Castle in 1667, almost certainly to the Hurlbutts' design. That provincial master craftsmen should have designed house and stable at Tredegar is inherently more likely than that a London-based architect should have been called in, for both buildings are fashionable but provincial, rather than metropolitan in style. We know too little about William Morgan to hazard a guess as to why he chose to employ the Hurlbutts, but we can feel that his house embodies a good deal of what must have been his own ebullient personality.

So now, after these preliminaries, detailed examination can start. Today visitors approach the house from the SE, through the service yard. In order to appreciate the house as William Morgan and his successors intended it to be seen, it is necessary to go round to the other side and stand in the entrance forecourt.

The two ranges built by William Morgan are of pale red brick with stone enrichments, of two storeys on a low rendered basement and crowned by a hipped roof. Both have recessed centres and slightly projecting angle pavilions. The rhythm of the NW, entrance, front is two-plus-seven-plus-two, while the NE front is by contrast of three-plus-three-plus-three bays, the centre bays more widely spaced than those in the pavilions. The W pavilion returns for three bays towards the SW and the E pavilion for two bays to the SE, showing clearly that a complete rebuilding of the earlier house was intended, with pavilions at all four corners. The hipped roof, though boldly projecting on the original carved wooden brackets, is a reconstruction made some time between 1793 and 1827 to a lower pitch, slated not tiled, and with idiosyncratic dormer windows, segment-headed and semicircular, the result of remodelling after 1853. The original steeper roof, balustraded platform and central lantern, flanked by tall chimneystacks, will have given a weightier look to the long, low entrance front.

What makes the exterior of Tredegar House unforgettable is the Bath stone enrichments, of a luxuriant bravura quite unlike the normally restrained Restoration style. The centrepiece is the
67 entrance doorway, its round-headed surround framed between twisted Corinthian columns up which bay fronds twine. Swagged pedestals below, pieces of frieze above, carved and curvaceous in profile, supporting a broken segmental pediment. The pediment ends are decorated with rosettes, and between them rests a many-quartered shield of arms held by the Morgan supporters, a lion and a gryphon, which bound up the pediment slopes to l. and r. Ten pairs of similar, smaller heraldic beasts support shields of arms, all of them different, on the broken triangular pediments over the ground-floor windows.* These windows and the windows above are equal in size, and all have broad, eared surrounds of stone, with correctly proportioned architrave mouldings, and, a happy survival, stone mullion-and-transom crosses. Pulvinated friezes to the window surrounds at both levels. The

* The armorial bearings may be an antiquarian restoration under the influence of Octavius Morgan, as they relate to family alliances going as far back as the C15.

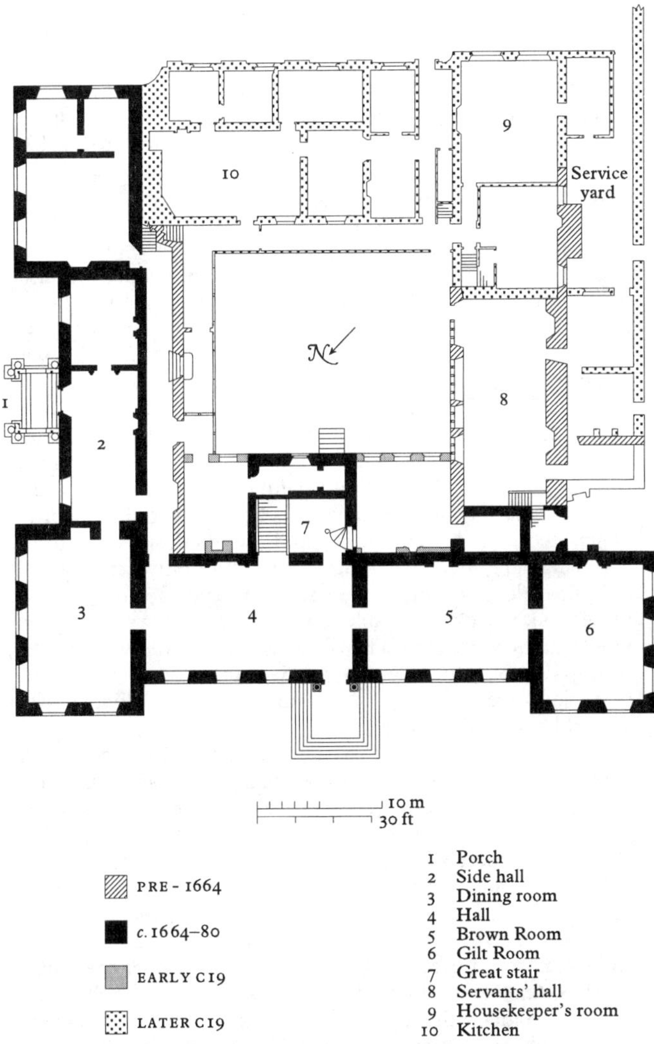

Tredegar House. Ground-floor plan

upper surrounds are topped by plain cornices, but have panels below them carved with swags of fruit in relief, and end drops which may be meant for a pine cone and a pomegranate. Finally, all this carved enrichment is anchored into a rhythmical composition by raised, alternating quoins, and by the stone cornice moulding which runs all the way across the façade at the level of the lower window heads. This last item has the effect of making the upper storey appear loftier than the lower, even though the enriched pediments of the lower windows signal that the state rooms are down on the ground floor.

The NE front is detailed in an identical manner, though the projecting stone porch is of 1877–9 by *Habershon & Fawckner*, over-emphasizing the motif of twisted columns in typical Victorian fashion. On both fronts the carved eaves brackets are paired every so often, and set on the diagonal in pairs at the corners. Whether this is a C17 or a C19 arrangement is not clear.

The SE front, after the two-bay return of the E pavilion, is wholly of 1877–9. *Habershon & Fawckner* devised for this, the service side, an elevation which echoed the C17 style without aping it. The centre four bays are three-storeyed, of red brick above a rendered ground storey which has mullioned windows within a blank arcade. Mullion-and-transom cross-windows in the top storey and plain cornice brackets. At the S end, two more bays under a gable, the windows very wide and long, with a transom and two mullions. The SW range shows work of all three periods. The S end is C17 remodelled in the C19; the W end is the three-bay return of the 1670s W pavilion, with next to it, in a plane further back, a four-storey bay with openings of the same period, a doorway with an eared surround, and above it a tier of windows of various late C17 vernacular forms. Decorated eaves brackets here too. Between these two ends the surviving late medieval range looks diminutive in scale. It is built of local rubble-stone. At the W end, a three-storeyed projection, narrow and gabled. Two-light windows with chamfered mullions at all levels in its NW face, the lower two renewed. Stump of a big chimneystack beside it to the r., and a second, more massive chimney-breast further along. (Evidence of a third beneath the roof.)

To see the front of the C16 range it is necessary to go into the courtyard. Here the walling is of squared, coursed local limestone, and there are impressively tall mullioned windows on two storeys. Above, they are of five, five and four lights, below of five, five, three and five (two visible) lights. All have arched lights and hollow chamfer mouldings, and all have hoodmoulds, the lower ones hacked back *c.* 1828, to make way for a covered walkway on iron posts. Clearly there were important rooms in this range. Some late medieval evidence remains inside. On the ground storey, in the present servants' hall, a four-centred-headed fireplace opening with hollow-and-wave-moulded surround and spandrels decorated with ribbon and shield. In the room above, a fragment of a similar, blocked fireplace opening, and, beside it, a large, broadly hollow-chamfered doorway.

The INTERIOR of the main house is entered through the C19 porch in the centre of the NE range. The first room, the SIDE HALL, was entirely refitted in 1879. It has a timber chimneypiece and door-cases in a sober late C17 style, and a beamed plaster ceiling and bracketed plaster cornice which are also a passable imitation of late C17 work. The small panels of gilt leather framed on the wall above the NW doorway have been brought in from Octavius Morgan's house in Newport, The Friars, and date from *c.* 1720. Yet in the inventory of 1688 this room is already named as 'the Drawing Room that is hang'd with Gilt Leather'. The NW doorway opens into the DINING ROOM (the New Parlour in 1688), the room which occupies the N pavilion. The panelling of the dining room is much more elaborate and genuinely of the late C17, with a full entablature all round, its frieze enriched with swags of fruit. The door-case surrounds are convex, eared and carved with foliage. The principal doorway also carries a frieze and broken pediment. Carved acanthus frieze to the chimneypiece, and a white marble bolection fireplace surround, may be of the C19. The wreathed plaster ceiling is a C19 replacement for the C17 one which had collapsed, convincing except for the Neoclassical husks in the centre.

The next room, entered through the pedimented doorway, is the HALL, i.e. the late C17 entrance hall. There was an original enriched plaster ceiling here too, but after its removal in the 1950s no attempt was made to replicate it. The plain black and white marble chimneypiece is probably early C19. The slate-flagged edging to the floor dates from 1994. The major survival of the C17 decoration is the panelling. Note its strong bolection mouldings. Spatially, there are two significant points. The first is that the C17 front door opens into the room not axially, but into its r.-hand corner. Secondly, the principal stair rises from the back of the hall, opposite the entrance doorway. But before examining and ascending the staircase, the two climactic ground-floor rooms remain to be entered.

The Brown Room and Gilt Room, occupying the ground storey of the entrance range W of the hall, were clearly conceived as the principal reception rooms, a state dining room and state withdrawing room beyond. The BROWN ROOM is architecturally the most successful room, if not wholly so. Its chimneypiece, almost central in the long wall, faces the central of the three windows; its two doorways – one larger than the other – are set almost central in the short end walls. This formality is reinforced with sonorous emphasis by magnificent carved oak panelling. The greatest weight of decoration is applied to the door-cases, which have massive broken scrolly pediments within which are carved high-relief trophies supporting painted plaster busts. The trophy at the hall end is of arms and armour and the bust of the emperor Augustus, the trophy at the opposite end of musical instruments, supporting a bust of the emperor's wife, Livia. Massive carved consoles support the pediments, and a bound olive wreath extends between the brackets, bearing superimposed central panels, with wreaths in egg-and-dart frames. The door-frames themselves have ears and a bold wave moulding carved with upright leaves. In the narrow outer panels drops of leaves and flowers hang from the consoles, providing visual support for what would otherwise look a precariously heavy superstructure. The walls are densely packed with raised vertical panels under scrolly broken pediments, all with busts within the pediment scrolls. The panels are lugged at all four angles and enclose wave-moulded inner frames. Below each panel runs a deep band of scrolling acanthus foliage inhabited by putti, dragons and serpents, between snarling animal and wild-man masks. Flanking the chimneypiece, the panels alternate with narrow vertical strips of foliage up which putti scramble. To crown everything a full entablature extends round the room, the frieze carved with a continuous acanthus scroll. A plaster ceiling of matching richness fell down in 1848. The present mid-C19 ceiling is quite a convincing replacement, though the central painting of the Tribute of the Gods to Flora and Zephyr was not replaced. Simple C19, white veined marble chimney-piece with side consoles.* An overmantel painting of Diana and Callisto was removed in the 1950s.

66 The last room on the ground floor, the GILT ROOM, which occupies the W pavilion, is equally spectacular, but also a calculated contrast to what has gone before. It is the only room in the house which retains its complete C17 decoration. The panelled walls are grained to imitate figured walnut, with all raised mouldings and carvings gilt. The heaviest concentration of carving, and so of gilding, occurs in the chimneypiece and its overmantel, which extends right up to the ceiling. The fireplace surround, broad and elaborately wave-moulded, is of exotic black veined marble. Continuous undercut gilt carving frames and crowns it. To l. and r. putti struggle to climb up fat swags of fruit. In the middle is a deep, segment-headed panel with a central circular wreath enclosing William Morgan's initials partly hidden behind a spray of roses, and flanking lions which playfully stick up their rumps and wave their tails. The overmantel is dominated by a pair of Corinthian columns, their twisted shafts painted to resemble black veined marble. Narrow outer panels with more scrambling putti. Central rectangular carved frame for a picture. The columns carry a mighty entablature of maximum elaboration. Undercut flowers in the pulvinated frieze. Undercut modillions in the cornice. The panelling is, by comparison, restrained, in three tiers, the top one deepest and framed above by tight-stretched swags of drapery and below by ribbon-tied swags of fruit. Narrow vertical panels enclosing straight laurel drops emphasize the rhythm of the panelling. The main panels on the entrance wall enclose contemporary paintings of allegorical figures. To the l. of the doorway are three of the four cardinal virtues, Justice, Temperance and Prudence, copied from engravings published 1665–8 of the sculptural decoration of Amsterdam Town Hall. Above the doorway is a reclining figure of Venus derived from a famous Titian composition. To the r. of it appear Summer and Winter from a set of the seasons of unknown derivation. In the centre of the ceiling is a much larger painting, representing the surprising subject of Pope Urban VIII overcoming lust and intemperance. This too has an engraved source, Tetius's print (1647) of *Pietro da Cortona*'s celebrated ceiling in the *gran salone* of the Palazzo Barberini in Rome. It is difficult to imagine that a coherent overall programme was intended. The plasterwork

* David Freeman suggests that the pink marble chimneypiece in the housekeeper's room may originally have belonged here.

consists of a wreath of tight-packed fruit and flowers encircling the painting, a scrolling acanthus border, and tufts of foliage in the spandrels.

It is now necessary to return to the hall and mount the GREAT STAIR. The stair is of the most sumptuous sort which English joiners could produce in the mid to late C17. Instead of balustrades it has panels of majestically proportioned acanthus scrolls, and on the newels are drops of fruit in relief. The upper parts of the stairwell were altered in the early C19, and the cupola which lit it from above removed. Sparse Neoclassical plasterwork. Upstairs, the NW and NE ranges provided suites of chambers. The corridor on the courtyard side of the NW range was formed in the early C19, and originally the rooms opened out of one another. The room above the Gilt Room in the W pavilion, at the end of the enfilade, is called the BEST CHAMBER in the 1688 inventory. Its handsome decoration is largely intact. The wave-moulded fireplace surround is of red veined marble, the overmantel decorated with gilt drops. Plain, full-height wainscot and top entablature. The plaster ceiling is original, with a central oval wreath of leaves and berries, outer panels bearing trophies of palm, olive, ivy etc., and acanthus at the ends. Close by, in the SE range, the contemporary BACK STAIR descends in a series of straight flights. Bulbous turned balusters, and ball finials on the newels. In the rooms which occupy the centre of the NW range there is nothing to note. In the N pavilion, the so-called KING'S ROOM. Wainscot with rounded tops to the main fields, black marble chimneypiece, swags in the overmantel, perhaps made up, and a plaster ceiling which looks a C19 pastiche. The corridor which runs the length of the NE range may be part of the late C17 plan. Note that the doorways of the rooms in this range are arranged *en enfilade*, in the late C17 manner. The three rooms in the centre of the range have panelling of indeterminate date and C19 plaster friezes. The third seems to have been the dressing room of the master of the house. Beyond it, in the E pavilion, his bedchamber and two closets. The MASTER'S BEDCHAMBER is soberly panelled below a plain plaster entablature, and what decoration there is concentrates on the chimneypiece. Black veined marble fireplace surround with the usual bold wave moulding, so presumably late C17. A band of upright leaves supports the mantelshelf, and a landscape painting above is inset between scrolls and swags. The tiny CEDAR CLOSET, by contrast, provides one of the most overpowering experiences of Tredegar. Full-height cedar panelling incorporates a series of cupboards framed with twisted Corinthian colonnettes. Red mottled marble fireplace surround. Ceiling crudely painted with flying putti and garlands. The single window is strongly barred, and in one light is the painted sundial previously mentioned for its date, 1672. So this must have been intended as the storeroom for the master's valuables, next door to his study. This, the corner closet, was fitted up in 1905 as a bathroom, with a formidable free-standing bath. Within the space of the corridor at its W end, a back stair with fluted bulbous balusters and ball finials on the newels. It is of the late C17, but has been somewhat rearranged.

The SE and SW ranges are occupied by service rooms, with nurseries and other minor family rooms in the upper storey of the SE range. The major rooms are the SERVANTS' HALL, at the W end of the SW range, formerly part of the late medieval house, the HOUSEKEEPER'S ROOM at the S end of the SW range, and the single-storey KITCHEN at the E end of the SE range.

68 The great STABLE, built, as has been shown above, *c.* 1684–8, flanks the SW side of the forecourt, so that every visitor to the house would see it. It is clearly intended as a showpiece – and doubtless the horses stalled in it were also prized objects of display. Red brick walls and Bath stone dressings, echoing those of the house. Eleven-bay façade, the bay at each end wider than the rest and brought forward slightly. Hipped, slated roof with early C19 dormers matching those on the house. The central three-bay pediment, rendered white and visually unrelated to the rest of the building, with its coved cornice, may also not be original. The clock in the centre of the pediment is dated 1766. What makes the stable so memorable is its enrichments, largely of cut stone. The main windows have architrave surrounds, small cornices and cross mullions and transoms, but above them is a row of flattened oval windows lighting the hay lofts. Most idiosyncratic are the pine-cone-carrying Ionic pilasters which demarcate the bays. They have brick shafts and extend little more than half the height of the façade. They are not in fact pilasters in the normal sense, but imitate the decorative heel-posts common in well-appointed C17 stables, and so are a sign of the function of the building. The major mark of distinction is the grandly scaled central carriage arch, framed by Corinthian half-columns on pedestals and crowned by a broken triangular pediment reaching up to the eaves. Bust of a Roman emperor between the pediment ends, and piles of armour on their slopes. Continuous wave-moulded arch surround with idiosyncratically shaped imposts, and in the entablature a boldly pulvinated frieze. Inside, the stalls which occupy the l. half are probably mid-C19, with cast-iron railings. The r. half is completely empty and open to the roof, and may have served as a riding school. The C17 roof structure remains, with tie-beams at two levels, kingposts and diagonal struts secured by iron straps. At the back, an original, central three-bay projection, with early flanking brick additions: a row of four COACHMEN'S HOUSES to the l., their stone doorways and windows matching those in the front façade, a seven-bay lean-to ORANGERY to the r., quite plain except for its shaped half gable-end in which an oval window has been reset. The GARDEN in front of it, with paths of coloured gravels, was first laid out soon after 1713, and re-created *c.* 1990.

69 The wrought-iron RAILINGS and GATES which enclose the forecourt in line with the outer, NW end of the stables, were made in 1714–18 by *William* and *Simon Edney* of Bristol. The railings are enlivened by decorative pilasters of wrought iron at intervals. The gates themselves (though much restored) are a

tour de force. The central double gates and flanking *claires-voies* are separated by densely patterned pilasters, which rise higher to solid Corinthian capitals crowned by openwork four-way scrolls and what look like miniature olive bushes. Frolicsome overthrows. In the brick forecourt walls which flank the house there are smaller, less elaborate wrought-iron gates.

The PARK, though drastically reduced from its former size, retains three crucial features. The OAK AVENUE continues the axis of the NW forecourt for a further ½ m. (1 kilometre) beyond the Edney gates. It was the spine of a typical late C17 planting of radiating avenues. Thanks to the rising ground on which its further extent is planted, the savage interruption caused by the M4 is barely noticed. The other two features belong to the landscaping of the grounds in accordance with a plan drawn up by *Adam Mickle* c. 1788. His is the long, narrow and slightly sinuous LAKE to the N of the house, and his was the mounding to the NW (now gone) which was intended to hide the new turnpike road (A48) from the house. In the park wall, near the N end of the lake, a pair of GATE LODGES was inserted by *Habershon & Fawckner* c. 1879, for the new drive leading to the NE front and its new entrance porch. The gate lodges, of red brick, single-storeyed under high hipped roofs with swept eaves and crowning chimneystack, provide a foretaste of the style of the house. They also suggest acquaintance with W.E. Nesfield's pioneering Queen Anne style lodge at Kew, 1867.

Finally, there is a little to say about the OUTBUILDINGS to the SE of the house. They are loosely grouped round a cobbled yard and were constructed at a variety of dates from the C17 to the C19. The former BREWHOUSE (now restaurant), facing the house, incorporates early stone walling. The GREATER and LESSER BARNS, to the E of the yards, were originally a single enormous barn, no less than 255 ft (78 metres) long, built in the C17 but reconstructed as two after a fire in the C19, when a passage was formed between them. Further E are low, red brick buildings of the mid C19, STABLES and MILL.

HILL-FORT, ¾ m. N (ST 289 869). In a good strategic position overlooking the mouth of the Usk. Its circuit of widely spaced banks and ditches covers the top of a rounded hill, which became the focus for the design of avenues radiating from Tredegar House below. Nothing is known of the history of the fortifications. They are assumed to belong to the late prehistoric period, though there has been speculation about a possible refortification in the medieval period. Field analysis is hampered by the remains of golf tees and bunkers. The defences consist of a rather angular innermost enclosure defended by a substantial bank and ditch. The second rampart is not concentric with it, being more widely spaced on the SW, where a third bank and ditch form a broad annexe. Modern tracks cut the defences at several points but the original entrance would seem to have been near the SW corner. COED Y DEFAID (ST 274 862), a small circular fort with well-preserved bank and ditch, can be easily seen across the river from here.

3090 TREDUNNOCK/TREDYNOG

St Andrew. The church lies back from the road, beyond a white-painted iron gateway dated 1902, and clipped rhododendron hedges. Norman nave and lower, square-ended chancel, to which a w tower was added, probably in the C14, a Perp s porch, and a N vestry, probably in 1877. Walls of Old Red Sandstone, with much old render adhering on the chancel. The Norman evidence consists of one tiny, tapering N window (now blocked) in the nave, and in the chancel a tiny window N and another s (the latter visible inside only). Extra light was provided for the chancel in the C15 by a three-light, pointed-headed E window, and for the nave by a three-light, square-headed s window. They are recognizably by the same mason, see the deep hollow reveals and in particular the minute lozenge tips to the cusping of the tracery. The square, mullioned N window cut through the rood-stair projection is part of *Arthur Grove*'s restoration of 1910. Late Perp depressed arches to the s priest's doorway and to the s porch arch and s doorway. The porch retains its original roof of arched braces and moulded purlins. Polygonal stoup, its bowl snapped off. Finally, the tower. This is short and thick, its corbelled parapet and rectangular belfry openings looking post-medieval. But the w doorway, with two broad continuous chamfers, suggests its origin in the C14. This is reinforced inside, where the broad tower arch is moulded with three continuous hollow chamfers. The only other structural feature of note inside is the off-axis chancel arch, wide and high, and formed of mottled Old Red Sandstone ashlar blocks. Three continuous chamfers, the inner one barely interrupted by token imposts. – FONT. Dated 1662, with the names of the churchwardens in deeply incised letters. Boldly gadrooned circular bowl on an octagonal shaft with flame-like stops. – PEWS. In the nave, with simplified poppyheads, surely by *Arthur Grove*, 1910. – STAINED GLASS. Chancel E. Early C19 heraldic glass in the tracery lights. Ascended Christ below, 1906 by *Joseph Bell & Son*. – MONUMENTS. Roman grave-slab (set in the wall above the font). Splendidly lettered and well-preserved inscription commemorating Julius Julianus, a soldier with the Second Augustan Legion, stationed at Caerleon (q.v.). – Panel in the porch dated 1910, recording the restoration. An early work by *Eric Gill*. The comparison with the Roman lettering is instructive.

In the CHURCHYARD, the broached base and lowest shaft-stone of a CROSS, set on new steps in 1910. (Also the base of a CROSS from Kemeys Inferior.)

Rectory, E of the church. Dour and substantial, of Old Red Sandstone, with gables and pointed doorways. 1857 by *Charles Fielding* of Huddersfield, extended by *Middleton, Prothero & Phillot* c. 1883.

Newbridge, $\frac{1}{2}$ m. E. Three-arch bridge spanning the tidal River Usk. Said to have been built in 1779 by a member of the celebrated *Edwards* family of bridge-builders. An extremely fine design beautifully executed in Old Red Sandstone masonry. Below high-water mark all is ashlar, in contrast to the slabby coursed masonry above. Piers with sharply pointed cutwaters carried up with two small set-offs to form triangular refuges at the level of the roadway. Wide segmental arches formed with a single ring of thin voussoir slabs.

GARN FAWR, 1¼ m. SW. The L-plan, two-storeyed house is a puzzle to interpret. The E-facing main range seems to have formed a plain three-unit house typical of the late C16. Three stone chimneypieces downstairs with chamfered jambs, a newel stair beside the central one, rising in a projecting rear stair-turret. The S cross range was added to provide improved accommodation at the parlour end of the house, with a stair rising in short, straight flights up a solid core. The doorway from the stair to the upper SE room has a shaped timber head, of the sort so plentiful from the second quarter of the C17. This means that the most conspicuous feature of the house, the complete set of three-light stone windows, cannot belong to it. With their arched lights and hollow-chamfered mouldings, they are of C16 character, too early for the S range at least. They are of Bath stone and must have been brought in from another house. The fine C16 chimneypiece, also of Bath stone, in the upper SE room must also be imported, but the plaster inscription above it, A.N.D.N. 1581, a half-century or so too early for the room, appears to be C19, though already in place by 1853. In 1860 it was noted that recent alterations had 'put an entire new face on the old structure'. The little battlemented turret at the N end, with arrow loops at the top, proclaims itself a piece of Victorian antiquarianism. Finally, inside, one more importation, the small-fielded early C17 wainscot in an upper room. Next door, at the N end, C17 plaster has been exposed, painted with *trompe-l'oeil* wainscot.

TREGARE/TREGAER *4010*

ST MARY. Small, Dec nave with lower chancel, and low unbuttressed W tower, its details all C19, under a pyramid roof. Restored in 1900 by *G. E. Halliday*. Unusual S porch, just stone side walls carrying a timber-framed eaves section and arch-braced and wind-braced roof. Two-light Dec N window in the nave, a quatrefoil under an ogee head. Big, square-headed S windows, the one which would have lit the rood completely plain with mullions. Simple square N and S windows in the chancel, one dated 1638. The delights are inside. Here it appears that the C14 mason was a man of delicate imagination. Slender keeled shafting to the nave N window. W window similarly treated, but cut down and deprived of its tracery when converted into the arch for the later tower. Most arresting, the chancel arch, or rather the high and bold cinquefoiled superarch above it. Roofs of the C15 or early C16. That in the nave is of the usual ribbed and plastered wagon form, on moulded, embattled wall-plates. Small lozenge bosses at the intersections of the ribs.

Chancel roof of single-rafter construction, arched, with a collar purlin. – FONT. A most remarkable C15 conceit, the shaft original, the bowl a C19 copy. Covered in hearts outlined by rolls, each heart enclosing IHS. – MONUMENT. John Evans †1704 (chancel N). Hanging wall monument of stone, with typical broken segmental pediment and cherub head at the foot.

In the CHURCHYARD, the three moulded steps for a CROSS and a section of shaft set in a base part octagonal, part square.

BOARD SCHOOL, 1 m. E. Small and lonely, built for the Dingestow and Tregaer school board in 1875–6, to the design of *Lawrence & Goodman* of Newport. Single-storey school range towards the road, boldly proclaiming its name beside the pointed entrance doorway, and tall teacher's house at r.-angles behind to the l. Both parts are of mauve Old Red Sandstone, dressed and banded with buff brick. The gables have jagged white barge-boards, the steep roofslopes are covered with fish-scale tiles. Only one feature is lost, the top of the red brick slab of a chimney-stack shared by house and school.

(HENLLYS, ¼m. SW. The house has an early C17 two-storeyed parlour wing at the N end with sunk-chamfered three-light N windows at both levels. Shaped head to the stair doorway.)

COED CEFN, ¾m. E. A long, thin range of several periods, thought to incorporate a small, late medieval cruck-trussed house. Panelling dated 1661 brought in from Penrhos Church in 1847.

ARTHA, ¾m. SE. A C17 farmhouse of exceptional pretension. From the N one sees the full length of a typical three-unit, two-storey house of *c.* 1600, the massive hall chimney-breast set, unusually, in the long wall. Second projecting chimney-breast to the r. This and the hipped roof are the immediately apparent evidence of the fashion-conscious enlargement and improvement made in the late 1670s by Isaac Williams. Round the corner to the E handsome channelled stone gatepiers carrying chunks of entablature with bolection frieze, the first sign of Williams's only slightly countrified awareness of the classical vocabulary. The square-headed stone S doorway into the hall is also his, moulded with wave and ovolo, on wine-jar-shaped stops. The SW parlour wing at r.-angles to the original range, built of brick on stone footings, is all of the 1670s.

Inside, the original hall and the parlour to its E now form a single room. The hall fireplace is crudely detailed, of stone, with monolithic lintel. The kitchen in the NW angle has a wide segment-headed fireplace with continuous chamfer, presumably of the 1670s. Then comes the dog-leg stair, rising to the roof and dated 1678 on the bottom newel. Flat, shaped balusters. Pairs of plaster roses in the ceilings here. The parlour, beyond, has the most impressive chimneypiece, framed with its overmantel in an architrave surround, top cornice under the ceiling decorated with all the proper Corinthian components: dentils, egg-and-dart and little modillions, the frieze boldly embossed with the date 1676 and Williams's initials, and supported on big carved brackets. Upstairs, the room over the parlour is dominated by the alarmingly low-slung plaster ceiling (reconstructed

1986), with moulded ribs, central rose and flattened cherub heads in the angles. Four symmetrically placed doors with matching miniature pediments. In the room over the kitchen, plaster chimneypiece with enriched frieze and the date 1679.

THE PWLL, ¾m. SW. Two-unit cruck-trussed hall house rescued from dereliction 1990–5. Complete N gable, with cruck blades visible and also the junction between wall-post and spur-tie supporting the wall-plate. Original sole-plate and vertical timbers exposed in the W wall. Inside, the upper parts of all three trusses can be seen. A crude post-and-panel partition forms an unheated room at the N end. Inserted chimneystack for the hall fireplace and beside it a spiral stair to an inserted upper floor. Entry passage and S bay all recently reconstructed.

LLWYN-Y-GAER, 1¼m. NW. The site is moated towards the N, so must be medieval, but the house is entirely mid-C17, of two dates, probably the 1630s and the 1670s. Before the W end was reduced in height *c.* 1950 and the N porch demolished, it was one of the largest and finest Monmouthshire farmhouses of its period, almost of gentry scale and pretension. Walls are of an unusual brown local rubble-stone, the windows have much-renewed timber frames under slate hoodmoulds, and the trios of typical lozenge chimneystacks are reconstructed in brick. Ovolo-moulded mullioned windows, two in the centre of the N front, above and below, unusually tall and transomed. The plan is an L, the E–W range much longer than the range which extends S from its E end. The W half of the longer range was clearly an addition, originally entered through the now demolished N porch. The timber door-frame of the porch, reused at the present S entrance, has relief decoration very similar to that on the porch dated 1675 at High House, Penrhos. The purpose of the 1670s extension seems to have been to improve the servicing of the house. The earlier kitchen was in the S range, to judge by the big oven projecting from its S wall.

Inside there is impressive decoration of both periods. The hall, lit by the lower transomed window, has ceiling beams moulded with a double ovolo and ovolo-moulded joists, typical of the second quarter of the C17. The parlour in the NE corner retains its moulded stone chimneypiece but is otherwise plain. The two rooms above these were richly decked with plasterwork in the 1670s, perhaps by the craftsman who was working at Artha (*see* above) at the same time. The best chamber, lit by the upper transomed window, is now subdivided. Here the earlier ovolo-moulded beams have been allowed to remain visible, but the fireplace is flanked by twisted, vine-clad columns and the overmantel decorated with large raspberry pendants and a central cherub head. In the square NE room the plaster decoration is on the ceiling: five circular fruit and leaf wreaths, a large one in the centre, surrounding a rosette, and smaller ones in the corners. A decorated plaster frieze is all that survives of the fireplace overmantel.

THE WAUN, 1m. N. A remarkable survival, a late C16 and C17 farmhouse of several periods, little altered subsequently and at the time of writing disused. T plan. Two-bay N range at the head of the T, originally timber-framed between stone-gabled end walls. In maybe the 1670s the timber-framing was replaced by a single-storey stone N front of two bays, with timber-framed semi-dormers tipped by cut-out pendants. Three-light ovolo-moulded windows of timber under slate hoods, and similarly detailed dormer windows aligned above them. Similar windows inserted at two levels in the E gable wall. The W gable wall has a doorway at its N end, a central chimney-breast and a big square stair projection added in the later C17. The S range, forming the upright of the T, is two-storeyed. The E entrance doorway, of timber, square-headed and multimoulded, looks like work of *c.* 1670. To the W, a broad projecting chimney-breast, and against its S flank a flight of steps to an upper storeroom.

5000

TRELLECH/TRELECH

The name Trellech, 'town of the stones', refers to the prehistoric Harold's Stones (*see* below) which were believed to mark the site of Harold Godwinson's victory over the Welsh in 1063. The splendid church stands in the centre of a varied group of buildings: vicarage, farm and modest endowed school. But the church recalls a much more impressive past, for Trellech was a planted town of the de Clares, and by the late C13 had become the largest Gwent borough, considerably larger than Chepstow. In 1296 there was a serious fire, and although the church was soon handsomely rebuilt, the town began to decline. Its situation, in uplands far from a river, must have told against it. By 1696 the one-time borough and market town was reduced to 'a poore inconsiderable village'. In 1901 there were just seventeen inhabited houses in the village.

17 ST NICHOLAS. One of the finest churches in the county. It is built entirely of the local Old Red Sandstone, its pinks and mauves mottled with grey lichen. Proud W steeple, a three-stage tower and lofty stone spire. Aisled and clerestoried nave to the same scale, a much lower and by comparison almost humble chancel. However, the round-headed priest's door here cannot be taken as evidence of Norman fabric, and the whole building was probably put up together in the early years of the C14. *E. H. Lingen Barker*'s restoration of 1893–4 reconstructed the roofs, not quite to the original line (see the crease in the E face of the tower), inserted an E window to a new design, and reinstated two windows in the N aisle.

Clearly the steeple was the town's pride and joy. It is of squared masonry, not the rubble walling used in nave and chancel, and it stands on a wave-and-chamfer base moulding. W doorway with three continuous sunk waves. Splendid four-light window over it, its tracery all cusped reticulation, in a wave-moulded frame. The top stage of the tower steps in significantly, its belfry lights two tiers of trefoil-headed lancets. The octagonal spire rises from behind a battlemented parapet, and has gabled lucarnes with paired lights at the base of alternate faces. The lean-to nave aisles have strong buttresses, dying in at the height of the window heads. The W bay to N and S clasps the tower and is windowless, an odd arrangement. The tracery patterns elsewhere are disappointingly simple. Two-light side windows with cusped Y-tracery and surrounds moulded with two thin hollows. Three-lighters at the E end. Small trefoil-headed lancets in the clerestory, only the E-most and W-most original. In the chancel, two-light side windows with Y-tracery and cinquefoiled lights.

The interior is also impressive. The tower arch is splendidly high and steeply pointed, with two-plus-two-plus-two continuous sunk waves. The five-bay nave has arcades on octagonal piers with moulded octagonal caps, and stilted arches given two-plus-two hollow mouldings. Cusped rere-arches to two N aisle windows, apparently at random. The chancel arch, moulded with two-plus-two hollows, was slightly heightened in 1893–4. – PISCINAS. That in the chancel under a plain ogee arch, that in the S aisle under a trefoiled arch carrying an elaborately patterned blind triangle, clearly an original feature. – ALTAR RAILS. C17. A remarkable survival, forming a spacious three-sided enclosure for the altar, a Laudian plan. Twisted balusters, in the round towards the W, flat to N and S. – PULPIT. Of the Laudian period. Decorated with the usual arcading above panels with circles and fleurs-de-lys. Clearly part of a more elaborate ensemble, some of which has been made up into a wall panel behind the reading desk, including the date 1639. – ROYAL ARMS. Of Charles II, dated 1683. Boldly carved and brightly coloured. – SUNDIAL (S aisle). The head of the sundial set up in 1689 by Lady Magdalen Probert of The Argoed, Penallt. Carved on three sides with reliefs of Trellech's three celebrated antiquities and labelled MAGNA MOLE (Great in its Mound – the Norman motte, thought to be the burial place of Harold Godwinson's troops), MAIOR SAXIS (Greater in its Stones – the three prehistoric stones, thought to mark the site of Harold's victory), MAXIMA FONTE (Greatest in its Well – the so-called Virtuous Well). (For all these *see* below.) Also incised flowers, identical with those of the font of 1661 at Llandenny. – STAINED GLASS. Chancel E, Risen Christ and angels with flame-like wings, quite arresting. Chancel NE and SE, saints. All inserted in 1894 by *Heaton, Butler & Bayne*. – Chancel NW and SW, 1909 by *Joseph Bell & Son*. – MONUMENT. Medieval effigy (sanctuary S). Of a priest? Worn and faceless.

In the CHURCHYARD, part of a CROSS SHAFT set on a spurred base and five steps. – LYCHGATE. Pyramid-roofed and ingeniously sprung off the wall of the adjoining house. The HOUSE itself served as the schoolhouse 1691–1820.

ENDOWED SCHOOL, N of the church. Small, of stone. 1820.

VICARAGE, E of the church. Erected shortly before 1828, but still entirely Georgian in character. Three storeys, three bays, the central one slightly advanced. Boldly fluted semicircular tympanum over the doorway.

3 HAROLD'S STONES. A landmark at the entrance to the village from the SW. The three tall stones form a line along the summit of the ridge; they now lean at different angles, but would originally have stood straight – a rare example of a Bronze Age alignment in this eastern part of Wales. The central stone is said to have been dressed to shape, and the two large hollows on its southern side are thought to be artificial 'cup marks', though in this sandstone conglomerate they may be natural depressions.

MOTTE, 200 yds (180 metres) S, approached from Court Farm. Known as Tump Terret. Of the late C11 or C12. Large and well-preserved, with clear traces of the surrounding ditch. A pine tree springs from the flattened top. The idea current in the C17 that this was an enormous tumulus is, of course, mythical.

THE VIRTUOUS WELL, ½ m. SE. Traditionally this is the only survivor of nine holy wells at Trellech. During the C17, according to Sir John Llwyd, it was still 'much frequented and reputed to cure the scurvy, colic and other distempers'. A low D-shaped wall encloses the curative spring. Segment-headed opening, rebated for a shutter, in the straight wall, where the water bubbles up. Square recesses to l. and r., in which cups could be placed, it is suggested. Stone benches round the curved sides, now only a few inches above the level of the paving.

COUNTY PRIMARY SCHOOL, Monmouth Road. 1986–7 by *Gwent County Architect's Department*, design architect *Michael Yearsley*. Typical low group clustered round a pyramid-roofed hall. But white walls and monopitch roofs to the classroom ranges give it an unexpected crispness.

HYGGA, 2 m. SW. The mansion has disappeared, but impressive early service buildings remain. The circular DOVECOTE retains its stone-slated conical roof, and rows of nesting holes on the outer face of the wall. A little higher up the hill, a remarkable seven-bay, C16 BARN with four-centred stone arch to the threshing bay, and, facing it across the farmyard a contemporary stone STABLE-CUM-SHIPPON range. This has three arched doorways and two mullioned windows towards the yard and a single outward-facing doorway.

PANT-GLAS, 1½ m. SW. Beautifully, if ruggedly, sited on a spur with distant views across the Vale of Usk. The house is a fascinating puzzle. Pant-glas was, according to Bradney, the seat of the Probert family for many centuries, until 1680, after which it was let as a farmhouse, Sir George Probert (†1677) having built The Argoed, Penallt, in the mid C17. The date over the front door is 1752, well into the tenant farmer's time. The plan is an L, the entrance in the S-facing range, the second range facing W. Of a third, N-facing, range only the lowest courses of the outer wall are in place. There survives of the medieval house one fragment, a segmentally vaulted undercroft at the SW corner, entered from the W through a two-centred-headed arch with a broad chamfer. All the outer walls and gable-ends of the house itself are faced with reused ashlar blocks. Both late medieval cut stonework and an Elizabethan door surround have been pressed into service to frame windows and doorways. Altogether it would be hard to find another such comprehensive use of robbed masonry. The suggestion that the stonework came from Raglan Castle, 4 m. W, deserves to be taken seriously. The three-bay S front can be taken as a composition of 1752, with central doorway and sash windows with keystones. But the bays are unusually wide and not equal, so this must be a thorough remodelling of an earlier range. Most remarkable is the entrance, made up of a late medieval, four-centred-headed doorway in which the date of 1752 is cut, flanked by handsome late C16 Doric columns, their shafts fluted above and carved below with a pattern of interlinked squares. The columns carry a pedimental feature insouciantly made up from sections of late C16 triglyph frieze. On the W front the fenestration is irregular, and here are reused other late medieval pieces, a doorway and three square, originally two-light windows with step and hollow moulding. The walls of the W front and what there is of the N front are set on a deep projecting plinth, formed of the same reused ashlar blocks as elsewhere. Inside there are more, presumably reused, medieval pieces. The most handsome is a late medieval fireplace surround, its jambs and flattened segmental head moulded with continuous hollow, wave, hollow. This is at the S end of the W wall. A narrow corridor runs along the inner side of the W range, and here are two large segment-headed stone doorways, broadly chamfered.

The lofty eight-bay BARN to the NE of the house provides further food for thought. It has one generously wide porch and originally had a second. On this, the roadward, side, but not elsewhere, the masonry is finely laid, and the angles are provided with squared quoin stones. So the barn has a show front, intended to impress those who passed by on their way to the house. Inside, the handsome roof trusses are of queenpost construction, suggesting a late C16 or early C17 date. The barn, then, is the best indicator of the substance and prestige of the Proberts, and presumably of their ancestral house.

FURNACE, 1 m. SW (SO 491 049), on the N bank of the Penarth Brook. Rubble masonry remains of an early BLAST FURNACE, probably of pre-Civil War date and thus one of the earliest to survive in England and Wales. The Proberts of Pant-glas probably worked it. The S and W walls rise largely intact from a 25 ft (8 metre) square base, capped by a smaller upper section. On the N and E sides the blowing- and tapping-arches have collapsed, allowing a view of the interior. Remains of the wheel pit and tail-race of the water-power system. On the hillside above, rubble-stone walls of a CHARCOAL STORE. To the E of this a leat leads from a storage pond which provided water to power the furnace.

Y GAER, 1½ m. SW (SO 493 037). A small enclosure on the nose of the ridge, overlooked by higher ground to the N but otherwise in a very commanding position. It is sub-rectangular in shape, enclosed by a wide clay bank without any sign of an external ditch; the entrance is near the SW corner, and in the N half the setting for a circular hut can be recognized.

4000 TRELLECH GRANGE

The name recalls a grange of Tintern Abbey. It is possible that the church was first built as a chapel to the grange.

CHURCH (dedication unknown). Tiny, behind farm buildings and a row of cottages. Basically medieval, the walls of coursed Old Red Sandstone, the nave and chancel under a continuous ribbed and plastered wagon vault on moulded and embattled wall-plates. All windows and the top-heavy W bellcote belong to *Prichard & Seddon*'s restoration of 1860–1. – PULPIT, ALTAR RAIL and PEWS appear to be theirs. – STAINED GLASS. N war memorial window, the Crucified Christ appearing to a dying soldier. 1922.

2000 TREVETHIN

ST CADOC. At the top corner of a huge churchyard, commanding the view S over Pontypool. The Hanburys of Pontypool Park used it as their estate church. The W tower is medieval, the cruciform church, with aisled nave, of 1846–7 by *T. H. Wyatt* of *Wyatt & Brandon*. The tower looks strong and massive, built of large squared blocks of local sandstone. No buttresses, three stages defined by set-offs rather than stringcourses. Square NE turret. Simple Perp W doorway and square-headed, two-light belfry windows. Wyatt's church is also Perp, and for its date impressively convincing in form and detail. The interior convinces less, the nave dominated by its starved-looking arch-brace and collar roof. N and W galleries, their timber fronts pierced and fringed with outsize pendant cusping. The N transept served as the family pew for the owners of Pontypool Park. – PEWS. With coarse poppyheads, doubtless of *c.* 1847. – WAR MEMORIAL ALTAR AND REREDOS. 1922 by *Gerald Cogswell*. – STAINED GLASS. S transept W (originally chancel E), scenes from the life of Christ, and lancet over the pulpit, St John preaching. Both of 1847 by *Thomas Willement*. Small, strongly coloured scenes, painted not stained, against quarry backgrounds. – S transept S, Faith, 1865 by *Charles A. Gibbs*. Old-fashioned for that date. – Nave S, Christ carrying the cross and Crucifixion, 1888–9 by *Alexander Gibbs*. – Chancel E, memorial of an explosion at Llanerch, 1890 by *Heaton, Butler & Bayne*. – N transept, Works of Mercy in two windows, *c.* 1888, also apparently by *Heaton, Butler & Bayne* (A. Brooks). – Tower W, King David and Saint Cecilia, probably by *Jones & Willis* (A. Brooks). – S transept E, by *F. C. Eden c.* 1922. Crucified Christ blessing between SS David and Cadoc. Exquisitely and freshly detailed. Designed as part of the war memorial which includes the reredos and altar below. – MONUMENTS. The most important are in the N
77 transept. – John Hanbury †1734. Excellent marble standing wall monument. The bow-fronted inscription panel supports a first-rate bust, dramatically white against a black veined back

panel. Scrolly top pediment. The bust is characteristic of *Rysbrack*, and the design of the monument can confidently be attributed to *Gibbs*, on the basis of comparison with their monument in Westminster Abbey to Dr John Freind †1728. – Capel Hanbury †1765, John Capel Hanbury †1795 and John Hanbury †1834. Large wall tablet in a coarsely detailed Gothic stone frame, typical of the 1830s. – Capel Hanbury Leigh †1861. Frontal white marble bust in an early Renaissance frame. – John Capel and Louisa Hanbury. Well-lettered slate tablet, erected *c.* 1970. – Patrick John Hanbury Tenison †1989. A second slate tablet, equally good. – In the nave, a variety of tablets. Two are worth mentioning. Anne Morrison †1843. Grecian. A draped urn on a pedestal against a stele-shaped background. Signed *T. Smith*, Savoy St, London. – Robert †1823 and Anna Maria Smith †1850. Gothic canopied wall monument signed by *R. Brown*, Russell St, London.

VICARAGE, opposite the church. White, three-bay, two-storey villa. Full-width iron veranda across the garden front. 1845–6 by *Robert Carter* of Pontypool.

TABERNACLE BAPTIST CHAPEL, Penygarn Road. The chapel originated in 1727. (The date was cut into the lintel of a fire-place.) The present much-modernized building has a house-like appearance, characteristic of early chapels. Rectangular windows in two storeys. Porch dated 1925. The interior has been altered, but retains a simple early C19 pulpit and flanking box pews. Much brought-in STAINED GLASS, with a repeated design of bunches of grapes, made in 1931. Far-extending BURIAL GROUND.

PENYGARN JUNIOR AND INFANT SCHOOL, St Cadoc's Road. 1962–3 by *Monmouthshire County Architect's Department*, County Architect *Sydney Leyshon*. Quite an extensive single-storeyed group, with curtain walling and slightly inclined monopitch roof. Red window panels for the infants, blue for juniors.

TREVETHIN COMMUNITY EDUCATION CENTRE, Folly Road. Of *c.* 1957–8 and *c.* 1990, the two parts at r.-angles to one another and instructively contrasted. Pitched green copper roofs on both. The earlier ranges, built across the slope, are simple and undemonstrative, two-storeyed, with brown brick end walls and windows in continuous bands typical of *Monmouthshire County Architect's Department* when led by *Colin Jones*. The later range, built down the slope, of brown brick below, buff above, has its fenestration in many varieties: as a clerestory, as an oriel, as a full-height strip at one angle.

PONTYPOOL UPPER PARK, approached from Channel View, Penygarn. The drive twists through the rhododendrons, redwoods and Wellingtonias of the American Garden laid out in the 1850s at the upper end of the park, and passes an extraordinary RUSTIC LODGE of 1841. Constructed of limestone boulders and bedecked with scalloped bargeboards.

TWYN GWYN FARM, beyond the park. The farmhouse is isolated on the bare hillside. It is a characteristic C17 upland building of two periods, subsequently much altered. What is of special interest is the survival of the pentice sheltering the doorway, and the fact that the house has never been heightened to a full two storeys.

CHURCH FARM, off Mount Road. Much-modernized, early C17 farmhouse, mostly of one storey plus a habitable roof space. T-plan of three periods, still retaining three spiral stairs, several internal doorways of timber with arched heads, and the horizontal beams to support an external pentice.

FOLLY TOWER, ¾m. NE, beyond the end of Folly Lane. On the ridgetop. The present octagonal, battlemented tower with round-headed windows in two storeys was constructed 1993–4 as a replica of the eyecatcher built by John Hanbury of Pontypool Park in 1762. This had been renovated in 1831, but demolished at the beginning of the Second World War lest it should serve as a marker to German bombers.

3000

TROSTRE

ST DAVID. A small Perp church alone on the sloping hillside, of grey rubble-stone with pink Old Red Sandstone dressings. Nave and chancel in one. Fine W double bell gable, of ashlar, slightly corbelled out to N and S. Added W porch with arch-brace and wind-brace roof, its S wall slightly overlapping the trefoiled stoup. S rood-loft stair projection. Simple Perp S windows, those on the N side inserted in the C19, presumably as part of the restoration of 1872. Late C14 or C15 E window of three lights, its arched head two-centred, with panel tracery, but ogee heads to the lights. Set in a deep hollow-moulded surround. Inside, the ribbed wagon roof is much reconstructed. Are any of the unusually large foliage bosses old? – SCREEN. Perp, with six panel-traceried lights each side of the entrance arch. Much reconstructed. Evidence for the rood-loft arrangements in the original beam at the top of the screen, and slots cut in the wall-plates supporting the roof, indicating that there was a solid tympanum over the screen, as at Bettws Newydd, and that the present continuity of nave and chancel roof is misleading. – FONT. Oddly proportioned. Illtyd Gardner suggested that a C12 tub had been set on a late medieval panelled foot, and the whole thing inverted some time in the C19, and the foot hollowed out to become the bowl. – STAINED GLASS. Chancel E, *c.* 1855. Christ blessing children, Agony in the Garden, Noli me Tangere. No doubt by *Wailes* (A. Brooks). – MONUMENT. Charles Hughes †1676. Hanging wall monument under a broken segmental pediment, the two halves reversed. Inscription recut.

In the CHURCHYARD, four medieval steps and a large, plain modern CROSS.

CASTLE, 200 yds (180 metres) S. Excavation has established that there was a late C11 ringwork, converted to a simple stone castle in the C13.

TROSTREY COURT, ½m. E. A small manor house with a complex building history and a none too attractive exterior, now that the main range of stone has been crudely repointed and the brick cross wing greyly rendered. Late C20 standard windows. Most remarkable is the three-storey N porch. This must be early C17, see the four-centred outer arch and the big pendants under the overhang. The top two storeys are timber-framed but have been weatherboarded. Inner timber doorway with four-centred head and contemporary door.

Inside, there is an unexpectedly extensive array of C17 joinery. The earliest feature is the richly moulded post-and-panel partition in the room l. of the porch entrance, which must have been the original hall. More exceptional is the completely panelled porch room, its chimneypiece and overmantel with two tiers of fluted Tuscan pilasters on rusticated pedestals, and a central perspectival arched recess in the overmantel. In line with the porch, at the back of the house, a mid-C17 staircase rising on a dog-leg plan up to the roof space. Flat cut-out balusters of fussy outline, newels carrying pyramidal finials. The secondary stair in the SE wing has a dado with eared fields. Beyond it, a large square room lined with small-fielded panelling under a dentilled and bracketed entablature, in a pattern similar to that which encases the ceiling beams.

Immediately to the E, a large rubble-stone OX-BARN, dated 1667 on the gable-end towards the house.

UPPER BERTHLLWYD, 1½ m. NE. Fine farmhouse of two dates. The white-rendered W range of two storeys looks early C19, though its massive stone chimneystack may suggest an earlier origin. The higher E part, gabled in three directions with a rear stair projection, seems to be an early C17 parlour wing. Stone mullioned windows renewed in the late C20. (Inside, a post-and-panel partition and timber doorway with shaped head.)

UNDY/GWNDY

4080

ST MARY. A small church but a puzzle. Nave and lower chancel, S porch. The oldest feature is the W window, of *c.* 1300, with two trefoiled lancets. *John Prichard* in 1880 rewindowed the rest of the nave with similar trefoiled lancets and erected the bell gable over the chancel arch. He also restored the chancel – see the dated rainwater head – but spared its Perp two-light S window and its Tudor three-light E window. In the mid C19 (1860, says Kelly) a short tower at the E end of the nave had been removed. The S porch is dated 1790. The round-headed S doorway, just chamfered, may be of that date or of *c.* 1500. That leaves two incongruous items. First, the Perp W doorway is oddly displaced to the S and oddly handsome for this simple building. It has a continuous hollow and double wave and a panelled soffit, a local feature – *see* the W doorway at Caldicot. Hood on headstops. Secondly, the chancel arch, also Perp, is made up of a steep two-centred arch with double roll moulding which does not fit the imposts, a demi-lozenge in plan with angle rolls. This presumably belonged to the arches which supported the tower. – FONT.

A fine early C13 piece. Square bowl, its underside boldly scalloped, on a thick circular stem with four attached circular shafts. – PULPIT. Of timber, by *Prichard*, as are the PEWS. – STAINED GLASS. Chancel E, Crucifixion with Mary and John. Demi-angels in roundels below, and much Germanic foliage. Of *c.* 1884, and typical of the exquisite style of *Burlison & Grylls*. – Nave N, emblematic lancet. 1982 by *Celtic Studios*.

3000 USK/BRYNBUGA

The town occupies a strategic position in the centre of the Vale of Usk, so it is not surprising that when the Romans first penetrated into South Wales they established a legionary fortress here. Even though it was soon replaced by the fortress at Caerleon (q.v.), excavations since 1965 have recovered much of its layout (*see* below). The Usk that we see today, however, is a Norman foundation. The de Clares, who were *c.* 1119 granted the lordship of Netherwent, with its principal castle and borough at Chepstow, established a secondary centre of power here, though Usk was in Welsh hands 1138–74. A castle was constructed on the escarpment, and, in the course of time a borough and a monastic house, in this case a Benedictine nunnery, were established to the S of it. After the Dissolution the nave and aisle of the nunnery church became the parish church. Twyn Square, between castle and church, was presumably the original market place. But in 1598 a new market place was designated to the W, close to the river, and that is where the town hall came to be situated.

Subsequently, Usk hardly developed. In 1801 the population was still under 750, and although it had doubled by 1861, it was in decline during the agricultural depression of the last quarter of the century. Though revealing traces of C16–C18 buildings can be found here and there, it is the first half of the C19 that has left the strongest mark. Since the 1950s there has been another spate of building, but this has consisted of tucking groups of houses into vacant spaces within the boundaries of the medieval town. So even today Usk remains tightly defined, and in every direction there is open countryside a few hundred yards away from the town centre.

ROMAN FORTRESS. Although no remains are now visible, excavations have shown Usk to be the site of the earliest legionary fortress in South Wales, the precursor by some twenty years of Caerleon. Begun *c.* A.D. 55, probably by the Twentieth Valeria Victrix Legion, and constructed mainly in timber with earthwork defences, the site covered *c.* 48 acres (19.4 hectares). It lies mainly under the southern side of the town, with its northern defences almost on the line of Church Street, extending as far as the field to the S of the Gaol (*see* below, p. 593). From a Roman military viewpoint the site would appear to have major disadvantages: it is constricted by hills and rivers; it is too far upstream to be accessible to large ships; and it is liable to severe flooding. Despite this, it has a number of strategic advantages which led to its being chosen as the main base for the conquest of South Wales. It totally controls the Usk Valley, always a major route of penetration into the uplands of Breconshire, and it offers an excellent route of communication with England along the Olway Valley. But by A.D. 75 these advantages no longer prevailed, and it was closed, to be replaced by a new establishment at Caerleon.

Excavations to the E of the Gaol have revealed the remains of the defences and E gate, and of a series of large timber granaries; on the site of the former cattle market opposite the Gaol, the plans of various workshops and part of an officer's house were recovered. After the demolition of the fortress, the site continued to be occupied, initially by a small fort, and later by an extensive civilian settlement, apparently the centre of a thriving iron industry.

A possible EARTHWORK DEFENCE of the medieval town, consisting of a wide bank and ditch, has been located running on the western side of the cattle market. Fragments of another medieval earthwork, which may have been a mill-leat, can be seen on the edge of the field to the E of the Gaol and in the meadows beyond it.

ST MARY. Nave, N aisle and crossing tower of the church of Usk Priory, a Benedictine nunnery founded by Richard 'Strongbow' de Clare, probably in the years shortly before his death in 1176. The N aisle of the conventual church had been added in the C13 for the use of the townspeople, and widened in the C15, so it was natural that after the Dissolution of the nunnery in 1536, the town should take over the nave as well. The crossing tower was retained for secular use until 1844, when *T. H. Wyatt* vaulted the crossing space to be the sanctuary. He also added an extra W bay to the nave. Gallery removed 1875. *G. E. Halliday* of Llandaff, in a second major restoration, in 1899–1900, inserted Perp N and S windows and introduced ribbed and boarded wagon roofs over nave and aisle.

Inspection of the exterior should begin at the E end. Here the outline of the E crossing arch is apparent, arch and jambs plain and square-angled, with the simplest of imposts. Traces of a tunnel vault for the presbytery. Crease-line of the C12 gable above. Similar evidence to the N (partly obscured by the vestry) and to the S (visible only from the private garden of Usk Priory – *see* below). Crossing tower of two stages with simple chamfered C12 windows and bow-ended NW stair-turret. Battlements on a corbel table shared by tower and turret. (The S wall of the C12 nave survives with a blocked doorway; this too can be seen only from the priory garden.) Perp N aisle walls with two splendid two-storeyed Perp porches to N and W. Walls and porches were built together, as the shared plinth-moulding shows, though the aisle is of coursed Old Red Sandstone, the porches of limestone ashlar. The most likely builder is Sir William Herbert †1469.
Four-light aisle windows by *Halliday*. The porches are almost 31
identical, two-storeyed and two bays deep, lierne-vaulted. Angle buttresses to the N porch, diagonal buttresses to the W porch.

Each has an entrance arch richly moulded, and flanked by slender shafts which are clasped by the ends of the crocketed hoodmould. Deep, unpierced parapet, decorated with cusped Xs (N porch) or encircled quatrefoils (W porch). Bascule badge of the Herbert family in the parapet of the N porch, and grinning bearded king over. Skyline pinnacles lost. Vaults with big foliage corbels, the ribs enriched with cusps. Each porch has an image niche over the doorway, and the W porch has an unusually fine and well-preserved stoup on a head corbel. The W front is an awkward composition, with *Wyatt*'s nave extension, buttressed by *Halliday*, extending forward of the W porch of the aisle. In the late Middle Ages the town's aisle no doubt looked much more splendid and prominent than the nunnery's nave.

Inside, it is again best to go straight to the E end. Here the early C12 crossing is completely preserved, an impressive demonstration of Norman austerity. The piers consist of plain stepped imposts against which triplets of circular half-shafts abut. Plain scallop caps. Arches in two square-angled orders. That is all. The pier bases are below floor level. Neo-Norman plaster vault and E triple lancet of 1844. The four-bay N aisle is an equally direct expression of a mid-C13 aesthetic. Strong, circular piers (their moulded bases largely hidden), their circular moulded caps boldly projecting. Double-chamfered arches. The E-most free-standing pier has four slender attached shafts. It now stands at the junction between chancel and nave, but it is suggested that it originally marked the division between the nuns' E bay and the townspeople's three W bays of the aisle. The late medieval reconstruction of the aisle gave it a width equal to the nave. The rere-arches of the Perp windows appear to be original, so Halliday was reinstating the late medieval fenestration.

FURNISHINGS. – SCREENS. Perp, across chancel and aisle. Of Devon–Somerset type, with broad, traceried openings and bold ribbed cove to support a loft. The two parts are identical in design, the part across the chancel restored and coloured by *Halliday*. – FONT. Late C12. Square bowl with chamfered angles, chamfered down to a circular stem surrounded by four attached shafts with scallop caps. – ALTAR RAILS. C18. Twisted balusters rising from bulbs. – PULPIT. Of the C18, cut down from a three-decker. Stair rails similar to the altar rails. – LECTERN. Brass. A handsome piece, of *c.* 1860. – ORGAN. A magnificent object, designed in 1862 by *Prichard & Seddon* for Llandaff Cathedral and brought here in 1900. Polychromed pipes, most in the normal upright ranks, but some, dragon-like, pointing blaringly forward. Characteristic timber case, inset and pierced with foiled motifs and discs. Witty inscription from the Benedicite: 'O all ye beasts and cattle, bless ye the Lord and magnify him for ever'. – STAINED GLASS. Nave W, 1886 by *Joseph Bell & Son*. Ascension between the Virgin and Mary Magdalene. Small figures in grisaille-work with roundels of naturalistic flowers. The window commemorates the abolition of the town corporation. – Chancel S, Mary Magdalene scenes. 1889 by *Joseph Bell & Son*. – Nave SE. Raising of Lazarus etc. Of the four dates of death commemorated, 1863 is probably the relevant one. – Chancel E. Christ between Virgin Annunciate and St John. 1913. Sentimental. Probably by *Percy Bacon* (A. Brooks). – Nave S. Good Samaritan between saints. 1925 by *R. J. Newbery*, reusing a favourite design. – CURIOSUM (S porch). Large painted board recording the seating plan in the church in 1726, and listing the names of pewholders, an important social document. – MONUMENTS. Brass (fixed to the chancel screen). Early C15 inscription in Welsh, the earliest to survive, commemorating Adam of Usk (†1430), chronicler of the town and benefactor of the priory. – Walter Jones †1656. Gravestone with inscription surmounted by a device of encircled concave-sided lozenges, and flanked by a sword. – The Neoclassical wall monuments grouped at the W end demonstrate the mass-production of workshops such as *Tyley* of Bristol. – Samuel Browne †1790. Draped urn. Signed *Tyley*. – Thomas Prothero †1819. Weeping willow, falling Ionic column and oval panel commemorating three more deaths in 1819–20. Signed *Tyley*. – Tablet commemorating the benefactions of Roger Edwards. 1822. Inscription scroll and draped urn. Signed *Tyley*. – Henry Penoyre and two sons. Stele with dove descending above, olive branch below. Undated and unsigned.

In the CHURCHYARD (beside the path to the W door), a stone EFFIGY, extremely worn, just recognizable as of a recumbent figure in civilian dress, datable to the C14. In the NW corner, a group of polished granite GRAVESTONES surrounded by low ironwork enclosures. – Eleanor Nicholl †1850 and Augusta Jane Nicholl †1851. A pair, designed by *Sir Matthew Digby Wyatt*. The stylized forms of the ironwork reminiscent of Wyatt's iron roof trusses at Paddington Station. – William Nicholl †1874, probably also by *Wyatt*. – Sir Matthew Digby Wyatt †1877, who had married a Nicholl. By his brother *T. H. Wyatt*. Ironwork of conventional stiff-leaf character.

PRIORY GATEHOUSE. Beside the main entrance to St Mary's churchyard. Two-storeyed, gable-ended, with wide, round-headed inner and outer arches, simply chamfered. Square-headed windows to light, and W stack for the hearth to heat the room above. Uncusped lights, suggesting a C16 date, perhaps even post-Dissolution.

PRIORY HOUSE. Quite a large Victorian house, of stone, gabled, with lozenge-plan stacks. Built in 1868 by *J. Nevill* of Abergavenny, enlarged in 1894 by *Veall & Sant* of Cardiff. Whether anything earlier survives is not clear. (Inside, part of a timber frieze datable between 1530 and 1533, put up by the last prioress. For the rest of it, *see* Cefntilla, Llandenny.)

ST FRANCIS XAVIER AND ST DAVID LEWIS (R.C.), Porthycarne Street. 1847 by *Charles Hansom*, with a N tower added by him in 1865. Quite a scholarly performance, Geometrical. Nave with N porch and S aisle, slightly lower chancel and N vestry. Coursed Old Red Sandstone with Bath stone dressings. The tower is quite idiosyncratic, almost a campanile, the belfry stage recessed with angle pilaster buttresses and Dec two-light openings. Steep slated roof. The interior lacks character. Conventional four-bay arcade with octagonal piers. Thin scissor-brace roof in the nave. – STAINED GLASS. Chancel E, Risen Christ between (apparently) St Charles Borromeo and St Francis. 1857 by *Hardman*. Boldly coloured. – Chancel S, a boy presented to the Virgin. By *Hardman*, *c*. 1862. – S aisle E. Annunciation, clearly by *Wailes*, of the 1850s. – S aisle SE, saints. Of *c*. 1908, signed by *H. Beiler* of Heidelberg.

BAPTIST CHURCH, Old Market Street. Gable-ended front boldly dated 1842. Long square-headed windows and central Doric porch. Inside, the original W gallery survives.

WESLEYAN METHODIST CHURCH, Maryport Street. Dated 1817. Small, rendered. Two outsize round-headed windows towards the road. Drastically modernized.

TOWN HALL, New Market Street. Originally built at the end of the C16, after the Earl of Pembroke had in 1598 granted the town a new site for a market and market house. The present building consists of two parts. The S range, facing Old Market Street, has the characteristic arrangement of an arcaded ground storey with lofty council chamber above. The N range, although as wide, is lower and clearly subordinate. It is tricky to work out the constructional history. The arcaded ground storey, of five Old Red Sandstone arches by two, was probably constructed in 1771. The ground storey of the N half is also of Old Red Sandstone, as the E end shows, and clearly later than the arcade. It is presumably the extension made in 1816. Both halves are bound together by a continuous plain stringcourse above the ground storey. The rebuilding carried out in 1835 must only have been of the upper storey. As the walls here are rendered, it is impossible to confirm that they are all of one date. The council chamber windows are large, segment-headed sashes, above which are bold, blind oculi. The N elevation towards the broad end of New Market Street is composed as one-plus-four-plus-one bays, but here the sash windows are rectangular. Meagrely detailed four-bay central pediment enclosing a clock. In 1859 the County Surveyor made modifications, which probably included the blocking of the arcade arches with idiosyncratic tripartite stone windows.

CASTLE

The castle ruins stand on the high ground immediately to the N of the town, looking down on to Twyn Square and far over the countryside beyond, yet it is only in the winter when the trees are leafless that even the most prominent tower is visible. An inconspicuous lane swings up to it from the E end of Castle Parade, and since the castle remains in private ownership (though regularly open to the public), the walls have not been ruthlessly stripped of plant growth, and the outer and inner wards form a two-level garden and paddock.

The first record of a castle at Usk dates from 1138, when it was seized by the Welsh from the de Clares, who owned it as part of their great lordship of Netherwent. It will then have consisted of a substantial earthwork enclosure, with a barbican to the N, where the site was weakest. The earliest stone structure, the keep, was probably built by Richard 'Strongbow' de Clare, after he recovered it from Welsh control in 1174. In 1189 Usk came by marriage to William Marshal. His was the major campaign of fortification. He built the stone enclosure wall of the inner ward, formalizing the earthworks as a nearly regular rectangle with an obtuse angle near the centre of each face, and he strengthened the angles by means of towers, particularly the circular Garrison Tower on the townward side. To judge by their character, he must have put these works in hand at the end of his life, 1212–19, when he was in royal favour but his South Wales estates were threatened by the Welsh prince Llewelyn the Great. The keep was remodelled as a comfortable residence by one of Marshal's sons before 1245. By the late C13 Usk Castle was back in de Clare hands, and a document of 1289 shows that Gilbert de Clare had then just built the N tower, to serve as a treasury, and formed a chamber in the top storey of the Garrison Tower. By the early C14 considerations of defence were slackening, Llangibby Castle, 2½ m. S, being expected to take over as the major fortress in the area. So a large hall and chapel were built, probably by Elizabeth de Burgh, sister of the last de Clare, against the N curtain wall, with a chamber block added outside the wall. Consequently, the C12 keep was remodelled again to provide three storeys of household accommodation. But Llangibby was never completed, so later in the C14, probably between 1368 and 1425, when the Mortimers, Earls of March, held the lordship, the outer ward, at a lower level to the S, was fortified with an imposing gatehouse, wall and circular mural tower. The castle survived a Welsh attack in 1405, but did not again serve as the residence of the lord of Usk. In 1431 William ap Thomas of Raglan was created steward of the lordship. His son, Sir William Herbert, must have been responsible for the final remodelling of the keep as a handsome steward's lodging, with fireplaces and a window which match his work at Raglan Castle. But by the early C16 the steward was living in the gatehouse, and the rest of the castle was in decay. In 1556 Roger Williams of Usk (*see* p. 595) was accused of pulling down the great hall and a great barn within the castle. From the mid C18 Usk Castle belonged to the Dukes of Beaufort, but it was only after 1899, when the Addams-Williams family of Llangibby Castle bought it, that the first attempts were made to conserve the ruins. At all periods the main building stone was the local Old Red Sandstone.

Since it is impossible to walk round the exterior of the castle walls, close inspection can begin at the highest level, the inner ward, starting at the entrance in the NE wall, then proceeding from the keep anticlockwise. The gatehouse and outer ward, which are separately approached from the W, can be examined afterwards.

The INNER WARD is entered through what is no more than a GATEWAY in the NE side of the C13 enclosure wall. It has a pointed arch and a chamfered order on its inner face. Part of the portcullis groove remains. It was protected originally only

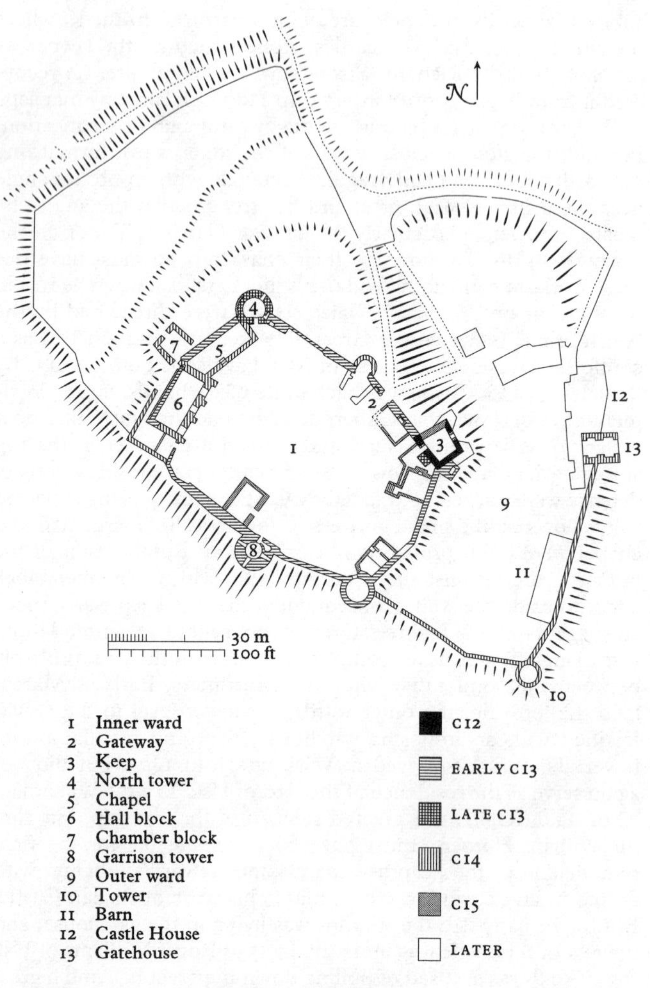

Usk Castle. Plan

by the earthwork barbican to the N. Foundations only of the D-shaped stone tower later added to the angle of the curtain wall a few yards to the NW, to cover the gateway. The C12 KEEP SE of the gateway was incorporated into the C13 enclosure wall. It may have helped to provide cover for the gateway. But since the wall of the keep facing the gateway was entirely rebuilt in the C15, it is impossible to tell how this was managed. The other three, late C12, walls of the keep stand virtually to their full height, reinforced externally by a massive battered plinth at basement level, cut away for a later E doorway. The keep is neither large nor regular, being a trapezoid in plan, so was clearly of minor importance among the de Clares' strongholds. Two blocked original windows in the S wall, splayed outside as well as inside, and part of another at a slightly higher level in the E wall, evidence of an upper hall. Note that the surrounds to the S window openings are of yellow Triassic sandstone. C13 S doorway providing access to the large, rectangular C13 garderobe projection, built integrally with the curtain wall. The evidence of a mid-C13 remodelling to create a more impressive hall within the keep is the large blocked doorway at the S end of the W wall, and the large blocked window beside it. The W wall also reveals most clearly the mid-C14 remodelling, when the status of the keep was reduced, and heightening of the walls and rearrangement of the floors produced three storeys. Double-chamfered, two-centred-headed W doorway at ground level, and, visible inside the keep, doorways in the centre of the W wall at both upper levels. The lancet window high in the S wall must also be of this period. The last, mid-C15 phase of work has left its mark most obviously in the E wall and the new-built N wall. E basement doorway, and above it the opening for a large mullioned window with four-centred head. Fireplace at this level in the N wall. The top storey has a similar N fireplace, and another fragmentary E window, this with finely moulded rere-arch and external hood on square stops. These details are comparable with Sir William Herbert's work at Raglan Castle (q.v.). In the curtain wall l. and r. of the gateway, fireplace openings, now robbed, show that mid-C15 structures were built up against the wall.

The NORTH TOWER, built by Gilbert de Clare shortly before 1289, is more than a semicircle in plan, the W half externally refaced in the C15. As befitted the tower 'where the Lord Earl's treasure is placed for safe keeping', it has extremely thick walls, and cross arrow slits to the E, where the wall has not been refaced. Reconstructed steps from the ward lead to a first-floor chamber, through a doorway in the flat back wall of the tower. The doorway has bull-nose jambs, typical of the de Clare work of the late C13, e.g. at Caerphilly Castle. Adjoining the doorway, a fireplace with corbelled lintel and traces of a window recess. The corbelled-out top storey of the tower has disappeared, but is recorded in the Bucks' engraving of 1732.

The early C14 CHAPEL and HALL BLOCK, immediately to the W of the N tower, were the major buildings erected within the curtain wall of the inner ward, though now incorporated into garden planting. The chapel is fitted with a modern altar. The hall is emphatically divided into three bays by thick projecting buttresses in its S wall. The ground-level doorway in the W bay has renewed jambs. The windows in the central bay here have largely gone, but the seats in the splays survive. Later fireplace in the E bay. The hall itself was at upper-floor level, with a doorway into the screens passage in the W bay. Doorway in the W gable-end to the service rooms, now demolished. The CHAMBER BLOCK is a small rectangular projection outside the curtain wall, overlapping the junction of chapel and hall block. The newel stair, in the thickness of the wall at the junction, presumably gave access from the dais end of the hall. It certainly provides the vertical link between the chambers on two levels. Fireplace in each chamber, and evidence of hollow-moulded windows. Doorways E and W give access to the outer face of the curtain wall.

The mighty circular GARRISON TOWER of the early C13, midway along the SW extent of the curtain wall, survives almost complete. It was the main defensive element of William Marshal's castle, and although it is built integrally with the curtain wall, it is a close relative of the free-standing round keep-towers at Skenfrith, and at Bronllys and Tretower across the border to the N in Powys. The tower rises four-storeyed on a battered base from the precipitous slope of the escarpment. Continuous set-offs mark the floor levels. At third-floor level is a row of sockets for beams intended to support a timber hoard, or fighting gallery, at the wall-head. The early C13 entrance, tall and round-headed, at first-floor level, would originally have been reached by an external timber porch. The top courses of the tower, of yellow sandstone, the corbelled battlements and remodelled lancets in the top storey, date to *c.* 1289, when the tower top was remodelled. Of the same date is the doorway with bull-nose jambs from the inner ward into the tower. Inside the tower the rationale of the early C13 design is clear, with arrow slits in three directions in the two lower storeys, and lancets in three directions in the upper two. The spiral stair to the l. of the doorway links all four levels. The third level intercommunicates with the wall-walk, and has a garderobe, part of the improvements of *c.* 1289. The top storey was at that time given not only improved lighting but also the comfort of a hooded fireplace. Immediately to the W, traces of a two-storeyed later medieval structure, for which apertures at both levels were cut through the curtain wall. At the S angle of the inner ward, the foundations of a smaller, early C13 round tower and an abruptly snapped-off stretch of curtain wall. The corbelled chimney-breast served yet another late medieval structure built against the curtain wall.

From here it is possible to descend to the level of the OUTER WARD. This was enclosed in the late C14 with a stone curtain wall on its SW and SE sides, with a drum tower at its S angle, and a gatehouse at the E end. Traces of a postern gate at the W end of the SW wall. The SOUTH TOWER is of two storeys over a basement and survives up to the corbelling below its battlements. Towards the ward, doorways at two levels, both chamfered and roughly round-headed. Outward-facing slit windows, with panelled jambs to their rere-arches. The tower was later converted into a dovecote. To the NE, an eight-bay BARN, built on to the wall-walk of the curtain. It has a queen-strut roof and is clearly post-medieval. The gabled rear range of CASTLE HOUSE appears just beyond to the NE. This incorporates the inner half of the upper stage of the late C14 gatehouse.

The GATEHOUSE itself both projects boldly forward of the curtain wall and stands at a lower level. To see its external elevation it is necessary to leave the outer ward and descend to the level of what was formerly the public highway. Here it is seen to be three-storeyed, tricked out with mid-C19 window labels and ochre render. A gawky C19 oriel cuts through the medieval corbel table. The bottom storey is open as a vaulted entrance-way. This has a chamfered, two-centred outer arch, a shaly rubble vault, and an inner arch of two chamfered orders flanking a portcullis slot. So the middle storey was the portcullis room. Within, a steep flight of steps leads up to the top storey and the level of the outer ward.

PRIMARY SCHOOL, Monmouth Road. By *Gwent County Architect's Department*, County Architect *K. P. Jones*, 1983–5. Low under long slopes of tiled roof.

GAOL, Maryport Street. 1841–2 by *T. H. Wyatt*. A high, battered sandstone wall with pilaster buttresses faces the road. Recessed centre between bold polygonal turrets. Round-headed entrance arch. (Internally, there are radiating cell-blocks within a semi-polygonal enclosure, i.e. the Benthamite panopticon plan as embodied in Pentonville Prison, London, in 1840, which became the model for prison layout for a generation.) Enlarged *c.* 1868 by *W. P. James*, the County Surveyor.

SESSIONS HOUSE, Maryport Street. Built 1875–7 to designs by *T. H. Wyatt*. Italianate. Mauve local sandstone with buff Bath stone dressings. Single-storeyed, seven-bay façade demarcated by Tuscan pilasters. Three-bay central arcaded loggia under a balustrade. Broad end bays with coupled pilasters framing the large rounded-headed windows for the two courts. Very old-fashioned for its date: Wyatt's first designs for the site had been made in 1858. (Inside, one of the two courtrooms survives little altered.)

BRIDGE, over the River Usk. Of stone. Five segmental arches on piers with pointed cutwaters. Traditional but well-proportioned. Built *c.* 1750 to the design, says Malkin's guide book of 1804, of William Edwards the celebrated South Wales bridge-builder, and in 1836 widened on both sides, as the soffits of the arches clearly reveal.

PERAMBULATION

The town is small and modest, hardly revealing its medieval importance. It is also oddly diffuse, the church at the SE corner, the Town Hall at the SW. Nevertheless, St Mary's Church and the Priory gatehouse make a logical starting point for an exploration. PRIORY STREET leads to the N into TWYN SQUARE. In the centre of the square, the minuscule CLOCK TOWER, dated 1887. The E and W sides of the square are lined by a medley of low, rendered houses, the very modest centrepiece to the E being the CASTLE INN, and to the W the NAG'S HEAD. At the far NE corner, something more eye-catching, the former CONGREGATIONAL CHAPEL, 1861–2 by *Habershon & Pite*. Mauve Old Red Sandstone and buff Bath stone ashlar. Large Geometrical window over a gabled porch. Stair-turret to the l. carried up to a broached ashlar stage and slated spirelet.

Plate-traceried windows down the long side. Opposite, at the NW corner, MIDLAND BANK, a big, four-square, sash-windowed house of *c.* 1800, heavily modernized. The castle should dominate the square from the heights to the N, but trees envelop its keep and towers, so that its presence is hardly noticed. Instead, the traffic of the A472 interrupts. There are things to see to the W along the main road. Nothing at first, where it is called CASTLE PARADE. Then beyond Porthycarne Street on the r. and Maryport Street on the l. (*see* below), where the name changes to BRIDGE STREET, several buildings worth comment. No. 4, on the r., prominent with its two window bays under strongly projecting gables, must be of *c.* 1900. No. 49, further along on the l., has a characteristic frontage of the 1830s, of five bays and three storeys under bracketed Tuscan eaves. Beyond it, the NATIONAL WESTMINSTER BANK, built in 1848 by *R. G. Thomas* of Newport for the Monmouthshire and Glamorgan Bank, its porch on pairs of gross columns, fluted, baseless but with lotus capitals. No. 28, opposite, set back from the street-line, is a fragment of a two-storeyed stone building of *c.* 1500, identifiable as part of the medieval bridge-side hospital belonging to Usk Priory. The hoodmould of one upper window and part of a second, with idiosyncratic spurred stops, are the datable features.

Just before Usk Bridge* NEW MARKET STREET opens up on the l. This is the most attractive street in the town, its rendered and colour-washed frontages apparently of the late C18 and early C19. Its shape, however, widening and narrowing, and then fanning out in front of the Town Hall, suggests a much earlier origin and reflects its market function. The first house to reveal its early origins is OLDE MALTSTERS on the l. near the W end. Towards the street the front door is set in a two-centred-headed doorway with a broad chamfer, probably of the C16. Round the corner, behind the early C19 front block, a tiny cusped-headed lancet, and a small, upper square-headed window, much mutilated, its hoodmould with square stops, reveal the building's late medieval origins. Next door, a three-bay stone barn, now GWENT RURAL LIFE MUSEUM. Across the road, THE LAWNS is a three-bay, three-storey villa, built for the vicar of Usk after 1785. Then No. 18, another, more powerful reminder of what much of Usk may have looked like in the C16. The gabled end towards the street has a jettied upper storey, timber-framed with regularly spaced uprights. The long stone range beyond, MIN YR AFON and YNYS HAFOD, is sash-windowed and set behind early C19 railings. But radiating voussoirs in the wall show that there were originally wider windows. The whole range may date back to the early C17. For the Town Hall *see* above, p. 588.

OLD MARKET STREET, which leads off to the l. immediately beyond the Town Hall, contains the most remarkable early house in the town. Nos. 17–27, apparently a two-storeyed terrace of

* For what lies immediately across the bridge, *see* Llanbadoc, p. 267.

exceptional height, is the principal range of the town mansion built by Roger Williams in the mid C16, with stone plundered from the castle (*see* above, p. 589). The rubble-stone walling is partly colour-washed, partly rendered over. The only informative features on the street side are a much-mutilated doorway in No. 19, with a hollow chamfer, and a small chimney-breast corbelled out above it. There is a good deal to see at the back, parts of four-light upper windows in Nos. 19, 21 and 23. All three have hoodmoulds, the first has arched lights, the second ovolo-moulded, straight-topped lights, the third hollow-moulded, straight-topped lights. So the range may not have been built all at one time. There are relieving arches for equally large upper windows in Nos. 25 and 27, of which the former projects forward slightly, but not enough to indicate that this was the original porch. The real surprise is inside No. 27, decorated plaster ceilings on both floors. The lower ceiling has thick ribs with decorated soffits, forming patterns of interlocking pointed quatrefoils. Rosettes, shields and floral sprigs enrich the fields. Rose and thistle in the four corners, suggesting a date for the ceiling after the Union of the Crowns in 1603. The upper ceiling has thin moulded ribs in yet more complicated patterns, and sprigs of flowers in the fields. Also a deep frieze decorated with shields and affronted wyverns. Plain plaster cove over the roof space above.

Nothing more in Old Market Street except the Baptist Church (*see* above, p. 588). At the end MARYPORT STREET cuts across. Here, to the r., at the S edge of the town, the Sessions House and Gaol (*see* above, p. 593). To the l., first another attractive run of colour-washed frontages, in particular Nos. 24–30, single-storey cottages interrupted by ASHLEY HOUSE, Tudoresque of the 1850s, and followed by the Wesleyan Methodist Church of 1817 (*see* above, p. 588). Then, on the r., the CHURCH SCHOOL of 1869 by *W. P. James*, the County Surveyor. Single-storeyed, gabled. Red brick with yellow brick chimneystacks and notched bargeboards. Timidly High Victorian, that is to say. Note the foundation stone bearing the date and inscribed 'To the glory of God' in Greek. A short way further along on the other side, a second school. This (now Adult Education Centre) is the successor to the historic GRAMMAR SCHOOL of Usk, founded in 1621 by Roger Edwards of Allt-y-bela, Llangwm Uchaf. The present Tudor-style building, of local stone, is of two dates. The two-storeyed schoolroom range to the S, with large mullioned windows, those below given a transom, was rebuilt in 1863–4 to the plans of *Judge Falconer*. The gabled master's house to the N is of *c.* 1843 by *Joshua Daniel*. Entrance porch in the angle between the two parts.

Maryport Street leads back to Bridge Street. Opposite, PORTHYCARNE STREET continues. On the l. corner, THREE SALMONS HOTEL, large, rendered and painted black and white, a debased and confused classical design of, perhaps, *c.* 1840. Fat Tuscan pilasters on the upper storey. The STABLES opposite, of squared brown stone, are almost as large. Beyond this, several more pleasant early C19 stuccoed houses. Embedded in THE LAURELS, on the l., is a C17 farmhouse. Further along on the r., the R.C. church (*see* above, p. 587), and just before it No. 24, an elegant and considered piece of early C19 architecture. Just a two-storeyed, three-bay villa, the centre brought slightly forward. Central doorway framed by Greek Doric columns *in antis* and round-headed windows under round-headed relieving arches. Two more substantial houses set back behind trees, one on each side of the road, make an instructively contrasted pair, both built *c.* 1834–5. PORTHYCARNE HOUSE, on the l., is another restrained white Grecian villa, of three bays. Two-storeyed, the roof behind a plain blocking course. The single-storey central porch set forward a little with two baseless Doric columns *in antis* and a heavy entablature. Large tripartite flanking windows set in shallow, full-height projections. Identical rear elevation. The house was built for Thomas Reece, agent of the great ironmaster Crawshay Bailey. PLAS NEWYDD, on the r., tightly set below the castle, is irregular, gabled, Tudor Gothic. Veranda with ogee arches. Francis McDonnell, J.P., leader of the town's Roman Catholics, built the house.

3010

WHITE CASTLE

1¾ m. NW of Llantilio Crossenny

The largest and loneliest of the Three Castles, commanding panoramic views over the border country of North Gwent. Its purpose and building history seem to have differed from those of Grosmont and Skenfrith, and explain its continuing isolation. The two main phases of building in stone belong to periods when White Castle was in royal hands. The early Norman earthwork castle was strengthened at the end of the C12 with a masonry keep and walls enclosing a bailey. The sum of £128 16s expended 1184–6 on White Castle (or Llantilio Castle, as it was then called) by the royal official Ralph of Grosmont, sheriff of Hereford, probably paid for them. Nothing more was done until the third quarter of the C13, when, probably in the face of the threat posed by the burgeoning power of the Welsh prince Llewelyn ap Gruffudd, who in 1263 attacked Abergavenny, the defences were drastically modernized and extended. Already in 1256–7 expenditure was recorded on an outer gate and portcullis and a new bridge. Virtually a new castle was constructed, consisting of a new outer ward to the N, protected by a dry moat and masonry walls along which were placed a twin-towered gatehouse and four mural towers, and an inner ward, protected by a wet moat and the pre-existing masonry walls strengthened by a second, twin-towered gatehouse and four further mural towers. A second outer enclosure to the E, protected only by earthen ramparts, and the slightness of the residential buildings in the inner ward suggest that White Castle was never a residence of the Lord of the Three Castles, but was intended to function as a garrison, if necessary for large numbers of troops. This must be the reason why no church and no village were planted beside it. The castle was kept in repair at least until the mid C15, but by 1538, when Leland saw it, it was disused and abandoned. In 1922 the ruins came into the guardianship of the state, and today they are cared for by Cadw: Welsh Historic Monuments.

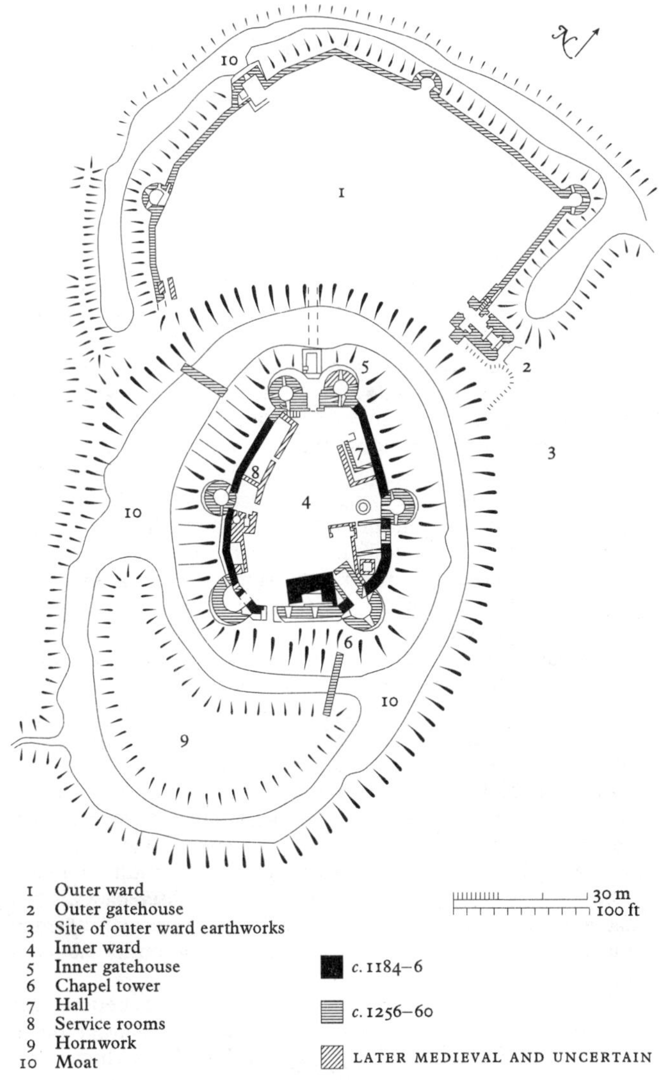

White Castle. Plan

PERAMBULATION

The castle is constructed of mauve Old Red Sandstone rubble. Traces of the white lime render which covered the walls and gave the castle its name are difficult to spot today.

The OUTER WARD is entered through an E-facing, twin-towered GATEHOUSE, probably the one under construction in 1256–7. It is a deep rectangle in plan, fronted by two solid, bow-fronted turrets, with tentatively battered bases. The gatehouse can never have been of particularly threatening aspect, and its impact is today much reduced by the disappearance of the vault over the central passage, and all but traces of the drawbridge, portcullis and doorway that protected it. Under the modern timber bridge, the drawbridge pit with two vertical slits in its front wall. At the inner end of the entrance passage, traces of a heated guardroom on the l., and on the r. an arrow loop and steps leading on to the curtain wall for a latrine.

The outer ward itself is a very large, roughly rectangular space enclosed by a dry ditch, stone walls which stand nearly to full height and four well-preserved towers. To the E and N the wall runs straight, but to the W it describes a shallow faceted bow, where it seems to have followed the line of the C12 bailey rampart. The towers are two-storeyed and extremely plain. The lower storey of each was a windowless basement. The upper storey is provided with arrow loops facing in three directions. Three of the towers are cylindrical, but the NW tower is rectangular, and has a faceted projection for a latrine. Traces of a hooded fireplace too. So there were living quarters in this tower. The recess at the SW end of the curtain wall has been identified as another latrine. It raises the question of what more ephemeral structures stood in the outer ward. A resistivity survey has identified the buried foundations of a very large rectangular structure, probably an aisled barn.

The defences of the INNER WARD to the S are much more formidable. It is surrounded by a wide and deep moat with steep, stone-revetted outer side. Low stone walls at the foot of the moat to W and S were intended to regulate the height of water in it. Across the moat rise the twin drum towers of the INNER GATEHOUSE. They are high, broad and completely plain, rising from deep aprons constructed on the sloping side of the moat. In the W tower, arrow loops to front, left and right at the base of the vertical wall. In the E tower no loops, but walling punctuated by many putlog holes. The reason for this discrepancy is that the front half of the E tower collapsed and was reconstructed in the later Middle Ages when all-round protection by archers was no longer important.

The ruined rectangular structure which projects between the towers on the sloping side of the moat is what remains of the pit for the drawbridge. The drawbridge itself must have linked to a fixed timber bridge extending across half the moat from the outer ward.

The CURTAIN WALL which encloses the roughly oval inner

ward survives from the first masonry castle. It is typical of late C12 castle-building in its construction as a series of short straight stretches. But to understand the character of the earlier castle it is best to wait until one can examine what remains inside the ward. The mid-C13 strengthening of the C12 curtain involved the addition of four regularly spaced D-shaped towers. These, like the gate-towers, rise high above the curtain wall but are devoid of any offset, moulding or aperture, except for three arrow loops in each, one facing forward, the others placed to cover the intervening stretches of curtain wall. At the S end the curtain wall was also rebuilt and provided with two further arrow loops. These, like all the others, are to a design unique to the castle, with horizontal sighting slits at two different levels, rather than forming a cruciform opening in the usual way.

On entering the INNER WARD across the modern bridge, one sees that the inner gatehouse was further protected, as was normal, with a portcullis – see the remains of one of the grooves in which it was raised and lowered. Also in the W tower, two slots for draw-bars to protect the door within the entrance passage. The E tower was entered through a doorway in the passage. The W tower, on the other hand, is entered from the ward itself up a short flight of steps and through a restored stone doorway. This leads both to the chamber with the arrow loops and to a stair spiralling up in short flights to the top storey, and to the roof and wall-walk, but bypassing the intermediate storey. The space at this level can only have been used for storage, and was included, it has been suggested, primarily in order to increase the height of the towers.

The interiors of the towers in the curtain wall are designed along similar lines, but without internal stairs. In each, the lowest chamber is entered from the ward, the middle one was again an unlit storage area, and the topmost chamber could be reached from the wall-walk, which remains in part along the top of the C12 curtain walls. The SE tower, however, has a piscina at the level of the arrow loops. So here there was a chapel, and the appearance of defence was misleading. The footings of the rectangular nave of the chapel have been exposed in the ward.

Other stone footings within the ward show that buildings, probably timber-framed above their stone base courses, were erected against the long walls. The fireplace cut into the wall S of the E tower has chamfered jambs with pyramid stops, a characteristic late C13 form. It must have heated a comfortable private room. The square structure S of it has been interpreted as a communal latrine, presumably made after the C13 room had gone out of use. Traces further N of a small rectangular hall, and its subsequent rebuilding larger. The service rooms were probably built against the W wall.

That leaves the much broader footings at the S end of the ward, close to the chapel tower. These clearly formed the foundations of the N half of a rectangular tower or small keep. The S half of this structure was destroyed by the C13 works, and it is clear that it must originally have straddled the line of the C12 curtain walls. Thus the plan of the masonry castle of 1185–7, a ward enclosed by a faceted curtain with a small rectangular keep astride it, conforms to a type of which several examples have been identified in Glamorgan, e.g. Coity, Ogmore. The keep was demolished, and the entrance gateway which must have been close to the keep eliminated by the rebuilding of the castle in the C13, when the curtain wall was reconstructed at this point. The C12 castle therefore must have been approached from the S, not the N. This means that the crescent-shaped earthen mound, the HORNWORK, which survives to the S enclosed by an arm of the moat, was originally part of the defences at the entrance to the castle. The C13 re-orientation of the castle left the hornwork as little more than an irrelevant excrescence. It will, however, have been protected by a palisade or even a masonry wall. Traces remain of a rectangular stone turret to the SE.

3080 WHITSON

One of the most evocative places on the Gwent Levels. The church stands to the SE, and the Court a mile away to the NW. Set back to the E of the road which joins them is what almost amounts to a row of substantial, largely C18 farmhouses, suggesting vividly the richness of the meadowlands drained by a network of willow-lined ditches.

CHURCH (dedication unknown). The Perp W tower, its NE stair-turret capped with a stone spike, is a veritable Leaning Tower of Pisa. Though the lower stage settled towards the S, the builders managed to construct a vertical upper stage. Norman nave, as the S doorway demonstrates. Its arch, segmental rather than semicircular, is outlined by two fat rolls, the inner carried down the imposts, the outer set on roll-like shafts with carved capitals, the l. with scallops, the r. with leaves. The chancel, the nave S windows, the S porch and the prominent S vestry chimney belong to what seems to have been an unfinished restoration by *Prichard & Seddon* of 1861. (Further restoration in 1909 by *Arthur Grove.*) Inside, tower arch with two broad chamfers, an inner order dying into the imposts. The chancel arch is of 1861. – FONT. An impressive Norman piece. Square bowl, the N face decorated with a lattice pattern, the undersides of all four faces boldly scalloped. – PEWS. In the nave, open benches to *Prichard & Seddon*'s typical pattern. – STAINED GLASS. Chancel E, Crucified Christ with Mary and John, 1884. C15 Netherlandish style. Clearly by *Burlison & Grylls* (A. Brooks). – Nave S, Baptism of Christ. 1962, signed by *A.E. Buss* of *Goddard & Gibbs*. – MONUMENTS. Four simple Neoclassical tablets in the nave, for the Phillips family of Whitson Court. The series begins with one to William Phillips †1789 aged 100, and earlier members. – Matilda Louise Phillips †1850. With the familiar willow weeping over an urn.

WHITSON COURT, 1 m. NW. Built for William Phillips, and attributed at the time of building to John Nash, though this is hard to believe. Four-square and formal red brick house of three storeys, which was nearing completion in 1795. It is flanked by matching dairy and stable ranges. The five-bay entrance front faces W; the three-bay return fronts have dummy windows where the chimney-breasts rise. Across all three the ground-floor windows are set under round-headed relieving arches of rubbed brick on stone impost blocks. Flat stone string-course above. Dentilled top cornice. The single-storey, pilastered porch is a mid-C19 addition. The one-bay ends of the service ranges have false windows and relieving arches to match those on the house. The W front of the house springs a surprise. It is of only three wide bays, the tripartite lower windows set under semicircular, rendered tympana with rubbed brick outer arches. The spacious rhythm of the façade has been upset by the irregular insertion of extra upper windows.

Inside, the plan is straightforward, with rectangular rooms l. and r. of the narrow entrance hall. At the back of the hall, a segmental arch, and beyond it the cantilevered stone stairs, which sweep up in a tight curve under a circular balcony at top-floor level and a glazed oculus. Fluted vertical surfaces surround both apertures. Further square rooms flank the stairs, entered through enriched round-headed arches. That to the l. was originally the kitchen. Reticent plaster cornices.

Contemporary single-storey STABLE, also of red brick, set at r.-angles to the SW.

Further S, beside the road, THE LODGE, a symmetrical *cottage orné* with timber verandas flanking the central porch. The attribution to *Nash*, *c.* 1800, is plausible. Its cast-iron window casements have unfortunately been replaced.

WILCRICK 4080

ST MARY. The little building, at the foot of Wilcrick Hill, is heavily overshadowed by a pair of yew trees. Nave with W bellcote, lower chancel, all virtually reconstructed in 1860. Stone dated 1621 apparently randomly set in the E wall. Inside, the nave has a plastered wagon vault of late medieval type with the usual moulded ribs. – FONT. C12. Circular bowl with raised rim. Telling evidence of the church's early origin. – ALTAR RAILS. Late C17 or early C18. Turned balusters. – STAINED GLASS. Chancel E, four Evangelists. Strongly coloured figures naively drawn. Mid-C19.

WOLVESNEWTON 4090

ST THOMAS A BECKET. The view from the S is dominated by the war memorial, which incorporates the broached base and part of the spurred shaft of the medieval churchyard CROSS. The church is built of slabs of Old Red Sandstone. Nave with S porch and lower chancel, drastically restored by *John Norton* 1855–7. The N wall was until the C19 entirely windowless. A straight joint on this side shows where the nave was lengthened, with a blocked two-centred-headed doorway immediately W of the joint. The small saddlebacked W tower has Tudor details. The Dec S windows were all introduced by Norton, the late Perp square-headed ones much renewed. The chancel arch must be his too. – SANCTUARY FITTINGS. 1924 by *Thomas W. Camm* of Smethwick. – STAINED GLASS. Sanctuary E and S, 1924, signed by *Florence Camm* of the above firm. Bright, harsh colours, but maudlin sentiment. The scheme forms a unified war memorial. – Nave N and S, also a war memorial, routine work by *R.J. Newbery*.

At CWRT-Y-GAER, ⅓m. W, a platform S of the house, interpreted by Cathcart King as a large ringwork. The modern-looking house incorporates a small, late C16, two-bay, two-storey house, entered at the gable-end in the characteristic way.

GREAT HOUSE, ¾m. NE. Long, white, single-pile farmhouse, constructed in the mid C17 but drastically modernized in 1944. For Fox and Raglan it was a classic example of the three-room plan, of hall and inner parlour, and service room beyond the cross-passage. The three rooms are roughly equal in size, all heated. Unusually the hall fireplace is in the long rear (N) wall, next to the two-storey, gabled newel-stair tower.

4010

WONASTOW/LLANWARRW

ST WONNOW. The chancel is Perp, of Old Red Sandstone, with square-headed windows in all three walls, the ogee lights cinquefoiled, the surrounds deeply hollowed. Priest's door, unusually, in the N wall. Short nave, probably of 1863, to which *Arthur Grove* added a charming N porch in 1909. Arts and Crafts detail in the timber gates and entrance door, in the glazed side windows, and in particular in the sculpture round the arch. Pink sandstone. Virgin and Child above, the springers at eye level carved in low relief with a thrilling Annunciation. Stout W tower dated 1865. Inside, nave roof of spindly hammerbeam trusses on leaf corbels. C19 arches to tower and chancel with two continuous sunk waves. The chancel is a remarkable ritualistic shrine, created by the benefactions of Lady Seale (donor also of the N porch). CHANCEL SCREEN by *G.E. Halliday*. – SANCTUARY STEPS. Squared in green and grey marble. – REREDOS. Of timber, full-width, with figures under pinnacled canopies. – SACRAMENT HOUSE (chancel N wall). Timber canopy 1922 by *J. Coates Carter*. – CHANDELIERS. Five, of brass, in the sanctuary. – STAINED GLASS. Chancel E, 1903 by *Comper*. Virgin and Child between St Michael and a bishop. Clean draughtsmanship and cool colours. – Nave S, two windows the gift of Lady Seale. Adoration of the Shepherds, 1897 by *Kempe*, unusually convincing. St Anne between SS Francis and Winwalo, *c.* 1914, by *Herbert W. Bryans*.

– MONUMENT. George Milborne †1637 (chancel S). An astonishingly late date for the Elizabethan character of this standing wall monument. Bold strapwork frames at top and bottom. Corinthian side columns carrying an entablature and strapwork cresting. Small kneeling figures of four sons and seven daughters below. Blank area in the middle, apparently for a full-scale recumbent figure.

In the CHURCHYARD, a CROSS on steps, of which only the broached base is medieval.

WONASTOW COURT. Plain classical S range, rendered, of three storeys and five bays, with Doric porch. Built for Thomas Swinnerton in 1803. At r.-angles to the W, a three-storey stone pseudo-gatehouse in Tudor style, which, confusingly, bears this date though it looks half a century later. Lower, two-storey stone range to the r., probably of the C17, all that remains of the seat of the Milbornes.

At WORTHYBROOK, 1½ m. NW, a tiny Primitive Methodist Chapel, GWERN-Y-SAINT, dated 1850. Front with two segment-headed windows under a bargeboarded gable. Modernized interior.

TREOWEN, 1¾ m. W. The most important early C17 gentry house 53
in the county. Built for William Jones between *c.* 1615 and 1627, the date on the hall screen now at Llanarth Court (*see* p. 264). Of pink Old Red Sandstone rubble, with caramel-coloured ashlar blocks for the S entrance front and dressings largely of green Bridgend (Quarella) sandstone. As originally built, the height of the house must have been as daunting as the sheer repetitiveness of its design. In plan a rectangular double pile, four generous

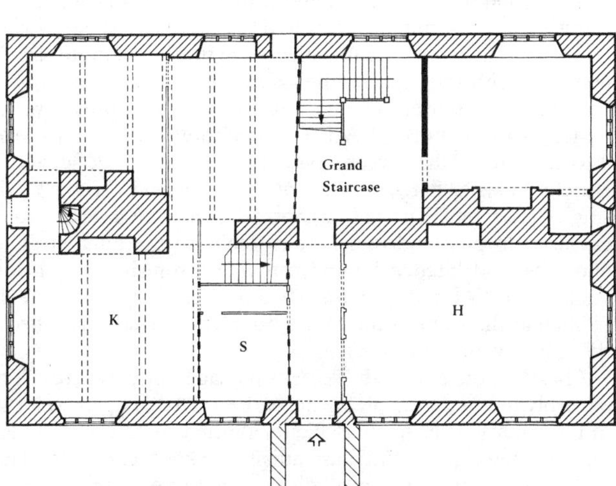

Wonastow, Treowen. Plan

bays wide. Three-and-a-half storeys reduced to two in the front pile, with three massive chimneystacks spaced across the spine wall, and in the rear pile a plain gable over every bay. The two-storey entrance porch was clearly an afterthought – see how it overlaps the window frames to the r. Much more upsetting is the partial removal in the C18 of the top storey-and-a-half, giving arbitrary irregularity where none was intended.

Closer inspection reveals some subtleties. On the S-facing entrance front, mullioned four-light windows, with mid-height transom. Ovolo mouldings. Small hoodmoulds fused with continuous stringcourses at both levels. The porch has a two-storey classical frontispiece of distressing crudity. Siamese twin-like columns, Doric below, Ionic above, carry entablatures, which continue round the sides of the porch, out of step with the adjoining stringcourses. Porch arch of flattened form on moulded imposts. Above, at the Ionic level, mantled and helmeted armorial shield with many quarterings, flanked by positively barbaric terms. Three-light mullion-and-transom window above for the porch room, and triangular gable decorated with strapwork, doubtless copied from a de Vries engraving. Timber bargeboard, probably early C19. The E front is partly ashlar-faced, in small blocks, partly of rubble. To the N rubble walling takes over entirely, and in other ways it has a more utilitarian aspect. Mullioned windows without transoms, four-light in the two lower storeys, then three-light, with two-lighters in the gables. Hoodmoulds but no stringcourses. Rigorous vertical alignment, taking no account of the great staircase inside and upset only by a practically sited service doorway. W front of similar character, the central doorway and six storeys of two-light windows above serving the back stairs.

The mood of the interior is as austere as that outside, but this is misleading, for much joinery and plasterwork has been lost or removed. The stone chimneypieces are indeed all quite simple, openings with four-centred heads in the major rooms, square-headed in the minor. The entrance doorway is similar, with a flattened four-centred head. Contemporary door. This leads into the site of the screens passage, where a short section of enriched plaster frieze survives at the inner end. To the r., the single-storey hall. To the l., a short passage, past a service room enclosed in post-and-panel walls, leads to the kitchen. This, and a second kitchen behind, provide astonishingly spacious cooking areas for the house. (It has been suggested that the kitchen at the front of the house doubled as what was called at the time a winter parlour.)

54 Ahead, at the end of the screens passage, the great stair. This superbly monumental piece, the earliest datable open-well stair in the county, rises in short flights all the way to the roof. The tapering newel posts with vase finials, the knob-ended pendants and the tapering balusters all display the turner's art. Above the hall lies the great chamber, and this retains part of its plaster frieze and ceiling. Broad enriched bands radiate from pendants. Cusping in the fields, an unusual feature. Next door, the NE

room, the only one to retain its wainscoting and carved top frieze. Coarsely detailed timber overmantel carried on thick, fluted Doric pilasters. Turned pendants in arcading.

Square C17 GARDEN to the N, with slightly raised walls.

WYESHAM 5010

The only parish in the county on the E side of the River Wye, but almost an outer suburb of Monmouth. The church is surrounded by typical 1950s HOUSING, by *John H. Evans* for Monmouth Borough Council. On the summit of the Kymin behind is something much more unexpected, a late Georgian summer-house and patriotic temple erected for a club of Monmouth gentlemen.

ST JAMES. Built 1873–5 by *J. P. Seddon*. Tower completed 1890. Boldly grouped, and rather aggressive. Purple snecked Old Red Sandstone dressed with greenish Forest ashlar. The chancel presents its three-light Geometrical window towards the road. Higher nave. Trefoil-headed lancets N and S, singletons, pairs and trios. W composition of long, paired plate-traceried lights and encircled hexfoil above. Most dramatic is the sheer, saddleback N porch-tower. Shafted, plate-traceried belfry openings. The interior is straightforward and well-integrated, the spaces broad and not high. Boarded roofs, with iron tie-rods in the nave. The chamfered chancel arch is wide, just pointed, set on moulded caps, and corbels formed of two tiers of upright leaves. Rendered walls, tiled floors, and a goodly complement of appropriate fittings. – FONT. Plain, octagonal, from Rockfield Church. – PULPIT. 1875, so presumably by *Seddon*. Octagonal on a stem. Blind arcading with stiff-leaf foliage in the spandrels. – PEWS. In the nave, typical of *Seddon* in their prominent carpentry details. – REREDOS. A heavy alabaster piece, decorated with sunk, mosaic-backed quatrefoils. Clearly a later insertion. – STAINED GLASS. Chancel E, Transfiguration between the Calling of the Apostles and the Agony in the Garden. 1875 by *Cox & Co.* – Nave W, 'Come unto me ...' and Christ with Martha and Mary. 1882 by *Ward & Hughes*. – Chancel S, Good Shepherd. Signed by *Ward & Hughes*. – Nave NW, SS James and Peter. 1906 by *Comper*. Typically exquisite draughtsmanship. – Nave NE, Nunc Dimittis. By *A. L. & C. E. Moore*. – Nave S, Adoration of the Kings. 1926 by *A. J. Davies* of the *Bromsgrove Guild*. Arresting in its coloration and naturalism.

NATIONAL SCHOOL (now Community Hall). Also by *Seddon*, 1873. W of the church, contrastingly low and modest. Old Red Sandstone, with timber details. Single-storey gabled schoolrooms. The teacher's house set crosswise to the N is allowed some polychromy on the porch.

THE CELL, $\frac{1}{4}$m. SW, beside the A466. Formed out of the medieval CHAPEL of St Thomas. The present entrance front was clearly the buttressed side elevation of the chapel. Small, trefoil-headed window in the gable-end.

THE KYMIN, ½m. E, is approached from the A4136, up a switchback lane. The hilltop view, giving a panorama to the W of all the hills in Monmouthshire, attracted members of the Kymin Club, led by Philip Meakins Hardwick, in 1794 to erect a circular SUMMER-HOUSE here. The two storeys provided for a kitchen below and a banqueting house above. Sash windows, but top battlements. Rendered white. Irregular practical extension to the E. Was the flat grass-plot to the E, partly enclosed by a low wall, a BOWLING GREEN?

At a lower level, 200 yds (183 metres) to the S, the Club in
90 1800 erected the NAVAL TEMPLE, an extraordinary jingoistic gesture, commemorating the admirals whose naval victories since 1793 had just culminated in Nelson's rout of Napoleon at the Battle of the Nile. It consists of two two-column porticoes *in antis* back to back. Columns of the heroically austere primitivist Doric, without either bases or fluting, carry entablatures inscribed BRITAIN'S GLORY (W) and GLORIOUS VICTORY (E). Above this, a blind attic to which are attached discs naming the admirals and recording the dates of their victories. A pitched stone-slate roof supports an arch on which sits, in replica, a bronzed figure of seated Britannia. Oval marble inscription panels explain the purpose of the monument, and refer to two paintings, now lost, one representing 'The Standard of Great-Britain, waving triumphant over the fallen and captive of France, Spain and Holland', the other 'The Glorious and Ever Memorable Battle of the Nile'. Sir Richard Colt Hoare, who saw the temple in 1803, thought it 'in very bad taste'. Today, restored to its pristine condition, it is even harder to come to terms with.

RAILWAY VIADUCT, W of the A466. This splendid viaduct of twenty-two tall semicircular arches, faced with rock-faced Old Red Sandstone, was built in 1861 as an extension of the single-track Coleford, Monmouth, Usk and Pontypool Railway, a line begun in 1853 but completed only in 1883. A large metal truss spanned the River Wye, and the approach viaduct extends far across its floodplain to the W.

RAILWAY BRIDGE, immediately N of the viaduct. Large, three-span iron bridge constructed in 1874 to take the Ross and Monmouth Railway across the River Wye. The main iron bow-string truss and two side trusses together with the deck are carried on four tall iron columns. The railway line closed in 1959.

At HADNOCK, 2½m. NE (SO 536 152), series of Roman buildings have been located in recent excavations. At least some of them appear to have been connected with ironworking.

1090

YNYSDDU

ST THEODORE. Alone below the bracken-covered hillside at the S end of the settlement. Dated 1925, but easy to mistake for one of E.M. Bruce Vaughan's churches at the turn of the century. The architect was *W.A. Griffiths* of Pontllanfraith. Long nave and lower chancel, NE tower not built. Inside, the nave roof trusses are unusually complicated. – IMMERSION FONT. In the SW corner. A late example of this South Wales fashion. – STAINED GLASS. Chancel E, and centre two lights, Christ and the Virgin, 1953 by *Howard Martin* of *Celtic Studios*. Outer lights SS Theodore and David, from a war memorial, by an unknown maker.

At CWMFELINFACH, 1 m. SE, the towering roadside MINERS' INSTITUTE, 1913 by *R. L. Roberts* of Abercarn, was demolished in 1997. That leaves the contemporary, rather impressive PIONEER HOTEL, faced with rough Pennant sandstone and smooth white render, and full of intriguing Art Nouveau reminiscences.

ARCHITECTURAL GLOSSARY

Numbers and letters refer to the illustrations (by John Sambrook) on pp. 618–25.

ABACUS: flat slab forming the top of a capital (3a).

ACANTHUS: classical formalized leaf ornament (3b).

ACCUMULATOR TOWER: *see* Hydraulic power.

ACHIEVEMENT: a complete display of armorial bearings.

ACROTERION: plinth for a statue or ornament on the apex or ends of a pediment; more usually, both the plinth and what stands on it (4a).

AEDICULE (*lit.* little building): architectural surround, consisting usually of two columns or pilasters supporting a pediment.

AGGREGATE: *see* Concrete.

AISLE: subsidiary space alongside the body of a building, separated from it by columns, piers, or posts.

AMBULATORY (*lit.* walkway): aisle around the sanctuary (q.v.).

ANGLE ROLL: roll moulding in the angle between two planes (1a).

ANSE DE PANIER: *see* Arch.

ANTAE: simplified pilasters (4a), usually applied to the ends of the enclosing walls of a portico *in antis* (q.v.).

ANTEFIXAE: ornaments projecting at regular intervals above a Greek cornice, originally to conceal the ends of roof tiles (4a).

ANTHEMION: classical ornament like a honeysuckle flower (4b).

APRON: raised panel below a window or wall monument or tablet.

APSE: semicircular or polygonal end of an apartment, especially of a chancel or chapel. In classical architecture sometimes called an *exedra.*

ARABESQUE: non-figurative surface decoration consisting of flowing lines, foliage scrolls etc., based on geometrical patterns. Cf. Grotesque.

ARCADE: series of arches supported by piers or columns. *Blind arcade* or *arcading*: the same applied to the wall surface. *Wall arcade*: in medieval churches, a blind arcade forming a dado below windows. Also a covered shopping street.

ARCH: Shapes *see* 5c. *Basket arch* or *anse de panier* (basket handle): three-centred and depressed, or with a flat centre. *Nodding*: ogee arch curving forward from the wall face. *Parabolic*: shaped like a chain suspended from two level points, but inverted. Special purposes. *Chancel*: dividing chancel from nave or crossing. *Crossing*: spanning piers at a crossing (q.v.). *Relieving* or *discharging*: incorporated in a wall to relieve superimposed weight (5c). *Skew*: spanning responds not diametrically opposed. *Strainer*: inserted in an opening to resist inward pressure. *Transverse*: spanning a main axis (e.g. of a vaulted space). *See also* Jack arch, Triumphal arch.

ARCHITRAVE: formalized lintel, the lowest member of the classical entablature (3a). Also the moulded frame of a door or window (often borrowing the profile of a classical architrave). For *lugged* and *shouldered* architraves *see* 4b.

ARCUATED: dependent structurally on the arch principle. Cf. Trabeated.

ARK: chest or cupboard housing the

tables of Jewish law in a synagogue.

ARRIS: sharp edge where two surfaces meet at an angle (3a).

ASHLAR: masonry of large blocks wrought to even faces and square edges (6d).

ASTRAGAL: classical moulding of semicircular section (3f).

ASTYLAR: with no columns or similar vertical features.

ATLANTES: *see* Caryatids.

ATRIUM (plural: atria): inner court of a Roman or C20 house; in a multi-storey building, a toplit covered court rising through all storeys. Also an open court in front of a church.

ATTACHED COLUMN: *see* Engaged column.

ATTIC: small top storey within a roof. Also the storey above the main entablature of a classical façade.

AUMBRY: recess or cupboard to hold sacred vessels for the Mass.

BAILEY: *see* Motte-and-bailey.

BALANCE BEAM: *see* Canals.

BALDACCHINO: free-standing canopy, originally fabric, over an altar. Cf. Ciborium.

BALLFLOWER: globular flower of three petals enclosing a ball (1a). Typical of the Decorated style.

BALUSTER: pillar or pedestal of bellied form. *Balusters*: vertical supports of this or any other form, for a handrail or coping, the whole being called a *balustrade* (6c). *Blind balustrade*: the same applied to the wall surface.

BARBICAN: outwork defending the entrance to a castle.

BARGEBOARDS (corruption of 'vergeboards'): boards, often carved or fretted, fixed beneath the eaves of a gable to cover and protect the rafters.

BAROQUE: style originating in Rome *c.* 1600 and current in England *c.* 1680–1720, characterized by dramatic massing and silhouette and the use of the giant order.

BARROW: burial mound.

BARTIZAN: corbelled turret, square or round, frequently at an angle.

BASCULE: hinged part of a lifting (or bascule) bridge.

BASE: moulded foot of a column or pilaster . For *Attic* base *see* 3b.

BASEMENT: lowest, subordinate storey; hence the lowest part of a classical elevation, below the piano nobile (q.v.).

BASILICA: a Roman public hall; hence an aisled building with a clerestory.

BASTION: one of a series of defensive semicircular or polygonal projections from the main wall of a fortress or city.

BATTER: intentional inward inclination of a wall face.

BATTLEMENT: defensive parapet, composed of *merlons* (solid) and *crenels* (embrasures) through which archers could shoot; sometimes called *crenellation*. Also used decoratively.

BAY LEAF: classical ornament of overlapping bay leaves (3f).

BAY: division of an elevation or interior space as defined by regular vertical features such as arches, columns, windows, etc.

BAY WINDOW: window of one or more storeys projecting from the face of a building. *Canted*: with a straight front and angled sides. *Bow window*: curved. *Oriel*: rests on corbels or brackets and starts above ground level; also the bay window at the dais end of a medieval great hall.

BEAD-AND-REEL: *see* Enrichments.

BEAKHEAD: Norman ornament with a row of beaked bird or beast heads usually biting into a roll moulding (1a).

BELFRY: chamber or stage in a tower where bells are hung.

BELL CAPITAL: *see* 1b.

BELLCOTE: small gabled or roofed housing for the bell(s).

BERM: level area separating a ditch from a bank on a hill-fort or barrow.

BILLET: Norman ornament of small half-cyclindrical or rectangular blocks (1a).

BLIND: *see* Arcade, Baluster, Portico.

BLOCK CAPITAL: *see* 1a.

BLOCKED: columns, etc. interrupted by regular projecting blocks (*blocking*), as on a Gibbs surround (4b).

BLOCKING COURSE: course of stones, or equivalent, on top of a cornice and crowning the wall.

BOLECTION MOULDING: covering the joint between two different planes (6b).

BOND: the pattern of long sides (*stretchers*) and short ends (*headers*) produced on the face of a wall by laying bricks in a particular way (6e).

BOSS: knob or projection, e.g. at the intersection of ribs in a vault (2c).

BOW WINDOW: *see* Bay window.

BOX FRAME: timber-framed construction in which vertical and horizontal wall members support the roof (7). Also concrete construction where the loads are taken on cross walls; also called *cross-wall construction*.

BRACE: subsidiary member of a structural frame, curved or straight. *Bracing* is often arranged decoratively e.g. quatrefoil, herringbone (7). *See also* Roofs.

BRATTISHING: ornamental crest, usually formed of leaves, Tudor flowers or miniature battlements.

BRESSUMER (*lit.* breast-beam): big horizontal beam supporting the wall above, especially in a jettied building (7).

BRICK: *see* Bond, Cogging, Engineering, Gauged, Tumbling.

BRIDGE: *Bowstring*: with arches rising above the roadway which is suspended from them. *Clapper*: one long stone forms the roadway. *Roving*: *see* Canal. *Suspension*: roadway suspended from cables or chains slung between towers or pylons. *Stay-suspension* or *stay-cantilever*: supported by diagonal stays from towers or pylons. *See also* Bascule.

BRISES-SOLEIL: projecting fins or canopies which deflect direct sunlight from windows.

BROACH: *see* Spire and 1c.

BUCRANIUM: ox skull used decoratively in classical friezes.

BULLSEYE WINDOW: small oval window, set horizontally (cf. Oculus). Also called *oeil de boeuf*.

BUTTRESS: vertical member projecting from a wall to stabilize it or to resist the lateral thrust of an arch, roof, or vault (1c, 2c). A *flying buttress* transmits the thrust to a heavy abutment by means of an arch or half-arch (1c).

CABLE or ROPE MOULDING: originally Norman, like twisted strands of a rope.

CAMES: *see* Quarries.

CAMPANILE: free-standing bell tower.

CANALS: *Flash lock*: removable weir or similar device through which boats pass on a flush of water. Predecessor of the *pound lock*: chamber with gates at each end allowing boats to float from one level to another. *Tidal gates*: single pair of lock gates allowing vessels to pass when the tide makes a level. *Balance beam*: beam projecting horizontally for opening and closing lock gates. *Roving bridge*: carrying a towing path from one bank to the other.

CANTILEVER: horizontal projection (e.g. step, canopy) supported by a downward force behind the fulcrum.

CAPITAL: head or crowning feature of a column or pilaster; for classical types *see* 3a; for medieval types *see* 1b.

CARREL: compartment designed for individual work or study.

CARTOUCHE: classical tablet with ornate frame (4b).

CARYATIDS: female figures supporting an entablature; their male counterparts are *Atlantes* (*lit*: Atlas figures).

CASEMATE: vaulted chamber, with embrasures for defence, within a castle wall or projecting from it.

CASEMENT: side-hinged window.

CASTELLATED: with battlements (q.v.).

CAST IRON: hard and brittle, cast in a mould to the required shape. *Wrought iron* is ductile, strong in tension, forged into decorative patterns or forged and rolled into e.g. bars, joists, boiler plates; *mild steel* is its modern equivalent, similar but stronger.

CATSLIDE: *See* 8a.

CAVETTO: concave classical moulding of quarter-round section (3f).

CELURE OR CEILURE: enriched area of roof above rood or altar.

CEMENT: *see* Concrete.

CENOTAPH (*lit.* empty tomb): funerary monument which is not a burying place.

CENTRING: wooden support for the building of an arch or vault, removed after completion.

CHAMFER (*lit.* corner-break): surface formed by cutting off a square edge or corner. For types of chamfers and *chamfer stops see* 6a. *See also* Double chamfer.

CHANCEL: part of the E end of a church set apart for the use of the officiating clergy.

CHANTRY CHAPEL: often attached to or within a church, endowed for the celebration of Masses principally for the soul of the founder.

CHEVET (*lit.* head): French term for chancel with ambulatory and radiating chapels.

CHEVRON: V-shape used in series or double series (later) on a Norman moulding (1a). Also (especially when on a single plane) called *zigzag*.

CHOIR: the part of a cathedral, monastic or collegiate church where services are sung.

CIBORIUM: a fixed canopy over an altar, usually vaulted and supported on four columns; cf. Baldacchino. Also a canopied shrine for the reserved sacrament.

CINQUEFOIL: *see* Foil.

CIST: stone-lined or slab-built grave.

CLADDING: external covering or skin applied to a structure, especially a framed one.

CLERESTORY: uppermost storey of the nave of a church, pierced by windows. Also high-level windows in secular buildings.

CLOSER: a brick cut to complete a bond (6e).

CLUSTER BLOCK: *see* Multi-storey.

COADE STONE: ceramic artificial stone made in Lambeth 1769–*c.*1840 by Eleanor Coade (†1821) and her associates.

COB: walling material of clay mixed with straw. Also called *pisé*.

COFFERING: arrangement of sunken panels (coffers), square or polygonal, decorating a ceiling, vault, or arch.

COGGING: a decorative course of bricks laid diagonally (6e). Cf. Dentilation.

COLLAR: *see* Roofs and 7.

COLLEGIATE CHURCH: endowed for the support of a college of priests.

COLONNADE: range of columns supporting an entablature. Cf. Arcade.

COLONNETTE: small medieval column or shaft.

COLOSSAL ORDER: *see* Giant order.

COLUMBARIUM: shelved, niched structure to house multiple burials.

COLUMN: a classical, upright structural member of round section with a shaft, a capital, and usually a base (3a, 4a).

COLUMN FIGURE: carved figure attached to a medieval column or shaft, usually flanking a doorway.

COMMUNION TABLE: unconsecrated table used in Protestant churches for the celebration of Holy Communion.

COMPOSITE: *see* Orders.

COMPOUND PIER: grouped shafts (q.v.), or a solid core surrounded by shafts.

CONCRETE: composition of *cement* (calcined lime and clay), *aggregate* (small stones or rock chippings), sand and water. It can be poured into *formwork* or *shuttering* (temporary frame of timber or metal) on site (*in-situ* concrete), or *pre-cast* as components before construction. *Reinforced*: incorporating steel rods to take the tensile force. *Pre-stressed*: with tensioned steel rods. Finishes include the impression of boards left by formwork (*board-marked* or *shuttered*), and texturing with steel brushes (*brushed*) or hammers (*hammer-dressed*). *See also* Shell.

CONSOLE: bracket of curved outline (4b).

COPING: protective course of masonry or brickwork capping a wall (6d).

CORBEL: projecting block supporting something above. *Corbel course*: continuous course of projecting stones or bricks fulfilling the same function. *Corbel table*: series of corbels to carry a parapet or a wall-plate or wall-post (7). *Corbelling*: brick or masonry courses built out beyond one another to support a chimney-stack, window, etc.

CORINTHIAN: *see* Orders and 3d.

CORNICE: flat-topped ledge with moulded underside, projecting along the top of a building or feature, especially as the highest member of the classical entablature (3a). Also the decorative moulding in the angle between wall and ceiling.

CORPS-DE-LOGIS: the main building(s) as distinct from the wings or pavilions.

COTTAGE ORNÉ: an artfully rustic small house associated with the Picturesque movement.

COUNTERCHANGING:of joists on a ceiling divided by beams into compartments, when placed in opposite directions in alternate squares.

COUR D HONNEUR: formal entrance court before a house in the French manner, usually with flanking wings and a screen wall or gates.

COURSE: continuous layer of stones, etc. in a wall (6e).

COVE: a broad concave moulding, e.g. to mask the eaves of a roof. *Coved ceiling*: with a pronounced cove joining the walls to a flat central panel smaller than the whole area of the ceiling.

CRADLE ROOF: *see* Wagon roof.

CREDENCE: a shelf within or beside a piscina (q.v.), or a table for the sacramental elements and vessels.

CRENELLATION: parapet with crenels (*see* Battlement).

CRINKLE-CRANKLE WALL: garden wall undulating in a series of serpentine curves.

CROCKETS: leafy hooks. *Crocketing* decorates the edges of Gothic features, such as pinnacles, canopies, etc. *Crocket capital*: *see* 1b.

CROSSING: central space at the junction of the nave, chancel, and transepts. *Crossing tower*: above a crossing.

CROSS-WINDOW: with one mullion and one transom (qq.v.).

CROWN-POST: *see* Roofs and 7.

CROWSTEPS: squared stones set like steps, e.g. on a gable (8a).

CRUCKS (*lit.* crooked): pairs of inclined timbers (*blades*), usually curved, set at bay-lengths; they support the roof timbers and, in timber buildings, also support the walls (8b). *Base*: blades rise from ground level to a tie- or collar-beam which supports the roof timbers. *Full*: blades rise from ground level to the apex of the roof, serving as the main members of a roof truss. *Jointed*: blades formed from more than one timber; the lower member may act as a wall-post; it is usually elbowed at wall-plate level and jointed just above. *Middle*: blades rise from halfway up the walls to a tie- or collar-beam. *Raised*: blades rise from halfway up the walls to the apex. *Upper*: blades supported on a tie-beam and rising to the apex.

CRYPT: underground or half-underground area, usually below the E end of a church. *Ring crypt*: corridor crypt surrounding the apse of an early medieval church, often associated with chambers for relics. Cf. Undercroft.

CUPOLA (*lit.* dome): especially a small dome on a circular or polygonal base crowning a larger dome, roof, or turret.

CURSUS: a long avenue defined by two parallel earthen banks with ditches outside.

CURTAIN WALL: a connecting wall between the towers of a castle. Also a non-load-bearing external wall applied to a C 20 framed structure.

CUSP: *see* Tracery and 2b.

CYCLOPEAN MASONRY: large irregular polygonal stones, smooth and finely jointed.

CYMA RECTA and CYMA REVERSA: classical mouldings with double curves (3f). Cf. Ogee.

DADO: the finishing (often with panelling) of the lower part of a wall in a classical interior; in origin a formalized continuous pedestal. *Dado rail*: the moulding along the top of the dado.

DAGGER: *see* Tracery and 2b.

DEC (DECORATED): English Gothic architecture *c.* 1290 to *c.* 1350. The name is derived from the type of window Tracery (q.v.) used during the period.

DEMI- or HALF-COLUMNS: engaged columns (q.v.) half of whose circumference projects from the wall.

DENTIL: small square block used in series in classical cornices (3c). *Dentilation* is produced by the projection of alternating headers along cornices or string courses.

DIAPER: repetitive surface decoration of lozenges or squares flat or in relief. Achieved in brickwork with bricks of two colours.

DIOCLETIAN or THERMAL WINDOW: semicircular with two mullions, as used in the Baths of Diocletian, Rome (4b).

DISTYLE: having two columns (4a).

DOGTOOTH: E.E. ornament, consisting of a series of small pyramids formed by four stylized canine teeth meeting at a point (1a).

DORIC: *see* Orders and 3a, 3b.

DORMER: window projecting from the slope of a roof (8a).

DOUBLE CHAMFER: a chamfer applied to each of two recessed arches (1a).

DOUBLE PILE: *see* Pile.

DRAGON BEAM: *see* Jetty.

DRESSINGS: the stone or brickwork worked to a finished face about an angle, opening, or other feature.

DRIPSTONE: moulded stone projecting from a wall to protect the lower parts from water. Cf. Hoodmould, Weathering.

DRUM: circular or polygonal stage supporting a dome or cupola. Also one of the stones forming the shaft of a column (3a).

DUTCH or FLEMISH GABLE: *see* 8a.

EASTER SEPULCHRE: tomb-chest used for Easter ceremonial, within or against the N wall of a chancel.

EAVES: overhanging edge of a roof; hence *eaves cornice* in this position.

ECHINUS: ovolo moulding (q.v.) below the abacus of a Greek Doric capital (3a).

EDGE RAIL: *see* Railways.

E. E. (EARLY ENGLISH): English Gothic architecture *c.* 1190–1250.

EGG-AND-DART: *see* Enrichments and 3f.

ELEVATION: any face of a building or side of a room. In a drawing, the same or any part of it, represented in two dimensions.

EMBATTLED: with battlements.

EMBRASURE: small splayed opening in a wall or battlement (q.v.).

ENCAUSTIC TILES: earthenware tiles fired with a pattern and glaze.

EN DELIT: stone cut against the bed.

ENFILADE: reception rooms in a formal series, usually with all doorways on axis.

ENGAGED or ATTACHED COLUMN: one that partly merges into a wall or pier.

ENGINEERING BRICKS: dense bricks, originally used mostly for railway viaducts etc.

ENRICHMENTS: the carved decoration of certain classical mouldings, e.g. the ovolo (qq.v.) with *egg-and-dart*, the cyma reversa with *waterleaf*, the astragal with *bead-and-reel* (3f).

ENTABLATURE: in classical architecture, collective name for the three horizontal members (architrave, frieze, and cornice) carried by a wall or a column (3a).

ENTASIS: very slight convex deviation from a straight line, used to prevent an optical illusion of concavity.

EPITAPH: inscription on a tomb.

EXEDRA: *see* Apse.

EXTRADOS: outer curved face of an arch or vault.

EYECATCHER: decorative building terminating a vista.

FASCIA: plain horizontal band, e.g. in an architrave (3c, 3d) or on a shopfront.

FENESTRATION: the arrangement of windows in a façade.

FERETORY: site of the chief shrine of a church, behind the high altar.

FESTOON: ornamental garland, suspended from both ends. Cf. Swag.

FIBREGLASS, or glass-reinforced polyester (GRP): synthetic resin reinforced with glass fibre. GRC: glass-reinforced concrete.

FIELD: *see* Panelling and 6b.

FILLET: a narrow flat band running down a medieval shaft or along a roll moulding (1a). It separates larger curved mouldings in classical cornices, fluting or bases (3c).

FLAMBOYANT: the latest phase of French Gothic architecture, with flowing tracery.

FLASH LOCK: *see* Canals.

FLÈCHE or SPIRELET (*lit.* arrow): slender spire on the centre of a roof.

FLEURON: medieval carved flower or leaf, often rectilinear (1a).

FLUSHWORK: knapped flint used with dressed stone to form patterns.

FLUTING: series of concave grooves (flutes), their common edges sharp (arris) or blunt (fillet) (3).

FOIL (*lit.* leaf): lobe formed by the cusping of a circular or other shape in tracery (2b). *Trefoil* (three), *quatrefoil* (four), *cinquefoil* (five), and multifoil express the number of lobes in a shape.

FOLIATE: decorated with leaves.

FORMWORK: *see* Concrete.

FRAMED BUILDING: where the structure is carried by a framework – e.g. of steel, reinforced concrete, timber – instead of by load-bearing walls.

FREESTONE: stone that is cut, or can be cut, in all directions.

FRESCO: *al fresco*: painting on wet plaster. *Fresco secco*: painting on dry plaster.

FRIEZE: the middle member of the classical entablature, sometimes ornamented (3a). *Pulvinated frieze* (*lit.* cushioned): of bold convex profile (3c). Also a horizontal band of ornament.

FRONTISPIECE: in C16 and C17 buildings the central feature of doorway and windows above linked in one composition.

GABLE: For types *see* 8a. *Gablet*: small gable. *Pedimental gable*: treated like a pediment.

GADROONING: classical ribbed ornament like inverted fluting that flows into a lobed edge.

GALILEE: chapel or vestibule usually at the W end of a church enclosing the main portal(s).

GALLERY: a long room or passage; an upper storey above the aisle of a church, looking through arches to the nave; a balcony or mezzanine overlooking the main interior space of a building; or an external walkway.

GALLETING: small stones set in a mortar course.

GAMBREL ROOF: *see* 8a.

GARDEROBE: medieval privy.

GARGOYLE: projecting water spout often carved into human or animal shape.

GAUGED or RUBBED BRICKWORK: soft brick sawn roughly, then rubbed to a precise (gauged) surface. Mostly used for door or window openings (5c).

GAZEBO (jocular Latin, 'I shall gaze'): ornamental lookout tower or raised summer house.

GEOMETRIC: English Gothic architecture *c.* 1250–1310. *See also* Tracery. For another meaning, *see* Stairs.

GIANT or COLOSSAL ORDER: classical order (q.v.) whose height is that of two or more storeys of the building to which it is applied.

GIBBS SURROUND: C18 treatment of an opening (4b), seen particularly in the work of James Gibbs (1682–1754).

GIRDER: a large beam. *Box*: of hollow-box section. *Bowed*: with its top rising in a curve. *Plate*: of I-section, made from iron or steel plates. *Lattice*: with braced framework.

GLAZING BARS: wooden or sometimes metal bars separating and supporting window panes.

GORSEDD CIRCLE: modern stone circle; one is erected annually at different Welsh sites in connection with the national Eisteddfod.

GRAFFITI: *see* Sgraffito.

GRANGE: farm owned and run by a religious order.

GRC: *see* Fibreglass.

GRISAILLE: monochrome painting on walls or glass.

GROIN: sharp edge at the meeting of two cells of a cross-vault; *see* Vault and 2b.

GROTESQUE (*lit.* grotto-esque): wall decoration adopted from Roman examples in the Renaissance. Its foliage scrolls incorporate figurative elements. Cf. Arabesque.

GROTTO: artificial cavern.

GRP: *see* Fibreglass.

GUILLOCHE: classical ornament of interlaced bands (4b).

GUNLOOP: opening for a firearm.

GUTTAE: stylized drops (3b).

HALF-TIMBERING: archaic term for timber-framing (q.v.). Sometimes used for non-structural decorative timberwork.

HALL CHURCH: medieval church with nave and aisles of approximately equal height.

HAMMERBEAM: *see* Roofs and 7.

HEADER: *see* Bond and 6e.

HEADSTOP: stop (q.v.) carved with a head (5b).

HELM ROOF: *see* 1c.

HENGE: ritual earthwork.

HERM (*lit.* the god Hermes): male head or bust on a pedestal.

HERRINGBONE WORK: *see* 6e (for brick bond). Cf. Pitched masonry.

HEXASTYLE: *see* Portico.

HILL-FORT: Iron Age earthwork enclosed by a ditch and bank system.

HIPPED ROOF: *see* 8a.

HOODMOULD: projecting moulding above an arch or lintel to throw off water (2b, 5b). When horizontal often called a *label.* For label stop *see* Stop.

HUSK GARLAND: festoon of stylized nutshells (4b).

HYDRAULIC POWER: use of water under high pressure to work machinery. *Accumulator tower*: houses a hydraulic accumulator which accommodates fluctuations in the flow through hydraulic mains.

HYPOCAUST (*lit.* underburning): Roman underfloor heating system.

IMPOST: horizontal moulding at the springing of an arch (5c).

IMPOST BLOCK: block between abacus and capital (1b).

IN ANTIS: *see* Antae, Portico and 4a.

INDENT: shape chiselled out of a stone to receive a brass.

INDUSTRIALIZED OR SYSTEM BUILDING: system of manufactured units assembled on site.

INGLENOOK (*lit.* fire-corner): recess for a hearth with provision for seating.

INTERCOLUMNATION: interval between columns.

INTERLACE: decoration in relief simulating woven or entwined stems or bands.

INTRADOS: *see* Soffit.

IONIC: *see* Orders and 3c.

JACK ARCH: shallow segmental vault springing from beams, used for fireproof floors, bridge decks, etc.

JAMB (*lit.* leg): one of the vertical sides of an opening.

JETTY: in a timber-framed building, the projection of an upper storey beyond the storey below, made by the beams and joists of the lower storey oversailing the wall; on their outer ends is placed the sill of the walling for the storey above (7). Buildings can be jettied on several sides, in which case a *dragon beam* is set diagonally at the corner to carry the joists to either side.

JOGGLE: the joining of two stones to prevent them slipping by a notch in one and a projection in the other.

KEEL MOULDING: moulding used from the late C12, in section like the keel of a ship (1a).

KEEP: principal tower of a castle.

KENTISH CUSP: *see* Tracery and 2b.

KEY PATTERN: *see* 4b.

KEYSTONE: central stone in an arch or vault (4b, 5c).

KINGPOST: *see* Roofs and 7.

KNEELER: horizontal projecting stone at the base of each side of a gable to support the inclined coping stones (8a).

KNOTWORK: *see* Interlace. Used on early Christian monuments.

LABEL: *see* Hoodmould and 5b.

LABEL STOP: *see* Stop and 5b.

LACED BRICKWORK: vertical strips of brickwork, often in a contrasting colour, linking openings on different floors.

LACING COURSE: horizontal reinforcement in timber or brick to walls of flint, cobble, etc.

LADY CHAPEL: dedicated to the Virgin Mary (Our Lady).

LANCET: slender single-light, pointed-arched window (2a).

LANTERN: circular or polygonal windowed turret crowning a roof or a dome. Also the windowed stage of a crossing tower lighting the church interior.

LANTERN CROSS: churchyard cross with lantern-shaped top.

LAVATORIUM: in a religous house, a washing place adjacent to the refectory.

LEAN-TO: *see* Roofs.

LESENE (*lit.* a mean thing): pilaster without base or capital. Also called *pilaster strip*.

LIERNE: *see* Vault and 2c.

LIGHT: compartment of a window defined by the mullions.

LINENFOLD: Tudor panelling carbved with simulations of folded linen. *See also* Parchemin.

LINTEL: horizontal beam or stone bridging an opening.

LOGGIA: gallery, usually arcaded or colonnaded; sometimes free-standing.

LONG-AND-SHORT WORK: quoins consisting of stones placed with the long side alternately upright and horizontal, especially in Saxon building.

LONGHOUSE: house and byre in the same range with internal access between them.

LOUVRE: roof opening, often protected by a raised timber structure, to allow the smoke from a central hearth to escape.

LOWSIDE WINDOW: set lower than the others in a chancel side wall, usually towards its W end.

LUCARNE (*lit.* dormer): small gabled opening in a roof or spire.

LUGGED ARCHITRAVE: *see* 4b.

LUNETTE: semicircular window or blind panel.

LYCHGATE (*lit.* corpse-gate): roofed gateway entrance to a churchyard for the reception of a coffin.

LYNCHET: long terraced strip of soil on the downward side of prehistoric and medieval fields, accumulated because of continual ploughing along the contours.

MACHICOLATIONS (*lit.* mashing devices): series of openings between the corbels that support a projecting parapet through which missiles can be dropped. Used decoratively in post-medieval buildings.

MANOMETER or STANDPIPE TOWER: containing a column of water to regulate pressure in water mains.

MANSARD: *see* 8a.

MATHEMATICAL TILES: facing tiles with the appearance of brick, most often applied to timber-framed walls.

MAUSOLEUM: monumental building or chamber usually intended for the burial of members of one family.

MEGALITHIC TOMB: massive stone-built Neolithic burial chamber covered by an earth or stone mound.

MERLON: *see* Battlement.

METOPES: spaces between the triglyphs in a Doric frieze (3b).

MEZZANINE: low storey between two higher ones.

MILD STEEL: *see* Cast iron.

MISERICORD (*lit.* mercy): shelf on a carved bracket placed on the underside of a hinged choir stall seat to support an occupant when standing.

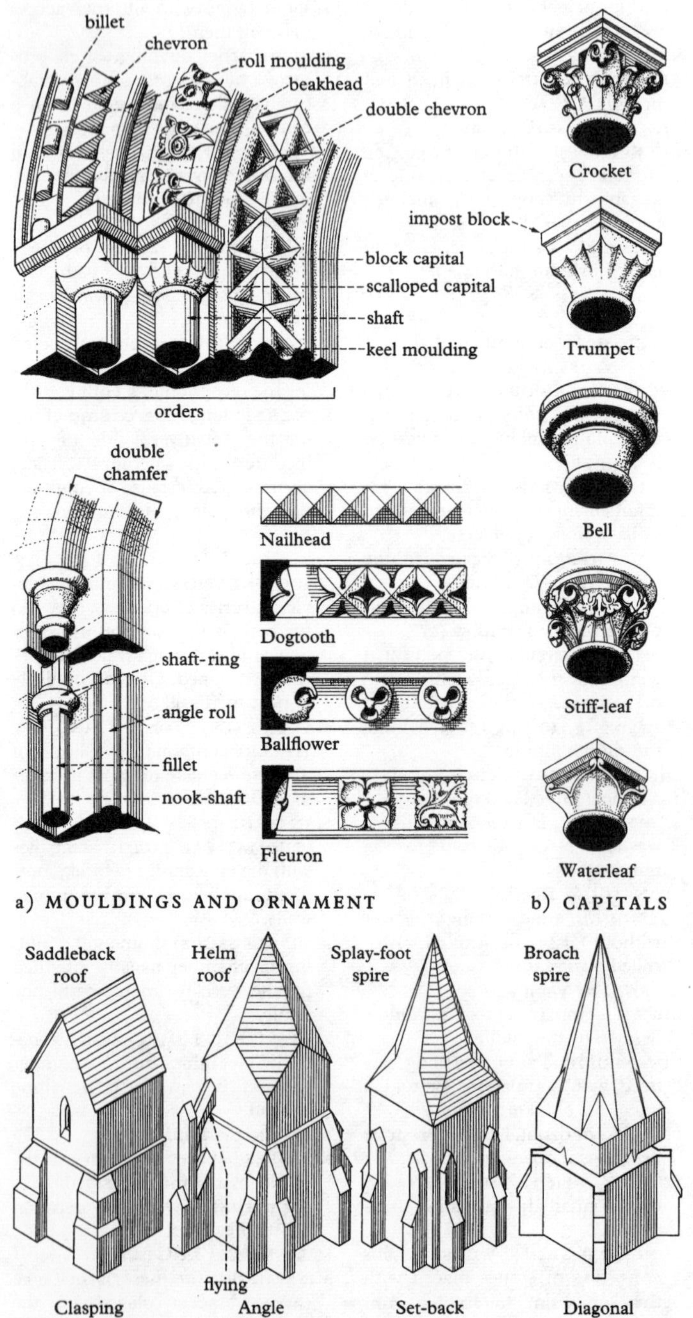

a) MOULDINGS AND ORNAMENT

b) CAPITALS

c) BUTTRESSES, ROOFS AND SPIRES

FIGURE 1: MEDIEVAL

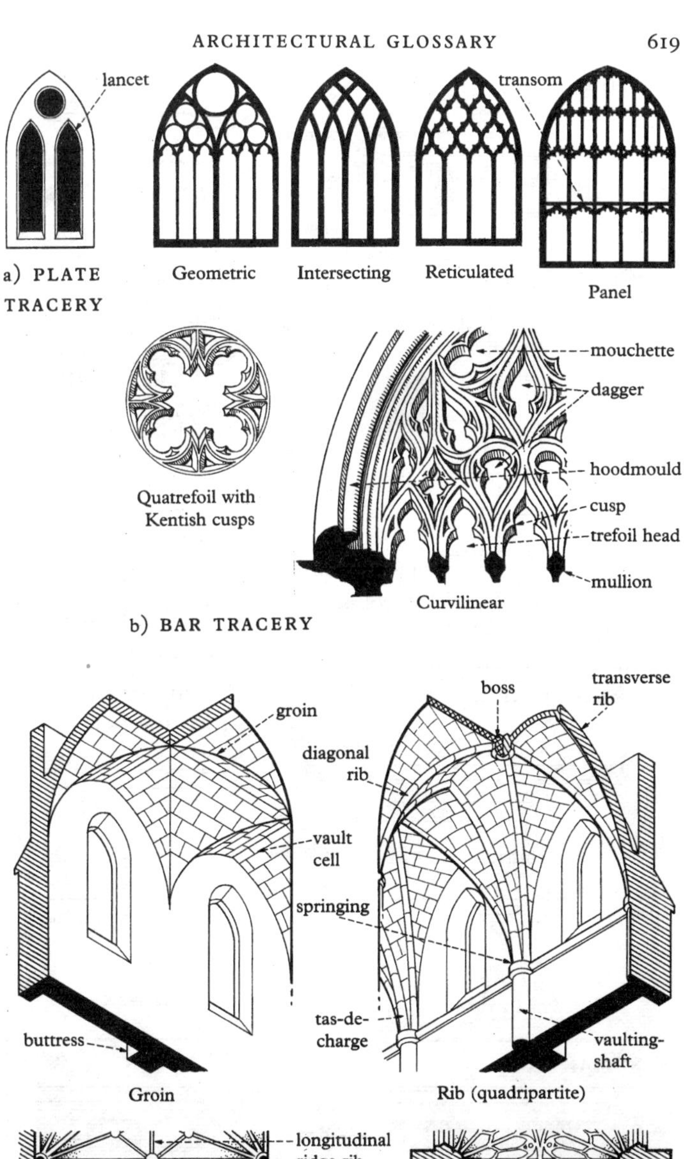

FIGURE 2: MEDIEVAL

ORDERS

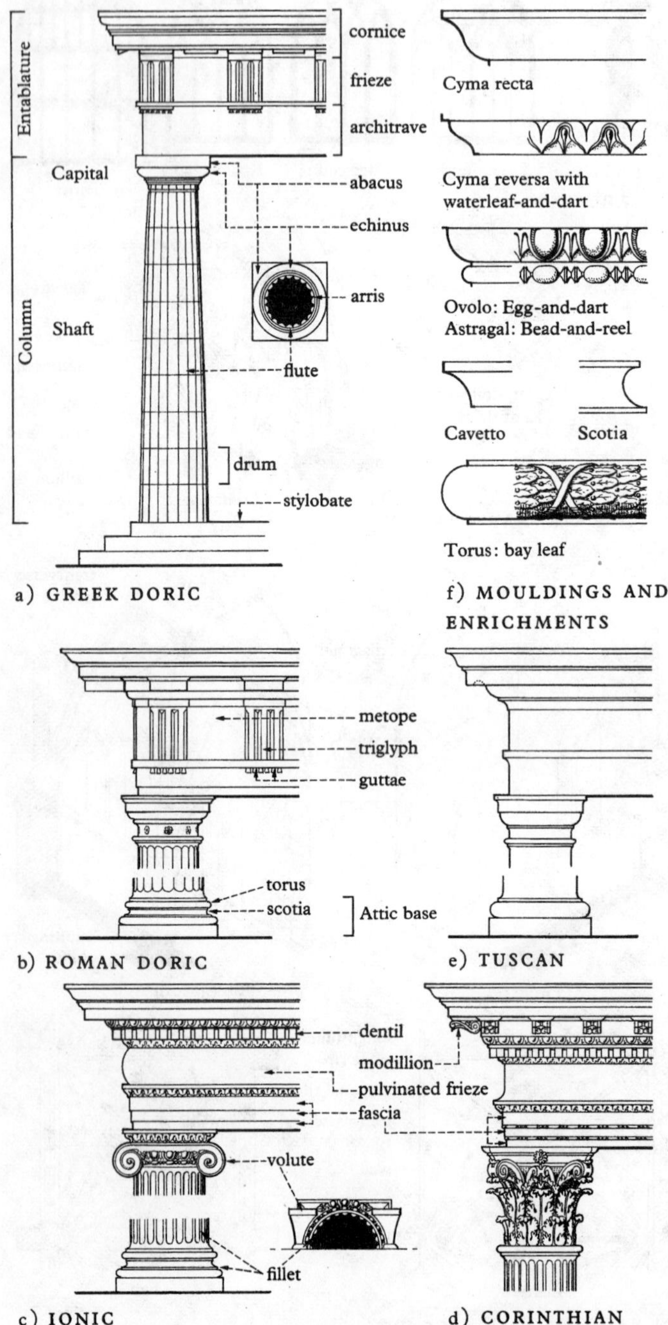

FIGURE 3: CLASSICAL

FIGURE 4: CLASSICAL

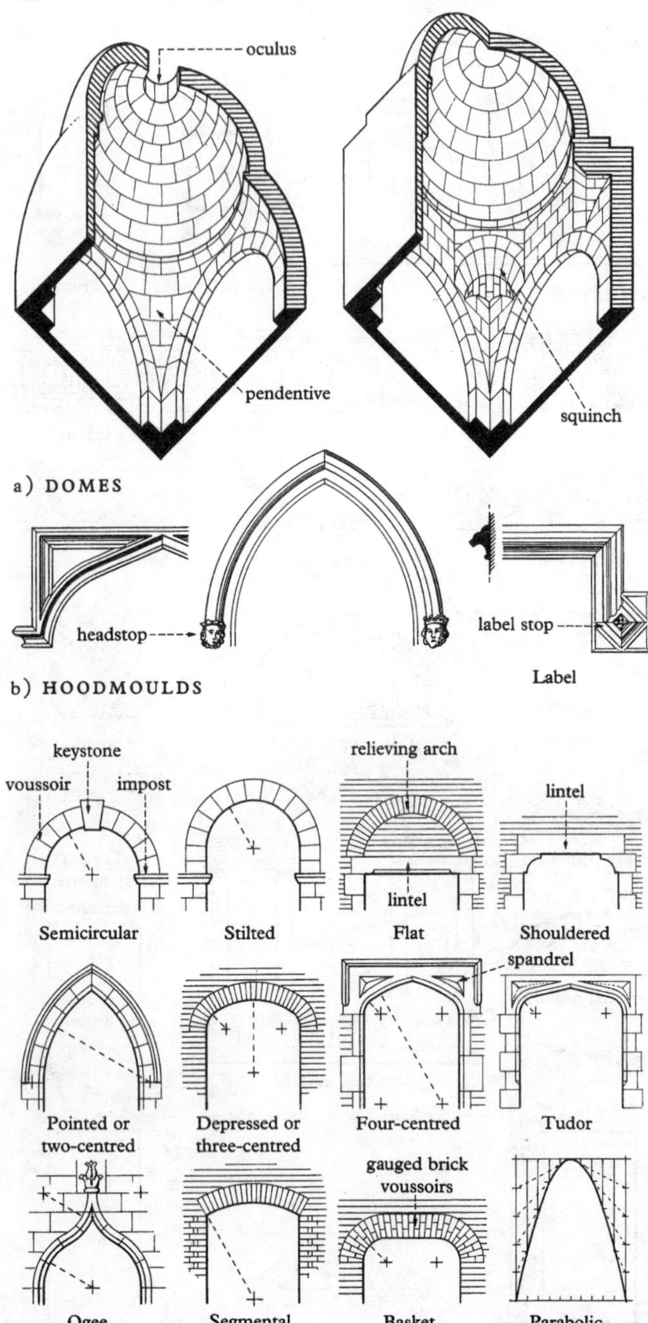

FIGURE 5: CONSTRUCTION

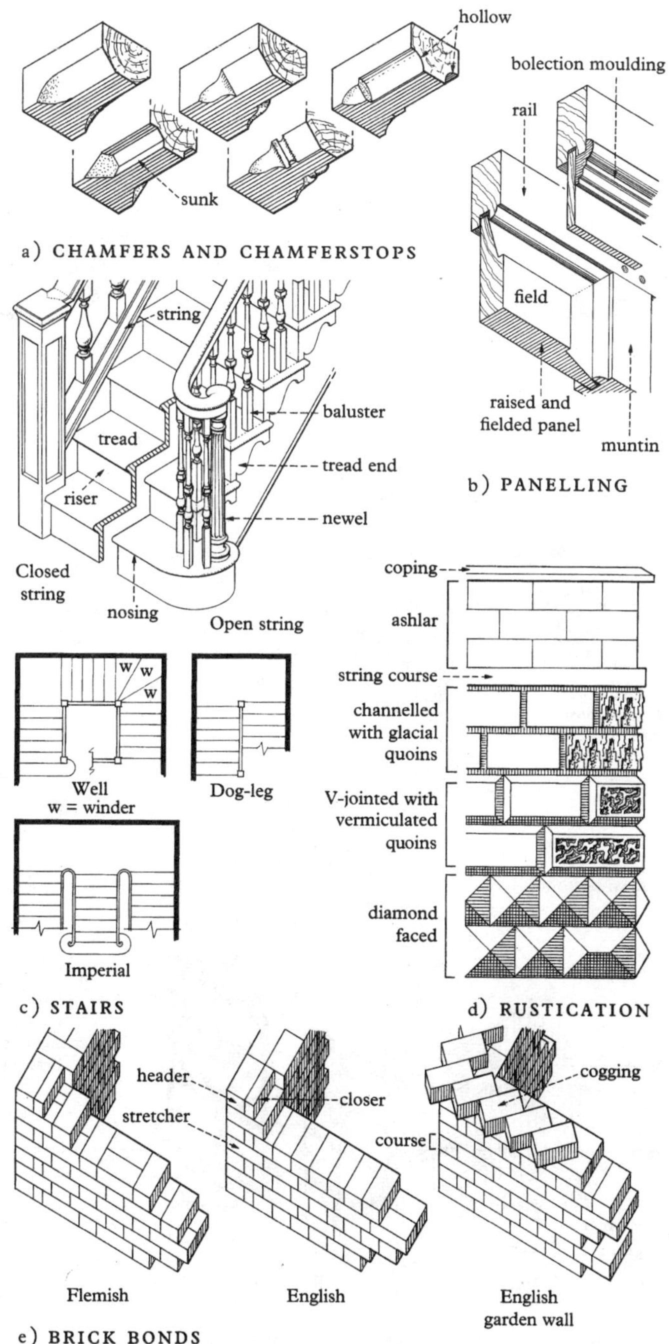

FIGURE 6: CONSTRUCTION

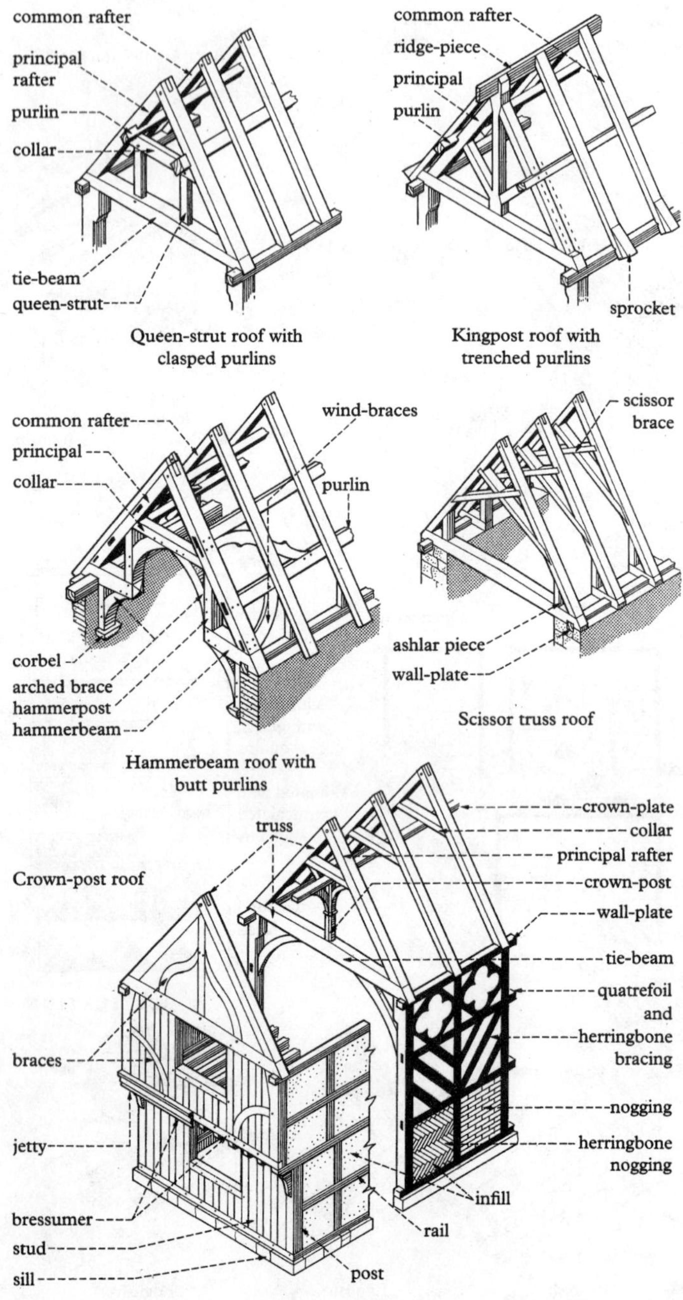

FIGURE 7: ROOFS AND TIMBER-FRAMING

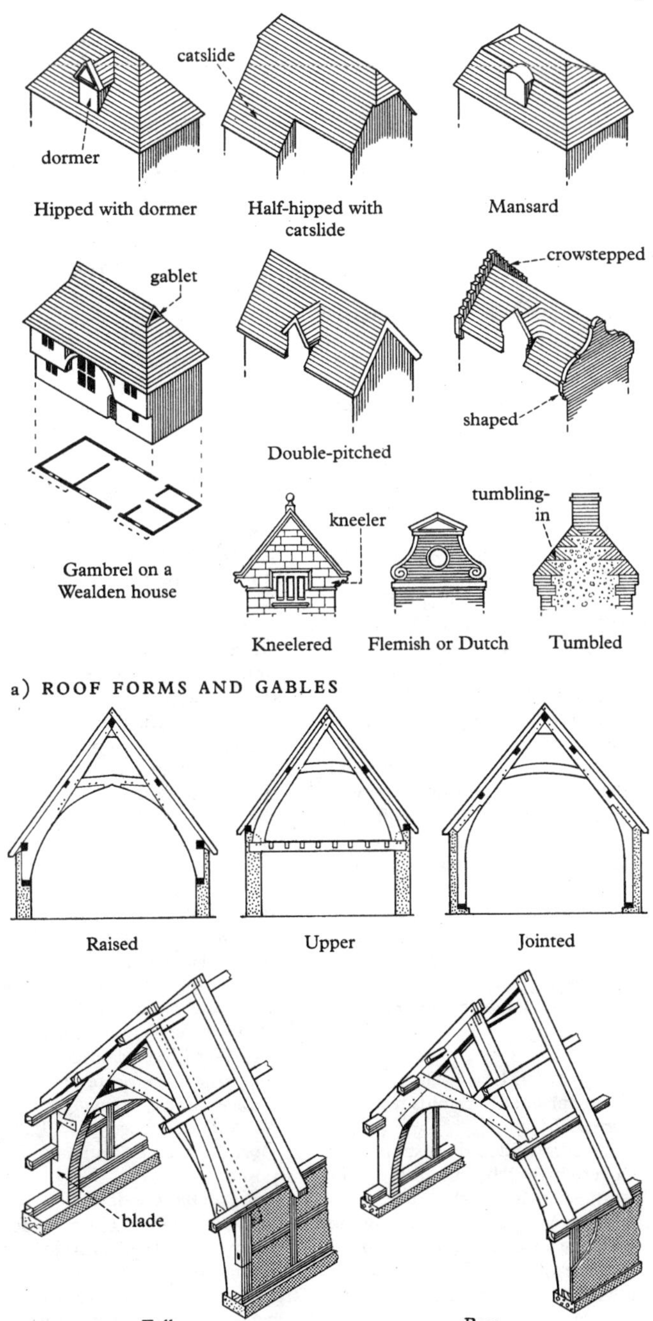

FIGURE 8: ROOFS AND TIMBER-FRAMING

MIXER-COURTS: forecourts to groups of houses shared by vehicles and pedestrians.

MODILLIONS: small consoles (q.v.) along the underside of a Corinthian or Composite cornice (3d). Often used along an eaves cornice.

MODULE: a predetermined standard size for co-ordinating the dimensions of components of a building.

MOTTE-AND-BAILEY: post-Roman and Norman defence consisting of an earthen mound (motte) topped by a wooden tower within a bailey, an enclosure defended by a ditch and palisade, and also, sometimes, by an internal bank.

MOUCHETTE: *see* Tracery and 2b.

MOULDING: shaped ornamental strip of continuous section; *see* Cavetto, Cyma, Ovolo, Roll.

MULLION: vertical member between window lights (2b).

MULTI-STOREY: five or more storeys. Multi-storey flats may form a *cluster block*, with individual blocks of flats grouped round a service core; a *point block*: with flats fanning out from a service core; or a *slab block*, with flats approached by corridors or galleries from service cores at intervals or towers at the ends (plan also used for offices, hotels etc.). *Tower block* is a generic term for any very high multi-storey building.

MUNTIN: *see* Panelling and 6b.

NAILHEAD: E.E. ornament consisting of small pyramids regularly repeated (1a).

NARTHEX: enclosed vestibule or covered porch at the main entrance to a church.

NAVE: the body of a church W of the crossing or chancel often flanked by aisles (q.v.).

NEWEL: central or corner post of a staircase (6c). Newel stair *see* Stairs.

NIGHT STAIR: stair by which religious entered the transept of their church from their dormitory to celebrate night services.

NOGGING: *see* Timber-framing (7).

NOOK-SHAFT: shaft set in the angle of a wall or opening (1a).

NORMAN: *see* Romanesque.

NOSING: projection of the tread of a step (6c).

NUTMEG: medieval ornament with a chain of tiny triangles placed obliquely.

OCULUS: circular opening.

OEIL DE BOEUF: *see* Bullseye window.

OGEE: double curve, bending first one way and then the other, as in an *ogee* or *ogival arch* (5c). Cf. Cyma recta and Cyma reversa.

OPUS SECTILE: decorative mosaic-like facing.

OPUS SIGNINUM: composition flooring of Roman origin.

ORATORY: a private chapel in a church or a house. Also a church of the Oratorian Order.

ORDER: one of a series of recessed arches and jambs forming a splayed medieval opening, e.g. a doorway or arcade arch (1a).

ORDERS: the formalized versions of the post-and-lintel system in classical architecture. The main orders are *Doric*, *Ionic*, and *Corinthian*. They are Greek in origin but occur in Roman versions. *Tuscan* is a simple version of Roman Doric. Though each order has its own conventions (3), there are many minor variations. The *Composite* capital combines Ionic volutes with Corinthian foliage. *Superimposed orders*: orders on successive levels, usually in the upward sequence of Tuscan, Doric, Ionic, Corinthian, Composite.

ORIEL: *see* Bay window.

OVERDOOR: painting or relief above an internal door. Also called a *sopraporta*.

OVERTHROW: decorative fixed arch between two gatepiers or above a wrought-iron gate.

OVOLO: wide convex moulding (3f).

PALIMPSEST: of a brass: where a metal plate has been reused by turning over the engraving on the back; of a wall-painting: where one overlaps and partly obscures an earlier one.

PALLADIAN: following the examples and principles of Andrea Palladio (1508–80).

PALMETTE: classical ornament like a palm shoot (4b).

PANELLING: wooden lining to interior walls, made up of vertical members (*muntins*) and horizontals (*rails*) framing panels: also called *wainscot*. *Raised-and-fielded*: with the central area of the panel (*field*) raised up (6b).

PANTILE: roof tile of S section.

PARAPET: wall for protection at any sudden drop, e.g. at the wall-head of a castle where it protects the *parapet walk* or wall-walk. Also used to conceal a roof.

PARCHEMIN PANEL:with a vertical central rib or moulding branching in ogee curves to meet the four corners of the panel; sometimes used with linenfold (q.v.).

PARCLOSE: *see* Screen.

PARGETTING (*lit.* plastering): exterior plaster decoration, either in relief or incised.

PARLOUR: in a religious house, a room where the religious could talk to visitors; in a medieval house, the semi-private living room below the solar (q.v.).

PARTERRE: level space in a garden laid out with low, formal beds.

PATERA (*lit.* plate): round or oval ornament in shallow relief.

PAVILION: ornamental building for occasional use; or projecting subdivision of a larger building, often at an angle or terminating a wing.

PEBBLEDASHING: *see* Rendering.

PEDESTAL: a tall block carrying a classical order, statue, vase, etc.

PEDIMENT: a formalized gable derived from that of a classical temple; also used over doors, windows, etc. For variations *see* 4b.

PENDENTIVE: spandrel between adjacent arches, supporting a drum, dome or vault and consequently formed as part of a hemisphere (5a).

PENTHOUSE: subsidiary structure with a lean-to roof. Also a separately roofed structure on top of a C20 multi-storey block.

PERIPTERAL: *see* Peristyle.

PERISTYLE: a colonnade all round the exterior of a classical building, as in a temple which is then said to be *peripteral*.

PERP (PERPENDICULAR): English Gothic architecture *c.* 1335–50 to *c.* 1530. The name is derived from the upright tracery panels then used (*see* Tracery and 2a).

PERRON: external stair to a doorway, usually of double-curved plan.

PEW: loosely, seating for the laity outside the chancel; strictly, an enclosed seat. *Box pew*: with equal high sides and a door.

PIANO NOBILE: principal floor of a classical building above a ground floor or basement and with a lesser storey overhead.

PIAZZA: formal urban open space surrounded by buildings.

PIER: large masonry or brick support, often for an arch. *See also* Compound pier.

PILASTER: flat representation of a classical column in shallow relief. *Pilaster strip*: *see* Lesene.

PILE: row of rooms. *Double pile*: two rows thick.

PILLAR: free-standing upright member of any section, not conforming to one of the orders (q.v.).

PILLAR PISCINA: *see* Piscina.

PILOTIS: C20 French term for pillars or stilts that support a building above an open ground floor.

PISCINA: basin for washing Mass vessels, provided with a drain; set in or against the wall to the S of an altar or free-standing (*pillar piscina*).

PISÉ: *see* Cob.

PITCHED MASONRY: laid on the diagonal, often alternately with opposing courses (*pitched and counterpitched* or herringbone).

PLATE RAIL: *see* Railways.

PLATEWAY: *see* Railways.

PLINTH: projecting courses at the

foot of a wall or column, generally chamfered or moulded at the top.

PODIUM: a continuous raised platform supporting a building; or a large block of two or three storeys beneath a multi-storey block of smaller area.

POINT BLOCK: *see* Multi-storey.

POINTING: exposed mortar jointing of masonry or brickwork. Types include *flush*, *recessed* and *tuck* (with a narrow channel filled with finer, whiter mortar).

POPPYHEAD: carved ornament of leaves and flowers as a finial for a bench end or stall.

PORTAL FRAME: C20 frame comprising two uprights rigidly connected to a beam or pair of rafters.

PORTCULLIS: gate constructed to rise and fall in vertical gooves at the entry to a castle.

PORTICO: a porch with the roof and frequently a pediment supported by a row of columns (4a). A portico *in antis* has columns on the same plane as the front of the building. A *prostyle* porch has columns standing free. Porticoes are described by the number of front columns, e.g. tetrastyle (four), hexastyle (six). The space within the temple is the *naos*, that within the portico the *pronaos*. *Blind portico*: the front features of a portico applied to a wall.

PORTICUS (plural: porticūs): subsidiary cell opening from the main body of a pre-Conquest church.

POST: upright support in a structure (7).

POSTERN: small gateway at the back of a building or to the side of a larger entrance door or gate.

POUND LOCK: *see* Canals.

PRESBYTERY: the part of a church lying E of the choir where the main altar is placed; or a priest's residence.

PRINCIPAL: *see* Roofs and 7.

PRONAOS: *see* Portico and 4a.

PROSTYLE: *see* Portico and 4a.

PULPIT: raised and enclosed platform for the preaching of sermons. *Three-decker*: with reading desk below and clerk's desk below that.] *Two-decker:* as above, minus the clerk's desk.

PULPITUM: stone screen in a major church dividing choir from nave.

PULVINATED: *see* Frieze and 3c.

PURLIN: *see* Roofs and 7.

PUTHOLES or PUTLOG HOLES: in the wall to receive putlogs, the horizontal timbers which support scaffolding boards; sometimes not filled after construction is complete.

PUTTO (plural: putti): small naked boy.

QUARRIES: square (or diamond) panes of glass supported by lead strips (*cames*); square floor-slabs or tiles.

QUATREFOIL: *see* Foil and 2b.

QUEENSTRUT: *see* Roofs and 7.

QUIRK: sharp groove to one side of a convex medieval moulding.

QUOINS: dressed stones at the angles of a building (6d).

RADBURN SYSTEM: vehicle and pedestrian segregation in residential developments, based on that used at Radburn, New Jersey, U.S.A., by Wright and Stein, 1928–30.

RADIATING CHAPELS: projecting radially from an ambulatory or an apse (*see* Chevet).

RAFTER: *see* Roofs and 7.

RAGGLE: groove cut in masonry, especially to receive the edge of a roof-covering.

RAGULY: ragged (in heraldry). Also applied to funerary sculpture, e.g. *cross raguly*: with a notched outline.

RAIL: *see* Panelling and 6b; also 7.

RAILWAYS: *Edge rail:* on which flanged wheels can run. *Plate rail:* L-section rail for plain unflanged wheels. *Plateway:* early railway using plate rails.

RAISED-AND-FIELDED: *see* Panelling and 6b.

RAKE: slope or pitch.

RAMPART: defensive outer wall of stone or earth. *Rampart walk:* path along the inner face.

REBATE: rectangular section cut out of a masonry edge to receive a shutter, door, window, etc.

REBUS: a heraldic pun, e.g. a fiery cock for Cockburn.

REEDING: series of convex mouldings, the reverse of fluting (q.v.). Cf. Gadrooning.

RENDERING: the covering of outside walls with a uniform surface or skin for protection from the weather. *Lime-washing:* thin layer of lime plaster. *Pebble-dashing:* where aggregate is thrown at the wet plastered wall for a textured effect. *Roughcast:* plaster mixed with a coarse aggregate such as gravel. *Stucco:* fine lime plaster worked to a smooth surface. *Cement rendering:* a cheaper substitute for stucco, usually with a grainy texture.

REPOUSSÉ: relief designs in metalwork, formed by beating it from the back.

REREDORTER (*lit.* behind the dormitory): latrines in a medieval religious house.

REREDOS: painted and/or sculptured screen behind and above an altar. Cf. Retable.

RESPOND: half-pier or half-column bonded into a wall and carrying one end of an arch. It usually terminates an arcade.

RETABLE: painted or carved panel standing on or at the back of an altar, usually attached to it.

RETROCHOIR: in a major church, the area between the high altar and E chapel.

REVEAL: the plane of a jamb, between the wall and the frame of a door or window.

RIB-VAULT: *see* Vault and 2c.

RINCEAU: classical ornament of leafy scrolls (4b).

RISER: vertical face of a step (6c).

ROCK-FACED: masonry cleft to produce a rugged appearance.

ROCOCO: style current *c.* 1720 and *c.* 1760, characterized by a serpentine line and playful, scrolled decoration.

ROLL MOULDING: medieval moulding of part-circular section (1a).

ROMANESQUE: style current in the C11 and C12. In England often called Norman. *See also* Saxo-Norman.

ROOD: crucifix flanked by the Virgin and St John, usually over the entry into the chancel, on a beam (*rood beam*) or painted on the wall. The *rood screen* below often had a walkway (*rood loft*) along the top, reached by a *rood stair* in the side wall.

ROOFS: Shape. For the main external shapes (hipped, mansard etc.) *see* 8a. *Helm* and *Saddleback*: *see* 1c. *Lean-to*: single sloping roof built against a vertical wall; lean-to is also applied to the part of the building beneath.

Construction. *See* 7.

Single-framed roof: with no main trusses. The rafters may be fixed to the wall-plate or ridge, or longitudinal timber may be absent altogether.

Double-framed roof: with longitudinal members, such as purlins, and usually divided into bays by principals and principal rafters.

Other types are named after their main structural components, e.g. *hammerbeam*, *crown-post* (*see* Elements below and 7).

Elements. *See* 7.

Ashlar piece: a short vertical timber connecting inner wall-plate or timber pad to a rafter.

Braces: subsidiary timbers set diagonally to strengthen the frame.]

Arched braces: curved pair forming an arch, connecting wall or post below with tie- or collar-beam above. *Passing braces:* long straight braces passing across other members of the truss. *Scissor braces:* pair crossing diagonally between pairs of rafters or principals. *Wind-braces:* short, usually curved braces connecting side purlins with principals; sometimes decorated with cusping.

Collar or *collar-beam:* horizontal transverse timber connecting a pair of rafter or cruck blades (q.v.), set between apex and the wall-plate.

Crown-post: a vertical timber set centrally on a tie-beam and supporting a collar purlin braced to it longitudinally. In an open truss lateral braces may rise to the collar-beam; in a closed truss they may descend to the tie-beam.

Hammerbeams: horizontal brackets projecting at wall-plate level like an interrupted tie-beam; the inner ends carry *hammerposts*, vertical timbers which support a purlin and are braced to a collar-beam above.

Kingpost: vertical timber set centrally on a tie- or collar-beam, rising to the apex of the roof to support a ridge-piece (cf. Strut).

Plate: longitudinal timber set square to the ground. *Wall-plate:* plate along the top of a wall which receives the ends of the rafters; cf. Purlin.

Principals: pair of inclined lateral timbers of a truss. Usually they support side purlins and mark the main bay divisions.

Purlin: horizontal longitudinal timber. *Collar purlin* or *crown plate:* central timber which carries collar-beams and is supported by crown-posts. *Side purlins:* pairs of timbers placed some way up the slope of the roof, which carry common rafters. *Butt* or *tenoned purlins* are tenoned into either side of the principals. *Through purlins* pass through or past the principal; they include *clasped purlins*, which rest on queenposts or are carried in the angle between principals and collar, and *trenched purlins* trenched into the backs of principals.

Queen-strut: paired vertical, or near-vertical, timbers placed symmetrically on a tie-beam to support side purlins.

Rafters: inclined lateral timbers supporting the roof covering. *Common rafters:* regularly spaced uniform rafters placed along the length of a roof or between principals. *Principal rafters:* rafters which also act as principals.

Ridge, ridge-piece: horizontal longitudinal timber at the apex supporting the ends of the rafters.

Sprocket: short timber placed on the back and at the foot of a rafter to form projecting eaves.

Strut: vertical or oblique timber between two members of a truss, not directly supporting longitudinal timbers.

Tie-beam: main horizontal transverse timber which carries the feet of the principals at wall level.

Truss: rigid framework of timbers at bay intervals, carrying the longitudinal roof timbers which support the common rafters. *Closed truss:* with the spaces between the timbers filled, to form an internal partition.

See also Cruck, Wagon roof.

ROPE MOULDING: *see* Cable moulding.

ROSE WINDOW: circular window with tracery radiating from the centre. Cf. Wheel window.

ROTUNDA: building or room circular in plan.

ROUGHCAST: *see* Rendering.

ROVING BRIDGE: *see* Canals.

RUBBED BRICKWORK: *see* Gauged brickwork.

RUBBLE: masonry whose stones are wholly or partly in a rough state. *Coursed*: coursed stones with rough faces. *Random:* uncoursed stones in a random pattern. *Snecked:* with courses broken by smaller stones (snecks).

RUSTICATION: *see* 6d. Exaggerated treatment of masonry to give an effect of strength. The joints are usually recessed by V-section chamfering or square-section channelling (*channelled rustication*). *Banded rustication* has only the horizontal joints emphasized. The faces may be flat, but can be *diamond-faced*, like shallow pyramids, *vermiculated*, with a stylized texture like worm-casts, and *glacial* (frost-work), like icicles or stalactites.

SACRISTY: room in a church for sacred vessels and vestments.

SADDLEBACK ROOF: *see* 1C.

SALTIRE CROSS: with diagonal limbs.

SANCTUARY: area around the main altar of a church. Cf. Presbytery.

SANGHA: residence of Buddhist monks or nuns.

SARCOPHAGUS: coffin of stone or other durable material.

SAXO-NORMAN: transitional Romanesque style combining Anglo-Saxon and Norman features, current *c.* 1060–1100.

SCAGLIOLA: composition imitating marble.

SCALLOPED CAPITAL: *see* 1a.

SCOTIA: a hollow classical moulding, especially between tori (q.v.) on a column base (3b, 3f).

SCREEN: in a medieval church, usually at the entry to the chancel; *see* Rood (screen) and Pulpitum. A *parclose screen* separates a chapel from the rest of the church.

SCREENS or SCREENS PASSAGE: screened-off entrance passage between great hall and service rooms.

SECTION: two-dimensional representation of a building, moulding, etc., revealed by cutting across it.

SEDILIA (singular: sedile): seats for the priests (usually three) on the S side of the chancel.

SET-OFF: *see* Weathering.

SGRAFFITO: decoration scratched, often in plaster, to reveal a pattern in another colour beneath. *Graffiti*: scratched drawing or writing.

SHAFT: vertical member of round or polygonal section (1a, 3a). *Shaft-ring:* at the junction of shafts set *en delit* (q.v.) or attached to a pier or wall (1a).

SHEILA-NA-GIG: female fertility figure, usually with legs apart.

SHELL: thin, self-supporting roofing membrane of timber or concrete.

SHOULDERED ARCHITRAVE: *see* 4b.

SHUTTERING: *see* Concrete.

SILL: horizontal member at the bottom of a window or door frame; or at the base of a timber-framed wall into which posts and studs are tenoned (7).

SLAB BLOCK: *see* Multi-storey.

SLATE-HANGING: covering of overlapping slates on a wall. *Tile-hanging* is similar.

SLYPE: covered way or passage leading E from the cloisters between transept and chapter house.

SNECKED: *see* Rubble.

SOFFIT (*lit.* ceiling): underside of an arch (also called *intrados*), lintel, etc. *Soffit roll:* medieval roll moulding on a soffit.

SOLAR: private upper chamber in a medieval house, accessible from the high end of the great hall.

SOPRAPORTA: *see* Overdoor.

SOUNDING-BOARD: *see* Tester.

SPANDRELS: roughly triangular spaces between an arch and its containing rectangle, or between adjacent arches (5c). Also non-structural panels under the windows in a curtain-walled building.

SPERE: a fixed structure screening the lower end of the great hall from the screens passage. *Spere-truss*: roof truss incorporated in the spere.

SPIRE: tall pyramidal or conical feature crowning a tower or turret. *Broach:* starting from a square base, then carried into an octagonal section by means of triangular faces; and *splayed-foot:* variation of the broach form, found principally in the south-east, in which the four cardinal faces are splayed out near their base, to cover the corners, while oblique (or intermediate) faces taper away to a point (1c). *Needle spire:* thin spire rising from the centre of a tower roof, well inside the parapet: when of timber and lead often called a *spike*.

SPIRELET: *see* Flèche.

SPLAY: of an opening when it is wider on one face of a wall than the other.

SPRING OR SPRINGING: level at which an arch or vault rises from its supports. *Springers:* the first stones of an arch or vaulting rib above the spring (2c).

SQUINCH: arch or series of arches thrown across an interior angle of a square or rectangular structure to support a circular or polygonal superstructure, especially a dome or spire (5a).

SQUINT: an aperture in a wall or through a pier usually to allow a view of an altar.

STAIRS: *see* 6c. *Dog-leg stair:* parallel flights rising alternately in opposite directions, without an open well. *Flying stair:* cantilevered from the walls of a stairwell, without newels; sometimes called a *Geometric* stair when the inner edge describes a curve. *Newel stair:* ascending round a central supporting newel (q.v.); called a *spiral stair* or *vice* when in a circular shaft, a *winder* when in a rectangular compartment. (Winder also applies to the steps on the turn). *Well stair:* with flights round a square open well framed by newel posts. *See also* Perron.

STALL: fixed seat in the choir or chancel for the clergy or choir (cf. Pew). Usually with arm rests, and often framed together.

STANCHION: upright structural member, of iron, steel or reinforced concrete.

STANDPIPE TOWER: *see* Manometer.

STEAM ENGINES: *Atmospheric:* worked by the vacuum created when low-pressure steam is condensed in the cylinder, as developed by Thomas Newcomen. *Beam engine:* with a large pivoted beam moved in an oscillating fashion by the piston. It may drive a flywheel or be *non-rotative*. *Watt* and *Cornish:* single-cylinder; *compound:* two cylinders; *triple expansion:* three cylinders.

STEEPLE: tower together with a spire, lantern, or belfry.

STIFF-LEAF: type of E.E. foliage decoration. *Stiff-leaf capital see* 1b.

STOP: plain or decorated terminal to mouldings or chamfers, or at the end of hoodmoulds and labels (*label stop*), or string courses (5b, 6a); *see also* headstop.

STOUP: vessel for holy water, usually near a door.

STRAINER: *see* Arch.

STRAPWORK: late C16 and C17 decoration, like interlaced leather straps.

STRETCHER: *see* Bond and 6e.

STRING COURSE: horizontal course or moulding projecting from the surface of a wall (6d).

STRING: *see* 6c. Sloping member holding the ends of the treads and risers of a staircase. *Closed string:* a broad string covering the ends of the treads and risers. *Open string:* cut into the shape of the treads and risers.

STUCCO: *see* Rendering.

STUDS: subsidiary vertical timbers of a timber-framed wall or partition (7).

STUPA: Buddhist shrine, circular in plan.

STYLOBATE: top of the solid platform on which a colonnade stands (3a).

SUSPENSION BRIDGE: *see* Bridge.

SWAG: like a festoon (q.v.), but representing cloth.

SYSTEM BUILDING: *see* Industrialized building.

TABERNACLE: canopied structure to contain the reserved sacrament or a relic; or architectural frame for an image or statue.

TABLE TOMB: memorial slab raised on free-standing legs.

TAS-DE-CHARGE: the lower courses of a vault or arch which are laid horizontally (2c).

TERM: pedestal or pilaster tapering downward, usually with the upper part of a human figure growing out of it.

TERRACOTTA: moulded and fired clay ornament or cladding.

TESSELLATED PAVEMENT: mosaic flooring, particularly Roman, made of *tesserae*, i.e. cubes of glass, stone, or brick.

TESTER: flat canopy over a tomb or pulpit, where it is also called a *sounding-board*.

TESTER TOMB: tomb-chest with effigies beneath a tester, either free-standing (tester with four or more columns), or attached to a wall (*half-tester*) with columns on one side only.

TETRASTYLE: *see* Portico.

THERMAL WINDOW: *see* Diocletian window.

THREE-DECKER PULPIT: *see* Pulpit.

TIDAL GATES: *see* Canals.

TIE-BEAM: *see* Roofs and 7.

TIERCERON: *see* Vault and 2c.

TILE-HANGING: *see* Slate-hanging.

TIMBER-FRAMING: *see* 7. Method of construction where the structural frame is built of interlocking timbers. The spaces are filled with non-structural material, e.g. *infill* of wattle and daub, lath and plaster, brickwork (known as *nogging*), etc. and may be covered by plaster, weatherboarding (q.v.), or tiles.

TOMB-CHEST: chest-shaped tomb, usually of stone. Cf. Table tomb, Tester tomb.

TORUS (plural: tori): large convex moulding usually used on a column base (3b, 3f).

TOUCH: soft black marble quarried near Tournai.

TOURELLE: turret corbelled out from the wall.

TOWER BLOCK: *see* Multi-storey.

TRABEATED: depends structurally on the use of the post and lintel. Cf. Arcuated.

TRACERY: openwork pattern of masonry or timber in the upper part of an opening. *Blind tracery* is tracery applied to a solid wall.

Plate tracery, introduced *c.* 1200, is the earliest form, in which shapes are cut through solid masonry (2a).

Bar tracery was introduced into England *c.* 1250. The pattern is formed by intersecting moulded ribwork continued from the mullions. It was especially elaborate during the Decorated period (q.v.). Tracery shapes can include circles, *daggers* (elongated ogee-ended lozenges), *mouchettes* (like daggers but with curved sides) and upright rectangular *panels*. They often have *cusps*, projecting points defining lobes or *foils* (q.v.) within the main shape: *Kentish* or *split-cusps* are forked (2b).

Types of bar tracery (*see* 2b) include *geometric(al)*: *c.* 1250–1310, chiefly circles, often foiled; *Y-tracery*: *c.* 1300, with mullions branching into a Y-shape; *intersecting*: *c.* 1300, formed by interlocking mullions; *reticulated*: early C14, net-like pattern of ogee-ended lozenges; *curvilinear*: C14, with uninterrupted flowing curves; *panel*: Perp, with straight-sided panels, often cusped at the top and bottom.

TRANSEPT: transverse portion of a church.

TRANSITIONAL: generally used for the phase between Romanesque and Early English (*c.* 1175–*c.* 120ffl).

TRANSOM: horizontal member separating window lights (2b).

TREAD: horizontal part of a step. The *tread end* may be carved on a staircase (6c).

TREFOIL: *see* Foil.

TRIFORIUM: middle storey of a church treated as an arcaded wall passage or blind arcade, its height corresponding to that of the aisle roof.

TRIGLYPHS (*lit.* three-grooved tablets): stylized beam-ends in the Doric frieze, with metopes between (3b).

TRIUMPHAL ARCH: influential type of Imperial Roman monument.

TROPHY: sculptured or painted group of arms or armour.

TRUMEAU: central stone mullion supporting the tympanum of a wide doorway. *Trumeau figure:* carved figure attached to it (cf. Column figure).

TRUMPET CAPITAL: *see* 1b.

TRUSS: braced framework, spanning between supports. *See also* Roofs and 7.

TUMBLING or TUMBLING-IN: courses of brickwork laid at right-angles to a slope, e.g. of a gable, forming triangles by tapering into horizontal courses (8a).

TUSCAN: *see* Orders and 3e.

TWO-DECKER PULPIT: *see* Pulpit.

TYMPANUM: the surface between a lintel and the arch above it or within a pediment (4a).

UNDERCROFT: usually describes the vaulted room(s), beneath the main room(s) of a medieval house. Cf. Crypt.

VAULT: arched stone roof (sometimes imitated in timber or plaster). For types *see* 2c.

Tunnel or *barrel vault:* continuous semicircular or pointed arch, often of rubble masonry.

Groin-vault: tunnel vaults intersecting at right angles. *Groins* are the curved lines of the intersections.

Rib-vault: masonry framework of intersecting arches (ribs) supporting *vault cells*, used in Gothic architecture. *Wall rib* or *wall arch:* between wall and vault cell. *Transverse rib:* spans between two walls to divide a vault into bays. *Quadripartite* rib-vault: each bay has two pairs of diagonal ribs dividing the vault into four triangular cells. *Sexpartite* rib-vault: most often used over paired bays, has an extra pair of ribs springing from between the bays. More elaborate vaults may include *ridge ribs* along the crown of a vault or bisecting the bays; *tiercerons:* extra decorative ribs springing from the corners of a bay; and *liernes:* short decorative ribs in the crown of a vault, not linked to any springing point. A *stellar* or *star* vault has liernes in star formation.

Fan-vault: form of barrel vault used in the Perp period, made up of halved concave masonry cones decorated with blind tracery.

VAULTING SHAFT: shaft leading up to the spring or springing (q.v.) of a vault (2c).

VENETIAN or SERLIAN WINDOW: derived from Serlio (4b). The motif is used for other openings.

VERMICULATION: *see* Rustication and 6d.

VESICA: oval with pointed ends.

VICE: *see* Stair.

VILLA: originally a Roman country house or farm. The term was revived in England in the C18 under the influence of Palladio and used especially for smaller, compact country houses. In the later C19 it was debased to describe any suburban house.

VITRIFIED: bricks or tiles fired to a darkened glassy surface.

VITRUVIAN SCROLL: classical running ornament of curly waves (4b).

VOLUTES: spiral scrolls. They occur on Ionic capitals (3c). *Angle volute:* pair of volutes, turned outwards to meet at the corner of a capital.

VOUSSOIRS: wedge-shaped stones forming an arch (5c).

WAGON ROOF: with the appearance of the inside of a wagon tilt; often ceiled. Also called *cradle roof.*

WAINSCOT: *see* Panelling.

WALL MONUMENT: attached to the wall and often standing on the floor. *Wall tablets* are smaller with the inscription as the major element.

WALL-PLATE: *see* Roofs and 7.

WALL-WALK: *see* Parapet.

WARMING ROOM: room in a religious house where a fire burned for comfort.

WATERHOLDING BASE: early Gothic base with upper and lower mouldings separated by a deep hollow.

WATERLEAF: *see* Enrichments and 3f.

WATERLEAF CAPITAL: Late Romanesque and Transitional type of capital (1b).

WATER WHEELS: described by the way water is fed on to the wheel. *Breastshot*: mid-height, falling and passing beneath. *Overshot*: over the top. *Pitchback*: on the top but falling backwards. *Undershot*: turned by the momentum of the water passing beneath. In a *water turbine*, water is fed under pressure through a vaned wheel within a casing.

WEALDEN HOUSE: type of medieval timber-framed house with a central open hall flanked by bays of two storeys, roofed in line; the end bays are jettied to the front, but the eaves are continuous (8a).

WEATHERBOARDING wall cladding of overlapping horizontal boards.

WEATHERING or SET-OFF: inclined, projecting surface to keep water away from the wall below.

WEEPERS: figures in niches along the sides of some medieval tombs. Also called *mourners*.

WHEEL WINDOW: circular, with radiating shafts like spokes. Cf. Rose window.

WROUGHT IRON: *see* Cast iron.

LANGUAGE GLOSSARY

Adapted, with omissions and a few augmentations, with the permission of the Director General of the Ordnance Survey, from the OS publication *Place Names on Maps of Scotland and Wales*. Crown copyright reserved.

a = adjective
ad = adverb
f = feminine
n = noun masculine
nf = noun feminine
np = noun plural
pl = plural
pr = preposition

abad, *n* abbot
abaty, *n* abbey
aber, *n & nf* estuary, confluence, stream
adeiladu, *verb* to build
aderyn, *pl* adar, *n* bird
ael, *nf* brow, edge
aelwyd, *nf* hearth
aethnen, *nf* aspen, poplar
afallen, *nf* apple tree
afon, *nf* river
ailadeiladu, *verb* to rebuild
allt, *pl* elltydd, alltau, *nf* hillside, cliff, wood
Annibynnol, *a* Independent
ar, *pr* on, upon, over
ardd, *n* hill, height
argoed, *nf* wood, grove

bach, *a* small, little, lesser
bach, *pl* bachau, *nf* nook, corner
bala, *n* outlet of a lake
banc, *pl* bencydd, *n* bank, slope
bangor, *nf* monastery originally constructed of wattle rods
banhadlog, *nf* broom patch
banw, *n* young pig
bar, *n* top, summit
bechan, *a* *see* bychan
bedd, *pl* beddau, *n* grave
Bedyddwyr, *a* Baptist
beidr, *nf* lane, path
beili, *pl* beiliau, *n* bailey, court before a house bailiff
bellaf, *a* far
bendigaid, *a* blessed
betws, *n* oratory, chapel
beudy, *n* cow-house
blaen, *pl* blaenau, *n* end, edge; source of river or stream; highland
bod, *n & nf* abode, dwelling
bôn, *n* stock, stump
bont, *nf* *see* pont
braich, *n & nf* ridge, arm
brân, *pl* brain, *nf* crow
bre, *nf* hill
brith, *f* braith, *a* speckled; coarse
bro, *nf* region; vale, lowland
bron, *pl* bronnydd, *nf* hillbreast (breast)
bryn, *pl* bryniau, *n* hill
bugail, *pl* bugelydd, bugeiliaid, *n* shepherd
bwla, *n* bull
bwlch, *pl* bylchau, *n* gap, pass
bwth, bwthyn, *n* cottage, booth
bychan, *f* bechan, *pl* bychain, *a* little, tiny

caban, *n* cottage, cabin
cader, cadair, *nf* seat, stronghold
cadlas, *nf* close, court of a house
cae, *pl* caeau, *n* field, enclosure
caer, *pl* caerau, *nf* stronghold, fort
cafn, *n* ferry-boat, trough
canol, *n* middle
cantref, *n* hundred (territorial division)
capel, *n* meeting house, chapel
carn, *pl* carnau, *nf* heap of stones, tumulus
carnedd, *pl* carneddau, carneddi, *nf* heap of stones, tumulus

carreg, *pl* cerrig, *nf* stone, rock
carrog, *nf* brook
carw, *n* stag
cas (in Casnewydd etc.), *n* castle
castell, *pl* cestyll, *n* castle; small stronghold; fortified residence; imposing natural position
cath, *nf* cat. (In some names it may be the Irish word cath meaning 'battle'.)
cau, *a* hollow; enclosed
cawr, *pl* ceiri, cewri, *n* giant
cefn, *pl* cefnydd, *n* ridge
cegin, *nf* kitchen
ceiliog, *n* cock
ceiri, *np* *see* cawr
celli, *nf* grove
celynen, *pl* celyn, *nf* holly tree
celynog, clynnog, *nf* holly grove
cemais, *n from np* shallow bend in river, or coastline
cennin, *np* leeks
cerrig, *np* *see* carreg
cesail, *nf* hollow (arm- pit)
ceunant, *n* ravine, gorge
cewri, *np* *see* cawr
chwilog, *nf* land infested with beetles
cil, *pl* ciliau, *n* retreat, recess, corner
cilfach, *nf* nook
clas, *n* quasi-monastic system of the Celtic Church, existing in Wales, Cornwall and Ireland from the Dark Ages to *c.* 1200. *Clasau* comprised a body of secular canons
clawdd, *pl* cloddiau, *n* ditch, hedge
cloch, *nf* bell
clochydd, *n* sexton, parish clerk
cloddiau, *np* *see* clawdd
clog, *nf* crag, precipice
clogwyn, *n* precipice, steep rock hanging on one side
clwyd, *pl* clwydydd, *nf* hurdle, gate
clynnog, *nf* *see* celynog
coch, *a* red
coeden, *pl* coed, *nf* tree
collen, *pl* cyll, coll, *nf* hazel
colwyn, *n* whelp
comin, *pl* comins, *n* common
congl, *nf* corner
cornel, *nf* corner
cors, *pl* corsydd, *nf* bog
craf, *n* garlic
craig, *pl* creigiau, *nf* rock
crib, *n* crest, ridge, summit
crochan, *n* cauldron
croes, *nf* cross
croesffordd, croesheol, croeslon, *nf* cross-roads
crofft, *pl* crofftau, *nf* croft
croglofft, *nf* garret, low cottage with loft under the roof
crug, *pl* crugiau, *n* heap, tump
cwm, *pl* cymau, cymoedd, *n* valley, dale
cwmwd, *n* commote (territorial division)
cwrt, *n* court, yard
cyffin, *n* boundary, frontier
cyll, *np* *see* collen
cymer, *pl* cymerau, *n* confluence
Cynulleidfaol, *a* Congregational
cywarch, *n* hemp

dan, *pr* under, below
derwen, *pl* derw, *nf* oak
diffwys, *n* precipice, abyss
dinas, *n & nf* hill-fortress (city)
diserth, *n* hermitage
disgwylfa, *nf* place of observation, look-out point
dôl, *pl* dolau, dolydd, *nf* meadow
draw, *ad* yonder
du, *a* black, dark
dwfr, dŵr, *n* water
dyffryn, *n* valley

eglwys, *nf* church
(ei)singrug, *n* heap of bran or corn husks
eisteddfa, *nf* seat, resting place
eithinog, *nf* furze patch
elltyd, *np* *see* allt
ellyll, *n* elf, goblin
eos, *nf* nightingale
erw, *pl* erwau, *nf* acre
esgair, *nf* long ridge (leg)
esgob, *n* bishop
ewig, *nf* hind

-fa, *nf* *see* ma-
fach, *a* *see* bach
faenor, *nf* Vaynor. cf. maenor
fawr, *a* *see* mawr
felin, *nf* *see* melin
ffald, *pl* ffaldau, *nf* sheep-fold, pound, pen, run
ffawydden, *pl* ffawydd, *nf* beech tree
fferm, *nf* farm
ffin, *nf* boundary

ffordd, *nf* way, road
fforest, *nf* forest, park
ffridd, ffrith, *pl* ffriddoedd, *nf* wood; mountain enclosure, sheep walk
ffrwd, *nf* stream, torrent
ffynnon, *pl* ffynhonnau, *nf* spring, well
fron, *nf* *see* bron
fry, *ad* above

gaer, *nf* *see* caer
ganol, *n* *see* canol
gardd, *pl* gerddi, garddau, *nf* garden; enclosure or fold into which calves were turned for first time
garreg, *nf* *see* carreg
garth, *n* promontory, hill enclosure
garw, *a* coarse, rough
gefail, *nf* smithy
(g)eirw, *np* rush of waters
gelli, *nf* *see* celli
glan, *nf* river bank, hillock
glas, *a* green
glas, glais (as in dulas, dulais), *n & nf* brook
glo, *n* charcoal, coal
glyn, *n* deep valley, glen
gof, *n* smith
gogof, *pl* gogofau, *nf* cave
gorffwysfa, *nf* resting place
gris, *pl* grisiau, *n* step
grug, *n* heath, heather
gwaelod, *n* foot of hill (bottom)
gwastad, *n* plain
gwaun, *pl* gweunydd, *nf* moor, mountain meadow, moorland field
gwely, *n* bed, resting place, family land
gwen, *a* *see* gwyn
gwerdd, *a* *see* gwyrdd
gwernen, *pl* gwern, *nf* alder tree
gwersyll, *n* encampment
gwrych, *n* hedge, quickset hedge
gwryd, *n* fathom
gwyddel, *pl* gwyddyl, gwyddelod, *n* Irishman
gwyddrug, *nf* mound, wooded knoll
gwyn, *f* gwen, *a* white
gwynt, *n* wind
gwyrdd, *f* gwerdd, *a* green

hafn, *nf* gorge, ravine
hafod, *nf* shieling, upland summer dwelling
hafoty, *n* summer dwelling
helygen, *pl* helyg, *nf* willow
hen, *a* old
hendref, *nf* winter dwelling, old home, permanent abode
heol, hewl, *nf* street, road
hir, *a* long

is, *pr* below, under
isaf, *a* lower (lowest)
isel, *a* low
iwrch, *pl* iyrchod, *n* roebuck

lawnd, lawnt, *nf* open space in woodland, glade
llaethdy, *n* milkhouse, dairy
llan, *nf* church, monastery; enclosure
Llanbedr St Peter's church
Llanddewi St David's church
Llanfair St Mary's church
Llanfihangel St Michael's church
llannerch, *nf* clearing, glade
lle, *n* place, position
llech, *pl* llechau, *nf* slab, stone, rock
llechwedd, *nf* hillside
llethr, *nf* slope
llety, *n* small abode, quarters
llidiard, llidiart, *pl* llidiardau, llidiartau, *n* gate
llom, *a* *see* llwm
lluest, *n* shieling, cottage, hut
llumon, *n* stack (chimney)
llwch, *n* dust
llwch, *pl* llychau, *n* lake
llwm, *f* llom, *a* bare, exposed
llwyd, *a* grey, brown
llwyn, *pl* llwyni, llwynau, *n* grove, bush
llyn, *n & nf* lake
llys, *n & nf* court, hall
lôn, *nf* lane, road

ma-, -fa, *nf* plain, place
maen, *pl* meini, main, *n* stone
maenol, maenor, *nf* stone-built residence of chieftain of district, rich low-lying land surrounding same, vale
maerdref, *nf* hamlet attached to chieftain's court, lord's demesne (maer, steward + tref, hamlet)
maerdy, *n* steward's house, dairy

maes, *pl* meysydd, *n* open field, plain
march, *pl* meirch, *n* horse, stallion
marchog, *n* knight, horseman
marian, *n* holm, gravel, gravelly ground, rock debris
mawnog, *nf* peat-bog
mawr, *a* great, big
meillionen, *pl* meillion, *nf* clover
meini, *np* *see* maen
meirch, *np* *see* march
melin, *nf* mill
melyn, *f* melen, *a* yellow
menych, *np* *see* mynach
merthyr, *n* burial place, church
Methodistaidd, *a* Methodist
meysydd, *np* *see* maes
mochyn, *pl* moch, *n* pig
moel, *nf* bare hill
moel, *a* bare, bald
môr, *n* sea
morfa, *n* marsh, fen
mur, *pl* muriau, *n* wall
mwyalch, mwyalchen, *nf* blackbird
mynach, *pl* mynych, menych, myneich, *n* monk
mynachdy, *n* monastic grange
mynwent, *nf* churchyard
mynydd, *n* mountain, moorland

nant, *pl* nentydd, naint, nannau, *nf* brook
nant, *pl* nentydd, naint, nannau, *n* dingle, glen, ravine
neuadd, *nf* hall
newydd, *a* new
noddfa, *nf* hospice
nyth, *n & nf* nest, inaccessible position

oen, *pl* ŵyn, *n* lamb
offeiriad, *n* priest
onnen, *pl* onn, ynn, *nf* ash tree

pandy, *n* fulling mill
pant, *n* hollow, valley
parc, *pl* parciau, parcau, *n* park, field, enclosure
pen, *pl* pennau, *n* head, top; end, edge
penrhyn, *n* promontory
pensaer, *n* architect
pentref, *n* homestead, appendix to the real 'tref', village
person, *n* parson
pistyll, *n* spout, waterfall
plas, *n* gentleman's seat, hall, mansion
plwyf, *n* parish
poeth, *a* burnt (hot)
pont, *nf* bridge
porth, *n* gate, gateway
porth, *nf* ferry, harbour
pwll, *pl* pyllau, *n* pit, pool

rhaeadr, *nf* waterfall
rhandir, *n* allotment, fixed measure of land
rhiw, *nf & n* hill, slope
rhos, *pl* rhosydd, *nf* moor, promontory
rhyd, *nf & n* ford

saeth, *pl* saethau, *nf* arrow
sant, san, *pl* saint, *n* saint, monk
sarn, *pl* sarnau, *nf* causeway
simnai, simdde, *nf* chimney
siop, *nf* shop
sticil, sticill, *nf* stile
swydd, *nf* seat, lordship, office
sych, *a* dry

tafarn, *pl* tafarnau, *n & nf* tavern
tai, *np* *see* tŷ
tâl, *n* end (forehead)
talwrn, *pl* talyrni, tylyrni, *n* bare exposed hillside, open space, threshing floor, cockpit
tan, dan, *nf* under, beneath
teg, *a* fair
tir, *n* land, territory
tom, tomen, *nf* mound
ton, *pl* tonnau, *nf* wave
ton, tonnen, *pl* tonnau, *n & nf* grassland, lea
torglwyd, *nf* door-hurdle, gate
towyn, *n* *see* tywyn
traean, traen, *n* third part
traeth, *n* strand, shore
trallwng, trallwm, *n* wet bottom land
traws, *a & n* cross, transverse
tref, *nf* homestead, hamlet, town
tros, *pr* over
trwyn, *n* point, cape (nose)
tŵr, *n* tower
twyn, *pl* twyni, *n* hillock, knoll
tŷ, *pl* tai, *n* house
tyddyn, ty'n, *n* small farm, holding
tylyrni, *np* *see* talwrn
tywyn, towyn, *n* sea-shore, strand

uchaf, *a* higher, highest
uchel, *a* high

uwch, *pr* above, over

ŵyn, *np* *see* oen

y, yr, 'r (definite article) the
yn, *pr* in
ynn, *np* *see* onnen
ynys, *pl* ynysoedd, *nf* island; holm, river-meadow
ysbyty, *n* hospital, hospice
ysgol, *pl* ysgolion, *nf* school
ysgubor, *pl* ysguboriau, *nf* barn
ystafell, *nf* chamber, hiding place
ystrad, *n* valley, holm, river-meadow
ystum, *nf & n* bend shape

INDEX OF ARTISTS

INDEX OF PATRONS, RESIDENTS AND TOURISTS

INDEX OF PLACES

Principal references are in **bold** type; demolished buildings are shown in *italic*.